I0325331

Antonio Loprieno, Matthias Müller, Sami Uljas
**Non-Verbal Predication in Ancient Egyptian**

# The Mouton Companions to Ancient Egyptian

Editors
Eitan Grossman
Stéphane Polis
Jean Winand

## Volume 2

Antonio Loprieno,
Matthias Müller, Sami Uljas

# Non-Verbal Predication in Ancient Egyptian

DE GRUYTER
MOUTON

ISBN 978-3-11-065157-7
e-ISBN (PDF) 978-3-11-040989-5
e-ISBN (EPUB) 978-3-11-040994-9
ISSN 1861-4302

**Library of Congress Cataloging-in-Publication Data**
A CIP catalog record for this book has been applied for at the Library of Congress.

**Bibliografische Information der Deutschen Nationalbibliothek**
The Deutsche Nationalbibliothek lists this publication in the Deutschen Nationalbibliografie; detailed bibliographic data are available on the internet http://dnb.dnb.de.


This volume is text- and page-identical with the hardback published in 2017.
Cover image: Dimitri Laboury
Typesetting: Compuscript Ltd., Shannon, Ireland
Printing and binding: CPI books GmbH, Leck
♾ Printed on acid-free paper
Printed in Germany

www.degruyter.com

# Preface

This book is the first monograph resulting from the work on a *Diachronic Grammar of Egyptian and Coptic*, a common research project that has been conducted at the University of Basel by many scholars over the past decade. Two of the three authors alternated in securing the project's leadership, and the third was so intensely associated with it from its very inception that he probably ended up contributing to its development and success to an equal extent, if not more. At different times and to varying degrees, other scholars were also associated with our endeavour and provided documentary and methodological contributions: *pars pro toto* we would like to mention Andréas Stauder for Earlier Egyptian and Ghislaine Widmer for Demotic, without whom our project would not have been able to address the historical breadth of the documentary evidence in the way we wanted to. Whilst the book is a common scholarly product, it is fair to state that Sami Uljas is the primary author of the sections on Earlier Egyptian, whereas Matthias Müller, the current director of the project, bears the main responsibility for the sections on Later Egyptian, and especially for the Coptic evidence. While typological studies usually treat Coptic as a more or less well-documented appendix to earlier periods, the analysis of the Coptic evidence is derived here from an extensive first-hand study of the material.

Linguistic treatises on the Egyptian language are neither easy to conceive nor to read, and this book is no exception. The main reason for this is that the intended audience of an Egyptological linguistic analysis is doomed to remain underdetermined: if the model reader is the Egyptologist, the philological encyclopaedia can indeed be considered given, but knowledge of theoretical linguistics mostly wanting; if she is a linguist, one never knows how far to go when explaining the idiosyncratic intricacies of the philological evidence, especially in terms of graphemic, and hence morphological opaqueness. We opted for what we might call 'an Egyptologically sensitive linguistic approach', in hopes of making some readers happy rather than making all of them unhappy: our model reader is a linguist who displays the necessary trust in the authors' didactic skills not to need to go through years of philological drill before delving into our presentation of non-verbal grammar. The introduction is meant to offer readers a quick orientation on history and structure of the Egyptian language, detailed enough to provide them with the necessary contextual background before facing the syntactic and semantic study of a particular aspect of Egyptian grammar treated in Parts I–III, and the interlinear translation is as user-friendly as possible and seeks to address primarily the needs of the typological analysis. However, although our intended audience consists mainly of linguists, we would

https://doi.org/10.1515/9783110409895-202

be very sad if fellow Egyptologists and Coptologists – who are in fact the main addressees of the footnotes – renounced reading this book altogether, for we believe that we also provide in it new information for a better understanding of the Egyptian and Coptic sources. Inevitably, trying to serve one audience without forgetting the other will at times generate informational redundancies and organisational unevenness. To allow a quick conceptual grasp of the argument, we have opted – when contextually needed – for a concise summary of information even if it has already been mentioned in a preceding section. This is particularly true in the references to Later Egyptian, where the most relevant points of the Earlier Egyptian treatment are often repeated in concise form before addressing the developments in the later stages of the language. So, whilst not aiming at stylistic elegance (especially since it starts and ends in a rather abrupt manner), this book will hopefully allow readers who are interested in a particular linguistic issue or historical period to go back from the index to a treatment in the main body of the text in which they will find a coherent presentation without too much browsing through the entire book.

Over the years, and especially in recent times, we have benefited from the Egyptological help of a number of colleagues who have devoted their time and energy to answering our queries, reviewing the first version of our texts, or simply providing important editorial assistance. Of these, our friends and colleagues at the University of Liège and the Hebrew University of Jerusalem, Eitan Grossman, Stéphane Polis, and Jean Winand, should be singled out for being not only the editors of the *Mouton Companions to Ancient Egyptian*, but also our endeavour's sparring partners from the very beginning. We are very much indebted to their competence and their patience. We are equally grateful to Heike Behlmer, Nathalie Bosson, Anne Boud'hors, Robert J. Demarée, Stephen Emmel, Alin Suciu, Karsten Knigge, Nicolas Sartori, and Günter Vittmann for insightful assistance. Finally, our gratitude goes to the funding agencies that have supported our project, in particular the Gertrud Mayer Stiftung and the Research Fund of the University of Basel, and to our academic homes, the Rectorate and the Department of Ancient Studies at the University of Basel, and particularly to Susanne Bickel, as well as the Department of Archaeology and Ancient History at the University of Uppsala for offering us the ideal financial and infrastructural context for our work. It goes without saying that despite their manifold help, these colleagues and institutions cannot be held responsible for any error contained in our book.

Antonio Loprieno, Matthias Müller and Sami Uljas
Basel, December 2016

# Contents

**Preface —— v**
**Index of non-standard glosses used —— xiii**

**Introduction —— 1**
1 The language of Ancient Egypt —— 1
1.1 Earlier Egyptian —— 1
1.2 Later Egyptian —— 2
1.3 Dialects —— 3
1.4 Writing —— 4
2 Phonology —— 5
3 Morphology —— 6
3.1 Nouns —— 7
3.2 Articles and demonstratives —— 8
3.3 Adjectives —— 9
3.4 Personal pronouns —— 9
3.5 Relative and interrogative pronouns —— 10
3.6 Verb —— 10
3.7 Negation —— 12
3.8 Numerals and quantifiers —— 13
3.9 Prepositions —— 13
4 Syntax —— 14
5 Sentence types and word order —— 15
5.1 Adverbial sentences —— 15
5.2 Nominal sentence —— 16
5.3 Adjectival sentence —— 17
5.4 Verbal sentence —— 18
5.5 Coordination and subordination —— 18
5.6 Relativisation —— 19
6 About this book —— 20

## Part I: **The adverbial sentence**

**1 Internal morpho-syntax —— 23**
1.1 Earlier Egyptian —— 23
1.2 Later Egyptian —— 36
1.2.1 Late Egyptian —— 40
1.2.2 Demotic —— 47
1.2.3 Coptic —— 55

| | |
|---|---|
| 2 | **Clausal morpho-syntax — 65** |
| 2.1 | Earlier Egyptian — 65 |
| 2.1.1 | Initial and coordinated clauses — 65 |
| 2.1.2 | Adjunct clauses 1: Unmarked constructions — 70 |
| 2.1.3 | Adjunct clauses 2: marked constructions — 77 |
| 2.1.4 | Adjunct clauses 3: control constructions — 81 |
| 2.1.5 | Complement clauses — 85 |
| 2.1.6 | Relative clauses 1: constructions with a relative adjective/ auxiliary — 90 |
| 2.1.7 | Relative clauses 2: 'virtual' relative clauses — 100 |
| 2.2 | Later Egyptian — 102 |
| 2.2.1 | Initial and coordinated clauses — 102 |
| 2.2.1.1 | Late Egyptian — 102 |
| 2.2.1.2 | Demotic — 105 |
| 2.2.1.3 | Coptic — 107 |
| 2.2.2 | Adjunct clauses — 108 |
| 2.2.2.1 | Late Egyptian — 108 |
| 2.2.2.2 | Demotic — 112 |
| 2.2.2.3 | Coptic — 115 |
| 2.2.3 | Complement clauses — 118 |
| 2.2.3.1 | Late Egyptian — 118 |
| 2.2.3.2 | Demotic — 122 |
| 2.2.3.3 | Coptic — 123 |
| 2.2.4 | Relative clauses — 125 |
| 2.2.4.1 | Late Egyptian — 125 |
| 2.2.4.2 | Demotic — 129 |
| 2.2.4.3 | Coptic — 133 |
| | |
| 3 | **Semantics and pragmatics — 139** |
| 3.1 | Earlier Egyptian — 139 |
| 3.1.1 | Core — 139 |
| 3.1.2 | Bare adverbial sentences — 141 |
| 3.1.2.1 | Independent clauses — 141 |
| 3.1.2.2 | Subordinate clauses — 147 |
| 3.1.3 | Introduced adverbial sentences — 152 |
| 3.1.3.1 | Auxiliary-headed constructions — 152 |
| 3.1.3.1.1 | Combinations with *iw* — 153 |
| 3.1.3.1.2 | Combinations with *wn/wnn* — 157 |
| 3.1.3.2 | Adverbial sentences introduced by initial particles — 173 |
| 3.1.3.3 | Adverbial sentences introduced by subordinating elements — 178 |
| 3.1.4 | Semantic extensions of the adverbial sentence — 185 |

3.2 Later Egyptian — 193
3.2.1 Core — 193
3.2.2 Temporal and information structure operators — 212
3.2.2.1 Late Egyptian — 212
3.2.2.2 Demotic — 217
3.2.2.3 Coptic — 219
3.2.3 Subordinate adverbial sentences — 226
3.2.4 Semantic extensions of the adverbial sentence — 235

**4 Negation — 255**
4.1 Earlier Egyptian — 255
4.2 Later Egyptian — 266
4.2.1 Late Egyptian — 266
4.2.2 Demotic — 273
4.2.3 Coptic — 278

## Part II: **The nominal sentence**

**1 Internal morpho-syntax — 289**
1.1 Bipartite nominal sentences without grammaticalised subject element — 289
1.1.1 Earlier Egyptian — 289
1.1.2 Later Egyptian — 301
1.1.2.1 Late Egyptian — 301
1.1.2.2 Demotic — 317
1.1.2.3 Coptic — 332
1.2 Bipartite nominal sentences with grammaticalised subject element — 367
1.2.1 Earlier Egyptian — 367
1.2.2 Later Egyptian — 381
1.2.2.1 Late Egyptian — 381
1.2.2.2 Demotic — 385
1.2.2.3 Coptic — 392
1.3 Tripartite nominal sentences — 406
1.3.1 Earlier Egyptian — 406
1.3.2 Later Egyptian — 414
1.3.2.1 Late Egyptian — 414
1.3.2.2 Demotic — 418
1.3.2.3 Coptic — 421
1.4 Bipartite nominal sentences with ellipsis of the subject element — 462

**2 Clausal syntax — 469**
2.1 Initial and coordinated clauses — 469
2.1.1 Earlier Egyptian — 469
2.1.2 Later Egyptian — 477
2.2 Adjunct clauses — 493
2.2.1 Earlier Egyptian — 493
2.2.2 Later Egyptian — 495
2.3 Complement clauses — 507
2.3.1 Earlier Egyptian — 507
2.3.2 Later Egyptian — 511
2.4 Relative clauses — 513
2.4.1 Earlier Egyptian — 513
2.4.2 Later Egyptian — 514

**3 Semantics and pragmatics — 519**
3.1 Earlier Egyptian — 519
3.1.1 Grammatical relations: subject and predicate I — 519
3.1.2 Semantic typology of Earlier Egyptian nominal sentences: subject and predicate II — 523
3.1.3 Nominal sentences with non-canonical information structure — 531
3.1.4 Tense and modality — 550
3.1.5 The limits of the nominal sentence — 556
3.2 Later Egyptian — 560
3.2.1 Subject and predicate — 560
3.2.2 The core semantic functions of Later Egyptian nominal sentences — 567
3.2.2.1 Late Egyptian — 571
3.2.2.2 Demotic — 574
3.2.2.3 Coptic — 580
3.2.3 Temporal modification — 594
3.2.4 Pragmatics of subordinated nominal sentences — 596

**4 Negation — 601**
4.1 Earlier Egyptian — 601
4.2 Later Egyptian — 613
4.2.1 Late Egyptian — 613
4.2.2 Demotic — 622
4.2.3 Coptic — 626

## Part III: **The adjectival sentence**

**1 Internal morpho-syntax — 649**
1.1 Earlier Egyptian — 649
1.2 Later Egyptian — 668
1.2.1 Late Egyptian — 668
1.2.2 Demotic — 679
1.2.3 Coptic — 685

**2 Clausal syntax — 699**
2.1 Initial and coordinated clauses — 699
2.1.1 Earlier Egyptian — 699
2.1.2 Later Egyptian — 701
2.2 Adjunct clauses — 703
2.2.1 Earlier Egyptian — 703
2.2.2 Later Egyptian — 707
2.3 Complement clauses — 710
2.3.1 Earlier Egyptian — 710
2.3.2 Later Egyptian — 714
2.4 Relative clauses — 718
2.4.1 Earlier Egyptian — 718
2.4.2 Later Egyptian — 719

**3 Semantics and pragmatics — 723**
3.1 Earlier Egyptian — 723
3.2 Later Egyptian — 734

**4 Negation — 747**
4.1 Earlier Egyptian — 747
4.2 Later Egyptian — 751

**Bibliography — 759**

**Index of cited sources — 803**

**Index of topics — 837**

# Index of non-standard glosses used

The glosses used in the examples follow broadly the modified Leipzig Glossing System proposed in Biase-Dyson, Kammerzell and Werning 2009, "Glossing Ancient Egyptian: suggestions for adapting the Leipzig Glossing Rules", *Lingua Aegyptia* 17, 343–66. Note, however, the following:

| | |
|---|---|
| ADM | admirative |
| APR | approximate |
| CFT | counterfactual |
| CNJ | conjunctive verb form |
| COM | comitative preposition |
| CONC | concessive conditional |
| DAM | demonstrative, above-mentioned |
| DIM | diminutive |
| DPR | determinative pronoun |
| GEM | geminating |
| HORT | hortative |
| IP | interrogative particle |
| IPF | imperfective |
| NC | negatival complement |
| NCO | negative completive |
| PIA | imperfective active participle |
| PIP | imperfective passive participle |
| PPA | perfective active participle |
| PPP | perfective passive participle |
| PREF | prefix |
| PTC | particle |
| PTL | participle |
| QU | quantifier |
| RLT | relational (*nisbe*) |
| SE | subject element |
| SEQ | sequential |
| ST | second tense |
| STA | stative |
| SUB | subjunctive |
| TERM | terminative ('*sḏm-t-f*') |
| WH | interrogative 'wh'-element |

https://doi.org/10.1515/9783110409895-204

# Introduction

## 1 The language of Ancient Egypt

This book presents a typological study of the non-verbal syntax of Ancient Egyptian and Coptic, together a branch of the Afroasiatic language family. This introduction is meant to provide readers with the basic historical and structural information needed about the language itself to tackle the linguistic issues addressed in the main sections of the book.

Within the Afroasiatic family (which has also been called Hamito-Semitic or Semito-Hamitic), Egyptian, whose productive history as a written language spans from approximately 3000 BC to AD 1300, shows the closest relations to Semitic and Berber languages. As a spoken language, it was used in the Nile valley and the Nile delta, broadly within the borders of present-day Egypt. In certain periods from the Early Bronze to the Iron Age, Egypt's political supremacy exceeded these natural borders, and Egyptian came to be used as written language of the ruling elite in the occupied territories such as Nubia, which corresponds to modern Sudan, or the southern Levant. However, Egyptian, unlike its contemporary Akkadian from Mesopotamia, never established itself as a lingua franca, although it left a few traces of language contact in the Nilotic and Semitic languages of the adjacent regions. In recent years, scholars have also pointed to some prehistoric contacts between Egyptian and Indo-European.

In terms of language history, Egyptian divides into two main stages, called 'Earlier Egyptian' and 'Later Egyptian', separated by a major typological change from synthetic to analytic patterns. Further historical subdivisions within each of these two stages are determined mainly by changes in the writing conventions and in patterns of standardisation.

### 1.1 Earlier Egyptian

Earlier Egyptian is the language of all written texts from 3000 BC to approximately 1400 BC and survives in formal religious texts down to the third century AD. It is usually subdivided as follows:

1. *Old Egyptian*, the language of the Early Bronze Age (a politically centralised period called the 'Old Kingdom' followed by a decentralised 'First Intermediate Period', 3000–2000 BC). The main documents of this stage of the language are royal rituals, funerary texts and private biographies with accounts of professional achievements inscribed in the rock-cut tombs of

https://doi.org/10.1515/9783110409895-001

the administrative elite. Additionally, a limited number of letters and business documents survive from this period.

2. *Classical (or Middle) Egyptian*, from the Middle Bronze Age to the early part of the Late Bronze Age (a politically centralised period called 'Middle Kingdom', a less centralised 'Second Intermediate Period', and the first portion of the 'New Kingdom', 2000–1400 BC). Classical Egyptian is the language of religious texts, of wisdom texts conveying the educational and professional expectations of Egyptian society, of narratives relating the adventures of the tale's hero and voicing individual concerns, and of administrative and historical records.
3. *Traditional Egyptian* (often referred to with the French expression *égyptien de tradition*), the standardised language of most monumental texts from the Late Bronze Age to the end of the Egyptian writing tradition in Late Antiquity. For more than a millennium, Traditional Egyptian coexisted with the various stages of Later Egyptian (see below) in a situation of diglossia, maintaining the linguistic structures of the classical language, but displaying, especially in the Hellenistic and Roman periods, an expansion of its graphic inventory. Because of its explicitly artificial character, Traditional Egyptian is not treated in this book.

Earlier Egyptian is characterised by a preference for *synthetic* grammatical structures: it displayed a full set of morphological suffixes indicating gender and number; it exhibits no definite article; it prefers the VSO order in verbal formations:

(1) *wꜥb* *rn-k*
purify.SUB.PASS name-2MS
May your name be purified.

## 1.2 Later Egyptian

Later Egyptian is documented from the Late Bronze Age (the second part of the New Kingdom) down to the Middle Ages (1400 BC–1300 AD). It is further subdivided as follows:

1. *Late Egyptian* (1300–700 BC), during the late New Kingdom and the so-called 'Third Intermediate Period'. It has a rich literature consisting of wisdom texts and tales, as well as new literary genres, such as mythology or love poetry. Late Egyptian was also the vehicle of bureaucracy, such as administrative archives, and of school texts. Late Egyptian is not very homogeneous: the texts display varying degrees of interference with the classical language, with

the tendency of older or more formal texts, such as historical records or literary tales, to display a higher degree of overlapping than later or administrative texts, where classical forms become rarer.

2. *Demotic* (seventh century BC to fifth century AD) is the language of administration and literature from the Pharaonic 'Late Period' down to late antiquity. Although grammatically close to Late Egyptian, it radically differs from it in its graphemic system. Important texts in Demotic, especially during the Hellenistic period, are narrative cycles, moral instructions, and economic and administrative documents.
3. *Coptic* (300–1300 AD), the language of Christian Egypt, was written in a variety of the Greek alphabet with the addition of Demotic signs to indicate Egyptian phonemes absent from Greek. As a spoken, and gradually also as a written language, Coptic was superseded by Arabic by the ninth century, but it survived as the liturgical language of the Christian (Coptic) Church and in the traces it left in spoken Egyptian Arabic.

Besides having undergone numerous phonological changes, Later Egyptian diverges from Earlier Egyptian in its preference for *analytic* patterns: suffixal morphological markers tend to be dropped and functionally replaced by prefixal deictic compounds; the demonstrative pronoun 'this' and the numeral 'one' evolve into the definite and indefinite article, respectively; periphrastic SVO patterns supersede VSO verbal forms, as in the following Coptic example:

(2) *mare-pe-k-ran* *uop*
JUSS-POSS.M-2MS-name pure.STA
Hallowed be thy name.

## 1.3 Dialects

Owing to the centralised nature of the political and cultural models underlying the evolution of Ancient Egyptian society, there is hardly any evidence of dialect differences in pre-Coptic Egyptian. Although the patterns of the hieroglyphic writing system probably originated in the south of the country, the origins of the linguistic type represented by Earlier Egyptian are to be seen in northern Egypt, around the city of Memphis, which was the capital during the Old Kingdom. The linguistic origins of Later Egyptian lie in southern Egypt, in the region of Thebes, which was the cultural, religious, and at times also political centre during the New Kingdom. Coptic, on the contrary, is known through a variety of dialects differing primarily in the graphic rendition of Egyptian phonemes, to a lesser extent in morphology, syntax, and lexicon. The most important dialects were Sahidic (from the Arabic word for 'Upper Egypt'), the written standard of the Theban area, and Bohairic (from the Arabic word for 'Lower Egypt'), the dialect of Alexandria, which eventually became the language of the liturgy of the Coptic Church. Other important dialects are Akhmimic (assumed to be from the city of Akhmim in Upper Egypt), Lycopolitan (earlier called Subakhmimic), the dialect in connection with the city of Assiut in Middle Egypt, and Fayyumic, the variety of Coptic from the Fayyum oasis.

## 1.4 Writing

The basic graphemic system of the Egyptian language from about 3000 BC to the first centuries AD consists of a set of pictographic signs called *hieroglyphs*, in Egyptian *mdw-w-nṯr* 'divine words'. This writing was used primarily on stone for monumental purposes. Two handwritten varieties eventually emerged for cursive uses: *Hieratic*, documented from the Old Kingdom, in which hieroglyphic signs maintain their pictorial features, and *Demotic*, from the seventh century BC, which displays standardised sign groups. Starting in Hellenistic times, hieroglyphs and their cursive varieties were gradually superseded by alphabetic transcriptions of words, and then of texts, inspired by Greek with the addition of Demotic signs for Egyptian phonemes unknown to Greek. The final result of this process was the emergence of the Coptic alphabet.

Egyptian hieroglyphs are pictographic signs representing human and divine entities, animals, plants, objects and buildings. The signs are not purely logographic, but convey different combinations of phonological and semantic contents. An Egyptian word usually consists of two components: (a) a sequence of phonograms, each of which represents a sequence of one, two, or three phonemes containing the consonantal skeleton of the word. The phonological value of a sign is usually derived from the name of the represented entity by means of the rebus principle, i.e. by applying the same phonological sequence to semantically unrelated words. (b) The sequence of phonograms is usually followed by a semogram, called a determinative (or classifier), which refers to the semantic sphere and also functions as word boundary: for example, a sitting man touching his mouth indicates the domain of eating, speaking, thinking, or sensing 𓀁 ; a scribe's equipment defines the area of writing 𓏞 ; a stylised settlement identifies the word as a toponym 𓊖 ; a vertical stroke ('one') indicates the logographic use of the sign.

Unlike most other complex writing systems, such as Mesopotamian cuneiform or Chinese logograms, Egyptian hieroglyphs maintained their original iconicity throughout their entire history and entertained a culturally negotiable distinction between phonetic and semantic content of many signs. For this reason, it is more difficult than in other writing traditions to draw a clear line between the use of a sign as logogram and as determinative. This analogical nature of the writing system has also complicated the development of universally accepted conventions of transliteration and transcription. In the system adopted in this book, the most widespread among Egyptologists, only the consonantal skeleton of the word is transliterated, with the occasional integration of morphologically distinctive glides or of grammatically significant vocalic reconstructions or pictorial devices, e.g.:

(3)  <*s-sḏm*$^{\text{ear}}$-*m*-papyrus roll-sitting man> =
*/sḏm-i̯/*
hear.SUB-1S
I shall hear.

## 2 Phonology

Although all the consonantal phonemes of the language (except */l/*) are distinctly recognisable in Egyptian writing, their phonetic value can remain opaque because of the lack of reliable Afroasiatic correspondences. However, transcriptions of Egyptian words and phrases in other languages (mainly Akkadian and Greek) and the Coptic evidence provide sufficient evidence to gain a coherent picture not only of consonantal values, but also – at least partially – of vocalism and prosody, despite a considerable number of graphic idiosyncrasies.

A certain number of features is typical for Egyptian phonology as opposed to other Afroasiatic languages: (1) in prehistoric times, a palatalisation process led to the emergence of palatal stops, conventionally transcribed with *ṯ* (for */c/*) and *ḏ* (for */c'/*); (2) the opposition between voiceless and voiced phonemes is limited to bilabial stops, whereas in other series, the articulatory opposition is between voiceless and ejective stop or affricate, e.g. *t* (for */t/*) and *d* (for */t'/*); (3) the Egyptian phoneme conventionally transcribed *ꜥ* (*'ayin*) displays an etymological connection with Semitic *d*, e.g. Egyptian *ḥnꜥ* = Arabic *'inda* 'with', the Egyptian phoneme conventionally transcribed *ꜣ* (*aleph*) with Semitic *r*, e.g. Egyptian *ḥꜣy* = Semitic **ꜥry* 'naked'; (4) during the late second millennium BC, uvulars and velars became palatals, palatals became dentals, and dentals were dropped in the final position; (5) in stressed syllables, plain stops are aspirated; (6) the liquid *l* is not unambiguously indicated in pre-Coptic Egyptian writing and does not, therefore, appear in transcribed texts.

The set of vowels posited for the Egyptian is the same as for other Afroasiatic languages in their earliest stage of development (i.e. *a*, *i*, *u*), but underwent many historical changes: (1) unstressed vowels gradually lost phonological status and were eventually realised as *schwa*; (2) stressed vowels underwent a *Lautverschiebung* during the second millennium BC: /*u:*/ > /*e:*/; /'*i*/, /'*u*/ > /'*e*/. In the two main Coptic dialects and unless followed by glottal stop, this /'*e*/ then evolved into /'*a*/; (c) around 1000 BC, /*a:*/ > /*o:*/, /'*a*/ > /'*o*/, this change being limited to the portion of the linguistic domain to which /'*i*/, /'*u*/ > /'*e*/ applied.

In Earlier Egyptian, the stress lay on the ultimate or penultimate syllable of a word. Closed (CVC) and open (CV) syllables could be found in pre-tonic, tonic, and post-tonic positions. The stressed vowel of a penultimate open syllable was always long (CV:). These syllabic structures were modified under the influence of a strong expiratory stress and prompted significant typological changes in morphology and syntax. In Coptic, the loss of short unstressed vowels led to the emergence of word-initial consonantal clusters.

## 3 Morphology

Earlier Egyptian was a language of the flectional type: morphemes are non-segmentable units combining many grammatical functions. Morphological forms exhibited a certain number of correspondences with the patterns of word formation in other Afroasiatic languages.

The basic structure of an Egyptian word was a lexical *root*, an abstract linguistic entity consisting of a sequence of consonants or glides varying in number from one to four, with an overwhelming majority of bi-consonantal and tri-consonantal roots. Within the root, rules of compatibility prevented the combination of homorganic phonemes, e.g. the clustering of *b* and *p* was not allowed. Superimposed on the root there was a vocalic or semi-vocalic pattern, which together with the root formed the so-called *stem*, the surface form acquired by the root; the stem determined the functional class to which the word belonged. Actual word-forms were derived from the stem by means of inflectional affixes, which conveyed deixis and other grammatical functions such as gender, number, tense and aspect, and voice.

Vocalic patterns generally determined the structure of nouns and of basic conjugational forms, with suffixes conveying the expression of the plural, of participles and relative forms, and of conjugational patterns. Examples of consonantal additions prefixed to a root are *s*- for causative stems, *n*- for detransitive stems, and *m*- for nouns of instrument, place, or agent. Egyptian stems resulting from the addition of a consonantal phoneme to a root tended to be lexicalised rather than treated as grammatical forms of the basic root: Egyptian, therefore, did not possess a full-fledged paradigm of verbal stems conveying semantic nuances of a verbal root similar to the ones known in Semitic.

Common modifications of the root were: (1) the reduplication of the entire root or of a segment thereof. This pattern affected the semantic sphere, creating new lexemes: *sn* 'brother' > *snsn* 'to befriend'; (2) the reduplication (Egyptologists call it 'gemination') of the last or penultimate consonantal radical, affecting the grammatical sphere: *mri* 'to love' > *mrr-f* 'he loves'; *sḏm* 'to hear' > *sḏmm-f* 'he will be heard'.

### 3.1 Nouns

In Earlier Egyptian, nouns were built by adding a suffix to the stem: if the stem ended in a consonant, the suffix was zero; if it ended in a vowel, a *w*-suffix was added. Nouns inflected for gender (masculine vs. feminine) and number (singular, dual, and plural). Case marking might have been present in prehistoric Egyptian, but no traces are left in writing. The feminine marker was a *t*-suffix added to the masculine noun; the plural displayed a *w*- or *ww*-suffix; the dual had a *wi*-suffix added to the stem of the singular.

Under the pressure of a strong expiratory stress, which reduced the distinctive function of unstressed vowels, the flectional system underwent a profound crisis in Later Egyptian, which prompted a reorganisation of the morphological information. The general trend was then to replace synthetic by analytic constructions, e.g. participles and abstract nouns were replaced by relative constructions or lexicalised nominal classifiers:

| | | | | |
|---|---|---|---|---|
| (4) | PARTICIPLE | | > | RELATIVE CONSTRUCTION |
| | *sḏm* | | | *p-et-sôtm* |
| | hear.PIA | | | DEF.M-REL-hear |
| | the hearer | | | |
| (5) | PARTICIPLE | | > | 'MAN-WHO'-V |
| | *mwt* | | | *ref-mout* |
| | die.PIA | | | AGT-die.STA |
| | dead | | | |
| (6) | ABSTRACT NOUN | | > | 'THING-OF'-N |
| | *rꜣ* | *n(y)-kmt* | | *mnt-rm-n-kême* |
| | speech | of[-M]-Egypt | | ABST-man-of-Egypt |
| | Egyptian language | | | |

Thus, because of the loss of regular flectional patterns, the only device by which Coptic eventually conveyed the distinction between morphological categories was through markers preceding the noun: *p-rôme* 'the man' vs. *n-rôme* 'the men'; *ref-mout* 'dead' vs. *f-mout* 'he is dead'. In some prosodic environments, oppositions by means of suffixes (masculine vs. feminine, singular vs. plural) were maintained, but were not any more recognizable due to the underlying phonetic evolution: *son* 'brother' vs. *sône* 'sister', *hto* 'horse' vs. *htôôr* 'horses'.

### 3.2 Articles and demonstratives

Although Earlier Egyptian displays neither a definite nor an indefinite article, Later Egyptian developed both. The definite article derives from the demonstrative pronoun 'this', the indefinite article from the numeral *wꜥꞽ* 'one':

| | | | |
|---|---|---|---|
| (7) | *rmṯ* | > | *pꜣ-rm(t)* |
| | N[+SPEC] | | DEF.M-N |
| | the.man | | the-man |

| | | | |
|---|---|---|---|
| (8) | *sn-t* | > | *wꜥ(-t)-sn(-t)* |
| | N-F[−SPEC] | | IDF[-F]-N[-F] |
| | a.sister | | a-sister |

The definite article also attracted the pronominal affix indicating the possessor, which in Earlier Egyptian followed the head noun:

| | | | |
|---|---|---|---|
| (9) | *sn-f* | > | *pe-f-son* |
| | N-3MS | | DEF.M-POSS-N |
| | brother-his | | the-his-brother |

Demonstratives are characterised by a deictic element preceded by the indicator of gender and number: masculine *pn, pf, pw*; feminine *tn, tf, tw*. The plurals (originally neuter) *nw, nf, nn* were also used as pronouns in partitive constructions with the determinative pronoun *n-*: *nn n(-y)-sr-w* 'this of officials' > 'these officials'. The determinative pronoun **n-y*, feminine **n-t*, plural *n-w* was used as a marker of genitival relation: *rmṯ-w n-w-kmt* 'men of Egypt' > 'Egyptians'. Although the demonstratives followed the noun they refer to in Earlier Egyptian, in Later Egyptian they precede it:

| | | | |
|---|---|---|---|
| (10) | N-DEICTIC | > | DEICTIC-N |
| | *ḥm-t=tn* | | *tei-shime* |
| | woman-F=DEM.F | | DEM.F-woman |

From Late Egyptian on, the demonstratives were used regularly in absolute function: *pꜣy, tꜣy, nꜣy* 'this one, those ones'. For the expression of the distal function, Coptic employs an etymological relative clause ('which is there'):

(11) *n-hmhal* *et-mmau*
DEF.P-servant REL-there
those servants

### 3.3 Adjectives

Adjectives were morpho-syntactically treated like nouns. However, since they could be expanded by adverbs, they do constitute a separate word class. In a common derivational pattern, called nisbation, a morpheme masculine **y*, feminine **yt* was added to the stem: *nṯr* 'god' > *nṯr-y, nṯr-yt* 'divine'. In Later Egyptian, adjectival specification was more or less completely confined to the syntactic sphere.

### 3.4 Personal pronouns

Egyptian had a rich system of personal, demonstrative, relative and interrogative pronouns. Reflexive and reciprocal pronouns are not attested.

There were three sets of personal pronouns (plus the endings of the Stative verbal form): (1) stressed absolute pronouns used as full lexemes:

(12) *ink* *it-k*
1S father-2MS
I am your father.

(13) *nts* *sꜥnḫ* *rn-i*
3FS enliven.PIA name-1S
It is she who makes my name live.

(2) Unstressed clitic pronouns used as object of verbal forms and as subject of nominal and adjectival sentences (cf. Parts II–III):

(14) *hꜣb-n-f=wi*
send-PST-3MS=1S
He sent me.

(15) *nfr=tw* *ḥnꜥ-i*
good=2MS with-1S
You are happy with me.

(3) Suffix pronouns used as subjects of verbs, complements of prepositions, and possessives:

(16) *di-k=rk=n-i* *ḫ-t-i*
give.SUB-2MS=PTC=to-1S thing-F-1S
May you give me my possessions.

### 3.5 Relative and interrogative pronouns

The relative pronoun was masculine *nt-y*, feminine *nt-t*, plural *nt-w* 'who, which, that.' It was morphologically derived from the determinative pronoun (genitive marker) *n-* 'that of'. In Earlier Egyptian, these pronouns agreed in gender and number with the head noun, which had to be semantically specific. Earlier Egyptian also displays a negative relative pronoun masculine *iwt-y*, *iwt-t*, *iwt-w* 'that not'. In Later Egyptian, the gender-number agreement is lost and only one morpheme *nty* is employed in affirmative and negative constructions.

Interrogative pronouns were mostly generic, e.g. *m* 'who, what?'. They could be combined with prepositions or particles to form complex pronouns: *in-m* 'who?' (agent), lit. 'by-who?'; *ḥr-m* 'why?' lit. 'on-what?' Interrogative pronouns could not be used as relative pronouns.

### 3.6 Verb

Earlier Egyptian finite verb phrases displayed a limited number of stems (three or four) indicating tense, aspect, and voice, followed by the nominal subject or a pronominal suffix:

(17) *hꜣb=wi* *ḥm-f*
send.PRF=1S majesty-3MS
His Majesty sent me.

(18) *pr-k*
come.SUB-2MS
May you come.

In addition to stem variations, temporal and aspectual features could be conveyed by infixes inserted between the stem and the subject: the most important indicators were *n* for the preterite (*sḏm-n-f* 'he heard'), *w* for prospective tense (*mri-w-f* 'he will love') and passive voice in perfective stems (*sḏm-w N* 'N was heard'), *tw* for passive in non-perfective stems (*sḏm-tw-f* 'he is heard'), *t* for a few bound occurrences of the perfective (*n sḏm-t-f* 'before he had heard') and some prospective forms (e.g. *ỉn-t-f* 'may he bring').

A particular verbal stem displayed in weak verbal classes the reduplication of the second radical: *mrỉ* > *mrr-*. A similar morphological feature indicates in Semitic languages the imperfective aspect; in Egyptian, this may have indeed been the original meaning, but in the literary language its main function was to signal that the 'pivot' of the information provided by the sentence is not the verb itself, but rather a subsequent (typically adjunct) expression:

| | | | |
|---|---|---|---|
| (19) | *ỉrr* | *ḥm-k* | *r-mr-t-f* |
| | do.GEM | majesty-2MS | to-want.REL-F-3MS |
| | Your Majesty acts indeed as he pleases. | | |

The imperative had no suffix element in the singular, but sometimes, especially with weak verbs, a semi-vocalic suffix in the plural.

Egyptian also exhibited a verbal form, variously called the Old Perfective, Stative, or Pseudoparticiple, which indicated the semantic range of perfectivity, from perfect aspect with intransitive verbs to passive voice with transitive verbs. This form was built with a special set of personal pronouns etymologically linked to the forms of the Semitic suffix conjugation:

| | | |
|---|---|---|
| (20) | *mk=wỉ* | *ỉy-kw* |
| | PTC=1S | come-STA.1S |
| | Look, I have come. (i.e. 'I am here') | |

In Later Egyptian, finite VSO forms were replaced by SVO constructions, called 'sentence conjugations' or 'clause conjugations', which resulted from the grammaticalisation of a form of the verb *ỉr(ỉ)* 'to do' followed by the infinitive:

| | | | |
|---|---|---|---|
| (21) | VSO | > | SVO |
| | EARLIER Egyptian | LATE EGYPTIAN | COPTIC |
| | *sḏm-ḫr-f* | *ḫr-ỉr-f-sḏm* | *ša-f-sôtm* |
| | hear-SEQ-3MS | AOR-do.AUX-3MS-hear | AOR-3MS-hear |
| | Then he hears > He can hear | | |

The outcome of this typological trend was that Coptic eventually maintained only two flectional patterns from most verbal roots: the *infinitive* for processes (whether activities such as *i* 'to come', accomplishments such as *ôô* 'to conceive', or achievements such as *cine* 'to find'), and the *Stative*, derived from the Old Perfective, for states (e.g. *eet* 'to be pregnant'):

| | | | |
|---|---|---|---|
| (22) | *f-kôt* | vs. | *f-kêt* |
| | 3MS-build.INF | | 3MS-build.STA |
| | he builds | | it is built |

Moreover, Coptic also displayed an inflected form of the infinitive (*p-tre-f-sôtm* 'the fact that he hears', 'his hearing') that could also be used after prepositions (*hm-p-tre-f-sôtm* 'in his hearing' > 'while he heard').

Thus, with the productivity of root and stem variations massively reduced, Later Egyptian linguistic typology gradually moved from the original flectional towards the polysynthetic type, which to a large extent characterises Coptic:

(23)

| | | | | | |
|---|---|---|---|---|---|
| EARLIER EGYPTIAN | | | > LATE EGYPTIAN | | > COPTIC |
| *ỉw* | *sḏm-n-ỉ* | *ḫrw* | *ỉir-ỉ-sdm* | *wꜥ-ḫrw* | *a-i-setm-ou-hrou* |
| AUX | hear-PST-1S | voice | do.AUX-1S-hear | IDF.S-voice | PST-1S-hear-IDF.S-voice |
| I heard a voice. | | | | | |

This evolution towards a lexicalisation of compound expressions also affected verbal semantics. In many instances, an Earlier Egyptian verb was replaced in Later Egyptian, and particularly in Coptic, by an auxiliary of generic meaning ('to do', 'to give', 'to take', etc.) followed by the verbal infinitive or by a noun object:

(24)

| | | |
|---|---|---|
| VERBAL LEXEME | > | AUXILIARY + NOUN |
| *wḏꜥ* | | *r-hap, ti-hap* |
| judge.INF | | do.INF-law, give.INF-law |
| to judge | | |

### 3.7 Negation

The basic negative particle was *n*, which was used for unmarked (contradictory) negation:

(25)

| | |
|---|---|
| *n-rdỉ-f=n-ỉ* | *mw* |
| NEG-give-3MS=to-1S | water |
| He did not give me water. | |

A morphological variant of *n*, conventionally transcribed *nn*, is used in noun clauses to negate the existence and in verb clauses to negate the future:

(26)

| | |
|---|---|
| *nn* | *mꜣꜥty-w* |
| NEG | righteous-P |
| There are no righteous people. | |

(27)

| | |
|---|---|
| *nn* | *mwt-k* |
| NEG | die.SUB-2MS |
| You shall not die. | |

### 3.8 Numerals and quantifiers

Numerals preceded the noun they refer to. The number 5 was etymologically derived from the word for 'hand'; 20 is the dual of 10; 50 through 90 represent the plural forms of the respective units 5 through 9. Ordinals were derived from cardinals through the addition of a suffix *-nw* (from 2 to 9: *ḫmt-nw* 'third'), later through the prefixation of the participle *mḥ* 'filling' to the cardinal number: *mḥ-20* 'filling twenty' > 'twentieth'). An exception was the ordinal number 'first,' for which discrete lemmas derived from nouns were used in place of a derivation: *tpy* 'first' in Earlier Egyptian, *ḥ3w-ti* in Later Egyptian. Multiples were derived by the help of the noun *sp* 'time' following the number (*4 sp* 'four times'). The derivation of fractions was achieved via the prefix *r* (from *r* 'part') plus the number of the fraction (*r-5* '1/5'). Only for 'half' a specific word *gs* was used. Fractions other than 1/*x* could be expressed only for 2/3 (*r-wy* 'the two parts' [part-DU]) and 3/4 (*ḫmt r-w* 'three parts (out of four)' [three part-P]). All other fractions were obtained by addition: 5/8 = 1/2 + 1/8.

Egyptian had a universal quantifier *nb*: morphologically an adjective, this quantifier was originally inflected for gender and number (M *nb*, F *nb-t*, MP *nb-w*, FP *nb-w-t*). The numeral 'two' was also employed to express the meaning 'other'. The function of scalar quantifiers was usually fulfilled by adjectives such as *ꜥš3* or *qnw*, which meant 'many,' or by genitive constructions with the noun *nhy* 'a little', also used for the plural of the indefinite article (*nhy n(-y)-ḥbs-w* 'some clothes').

### 3.9 Prepositions

The most frequent prepositions were *m* 'in, with'; *n* 'to, for'; *r* 'toward'; *mi* 'as, like'; *ḥr* 'on'; *ẖr* 'under'; *ḥnꜥ* 'with'; *ḫft* 'according to'; *ḫnt* 'before.' Prepositional phrases followed the noun or the verb they modified. Noteworthy is the presence of the preposition *ḫr* 'near', used whenever the two nouns A and B belonged to socially different hierarchical levels:

(28) *ḏd-f* *ḫr-ms-w-f*
say.SUB-3MS near-child-P-3MS
He will say to his children.

(29) *im3ḫy* *ḫr-nṯr* *ꜥ3*
honour.PIP near-god great
honoured by the great god

## 4 Syntax

Egyptian phrasal syntax was head-initial. This distribution was obligatory with nominal, adjectival and prepositional phrases. In Earlier Egyptian, however, quantifiers and demonstrative pronouns followed the noun they referred to. From a diachronic point of view, the evolution of the typological hierarchy within nominal phrases is as follows:

| EARLIER EGYPTIAN | > | LATER EGYPTIAN |
|---|---|---|
| HEAD – DEM– QU – ADJ – GEN | | DEM– HEAD – QU – ADJ – GEN |

In Earlier Egyptian, all numbers except the numeral '2' preceded the noun, which itself appeared in the singular: up to 299, they display gender agreement with the noun they refer to, but from 300 up they always appear as feminine. In Coptic, numbers are generally treated as masculine.

The typical coordination pattern of Earlier Egyptian was juxtaposition. Later Egyptian developed conjunctions, initially limited to NP coordination, out of prepositions such as *ḥnꜥ* or *ỉrm* 'with'. The expression of disjunction was achieved by means of a postpositional element *r-pw* 'or' or by juxtaposition.

Complement clauses could be finite or non-finite, in which case infinitive constructions were used. Finite complement clauses were introduced by a complementiser (*ntt*, *ỉwtt*, or *r-ḏd*) or directly juxtaposed to the main clause depending on the speaker's attitude towards the propositional content of the reported sentence. The difference between direct and indirect speech was expressed through deictic reference shift, which in Earlier Egyptian affected all referents, in Later Egyptian usually only one:

Earlier Egyptian:

(30) *ḏd-n-f* *ꜥḥꜣ-f* *ḥnꜥ-ỉ*
say-PST-3MS fight.SUB-3MS with-1S
He said he would fight with me.

Later Egyptian:

(31) *ṯ-j* *ḥr-ḏd* *n-pꜣrꜥḥrꜣḫty*[...] *ỉmỉ=n-k* *snb*
PTC-1S PRP-say to-N[...] give.IMP=to-2MS health
I pray to (god) Pra-Harakhty [...] that he may give you health.

Because of this kind of agreement marking, deletion of anaphoric pronouns in subject position was usually not allowed. Adverbial and complement clauses showed similar limitations except in non-finite structures.

Questions are usually introduced by particles. Although there is generally no WH-fronting in unmarked sentences, questions generally give rise to focalisation patterns such as cleft sentences if the interrogative scope was a pronoun, or the so-called second tenses if the interrogative scope was an adverb or a prepositional phrase:

(32) *i͗ḫ* *nꜣ-nty-ṯ-tn* *ḥr-ḏd-t-w*
WH DEM.P-REL-PTC-2P on-say.INF-OBJ-3P
What are you saying?

(33) *i͗-i͗ri͗-k* *gm-s* *mi͗-i͗ḫ*
ST-AUX-2MS find.INF-3C like-WH
How is it that you discovered it?

In comparative expressions, the second element of the comparison was introduced by the preposition *r* 'to' for inequality and *mi͗* 'like' for equality.

## 5 Sentence types and word order

Egyptian syntax knew four types of sentences, depending on the phrase in the predicate position: adverbial, nominal, adjectival, and verbal sentences. These four syntactic patterns are rather stable throughout the history of Egyptian.

### 5.1 Adverbial sentences

In adverbial sentences (cf. Part I), the predicate is an adverbial or prepositional phrase: S > [NP AP]. Throughout the history of the language, the word order is always SUBJ-PRED (as we shall see, some restrictions apply for the subject position):

(34) *ti-hm-pa-iôt*
1S-in-POSS.1S-father
I am in my father.

In Earlier Egyptian, adverbial sentences are often introduced by particles functioning as discourse markers:

(35) *i͗w* *nzw* *i͗r-p-t*
AUX king to-heaven-F
The king is going towards heaven.

(36) *ḫr-t-k* *m-pr-k*
ration-F-2MS in-house-2MS
(because) your rations are in your house.

The adverbial predicate can be an adverb proper or a prepositional phrase, whose head noun can also be a relative verb form:

(37) *wdi* *r-k* *m-ḫbd-n-sn*
act.PIA against-2MS as-reject.REL-PST-3P
He who acts against you is someone whom they have rejected.

Since the part of speech 'adverb' is [-N] and [-V], i.e. it has neither nominal nor verbal properties, the time setting of adverbial sentences is determined by contextual references. Some prepositions, however, naturally evoke a time reference, as in the case of *m* 'in, as', which expresses simultaneity, or *r* 'toward, to', which often implies a future reference. In a common syntactic pattern, which belongs to the verbal syntax (Egyptologists call this pattern 'pseudo-verbal') and therefore is not extensively discussed in this book, the predicate is not an adverbial phrase in the narrower sense, but rather a prepositional phrase in which the head noun is a verbal infinitive and conveys aspectual features:

(38) *nhpw* *ḥr-ḫpr* *rꜥ=nb*
dawn on-happen.INF day=QU.M
Dawn comes daily.

(39) *mk=tw* *r-irt* *ꜣbd* *ḥr-ꜣbd*
PTC=2MS to-do.INF month on-month
Look, you are going to spend many months.

### 5.2 Nominal sentence

In nominal sentences (cf. Part II), the predicate is a noun: S > [NP NP]. Any NP could occur in either position; pronouns, however, had a tendency to occupy the initial position. Typical are bipartite pattern with juxtaposed NPs and tripartite patterns with a copula as the third element:

(40) *dmi=pw* *imn-t*
harbour=COP west-F
The West is a harbour.

The distribution of PRED and SUBJ will be dealt with at length in Part II of this book. Generally speaking, both patterns S > [$NP_S$ $NP_P$] and S > [$NP_P$ $NP_S$] are possible:

(41) *ntk* *it* *n-nmḥw*
2MS father to-orphan
You are a father to the orphan.

(42) *zš-f=pw ḥr*
scribe-3MS=COP N
His scribe is the god Horus.

(43) *ỉn sn-t-ỉ sꜥnḫ rn-ỉ*
PTC sister-F-1S enliven.PIA name-1S
It is my sister who makes my name live.

Later Egyptian displays typologically similar bipartite or tripartite patterns:

(44) *u-me=te te-f-mnt-mntre*
IDF.S-truth=COP.F DEF.F-3MS-ABST-witness
His testimony is true.

### 5.3 Adjectival sentence

The predicate position of adjectival sentences (cf. Part III) is occupied by an adjective or a participle: S > [AdjP NP]. In the subject position a nominal phrase or clause may appear. The normal order of constituents is PRED-SUBJ:

(45) *nfr mtn-ỉ*
good path-1S
My path is good.

(46) *bỉn=wy ỉy-k ꜥḏ-tỉ wḏꜣ-tỉ*
bad=ADM come-2MS safe-STA sound-STA
How very unfortunate that you have come safe and sound!

In Later Egyptian, adjectival sentences become rare; in Demotic and Coptic, they are replaced by nominal or verbal patterns:

(47) *ang-u-agathos*
1S-IDF.S-good
I am good.

(48) *pꜣ-ḫm nm nꜣ-ꜥꜣ-f ỉwḏbꜣ-rn-f*
DEF.M-little dwarf ADJ-great-3MS because-name-3MS
'The little dwarf is big because of his name.'

Since the part of speech *noun* is [+N] but [-V], i.e. it has nominal but not verbal properties, patterns with nominal predicate will be less sensitive to the typically verbal tense/aspect dialectics and will always adjust to the contextual frame of reference, expressing a so-called relative present. The *adjective*, on the other hand, is [+N] and [+V], i.e. it combines nominal and verbal properties; patterns with adjectival predicate are therefore able to convey to some extent temporal or modal references.

### 5.4 Verbal sentence

In verbal sentences, the predicate is a verbal phrase; the basic word order is PRED-SUBJ:

(49) *ꞽꞽ-n-ꞽ* *m-nw-t-ꞽ*
come-PST-1S from-town-F-1S
I came from my town.

Unmarked verb clauses not introduced by discourse markers are in Egyptian less frequent than in related languages. They mostly function as dependent or modal clauses:

(50) *ḫꜥy-k*
appear.SUB-2MS
May you appear.

In Later Egyptian, the verbal predicate is most frequently conveyed by periphrastic SVO-patterns resulting from the grammaticalisation of an inflected form of the verb *ꞽri* 'to do' followed by the infinitive. In Coptic verbal sentences, the relative converter *nty* > *ete* and the dependency marker *ꞽw* > *e* are used to indicate changes in the informational 'pivot' of the sentence. Typically, the relative converter signals that the 'pivot' of the sentence is not the verbal form (which is described in Egyptological literature as 'Second Tense'), but rather a subsequent adjunct; conversely, the dependency marker (described by Egyptologists as 'circumstantial') frequently introduces the informational 'pivot' itself:

(51) *nt-a-n-cpo-f* *e-f-o* *n-blle*
ST-PST-3P-beget-3MS DEP-3MS-be.STA as-blind
He was born to us blind. (lit. 'that-we-begot-him is while-he-is as-blind')

### 5.5 Coordination and subordination

The presence or absence of morphemes indicating initiality was an important syntactic feature of Egyptian adverbial and verbal sentences. The general rule in Earlier Egyptian is that adverb clauses and verb clauses introduced by a discourse particle were initial main clauses, whereas bare patterns were non-initial clauses, either paratactically linked to it as non-initial coordinate main clauses or controlled by it as subordinate clauses.

In this respect, it is important to appreciate the difference between initiality as a property of *discourse* and coordination (and subordination) as syntactic features of the *sentence*. Sentences introduced by a particle were typically (but not always) main sentences; non-initial clauses could be paratactically linked to or syntactically dependent on the main clause. Rather than operating with the traditional two levels of clausal linkage (parataxis vs. hypotaxis, or coordination vs. subordination), it seems therefore suitable to analyse Egyptian syntactic phenomena by positing three forms of linkage between sentences:

1. *Parataxis*, i.e. the linkage between main clauses. Later Egyptian restricted parataxis to verb sentences in the perfective aspect.
2. *Hypotaxis*, i.e. a discourse-, rather than sentence-based, dependency on the informational nucleus. Hypotactically linked clauses could be bare or introduced by particles.
3. *Subordination*, i.e. the syntactic dependency of a clause on a higher node, which itself could be a main or a subordinate clause. Subordination is usually signalled by morphological markers such as prepositions governing verbal phrases, conjunctions or particles. In the absence of an overt marker of dependency, subordination could also be determined by syntactic control ('embedding').

## 5.6 Relativisation

As an example of the complex interface between overt and embedded subordination in Egyptian, let us consider relativisation. Specific antecedents were resumed by an overt marker of relativisation: the relative pronoun in adverb clauses or an agreement-marker inflected in the (restrictive) relative verb form:

(52) *ḫꜣs-t=nb-t* *rwꞽ-t-n-ꞽ* *r-s*
foreign_country-F=QU-F advance.REL-F-PST-1S against-3FS
Every country against which I advanced.

Non-specific antecedents, on the other hand, were modified by relative clauses without overt agreement-markers, but by means of embedding into the main clause:

(53) *k-t* *n-t-msḏr* *dꞽ-f* *mw*
other-F of-F-ear give-3MS water
Another (remedy) for an ear that gives off water.

## 6 About this book

This book offers an overview of the typology of Egyptian non-verbal syntax. It presents all its morpho-syntactic patterns, discussing first the Earlier Egyptian, and then the Later Egyptian evidence. Although a certain familiarity with issues and conventions of typological linguistics is expected, the historical and grammatical information provided in the preceding pages should be sufficient to read this book even without previous exposure to the language.

In the following sections, we shall begin our analysis with a discussion of adverbial sentences (Part I), arguably the most elementary sentence type, and then move on to nominal sentences (Part II), and finally to adjectival sentences (Part III). In developing our argument, we follow the same pattern: we begin by describing the internal morpho-syntax of the constructions, then move on to clausal syntax, and finally to the semantic and pragmatic properties, integrating whenever possible a treatment of diverging scholarly approaches.

The reader, however, should be aware that two main additional competences would be required for a more thorough study of the linguistic issues discussed in this book. The first is writing: because of the purely consonantal nature of the logographic or phonographic sequences expressed by the Egyptian scripts, morphology is doomed to remain partially opaque. Since a few graphemic features might contain information on vocalic patterns, knowing Egyptian writing is essential for further study.

The second issue is philology: a more thorough study of Egyptian linguistic features than is possible in an introductory book presupposes a detailed discussion of textual problems and of apparently marginal diachronic changes that require a familiarity with the textual tradition. Keeping these two provisions in mind, we have tried to offer a linguistically complete study, while avoiding erudite discussions of little relevance for the typological analysis and concentrating on the salient features and constraints of the syntactic patterns under consideration. We hope that our readership will not be disappointed.

# Part I: **The adverbial sentence**

# 1 Internal morpho-syntax

## 1.1 Earlier Egyptian

Adverbial sentences[1] represent the statistically most common type of Earlier Egyptian non-verbal sentence patterns. According to a somewhat more descriptive than analytic definition borrowed from functional grammar, an adverbial sentence is a construction whose predicate is an expression that can, without further (morphological etc.) measures being taken, also be used as a modifier (adjunct) of a functionally non-nominal head[2]:

(1a) Questions in a spell against a dangerous animal:
*ı͗(w)-k=trr* *ꜥꜣ* *ı͗(w)-k=trr* *ı͗m*
AUX-2MS=PTC here AUX-2MS=PTC there
Are you here? Are you there? (PT 248b)

(1b) The narrator describes his attire for a hunting-trip to the marshes:
*sṯs-w* *ḥr-rmn* *ꜥ-ı͗*
staves-P on-shoulder arm-1S
...with staves being upon the shoulder of my arm. (*Lit. Fragm.* pl. 3, 4.6)

(1c) Sinuhe tells of his fortunate position:
*sḫꜣwy-ı͗* *m-ꜥḥ*
memory-1S in-palace
The memory of me is in the palace. (Sin B, 156)

In Earlier Egyptian, constructions of the sort exemplified above represent the structural and semantic-pragmatic core of adverbial sentences. They are strictly non-verbal, there is no copular or auxiliary element, and the predication concerns a location in space. The predicate follows the subject, understood here as the morpho-syntactically most 'prominent' and least oblique participant that semantically scores highest on the hierarchies of definiteness (definite > other specific > non-specific), person (first/second person > third person), agentivity (agent > goal > recipient > instrumental > locative > temporal), and animacy (human > other animate > inanimate) as well as pragmatically commands the 'main vantage point' and 'principal perspective' from which

1 Historically, the constructions discussed below have been classified as 'adverbial nominal sentences'. This label arises from the traditional dichotomic perception of predication as divisible into 'verbal' and 'nominal', with the latter term encompassing all non-verbal varieties.
2 This definition is borrowed from Hengeveld (1992: 58).

https://doi.org/10.1515/9783110409895-002

a given state of affairs is described.[3] This core construction and sense could be altered and extended considerably by various means. For example, in Earlier Egyptian adverbial sentences could be preceded by auxiliary or introductory particles so as to modify their very rudimentary TAM-properties. Similarly, in this phase of the language adverbial sentences were a *radial* class of constructions both in terms of morpho-syntax and meaning. There were various synchronic and diachronic extensions from the semantic and constructional prototype shown in the above examples, which show structural and/or semantic-pragmatic parallelism and overlap with other sentence types. As will be shown later, the basic or most fundamental meaning of adverbial sentences was from very early on employed metaphorically for the *classification* of the subject, thus aligning them with nominal sentence semantics, and for defining its *temporal* location, a typically verbal function.[4] In the first case, the construction was still grammatically very much an adverbial sentence, and the same holds for some of its temporal extensions as well. However, these latter in particular already occupy a semantic position mid-way between adverbial and verbal sentences, and a full demarcation takes place in sentences of the type [subject + preposition + infinitive], which are purely verbal constructions both semantically and structurally. Nevertheless, they are undeniably related to adverbial sentences both diachronically and in terms of morpho-syntax.

In Earlier Egyptian, as in the later stages of the language, adverbial sentences display a rather rigid internal syntax, word order, and ordering of the grammatical roles, which changed remarkably little during the thousand years of linguistic history between the late Fourth and early Eighteenth Dynasties. The basic schema of the sentence pattern is S > [NP AP]. The *predicate* of an adverbial sentence may be either lexical or phrasal 'adverbial' expression. In the first case, it consists of a single lexeme: in practise, a spatial, temporal, or interrogative adverb. Of the small number of Earlier Egyptian 'real' or 'primary' adverbs – i.e. expressions only used thus (as attributes and/or predicates) and specialised for this syntactic and semantic function – only

**3** This definition of *subject*, a concept that has a notably complex history in Egyptological linguistics, is essentially a combination of definitions proposed in functional and cognitive approaches to language. See e.g. Dik (1997: 266); Grimshaw (1990: 31–33); Langacker (1991: 305–13); Givón (2001 vol. I: 108–09, 196–97). Cf. also Loprieno (1988a: 92–93).

**4** For classifying nominal sentences, see Part II 3.1.2.

the interrogative *ṯn(ỉ)* 'where' and the spatial *ꜥꜣ* 'here' are attested in predicative use:

(2a) A question by a fieldworker to his comrade:
*ỉ(w)-k* *ṯn* *ṯꜣy* *srf–ỉb*
AUX-2MS WH male hot-heart
Where are you, O zealous man? (Junker, *Giza* VI, fig. 43)

(2b) After enduring Sinuhe's eulogy of the pharaoh, Ammunenshi begins his reply by stating the obvious:
*mk=tw* *ꜥꜣ*
PTC=2MS here
Look, you are here. (Sin B, 77)

The interrogative adverb *ṯn(ỉ)* is rarely placed in the initial position before the subject, which, if a personal pronoun, takes the form of a *clitic* pronoun.[5] The resulting construction represents the sole (true) exception to the rule that in Earlier Egyptian adverbial sentences the predicate follows the subject (see below for another apparent exception):

(3a) The opening of PT Spell 388:
*ṯn* *ḥr* *pr* *m-šn-t*
WH N go.PPA from-serpent-F
Where is Horus, who escaped from the serpent? (PT 681a)

(3b) A question asked concerning the deceased:
*ṯn=sw* *pr*
WH=3MS go.forth.PPA
Where is he who has gone forth? (CT II 292a)

More common than predicatively used 'primary' adverbs are 'secondary' lexical adverbials, or lexemes that usually do not outwardly differ from verbal, nominal, adjectival, or prepositional expressions but that may sometimes display extra derivational and/or function-indicating morphology.[6] The latter does not, however, appear in the predicative use of these expressions but

---

5 'Dependent pronoun' in traditional Egyptological terminology. The most thorough discussion of Earlier Egyptian personal pronouns and their etymology and mutual relations is Kammerzell (1991). For the topic at hand, see also Loprieno (1991b: 205–08); *id.* (1995: 144); Gundacker (2010: 59–63) and Uljas (2012a: 255, 264–65).

6 Cf. here the argument of such morphology as 'adverbial transpositor' made by Kammerzell (1990: 188).

only in adjunction, and overall in Earlier Egyptian predicative use of secondary lexical adverbials seems to be restricted to the expressions *ỉm* 'there', *mm* 'among', *ḥnꜥ* 'with', and *ḏr* 'at the limit' derived from – or otherwise functioning as – prepositions (for the negations, sentence-initial elements, and the position of *ỉm* in 4a, see below):

(4a) The shipwrecked sailor describes the wonders of the Phantom Island:

| | | |
|---|---|---|
| *rm-w* | *ỉm* | *ḥnꜥ-ꜣpd-w* |
| fish-P | there | with-bird-P |

There were fish and birds. (Sh.S. 50–51)

(4b) Thutmosis III assures his audience of the trustworthiness of his words:

| | | | |
|---|---|---|---|
| *nn* | *ṯs* | *n(-y)-ỉwms* | *mm* |
| NEG | phrase | of[-M]-lie | there |

There is not a false phrase therein. (*Urk.* IV 835, 14)

(4c) The snake tells why he avoided the fate of his family:

| | | |
|---|---|---|
| *ḫpr-n=rs* | *nn=wỉ* | *ḥnꜥ* |
| happen-PST=PTC | NEG=1S | with |

It so happened that I was not therewith. (Sh.S. 130)

(4d) The sage exclaims at the face of the horrors he describes:

| | | |
|---|---|---|
| *ỉw-ỉ* | *ḏr* | *rsy* |
| AUX-1S | end | completely |

I am completely at end! (lit. 'ended') (Ipuwer 6, 4–5)

Rather than a bare lexical adverb, the predicate of an adverbial sentence was in Earlier Egyptian more often a prepositional phrase, which is syntactically equivalent to an adverb. The element governed by the preposition was typically a suffixed personal pronoun or a noun phrase:

(5a) The shipwrecked sailor says to the snake-god:

| | |
|---|---|
| *ỉw-ỉ* | *m-bꜣḥ-k* |
| AUX-1S | in-front-2MS |

I am before you. (Sh.S. 75)

(5b) The herdsman describes his fear upon seeing a naked goddess:

| | |
|---|---|
| *šfšf-t-s* | *ḫt-ḥꜥ-ỉ* |
| fear-F-3FS | throughout-body-1S |

The fear of her was throughout my body. (Herdsman 7)

(5c) Sinuhe describes his awe before the king:

| | | | |
|---|---|---|---|
| *ỉw-ỉ* | *mỉ-s* | *ỉt-w* | *m-ꜥḫḫw* |
| AUX-1S | like-man | seize.PPP-M | in-twilight |

I was like a man seized in the twilight. (Sin B, 254)

Less often, the governed expression could also be an interrogative pronoun (exx. 6a and 6b), a preposition-derived 'relational' noun[7] (ex. 6c), a participle (6d), or a relative form – a finite verb form inflected, like a participle, for number and gender and used, amongst other things, as a modifier of an (overt or covert) NP antecedent (6e; see Loprieno 1995: 203–204). However, the last three of these are attested only with the so-called *m* of predication and *r* of futurity in semantically specialised adverbial sentences used for classification of the subject and for the expression of tense (see 3.2.4):

(6a) A question in a mathematical puzzle for finding the need of daily bread rations:
*ỉw-f* *r-wr*
AUX-3MS to-WH
What does it amount to? (lit. 'It corresponds to how much?')
(pMoscow Math. n.23, 5)

(6b) A divine being asks the deceased:
*ỉw-k=tr* *r-ṯn*
AUX-2MS=PTC to-WH
Where are you off to? (CT V 68e)

(6c) The peasant comments upon the character of a dishonest judge:
*ỉw-f* *m-ỉm(-y)-ḥꜣ-t* *n-ỉrr*
AUX-3MS as-in.RLT[-M]-front-F to-do.PIA
He is a model for a criminal. (Peas B1, 249)

(6d) Ptahhetep stresses the universality of obedience:
*mꜣ-w* *m-sḏm-w*
see.PPA-M as-hear.PIA-M
He who has seen is he who hears. (Ptahhetep 569)

(6e) Ptahhetep says of a disobedient son in relation to the gods:
*wd* *r-k* *m-ẖbd-n-sn*
struggle.PIA against-2MS as-reject.REL-PST-3P
He who struggles against you is one whom they have rejected.
(Ptahhetep 216)

7 These are the so-called *nisbes* of traditional Arabic grammar; see Loprieno (1995: 56).

Infinitives are also found in adverbial sentences of this type:

(7) Heqanakhte begins his letter to a superior with a standard epistolary cliché:
*ỉw* *ḫr-t-k* *mỉ-ꜥnḫ* *ḥḥ* *n(-y)-sp*
AUX condition-F-2MS like-live.INF million of[-M]-occasion
Your condition is like living a million times. (Heqanakhte III, r° 3)

The *subject* of an Earlier Egyptian adverbial sentence (see also Loprieno 1995: 146–147) can be any expression capable of assuming the function of an NP found in the language. This class naturally includes bare nouns (ex. 8a) and noun phrases (8b), but also infinitives (8c), participles (8d), and relative forms (8e). The last two are again attested only with the *m* of predication and *r* of futurity (see 3.2.4):

(8a) The man laments his weariness of life:
*ỉw* *m-t* *m-ḥr-ỉ* *m-mỉn*
AUX death-F in-face-1S in-today
Death is before me today (Man and Ba 130)

(8b) Wepwawetaa says that he found special favour with the king:
*mr-w-ỉ* *m-sṯpsꜣ*
love-M-1S in-residence
The love of me was in the residence. (*Lesestücke* 74, 16–17)

(8c) Ptahhetep argues that nourishment is god-given:
*ỉw* *wnm* *tꜣ* *ḫr-sḫr* *nṯr*
AUX eat.INF bread under-plan god
Eating bread depends on god's plan. (Ptahhetep 142)

(8d) Neferty describes the prevailing chaos:
*ỉry-t* *m-tm-t=ỉrỉ*
do.PPP-F as-AUX.NEG.PP-F=do.NC
What has been done is what should not be done. (Neferty IVc)

(8e) The loyalist teacher says concerning the king:
*ỉw* *ḥsy-f* *r-nb* *ꜥꜣb-t* *ỉw*
AUX favour.REL.FUT-3MS to-lord offering-F AUX
*rqy-f* *r-ỉwt-y-f*
reject.REL.FUT-3MS to-REL.NEG-M-3MS
The one whom he favours will be a lord of offerings; the one whom he rejects will be a pauper. (*Loyaliste* §3, 9–10)

The degree of definiteness of the nominal subject of the adverbial sentence does not affect the overall construction in Earlier Egyptian. However, as will be shown below, this situation changes gradually in Later Egyptian (1.2.1). Potential instances of the later syntactic marking of indefinite subjects by means of the existential auxiliary *wn* appear already in early New Kingdom monumental texts:

(9) The background of a rebellion in Nubia is reported to King Thutmosis II:

*sṯ* *wn* *wr* *ḥr-mḥt-t* *kš* *ẖs-t* *wꜣ-f* *r-ṯr*
PTC AUX chief on-north-F N vile-F fall-3MS to-season
*n(-y)-rt-t*
of[-M]-disobedience-F
There is now a chief north of vile Kush involved in a conspiracy.
(*Urk.* IV 139, 2–3)

Of personal pronoun subjects of adverbial sentences, clitic pronouns (ex. 10a) are most common alongside the so-called suffix pronouns, which appear to represent incorporated person-marking endings (10b and 10c):

(10a) The shipwrecked sailor says to the snake-god:
*mk=wỉ* *r-gs-k*
PTC=1S to-side-2MS
See, I am beside you. (Sh.S. 108)

(10b) Amenemhab says that he took part in the Syrian wars of Thutmosis III:
*ỉw-ỉ* *m-šmsw-t-f*
AUX-1S in-following-F-3MS
I was in his following. (*Urk.* IV 892, 7)

(10c) Sinuhe ends his tale by telling how he once again became a royal courtier:
*ỉw-ỉ* *ẖr-ḥs-w-t* *n-t-ẖrnsw* *r-ỉw-t* *hrw*
AUX-1S under-praise-P-F of-F-before king to-come-TERM day
*n(-y)-mnỉ*
of[-M]-moor.INF
I remained in the king's favour until the day of passing away arrived.
(Sin B, 309–10)

In certain instances, the personal pronoun subject may also be coded as the agreement ending of the so-called Stative verb form, but this seems to occur mostly when the adverbial sentence is assigned a special information structure by means of the auxiliary *wn/wnn* (see section 3.1.3.1.2):

(11) Queen Hatshepsut says of her status as a daughter of god:
*wn-kw=[r]f* *m-ḥꜥ* *wꜥ* *ḥnꜥ-f* *sẖpr-n-f=wỉ*
AUX-STA.1S=PTC in-flesh one with-3MS create-PST-3MS=1S
*r-rdỉt* *wsr* *qꜣ-w-t-f* *m-tꜣ=pn*
to-cause.INF mighty power-P-F-3MS in-land=DEM.M
Having been of one flesh with him, he created me to impose the might of his power over this land. (*Urk.* IV 385, 3–4)

Both suffix and clitic personal pronouns required some preceding host-expression. In the case of the clitic pronouns, which are grammatically analysable as second position 'Wackernagel' clitics, this was often one of the so-called initial particles, the most common being the presentative element *mk/mṯ/mṯn* 'look' in ex. 10a.[8] Earlier Egyptian also displays a set of auxiliary elements, the most common of which is the element *ỉw*. As will be discussed in more detail later, this element typically appeared in initial main clauses and, as in exx. 10b and 10c, provided a readily available incorporation-base (locus of attachment) for suffix pronoun subjects of adverbial sentences. It is often assumed that the use of these introductory elements was motivated solely by the affix and clitic status of the suffix and clitic pronouns and that they had to be used so that the adverbial sentence could have a pronominal subject (e.g. Depuydt 1999: 225). However, there are various indicators showing that rather than as part of syntax, initial particles and auxiliaries should primarily be seen as part of the array of semantic-pragmatic modifiers associated with adverbial sentences. As can be seen from many of the above examples, initial particles and auxiliaries are commonly used in adverbial sentences with noun subjects as well. This shows that the use of such an element was not, even in case of pronouns, only or even primarily motivated by the structural requirement of providing a host expression for suffixing or cliticising. Further sure signs of this are subordinate adverbial sentences, discussed in 2.1.2. It will be seen that relative past and present adverbial sentence adjunct clauses with noun subjects could be 'embedded' directly without introducing elements, whereas in ones with pronominal subjects, the appearance of a host particle was obligatory – rather in line with the idea of the structural motivation for the use of the latter. Yet in adjunct clauses with future reference (e.g. final clauses), no direct 'embedding' was allowed, and all adverbial sentences had to be preceded by the auxiliary element *wn/wnn*, regardless of the type of their subjects. There are also instances of independent adverbial sentences where a pronominal subject is coded with an initial ***absolute*** personal pronoun (see also Allen 1994: 6):

(12a) The king is on his way to heaven:

| | | | | | |
|---|---|---|---|---|---|
| *ỉr-p-t* | *ỉr-p-t* | *m-ꜥb-nṯr-w* | *prwt-w* | *ỉnk* | *ỉr-p-t* |
| to-sky-F | to-sky-F | in-midst-god-P | emergent-P | 1S | to-sky-F |
| *m-ꜥb-nṯr-w* | *prwt-w* | | | | |
| in-midst-god-P | emergent-P | | | | |

To sky, to sky, amidst the emergent gods! *I* am to the sky, among the emergent gods! (PT 1114a–b/P)

**8** For 'initial particles' in general, see Oréal (2011: *passim*).

(12b) Mery says that his work on religious buildings was met with approval:

| | | | | |
|---|---|---|---|---|
| *wsỉr* | *ḫnt(-y)ỉmntw* | *ḥꜥ* | *m-mn-w* | *n-w-nb(-ỉ)* |
| N | N | jubilate.STA.3MS | in-monument-P | of-P-lord[-1S] |

| | | |
|---|---|---|
| *ỉnk* | *ḏs(-ỉ)* | *m-ḥꜥ-w-t* |
| 1S | self[-1S] | in-jubilation-P-F |

Osiris Foremost of Westeners was jubilant with the monuments of my lord, and *I myself* was in jubilation. (Louvre C3, 7)

Constructions of this sort are quite rare, but they are nevertheless grammatically well formed and have a clearly defined pragmatic role within the category of adverbial sentences (see 3.1.2.1). Finally, it is clear that initial particles stand at the far left-periphery of the clause; witness, in the following example, the use of the particle *ỉst* before an adverbial sentence whose subject is ante-posed outside the clausal frame by means of the element *ỉr* (see also 3.1.3.2):

(13) In a description of a pool in a narrative story:

| | | | | | | |
|---|---|---|---|---|---|---|
| *ỉst=rf* | *ỉr* | *pꜣ-mw* | *ỉw-f* | *m-mḥ* | *12* | *ḥr-ỉꜣ-t-f* |
| PTC=PTC | PTC | DEM.M-water | AUX-3MS | as-cubit | 12 | on-back-F-3MS |

Now, as for this water, it was 12 cubits deep (lit. 'on its back'). (pWestcar 6, 10–11)

As will be discussed in 1.2.1, Late Egyptian saw a thorough reorganisation of the adverbial and verbal syntax, and an important part of this process was the grammaticalisation of a set of prefixed ('preformative') personal pronouns used in the group of conjugations known in descriptive Egyptian-Coptic linguistics as Present I. First instantiations of these pronouns are found in late Seventeenth/early Eighteenth Dynasty texts; below are two early examples of their use in adverbial sentences:

(14a) The pharaoh's courtiers, fearful of attacking the Hyksos king, express their preference for the status quo:

| | | | | |
|---|---|---|---|---|
| *sw* | *ẖr-tꜣ* | *[n(-y)]-ꜥꜣm-w* | *tw-n* | *ẖr-kmt* |
| 3MS | under-land | of[-M]-Asiatic-P | PTC-1P | under-Egypt |

He controls (lit. 'is under') the land of the Asiatics, but we hold sway over Egypt. (Carnarvon Tablet 7)

(14b) Emheb says of his lord:

| | |
|---|---|
| *sw* | *m-nṯr* |
| 3MS | as-god |

He is a god. (Cairo JE 49566, 11)

As in the other members of the Present I group, in Late Egyptian the prefix pronouns completely replace the suffix and clitic personal pronouns as subjects of adverbial sentences (see again 1.2.1 for discussion and examples).

In Earlier Egyptian, the subject of an adverbial sentence may also be a demonstrative pronoun:

(15a) Words said by a fowler with a mighty catch of netted birds:
*ı͗w nn n-kꜣ n(-y)-ṯy*
AUX DEM.M to-soul of[-M]-N
This is for the soul of Ti (*Ti* pl. 116)

(15b) After citing some wise words, Rekhmira notes:
*ı͗w nꜣ m-sbꜣy-t*
AUX DEM.M in-instruction-F
This is from an instruction (i.e. a wisdom text). (*Urk.* IV 1090, 3)

Interrogative pronouns appear only as predicates in adverbial sentences. The adverbial sentence subject could also be a target of ellipsis if it had an indeterminate, strongly situational (and hence obvious), and/or anaphorically highly continuous reference[9]:

(16a) Sinuhe tells Ammunenshi: 'I do not know what separated me from my abode...'
*ı͗w-ø mı͗-sšm rsw-t*
AUX-Ø like-manner dream-F
(It) was like a manner of a dream. (Sin B, 224–25)

(16b) Words of a priest presenting offerings:
*ı͗w-ø n-kꜣ-ṯ*
AUX-Ø to-soul-2FS
(It) is for your soul. (Junker, *Giza* XI, fig. 105)

(16c) A magician has just told the king that he knows where a certain charm is; then:
*ḏd-ı͗n ḥm-f ı͗w-ø=ı͗rf tn*
say-SEQ majesty-3MS AUX-Ø=PTC WH
*ḏd-ı͗n ḏdı͗=pn ı͗w ꜥfd-t ı͗m n-t-ds m-ꜥ-t*
say-SEQ N=DEM.M AUX chest-F there of-F-flint in-room-F
*sı͗pty rn-s m-ı͗wnw*
inventory name-3FS in-N
*ø m-tꜣ-ꜥfd-t*
ø in-DEM.F-chest-F
Said his majesty: 'So, where is (it)?' This Djedi said: 'There is a chest of flint in a room called "Inventory" in Heliopolis. (It) is in this chest'.
(pWestcar 9, 4–5)

9 Subject omission has been much studied in Egyptology. Of the many discussions, the most recent and extensive is Vernus (2014).

With interrogative predicates, the subject of an adverbial sentence can also occur as overt or covert cataphoric pronoun semantically co-indexed with an appositive NP in the sentence[10]:

(17a) It is asked of Horus:

| | | | |
|---|---|---|---|
| *ı͗(w)-f* | *ṯn* | *ı͗h=pn* | *ꜥꜣ* |
| AUX-3MS | WH | shouter=DEM.M | great |

Where is he$_i$, (namely) [this great shouter]$_i$? (CT VI 212b/S11C)

(17b) A question in a mathematical text:

| | | | | |
|---|---|---|---|---|
| *ı͗w-ø=tr* | *ṯn* | *ẖtm* | *ı͗wꜣ-w-k* | *ꜥšꜣ* |
| AUX-Ø=PTC | WH | N | COW-P-2MS | many |

Where is (it)$_i$ then, [the *ẖtm* of your many cows]$_i$? (pRhind math. n.67, 3)

Deviations from the basic ordering of the subject and predicate as S–P are very rare in Earlier Egyptian. Personal pronoun datives built with the preposition *n* 'to' + suffix pronoun are in Earlier (and most of the Later) Egyptian treated as second position clitics. In bare adverbial sentences consisting of nothing but an NP subject and a personal pronoun dative predicate, the former naturally precedes the latter (for the possessive sense, see 3.1.4):

(18) The deceased is told:

*bꜣ-k=n-k*

soul-2MS=to-2MS

You (shall?) have your soul. (CT I 162e)

Yet when an adverbial sentence of this sort is preceded by e.g. an auxiliary, the order of the two constituents is reversed:

(19) A harpist sings to his deceased master:

| | | | |
|---|---|---|---|
| *ı͗w=n-k* | *ṯꜣw* | *nḏm* | *n(-y)-mḥy-t* |
| AUX=to-2MS | wind | sweet | of[-M]-north.RLT-F |

Yours is the sweet northern wind. (*Lesestücke* 87, 7)

However, this is wholly in accord with the regular word order rules of Earlier Egyptian and not a true 'exception' to the S–P rule in adverbial sentences. The pronominal dative has to cliticise to the first prosodic unit of the clause, which in ex. 19 is the initial auxiliary, but as ex. 18 shows, the dative follows the subject just like any other prepositional phrase when no such element is present. Nevertheless, a short predicative adverb or prepositional phrase may sometimes break the phrasal

10 This is the standard Late Egyptian pattern; see section 1.2.1.

continuity of a syntactically more complex subject, such as a noun phrase with the indirect genitival element *n(y)* 'of' in the following examples (cf. Gardiner 1957: §121):

(20a) Sinuhe describes the house of the king's son:

*sḏꜣ-w-t* *im-f* *n-t-prḥḏ*
valuable-P-F in-3MS of-F-treasury
There were valuables of the treasury in it. (Sin B, 287–88)

(20b) Henu tells of his expedition to the mines:

*ʿḥʿ-n(-i)* *pr-kw* *m-gbtw* *ḥr-mtn* *wḏ-n=n(-i)*
AUX-PST[-1S] go-STA.1S from-N on-road order.REL-PST=to[-1S]
*ḥm-f* *mšʿ* *ḥnʿ(-i)* *n(-y)-šmʿ*
majesty-3MS army with[-1S] of[-M]-N
Then I set forth from Coptos on the road, which his majesty had ordained to me, with an expeditionary force of Upper Egypt being with me.
(*Hammamat* 114, 10–11)

This phenomenon is seemingly motivated by the mutual syntactic and prosodic 'weight' of the subject and predicate. In cases such as ex. 20a, where there is an apparent dissonance between the structural complexity of these constituents, the predicate *im-f* behaves like a clitic and separates the subject head noun *sḏꜣ-w-t* 'valuables' from its attributive genitive *n-t-pr-ḥḏ* 'of the treasury'. Again, one can scarcely speak of true reversal of the ordering of grammatical roles here. The only instance where this actually occurs is when the predicate of the adverbial sentence is the interrogative adverb *ṯn*, which, as noted, sometimes appears before the subject:

(21) In an obscure context:

*ṯni=sw=irf* *iri* *nšn* *wd* *šd*
WH=3MS=PTC do.PPA strife put.PPA fire
Where is he, (namely) the one who created strife and cast forth fire?
(CT VII 961)

Similar examples do not occur in adverbial sentences with predicative interrogative phrases (e.g. *mi-m* 'like what'), but there are some rare instances of verbal constructions where interrogative expressions of this sort indeed appear sentence-initially.[11] It would thus seem that this represents one of the means by which the information structure of the proposition could affect the relatively static syntax of all these sentence types (see 3.1.2.1 for further discussion).

Finally, adverbial sentences occasionally incorporate various kinds of clitic particles that modify the illocutionary force of the sentence (Oréal 2011). A good

11 See Uljas (2012a: 257) for examples.

number of such elements are attested in Earlier Egyptian, but with adverbial sentences only some have been documented. The clitic particle =*ꜣ*, which in statements seems to imply a degree of speaker incredulity and disbelief, occurs with adverbial sentences only after the desiderative initial element *ḥꜣ*/*ḥw* 'would that/if only':

(22) The deceased expresses his desire to be in the retinue of Hathor:
*ḥw=ꜣ=wỉ* *ỉm*
PTC=PTC=1S there
If only I were there! (CT IV 48d)

The contrastive clitic particle =*swt* 'but' is also rare, as are the dubitative element =*tr*, the additive =*gr*(*t*) 'moreover', and the slightly obscure =*ms*, which perhaps means 'alas':

(23a) The peasant remarks, implying contrast with the high steward's conduct:
*ỉw=swt* *mꜣꜥ-t* *r-nḥḥ*
AUX=but justice-F to-eternity
But justice is forever. (Peas B1, 338)

(23b) In a damaged context:
*ỉw-k=tr* *m-m* *n(-y)-nṯr*
AUX-2MS=PTC as-WH of[-M]-god
Which god are you, in fact? (pRamesseum I, A15)

(23c) The sage recalls times when the Egyptian army was respected abroad:
*ỉw=grt* *ḫꜣs-w-t=nb* *ḫr{t}-snḏ-w-f*
AUX=PTC foreign land-P-F=QU.M under-fear-M-3MS
Moreover, all foreign lands were in fear of it. (Ipuwer 15, 2)

(23d) The sage describes the people of Egypt in chaos:
*ỉw=ms* *rmṯ* *mỉ-gm-w*
AUX=PTC people like-black_ibis-P
Alas, people are like black ibises. (Ipuwer 2, 8)

The various versions of the clitic =(*ỉ*)*r* + suffix (e.g. =(*ỉ*)*rk*, =(*ỉ*)*rf*), which signals whether the clause relates primarily to some of the speech participants or to the entire context, are also found with adverbial sentences:

(24) A question concerning the yon ferry:
*ỉw-s=ỉrf* *m-ỉšst*
AUX-3FS=PTC as-WH
So, what is it? (CT V 91d/T1Be)

Adverbial sentences with the clitic particle =*ỉs* are also commonly found, but, as will be shown later, this element is best understood functionally within the clausal syntax of these constructions (see 2.1.3 and 2.1.5).

## 1.2 Later Egyptian

As in Earlier Egyptian, predicative constructions in which the predicate is an adverb or an adverbial phrase are common in Later Egyptian, but they are no longer the dominant type of non-verbal sentences in the language. As will be observed later, this role was gradually assumed by the nominal sentences, which took over several semantic functions that had earlier been fulfilled by the adverbial sentence. Similarly, the general template of the Later Egyptian adverbial syntagm is still S > [NP AP], but, unlike in the earlier language, the use of introductory particles is much less frequent. As in earlier phases, the subject position is occupied by a nominal phrase, typically a noun or a pronoun. If the subject is an indefinite noun, in Late Egyptian and Demotic one observes a split system of morphological versus syntactic marking, of which only the latter survives in Coptic. The morphological pattern makes use of the indefinite articles with the subject NP (*wꜥ-* for singular, *nhi n-/hyn-* for plural) without any further introductory particle, whereas in the syntactic pattern, the bare subject is preceded by the initial element *wn* (Late Egyptian and Demotic) or *un/uon* (Coptic):

S > [*wn*-ø-$\text{NP}_{\text{-DEF}}$ AP]
S > [ø-IDF-$\text{NP}_{\text{-DEF}}$ AP]

As in the earlier language, the predicate position of Later Egyptian adverbial sentences may be occupied by adverbs and prepositional phrases:

- Adverb
  [*pek-son*]$_\text{S}$ [*tai*]$_\text{P}$ Your brother (*pek-son*) is here (*tai*).
- Prepositional phrase
  [*ṯ-k*]$_\text{S}$ [*mi-ꜥꜣ*]$_\text{P}$ You (*ṯ-k*) are like a donkey (*mi-ꜥꜣ*).

The use of morphologically identified adverbs is still rare in Later Egyptian, and the category itself has a rather limited number of specimens. Instead, prepositional phrases are mostly employed in place of adverbs. In Coptic, several prepositional phrases are no longer segmentable and have thus acquired the status of lexical adverbs.

The identification of subject and predicate presents no difficulty in Later Egyptian adverbial sentences. There are, however, no syntactic rule(s) for determining the predicative AP in cases where more than one appears. Instead, this must be deduced from the context; cf. the following Late Egyptian sentences:

*Late Egyptian*

(25a) A note added to a list of thirteen thieves given by a suspected tomb robber:

| | | | |
|---|---|---|---|
| *ḏd-f* | *wn-w* | *irm-i* | *m-tꜣ-s-t* |
| say.PST-3MS | IPF-3P | with-1S | in-DEF.F-place-F |

He said: 'They were with me in the place.' (*KRI* VI 770, 7)

(25b) After first wanting to kill him, the Syrian chief is won over by the Egyptian prince and says:

| | | | | | |
|---|---|---|---|---|---|
| *i͗-dd=n-i͗* | *qꜣi͗-k* | *ptr* | *ṯ-k* | *mdi͗-i͗* | *m-šri͗* |
| IMP-say=to-1S | background-2MS | look | PTC-2MS | with-1S | as-child |

Tell me your background! Look, you are a child to me. (*LES* 6, 5)

(25c) The pharaoh acclaims his right to the throne:

| | | | |
|---|---|---|---|
| *ṯ-i͗* | *m-s-t* | *wtt-i͗* | *mi͗-sꜣ-ist* |
| PTC-1S | in-place-F | progenitor-1S | like-son-N |

I am in the place of my progenitor like the son of Isis. (*KRI* VI 23, 6)

In ex. 25a, the first adverbial phrase *irm-i͗* 'with me' is the predicate rather than the following locative adjunct *m-tꜣ-s-t* 'in the place'. In ex. 25b, neither *mdi͗-i͗* 'with/ to me' nor *m-šri͗* 'as a child' alone is the predicate, but the complex *mdi͗-i͗ m-šri͗* as a whole. Finally, in ex. 25c, the location of the pharaoh seems more central than the equative adverbial. These criteria are, however, based purely on contextual deductions of a rather intuitive sort.

In Coptic, pronominal subjects and the adverbial predicate form a phonological unit, as we can infer from the fact that clitic particles cannot intervene between the two. If the subject is a noun, this is not the case, and clitics appear freely between the subject and the predicate. The situation in the earlier stages of Later Egyptian is more difficult to discern because of the relative rarity of examples with clitisation of the adverb *dy* 'here', which in Late Egyptian cliticises to the pronoun even when it is not the predicate – showing that the subject and the predicate do not form a prosodic word. In Demotic, *dy* appears to lose its clitic properties. If it appears immediately after the pronoun, it usually functions as predicate. In what follows, Late Egyptian examples will be cited with pronominal subjects separated from the adverbial predicates and Demotic and Coptic examples will be glossed with their pronominal subjects combined with their predicates.

A further problem is raised by the opaque distinction between adverbial sentences with indefinite subjects and existential sentences. Clearly existential are, of course, sentences that contain no adverbial phrase whatsoever. Yet if an adverb or an adverbial phrase is involved, the decision between the two sentence types is impossible on syntactic grounds, and it is often problematic semantically as well:[12]

**12** Note that in the attempt to be as descriptive as possible, both existential *un-* and the marker of indefinite subjects *un-* are glossed as particle (PTC) here, since a decision, which of the functions is intended, is at times rather difficult.

*Coptic*

(26a) The idols of the heathen are described as inferior works of human hands:
*mn-pn(eum)a* *hn-rô-u*
NEG-breath in-mouth-3P
No breath is in their mouths. ($^{S}$Ps 134 [135]:17)

(26b) The inscription upon a Coptic tombstone declares:
*mn-at-mu* *hicn-p-kah*
NEG-NEG-die upon-DEF.M-earth
There is no immortality upon earth. ($^{S}$CG 8631, 2–3)

(26c) Salome told Jesus that she would not be in doubt:
*mn-meue* *hn-pa-hêt* *e-f-pats*
NEG-thought in-POSS.M.1S-heart DEP-3MS-split.STA
*e-f-parc*
DEP-3MS-divide.STA
There is no thought in my heart that is split or divided.
($^{L}$*Psalms of Thomas* 223, 3)

(26d) When questioned about divorce, Jesus argues:
*un-sior=gar* *ncin-t-kalahê* *n-te-u-meu*
PTC-eunuch=for since-DEF.F-womb of-POSS.F-3P-mother
*e-ha-u-cpa-u* *n-tei-hê*
DEP-PST-3P-bear-3P in-DEM.F-way
*auô* *un-sior* *e-ha-u-e-u* *n-sior* *ebal* *hitn-n-rome*
and PTC-eunuch DEP-PST-3P-do-3P as-eunuch out by-DEF.P-man
*un-sior* *e-ha-f-e-f* *n-sior* *ebal* *hitat-f* *mmin* *mma-f*
PTC-eunuch DEP-PST-3MS-do-3MS as-eunuch out by-3MS own of-3MS
*etbe-t-mnt-era* *n-m-pê*
because-DEF.F-ABST-king of-DEF.P-heaven
For there are eunuchs who were born like this since the womb of their mother; there are eunuchs who were made eunuchs by men, and there are eunuchs who choose to live like that for the sake of the kingdom of heaven.
($^{M}$Mt 19:12 mae 1)

(26e) The proverbs speak about wealth:
*uon-han-uon=de* *e-u-sôrem* *n-nê* *ete-nu-u*
PTC-IDF.P-one=yet DEP-3P-lose OBJ-DEF$_{3}$.P REL-POSS.P-3P
*uoh* *a-u-nêu* *n-er-huo*
and ST-3P-come.STA in-do-more
There are some who lose what they possess and yet come out wealthier.
($^{B}$Prv 11:24)

Both readings 'No breath exists in their mouths' and 'No breath is in their mouth' seem plausible in ex. 26a. However, syntactic differences between the two patterns may have played a role. For instance, a Coptic existential sentence can be coordinated with a verbal sentence with a verb in the Conjunctive form whereas adverbial sentences cannot:

*Coptic*

(27) St John asks the Cherub:

| | | | |
|---|---|---|---|
| *pa-c(oi)s* | *un-u-rompe* | *nte-p-mou* | *sbok* |
| POSS.M.1S-lord | PTC-IDF.S-year | CNJ-DEF.M-water | be_few |

| | |
|---|---|
| *nte-p-he-nufe* | *šôpe* |
| CNJ-DEF.M-season-good | happen |

| | | | |
|---|---|---|---|
| *un-u-rompe* | *on* | *nte-p-mou* | *r-nok*$^{j}$ |
| PTC-IDF.S-year | again | CNJ-DEF.M-water | make-great |

| | |
|---|---|
| *nte-p-hebôôn* | *šôpe* |
| CNJ-DEF.M-season-bad | happen |

My lord, there is a year when water is scarce and there is plenty. And then again there is a year when water is abundant and there is famine.

($^{S}$*Mysteries of St John Evangelist* [Budge, *Apocrypha* 60, 33–61, 1]

In most grammatical works on Later Egyptian, adverbial sentences are treated as a member of a conjugation pattern known as Present I (see Loprieno 1995: 93), which includes also purely verbal patterns. However, such an approach ignores the differences in temporal function(s) between verbal and adverbial constructions. Syntactically, the verbal constructions subsumed under the label Present I and its derivations seem to be identical with sentences with adverbial predicates treated here, but the former show fully verbal behaviour already in Earlier Egyptian (see 3.1.4). Similarly, the verb forms used in the Later Egyptian Present I formation (infinitives and the stative) are not used as adverbials outside this particular construction. Moreover, while the infinitival Present I construction *sw-ḥr-irt* 'He does/is doing' expresses a temporal relationship, sentences with adverbial predicate do not. That is, propositions such as *sw-m-bwt n-rmṯ* 'He is the abomination of mankind' are not temporally limited to the context of the utterance situation but rather should be regarded as (relatively) atemporal, although, in principle, susceptible to change.[13] For these reasons, Later Egyptian adverbial sentences are here considered separately from the verbal patterns belonging to the Present I formation.

**13** See section 3.1.3.1.1 for the importance of this notion in Earlier Egyptian.

### 1.2.1 Late Egyptian

In Late Egyptian, the structure of adverbial sentences does not differ greatly from Earlier Egyptian. The sentence *subject*, if marked for definiteness, occupies the absolute initial position:

(28a) The pharaoh quarrels with his washermen:
*stj sgnn m-nꜣ-n-ḥbs n-prꜥꜣ*
[scent ointment]$_S$ [in-DEF.P-PTC-garment of-pharaoh]$_P$
The scent of ointment is in the garments of the pharaoh. (*LES* 20, 12)

(28b) During the nocturnal journey of the sun god, the land is at peace:
*s=nb m-ḏbꜣ-t-f*
[man=QU]$_S$ [in-coffin-F-3MS]$_P$
Everyone is in his coffin. (CG 25206, 10)

(28c) A woman in charge of foreigners at the harim at Miwer complains of them in a letter to the pharaoh:
*pꜣwn nꜣ-nty=dy m-ẖrd-w ꜥꜣ-y*
because [DEF-REL=here]$_S$ [as-children-P great-P]$_P$
...for those that are here are big children! (*RAD* 14, 9)

(28d) The victory of the Egyptians has a devastating effect on their Libyan foes:
*nry ꜥꜣ m-ḥꜣty-w-sn n-tꜣmry*
fear great in-heart-P-3P for-Egypt
The great fear for Egypt is in their hearts. (*KRI* IV 14, 4)

(28e) The sender of a letter repeats instructions the adressee had given him earlier to enter a stable at a house. Opposite two millstones, he is told, should be two pits:
*nꜣ-n-ḫꜥ-w n-ḥmtı m-ẖnw-sn*
DEF.P-of-tool-P of-copper in-inside-3P
The copper tools are in them. (*HO* 88 r° 4)

(28f) Pharaoh Ramesses III reports to the God Amun about his deeds for the god for his temple at Karnak. He erected a large jar stand for him:
*nꜣy-f-stı-y n-nbw ẖr-ırp ḥnq-t r-ḥnk-w*
POSS.P-3MS-pitcher-P of-gold under-wine beer-F to-present-3P
*r-ḫft-ḥr-k r-tnı dwꜣ-t*
to-opposite-face-2MS to-every morning-F
Its pitchers of gold are filled with wine and beer to offer them in front of you each morning. (pHarris I 6, 1)

If the subject was indefinite, it could be marked using either a morphological or a syntactic pattern. In the former the subject NP was prefixed with the indefinite article, *wꜥ-* in the singular (with additional gender-marking) and *nhꞽ n-* in the plural without any introductory particle (for further examples in subordinate clauses, see below):

(29a) After being repeatedly interrogated with the help of a bastinado, a suspected tomb robber says:
*sḏm-ꞽ* *rḏd-wꜥ-ksks-t* *mdꞽ-N* *ꞽw-s* *mḥ-tꞽ*
hear.PST-1S COMP-IDF.S-basket-F with-N DEP-3FS fill-STA.3FS
*m-nbw* *ꞽw-ns-sw-pꜣ-ẖr*
in-gold DEP-belong-3S-DEF.M-tomb
I heard that a basket filled with gold belonging to 'the tomb' is with the chief-doorkeeper Thutmosis. (K*RI* VI 776, 2–3)

(29b) A boy brought his blinded father into a house:
*ꞽw-f* *ḥr-dꞽ-ḥms-f* *wꜥ-qnꞽ* *ẖr-f*
DEP-3MS PRP-give-sit-3MS IDF.S-chair under-3MS
...and he made him sit down. He sat upon a chair (*lit.* a chair was under him). (*LES* 33, 7–8)

In the syntactic marking pattern, the sentence was usually introduced by the particle *wn*. This particle had an existential verbal origin, but in adverbial sentences, it had no verbal or predicative function but rather marked the bare (article-less) indefinite subject:

(30a) The sister-in-law tells the younger brother:
*wn-pḥty* [*ꜥꜣ*] *ꞽm-k*
[PTC-power great]$_S$ [in-2MS]$_P$
You are very strong! (lit. 'there is great strength in you') (*LES* 12, 8)

(30b) The ascension of King Merenptah is described:
*wn-pḥty* *ꞽm-f* *r-ꞽrt*
[PTC-power]$_S$ [in-3MS to-act.INF]$_P$
He has the ability to act (lit. 'there is strength in him to act'). (K*RI* IV 3, 11)

(30c) After giving orders to his family at home, Thutmosis ends his letter with the following remark:
*yꜣ* *wn-hrw=dy* *r-ḥꜣ-t-tn*
PTC [PTC-day]=[t/here to-front-F-2P]
So, there is a day ahead of you there. (*LRL* 10, 8–9)

One might expect the particle *wn* to be mandatory also in existential sentences whose subject is indefinite, but genuine examples without any further adverbial adjunct and clearly analysable as existentials are rare. The predicative analysis of *wn* has led various scholars to view some of the examples above as existential – i.e. verbal – rather than non-verbal adverbial sentences. This difficulty of differentiating between existential and adverbial sentences is a consistent feature of adverbial sentence syntax and semantics.

The subject of a sentence with an adverbial predicate may also be pronominal; below is an example with the interrogative pronoun *nym* 'who':

(31) After some advise on how to behave towards elder or higher ranking persons, the reader is told:
*nym=dy* *ḫr-ṯ* *rꜥ=nb*
[WH]$_S$=[here]$_P$ say-one day=QU
'Who is here?' they say daily. (Ani B 19, 13–14)

For personal pronoun subjects of adverbial sentences, Late Egyptian and the subsequent stages of the language employed a specific set of prefixed ('preformative') pronouns (see exx. 14a and 14b for early Eighteenth Dynasty instances):

**Tab. I.1:** Late Egyptian pronominal preformatives in adverbial sentences (common forms only).

| | Singular | Plural |
|---|---|---|
| 1C | *ṯ-i* | *ṯ-n* |
| 2M | *ṯ-k* | *ṯ-tn* |
| 2F | *ṯ-ṯ* | |
| 3M | *sw* | *st* |
| 3F | *st* | |

Except in the third person, these pronouns were etymologically built from the element *ṯ* (usually written 𓏏𓅱 *tw*) of an obscure origin,[14] followed by the corresponding suffix pronoun. For impersonal expressions *ṯ-ṯ* 'one' with *ṯ* plus the indefinite pronoun *ṯ* (also usually written 𓏏𓅱 *tw*) is used. The third person forms *sw* (3MS), *st* (3FS), and *st* (3C) are commonly confused in writing, apparently due to

14 See, however, Vernus (1998: 200–209), for an etymological suggestion concerning the homographic passive morpheme -*ṯ* as the origin of the morpheme. Loprieno (1995: 67), considered the grammaticalisation of the conjunction *ti* > *is* 'while' followed by a suffix pronoun to be the etymological predecessor of this morpheme.

their closely similar phonetic realisation.[15] As the comparison of the third person forms with those of first and second person shows, the element *ṯ* may originally have been a particle. Yet already when the 'preformatives' are first attested in the sources, their etymological constituents are no longer segmentable. Nevertheless, for practical purposes, the element *ṯ* will be glossed here as a particle to allow comparison with the patterns found in subordinate adverbial sentences discussed in 2.2.2.

In Late Egyptian adverbial sentences, the preformative pronouns occupy the subject position in main clauses:

(32a) The younger brother retorts to his sister-in-law's attempts to seduce him:
*ḫr mk ṯ-ṯ mdỉ-ỉ m-sḫr n-mw-t*
PTC PTC [PTC-2FS]$_S$ [with-1S in-state of-mother-F]$_P$
But look, you are like a mother to me. (*LES* 12, 15)

(32b) The plight of the soldier in summer is described:
*ỉw-pꜣ[y-k-š]m m-bꜣw n-ỉmn sw m-bwt n-rmṯ-w*
DEP-POSS.M-2MS-heat as-might of-N [3MS]$_S$ [as-abomination to-people-P]$_P$
Your heat is like the might of Amun; it is an abomination for the people. (*LEM* 59, 4)

In Late Egyptian adverbial sentences, any semantic type of adverbials may appear in the predicate position. As noted, genuine morphological adverbs are rather few in number, although interrogative adverbs form a partial exception to this generalisation; note that in these cases the sentence subject is generally a cataphoric personal pronoun coreferential with an appositional NP following the adverbial predicate:

(33a) The recipient of a satirical letter is questioned about Syrian geography:
*pꜣ-ḫd n-nṯn tnw ỉṯ mỉ-ỉḫ*
[DEF.M-river of-N]$_S$ [WH]$_P$ [N]$_S$ [like-WH]$_P$
Where is Litani river? What is Usu like? ($^{2}$*pAnastasi I* 131, 3–4)

15 See the list given by Junge (2008: 118). Most stable in its graphemic representation appears to be the masculine third person singular form, which is only attested as *sw*. More variation occurs with the feminine third person singular, which varies between *st* (e.g., *KRI* IV 417, 7), *sw* (*KRI* VI 808, 9), *st*$^{\text{PLUR}}$ (*LRL* 28, 11) and *sy* (*Paheri* pl. 3, middle register). However, *sy* is rare both early on and later, but see *KRI* II 87, 12 and 13 *sy m-di-f* 'She is with him'. The same holds also for the third person plural for which sometine the spelling *sn* (*RAD* 77, 3) occurs.

(33b) The Prince of Byblos demands that Wenamun provide official documents to support his claims:

| | | | | | |
|---|---|---|---|---|---|
| *sw* | *tnw* | *pꜣ-wḫꜣ* | *n-ỉmn* | *nty-m-dr-ṯ-k* | |
| [3MS]$_S$ | [WH]$_P$ | DEF.M-document | of-N | REL-in-hand-F-2MS | |
| *sw* | *tnw* | *tꜣ-šꜥ* | *n-pꜣ-ḥmnṯr* | *tpy* | *n-ỉmn* |
| [3MS]$_S$ | [WH]$_P$ | DEF.F-letter-F | of-DEF.M-priest | first | of-N |
| *nty-m-ḏr-ṯ-k* | | | | | |
| REL-in-hand-F-2MS | | | | | |

Where is the rescript of Amun that you (should) have? Where is the letter of the High Priest of Amun that you (should) have? (*LES* 66, 9–10)

(33c) The pharaoh's general concedes to the actions of his correspondent:

| | | |
|---|---|---|
| *sw* | *m-šs* | *pꜣ-ỉ-ỉr-k* |
| [3MS]$_S$ | [in-state]$_P$ | DEF.M-REL-do-2MS |

What you have done is fine. (*LRL* 34, 11–12)

Although interrogative adverbs constitute the majority of examples, other adverbs are also attested as adverbial sentence predicates:

(34) The addressee of a letter is told:

| | |
|---|---|
| *ky-ḏd* | *nꜣ-ꜥr-w=dy* |
| other-say | [DEF.P-scroll-P]$_S$=[here]$_P$ |

Further: The papyrus scrolls are here. (pSt. Petersburg 1118, 6)

A predicative adverbial phrase may be expanded by further adverbials:

(35a) The abridged version of the story about the Battle of Kadesh begins:

| | | | | |
|---|---|---|---|---|
| *ỉst* | *ḥm-f* | *ḥr-ḏꜣhy* | *m-wḏ-t-f* | *sn-nw-t* |
| PTC | majesty-3MS | upon-N | in-expedition-F-3MS | two-ORD-F |
| *n-t-nḫt* | | | | |
| of-F-victory | | | | |

(Date...) when his majesty was in Palestine on his second campaign of victory. (*KRI* II 102, 8)

(35b) In his First Marriage stela, Ramesses II is presented as a hero towering over his opponents:

| | | | |
|---|---|---|---|
| *bꜣ-w-f* | *ỉm-sn* | *mỉ-tkꜣ* | *ḥr-nbỉ* |
| might-P-3MS | in-3P | like-torch | upon-flame |

His might is in them like a burning torch. (*KRI* II 244, 6)

As noted, and unlike in the examples just cited, on basis of syntax alone, it is not always apparent which one of the adverbial phrases following the subject is the actual predicate:

(36) After first wanting to kill him, the Syrian chief is won over by the Egyptian prince and says:

*i-dd=n-i* *qꜣi-k* *ptr* *ṯ-k* *mdi-i* *m-šri*
IMP-say=to-1S background-2MS PTC PTC-2MS with-1S as-child
Tell me your background! Look, you are a child to me. (*LES* 6, 5)

Coordinated predicative adverbial expression can be simply juxtaposed:

(37) In a purification ritual the God Khnum of Elephantine asks his namesake deity from another town to send an amulet for the patient to be treated:

*iw-pꜣy-f-mnḫ* *nty-r-f* *mi-ssn* *n-ist* *msn*
DEP-POSS-3MS-cord REL-to-3MS like-string of-N thread
*n-nbḥwt* *m-sẖt* *ḥdḥtp*
of-N as-fabric of-N
*m-kꜣ-t* *n-ptḥ* *m-ir-(t-)n-ist* *nṯr-t* *mẖny-rsi* *nt* *mḥti*
as-work-F of-N as-do-F-PST-N god-F inside-south water northern
*m-ṯs-t* *n-nt* *r-ḥꜣ-t-s*
as-knot-F of-N to-front-3FS
...while his cord that pertains to it is like the string of Isis, the thread of Nepthys, as the fabric of Hedjhotep, as the work of Ptah, as that what the goddess Isis made in the south and the northern water, and as the knot of Neith in front of her. (Roccati, *Mag. taur.*, 24, 2–3)

In prepositional phrases, the preposition is sometimes omitted in writing. Although this development has a phonetic background for prepositions such as *ḥr* or *r*, which in Late Egyptian had been wholly or partly reduced to vowels, such an explanation is not applicable to the so-called *m* of predication used in adverbial sentences expressive of classification of the subject. Omission of this preposition is common (albeit not typical) in texts of the first millennium BC (cf. exx. 38c and 38d); here, the use of the preformative pronouns confirms the analysis of the construction as an adverbial sentence:

(38a) The younger brother warns his new wife to leave the house lest the sea catch her:

*ḫr* *nn-iw-i* *rḫ* *nḥm-ṯ* *mdi-f* *pꜣwn-ṯ-i*
for NEG-FUT-1S know rescue-2FS with-3MS because-PTC-1S
*(m)-sḥm-t* *mi-qd-ṯ*
(as)-woman-F like-form-2FS
...for I will not be able to save you from it, because I am a woman like you. (*LES* 19, 14–15)

(38b) A wisdom text advises:
*mỉr-ỉrỉ=n-k* *hꜣ* *n-ꜥḏꜣ* *st* *(m)-štm* *ꜥꜣ* *n-mwt*
NEG.IMP-make=for-2MS list of-wrong 3P (as)-defamation great of-death
*st* *(m)-ꜥnḫ* *ꜥꜣ* *n-sḏfꜣtr* *st* *n-smtr* *n-wḥm*
3P (as)-oath great of-allegiance 3P for-interrogation of herald
Do not make for yourself false enrolment lists! They are a great defamation worthy of death. They are a great oath of allegiance. They belong to the interrogation of the herald. (Amenemope 21, 9–12)

(38c) The recipient of a petition is informed that a servant had fled:
*sw* *(m)-ẖnw* *tꜣdhnt* *pꜣy-k-dmỉ*
3MS in-inside N POSS.M-2MS-city
He is in The Promontory, your town. (Jansen-Winkeln, *IdS* I, 203, 12)

(38d) The addressee of a letter is ordered to send a guard onto the walls because the sender has received an oracle saying:
*mỉr-dỉt-ḥn-rmṯ=nb* *(r)-sḫ-t* *ỉw-f* *(m)-wꜥw*
NEG.IMP-give.INF-go-man=all (to)-field-F DEP-3MS (as)-soldier
*ỉw-f* *(m)-sḫ-t*
DEP-3MS (as)-bird catcher
*ỉw-f* *(m)-rmṯ* *wnḏw=nb*
DEP-3MS (as)-man common=QU
Do not let anyone go outside to the fields, be it a soldier, a bird catcher, or any person! (Jansen-Winkeln, *IdS* I, 200, 12–14)

(38e) In a decree, the gods of Thebes are asked to guarantee the property of Lady Makare:
*ẖdb* *rmṯ=nb* *n-wnḏw=nb* *n-pꜣ-tꜣ* *ḏr-f* *ỉw-w*
kill.IMP man=QU of-sort=QU of-DEF.M-land all-3MS DEP-3P
*n-ꜥḥꜣt-w* *ỉw-w* *n-ḥm-w-t*
as-male-P DEP-3P as-female-P-F
Kill any people of every kind of the entire land, be they men or women...
(Jansen-Winkeln, *IdS* I, 183, 1–2)

Note that the adverb *dy* 'here' is often treated like a second position clitic[16]:

16 The adverb *dy* is a characteristically Later Egyptian lexeme and might merely represent a new written form of the old adverb *ꜥꜣ* 'here', where the initial *ꜥ* might in reality have had the phonemic value /d/; see Kammerzell (1998: 34–35). According to Jean Winand (personal communication), in Late Egyptian *ꜥꜣ* appears to be used in northern Egypt and *dy* in the south, which would indicate a diatopic alternance <ꜥ>/<d>. In the variety of Earlier Egyptian in use in the first half of the 1st millennium BCE, *dy* is the only lexical adverb found as the predicate of adverbial sentences.

(39a) The recipient of a letter is asked to bring a basket to carry soil:

*iw-mir-ꜥn=n-i* *smy*
DEP-NEG.IMP-return=to-1S report
*yꜣ* *ṯ-i* *ꜣs-k(wi)* *r-fꜣy* *nꜣ-iwtn* *nty=dy*
PTC PTC-1S hurry-STA.1S to-carry.INF DEF.P-soil REL=here
*mdi-i* *m-pꜣ-pr*
with-1S in-DEF.M-house

So do not report to me: 'Surely I have hurried to carry out that soil that is with me here in the house'. (*KRI* IV 416, 8–10)

(39b) In a document concerning the renewal of earlier treaties between Egypt and Hatti, the Hittite king Hattusili is quoted as having stated:

*ir* *pꜣ-ntꜥ* *mty* *wn=dy* *m-hꜣw* *spll* *pꜣ-wr*
as_for DEF.M-treaty agreed AUX.REL=here in-time N DEF.M-chief
*ꜥꜣ* *n-ḫt*
great of-N
*m-mit-t* *pꜣ-ntꜥ* *mty* *wn* *m-hꜣw* *mwtl*
in-likeness-F DEF.M-treaty agreed AUX.REL in time N
*pꜣ-wr* *ꜥꜣ* *n-ḫt*
DEF.M-chief great of-N
*pꜣy-i-it* *mḥ-i* *im-f*
POSS.M-1S-father take.PROS-1S OBJ-3MS

Regarding the agreed treaty that was here at the time of Suppiluliuma, the great chief of Hatti, as well as the agreed-upon treaty that was in the time of Muwatalli, the great chief of Hatti, my father, I take it up (again). (Edel, *Vertrag*, 28*, 1–3)

(39c) A son is quoted as having written after his mother's death:

*imi* *di-tw* *pꜣ-ḥtr* *wn* *ḥr-pri* *n-s*
give.IMP give-PASS DEF.M-ration AUX.PST on-go_out for-3MS
*n-tꜣy-i-sn-t* *wn=dy* *m-ḫꜣr-t* *ḥr-mn* *n-rnp-t*
to-POSS.F-1S-sister-F AUX.IPF=here as-widow-F for-period of-year-F
*r-tꜣy*
to-DEM.F

Let the rations that were used to be given to her be given to my sister, who has been a widow here for nearly a year until now. (pTurin 1977, 5–6 [Bakir, *Epist.*, pl. 26])

### 1.2.2 Demotic

The structure of Demotic adverbial sentences differs only marginally from that of Late Egyptian. The basic syntactic template remains S > [NP AP]. If the subject is a definite NP, it appears before the predicate:

(40a) The goddess insists on her primacy:
*twwst* *pꜣ-tꜣ* *ỉỉrḥr-y* *m-qdty-t-wꜥ-t-ꜥfṯy-t*
behold [DEF.M-earth] [before-1S in-likeness-F-IDF.S-F-chest-F]
Behold, the earth is before me like a chest. (Myth of the Sun's Eye 9, 21–22)

(40b) Setne has just assigned all his possessions to Tabubu when he is told:
*nꜣy-k-ẖrṯ-w* *ẖry*
[POSS.P-2MS-child-P] [below]
Your children are below. (Setne I 5, 21)

(40c) The deceased is assured:
*šꜥ* *n-snsn* *n-ḏḥwty* *m-sꜣ-k*
[book of-breath of-N] [as-protection-2MS]
Thoth's book of breathing is your protection. (pRhind I 8, d1)

(40d) The king is addressed in an encomium to his praise:
*ḏḥwty* *ỉrm-k* *ỉw-f* *ꜥš* *n-k* *sẖ* *(n)-dy*
N with-2MS DEP-3MS read for-2MS writing of-give.INF
*n-k* *pꜣ-ḏre*
for-2MS DEF.M-strength
*pꜣ-sbty* *(n)-pꜣy-k-mšꜥ* *pꜣ-wḏꜣ* *(n)-tꜣy-k-dnyḥry*
DEF.M-readiness of-POSS.M-2MS-army DEF.M-weal of-POSS.F-2MS-dominion
Thoth is with you, while he reads for you a document to provide you with the strength and the readiness of your army and the prosperity of your dominion. (*Archive of Hor* #3, 8–9)

The split system of marking indefiniteness seen in Late Egyptian (1.2.1) is basically still valid. Indefinite subject NPs continue to be marked morphologically by the indefinite articles (singular *wꜥ-*, plural *hyn-*) without any introductory particle, but this pattern is now mainly limited to dependent clauses. However, first signs of a collapse of the system can be witnessed (ex. 41c):

(41a) Description of the objects to be placed at the top of a naos:
*mtw-w-ẖꜣꜥ* *wꜥ-t-ꜥrꜥy* *r-wꜥ-t-nbw* *ẖrr-s* *ḥr-wꜥ-wt*
CNJ-3P-set IDF.S-F-uraeus DEP-IDF.S-F-basket under-3FS on-IDF.S-papyrus
A uraeus, with a basket under it, should be set on a papyrus...
(Rosetta Decree 27)

(41b) Setne sees Tabubu for the first time:
*nꜣw-ꜥn-s* *ỉw-hyn-w-wpw-t-w* *n-nb* *ꜥšꜣy* *nỉm-s*
PTC-beautiful-3FS DEP-IDF-P-work-F-P of-gold many in-3FS
*ỉw-hyn-w-ẖmẖl-w* *sḥm-t-w* *mšꜥ* *msꜣ-s*
DEP-IDF-P-servant-P female-F-P walk.STA after-3FS

*ỉw-wn-rmt    ẖ-nꜣw-pr    s    2    ỉp    rr-s*
DEP-PTC-man    body-POSS.P-house    man    2    count    for-3FS
She was beautiful, with numerous golden ornaments (i.e. jewelry) upon her, while maidservants walked behind her and there were two male servants from her household assigned to her. (Setne I 4, 39)

(41c) The judgement scene of the deceased is given in description.
It contains:
*ḏḥwty    ỉw-f-ꜥš-sẖ    ỉw-wꜥ-ḏꜥm*
N    DEP-3MS-read-written_document    DEP-IDF.S-papyrus
*n-ḏr-ṯ-f    n-tꜣ-ꜥme-t    ỉw-wn-mḥy-t    2-t*
in-hand-F-3MS    for-DEF.F-devourer-F    DEP-PTC-feather-F    two-F
*nḥr-ḏꜣḏꜣ-s    ỉw-wn-tmꜣ-t    2-t    ỉỉr-ḏr-ṯ-s*
on-head-3FS    DEP-PTC-knife-F    two-F    to-hand-F-3FS
*ỉw-wn-wꜥ-syf    ḥr-wꜥ-ḥq    ỉỉr-ḥr-s*
DEP-PTC-IDF.S-child    on-IDF.S-sceptre    to-face-3FS
Thoth, who recites having a papyrus in his hand to the devourer, who has two plumes on her head, two knives in her hand and a (divine) child on a sceptre in front of her. (pBN 149 1, 20–21)

Alternatively, the bare subject is marked syntactically with the particle *wn-*:

(42a) Tabubu describes her house to Setne:
*wn-sbte=nb    ẖn-f*
PTC-equipment=QU    in-3MS
It is furnished with everything. (*lit:* every equipment is in it.)
(Setne I 5, 9)

(42b) In a letter of broken context the following utterance of certain priests is quoted:
*wn-ꜣrry    ẖn-f    mtw-w    dy=n-y    ḥḏ    1000*
PTC-vine    in-3MS    CNJ-3P    give=to-1S    silver    1000
There are vines within, and I have been given 1000 (pieces of) silver.
(pLoeb 17, 47–48 = v° 16–17)

(42c) Moral precepts state:
*wn-ꜥwnḥꜣtyṯ    (n)-ẖn    m-qdy-tꜣ-sty-t    ỉw-s-pr*
PTC-patience    of-stupid    in-likeness-DEF.F-flame-F    PTC-3FS-go
*mtw-s-ꜥẖm*
CNJ-3FS-extinguish
An idiot's patience is like the flame: it lights up and goes out.
(pInsinger 21, 20)

The particle *wn* is also used when an indefinite NP functioning as subject is followed by a number or a quantifier, although exceptions do occur:

(43a) Setne found the upper room of Tabubu's house swept and adorned:

| *ỉw-wn-glg* | *ꜥšꜣy* | *ẖn-s* |
|---|---|---|
| DEP-PTC-bed | many | in-3FS |

... there being many beds in it. (Setne I 5, 16)

(43b) The spell recited by Naneferkaptah allowed him to see the fish of the deep:

| *ỉw-wn-mḥ-ntr* | *21* | *n-mw* | *ḥr-ḏꜣḏꜣ-w* |
|---|---|---|---|
| DEP-PTC-cubit-divine | 21 | of water | on-head-3P |

... although there were 21 divine cubits of water above them.
(Setne I 3, 37)

Yet in Demotic, a shift towards the syntactic marking is witnessed, which may now appear with subjects marked also by the indefinite article as well:

(44a) The author of a letter quotes the utterance of the god Amenothes saying:

| *wn-wꜥ-ẖmm* | *n-ẖe-ṯ-f* | *n-ḏdḥr* | *sꜣ* | *pꜣšrỉmn* |
|---|---|---|---|---|
| PTC-IDF.S-fever | in-body-F-3MS | of-N | son | N |

There is a fever in the body of Teos the son of Pseamunis.
(oPSBA 35, pl. 27, 2–3)

(44b) King Amasis suffered from the effects of a nightly diversion and an over-indulgence with strong beverages. He was unable to focus on daily business. However:

| *wnnꜣw-wn-wꜥ-wꜥb-(n)-nyt* | *ẖn-nꜣ-sre-w* | *r-pꜣsnmṯk* | *rn-f* |
|---|---|---|---|
| PRT-PTC-IDF.S-priest-of-N | in-DEF.P-magistrate-P | DEP-N | name-3MS |

Among the magistrates was a priest of Neith whose name was Psamtek...
(pBN 215, v° a12)

However, most examples of this sort could also be analysed as existential sentences. As in Late Egyptian, the line of demarcation between adverbial sentences with an indefinite subject and existential sentences is not easy to draw, and ambiguous cases are common:

(45) The pharaoh asks his courtiers:

| *ỉn-wn-rmt* | *nỉm-tn* | *mtw-f* | *rḫ-ỉr* | *wꜥ-sḏy* | *ỉỉrḥr-y* |
|---|---|---|---|---|---|
| IP-PTC-man | in-2P | CNJ-3MS | know-make | IDF.S-story | to-1S |

Is there someone among you who could tell me a story?
(pBN 215, v° a11)

Demotic preformative personal pronouns show some evolution from Late Egyptian (see Tab. I.2):

**Tab. I.2:** Demotic pronominal preformatives in adverbial sentences (common forms only).

| | Singular | Plural |
|---|---|---|
| 1C | *tw-ỉ*<br>*dy-ỉ* | *tw-n* |
| 2M | *dy-k*<br>*ỉw-k* | *tw-tn* |
| 2F | *tw-t* | |
| 3M | *ỉw-f* | *st* |
| 3F | *ỉw-s* | |

The second person masculine singular exhibits variation between an adjusted version of the old form (*dy-k*) and a new form (*ỉw-k*), and the third person singular forms show a dummy marker *ỉw* followed by the suffix pronoun (note that the forms are partly taken from the similar Present I patterns, since not all forms are attested as pronominal subjects of adverbial sentences). The reason for this might be that the Late Egyptian third person pronouns *sw/st* had been reduced to [se] (or simple [s]) and thus become indistinguishable from the suffix pronoun -*s*. The new forms with *ỉw* were probably first introduced here to reduce ambiguity, and the former then served as a model for analogous change in the second person (see Winand 1992: 428–439 for the general development of the pronominal subject marking in this and the syntactically similar Present I pattern). The syntactic features of these pronouns remained unchanged:

(46a) God Thoth complains to god Pre about Naneferkaptah's misbehaviour and receives the following answer:

| | | | | |
|---|---|---|---|---|
| *ỉw-f* | *ỉỉrḥr-k* | *ỉrm-rmt=nb* | *nty-mtw-f* | *ḏr-w* |
| PTC-3MS | before-2MS | with-man=QU | REL-with-3MS | all-3P |

He is in your hands together with every person who belongs to him.

(Setne I 4, 7)

(46b) At the end of a lease document about 'beer-work', the lessees swear:

| | | | | |
|---|---|---|---|---|
| *ỉw-n* | *ỉr* | *r-ẖ-pꜣ-ꜥnḫ* | *nty-ḥry* | *tw-n* |
| DEP-1P | do | as-way-DEF.M-oath | REL-above | PTC-1P |

| | |
|---|---|
| *ẖn-nꜣ-ḥs-w* | *n-prꜥꜣ* |
| in-DEF.P-praised_one-P | of-pharaoh |

If we act according to the oath above, we are among the praised ones of the pharaoh. (pLüddeckens 13 B19)

(46c) Neithemhat is told concerning certain slain young men:

| | |
|---|---|
| *st* | *n-ḥw-t-nṯr* |
| 3P | in-house-F-god |

They are in the temple. (pRylands IX 14, 2)

(46d) The small dog-ape tells the goddess:

| | | | | | | |
|---|---|---|---|---|---|---|
| *tw-y* | *ỉrm-t* | *bn-ỉw-y* | *wy* | *rḥr-t* | *ꜥn* | *spsn 2* |
| PTC-1S | with-2FS | NEG-FUT-1S | be far | from-2MS | again | twice |

I am with you. I shall never leave you! (Myth of the Sun's Eye 16, 30)

The variants with *ỉw* in the second singular masculine and both third person singular pronouns reflect the gradual development of the later Coptic prefix pronouns (see 1.2.3):

(47a) Setne calls upon Naneferkaptah who has taken the appearance of a very old priest:

| | | | | | |
|---|---|---|---|---|---|
| *ỉw-k* | *n-smte* | *n-rmṯ* | *ỉw-f* | *ꜥ(ꜣ)y* | *n-ms* |
| PTC-2MS | in-manner | of-man | DEP-3MS | long | of-birth |

You seem to be an old man. (Setne I 6, 11)

(47b) Moral precepts state the obvious:

| | | |
|---|---|---|
| *tꜣ-nty-ḥr-ḥꜣtyṯ-f* | *ỉw-s* | *ḥr-ḥꜣtyṯ-f* |
| DEF.M-REL-on-heart-3MS | PTC-3FS | on-heart-3MS |

What is in his heart is in his heart. (Onkhsheshonqy 27, 10)

However, a new ambiguity was introduced by the replacement of *tw* with *ỉw*; the latter forms had now become graphically indistinguishable from subjects in adjunct clauses introduced by the adjunct marker *ỉw* (see 2.2.2.2).

The predicate of Demotic adverbial sentences is usually a (mostly locative) prepositional phrase[17]:

(48a) In a partition of a piece of real estate, the location of this is described in relation to its neighbours and the cardinal points:

| | | | | |
|---|---|---|---|---|
| *ỉmnṯ* | *pꜣ-sbt* | *n-sꜣwt* | *ỉw-pꜣ-ẖr* | *ỉwt-w* |
| west | DEF.M-wall | of-N | DEP-DEF.M-street | between-3P |

West: the wall of Assiut with the street between them. (pCG 50058, 6)

(48b) In an unclear explanation of mythological details, it is stated:

| | |
|---|---|
| *ỉw-f* | *msꜣ-ỉ* |
| PTC-3MS | behind-1S |

He is behind me. (Myth of the Sun's Eye 9, 5)

17 It should also be noted that certain previously common constructions such as the pattern *ỉw-f=n-ỉ* 'It is (= it belongs) to me' are no longer attested in Demotic.

(48c) The author of a letter informs the addressee about his latest achievements and says:
*dy-y* *r-pꜣ-ꜥwy-n-ḥtp* *ẖnm*
PTC-1S to-DEF.M-house-of-rest N
I am at the resting place of Khnum. (pBerlin P 13579, x+9)

A few adverbs are also encountered, particularly the relatively frequent interrogative *tn* 'where?' and the locative *dy* 'here', the latter often occurring in relative clauses. Besides the use of unmarked sentences the employment of marked forms known as Second Tenses is commonly attested with the interrogative *tn* (for Second Tenses, see 3.1.3.1.2).

(49a) Horudja asks:
*ỉw-f* *tn* *pꜣy-f-šr*
PTC-3MS WH POSS.M-3MS-son
Where is he (then), his son? (pRylands IX 15, 4)

(49b) In a literary text of broken context:
*ỉir-k* *tn*
ST-2MS WH
Where are you? (*Saqqara Dem. Texts* #2 6, 30)

(49c) The author of a letter asks for some copper to be handed over:
*(r)ḏbꜣḫpr-wꜥ-ꜥšsḥn* *nỉm-w=dy*
because-IDF.S-order in-3P=here
... because an order concerning it is here. (pBresciani 33, 7–8)

(49d) Horudja warns Peteese, son of Ireturu:
*[mỉr]-dyt-sḏm-s* *nꜣy-wꜥb-w* *nty=dy*
NEG.IMP-give.INF-hear-3MS DEM.P-priests-P REL=here
*rmt-swg-w* *nꜣw*
man-insane.P SE.P
[Do not let] these priests who are here hear that. They are insane! (pRylands IX 10, 21)

Note that *dy*, therefore, is not a clitic in all cases. As in Late Egyptian, this adverb is often followed by further adverbials that may be understood as predicates:

(50a) After the troubles announced by the Lamb, order and justice will return and people will say:
*hmyr* *pꜣy(-y)-ỉṯ* *pꜣ-ỉṯ* *n-pꜣy(-y)-ỉṯ* *dy* *ỉrm-y*
PTC POSS.M-1S-father DEF.M-father of-POSS.M-1S-father here with-1S
*n-pꜣ-hꜣy* *nfr{w}* *nty-ỉw-f* *ḫpr*
in-DEF.M-time good REL-PTC-3MS happen
Would that my father and the father of my father were here with me in the good times that will come! (pVienna D 10000 3, 4–5)

(50b) The hero is urged to come south:
*ỉwḏbꜣ-hyn-w-ꜥꜣm* *n-pr-ḏwf* *ỉw-w=dy* *n-nw-t*
because-IDF-P-shepherds of-district-reed DEP-3P=here in-town-F
...due to some shepherds from the Delta, who are here at Thebes.
(pSpiegelberg 12, 23)

The position of *dy* in the following example seems rather unusual, but as the Roman Period funerary text in question presents several unetymological writings, *dy* could stand for some other word (in particular the demonstrative pronoun *tꜣy*)[18]:

(51) Animals of the desert say:
*ỉn=dy* *tꜣy-n-mw-t*
IP=here POSS.F-1P-mother-F
Is our mother here? (pLouvre N 2420, c4–5)

As in some Late Egyptian texts, the preposition *n* is often omitted in Demotic, even when it is part of the predicate. The example below shows that absence and presence of the preposition can be found in adjacent sentences.

(52) The goddess Isis is addressed with words of praise. She is asked:
*ỉn* *tw-t* *(n)-tꜣ-p-t* *ỉn* *tw-t* *n-pꜣ-ỉtn*
IP PTC-2FS (in)-DEF.F-sky-F IP PTC-2FS in-DEF.F-earth
Are you in heaven? Are you in the ground/on earth? (grTheben 3156, i, 11)

Once again, several adverbial phrases are allowed within a sentence, and identifying the predicate may be difficult at times[19]:

(53a) In a dream text the following description of a dream is given:
*tw-y* *ḫn-pꜣ-ꜥwy* *ỉrm-pꜣy-(y)-sn* *ꜥꜣ* *ỉw-f*
PTC-1S in-DEF.M-house with-POSS.M-1S-brother great DEP-3MS
*rmy* *ỉỉrḥr-y*
weep before-1S
I am in the house with my older brother who weeps before me...
(pBologna 3173, 13–14)

(53b) The small dog-ape informs the goddess about Egypt's state of devastation:
*qmy* *n-ḫneyn-t* *ḥr-rd-wy-t*
Egypt in-despair-F on-feet-DU-2FS
Egypt is in despair at your feet. (Myth of the Sun's Eye 11, 3–4)

---

18 Cf. the translation by Chauveau (1991: 7 note n).
19 An analysis positing ellipsis of the second clausal subject can be excluded in the examples below.

### 1.2.3 Coptic

In Coptic, the development of the syntax of the adverbial sentence continued along the track observed in Demotic. The split system according to the definiteness of the subject NP was still observed, and the preformative personal pronoun subjects underwent further morphological change. The category 'adverb' grew in size as some etymological PPs were reanalysed as adverbs.

As in earlier phases of Later Egyptian, in Coptic, definite *subjects* of adverbial sentence occupy the initial position before the predicate (the brackets [] in the interlinear glossing indicate the constituents):

(54a) God is the Lord:
*pe-f-hap* *hm-p-kah* *têr-f*
[POSS.M-3MS-law]$_S$ [in-DEF.M-world whole]$_P$
His judgement is on all earth. ($^S$Ps 104 [105]:7)

(54b) In the first letter of Clemens, Jesus is cited as having assured:
*n-bel* *m-p-cais* *acn-n-dikaios*
[DEF.P-eye of-DEF.M-lord]$_S$ [upon-DEF.P-righteous]$_P$
The eyes of the Lord rest upon the righteous. ($^A$1Cl 22:6)

(54c) The sender of a letter informs the addressee:
*t-ke-lekme=an* *n-hno* *n-hamt*
[DEF.F-other-piece=again of-vessel of-copper
*et-a-tetn-tnnau-s=nê-i* *ishête* *n-ni-ma*
REL-PST-2P-send-3FS=for-1S]$_S$ behold [in-DEM.P-place]$_P$
Also, the other piece of copper vessel that you
sent me is here. ($^L$*P.KellisCopt.* 64, 9–11)

(54d) In a penitential prayer, David asks the Lord to have mercy on him:
*ce-ti-saun* *anak* *n-ta-anomia*
for-1S-know 1S OBJ-POSS.F.1S-transgression
*auô* *pa-nabe* *m-pa-mta* *ebal* *n-uaiš* *nim*
and [POSS.M.1S-sin]$_S$ [in-POSS.M.1S-presence out in-time QU]$_P$
For I acknowledge my transgressions. My sin is continually before me.
($^M$Ps 50 [51]:5 [3])

(54e) The psalmist sings the praise of the Lord:
*p-c$^h$(ôi)s* *ḫen-pe-f-erp$^h$ei* *et$^h$uab*
[DEF.M-lord]$_S$ [in-POSS.M-3MS-temple holy]$_P$
The Lord is in his holy temple. ($^B$Ps 10 [11]:4)

Noteworthy seems the intrusion of the presentative particle *ishête* in 54c, which might be due to a slip in the drawing up of the letter.

Any kind of definite NP can appear in the subject position, including relative phrases:

(55a) Jesus answers the pharisees' complaints about his disciples eating on the Sabbath:

*ti-cô=de* *mmo-s* *nê-tn* *ce-p-et-o* *n-nok*$^j$
1S-say=yet OBJ-3FS for-2P COMP-DEF.M-REL-be.STA as-great
*e-p-rpe* *m-pei-ma*
to-DEF.M-temple in-DEM.M-place
I tell you that the one who is greater than the temple is here. ($^S$Mt 12:6)

(55b) Again, the pharisees ask for a sign. Jesus likens his appearance to Old Testament characters:

*auô* *hi* *p-et-uatb* *e-solomôn* *m-pei-me*
and see DEF.M-REL-great.STA than-N in-DEM.M-place
And behold, the one greater than Solomon is here. ($^M$Mt 12:42)

Coordinated subjects may appear successively (ex. 56a) or separated and following the predicate phrase (56b):

(56a) In a prayer for the house of David, the Lord is quoted to have assured:

*ta-mee* *nem-pa-nee* *neme-f*
POSS.F.1S-truth CNJ-POSS.M.1S-mercy with-3MS
My faithfulness and my mercy shall be with him. ($^M$Ps 88 [89]:25 [24])

(56b) Many beheld the death of Jesus from afar:

*nai* *ete-nare-maria* *ebol* *nḫêt-u* *pe* *ti-magdalinê*
DEM.P REL-IPF-N out inside-3P PTC DEF$_2$.F-N
*nem-maria* *t*$^h$*a-iakôbos*
and-N POSS.F-N
*nem-t*$^h$*-mau* *n-iôsêph* *nem-t*$^h$*-mau* *n-nen-šêri* *n-zebedeos*
and-DEF.F-mother of-N and-DEF.F-mother of-DEF.P-child of-N
Among them was Mary Magdalene, Mary the mother of James and Joseph, and the mother of the children of Zebedaios. ($^B$Mt 27:56)

Identical subjects of coordinated clauses may undergo ellipsis; cf. the following examples:

(57a) Jesus warns against believing people who would claim:

*is* *p-kh(risto)s* *ha-mnai* *ie* *ha-mnê*
PTC DEF.M-Christ under-here or under-there
Lo, the Christ is here or there. ($^B$Mk 13:21)

(57b) The apostle Paul asks the Romans: *What then? Shall we sin*:

*ce-ten-k*$^h$*ê* *ḫa-p*$^h$*-nomos=an* *alla* *ḫa-pi-hmot*
for-1P-AUX under-DEF.M-law=NEG but under-DEF$_2$.M-grace
... because we are not under the law, but under the grace? ($^B$Rm 6:15)

(57c) Jesus answers to the Pharisees that the kingdom of God does not come in any observable way:

| | | | | |
|---|---|---|---|---|
| *ude* | *se-na-co-s=an* | *ce-s-tai* | *ie* | *s-tê* |
| nor | 3P-FUT-say-3FS=NEG | COMP-3FS-here | or | 3FS-there |

Nor shall they say "It is here or it is there." ($^{B}$Lk 17:21)

Contrary to the situation in earlier Later Egyptian, any indefinite subject with or without explicit morphological marking was now introduced by the initial particle $^{S}$*un*/$^{B}$*uon*.[20] Hence, both subjects lacking an article (exx. 58a and d) and subjects marked with the indefinite article (58b and f) after the introductory $^{S}$*un*/$^{B}$*uon* are found in all dialects:

(58a) Invading barbarians ask a wise old monk whose cell they pass by:

| | |
|---|---|
| *un-rôme* | *m-pei-ma* |
| PTC-man | in-DEM.M-place |

Is anyone here? ($^{S}$*AP* Chaîne 80, 5)

(58b) Tobit prays to teh Lord in his affliction bewailing his situation:

| | | |
|---|---|---|
| *un-u-nok$^{j}$* | *n-lupê* | *nmma-i* |
| PTC-IDF.S-great | of-grief | with-1S |

...and great grief is with me. ($^{S}$Tb 3:6)

(58c) A proverb of Solomon about wise versus foolish behaviour:

| | | | |
|---|---|---|---|
| *un-u-pêgê* | *n-ônḫ* | *hi-n-hou* | *n-t-sophia* |
| PTC-IDF.S-fountain | of-life | in-DEF.P-ways | of-DEF.F-wisdom |

A fountain of life is in the ways of wisdom. ($^{A}$Prv 13:14)

(58d) In the Gnostic *Gospel of Philip* the writer speaks of his maxims in metaphoric terms:

| | | | |
|---|---|---|---|
| *um-mou* | *hn-u-mou* | *un-kôht* | *hnn-u-khrisma* |
| PTC-water | in-IDF.S-water | PTC-fire | in-IDF.S-oil |

There is water in water. There is fire in oil. ($^{L}$*GospPh.* 57, 27–28)

(58e) The leaders of the synagogue send a message to Paul and Barnabas saying "You men and brethren"

| | | | | | | | |
|---|---|---|---|---|---|---|---|
| *ešope* | *un-sophia* | *hn-uan* | *mmo-tn* | *ê* | *sece* | *n-tok* | *n-hêt* |
| if | PTC-wisdom | in-one | of-2P | or | word | of-thick | of-heart |

| | |
|---|---|
| *a-ci-s* | *m-p-laos* |
| IMP-say-3FS | to-DEF.M-people |

If wisdom is in one of them or a word of encouragement, speak to the people. ($^{M}$Acts 13:15)

20 Occasional omissions here are probably no more than slips by the copyist.

(58f) The prophet warns the Israelites not to seek aid in Egypt:
*ce-uan-hen-faišini* *n-ancôc* *e-u-hau* *hn-t-ceeni*
for-PTC-IDF.P-messenger of-leader DEP-3P-evil.STA in-DEF.F-N
...for in Tanis there are evil leading messengers. ($^{F}$Is 30:4)

(58g) The fullness of wisdom is to fear the Lord:
*uoh* *uon-u-unof* *ḫen-ne-s-karpos*
and PTC-IDF.S-joy in-POSS.P-3FS-fruit
And joy is in their fruit. ($^{B}$Eccl 1:16)

It should be noted that there is thus no structural difference between adverbial (58a) and existential sentences (59):

(59) In his Canons, Athanasius describes a certain case:
*ešôpe* *un-ua* *hm-pe-kleros* *ere-p-pn(eum)a* *etuaab* *me*
if PTC-one in-DEF.M-clergy REL-DEF.M-spirit holy love
*mmo-f* *ehuo* *etbe-te-f-mnt-rôme* *et-nanu-s*
OBJ-3MS more because-POSS.F-3MS-ABST-man REL-be good-3FS
If there is someone within the clergy whom the Holy Ghost loves more because of his good humanity. (*Canons Athan.* [*ASAE* 19, 239, 5–10])

However, when the sentence is introduced by *is* 'behold' an indefinite subject is not additionally marked with *un-*[21]:

(60a) Shenute speaks about the work of doctors and then says:
*is-sain* *hm-ma* *nim* *hm-p-kah* *têr-f*
PTC-ø-doctor in-place all in-DEF.M-world all-3MS
There are doctors everywhere in the world.
($^{S}$Shenute, *God Who Alone Is True* [L IV 161, 2–3])

(60b) After the angel asked him what he saw, Zachary answers:
*a-i-no* *au* *este* *is-u-lukhnia* *n-nub* *têr-s*
PST-1S-see and behold lo-IDF.S-lamp-stand of-gold all-3FS
*au* *t-s-lampas* *na-s-hicô-s* *na-un-saḫf* *n-ḫêbs* *hicô-s*
and POSS.F-3FS-lamp PRT-3FS-upon-3FS PRT-PTC-seven of-light upon-3FS
*au* *saḫf* *n-ḫlap* *n-n-ḫêbs* *et-hicô-s*
and seven of-vessel for-DEF.P-light REL-upon-3FS
I have seen and behold, there is a lamp-stand all of gold and ist torch it was on it and there were seven lamps upon it and seven pouring vessels for the lamps which were upon it. ($^{A}$Zec 4:2)

21 However, this does not seem to hold with the Mesokemic equivalent *hi*. Similar structural rules are applied to Present I constructions in which the particle *un* is retained. For *is*, see further Shisha-Halevy (1984a: 73–76).

(60c) A woman informs her family in a letter about her well-being as well as that she has sent an item:
*is-u-clk$^{j}$e* *a-ue*
lo-IDF.S-bag for-one
Here is a cloth bag for one (of you). ($^{L}$*P.KellisCopt*. 64, 26–27)

(60d) Jesus says that the queen of the south will come to hear the Son of Man as she did for Solomon's wisdom:
*uoh is-huo e-solomôn m-pai-ma*
and lo-more than-N in-DEM.M-place
And, behold, one greater than Solomon is here. ($^{B}$Lk 11:31)

The prefixed preformative personal pronouns are further developed in Coptic. Remains of the original element *ṱ*- are retained only in the first-person forms as well as in the second singular feminine and the second plural. The variant element *iw* seen in Demotic is dropped, and the resulting forms appear similar to simple suffix pronouns:

**Tab. I.3:** Coptic pronominal preformatives in adverbial sentences (common forms only; dialectal variation only marked if attested). Note that B shows the aspirated allomorph k$^{h}$ (2MS) before sonorants.

| | **Singular** | **Plural** |
|---|---|---|
| 1C | *ti* | *t(e)n* |
| 2M | *k* | *tet(e)n* |
| 2F | *te(r/l)* | |
| 3M | *f* | *se* |
| 3F | *s* | |

The use of these pronouns is the same as before:

(61a) Jesus tells his disciples that a day will come when people will long to see the Son of Man:
*n-se-coo-s nê-tn ce-eishêête f-hm-pei-ma ê hm-pai*
CNJ-3P-say-3FS to-2P COMP-look [3MS]-[in-DEM.M-place or in-DEM.M]
And they will say to you, 'Look, He is here or there!' ($^{S}$Lk 17:23)

(61b) Prayer and curse are to be said on two mountains:
*se-hm-pe-kro m-p-iordanês*
[3P]-[in-DEF.M-side of-DEF.M-N]
They are on the other side of the Jordan. ($^{S}$Dt 11:30 [Ciasca])

(61c) Jesus tells his disciples:
*ari-pist[eue nê-i ce]-an[ak] ti-hn-pa-iôt*
AUX.IMP-believe for-1S COMP-1S [1S]-[in-POSS.M.1S-father]
Believe me, that I, I am in my father. ($^{L}$Jn 14:11)

(61d) The Psalmist says that he always saw the Lord before him:
*ce-f-hi-uinem* *mma-i* *ce-nna-nain*
for-3MS-on-right of-1S so_that-NEG.FUT.1S-shake
... for he is on the right of me so that I might not be shaken. (MPs 15[16]:8)

(61e) The skull of a pagan tells Macarius about the punishment inflicted on someone in hell who has with a fiery river above him:
*uoh* *f-sapesêt* *mmo-n*
and 3MS-beneath in-1P
And he is beneath us. (B*AP Macarius* B30 [MG 25, 226, 4])

Note the omission of the subject in ex. 61a with coordinated predicates, a feature that would have been impossible in earlier stages of the language. A nominal subject could be placed at the beginning of the sentence and resumed by a pronoun:

(62a) The author urges humility and restraint:
*t-hote* *m-p-nute* *s-nmma-k* *n-uoiš* *nim*
DEF.F-fear of-DEF.M-god [3FS]-[with-2MS in-time QU]
The fear of god is always with you. (S*Shenute?* [L III 101, 6–7])[22]

(62b) After he struck Israel with a plague of locusts, the Lord assured his people of his mercy:
*tetn-mme* *ce-anak* *ti-hn-t-mête* *m-p-i(sra)êl*
2P-know COMP-1S [1S]-[in-DEF.F-middle of-DEF.M-Israel]
You shall know that I am amidst Israel. (AJl 2:27 [Till])

(62c) The designations 'Father', 'Son', and 'Holy Ghost' are explained in the Gnostic *Gospel of Philip*: they (i.e. the names) are everywhere:
*p-pn(eum)a* *etuaab* *f-hm-p-uônh* *ebol* *f-hm-p-sa*
DEF.M-spirit holy [3MS]-[in-DEF.M-reveal out] [3MS]-[in-DEF.M-side
*m-p-itn* *f-hm-p-et-hêp* *f-hm-p-sa*
of-DEF.M-ground] [3MS]-[in-DEF.M-rel-hide.STA] [3MS]-[in-DEF.M-side
*n-t-pe*
of-DEF.F-heaven]
The Holy Ghost, it is in the revealed; it is below. It is in the concealed; it is above. (L*GospPh.* 59, 16–18)

(62d) The Lord appears in his might:
*uoh* *han-tap* *se-nhrêi* *ḫen-ne-f-cic*
and IDF.P-horn 3P-within in-POSS.P-3MS-hand
Horns are in his hands. (BHeb 3:4)

22 The attribution of this text to Shenute's authorship has been doubted, see Emmel (2004: II, 918 sub #33).

The examples cited above already illustrate the positioning of the predicate of the adverbial sentence in Coptic rather adequately. The majority of the latter are prepositional phrases, but some of these have probably been reanalysed as compounds and are no longer segmentable into their etymological parts. Actual adverbs are seldom attested due to the generally low number of such expressions in Coptic, where even the usually unsegmentable adverbs go back etymologically to prepositional phrases, such as e.g., *mpaima* 'here' (< *m-pai-ma* in-DEF.M-place) or *sapesêt* 'below' (< *sa-p-esêt* side-DEF.M-floor):

(63a) Victor tells of his ascetic lifestyle:
*hn-u-me pa-son pa-meh-hme pou*
in-IDF.S-truth POSS.M.1S-brother POSS.M.1S-ORD-40 today
*mpe-lau bôk ehun*
NEG.PST-any go into
*e-ta-tapro ude mpe-i-kaa-t kaheu n-na-hoite*
to-POSS.F.1S-mouth nor NEG.PST-1S-give-1S naked of-POSS.P.1S-cloth
*et-hiôô-t*
REL-upon-1s
Truly my brother, today is the fortieth (day) while nothing has entered my mouth, nor have I taken off the garment that I am wearing.
($^{S}$*Mart. St Victor the General* [Budge, *Martyrdoms* 31, 19–22])

(63b) Once a group of elders paid a visit to Apa Poemen:
*un-u-rôme=de mmau*
PTC-IDF.S-man=yet there
But there was a man. ($^{S}$*AP* Chaîne 67, 18–19)

(63c) An angel appeared in a glorious form:
*ne-f-urête n-t-ḫe n-u-amt barôt*
POSS.P-3MS-foot in-DEF.F-way of-IDF.S-metal brass
*e-f-pase ḫn-u-koht*
DEP-3MS-cook.STA in-IDF.S-fire
His feet were like brass glowing in fire.
($^{A}$*ApSoph.* [Steindorff, *Apokalypse des Elias* 50 9, 19–10, 1])

(63d) Having reached a well surrounded by palm trees and plants on his journey through the desert, Paphnutius took a rest and wondered who could have planted the trees:
*ne-uon-han-beni=gar mmau pe nem-han-kithri*
PRT-PTC-IDF.P-palm=for there PTC COM-IDF.P-lemon
*nem-han-erman nem-han-kente*
COM-IDF.P-pomegranate COM-IDF.P-fig
*nem-han-emp*$^{h}$*eh nem-han-aloli nem-han-dôrakion nem-han-sisiphos*
COM-IDF.P-apple COM-IDF.P-vine COM-IDF.P-nectarine COM-IDF.P-jujube

*nem-han-ke-mêš* *n-šên* *e-nese-pu-karpos*
COM-IDF.P-other-multitude of-tree DEP-beautiful-POSS.M.3P-fruit
*ere-tu-tipi* *holc* *m-p$^h$-rêti* *m-pi-ebiô*
DEP-POSS.F.3P-taste sweet.STA in-DEF.M-way of-DEF$_2$.M-honey
For there were palm and lemon trees, pomegranate and fig trees, apple trees and vine, nectar and jujube trees, as well as many other trees with beautiful fruit whose taste was sweeter than honey.
($^B$Papnute, *Wanderings* [*RecTrav* 6, 185, 7–9; collated])

In some Coptic dialects, but especially in Bohairic, certain etymological noun phrases can function as adverbials, typically with the location adverbs construed with the locative noun *sa-* (lit. 'side'):

(64a) Macarius spent a night in an ancient tomb filled with corpses of long deceased heathens. He used one of them as a pillow. Demons tried to frighten him by calling out to the corpse, which replied:
*uon-u-šemmo* *sa-p-šôi* *mmo-i* *mmon-š-com*
PTC-IDF.S-stranger side-DEF.M-height from-1S NEG.have-can-power
*mmo-i* *e-i*
OBJ-1S to-go
There is a stranger on top of me, and I cannot leave.
($^B$*AP Macarius* [*MG* 25, 212, 15; collated])

(64b) Jesus tells the Pharisees that the kingdom of God will not come in any observable way, and no-one will be able to say that it would be here or there:
*hêppe=gar* *is* *ti-met-uro* *nte-p$^h$-(nu)ti* *sa-ḫun* *mmô-ten*
behold=for lo DEF$_2$.F-ABST-king of-DEF.M-god side-within of-2P
For, behold, the kingdom of God is within you. ($^B$Lk 17:21)

Coptic shows free positioning of non-predicative adverbial phrases in the sentence; in the following example a temporal adverbial appears initially:

(65) Apa Sisoi met a hunter in the wilderness and asked him:
*e-k-nêu* *tôn* *auô* *eis-uêr* *n-uoiš*
ST-2MS-come.STA WH and look-how_long of-time
*k-m-pei-ma*
2MS-in-DEM.M-place
*ntof=de* *peca-f* *ce-phusi* *pa-iôt*
3MS=yet said-3MS COMP-truly POSS.M.1S-father
*eis-mnt-ue* *n-ebot* *ti-hm-pei-tou*
look-ten-one of-month 1S-in-DEM.M-mountain
'Where do you come from, and for how long have you been here?' He replied: 'To be honest my father, it is eleven months now that I am in these mountains'. ($^S$*AP* Chaîne 81, 1–2)

Even though adverbial sentences do occur in Bohairic, this dialect shows a specific development in the form of a dummy predicate *$k^h$ê* inserted before the actual predicative adverbial. This *$k^h$ê* is the stative form of the verb *$k^h$ô* 'to place' but is completely devoid of its original semantic value (quite similar to Late Egyptian use of *ꜥḥꜥ* in comparable sentences, as J. Winand pointed out to us). However, the auxiliary is less often attested in sentences with an indefinite subject:

(66a) God reveals himself to Isaac and says:

| | | |
|---|---|---|
| *mper-er-hoti* | *ti-$k^h$ê=gar* | *nema-k* |
| NEG.IMP-do-fear | 1S-AUX=for | with-2MS |

Fear not, for I am with you. ($^{B}$Gn 26:24)

(66b) The narrative inserts some biographical data:

| | | | | |
|---|---|---|---|---|
| *e-na-f-$k^h$ê=gar* | *ḫen-20* | *n-rompi* | *pe* | *et-a-f-saci* |
| DEP-PRT-3MS-AUX=for | in-20 | of-year | PTC | REL-PST-3MS-speak |

| | |
|---|---|
| *nema-f* | *nce-p-uro* |
| with-3MS | PVS-DEF.M-king |

He was twenty years old when the emperor spoke to him.
($^{B}$*Mart. Macarius of Antioch* [*AdM* 40, 17])

(66c) A description of the setting of the Ark of the Covenant and related items in the temple ends:

| | | | | | |
|---|---|---|---|---|---|
| *uoh* | *na-u-$k^h$ê* | *mmau* | *pe* | *ša-eḫun* | *e-$p^h$ou* |
| and | PRT-3P-AUX | there | PTC | until-down | to-today |

And there they were up until today. ($^{B}$2Chr 5:9)

(66d) Amphilochius starts his sermon on the patriarch Abraham with the sentence:

| | | | | |
|---|---|---|---|---|
| *uon* | *niben* | *$k^h$ê* | *ḫa-$p^h$-nomos* | *nte-te-f-phusis* |
| each | all | AUX | under-DEF.M-law | of-POSS.F-3MS-nature |

| | | | | | | |
|---|---|---|---|---|---|---|
| *uoh* | *e-f-oi* | *m-bôk* | *na-s* | *f-uôš* | *f-uôš* | *an* |
| and | DEP-3MS-be.STA | as-servant | for-3FS | 3MS-wish | 3MS-wish | NEG |

| | | | | |
|---|---|---|---|---|
| *ša-f-côk* | *ebol* | *n-nê* | *ete-te-f-phusis* | *uaš-u* |
| AOR-3MS-complete | out | OBJ-DEF$_3$.P | REL-POSS.F-3FS-nature | wish-3P |

Every man is subject to the law of his nature, and, being a slave of it and whether agreeing or not, he performs all that his nature wants.
($^{B}$Amphilochius of Iconium, *On Abraham* [Datema 275, 5–7])

(66e) St Anthony reasons:

| | | | | | |
|---|---|---|---|---|---|
| *uon-3* | *n-hôb* | *$k^h$ê* | *ḫen-pi-kosmos* | *uoh* | *se-$k^h$ê* |
| PTC-3 | of-thing | AUX | in-DEF$_2$.M-world | and | 3P-AUX |

*hi-pi-tôu=an*
on-DEF$_2$.M-mountain=NEG

Three things are in this world, and they are not in the desert.
($^{B}$*AP St Anthony* [Amélineau, MG 25 36, 12–13 collated])

The use of *$k^{h}$ê* is occasionally attested in other dialects, but much less often than in Bohairic:

(67a) In the parable of the ten pieces of silver the third servant comes back and returns the money to his master:

| | | | | |
|---|---|---|---|---|
| *p-cois* | *te-k-mna* | *e-ne-s* | *ntoot-ø* | *s-kê* |
| DEF.M-lord | POSS.F-2MS-mina | DEP-PRT-2FS | with-1S | 3FS-AUX |
| *hn-u-sudarion* | | | | |
| in-IDF.S-napkin | | | | |

My Lord! (Here is) your money that has been with me! It is in a napkin. ([S]Lk 19:20)

(67b) Asked by Anthimus what a man who has given out alms should do if accused of having forgotten the recipients, Cyril answers:

| | | | | |
|---|---|---|---|---|
| *p-et-k-šine* | *nsô-f* | *kê* | *hn-šomnte* | *n-hupothesis* |
| DEF.M-REL-2MS-look | after-3MS | AUX | in-3 | of-possibility |

There are three possibilities for what you ask for.

([S]Cyril of Alexandria, *Erotapokrisis* [Crum, pCheltenham 10, 1])

(67c) Hosea castigates the Israelites and accuses them of false oaths and lying:[23]

| | | | | |
|---|---|---|---|---|
| *au* | *n-t-ẖe* | *n-u-ntê$k^{j}$* | *e-f-ẖn-u-kaie* | |
| and | in-DEF.F-way | of-IDF.S-weed | DEP-3MS-in-IDF.S-field | |
| *e-s-ki* | *a-p-šô* | | | |
| DEP-3FS-AUX | to-DEF.F-sand | | | |
| *tei* | *te* | *t-ẖe* | *et-f-na-ti-uu* | *n$k^{j}$i-p-hep* |
| DEM.F | COP.F | DEF.F-way | REL-3MS-FUT-give-loose | PVS-DEF.M-law |

...and like a weed, which is in a sandy field, thus springs up the law.

([A]Hos 10:4 [Till])

(67d) The apostle tells the Thessalonians that he has sent Timothy for their encouragement and to comfort them in their faith:

| | | |
|---|---|---|
| *teten-soun=gar* | *ce-a-n-kê* | *e-pei-hôb* |
| 2P-know=for | COMP-ST-1P-AUX | to-DEM.M-thing |

For you know that we are appointed thereunto. ([F]1Th 3:3)

23 In this example, the use of *$k^{h}$ê* might also represent the lexical expression *ki apšo* 'be sandy' rather than an auxiliation process; cf. Crum (1939: 549b bottom).

# 2 Clausal morpho-syntax

## 2.1 Earlier Egyptian

### 2.1.1 Initial and coordinated clauses

Adverbial sentences are found in a wide variety of clausal configurations in Earlier Egyptian. Contrary to what is usually stated or implied in grammatical works on this language (e.g. Graefe 2001: 49), bare constructions of this kind without any introducing elements are widely used in independent clauses. If the subject of such a sentence is a noun (-phrase), it occupies the absolute initial position, as in the following examples that set off sections of direct speech or description and where there is thus no doubt of their syntactic status (cf. Vernus 1997: 45–58):

(68a) Beginning of CT spell 767:

| *ḥtp-w* | *m-p-t* | *ḥꜥ-w* | *m-tꜣ* |
|---|---|---|---|
| content.PIA-P | in-heaven-F | joy.PPA-P | in-earth |

The content ones are in heaven; the joyful ones are on earth. (CT VI 398f)

(68b) Appeal to the Living of Qay:

| *mrr* | *ḥss=sw* | *ḫntyimntw* | *ḏd-t(y)-f(y)* |
|---|---|---|---|
| desire.IP | favour=3MS | N | say-FUT.REL-AGR |

| *ḫꜣ* | *m-ḫ-t=nb* | *n-imꜣḫ* | *qꜣy* |
|---|---|---|---|
| 1000 | in-thing-F=QU.M | to-revered | N |

He who desires that Khentyamenty favours him (is) one who will say:
'A thousand of everything to the revered Qay'. (CG 20567, 1–2)

(68c) The deceased says to Seth:

| *m=ḏd=rk* | *ḥr-k* | *n-ḫr-k* |
|---|---|---|
| AUX.NEG.IMP=say.NC=PTC | face-2MS | to-testicles-2MS |

Do not say: 'May your face be against your testicles!' (BD 90/*Nu* pl. 22, 7)

Less often, if the subject of such a clause is pronominal, it is coded by an absolute pronoun (see exx. 12a and 12b). Nevertheless, the information structure and illocutionary status of such bare adverbial sentences differs markedly from that of their counterparts preceded by an initial particle or especially by an auxiliary (see 3.1.2.1 for discussion). Broadly speaking, in initial environments Earlier Egyptian adverbial sentences are usually preceded by an initial particle or an auxiliary – regardless of the nature of its subject expression. Examples of some of these elements have already been cited above, but here one should note the less common combinations. As for initial particles, aside from the common *mk/mṯ/mṯn*,

https://doi.org/10.1515/9783110409895-003

one often finds the elements *ỉsṯ/ỉst/ỉsk* and *tỉ*, whose function was in origin to mark the following adverbial (or some other type of) sentence as consisting of background information that is nevertheless important to the understanding of the overall discourse context:

(69a) Having told how he had served 'his mistress' Rediu-Khnum clarifies:

| | | | | | |
|---|---|---|---|---|---|
| *ỉsṯ=s(y)* | *m-sꜣ-t* | *nsw* | *m-ḥm-t* | *nsw* | *mr-t-f* |
| PTC=3FS | as-daughter-F | king | as-wife-F | king | love.PPP-F-3MS |

Now, she was the king's daughter and his beloved royal wife. (CG 20543, 9)

(69b) Thutmosis III tells of his youth in the temple of Amun:

| | | | | |
|---|---|---|---|---|
| *tỉ=w(ỉ)* | *m-wḏḥỉ* | *m-rpr* | *nw-t-f* | *n-ḫpr[-t]* |
| PTC=1S | as-youth | in-temple | city-F-3MS | NEG-happen-TERM |
| *bs-ỉ* | *r-ḥmnṯr* | | | |
| initiation-1S | to-priest | | | |

Now, I was a youth in the temple of his city when my initiation as a priest had not taken place. (*Urk.* IV 157, 8–9)

The initial particles *nḥmn* 'certainly' and *ḥꜣ/ḥw* 'if only' mentioned at the end of section 1.1, are rare with adverbial sentences, as is the alternative (yes/no) question marker *ỉn/ỉnỉw*:

(70a) Sinuhe boasts:

| | |
|---|---|
| *nḥmn=wỉ* | *mỉ-kꜣ* |
| PTC=1S | like-bull |

I am certainly like a bull! (Sin B, 117–18)

(70b) Khakheperraseneb longs for personal fortitude in the face of misfortune:

| | | | |
|---|---|---|---|
| *ḥꜣ=n-ỉ* | *ỉb* | *m-rḫ* | *wḫdw* |
| PTC=to-1S | heart | as-know.PIA | suffering |

If only I had a heart that knew suffering. (Khakheperraseneb r° 13–14)

(70c) The deceased asks:

| | | | |
|---|---|---|---|
| *ỉnỉw=tr* | *ỉt(-ỉ)* | *ꜥꜣ* | *ḥnꜥ(-ỉ)* |
| IP=PTC | father[-1S] | here | with[-1S] |

Is my father really here with me? (CT I 227c)

A characteristic feature of Earlier (as well as later) Egyptian syntax is the grammatical marking of clauses as sequential or 'contingent' in character.[24] With the

24 See Depuydt (1993: 201–55) for a general discussion; cf. also Vernus (1990: 61–99); Polis (2005: 301–22).

adverbial sentence, there are some examples with the particle *ḫr* 'then', which signals generic and often 'processual' states of affairs unfolding in a sequence[25]:

(71) A mortuary text reveals what to say to the yon ferryman and adds:
*ḫr* *ḥr-f* *r-nṯr-w=ipn* *wn-w* *ḥr-pf* *gs*
PTC face-3MS to-god-P=DEM.P AUX.PP-P on-DEM.M side
*n(-y)-itrw*
of[-M]-river
Then his face is towards those gods who are on that side of the river.
(CT V 187d/B7C)

The synthetic equivalent (and diachronic predecessor) of *ḫr* + sentence is the pattern predicate/AUX + *ḫr-f* + clause, where *ḫr* is affixed to a lexical verb or, in case of S–P patterns such as adverbial sentences, a form of the auxiliary *wn/wnn*:

(72) A general point concerning kingship:
*isṯ* *nsw* *dni-t=pw* *n(-y)-inr* *wn-ḫr-f* *m-ḥs*
PTC king dam-F=SE of[-M]-stone AUX-SEQ-3MS in-opposition
*r-wry-t*
to-flood-F
Now the king, he is a stone dam; and thus he stands in opposition to a flood. (Red Chapel 126, 16–17)

In past sequential contexts, the corresponding construction is introduced by *wn-in*:

(73) The courtiers have just entered before the king:
*wn-in-sn* *ḥr-ẖ-t-sn* *m-bꜣḥ-ḥm-f* *ꜥ.w.s.* *m-wḥmꜥ*
AUX-SEQ-3P on-belly-F-3P in-presence-majesty-3MS l.p.h. in-again
Then they were again on their bellies in the presence of his majesty l.p.h.
(Neferty Ii)

Of the sequential particles *kꜣ* and *iḫ*, only examples in which the adverbial sentence is preceded by the auxiliary *wn/wnn* are attested for certain (see 3.1.3.1.2). There are serious doubts concerning the representativeness and grammaticality of the following rare instances in which these particles appear to precede bare adverbial sentences:

---

**25** That is, *ḫr* and its earlier equivalent *sḏm-ḫr-f* noted below characteristically describe sequential situations that are parts of a larger process such as preparing medical potions, conducting mathematical calculations, and the like. The overall effect resembles that of modern travel guides: 'You walk forward and come across a large court. You turn right and enter the temple of Ramesses III ...' etc.

(74a) In a broken context:
*k3=rf* *ḏḥwty* *m-gs[-i]*
PTC=PTC N in-side-1S
Then Thoth will be by my side. (pLondon med. 7, 12)

(74b) After informing the temple overseer of an expected heliacal rising of Sirius, the author of a letter adds:
*iẖ* *ḥr* *im* *[n-y?]-wnw-t* *ḥwtnṯr*
PTC face there (of-M)-priesthood-F temple
Then the attention (of?) the priesthood of the temple should be (directed) thereto. (pBerlin P 10012, 4 –5)

Of the auxiliaries, the otherwise very common element *ʿḥʿ-n* 'then' is rare with adverbial sentences, although some examples with it are documented[26]:

(75) Nehri, referring to himself in the third person, says that he received his rule through royal recognition:
*ʿḥʿ-n* *t3=pn* *r-ḏr-f* *ẖr-sẖr=nb* *ḏdy-f*
AUX land=DEM.M to-limit-3MS under-plan=QU.M say.REL.FUT-3MS
Then all this land was subject to any scheme that he might announce. (Hatnub 20, 5–6)

Much more common with adverbial sentences are the auxiliaries *iw* and *wn/wnn*. However, the latter in particular has little to do with clausal initiality, although it may occur in absolute initial adverbial sentences that, for example, set off sections of direct speech or provide the opening title for religious spells:

(76a) Having heard of the death of Amenemhat I, Ammunenshi asks:
*wnn=irf* *t3=pf* *mi-m* *m-ẖmt-f*
AUX=PTC land=DEM.M like-WH in-ignorance-3MS
How, then, is that land without him? (Sin B, 43–44)

(76b) Title of a CT spell:
*wnn* *s* *mm-ʿnẖ-w*
AUX man among-living-P
The man is among the living. (CT VI 333a)

(76c) In a funerary formula of a Memphite official:
*wn* *im3ẖ-f* *ẖr-inpw*
AUX reverence-3MS before-N
May his reverence be before Anubis! (*Teti Cemetery* III, pl. 18)

26 See ex. 196 for another occurrence.

Instead, *wn/wnn* is rather used to modify the illocutionary and temporal profile of the adverbial sentence in various ways that will be described later (3.1.3.1.2). As for *ỉw*, it is a common working practise amongst scholars and students alike to interpret this element as a signal of clausal initiality, at least when the grammatical pattern introduced by it is of the order S–P and the subject is a noun (e.g., Polotsky 1971: 90). Although there is much to be said for this rule of thumb, it cannot always be applied mechanically; for example:

(77a) The peasant draws the high steward's attention to his own fortunate position:

| | | | | | |
|---|---|---|---|---|---|
| *ỉw* | *šd-w-k* | *m-sẖ-t* | *ỉw* | *fqꜣ-k* | *m-spꜣ-t* |
| AUX | field-P-2MS | in-country-F | AUX | reward-2MS | in-nome-F |
| *ỉw* | *ꜥq-w-k* | *m-šnꜥ* | | | |
| AUX | ration-P-2MS | in-storehouse | | | |

Your fields are in the country, your rewards are in the estate, and your rations are in the storehouse. (Peas B2, 65–66)

(77b) The deceased is told of his food provisions in the hereafter:

| | | | | | | | |
|---|---|---|---|---|---|---|---|
| *ỉw* | *tꜣ* | *3* | *r-p-t* | *ỉw* | *tꜣ* | *2* | *r-tꜣ* |
| AUX | bread | 3 | to-heaven-F | AUX | bread | 2 | to-earth |

Three loaves are for the sky, and two loaves are for the earth.

(CT VI 208g–h)

It is of course perfectly possible that each of the *ỉw*-introduced clauses in 77a is an 'independent' initial main clause used to give the words of the exasperated speaker a distinct rhetorical contour. Yet for 77b, the same argument would not seem to be equally applicable. It might also be pointed out that, like *wn/wnn*, *ỉw* is not primarily a marker of syntactic status of the clause but rather, as will be discussed in 3.1.3.1.2, of illocutionary force and information structure. Accordingly, the clauses in 77a and 77b could just as well be read as coordinated, as in the translation (cf. Collier 1991c: 46–47). Such an analysis is often unavoidable in instances where a particle-introduced clause precedes a string of *bare* adverbial sentences that are easily understood as asyndetic coordinated clauses, particularly when the successive clauses display tight thematic continuity (Collier 1996; Uljas 2007b):

(78a) The peasant approached the house of the villain Nemtynakht on a road described thus:

| | | | | | |
|---|---|---|---|---|---|
| *ỉw* | *wꜣ-t-f* | *wꜥ-t* | *ẖr-mw* | *k-t* | *ẖr-ỉt* |
| AUX | side-M | one-F | under-water | other-F | under-corn |

Its one side was under water, and the other was under barley.

(Peas R, 7.5–6)

(78b) The effect of the death of Amenemhat I is described:

| | | | | |
|---|---|---|---|---|
| *ỉw* | *ḫnw* | *m-sgr* | *ỉb-w* | *m-gmw* |
| AUX | residence | in-silence | heart-P | in-mourning |

The residence was in silence, and hearts were in mourning. (Sin R, 8–9)

(78c) Beginning of a magical spell in a medical text:

| | | | | |
|---|---|---|---|---|
| *ỉw* | *ḫrw* | *m-p-t* | *rs-t* | *ḏr-ḫꜣw* |
| AUX | voice | in-heaven-F | southern-F | since-night |
| *ḫnnw* | | *m-p-t* | *mḥt-t* | |
| disturbance | | in-heaven-F | northern-F | |

A tumult is in the southern sky through the night and a commotion in the northern sky. (pEbers 58, 7–8)

The key point is that, on the whole, a coordinated status of adverbial sentences, like that of many verbal sentence types, is usually not grammatically marked in Earlier Egyptian, and even *ỉw*-introduced clauses cannot simply be treated as 'wholly independent' even when their subjects are not pronominal. Most remarkably, however, coordination is by and large not marked separately from adjunction either. Indeed, adverbial sentences could clearly be used or 'embedded' directly as adjunct (in Egyptology, the traditional term is 'circumstantial') clauses without explicit grammatical marking. By this token, in 78a and 78b, an alternative and contextually perhaps equally feasible analysis would be to read the clauses *k-t ḫr-ỉt* and *ỉb-w m-gm-w* as relative present adjuncts '*while* the other was under water' and '*while* hearts were in mourning'. This ambiguity is a characteristic feature of Earlier Egyptian clausal syntax of bare adverbial sentences, which very often function as grammatically unmarked adjuncts. In addition, adverbial sentences could also be used in adjunct clauses preceded by various preposition-conjunctions, but their form was then radically different from that of the bare adverbial sentence 'circumstantials'. Finally, Earlier Egyptian adverbial sentences also occur in adjuncts exhibiting semantic control of the sentence 'actor', which was then omitted as a rule. These three types of adverbial sentence adjuncts must now be considered in turn.

### 2.1.2 Adjunct clauses 1: Unmarked constructions

In Egyptological studies predating the mid-1960s, the common type of Earlier Egyptian adjunct clauses whose 'circumstantial' status was not marked overtly and where the clause had 'nothing to distinguish it from a complete sentence except its meaning and its syntactic function' were viewed as having this status only 'virtually' (Gardiner 1957: §182). This analysis was later replaced by a theory according to which the adjunct use of the forms and constructions found in 'virtual' adjuncts was in fact a reflection of their adverbial status.[27] Nevertheless, it seems that the earlier hypothesis of Earlier Egyptian 'virtual' adjuncts as essentially unmarked rather than formally subordinate constructions is indeed broadly correct.[28] They appear to represent a category of co-textually connected clauses merely linked to another clause in a structurally and semantic-pragmatically maximally schematic and indeterminate manner. Consequently, their relationship may be understood and interpreted as one between a 'main' and an adjunct clause, but this is not the only alternative.[29] Indeed, the exact semantic interpretation of the combined clauses is left largely open and to be inferred by the hearer/reader.

Bare adverbial sentences are one of the most ubiquitous construction types found in Earlier Egyptian unmarked adjunct clauses. In cases where the subject of the construction is a noun and the state of affairs described is concomitant with that of the superordinate clause, the adjunct consists of nothing but the bare adverbial sentence that occupies the canonical position of adjuncts in Earlier Egyptian after the main clause:

(79a) The shipwrecked sailor advises his captain:

| *mdw-k* | *n-nsw* | *ỉb-k* | *m-ꜥ-k* |
|---|---|---|---|
| speak.SUB-2MS | to-king | heart-2MS | in-hand-2MS |

You should speak to the king with your mind in control. (Sh.S. 15–16)

(79b) The snake tells the shipwrecked sailor what will happen soon:

| *ỉw* | *dp-t* | *r-ỉỉt* | *m-ẖnw* | *sqd-w* | *ỉm-s* |
|---|---|---|---|---|---|
| AUX | boat-F | FUT-come.INF | from-residence | sailor-P | in-3FS |

| *rḫ-n-k* |
|---|
| know.REL-PST-3MS |

A boat will come from the residence, with sailors in it whom you know. (Sh.S. 119–21)

(79c) Sinuhe is welcomed at the border by a royal envoy:

| *rdỉ-ỉn* | *ḥm-f* | *ỉw-t* | *mr* | *sḫt-w* | *mnḫ* |
|---|---|---|---|---|---|
| cause-SEQ | majesty-3MS | come-SUB | overseer | peasant-P | efficient |

| *n(-y)-prnsw* |
|---|
| of[-M]-palace |

| *ꜥḥꜥ-w* | *ꜣtp* | *m-ḫt-f* |
|---|---|---|
| boat-P | load.STA | after-3MS |

His majesty caused the overseer of the elite royal peasants to come, with laden boats in his charge. (Sin B, 243–44)

---

27 The principal discussion here is Polotsky (1971: 71–96).

28 Collier (1990; 1991c; 1999) provides the fundamental analysis here.

29 Indeed, adverbial sentences, along with the other 'circumstantially' used patterns, may also be used in the so-called virtual *relative* clauses; see 2.1.7.

If the subject of an adjunctive adverbial sentence of this type is a personal pronoun, it appears either as a suffix or clitic personal pronoun, both of which require some preceding ‘supporting’ host expression. In case of clitic pronouns, this was some form of the particles *(ỉ)sṯ/(ỉ)sk* or *tỉ* whose ‘backgrounding’ character made them ideally suited for the purpose[30]:

(80a) Thutmosis III says of his father Amun:
*wḏ-n-f=n(-ỉ)* *wnn(-ỉ)* *ḥr-ns-t-f* *ỉsk=wỉ*
order-PST-3MS=to[-1S] AUX[-1S] on-throne-F-3MS PTC=1S
*m-ỉm(-y)* *sš-f*
as-in.RLT[-M] nest-3MS
He ordered me to remain on his throne when I was (still) a fledgling.
(*Urk.* IV 157, 2–3)

(80b) The king says to Amenemhab:
*rḫ-n(-ỉ)* *qd-k* *tỉ=wỉ* *m-sšy*
know-PST[-1S] character-2MS PTC=1S in-nest
I came to know your character when I was (still) in the nest.
(*Urk.* IV 897, 11–12)

With suffix pronouns, the incorporation-base was, as noted in 1.1, the element *ỉw*:

(81a) Heqanakhte asks his addressee:
*(ỉ)n* *ḫr* *nfr=tw* *ḥr-wnm* *ỉt* *nfr* *ỉw-ỉ*
IP PTC good=2MS PROG-eat.INF barley good DEP-1S
*r-tꜣ*
to-earth
Now, are you not happily eating good barley when I am cast out?
(Heqanakhte I, v° 2)

(81b) The shipwrecked sailor has just encountered a fantastic snake; then:
*ỉw* *wp-n-f* *rꜣ-f* *r-ỉ* *ỉw-ỉ* *ḥr-ẖ-t-ỉ*
AUX open-PST-3MS mouth-3MS to-1S DEP-1S on-belly-F-1S
*m-bꜣḥ-f*
in-presence-3MS
He opened his mouth to me as I was on my belly before him.
(Sh.S. 67–68)

30 Cf. Ritter (1992: 136) and the term ‘flashback’ used of this in Winand (2006: 377).

Interestingly, it seems as if this '*i͗w*-support' took place also with demonstrative pronoun subjects (cf. Borghouts 2010: 98.e.ii):

(82) The man says in reference to his wealth:
*n-šm-i͗* *i͗w* *nfꜣ* *r-tꜣ*
NEG-go-1S DEP DEM.M to-earth
I have not passed away, although that is lost. (Man and Ba 33–34)

This supportive role of *i͗w* appears to have a major contributing factor in its subsequent Late Egyptian re-categorisation as a marker of syntactic dependency.[31] Earliest instances of this use seem to occur during the First Intermediate Period; below is an example with an adverbial sentence[32]:

(83) Khety boasts of his wealth during difficult times:
*i͗nk* *ꜥꜣ* *i͗tmḥ* *i͗w* *tꜣ* *m-ṯs*
1S great.PP grain DEP land in-sandbank
I was one plentiful of grain when there was a drought in the land.
(Siut V, 9)

In the following example, the two 'support'-constructions vary mutually:

(84) The deceased has asked his soul to come and see the 'yon man'; he adds:
B1C: *ꜥḥꜥ-f* *ḥms-f* *i͗w-k* *ẖft-ḥr-f*
stand.SUB-3MS sit.SUB-3MS DEP-2MS before-face-3MS
B2L: *ꜥḥꜥ-f* *ḥms-f* *sk=ṯw* *ẖft-ḥr-f*
stand.SUB-3MS sit.SUB-3MS PTC=2MS before-face-3MS
He will stand up and sit down whilst you are before him. (CT II 108c)

It is important to bear in mind that the *i͗w*-clauses in 81a and 81b are not formally subordinate any more than the bare adverbial sentences in 79a–79c, nor does *i͗w*, which here is a mere morphological supporting element, have its usual function as a predication-level operator used to fix the illocutionary force and information structure of the following proposition (see 3.1.3.1). The same largely holds also for clauses with (*i͗*)*sṯ* etc., which are similarly not marked as subordinate. However, with the latter elements, the situation is more complex than with *i͗w*. It is common for (*i͗*)*sṯ* and related particles to introduce clauses where the subject of the

---

**31** See 2.2.2.1 as well as Kroeber (1970: 106–26).

**32** See also Loprieno (2006) and Uljas (2010) for further examples from Earlier Egyptian sources. For counterarguments against the adjunct analysis of the relevant examples, see Schenkel (2007).

adverbial sentence is a noun, but which are still most straightforwardly rendered as adjuncts:

(85a) Weni says that it was exceptional that he was appointed to lead a huge army:

*ỉnk wn ỉrỉ(-ỉ)=n-sn sẖr sṯ ỉꜣ-t(-ỉ) m-mr*
1S AUX.PP do[-1S]=to-3P plan PTC office-F[-1S] as-overseer
*ẖnt(-y)š pr-ꜥꜣ*
tenant house-great
It was me who used to make plans for them, although my office was (only) that of overseer of royal tenants. (*Urk.* I 102, 9–10)

(85b) Young King Pepi II writes to his envoy Harkhuf, anxious to receive an unusual gift:

*ỉr spr-k r-ẖnw sk dng=pw m-ꜥ-k*
CND arrive-2MS to-residence PTC dwarf=DEM.M in-hand-2MS
*ꜥnẖ wḏꜣ snb*
live.STA prosper. STA healthy.STA
*ỉw ḥm(-ỉ) r-ỉrt=n-k ꜥꜣ-t*
AUX majesty[-1S] FUT-do.INF=to-2MS great-F
If you arrive at the residence with this dwarf with you alive, healthy, and prosperous, my majesty will do something great for you. (*Urk.* I 130, 16–131, 1)

Yet equally often, formally identical clauses occur in environments where an adjunct interpretation is unlikely if not impossible. Consider, for example, the following instance:

(86) Nemtynakht has just eyed the goods of the peasant greedily; the narrative proceeds:

*ỉst=rf pr nmtynẖt=pn ḥr-smꜣ-tꜣ n(-y)-rꜣ*
PTC=PTC house N=DEM.M on-join-land of[-M]-mouth
*n(-y)-wꜣ-t*
of[-M]-road-F
Now, the house of this Nemtynakht was at the junction by an opening of a road. (Peas Bt, 27–28)

Here the adverbial sentence actually follows a section of direct speech by one of the protagonists of the tale. It also sets off a new thematic section that represents one of the most pivotal episodes of the story in which the peasant is deprived of his goods. However, rather than part of the main narrative thread, the geographical locus of the villain Nemtynakht's house is nevertheless merely necessary background for the understanding of his method of robbing the peasant.

Accordingly, this and other clauses introduced by *(ỉ)sṯ* are not ‘really’ syntactically adjuncts, but since they convey supportive material to the main narrative or descriptive thread, they may often be *translated* as such (cf. Loprieno 1995: 152–153). In Old Egyptian, adverbial (and other) sentences with *(ỉ)sṯ/(ỉ)sk* are not bound to occur in the canonical adjunct position after a main clause, but may also appear in absolute initial position:

(87a) Weni tells of his rapid promotion:
*sṯ=w(ỉ)* *m-zꜣb* *r-nḫn* *rdỉ=w(ỉ)* *ḥm-f*
PTC=1S as-judge warden-N put.PRF=1S majesty-3MS
*m-smr-wꜥt(y)* *mr* *ḫnt(-y)š* *pr-ꜥꜣ*
as-friend-sole overseer tenant house-great
When I was a judge and warden of Nekhen, his majesty appointed me a unique friend and overseer of royal tenants. (*Urk.* I 100, 6–7)

(87b) Hezi tells of his exalted position in the court:
*sk=w(ỉ)* *m-zꜣb* *sḥḏ* *sš* *n(-y)-rḫ* *nsw*
PTC=1S as-judge overseer scribe of[-M]-know.INF king
*rn(-ỉ)* *ṯn-y*
name[-1S] distinguish-STA
*r-bꜣk=nb*
to-servant=QU.M
Now, although I was (only) a judge and an overseer of scribe(s) of the king’s knowing, my name was more distinguished than (that of) any servant. (Hezi A5 [*JARCE* 37, 1–13])

Similar constructions are not attested later on, although in the following example an adverbial sentence introduced by *ỉst* is inserted parenthetically in the middle of the main clause:

(88) Description of part of Neferperet’s foreign plunder:
*ỉn-n* *wdpw* *nsw* *nfrprt* *ỉst=sw* *m-šmsw-t*
bring-PST butler king N PTC=3MS in-following-F
*ḥm-f* *ḥr-ḫꜣs-t* *rṯnw*
majesty-3MS on-foreign land-F N
*mnmn-t* *n-ḏꜣhy* *ḥm-t* *4*
cattle-F of-Syria cow-F 4
The royal butler Neferperet brought, when he was in his majesty’s train in the country of Retenu, Syrian cattle, (including) four cows...
(*Urk.* IV 1020, 7–9)

This might be seen as supporting the hypothesis that *(ỉ)sṯ* was originally an adjunct marker that subsequently acquired the role of a more general marker of dependence.[33] However, the diachronic development of comparable elements normally proceeds in the reverse order; i.e. connectors of a more semantic and pragmatic function become 'syntacticised' and acquire a structural role – as seen e.g. from the development of *ꞽw* from Earlier to Later Egyptian, which furnishes a very good example of this (see 2.2.2.1).

The final formally separate class of unmarked adverbial sentence adjuncts, i.e. constructions where adjunctive status is not marked by any specific means, are bare final ('so that') clauses. In these constructions, the situation described is not concomitant with the main clause, but rather portrayed as a relative future expectation that typically describes the motive for the state of affairs described in the latter (cf. Palmer 2000: 131). Adverbial sentences of this type are headed by the form *wn* of the auxiliary element *wn/wnn*:

(89a) The goddess Hathor says to Queen Hatshepsut:

| | | |
|---|---|---|
| *ꞽꞽ-n(-ꞽ)* | *wn(-i)* | *m-sꜣ-ṯ* |
| come-PST[-1S] | AUX[-1S] | as-protection-2FS |

I have come so that I may be your protection. (*Urk*. IV 239, 16–17)

(89b) The deceased is said to be deserving of entry to the underworld:

| | | | | | | |
|---|---|---|---|---|---|---|
| *ꞽw* | *N* | *rḫ* | *wꜣ-w-t* | *štꜣ(-t)* | *sbꜣ-w* | *n-w-sḫtꞽꜣrw* |
| AUX | N | know.STA | road-P-F | hidden[-F] | gate-P | of-P-N |
| *wn* | *N* | *ꞽm* | | | | |
| AUX | N | there | | | | |

N knows the hidden roads and the gates of the Field of Reeds, so that N may be there. (CT IV 49p–q)

The second example above shows that *wn* is required regardless of whether the subject of the final clause here is a noun or a pronoun. Its appearance is thus not determined by the morpho-syntactic properties of pronominal subjects of the adjunct clause. Instead, and as shown in 3.1.3.1, the use or non-use of auxiliary elements in adverbial sentences and the choice of the specific auxiliary is a complex matter based on temporal, modal, and information-structuring decisions by the users of the language.

**33** Oréal (2011: 249–50 and *passim*). More particularly, Oréal argues that *(ꞽ)sk/(ꞽ)sṯ* were used in Old Egyptian to introduce subordinate adjunct clauses whose content, however, need not be backgrounded. During the First Intermediate Period the particles developed a rather more pragmatically-based information structuring and backgrounding function typical of the Middle Egyptian *(ꞽ)st* and particularly *tꞽ*.

### 2.1.3 Adjunct clauses 2: marked constructions

Besides appearing in unmarked adjunct clauses lacking special formal indications of subordinate status, Earlier Egyptian adverbial sentences are also commonly found in *marked* adjuncts preceded by subordinating elements. Interestingly, Earlier Egyptian did not possess a specialised class of grammaticalised conjunctions for introducing adjunct clauses. Instead, and in keeping with the tendency of this language to form clausal adjuncts without specialised means, expressions usually classified as prepositions were employed for this task (Gardiner 1957: §§222–223; Uljas 2007c: 221–263, 266–268; Stauder-Porchet 2009: 42–50). Adverbial sentence adjunct clauses of this type, and, indeed, all adjuncts preceded by a preposition-conjunction, are divisible into two structural types. In the first type, the preposition-conjunction is directly followed by the adverbial sentence that is invariably preceded by a form of the auxiliary *wn/wnn*. Although a great many preposition-conjunctions are attested in Earlier Egyptian, examples with a directly following adverbial (rather than verbal) sentences are documented only with the elements *m* 'when', *mi͗* 'like', *r* '(in order) to', *ḏr* 'since', and *n-mrwt* 'so that' (lit. 'for love of'):

(90a) Idi says that he took revenge at his dead father's enemies:

| | | | |
|---|---|---|---|
| *mꜣ-n(-i͗)=nb* | *sfꜣ=sw* | *srḫ=n-f=nb* | *i͗m-sn* |
| see.REL-PST[-1S]=QU.M | hate.PPA=3MS | accuse.PPA=to-3MS=QU.M | in-3P |

| | |
|---|---|
| *m-wn-f* | *m-pr-f* |
| as-AUX-3MS | in-house-3MS |

| | | |
|---|---|---|
| *i͗w* | *sḫr-n(-i͗)=sn* | *mi͗-qd-sn* |
| AUX | fell-PST[-1S]=3P | like-form-3P |

Anyone I saw who had hated him or laid accusations against him among them when he was in his house – I overthrew them all.

(Kom el-Koffar A9 [*ASAE* 70, 419–29])

(90b) The coda of a spell contains an assurance of its benefits to the deceased:

| | | | |
|---|---|---|---|
| *wnn-ḫr-f* | *wḏꜣ* | *mi͗-wnn-f* | *tp-tꜣ* |
| AUX-SEQ-3MS | flourish.STA | like-AUX-3MS | on-earth |

Consequently he flourishes, just as when he was on earth.

(BD 72/*Nu* pl. 20, 14)

(90c) The deceased is one of the divinities:

| | | | |
|---|---|---|---|
| *sḫpr-w-n* | *tm* | *sꜣḫ-w-n-f* | *ṯn-w-n-f* |
| create.REL-P-PST | N | enspirit.REL-P-PST-3MS | distinguish.REL-P-PST-3MS |

| |
|---|
| *ṯs-w-n-f* |
| lift.REL-P-PST-3MS |

| | | | | |
|---|---|---|---|---|
| *ḥr[-sn]* | *r-wnn-sn* | *ḥnꜥ-f* | *wꜥ-y* | *m-nw* |
| face-3P | to-AUX-3P | with-3MS | alone-STA | in-N |

...whom Atum created and made spiritual and whose faces he distinguished and lifted up so that they might be with him alone in Nu. (CT IV 75d–f/B6C)

(90d) Queen Hatshepsut claims to have restored damage done by the Hyksos:
*i͗w ṯs-n-i͗ stp-t ḥꜣt ḏr-wn ꜥꜣm-w*
AUX erect-PST-1S break.PPP-F earlier since-AUX Asiatic-P
*m-qꜣb-n(-y)-tꜣmḥw ḥwtwꜥrt*
in-middle-of[-M]-N N
I have (re-)erected what had been in pieces earlier, since the Asiatics were in the midst of Avaris of Lower Egypt. (*Urk*. IV 390, 6–7)

(90e) The deceased is assigned awesome powers by a god:
*i͗w rdi͗-n-i͗ ꜣ-t-k mm-ꜣḫ-w*
AUX put-PST-1S dread-F-2MS among-spirit-P
*n-wr-n(-y)-pḥty-k*
through-greatness-of[-M]-might-2MS
*n-mrwt-wnn snḏ-k m-ḫ-t-sn*
for-love-AUX fear-2MS in-body-3P
I have put the dread of you among the spirits due to the greatness of your might, in order that the fear of you might be in their bodies. (CT I 77f–78a/B6C)

The introducing elements here perform a function of clausal conjunctions, but the adverbial sentence is apparently treated as a complement clause of a preposition. Consequently, rather than by the auxiliary *wn/wnn*, the clause could also be preceded by a specialised complementiser after the preposition. In this second type of marked adjuncts, which is found only with causal preposition-conjunctions, in affirmative clauses the complementiser is the element *ntt*. With adverbial sentences the combination [preposition + complementiser] is attested mostly with the elements *ḥr* 'because' and *ḏr* 'since'[34]:

(91a) A medical handbook explains why a physician may feel a pulse everywhere in the patient's body:
*ḫꜣꜣ-f n-ḥꜣ-t ḥr-ntt mt-w-f*
examine-3MS to-heart-F because-COMP vessel-P-3MS
*n-ꜥ-t-f=nb-t*
to-member-F-3MS=QU-F
It is the heart that he feels, because its vessels pertain to his (the patient's) every member. (pEbers 99, 4)

34 With other constructions the range of causal preposition-conjunctions is wider. In many Egyptological works, the complementiser and the preposition are analysed as non-isomorphic 'preposition-*ntt* connectors'; for arguments against this analysis, see Uljas (2007c: 248–50).

(91b) Ptahhetep warns against taking pride of one's own learning:

*m=mḥ* *ib-k* *ḥr-ntt=tw* *m-rḫ*
AUX.NEG.IMP=full.NC heart-2MS because-COMP=2MS as-know.PIA
Do not be cocksure because you are wise. (Ptahhetep 53)

(91c) It is said of the deceased and his relationship to Osiris:

*s3w-t(w)* *ib* *n(-y)-wsir* *ḏr-ntt-f*
expand.SUB-PASS heart of[-M]-N since-COMP-3MS
*m-wꜥ* *n-w-ḏm* *r-f*
as-one of-P-suffer.PPA to-3MS
The heart of Osiris will be gladdened, since he is one of those who suffered for him. (CT VII 385b–c/B3C)

(91d) The deceased moves freely on the waterways of the netherworld:

*n* *iw-y-s* *d3-t* *ꜥ3-t* *in* *ḥrfmrdw3ḥꜥ*
NEG boatless-PROSP-3FS barque-F great-F AGT N
*ḏr-ntt* *rn* *n(-y)-rꜥ* *m-ẖ-t* *n-t-N=tn*
since-COMP name of[-M]-N in-body-F of-F-N=DEM-F
She will not be deprived of the great barque by He Whose Face is at His Knees and Who Acts with His Arm, since the name of Ra is in the body of this N. (CT VII 398c–399a/B3C)

Examples 91b and 91c show that if the adverbial sentence had a pronominal subject after *ntt*, in case of the second-person singular, this took the form of a clitic pronoun, whereas suffix pronouns were used in the corresponding third person. In the first-person singular, there is variation between the two types of pronouns (note the haplography (*n*)-*ntt* in 92b)[35]:

(92a) The deceased says that he will not become an offering for the guardians of the underworld:

*ḥr-ntt=wi* *m-šms* *n(-y)-nb* *ḫ-t*
because-COMP=1S in-train of[-M]-lord thing-F
...because I am in the train of the lord of offerings. (CT IV 310a/M54C)

(92b) After a long list of epithets, Intef gives his reason for asking for offerings:

(*n*)-*ntt-i* *m-b3k* *mrr-w*
because-COMP-1S as-servant love.IP-M
...because I was a beloved servant. (BM 572, 8)

**35** The complementiser *ntt* had, in the early language, a negative counterpart *iwt*. Examples of this element after prepositions are very rare, but some instances occur in the Pyramid Texts the preposition-conjunct *n* 'because'. Some of these would, at first sight, seem to be analysable as adverbial sentences, but a closer scrutiny shows that they actually represent existential constructions. See Uljas, forthcoming.

Under the heading of marked adverbial sentence adjuncts, one may also include conditional protases with the element *ir*.[36] In these relatively common constructions, the adverbial sentence is always introduced by the auxiliary *wn/wnn*, which in the vast majority of instances shows the writing *wnn*, the non-reduplicated *wn* being much less frequent[37]:

(93a) Sinuhe says of his adversary's possible intentions:

| | | | | | |
|---|---|---|---|---|---|
| *ir* | *wnn* | *ib-f* | *r-ꜥḥꜣ* | *imi* | *ḏd-f* |
| CND | AUX | heart-3MS | to-fight.INF | cause.IMP | say.SUB-3MS |

*ḫr-t-ib-f*
state-F-heart-3MS

If his mind is set for a fight, let him speak out his mind. (Sin B, 125)

(93b) Suspecting his addressee of causing mishap, the author of a letter to a dead person utters in desperation:

| | | | | |
|---|---|---|---|---|
| *ir* | *wn* | *srḫ* | *m-ẖ-t-ṯ* | *smḫ=sw* |
| CND | AUX | grief | in-body-F-2FS | forget.IMP=3MS |

*n-ib-n(-y)-ẖrd-w-ṯ*
for-heart-of[-M]-child-P-2FS

If there be a grievance in your body, forget it for the sake of your children! (Berlin Bowl, 2)

Finally, in the earlier stages of the language, there are some rare examples of adverbial sentence adjuncts with the clitic particle *=is*:

(94) The king, as Osiris, lies (metaphorically) on the hands of the ritualist:

| | | | | |
|---|---|---|---|---|
| *sbḥ=n-k* | *mn-t* | *wr-t* | *wsir=is* | *m-s-t* |
| cry.PRF=to-2MS | nurse-F | great-F | N=PTC | in-place-F |

*ꜥ-wy-f(y)*
hand-P:DU=3MS:DU

The Great Nurse has cried for you, with Osiris being in the place of his arms. (PT 884)

This particle appears to be an early marker of general clausal 'dependency'.[38] It does not seem to have been specialised to signal any particular type thereof, or even subordination. Since adverbial sentences could, as seen, be used directly as adjuncts, *=is* probably does not here so function as an operator/subordinator

---

**36** For general discussions, see e.g. Malaise (1985); Satzinger (1993); Kruchten (1994); Allen (2002: 91–93).

**37** Cf. Collier (1994: 17).

**38** However, this holds only insofar *affirmative* propositions are concerned. For the use of *=is* with the negative morpheme *n*, see the discussion on negated nominal sentences in Part II. A rather different analysis of *=is* is proposed in Loprieno (1995: 153–55).

in ex. 94 but rather just provides an overt signal of the subordinate status of the clause. Nevertheless, it shall be shown that the same particle is found also in nominal sentences serving as adjunct or complement clauses, and there the 'general dependency' of =*is* indeed seems to have functioned as a syntactic subordinator (see 2.1.5).

### 2.1.4 Adjunct clauses 3: control constructions

Besides fully clausal adjuncts of the sort illustrated above, Earlier Egyptian displays extensive adjunct use of adverbial sentences whose subject is semantically controlled by some previous expression.[39] In Earlier Egyptian, semantic control of adjunct clause subjects involves various verbal constructions and may be divided into subtypes, but with adverbial sentences control in adjuncts only occurs in oblique object environments comparable to English *I saw him walking in the street*, where the 'primary' object of the matrix verb is understood to be the subject of the following gerundive oblique object or 'predicative adjunct'. As in the example just cited, in English this construction is common with various kinds of transitive verbs, such as verbs of perception. In Earlier Egyptian, the oblique object may be a fully clausal suffix conjugation form, a bare subjectless Stative, or an adverbial sentence, but control in such environments is in this language restricted to verbs of visual perception and physical manipulation, both of which imply (but do not necessarily entail) direct contact between the perceiver or manipulator and the entity perceived or manipulated. Examples with adverbial sentences are commonest after the verbs *mꜣꜣ* 'see', *siꜣ* 'perceive, identify', and *gmi* 'discover' describing or implying visual perception. The oblique object is usually built with the so-called *m* of predication. Because in these instances the issue is often that of 'conceptual' rather than strictly perceptual 'finding', 'seeing', etc. (see here Collier 2007; Polis 2009: 351–52), the translation of the governing verb may vary between regarding, recognising, and identifying:

(95a) The king tells Ikhernefret why he has decided to send him on a mission:

| | | | | |
|---|---|---|---|---|
| *iri-n* | *ḥm(-i)* | *nw* | *mꜣ-n-i=ṯw* | *m-iqr-sḫr* |
| do-PST | majesty[-1S] | DEM | see-PST-1S=2MS | as-skilled-plan |

The reason why my majesty has done this is because I have recognised you as highly competent. (Berlin 1204, 7–8)

39 To date, the most thorough discussion of control in Earlier Egyptian is Uljas (2014).

(95b) Amenemhab tells that the king promoted him on account of his skills:

| | | |
|---|---|---|
| *si3-f=sw* | *m-ir-w* | *3ḫ-t* |
| identify.PRF-3MS=3MS | as-do.PPA-M | useful.P-F |

...because he identified him as one who does what is useful.

(*Urk.* IV 898, 14)

(95c) The snake tells of his feelings after the death of his siblings:

| | | | | |
|---|---|---|---|---|
| *ꜥḥꜥ-n-i* | *mt-kw=n-sn* | *gm-n-i=st* | *m-ẖ3y-t* | *wꜥ-t* |
| AUX-PST-1S | die-STA.1S=to-3P | find-PST-1S=3C | as-corpse-F | one-F |

Then I (nearly) died for their sake, after I found them in one heap of corpses.

(Sh.S. 131–32)

In principle, one could argue that constructions such as those above be analysed as fully clausal object complement adverbial sentences (i.e. *m3-n-i* [*=ṯw m-iqr-sḫr*]) rather than as involving a 'primary object' cleft apart from a merely phrasal 'secondary' oblique object (i.e. *m3-n-i* [*=ṯw*][*m-iqr-sḫr*]). However, bare adverbial sentences are not otherwise used as complements in Earlier Egyptian without a preceding auxiliary or complementiser (see 2.1.5). Furthermore, the controlling participant need not be immediately local to the 'oblique' object, as can be seen from ex. 96, where the clitic pronoun 'primary' object *=wi* cliticises to the first prosodic unit of the matrix clause and precedes the noun subject *ḥm-f* of the latter:

(96) Nekhebu tells of the beginning of his career:

| | | | |
|---|---|---|---|
| *gm-n=w(i)* | *ḥm-f* | *m-qd* | *n(-y)-ꜥš3-t* |
| find-PST=1S | majesty-3MS | as-builder | of[-M]-mass-F |

His majesty found me as an ordinary builder. (*Urk.* I 216, 1)

The full clausal analysis would somehow have to explain the now very discontinuous structure of the assumed clause where *=wi* is a member.[40] Finally, the following unique example seems to exhibit control with an adverbial sentence without zeroing of the adjunct subject, seemingly because the governing predicate is not a verb of visual perception:

(97) The snake threatens the shipwrecked sailor:

| | | | | |
|---|---|---|---|---|
| *ir* | *wdf-k* | *m-ḏd=n-i* | *in=tw* | *r-iw=pn* |
| CND | delay-2MS | in-say.INF=to-1S | bring.PP=2MS | to-island=DEM.M |

| | | | |
|---|---|---|---|
| *rdi-i* | *rḫ-k =tw* | *iw-k* | *m-ss* |
| cause-1S | know.SUB-2MS=2MS | DEP-2MS | as-ash |

If you delay in telling me who brought you to this island, I will make you feel (lit. 'know') yourself as ashes. (Sh.S. 70–72)

40 As correctly noted by Collier (1991c: 48 n.101).

Here the controlled adjunct is, of course, fully clausal, and the division between the 'primary' and 'oblique' objects quite obviously *rḫ-k* [=*tw*][*iw-k m-ss*]. Besides casting further doubt on the 'full clause' analysis of examples such as 95a–95c above, this last example also seems to show that omission of the controlled subject was not mandatory in instances not involving perception. However, although data here are woefully sparse, the following (partly corrupt) adverbial sentence example may suggest that, conversely, the overt expression of the subject was not mandatory either:

(98) Horemkhauef tells why he was promoted by his superior:

| | | | |
|---|---|---|---|
| *isṯ=grt* | *rḫ-n-f=(w)i* | *m-sr* | *mnḫ* |
| PTC=PTC | know-PST-3MS=1S | as-official | efficient |

He had identified me as an efficient official. (MMA 35.7.55, 7–8)

Then again, the verb *rḫ* does not mean simply 'know' here but rather 'to have learnt' or 'identified', which perhaps implies knowledge based on observation.[41] In any case, it seems that oblique control was in Earlier Egyptian a property associated with lexical entries and was thus a fundamentally semantic rather than a syntactic phenomenon. The construction is also common with the verbs of creating and placing *iri* and *rdi* and may represent an analogical formation based on the verbs of perception and the notion that the former situations prototypically take place 'under the eyes' of the manipulator or creator and imply direct visual observance. The direct object is usually followed by an adverbial phrase construed with the *m* of predication or *r* of futurity and corresponds to English predicative adjunct of the matrix verb:

(99a) Paheri profiles himself as a recognised intellectual:

| | | |
|---|---|---|
| *iri-n=wi* | *ʿry-i* | *m-rḫḫy* |
| make-PST=1S | pen-1S | as-know.PPP |

My pen made me known. (*Urk.* IV 119, 3)

(99b) Ptahhetep gives advice concerning an opponent:

| | | |
|---|---|---|
| *m=iri=sw* | *r-tkn* | *im-k* |
| AUX.NEG.IMP=do.NC=3MS | to-intimate | in-2MS |

Do not make him an intimate to you. (Ptahhetep 486)

41 A similar, but perhaps less easily accountable instance with the stative is Hezi A5 [*JARCE* 37, 1–13].

(99c) Khnumhetep relates the highpoint of his career:

| | | | | |
|---|---|---|---|---|
| *ꜥḥꜥ-n* | *rdi-n=wi* | *ḥm-f* | *m-ḥ3tyꜥ* | *n(-y)-mnꜥtḫwfw* |
| AUX | put-PST=1s | majesty-3MS | as-mayor | of[-M]-N |

Then his majesty appointed (lit. 'put') me as the mayor of Menat-Khufu.

(*Beni Hasan* I, pl. 44, 7)

(99d) Khnumhetep tells of his father's promotion by the king:

| | | | |
|---|---|---|---|
| *ꜥḥꜥ-n* | *rdi-n-f=sw* | *r-rpꜥt* | *ḥ3tyꜥ* |
| AUX | put-PST-3MS=3MS | to-elite member | mayor |

Then he appointed (lit. 'put') him an elite-member and a mayor.

(*Beni Hasan* I, pl. 25, 46–47)

Seeing that in 99a and 99c the clitic personal pronoun direct objects again precede the noun subject of the matrix verb *iri*, the correct syntactic division here is clearly [=*wi*][*m-rḫḫy*] and [=*wi*][*m-ḥ3tyꜥ*] rather than [=*wi m-rḫḫy*] and [=*wi m-ḥ3tyꜥ*]. However, this division is in conflict with the semantics of the sentences. In 99a, the idea is obviously not that 'my pen' 'made me' plain and simple, but, of course, that it 'made me famous'. The adverbial phrase is, in other words, very much a controlled predicative adjunct. Yet, whilst in 99a and 99b the latter seems still relatively omissible from a syntactic point of view (both *iri-n=wi ꜥry-i* 'My pen made me' and *m=iri=sw* 'Do not make him' would still be well-formed sentences), in 99c and 99d, omitting *m-ḥ3tyꜥ* 'as the mayor' and *r-rpꜥt* '(as) an elite-member' would lead to ungrammaticality. These phrases are thus no longer simply predicative adjuncts, but in fact non-omissible semantic arguments of the matrix verbs. That is, the issue is not only that of the semantic cohesion between the primary and oblique objects, but also between the latter and the matrix verb. Consider also the following examples:

(100a) Neferty announces what will follow next in his prophecy:

| | | | | |
|---|---|---|---|---|
| *di-i=n-k* | *s3* | *m-ḫrwy* | *sn* | *m-ḫft(y)* |
| give.SUB-1S=to-2MS | son | as-enemy | brother | as-opponent |

I will show (lit. give) you son as an enemy and brother as an opponent.

(Neferty IXf)

(100b) Djehutihetep tells how he received his position from his father:

| | | |
|---|---|---|
| *rdi-n-f=wi* | *m-ḥr(y)* | *nw-t-f* |
| put-PST-3MS=1S | as-chief | town-F-3MS |

He appointed (lit. 'put') me a chief over his town. (*El Bersheh* I, pl. 33)

Truncating 100a into mere *di-i=n-k s3* 'I will give you a son' would be completely beside the point, but it would still be grammatical, because the oblique expression is not an argument of the matrix verb. In 100b, however, it again has that status, rendering it both semantically and syntactically obligatory. What all this suggests is that besides being variously linked to the 'primary' object, controlled oblique expressions also form a scale of interconnections with the matrix verb that extends from 'free' attributes via semantically indispensable 'predicative' adjuncts to semantically *and* syntactically necessary arguments. Syntax, however, is considerably more static than meaning, and the same structural blueprint is generalised across a range of semantically divergent propositions.

### 2.1.5 Complement clauses

Adverbial sentences are common in all the different types of clausal complementation in Earlier Egyptian, and one of these types was already illustrated in 2.1.3. As shown earlier, in this phase of Egyptian adjunct clauses are usually formed using prepositions or 'preposition-conjunctions' as adjunctors. From a syntactic point of view, clauses following these elements serve as complements of the latter, and adverbial sentences serving this function are preceded either by a form of the auxiliary element *wn/wnn* or, in causal contexts, by the specific complementiser *ntt*. It suffices here to cite one more example of each of these two types of construction:

(101a) Sabu tells how the king singled him out for special favours:

| | | |
|---|---|---|
| *n-wn* | *ỉmꜣḫ(-ỉ)* | *m-ỉb-f* |
| because-AUX | reverence[-1S] | in-heart-3MS |

...because the reverence for me was in his heart. (*Urk*. I 84, 3)

(101b) Part of the dialogue between the deceased and gods, who try to force him to eat excrement:

| | | | | |
|---|---|---|---|---|
| *wnm=ỉrk* | *ỉn-sn* | *r-ỉ* | *n* | *wnm-ỉ=n-ṯn* |
| eat.IMP=PTC | QUOT-3P | to-1S | NEG | eat.PROSP-1S=to-3P |
| *ḥr-ỉšst* | *ỉn-sn* | *r-ỉ* | *ḥr-ntt* | *mdw=pw* |
| because-WH | QUOT-3P | to-1S | because-COMP | staff=DEM.M |
| *m-ꜥ-ỉ* | | | | |
| in-hand-1S | | | | |

'Eat!' they say to me. 'I will not eat for you'. 'Why?' they say to me. 'Because this staff is in my hand'. (CT III 49b–e/B1C)

Exactly the same division between *wn/wnn-* and complementiser-introduced adverbial sentence complements is found after governing verbs. Examples of the complementiser *ntt* and the diachronically earlier but functionally identical element *wnt* are largely restricted to object complement clauses of verbs of saying, knowing, and perception[42]:

(102a) The king tells his addressee what he thinks of the latter's skills as an organiser:
*sk=ḥm* *ḥm(-ꞽ)* *rḫ* *wnt* *ḥꜥw=nb*
PTC=PTC majesty[-1S] know.STA COMP ship=QU.M
*ḥr-nfr-w-f*
on-good-M-3MS
Now, my majesty knows that every ship is on an even keel. (*Urk.* I 61, 9)

(102b) Horus quotes what Ra told him to say concerning certain deities:
*ꞽw-sn* *ḥnꜥ-ꞽ* *kꜣ-k* *ḏr-kꜣ-sn* *ḥnꜥ-k*
AUX-3P with-1S QUOT-2MS limit-SEQ-3P with-2MS
*r-rḫ-t* *stẖ* *wnt-sn* *ḥnꜥ-k*
until-know-TERM N COMP-3P with-2MS
'They are with me' – so you shall say. Then they will end up with you well before Seth knows that they are with you. (CT II 359c–360a/S2P)

(102c) It is decreed in a directive outlining offences for which individuals are entered to criminal dockets:
[*ꞽr* *ꞽw*] *sp-sn* *k-y* *sp* *ḫr-t(w)* *smꞽ-t(w)*
CND come case-3P other-M time SEQ-PASS report-PASS
*swḏ-t(w)* *ntt=st* *ḥr-šfd*
inform-PASS COMP=3C on-papyrus
*n(-y)-ḫbnty* *sšr* *mdw-t* *wꜣḥ=st* *ḥr-s*
of[-M]-criminal utterance matter-F place.PP=3C on-3FS
*ḥr-pꜣ-šfd*
on-DET.M-papyrus
[Should] a case involving them [arise] again, then a report is made and it is informed that they are on the criminal docket with a statement on the matters because of which they were entered on the said dockets.
(*Urk.* IV 1109, 5–8)

In the following example, the complement clause is analysable as a subject of the main verb of saying passivised by the element *-t(ꞽ)*, but the constructions following *wnt*, rather than as adverbial sentences, may also be understood as containing

**42** Differences between *ntt* and *wnt* have been suggested by Polotsky (2007: 30–31); Gilula (1971: 16), and more recently Borghouts (2010: §32.b.3–4).

a Stative predicate (*wnt btk-w nḫ-t(ỉ) m-ḫꜣs-t-w=pn*) '... that troublemakers were strong among these hill-dwellers'[43]:

(103) Weni relates the background of a punitive campaign he orchestrated:
*ḏd-t(ỉ)* *wnt* *btk-w* *nḫt* *m-ḫꜣs-t-w=pn*
say.PRF-PASS COMP troublemaker-P strong in-hill.RLT-F-P=DEM.P
It was said that there were strong troublemakers among these hill-dwellers.
(*Urk.* I 104, 12)

In other complement environments the adverbial sentence is preceded by a form of the auxiliary verb *wn/wnn*:

(104a) The deceased is told of his status in the netherworld:
*ỉw* *wḏ-n* *rʿ* *wnn-k* *ỉm* *m-ḥqꜣ* *ns-w-t-f*
AUX order-PST N AUX-2MS there as-ruler throne-P-F-3MS
Ra has ordered that you be there as the ruler of his thrones. (CT VI 393h)

(104b) Idu claims to have lived according to superb standards:
*n* *zp* *ḏd(-ỉ)* *ḫ-t=nb* *ḏw* *ỉw* *ḫꜣb*
NEG occasion say[-1S] thing-F=QU.M evil unjust crooked
*r-rmṯ=nb-w*
against-man=QU-P
*n-mrr(-ỉ)* *hr-t* *bꜣq-t(ỉ-ỉ)* *wnn* *ỉmꜣḫ(-ỉ)*
because-want[-1S] happiness-F clear-PASS[-1S] AUX reverence[-1S]
*ḫr-nṯr* *ḫr-rmṯ* *ḏt*
before-god before-man forever
I never said anything evil, unjust or crooked against anyone, because I desired happiness, vindication, and reverence before god and men forever.
(*Urk.* I 204, 9–10)

The auxiliary is also regularly used in the causative construction *rdi* + Subjunctive *sḏm-f* verb form, the latter of which shows the non-reduplicated written form *wn*:

(105a) Meryra-nefer boasts of his achievements in animal husbandry:
*ỉw* *rdi-n(-ỉ)* *wn* *ỉwꜣ-w* *n-w-spꜣ-t=tn* *r-ḥr*
AUX cause-PST[-1S] AUX OX-P of-P-nome-F=DEM.F to-face
*n(-y)-ỉwꜣ-w*
of[-M]-OX-P
I caused the oxen of this nome to be the best (lit. 'to front') of oxen.
(*Urk.* I 254, 8)

43 So Osing (1977: 173). This, however, changes the historical interpretation of the passage.

(105b) The author of a letter informs his addressee:
*mk* *bꜣk-ꞽ[m]* *dꞽ-n-f* *wn-k* *ḥnꜥ-pꜣ[y-k]*
PTC servant-there give-PST-3MS AUX-2MS with-POSS.M-2MS
*ḫrw*
household
Look, yours truly has ensured that you will be with your household.
(pUC 32213, v° 10–11)

(105c) Djehuty says that he was especially favoured by the king:
*rdꞽ-n-f* *wn-ꞽ* *m-ꞽb-w* *rmṯ*
give-PST-3MS AUX-1S in-heart-P people
He caused me to be in the hearts of people. (*Urk.* IV 132, 16)

*wn/wnn*-introduced adverbial sentence *subject* complements are extremely rare, but in the following instance the clause *wnn ꞽmꜣḫ-ṯn ḫr-N* seems to represent a second clausal subject of the passive participle adjectival predicate *mry* (Edel 1955/1964: §509):

(106) Nekhebu asks the functionaries of the necropolis:
*ꞽ* *ḥm-w* *kꜣ* *n-w-ꞽmꜣḫ-w* *ꞽnꞽw* *mry=n-ṯn*
VOC priest-P soul of-P-revered-P IP desire.PPP=to-2P
*ḥz=ṯn* *nzw*
praise.SUB=2P king
*wnn* *ꞽmꜣḫ-ṯn* *ḫr-nb-w-ṯn* *ꞽt-w-ṯn* *m-ẖrtnṯr*
AUX reverence-2P before-lord-P-2P father-P-2P in-necropolis
O the soul-priests of the blessed dead. Is it desirable to you that the king favour you and that your reverence remain before your lords and forefathers in the necropolis? (Then say to your children ... etc.)
(*Urk.* I 217, 15–17)

Examples of the other types of adverbial sentence complementation are more common. These constructions are relatively frequent in clauses serving as the *predicate* of the subject element =*pw* in bipartite nominal sentences, where the use of *wn/wnn* (always in its reduplicated form) is standard:

(107a) A gloss explaining an expression in a medical work:
*ꞽr* *ꞽb-f* *sš-f* *wnn* *mt-w=pw* *n(-y)-ḥꜣ-t*
PTC heart-3MS spread-3MS AUX vein-P=SE of[-M]-heart-F
*ḫr-ḥs*
under-excrement
As for 'his heart spreads out'; this means that the veins of the heart carry (lit. 'are under') excrement. (pEbers 100, 17–18)

(107b) As above:

| | | | | | |
|---|---|---|---|---|---|
| *ỉr* | *s-t* | *ḥn* | *n(-y)-tp-f* | *mỉ-bk* | *n(-y)-ʿwt* |
| PTC | smell-F | chest | of[-M]-head-3MS | like-urine | of[-M]-small cattle |
| *wnn* | *s-t* | *wp-t-f=pw* | *mỉ-wsš-t* | *n-t-ʿwt* | |
| AUX | smell | forehead-F-3MS=SE | like-urine-F | of-F-small cattle | |

As for 'the smell of the "chest" of his head is like (that of) the urine of small cattle'; this means that the smell of his forehead is like (that of) the urine of small cattle. (pEdwin Smith 3, 21–4, 1)

However, there are also instances where no *wn/wnn* is used, but instead the bare adverbial sentence is embedded as a predicate complement clause:

(108) The king's soul is told to arise before gods and spirits:

| | | | |
|---|---|---|---|
| *snḏ-k=pw* | *ỉr-ḥꜣ-t-w-sn...* | *šʿ-t-k=pw* | *ỉr-ḥꜣ-t-w-sn* |
| fear-2MS=SE | to-heart-F-3P | dread-F-2MS=SE | to-heart-F-P-3P |

The fear of you, it will be in their hearts ... the dread of you, it will be in their hearts. (PT 763a–d)

As will be discussed in section 3.1.2.2, the semantic and pragmatic characteristics of these two types of predicate complements are rather different (see also Part II 1.2.1 and 3.1.5).

Adverbial sentence complements of the *genitival* element *n-* are not altogether rare (see most recently Uljas 2012b). Here again, the auxiliary element *wn/wnn* makes a regular appearance in both its reduplicated and non-reduplicated forms:

(109a) Heqanakhte scorns his household:

| | | | | | |
|---|---|---|---|---|---|
| *ptr* | *ky* | *n(-y)-wnn-ỉ* | *ḥnʿ-ṯn* | *m-ṯ-t* | *wʿ-t* |
| WH | form | of[-M]-AUX-1S | with-2P | in-table-F | one-F |

What is the point of me being at the same table with you? (Heqanakhte II, r° 43)

(109b) The deceased is told:

| | | | |
|---|---|---|---|
| *ỉỉ-tỉ* | *m-qmꜣ-k* | *n(-y)-pḥty-k* | *m-ḥwn-k* |
| come-STA | in-form-2MS | of[-M]-strenght-2MS | in-youth-2MS |
| *n(-y)-wn-k* | *ỉm-f* | | |
| of[-M]-AUX-2MS | in-3MS | | |

You have come in your form of vigour, in your youthful state of your (former) being. (*Urk.* IV 497, 9–10)

Contrary to the situation in nominal sentences (see Part II), examples of bare adverbial sentences serving as complements and displaying the clitic particle =*ỉs* do not seem to occur. In the following unique example, the *wnn*-introduced subordinate adverbial sentence with =*is* appears to represent a type of sentence known in Egyptology as 'emphatic Second Tense', which will be described in 3.1.2.2:

(110) The king addresses Horus:
*ḏd-k* *wnn=is* *N=(p)n* *m-ʿb-sn* *nṯr-w* *im-w* *p-t*
say-2MS AUX=PTC N=DEM.M in-among-3P god-P in.RLT-P heaven-F
May you say that the king is truly among them – the gods who are in heaven. (PT 1489b–1490a)

Nevertheless, on the basis of examples such as the following where the adverbial sentence complement clause of the preposition *n* 'because' that contains the clitic =*is* is preceded by the complementiser *ntt*, it may be surmised that this was once a grammatical construction:

(111) The king, as a mighty bull, is entitled to offerings:
*n-ntt* *N=is* *ir-5-t* *išt-t* *m-ḥw-t*
because-COMP N=PTC to-5-F thing.P-F in-mansion-F
...because king N is due (lit. 'toward') five meals in the mansion. (PT 121c)

It shall be shown later in connection with the nominal sentence that co-occurrence of =*is* and *ntt* appears to reflect a gradual diachronic replacement of the former by the latter and a shift from marking complementation simply as 'dependency' to a more structurally and semantic-pragmatically specific manner (Gilula 1972: 59).

### 2.1.6 Relative clauses 1: constructions with a relative adjective/auxiliary

Adverbial sentences are widely attested in Earlier Egyptian relative clauses. There are two types of such constructions. In the first type, described in this section, the relative clause status of the adverbial sentence receives overt grammatical marking. The most common marker is the relative adjective *nt-*, which stands at the head of the relative clause[44]:

(112a) The king is about to order his officials back to him:
*ḏd-in* *ḥm-f* *ʿ.w.s.* *n-ḫtmw* *nt-y* *r-gs-f*
say-SEQ majesty-3MS l.p.h. to-sealbearer REL-M to-side-3MS
Then his majesty l.p.h. said to the sealbearer who was at his side (a quote follows) (Neferty 1f)

44 Etymologically, *nt-* is probably derived from the same determinative pronoun *n-* used as a predicate in possessive nominal sentences – see Part II.

(112b) Sinuhe expresses his desire to enter the service of the queen of Egypt:
*nḏ-ỉ* *ḫr-t* *ḥnw-t* *tꜣ* *nt-t* *m-ꜥḥ-f*
greet.SUB-1S state-F mistress-F land REL-F in-palace-3MS
I will inquire about the health of the mistress of the land who is in his (the king's) palace. (Sin B, 166)

(112c) Sinuhe tells why a Syrian chieftain treated him with kindness:
*mtr-n=wỉ* *rmṯ* *kmt* *nt-w* *ỉm* *ḥnꜥ-f*
vouch-PST=1S people Egypt REL-P there with-3MS
The Egyptians who were there with him vouched for me. (Sin B, 33–34)

The element *nt-* shows gender- and number agreement with its antecedent:

**Tab. I.4:** Distribution of gender and number marking with the relative adjective *nt-*.

| | **Singular** | **Plural** |
|---|---|---|
| Masculine | *nt-y* | *nt-w* |
| Feminine | *nt-t* | *nt-t* |

Dual forms are rare, although some examples may be cited from religious texts:

(113a) The deceased is cleansed of all evil:
*wꜥb-n-ỉ* *m-sš-wy* *ỉp-w(y)* *wr-w(y)* *ꜥꜣ-w(y)* *nt-wy*
bathe-PST-1S in-pool-DU DEM-DU great-DU mighty-DU REL-DU
*m-nnnsw*
in-N
I have bathed in these two great and mighty pools, which are in Heracleopolis. (CT IV 210b–212a/T1C$^{b}$)

(113b) The king arrives before gods:
*ỉw-n* N *ḫr-ṯny* *rḥ-tỉ* *wr-tỉ* *ꜥꜣ-tỉ*
come-PST N before-2DU goddess-DU great-DU mighty-DU
*nt-tỉ* *m-gs* *ỉꜣb(-ty)* *n(-y)-p-t*
REL-DU in-side east[-RLT] of[-M]-sky-F
King N has come before you, O you two great and mighty goddesses who are on the eastern side of sky. (PT 2200a–b)

In some, and particularly later Middle Egyptian texts, the form *nty* may be used invariably, anticipating its Late Egyptian use as an uninflecting relative particle (see 2.2.4.1):

(114a) The children of Kagemni accepted his instruction:

| | | | | |
|---|---|---|---|---|
| *wn-in* | *nfr=st* | *ḥr-ib-sn* | *r-ḫ-t=nb-t* | *nty* |
| AUX-SEQ | good=3C | on-heart-3P | to-thing-F=QU-F | REL |
| *m-tꜣ=pn* | *r-ḏr-f* | | | |
| in-land=DEM.M | to-limit-3MS | | | |

Then it was more pleasant in their minds than anything that is in this entire land. (Kagemni II, 6–7)

(114b) Wepwawetaa tells how he used to arrive at the palace to offer salutations to the king:

| | | | | | |
|---|---|---|---|---|---|
| *ḫtmt-w* | *nty* | *m-pr-nsw* | *ꜥnḫ-w* | *nt(y)* | *r-ꜥrry-t* |
| sealbearer-P | REL | in-king-house | soldier-P | REL | to-gate-F |
| *ḥr-mꜣꜣ* | *stꜣ-i* | | | | |
| PROG-see.INF | introduce.INF-1S | | | | |

...with the sealbearers who were in the palace and the soldiers serving at the gates witnessing my introduction. (*Lesestücke* 74, 13–14)

The use in the relative clause of resumptive pronouns referring back to the antecedent follows the basic rules of resumption in Earlier Egyptian relative constructions.[45] In general, resumption does not take place if the resumptive pronoun would, in terms of word order, have been immediately local to (i.e. would have appeared directly after) the lexical unit containing the agreement, in this case the element *nt-*.[46] The examples above are instances of subject relativisation, where the antecedent and the subject of the relative clause have identical reference. The latter does not appear as a resumptive pronoun because this would have followed immediately after *nt-*. By contrast, in the following example with a negated adverbial sentence, the negative lexeme *nn* intervenes

45 These have been worked out by Collier (1991b: 37–41) and complemented by Uljas (2012b).

46 In fact, a more precise definition would postulate omission following locality to the *agreement domain*, which consists of the agreement carrier and any following expression that constitutes a single prosodic unit with the former. Agreement domains of this sort are, e.g., relative expression + pronominal dative, and the genitival *n-* + its complement; see Uljas (2012b).

between the agreement-carrying relativiser and the relative clause subject; the latter is consequently expressed as a resumptive pronoun (see section 4 for negative adverbial sentences):

(115) The sailor describes the luxury of the Phantom Island:

| | | | |
|---|---|---|---|
| *nn* | *nt-t* | *nn=st* | *m-ẖnw-s* |
| NEG | REL-F | NEG=3C | inside-3FS |

There was nothing that was not in it. (Sh.S. 51–52)

This example also provides an instance of the non-attributive ('nominal') use of relativised adverbial sentences. For the equivalent of the neuter '(some) thing that' Earlier Egyptian uses the feminine form *nt-t*. Otherwise, the masculine singular and plural forms *nt-y* and *nt-w* are common (note the quantifier =*nb* in ex. 116a):

(116a) Nakhti asks the offering formulae to be read:

| | |
|---|---|
| *n-nt-y=nb* | *ḥr-ḥḏ=pn* |
| to-REL-M=QU.M | on-stela=DEM.M |

...to everyone on this stela. (CG 20057s)

(116b) The shipwrecked sailor climbs a tree to get a better look of a ship approaching:

| | | |
|---|---|---|
| *sỉꜣ-n-ỉ* | *nt-w* | *m-ẖnw-s* |
| recognise-PST-1S | REL-P | in-inside-3FS |

I recognised the ones in it. (Sh.S. 156)

In instances where the antecedent was not co-referential with the relative clause subject, it would not, according to the rules of word order, appear locally to the agreement-carrying relativiser. Consequently, the use of resumptive pronouns is obligatory in *nt*-introduced adverbial sentences not representing subject relativisation. In the examples below, the antecedent performs a locative or genitival role in the relative clause, and the occurrence of a resumptive pronoun is mandatory:

(117a) Sinuhe's exile is about to end:

| | | | | | |
|---|---|---|---|---|---|
| *ỉst=rf* | *ḏd* | *n-ḥm* | *nswbỉt(y)* | *ḫprkꜣwrʿ* | *mꜣʿ-ḫrw* |
| PTC=PTC | say.PASS | to-majesty | dual_king | N | true-voice |

| | | |
|---|---|---|
| *ḥr-ssm=pn* | *nt-y=wỉ* | *ẖr-f* |
| on-condition=DEM.M | REL-M=1S | under-3MS |

Now, the majesty of the dual king Kheperkaura the justified had been told about this condition under which I was (suffering).

(Sin B, 173–74)

(117b) The magician Djedi joined prince Hardjedef on a journey to the residence:
*ỉwt=pw ỉr-n ḏdi m-ḫd m-wsḫ nt-y*
come.INF=SE do.REL-PST N in-sail_north in-boat REL-M
*sꜣ-nsw ḥrddf ỉm-f*
son-king N in-3MS
Djedi went northwards in the boat in which the king's son Hardjedef was. (pWestcar 8, 4–5)

(117c) The snake demands to know how the sailor arrived on the Phantom Island:
*(ỉ)n m ỉn=tw r-ỉw=pn n(-y)-wꜣḏwr nt-y*
PTC WH bring.PP=2MS to-island=DEM.M of[-M]-sea REL-M
*gs-fy m-nwy*
side-3DU in-wave
Who brought you to this island of the sea whose two sides are in the water? (Sh.S. 84–86)

(117d) The decease prays to Atum:
*nḥm-k=wi m(-ꜥ)-nṯr=pw ... nt-y ḥr-f*
rescue.SUB-2MS=1S from-hand-god=DEM.M REL-M face-3MS
*m-ṯsm*
as-dog
Rescue me from that god... whose face is that of a dog. (CT IV 312b–313a/M4C)

Omission of the resumptive pronoun occurs only with the locative adverb *ỉm* 'there' (compare this example with 117b):

(118) The deceased says:
*ỉi-n=ỉ min r-bw nt(-y) wsỉr ỉm*
come-PST=1S today to-place REL[-M] N there
Today I have come to the place where Osiris is. (CT VI 218k)

When a first-person singular pronoun follows *nt-y/nt-t/nt-w*, it assumes the form of a clitic pronoun, as in 117a with *nt-y=wi*. By contrast, suffix pronouns are used with the corresponding second and third persons, of which only the following kind of examples seems to be attested:

(119a) A divinity is told not to oppose the king:
*ỉw-f ỉr-bw nt(-y)-k ỉm*
AUX-3MS to-place REL[-M]-2MS there
...when he comes to the place where you are. (PT 1436d/P)

(119b) The deceased says to a divinity:

*dỉ-k* *ỉw-t=n-ỉ* *bꜣ-ỉ=pn* *m-bw=nb*
give.SUB-2MS come-SUB=to-1S soul-1S=DEM.M in-place=QU.M
*nt-y-f* *ỉm*
REL-M-3MS there
Allow my soul to come from any place where he is. (BD 89/*Nu* pl. 51, 2–3)

For the neuter 'it' =*st* is common (see ex. 115), and the same pronoun is also often used for third person plural, particularly in later texts[47]:

(120) The magician Djedi says that he does not know the number of certain magical chambers; however:

*ỉw-ỉ=swt* *rḫ-kw* *bw* *nt-y=st* *ỉm*
AUX-1S=PTC know-STA.1S place REL-M=3C there
But I do know the place in which they are. (pWestcar 9, 3–4)

This behaviour of the pronouns is identical with the pattern exhibited by the complementiser *ntt* seen in 2.1.5, which etymologically is clearly a feminine form of the same element *nt-* serving also as a relative adjective (see most recently Borghouts 2010: §32.b.3). In addition, like the complementiser *ntt*, the relative adjective *nt-* had a negative counterpart *ỉwt-*, which, unlike its complementiser version, is found introducing adverbial sentences:

(121) The deceased addresses a locality in the hereafter:

*ỉ* *ỉꜣ-t=ṯwy* *n-t-ꜣḫ-w* *ỉwt-t*
VOC mound-F=DEM.F of-F-blessed-P NEG.REL-F
*swꜣ* *ḥr-s*
pass.INF on-3FS
O mound of the blessed dead over which there is no passing.
(BD 149/*Nu* pl. 83, 34)

The commonest occurrence of adverbial sentences after *ỉwt-* is in the standard expression *ỉwt-y=n-f*, lit. 'which is not to him' used to express negative possession 'who has/had not', with the generic possessed subject of the relative clause omitted as a rule:

**47** Early examples of the use of =*st* for third person plural are Qaw Bowl, outside 3 *m-wnm-ṯ=st* (in-eat-2FS=3C) 'when you ate them' and Haskell Mus. 13945, 6 *shꜣ=st* (confound.IMP=3C) 'Confound them!', both dating to the First Intermediate Period (ca. 2160–2055 BC).

(122) Intef characterises himself:

| | | | | | |
|---|---|---|---|---|---|
| *ỉnk* | *ḥnms* | *n-mꜣr-w* | *bnr-(ỉ)mꜣ-t* | *n-ỉwt-y=n-f* | ø |
| 1s | friend | to-poor-P | sweet-character-F | to-NEG.REL-M=to-3ms | ø |

I was a friend to the poor and one well-disposed towards him who had not. (BM 581, 16)

The following example displays *ỉwt-y=n-f* in close co-occurrence with its affirmative counterpart *nt-y=n-f* 'which is to him', i.e. 'who has/had' and shows the correspondence of the relative element *nt-* and the complementiser *ntt*:

(123) Opening of the PT Spell 507:

| | | | | | | |
|---|---|---|---|---|---|---|
| *ỉḫmti* | *ḏd* | *n-nt-ỉ=n-f* | ø | *ntt* | *ỉwt-ỉ=n-f* | ø |
| N | say.IMP | to-REL-M=to-3MS | ø | COMP | NEG.REL-M=to-3MS | ø |
| *ꜥꜣ* | | | | | | |
| here | | | | | | |

O Ikhemty; say to the one who has that he who has not is here. (PT 1102a)

In the above examples with *ỉwt*, the adverbial sentence is, of course, affirmative and the relative connector negative. In ex. 115, the adverbial sentence itself is negated.

In addition to being preceded by relative adjectives, Earlier Egyptian adverbial sentences functioning as relative clauses are also often introduced by a form of the auxiliary verb *wn/wnn*. In this second type of grammatically marked relative clause, the auxiliary is conjugated in the appropriate relative clause form. Below are examples of the reduplicated imperfective participle *wnn* (+/- gender/number-marker) and of the non-reduplicating perfective participle *wn* (+/- gender/number marker):

(124a) A title of a prescription in a medical text:

| | | | | |
|---|---|---|---|---|
| *k-t* | *dr* | *mr-t* | *wnn-t* | *m-ẖnw-ḥꜥ* |
| another-F | remove.INF | illness-F | AUX.IP-F | in-inside-body |

Another (prescription) for removing a disease that is in the body (pEbers 76, 12)

(124b) The young Pepi II gives orders to his envoy on the protection of a precious dwarf:

| | | | | | | |
|---|---|---|---|---|---|---|
| *ỉr* | *hꜣ-f* | *m-ꜥ-k* | *r-dp-t* | *ỉri* | *rmṯ* | *ỉqr-w* |
| CND | descend-3MS | in-hand-2MS | to-boat-F | do.IMP | people | excellent-P |
| *wnn-w* | *ḥꜣ-f* | *ḥr-gs-wy* | *dp-t* | | | |
| AUX.IP-P | behind-3MS | on-side-DU | boat-F | | | |

Should he go down to a boat with you, provide skilled people who keep watch on him (lit. 'are behind him') on the sides of the boat (*Urk.* I 130, 6–8)

(124c) Sinuhe tells that Senwosret I was not the sole person informed of the death of Amenemhat I:

*ı͗st=rf* *hꜣb* *r-msw-nsw* *wn-w* *m-ḫt-f*
PTC=PTC send.PASS to-children-king AUX.PP-P after-3MS
*m-mšꜥ=pn*
in-expedition=DEM.M
Now, there had also been sent to the king's children who were in his following on this expedition. (Sin R, 22–23)

(124d) Tjetji says his official position was recognised under a new king:

*dı͗-n-f=n(-ı͗)* *šmt=nb* *wn-t* *m-ꜥ(-ı͗)* *m-rk*
give-PST-3M= to[-1S] go.INF=QU.M AUX.PP-F in-arm[-1S] in-time
*ı͗t-f*
father-3MS
He passed on to me all the business that had been under my responsibility at the time of his father. (BM 614, 13–14)

(For the time-reference in the above examples, see 3.1.1). Examples of the future participle form *wnn-ty-fy* are also attested:

(125) Sinuhe urges Ammunenshi to pledge allegiance to the pharaoh:

*nn* *tm-f=ı͗rı͗* *bw* *nfr* *n-ḫꜣs-t*
NEG AUX.NEG-3MS=do.NC place good to-foreign_land-F
*wnn-ty-sy* *ḥr-mw-f*
AUX-REL.FUT-AGR on-water-3MS
He will not fail to do good for a land that will be loyal to him (lit. 'on his water') (Sin B, 74–75)

In instances of non-subject relativisation where the subject of the relativised adverbial sentence is not identical with the antecedent, the auxiliary *wn/wnn* occurs in inflected verbal forms that in Egyptological linguistics are called 'Relative Forms'. Examples with the reduplicated form *wnn-f* are rare:

(126) Ammunenshi describes the recently deceased Amenemhat I:

*nṯr=pf* *mnḫ* *wnn-w* *snḏ-f*
god=DEM.M potent AUX.IPF.REL-M fear-3MS
*ḫt-ḫꜣs-w-t*
through-foreign land-P-F
That potent god, the fear of whom used to pervade foreign lands (Sin B, 44–45)

When no ending is present, the non-reduplicating writing *wn-f* should probably be understood as a haplographic writing of a *sḏm-n-f* relative form *wn-n-f* resulting from the two *n*-formants of *wn-n* not being separated by a vowel or some other element:

(127a) The snake promises that the shipwrecked sailor will return home:
*pḥ-k* *ḫnw* *wn-k* *im-f*
reach.SUB-2MS home AUX.REL-2MS in-3MS
*m-qꜣb-n(-y)-sn-w-k*
in-midst-of[-M]-sibling-P-2MS
You will reach home, where you were amidst your siblings.
(Sh.S. 135–36)

(127b) A (male!) divinity is addressed on behalf of the deceased:
*n* *N=tn=is* *dbḥ-t* *mꜣ-s=ṯn* *m-qd-ṯ=pw*
NEG N=DEM.F=NEG ask.PIA-F see.SUB-3FS=2FS in-form-2FS=DEM.M
*wn-ṯ* *im-f*
AUX.REL-2FS in-3MS
*in* *ḥr* *dbḥ* *mꜣ-f=ṯw* *m-qd-k=pw*
PTC N ask.PIA see.SUB-3MS=2MS in-form-2MS=DEM.M
*wn-k* *im-f*
AUX.REL-2MS in-3MS
It is not this N who asks whether she may see you in this your form in which you were; it is Horus who asks whether he might see you in this your form in which you were. (CT VI 353l–m)

This is suggested by examples such 128a, where the rather rare ending *-w* of the *sḏm-n-f* relative form is attached to *wn* and the form is written *wn-w-n-f* (cf. Edel 1955/1964: §676), as well as ex. 128b, where the inclusion of the feminine ending *-t* results in a similar written form:

(128a) It is ordered in a royal decree:
*iw* *wḏ-n* *ḥm(-i)* *nfrn* *iṯ* *ḫntš=nb*
AUX order-PST majesty[-1S] NEG take tenant.P=QU.P
*n-w-nw-(t)y* *(i)ptn...*
of-P-town-F:DU DEM.P
*in* *rmṯ=nb* *in* *nḥs-ḥtp-w=nb(-w)*
AGT people=QU.M AGT Nubian-pacified-P=QU-P
*n-wn-w-n-sn* *ḫr-sn*
to-AUX.REL-P-PST-3P before-3P
My majesty has ordered that no royal tenants of these two (pyramid-) towns may be seized by any people or 'pacified Nubians' to those with whom they were (previously). (*Urk.* I 211, 5–11)

(128b) Djadjai describes his unassailable conduct as an official:

| | | | | | |
|---|---|---|---|---|---|
| *n* | *zp* | *ns* | *ꜥꜣ* | *n-nb-f* | *m-ꞽꜣ-t* |
| NEG | occasion | appeal | great | to-lord-3MS | in-office-F |
| *wn-t-n(-ꞽ)* | *ꞽm-s* | | | | |
| AUX.REL-F-PST[-1S] | in-3FS | | | | |

Never did a magnate appeal to his lord concerning the office in which I was. (*Hamra Dom* pl. 47, 5)

However, the writing *wn-f* is potentially ambiguous between the Relative *sḏm-n-f* and the Perfective Relative Form, an archaic construction that in general displays no gemination or reduplication and whose occasional presence (at least in earlier texts) seems confirmed by examples such as the following showing an ending -*w* but no additional *n* (Schenkel 2010):

(129) Horus says to his father Osiris:

| | | |
|---|---|---|
| *ngꜣ-n(-ꞽ)=n-k* | *ngꜣ=ṯw* | *m-ng(ꜣ)* |
| break-PST[-1S]=to-2MS | break.PPA=2MS | as-long_horn |
| *wn-w-k* | *ḥr-sꜣ-f* | |
| AUX.REL-M-2MS | on-back-3MS | |

As the long-horn on whose back you were, I have broken for you the one who broke you. (PT 1544c–d)

Like *nt*-, *wn/wnn* shows gender and number agreement with the antecedent and observes the same rules of resumption. In exx. 124a–124d, the adverbial sentence subject, co-referential with the antecedent, would have been strictly local to the agreement-carrying auxiliary and is not expressed. In exx. 126–129, this is not the case, and resumptive pronouns appear. As with *nt*-, in subject relativisation, the rules of word order usually result in strict locality between the agreement carrier and the relative clause subject. Examples such as the following, where the negative element *nn* intervenes between the two and necessitates overt expression of the relative clause subject, are rare (cf. the analogous 115):

(130) Senemyah says in reference to the king (?):

| | | | | |
|---|---|---|---|---|
| *ḫmt-n-f* | *smnḫ* | *mnw* | *wn-w* | *nn=st* |
| plan-PST-3MS | restore.INF | monument(s) | AUX.REL-P | NEG=3C |
| *ḥr-pd-w-sn* | | | | |
| on-foot-P-3P | | | | |

He planned to restore monuments that were no longer standing. (*Urk.* IV 501, 10)

### 2.1.7 Relative clauses 2: 'virtual' relative clauses

As will be discussed in 3.1.2.2, the form of the relative clause in Earlier Egyptian sems to depend on its character as either restrictive or non-restrictive, which very often correlates with the degree of definiteness of the (overt or covert) antecedent that the clause modifies.[48] By and large, *marked* relative clauses employing specialised relative verb forms (participles, relative forms, the Future Participle *sḏm-ty-fy*) and the relative adjectives *nt-* and *ỉwt-* were used in restrictive relative clauses, usually with definite antecedents, whereas otherwise Earlier Egyptian had recourse to what in Egyptology has traditionally been called a 'virtual' relative clause. These clauses are *unmarked* in the sense that they exhibit grammatical patterns that are not specialised for occurrence in relative clauses, but have other uses as well. In principle, any verbal or non-verbal form or construction could in Earlier Egyptian be used as an unmarked or 'virtual' relative clause, but some patterns are more frequently found in this function than others. Adverbial sentences are relatively often attested; below are some representative examples:

(131a) In a description of a medical procedure:

| | | | | |
|---|---|---|---|---|
| *ỉr* | *mꜣꜣ-k* | *s* | *st-w-t* | *m-nḥb-t-f* |
| CND | see-2MS | man | swelling-P-F | in-neck-F-3MS |

If you see a man on whose neck are swellings... (pEbers 51, 19–20)

(131b) Sinuhe tells how he was provided accommodation courtesy of the palace:

| | | | | |
|---|---|---|---|---|
| *rdỉ-kw* | *r-pr* | *sꜣ-nsw* | *špss-w* | *ỉm-f* |
| put-STA.1S | to-house | son-king | valuable-P | in-3MS |

I was settled in a princely house in which there were riches. (Sin B, 286)

(131c) An item is described in a mathematical text:

| | | | |
|---|---|---|---|
| *mr* | *prmsw* | *n-f-ỉmy* | *m-93 1/3* |
| pyramid | height | to-3MS-POSS | as-93 1/3 |

A pyramid whose height is 93 1/3 (cubits) (pRhind math. n.58, 1)

Outwardly, adverbial sentences functioning as 'virtual' relative clauses are identical with the unmarked adjuncts seen earlier on and show exactly the same structural properties. Ex. 131a resembles the control constructions after verbs of direct visual perception described in section 2.1.4, whereas 132a is similar to corresponding structures with verbs of direct physical manipulation, and in 132b, the auxiliary element *ỉw* provides an incorporation-base for the suffix pronoun subject of the 'virtual' relative clause:

48 See Malaise and Winand (1999: §§1002, 1021–27) for this analysis in Earlier Egyptian and Müller (2015b) for a detailed argument for Later Egyptian. The syntactic properties of 'virtual' relative clauses are most thoroughly studied by Collier (1991b).

(132a) In a description of a medical procedure:
*ir* *ḫꜣ-w-k* *s* *inw(t)* *n-t-wḫdw* *m-tp-ʿ-wy-fy*
CND examine-2MS man N of-F-pain in-upon-hand-DU-3DU
If you should examine a man on whose hands there are painful symptoms of *inwt* ... (pBerlin med. 14, 7)

(132b) A title of a medical instruction:
*irr-t* *r-šdt* *sr-t* *iw-s* *m-ḥʿ*
do.IPP-F to-remove.INF thorn-F DEP-3FS in-flesh
What is to be done to remove a thorn that is in the flesh. (pEbers 88, 4)

As shall be discussed in more detail in connection with nominal sentences in Part II, it would seem that the antecedent of an adverbial sentence 'virtual' relative clause could also be omitted under relevance[49]:

(133a) The deceased says:
*ink* ø *rd-f* *r-p-t* *ʿ-f* *r-tꜣ*
1S ø foot-3MS to-heaven-F arm-3MS to-earth
I am (someone) whose foot is toward heaven and whose arm is toward ground. (CT V 259c/B2Bo)

(133b) In a description of a medical procedure:
*ir* *ḫꜣ-k* ø *šnʿ* *n(-y)-rib-f*
CND examine-2MS ø blockage of[-M]-stomach-3MS
If you examine (someone) who has a blockage in his stomach...
(pEbers 40, 14–15)

The difference between the unmarked adjuncts of section 2.1.2 and exx. 131a–132b is that in the latter the clause is not understood as 'ad-verbial' or more generally predication-modifying in character, but as functionally *ad-nominal.* This correspondence between adjunctive and adnominal is, of course, not coincidental since both adverbial sentence adjuncts without introducing elements and 'virtual' relative clauses are examples of precisely the same unmarked construction type whose semantic-pragmatic interpretation and syntactic function(s) are not predetermined. Just as an unmarked adverbial sentence adjunct clause does not display any overt formal sign of its adjunctive or 'adverbial' status, an adverbial sentence 'virtual' relative clause is not *formally* a relative clause. This is clear from the fact that such clauses do not display the most fundamental characteristics of 'real' relative constructions with specialised relative patterns, viz., they cannot be used non-attributely, are not preceded by a relativising morpheme or a relative-inflected auxiliary, do not show agreement with the antecedent, and

**49** Cf. here Loprieno (1994: 377–78). For examples akin to 133a, a rather different analysis is proposed by Borghouts (1994).

do not observe the rules governing the use of resumptive expressions in 'real' relative clauses (cf. Collier 1991b). Nevertheless, they are clearly relative clauses *functionally*. This is apparent not only from the fact that in each case above, the clauses indisputably exhibit the characteristic adnominal role of relative clauses – resulting in the impossibility of an adjunct reading. The bare adverbial sentence can be used 'relatively', firstly, because as a construction, it is syntactically undetermined *vis-à-vis* relative and adjunctive functions, just as it is unmarked for coordinate (and thus 'main') clause role *vis-à-vis* the two subordinate clause types just mentioned. Secondly, and as will be seen in section 3.1.1, adverbial sentences are also *pragmatically* unmarked. Indeed, it is this latter feature that accounts for many of their structural properties in Earlier Egyptian.

## 2.2 Later Egyptian

### 2.2.1 Initial and coordinated clauses

#### 2.2.1.1 Late Egyptian

In Late Egyptian – and in the subsequent diachronic stages of the language – the question of clausal initiality and non-initiality is much less controversial than in Earlier Egyptian. The reasons for this state of affairs are manifold, but most decisive for the fate of the adverbial sentence were, on the one hand, the development of the 'preformative' series of personal pronouns and, on the other hand, the functional 'syntactisation' of the all-important element *iw*, which from Late Egyptian onwards was no longer primarily associated with initial main clauses but, as will be seen, regularised the opposite role of marking subordination.

As discussed before, in Late Egyptian, bare adverbial sentences with noun and pronominal subjects often stand alone, without any introductory particle or auxiliary:

(134a) In a love-song the adored person is described as a sycamore tree:
*nꜣy-s-gꜣb* *mi-mfkꜣ-t*
POSS.P-3FS-leaf like-turquoise-F
Its/Her leaves are like turquoise. (Mathieu, *Poesie*, pl. 16, 3)

(134b) The author quotes from an earlier letter of the addressee and resumes:
*sw* *m-sš* *pꜣy-i-ir-k*
3MS in-state DEM.M-REL-do-2MS
What you did is excellent. (*LRL* 9, 10–11)

The following examples show the morphological vs. syntactic marking of indefinite noun subjects discussed in 1.2.1:

(135a) A boy brought his blinded father into the house and had him sit:
*wꜥ-qnỉ* *ẖr-f*
IDF.S-chair under-3MS
He sat upon a chair (*lit.* a chair was under him). (*LES* 33, 8)

(135b) Paneb is accused of having planned a robber's shaft into a tomb:
*ỉw-wn-wḏ-t* *r-ỉwd-s*
DEP-PTC-stela-F to-separation-3FS
...that was covered by a stela (*lit.* there being a stela between it.)
(*KRI* IV 412, 15–16)

In Late Egyptian, coordination of two adverbial sentences is asyndetic, i.e. it does not display any marker or conjunct:

(136a) A letter of congratulations to a promoted officer ends with the words:
*ṯ-ỉ* *m-sš* *pꜣ-tꜣ* *(n)-prꜥꜣ* *ꜥ.w.s.* *[m-sš]*
PTC-1S in-order DEF.M-land of-pharaoh l.p.h. in-order
*m-dỉ-ḥꜣtỉ-k* *msꜣ-ỉ*
NEG.IMP-give-heart-2MS after-1S
I am fine and the land of the pharaoh, l.p.h., [is fine]. Do not worry about me. (*LEM* 62, 13–14)

(136b) In a love poem, the beauty of the adored woman is praised with the words:
*[ptr]* *dhn-t-st* *(m)-pꜣ-pẖꜣ* *n-mry* *ṯ-ỉ* *m-gb*
look front-F-3FS in-DEF.M-trap of-cedar PTC-1S as-duck
*krṯ*
fledgling
*nꜣy-ỉ-[...* *m]-šn-w-<s>* *m-wꜥy* *ẖr-pꜣ-pẖꜣ*
POSS.P-1S-[... in]-hair-P-<3SF> in-worm under-DEF.M-trap
*n-mr[y]*
of-cedar
Look, her front is like the bird trap of cedar wood, and I am a duckling. My [... are] in <her> hair, in a bait under the bird trap of cedar wood.
(Mathieu, *Poesie*, pl. 8, 12–pl. 9, 1)

(136c) The author of a letter states:
*ḫr* *nfr-pꜣ-hꜣb* *ỉr-k=n-ỉ* *rḏd-ṯ-ỉ*
PTC good-DEF.M-send (REL)-do.PST-2MS=to-1S COMP-PTC-1S
*m-sš* *tꜣ-ỉs-t* *m-sš*
in-order DEF.F-gang-F in-order
It is good that you wrote to me: 'I am doing fine and the gang is doing fine'. (pTurin 1977, 9–10 [Bakir, *Epistolography*, pl. 33])

(136d) The gods affirm Horus' claim to the throne of his father and say:

*ṯ-k m-nsw nfr n-tꜣmrỉ*
PTC-2MS as-king good in-N
*ṯ-k m-nb ꜥ.w.s. nfr n-tꜣ=nb r-šꜣꜥ-ḥḥ*
PTC-2MS in-lord l.p.h. good of-land=QU to-until-eternity
*ḥnꜥ-ḏ-t*
and-infinite time-F

You are the good king of Egypt and you are the good lord, l.p.h., of every land up until eternity and infinite times. (*LES* 59, 11–12)

(136e) People chant a paean of joy:

*ṯ-k mỉ-mntw spsn pꜣ-ḥqꜣ ṯ-k mỉ-mntw*
PTC-2MS like-N twice DEF.M-ruler PTC-2MS like-N
*ṯ-k mỉ-mntw m-ẖnw-wꜣst ḏr-ẖn-k ỉmn*
PTC-2MS like-N in-inside-N since-row-2MS N
*ẖn-k nsw m-ḥḥ-rnp-t ỉw-k m-ḥqꜣ*
row.2MS king in-million-years DEP-2MS as-ruler
*šmꜥ wꜣḏ*
Upper Egypt Lower Egypt

You are like Monthu, you are like Monthu, O you ruler. You are like Monthu, you are like Monthu in Thebes when you row Amun, when you row him during the millions of years that you are ruler of Upper and Lower Egypt. (*OIP* 100, pl. 20)

(136f) The king reports that the temple for the gods has been excavated into living rock:

*ỉmn ỉm-s rꜥ m-ẖnw-s ptḥ wsỉr m-ḥw-t-ꜥꜣ-t-s*
N in-3FS N in-inside-3FS N N in-house-F-great-F-3FS
*ḥr ỉst mnmꜣꜥtrꜥ*
N N N

Amun is in it, Ra is within it, Ptah and Osiris are in its temple and Horus, Isis and Menmaatra (Sety I). (*KRI* I 67, 3)

(136g) Nebwennef tells that he was introduced into the presence of his Lord, the pharaoh:

*ỉst sw m-ḥmnṯr tpy n-ỉnỉḥrt ḥmnṯr tpy n-ḥwtḥr*
PTC 3MS as-priest first of-N priest first of-N
*nb-t ỉwnw*
lord-F N
*mr-ḥm-w-nṯr n-nṯr-w=nb-w rsy-f r-ḥrỉḥrỉmn*
overseer-priest-P-god of-god-P=QU-P south-3MS to-N
*mḥti-f r-ṯnw*
north-3MS to-N

*ḏd-in=n-f* *ḥm-f* *ṯ-k* *m-ḥmnṯr* *tpy* *n-imn*
say-SEQ=to-3MS majesty-3MS PTC-2MS as-priest first of-N
*pr-wi-ḥḏ-f*
house-DU-silver-3MS
*šnw-t-f* *ḥr-ḏbˤ-k* *ṯ-k* *m-r3* *ḥri*
granary-F-3MS on-seal-2MS PTC-2M as-mouth upper
*n-rpr-f* *sḏf3-f=nb*
for-temple-3MS provision-3MS=QU
*r-ḫt-k* *pr-ḥwtḥr* *nb-t* *iwnt* *r-ḫt-[k]*
to-authority-2MS house-N lord-F N to-authority-2MS
... while he was high priest of Onuris and high priest of Hathor, Lady of Dendereh, his south at Hraihiamon, his north at This. Then his majesty said to him: 'You will be/are the high priest of Amun; his storehouses and his granary will be/are upon your seal; you will be/are head of his temple; all his provisions will be/are under your authority, and the temple of Hathor, Lady of Dendereh, will be under your authority'.
(*KRI* III 283, 6–9)

Examples such as 136b might suggest a similar omission strategy, as is known from the Present I pattern, where the subject of a coordinated clause may be omitted if identical with the subject of the preceding clause. This phenomenon also seems to be illustrated also by the following example:

(137) The king describes his skills as a warrior:
*ṯ-i* *ḥr-stt* *ḥr-wnm-i* *ḥr-kfˤ* *m-smḥ-i*
PTC-1S PRP-shoot on-right-1S PRP-capture in-left-1S
I shoot to my right and capture with my left. (*KRI* II 44, 12)

### 2.2.1.2 Demotic

As in Late Egyptian, Demotic adverbial sentences usually occur without introductory particles:

(138a) A letter begins with an introductory wish and then continues:
*t3-ḫm* *ḫry*
DEF.F-small below
The little one is below. (pSaqqara H5-DP 265 , 1–2)

(138b) A tenant swears an oath by the king and says:
*iw-y* *ir-f* *(n)-ˤnḫ* *(n)-ˤd* *tw-y* *ḫn-p3-lˤ*
DEP-1S do-3MS as-oath of-false PTC-1S in-DEF.M-punishment
*n-p3-ˤnḫ-prˤ3*
of-DEF.M-oath-pharaoh

Should I swear it as a false oath, I am in the punishment of the oath of the pharaoh. (pBerlin P 3080, 25–26)

(138c) The deceased is assured of a beautiful afterlife:
*tw-t* *ẖn-nꜣ-sm-w* *n-nꜣ-nṯr-w* *n-p-t* *tꜣ*
PTC-2FS in-DEF.P-blessing-P of-DEF.P-god-P of-sky-F land
*tꜣ-dwꜣ-t*
DEF.F-netherworld-F
You are in the blessings of the gods of heaven and earth and of the netherworld. (BM 35464, 19–20)

(138d) The small dog-ape tries to soothe the goddess by saying that he is like a sacrificial bird before her:
*tw-y* *m-qdy-t-ṯrp* *rἰw-f* *rd* *r-nꜣy-f-mꜣḥy*
PTC-1S in-likeness-F-goose DEP-3MS grow DEP-POSS.P-3MS-feather
*ꜥꜣy-w* *n-tqm*
great-P in-pinch
I am (for you) like a fattened goose whose great feathers have been plucked out. (pMag. London&Leiden 9, 18–19)

Indefinite subjects could still be marked morphologically using the indefinite article or syntactically by means of the introductory auxiliary (or particle) *wn*. Yet, from rather early on, a combination of the two procedures takes place, anticipating the situation in Coptic. In Demotic, the morphological pattern is mainly limited to dependent clauses:

(139a) A question in a broken context:
*ἰn-wn-nṯr* *m-qdy-pꜣ-rꜥ*
IP-PTC-god in-likeness-DEF.M-N
Is there a god like Re? (*Petubastis-Cycle* tCambridge 5)

(139b) A report on the activities of local priests at el-Hibeh begins:
*wn-wꜥ-t-mꜣy* *ẖr-nꜣ-wꜥb-w* *n-ἰmn* *(n)-tꜣywḏy*
PTC-IDF.S-F-island under-DEF.P-priest-P of-N of-N
There is an island under the authority of the Amun-priests of el-Hibeh. (pRylands IX 16, 6–7)

No unambiguous examples of coordinated adverbial sentences are attested in Demotic, and there was probably no morpho-syntactic feature to differentiate between two unconnected main sentences and two coordinated ones. The following examples could be read either way:

(140) The deceased is reassured that Osiris will receive her and let her enter his house:
*tw-t* *(n)-pꜣ-ẖn* *(n)-tꜣ-psd-t* *(n)-pꜣ-wr*
PTC-2FS (in)-DEF.M-midst (of)-DEF.F-ennead-F (of)-DEF.M-prince

*ꜥꜣ* *imnṯ*
great western
*tw-t* *m-bꜣḥ-pꜣ-kꜣ* *syt* *ꜥꜣ* *(n)-mn*
PTC-2FS in-presence-DEF.M-bull beget great in-daily
*tw-t* *(n)-pꜣ-ẖn* *(n)-nꜣy-f-ḥs-w*
PTC-2FS (in)-DEF.M-midst (of)-POSS.P-3MS-praised-P
*tw-t* *(n)-pꜣ-bnr* *(n)-nꜣy-f-ḫr-w*
PTC-2FS (in)-DEF.M-outside (of)-POSS.P-3MS-wrath
*tw-t* *(n)-pꜣ-ẖn* *(n)-nꜣy-f-smš-w*
PTC-2FS (in)-DEF.M-midst (of)-POSS.P-3MS-following-P
*tw-t* *(n)-pꜣ-bnr* *(n)-nꜣy-f-ḫfṯ-w*
PTC-2FS (in)-DEF.M-outside (of)-POSS.P-3MS-enemy-P
You are among the ennead of the great western prince; you are daily in the presence of the great begetting bull; you are among his praised ones; you are outside of his wrath; you are among his followers, and you are outside of his enemies. (pHarkness 2, 34–35)

#### 2.2.1.3 Coptic

Finally, as in the preceding stages of Later Egyptian, Coptic adverbial sentences do not require any initial particle to mark the sentence as a main clause (note that the connectors 'and' in the examples below are not required by syntax but rather appear for pragmatic reasons):

(141a) David acknowledges his transgressions:
*auô* *pa-nobe* *m-pa-mto* *ebol* *n-uoiš* *nim*
and POSS.M.1S-sin in-POSS.M.1S-presence out in-time QU
And my sin is continually before me. ([S]Ps 50 [51]:5 [3])

(141b) The devil told the Lord that he had been roaming the earth:
*uoh* *ti-m-pai-ma*
and 1S-in-DEM.M-place
...and (now) I am here. ([B]Job 1:7)

In Coptic, however, indefinite subjects must now be introduced by the particle *un-/uon-*, the direct descendent of *wn*, regardless of whether they are accompanied by an indefinite article or not:

(142a) The apostle assures the Romans that he is speaking the truth and that his conscience tells him:
*ce-un-u-nokʲ* *n-lupe* *nmma-i* *mn-u-mkah* *n-hêt*
COMP-PTC-IDF.S-great of-sorrow with-1S and-IDF.S-pain of-heart

*n-at-ôcn* *hm-pa-hêt*
of-un-cease in-POSS.M.1S-heart
...that I have great sorrow, and continuous grief is in my heart. ($^{S}$Rm 9:2)

(142b) The soul tells how she walked the earth and reached the banks of a river:
*un-u-lilu* *mmeu* *e-f-hmast* *e-f-r-psale*
PTC-IDF.S-boy there DEP-3MS-sit DEP-3MS-AUX-sing
There was a boy sitting and making music.
($^{L}$*Psalms of Thomas* 211, 15–16)

(142c) After several days wandering in the desert, Onnophrius reached a small cave and went to see:
*ce-uon-rômi* *nḫêt-f* *šan-mmon*
COMP-PTC-man inside-3MS or-not
...whether there was someone in it or not.
($^{B}$Papnute, *Wanderings* [*RecTrav* 6, 177, 15, collated])

Coptic adverbial sentences are conjoined asyndetically rather than by means of conjunctions, as in ex. 142a cited above. Identical subjects of coordinated clauses may be either omitted or expressed overtly:

(143a) A citizen speaks for the apostles who are in his house:
*se-ḫen-pi-šteko=an* *et$^{h}$-uonh* *ebol* *alla* *ḫen-u-êi*
3P-in-DEF$_2$.M-jail=NEG REL-reveal out but in-IDF.S-house
*e-f-hêp*
DEP-3MS-hide.STA
They are not in a public prison, but in a private house.
($^{B}$*Apocr. Acts of the Apostles* [*Mon. Wadi Natrun* I 22, 28])

(143b) The designations 'Father', 'Son', and 'the Holy Ghost' are said to be manifest everywhere:
*se-m-p-sa* *n-t-pe* *se-m-p-sa* *m-p-itn*
3P-in-DEF.M-side of-DEF.M-sky 3P-in-DEF.M-side of-DEF.M-ground
*se-hn-p-et-hêp* *se-hn-n-et-ouonh* *ebol*
3P-in-DEF.M-REL-hide.STA 3P-in-DEF.M-REL-reveal.STA out
They are above. They are below. They are in the concealed. They are in the revealed. ($^{L}$*GospPhil.* 59, 13–16)

### 2.2.2 Adjunct clauses

#### 2.2.2.1 Late Egyptian

In Late Egyptian, adjunct clauses are marked by the subordinator *iw*. Although certainly stemming from the identically written Earlier Egyptian auxiliary, the

Late Egyptian *ỉw* differs from the former in various important ways. First and foremost, it is only used to mark subordinate clauses.[50] The second main distinction lies in its prefixing behaviour. Whereas in Earlier Egyptian Wackernagel clitics could be attached to the main clause marker *ỉw*, no such cliticisation is allowed in Later Egyptian. Here, the leftmost landing site for a second-position clitic is after the compound [*ỉw* + subject]. In Late Egyptian, the element had therefore probably lost its full-fledged prosodic form, and the conventional transcription *ỉw* no longer reflects its actual phonetic realisation, which might have been reduced to a mere vowel, as later in Coptic. Writings with <*ỉꜣ*> or <*r*> seem to point to a similar explanation. Below are examples of *ỉw* in adverbial sentence adjunct clauses:

(144a) King Seqenenra ruled at Thebes:
*ỉw-wr* *ỉppy* *ꜥ.w.s.* *m-ḥwtwꜥrt*
DEP-prince N l.p.h. in-N
...while the prince Apophis, l.p.h., was in Avaris. (*LES* 85, 6–7)

(144b) In an instruction for the repair of a boat the addressees are told to supply a gunwale for a boat in the shipyard:
*ỉw-ỉswꜣṯ* *2* *ỉm-sn* *ḥr-rwỉ*
DEP-plank 2 in-3P on-side
...having two planks in it on the side. (*LEM* 43, 5–6)

(144c) The king praises god Amun:
*rdỉ-n-k=(w)ỉ* *r-nsw* *ỉw-ỉ* *m-swḥ-t* *ỉw-bn-ḏr-t*
give-PST-2MS=1S to-king DEP-1S in-egg-F DEP-NEG-hand-F
*n-ky* *ỉm-ỉ*
of-other in-1S
You appointed me a king while I was still unborn (lit: in the egg), while the hand of no other having yet touched me. (*KRI* V 239, 5–6)

(144d) The author of a letter tells his addressee:
*ỉw-ỉr-wỉ-ỉ* *mỉ-ꜥꜣ* *mnnfr* *pꜣwn* *ṯ-ỉ*
DEP-eyes-DU-1S like-greatness N because PTC-1S
*ḥqr-k(wỉ)* *m-ptr-k*
starve-STA.1S in-see.INF-2MS
...while my eyes are as big as Memphis because I hunger to see you.
(*KRI* I 239, 14–15)

---

**50** Note that the similar-looking initial particle of futurity *ỉw* appears in a 'sandwich form' with an *r* surrounding the subject, thus *ỉw*-SUBJ-*r*-.... In addition, the future form in front of a noun subject may appear as *ỉrỉ* which is never the case with the subordinating *ỉw*. Thus, although all the various Late Egyptian morphemes written as *ỉw* might originate in a single form, their functional development lead to more specific form-function matches.

(144e) The commission to inspect the tombs in the necropolis gives a description of features of the partly ruined tomb of King Intef. At the tomb is a stela upon which the king is depicted standing:

| | | |
|---|---|---|
| *ỉw-pꜣy-f-ṯsm* | *r-ỉwd-rd-wỉ-f* | *ḏd=n-f* |
| DEP-POSS.M-3MS-hound | to-parting-leg-DU-3MS | say.PST.PASS=to-3MS |
| *bḥk* | | |
| N | | |

...while his hound called Behek is between his legs. (*KRI* VI 470, 8–9)

In adjuncts, the use of morphological marking of indefinite subjects by the indefinite article seems to have been preferred:

(145a) A person is reported as having removed the signs of ownership on some cattle:

| | | | | |
|---|---|---|---|---|
| *ỉw-f* | *ṯꜣ* | *pꜣ-gstỉ* | *m-ḏr-t-f* | |
| DEP-3MS | take | DEF.M-palette | in-hand-F-3MS | |
| *ỉw-f* | *ỉr* | *wꜥ-rwḏ* | *ỉw-wꜥ-ỉwn* | *m-ẖnw-f* |
| DEP-3MS | make | IDF.S-whip | DEP-IDF.S-pillar | in-inside-3MS |

...and he took the scribal palette and made a whip-sign with a pillar in it. (*RAD* 59, 16–60, 1)

(145b) The goddess Isis appears to the ferryman Nemty disguised as a crone:

| | | | |
|---|---|---|---|
| *ỉw-wꜥ-ḫtm* | *šrỉ* | *n-nbw* | *r-ḏr-t-s* |
| DEP-IDF.S-ring | small | of-gold | to-hand-F-3FS |

...with a little golden ring in her hand. (*LES* 43, 8–9)

In adjunct clauses, the subject pronoun clitisises to the subordinator *ỉw*. The forms for pronominal subject are as follows:

**Tab. I.5:** Late Egyptian forms of personal pronouns attached to the subordinator *ỉw* (common forms only).

| | Singular | Plural |
|---|---|---|
| 1C | *ỉw-ỉ* | *ỉw-n* |
| 2M | *ỉw-k* | *ỉw-tn* |
| 2F | *ỉw-ṯ* | |
| 3M | *ỉw-f* | *ỉw-sn* |
| 3F | *ỉw-s* | |

(146a) The king states that he will not change the location of his new residential city even if advised that some other place might be better suited:

*ỉw-s* *n-ḫd* *ỉw-s* *n-rsy* *ỉw-s* *n-ỉmnty*
DEP-3FS for-downstream DEP-3FS for-south DEP-3FS for-west
*ỉw-s* *n-wbnw*
DEP-3FS for-rising

...whether it (the new place) be downstream, whether it be in the south, whether it be in the west, or whether it be in the orient.
(*Boundary Stelae* 24, 16)

(146b) The king addresses his intended future audience:

*sḏm-n* *dỉ-ỉ* *ꜥm-tn* *m-nꜣy-ỉ-ꜣḫ-w* *ỉ-ỉr-ỉ*
listen.IMP-P give-1S swallow-3P OBJ-POSS.P-1S-benefit-P REL-do-1S
*ỉw-ỉ* *m-nsw* *n-rḫy-t*
DEP-1S as-king of-mankind-F

Listen, and I will let you understand the beneficial deeds which I accomplished when I was a king of mankind. (pHarris I 75, 2)

(146c) The king tells the audience about the Libyan tribes:

*ntw* *ỉ-fḫ* *nꜣ-dmỉ-w* *n-ḫꜣsww* *m-rnp-w-t* *qnw-w*
3P PPA-destroy DEF.P-city of-N in-year-P-F plenty-F
*ꜥšꜣ-w* *ỉw-sn* *ḥr-kmt*
many-P DEP-3P on-Egypt

And it is *they* who destroyed the cities of Xois in many uncountable years when they were in Egypt. (pHarris I 77, 2)

(146d) The author of a letter asks for the consignment of a document and states that he will enjoy the pleasures of accounting. Then he adds:

*ḫr* *dỉ-ptḥ* *ỉr-y-k* *ꜥḥꜥ* *qꜣ* *ỉꜣw-t* *nfr*
and give-N do-SUB-2MS lifetime high old age-F good
*ỉw-k* *mdỉ-ỉ* *m-ỉt* *r-nḥḥ*
DEP-2MS with-1S as-father for-eternity

Then Ptah will let you achieve a long lifetime and a perfect old age, while you are with me as a father forever. (*KRI* V 565, 5–6)

Causal clauses may be introduced by *pꜣwn* 'because' followed by a main clause pattern:

(147a) The author of a letter begs his addressee:

*ỉḫ* *hꜣb-k* *n-ỉ* *ḥr-ꜥ-k* *pꜣwn* *ḥꜣty-ỉ* *msꜣ-k*
PTC send-2MS to-1S on-state-2MS because heart-1S after-2MS

Please write to me about your state, because my heart longs for you.
(*KRI* III 231, 7)

(147b) In his hymn to the promontory, a man says that the deity of the place punishes slackness. He then calls out to his audience:
*sꜣw* *tꜣ-dhn* *pꜣwn* *mꜣyw* *m-ẖnw-s*
guard DEF.F-promontory because lion in-inside-3FS
Beware of The Promontory, for a lion is within it. (Turin 50058, 8–9)

(147c) The author of a letter urges the recipient to beg the god Amun to grant him safe return:
*pꜣwn* *ṯ-ỉ=dỉ* *m-ẖnw-pꜣ-ḫrỉw*
because PTC-1S=here in-inside-DEF.M-enemy
...because I am here amidst the enemy. (pSt. Petersburg 1119, 12)

Here the appearance of the pronominal subject with the particle *ṯ* shows that it does not suffix to *pꜣwn*. However, the connection seems to have been rather close in view of the fact that the adverb *dy* 'here', which often behaves like a second-position clitic, does not move into the position immediately after *pꜣwn*.[51]

#### 2.2.2.2 Demotic

As in Late Egyptian, Demotic adverbial sentence adjunct clauses are marked by *ỉw*. Due to its phonological reduction to a mere vowel (if there ever was any consonant at all, see the deliberations in the preceding Late Egyptian part), *ỉw* is in Middle and Late Demotic almost always written *r* before noun subjects. If the subject is a personal pronoun, the suffix pronouns rather than the preformative pronouns appear:

**Tab. I.6:** Demotic forms of personal pronouns attached to the subordinator *ỉw* (common forms only).

<table>
<tr><th></th><th>Singular</th><th>Plural</th></tr>
<tr><td>1C</td><td>ỉw-ỉ</td><td>ỉw-n</td></tr>
<tr><td>2M</td><td>ỉw-k</td><td rowspan="2">ỉw-twtn</td></tr>
<tr><td>2F</td><td>ỉw-t</td></tr>
<tr><td>3M</td><td>ỉw-f</td><td rowspan="2">ỉw-w</td></tr>
<tr><td>3F</td><td>ỉw-s</td></tr>
</table>

In later texts such as the *Myth of the Sun's Eye*, a redundant *r* is attached to *ỉw*, which thus appears as *rỉw* (see ex. 148g)

51 See also the very fragmentary pCG 58060 r° 12: [...] *ꜣs sp-2 pꜣwn ṯ-k=dy* [...] '[...] very fast, because you are here [...]'.

(148a) A legal formula found in cession documents:
*ỉw-y msꜣ-k n-pꜣ-sẖ n-wy 2*
DEP-1S after-2MS in-DEF.M-document of cession 2
*r-ỉr-k=n-y*
REL-do-2MS=for-1s
...I having a claim over you with both cession documents which you made for me. (pBrooklyn 37.1839 A, r° 8)

(148b) A deity addresses the deceased:
*tw-y wḏꜣ nꜣy-k-ꜣty-w ỉw-y m-ỉnp n-pꜣy-y-ḫbr*
PTC-1S safe POSS.P-2MS-limb-P DEP-1S as-N in-POSS.M-1S-form
*n-ẖrḥb*
of-lector_priest
I will let your limbs be safe, as I am Anubis in my form of a lector-priest. (pRhind I 2, d9)

(148c) A person writes from Memphis back to his people at home on Elephantine:
*gm-y pꜣ-ꜥḥꜥrd ḏd-r-rḫ-nꜣ-md-w mtw-y*
find-1S DEF.M-proof COMP-FUT-can-DEF.P-thing-P with-1S
*drꜥ ỉw-y=dy (n)-mnnfr*
strengthen DEP-1S=here in-N
I found the proof that my affairs can be strengthened while I am here in Memphis. (pBerlin P 15617, 3)

(148d) Stipulations to provide for the contingencies resulting from the purchase of a cow:
*ỉw-w ṯꜣyṯ-s ỉw-wn-kꜣ-ḥwṯ msꜣ-s*
PTC-3P take-3FS DEP-PTC-bull-male after-3FS
If it (the cow) is taken while a bull follows her... (pRylands VIII, 9)

(148e) The lamb answers to the question of whether its prophecies will be realised in its own lifetime:
*ỉỉr-ỉw-w ḫpr ỉw-y n-ỉꜥry n-ḏꜣḏꜣ prꜥꜣ*
AUX-FUT-3P happen DEP-1S as-uraus in-head pharaoh
*ntyỉw-f ḫpr (n)-pꜣ-mnq rnpt 900*
REL-3MS happen in-DEF.M-completion year 900
I will be a uraeus upon the brow of the pharaoh that will exist after 900 years have been completed. (pVienna D 10000 2, 20–21)

(148f) In a document over a trial marriage, the following stipulation is found:
*mtw-t-ḫpr n-pꜣy-(y)-ꜥwy ỉw-t mtw-y n-ḥm-t*
CNJ-2FS-happen in-POSS.M-1S-house DEP-2FS with-1S as-wife-F
*n-ṯꜣy-n-pꜣ-hrw*
in-take-of-DEF.M-day
...and you will be in my house, being my wife from today.
(oStrasbourg 1845 r° 7)

(148g) Trying to regain the favour of the goddess for Egypt, the small dog-ape soothes her with fair words:
*ḫꜥ-pꜣ-rꜥ n-dwꜣe rỉw-f m-ỉtn ꜥꜣ nbꜥꜣ-t*
rise-DEF.M-N in-morning DEP-3MS as-disc great flame-F
*r-nꜣy-f-nw-w ḫr-ršy*
DEP-POSS.P-3MS-look-P under-joy
*r-nꜣy-f-sꜣtw-w ḫr-ꜥnḫ r-bn-šn ḥr-tꜣ-ỉmy-t-spdt*
DEP-POSS.P-3MS-ray-P under-life DEP-NEG-cloud on-DEF.F-way-F-N
May the Sun-god rise, being a great blazing disc and with his looks full of joy, his rays full of life, and no cloud upon the way of Sothis.
(Myth of the Sun's Eye 16, 5–7)

The distribution of syntactic marking (with the particle *wn*) and morphological marking (with the indefinite articles) to introduce an indefinite subject is, as in main clauses, still observable, but examples such as 149d, in which both patterns appear combined, suggest that the alternation was gradually eroding:

(149a) The addressee of a letter is urged to be scrupulous with his duties:
*mỉr-wrr-wꜥ-t-wnw-t r-wn-bd-t n-pꜣ-ḫyr*
NEG.IMP-hesitate-IDF.S-F-hour-F DEP-PTC-emmer-F in-DEF.M-street
Do not hesitate even for a single moment when emmer is on the street.
(pBerlin P 15522, 20–21)

(149b) A petitioner argues that stored grain should be guarded by night as brigands are in the nearby mountains:
*ḫr ḫpr-f ỉw-w ḥms wbꜣ-n n-mtr*
and happen-3MS DEP-3P sit opposite-1P in-noon
*msꜣ-ḫpr ỉw-wn-wš qy ỉwt-n ỉwṯ-w*
after-happen DEP-PTC-gap high between-1P between-3P
And it happened that they camped opposite to us, but with a large distance between us and them. (pLoeb 1, 9–10)

(149c) Setne beheld Lady Tabubu for the first time:
*nꜣw-ꜥn-s ỉw-hynw-wpw-t-w n-nb ꜥšꜣy nỉm-s*
ADJ-beautiful-3FS DEP-IDF.P-work-F-P of-gold plenty in-3FS
She was beautiful, with numerous golden ornaments (i.e. jewelry) upon her. (Setne I 4, 39)

(149d) The demarcation lines of a piece of real estate are noted down according to the cardinal points. South of the said building is another house:
*ỉw-wn-wꜥ-t-ḏyꜣ-bk-t ỉwṯ-tn ỉwṯ-pꜣ-ꜥwy*
DEP-PTC-IDF.S-F-wall-sustain-F between-2P between-DEF.M-house
*n-shm-t taỉmn ta-nsmn*
of-woman-F N POSS.F-N

...with a sustaining wall between you and the house of the lady Taminis, daughter of Sminis. (pPhiladelphia 1, 2–3)

(149e) When Setne left the netherworld, his deceased wife was weeping. Naneferkaptah consoled her by saying:

*ỉw-y* *dy-ỉn-f* *pȝy-ḏmʿ* *rbwnȝy*
FUT-1S let-bring.SUB-3MS DEM.M-book here
*ỉw-wn-wʿ-t-šlt-t* *šbte* *n-ḏr-ṯ-f*
DEP-PTC-IDF.S-F-forked-F rod in-hand-F-3MS
*ỉw-wn-wʿ-ʿḫ* *n-ste-t* *ḥr-ḏȝḏȝ-f*
DEP-PTC-IDF.S-brazier of-fire on-head-3MS

I will make him return with a forked stick in his hand and a fire-brazier upon his head. (Setne I 4, 35–36)

Causal clauses are marked by the introductory particle *ḏd* or by *(r)-ḏbȝ-ḫpr* followed by a dependent clause:

(150a) A woman is reviled in a literary(?) text and evil is wished upon her:

*ḏd-pȝ-shne-wrȝt* *pȝ-hrw*
for-DEF.M-inspection-N DEF.M-day

...for the inspection of the netherworld demon takes place today. (pVienna D 70, 10)

(150b) The author of a letter urgently waits for some goods and exhorts his addressee:

*mỉr-dy-ỉỉr-w* *wrr* *ḏbȝ-ḫpr* *ỉw-y*
NEG.IMP-let-AUX-3P delay because-happen DEP-1S
*(n)-pȝy-w-ḏf* *mšs*
(in)-POSS.M-3P-burning very

Do not let them be delayed for I am longing for them. (pBerlin P 13564, 14–15)

#### 2.2.2.3 Coptic

In Coptic, adjunct marking is carried out by initial connectors and usually does not involve specific syntactic or other adjustments within the clause itself. Adverbial sentence adjuncts are typically introduced by the marker *e* (*ere* before noun subjects), the descendant of the earlier *ỉw*:

(151a) The Lord's anger is described. He sloped heaven and came down:

*ere-u-kʲosm* *ha-ne-f-uerête*
DEP-IDF.S-darkness under-POSS.P-3MS-feet

...while darkness was under his feet. (SPs 17 [18]:10 [9])

(151b) A great angel approaches:
*ere-t-salpigks* *n-(n)ub* *n-toot-f*
DEP-DEF.F-trumpet of-gold in-hand-3MS
...holding a golden trumpet.
([A]*ApSoph.* [Steindorff, *Apokalypse des Elias* 58 14, 15–16])

(151c) St Paul sees Hermippos approaching:
*ere-u-sêfe* *n-toot-f* *[e-s-t]akm*
DEP-IDF.S-sword in-hand-3MS DEP-3FS-draw.STA
...with a drawn sword in his hand. ([L]*Acta Pauli* 22* 31, 12–13)

(151d) Isaiah prays to the Lord for the Israelites to be spared from destruction:
*ere-pe-n-ucei=de* *hm-pe-uaiš* *n-te-thlipsis*
DEP-POSS.M-1P-salvation=yet in-DEF.M-time of-DEF.F-affliction
...but our salvation is in the time of affliction. ([F]Is 33:2)

(151e) Having healed a lame man, Jesus withdrew:
*e-uon-u-mêš* *m-pi-ma* *etemmau*
DEP-PTC-IDF.S-multitude in-DEF$_2$.M-place that
...whilst a multitude was present there. ([B]Jn 5:13)

(151f) A demon assumed the form of a herd of wandering camels:
*ere-nu-šêri* *ḫen-t-herimos*
DEP-POSS.P.3P-son in-DEF.F-desert
...with their young in the desert.
([B]Theodore of Antioch, *On the Theodores* [Win. 29, 1])

As can be seen, the use of *un* is not obligatory in adjunct clauses with indefinite subjects. As in the earlier stages of Later Egyptian, personal pronoun subjects are suffixed directly to the marker *e-*:

**Tab. I.7:** Coptic forms of personal pronouns attached to the subordinator e- (common forms only; dialectal variation only marked if deviating).

<table>
<tr><th></th><th>Singular</th><th>Plural</th></tr>
<tr><td>1C</td><td>e-i-</td><td>e-n</td></tr>
<tr><td>2M</td><td>e-k-</td><td rowspan="2">[S]e-tetn/<br>[B]ere-ten</td></tr>
<tr><td>2F</td><td>ere-</td></tr>
<tr><td>3M</td><td>e-f-</td><td rowspan="2">e-u-</td></tr>
<tr><td>3F</td><td>e-s-</td></tr>
</table>

Note that especially the forms of the first person plural (but also others) graphically dispense with *e* due to the following nasal, i.e. the articulatory proximity of $^{e}n$ and syllabic *n*. However, as the form of the pronoun was already sufficient to signal the status of the clause as an adjunct (i.e. *(e)-n-* for the dependency marking versus *t(e)n-* for the main clause pattern), no ambiguity arose.

(152a) Theodore asks an apparition:

*ntk-nim pa-cois e-k-hn-pei-nok$^{j}$ n-eou*
2MS-WH POSS.M.1S-lord DEP-2MS-in-DEM.M-great of-glory
*ntari-cô m-pe-k-ran e-leontios*
CNJ.FUT.1S-say OBJ-POSS.M-2MS-name to-N
Who are you, my lord, who is in such great glory, so that I can tell your name to Leontius?
($^{S}$*Mart. Theodore et al.* [Müller and Uljas, *Martyrs & Archangels* §99])

(152b) Jesus advises to appease an adversary:

*hoson e-k-hi-te-hiê neme-f*
while DEP-2MS-on-DEF.F-way with-3MS
...while you are still on the way with him. ($^{M}$Mt 5:25 mae 1)

(152c) St Paul calls out to the Romans:

*ḫen-ti-met-mai-son ere-ten-k$^{h}$ê ḫen-u-mei eḫun*
in-DEF$_{2}$.F-PIA-brother DEP-2P-AUX in-IDF.S-love into
*e-ne-ten-erêu*
to-POSS.P-2P-fellow
...brotherly, with affection to each other. ($^{B}$Rm 12:10)

As can be seen from ex. 152c, Bohairic makes use of the auxiliary *k$^{h}$ê* here as well (see above section 1.2.3). Besides *e/ere*, Coptic also makes use of various more specialised adjunctors such as the causal *ebolce-* or *ce-*; below are examples with adverbial sentences:

(153a) After Moses' death the Lord addressed Joshua and ordered him to lead His people to the Promised Land. He told him not to fear:

*ebolce-f-nmma-k nk$^{j}$i-p-cois pe-k-nute hn-ma*
because-3MS-with-2MS PVS-DEF.M-lord POSS.M-2MS-god in-place
*nim et-k-na-bôk ero-u*
all REL-2MS-FUT-go to-3P
...for the Lord, your God, is with you wherever you go.
($^{S}$Jo 1:9 [Thompson])

(153b) God accuses Israel of having turned away from him:
*ce-un-pn(eum)a n-pornia nḫrêi nḫêt-u*
for-PTC-spirit of-fornication inside within-3P
...because a spirit of whoredom is among them. ([A]Hos 5:4 [Till])

### 2.2.3 Complement clauses

#### 2.2.3.1 Late Egyptian

In Late Egyptian, the standard pattern of complementation with adverbial sentences is with the complementiser *(r)ḏd* prefixed to the clause. The adverbial sentence itself is bare, unless – as in the last example below – it is marked for past tense by the preterite marker *wn* (see section 3.2.2.1 for the latter):

(154a) Ramesses II interrogated captured enemy scouts, asking them for the location of the king of Hatti:
*mk sḏm-i rḏd-sw m-tꜣ n-ḫlb*
PTC hear.PST-1S COMP-3MS in-land of-N
Behold, I heard that he was in the land of Aleppo. (*KRI* II 110, 15)

(154b) The pharaoh's valiance amidst the more numerous enemy forces did not go unnoticed by his own formerly cowardly host:
*ḫr-ir mḏr-ptr-pꜣy-i-mšꜥ tꜣy-i-ṯntḥtr (r)ḏd-ṯ-i*
PTC-PTC TMP-see-POSS.M-1S-army POSS.F-1S-chariotry COMP-PTC-1S
*mi-mnṯ ḫpš wsr*
like-N arm strong.STA
*pꜣ-rꜥ pꜣy-i-it ḥnꜥ-(i) (n)-sp*
DEF.M-N POSS.M-1S-father with-1S in-time
Now when my army and my chariotry saw that I was like Montu, with (my) arm powerful, and my father the sun-god suddenly with me...
(*KRI* II 71, 16–72, 9)

(154c) The Hittite king and all his allies attacked the Egyptian army from their place of ambush:
*iw-n-rḫ ḥm-f rḏd-st im*
DEP-NEG-know.PST majesty-3MS COMP-3P there
...while his majesty was not aware that they were there. (*KRI* II 108, 6)

(154d) Words said concerning another person by a man interrogated by officials:
*sḏm-i rḏd-wn-f m-nꜣw-s-w-t iw-bpw-i*
hear.PST-1S COMP-PRT-3MS in-DEM.P-place-P-F DEP-NEG.PST-1S
*ptr-f m-ir-t-i*
see-3MS in-eye-F-1S
I heard that he had been in those places, although I did not see him with my own eyes. (*KRI* VI 810, 2–3)

(154e) The sender of a letter tells his correspondent about a woman:

*bpy-ỉ* *di-t-ꜥmꜣ-s* *rḏd-hꜣb-ỉ=n-k*
NEG.PST-1S give-INF-know.SUB-3FS COMP-send.PST-1S=for-2MS
*rḏd-sw=dy*
COMP-3C=here
I did not let her know that I wrote to you that she is here.

(*KRI* VI 267, 6–7)

However, some verbs such as *gmi* 'find' can mark the difference in the speaker's evaluation of the proposition in terms of perceptual vs. conceptual discovery, i.e. whether the speaker actually witnessed the find, in which case the complement appears as an *ỉw*-headed clause, or whether he did not attend the discovery but merely assesses the truth values of the proposition, in which case the clause is introduced by *rḏd* (see Collier 2007: 33–46). Alas, the surviving textual material does not seem to supply constrasting examples with adverbial sentences:

(155) In a list of thieves interrogated a note is added:

*gm-yt* *ỉw-wn-w* *m-nꜣw-s-w-t*
find-PPP DEP-PRT-3P in-DEM.P-place-P-F
...of whom it was discovered that they were in those places.

(*KRI* VI 824, 15)

In oblique environments, e.g., after verbs of perception, the oblique complement is often an *ỉw*-clause with its own overt controlled subject:

(156a) An interrogated thief reports:

*ỉw-n* *gm-pꜣ-mḥr* *n-nsw* *N* *ỉw-bn-sw*
DEP-1P find-DEF.M-pyramid of-king N DEP-NEG-3MS
*mỉ-qd-nꜣ-mḥr-w*
in-likeness-DEF.P-pyramids-P
*mꜥḥꜥ-w-t* *n-nꜣ-sr-w* *nty-ṯ-n* *šm* *r-ṯꜣṯ* *ỉm-w*
tomb-P-F of-DEF.P-notable-P REL-PTC-1P go to-steal in-3P
*m-dwn* *spsn* *ỉn*
in-stretch twice NEG
We found the pyramid of king N not being at all like the pyramids and tombs of the nobles which we have usually entered to steal in them.

(*KRI* VI 483, 13–484, 1)

(156b) A man made a statement that thirteen persons were involved with him in robberies; he swore an oath on the god Amun and the ruler:

*mṯ-ṯ* *gm-rmṯ* *ỉw-wn-f* *ỉrm-ỉ* *ỉw-ḥꜣp-ỉ=sw*
CNJ-PASS find-man DEP-PRT-3MS with-1S DEP-hide.PST-1S=3MS

*ỉw-ỉr-w=n-f* *tꜣy-f-sbꜣy-t*
DEP-do-pass=to-3MS POSS.F-3MS-punishment
...if it is discovered that anyone else was with him and he hid him, his punishment shall be inflicted upon him. (*KRI* VI 770, 8–9)[52]

(156c) As the other scribe had claimed the author that is not inscribed into the official documents, the latter responds that he rather should look closer and he would find the author's name upon the lists of the royal stable and:
*mtry-k* *ḥr-pꜣ-sḥn* *n-pꜣ-ỉḥ* *ỉw-ḏrwt*
witness.PROSP-2MS on-DEF.M-order of-DEF.M-stable DEP-ration.PL
*m-sš-w* *ḥr-rn-ỉ*
in-writing-PL on-name-1S
And you will witness on "the order of the stable" that rations are booked under my name. ([2]*pAnastasi I* 101, 6–7)

However, covert controlled subjects are also common:

(157a) A note in an administrative journal says about a court case:
*ỉw-ṯ* *ḥr-gm* *pꜣ-sš* *2* *m-ꜥḏꜣ* [...] *gm*
DEP-PASS PRP-find DEF.M-scribe 2 in-wrong [...] find
*tꜣ-ỉs-t* *m-mꜣꜥ-t*
DEF.F-gang-F in-truth-F
...and one found the two scribes being wrong [...] found the gang being right. (*KRI* V 533, 16–534, 1)

(157b) A consignment of galena was examined by doctors:
*ỉw-ṯ* *gm-ṯ-f* *m-msdm-t* *wỉꜣwỉꜣ*
DEP-PASS find-INF-3MS as-galena mixed
...and it was discovered to be mediocre galena. (*KRI* VI 519, 1)

(157c) The sorrows of the recipient of a letter concerning his father are assuaged with the words:
*sḏm-ỉ* *ꜥ-f* *m-sš* *spsn*
hear.PST-1S state-3MS in-order twice
I heard that he is doing very well. (*LRL* 59, 1–2)

One could probably interpret the following example along similar lines:

(158) An entry in a journal drawn up by the commission examining the robberies in the Theban necropolis states of a royal tomb:
*sw* *gm-yt* *m-rꜥ-wtn* *m-ḏr-t-nꜣ-ỉṯꜣ-w*
3MS find-PPP in-state-break in-hand-F-DEF.P-thief

52 For an interpretation of this passage as indirect speech, see Peust (1996: 111 n.409).

*m-s-t-smn-p3y-f-wḏ* *n-p3y-f-mḥr*
in-place-F-erect-POSS.M-3MS-stela of-POSS.M-3MS-pyramid
It was discovered in the state of being broken in by the thieves at the site of his stela of his pyramid. (*KRI* VI 471, 2–3)

Occasionally, other particles such as *is* are found introducing full oblique clauses:

(159) The deceased is far from the misery of the unfortunate dead:
*n-m33-sn=tw* *is* *ṯ-k* *m-ḥr-(t)*
NEG-see-3P=2MS PTC PTC-2MS in-sky-F
They could not see you while you were in the sky,
(*Tomb of Tjanefer* pl. 10, 1)

With a negated clause, the complementiser can be omitted:

(160) The addressee of a letter confirms receipt of the letter and his pleasant anticipation; yet:
*gm-i* *bn-st* *m-ḥsw-t* *bn-st* *m-sḥwr*
find.PST-1S NEG-3FS as-praise-F NEG-3FS as-curse
I discovered that it was made neither of praises nor of curses.
([2]*pAnastasi I* 56, 3–4)

In cases where the truth-value of the complement was yet to be discovered, Late Egyptian used the interrogative particle *n* 'whether' as the introducing element[53]:

(161a) Wenamun tells the Prince of Byblos that he has the image of Amun with him:
*iw-bw-rḫ-k* *n-sw=dy* *n-bn-sw*
DEP-NEG.AOR-know-2MS IP-3MS=here IP-NEG-3MS
*(m)-p3-nty-wn-f*
as-DEF-REL-AUX.PRT-3MS
But you never had any idea whether he is here and whether he is what he used to be. (*LES* 69, 12–13)

(161b) The adressees are told to send out their scribes and man:
*mṯ-tn-ptr* *n-wn-sš-w* *is-w* *n-p3-ḫr*
CNJ-2P-look IP-be-writing-P old-P of-DEF.M-tomb
...and then you look whether there are old documents of 'The Tomb.'
(pTurin 1978/208, r° 2–3)

53 For examples with an existential sentence, see *LEM* 43, 6–7.

### 2.2.3.2 Demotic

As in Late Egyptian, the standard construction in Demotic for adverbial sentences used as complement clauses is with the complementiser *(r)ḏd*:

(162a) Two warriors fought for many days:
*ỉw-pꜣ-mšꜥ* *n-kmy* *sḏy* *wbꜣ-nꜣy-w-ỉry-w*
DEP-DEF.M-host of-Egypt tell against-POSS.P-3P-fellow-3P
*ḏd-mn-mhw-t* *n-rmt-qnqn* *ẖn-kmy*
COMP-NEG-family-F of-man-warrior in-Egypt
*m-qdy-tꜣ-mhw-t* *wsỉr* *nsw* *ỉỉrtḥrrw*
in-likeness-DEF.F-family-F deceased king N
...while the host of Egyptians told each other that there was no family of warriors in Egypt like the family of the deceased King Inaros.
(pSpiegelberg 17, 14–17)

(162b) The deceased Naneferkaptah beseeched Setne in the netherworld by telling him about his family:
*stne* *dy-k* *ỉrrẖ=s* *ḏd-ỉhwret* *ỉrm-mrỉbptḥ* *pꜣy-s-šr*
N PTC-2MS know=3FS COMP-N with-N POSS.M-3FS-son
*st* *n-qbṯ*
3P in-N
*ỉw-w=dy* *ẖn-tꜣy-h-t* *n-wp-t* *n-sẖ-nfr*
DEP-3P=here in-DEM.F-tomb-F in-work-F of-scribe-good
Setne, you know that Ahure and her son Meribptah are in Coptos, whilst they are (at the same time) here in this tomb through the art of a capable scribe. (Setne I 6, 3)

(162c) In a broken context: Something urges the protagonists to go to a certain place but:
*bn-ỉw-w* *nḥṯy-s* *ḏd-tw-n* *nỉm*
NEG-PTC-3P believe-3FS COMP-PTC-1P there
They will not believe that we are there. (pSaqqara I 1 9, 16)

As in Late Egyptian, in oblique environments clausal 'secondary' objects[54] often take the form of *ỉw*-clauses (ex. 163a), but omission of the controlled subject is also common (163b):

(163a) After a set of instructions to the ritualist, a magical text reveals the result of the procedure described:
*ẖr* *nw-k* *r-pꜣ-nṯr* *ỉw-f* *n-pꜣ-smte*
PTC see-2MS OBJ-DEF.M-god DEP-3MS in-DEF.M-likeness

54 I.e., the object appears twice: Once as direct object and once as subject within the object clause.

*n-wʿ-wʿb*
of-IDF.S-priest
*iw-f ṯꜣy ḥbs n-šs-n-nsw ḥr-ꜣṯ-f*
DEP-3MS carry clothes of-byssos-of-king on-back-3MS
Then you will see that the god has the appearance of a priest clothed in royal byssos. (pMag. London&Leiden 4, 8)

(163b) The god Anubis will grant certain things to the deceased, among them:
*tw-f ḫpr-t m-wʿ-t n-ḥm-t-w nfr-t-w*
give-3MS happen-2FS as-one-F of-woman-F-P beautiful-F-P
*n-tꜣ-ḥnw-t-imnṯ*
of-DEF.F-mistress-F-west
He lets you become one of the beautiful women of the lady of the West. (pRhind II 5, d3)

### 2.2.3.3 Coptic

Coptic adverbial sentences functioning as complement clauses are introduced by *ce*, which is the outcome of the earlier *rḏd*:

(164a) Phinehas the priest said to the sons of Ruben and Gad and to the half of the tribe of Manasse:
*mpou a-n-ime ce-p-cois nmma-n*
today PF-1P-know COMP-DEF.M-lord with-1P
Today we know that the Lord is with us. ([S]Jo 22:31 [Thompson])

(164b) The pharaoh told the Israelites that they should make bricks without straw:
*a-u-nau=de ero-u nkʲi-ne-grammateus n-n-šêre*
PF-3P-see=yet OBJ-3P PVS-DEF.P-scribe of-DEF.P-child
*m-p-is(raê)l*
of-DEF.M-Israel
*ce-se-hn-p-et-hou*
COMP-3P-in-DEF.M-REL-bad.STA
Now the recorders of the sons of Israel saw that they were in trouble. ([S]Ex 5:19)

(164c) After Tobit has buried a dead fellow Hebrew in the night, he returns home. Since he is defiled from his work, he decides to sleep outside by the wall in the courtyard with his face uncovered:
*auô ne-i-soun=an ce-un-hen-cac*
and PRT-1S-know=NEG COMP-PTC-IDF.P-sparrow
*hi-t-coe*
on-DEF.F-wall
And I was unaware that there are sparrows on the wall. ([S]Tb 2:10)

(164d) Jesus made Lazarus rise from the death:

| | | | |
|---|---|---|---|
| *u-mêše=de* | *e-anšô-f* | *abal* | *hn-ni-iutai* |
| IDF.S-multitude=yet | DEP-be_plenty-3MS | out | in-DEF.P-Jew |

| | |
|---|---|
| *a-u-sôtem* | *ce-f-mmeu* |
| PST-3P-hear | COMP-3MS-there |

Now many of the Jews heard that he was there. ([L]Jn 12:9)

(164e) Tabitha had died in the town of Joppe:

| | | | |
|---|---|---|---|
| *etha-ne-snêu=de* | *sotm* | *ce-petros* | *hn-lunda* |
| TMP-DEF.P-brothers.P=yet | hear | COMP-N | in-N |

...when the brothers heard that Peter was in Lydda. ([M]Acts 9:38)

(164f) Jesus chides Philip who had said that Jesus should show the Father to the disciples:

| | | | |
|---|---|---|---|
| *$k^h$-nahti=an* | *ce-anok* | *ti-ḫen-pa-iôt* | *uoh* |
| 2MS-believe=NEG | COMP-1S | 1S-in-POSS.M.1S-father | and |

| | |
|---|---|
| *pa-iôt* | *nḫêt-ø* |
| POSS.M.1S-father | inside-1S |

Do you not believe that I am in my Father and my Father is in me?
([B]Jn 14:10)

(164g) The Theodores address the archbishop supposedly holding a Persian prince in custody, saying:

| | |
|---|---|
| *a-u-tamo-n* | *ce-f-ḫen-pi-polemos* |
| PST-3P-teach-3P | COMP-3MS-in-DEF$_2$.M-war |

We have been told that he is in the war.
([B]Theodore of Antioch, *On the Theodores* [*AM* II 139, 21])

Certain verbs such as [SB]*nau* 'see' are attested with *e*-marked oblique complements, but this pattern is more common with verbal complements[55]:

(165) The narrator sees an angel and tells:

| | | | |
|---|---|---|---|
| *a-i-sônt-$k^j$e* | *a-i-no* | *ara-f* | *e-un-u-kheirographon* |
| PF-1S-behold-then | PF-1S-see | OBJ-3MS | DEP-PTC-IDF.S-scroll |

*n-toot-f*
in-hand-3MS

I looked and I saw that he had a scroll in his hand.
([A]*Ap Soph.* [Steindorff, *Apokalypse des Elias* 53 10, 21–11, 1])

55 At least from the example [A]*ApSoph.* [Steindorff, *Apokalypse des Elias* 52 11, 8] using a Present I pattern, it seems probable that the non-occurrence of examples without a complementiser after the verb *$k^j$ine* is due to a chance of preservation.

### 2.2.4 Relative clauses

#### 2.2.4.1 Late Egyptian

As in Earlier Egyptian, also in Later Egyptian, a formal demarcation is made between restrictive and non-restrictive relative clauses (cf. 2.1.6 and 2.1.7). In Late Egyptian restrictive relative clauses with the relative operator *nty*, which is by now uninflected (see the description of the development in Earlier Egyptian above), the subject pronoun is usually omitted if it is coreferential with the antecedent[56]:

(166a) An oracle is quoted in a letter:

| *rwi* | *rmṯ-w=nb* | *nty-n-pꜣ-ḥꜣṯ* |
|---|---|---|
| remove.IMP | men-P=QU | REL-for-DEF.M-captain |

| *nty-m-ẖnw-pꜣy-pr* | *n-swpꜣꜥnḫ* |
|---|---|
| REL-in-inside-DEM.M-house | of-N |

Remove all the men who are for the captain and who are in the house of Saupeankh! (Jansen-Winkeln, *IdS* I, 199, 8–9)

(166b) Paneb is accused of having entered a tomb of a deceased workman and:

| *iw-f* | *iṯꜣ* | *tꜣ-s-t* | *sḏr* | *nty-ẖr-f* |
|---|---|---|---|---|
| DEP-3MS | take | DEF.F-place-F | lie | REL-under-3MS |

He took the bed that was beneath him. (*KRI* IV 413, 1)

(166c) In an instruction for the repair of a boat the addressees are told to supply a gunwale:

| *n-pꜣ-skṯ* | *n-šnṯ* | *nty-mdi-tn* | *ḥr-wḫr* |
|---|---|---|---|
| for-DEF.M-boat | of-acacia wood | REL-with-2P | on-shipyard |

...for the boat of acacia wood that is with you in the shipyard. (*LEM* 43, 5)

In cases in which the subject of the relative clause is not coreferential with the antecedent, it must be expressed:

(167a) In a broken context, the story of the protagonist's exploits continues:

| *iw-f* | *ḥr-šm* | *r-pꜣ-nty-pꜣ-bik* | *[im]* |
|---|---|---|---|
| DEP-3MS | PRP-go | to-DEF.M-REL-DEF.M-falcon | in |

...and he went to (the place) where the falcon was. (pDeM 39 r° 7)

56 In most descriptions of Late Egyptian relative clauses, the factor determining the form of the relative clause is assumed to be definiteness of the antecedent. The sole exception here is Korostovtsev (1973: 446–447), who opts for restriction as explanation; see now also Müller 2015b.

(167b) The Lord of All sent a letter to Osiris who in his reply begins a description of his abode:

*ir* *pꜣ-tꜣ* *nty-ṱ-i* *im-f*
PTC DEF.M-land REL-PTC-1S in-3MS
As to the land in which I am... (*LES* 58, 2–3)

(167c) Deities are invoked to come and purify the patient as they did for their father Rahorakhty upon the great hills of the eastern mountains, at the appearance of:

*pꜣ-mḥy* *wr* *nty-pꜣ-30* *n-mḥ* *n-inr*
DEF.M-serpent great REL-DEF.M-30 of-cubit of-stone
*n-ds* *m-ḥꜣt-ḫpr-f*
of-knife in-front-manifestation-3MS
...the great serpent that has the thirty cubit stone knife in front of his manifestation. (Roccati, *Mag. taur.*, 24, 6)

(167d) The prince of Byblos asks Wenamun:

*wr* *r-pꜣ-hrw* *mḏr* *iw-k*
great to-DEF.M-day since come.PST-2MS
*n-pꜣ-nty-imn* *im*
from-DEF.M-REL-N there
How long is it since you came from where Amun is? (*LES* 66, 7)

(167e) A man reports in court about troubles with his tomb, which found the interest of other people as well. However, one day he has at the spot with two other gentlemen:

*iw-bw-rḫ(-i)* *pꜣ-nty-pꜣ-ꜣḥmr* *n-tꜣy-i-(m)ꜥḥꜥ*
DEP-NEG.AOR-know-1S DEF.M-REL-DEF.M-entrance of-POSS.F-1S-tomb
*m-im*
in-there
...but I did not know where the entrance of my tomb there is.
(oBM EA 5624 v° 6)

(167f) A person narrates that he has been apprehended once:

*iw-ink* *ms-ḫr* *iw-f* *mtn* *r-pꜣ-nty-iw-w*
DEP-1S child-necropolis DEP-3MS enlist.STA to-DEF.M-REL-DEP-3P
*m-im*
in-there
although I am a member of the necropolis personnel, who is enlisted at the place where they are. (*HO* 88 r° 14)

(167g) Context broken:

[...] *pꜣ-ntyiw-k* *i[m]*
... DEF.M-REL-2MS there
How long is it since you came from where Amun is? (*LES* 63, 9)

(167h) The address line of a petition runs as follows:

*pꜣ-ḫrw* *n-ỉtnṯr* *N* *sš N* *ntyỉw-f* *n-ỉtnṯr*
DEF.M-voice of-priest N scribe N REL-3MS for-priest
*sš-ḥwtnṯr* *N* *n-Pnpꜣỉhꜣy*
scribe-temple N of-N
The petition of the priest of the god Onuris and scribe Bakenkhons which is intended for the priest and temple scribe of the god Pepohe Horemachbit.
(Jansen-Winkeln, *IdS* I, 203, 9–10)

As can be seen from ex. 167b above, personal pronouns are not directly attached to the relative particle *nty*, which is rather followed by the preformative pronouns of the *ṯ*-series or, in the case of the 3rd person pronouns, direct adjacency (Winand 1992: 428–39). This picture changes in the Third Intermediate Period (with isolated examples as early as the 19th dynasty), when forms with *nty-ỉw*-PRN appear as exemplified by exx. 167f–h above, a feature that probably foreshadows the common Demotic marking of what later appears in Coptic as *ete-*.

As in Earlier Egyptian, adverbial sentences may also be used in relative clauses formed with a participle or a relative form of the auxiliary *wn/wnn*:

(168a) In a letter of complaint, a village foreman is accused of having had clandestine business with:

*pꜣrʿmḥb* *wn* *m-ṯꜣty*
N AUX.PTL as-vizier
...Pramheb, who was the vizier (*KRI* IV 408, 13–14)

(168b) A person in a list of accused thieves:

*pꜣ-sš* *n-pꜣ-ỉmyr* *prḥḏ* *wn* *ỉrm-w*
DEF.M-scribe of-DEF.M-overseer treasury AUX.PTL with-3P
The scribe of the treasury, who has been with them (i.e. the suspects)
(*KRI* VI 473, 8)

(168c) In a legal case between a father and daughter, the former reports:

*ỉw-ỉ* *ḥr-hꜣb* *n-pꜣ-rmṯ* *wn* *pꜣy-ỉ-sḏy*
DEP-1S PRP-send to-DEF.M-man AUX.PTL POSS.M-1S-shawls
*2* *m-dỉ-f*
2 with-3MS
So I wrote to the (work-)man with whom my two shawls were.
(*KRI* IV 417, 12–13)

(168d) In a letter a man reports about a woman is a relative of a certain man from the tomb builders community. To refresh the addressee's memory he adds:

*pꜣ-wn=dy* *ḥr-ỉmnti* *pꜣ-ỉnti* *ḥb-Imn*
DEF.M-AUX.PTL=here on-west (at)-DEF.M-valley_feast feast-N

...the one who was here on the west(-bank during) the Feast of the Valley, Amun's feast, .... (*KRI* IV 330, 13–14)

(168e) The patient is likened to the gods to convince the healing deities that he is one of them:
*ḫr mntf nmmwỉ n-ṯḥn-t wnn-f r-ḫḫ n-gb*
PTC 3MS dwarf of-fayence AUX.REL-3MS to-neck of-N
For he is the dwarf of fayence that was at the neck of Geb.
(Roccati, *Mag. taur.*, 26, 14)

Again, in 168a and 168b, the subject of the relativised participial adverbial sentence is coreferential with the antecedent and remains covert. Examples like the last one might point to a gradual replacement of the participle by relative clauses over time.

Late Egyptian non-restrictive relative clauses take the form of simple *ỉw*-introduced constructions (whence the appellation 'virtual'). Below are examples of this kind with adverbial sentences:

(169a) The recipient of a letter is told:
*ḥnʿ ntk dỉt ḥr-k n-mryms ỉw-f=dy*
and 2MS give.INF face-2MS to-N DEP-3MS=there
*mdỉ-k*
with-2MS
...and take care of Merymose, who is there with you. (*KRI* I 239, 10–11)

(169b) One of the accusations against the village foreman Paneb:
*nk pꜣnb ʿnḫ ṯy ỉw-s m-ḥm-t n-rmṯ-ỉs-t qnnꜣ*
copulate N lady N DEP-3FS as-wife-F of-man-gang-F N
*nk-f ʿnḫ ḥl ỉw-s mdỉ-pntꜣwrt*
copulate-3MS lady N DEP-3MS with-N
Paneb had sex with Lady Ty, who is the wife of the workman Qenna, and he had sex with Lady Hal, who is with Pentawere. (*KRI* IV 410, 14–16)

(169c) The patient is likened to the gods to convince the healing deities that he is one of them:
*mntf ḥr m-sš-t n-t-ꜣḫbỉt m-bỉk n-mḥ-1 ỉm-f*
3MS N in-nest-F of-F-N as-falcon of-cubit-1 in-3MS
*ỉw-f m-ỉḥwny pwy n-sꜣ-ḥwtḥr ỉw-ḥqꜣy nḫnḫ*
DEP-3MS as-child DEM.M of-son-N DEP-sceptre flail
*m-ḏr-t-f*
in-hand-F-3MS
He is Horus in the nest of Chemmis as a falcon of one cubit, who is that child of the son of Hathor and holds the sceptre and the flail.
(Roccati, *Mag. taur.*, 25, 5–7)

(169d) The young prince stood at the roof of a building and saw:

| | | | | | |
|---|---|---|---|---|---|
| *wꜥ* | *n-ṯsm* | *iw-f* | *msꜣ-wꜥ* | *n-s* | *ꜥꜣ* |
| IDF.S | of-dog | DEP-3MS | behind-IDF.S | of-man | great |

...a dog, that followed an adult man. (*LES* 2, 2–3)

It should be noted that even if the subject of the relative clause is here coreferential with the antecedent, it cannot be omitted. The same restriction was also observed in Earlier Egyptian 'virtual' relative clauses (see 2.1.7). Even without corroborating examples, the syntactic behaviour of adjunct *iw*-clauses can lead us to assume that the same distribution of patterns (morphologically by means of the indefinite article vs. syntactically with the particle *wn-*) also applies to 'virtual' relative clauses with a subject marked for indefiniteness.

### 2.2.4.2 Demotic

As in the earlier as well as later stages of the language, the strategy for relativisation in Demotic depended on the difference between restrictive and non-restrictive relative clauses. Restrictive relative clauses were introduced by the relativiser *nty* or expressed with the help of a participle or a relative form:

(170a) The author of a letter reassures his addressee on Elephantine that he is being informed about all the good things by a certain Lesonis:

| | |
|---|---|
| *irm-nꜣ-wꜥb-w* | *nty-irm-f* |
| with-DEF.P-priest-P | REL-with-3MS |

...and the priests who are with him. (pBerlin P 15617, 5)

(170b) A note in a receipt:

| | | |
|---|---|---|
| *pꜣ-šmw* | *n-nꜣ-ꜣḥ* | *nty-ẖr-pꜣ-ẖbs* |
| DEF.M-harvest tax | of-DEF.P-field | REL-under-DEF.M-flame |

The harvest-tax of the fields that are under the authority of the flame (endowment of the temple) .... (pSaqqara-Sekhemkhet, 5)

(170c) In a description of a locality:

| | | | |
|---|---|---|---|
| *pꜣ-prḥḏ* | *10* | *nty-ẖn-w* | *nty-ḥr-pꜣ-mꜣꜥ-rsy* |
| DEF.M-treasury | 10 | REL-in-3P | REL-on-DEF.M-place-south |
| *n-tꜣ-ḫꜣs-t* | *n-mnnfr* | | |
| of-DEF.F-desert-F | of-N | | |

...and the ten treasuries therein which are in the southern area of the necropolis of Memphis. (pLeiden I 379, 3)

(170d) The sun-god praises Thoth in form of the small dog-ape:

| | | | | | |
|---|---|---|---|---|---|
| *ꜣn* | *ṯꜣy-k* | *qmqm* | *r-nhm* | *n-tꜣy* | *nty-m-ḫnmn* |
| IP | take-3MS | cymbal | to-jubilate | for-DEM.F | REL-in-N |

Have you not taken a cymbal to jubilate for that one who is in Akhmim? (Myth of the Sun's Eye 22, 28)

(170e) The text accompanying the judgement of the deceased scene are given. The deceased has to say:

*tw-y irrḫ pꜣy-k-42 n-nṯr nty-ḫpr irm-k*
PTC-1S know POSS.M-2MS-42 of-god REL-happen with-2MS
*ḫn-tꜣ-wsḫꜣ-t nty-wpy*
in-DEF.F-hall-F REL-judge
I know your 42 gods who are with you in the hall and who judge.
(pBN 149 1, 27)

(170f) Someone complains about having been marred by:

*tꜣ-sḥm r-wn irm-pꜣy(-y)-iṯ*
DEF.F-woman PTL-PST with-POSS.M-1S-father
...the woman who was with my father. (oIFAO D 632, 3)

(170g) Pakrur urges the general Werdiamunno to attack by sending into battle:

*pꜣy-f-27 n-rmṯ-qnqn irm-f rwnnꜣw*
POSS.M-3MS-27 of-man-fight with-3MS PST.PTL
*ḫn-pꜣ-40 tl*
in-DEF.M-40 hero
...his 27 warriors who were among the 40 heroes ... (pKrall 18, 32)

(170h) The priests of el-Hibeh are supposed to deliver a certain amount of grain:

*n-pꜣ-šmw n-tꜣy-mꜣy iwnnꜣw ḫrr-w*
of-DEF.M-harvest of-DEM.F-island PST.PTL under-3P
...of the harvest of that island which was under their authority.
(pRylands IX 16, 13)

If the subject of the relative clause, as in the examples cited above, is coreferential with the antecedent, it is omitted. Otherwise, as in the examples below, the relative clause subject appears overtly. In this latter case, the relative particle appears now commonly in the form *ntyiw*, a spelling that undoubtedly represents the predecessor of the later Coptic relativiser *ete*. Hence, it may be safely assumed that the appearance of *iw* after *nty* is not an additional marking of subordination. In Later Demotic texts written in the Roman period the usual way to write *ntyiw* is *mtw* (see ex. 171e) and in Old Coptic texts the outcome is already *ete-* (as in ex. 171f):

(171a) A formula in a sales document states that no-one can appeal against the matter by asking for a witness:

*pꜣ-bnr n-pꜣ-dmy ntyiw-pꜣ-mtr nim-f*
DEF.M-outside of-DEF.M-city REL-DEF.M-witness in-3MS
...outside the city in which the witness is. (pRylands I, 7)

(171b) A man complains to a deity in a letter:
*tw-y ꜥwy-ṯ n-ms r-nꜣ-stbe ntyỉw-(y) nỉm-w*
PTC-1S old-STA for-birth to-DEF.P-rigours REL-1S in-3P
I am too old for all the rigours in which I am. (pBM 73785, 3–4)

(171c) Isis has asked a question that is to be answered via an ordeal by a stone. One of the answers states:
*mỉr tḥꜣ n-ḥꜣty n-nꜣ-ntyỉw-(ṯ) ẖn-w*
NEG.IMP suffer in-heart for-DEF.P-REL-2FS in-3P
Do not be sad over the situation in which you are!
(pVienna D 12006 3, 29–30)

(171d) Osiris is addressed as:
*pꜣ-ntyỉw-ḥr-f m-sn n-ḥr n-bk n-šs-nsw*
DEF.M-REL-face-3MS as-image of-N as-falcon of-linen-king
He whose face is the face of the falcon of byssus.
(pMag. London&Leiden 21, 4)

(171e) The hero of a literary story has fallen in love with a woman he beheld in the temple. So when evening comes:
*ỉw-f ỉw r-pꜣ-mꜣꜥ mtw-s nỉm-f*
PTC-3MS go to-DEF.M-place REL-3FS in-3MS
...he was going to the place where she was.
(pCarlsberg 159+PSI inv. D 10 v° 1, 13)

(171f) In a love spell to conjure a woman the aim is to arouse her heart:
*še-e-i-emmi (n)-n-ete-n-pe-s-hêt ero-i*
SO-DEP-1S-know OBJ-DEF.P-REL-in-POSS.M-3FS-heart to-1S
...so that I know what is in her heart for me...
($^{OC}$Great Mag. P. Paris [*ZÄS* 21, 104, 15])

If the subject of the relative clause is marked as indefinite, only the syntactic marking with the particle *wn* after the relativiser is attested. Yet, examples with the formally similar Present I formation suggest that this is due to the accident of preservation rather than to a morpho-syntactic rule:

(172) Moral precepts state:
*ỉỉr-pr wn r-pꜣ-ntyỉw-wn-nkt (n)-ḏrṯ-f*
AUX-house open.STA to-DEF.M-REL-PTC-something in-hand-3MS
A house is open for the one who owns something.
(Onkhsheshonqy 14, 13)

As in the earlier stages of the language, non-restrictive relative clauses are marked as *ỉw*-introduced 'virtual' relative clauses. As before, subjects of such clauses could not be omitted even if they were coreferential with the antecedent:

(173a) After being severely beaten and with his life threatened, Petese was carried into his house:
*ir-(y) hrw 4 iw-bw-rḫ-(y) md-t n-pꜣ-tꜣ*
do.PST-1S day 4 DEP-NEG.AOR-know-1S thing-F of-DEF.M-land
*iw-(y) ẖn-s*
DEP-1S in-3FS
I spent four days not knowing any earthly matter, in which I was involved.
(pRylands IX 3, 2)

(173b) A description in a narrative:
*mšʿ-f r-wʿ-k(ꜣ)m iw-f (n)-bnr n-pꜣ-dmy*
walk-3MS to-IDF.S-garden DEP-3MS (in)-outside of-DEF.M-city
*iw-f fḫ*
DEP-3MS ragged.STA
He walked to a ragged garden, which was outside the city.
(*Saqqâra Demotic Papyri I*, text 01 9, 17)

(173c) The Greek word *phêklês* 'wine yeast' is explained:
*wʿ-iny iw-f wbḫe pꜣy iw-f*
IDF.S-stone DEP-3MS white SE.M DEP-3MS
*m-qdy-gʿrbꜣnʿ*
in-likeness-galbanum
It is a white stone, which looks like galbanum.
(pMag. London&Leiden v° 3, 4–6)

If the subject of the 'virtual' relative clause is marked as indefinite, only the syntactic marking by *wn* after the initial *iw* is attested, but as with the *nty*-clauses, this is probably due to accidents of preservation:

(174a) An advertisement of a beast of burden:
*wʿ-t-ʿꜣ-t ḥꜣ tꜣy wʿ-t-ʿꜣ-t iw-wn-ḏnf*
IDF.S-F-donkey-F first SE.F IDF.S-F-donkey-F DEP-PTC-accuracy
*nim-s*
in-3FS
She is a first-class she-ass; a she-ass in which there is proportion.
(pBerlin P 3093, 26–27)

(174b) The harpist is said to be morally depraved:
*m-qdy-sg iw-f mḥṯ ḏmʿ iw-wn-sbꜣ-t nb-t*
in-likeness-fool DEP-3MS grasp book DEP-PTC-teaching-F QU-F
*ḥr-ꜣtṯ-f*
on-back-3MS
...like a fool grasping a book in which there is (just) any kind of teaching.
(Depraved Harpist 3, 13)

Adverbial sentence relative clauses with a past reference are marked by initial *(r)-wnnꜣw* (or its graphemic variants):

(175a) The narrator of the story relates how he came to El-Hibeh to claim his rights against the local priests. These were not amused about this intrusion by an outsider and threw him into prison, beating him and his son. Then they dismissed the local priest in charge of the temple's administrative affairs:

| | | | | |
|---|---|---|---|---|
| *dy-f* | *ḥwy-w=s* | *r-tꜣ-s-t* | *i͗-wnnꜣw-i͗w-n* | *ni͗m-s* |
| give.PST-3MS | throw-3P=3MS | to-DEF.F-place-F | REL-PRT-PTC-1P | in-3FS |

He caused him to be thrown to the place where we are.

(pRylands IX 2, 8–9)

(175b) In a broken context the hero causes something or someone to retreat from the person speaking:

| | | | | |
|---|---|---|---|---|
| *bnpw-w* | *wy* | *r-pꜣ[srʿšꜣi͗]ḫy* | *r-wnnꜣw* | *i͗rm-y* |
| NEG.PST-3P | be_far | from-N | REL-PST | with-1S |

But they did not retreat from Psenasychis who was with me.

(CG 30692, 4)

(175c) The king enclosed the fortress of *Škꜣn* with a wall:

| | | | |
|---|---|---|---|
| *(r)ḏbꜣ* | *nꜣ-sbꜣ-w* | *r-wnnꜣw* | *(n)-pꜣy-s-ḫn* |
| because | DEF.P-rebel-P | REL-PST.REL | (in)-POSS.M-3FS-inside |

...because of the rebels who were inside it. (Rosetta Decree 13)

#### 2.2.4.3 Coptic

Coptic adverbial sentences are relativised by means of the relative operator *et(e)-*, a direct descendent of the earlier *nty* (and Demotic *ntyi͗w*) when they are restrictive. In non-restrictive cases the clause was simply marked as dependent (or 'circumstantial'). Almost all Coptic dialects use the relative operator *etere-* if the subject of the relative clause is a noun and *et(e)-* if it is a pronoun. Only Bohairic always employs *ete-* (with occasional exceptions in its Nitrian variety) thus disregarding the subject's word class. In addition, some dialects include a specific determiner before the relative clause (as in ex. 176e) even if the latter follows the antecedent more or less immediately:

(176a) After he had risen from the dead, the Saviour came to the Mount of Olives and made a cloud to cover:

| | | | |
|---|---|---|---|
| *e-ne-khôra* | *têr-u* | *etere-n-apostolos* | *nhêt-u* |
| OBJ-DEF.P-land | all-3P | REL-DEF.P-apostle | inside-3P |

...all the lands where the apostles were.

($^{S}$*Mysteries of St John Evangelist* [Budge, *Apocrypha*, 59, 7–8])

(176b) When Jewish sorcerers tried to expel demons in the name of Jesus and Paul, the demon answered that he knew Jesus and Paul, but not them; then:

*a-f-fôkʲe* *ehrai* *ecô-u* *nkʲi-p-rôme* *etere-pe-pn(eum)a*
PST-3MS-leap down upon-3P PVS-DEF.M-man REL-DEF.M-spirit
*m-ponêron* *hiôô-f*
of-evil on-3MS

The man in whom the evil spirit was leaped on them. ([S]Acts 19:16)

(176c) Clement quotes the words of God in the Old Testament when He told Abraham to raise his eyes and look:

*cnm-p-ma* *et-k-nh̯ê[t]-f*
from-DEF.M-place REL-2MS-inside-3MS

...from where you are. ([A]1Cl 10:4 [Schmidt 45, 22–23])

(176d) The supremely mighty being tells Adamas to help:

*a-p-lilu* *et-ha-p-lekh* *et-m-p-itne*
OBJ-DEF.M-youth REL-under-DEF.M-pit REL-in-DEF.M-ground
*n-emnte*
of-Hades

...the youth who is beneath the pit which is at the bottom of Hades. ([L]*Psalms of Thomas* 209, 28)

(176e) Speaking about the arrangement of the earthly ritual, the author mentions:

*t-skynê* *n-šarp* *tê* *etere-ti-lykhnia* *nhêt-s*
DEF.F-tent of-first DEF.F REL-DEF.F-candlestick in-3FS

...the first tabernacle within which is the candlestick. ([F]Heb 9:2)

(176f) In the introduction to a story, Ari is described as a godly man who healed everyone, particularly:

*ni-rômi* *ete-ni-demôn* *nemô-u*
DEF.P-man REL-DEF.P-demon with-3P

...people possessed by demons. ([B]*Mart. Ari* [*AdM* 203, 10–11])

If the subject of the relative clause is coreferential with the antecedent, no resumptive pronoun appears:

(177a) The Christ is explained as being one who died and was resurrected; furthermore:

*pai-on* *et-hi-unam* *m-p-nute*
DEM.M-PTC REL-upon-right of-DEF.M-god

This is also the one who is on the right side of god. ([S]Rm 8:34)

(177b) Boas publicly claims to have bought Elimelech's possessions from Naomi:

*auô* *p-laos* *têr-f* *et-hn-t-pulê* *peca-u*
und DEF.M-people all-3MS REL-in-DEF.F-gate said-3P

*ce-tn-o* *m-mntre*
COMP-1P-be.STA as-witness
And all the people that were at the gate said: 'We are witnesses'.
($^{S}$Ru 4:11)

(177c) The Apocalypse of Elijah starts with the words of the Lord containing a quote from 1Jn 2:15:
*mn-mrre-p-kosmos* *ude* *n-et-ḫm-p-kosmos*
NEG.IMP-love-DEF.M-world nor DEF.P-REL-in-DEF.M-world
Love not the world, nor what is in it!
($^{A}$*ApEl* [Steindorff, *Apokalypse des Elias* 67 19, 6–7])

(177d) Clement narrates that Lot has been saved due to hospitality and piety. Yet:
*tare-t-f-shime=gar* *i* *abal* *neme-f*
TMP-POSS.F-3MS-woman=for go out with-3MS
*ete-n-u-gnômê=en* *n-uôt*
REL-in-IDF.S-mind=NEG of-single
*alla* *ete-n-hêt* *sno*
but REL-in-heart two
When his wife left with him who was did not agree but was doubtful, ...
($^{A}$1Cl 11:2 [Schmidt])

(177e) Deceived by the three wise men, King Herod resorted to drastic measures:
*ha-f-ḫotb* *n-n-kui* *n-lulaue* *et-hn-bethleem*
PST-3MS-slay OBJ-DEF.P-small of-child REL-ø-in-N
*mn-n-et-hn-ne-s-tešêu* *têr-u* *ncin-rampe*
and-DEF.P-REL-ø-in-POSS.P-3FS-border all-3P from-year
*snte* *e-p-esêt*
2.F to-DEF.M-bottom
He slew the little children that were in Bethlehem and all its surrounding areas from two years old and under. ($^{M}$Mt 2:16)

(177f) Wandering in the desert, Papnute reached a cave in which an anchorite had once lived. He found its former occupant dead and decided to bury him:
*uoh* *a-i-ôli* *n-ta-stolê* *et-hicô-i*
and PST-1S-take OBJ-POSS.F.1S-garment REL-upon-1S
And I took my garment that I was wearing.
($^{B}$Papnute, *Wanderings* [*RecTrav* 6, 169, 3, collated])

Bohairic again shows the insertion of the dummy predicate $k^{h}$ê both in clauses with and without subject omission:

(178a) Addressing the angel of Pergamos, John says that he knows the angel's abode:

*pi-ma* *ete-pi-thronos* *m-p-satanas* *k$^h$ê* *mmo-f*

DEF$_2$.M-place REL-DEF$_2$.M-throne of-DEF.M-Satan AUX in-3MS

...the place wherein is the throne of Satan. ($^B$Rev 2:13)

(178b) Moses is told to go to the pharaoh and tell him that he will strike the waters:

*ḫen-pi-šôbt* *p$^h$ê* *ete-k$^h$ê* *ḫen-ta-cic*

in-DEF$_2$.M-rod DEF$_3$.M REL-AUX in-POSS.F.1S-hand

...with the rod that is in my hand. ($^B$Ex 7:17)

(178c) Describing the area that the Israelites plundered, Moses begins:

*aroêr* *t$^h$ê* *et-k$^h$ê* *esken-nen-sp$^h$otu* *m-pi-mu-n-sôrem*

N DEF.F REL-AUX beside-DEF.P-edge.P of-DEF$_2$.M-water-of-lose

*nte-arnon*

of-N

...Aroer, which is along the edge of Wadi Arnon. ($^B$Dt 2:36)

Relative clauses with *ete(re)-* mark the clause as restrictive relative clauses. For non-restrictive relative clauses, the 'virtual' relative clause was simply marked as dependent with *e-*, but see Müller 2015b for an explanation within a restriction-marking system:

(179a) The first of the four streams out of Eden is the river Pishon running through:

*p-kah* *têr-f* *n-neuilat* *e-f-mmau* *nk$^j$i-p-nub*

DEF.M-land all-3MS of-N DEP-3MS-there PVS-DEF.M-gold

...the whole land of Heuilat, where the gold is. ($^S$Gn 2:11)

(179b) The prophet looked up and saw:

*is* *u-rôme* *e-un-u-nuh* *n-ḫi-ôhe* *n-toot-f*

PTC IDF.S-man DEP-PTC-IDF.S-rope of-measure-field in-hand-3MS

Behold, a man, who has a measuring line in his hand. ($^A$Zec 2:1 [Till])

(179c) Jesus continued his journeys and:

*ha-f-ne* *e-u-rome* *e-f-hmas*

PST-3MS-see OBJ-IDF.S-man DEP-3MS-sit

*hicn-p-ma-n-telônês*

upon-IDF.S-place-of-tax_collector

*e-pe-f-ren=pe* *maththaios*

DEP-POSS.M-3MS-name=COP.M N

He saw a man, who was sitting by the tax booth, and whose name was Matthew. ($^M$Mt 9:9)

(179d) As the apostles approached the city, they met:
*u-lômi* *ele-u-p[n(eum)a]* *n-lef-šini* *nem[ê-f]*
IDF.S-man DEP-IDF.S-spirit of-AGT-search with-3MS
...a man, possessed by a spirit with magical properties.
([F]*Acts of Philip* [von Lemm I 524, 22–23])

(179e) Shenute says of God's work of creation:
*uoh* *et-a-f-c$^{h}$ô-f=an* *ḫen-han-ššên* *n-at-utah*
and ST-PST-3MS-plant-3MS=NEG in-IDF.P-tree of-NEG-fruit
*ie* *e-f-hôu* *nce-pu-utah*
or DEP-3MS-bad PVS-POSS.M.3P-fruit
And he planted neither fruitless trees nor those of bad fruit.
([B]Shenute [*Le Muséon* 45 26 #4, 7–8])

Examples such as 180a and 180b are usually described as reflecting a collapse between the assumed difference between 'real' relative clauses with definite antecedents and their 'virtual' counterparts with indefinite antecedents (see Erman 1897: 64; Junker 1908–1911: I 93; Richter 1999: 91):

(180a) In the Epistle to the Colossians, the apostle urges people to seek things that are above:
*pi-ma* *ete-p-kh(risto)s* *mmo-f*
DEF$_2$.M-place REL-DEF.M-Christ in-3MS
...the place where Christ is. ([B]Col 3:1 [*var.*])

(180b) Theodore quotes from the Epistle to the Colossians (3:1) where the apostle urges people to seek things that are above:
*pi-ma* *ere-p-kh(risto)s* *mmo-f*
DEF$_2$.M-place DEP-DEF.M-Christ in-3MS
...the place, where Christ is.
([B]Theodotus of Ancyra, *In S. Georgem Diosp.* [*AM* II 184, 22–23])

# 3 Semantics and pragmatics

## 3.1 Earlier Egyptian

### 3.1.1 Core

As a semantic category, adverbial sentences may be viewed as a *radial* class centred on the core idea of expressing *locus* (cf. Stassen 1997: 15 and *passim*; Winand 2006: 158; Gracia Zamacona 2010: 13–15; Borghouts 2010: §§97.a.1, 97.b). This locative meaning represents its 'prototype value' that is shared in some sense by all but one of the representatives of the class. The core spatial relations may be expressed schematically as follows:

**Table I.8:** The core spatial relations expressed by adverbial sentences.

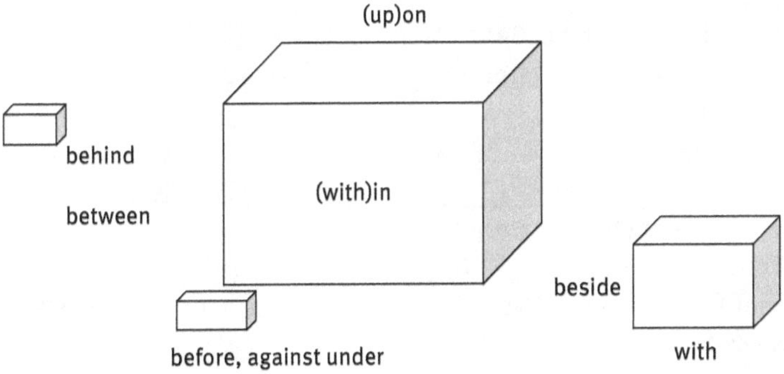


There is no need here to provide an exhaustive illustration of all these and other locative meanings expressed by Earlier Egyptian adverbial sentences seeing that in most cases the predicate is a prepositional phrase, and this is then largely a matter of semantics of the prepositions occurring in the predicative segment. Nevertheless, below are examples covering most of the relations seen in the above table:

(181a) A maidservant tells her mistress about a certain sack of grain belonging to a group of singers:

| | | |
|---|---|---|
| *ỉw-f* | *m-ꜥ-t* | *ḥr-ḫtm-sn* |
| AUX-3MS | in-room-F | on-seal-3P |

It is in a room and behind their seal. (pWestcar 11, 24)

https://doi.org/10.1515/9783110409895-004

(181b) The sage laments the deprived state of elite women:
*mtn šps-w-t ḥr-šd-w*
PTC noble-P-F on-raft-F
Look, noble ladies are on rafts. (Ipuwer 7, 10)

(181c) The road near the house of the villain Nemtynakht is described:
*iw w3-t-f wʿ-t ẖr-mw*
AUX side-F-3MS one-F under-water
Its one side was under water. (Peas B1, 26)

(181d) The sailor says to the snake:
*mk=wi r-gs-k*
PTC-1S to-side-2MS
Look, I am beside you. (Sh.S. 108)

(181e) As above:
*iw-i m-b3ḥ-k*
AUX-1S in-presence-2MS
I am before you. (Sh.S. 75)

(181f) The author of a *Letter to the Dead* points out to his addressee that he is sharing the abode with his father:
*mk=sw ḥnʿ-k*
PTC=2MS with-2MS
Look, he is with you. (Qaw Bowl inside, 8)

(181g) The king appears in his full glory:
*iw k3-w N ḥ3-f iw ḥms-w-t-f ẖr-rd-wy-f*
AUX soul-P N behind-3MS AUX N-P-F-3MS under-foot-DU-3MS
*iw nṯr-w-f tp-f*
AUX god-P-3MS upon-3MS
The souls of King N are behind him; his *ḥmswt* are under his feet; his gods are upon him. (PT 396a–b)

Locative are, of course, also sentences whose predicate is *ʿ3* 'here' or the interrogative *ṯn(i)* 'where', two of the rare genuine adverbs in Earlier Egyptian:

(182a) The Hyksos king tells his Nubian colleague that the latter need not fear the Egyptian pharaoh:
*mk=sw ʿ3 m-ʿ-i*
PTC=3MS here in-hand-1S
Look, he is here, with me. (Kamose Stela II, 23)

(182b) Words of an overseer to a group of men harvesting:
*i(w)-k ṯn wb3 m-hw-t-f*
AUX-1S WH skilled.PPA in-task-F-3MS
Where are you, one skilled in his task? (Junker, *Giza* VI, fig. 43)

The only clear exception to locative sense is *similes* expressed by means of the preposition *mi* 'like' seen in many examples cited earlier on.

The adverbial sentence is tenseless and may thus, depending on context, be translated as past, present, or future.[57] However, the core sense of something occupying a position in space entails also the idea of occupying a locus in time, and this in turn entails the kinetic idea of potential and susceptibility for development and change. In Earlier Egyptian, this network of concepts pertaining to adverbial sentence semantics had important repercussions on the grammatical marking of these constructions for features of TAM, illocution, and information structure, which differ radically from what is seen with the other non-verbal sentence types. In addition, the basic locative meaning prompted several semantic extensions, some of which may be viewed as broadly synchronic in character, whereas others were clearly diachronic developments. This historical setting would play a major role in the subsequent evolution of the Egyptian verbal system, which eventually led to the amalgamation of verbal and adverbial syntax.

The various meanings associated with adverbial sentences are so intertwined with, and dependent on, the syntactic uses of these constructions that a description of the former must by necessity be principally founded on the latter. Accordingly, in what follows the semantic-pragmatic nature of Earlier Egyptian adverbial sentences will be examined first in the 'bare' constructions consisting of nothing but subject and predicate, in their independent and syntactically bound uses. This will then be followed by an inquiry into the various ways in which the semantic-pragmatics and information structure of the adverbial sentence could be determined, enhanced, and modified by means of association with various auxiliary and, to a lesser extent, initial and clitic elements. The final section provides a brief overview of the various extensions of the core semantics of these constructions and of their diachronic significance.

### 3.1.2 Bare adverbial sentences

#### 3.1.2.1 Independent clauses

As noted in section 1.1, and contrary to what is often stated or implied in classical Egyptological studies, bare adverbial sentences without introductory particles

57 The most succinct Egyptological discussion to date is Winand (2006: 158–65).

are not at all rare in Earlier Egyptian 'independent' clauses.[58] They are, however, nevertheless slightly exceptional. Broadly speaking, constructions of this sort were used independently for a number of *non-assertive* speech acts as well as situation-descriptions whose information structure properties set them conceptually close to non-assertion. Most common are instances where bare adverbial sentences are used to carry out desiderative, directive, exhortative, or promissive speech acts (cf. Gardiner 1957: §118.1; Grapow 1941: 65–70):

(183a) Meni casts a curse against those who may damage his memorial:
*mzḥ i͗r-f m-mw ḥfȝ i͗r-f*
crocodile against-3MS in-water snake against-3MS
*ḥr-tȝ i͗r-t(y)-f(y) ḫ-t i͗r-nw*
on-land do.REL-FUT-AGR thing-F against-DEM
A crocodile in water and a snake on land against him who will do something against this! (*Urk.* I 23, 12–14)

(183b) Ankhreni bequeaths his property to his brother in his last will:
*ḫ-t-i͗=nb-t m-šȝ m-nw-t n-sn-i͗*
thing-F-1S=QU-F in-country in-town-F to-brother-1S
All my property in the country and in town shall belong to my brother. (pUC 32058, 4)

(183c) The gods are addressed on behalf of the deceased who is identified as Horus:
*mw n-ḥr mw n-ḥr i͗mi͗=n-f mw*
water to-N water to-N give.IMP to-3MS water
*n(-y)-i͗t-f wsi͗r*
of[-M]-father-3MS N
*hȝ N=pn mw-k=n-k qbḥ-k=n-k*
VOC N=DEM.M water-2MS=to-2MS refreshment-2MS=to-2MS
Water for Horus! Water for Horus! Give him the water of his father Osiris! Ho N; you shall have your water; you shall have your refreshment. (CT VII 34 g–i)

58 Given the multitude of examples of the bare use of these patterns in Earlier Egyptian, it is difficult to see how this old axiom, based on the allegedly 'adverbial' character of the said constructions, could have been so popular (cf. Allen 2000: 407; Vernus 1997: 23). Judging from H.-J. Polotsky's comments on this matter (1971: 94), the original idea seems to have been that the issue could be left on the level of historical linguistics and proto-Egyptian.

(183d) The deceased says to a malevolent being in the underworld:

| | | | |
|---|---|---|---|
| *ns-k* | *m-ṯ-t-k* | *ḥnn-k* | *m-rꜣ-k* |
| tongue-2MS | in-rectum-F-2MS | penis-2MS | in-mouth-2MS |

May your tongue be in your rectum (?) and your penis in your mouth! (CT VI 332g–h)

Particularly frequent here are utterances with the dative preposition *n* corresponding to similar expressions in other languages (e.g. English *Power to the people!*). Rather common are also exclamative utterances expressing the speaker's subjective feelings (surprise, elation, etc.) with respect to states of affairs whose actuality is presupposed in the speech context.[59] Examples are not always easy to distinguish from desiderative and directive uses:

(184a) Words by a sculptor gazing at his work:

| | | | | | |
|---|---|---|---|---|---|
| *ꜣbd* | *r-nn* | *n(-y)-hrw* | *ḏr-wd(-i)* | *ꜥ(-i)* | *m-twt=pn* |
| month | to-DEM | of[-M]-day | since-put[-1S] | arm[-1S] | in-statue=DEM.M |

| | | |
|---|---|---|
| *m-twt=pn* | *nt(-y)* | *m-ꜥ(-i)* |
| in-statue=DEM.M | REL[-M] | in-arm[-1S] |

It is a whole month until today since I laid my hand upon this statue that I have! (Hassan, *Giza* II fig. 219)

(184b) Words by a group of soldiers dragging a statue:

| | |
|---|---|
| *imnt-t* | *m-ḥb* |
| west-F | in-joy |

The West is in joy! (*El Bersheh* I, pl. 15, 2. reg.)

In terms of illocution, both these types of utterances are, for different reasons, rather obviously non-assertive in character: deontic statements do not assert but express the speaker's will, whereas exclamatives do not simply pass on information, but rather 'comment on' presupposed states of affairs (cf. Sadock and Zwicky 1985: 162). More complex are bare adverbial sentences used for descriptions of states of affairs with a thetic information structure[60]:

(185a) The opening of a PT spell:

| | |
|---|---|
| *ẖnw* | *m-p-t* |
| commotion | in-heaven-F |

There is a commotion in heaven. (PT 304a/W)

59 Cf. Vernus (1997: 45–51); for exclamatives generally, see Michaelis (2001).

60 What follows will be discussed in more detail in Stauder and Uljas (in preparation), but for thetic information structure in general, see e.g. Sasse (1987); Lambrecht (1994: 124, 137–46); Rosengren (1997). Earlier Egyptological discussions of theticity are e.g. Loprieno (1991b: 214); *id.* (1995: 110–11, 153); Uljas (2007c: 298–301).

(185b) Having finished the story of his father, Khnumhetep moves on in his self-presentation:

| | | |
|---|---|---|
| *sꜥḥ-ỉ* | *tp(-y)* | *n-msw-t-ỉ* |
| distinction-1S | head[-RLT] | to-birth-F-1S |

My first distinction related to my birth. (*Beni Hasan* I pl. 25, 62–63)

(185c) The opening of Coffin Texts Spell 636:

| | | | | | | | |
|---|---|---|---|---|---|---|---|
| *sbk* | *m-mw* | *ddwn* | *m-tꜣst* | *ḥꜣ* | *m-ỉmn-t* | *spdw* | *m-ỉꜣb-t* |
| N | in-water | N | in-N | N | in-west-F | N | in-east-F |

Sobek is in the water, Dedwen is in *tꜣ-st*, Ha is in the west, and Sopdu is in the east. (CT VI 259b–c)

(185d) The peasant says to the high steward:

| | | | |
|---|---|---|---|
| *mꜣꜣ* | *m-ḥr-k* | *psš-w* | *m-ꜥwn-w* |
| see.IMP | with-face-2MS | distributor-M | as-greedy-M |

See for yourself: the distributor is a greedy man. (Peas B1, 278–79)

Take ex. 185a, which serves as a 'dramatic' setting for a mythological narrative. Here, the communicative *raison d'être* of the sentence is not to make a categorical statement – or, more freely speaking, to say anything about – the 'commotion'.[61] Rather, the proposition presents the entire state of affairs [commotion-is-in-heaven] as an indivisible block of information for acceptance, denial, or, as here, for the purposes of providing a 'stage' on which to build further discourse. Similarly, in 185d, the peasant does not in fact make a statement whose purpose is to inform the high steward about the rapaciousness of some (in any case wholly metaphorical and non-referential) 'distributor'. Instead, he merely presents a complete state of affairs for the hearer to observe: 'See for yourself: this is the status quo in the world' (compare Junge 1989: 105). Utterances such as these are, in other words, not intended to enhance the hearer's knowledge or idea of some participant. Rather, they represent presentational propositions that merely announce, recognise, acknowledge, or state the existence of a situation *en bloc* without viewing it from the vantage point of any entity or individual engaged therein. Such situation-thetic expressions are not necessarily strictly non-assertive, but inasmuch as they do not profile the predication between the sentence subject and predicate as the most salient information in what is said, they share more in common with non-assertions such as presuppositions than they do with assertions, where the predication itself is by definition the informative pivot of the proposition.

**61** This is what 'categorical' statements do instead – see Sasse (1987: 559, 563, *passim*); Lambrecht (1994: 144).

It should be stressed that in all the instances above, the non-assertive or thetic reading is merely an interpretation arising from the discourse or situational context in which the bare adverbial setting is used. None of these values is an inherent feature associated with the adverbial sentence as a construction and none is grammatically marked. However, as seen in section 1.1, there are adverbial sentences where a pronominal subject is an absolute pronoun:

(186a) The king ascends to heaven in the retinue of gods:
*ỉr-p-t* *ỉr-p-t* *m-ꜥb-nṯr-w* *pr-wt* *ỉnk*
to-heaven-F to-heaven-F in-midst-god-P emerge.PP-P 1S
*ỉr-p-t* *m-ꜥb-nṯr-w* *prwt*
to-heaven-F in-midst-god-P emerge.PPA
To heaven, to heaven, among the emergent gods! *I* am (also) on a way to heaven, among the emergent gods. (PT 1114a–b/P)

(186b) The king traverses heaven in the company of the four sons of Horus:
*snw* *ḥr-gs* *snw* *ḥr-gs* *ỉnk* *m-ḥm*
two on-side two on side 1S as-oar
Two are on (one) side and two are on (the other) side, but *I* am at the steering oar. (PT 1092d–1093a/P)

(186c) The deceased states about his relationship with Osiris:
*wḏꜣ-f* *m-ꜥ-ỉ* *wḏꜣ-ỉ* *m-ꜥ-f*
proceed-3MS in-arm-1S proceed-1S in-arm-3MS
*ỉnk* *ḥr-fnḏ* *wsỉr*
1S under-nose N
He proceeds with my assistance, and I proceed with his assistance; but only *I* am under the nose of Osiris. (CT III 348a–b/S1C[b])

In examples of this sort, which are relatively rare in Earlier Egyptian, the subject of the adverbial sentence is assigned special pragmatic prominence.[62] This sort of participant or constituent focus is best understood as resulting from a particular kind of presuppositional structure brought into effect by a presupposition trigger that launches the presupposition and may be a single lexeme or some specific construction. It will be argued later in connection with the discussion of nominal sentences that first- and second-person absolute pronouns are not in fact themselves such triggers (see Part II below). However, *constructions* in which they appear may be, and this is precisely what is at issue with adverbial sentences such as those above. The subject focus here results from the

62 See Allen (1994: 6). No examples at all are attested in the Traditional Egyptian of the Twenty-First to Twenty-Fifth dynasties.

construction [absolute pronoun + adverbial predicate] triggering a special set of presuppositions. For example, in 186c this is '*x* is under the nose of Osiris', and the actual information then conveyed (or, as it is often said, 'asserted') by the sentence is the link between the subject and the empty slot in the presuppositional structure (*x* = me) rather than the simple subject-predicate relation (cf. Lambrecht 1994: 228–33). Indeed, the predicative relation between 'I' and 'being under the nose of Osiris', which is the main information content of the non-focal allo-sentences of the present construction, forms part of the presupposition of the proposition. It does not represent its informational high point and remains unasserted. In a sense, then, the subject-focus adverbial sentences are the polar opposite of the situation-thetic propositions seen above: the former single out one participant in the information structure, the latter level off the differences in their prominence. Nevertheless, in both the subject-predicate relation is either clearly unasserted or bears a family resemblance to non-assertion.

Finally, a note should be made on adverbial sentences with left-dislocated interrogative predicates. As seen above, the order S–P is rigidly adhered to in most Earlier Egyptian evidence, but one also finds examples of the interrogative adverb *ṯn*(*ỉ*) used as a predicate and occupying the initial position (cf. Loprieno 1991b: 205–206):

(187) The spirits of the underworld ask the deceased:
*wꜣ-t-k=tn* *ṯn* *wꜣ-t-k=tn*
road-F=2MS=DEM.F WH road-F=2MS=DEM.F
This your road; where is this your road? (CT VI 57e/S1C)

Instances of this phenomenon are more common in early texts – cf. the Pyramid Texts ex. 188a with its later Coffin Texts version 188b:

(188a) The priest offering a royal funerary libation says:
*mrḥ-t* *mrḥ-t* *ṯn* *wn-ṯ* *ỉm-t* *ḥꜣ-t* *ḥr* *ṯn* *wn-ṯ*
oil-F oil-F WH AUX-2FS in.RLT-F front-F N WH AUX-2FS
Oil, oil, where have you been? You who are on the brow of Horus; where have you been? (PT 52a/N)

(188b) As above:
*mrḥ-t* *wn-t* *ṯn* *ỉm-t* *ḥꜣ-t* *wn-t* *ṯn*
oil-F AUX-2FS WH in.RLT-F front-F AUX-2FS WH
Oil, where have you been? You who are on (one's) brow; where have you been? (CT VII 105o–p)

The idea behind this positioning is the same as in the so-called WH-movement seen e.g. in English WH-questions, i.e. to mark the special information structure brought about by the presupposition-triggering interrogative expression constructionally by 'moving' the former into the first position in the clause (see Uljas 2012b: 264–265). The rarity of this construction appears to relate to the strong association of adverbials with the sentence-final position in Earlier Egyptian, but in adverbial sentences the fronting also violated the otherwise strongly enforced S–P rule. Consequently, WH-fronting was in these constructions limited to rare 'moving' of the relatively 'light' element *ṯn*(*i*).

#### 3.1.2.2 Subordinate clauses

The adverbial sentences described in the previous section are all independent, in the sense that they seem to represent (relatively) self-standing propositions. However, in Earlier Egyptian bare adverbial sentences were also, as seen, used in adjunct- and relative clauses without any grammatical marker of their adjunct- or relative clause status. Once again, it is clear that functionally adverbial sentences found in such unmarked subordinate clauses are indeed attributive adjuncts and relative clauses, but equally clearly they are nothing of the sort formally. It is as yet unknown what precisely allowed adverbial sentences to display such syntactic flexibility in Earlier Egyptian, but it seems that the most straightforward (if not entirely satisfactory) explanation is to assume that these constructions were simply unmarked for syntactic function in this respect.[63] Yet, overall, this disregard of syntactic boundaries seems to reflect the semantic vacuity of the category 'adjunction' as a whole. Consider the following example:

(189) The shipwrecked sailor describes the delights of the Phantom Island:
*gm-n-i* *d3b-w* *i3rr-t* *im* *i3q-w-t=nb-t* *šps-t*
find-PST-1S fig-P grape-P there vegetable-P-F=QU-F excellent-F
*k3-w* *im* *ḥnʿ-nq-w-t* *šsp-w-t* *mi-iri-t*(*w*)-*s*
sycamore_fig-P there with-ripe-P-F cucumber-P-F like-do-PASS-3FS
I found figs and grapes there and all (sorts) of excellent vegetables: there were sycamore figs – ripened-ones as well – and the cucumbers were as if (ready-) made. (Sh.S. 47–50)

Here the status of the successive adverbial sentences after *gm-n-i d3b-w i3rr-t im* 'I found figs and grapes there' is not particularly obvious. Rather than describing 'adjunctive' concomitant circumstances *stricto sensu*, the clauses seem to serve a

63 This is in essence the hypothesis proposed by Collier (1991c).

broader enhancing function, itemising and fleshing out the situation described in the preceding encapsulating main clause in an almost coordinated fashion. The problem of distinguishing between unmarked coordinated and adjunctive adverbial sentences was already noted above (2.1.1), but at its root there seems to lay the general difficulty of drawing a hard and consistent semantic line between coordination and adjunction. Indeed, it has been argued both in linguistics and in Egyptology that the semantics of hypotactic main-adjunct and paratactic main-main clausal combinations are merged and that the two form one unbroken semantic continuum of clausal linkage where cut-off points are more or less arbitrary (see Uljas 2007b; Matthiessen and Thompson 1988; cf. also Collier 1996). It has been suggested that in Earlier Egyptian, the lack of marking between e.g. adjunct and coordinate adverbial sentences (as well as several verbal patterns) reflects the semantic intermingling of the two classes.

All this should be kept in mind particularly when attempting to provide an inventory of the different semantic types of Earlier Egyptian unmarked adjunct clauses formed by using directly subordinated adverbial sentences. Just as the syntactic status of such clauses is not explicitly marked, the same also applies to their semantic nature, whose interpretation depends on judgements made by individual readers/hearers and is based on their understanding of the discourse context and the interrelations of states of affairs therein. Usually, the most straightforward interpretation is to read the clause in terms of temporal simultaneity (e.g. 'He spoke to me *when he was here*' or '...*while being here*' etc.):

(190a) At the time of his father's death, Senwosret I was campaigning abroad:

| | | | | | |
|---|---|---|---|---|---|
| *ꞽst=rf* | *sb-n* | *ḥm-f* | *mšꜥ* | *r-tꜣ* | *ṯmḥi* |
| PTC=PTC | send-PST | majesty-3MS | expedition | to-land | N |

| | | |
|---|---|---|
| *sꜣ-f* | *smsw* | *m-ẖry=ꞽr-y* |
| son-3MS | eldest | as-leader=to.RLT-M |

Now, his majesty had sent an expedition to the Tjemehi-land, with his eldest son as its leader. (Sin R, 11–13)

(190b) Goddesses set out to meet the family of Redjedet in disguise:

| | | | | | |
|---|---|---|---|---|---|
| *wḏꜣ=pw* | *ꞽri-n* | *nn* | *nṯr-w* | *ꞽri-n-sn* | *ḫpr-w-sn* |
| proceed.INF=SE | do.REL-PST | DEM | god-P | do-PST-3P | form-P-3P |

*m-ḫny-w-t*
as-singer-P-F

| | | |
|---|---|---|
| *ẖmnw* | *ḥnꜥ-sn* | *ẖr-qni* |
| N | with-3P | under-palanquin |

These gods went forth, having made their appearance as (that of) musicians, whilst Khnum was with them carrying a palanquin.
(pWestcar 9, 27–10, 1)

(190c) Iti tells how he accumulated material wealth during difficult times:
*ỉw* *ḥb-n(-ỉ)* *ỉdr* *10* *m-ꜥnḫ-w-t* *mnỉ-w*
AUX acquire-PST[-1S] herd 10 in-goat-P-F herdsman-P
*m-sꜣ-ỉdr=nb*
in-back-herd=QU.M
I acquired ten herds of goats, with herdsmen for (lit., 'behind') each herd. (CG 20001, 5–6)

This is also the case in constructions in which the element *ỉw* provides an incorporation-base for suffix pronouns. Because of their purely morphological function, these constructions may be loosely characterised as 'bare' despite the presence of *ỉw*[64]:

(191) The sailor tells the story of his shipwreck:
*ḏꜥ* *pr* *ỉw-n* *m-wꜣḏwr*
storm come.STA DEP-1P in-sea
A storm came when we were at sea. (Sh.S. 32–33)

A more precise interpretation of the clause is seldom possible, although the following instances showing the pronominal subject attached to the element *ỉw* might be interpreted as clauses of result ('Do that *and you'll be in trouble*') and concession ('the fuse blew *although it was in the right slot*'):

(191a) The peasant warns the high steward of the dangers of inaction:
*swꜣ* *ḥr-sp* *ỉw-f* *r-snw*
pass.IMP over-case DEP-3MS to-two
Pass over a case and it will become two. (Peas B1, 246)

(191b) Ahmose tells how he took over the profession of marine from his father:
*ꜥḥꜥ-n-ỉ* *ḥr-ỉrt* *wꜥw* *r-ḏbꜥ-f* *m-pꜣ-ꜥḥꜥ*
AUX-1S PROG-do.INF soldier to-replace-3MS in-DET.M-ship
*n(-y)-pꜣ-smꜣ* *m-hꜣw* *nb* *tꜣ-wy*
of[-M]-DET.M-N in-era lord land-DU
*nbpḥtyrꜥ* *mꜣꜥ-ḫrw* *ỉw-ỉ* *m-šrỉ*
N true-voice DEP-1S as-child
Then I became a soldier in his stead in the ship 'Raging Bull' in the time of King Nebpehtijra, justified, although I was (merely) a young boy. (*Urk.* IV 2, 12–14)

64 For reasons explained in section 1.1, clauses with the particle *ỉsṯ* etc. cannot be similarly characterised.

Overall, however, the adjunct interpretation in general, and the semantic value of the adjunct in particular, depend on inferences drawn by the hearer or the reader. Similarly, it is delegated to the hearer to interpret the clause as either attributive of a verbal or even non-verbal predication, or else as an adnominal 'virtual' relative clause. The choice between the two is not always wholly obvious:

(192) An instruction in an incantation:

| | | | | | |
|---|---|---|---|---|---|
| *ḏdmdw* | *ỉn* | *s* | *ḫt* | *ds* | *m-ꜥ-f* |
| recitation | AGT | man | stick | N | in-hand-3MS |

To be recited by a man when he has/who has a stick of *ds*-wood in his hand. (pEdwin Smith 18, 15)

As noted in section 2.1.7, 'virtual' relative clauses are in general preferred when the antecedent is indefinite, even though Earlier Egyptian mostly did not mark definiteness overtly. There are, however, exceptions to this rule of thumb (cf. Gardiner 1957: §198):

(193) A heading of an administrative document:

| | | | | | | |
|---|---|---|---|---|---|---|
| *mỉt(y)* | *n(-y)-wpw-t* | *n-t-ꜥḥꜣwty* | *ḥri* | *sꜣ* | *snfrw* | *ỉt-f* |
| copy | of[-M]-report-F | of-F-soldier | N | son | N | father-3MS |
| *ḥr-snw-t* | *n-t-ḏꜣm-w* | | | | | |
| on-second-F | of-F-troop-P | | | | | |

Copy of the household census of the soldier Hori's son Sneferu, whose father is in the second (list?) of troops. (pUC 32163, r° 2)

Here, the antecedent 'Hori's son Sneferu' is clearly definite. Conversely, as will be shown below, clauses with the relative adjective *nt-* are often used with apparently generic and indefinite antecedents. It is precisely because of such anomalies that 'virtual' relative clauses have been suggested to be specifically used for non-restrictive relative propositions providing mere parenthetic information that is not essential to the identification or specification of the antecedent (as in *Sean Connery, who is a Scottish nationalist, is best remembered for his role as a British secret agent*; see Malaise and Winand 1999: §§1002, 1021–27; Müller 2015b). This proposal seems rather cogent for at least most of the examples cited in 2.1.7, but examples such as (194) show that matters are more complex:

(194) An item is described in a mathematical text as follows:

| | | | | | | |
|---|---|---|---|---|---|---|
| *qrf-t* | *nbw* | *ỉm-s* | *ḥḏ* | *ỉm-s* | *ḏḥty* | *ỉm-s* |
| container-F | gold | in-3FS | silver | in-3FS | lead | in-3FS |

A container in which there is gold, silver, and lead. (pRhind math. n.62, 2)

Here the antecedent *qrf-t* 'container' is, of course, generic and non-referential, but its interpretation is nevertheless restricted to such a 'container' that has the specific characteristics described by the modifying relative clauses (the text concerns calculating the value of a vessel of the said type).

Finally, in Earlier Egyptian, bare adverbial sentences were not commonly used in complement clauses, but the one exception to this rule was seen in 2.1.5, where it was noted that they could occasionally be embedded as predicative complements of the subject element =*pw* in a bipartite nominal sentence:

(195a) The king's soul is told to arise before gods and spirits:
*snḏ-k=pw* *ỉr-ḥꜣ-t-w-sn* ... *šʿ-t-k=pw* *ỉr-ḥꜣ-t-w-sn*
fear-2MS=SE to-heart-F-3P dread-F-2MS=SE to-heart-F-P-3P
The fear of you, it will be in their hearts... the dread of you, it will be in their hearts. (PT 763a–d)

(195b) Amun says to Queen Hatshepsut:
*rn(-ỉ)=pw* *ḫnt-nṯr-w* *[r]n-ṯ=pw* *ḫnt-ʿnḫ-w=nb-w*
name[-1S]=SE before-god-P name-2FS=SE before-living-P=QU-P
*ḏt*
forever
My name, it is before gods. Your name, it is before all the living forever. (*Urk.* IV 347, 2–3)

In this special construction, =*pw* topicalises the subject of the embedded adverbial sentences by separating it from the rest of the construction (see Part II 1.2.1). Yet the topicalisation thus achieved takes place without removing the left-dislocated adverbial sentence subject from its original clausal frame.[65] This

65 Rare though constructions such as this may be, they are attested even in the so-called Traditional Egyptian of the Third Intermediate Period. An example is

(FNa) Djedkhonsuefankh addresses his descendents:
*gs* *ḏ-t-ṯn=pw* *ỉm-ỉ* *mỉ-dwꜣ-t* *ḫpr-f* *m-sf*
half body-F-2P=SE in-1S like-dawn-F happen-3MS from-yesterday
A half of your body originates (lit. 'is in') me, just like dawn appearing from yesterday. (CG 42210, d1–2)

However, one also finds instances of subjects anteposed by means of absolute pronouns – a strategy wholly alien to Earlier Egyptian but much used in Late Egyptian:

(FNb) Harsiesi tells of his respectful conduct upon earth:
*ỉnk* *mḏr* *wn-ỉ* *ḥr-tp-tꜣ* *trỉ-ỉ* *wr-w*
1S when AUX-1S on-upon-earth respect-1S noble-P
As for me, when I was upon earth, I used to pay respect to notables. (CG 42254, left 9–10)

contrasts with the more widely used alternative strategy of topicalisation of adverbial sentence subjects with or (less often) without the element *ỉr* (see section 3.1.3.2).

### 3.1.3 Introduced adverbial sentences

The term 'introduced' is here used, for want of a better label, to designate Earlier Egyptian adverbial sentences preceded by one or several functional element(s) that determine, modify, or alter its semantic-pragmatic and/or syntactic status. The following constructions may be distinguished:

1. Adverbial sentences introduced by auxiliary elements such as *ỉw* or *wn/wnn*
2. Bare or auxiliary-headed adverbial sentences introduced by initial particles
3. Bare or auxiliary-headed adverbial sentences introduced by various subordinating elements such as preposition-conjunctions, relative adjectives, and/or complementisers.

#### 3.1.3.1 Auxiliary-headed constructions

Earlier Egyptian adverbial sentences are characteristically preceded by clause-initial auxiliary expressions that contribute to their semantic-pragmatic and syntactic character. Until the early 1990s, studies on Earlier Egyptian tended to view elements belonging to this class such as *ỉw* and *ꜥḥꜥ-n* as serving primarily structural functions (*Locus classicus* is Polotsky 2007: 94; for a summary, see Schenkel 1990: 187–88). The form and meaning of adverbial sentences, as well as the other types of grammatical forms and patterns attested with auxiliaries, were viewed largely through the prism of the assumed syntactic role of the latter. Nowadays, however, it is widely accepted that the presence or absence of an auxiliary before an adverbial sentence is semantic-pragmatically rather than structurally motivated. Indeed, the earlier view, noted in section 1.1, of the use of auxiliaries before adverbial sentences as based on the morpho-syntactic requirements of pronominal subjects and claims on the structural anomality of these constructions without the said elements must be considered erroneous. As seen in 3.1.2.1, bare adverbial sentences with noun or pronoun subjects are commonly used in independent utterances. There are also other more marginal indicators of this such as the mandatory occurrence of the auxiliary *wn/wnn* in all adverbial sentence final clauses regardless of the nature of their subject (see 2.1.2). The situation is clearer in independent than in subordinate clauses, but even in the former case opinions diverge on the exact contribution of the auxiliaries to the meaning and profile of the construction.

Overall, Earlier Egyptian auxiliaries may be characterised as core-level operators whose functional scope is the *predication* of the proposition to which they relate (including its arguments).[66] Of the various expressions belonging to this category, adverbial sentences are found after the auxiliaries *iw*, *wn/wnn*, and *ʿḥʿ-n*. As noted in section 1.1, combinations with the last of these elements are very rare[67]; below is another example with *ʿḥʿ-n* in addition to ex. 75 cited earlier:

(196) It is told how Horus and Seth entered into east:

| | | | |
|---|---|---|---|
| *ʿḥʿ-n* | *ʿḥȝ-ʿ* | *m-tȝ* | *r-ḏr-f* |
| AUX | fighting | in-land | to-limit-3MS |

Then there was fighting throughout the entire land. (CT IV 292a/T1C[b])

The rarity of *ʿḥʿ-n* before adverbial sentences is understandable given the narrative character of this auxiliary and the fact that the prototypical semantic value(s) of adverbial sentences such as spatial loci are more common in descriptions than in narration. By contrast, adverbial sentences introduced by the auxiliaries *iw* and *wn/wnn* are extremely common in Earlier Egyptian. The semantic-pragmatic contribution of these elements is difficult to characterise briefly, and both display several related functions that form a complex lattice of distinct but nonetheless related meanings with adverbial sentences as well as in general.

#### 3.1.3.1.1 Combinations with *iw*

The most common auxiliary element found with adverbial sentences is *iw*.[68] Its use in adjuncts as a purely morphological incorporation-base for suffix pronouns has already been noted several times, but its main employment with adverbial sentences as well as elsewhere is in syntactically independent (initial and possibly coordinated) clauses, where it functions as a predication-level operator, signalling that the predication it introduces has a particular kind of temporal-modal and information-structuring value. As seen in section 3.1.1, bare independent adverbial sentences are commonly used for exclamative and various sorts of deontic speech acts as well as for descriptions of states of affairs profiled as situation-thetic. These speech act and pragmatic features set such propositions either clearly within or close to the domain of non-assertion. By contrast,

66 This definition is based on the idea of the layered structure of the clause and of each of the layers potentially under the scope of various operators with varying scope-properties presented in Role and Reference Grammar (summary by van Valin 2010: 703–38, particularly 709).

67 For the semantics of *ʿḥʿ-n*, see Collier (1994: 82–86).

68 *iw* is by far the most discussed grammatical element in Earlier Egyptian and the literature on it is very extensive. For overviews and bibliographical details, see Doret (1986: 98, 125–26); Schenkel (1990: 134–35, 186–88, 192–93); Vernus (1997: 26–28); Depuydt (1998: 20–21).

introducing an adverbial sentence with *ỉw* serves as an explicit signal that the predicative relation has illocutionary and informative properties that characterise it as an *asserted* statement. For example:

(197a) Sinuhe describes his new Syrian estate:

*ỉw dbꜣ-w ỉm-f ḥnꜥ-ỉꜣrr-w-t ... ỉw ỉt ỉm*
AUX fig-P in-3MS with-grape-P-F AUX barley there
*ḥnꜥ-bd-t*
with-emmer-F
There were figs and grapes... there was barley and emmer. (Sin B, 81–84)

(197b) The peasant draws the high steward's attention to his own fortunate position:

*ỉw šd-w-k m-sḫ-t ỉw fqꜣ-w-k m-spꜣ-t*
AUX field-P-2MS in-country-F AUX reward-P-2MS in-nome-F
*ỉw ꜥq-w-k m-šnꜥ*
AUX ration-P-2MS in-storehouse
Your fields are in the country, your rewards are in the estate, and your rations are in the storehouse. (Peas B2, 65–66)

(197c) Heqanakhte issues a stark warning to his household:

*ꜥnḫ=n-ỉ s=pn... ỉr-t(y)-f(y) sp=nb ḥr-pgꜣ*
live=to-1S man=DEM.M do.REL-FUT-AGR occasion=QU.M on-enter.INF
*n-ḥbsw-t(-ỉ)*
to-new wife[-1S]
*ỉw-f r-ỉ ỉw-ỉ r-f*
AUX-3MS against-1S AUX-1S against-3MS
As this man lives for me... he who will make a sexual advance against my new wife, he is against me; I am against him. (Heqanakhte II, r° 40–41)

Rather than being a mere inventory of the agricultural produce of Sinuhe's estate, the information presented in ex. 197a is profiled as factual, in the sense that the speaker is fully committed to its correctness and reliability.[69] Similarly, in ex. 197b the speaker presents a more or less clearly itemised series of what are intended as (either coordinated or fully independent) statements of undeniable facts that in this instance are particularly salient, since they are implied to stand in contrast with the speaker's own position. Finally, in 197c, the speaker's final words are part of an oath; thus, they are certainly meant as illocutionary acts to be taken as an expression of absolute personal

69 For this role of *ỉw*, cf. e.g. Winand (2006: 165–66); Malaise and Winand (1999: §408); Loprieno (1995: 166); Ritter (1995: 99), and numerous others.

commitment. In addition, the adverbial sentences in exx. 197a–197c are uniformly categorical in terms of their information structure: their communicative function is precisely to widen the audience's understanding of the subjects by presenting the sentence predication as optimally relevant information. These meanings are signalled by the operator *ỉw*. Thus, an adverbial sentence introduced by this element is grammatically marked as representing a statement towards which the speaker entertains a high degree of commitment and whose predicative relation is presented as highly relevant and newsworthy information, i.e. as an assertion.[70] Therefore, notwithstanding one single exception to be described shortly (and which may be seen to confirm the rule), an *ỉw*-sentence never has a deontic, exclamative, or otherwise non-assertive illocutionary force. Similarly, its predication is the communicative key to the entire statement and never part of the presuppositions underlying the proposition or profiled as thetic. In other words, *ỉw*-sentences fulfil also the information structuring requirements of assertion.[71]

The role of *ỉw* as a marker of maximal speaker commitment and informative salience of the proposition predicative relation explains its absence in the bare adverbial sentences of section 3.1.1 and, as will be seen shortly, in other instances where these constructions fail the essential conditions for assertive illocution and information structuring. However, it also helps to understand the interconnections between *ỉw*, adverbial sentences, and the abstract concept of temporality, which has dominated discussions on this element.[72] On the whole, *ỉw* is not a temporal operator *per se* and does not directly modify the time reference of the adverbial sentence. This may be seen from the way in which adverbial sentences introduced by *ỉw* may, in appropriate circumstances, be read as past, present, or even future:

(198a) Sinuhe describes the effects of the pharaoh's death at the court:

| | | |
|---|---|---|
| *ỉw* | *ẖnw* | *m-sgr* |
| AUX | residence | in-silence |

The residence was in silence. (Sin R, 8)

70 For this definition of assertivity, see e.g. Searle (1969: 67), amongst others.

71 In the analysis proposed by Collier (1994: 78–87), inspired by Cognitive Grammar, *ỉw* and other auxiliaries perform 'grounding functions' that include modality, presupposition, and speech acts. However, it is unclear whether the model proposed can explain the non-occurrence of these elements before nominal and adjectival sentences (see below).

72 In many works, the role of *ỉw* is also considered to be that of marking the following proposition as related to the temporal position of the speaker (most notably Allen 1986b: 8–11). In the present analysis, this alleged temporal role of *ỉw* is viewed as an adjunct to its assertive function that perforce relates the statement to the 'sphere of interest' or 'here and now' of the speaker. However, the situation must then also contain a temporal element, see below.

(198b) Prince Hardjedef salutes the magician Djedi:
*i͗w ḫr-t-k mi-ꜥnḫ tp-m-tni*
AUX condition-F-2MS like-live.INF front-in-senility
Your condition is like living beyond senility! (pWestcar 7, 17)

(198c) The words of the king in a royal decree to a provincial official:
*i͗(w)-k m-ḥꜣtyꜥ mr šmꜥw mr ḥm-nṯr*
AUX-2MS as-mayor overseer N overseer servant-god
*m-šmꜥw=pw n[t-y ḫr]-ḥr-k*
in-N=DEM.M REL-M under-face-2MS
You will be a mayor, overseer of Upper Egypt, and the overseer of priests in this Upper Egypt that is under your jurisdiction. (*Urk.* I 299, 6)

Example 198a is from a past description of the events that led to the narrator's subsequent exile and adventures abroad, whereas ex. 198b describes a gnomic state of affairs. In ex. 198c, the king's words are not *grammatically* a description of future states of affairs, but rather simple assertions of the type 'You are a mayor' intended to confirm the appointment of the addressee through a royal announcement of them as established facts. Yet there is nothing here that excludes a future reading, which, in fact, seems to be almost required. Thus, introducing the adverbial predication by *i͗w* does not alter its fundamentally timeless character. What it does is to add a strong personal perspective to the description and to relate it to the speaker's subjective attitudes, opinions, and communicative intentions. All these aspects are in some sense connected to the speaker's individual temporal sphere. If defined in this way, temporality is perhaps the main ingredient that makes the use of *i͗w* possible with adverbial sentences. Conceptually, adverbial sentences, which prototypically concern the expression of locus, present states of affairs involving at least one locus in both space and time. Thus, they are ideationally akin to verbal predications in that both describe situations (potentially) transitory and susceptible to change. This allows for adverbial predication greater latitude to be assigned such typically verbal properties as TAM. Consider, for example, the case of modality, which concerns the speaker's attitude towards and evaluation of propositions and the information they convey. Its grammatical expression is more likely to be associated with descriptions of situations where (real or imaginary) participants interact with others, function in some real or possible world, or exist and occupy a locus in time and space that changes or may change. Verbal and adverbial constructions describe just such states of affairs (cf. the discussion in Winand 2006: 159–65), and consequently, they tend to be associated with grammatical markers such as the auxiliaries, whose functional profiles are fundamentally associated with temporality, modality, and illocution. By contrast, in states of affairs that are not profiled as undergoing sudden or gradual development, as resulting from anything, or as having a beginning or an end, there is less room for modality and illocution than in more contingent and transitory descriptions. It will be observed later that the other non-verbal predication types are conceptually of this latter type, and, consequently, far less likely to be combined with auxiliaries.

Before leaving *ἰw*, a note should be made on its use in interrogative adverbial sentences (see Uljas 2009b). This use represents the sole exception to the rule that the predicative relation of propositions introduced by *ἰw* is assertive. As can be seen from the examples below, in these cases *ἰw* clearly does not represent a mere host for suffix pronouns, since noun subjects are equally common. Neither does *ἰw* function as a precursor of the later Coptic Second Tense marker ^S^*e*-/^B^*a*-, since examples are documented already in Old Kingdom texts:

(199a) A question by a fieldworker to his comrade:
*ἰ(w)-k* *ṯn* *ṯ3* *srf-ἰb*
AUX-2MS WH man hot-heart
Where are you, O zealous man? (Junker, *Giza* VI, fig. 43)

(199c) A question concerning the yon ferry:
*ἰw-s=ἰrf* *mi-ἰšst*
AUX-3FS=PTC like-WH
What is she like? (CT V 91d/T1Be)

(199b) The sage asks:
*ἰw* *pr-ḥḏ* *r-m* *m-ḫmt-b3k-w-f*
AUX house-silver to-WH in-absence-due-P-3MS
What good is a treasury without its dues? (Ipuwer 3, 12)

At present, the appearance of *ἰw* in interrogative adverbial sentences remains unexplained. This highlights the fact that the semantic-pragmatic character of this most discussed of Earlier Egyptian auxiliaries has not yet been exhaustively defined.

#### 3.1.3.1.2 Combinations with *wn/wnn*

It is fair to say that Earlier Egyptian does not know any other grammatical element that formally and functionally is as complex as the auxiliary *wn/wnn*, which is a grammaticalised form of the lexical root *wnn* 'exist'.[73] *wn/wnn* displays two *written* forms: a reduplicating *wnn* and a shorter form *wn* without reduplication, but it is not clear how many inflected forms are hidden behind these writings, since the functions of both are so diverse that one is often at a loss to find some common denominator for all of them. Because of this difficulty, in the following account of the functions of the auxiliary *wn/wnn* in adverbial sentences, the starting point will be written morphology, and speculations about the underlying forms will be postponed until the uses of the two writings with the latter have been described.

Overall, *wn/wnn* functionally behaves in many ways as the opposite of *iw*. It is used to modify the temporal character of construction in which it appears and apparently also its illocutionary force or information structure. These functions are observable also in combinations with adverbial sentences. In independent clauses the form *wn* is used for clearly future deontic speech acts such as orders, wishes, and requests:

(200a) It is ordered in a transfer document donating a priestly office to Queen Ahmes Nefertari:

*wn-s=n-s* *m-sꜣ* *n-sꜣ*
AUX-3FS=to-3FS as-son to-son
It shall be hers from son to son. (*Texte 2. Zwischenzeit* n.122, 24)

(200b) In a funerary formula of a Memphite official:

*wn* *imꜣḫ-f* *ḫr-inpw*
AUX reverence-3MS before-N
May his reverence be before Anubis!
(*Teti Cemetery* III, pl. 18, middle jamb left, 1)

---

73 Save for Vernus (1990: 45–52) and Winand (2006: 383–86 for the past marker), no general discussion of *wn/wnn* in Earlier Egyptian, let alone in Egyptian generally, has appeared thus far. Here a word is in order on the predicative relations in *wn/wnn*-introduced adverbial sentences (for what follows, see Uljas 2009b: 152–53). It has been sometimes thought that in these constructions *wn/wnn* is the predicate (so e.g. Allen (1986a: 19; Loprieno 1995: 147). Yet despite their deceptively 'verbal' appearance, all *wn/wnn*-introduced adverbial sentences in fact still express adverbial, i.e. non-verbal, predication and the auxiliary plays no role in this. Consider e.g. the following sentences:

| | | |
|---|---|---|
| *iw s 10 im* | *wnn s 10 im* | The ten men are/will be there |
| *iw s 10 r-fnḏ-i* | *wnn s 10 r-fnḏ-i* | ?The ten men are/will be to my nose |

The semantic weirdness of the propositions marked with '?' shows that both in sentences introduced by *wn/wnn* and in those without *wn/wnn*, it is the adverbial expression that sets the selectional restrictions on the type of suitable arguments. In addition, in e.g. *wnn tꜣy-i ḥm-t im* in ex. 203a, the expression *im* cannot be omitted without destroying the sense of the utterance. Thus, *im* does not represent a modifying adjunct but rather the predicate of the proposition.

(200c) Invocation to gods on behalf of the dead king:

*wn N ḥnꜥ-ṯn nṯr-w wn-ṯn ḥnꜥ-N nṯr-w*

AUX N with-2P god-P AUX-2P with-N god-P

Let King N be with you, O gods; may you be with King N, O gods. (PT 377b)

As in the examples above, the futurity expressed by *wn* appears to be of a remote sort characterised by a period of time separating the situation described and the temporal locus (or the 'here and now') of the time of speaking. However, *wn* is also used to profile the adverbial sentence situation as completed in the past. Except for instances where the described state of affairs is also associated with non-canonical information structure and in complement clauses of prepositions (see below), this use is relatively infrequent in Earlier Egyptian; note the internal contrast in 201b with the apparently future *wnn*:

(201a) The speaker describes his bonhomie during a difficult period:

*wn-ỉ m-mnꜥ-t ḥr-ꜣty n-ỉỉ=nb ỉnḏ-w*

AUX-1S as-nurse-F PROG-care.INF to-come.PP=QU.M afflict-STA

I was a nurse taking care of all who arrived afflicted. (Hatnub 16, 9–10)

(201b) Reply by the ceremonial oil to a question concerning its whereabouts:

*wn-ỉ m-ḥꜣ-t ḥr wnn-ỉ m-ḥꜣ-t N*

AUX-1S in-brow-F N AUX-1S in-brow-F N

I was on the brow of Horus, and I will be on the brow of N. (CT VII 105q)

In the first person singular, the suffix pronoun *-ỉ* could rarely be replaced by the corresponding Stative ending, which in Middle Egyptian usually appears in its archaic form *-kỉ* (for further examples, see Stauder 2013: 22–23, 246):

(202) Khentyemsmyt tells of his notable status in the court:

*wn-k(ỉ)=rf m-ỉw-f ꜥꜣ-f*

AUX-STA.1S=PTC as-come-3MS great-3MS

I was a coming and growing man. (BM 574, 4)

Also the reduplicating written form *wnn* is seemingly used to signal that the adverbial sentence has a future value:

(203a) A decree in the will of Ankhreni:

*ỉr=grt nꜣ-n-ꜥ-w-t qd-n=n-ỉ sn-ỉ ... wnn*

PTC=PTC DET.P-of-room-P-F build.REL-PST=to-1S brother-1S AUX

*tꜣy-ỉ ḥm-t ỉm*

POSS.F-1S wife-F there

Now, concerning the living quarters which my brother built for me... my wife shall be/remain there. (pUC 32058, 13)

(203b) Nebipusenwosret promises royal favours to those who recite the offering formula on his behalf:

| | | |
|---|---|---|
| *wnn-ṯn* | *ẖr-ḥsw-t* | *n-t-ỉty-ṯn* |
| AUX-2P | under-favour-F | of-F-sovereign-2P |

You will remain under the favour of your sovereign.

(BM 101, horizontal, 2)

(203c) Ammulanenshi accepts Sinuhe as his guest:

| | | | |
|---|---|---|---|
| *mk=tw* | *ꜥꜣ* | *wnn-k* | *ḥnꜥ-ỉ* |
| PTC=2MS | here | AUX-2MS | with-1S |

Look, you are here, and you will stay with me. (Sin B, 77)

The difference *vis-à-vis* the corresponding constructions with *wn* seems to be that *wnn* often appears to profile the situation as either continuing unbroken from the speaker's current temporal locus (exx. 203a–203c), or when this continuity is definitely excluded, and the situation is portrayed as durative and/or ongoing (ex. 201b). Futures with *wnn* also seem to have a rather indeterminate illocutionary value: exx. 203a–203c may well be read as orders and promises, whereas 201b appears to have a plain indicative sense. Accordingly, in exx. 203a–203c, the semantic contribution of *wn* to the adverbial sentence seems to be of temporal-modal character, whereas in ex. 201b, it appears purely temporal.

Besides bearing on temporal and/or illocutionary properties, *wn/wnn* was also used to signal that the information structure of an adverbial sentence predicate is non-canonical. As seen, in constructions with the auxiliary *ỉw*, the informational pivot of the proposition is the relation between the sentence subject and predicate. This can be viewed as the canonical or statistically most frequent state of affairs. By contrast, the auxiliary *wn/wnn* could be used to signal that such a 'standard' organisation of information did not obtain. This parallels the corresponding strategy seen in the domain of lexical verbs and represents the most complex and sophisticated use of the auxiliary *wn/wnn*. Earlier Egyptian had a set of verbal constructions, known collectively as 'Second Tenses' (see Introduction 3.6), in which various morphological and/or syntactic means were used to indicate that the predicative relation between the verb and its subject did not represent the most salient segment of information, as in the canonical case.[74] For example, in the verbal formation known as the *sḏm-f*, this special role of the verb in the information structure was, at least in a number of root-classes, signalled by the morphological phenomenon of reduplication ('gemination' in

74 The literature on Second Tenses is of unparalleled quantity in Egyptology. The seminal works are H-J. Polotsky's 1944 *Études de Syntaxe Copte* as well as his 1965 and 1976 articles "Egyptian tenses" and "Les transpositions du verbe en Égyptien Classique" (see Polotsky 1971: 102–207, 71–96, and 2007: 55–104). The most thorough summaries to date are Depuydt (1983); Schenkel (1990: 149–52, 156) and Cassonet (2000: 4–8).

Egyptology) of the penultimate consonant of the root (e.g., the root *mrỉ* 'love' → *mrr-f*).[75] Besides verbal propositions, Second Tenses could also be formed from adverbial sentences, where prefixing *wn/wnn* was used to indicate that the predicative relation of the following proposition was non-canonical and either did not consist of maximally salient information or, alternatively, carried an exceptionally high degree of salience. These two functions were based on the same underlying principle and were not mutually contradictory. There were three types of Second Tense constructions in Earlier Egyptian, two of which are attested also with *wn/wnn*-headed adverbial sentences.[76] The so-called 'protatic' Second Tenses appear to be syntactically paratactic pairings where an initial clause is understood to provide a past or generic (usually best viewed as general concessive conditional) setting to a following full clause[77]:

(204a) Sinuhe tells how he ended up in the Syrian town of Qedem; then:

| | | | | | |
|---|---|---|---|---|---|
| *ỉri-n-ỉ* | *rnp-t* | *gs* | *ỉm* | *ỉn-[n]=wỉ* | *ꜥmwnnš* |
| do-PST=1S | year-F | half | there | bring-PST =1S | N |

After I had spent half a year there, Ammulanenshi brought me away. (Sin R, 54)

(204b) Mentuhetep tells of his elation after royal receptions at the palace:

| | | | | |
|---|---|---|---|---|
| *prr(-ỉ)* | *ỉm* | *ỉb(-ỉ)* | *wꜣš* | *ḥsw-t(-ỉ)* |
| exit.GEM[-1S] | there | heart[-1S] | exalt.STA | praise-F[-1S] |
| *m-ḥr* | *n(-y)-bw=nb* | | | |
| in-face | of[-M]-place=QU.M | | | |

Whenever I exited from there, my mind was exalted, and admiration of me was on everyone's face. (UCL 14333, 4)

The idea behind this mechanism is the informational back-grounding of the predication into what is in fact (intended to be *accommodated as*) part of the presuppositional structure of the overall proposition, at the expense of whatever

75 In some root classes, no similar morphological signal is visible, and it is unclear whether a corresponding formal split existed for them; see Uljas (2011) for a tentative negative answer. It may be that in roots where no morphological differences are observable in the writings, the 'Second Tense' function of the verb was marked negatively by the absence of the auxiliary *ỉw*, whose (one) function, as seen, was precisely to signal that the information structure of the predication introduced by it was canonical. At least in case of the *sḏm-n-f* it is certain that no formal division was involved and that the same form was used for both 'first' and 'second' tense functions; see here Uljas (2010b) and Stauder (2014).

76 No examples of the so-called balanced sentences seem to be forthcoming with the auxiliary *wn/wnn*, although they occur with the lexical verb *wnn* 'exist' (e.g. *Urk*. IV 570, 6).

77 See Vernus (1981). The term 'protatic' Second Tense is borrowed from Coptic studies, where it is used of corresponding constructions (Shisha-Halevy 1987). It has been applied to similar (but not necessarily the same) Late Egyptian and Demotic constructions by Grossman (2007).

is understood to be in construction with the verb – in this instance, another full clause.[78] The initial clause is thus not syntactically an adjunct, although it is usually best translated as such. Exactly the same idea underlies also the so-called 'emphatic' Second Tenses, where the segment understood to be in construction with the demoted verbal clause is syntactically a mere adjunct. As a result, the latter appears to acquire a degree of pragmatic focus, which, however, results from the same defocusing of the initial verbal predication as seen in the protatic constructions:

(205a) The deceased is a divine falcon:
*ḫꜥꜥ* *rꜥ* *rꜥ=nb* *r-sdm*(sic) *mdw* *N=pn*
appear.GEM N day=QU.M to-hear.INF speak N=DEM.M
Ra appears daily only to hear the words of this N. (CT IV 591)

(205b) The deceased announces:
*bw-t-ỉ=pw* *prt* *m-grḥ* *prr-ỉ* *m-hrw*
abomination-F-1S=SE go.INF in-night go.GEM-1S in-day
My abomination is going forth at night. I go only at day-time.
(CT VI 86c–d/B9C)

In adverbial sentences, both *wn* and *wnn* were used to turn the sentence into a protatic Second Tense construction. The auxiliary acted then as a purely functional operator whose role was to provide a presupposed dummy (non-lexical and non-predicative) verbal head to the construction. The writing *wn*, which is more common in these constructions, was used when the protatic 'setting' clause had a completed past reference:

(206a) Weni tells of his promotion:
*wn(-ỉ)* *m-ꜣṯw* *ḥwt-ꜥꜣ* *ḥr(y)-ṯbt(y)* *rdỉ=w(ỉ)*
AUX[-1S] as-tutor estate-great bearer-sandal give.PRF=1S
*nzwbit(y)* *mrnrꜥ*
dual_king N
*nb(-ỉ)* *ꜥnḫ* *ḏt* *m-ḥꜣtyꜥ* *mr* *šmꜥ* ...
lord[-1S] live.STA eternity as-town governor overseer N
*wn(-ỉ)* *m-ꜣtt* *ḥr(-y)-ṯb-w-t(y)* *ḥz=w(ỉ)* *ḥm-f*
AUX[-1S] as-tutor bearer-sandal-P-DU praise.PRF=1S majesty-3MS
*ḥr-rsw(-ỉ)*
on-vigilance[-1S]
When I was a tutor of a great estate and a (royal) sandal-bearer, the dual king Merenra living forever, my lord, appointed me as a town-governor and the overseer of Upper Egypt... When I was a tutor and a sandal-bearer, his majesty praised me for my vigilance. (*Urk.* I 105, 11–18)

78 This formulation follows the analysis proposed in Uljas, in preparation.

(206b) Senemyah describes his ethical behaviour upon earth:

*wn(-ỉ)* *m-tꜣ* *n(-y)-ʿnḫ-w* *n-ỉrỉ-ỉ* *šnt[-t* *nṯr]*
AUX[-1S] on-land of[-M]-living-P NEG-do-1S object.REL-F god
When I was upon the land of the living, I did not do to what god objects.
(*Urk.* IV 511, 4–5)

Again, the suffix *-ỉ* after the initial *wn* could be replaced by the Stative ending. Middle Egyptian instances with adverbial sentences are not known, but corresponding examples with a following Stative show the archaic writing *-k(ỉ)* for the ending.[79] In the early Eighteenth Dynasty, examples with the adverbial sentence are attested, but the person ending now shows the more standard writing *-kw*:

(207) Queen Hatshepsut says of her status as a daughter of god:

*wn-kw=[r]f* *m-ḥʿ* *wʿ* *ḥnʿ-f* *sḫpr-n-f=wỉ*
AUX-STA.1S=PTC as-flesh one with-3MS create-PST-3MS=1S
*r-rdỉt* *wsr* *qꜣw-t-f* *m-tꜣ=pn*
to-give.INF might power-F-3MS in-land=DEM.M
Having been of one flesh with him, he created me to impose the might of his power over this land. (*Urk.* IV 385, 3–4)

The writing *wnn* occurs when the reference is to prolonged and generic states of affairs:

(208a) The deceased describes his journey to the underworld:

*wnn-ỉ* *m-tꜣ-ỉ* *ỉỉ-n-ỉ* *m-nw-t-ỉ*
AUX-1S in-land-1S come-PST-1S from-town-F-1S
When I was (still) upon my land, I came forth from my town.
(CT IV 207b/T3L)

(208b) Ptahhetep makes a generic point about corruption:

*ỉr* *sr* *wnn-f* *ḥꜣ-tp-t* ... *ỉw-f* *r-rdỉt*
PTC official AUX-3MS above-ration-F AUX-3MS FUT-give.INF
*n-ḥssy-f*
to-favour.REL-3MS
As for an official, whenever he is in charge of rations... he will give to his favourite. (Ptahhetep 135–37)

The auxiliary *wnn*, but not *wn*, also appears in 'emphatic' Second Tenses, where it again provides a dummy verb heading the downgraded or defocused part of the construction (for this and what follows see Vernus 1991: 340;

**79** E.g., Sh.S. 136–37.

Uljas 2009b: 153–54). The part left standing in relief subsequent to this operation seems in most cases to be the predicative adverbial expression itself:

(209a) The deceased reveals his knowledge of divine secrets:

| | | | | |
|---|---|---|---|---|
| *ỉw(-ỉ)* | *rḫ-kw* | *ḏw=pw* | *n(y)-bꜣḫw* | *nt(-y)* |
| AUX[-1S] | know-STA.1S | mountain=DEM.M | of[-M]-N | REL[-M] |

| | | |
|---|---|---|
| *p-t* | *rhn-s* | *ḥr-f* |
| heaven-F | lean-3FS | on-3MS |

| | | | | | | | |
|---|---|---|---|---|---|---|---|
| *wnn-f* | *m-tỉ* | … | *wnn* | *sbk* | *nb* | *bꜣḫw* | *m-ỉꜣb-t* |
| AUX-3MS | as-N | | AUX | N | lord | N | in-east-F |

*ḏw=pn*
mountain=DEM.M

| | | | | | |
|---|---|---|---|---|---|
| *wnn* | *ḥwtnṯr-f* | *m-ḥrs-t* | *wnn* | *ḥfꜣw* | *ḥr-wp-t* |
| AUX | temple-3MS | as-carnelian-F | AUX | snake | on-summit-F |

*ḏw=pf*
mountain=DEM.M

I know this mountain of Bakhu upon which the heavens rest. It is of *tỉ*… Sobek, lord of Bakhu is in the east of this mountain. His temple is of carnelian. At the summit of that mountain there is a serpent.

(CT II 375c–377c/S2P)

(209b) Explanation of a mythological setting in a religious text:

| | | | | | |
|---|---|---|---|---|---|
| *ỉ[r]* | *nṯr* | *ḥḏtꜣ* | *rn-f* | *wnn-f* | *ỉmty-nṯr-wy* |
| PTC | god | N | name-3MS | AUX-3MS | between-god-DU |

| | | |
|---|---|---|
| *ꜥꜣ-wy* | *ỉw-sny* | *m-p-t* |
| great-DU | AUX-3DU | in-heaven-F |

| | | | | | |
|---|---|---|---|---|---|
| *ỉw* | *wꜥ* | *ỉm-s(ny)* | *m-ỉmywr-t* | *[n-t-p-t]* | *ỉw* |
| AUX | one | in-3P:DU | in-starboard-F | of-F-heaven-F | AUX |

| | | |
|---|---|---|
| *wꜥ* | *m-tꜣwr* | *n(-y)-p-t* |
| one | in-larboard | of[-M]-heaven-F |

As for the god whose name is *ḥḏ-tꜣ*, he is *between two great gods*. They are in heaven. One is at the west of the sky; the other is at the east of the sky. (CT V 387b–f)

(209c) Words of a man being told to attend to his work:

| | | |
|---|---|---|
| *mk* | *wnn-ỉ* | *r-gs-f* |
| PTC | AUX-1S | beside-3MS |

See, I am right at (lit. 'beside') it! (*Tomb of Antefoqer* pl. 8)

The information structuring mechanism consisting in reducing an initial verb to a status of presupposition is the same here as in 'emphatic' sentences with lexical verbs. There, however, the segment left in relief is not the predicate of the construction, whereas in exx. 209a–209c, where the downgraded verb is a non-predicative auxiliary, it is. The effect of *wnn* in 'emphatic' adverbial sentences is thus usually a kind of predicate focus, or pragmatic highlighting of the predicate over and above its canonical information value. The highlighted segment may also be some non-predicative adjunct, but as with Second Tenses with lexical verbs, the difference between the two is usually a matter of extra-linguistic deduction:

(210) Horemkhauef says of himself:

| | | | | | | |
|---|---|---|---|---|---|---|
| *ink* | *s3b* | *iqr* | *tp-t3* | *wnn-i* | *m-3ḫ* | *iqr* |
| 1S | official | excellent | upon-earth | AUX-1S | as-spirit | excellent |

*m-ḫrtnṯr*
in-necropolis

I was an excellent official upon earth; I will be an excellent spirit in the necropolis. (MMA 35.7.55, 10)

Here the informationally prominent part could be argued to be the predicate *m-3ḫ* contrasting with 'an excellent official' in the previous nominal sentence, or else the adjunct *m-ḫrtnṯr* 'in the necropolis', contrasting with *tp-t3* 'upon earth'. Alternatively, the *wnn*-sentence could, of course, also be read as a 'normal' future without any special information structuring.

Other than the constructions described above, the use of *wn/wnn* with adverbial sentences in non-subordinate environments is relatively infrequent in Earlier Egyptian. The writing *wnn* appears in adverbial sentences functioning as labels, e.g., in titles of religious spells:

(211) Title of a CT spell:

| | | |
|---|---|---|
| *wnn* | *s* | *mm-ʿnḫ-w* |
| AUX | man | among-living-P |

The man is among the living. (CT VI 333a)

Constructions of this type seem to represent marked versions of the situation-thetic bare adverbial sentences seen in 3.1.2.1 (Stauder and Uljas in preparation). In the latter case, the thetic information structure is not a feature of the construction itself but merely a contextual deduction brought about by unsuitability of other (e.g. deontic) readings as well as by the absence of *iw*, which, as already shown, marks the sentence as categorical. In ex. 211, the situation is again presented or announced as a whole, without the intent of providing information about an abstract and non-referential 'man', but this information structure is now grammatically marked by the auxiliary *wnn*, which, although not the predicate itself, serves to signal that the informative status of the true predicate is contextually non-canonical. 'Label' statements are thus related to Second Tenses with *wn/wnn* described above.

The final use of *wn* and *wnn* with adverbial sentences in non-subordinate environments appears in the sequential verbal constructions *sḏm-ꞽn-f* and *sḏm-ḫr-f*, where the auxiliary occupies the place of the lexical verb (see Depuydt 1993; Polis 2005). The first of these constructions has an invariable past sense, and here the writing *wn* is always found:

(212) The courtiers have just entered before the king:
*wn-ꞽn-sn* *ḥr-ẖ-t-sn* *m-bꜣḥ-ḥm-f* *ꜥ.w.s.* *wḥmꜥ*
AUX-SEQ-3P on-belly-F-3P in-before-majesty-3MS l.p.h. again
Then they were again on their bellies in the presence of his majesty l.p.h.
(Neferty Ii)

The construction *sḏm-ḫr-f* is, in principle, wholly atemporal, but with *wn/wnn* one finds variation between past completed *wn-ḫr-f* and gnomic/generic *wnn-ḫr-f*[80]:

(213a) Djehuty says that his integrity was widely recognised:
*mtrw=pw* *ꞽb-ꞽ* *ḏs-ꞽ* *n-ꜥqꜣ(-ꞽ)* *n-ꜥbꜥ*
witness=COP heart-1S self-1S NEG-excel[-1S] through-boast
*m-grg* *wꜥ* *s* *2* *s* *3* *ḫr-tw* *wn-ḫr-ꞽ*
in-falsehood one man 2 man 3 QUOT-PASS AUX-SEQ-1S
*m-ḥꜣ-t-w*
in-front.RLT-F-P
My own heart is a witness: I did not excel through false boasts of one, two, or three men – so it was said. And so I was among the foremost.
(*Studies Griffith* pl. 39, 16)

(213b) It is said that the gods recognise the deceased:
*wnn-ḫr-f* *mꞽ-wꜥ* *ꞽm-sn*
AUX-SEQ-3MS like-one in-3P
Thus he is like one of them. (BD 190/*Nu* pl. 45, 13)

80 It has been suggested that the instances of *wnn-ḫr-f* may represent Second Tense versions of this particular sequential pattern (Malaise and Winand 1999: §781). Yet this seems unlikely given the absence of similar variation in lexical verbs, which never display reduplication of the penultimate radical in *ult. inf.* classes (i.e. variance between *pr-ḫr-f* and **prr-ḫr-f* does not occur). Similarly, there is no such variance in the pattern *wn-ꞽn-f*, and practically all examples of *wnn-ḫr-f* derive from the *Book of the Dead of Nu* (pBM EA 10477).

As discussed above, the auxiliary *wn/wnn* is also used in many subordinate clauses formed of adverbial sentences. In relative clauses, it could help to relativise the adverbial sentence by assuming the form of a participle or a relative form, and like the relative adjective *nt-*, it then functioned as agreement carrier. However, unlike *nt-*, *wn/wnn* as auxiliary verb is capable of indicating tense and aspect. The temporal properties expressed are well known from the relative clauses with lexical verbs. The writing *wnn*, which represents the conjugated form of the imperfective participle or relative form, was used in reference to continuous, aorist, and habitual states of affairs:

(214a) Amenyseneb tells how he restored various pieces of cultic paraphernalia, including:

| | | | | |
|---|---|---|---|---|
| *ꜥš* | *ḫꜣy(-t)* | *wr-t* | *wnn-t* | *m-bꜣḥ* |
| cedar | altar-F | great-F | AUX.PIA-F | in-presence |

The great cedar altar, which is in the (god's) presence. (Louvre C11, 7)

(214b) The deceased will be taken:

| | | | | | | | |
|---|---|---|---|---|---|---|---|
| *r-bw* | *wnn* | *rꜥ* | *i͗m* | *rꜥ=nb* | *r-bw* | *wnn* | *ḥwthr* |
| to-place | AUX.REL | N | there | day=QU.M | to-place | AUX.REL | N |

| | |
|---|---|
| *i͗m* | *rꜥ=nb* |
| there | day=QU.M |

...to the place where Ra and Hathor stay every day. (CT VI 80g/B3L)

The non-reduplicating writing *wn* is found as a perfective participle, as *sḏm-n-f* relative form, and, although it can seldom be told apart from the former, as archaic perfective relative form, all of which are used for completed past descriptions:

(215a) The sage laments the sacrileges committed:

| | | | | |
|---|---|---|---|---|
| *i͗w=ms* | *wn-w* | *m-wꜥb-t* | *di͗-t(i͗)* | *ḥr-qꜣꜣ* |
| AUX=PTC | AUX.PPA-P | in-embalminghouse-F | place-STA | on-mountain |

Alas, those who were in the embalming house have been thrown on the mountains. (Ipuwer 6, 14)

(215b) The snake begins his tale about how he lost his family:

| | | | |
|---|---|---|---|
| *sḏd=i͗=rf=n-k* | *mi͗t-t=i͗r-y* | *ḫpr-w* | *m-i͗w=pn* |
| relate.SUB-1S=PTC=to-2MS | like.RLT-F to-RLT.M | happen.P-M | in-island=DEM.M |

| | | |
|---|---|---|
| *wn-i͗* | *i͗m-f* | *ḥnꜥ-sn-w-i͗* |
| AUX.PRF.REL-1S | in-3MS | with-sibling-P-1S |

I will tell you something similar that happened on this island in which I was with my siblings. (Sh.S. 125–26)

(215c) It is ordered in a royal decree:
*ỉw wḏ-n ḥm(-ỉ) nfrn ỉṯ ḫntš=nb(-w)*
AUX order-PST majesty[-1S] NEG take tenant=QU[-P]
*n-w-nw-(t)y=(ỉ)ptn...*
of-P-town-DU=DEM.P
*ỉn rmṯ=nb ỉn nḥs-ḥtp-w=nb(-w)*
AGT people=QU.M AGT Nubian-pacified-P=QU[-P]
*n-wn-w-n-sn ḫr-sn*
to-AUX.REL-P-PST-3P before-3P
My majesty has ordered that no royal tenants of these two (pyramid-) towns may be seized by any people or 'pacified Nubians' to those with whom they were (previously). (*Urk.* I 211, 5–11)

It has been argued that the perfective relative form should be distinguished from what is thought to be a prospective relative form (Schenkel 2010). No certain examples of future relative clauses are found with *wn/wnn* + adverbial sentence, the following late example with the writing *wn* being paralleled by two (equally very late) other versions where the writing *wnn* appear:

(216) Prince Hardjedef exhorts his son to see to his own funerary arrangements:
*qd-k pr-k {t}n-bꜣ(-k) ỉw ỉrỉ-n-k bw*
build-2MS house-2MS to-soul-2MS AUX make-PST-2MS place
*wn-k ỉm[-f]*
AUX.REL-2MS in-3MS
Build a house for your soul, and you (will) have created a place in which you will be. (Hardjedef II.1/Mü)

Nevertheless, examples of the Future Participle form *sḏm-ty-fy* used for future subject relativisation, are not altogether rare:

(217) Meru begins his Appeal to the Living:
*ỉ ꜥnḫ-w tp-w tꜣ wnn-t(y)-s(n) m-šms*
VOC living-P upon.RLT-P earth AUX.REL-FUT-AGR in-following
*n(-y)-ḫnt(y)ỉmntw*
of[-M]-N
O the living upon earth who will be in the following of (god) Khentyamenty. (Turin 1447, 2–3)

As noted above, the participles and relative forms formed by means of the auxiliary *wn/wnn* have been thought to occur only in restrictive relative clauses essential to the identification of the (overt or covert) antecedent. The principle seems to work reasonably well in adverbial sentences relativised with *wn/wnn*.

Among adverbial sentence functioning as adjuncts, *wn/wnn* is only used in final clauses. As noted, the auxiliary appears regardless of the nominal or pronominal status of the sentence subject, indicating that its presence is here based on semantic-pragmatics rather than morpho-syntax. Final clauses refer to states of affairs that, although potentially factual at the time of speaking, are presented as reasons of or motivations for the situation or action described in the accompanying matrix clause and hence are not asserted (Palmer 2000: 131). In these instances, many languages use a subjunctive or corresponding verb form. In Earlier Egyptian, clauses of this type provide one of the diagnostic syntactic environments for the so-called subjunctive *sḏm-f* paradigm, which is recurrently found also in many other non-assertive environments (Loprieno 1995: 82). Here the auxiliary *wn/wnn* is always written *wn*:

(218a) A god says to King Sahura:
*di-n(-i)=n-k* *ꜥnḫ* *wꜣs=nb* *snb=nb*
give-PST[-1S]=to-2MS life dominion=QU.M health=QU.M
*ꜣwtib=nb* *ḏd=nb*
joy=QU.M stability=QU.M
*wn-k* *ḫnt-kꜣ-w* *ꜥnḫ-w=nb*
AUX-2MS before-soul-P living-P=QU.P
I have given you all life and dominion, all health, all joy, and all stability, so that you might be before the souls of all the living.
(*Urk.* I 168, 9–10)

(218b) Atum says that he set out:
*n* *ir-t-i* *nwt* *wn-s* *ḥr-tp-i*
NEG make-TERM-1S N AUX-3FS upon-head-1S
...when I had not yet created Nut so that she might be above me.
(CT II 34b/B1C)

(218c) The funerary cortège of Amenmose prays to Osiris on his behalf:
*imi=n-f* *tꜣw* *nḏm* *im* *wn-f*
give.IMP=to-3MS wind sweet there AUX-3MS
*mm-ḥsy=nb* *m-tꜣ* *n(y-)-ꜥnḫ-w*
among-praise.PP=QU.M in-land of[-M]-living-P
Give him the sweet wind therein so that he might be among every praised-one in the land of the living. (*Urk.* IV 1024, 11–12)

Finally, *wn/wnn* is used in adverbial sentences functioning as complement clauses after notionally non-assertive verbs of, e.g., desiring, ordering, requesting, etc.

(219a) Henqu maintains his worth:
*ỉnk=ḥm* *wꜥb-w-n* *nṯr* *rꜣ-f* *rdỉ-w* *snḏ*
1S=PTC purify.REL-M-PST god mouth-3MS put.PPA-M fear
*r-[gs]-w-f*
to-peer-P-3MS
*ỉ-mr* *wn* *ỉ[mꜣḫ-f]* *ḫr-sn* *m-bw* *[nty-f* *ỉm]*
PREF-desire.PPA AUX reverence-3MS before-3P in-place REL-3MS there
I was truly one whose mouth the god purified, who inspired fear in his peers and who desired that his reverence be before them wherever he might be. (*Urk.* I 79, 26a–28a)

(219b) Appeal to the Living of Lady Nefertut:
*ỉ* *ꜥnḫ-w* *tp-w* *tꜣ* ... *m-mrr-ṯn* *wnn*
VOC living-P upon.RLT-P earth as-desire-2P AUX
*ỉmꜣḫ-ṯn* *ḫr-nṯr* *ꜥꜣ*
reverence-2P before-god great
*prtḫrw* *st-ṯn=n(-ỉ)* *mw*
invocation offerings pour.SUB-2P=to[-1S] water
O the living upon earth... as you desire that your reverence be before the great god and (that you have) invocation-offerings, pour water for me. (BM 152, 3–4)

(219c) Nebipusenwosret assures prospective visitors to his stela:
*ỉw* *wḏ-n* *nṯr* *ꜥꜣ* *wnn-ṯn* *tp-tꜣ* *ḫr-ḥsw-t-f*
AUX order-PST god great AUX-2P upon-earth under-favour-F-3MS
The great god has ordered you to be upon earth under his favour. (BM 101, horizontal 4)

(219d) The deceased is guaranteed provisions in the hereafter:
*ỉw* *wḏ-n* *ỉnpw* *ỉmy-ḥtp-t* *wn* *ḥtp-t* *n-N* *m-ꜥ-f*
AUX order-PST N in.RLT-offering-F AUX offering-F to-N in-arm-3MS
Anubis, who is in charge of offerings, has ordered that the offerings due to N will be with him. (BD 144/*Nu* pl. 75, 33–34)

(219e) Isis is on her way to meet her son in the entourage of gods:
*hꜣ* *ꜣst* *r-wḥꜥ* *ỉn* *ḥr* *dbḥ-n* *ꜣst* *wnn-f* *m-wḥꜥ*
descend N to-N bring.PPA N ask-PST N AUX-3MS with-N
*m-sšm-w* *nḥḥ*
as-leader-M eternity
Isis goes down to *wḥꜥ* who has brought Horus, for Isis had asked that he might be with *wḥꜥ* as the leader of eternity. (CT II 222b–c)

Complement clauses functioning as predicates, unlike the embedded topicalising examples in 195a–195b, are essentially situation-thetic.

(220) An explanatory gloss in a medical handbook:
*wnn šf-w-t=pw ḥr-qꜣb-t-f*
AUX swelling-P-F=SE on-breast-F-3MS
This means that there are swellings on his (the patient's) breast.
(pEdwin Smith 15, 17)

The predicative relation here is not presented as the informational pivot of the proposition. In this case, this semantic-pragmatic function is fulfilled by the syntactically higher relationship between the subject element =*pw* and the embedded clause. It was argued in 3.1.2.1 that this kind of information structuring is conceptually close to non-assertion. The choice between the writings *wnn* and *wn* in object complements is a complex and poorly understood matter that depends partly on the tense of the governing verb and partly on the innate semantics of the latter (see Uljas 2007c: 139, 148–51 for one tentative hypothesis). After the causative *rdi*, which again is one of the diagnostic environments of the subjunctive *sḏm-f*, the writing is always the non-reduplicating *wn*; examples from past contexts are[81]:

(221a) An official reports to his correspondent about administrative arrangements:
*mk bꜣk-ꞽ[m] dꞽ-n-f wn-k ḥnꜥ-pꜣ[y-k]*
PTC servant-there cause-PST-3MS AUX-2MS with-POSS.M-2MS
*ẖr-w*
underling-P
Yours truly has arranged that you may be with your household.
(pUC 32213, v° 10–11)

(221b) Goddess Nut has spread herself above the deceased:
*rdꞽ-n-s wn-k m-nṯr*
cause-PST-3FS AUX-2MS as-god
She has caused you to be a god. (Turin 4262)

An example from a future context is:

(222) Thutmosis III reveals his reasons for depicting specimens of plants from conquered lands:
*ꞽrꞽ-n ḥm-ꞽ nw n-mr(w)t-rdit wn-sn*
do-PST majesty-1S DEM.M for-love-cause.INF AUX-3P
*m-bꜣḥ-ꞽt-ꞽ ꞽmn*
in-front-father-1S N
My majesty has done this in order to cause them to be in the presence of my father Amun. (*Urk.* IV 776, 13–14)

**81** See again Uljas (2007c: 148–49) for an attempt to find order in the use of different writings here.

In conclusion, some remarks on the possible morphological realities concealed by the two writings *wnn* and *wn* are in order. Although the issue does not relate directly to the grammar of adverbial sentences per se, it has much occupied Egyptologists in the past. Moreover, understanding the morphology of *wn/wnn* bears directly on the meaning of constructions with which they are combined, and amongst these the adverbial sentences. In general, and like *ỉw*, *wn/wnn* seems in most cases to exhibit a clear connection with illocution and/or information structure, but both *wn* and *wnn* appear to have purely temporal uses as well. As for *wn*, in its future uses this writing coincides with the subjunctive *sḏm-f* of lexical verbs, but identifying this form elsewhere is more difficult. In protatic Second Tenses the function of *wn* is very much akin to the past/anterior form known as *sḏm-n-f* of lexical roots (cf. Doret 1979: 161–62; 1980: 40), and it is known from relative environments that *wn/wnn* could be conjugated in the (at least relative) *sḏm-n-f*. Yet in examples such as 201a and 201b, where the writing appears to serve as a mere 'backshifter', this interpretation seems less likely (but cf. Vernus 1990: 51). It will be seen in 3.1.3.3 that in preposition complement clauses, *wn* is also very commonly used in reference to completed past, but there the interpretation as the anterior form *sḏm-n-f* seems unlikely, since lexical verbs do not generally employ this form after prepositions. For *wn* to be the so-called Old Egyptian 'indicative' *sḏm-f* would not only be an anachronism, but seems excluded given the free use of *wn* with pronominal subjects, which did not combine with the indicative even in Old Egyptian. Thus, the writing *wn-f* may have concealed at least two different underlying non-relative forms, but the issue remains unclear. There is much uncertainty in the relative forms as well: *wn-f* is occasionally the undisputable writing of the *sḏm-n-f* Relative Form, but it may seemingly also stand for the archaic Perfective Relative Form. There is confusion also with the reduplicated writing *wnn*. In the 'emphatic' Second Tenses and label uses, the writing corresponds functionally to the 'geminating' *sḏm-f* of *ult. inf.* roots (*mrr-f*). Yet in 203a–203c and their ilk, the semantic contribution of the auxiliary seems again purely temporal, and it has been suggested that these might be examples of the so-called Prospective *sḏm-f* form of *wnn* (e.g., Allen 2000: 289–90). Indeed, the same writing appears also in future negations after *n*, which Egyptologists treat as a diagnostic environment for the latter:

(223) Khnumhetep says in reference to his memorial:

| | | | |
|---|---|---|---|
| *ỉr=grt* | *ḥm-kꜣ* | *rmṯ=nb-t* | *ẖnn-t(y)-sn=st* |
| PTC=PTC | priest-soul | man=QU-F | disturb-FUT.REL-AGR=3C |

| | | | | | |
|---|---|---|---|---|---|
| *n* | *wnn-f* | *n* | *wnn* | *sꜣ-f* | *ḥr-ns-t-f* |
| NEG | exist.PROSP-3MS | NEG | AUX | son-3MS | on-seat-F-3MS |

As for any soul-priest or anyone who will disturb it, he will not exist, and his son will not occupy his post. (*Beni Hasan* I pl. 25, 96–99)

Yet in classical Middle Egyptian and in sources later than the Middle Kingdom, it would be strange if the future *wnn* were the Prospective form, since this paradigm appears to have become less productive during the Old Kingdom or shortly thereafter. Accordingly, also the writing *wnn* may conceal two different forms, but again their identity remains uncertain. Ultimately, however, it may be that the writings of the grammaticalised auxiliary *wn/wnn* do not directly correspond to the inflectional scope of the lexical classes of the Earlier Egyptian verb. It is notable that in this language, the inflection of auxiliaries is generally minimal (e.g., *iw*) and/or fossilised (e.g., *ꜥḥꜥ-n*). In the case of an auxiliary, therefore, the number and character of forms concealed by the writings *wn* and *wnn* need not equal or match that of the lexical roots. Thus, it could very well be that the past uses of *wn* where the past form *sḏm-n-f* seems unlikely involve the same *perfective* form as in the future 'subjunctive' environments, whose different forms of employment resulted from its aspectually bounded character appropriate for both past complet*ed* as well as future complet*e* states of affairs that equally involve a degree of 'separation' and 'dissociation' from the vantage point of the conceptualiser (e.g., Satzinger [1968: 39] argues in favour of a single perfective form *wn-f*). The correct sense would be established by the context in which the *wn*-clause appears. Conversely, *wnn* could be an aspectually *unmarked* form, perhaps morphologically derived from the grammaticalisation of a 'geminating' or Prospective form.[82] This, however, is speculative. With adverbial sentences, as in other environments, the use of *wn/wnn* is motivated by a range of temporal-modal and information structuring reasons, which may have been shared by a number of forms. However, at the present stage of our knowledge, the morphology of this most complex of Earlier Egyptian auxiliaries seems to defy attempts for an exhaustive reconstruction.

#### 3.1.3.2 Adverbial sentences introduced by initial particles

Not much more needs to be said about adverbial sentences preceded by the so-called initial particles enumerated in 2.1.1. Overall, the contribution of these cotextual, illocutionary, and modal elements to the following adverbial sentence is the same as with all constructions with which they are found.[83] As operators, their functional scope is the entire proposition rather than, as with the

---

82 A single 'emphatic converter' *wnn* is postulated by Vernus (1990: 45–52).

83 See Oréal (2011: chapters 7, 8, and 12) for a synopsis of some of the more important of these elements.

auxiliaries, its predicative relation.[84] The particles *mk/mṯ/mṯn* serve to draw the hearer's attention to the introduced proposition (or sentence), which is profiled as consisting of information regarded as being of high interest/communicative value and part of the discourse foreground:

(224a) Hapdjefa tells his soul-priest of the latter's role in his mortuary fund:

| | | | | | |
|---|---|---|---|---|---|
| *mk* | *nn* | *n(-y)-ḫ-t* | *r-ḏr* | *ḫtm-n-ꞽ* | *m-ꜥ-nn* |
| PTC | DEM | of[-M]-thing-F | to-limit | seal.REL-PST-1S | in-hand-DEM |
| *n(-y)-wꜥb-w* | *ẖr-st-ḥr-k* | | | | |
| of[-M]-priest-P | under-place-face-2MS | | | | |

All these things of which I have made a contract with these priests are under your authority. (Siut I, 269)

(224b) Heqanakhte tells his family that they are in a fortunate position given the present food shortage:

| | | | | |
|---|---|---|---|---|
| *mṯn=ṯn* | *m-pꜣ-wnm* | *r-sꜣ-f* | *ḥqr* | *r-bꜣẖ[t]* |
| PTC=2P | as-DET.M-eat.PP | to-satisfaction-3MS | hungry.STA | to-white |
| *ꞽr-ty-fy* | | | | |
| eye-FDU-3MDU | | | | |

You are the one who ate to his satisfaction, being hungry to the white of his eyes! (Heqanakhte II, r° 3)

(224c) The king cunningly reminds his vizier about the latter's subordinate status:

| | | | | | | |
|---|---|---|---|---|---|---|
| *mk* | *wnn* | *s* | *m-ꞽꜣ-t-f* | *ꞽrꞽ-f* | *ḫ-t* | *ḫft-ḥr-dd=n-f* |
| PTC | AUX | man | in-office-F | do-3MS | thing-F | before-face-give.PIA=to-3MS |

A man remains in his office only if he carries out tasks for the one who provides for him. (*Urk.* IV 1092, 9 –10)

Sentences introduced by *mk* are seemingly always main clauses regardless of contextual factors. Conversely, and as already noted, *(ꞽ)sṯ/(ꞽ)sk/tꞽ* signal that the following proposition consists of supportive background material whose role in the thread of discourse is relatively subsidiary, and which may therefore be translated either as main or subordinate clauses, as befits the context:

84 This formulation again follows the Role and Reference Grammar conception of the layered structure of the clause, where each layer is potentially under the scope of one or more operators (see 3.1.3.1 above). Due to their sentence-, rather than predicate-level scope, initial particles can occur with practically all construction types. Sometimes, this can have unexpected effects. For example, the 'foregrounding' particle *mk* is compatible with Second Tenses even though in these constructions the predication expressed by the verb belongs to the presuppositional background in the overall information structure. Nevertheless, the *sentence* of which the latter forms a part can still be viewed as being foreground and be placed under the scope of *mk*.

(225a) Thutmosis II enjoyed the fruits of his success as a pharaoh:

| | | | | |
|---|---|---|---|---|
| *st* | *ḥm-f* | *m-ꜥḥ-f* | *bꜣw-f* | *sḫm* |
| PTC | majesty-3MS | in-palace-3MS | might-3MS | strong.STA |

| | |
|---|---|
| *snḏ-f* | *ḫt-tꜣ* |
| fear-3MS | throughout-land |

His majesty was in his palace, his divine might strong and the fear of him throughout the land. (*Urk.* IV 137, 16–138, 1)

(225b) Pepinakht tells how he smote Nubians:

| | | | | | | |
|---|---|---|---|---|---|---|
| *ỉw* | *ỉn-n(-ỉ)* | *ṯnw* | *ꜥꜣ* | *ỉm* | *r-ẖnw* | *m-sq(r)ꜥnḫ-w* |
| AUX | bring-PST[-1S] | number | great | there | to-residence | as-captive-P |

| | | | |
|---|---|---|---|
| *sk=w(ỉ)* | *ḫr-ḥꜣt-mšꜥ* | *ꜥšꜣ-w* | *wsr-w* |
| PTC=1S | under-front-troop | many-P | strong-P |

I carried off a great number of them as captives to the residence, whilst I was at the helm of numerous strong battalions. (*Urk.* I 133, 14–16)

As might be expected, there are no strict rules concerning the translational values of 'subordinate' (*ỉ*)*sṯ*-clauses, but a concessive reading often seems particularly suitable:

(226a) Weni tells how he was asked to conduct a delicate judicial process against the queen:

| | | | | | | |
|---|---|---|---|---|---|---|
| *ỉnk* | *ỉri* | *m-sš* | *wꜥ-k(ỉ)* | *ḥnꜥ-zꜣb* | *r-nḫn* | *wꜥ* |
| 1S | do.PPA | in-script | one-STA.1S | with-judge | warden-N | one |

| | | | | |
|---|---|---|---|---|
| *sṯ* | *ỉꜣ-t(-ỉ)* | *m-mr* | *ḫnt(-y)š* | *pr-ꜥꜣ* |
| PTC | office-F[-1S] | as-overseer | tenant(s) | king-house |

It was me who wrote the protocols alone with a single judge and warden of Nekhen, although my office was (only) that of overseer of royal tenants. (*Urk.* I 101, 2–3)

(226b) Hezi says that the king trusted his judgement over that of higher-ranking officials:

| | | | | |
|---|---|---|---|---|
| *wn* | *ḥm-f* | *nḏ-f* | *ḫ-t* | *m-ꜥ(-ỉ)* |
| AUX | majesty-3MS | inquire-3MS | thing-F | from-hand[-1S] |

| | |
|---|---|
| *m-rꜥ(-ỉ)* | *mm-sr-w* |
| in-standard[-1S] | among-official-P |

| | | | |
|---|---|---|---|
| *sk=w(ỉ)* | *m-zꜣb* | *sḥḏ* | *sš* |
| PTC=1S | as-judge | inspector | scribe |

His majesty used to ask my advice because of my efficiency among officials, although I was (only) a judge and an inspector of scribes. (Hezi A4–5 [*JARCE* 37, 1–13])

The effect of the sequential particles *ỉḫ*, *kꜣ*, and *ḫr* is different from prototypical coordination in that they are used, in principle, to signal that a situation follows from another in a specific way (Vernus 1990: 61–114). The particle *ḫr* marks it as typically, generally, and/or logically following from something else. This element is common e.g. in directions for procedural actions such as medical treatments and the like (cf. Green 1987: 89). The adverbial sentence follows directly after the particle:

(227) A conclusion in a mathematical presentation:
*ḫr r-5 r-10 m-wꜣḥ ḥr-f*
PTC 1/5 1/10 as-place.PPA on-3MS
Then 1/5 + 1/10 is what remains of it. (pRhind math. n. 22, 9)

With *iḫ* and *kꜣ*, the use of the auxiliary *wn/wnn* in its non-reduplicated form *wn*, which may or may not be the subjunctive, is apparently obligatory[85]:

(228a) Mentuhetep tells of his expectations concerning the afterlife:
*iḫ wn-i m-šms nṯr*
PTC AUX-1S in-retinue god
Then I will join the retinue of god. (CG 20539ii, b12)

(228b) Having told about certain agreements with a third party, the author of the letter commands his addressee:
*kꜣ wn-k ḥnꜥ-f m-s wꜥ*
PTC AUX-2MS with-3MS as-man one
Then you shall join him as one man. (pUC 32201, 20–21)

This may be because after *iḫ* and *kꜣ* the situation described is projected to the future, whereas with *ḫr* it is not. An even more probable explanation is that after the first two elements, the state of affairs characteristically represents the speaker's expectation, evaluation, injunction, or assessment of things to come, whereas after *ḫr*, it is portrayed as a natural or logical outcome. The former also holds true for the strongly modal desiderative elements *ḥꜣ* and *ḥw* 'if only', which signal the following proposition as something merely desired by the speaker, but after which no auxiliary appears:

(229a) The narrator wishes to join the company of the man of the marshes:
*ḥꜣ=wi m-ḫt-f*
PTC=1S after-3MS
If only I were in his following! (*Lit. Fragm.* pl. 2, 12)

(229b) The sun god is quoted as having said:
*ḥw=ꜣ=n-i sꜣ-i*
PTC=PTC=to-1S son-1S
If only I had my son! (CT III 334d)

85 See exx. 74a and 74b for some dubious exceptions to this.

The absence of *wn* is easier to understand after *nḥmn* 'certainly', which indicates that the speaker feels particularly committed to the following proposition:

(230) Sinuhe boasts:
*nḥmn=wỉ* *mỉ-kꜣ*
PTC=1S like-bull
I am certainly like a bull! (Sin B, 117–18)

The interrogative particle *ỉn*, which with adverbial sentences always appears in the (probably merely graphic) variant form *ỉnỉw*, marks alternative yes/no-questions:

(231) A sarcastic question of a sculptor to his colleague:
*(ỉ)nỉw* *ḫ-t* *mỉ-ꜥꜣ-t*
IP wood-F like-hard_stone-F
Is wood like hard stone? (Hassan, *Giza* II, fig. 219)

Finally, adverbial sentences may function as conditional protases when preceded by the conditional marker *ỉr*; the occurrence of *wnn*, which with very few exceptions appears here regularly in its reduplicated form, is mandatory:

(232) Ptahhetep recommends the cultivation of social contacts:
*ỉr* *wnn-k* *ḥnꜥ-rmṯ* *ỉrỉ=n-k* *mr-w* *n-pḥỉb*
CND AUX-2MS with-people make.IMP=to-2MS friend-P to-confidence
If you are together with people, acquire trusted friends.
(Ptahhetep 232–33)

Here, the presence of the auxiliary is probably connected to the fact that the element *ỉr* is related to (or even the same as) the preposition *ỉr/r* 'to' and syntactically the clause following it may represent a complement clause. As seen in 2.1.5, adverbial sentences subordinated as complements must be introduced by an auxiliary if not preceded by a complementiser. *ỉr* is also the standard means of extra-posing, and in adverbial sentences it is used for subject topicalisation much more commonly than the alternative construction where the adverbial sentence is embedded as a predicative complement of a bipartite =*pw*-sentence (see again 2.1.5):

(233a) The peasant comments upon the character of a dishonest judge:
*ỉr* *wḏꜥ* *rw-t* *m-ḫsf-w=n-f* *ỉw-f*
PTC judge case-F as-punish.IPP-M=to-3MS AUX-3MS
*m-ỉm(-y)-ḥꜣ-t* *n-ỉrr*
as-in.RLT[-M]-front-F to-do.PIA
As for a judge who ought to be punished, he is a model for a criminal (lit. 'doer'). (Peas B1, 248–49)

(233b) It is said of the yon sycamore and the fortunate dead:

*ỉr* *wnn* *ẖr-s* *ỉw-f* *m-nṯr* *ꜥꜣ*

PTC AUX.PIA under-3FS AUX-3MS as-god great

As for the one who is under it, he is a great god. (BD 189/*Nu* pl. 55, 11)

(233c) In a description of a pool in a narrative story:

*ỉst=rf* *ỉr* *pꜣ-mw* *ỉw-f* *m-mḥ* *12* *ḥr-ỉꜣ-t-f*

PTC=PTC PTC DEM.M-water AUX-3MS as-cubit 12 on-back-F-3MS

Now, as for the water, it was 12 cubits deep (lit. 'on its back').

(pWestcar 6, 10–11)

The difference between the two constructions is syntactic. With *ỉr*, the topicalised element is *extra*-posed outside the clausal frame, whereas in the =*pw*-construction, it is *ante*-posed and still within the clause but split from the rest of the construction by the 'gap' created by the subject element =*pw* of the higher nominal sentence. The fully clausal status of what follows the *ỉr*-extra-posed expressions is particularly clear in exx. 233a–233c.

#### 3.1.3.3 Adverbial sentences introduced by subordinating elements

Adverbial sentences introduced by relativisers, complementisers, and prepositional conjunctions do not form a coherent semantic-pragmatic class, but they do show a number of shared features. The relativiser *nt-* is etymologically and perhaps functionally related to the most common complementiser used with adverbial sentences. Also the grammar and semantic-pragmatics of adverbial sentence adjuncts introduced by preposition-conjunctions are inherently related to the syntax of complement clauses.

The semantic-pragmatics of adverbial sentence relative clauses introduced by the relative adjective *nt-* are in line with what is observed in corresponding constructions with the auxiliary *wn/wnn* (3.1.3.1.2). In principle, it seems that *nt*-relativisation is characteristically employed for restrictive relative clauses[86]:

(234a) Hapdjefa's contracts order priests to carry out cultic tasks including rites involving:

*ḫnt* *nt-y* *m-š-ỉ*

statue REL-M in-garden-1S

The statue, which is in my (tomb-)garden. (Siut I, 317)

(234b) Amenyseneb tells of his renovation work:

86 See 3.1.2.2 for further remarks.

| | | | | |
|---|---|---|---|---|
| *ỉw* | *rdỉ-n-ỉ* | *srwd-tw* | *mnqb=nb* | *n(-y)-nṯr=nb* |
| AUX | cause-PST-1S | restore-PASS | chapel=QU-M | of[-M]-god=QU.M |
| *nt-y* | *m-pꜣ-rpr* | | | |
| REL-M | in-DEM.M-temple | | | |

I caused one to restore every chapel of every god that is in this temple.

(Louvre C11, 5–6)

(234c) Sinuhe tells that the Egyptian king was told:

| | | |
|---|---|---|
| *ḥr-sšm=pn* | *nt-y=wỉ* | *ḥr-f* |
| about-condition=DEM.M | REL-M=1S | on-3MS |

...about this condition in which I was. (Sin B, 173–74)

(234d) In an instruction on the use of a medicine against a disease caused by a demon:

| | | | | |
|---|---|---|---|---|
| *swỉ* | *ỉn* | *s* | *nt-y* | *ẖr-nsyt* |
| drink.INF | AGT | man | REL-M | under-N |

To be drunk by someone who is suffering from the *nsyt*-illness.

(pEbers 89, 20)

In each of these cases, the relative clause restricts the interpretation or reference of the antecedent to some specific entity or class: the precise statue in the garden, every chapel specifically in the temple of Abydos, etc. In ex. 234d, the antecedent is, it seems, indefinite, but the relative clause with *nt-* signals that the medicine is to be drunk specifically by a person that suffers from the said demonic malady, and no one else. Exceptions to the restrictive nature of relative *nt-* clauses occur rarely, although the following example, where the relative clause appears to provide mere parenthetical information, would seem to be a candidate here:

(235) Thoth proclaims to other gods about Queen Hatshepsut:

| | | | | | | |
|---|---|---|---|---|---|---|
| *mꜣꜥtkꜣrꜥ* | *nt-t* | *m-nsw* | *ḫꜥ-tỉ* | *ḥr-s-t* | *ḥr* | *ḏt* |
| N | REL-F | as-king | appear-STA | on-throne-F | N | forever |

Maatkara, who is the king, has appeared on the throne of Horus forever!

(*Urk.* IV 289, 10)

Nevertheless, if one is ready assume that relative clauses with *nt-* are typically semantically restrictive, it is perhaps significant that in languages where the marking of modality plays a significant role in the grammatical organisation, restrictive and non-restrictive relative clauses are sometimes differentiated along these lines.[87] This is particularly interesting in view of the fact that *nt-* clearly also lies at the root of

87 For example, in Spanish, restrictive relative clauses employ the indicative whereas in non-restrictive environments the subjunctive is used (Butt & Benjamin 2000: 268–69).

the complementiser *ntt*, which in origin appears to be a feminine/neuter headless relative word, whereas the seemingly diachronically earlier complementiser *wnt* is etymologically almost certainly a neuter perfective participle of the lexical verb *wnn* 'exist'. It is probable that in complement environments, *ntt* and *wnt* originally stood for the actual complement of a verb with the meaning 'what is/exists', followed by an appositional content clause. Later, this syntactic construction was reanalysed as consisting of a complementiser + clause.[88] It is hardly coincidental then that *ntt* and *wnt* are used only after notionally assertive verbs such as those of locution, perception, and cognition – and then only if the complement is truly asserted:

(236a) It is said to those in the underworld:

| *ḏd-n=n-sn* | *wdnsḫmf* | *wnt* | *N=pn* | *m-wꜥ* | *ỉm-sn* |
|---|---|---|---|---|---|
| say-PST=to-3P | N | COMP | N=DEM.M | as-one | in-3P |

He whose might is overwhelming has told them that King N is one of them. (PT 2085a–b)

(236b) An instruction concerning the vizier's conduct in land-disputes:

| *ỉr* | *sprty=nb* | *n[t]-y* | *r-ḏd* | *mnmn* | *tꜣš-n* |
|---|---|---|---|---|---|
| PTC | petitioner=QU.M | REL-M | to-say.INF | move.PASS | boundary-1P |

| *ḫr* | *mꜣꜣ-t(w)* | *ntt=st* | *ḥr-ḫtm* |
|---|---|---|---|
| PTC | see-PASS | COMP=3C | upon-seal |

| *n(-y)-sr=ỉr-y* | *ḫr-f* | *šd-f* | *šd-w-t* |
|---|---|---|---|
| of[-M]-official=to.RLT-M | PTC-3MS | take-3MS | land-P-F |

| *n-tꜣ-ḏꜣḏꜣ-t* | *smnmn-t=st* |
|---|---|
| of-DET.F-council-F | move.PPA-F=3C |

As for any petitioner who shall say: 'Our boundaries have been moved' – when it is ascertained that they (i.e. land-register documents) carry the seal of the relevant official, then he (the vizier) can confiscate the *šd*-lands of that council which allowed them to be moved. (*Urk.* IV 1111, 9–13)

(236c) The king's superiority in battles against foreign foes is attributed to higher forces:

| *ỉỉ-n-sn* | *m-ḥḥ-w* | *n-rḫ-sn* | *ntt* | *ỉmnrꜥ* | *ḥr-mw-f* |
|---|---|---|---|---|---|
| come-PST-3P | in-million-P | NEG-know-3P | COMP | N | on-water-3MS |

Although they (the foreigners) came in millions, they did not know that Amun-Ra is his ally. (*Urk.* IV 1291, 1–3)

In each of the cases above, the speakers are fully committed to the complement propositions, which they present as highly relevant and salient information. Note that the

---

88 For what follows, see Uljas (2007c: 100). Similar processes have been attested in other languages, see e.g. Hopper & Traugott (1993: 185–89) for the history of the English complementiser *that*.

relevant individual is regularly the real speaker rather than the main clause subject: in ex. 236c, it is said that the subject(s) were not aware of the complement situation (which they thus could not assert), but this does not affect the grammatical marking. By contrast, as seen above, after notionally non-assertive verbs no complementiser appears; in the case of adverbial sentences, the complement clause is introduced by a form of the auxiliary verb *wn/wnn*.[89] This means that the complementiser is not used simply because adverbial sentences could not be used as complements, and the variance between the two patterns seems to belie an intricate, semantically and pragmatically based division. Corresponding signalling of the pragmatic status of complement clauses is found across a wide range of languages.[90]

The pragmatic role of the complementisers *ntt* and *wnt* after verbs seems to also provide insight into the variation between their presence and absence in adjunct clauses introduced by preposition-conjunctions. In most instances, the subordinating preposition is followed directly by an adverbial sentence headed by *wn/wnn*. The difference between the appearance of *wnn* and *wn* seems to be primarily temporal in character. In non-future adjuncts, *wnn* profiles the situation as imperfective, durative, or ongoing:

(237) The coda of Book of the Dead Spell 72 contains an assurance of its benefits to the deceased:

*wnn-ḫr-f* *wḏꜣ* *mỉ-wnn-f* *tp-tꜣ*
AUX-SEQ-3MS flourish.STA like-AUX-3MS upon-earth
Consequently he is flourishing just as he used to do upon earth.
(BD 72/*Nu* pl. 20, 14)

Similarly, in instances with future reference, the auxiliary seems to portray the situation as continuing from the present or again as durative or prolonged/extensive:

(238a) It is said that Atum created companion spirits:

*r-wnn-sn* *ḥnꜥ-f* *wꜥ-y* *m-nw*
to-AUX-3P with-3MS one-STA in-N
...so that they may stay with him alone in Nun. (CT IV 75f/B6C)

**89** Again, this situation parallels that found in other languages, where the use of subjunctives and other non-assertive forms is standard after non-assertive verbs.

**90** For example, in Spanish the indicative is used in complementation under exactly the same conditions – see Hooper and Terrell (1974: 484–94).

(238b) Queen Hatshepsut built a magazine for incense...
*n-mr(w)t-wnn* *pr=pn* *m-sṯ* *tꜣ-nṯr*
for-love-AUX house=DEM.M in-scent land-god
...in order that this temple may be (permeated) with the scent of the god's land. (*Texte 2. Zwischenzeit* n. 131, 2)

By contrast, *wn* is a past completed or 'detached' future involving a temporal gap between the time of reference and the time of the situation, both of which may, as noted (3.1.3.1.2), perhaps be viewed as manifestations of perfective (complet*ed*-ness vs. complet*e*ness) aspect:

(239a) Senenmut calls out to the living:
*m=wỉ* *m-ꜣḫ-ỉ=pn* *ḏbꜥ-ỉ* *m-sḫr(-ỉ)*
PTC=1S in-spirit-1S=DEM.M equipped-1S in-manner[-1S]
*ꜥpr-kw* *mỉ-wn-ỉ* *tp-tꜣ*
provide-STA.1S like-AUX-1S on-earth
See me in this my spiritual status, equipped in my (former) manner and provided as I was upon earth. (*Urk.* IV 547, 8–10)

(239b) Thutmosis III tells how he was blessed and favoured by his father Amun:
*ḏr-wn* *ḥm-ỉ* *m-ỉnp*
since-AUX majesty-1S as-toddler
...since my majesty was a toddler. (*Urk.* IV 157, 7)

(239c) Ikuded reveals his motivation for setting up a monument in Abydos:
*ꜥḥꜥ-n* *ỉrỉ-n(-ỉ)* *mꜥḥꜥ-t=tn* *r-rwd* *n(-y)-nṯr* *ꜥꜣ*
AUX make-PST[-1S] cenotaph-F=DEM.F to-terrace of[-M]-god great
*n-mr(w)t-wn(-ỉ)* *m-šmsw-f*
for-love-AUX[-1S] in-following-3MS
Then I constructed this cenotaph at the Terrace of the Great God, so that I might enter among his followers. (Berlin 1199, 8–9)

*wn* occurs also in such more abstractly 'remote' environments as counterfactuals:

(240) King Kamose tells how his troops sacked the enemy city of Avaris:
*mšꜥ-ỉ* *mỉ-wn* *mꜣỉ-w* *ḫr-ḥꜣq-t-sn*
army-1S like-AUX lion-P under-prey-F-3P
My army was as if lions were carrying their prey. (Carnarvon tablet 15)

Adjuncts of the above sort differ from their unintroduced and unmarked counterparts in 2.1.2 in that here the syntactic and semantic status of the clause is explicitly marked by the preposition-conjunction. But as noted earlier on, with causal preposition-conjunctions, the following clause, which syntactically represents a complement of the former, may be preceded by a complementiser, most commonly by the element *ntt*. With affirmative adverbial sentences, only examples with the prepositions *ḥr* and *ḏr* are attested:

(241a) The deceased addresses the guardians of the netherworld:

| | | | | | | |
|---|---|---|---|---|---|---|
| *nn* | *ḫtm-ṯn* | *ꜥꜣ-w-ṯn* | *ḥr-ỉ* | *ḥr-ntt* | *tꜣ-ỉ* | *m-p* |
| NEG | seal-2P | door-P-2P | on-1S | because-COMP | bread-1S | in-N |
| *ḥnq-t-ỉ* | *m-dpw* | | | | | |
| beer-F-1S | in-N | | | | | |

You will not seal your gates before me, because my bread is in (a place called) Pe, and my beer is in Dep. (BD 72/*Nu* pl. 20, 8–9)

(241b) The deceased salutes Ra and proclaims:

| | | | | | | |
|---|---|---|---|---|---|---|
| *mk=wỉ* | *ỉỉ-kw* | *m-sr* | *mꜣꜥ-t* | *ḏr-ntt* | *bỉꜣw* | *m-ỉmn-t* |
| PTC=1S | come-STA.1S | as-prophet | truth-F | since-COMP | N | in-west-F |

I have come as the prophet of truth, because the Distant One is in the west. (CT VII 401b–c/B3L)

The complementiser *ntt* cannot be freely substituted by the auxiliary *wn/wnn*; indeed, the former appears instead of the latter, exactly as in complements after verbs. Given this, it could be that the function of the complementiser is the same in both cases. Loosely speaking, adjunct clauses of the type [preposition + sentence] are specialised in that, as noted, their semantic and syntactic function is explicitly *marked* by the introducing preposition. In this respect, they contrast grammatically with unspecialised, directly embedded adjuncts, whose syntactic and semantic-pragmatic status is not specifically indicated. A number of linguistic theories equates subordination directly with non-assertion (e.g. Harris & Campbell 1995: 298–307; Cristofaro 2003: 29–40; cf. also e.g. Hopper 1981: 215–16; Lambrecht 1994: 67–69), arguing that it be defined as clausal linkage where one clause, namely the subordinated one, loses its autonomous profile and in essence becomes conceptually part of the profile of the main clause. This asymmetry involves loss of assertivity of the subordinate clause, which can be observed by tests such as negation, interrogation, preposing, and tag-questions. There are, however, certain important exceptions to this, notably in complementation and adjunction, the latter of which is of particular interest here. Adjunct clauses of time, manner, and concession present the situation as presupposed and thus do not assert, whereas final and conditional adjuncts refer to hypothetical states of affairs and neither presuppose nor assert (cf. Harris & Campbell 1995: 302–03). However, clauses of *cause* in particular are more complex in that they may either presuppose or assert. In English this difference is marked by the absence or presence of a pause, indicated by a comma in writing; tests such as tag-questions show that in the second example below the *because*-clause is asserted, whereas in the first instance, it is not:

I bought it because it has the best compatibility with THX-300 (*doesn't it?)
I bought it, because it has the best compatibility with THX-300 (doesn't it?)

This might also provide the key to the overall differences between the various types of Earlier Egyptian adjunct clauses. Leaving aside unmarked clauses where no grammatical marking took place, marked adjunct clauses introduced by preposition-conjunctions were in Earlier Egyptian perhaps not usually marked as assertions by means of a complementiser because as adjuncts they were mostly not asserted. Yet, the information in the adjunct could also belong to the discourse-pragmatic foreground and be asserted – but only in case of *causal* clauses, which almost alone among adjuncts fall into both asserted and non-asserted types and which in Earlier Egyptian alone exhibit a complementiser after the preposition-conjunction. Keeping in mind also that in complements of verbs the complementiser seems to signal the assertive status of the clause, this match is hardly a mere fortuitous coincidence. Instead, if it is taken seriously, the Earlier Egyptian typological and semantic-pragmatic organisation of affirmative adjunct clauses, including those with adverbial sentences, could be represented as follows[91]:

**Tab. I.9:** A possible typology of Earlier Egyptian affirmative adjunct clauses.

| INTRODUCED | UN-INTRODUCED |
| --- | --- |
| Assertion-marked<br>Causal preposition + complementiser | Bare clauses used as adjuncts |
| Not assertion-marked<br>Preposition + clause | |
| SEMANTIC-PRAGMATIC STATUS MARKED<br>SYNTACTIC STATUS MARKED | SEMANTIC-PRAGMATIC STATUS UNMARKED<br>SYNTACTIC STATUS UNMARKED |

91 There remains the question what conditions the choice between the specialised (i.e. introduced) semantic-pragmatically unambiguous and unspecialised (i.e. un-unintroduced) adjuncts, whose interpretation is seldom explicit. Here very little work has been carried out, but this seems to correlate, at least partly, with particular textual genres and registers. For example, unintroduced adjuncts predominate in literary works, whose linguistic idiom has a semi-artificial flavour and where the potential ambiguities and multiple interpretations of the former may even represent an artistic means of interacting more with the audience whose interpretative faculties are more heavily relied upon. By contrast, adjuncts introduced by prepositional conjuncts are ubiquitous, e.g., in the contracts of Hapdjefa, an early Middle Kingdom legal text, where avoidance of ambiguity and preciseness of expression are essential.

### 3.1.4 Semantic extensions of the adverbial sentence

In 3.1.1, the expression of location was taken to represent the 'basic', prototypical value of adverbial sentences in Earlier Egyptian and in general. Like all categories founded on (or rather around) a prototype, the concept of locus is sufficiently abstract and innately schematic to allow a number of semantic *extensions* of the core idea for the expression of more abstract notions (cf. here Collier 1994: 60–67; Nyord 2010; Gracia Zamacona 2010: 15–24). To use a consciously spatial metaphor to describe a phenomenon based on spatiality, the various extensions may be envisaged as occupying a position relatively closer to or more distant from the semantic core of expressing locus in three-dimensional space. For example, in Earlier Egyptian, one of the most widely encountered semantic extensions of the adverbial sentence meaning is the use of the dative or benefactive preposition *n* 'to' to convey predicative (as opposed to adnominal) *possession*:

(242a) In a harpist's song to his deceased master:
*i͗w=n-k* *tꜣw* *nḏm* *n(-y)-mḥy-t*
AUX=to-2MS wind sweet of[-M]-north-F
Yours is the sweet wind of the north. (*Lesestücke* 87, 7)

(242b) It is said of Queen Hatshepsut:
*i͗w=n-s* *tꜣ-w*
AUX=to-3FS land-P
(All) countries belong to her. (*Urk.* IV 244, 10)

(242c) The universal lordship of King Ahmose is stressed:
*tꜣ-w* *ḥr* *wnn-n=n-f*
land-P on AUX-1P=to-3MS
(All) countries say: 'We will belong to him/it is to him that we belong'. (*Urk.* IV 17, 14–15)

This pattern is used to express alienable possession, i.e. ownership in the restricted juridical-ethical sense as well as all kinds of temporary and momentary, but not inalienable possession, for which the adnominal direct genitive is used instead (e.g. *i͗b-f* 'his heart'). The grammatical use for this purpose of locational expressions in general or the dative in particular is a phenomenon very widely met across languages (see Heine 2006: 50–57, 60). The possessee is metaphorically profiled as being 'to' the possessor, which resembles a recipient of the possessee, as clearly seen in the examples above. Another less widely attested adverbial sentence pattern used as a possessive in Earlier Egyptian is with the preposition *m-ꜥ*, literally 'in the hand (of)':

(243) Paheri says that he has reached a content state at the end of his days:
*ẖr-t-i* *m-ʿ-i*
property-F-1S in-hand-1S
I have my property. (*Urk.* IV 123, 10)

Subsequently, this construction was grammaticalised in the form *m-di* > *mdi* (representing a graphemically adjusted successor of *m-ʿ*) as the principal possessive pattern of Late Egyptian, and in the Coptic expression *unt-* it becomes part of what is essentially a verb 'to have, possess' (see 3.2.4).

Possessive expressions such as those above may still in some sense be conceptualised as describing the locus of the possessed entities. However, there is a further, considerably more ubiquitous semantic extension of the adverbial sentence where this is no longer strictly possible, namely the constructions with what in Egyptology have been traditionally called the *m* of predication and *r* of futurity (Nyord 2010: 30–31, 41–42; Grossman and Polis 2014: 45–56; Grossman, Lescuyer and Polis 2014). Both these represent uses of the basic locative sense associated with the prepositions involved – 'in' in case of *m* and 'to/toward' with *r* – to express what corresponds semantically to temporally indeterminate and future classification respectively; thus, with *m*:

(244a) Meryra-nefer tells of the beginning of his career:
*wn(-i)* *m-ḥwnw* *ṯz* *mḏḥ* *m-rk* *tti*
AUX[-1S] as-youth tie.PPA fillet in-era N
In the era of King Teti, I was a youth who wore a fillet. (*Urk.* I 253, 18)

(244b) Neferty asks his heart to bear testimony to the coming horrors:
*gr* *m-iwḥ*
silent.PIA as-wrongdoer
He who is silent is a wrongdoer. (Neferty IIIg)

(244c) The sage laments the reversal of social roles:
*in=n-f* *ṯꜣb-t* *m-dd* *pr=st*
bring.PPA=to-3MS corn_load-F as-give.PIA go=3C
He who had to fetch a corn-load personally is (now) one who issues it. (Ipuwer 9, 5)

(244d) Sinuhe begins his eulogy of Senwosret I from the basics:
*iw-f* *m-nsw*
AUX-3MS as-king
He is a king. (Sin B, 68)

(244e) Ineni tells of his duties as an official:
*iw-i* *m-ḫrp* *ḥm-w-t=nb-t*
AUX-1S as-controller work-P-F=QU-F
I was a controller of all labour-undertakings. (*Urk.* IV 54, 4)

Examples with *r*:

(245a) A pair of unknown divinities is told about the king:
*ỉw-f* *r-ḫmnwt-ṯn* *m-ỉwnw*
AUX-3MS to-third-2P in-N
He will be your third one in Heliopolis. (PT 363f)

(245b) Sehetepibra remarks on the benefits of royal patronage:
*ỉw* *mr* *n(-y)-nsw* *r-ỉmꜣḫy*
AUX love.PPA of[-M]-king to-revered
One loved by the king will become one revered. (CG 20538ii, 18–19)

(245c) The king announces Sinuhe's imminent promotion:
*ỉw-f* *r-smr* *mm-sr-w*
AUX-3MS to-friend among-official-P
He shall be a royal favourite among officials. (Sin B, 280–81)

(245d) Words of a man to his superior in a fowling scene:
*ỉry(-ỉ)* *(r)-ḥs-t-k* *ỉw-k* *r-ḥsy*
do.SUB[-1S] to-praise.REL.FUT-F-2MS AUX-3MS to-favour.PPP-M
I will do as it pleases you; you will be pleased. (*Meir* III, pl. 8)

(245e) Ptahhetep notes that people of pleasant nature will be remembered by posteriority:
*ỉw* *qd* *nfr* *r-sḫꜣw*
AUX character good to-memory
A good character will become a memorial. (Ptahhetep 494)

In interrogative contexts the relevant properties are, of course, not stated, but inquired:

(246a) In a broken context:
*ỉw-k=tr* *m-m* *n(-y)-nṯr*
AUX-2MS=PTC as-WH of[-M]-god
What god are you, in fact? (pRamesseum I, A15)

(246b) The peasant asks the high steward:
*ỉnỉw-k* *r-s* *n(-y)-nḥḥ*
IP-2MS to-man of[-M]-eternity
Will you be a man of eternity? (Peas B1, 126–27)

Examples with *wn/wnn* occur mostly with *m*, where the auxiliary again has either a temporal-modal or an information structuring function. Many of these have already been cited, but below are some further instances of the writings *wn* and *wnn* in close correspondence mutually and with *ỉw*; the semantic-pragmatic and syntactic analysis of clause-combinations such as these is highly problematic[92]:

(247a) The *djed*-pillar is addressed:
*ỉ ḏdw ḏd ỉm-y grwbꜣf wn N m-wrwt-k wnn*
VOC N djed_pillar in.RLT-M N AUX N as-N-2MS AUX
*N m-wrwt-k*
N as-N-2MS
O Busirite, the djed-pillar who is in *grw-bꜣ-f*. King N was your *wrwt*, and King N will (continue to) be your *wrwt*. (PT 719a–b)

(247b) The deceased is told:
*wn-ṯ m-nṯr wnn-ṯ m-nṯr*
AUX-2FS as-god AUX-2FS as-god
You were and will remain a god. (CT III 300d)

(247c) The deceased is told:
*ỉw-k m-nṯr wnn-k m-nṯr*
AUX-2MS as-god AUX-2MS as-god
You are a god, and a god you will remain. (CT I 55b)

With *r* the use of *wn/wnn* is considerably less common. In the following example *wnn* probably heads an 'emphatic' Second Tense construction (see 3.1.3.1.2):

(248) The deceased is told:
*mk wnn rn-k r-nḥḥ m-ḥwtnṯr n-t-ỉnpw*
PTC AUX name-2MS to-eternity in-temple of-F-N
See, your name will be forever in the temple of Anubis. (Siut IV, 23–24)

In these examples, the prepositions *m* and *r* clearly do not determine the spatial position of the subject as actually within or toward the entity referred to by the noun governed by the preposition. Instead, these concrete loci are treated as metaphors for the subjects' status as being or becoming some entity through a purely imaginary internalisation with or movement towards the latter. Consequently, adverbial sentences with the *m* of predication profile the subject as an instance of or as amounting to something, by virtue of their schematic character as positing the subject, as it were, 'within' the status:

**92** More particularly, it is often difficult if not impossible to decide whether, e.g., the variation between *wn* and *wnn* in ex. 247a is that of past completed and continuous time reference or whether e.g. *wnn* should be understood as functioning as a head of a Second Tense. Similar problems arise in instances such as ex. 247c, where *ỉw* and *wnn* seem to stand in opposition, but it is unclear whether the contrast is that of time-reference or information structure.

(249a) The peasant gives free rein to his frustration with the high steward's inaction:

| | | |
|---|---|---|
| *mk=tw* | *m-ḥwrw* | *n(y)-bꜣty* |
| PTC=2MS | as-wretch | of[-M]-washerman |

You are one wretch of a washerman! (Peas B1, 199–200)

(249b) A note in a mathematical puzzle involving measures:

| | | | | |
|---|---|---|---|---|
| *ỉw* | *mḥ* | *1* | *m-šsp* | *7* |
| AUX | cubit | 1 | as-palm | 7 |

One cubit is (adds up to) seven palms. (pRhind math. n.56, 3)

The imaginary movement that lies at the root of the *r* of futurity is clear from examples of the 'ordinary' *r* such as the following:

(250a) It is said of the deceased king:

| | | | |
|---|---|---|---|
| *ỉw* | *N* | *r-ns-t* | *ỉt-f=tw* |
| AUX | N | to-throne-F | father-3MS=DEM.F |

King N is bound towards this throne of his father. (PT 270a)

(250b) Nemtynakht has had enough of the peasant's wailing and threatens him with death:

| | | | | | |
|---|---|---|---|---|---|
| *m* | *qꜣ* | *ḫrw-k* | *sḫty* | *mk=tw* | *r-dmỉ* |
| NEG.AUX.IMP | high.NC | voice-2MS | peasant | PTC=2MS | to-abode |
| *n(-y)-nb* | *sgr* | | | | |
| of[-M]-lord | silence | | | | |

Do not raise your voice, peasant. Look, you are (on the way) to the abode of Lord of Silence. (Peas B1, 57–58)

Overall, adverbial sentences with the *m* of predication and especially with the *r* of futurity describe dynamic, acquired or forthcoming 'sameness' between the subject and the entity expression in the predicate rather than static, unmodifiable identity between the two. Indeed, sentences with them seem almost always to concern the *classification* of the subject rather than its identification or specification.[93] These two latter relations have a tendency to be much more permanent states that, among other things, are not subject to change or development.

**93** There are, however, some rare exceptions to this, among them the following:

(FNc) The king is resurrected:

| | | | | | | |
|---|---|---|---|---|---|---|
| *ỉw* | *N* | *m-nn* | *ḫꜥ* | *ḫꜥ* | *ỉ-mn* | *ỉ-mn* |
| AUX | N | as-DEM.M | appear.IMP | appear.IMP | IMP-endure | IMP-endure |

King N is this: 'Appear appear; Endure, endure!' (PT 414a)

where the use of the demonstrative *nn* 'this' as the predicate excludes classifying reading.

It will be seen later that for the expression of such states of affairs Earlier Egyptian rather uses the nominal sentence (Part II).

Analogous extensions involved in adverbial sentences with the *m* of predication and the *r* of futurity seem to belie verbal patterns of the type preposition *ḥr/m/r* + infinitive. This is something that becomes immediately obvious when considering variations such as the following, where a commonly met Old Kingdom utterance is alternatively phrased with simple *r* of futurity + noun (ex. 251a) and *r* + infinitive of the auxiliary *wn/wnn* followed by *m* + noun (ex. 251b):

(251a) Iti says concerning someone who will read aloud the offering formula for him[94]:

| | | | | |
|---|---|---|---|---|
| *[ỉw](-ỉ)* | *r-ḥꜣ-f* | *[m-ḏꜣ]ḏꜣ-t* | *nṯr* | *ꜥꜣ* |
| AUX[-1S] | to-protector-3MS | in-council-F | god | great |

I will be his protector in the council of the great god. (*Urk.* I 197, 18)

(251b) A similar affirmation by Zezi:

| | | | | |
|---|---|---|---|---|
| *ỉw(-ỉ)* | *r-wnn* | *m-ḥꜣy-f* | *m-ẖrtnṯr* | *m-ḏꜣḏꜣ-t* |
| AUX[-1S] | FUT-AUX.INF | as-protector-3MS | in-necropolis | in-council-F |
| *n-t-nṯr* | *ꜥꜣ* | | | |
| of-F-god | great | | | |

I will be his protector in the necropolis and the council of the great god. (*Urk.* I 202, 11)

This is not the place to discuss the more precise semantics of these periphrastic verbal constructions, but something should be said of their relation to adverbial sentences. Although the constructions *ḥr/m/r* + infinitive do not represent a semantic or syntactic subcategory of adverbial sentences and their grammar cannot be reduced to identity with the latter,[95] etymologically they clearly represent grammaticalisations of adverbial sentences, and something of their historical origins is preserved also in their synchronic uses. Put in a different way, the constructions with *ḥr/m/r* + infinitive and adverbial sentences form a semantic spectrum whose various intermediary points continued to exist in the language also synchronically even after the grammaticalisation of the former sometime during the Old Kingdom.[96] For example, given the concrete, substantive, and strictly atemporal character of the nouns governed by the prepositions

94 *ḥꜣ-f* 'its protector' is followed by a sitting-man determinative, and thus the reading *r* + infinitive is excluded.

95 The classic paper demonstrating this (albeit focussing only on *ḥr*) is Collier (1994: particularly 60–67).

96 There are no instances of *ḥr*, *m*, or *r* + infinitive in the Pyramid Texts (Allen 1984: §722D).

*ḥr* and *m* in exx. 1b and 1c cited earlier on, only a spatial interpretation is possible: the staves are 'upon the shoulder of my arm', and 'the memory of me' is 'in the palace'. In the following instances, however, the nouns governed denote emotions, activities, and abstractions whose conceptualisation entails a temporal element. Consequently, the sentences are understood to refer not strictly to loci, but to the subjects' undergoing, being engaged in, or proceeding (at first intentionally, but later in general) towards states of affairs denoted by the nouns:

(252a) The peasant tries to stir the high steward into action:
*mk=wỉ m-nhw*
PTC=1S in-need
Look I am in need. (Peas B1, 102)

(252b) Sinuhe describes the busy scene with royal servants:
*ỉw wdpw=nb ḥr-ỉr-t-f*
AUX butler=QU.M on-duty-F-3MS
Every butler was about his duty. (Sin B, 246)

(252c) The peasant contrasts the momentary gains from crookedness with more pertinent values:
*ỉw=swt mꜣꜥ-t r-nḥḥ*
AUX=PTC right-F to-eternity
But righteousness will be forever (lit. 'to eternity'). (Peas B1, 338)

From this there is a short step to profiling the subject as 'situated' within or towards an activity, with the preposition now functioning as a full-fledged temporal marker fleshing out the subject's locus within the internal temporal structure of the situation, or towards it as a whole. This is precisely what the patterns *ḥr/m/r* + infinitive do. As innovative grammaticalisations of locative expressions in which the imagery of space and motion is applied to describe time, they 'locate' the subject 'within' and 'moving toward' a situation rather than an entity, as with the *m* of predication and the *r* of futurity, which is tantamount to defining their locus in the temporal dimension of the latter. The result of this is, in the first case, the specific or continuous progressive aspect *ḥr/m* + infinitive. In the second case it is the so-called *r* + infinitive allative future (see Grossman & Polis 2014):

(253a) A note in a memorandum:
*[ỉ]w nb ꜥ.w.s. m-ỉwt r-sḫmsnwsrt mꜣꜥ-ḫrw*
AUX lord l.p.h. PROG-come.INF to-N true-voice
The lord l.p.h. is coming to (the town of) Sekhem-Senwosret, Justified.
(pUC 32205, v° 4)

(253b) The peasant tells his wife that he is about to travel to the Nile Valley:

*mt=wi m-hꜣt r-kmt*
PTC=S PROG-descend.INF to-Egypt
Look, I am going down to Egypt. (Peas R, 2–3)

(253c) Pepiankh the Middle says of his life achievements:

*i͗ri-n(-i) ꜥḥꜥw(-i) rꜥ=nb... sk=w(i) ḥr-i͗rt*
do-PST[-1S] lifetime[-1S] day=QU.M PTC=1S PROG-do.INF
*bw-nfr ḥr-ḏd mrr-t*
ABST-good PROG-say love.IPP-F
I spent every day of my lifetime... doing good and saying what is loved. (*Urk.* I 222, 8–9)

(253d) Kebi confirms the transfer of his official post to his son:

*i͗w-i ḥr-rdi͗t pꜣy-i-mty-n(-y)-sꜣ n-sꜣ-i*
AUX-1S PROG-give.INF POSS.M-1MS-controller-of[-M]-phyle to-son-1S
I am giving my (office of) controller of a phyle to my son. (pUC 32037, r° 3–4)

(253e) The peasant accuses the high steward of corruption:

*i͗w sr-w ḥr-rdi͗t=n-k i͗w-k ḥr-i͗tt*
AUX official-P PROG-give.INF to-2MS AUX-2MS PROG-take.INF
Officials keep bribing you, and you accept. (Peas B1, 332–33)

(253f) Seneni says in reference to those who may steal parts of his tomb:

*i͗w(-i) r-wḏ[ꜥ ḥnꜥ]-sn i͗n nṯr ꜥꜣ nb*
AUX[-1S] FUT-judge.INF with-3P AGT god great lord
*p-t*
heaven-F
*i͗w(-i) r-i͗ṯt ṯz[-sn] mi-(ꜣ)pd*
AUX[-1S] FUT-seize.INF neck-3P like-bird
I shall be judged with them by the great god, lord of heaven; I shall seize their neck(s) like (those of) bird(s). (*Urk.* I 116, 6)

(253g) The snake tells the shipwrecked sailor what his fate will be:

*mk=tw r-i͗rt ꜣbd ḥr-ꜣbd r-km-t-k*
PTC=2MS FUT-do.INF month on-month to-complete-TERM-2MS
*ꜣbd 4 m-ẖnw n(y) i͗w=pn*
month 4 in-interior of-M island=DEM.M
You are going to spend month upon month until you have completed four months on this island. (Sh.S. 117–19)

(253h) The peasant warns the high steward of the consequences of his inaction:
*iw* *wsf-k* *r-tht-k* *iw* *ꜥwnib-k* *r-swḫꜣ-k*
AUX idleness-2MS FUT-fool.INF-2MS AUX greed-2MS FUT-fool.INF-2MS
*iw* *snm-k* *r-sḫpr* *ḫrwy-w-k*
AUX gluttony-2MS FUT-create.INF enemy-P-2MS
Your idleness is going to lead you astray; your greed is going to fool you; your gluttony will make you enemies. (Peas B2, 39–42)

The interrelation between adverbial and sentences and the verbal constructions with *ḥr/m/r* + infinitive is thus both synchronic and diachronic in character.

## 3.2 Later Egyptian

### 3.2.1 Core

In Later Egyptian, the most fundamental properties of adverbial sentences known from Earlier Egyptian remained largely unchanged. The construction was essentially devoid of temporal reference, which was based mostly on contextual information:

*Late Egyptian*

(254a) The introductory setting for a display of royal prowess:
*ist-ḥm-f* *m-dmi* *n-ḥwtkꜣptḥ* *ḥr-ir-t* *ḥss*
PTC-majesty-3MS in-town of-N PRP-do-INF praise-PIA
*it-f* *imnḥrꜣḫty*
father-3MS N
His majesty was in the city of Memphis doing what his father Amun-Harakhty praises. (*KRI* I 38, 4–5)

(254b) Ramesses III speaks to Amun:
*rdi-n-k=(w)i* *r-nsw* *iw-i* *m-swḥ-t* *iw-bn-ḏr-t*
give-PST-2MS=1S to-king DEP-1S in-egg-F DEP-NEG-hand-F
*n-ky* *im-i*
of-other in-1S
You appointed me a king while I was still unborn (lit: in the egg), while the hand of no other having yet touched me. (*KRI* V 239, 5–6)

*Demotic*

(254c) A wish in a series of moral precepts:
*hmy* *ỉw-pꜣy-ỉy-ỉry-ḏd* *m-rḫ-ḏḥwty*
PTC DEP-POSS.M-1S-fellow-speak as-adept-N
Would that my opponent were as adept as Thoth.
(Onkhsheshonqy 10, 12)

(254d) The small dog-ape begs the goddess to return to Egypt and states:
*ỉnky* *ḥ(ꜥ)-y* *tw-y=dy* *šꜥtw-pꜣ-ḏbꜣ* *sy* *nỉm-y*
1S self-1S PTC-1S=here until-DEF.M-revenge be sated in-1S
As for me, I (will) stay here until the revenge has sated itself with me.
(Myth of the Sun's Eye 12, 3)

*Coptic*

(254e) In a prayer for the house of David, the Lord is quoted as having assured:
*ta-me* *mn-pa-na* *nmma-f*
POSS.F.1S-truth and-POSS.M.1S-mercy with-3MS
My faithfulness and my mercy shall be with him. ([S]Ps 88 [89]:25 [24])

(254f) Judas narrates to Paul that Jesus refused to free him from Hell and, so Judas, says:
*anok=de* *ti-m-pei-ma* *cin-pe-hou* *et(m)mau*
1S=yet 1S-in-DEM.M-place since-DEF.M-DAY that
So I am here since that day. ([S]*Acts of Andrew & Paul* [Jacques 204, 129])

(254g) The author of the epistle finishes with the greeting:
*p-hmot* *nemô-ten* *têr-u*
DEF.M-grace with-2P all-3P
Grace be with all of you. ([B]Heb 13:25)

In ex. 254a, the situation is set in the past because it appears in a past narrative context. The same holds also for ex. 254b. In ex. 254d, the time reference of the state of affairs referred to is the future, but no explicit marking is used. The Coptic sentences in exx. 254e and 254f both refer to situations of future relevance. Perhaps partly because of this lack of temporal reference, Coptic often avoided the adverbial sentence pattern of the diachronically earlier stages in favour of a verbal pattern with the qualitative form of the verb [S]*šôpe* 'exist', i.e. *šoop*, or of the verb [S]*ire* 'make', i.e. *o* (note, however, that harbingers of that development can be found already in Late Egyptian, see Winand 1996: 121–24, whereas Demotic examples seem limited to relative clauses but probably by chance of preservation only, see above ex. 170e):

*Coptic*

(255a) Jesus sat at the deathbed of his mother:

| | | | | | | |
|---|---|---|---|---|---|---|
| *ere-mikhaêl* | *šoop* | *hi-unam* | *mmo-f* | *ere-gabriêl* | *hi-$k^{j}$bur* | *mmo-f* |
| DEP-N | be.STA | upon-right | of-3MS | DEP-N | upon-left | of-3MS |

...with Michael on his right and Gabriel on his left.

($^{S}$*Trans.Mariae* 49, r° a1–4)

(255b) In the Paraphrase of Shem, the supreme deity reveals to Shem:

| | | | | |
|---|---|---|---|---|
| *ne-un-uoin* | *šoop* | *mn-u-kake* | *auô* | *ne-un-u-pn(eum)a* |
| IPF-PTC-light | be.STA | and-IDF.S-darkness | and | IPF-PTC-IDF.S-spirit |
| *hn-tu-mête* | | | | |
| in-POSS.P.3P-midst | | | | |

There was light and darkness and among them a spirit.

($^{S}$*Paraph. Shem* 1, 25–28)

(255c) A Cherub explains to St John:

| | | | |
|---|---|---|---|
| *hathe* | *mpate-p-nute* | *tamie-t-pe* | *mn-p-kah* |
| before | NCO-DEF.M-god | create-DEF.F-heaven | and-DEF.M-earth |
| *m-mou* | *ne-u-šoop* | | |
| DEF.P-water | IPV-3P-be.STA | | |

Before God created Heaven and Earth, waters existed.

($^{S}$*Mysteries of St John Evangelist* [Budge, *Apocrypha*, 61, 23–24])

(255d) The narrator of the vision asks the accompanying angel:

| | | | |
|---|---|---|---|
| *ara-mn-keke* | *ḫoop* | *m-pei-ma* | *ute-u-ḫi* |
| IP-NEG-darkness | be.STA | in-DEM.M-place | nor-IDF.S-night |

Is there neither darkness nor night in this place?

($^{A}$*ApSoph.* [Steindorff, *Apokalypse des Elias* 37 2, 2–4])

(255e) The Lord's anger will be awe-inspiring:

| | | | | |
|---|---|---|---|---|
| *ere-p-$k^{j}$ônt* | *m-p-c(ai)s* | *ai* | *n-t-hê* | *n-u-iei* |
| DEP-DEF.F-wrath | of-DEF.M-lord | be.STA | in-DEF.F-way | of-IDF.S-ravine |
| *e-f-muh* | *hitn-u-thên* | | | |
| DEP-3MS-burn | by-IDF.S-brimstone | | | |

...while the Lord's wrath is like a ravine burning with brimstone.

($^{F}$Is 30:33)

(255f) The angel of the church in Pergamos is addressed:

| | | | | |
|---|---|---|---|---|
| *ti-sôun* | *ce-a-k-šop* | *$t^{h}$ôn* | | |
| 1S-know | COMP-FOC-2MS-be.STA | WH | | |
| *pi-ma* | *ete-pi-thronos* | *m-p-satanas* | *$k^{h}$ê* | *mmo-f* |
| $DEF_2$.M-place | REL-$DEF_2$.M-throne | of-DEF.M-Satan | AUX | in-3MS |

I know where you are and where Satan's throne is. ($^{B}$Rev 2:13)

Occasionally, the various dialects of Coptic show variance between the constructions:

(256) The Prophet asks whether the Lord is wroth with the rivers:

| | | | | |
|---|---|---|---|---|
| *ie* | *are-pe-k-mbon* | | *ḫen-han-iarôu* | B |
| or | ST-POSS.M-2MS-wrath | | in-IDF.P-rivers.P | |
| *ie* | *are-pe-k-uoi* | | *ḫen-p$^{h}$-iom* | |
| or | ST-POSS.M-2MS-run | | in-DEF.M-sea | |
| *ê* | *a-p-k-k$^{j}$ônt* | *ḫoop* | *hen-ierôu* | A |
| or | ST-POSS.M-2MS-wrath | be.STA | in-IDF.P-rivers.P | |
| *ê* | *a-t-k-uoi* | *ḫoop* | *en-thalassa* | |
| or | ST-POSS.M=2MS-run | be.STA | in-DEF.M-sea | |

Or is your wrath against rivers or your onslaught against the sea?

(Hab 3:8)

Whereas the Bohairic version here uses the adverbial sentence, the Akhmimic variant has a construction with *ḫoop*, the Akhmimic Stative form of the verb $^{S}$*šôpe*. In general, the Akhmimic variety of Coptic privileges the verbal pattern when compared with other Coptic dialects. Nevertheless, it will be seen that the various strategies of defining, determining, and modifying the temporal reference of propositions by means of external operators that had already existed in Earlier Egyptian were extended, developed, and, in some sense, simplified in the later language, gradually resulting in a system of 'converters' with well-defined temporal functions. An analogous evolution also took place in the domain of information structuring, where a corresponding system of operators arose over time. The use of these novel expressions was not restricted to adverbial sentences, but the latter were a major domain of their employment. This evolution also resulted in a syntactic intermingling of adverbial and verbal sentences, which is a characteristic feature of Later Egyptian as a whole.

In Later Egyptian, the expression of spatial locus remained the central semantic function of adverbial sentences. The same strictly locative senses as found in Earlier Egyptian continue to represent the core of the example basis. Instances conveying the relation 'in', usually by means of the prepositions *m* or *m-ḫnw* (in Coptic mainly $^{S}$*hen-/ nhêt-* and $^{B}$*ḫen-/nḫêt-*) or locative adverbs, are ubiquitous:

*Late Egyptian*

(257a) The scribal profession is better than that of a stable master, whose family members must work hard:

| | |
|---|---|
| *tꜣy-f-šri-t* | *m-pꜣ-dni* |
| POSS.F-3FS-daughter-F | in-DEF.M-dyke |

His daughter is in the dyke. (*LEM* 17, 4–5)

(257b) The same is said of the baker, who bakes bread and put loaves on fire:

*ỉw-ḏꜣḏꜣ-f* *m-ẖnw-tꜣ-trr*
DEP-head-3MS in-inside-DEF.F-oven
...with his head in the oven. (*LEM* 17, 7)

*Demotic*

(257c) A priest explains where a certain book with magical spells is to be found:

*pꜣ-ḏmꜥ* *n-rn-f* *ỉw-f* *n-tꜣ-mtry-t*
DEF.M-book of-name-3MS PTC-3MS in-DEF.F-midst-F
*n-pꜣ-ym* *n-qbṯ*
of-DEF.M-sea of-N
*ẖn-wꜥ-t-tbe-t* *n-bnpy* *ỉw-tꜣ-tbe-t* *n-bnpy*
in-IDF.S-F-chest-F of-iron DEP-DEF.F-chest-F of-iron
*ẖn-wꜥ-t-tbe-t* *[n-ḥm-t]*
in-IDF.S-F-chest-F of-copper
The said book is amidst the 'Sea of Coptos' within a chest of iron, while the chest of iron is in a chest of copper. (Setne I 3, 17–18)

(257d) In a declaration about lifestock, the owner swears:

*ỉỉr-y* *ỉr-pꜣ-ꜥnḫ* *nty-ḥrỉ* *mꜣꜥ* *tw-y* *ẖn-nꜣ-ḥs-w*
DEP-1S do-DEF.M-oath REL-above true PTC-1S in-DEF.P-praised-P
*(n)-prꜥꜣ*
of-pharaoh
*ỉỉr-y* *ỉr-f* *ꜥḏ* *tw-y* *ẖn-pꜣ-btw*
DEP-1S do-3MS false PTC-1S in-DEF.M-punishment
If I swear the above oath truthfully, I am among the praised ones of the pharaoh. If I swear it falsely, I am in the punishment (of the pharaoh).
(pInv. Sorbonne 1248, 7–8 [*Enchoria* 8])

*Coptic*

(257e) The angel of Lord calls Abraham, who replies:

*is* *hêête* *ti-hm-pei-ma*
PTC behold 1S-in-DEM.M-place
Look, I am here. ($^{S}$Gn 22:11)

(257f) The opening formula in a letter guaranteeing protection:

*is* *p-logos* *m-p-noute* *ntoot-k*
PTC DEF.M-word of-DEF.M-god with-2MS
Look, the guarantee of god is in your hand. ($^{S}$*O.Ashm.Copt.* 3, 4–5)

(257g) In invoked magical power is told to protect a woman:

*mn-pe-s-šêli* *e-f-hn-te-s-kalahê*
and-POSS.M-3FS-child DEP-3MS-in-POSS.F-3FS-womb
...and her child, which is in her womb. ($^{F}$Kropp, *Zaubertexte* I, 15, 12)

(257h) The members of Jacob's household follow his orders that he himself received from the Lord:

*uoh a-u-ti n-ni-nuti n-šemmo n-iakôb nê*
and PST-3P-give OBJ-DEF$_2$.P-god of-alien to-N DEF$_3$.P
*e-na-u-*$k^h$*ê ḫen-nu-cic*
DEP-IPF-3P-AUX in-POSS.P.3P-hand
*nem-ni-leon e-na-u-*$k^h$*ê ḫen-nu-mašc*
and-DEF$_2$.P-ring DEP-IPF-3P-AUX in-POSS.P.3P-ear
*uoh a-f-*$k^h$*op-u nce-iakôb ḫa-ti-terebinthos et-*$k^h$*ê*
and PST-3MS-hide-3P PVS-N under-DEF$_2$.F-terebinth REL-AUX
*ḫen-sikima*
in-N
And they gave to Jacob the foreign gods that were in their hands and the earrings in their ears, and Jacob hid them under the terebinth in Sikima.
($^{B}$Gn 35:4)

The same holds also for the relation 'upon' an object or an area, usually with *ḥr* 'on' (Coptic *hi-/hiôt*, ex. 258c) or some other preposition[97]:

*Late Egyptian*

(258a) The summoned courtiers approached the pharaoh:

*pd-w-sn ḥr-tꜣ m-hꜣy sn-tꜣ*
knee-P-3P on-earth in-jubilation kiss-earth
...with their knees on the ground in jubilation and prostration.
(*KRI* II 326, 8–9)

97 Location within a country is usually marked by this expression, whereas location within a city or an area such as the desert usually requires the preposition *m-* in Late Egyptian (e.g., *Insc. of Mose* S13 ed. Gaballa pl. 63 or *KRI* II 355, 3–4) and Demotic (e.g., Myth of the Sun's Eye 11, 5 or pBN 226a + pLouvre N 2412, 2); but see ex. 258b) or *ḫn-* in Demotic (BM 5661, a3 ed. Arlt #25) and *hen-* in Coptic (e.g., $^{L}$Jn 4:20 or $^{B}$*AP Macarius* B34 [*MG* 25 230, 16–231,2]).

*Demotic*

(258b) In a memorandum, a priest has jotted down his presence at different locations over a time:

*ḫpr-rnp-t* *21-t* *ỉbd-1* *šmw* *sw-2*
happen-regnal year-F 21-F month-1 harvest day-2
*tw-y* *ḥr-ỉwnw*
PTC-1S on-N
On the $2^{nd}$ of Pakhons in the $21^{st}$ regnal year I was in Heliopolis.
(oHor 1, 2)

*Coptic*

(258c) In a description of the first Christian community:

*nê=de* *têr-u* *et-a-u-nahti* *na-u-hi-u-ma* *pe*
DEF$_3$.P=yet all=3P REL-PST-3P-believe PRT-3P-upon-IDF.S-place PTC
All who believed were together in one place. ($^B$Acts 2:44)

Late Egyptian still makes occasional use of the preposition *n* to express benefactive meaning:

(259a) The king narrates his achievements for various deities and their temples' wealth:

*di-ỉ* *ḫpr-sn* *ỉw-ḥꜣ-w* *n-w* *r-pꜣ-ḫr-ḥꜣ-t*
cause.PST-1S be.SUB-3P DEP-surplus-3P for-3P to-DEF.M-under-front-F
I made them have more abundance than in earlier times.
(*KRI* V 245, 2)

(259b) The king narrates how he established temples and endowed them with the necessary benefits. All these:

*ỉw-w* *n-k* *r-nḥḥ*
DEP-3P for-2MS to-eternity
...being for your for eternity. (pHarris I 9, 5)

(259c) God Amun has decreed:

*pꜣ-nḫw* *n-pꜣ-ḥqꜣ* *ʿ.w.s.* *ỉni* *tꜣ=nb*
DEF.M-protection for-DEF.M-ruler l.h.p. bring.PPA land=QU
The protection is for the ruler, l.h.p., who brought every land.
(oTurin 57001 r° 9)

This use is absent from later material. Already in Late Egyptian and regularly so in Demotic, the usual means of expressing benefactive meaning is with an adverbial sentence with the preposition *r*:

*Late Egyptian*

(260a) Even the Asiatic foreigner finds life in Memphis comfortable:

*sqnn bq n[ḥb]-w-t nḏm r-ḫḫ-[f]*
oil moringa oil lotus-bud-P-F sweet for-throat-3MS
Fragrant oil, moringa oil, and lotus buds are for his throat. (*LEM* 90, 12)

*Demotic*

(260b) The deceased is assured that his body will be wrapped in costly bandages and treated with unguents:

*tšps sgne r-nꜣy-k-ỉf-w šꜥ-pḥ m-mnḫꜣ*
camphor ointment for-POSS.P-2MS-flesh-P until-end as-wrapping
*šps*
costly
Fragrance of the camphor tree and ointment are for your flesh at the end of a costly wrapping. (pRhind I 3, d9)

In Coptic, this construction is retained majorly to express possession, most often for the very specific sense of denoting debt or obligation:

(261a) St Paul argues that God's spirit dwells within the faithful, hence:

*ara=kʲe na-snêu n-s-ero-n=an e-tre-n-ônh*
PTC=now POSS.P.1S-brother.P NEG-3P-to-1P=NEG to-INFL-1P-live
*kata-sarks*
according-flesh
Therefore, my brethren, we do not owe to live according to the flesh.
($^{S}$Rm 8:12)

(261b) The writer of a letter asks the addressee about his sister:

*ešôpe=an e-k-saune ce-un-hneu ara-s*
if=also DEP-2MS-know COMP-PTC-thing to-3MS
*e-mp-u-ka-s a-i etbêt-f*
DEP-NEG.PST-3P-let-3FS to-come because-3MS
*eie te[e]-f ntak hara-s*
then give.IMP-3MS 2MS under-3FS
Also, if you know that she has a debt because of which she is not allowed to come, then pay it, you on her behalf. ($^{L}$*P.KellisCopt.* 72, 19–22)

(261c) Jesus likens the kingdom of heaven to a king who reckoned with his servants:

*ha-u-ine n-uai eret-f e-uon-u-mêše*
PST-3P-bring OBJ-one to-3MS DEP-PTC-IDF.S-multitude
*n-kʲinkʲôr era-f*
of-talent to-3MS
There was brought to him one who owed him many talents. ($^{M}$Mt 18:24)

(261d) Macarius asks a devil:
*mê* *uon-hli* *nta-k* *ero-i* *on*
IR PTC-any of-2MS to-1S also
Do I owe you also anything?
($^{B}$*Life of Macarius of Alexandria* ed. *MG* 25 254, 6)

(261e) Among the creatures not to be eaten by the children of Israel are winged creeping things:
*nê* *ete-uon-fto* *m-p*$^{h}$*at* *erô-u*
DEF$_3$.P REL-PTC-four of-foot to-3P
...which have four feet ... ($^{B}$Lev 11:23)

Other common spatial meanings expressed by adverbial sentences in Later Egyptian were locations 'toward', 'besides', 'with', 'behind', and 'before,' conveyed using various different simple and complex prepositions (the latter consist etymologically of a construction of preposition plus noun to which a pronoun is then attached either via suffix- or infixation):

*Late Egyptian*

(262a) Isis approaches the ferryman Nemty disguised as a frail old woman:
*iw-wꜥ-ḫtm* *šri* *n-nbw* *r-ḏr-t-s*
DEP-IDF.S-ring small of-gold to-hand-F-3FS
...with a small golden ring in her hand. (*LES* 43, 8–9)

(262b) The patient is likened to gods, including:
*pꜣ-nṯr-2* *ꜥꜣ-y* *nty-r-gs-pꜣ-rꜥḥrꜣḫty*
DEF.M-god-2 great-P REL-to-side-DEF.M-N
...the two great gods that are besides Prehorakhty.
(Roccati, *Mag. taur.*, 25, 5)

(262c) The female lover sings:
*ṯ-i* *mdi-k* *mi-pꜣ-ḫꜣntꜣ* *srwd=n-i* *m-ḥrr*
PTC-1S with-2MS like-DEF.M-garden plant.PASS=for-1S in-flower
*m-ḫꜣw=nb*
in-plant=QU
I am with you like the garden planted for me with flowers and every plant. (Mathieu, *Poésie*, pl. 9, 7–8)

(262d) Having cited a law of the pharaoh over inheritance, a claimant says:
*pꜣy-i-nb* *nfr* *ptr* *ṯ-i* *m-bꜣḥ-nꜣ-sr*
POSS.M-1S-lord good look PTC-1S in-presence-DEF.P-magnate
*imi* *ir-y-pꜣ-nfr*
give.IMP make-PASS-DEF.M-good
My good lord, see, I am before the officials; cause that the right thing be done! (*KRI* V 450, 5–6)

(262e) The king describes the new processional barque he had fashioned for the god Amun of Karnak:

*prwr ꜥꜣ m-ẖnw-f n-nbw nfr m-mḥ-w*
shrine great in-inside-3MS of-gold good in-inlay-P
*m-ꜥꜣ-t=nb mꞽ-ḥwtꜥꜣ*
in-precious_stone-F=QU like-sanctuary
*ḥr-w šfy-t m-nbw m-ḥꜣ-t r-pḥw mꜣwḏ*
face-P ram-F in-gold in-front-F to-back adorn.STA
*m-ꞽꜥrꜥ-w-t ẖr-ꜣtf*
with-uraeus-P-F under-crown

A great shrine is inside it of choice gold and with inlays of every precious stone like a sanctuary. Faces of rams of gold are on prow and stern, adorned with uraei underneath the Atef-crown. (pHarris I 7, 6)

*Demotic*

(262f) In the description of the diadem of the cult image of Berenice, it is stated that it consists of two ears of corn and a uraeus between them:

*r-wn-wꜥ-wt (n)-ḏwf ꞽw-f ḏnf ꞽnḥꜣ-s*
DEP-PTC-IDF.S-stalk (of)-papyrus DEP-3MS equal.STA behind-3FS

...with a papyrus stalk of commensurate size behind it.
(Canopus Decree A, 17)

(262g) The deceased is reassured of a goodly afterlife:

*dwꜣ-k wsꞽr ꞽrm-tꜣy-f-sn-t ꞽst*
worship-2MS N and-POSS.F-3MS-sister-F N
*ꞽwꞽ-s-ꞽhtwe-f*
DEP-3FS-beside-3MS

You will worship Osiris and his sister Isis while she is beside him.
(pRhind I 5, d5)

(262h) The barque of the deceased will by rowed by the god Horus Khentyirty:

*ꞽw-nfrtm mꜣy ꞽꞽr-ḏr-t-tꜣy-t-ḥṯ-t*
DEP-N lion to-hand-F-POSS.F-2FS-rope-F

...while Nefertem the lion is next to your prow-rope. (pHarkness 3, 22)

(262i) The depiction of the judgement of the deceased is given and it is said that the goddess Hathor is to be seen in the middle and the balance is in equilibrium:

*ꞽw-ḏḥwty ḥr r-smḥ wnmy nꞽm-s*
DEP-N N to-left right in-3FS

...while Thoth and Horus are to the left and right of her.
(pBN 149 1, 18)

*Coptic*

(262j) A messenger tells the hegemon a story:
*un-u-kui* *m-polis* *sa-p-imnt* *mmo-n* *ere-hen-erpe*
PTC-IDF.S-small of-town side-DEF.M-west in-1P DEP-IDF.P-temple
*nhêt-s*
inside-2FS
*e-s-hicn-u-pygê* *m-mou* *e-ša-u-mute* *ero-s* *ce-phaleks*
DEP-3FS-upon-IDF.S-well of-water DEP-AOR-3P-call OBJ-3FS COMP-N
*hen-u-ma* *e-ša-u-mute* *ero-f* *ce-pubastis*
in-IDF.S-place DEP-AOR-3P-call OBJ-3FS COMP-N
There is a small town west of us with temples within that is upon a spring of water called Phalex in a place called Bubastis.
($^{S}$*Mart. Shnube* [*ASAE* 17, 150, 4–7])

(262k) The psalmist bewails his pitiful situation. Only the Lord listens to him:
*ce-anak* *ti-sebtot* *e-hen-massigks*
for-1S 1S-be_ready.STA to-IDF.P-scourge
*auô* *ta-makhs* *se-m-pa-mêt* *ebal* *n-uaeiš* *nim*
and POSS.F.1S-pain 3FS-in-POSS.M-2MS-face out in-time QUA
...because I am ready for scourges and my pain is ever in front of me.
($^{M}$Ps 37[38]:18[17])

(262l) The Lord shall not pass in silence. A fire will burn before him:
*auô* *u-nok$^{j}$* *n-hatêu* *hm-pe-f-kôte*
and IDF.S-great of-tempest in-POSS.M-3MS-circle
And a great tempest is around him. ($^{S}$Ps 49[50]:3)

Widely encountered are also partitive senses expressed by *m/ỉm-* or *ḫr*:

*Late Egyptian*

(263a) The pharaoh sent out an army of numerous soldiers:
*ỉw-s-t-ḥm-t* *ỉm-sn*
DEP-woman-F-wife-F in-3P
...and among them was a woman. (*LES* 21, 14)

(263b) Ramesses III ends his speech against the accused conspirators by saying that their evil deeds will turn against them, for he is safe now and forever:
*ỉw-ỉ* *ḫr-nꜣ-nsw-y* *mꜣꜥ-ty* *nty-m-bꜣḥ-ỉmnrꜥ*
DEP-1S under-DEF.P-king-P righteous-ADJ REL-in-front-N
*nsw-nṯr-w* *m-bꜣḥ-wsỉr* *ḥqꜣ-ḏ-t*
king-god-P in-front-N ruler-eternity-F
...being among the righteous kings who are before Amun-Re, king of gods, and before Osiris, ruler of eternity. (*KRI* V 351, 9–10)

*Demotic*

(263c) The magician spits out the blood of a dog and says:
*p3y-whr* *nty-ḫn-p3-10* *n-whr* *ntyiw-wn-tw-rinp* *s3-f*
DEM.M-dog REL-in-DEF.M-10 of-dog REL-PTC-with-N son-3MS
*n-ḫe-ṯ-f*
of-body-F-3MS
O that dog among the ten dogs that belong to Anubis, his own son.
(pMag. London&Leiden 19, 3–4)

*Coptic*

(263d) Women watched Jesus' crucifixion from afar:
*e-s-nhêt-u* *nk$^j$i-maria* *t-magdalênê* *auô* *maria*
DEP-3FS-within-3P PVS-N DEF.F-N and N
*ta-p-kui* *n-iakôbos*
POSS.F-DEF.M-small of-N
*auô* *t-mau* *n-iôsê* *mn-salômê*
and DEF.F-mother of-N and-N
...and among them were Mary Magdalene, Mary the mother of James the younger, and the mother of Joseph and Salome. ($^S$Mk 15:40)

(263e) Joshua and Caleb report that although people are already inhabiting the Promised Land, the Israelites should not lose heart:
*p-c(ôi)s=de* *nḫrêi* *nḫêt-en*
DEF.M-lord=yet inside within-1P
For the Lord is among us. ($^B$Nm 14:9)

(263f) Jesus tells his disciples that although people might think that someone who is served is more exalted than he who serves:
*anok* *p-et-i-k$^h$ê* *ḫen-te-ten-mêti* *m-p$^h$-rêti* *m-p$^h$ê*
1S DEF.M-REL-1S-AUX in-POSS.F-2P-midst in-DEF.M-way of-DEF$_3$.M
*et-er-diakôn*
REL-AUX-serve
...still I am among you like the one who serves. ($^B$Lk 22:27)

Comitatives are attested with various prepositions:

*Late Egyptian*

(264a) The prince was bid farewell after being ferried across the Nile:
*[iw]-p3y-f-ṯsm* *ḥnʿ-f*
DEP-POSS.M-3MS-dog with-3MS
...whilst his dog was with him. (*LES* 3, 1–2)

(264b) The sender of a letter urges an old friend to tell him the reason for a falling-out between the two of them, which apparently started from the adressees reaction to something commited by the sender. He begs him to write what the matter would be since:

*nḏm* *rmṯ* *ỉw-f* *ỉrm-pꜣy-f-ỉrw* *(n)-wm* *ỉs*
sweet man DEP-3MS with-POSS.M-3MS-fellow of-eat old
A person is delighted when he is together with an old table companion.
(*KRI* VI 265, 6–7)

*Demotic*

(264c) A woman has sold herself into slavery and states in a document that should someone contest the case, that person will have to pay a fee:

*ỉw-(y)* *mtw-k* *n-bꜣk* *ꜥn* *ḥnꜥ-nꜣy-(y)-ḫrd-w*
DEP-1S with-2MS as-slave again with-POSS.P-1S-child-P
...while I am still with you as a slave with my children.
(pLouvre N 706 v° 2)

(264d) The author of a letter urges the recipient:

*mỉ* *ỉr-w* *ḥrḥ* *r-pꜣy-ḫmḫr* *nty-ỉỉrn-k*
IMP AUX-3P guard OBJ-DEM.M-boy REL-with-2MS
One should take care of that boy who is with you.
(pLouvre E 7855, 11–12)

*Coptic*

(264e) God's human host will fight with courage:

*ce-p-cais* *neme-u*
for-DEF.M-lord with-3P
...for the Lord is with them. ($^{A}$Zec 10:5)

As in earlier phases of the language, the sole notable exception to the rule that spatiality forms the semantic core of adverbial sentences were similes, which in Late Egyptian continued to be expressed by means of the preposition *mỉ*:

*Late Egyptian*

(265a) Viewing the captives of the battle against the Sea Peoples, Ramesses III boasts:

*ṯ-ỉ* *mỉ-bỉk* *m-ḫnw-ḫpt*
PTC-1S like-falcon in-inside-rock_dove
I am like the falcon among the rock doves. (*KRI* V 33, 8)

(265b) The god Amun is praised and it is said that the utterance of his name would be sweet. The text continues:

*sw* *mi-dp-t-ʿnḫ* *sw* *mi-dp-t-ʿq* *n-ẖrd* *dꜣiw*
3MS like-taste-F-life 3MS like-taste-F-bread for-child loincloth
*n-ḥꜣy*
for-naked

It is like the taste of life. It is like the taste of bread for the child and the loincloth for the naked. (*JEA* 14, pl. 5, 12–14)

Although *mi* is still attested in Demotic, it seems to have been largely replaced by *m-qdi* (lit. 'in likeness' also written *n-qd*), appearings as *mi-qd* already in Late Egyptian, a preposition we already observed in the Late Egyptian ex. 265b. Occasionally, other prepositions such as *r-ẖ* (lit. 'according to the manner') are attested:

*Late Egyptian*

(266a) The lady Naunakhte declares in court what she did for her children. She provided them with a household:

*m-ꜣḫ-w-t=nb* *nty* *ṯ-ṯ* *ḥr-ir-f* *n-nꜣ-nty*
in-thing-P-F=QU REL PTC-one PRP-do-3MS for-DEF.P-REL
*mi-qd-w*
like-likeness-3P

...with all things qhich are made for those of their kind. (*KRI* VI 237, 15)

*Demotic*

(266b) The deceased is assured of her sound condition in the afterlife:

*md-t=nb* *mw-ḥs-nṯr*
thing-2FS=QU like-praise-god

All your belongings are like (those of) a one praised by god. (pHarkness 5, 29)

(266c) Moral precepts state:

*lẖ* *ẖn-ʿwy* *m-qdy-pwr* *ẖn-pr-irp*
fool in-house in-likeness-vinegar in-house-wine

A fool in the house is like vinegar in a wine cellar. (Onkhsheshonqy 22, 13)

(266d) Since Pharaoh wants him to aks for a longer life time for him and Meryre knows that this means a shorter life time for in return:

*rrmi-f* *iw-f* *n-qd-mw*
cry.PST-3MS DEP-3MS in-likeness-water

He cried very tearfully. (pVandier 2, 1)

(266e) A text with 'ethnographic descriptions' of various peoples states of one them:

| | | |
|---|---|---|
| *pꜣy-w-hp* | *tꜣy-w-qs-t* | *r-ẖ-nꜣ-mdy-w* |
| POSS.M-3P-law | POSS.F-3P-burial-F | to-way-DEF.P-N-P |

Their laws and their burial(-custom)s are like those of the Medes.
(pFlorence PSI D 88, 7 [*Enchoria* 32])

In both Late Egyptian and Demotic, an equative preposition + interrogative pronoun can be used for questions of inquiring nature or quality ('... is like what?'):

*Late Egyptian*

(267a) Before all else, the author of a letter demands to know:

| | |
|---|---|
| *ṯ-k* | *mi-iḫ* |
| PTC-2MS | like-WH |

How are you? (*KRI* I 239, 4)

*Demotic*

(267b) The unsavoury habits of the harpist are narrated and the narrator poses the question:

| | | |
|---|---|---|
| *pꜣy-f-šm* | *r-hrwṯ* | *m-qdy-iḫ* |
| POSS.M-3MS-walk | to-feast | in-likeness-WH |

How does he go to the feast? (*lit.* His walking to the feast is like what?)
(Depraved Harpist 2, 5)

Although Coptic possesses comparative prepositions such as *kata-* or *m-p-smot* 'like', it more often employs verbs such as SB*ini* 'be like' or a construction with the Stative form of the verb 'be' followed by an expression 'in the manner' to express comparative states of affairs:

*Coptic*

(268a) The neighbours of a man whom Jesus healed of his blindness discuss whether it is really he, as some say, or as is stated by others:

| | | | | |
|---|---|---|---|---|
| *mmon* | *alla* | *e-f-ini* | *mmof* | S |
| no | but | ST-3MS-liken.STA | OBJ-3MS | |
| | | *e-f-ini* | *mmof* | L |
| | | ST-3MS-liken.STA | OBJ-3MS | |
| *mmon* | *alla* | *a-f-oni* | *mmof* | B |
| no | but | ST-3MS-liken.STA | OBJ-3MS | |

'No, but he is like him'. (SLBJn 9:9)

(268b) God expresses his disappointment over his chosen flock and accuses them:
*pe-tn-nae=de* *a-f-e* *n-t-ẖe* *n-kloole*
POSS.M-2P-mercy=yet ST-3MS-be.STA in-DEF.F-way of-cloud
*m-p-no* *hitaue*
of-DEF.M-hour dawn
*au* *n-t-ẖe* *n-u-iôte* *e-ẖare-s-heie* *n-ẖôrp*
and in-DEF.F-way of-IDF.S-dew DEP-AOR-3FS-fall in-morning
Your mercy is like a morning cloud and like dew falling in the morning.
($^{A}$Hos 6:4)

Patterns with a predicatively used adverbial phrase *m-p$^h$-rêti* 'in the manner (of)' are attested only in Bohairic. However, this construction as well displays the insertion of an additional verb *ire* 'be' in the Stative, as in the ex. 269b below:

*Coptic*

(269a) God expresses his disappointment over his chosen flock and accuses them:
*pe-ten-nai=de* *e-f-m-p$^h$-rêti* *n-u-k$^j$êpi* *nte-hanatoui*
POSS.M-2P-mercy=yet ST-3MS-in-DEF.M-way of-IDF.S-cloud of-dawn
*nem-m-p$^h$-rêti* *n-u-iôti* *e-s-moši* *n-šôrp*
and-in-DEF.M-way of-IDF.S-dew DEP-3FS-walk in-morning
Your mercy is like a morning cloud and like dew falling in the morning.
($^{B}$Hos 6:4)

(269b) Jesus was taken up to heaven and out of sight of the disciples:
*na-u-oi=de* *m-p$^h$-rêti* *e-na-u-iorem* *uai* *ube-uai*
PRT-3P-be.STA=yet in-DEF.M-way DEP-PRT-3P-stare one against-one
*mmô-u* *e-f-moši* *ehrêi* *e-t-p$^h$e*
in-3P DEP-3MS-walk up to-DEF.F-heaven
But they seemed to be gazing, one against the other, whilst he ascended up to heaven. ($^{B}$Acts 1:10)

(269c) Searching for young men in possession of blood of saints, the protagonist of a story went to a palace:
*a-f-cimi* *m-pi-ẖel-širi* *2* *e-u-hemsi*
PST-3MS-find OBJ-DEF$_2$.M-youth 2 DEP-3P-sit
*e-u-m-p$^h$-rêti* *hôs* *e-u-sobti* *n-han-p$^h$aẖri*
DEP-3P-in-DEF.M-way like DEP-3P-prepare OBJ-IDF.P-drug
And he found the two youths sitting and seemingly preparing medicaments.
($^{B}$Cyril of Alexandria, *Miracles of the Three Youth* [de Vis II 169, 8–9])

As the last example above shows, *m-p$^{h}$-rêti* acquired the special meaning of expressing what 'seems to be'. Some of the old genuine adverbs continued to be used as predicates of Later Egyptian adverbial sentences. Thus, e.g., the interrogative *ṯn(ỉ)* > $^{S}$*tôn* 'where?' survived all the way down to Coptic:

*Late Egyptian*

(270a) A wisdom text advises against trying to control an efficient mistress of the house:

| | | | |
|---|---|---|---|
| *mỉr-ḏd=n-s* | *sw* | *tnw* | *ỉ-ỉnỉ=n-n* |
| NEG.IMP-say=to-3FS | 3MS | WH | IMP-bring=to-1P |

Do not tell her: 'Where is it? Go get it!' (Ani B 22, 4)

*Demotic*

(270b) The queen of the Amazons is informed about the retreat of the Indians and wants to know:

| | |
|---|---|
| *st* | *n-tn* |
| 3P | ADV-WH |

Where are they? (Amazons A2 x+17)

*Coptic*

(270c) God asks Cain:

| | | |
|---|---|---|
| *a-f-t$^{h}$ôn* | *abel* | *pe-k-son* |
| ST-3MS-WH | N | POSS.M-2MS-brother |

Where is your brother Abel? ($^{B}$Gn 4:9)

However, various new patterns were created whilst old ones were replaced or modified to such an extent that the perception of their etymological origin was gradually lost. For example, the old adverb *dy* 'there', although still found in Coptic as *tai* or *tê*, was by then mostly replaced by $^{SB}$*mmau*:

*Coptic*

(271) When St Paul and Silas came to Derbe and Lystra:

| | | |
|---|---|---|
| *ne-un-u-mathêtês=de* | *mmau* | *e-pe-f-ran=pe* |
| PRT-PTC-IDF.S-disciple=yet | there | DEP-POSS.M-3MS-name=COP.M |
| *timotheos* | | |
| N | | |

...there was a certain disciple named Timothy. ($^{S}$Acts 16:1)

An example of a newly created expression is the novel preposition *r-ỉwd* > *ỉwṯ-* > *ute-* 'between,' which in adverbial sentences mostly denotes location between entities, but sometimes also temporal distance between events:

*Late Egyptian*

(272a) The king has built a residence named 'Great of Strength':
*sw* *r-ỉwd-ḏꜣhi* *r-tꜣmry*
3MS to-parting-Syria from-Egypt
It is between southern Syria and Egypt. (*LEM* 12, 8)

(272b) The author of a letter apologises:
*ỉ-ỉr-ỉ-hꜣb=n-k* *ỉw-20* *n-hrw* *r-ỉwd-f*
ST-AUX-1S-send=for-2MS DEP-20 of-day to-parting-3MS
It is twenty days since I have written to you. (pDeM 8 r° 9)

*Demotic*

(272c) The demarcation lines of a piece of real estate are noted down according to the cardinal points. On each of its sides there is another building:
*ỉw-pꜣ-ḫr* *ỉwt-w*
DEP-DEF.M-street between-3P
...while the street is between them. (pCG 50058, 5 & 6)

*Coptic*

(272d) After narrating a parable, St Cyril urges the audience to live in peace with one another and not to go to sleep at night:
*ere-u-ariki* *utô-f* *nem-uai*
DEP-IDF.S-reproach between-3MS and-one
...while there is a reproach between him and someone else.
($^{\mathrm{B}}$Cyril, *De Hora Mortis* [*MMAF* IV.1 187, 13–14 collated])

As can be observed from the above examples, the use of adverbial sentences is in Coptic generally limited to stative locative semantics with occasional residual uses in other domains. Apparently, this mirrors a narrowing of the functional domain of adverbial sentences. If adverbials of other semantic spheres are involved, Coptic either uses the constructions with the Stative of a verb 'to be' such as *šoop* or *o* as above or employs nominal sentence patterns, as in the following examples below (see now Müller 2015a: 89–118):

(273a) The disciples meet a man at Emmaus whom they do not recognise as Jesus and tell him all that had occurred in Jerusalem. They finish their story with the following words:
*p-meh-šomnt* *n-hou=pe* *pou* *ci-nt-a-nai* *šôpe*
the-ORD-3 of-day=COP.M today since-PST-DEM.P happen
Today is the third day since all this happened. ($^{\mathrm{S}}$Lk 24:21)

(273b) Judah approaches his brother Joseph, pleading to be heard:
*ce-nt$^h$ok=pe* *menensa-pharaô*
COMP-2MS=COP.M after-pharaoh
...for you are right after the pharaoh. ($^B$Gn 44:18)

(273c) The Egyptians notice that the Hebrew women still give birth to male children. As they accuse the midwives, the latter midwives tell Pharaoh why they were not able to kill the male offspring of the Hebrews at birth:
*m-p$^h$-rêti=an* *n-ni-hiomi* *nte-k$^h$êmi* *ne*
in-DEF.M-way=NEG of-DEF$_2$.P-women.P of-Egypt COP.P
*ni-hiomi* *nte-ni-hevreos*
DEF$_2$.P-women.P of-DEF$_2$.P-Hebrew
The Hebrew women are unlike the Egyptian women. ($^B$Ex 1:19)

(273d) John the Little prays to the Lord quoting Hb 13:8:
*iê(su)s* *p-kh(risto)s* *nt$^h$ok* *nsaf* *nt$^h$ok* *mp$^h$ou* *on* *pe*
N DEF.M-Christ 2MS yesterday 2MS today again PTC
*nt$^h$ok* *on* *pe* *ša-eneh*
2MS again PTC until-eternity
Jesus Christ; you were yesterday and you are also today, and you will be also for eternity. ($^B$Zachary of Sakha, *Vita John Kolobos* §63 [Mikhail and Vivian 176, 31–32])

(273e) Pisenthius explains to his disciple why he had denied blessing a certain man who came with his sick child. He had been told that he would denigrate a poor man:
*uoh* *pe-f-14* *n-ehou=pe* *mp$^h$ou* *iscen*
and POSS.M-3MS-14 of-day=COP.M today since
*eta-f-er-diabalin* *mmo-f*
TMP-3MS-AUX-denigrate OBJ-3MS
Today it is a fortnight since he denigrated him.
($^B$Moses of Quft, *Vita Pisenthius*, 115, 13–116, 1 [collated])

Finally, despite the fact that the expression of locus still constitutes the basic semantic function of Later Egyptian adverbial sentences, e.g., the expression of 'location' between situations in time noted for *r-iwd* above, a certain degree of deviation from a strictly spatial expression can be observed. Like Earlier Egyptian, Later Egyptian made use of a number of different semantic extensions of the core locative sense of adverbial sentences to convey more abstract notions that were only metaphorically connected to the concrete idea of position in space. It will be seen below that many of these extensions were the heirs of the earlier phases, whereas others were new, and some old patterns would disappear over the almost three thousand years of language history encompassed by Late Egyptian, Demotic, and Coptic.

### 3.2.2 Temporal and information structure operators

A characteristic feature of the Egyptian language from the mid-second millennium BCE onwards is the gradual but notable increase in the morphological marking of syntactic and semantic-pragmatic functions. Part of this development was the rise of a series of grammaticalised expressions that in Egyptological parlance are often called 'converters,' but for which a better term is 'operator,' used in combination with verbal and non-verbal predication types. Their function was, broadly speaking, to define and modify the temporal status and information structure of the predicate. Some of these operators were direct descendants of Earlier Egyptian expressions that had had a closely related function; such as the marker of anteriority *wn* (Coptic $^{S}$*ne*/$^{B}$*na*), that represented a functionally more restricted version of the earlier multi-faceted auxiliary *wn/wnn* (see 3.1.3.1.2). Others were new elements with old functions, e.g., the Late Egyptian-Demotic 'Second Tense' prefix *ꞽꞽr* and its later Coptic equivalents *e-* and *(e)nt-/et-*, used to modify the information structure of the following predication in a similar manner as the Earlier Egyptian geminating *sḏm-f* and – partially – the auxiliary *wn/wnn*. Other operators still were old elements whose function(s) had been completely altered over time, e.g. the prefix *ꞽw/ꞽrꞽ* (Coptic *e-/ere-*) of the so-called 'Future III' conjugation, or the adjunct-marker *ꞽw* that diachronically went back to the similar Earlier Egyptian auxiliary (see 3.1.3.1.1). The grammaticalisation of these and other operators was part of the gradual change undergone by the Egyptian language towards a more analytic system of grammatical marking based on functional operators and later prefixes. This development was largely motivated by the slow demise of the suffix conjugation as the fundamental category of inflection in the verbal system and the strategy of expressing TAM by means of modifications of the verbal root. However, the creation of these operators had repercussions on the entire grammatical system, including the adverbial sentence, which now could be combined with the various operators as well.

#### 3.2.2.1 Late Egyptian

Late Egyptian adverbial sentences could be marked for future by prefixing the initial operator *ꞽw/ꞽrꞽ* of the so-called Future III; many examples occur in curses and threat-formulae (for the pattern, see Loprieno 1994: 90–91 & 94; see also Grossman & Polis 2014; Grossman, Lescuyer & Polis 2014 and for analogical patterns see Winand 1996):

(274a) A curse on a donation stela of Osorkon III from Tehne/Akoris:

*ỉr* *pꜣ-nty-ỉw-f* *mnmn* *tꜣ-wḏ* *ỉw-f* *n-šꜥd*
PTC DEF.M-REL-FUT-3MS move DEF.F-stela FUT-3MS for-sword
*n-ỉmnrꜥ*
of-N
*ỉw-f* *n-hh* *n-ḥm* *n-sḫmt*
FUT-3MS for-fire of-majesty of-N
Whoever will move the stela, he will be to the sword of Amun-Ra and to the fire of the majesty of Sakhmet. (Jansen-Winkeln, *IdS* II, 296, 7–8)

(274b) The author of a letter tells of a group of youths destined to be priests but seized by others, claiming:

*ỉw-w* *r-wꜥ-w*
FUT-3P to-soldier-P
They will be soldiers. (*LEM* 5, 6)

(274c) Describing his victory over his Libyan foes, King Merenptah has the Libyans say about their leader:

*ỉr-bꜣnrꜥmrỉmn* *msꜣ-ms-w-f*
FUT-N after-child-P-3MS
Baenra-Meryamun (i.e. Merenptah) will be after his children. (*KRI* IV 15, 5)

(274d) It is said of anyone who shall neglect a decree:

*ỉrỉ-wsỉr* *msꜣ-f* *ỉw-ỉst* *msꜣ-ḥm-t-f* *ỉw-ḥr*
FUT-N after-3MS DEP-N after-wife-F-3MS DEP-N
*msꜣ-ẖrd-w-f*
after-child-P-3MS
Osiris will pursue (lit. 'be after') him, Isis will pursue his wife, and Horus will pursue his children. (*KRI* I 70, 3–4)

(274e) A woman has to take the following oath:

*bn-ỉw-ỉ* *r-ẖnw* *n-sšqd* *ỉmnḥtp* *mrꜥ*
NEG-FUT-1S to-inside of-painter N also
I as well shall not be inside (the house) of the painter Amenhotep. (*KRI* VI 431, 8)

Conversely, adverbial sentences could be assigned past reference by means of the anterior marker *wn*:

(275a) A note in a court protocol following a list of names of suspected tomb robbers given by a certain herdsman:

*wn-w* *m-tꜣy-f-ṯt* *ỉṯꜣ-w*
PST-3P in-POSS.M-3MS-gang thief-P
They were in his gang of thieves. (*KRI* VI 769, 12)

(275b) An accusation concerning a man brought before magistrates investigating tomb robberies:

*wn-f* *m-pꜣ-ḫr* *ḥnꜥ-pꜣ-pr* *n-sṯꜣ*
PST-3MS in-DEF.M-tomb and-DEF.M-house of-draw
He has been in the tomb and in the shrine. (*KRI* VI 823, 12)

(275c) A witness says about the activities of his father suspected of involvement in tomb robbery:

*wn-pꜣy-i-it=im* *n-mꜣꜥ-t* *iw-i* *m-ꜥḏd* *šri*
PST-POSS.M-1S-father=there in-truth-F DEP-1S as-boy small
My father was indeed there whilst I am merely a young boy.
(*KRI* VI 807, 6–7)

(275d) During the examination of a tomb in a dispute, a suspect is asked:

*n* *wn-k* *m-s-t=[tn]*
IP PST-2MS in-place-F=DEM.F
Have you been in there? (*KRI* V 480, 2–3)

(275e) The recipient of a letter is told not to worry about a charioteer:

*wn-f=dy* *irm-n* *m-tꜣmḫrpt*
PST-3S=here with-1P in-N
He was with us here in Tamekherpe. (*LEM* 7, 8–9)

(275f) Disguised as a beautiful woman, Isis tells the lecherous Seth about her supposed background:

*ir* *ink* *wn-i* *m-ḥm* *mdꜣy-wꜥ-mni-iḥ-w*
PTC 1S PST-1S as-wife with-IDF.S-herdsman-cow-P
As for me, I was the wife of a herdsman of cattle. (*LES* 44, 16–45, 1)

The subject pronoun clitisises to the marker *wn*. The forms for pronominal subject are as follows:

**Tab. I.10:** Late Egyptian forms of personal pronouns attached to the anterior marker *wn* (common forms only).

<table>
<tr><th></th><th>Singular</th><th>Plural</th></tr>
<tr><td>1C</td><td>wn-i</td><td>wn-n</td></tr>
<tr><td>2M</td><td>wn-k</td><td rowspan="2">wn-tn</td></tr>
<tr><td>2F</td><td>wn-ṯ</td></tr>
<tr><td>3M</td><td>wn-f</td><td rowspan="2">wn-sn/-w</td></tr>
<tr><td>3F</td><td>wn-s</td></tr>
</table>

There does not seem to be any example of *wn* introducing adverbial sentences with indefinite subjects (see 1.2.1). It is therefore not clear whether in Late Egyptian this syntactic marking pattern was compatible with the past operator *wn*, i.e. whether such a sentence would have acquired the form *$wn_{\text{PST}}$ $wn_{\text{PTC}}$-N (as later in Coptic, see below), or rather the form *$wn_{\text{PST}}$-*wꜥ*-N. The past reference of the adverbial sentence could also be conveyed by the emergent Temporalis operator *mḏr/nḏr/mdỉ* (Coptic *nter-*):

(276a) A priest tells a stable-master that a promissory note is no longer in his possession:
*nḏr-wn-s* *m-ḏr-t-ḥwy* *sfḫ(-ỉ)=sw*
since-PST-3FS in-hand-F-N loose[-1S]=3MS
...since it was with Haja and I negotiated it. (*KRI* III 252, 8–9)

(276b) A husband addresses his deceased wife who still seems to haunt him:
*ỉr-mḏr-wn-ỉ* *mꜥ-ṯ* *m-hꜣy* *r-šꜣꜥ-pꜣ-hrw* *ỉrỉ-ỉ*
ST-since-PST-1S with-2FS as-husband to-until-DEF.M-day do-1S
*ỉḫ* *r-ṯ* *pꜣ-ỉrỉ-ỉ-ḥꜣp*
WH to-2FS DEF.M-do-1S-hide
From the time I was living with you as a husband until today, what have I done against you that I should have to conceal it?
(pLeiden I 371, 3–4)

(276c) The teacher warns his pupil of laziness, pointing out that he himself used to be lazy in his youth:
*ỉw-ptr-k* *ỉm-ỉ* *r-ḥꜥ-ỉ* *mḏr-wn-ỉ* *m-ḏꜣm-k*
DEP-see-2MS OBJ-1S to-self-1S since-PST-1S as-youth-2MS
And you have an impression of myself when I was in your age.
(*LEM* 65, 13–14)

(276d) The addressee is asked to send something that the author had probably ordered previously:
*mdỉ-wn-ỉ* *ỉm*
since-PST-1S there
...when I was there. (pBM 75019+10302 v° 3)

(276e) The sender of a missive wants to understand what the matter with his old friend is but acknowledges:
*yꜣ* *šꜣꜥ-ỉw-ỉ* *m-šrỉ* *rꜥ-pꜣ-hrw* *ỉw-ỉ* *ỉrm-k*
PTC from-DEP-1S as-child until-DEF.M-day DEP-1S with-2MS
*ḫr* *bw-ỉr-ỉ-ꜥmꜣ* *pꜣy-k-qꜣỉ*
PTC NEG.AOR-AUX-1S-understand POSS.M-2MS-form
Indeed, ever since I was a child even until today, when I am with you, I cannot fathom your nature. (*KRI* VI 266, 2–3)

In Late Egyptian verbal sentences could be turned into so-called Second Tenses by prefixing the operator *ỉỉr*. This signalled a change in the canonical information structure of the verbal predicate and the pragmatic elevation of a subsequent adverbial adjunct. It was seen above (3.1.3.1.2) that in Earlier Egyptian, the auxiliary *wn/wnn* was on occasion used in adverbial sentences to give special 'highlighting' to the predicate expression. In Late Egyptian, similar examples with *ỉỉr* + adverbial sentence are very rare, although the following example seems to provide an instance of this construction (this will be discussed in detail in a forthcoming study by Jean Winand, who argues that it originated in a form of sub-standard Late Egyptian):

(277) A reply of a suspected thief to his interrogators concerning certain vessels:

| | | | | | |
|---|---|---|---|---|---|
| *ꜥḏꜣ* | *ỉỉr* | *nꜣ-ṯbw* | *r-pꜣy-ḥḏ* | *ꜥꜣ* | *ỉ-ḏd-ỉ=n-tn* |
| wrong | ST | DEF.P-vessel | to-DEM.M-silver | great | REL-say-1S=to-2P |
| *ꜥn* | | | | | |
| again | | | | | |

False! The vessels belong *to the main treasury*, as I told you already.
(*KRI* VI 781, 5–6)

The following examples with *ỉw* resemble the later Coptic adverbial sentence Second Tenses marked with the operator *e-*:

(278a) King Ramesses II tells that he sent his troops and magistrates to welcome a Hittite princess and her entourage at the border:

| | | | | |
|---|---|---|---|---|
| *ꜥḥꜥ-n* | *wꜣwꜣ-n* | *ḥm-f* | *sḥ* | *ḥnꜥ-ỉb-f* |
| AUX-PST | think-PST | majesty-3MS | plan | with-heart-3MS |
| *m-ḏd-ỉw-w* | *mỉ-m* | | | |
| as-saying-PTC-3P | like-WH | | | |

Then his majesty pondered: 'How are they?' (*KRI* II 249, 1)

(278b) Moral precepts demand accuracy from scribes:

| | | | | | |
|---|---|---|---|---|---|
| *ỉw-f* | *n-ỉḫ* | *swḥ* | *mk* | *ỉw-f* | *sḥꜣ* |
| PTC-3MS | for-WH | apron | quality | DEP-3MS | betray |
| *m-bꜣḥ-pꜣ-nṯr* | | | | | |
| in presence-DEF.M-god | | | | | |

What good is an apron of *miku*-quality when he (his wearer) behaves like a traitor in the presence of god? (Amenemope 18, 10–11)

However, as we saw above, unlike Later Egyptian (see 3.2.1), Earlier Egyptian adverbial sentences with interrogative predicates are usually introduced by *ỉw* (1.1), which cannot be analysed as the harbinger of the later Coptic *e-*. The text in ex. 278a displays numerous features of Traditional Egyptian, which arouses suspicions of grammatical archaism. The *iw* in the examples cited is unlikely to represent the later *e-*. It would thus seem that the use of Second Tenses in adverbial sentences was not yet as standard in Late Egyptian as it was to become in Demotic and Coptic, although ex. 277 may anticipate this later grammatical pattern.

Other than with operators of tempus and information structure, in Late Egyptian, adverbial sentences could appear also after modal 'initial particles' seen already in Earlier Egyptian; the example below shows the use of *hꜣnꜣ*, the later version of Earlier Egyptian *ḥꜣ* 'would that':

(279) The pharaoh exclaims in battle:

| | | | | | |
|---|---|---|---|---|---|
| *wꜣḥ-kꜣ* | *n-imn* | *itm* | *hꜣnꜣ* | *ṯ-i* | *ḥr-kmt* |
| endure-soul | of-N | N | PTC | PTC-1S | on-Egypt |

By Amun and Atum, would that I were in Egypt. (*KRI* II 61, 4)

### 3.2.2.2 Demotic

No examples of adverbial sentences marked for future tense appear to be attested in Demotic. Instead, it seems that these constructions were rather embedded as adjuncts of tense-marked main clauses, a pattern later common in Coptic:

(280) An old priest offers to read to Setne two magical formulae by the god of wisdom Thoth himself:

| | | | | |
|---|---|---|---|---|
| *iw-k* | *ꜥš-pꜣ-hp* | *mḥ-2* | *iw-f* | *ḫpr* |
| DEP-2MS | read-DEF.M-formula | ORD-2 | FUT | 3MS-happen |
| *iw-k* | *ḫn-imnṯ* | | | |
| DEP-2MS | in-west | | | |
| *iw-k* | *n-pꜣy-k-gy* | *ḥr-pꜣ-tꜣ* | *ꜥn* | |
| DEP-2MS | in-POSS.M.2MS-form | on-DEF.M-land | still | |

If you read the second formula, you will be in the netherworld, although you are in your appearance still upon earth. (Setne I 3, 14)

By contrast, adverbial sentences marked as past (so-called Imperfect or Preterite) by introducing them with the element *wnnꜣw* (or some of its graphemic variants) are common even though the majority of examples stems from subordinate clauses:

(281a) A person overhears a conversation on the plot to kill the pharaoh:

| | | | | |
|---|---|---|---|---|
| *wn-wꜥ-rmt* | *na-sꜣ-pr* | *ḥr-tbn* | *wꜥ-mꜣꜥ* | |
| PRT.REL-IDF.S-man | POSS.P-3P-body(-F)-house | PRP-close | IDF.S-place | |
| *iw-f* | *sḏm* | *r(?)-ḫrw-w* | *n-pꜣ-s* | 2 |
| DEP-3MS | hear | to voice-P | of-DEF.M-man | 2 |

Close to a place(?) there was a man of the household who could hear the voices of the two men. (Onkhsheshonqy 2, x+17)

(281b) The beginning of a parable by the small dog-ape:

*rhwnnꜣw-wn-wnš 2 ḥr-pꜣ-tw rỉw-w šnb mšs*
PRT-PTC-jackal 2 on-DEF.M-mountain DEP-3P join.STA very
Upon the mountain were two jackals very attached to each other.
(Myth of the Sun's Eye 16, 15)

(281c) A man takes an obligation in case he intends to build a house next to that of his fellow:

*ỉw-bnỉw-y dy-šm ḫt r-ḫn nỉm-s*
DEP-NEG.FUT-1S give-send timber to-inside in-3FS
*msꜣ-nꜣ-ḫt-w n-pꜣ-r*
after-DEF.P-timber-P of-DEF.M-door
*ỉw-wnnꜣw ḫn-s ḥꜣ-t-pꜣ-hrw*
REL-PRT in-3FS front-F-DEF.M-day
...while I will not add any timber in it (the neighbour's wall) besides the timbers of the door that have been in it already today. (pBM 10524, 3)

As in the earlier stages of the language, the subject pronoun clitisises to the marker *wnnꜣw* yet most often with the help of a graphemic addition in form of *ỉw*, thus *wnnꜣwỉw-*. Since the outcome of this will be *ne-* (or *na-*) only in Coptic, the cluster of consonants shown in the common transcription will have been probably not equalled by as many consonants in pronouncation. The forms for pronominal subject are as follows:

**Tab. I.11:** Demotic forms of personal pronouns attached to the anterior marker *wn* (common forms only)

| | Singular | Plural |
|---|---|---|
| 1C | *wnnꜣwỉw-ỉ* | *wnnꜣwỉw-n* |
| 2M | *wnnꜣwỉw-k* | *wnnꜣwỉw -tn* |
| 2F | *wnnꜣwỉw-ṯ* | |
| 3M | *wnnꜣwỉw-f* | *wnnꜣwỉw -sn/-w* |
| 3F | *wnnꜣwỉw-s* | |

The predicate of an adverbial sentence could be pragmatically highlighted through the use of the Second Tense operator *ỉỉr*. This construction is rather more frequent in Demotic than in Late Egyptian, but not yet as widespread as in Coptic:

(282a) The great-grandfather of the old man had told his grandfather that:

*ꞽꞽr-nꜣ-ʿwy-w* *n-ḥtp* *n-ꞽhwret* *ꞽrm-mrꞽbptḥ* *pꜣy-s-šr*
ST-DEF.P-place-P of-rest of-N and-N POSS.M-3FS-son
*ḥr-tw-n-pꜣ-qḥ* *rsy* *n-pꜣ-ʿwy*
at-bosom-of-DEF.M-corner southern of-DEF.M-house
*n-pꜣ-[ḥry-mšš]*
of-DEF.M-[chief-police]

The resting places of Ahweret and her son Merib are in the southern corner of the house of the [chief of the police]. (Setne I 6, 13)

(282b) The small dog-ape explains why the sun-god is called ‘cat’:

*ꞽꞽr-f* *n-ḥr* *n-ꞽmy-t*
ST-3MS as-face of-cat-F

He has the face of a cat. (Myth of the Sun’s Eye 7, 21–22)

(282c) Description of the diadem of the cult image of Berenice, daughter of Ptolemy III Euergetes:

*ꞽꞽr-f* *n-ẖms-2* *r-wn-wʿ-t-ʿrʿy* *n-tꜣy-w-mtry-t*
ST-3MS as-ear-2 DEP-PTC-IDF.S-F-uraeus in-POSS.F-3P-midst-F
*r-wn-wʿ-wt* *(n)-ḏwf* *ꞽw-f* *ḏnf* *ꞽnḥꜣ-s*
DEP-PTC-IDF.S-stalk (of)-papyrus DEP-3MS equal.STA behind-3FS

It should consist *of two ears of corn*, there being a uraeus between them, a papyrus stalk of commensurate size behind it ....
(Canopus Decree A, 17)

(282d) As above:

*ꞽꞽr-w* *ꞽw-ꞽꞽr-f* *n-ẖms-2* *r-wn-wʿ-t-ʿrʿy*
ST-3P to-do-3MS as-ear-2 DEP-PTC-IDF.S-F-uraeus
*n-tꜣy-w-mtry-t*
in-POSS.F-3P-midst-F
*r-wʿ-wt* *n-ḏwf* *ꞽw-f-snḥ* *nḥꜣ-s*
DEP-Ø-IDF.S-stalk of-papyrus DEP-3MS-bound behind-3FS

They should make it *of two ears of corn*, there being a uraeus between them, a papyrus (scepter) of similar size being bound behind it...
(Canopus Decree B, 62–63)

It is worth observing that the version of the text in the last example makes use of the verbal form *ꞽꞽr-w ꞽꞽr-f* instead of *ꞽꞽr* + subject + prepositional phrase, as in the version cited in ex. 282c.

#### 3.2.2.3 Coptic

Surprisingly, no examples of adverbial sentences marked as future by means of the standard Coptic future markers, the infix *-na-* and the prefix *e-/ere-*, seem to be attested. Instead, verbal patterns with the auxiliary [S]*šôpe*/[B]*šôpi* appear to have been used as a suppletive pattern:

(283a) John assures his addressees that if they listen from the beginning:
*ntôtn hôt-têutn tetn-(n)a-šôpe hm-p-šêre auô hm-p-iôt*
2P self-2P 2P-FUT-be in-DEF.M-son and in-DEF.M-father
...you yourselves shall be in the son and in the father. ([S]1Jn 2:24)

(283b) The bishop of Shmun writes to his flock that is has been reported to him that a theft was commited in a woman's house. Whoever the culprit, he says, whether man or woman, stranger or native:
*efe-šôpe ha-p-sahu m-p-nomos mn-ne-prophêtês*
OPT.3MS-be under-DEF.M-curse of-DEF.M-law and-DEF.P-prophet
... he shall be under the curse of the law and the prophets.
([S]Letter of Bishop of Shmun ed. *Cat. Ryl.* 267)

(283c) Judas narrates to Paul what happened during Jesus' visit in hell. When Judas begged him to free him from Hell, Jesus retorts him sharply that he would be here on his own doing:
*etbe-pai eke-šôpe hn-n-tartaros ša-pe-hou*
because-DEM.M OPT.2MS-be in-DEF.P-N until-DEF.M-day
*m-p-hap*
of-DEF.M-law
*etere-p-cois na-ti-hap ero-k*
REL-DEF.M-lord FUT-give-law to-2MS
Therefore you will be in the Tartarus until the day of judgement that the Lord will judge you. ([S]*Acts of Andrew & Paul* [Jacques 202, 127–128])

(283d) God tells reluctant Moses that his brother Aaron shall be by his side and speak to the people:
*f-ḫôpe ne-k n-paikʲe*
3MS-be for-2MS as-mouth
He is the mouth for you. ([A]Ex 4:16)

(283e) Jesus argues that should a man drink from a well of water, he will thirst again:
*alla p-mau et-i-na-tee-f ne-f*
but DEF.M-water REL-1S-FUT-give-3MS for-3MS
*f-na-šôpe hrêi nhêt-f n-u-pêgê m-mau*
3MS-FUT-be down inside-3MS as-IDF.S-spring of-water
*e-f-fôkʲe ahrêi auô ônh ša-anêhe*
DEP-3MS-spring up and life to-eternity
...but the water that I shall give to him shall be in a well of water springing up into everlasting life. ([L]Jn 4:14)

(283f) Paul tells Elymas the sorcerer:

*tenu hi t-k$^{j}$ic m-p-c(oi)s ne-šope ehrêi ecô-k*
now lo DEF.F-hand of-DEF.M-lord FUT-be down upon-2MS
And now, behold: the hand of the Lord shall be upon you. ($^{M}$Acts 13:11)

(283g) Jesus warns that the angels of the Son of Man will cast all offenders into the outer darkness:

*p-me ete-p-limi ne-šôpi mmeu*
DEF.M-place REL-DEF.M-weeping FUT-happen there
*mn-pe-skêlkel n-ne-abh*
and-DEF.M-gnashing of-DEF.P-tooth
...where there will be weeping and gnashing of teeth. ($^{F}$Mt 13:42)

(283h) The Lord gives his promise to Joshua that from this day on he will magnify him in front of his people:

*kata-p$^{h}$-rêti et-a-i-šôpi nem-môusês*
like-DEF.M-way REL-PST-1S-happen with-N
*pai-rêti ti-na-šôpi nema-k hô-k*
DEM.M-way 1S-FUT-happen with-2MS self-2MS
As I was with Moses, so I will be with you also. ($^{B}$Jo 3:7 [Lagarde])

As can be seen from the examples presented, the most of them have a future reference. But as shown by the first clause of ex. 283g, a past marking is possible as well. In addition, examples with the usual initial preterite marker $^{SL}$*ne(re)-*/$^{AMFB}$*na(re)-* are common (Note that Lycopolitain varies between *ne(re)-* and *na(-re)-*):

(284a) Having been baptised by John, Jesus was taken to the desert by the Holy Ghost:

*auô ne-f-hn-t-erêmos pe n-hme n-hou e-f-piraze*
and PRT-3MS-in-DEF.F-desert PTC for-40 of-day DEP-3MS-tempt
*mmo-f ebol hitm-p-satanas*
OBJ-3MS out by-DEF.M-satan
*auô ne-f-mn-n-thêrion ere-n-aggelos diakonei na-f*
and PRT-3MS-with-DEF.P-beast DEP-DEF.P-angels minister for-3MS
And he was in the desert for forty days while being tempted by Satan.
And he was with the wild beasts while the angels ministered unto him.
($^{S}$Mk 1:13)

(284b) The opening words of a story about a monk:

*ne-un-u-son hn-u-heneet*
PRT-PTC-IDF.S-brother in-IDF.S-monastery
There was a brother in a monastery. ($^{S}$*AP* Chaîne 33, 22)

(284c) The crucifixion of Christ is described:
*ne-un-u-epigraphê=de hicô-f ce-pai pe*
PRT-PTC-IDF.S-inscription=yet above-3MS COMP-DEM.M COP.M
*p-rro n-n-iudai*
DEF.M-king of-DEF.P-Jew
But there was an inscription above him saying: 'This is the king of the Jews'. ($^{S}$Lk 23:38)

(284d) The angel of the Lord tells Tobit and Tobias that he brought Tobit's and Sarra's supplication to the Holy One:
*auô n-ehou e-k-tôms n-n-et-mout*
and DEF.P-day.P DEP-3MS-bury OBJ-DEF.P-REL-die.STA
*ne-i-nmma-k on pe*
PRT-1S-with-2MS again PTC
And during those days, while you were burying the dead, I was likewise with you. ($^{S}$Tb 12:12)

(284e) Jesus explains to the disciples that he hasn't said certain things to them earlier:
*ce-ne-[i]-nmmê-tn*
for-PRT-1S-with-2P
...because I was with you. ($^{L}$Jn 16:4)

(284f) Having named all the sons of Israel who went into Egypt, the story of Exodus continues:
*iôseph=de ne-f-hn-kême*
N=yet PRT-3MS-in-Egypt
But Joseph was in Egypt. ($^{A}$Ex 1:5)

(284g) Wisdom stresses her early existence:
*e-f-na-sbte-t-pe na-i-neme-f pe*
DEP-3MS-FUT-create-DEF.F-heaven PRT-1S-with-3MS PTC
When he was about to prepare the sky, I was present with him. ($^{A}$Prv 8:27)

(284h) The sea-monster has swalloed Jonah:
*au nare-iônas nḫêt-f m-p-kêtos n-ḫamt*
and PRT-N inside-3MS as-DEF.M-sea_monster for-three
*n-houe mn-hamt [n]-uḫi*
of-day and-three of-night
And Jonah was inside the sea-monster for three days and three nights. ($^{A}$Jon 2:1 [1:17] [Malinine])

(284i) On the third day, a wedding took place at Cana in Galilee:
*ouoh nare-t$^{h}$-mau n-iê(su)s mmau pe*
and PRT-DEF.F-mother of-N there PTC
...and the mother of Jesus was there. ($^{B}$Jn 2:1)

(284j) Judah had left his brothers and begot children with a Canaanite woman:

| | | | | |
|---|---|---|---|---|
| *t$^h$ai=de* | *na-s-k$^h$ê* | *ḫen-k$^h$asbi* | *hote* | *eta-s-mas-u* |
| DEM.F=yet | PRT-3FS-AUX | in-N | when | TMP-3FS-bear-3P |

She was in Kezib when she gave birth to them. ($^{B}$Gn 38:5)

Here, Bohairic also makes use of the *k$^h$ê*-insertion described above.

Again, the subject pronoun clitisises to the marker $^{SL}$*ne-*/$^{AMFB}$*na-* also in Coptic and hence the forms for pronominal subject are as follows, while for nominal definite subjects the prefix $^{SL}$*nere-*/$^{AMFB}$*nare-* was used. If the clause had an indefinite subject, the preterite marker would appear as $^{SL}$*ne-*/$^{AMFB}$*na-*:

**Tab. I.12:** Coptic forms of personal pronouns attached to the anterior marker *ne-/na-*(common forms only).

<table>
<tr><th></th><th>Singular</th><th>Plural</th></tr>
<tr><td>1C</td><td>ne-i-/<br>na-i-</td><td>ne-n-/<br>na-n</td></tr>
<tr><td>2M</td><td>ne-k-/<br>na-k-</td><td rowspan="2">nete-ten-/<br>nare-ten</td></tr>
<tr><td>2F</td><td>ne-re-/<br>na-re-</td></tr>
<tr><td>3M</td><td>ne-f-/<br>na-f-</td><td rowspan="2">ne-u-/<br>na-u-</td></tr>
<tr><td>3F</td><td>ne-s-/<br>na-s-</td></tr>
</table>

Note that in Fayumic the 2FS forms appear as *nale-*, while some Fayumic varieties have a tendency to double the nasal, i.e. the forms appear as *nna-*PRN-.

In Coptic, the use of the Second Tense operators $^{S}$*e(re)-*/$^{B}$*a(re)-* and their dialectal forms has become commonplace before adverbial sentences. Note that the last example from Nitrian Bohairic shows the occasional writing *e-* instead of the expected *a-*, which is assumed to be a slip from translating Sahidic texts into Bohairic in the monasteries of the Scete:

(285a) The psalmist proclaims his trust in the Lord, for the Lord is in his holy temple:

| | | |
|---|---|---|
| *p-coeis* | *ere-pe-f-thronos* | *hn-t-pe* |
| DEF.M-lord | ST-POSS.M-3MS-throne | in-DEF.M-heaven |

The Lord, his throne is *in heaven*. ($^{S}$Ps 10 [11]:4)

(285b) The patriarch John concludes his deliberations on the humanity of the Christ with the remarks that his healing hands have been pierced on the cross and asks:

*mê ere-fto n-k*$^{j}$*ic mmo-f*
IR ST-four of-hand in-3MS
Or does he have four hands?
([S]*Questions of Theodore* [van Lantschoot 68, 20–21])

(285c) A series of natural phenomena is mentioned in non of which the Lord came though. Then a light breeze was to hear and:

*ere-p-cois mmau*
ST-DEF.M-lord there
There was the Lord. ([S]3Kg 19:12)

(285d) The Proverbs of Solomon state about wisdom and piety:

*a-t-pêgê m-p-ônḫ ḫn-t-k*$^{j}$*ic m-p-dikaios*
ST-DEF.F-fountain of-DEF.M-life in-DEF.M-hand of-DEF.M-righteous
The fountain of life is *in the hand of the righteous.* ([A]Prv 10:11)

(285e) The psalmist remembers the old times:

*are-te-k-hiê n-t-thalassa auô ne-k-hiê m-maše*
ST-POSS.F-2MS-way in-DEF.F-sea and POSS.P-2MS-way of-walk
*hn-hen-mau e-našo-u*
in-IDF.P-water DEP-plenty-3P
*auô ne-tek*$^{j}$*se n-se-ne-senuon-u=en*
and POSS.P-2MS-footprint NEG-3P-FUT-know-3P=NEG
In the sea is our way, and your path is in many
waters, and your footprints will not be known. ([M]Ps 76 [77]:20)

(285f) Proclaiming the might of the Lord, the prophet says:

*a-f-ḫen-u-ḫae uoh a-f-ḫen-u-monmen nce-pe-f-môit*
ST-3MS-in-IDF.S-end and ST-3MS-in-IDF.S-shaking PVS-POSS.P-3MS-way
His way is termination and upheaval. ([B]Na 1:3)

(285g) Theodore's mother did not know that he had gone to Egypt:

*alla na-u-cô mmo-s na-s ce-e-f-ḫen-pi-polemos*
but PRT-3P-say OBJ-3FS to-3FS COMP-ST-3MS-in-DEF$_2$.M-war
...but they told her that he was in the war.
([B]Theodore of Antioch, *On the Theodores* [*AM* II 129, 12–13])

Unlike in earlier stages of the language where the adverbial sentence remained unmarked, this construction is now standard with *in-situ* interrogative predicative adverbs. In Coptic, especially in Bohairic, the alternative of anteposing the adverb before an unmarked clause is more common than in earlier stages of the language:

(286a) Paul says that he will soon visit the community of Corinth in order to deal with arrogant members:
*t-mnt-ero=gar* *m-p-nute* *n-e-s-hn-šace=an*
DEF.F-ABST-king=for of-DEF.M-god NEG-ST-3FS-in-speak =NEG
*alla* *hn-u-k$^{j}$om*
but in-IDF.S-power
For the kingdom of God consists not in talk but in power. ($^{S}$1Cor 4:20)

(286b) Isaac is guided through Hell and asks the accompanying angel:
*ša-t$^{h}$nau=ce* *ere-nai* *ḫen-kolasis*
until-when=now DEP-DEM.P in-punishment
How long are these in punishment?
($^{B}$Ps. Athanasius, *TestPatr: Isaac* [Guidi 238, 18])

In the last example, the dependency marker *ere-* appears instead of the Second Tense operator, as is typical for Nitrian Bohairic. Occasionally, both strategies – the fronting of the adverbial and the use of an operator – occur simultaneously (see Uljas 2011b: 98). With noun subjects, the use of a cataphoric pronoun is common in interrogative adverbial constructions, but as the last example below shows, this was not mandatory. However, first traces of such a process can be discerned already in Late Egyptian (see Winand 2016):

(287a) Isaac asks his father:
*eis* *p-kôht* *mn-n-še* *mn-t-k$^{j}$orte* *e-f-tôn*
PTC DEF.M-fire and-DEF.P-wood and-DEF.P-dagger ST-3MS-WH
*p-esou* *e-p-talo*
DEF.M-sheep to-DEF.M-lift
Behold the fire, the wood, and the dagger; but where is the lamb for the sacrifice? ($^{S}$Gn 22:7)

(287b) The Lord demands to know of Israel, who would help them in their destruction:
*a-f-tô* *p-k-rro* *pei*
ST-3MS-WH POSS.M-2MS-king DEM.M
Where is this king of yours? ($^{A}$Hos 13:10 [Till])

(287c) Thekla's prospective husband asks his future mother-in-law:
*theoklia* *e-s-ton* *thekla* *ete-tô-i* *ce-e-i-na-neu*
N ST-3FS-WH N REL-POSS.F-1S so that-ST-1S-FUT-see
*ara-s*
OBJ-3FS
Theoclia, where is my Thekla so that I may see her?
($^{L}$*Acta Pauli* [Schmidt 7* 10, 17–18])

(287d) The psalmist bewails that tears are his daily bread and that he is constantly asked:
*a-f-ton* *pe-k-n(u)ti*
ST-3MS-WH POSS.M-2MS-god
Where is your God? ($^{M}$Ps 41 [42]:4 [3])

(287e) St Peter asks Jesus:
*pa-c(ai)s* *ie* *a-u-tôn* *ne-psykhau* *(e)-n-ten-neu*
POSS.M.1S-lord IP ST-3P-WH DEF.P-souls.P DEP-NEG-1P-see
*ela-u* *en*
OBJ-3P NEG
*mpau* *hn-ne-kolasis*
today in-DEF.P-punishment
My Lord, where are the souls, for we do not see them today in punishment?
($^{F}$John Evangelist, *Investiture of Archangel Michael* [Müller 39, 15–16])

(287f) The governor mocks the saint, a former captain of the Roman army:
*a-f-t$^{h}$ôn* *pe-k-ništi* *n-aksiôma* *nem-te-k-ništi*
ST-3MS-WH POSS.M-2MS-great of-honour and-POSS.F-2MS-great
*m-met-ramao*
of-ABST-rich
*e-našô-s*
DEP-be plenty-3FS
Where is your great honour and your immense wealth?
($^{B}$*Mart. Eusebius* [*AdM* 32, 15–16])

(287g) Speaking to St Cyril about human figures who according to the scriptures have been taken up to God, Anthimus asks:
*ere-enôkh* *tôn* *hôô-f*
ST-N WH self-3MS
But where is Enoch? ($^{S}$Cyril of Alexandria, *Eratopokrisis* [Crum, pCheltenham 6, 3])

### 3.2.3 Subordinate adverbial sentences

Following a general trend of increasing marking of grammatical functions, adjunction is overtly marked in Later Egyptian, and the earlier dichotomy between marked and unmarked has largely disappeared. In all three major stages of Later Egyptian, the marker of adjunct status is the operator *iw-* > *e-*. As noted earlier on, this element represents a functionally reanalysed version of the Earlier Egyptian auxiliary whose re-categorisation as an adjunctor was probably favoured by its use as an incorporation-base for suffix personal pronouns in adjuncts (see 3.1.2.2). From a temporal point of view, an adverbial sentence adjunct introduced by *ỉw* is usually temporally concomitant with the situation described in the preceding matrix clause:

*Late Egyptian*

(288a) The Egyptian victory had a devastating effect on the Libyan chief:
*spr-f* *r-ḫꜣs-t-f* *ỉw-f* *m-nḫw*
reach -3MS to-land-F-3MS DEP-3MS in-mourning
He reached his land in mourning (*lit.* while he was in mourning).
(*KRI* IV 14, 16)

(288b) The pharaoh addresses his frightened soldiers who flee in despair:
*ptr-tn* *pꜣy-ỉ-nḫt-w* *ỉw-ỉ* *wꜥ-kw*
behold-2P POSS.M-1S-victory-P DEP-1S be_alone-STA.1S
*ỉw-ỉmn* *m-nbyw-ỉ*
DEP-N as-protector-1S
*ỉw-dr-t-f* *ḥnꜥ-ỉ*
DEP-hand-F-3MS with-1S
Behold my victory, although I am alone with Amun as my protector and his hand with me. (*KRI* II 56, 1–6/K1)

(288c) In a legal document a man narrates how on a certain day another man violated his property rights of a slot in the necropolis:
*ỉw-f* *ḥr-wsf* *ỉw-f* *ḥr-gm* *pꜣ-ꜣḥḥw*
DEP-3MS PRP-idle DEP-3MS PRP-find DEF.M-shaft
*nty-m-ḫnw-s*
REL-in-inside-3FS
*ỉw-f* *ḥr-hꜣy* *mỉm* *ỉrm-N* *ỉw-bn-ṯ-ỉ* *mỉm*
DEP-3MS PRP-go there with-N DEP-NEG-PTC-1S there
... while he was off-duty he found the shaft that is in it (the tomb) and went into with the official Neferhotep while I was not there.
(*KRI* V 475, 6–9)

(288d) The adressee is reminded again of his failure in proper conduct of orders:
*ỉ-ỉr-k-dỉ-t-ỉw* *pꜣy-ỉmw* *ꜥꜣ* *spsn* *spsn*
ST-AUX-2MS-give-INF-come DEM.M-boat great twice twice
*ỉw-f* *šw-w*
DEP-3MS be_empty.STA
*ỉw-tꜣy-f-ỉs-t* *mỉm-f*
DEP-POSS.F-3MS-crew in-3MS
Otherwise would you have dared to send that extra large boat empty with only its crew in it? (*KRI* III 504, 3–5)

(288e) An event on a certain day has been noted down on an ostracon:

| | | | | |
|---|---|---|---|---|
| *hrw=pn* | *(n)-spr* | *r-tꜣ-ỉmnt-t* | *(n)-nw-t* | *ỉn-sḫprrꜥ* |
| day=DEM.M | of-arrive.INF | to-DEF.F-west-F | of-city-F | PTC-N |

| | |
|---|---|
| *ỉw-f* | *m-qrs* |
| DEP-3MS | in-funeral |

The day of the arrival of king Sekhepere (i.e. Ramesses V) at the west of The City, being in funeral. (*KRI* VI 343, 13–14)

*Demotic*

(288f) The deceased woman is addressed and praised:

| | | | |
|---|---|---|---|
| *ntm-t* | *m-ꜥnḫ* | *ỉw-pꜣy-t-by* | *(m)-nꜣ-gs-w-pr-w* |
| sweet-2FS | in-life | DEP-POSS.M-2FS-soul | in-DEF.P-side-P-house-P |

You will be pleasant in life, while your ba is in the temples. (pHarkness 4, 29)

(288g) A record in a graffito by a member of a group of travellers:

| | | | | |
|---|---|---|---|---|
| *ỉw-n* | *r-prỉwlqe* | *ỉw-nꜣ-qrnjꜣ-w* | *n-ꜣst* | *ỉrm-y* |
| come.PST-1P | to-N | DEP-DEF.P-qorones-P | of-N | with-1S |

We came to Philae with the Qorones of Isis with me. (grPhilae 416, 7)

*Coptic*

(288h) Archelaos narrates how he visited the holy land and stopped at a small monastery on his way back. He studied the books in the monastery library:

| | | | |
|---|---|---|---|
| *mnnsa-etre-n-mušt=de* | *hn-ne-côôme* | *etuaab* | *a-f-i* |
| after-INFL-1P-search=yet | in-DEF.P-book | holy | PF-1S-come |

| | |
|---|---|
| *e-toot-n* | *nkʲi-p-côôme* |
| to-hand-1P | PVS-DEF.M-book |

| | | | |
|---|---|---|---|
| *n-arkhaios* | *ere-hen-syntagma* | *nhêt-f* | *nte-ne-iote* |
| of-old | DEP-IDF.P-treatise | in-3MS | CNJ-DEF.P-fathers.P |

| | |
|---|---|
| *n-apostolos* | *etuaab* |
| of-apostle | holy |

After we had perused the holy books, we chanced upon the ancient tome containing treatises on our holy apostolic fathers.

(SArchelaos of Neapolis, *On Gabriel* [Müller and Uljas §15])

(288i) Tobit urges to acknowledge the Lord even in capitivy for he will raise Jerusalem and the scattered Hebrews again and:

| | | | |
|---|---|---|---|
| *un-u-mêêše* | *n-hethnos* | *na-i* | *m-p-ue* |
| PTC-IDF.S-multitude | of-nation | FUT-come | in-DEF.M-distance |

| | | |
|---|---|---|
| *erat-f* | *m-p-ran* | *m-p-šêre* |
| to-3MS | in-DEF.M-name | of-DEF.M-son |

| | | |
|---|---|---|
| *m-p-nute* | *ere-hen-dôron* | *hn-ne-u-kʲic* |
| of-DEF.M-god | DEP-IDF.P-gift | in-POSS.P-3P-hand |

Many nations from afar will come to the name of the son of God, bearing gifts in their hands. ($^{S}$Tb 13:11)

(288j) Contrasting the fate of the disobedient with that of those loyal to the Lord, the prophet says:

*se-ne-teit-u* *hm-p-nomos* *ere-pe-n-ucei*
3P-FUT-give-3P in-DEF.M-law DEP-POSS.M-1P-salvation
*hn-ne-ahôôr*
in-DEF.P-treasure

They will be handed over to the law, while our salvation is in the treasures. ($^{F}$Is 33:6)

(288k) Zachary tells the story of Jesus' childhood years:

*e-f-ḫen-kenf=de=on* *n-te-f-mau* *uoh*
DEP-3MS-in-bosom=yet=again of-POSS.F-3MS-mother and
*e-s-fai* *mmo-f*
DEP-3FS-carry OBJ-3MS
*ḫen-pe-s-amêr* *m-p$^{h}$-rêti* *n-u-alu* *kata-p-smot*
in-POSS.M-3MS-embrace in-DEF.M-way of-IDF.S-boy like-DEF.M-form
*m-pe-n-thebio*
of-POSS.M-1P-humility
*a-u-siur* *eta-f-šai* *ḫen-t-p$^{h}$e* *ḫen-u-šp$^{h}$êri*
PST-IDF.S-star TMP-3MS-shine in-DEF.F-heaven in-IDF.S-wonder
*e-f-šebiêut*
DEP-3MS-change.STA
*ḫen-pe-f-smot* *uoh* *e-f-uot* *e-ni-ke-siu*
in-DEF.M-3MS-form and DEP-3MS-be different.STA to-DEF.P-other-star
*têr-u*
all-3P
*e-u-met-ref-c$^{h}$i-môit* *n-ni-magos* *šaro-f* *e-hiôiš*
DEP-IDF.S-ABST-AGT-take-way for-DEF$_2$.P-wise to-3MS to-proclaim
*m-pi-hôb*
OBJ-DEF$_2$.M-thing
*uoh* *a-f-er-met$^{h}$re* *ḫen-u-uônh* *ebol*
and PST-3MS-do-witness in-IDF.S-reveal about

Yet when he was still at his mother's bosom and she carried him in her arms like a boy, in accordance with our humble way, a star, having wondrously risen in heaven, different in form and unequal to all the other stars as well as a guide for the wise men to him to proclaim the matter, gave witness in a revelation. ($^{B}$Zachary of Sakha, *De Praesentatione* [de Vis II 7, 2–7])

A few adjunct clauses introduced by *e-* express concessive meaning (see also the Late Egyptian exx. 43b, 154d, and 288b):

*Late Egyptian*

(289a) The reason given by a group of people for their having beaten up a man:

*8 ꜣbd n-hrw r-pꜣ-[...] ꞽw-f m-nk mdꞽ-tꜣy-rmṯ*

8 month in-days to-DEF.M-[...] DEP-3MS in-copulate with-DEM.F-person

*ꞽw-bn-sw m-hy[-s]*

DEP-NEG-3MS as-husband-3FS

For eight months now he sleeps with that woman, although he is not her husband. (pBM 10416 r°, 9–10)

(289b) A woman from the village stands convicted of larceny and apparently not for the first time:

*ṯꜣw ꜥnḫnnwt tꜣnḏmḥmsꞽ wꜥ-n-kṯ šrꞽ n-dbn*

take.PST lady N IDF.S-of-cup small of-weight

*1 ½ dy m-pꜣ-dmꞽ*

1 ½ here in-DEF.M-village

*ḫrḥꜣ.t ꞽ-hꜣy ṯꜣtꞽ nfrrnpt ḫr-ꞽw-s m-ḥm-t n-pꜣšd*

earlier to-times vizier N and-DEP-3FS as-wife-F of-N

*sꜣ-ḥḥ*

son-N

The Lady Tanedjemhemsi stole a small cup worth 1 ½ *diban* here in the village earlier, at the times of the Vizier Nuferompe, although she was the wife of Pashed, son of Heh. (*KRI* IV 317, 5–7)

*Demotic*

(289c) The spell recited by Naneferkaptah allowed him to see the fish of the deep:

*ꞽw-wn-mḥ-ntr 21 n-mw ḥr-ḏꜣḏꜣ-w*

DEP-PTC-cubit-divine 21 of water on-head-3P

...although there were 21 divine cubits of water above them. (Setne I 3, 37)

*Coptic*

(289d) Jesus chastises his disciples:

*ere-ne-tn-bal mmô-tn n-tetn-eiôrh an*

DEP-POSS.P-2P-eye with-2P NEG-2P-perceive NEG

*auô ere-ne-tn-maace mmô-tn n-tetn-sôtm an*

and DEP-POSS.P-2P-ear with-2P NEG-2P-perceive NEG

*n-tetn-r-pmeeue an*

NEG-2P-do-remember NEG

Although you have eyes, you do not perceive. And although you have ears, you do not listen, and you do not remember. ([S]Mk 8:18)

(289e) Elijah reasons over the need to keep the fastings:
*p-et-r-nêsteue n-uaiš nim ne-f-r-nabe*
DEF.M-REL-do-fast in-time all NEG.FUT-3MS-do-sin
*e-un-kôh hi-titôn nḫêt-f*
DEP-PTC-enmity CON-strife inside-3MS
He who is fasting all the time does not commit sin even if enmity and strife are in him. ([A]ApEl [Steindorff, *Apokalypse des Elias* 74 23, 15–24, 1)

(289f) When Simon Peter reeled in the net, it was full of fish:
*uoh ere-tai-êpi nḫêt-f mpe-f-pʰôḫ nce-pi-šne*
and DEP-DEM.F-number inside-3MS NEG.PST-3MS-burst PVS-DEF$_2$.M-net
And even though this large number was in it, the net did not burst.
([B]Jn 21:11)

With the help of various conditional particles adverbial clauses could be transferred into conditional protases. In Demotic and Coptic, adverbial sentences could be used in hypothetical conditional clauses marked by *ene-* (dependency marker *e-* + preterite *ne-*, see exx. 290 b, e–f):

*Late Egyptian*

(290a) In an adoption text it is stipulated by the adopting woman:
*ỉnn wn mdỉ-ỉ ꜣḥ-w-t m-sḫ-t ỉnn wn*
CND be with-1S field-P-F in-country-F CND be
*mdỉ-ỉ ḫ-w-t=nb n-pꜣ-tꜣ*
with-1S thing-P-F of-DEF.M-land
*ỉnn wn mdỉ-ỉ šwṯ ỉw-w (r)-pš-w*
CND be with-1S merchandise FUT-3P FUT-divide-3P
*n-pꜣ-4-ẖrd-w ỉw-pꜣdỉw m-wꜥ ỉm-w*
for-DEF.M-four-child-P DEP-N as-one in-3P
If I have fields in the conutryside, if I have anything in this land, if I have merchandise, they shall be divided for the four children, with Padiu being one of them. (*KRI* VI 738, 3–6)

*Demotic*

(290b) After a short vivid description of the pity state the town of el-Hibeh is in the administrative official of the temple says that the people who rule the town by violence:
*bn-wꜣḥ n-w ỉnỉw wn-rmṯ n-pꜣ-dmy bnr n-w*
NEG-put for-3P CND PTC-man in-DEF.M-town except for-3P
...it is not to their liking(?), if there would be anyone in this town but them. (pRylands IX 1, 6–7)

*Coptic*

(290c) Pisenthius bids farewell to two brethren and urges them to behave well in the villages in which they have business. They are not to engage with evil women there, nor to take away the ox of a poor man:

| | | | | | |
|---|---|---|---|---|---|
| *ešôpe* | *untê-tn* | *lau* | *e-rôme* | *hn-nei-meros* | *mpr-anagkaze* |
| CND | have-2P | any | to-man | in-DEM.P-part | NEG.IMP-force |

| | | |
|---|---|---|
| *mmo-f* | *ude* | *mpr-hchôc-f* |
| OBJ-3MS | nor | NEG.IMP-compel-3MS |

If you have anything against a man in these parts, do not force him or compel him. ($^{S}$John the Elder, *V. Pisenthius* [Budge, *Apocrypha* 77, 27–29])

(290d) The writer of a letter, probably the monk Frange, gets right to the point in his writ:

| | | | | |
|---|---|---|---|---|
| *ari-p-na* | *ešôpe* | *p-nomos* | *hahtê-k* | *auô* |
| do.IMP-DEF.M-mercy | CND | DEF.M-law | with-2MS | and |

| | | |
|---|---|---|
| *ešôpe* | *p-hôb* | *areske* |
| CND | DEF.M-thing | please |

| | | | | |
|---|---|---|---|---|
| *n-te-k-mnt-iôt* | *tnnou-f* | *na-i* | *ntoot-f* | *m-pahatre* |
| for-DEF. F-ABST-father | send.IMP-3MS | to-1S | with-3MS | as-N |

Be so kind, if The Law (i. e., the Pentateuch) is with you and if the matter pleases your fathership, send it to me with Pahatre. ($^{S}$*O.Frange* #74, 1–8)

(290e) Before the Egyptian clerics set sail to journey to the council of Chalcedon, Macarius sees a deacon, whose boastful attire is not to Macarius liking. He tells Peter, another deacon:

| | | | | |
|---|---|---|---|---|
| *ešôp* | *uon-20* | *n-rômi* | *ḫen-ne-n-caci* | *n-heretikos* |
| CND | PTC-20 | of-man | in-POSS.P-1P-enemy | of-heretic |

| | | | | |
|---|---|---|---|---|
| *p$^{h}$ai* | *na-er-mah-21* | *nḫêt-u* | *nte-f-tôun* | *nemô-u* |
| DEM.M | FUT-do-card-21 | in-3P | CNJ-3MS-rise | with-3P |

| |
|---|
| *ḫen-tu-heresis* |
| in-POSS.F.3P-heresy |

If our heretic enemies count up to twenty men, this one will be their twentyfirst and will rise with them in their heresy.

($^{B}$Dioscorus of Alexandria, *On Macarius of Tkow* [Amélineau 97, 18–98, 1])

(290f) When a man returned home with his son, his wife expressed resentment about their absence:

| | | | |
|---|---|---|---|
| *ene-teten-em-pei-ma* | *mmate* | *ne-tetn-na-meh-mou* | *n-n-et-uôš* |
| CNT-2P-in-DEM.M-place | only | PRT-2P-FUT-fill-water | for-DEF.P-REL-wish |

If only you had been here, you could have drawn water for whoever wishes (for it). ($^{S}$*Further Miracles of Apa Mena* [Drescher, *Mena* 81, b21–25])

(290g) Annoyed by the behaviour of his stubborn she-ass, Balaam says:
*ene-uon-u-sêfi* *ḫen-ta-cic* *na-i-na-ḫelḫôl-i* *pe*
CNT-PTC-IDF.S-knife in-POSS.F.1S-hand PRT-1S-FUT-slaughter-2FS PTC
If I had a knife in my hand, I would slaughter you. ($^{B}$Nm 22:29)

In Coptic, headless adverbial sentence relative clauses can appear in nominal sentences of the tripartite pattern as well as in cleft sentences (see 1.3.2.3 and 1.1.2.3 below respectively):

(291a) In explaining the Parable of the Sower, Jesus says:
*n-et-hicn-t-petra=de* *ne* *nai* *e-ša-u-sôtm*
DEF.P-REL-upon-DEF.F-rock=yet COP.P DEM.P REL-AOR-3P-hear
*nse-šep-p-šace* *ero-u* *hn-u-raše*
CNJ.3P-receive-DEF.M-word to-3P in-IDF.S-joy
Yet those on the rocky ground are those who listen and receive the word with joy. ($^{S}$Lk 8:13)

(291b) Having announced the coming of three Persian kings who will imprison the Jews of Egypt and take them to Jerusalem, Elijah says:
*tote* *ašateten-sôtme* *ce-pôrc* *p-et-ḫn-t-hierusalêm*
then CND.2P-hear COMP-division DEF.M-REL-in-DEF.M-N
Then, if you hear that there is division in Jerusalem...
($^{A}$*ApEl* [Steindorff, *Apokalypse des Elias* 83 29, 5–6])

(291c) The Jews accuse Jesus:
*tinu* *a-n-mme* *ce-u-daimonion* *p-et-nme-k*
now ST-1P-know COMP-IDF.S-demon DEF.M-REL-with-2MS
Now we do know that you are possessed (lit., a demon is with you).
($^{L}$Jn 8:52)

(291d) John urges to carefully examine any prophets whether they are true or false. Yet the Christians will overcome them:
*u-ništi* *pe* *p$^{h}$ê* *et-ḫen-t$^{h}$ênu* *ehot-e-p$^{h}$ê*
IDF.S-great COP.M DEF$_{3}$.M REL-in-2P more-to-DEF$_{3}$.M
*et-ḫen-pi-kosmos*
REL-in-DEF$_{2}$.M-world
The one who is in you is greater than the one who is in the world.
($^{B}$1Jn 4:4)

As shown above, the tense of the construction can be marked as past by introducing the verb $^{S}$*šôpe* and changing the adverbial sentence into a verbal one (see 3.2.2.3 for mainly future tense examples):

(292a) The historical situation between the Romans and the Persians is outlined. The Persians expect tribute from their subjugated peoples, including the Romans:

*epeidê* *ha-t-hê* *mpate-rro* *šôpe* *hn-t-antiokhia*
because under-DEF.F-front NCO-king be in-DEF.F-N
*nere-t-mnt-erro*
PRT-DEF.F-ABST-king
*n-nm-persos* *o* *n-cois* *e-te-hrômania* *têr-s*
of-DEF.F-Persian be.STA as-lord to-DEF.F-Rome all-3MS
*mn-ne-s-toš*
and-POSS.P-3FS-province

Since before there was a king in Antioch, the Persian Empire ruled over the whole of Roman Empire and all of its territories.

($^{S}$*Mart. Theodore et al.* §4)

(292b) Having announced the might of the Lord and his forces, the prophet asks:

*au* *nim* *p-et-na-ḫôpe* *ne-f* *n-hikanos*
and WH DEF.M-REL-FUT-be for-3MS as-sufficient

And who shall be sufficient for it? ($^{A}$Jl 2:11 [Malinine])

(292c) Philip preached the Gospel in Samaria, driving out unclean spirits and healing many:

*a-f-šôpi=de* *nce-u-ništi* *n-raši* *ḫen-ti-polis* *etemmau*
PST-3MS-be=yet PVS-IDF.S-great of-joy in-DEF$_2$.F-city that

And there was great joy in that city. ($^{B}$Acts 8:8)

For specific temporal clauses, Coptic makes use of a combination of a tense-marking particle $^{S}$*cin-*/$^{B}$*iscen-* followed by a dependent clause. The state of affairs expressed in the clause is marked as simultaneous with the main clause and shares in addition a common starting point with a commenced state of affairs ('since', 'when still'):

(293a) The Devil explains to the emperors why he hates the Christians and especially Jesus:

*kaigar* *ne-f-ti* *nmma-i* *pe* *cin-e-i-hn-t-pe*
for PRT-3MS-give with-1S PTC since-ST-1S-in-DEF.F-heaven
*nmma-f*
with-3MS

For he fought with me since I was with him in heaven.

($^{S}$*Mart. Theodore et al.* §37)

(293b) The psalmist assures the Lord that he has always set his hopes on him alone:

| | | |
|---|---|---|
| *ha-i-ccara-i* | *eco-k* | *ncin-e-i-hn-t-kalahy* |
| PST-1S-lean-1S | upon-2MS | since-ST-1S-in-DEF.F-womb |

Upon you I leaned since being in the womb. ($^{M}$Ps 70 [71]:6)

(293c) On their way to the temple to pray, Peter and John meet a man:

| | | | |
|---|---|---|---|
| *e-f-oi* | *n-k$^{j}$ale* | *iscen* | *e-f-ẖen-t$^{h}$-neci* |
| REL-3MS-be.STA | as-lame | since | ST.PRS-3MS-in-womb |
| *nte-te-f-mau* | | | |
| of-POSS.F-3MS-mother | | | |

who had been lame since he was in his mother's womb. ($^{B}$Acts 3:2)

### 3.2.4 Semantic extensions of the adverbial sentence

As in Earlier Egyptian, the core locative meaning of adverbial sentences was in Later Egyptian used as a basis for the expression of various more abstract notions that can be viewed as metaphorical extensions of the former. However, the number of such extensions is lower than before, and their importance within the overall grammatical system was less pronounced than in the earlier phases. This is largely because by the second millennium BCE, some of the most charateristic extensions of Earlier Egyptian had become grammaticalised verbal patterns in their own right and had consequently departed from the class of adverbial sentences. This was particularly the case for the earlier construction [subject + preposition *ḥr/m/r* + infinitive]. As discussed above, the origin of this pattern seems to lie in an extension of the locative idea of the subject occupying a 'position' either 'amidst' or 'towards' an event expressed by the infinitive. However, it was noted then that already in Earlier Egyptian this construction is fully verbal in character, and its grammar and meaning cannot be properly analysed within the frame of adverbial sentences. This is even truer in Later Egyptian, where the construction had become an integral part of the so-called Present I and Future III constructions. As such, it had, paradoxically, once again aligned syntactically with adverbial sentences, but had also assumed new properties that emphasise its completely verbal character. Most notable of these was the loss of the prepositions *ḥr* and *r* between the subject and the infinitive already during the later New Kingdom (see Winand 1992: 413–419 & 504–510),[98] the grammaticalisation of *ἰw* as the conjugation base (or

98 The preposition *m*, however, was rarely omitted. The *r* of *r* + infinitive is frequently omitted in Old Egyptian (see Edel (1955/1964: §937), but never in Middle Egyptian.

operator) of Future III, and the replacement of the former in case of noun subjects by *iri*; compare:

*Earlier Egyptian*

(294a) In a property transfer document:
*iw-i* *ḥr-ir-t* *imtpr* *n-ḥm-t-i*
AUX-1S PROG-do-INF transfer_document to-wife-F-1S
I am making a transfer-document to my wife. (pUC 32058, 7)

*Late Egyptian*

(294b) The author of a letter assures his addressee that a certain Medjay-officer has not been disturbed:
*sw* *ir* *m-p3y-f-sḥn*
3MS do.INF in-POSS.M-3MS-commission
He is working on his commission. (*LRL* 32, 13)

*Earlier Egyptian*

(294c) A conclusion in a medical prognosis concerning childbirth:
*iw-s* *r-mst* *wḏf*
AUX-3FS FUT-bear late
She will give birth late. (pUC 32057, 3.14)

*Late Egyptian*

(294d) Part of a stipulation in a will:
*inn* *iw-s* *ms* *bn-šri* *bn-šri*
CND FUT-3FS bear.INF IP-son IP-daughter.F
If she will bear a son or a daughter... (*KRI* VI 737, 5–6)

(294e) The author of a letter says that he and others are carrying out their commissions:
*ḫr-iri-imnrʿ* *nsw* *nṯr-w* *p3y-k-nb* *dit=n-n* *ḥs-t*
PTC-AUX-N king god-P POSS-2MS-lord give=to-1P favour-F
*r-ḥr-k* *m-mitt*
to-face-2MS in-like
Then Amun-Ra, king of gods and your lord, will favour us before you as well. (*LRL* 46, 15)

Similarly, some old and even quite important early patterns were lost over time. This was particularly the case with the expression of classification of the subject by means of the so-called *m* of predication, which, as seen, had played a major part in Earlier Egyptian adverbial sentence semantics (3.1.4). The construction is still productive in Late Egyptian, including the use of identifying the material something is made of (ex. 295e):

(295a) A scribe gives advice to an unwilling pupil:

*ṯ-k* *m-rmṯ* *n-šꜣw* *(n)-sš* *iw-bw-iri-ṯ-k*
PTC-2MS as-man of-fit (of)-write DEP-NEG-have-TERM-2MS
*nk*
copulate

You are a man fit to write even before you have had sexual intercourse. (*LEM* 101, 12–13)

(295b) Bata reveals his identity to his former wife:

*ptr* *ṯ-i* *ꜥnḫ-kw* *mrꜥ* *iw-i* *m-kꜣ*
look PTC-1S live-STA.1S still DEP-1S as-bull

Look, I am still alive as a bull (*lit.* while I am a bull). (*LES* 25, 13)

(295c) Describing his victory over his Libyan foes, King Merenptah has the Libyans as saying about their chief:

*mryw* *m-bwt* *n-inbwḥḏ* *wꜥ* *sꜣ* *wꜥ*
N as-abomination of-N one son one
*m-mhꜣ-f* *r-ḏt*
in-family-3MS to-eternity

Meryaw is an abomination of Memphis, and so is son after son of his kin forever. (*KRI* IV 15, 3–5)

(295d) The woman who adopted the former slaves and the husband of of them ends up her words with the statement that the text above is entrusted to that additional adopted husband, who treated her well:

*iw-i* *m-ḫꜣr-t* *iw-pꜣy-i-hꜣy* *mwt-ṯ*
DEP-1S as-widow-F DEP-POSS.M-1S-husband die-STA

...when I was a widow and my husband was dead. (*KRI* VI 738, 7–8)

(295e) The king narrates what he did for the gods of Heliopolis. He made an august chapel for the god Re-Atum-Horakhty:

*sw* *m-ꜣḫ-t* *ꜥꜣ-t* *štꜣ-t* *n-ḥrꜣḫty*
3MS as-horizon-F great-F secret-F for-N
*s-t* *wr-t* *m-nbw* *ꜥꜣ-w* *m-ktm-t*
place-F great-F as-gold door-P as-fine_gold-F

It is the great secret horizon for Horakhty; the throne is of gold and the doors are of fine-gold. (pHarris I 26, 1)

Yet, sentences with the '*m* of predication' (often displaying the development *m* > *n*) are attested in Demotic mainly in traditional texts and formulae. In Ptolemaic administrative documents, the pattern often introduces the name of the eponymous priests and priestesses:

(296a) In the dating formula of a cession document:
*i͗w-hrnꜣ sꜣ-t ptwlmys n-wꜥb n-ꜣrsnꜣ tꜣmriṯs*
DEP-N daughter-F N as-priest of-N N
Eirene, daughter of Ptolemy, is a priestess of Arsinoe Philopator.
(pBrooklyn 37.1781, 2)

(296b) The Ethiopian cat starts feeling nostalgic about Egypt:
*kmy r-hwnnꜣw n-sty n-bdt(?) n-ḥꜣṯ-y*
Egypt DEP-IPF as-scent of-emmer in-heart-1S
Egypt, which was as the scent of emmer in my heart.
(Myth of the Sun's Eye 8, 16–17)

The wisdom text of the Papyrus Insinger makes abundant use of this pattern:

(297) From a wisdom text:
*sḥm-t nꜣ-nfr i͗w-bnpw-s mr ky*
woman-F PTC-beautiful DEP-NEG.PST-3MS love other
*ḫn-tꜣ-mhw-t n-sḥm-t rmt-rḫ-t*
in-DEF.F-family-F as-woman-F man-know-F
A beautiful woman, who did not love another (man) in the family, is a wise woman. (pInsinger 8, 5)

In Coptic, a few functional domains previously associated with adverbial sentences have been taken over by other patterns. In this stage of the language, bipartite nominal sentences had become the sole means of expressing classification, and no etymological remnants of the '*m* of predication' survive. A partial exception might be the construction involving the Stative of the verb 'to do' followed by an *n*- and a noun without any definiteness marker (e.g. $^{S}$*o n-rro*/$^{B}$*oi n-uro* 'be king'); the insertion of the Stative could be a later adjustment of the pattern.

The semantic extensions of adverbial sentences found in Later Egyptian tend to be – if a spatial metaphor is allowed here – relatively close to the core locative schema, but they also display various degrees of abstraction. Commonly the locus where the subject is situated is not a concrete position in space, but for example a treaty binding an individual, or else an office or title held:

*Late Egyptian*

(298a) It is said in the preamble in the Egypto-Hittite peace treaty:
*ptr ḫtsl pꜣ-wr ꜥꜣ n-ḫt [m]-ntꜥ*
look N DEF.M-prince great of-N in-treaty
Hattusili, the great chief of the land of Hatti, is in the treaty.
(Edel, *Vertrag*, 23*, 6)

(298b) One of the accused conspirators is introduced as follows:

*ḫr ꜥꜣ pꜣybꜣkkmn wn m-ꜥꜣ n-ꜥ-t*
enemy great N PST.PPA as-great of-chamber-F
The great enemy Pebekkamen, who was a chamberlain... (*KRI* V 352, 2)

(298c) Describing his victory over his Libyan foes, King Merenptah has the Libyans say about their chief:

*sw m-bꜣ-w n-nṯr-w nb-w mnnfr*
3MS in-power-P of-god-P lord-P N
He is in the power of the gods, the lords of Memphis. (*KRI* IV 15, 1)

(298d) The Syrian chief locks up his daughter in a high tower and tells all the princes of Syria:

*ỉr pꜣ-nty-ỉw-f r-pḥ pꜣ-sšd n-tꜣy-ỉ-šrỉ*
PTC DEF.M-REL-FUT-3MS to-reach DEF.M-window of-POSS.F-daughter
*ỉw-s=n-f r-ḥm-t*
FUT-3FS=to-3MS to-wife-F
Whoever reaches my daughter's window, will have her as his wife.
(*LES* 3, 8–9)

*Demotic*

(298e) The author addresses god Amun and complains about the priests of el-Hibeh:

*bnpw-w-ỉr=n-k ỉw-w-ḫn-tꜣy-w-nw*(?)
NEG-PST-3P-act=for-2MS DEP-3P-in-POSS.F-3P-time
They did not act for you when they were in their service(?).
(pRylands IX 24, 12–13)

(298f) The author of a letter complains to a woman:

*tꜣ-ỉꜥbỉ ntỉỉw-y ḫn-s yꜥby ꜥꜣ-t tꜣy*
DEF.F-misery REL-1S in-3FS misery great-F COP.F
The misery in which I am is a great misery. (pSaqqara 71/2 DP 145, 21–22)

(298g) A man reports in a graffito how he and his comrades from Nubia celebrated the feast of Isis:

*ỉw-pꜣ-mšꜥ n-pꜣ-tyme ḏr-f n-ỉhꜥyꜣ*
DEP-DEF.M-multitude of-DEF.M-village all-3MS in-jubilation
...while the population of the whole village was in jubilation.
(grPhilae 416, 13)

(298h) The speaker swears an oath and adds:

*ỉw-y ỉr-pꜣ-ꜥnḫ n-ꜥḏ tw-y ḫn-pꜣ-btw prꜥꜣ*
DEP-1S do-DEF.M-oath as-false PTC-1S in-DEF.M-punishment pharaoh
Should I swear falsely, I am subject to the pharaoh's punishment.
(pBerlin P 13637, 13–15)

*Coptic*

(298i) The inhabitants of Gabaon, having tricked the Israelites by claiming to live afar from them, pay obeisance by saying:
*tenu-$k^{j}$e is-hêête tn-ha-toot-têutn*
now-then lo-behold 2P-under-hand-2P
And now, see, we are in your power. ($^{S}$Jo 9:31[24] [Thompson])

(298j) In a late Sahidic song the Ecclesiastes is quoted as saying:
*me-laau hi-p-bios e-pi-kosmos esa-hise hi-mkah*
NEG-anything on-DEF.M-life in-DEF.M-world after-pain and-grief
There is nothing in this world except pain and grief.
($^{S}$Junker, *Poesie* II 96, e13–14)

(298k) Simeon and Levi had convinced the Canaanites of Salem that only if their men were circumcised would marriage between Israelites and Canaanites be possible. They consented:
*a-s-šôpi=de nḫrêi ḫen-pi-ehou m-mah-3 e-u-nḫrêi ḫen-pi-mkah*
PST-3FS-happen=yet down in-$DEF_2$.M-day of-ORD-3 DEP-3P-down in-$DEF_2$.M-pain
Now it came about on the third day when they were in pain... ($^{B}$Gn 34:25)

(298l) Arriving in a town where his father lives, Theodore asks a man whether his father is still alive. He replies:
*se f-onḫ alla e-f-ḫen-u-šôni et-ḫosi*
yes 3MS-live.STA but ST-3MS-in-IDF.S-illness REL-toil.STA
Yes, he is alive, but in a grave condition.
($^{B}$Theodore of Antioch, *On the Theodores* [*AM* II 124, 14–15])

(298m) The saints tell the emperor:
*u-dikeon=an=pe nte-n-hemsi hicen-u-thronos ere-u-polemos hicô-n*
IDF.S-righteous=NEG=COP.M CNJ-1P-sit upon-IDF.S-throne DEP-IDF.S-war upon-1P
It is not right that we sit upon a throne while war is upon us.
($^{B}$Theodore of Antioch, *On the Theodores* [*AM* II 136, 4–5])

Conversely, the entity located might also represent an abstraction:

*Late Egyptian*

(299a) Obsequious remarks by officials to the pharaoh in reference to his might over the peoples of all lands:
*šfy-t-k n-ḥr-w rˤ=nb*
terror-F-2MS in-face-3P day=QU
Your terror is daily in their faces (*KRI* V 33, 12)

(299b) After the contendings of Horus and Seth, Horus is restored to his father's office:
*p-t* *m-ršw-t*
heaven-F in-joy-F
The heaven is in joy. (*LES* 60, 7)

(299c) After the Hittites had made contact with the Egyptians:
*st* *m-sẖr=pn* *qsn* *ẖr-bꜣ-w* *ꜥꜣ* *n-w-nb* *tꜣ-wy*
3P in-state=DEM.M pity under-might-P great of-P-lord land-DU
They are in this pitiful state under the great might of the Lord of the two lands. (*KRI* II 246, 4)

(299d) The pupil is advised to stay calm in all circumstances and not to rush around:
*ṯ-k* *m-tꜣ-s-t* *ꜥrꜥr-k*
PTC-2MS in-place-F perfection-2MS
You are in the place of your perfection. (*LEM* Caminos 508, 2)

(299e) The sender of a letter assures the addressee to be diligently pursuing the issue of a foreign slave:
*ṯ-i* *msꜣ-pꜣ-ḥry-skt* *m-mnt*
PTC-1S after-DEF.M-chief-assault_troop in-daily
I am after the captain of the assault officers daily ... (*KRI* IV 80, 10–11)

Frequently met is the idea of carrying or holding something that is derived from the notion of being located 'under' an entity; this relatively basic extension, which remained in use until Coptic, is known already from Earlier Egyptian:

*Late Egyptian*

(300a) In the description of the bellicose appearance of Ramesses II it is stated:
*ḥtr* *ꜥꜣ* *nty-ẖr-ḥm-f* *nḫtmwꜣst*
horse great REL-under-majesty-3MS N
The great horse under his majesty was named Nekhtemwêse.
(*KRI* II 29, 1–7/K1)

(300b) Among the wonders of Memphis:
*[p]ꜣy-s-bꜣḥ* *ẖr-sšny-w*
POSS.M-3FS-inundated_land under-lotus-P
Its inundated land carries lotus blossoms. (*LEM* 90, 9)

(300c) In a broken letter the author reports that a certain bailiff came:
*r-nḥm* *tꜣy-ꜣḥ-t* *n-pr-sbk* *nty-ẖr-i*
to-take DEM.F-field-F of-house-N REL-under-1S
...to confiscate that field of the temple of Sobek which is under my authority. (pBM 75016 r° x+1 [Demarée pl. 5])

(300d) A man takes an oath on the lord saying that if he should return to the issue:

*ỉw-ỉ* *ẖr-100* *n-sẖ*
DEP-1S under-100 of-blow
...I shall bear hundred blows... (*KRI* VI 253, 3)

*Demotic*

(300e) The small dog-ape tells the goddess about the misery of the humans since she left Egypt:

*nꜣy-w-ỉf-w* *ẖr-sꜣẖy-t*
POSS.P-3P-flesh-3P under-wound-F
Their bodies are full of wounds. (Myth of the Sun's Eye 11, 4)

(300f) The local priests use the absence of Petese to scheme against him by telling the regional governor that a certain prebend is in his family's possession illegally:

*tws* *ỉw-s* *ẖr-pꜣ-šr* *n-pꜣy-f-šr* *šꜥ-pꜣ-hrw*
behold PTC-3FS under-DEF.M-son of-POSS.M-3MS-son until-DEF.M-day
Behold, it is still in the possession of the son of his son until today.
(pRylands IX 3, 18)

(300g) In the division of a real estate property the borders are specified by mentioning the neighbours:

*mḥt-t* *pꜣ-qꜣ* *n-wꜣḥmw* *ḥrỉỉrꜥw* *sꜣ* *pꜣdyꜣst*
north-F DEF.M-shrine of-coachyte N son N
*nty-ẖr-nꜣy-f-ẖrṯ-w*
REL-under-POSS.P-3MS-child-P
North: the shrine of the coachyte Horirau, son of Petesi, which is in possession of his children. (pLeiden I 379, 3)

(300h) A description of an individual in a letter:

*ỉw-f* *ẖr-sḥḏ*
PTC-1S under-leprosy
He suffers from leprosy. (pLoeb 5, 11–12)

(300i) In an Old Coptic love charm, Isis is said to come down from the mountain with the heat of a summer's day:

*e-iat-s* *$k^{h}$a-ermê* *e-etê-s* *$k^{h}$a-eom*
DEP-eye-3FS under-tear-P DEP-heart-3FS under-sigh
...her eyes full of tears and her heart full of sighs.
($^{OC}$Great Mag. P. Paris [*ZÄS* 21, 100, 34])

*Coptic*

(300j) Shenute begins his sermon with the words:
*e-i-hmoos* *anok* *hicn-u-tou* *pece-p-et-cô*
DEP-1S-sit 1S upon-IDF.S-mountain said.PST-DEF.M-REL-say
*n-nai*
OBJ-DEM.P
*a-i-nau* *e-u-zôon* *e-f-ha-pa-êr*
PST-1S-see OBJ-IDF.S-animal DEP-3MS-under-DEF.M-air
*e-f-miše* *mn-ke-zôon* *e-f-hicm-p-kah*
DEP-3MS-fight with-other-creature DEP-3MS-upon-DEF.M-earth
'As I sat on a mountain', said the one who says these things, 'I saw a creature in the air fighting with another creature that was upon the earth'. ($^{S}$Shenute, *As I Sat on a Mountain* [L III 44, 18–20])

(300k) The prophet describes the allophyles and enemies of Israel who do not live according to the laws of the Lord and eat:
*hen-hieb* *e-u-ḫa-pu-erôte*
IDF.P-lamb DEP-3P-under-POSS.M.3P-milk
...suckling lambs (lit., lambs that are under milk)... ($^{A}$Am 6:4 [Till])

(300l) The Ecclesiastes expresses his world-weariness:
*mmn-lapti* *n-hôb* *m-mui* *ha-p-rê*
NEG-any of-thing of-new under-DEF.M-sun
There is nothing new under the sun. ($^{F}$Eccl 1:9 [Schenke])

(300m) The leader of the Pharisees says of people who do not know the law:
*se-*$k^{h}$*ê* *ḫa-p-sahui*
3P-AUX under-DEF.M-curse
They are accursed. ($^{B}$Jn 7:49)

There were, however, certain novel developments as well. Demotic and Coptic[99] use adverbial sentences to express the age reached, whereas the concept of spending a span of years is usually coded with verbal sentences:

*Demotic*

(301a) The age of the deceased upon a mummy label:
*ỉw-f* *ḥn-rnp-t* *72*
PTC-3MS in-year-F 72
He is 72 years old. (Louvre AF 10076, 5)

99 The absence in Late Egyptian is probably simply due to accidents of preservation as well as to the fact that the texts attested do not note down age regularly.

(301b) As above:

| | | |
|---|---|---|
| *iw-s* | *ḫn-rnp-t* | *39* |
| PTC-3FS | in-year-F | 39 |

She is 39 years old. (BM 23186, a6)

*Coptic*

(301c) A description of the Virgin:

| | | | | |
|---|---|---|---|---|
| *auô* | *nt-a-s-cpo-f* | *e-s-hn-a-mntê* | *n-rompe* | *n-ahe* |
| and | ST-PST-3FS-give birth-3MS | DEP-3FS-in-APR-15 | of-year | of-life |
| *a-f-r-mabšomte* | *n-rompe* | *mpat-u-st(au)ru* | *mmo-f* | |
| PST-3MS-make-33 | of-year | NCO-3P-crucify | OBJ-3MS | |
| *nt-a-u-st(au)ru* | *m-p-cois* | *i(êsu)s* | *ere-t-parthenos* | |
| ST-PST-3P-crucify | OBJ-the lord | N | DEP-DEF.F-virgin | |
| *hn-hmešmêne* | *n-rompe* | | | |
| in-48 | of-year | | | |

She was about 15 years old when she gave birth to him. Jesus Christ spent 33 years before he was crucified. The virgin was 48 years when the Lord Jesus was crucified. ([S]*Trans.Mariae* 13–14 r$^{o}$ a3–13)

(301d) The narrator tells about the healing of Tobit:

| | | | | |
|---|---|---|---|---|
| *ne-f-hn-taiu-šmêne* | *n-rompe* | *ntere-f-lo* | *e-f-nau* | *ebol* |
| PRT-3MS-in-fifty-eight | of-year | TMP-3MS-cease | DEP-3MS-see | out |
| *auô* | *mnnsa-šmune* | *n-rompe* | *a-f-nau* | *ebol* |
| and | after-eight | of-years | PST-3MS-see | out |

He was 58 years old, when he lost his sight, and after eight years, he saw (again). ([S]Tb 14:2)

(301e) The saviour tells his disciple John that John the Baptist had been beheaded on the second day of the month of Thoth:

| | | |
|---|---|---|
| *e-f-hn-34* | *n-lampi* | *n-ehi* |
| DEP-3MS-in-34 | of-year | of-age |

...while he was 34 years of age.

([F]John Evangelist, *Investiture of Archangel Michael* §12 [Müller 31, 12])

(301f) Jesus raised a young girl from the dead:

| | | |
|---|---|---|
| *na-s-ḫen-12=gar* | *n-rompi* | *pe* |
| PRT-3FS-in-12=for | of-year | PTC |

She was twelve years old. ([B]Mk 5:42)

(301g) The narrator resumes the story:
*a-iôsêph taho-f e-rat-f m-p-emt$^h$o n-pharaô*
PST-N stand-3MS to-foot-3MS in-DEF.M-face of-pharaoh
*e-f-k$^h$ê ḫen-130 n-rompi*
DEP-3MS-AUX in-130 of-year
*nem-ke-17 n-rompi e-a-f-ait-u ḫen-k$^h$êmi*
and-other-17 of-year DEP-PST-3MS-do-3P in-Egypt
*nai têr-u se-iri n-147 n-rompi*
DEM.P all-3P 3P-do as-147 of-year
Joseph was 130 years old when he stood before the pharaoh, and a further 17 years he spent in Egypt. In all, this makes 147 years.
($^B$Ps. Athanaius, *TestPatr: Jacob* [Guidi 255, 5–8])

The Bohairic dialect of Coptic shows both the pattern with and without the auxiliary *k$^h$ê*. Coptic also saw the creation of a pattern used to express a dynamic modal sense of ability that came to occupy an intermediate position between verbal and adverbial sentences. It was built with the introductory particle *un* (< *wn*) followed by the word *kʲom* 'power; possibility' followed by the predicate introduced by the prepositional phrase *n-/mmo-* 'in' and the entity with which the ability (or, in the negative, inability) was associated, lit. 'there is/no power in':

(302a) Do not say: Go and come back and tomorrow I will give to you:
*e-un-kʲom <m>mo-k e-r-p-et-nanu-f* ($^S$Worrell)
*e-un-kʲam mma-k n-r-p-et-nanu-f* ($^A$Boehlig)
*e-un-kʲom mmo-k e-r-p-et$^h$-nanu-f* ($^B$Burmester and Dévaud)
DEP-PTC-power in-2MS to-do-DEF.M-REL-good-3MS
...as you do not have the power to do good. (Prv 3:28)

(302b) Apa Nahrow challenges the king to have his pagan deity rescue him from the trouble that he is in:
*pa-cois-de ntof i(êsu)s un-kʲom mmo-f e-hôb nim*
POSS.M.1S-lord-yet 3MS N PTC-power in-3MS for-thing QU
My Lord Jesus, however, is able to do everything.
($^S$*Mart. Nahrow* [*ASAE* 19, 78, 18–21])

(302c) The sailors tell Gesios that they think it is in vain to sit and weep over a corpse:
*mê uen-kʲom mmo-k rô e-tunos-f n-ke-sop*
IP PTC-power in-2MS PTC to-raise-3MS for-other-time
Or is it perhaps possible for you to raise him again?
($^S$*Gesios and Isidorus* [*ZÄS* 21, 143, 10])

(302d) Hermippus sets his hopes on the one who saved his father and raised his brother again:

*un-kʲam* *mma-f* *hôô-t* *an* *a-tre-f-nahme-t*
PTC-power in-3MS self-1S again to-INFL-3MS-save-1S
It might be possible for him to save me as well. ([L]*Acta Pauli* 23* 32, 21)

(302e) The apostle says that people should not quarrel but accept the fate which God has set for everyone:

*alla* *kan* *ešôpi* *uan-kʲom* *mmo-k* *e-el-lemhe* *khrô*
but even if PTC-power in-2MS to-do-free use.IMP
*n-hua*
in-more
But if indeed you are able to be free, make the most of the opportunity. ([F]1Cor 7:21)

A possibly diatopic variant of this construction shows the insertion of *š*-, another auxiliary conveying the notion 'to be able to' (from Egyptian *rḫ* 'to know), between *un-* and *kʲom*; in B this insertion is almost mandatory:

(303a) A leprous man asks Jesus:

*p-cois* *ekšan-uôš* *un-š-kʲom* *mmo-k* *e-tbbo-i*
DEF.M-lord CND.2SM-wish PTC-can-power in-2MS to-cleanse-1S
Lord, if you wish, you can cleanse me. ([S]Mt 8:2)

(303b) The king of Assyria might supply a thousand horses:

*ešce* *uan-š-kʲam* *mma-ten* *e-ti-ref-alê* *ecô-u*
CND PTC-can-power in-2P to-give-AGT-mount on-3P
...if you can find enough riders for them! ([F]Is 36:8)

(303c) Judas objects to his master's feet being anointed with costly perfumed oil:

*ne-uon-š-com=gar* *pe* *e-ti* *m-p$^{h}$ai*
IPF-PTC-can-power=for PTC to-give OBJ-DEM.M
*ebol* *ḫa-u-mêš*
out under-IDF.S-multitude
*uoh* *e-têit-u* *n-ni-hêki*
and to-give-3P for-DEF.P-poor
For it could have been sold for a high price and given to the poor ([B]Mt 26:9)

The attestations of the construction with an impersonal *un-(š)-kʲom* may indicate development towards a verbalisation of the pattern, especially as they are used with conjunctive clauses and the purposive construction *e* 'to' + infinitive:

(304a) Jesus replies to the question over why his disciples do not fast:
*mê un-$k^j$om e-tre-n-šêre m-p-ma*
PTC PTC-power to-INFL-DEF.P-child of-DEF.M-place
*n-šeleet nêsteue*
of-bride fast
*hoson ere-pe-pa-t-šeleet šoop nmma-u*
as long as DEP-DEF.M-POSS.M-DEF.F-bride happen.STA with-3P
How could the children of the bridal chamber fast as long as the bridegroom is among them? ($^{S}$Mk 2:19)

(304b) God promises Abraham to make his seed as numerous as the sand of the earth:
*un-$k^j$am nt-u-ôp m-p-šu m-p-kah eia*
PTC-power CNJ-3P-count OBJ-DEF.M-sand of-DEF.M-earth then
*se-na-ôp (m)-p-k-sperma*
3P-FUT-count OBJ-POSS.M-2MS-seed
If someone can count the sand of the earth, then your seed can be counted. ($^{A}$1Cl 10:5 [Schmidt])

(304c) As the Lord has been gracious to hear about you again:
*ešôpe un-š-$k^j$am n-g-i ntak šara-n*
CND PTC-can-power CNJ-2MS-come 2MS to-1P
Would it be possible that you yourself came to us.
($^{L}$*Acta Pauli* 40* 46, 23–24)

(304d) Jesus prays:
*pa-iôt isce uon-š-com nte-pai-ap$^{h}$ot sen-t*
POSS.M.1S-father CND PTC-can-power CNJ-DEM.M-cup pass-1S
*ebêl nta-so-f mare-p-ete-hna-k šôpi*
except CNJ.1S-drink-3MS JUSS-DEF.M-REL-wish-2MS happen
My father, if it is possible that this cup pass me except I drink it, may your will be done. ($^{B}$Mt 26:42)

These expressions can appear in a protasis of a conditional sentence typically followed by a jussive:

(305a) Apa Nahrow stirs up a figure of a pagan deity and says to the king:
*ešce un-$k^j$om mmo-f mare-f-tuco-f hm-pei-$nok^j$ n-šipe*
CND PTC-power of-3MS JUS-3MS-save-3MS in-DEM.M-great of-trouble
*nt-a-f-taho-f*
REL-PST-3MS-touch-3MS
If it is possible for him, may he save himself from this great affliction that reached him. ($^{S}$*Mart. Nahrow* [*ASAE* 19, 78, 18–21])

(305b) Athanasius decrees that a bishop should serve his clergy in various ways:
*ešôpe=de un-kʲom mmo-f mare-f-iô n-ne-u-uerête*
CND=yet PTC-power of-3MS JUS-3MS-wash OBJ-POSS.P-3P-foot
*hn-ne-f-kʲic*
with-POSS.P-3MS-hand
If it is possible for him, he should wash their feet with his hands.
(ˢ*Canons of Athanasius* [Crum in Riedel §66])

However, the expression *ešôpe un-š-kʲom* 'if possible', which was originally a conditional protasis, may also appear alone[100]:

(306) If a prelate has some urgent business, he may leave:
*plên efe-šine m-pe-presbuteros mpate-f-bôk ešôpe*
yet FUT.3MS-ask OBJ-DEF.M-presbyter NCO-3MS-go CND
*un-š-kʲom*
PTC-can-power
Yet he should ask the presbyter before he leaves, if possible.
(ˢ*Canons of Athanasius* [Crum in Riedel §50])

Diachronically, the most important extension of the adverbial sentence was probably the evolution of the basic possessive construction of Later Egyptian. As seen before, in Earlier Egyptian, the idea of possession could sometimes be expressed by means of an adverbial sentence whose predicate was the compound preposition *m-ꜥ*, literally 'in the hand (of)' (see 3.1.4). In Late Egyptian *m-ꜥ* had been replaced by *m-di͗* > *mdi͗* 'with'[101] and adverbial sentences with the latter reanalysed as possessive constructions of the type [possessee *m-di͗*-possessor]. The possessors seem to have been initially restricted to pronominals, and the construction appears to have followed the expected pattern for syntactically marked definiteness. If the possessee was marked as definite, no additional marking occurred:

(307a) The oracle of the deified King Amenhotep I is asked of the whereabouts of two pieces of cloth. After reaching the house of the scribe Amennakht the oracle nods and proclaims:
*st mdi͗-tꜣy-f-šri͗*
[3P]$_S$ [with-POSS.F-3MS-daughter]$_P$
His daughter has them. (*KRI* VI 142, 8)

100 Here, it is obviously not the possibility to leave that should be asked for but the possibility to ask a presbyter.

101 This is in reality merely a case of graphemic adjustment as the sound represented in this (and other) case(s) by ꜥ was a stop rather than a fricative, see Kammerzell 1998: 34–35.

(307b) The author of a letter has been asked about a crown:
*ỉn* *sw* *mdỉ-k*
IP [3MS]$_S$ [with-2MS]$_P$
Do you have it? (*LRL* 15, 6)

(307c) The author of a letter cites a statement of the addressee when he had raised the question of the whereabouts of a certain donkey:
*mk* *pꜣ-ꜥꜣ* *mdỉ-ỉ*
PTC DEF.M-donkey with-1S
Look, I have the donkey. (*KRI* I 238, 12)

If, however, the possessee was marked as indefinite, the use of the syntactic pattern, with the introductory particle *wn* was mandatory:

(308a) A woman asks her sister to make some barley into bread because her husband argues:
*ḫr* *wn* *mdỉ-t* *sn-w* *ḫr* *bw* *ỉrỉ-w-nw* *r-t*
PTC PTC with-2FS sibling-P PTC NEG make-3P-care to-2FS
Although you have brothers and sisters, they do not take care of you! (*HO* 70, 2.6–7)

(308b) The addressee of a letter is ordered to join another man and to have a coppersmith make spears:
*wn-ḥmty* *ỉm* *mdỉ-k*
PTC-copper there with-2MS
You have copper there. (*LRL* 19, 15)

(308c) A workman has accused another workman of the theft of some tools belonging to the official adminstration of the tomb builders. Being asked whether he has witnesses of the theft he replies:
*wn* *mdỉ-ỉ* *mtr-y*
PTC with-1S witness-P
I do have witnesses. (*KRI* IV 318, 6)

(308d) Wenamun asks the prince of Byblos whether it was not an Egyptian boat and crew rowing for King Smendes and goes on:
*ỉn-wn* *(m)dỉ-f* *ỉs-t* *ḫꜣrw*
IP-PTC with-3MS crew-F Syria
Does he have a Syrian crew? (*LES* 67, 3–4)

Originally, the adverbial phrase *m-dỉ* > *mdỉ* + pronoun regularly occupied the final position in the sentence, but it was soon pre-posed before the original subject/possessee. Indeed, in Demotic the earlier preposition *m-dỉ* is written *mtw* and now also appears directly after the introducing *wn*; deviations such as in ex. 309c are to be viewed as exceptions:

(309a) A petitioner addresses the pharaoh, asking for a favour:
*wn-mtw(-y)* *wꜥ-sn* *pꜣdyꜣst* [*sꜣ*] *irtwrw* *rn-f*
PTC-with[-1S] IDF.S-brother N son N name-3MS
I have a brother. His name is Padiese, son of Irturu.
(pRylands IX 5, 20–6, 1)

(309b) A description of a person:
*wnnꜣw-wn-mtw-f* *wꜥ-sn* *šr* *n-pꜣ-sn*
PTC-be-with-3MS IDF.S-brother son of-DEF.M-brother
*ḫm* *n-pꜣy-f-it* *pꜣy*
little of-POSS.M-3MS-father SE.M
He had a male relative. He was the son of the younger brother of his father. (pRylands IX 5, 17)

(309c) The small dog-ape has managed to calm the furious goddess; she says:
*ꜣn-wn-bš-k* *mtw-y*
IP-PTC-saliva-2MS with-1S
Does your saliva not belong to me? (Myth of the Sun's Eye 8, 18)

(309d) In a deed of endowment, it is stipulated about a piece of real estate:
*iw-wn-mtw-t* *tꜣy-f-pš* *iw-wn-mtw-s*
DEP- PTC-with-2FS POSS.F-3MS-part DEP-be-with-3FS
*tꜣy-f-k-t-pš*
POSS.F-3MS-other-F-part
...while its one half belongs to you and its other half belongs to her.
(pPhiladelphia 1, 3–4)

As in the examples above, most instances show an indefinite possessed subject. In generic expressions the possessee can be omitted:

(310a) Moral precepts tell:
*mir-mqḥ* *iw-wn-mtw-k*
NEG.IMP-sad DEP- PTC-with-2MS
Do not be distressed when you have (possessions).
(Onkhsheshonqy 6, 22)

(310b) Moral precepts advise:
*tm-dy-t* *b(y)n* *nꜣy-k-if-w* *iw-wn-mtw-k*
NEG-give-INF bad POSS.P-2MS-flesh-P DEP-PTC-with-2MS
*n-pꜣ-pr-ḥḏ*
in-DEF.M-house-silver
Do not let your body suffer when you have (something) in your storehouse. (pInsinger 17, 4)

(310c) In a letter to god Thoth, the author tells of a debtor who refused to pay, saying:
*wn-mtw-y*
PTC-with-1S
I am wealthy (lit. 'I have') (pBM 73786, 4)

Unintroduced examples with definite subjects do not seem to occur. This has been explained as being due to the existence of a suppletive paradigm consisting of two patterns (Simpson 1996: 158). If the possessee was indefinite, the above construction was used. In case of definite possessees, one had recourse to a construction consisting of an independent pronoun possessor plus a dependent pronoun possessee, which in origin was an adjectival sentence. However, examples of the latter are scarce and the pattern does not seem to have been particularly productive. Furthermore, examples of *wn* with numbered – and thus definite – possessees do occur:

(311a) The author of a letter introduces his case:
*wnnꜣw-mtw-y (stꜣt) 10 ꜣḥ ḫn-pꜣ-ḥtp-nṯr sbk*
PTC-with-1S (aroura) 10 field in-DEF.M-offering-god N
I have 10 arouras of land in the provisioning establishment of Sobek.
(pLoeb 4, 10–11)

(311b) The author complains to the addressee that two priest approached him with the words:
*wn-mtw-n hrw-2 qd dy*
PTC-with-1P day-2 build here
We have here two days of building. (pBerlin P 13548, 2–3)

In Demotic, this reflects a general change in the syntactic structure of the construction. The introductory particle *wn*, previously mandatory only with indefinite subjects, had now been reanalysed and apparently considered to form a unit with the prepositional phrase *mtw*-POSS and meaning 'have', although it had probably not yet been wholly verbalised. Thus, it could now be used irrespective of the definiteness of the possessee. However, the change of position of the syntactic elements resulted in the possessor (marked through the comitative expression) now preceding the possessee, i.e. the original subject of the construction:

(312a) Writing to the king, Padiese recommends the son of the deceased Padiese, son of Onkhsheshonqy, as his fellow administrator of the southern district:
*wn-mḏr-pꜣdyꜣst sꜣ ꜥnḫššq pꜣ-ꜥꜣ-n-mr pꜣy-f-šr*
PTC-with-N son N DEF.M-great-of-ship POSS.M-3MS-son
The shipmaster Padiese, son of Onkhsheshonqy, has his son.
(pRylands IX 10, 3)

(312b) Moral precepts extol the benefits of praying to god:

*wn-mtw-f* *tꜣy-f-wnw-t* *n-sḏm*
PTC-with-3MS POSS.F-3MS-hour-F of-listen

He has his hour of listening. (Onkhsheshonqy 28, 10)

(312c) Moral precepts warn:

*mir-ḏd* *wn-mtw-i* *pꜣy-nkt*
NEG.IMP-say PTC-with-1S DEM.M-thing

*bn-iw-i* *šms-nṯr* *bn-iw-i* *šms-rmṯ* *ʿn*
NEG-FUT-1S follow-god NEG-FUT-1S follow-man again

Do not say: 'I have this property; I will not again follow god or man'.
(Onkhsheshonqy 18, 16)

This suggests a rather advanced grammaticalisation of the construction as a verbal rather than an adverbial predication. However, seeing that some late examples still allow *wn* and *mtw* to be separated, the construction has been included here instead of treating it solely as a verbal pattern. Nevertheless, in Coptic the possessive pattern had become grammaticalised to such an extent that its diachronic origins are only vaguely perceptible. The introductory particle *un* (< *wn*) and the former preposition *nte* (< *m-di*) now formed an inseparable unit *un-nt-* > *unt-*. Moreover, the pattern has been re-interpreted as a *verbal* construction, for which reason it will not be described here. Other adverbial sentence patterns could now be used to express the idea of possession, including locative patterns either with *n-/mmo-* or *hen-/nhêt-* both 'in':

(313a) The psalmist calls all heathen idols mere human works of silver and gold:

*un-bal* *mmo-u* *me-u-nau* *ebol* *un-maace* *mmo-u*
PTC-eye in-3P NEG.AOR-3P-look out PTC-ear in-3P

*me-u-sôtem*
NEG.AOR-3P-hear

*rô-u* *mmo-u* *me-u-šace* *šaant-u* *mmo-u*
mouth-3P in-3P NEG.AOR-3P-speak nose-3P in-3P

*me-u-šôlm*
NEG.AOR-3P-smell

Eyes they have but they do not see; ears they have but they do not listen; they have their mouths but they do not speak; they have their noses but they do not smell. ($^{S}$Ps 134 [135]:16–17 [Budge])

(313b) St Paul addresses the Jews and argues:

*uon-hêu=gar* *m-pi-sebi* *ešôp* *akšan-iri*
be-profit=for OBJ-DEF$_2$.M-cirumcision CND CND.2MS-make

*m-pi-nomos*
OBJ-DEF$_2$.M-law

Circumcision is profitable if you keep the law. ($^{B}$Rm 2:25)

(313c) Peter of Alexandria argues against heretics who stop him by the entrance to the church:
*isce uon-u-saci ḫen-rô-ten a-co-f*
CND be-IDF.S-word in-mouth-2P IMP-say-3MS
*isce=de mmon ie $t^{h}$ôm n-rô-ten e-štem-ceua*
if=yet NEG PTC shut OBJ-mouth-2P to-NEG-blaspheme
If you have something to say, say it! If not, then stay silent so as not to utter blasphemy!
($^{B}$Alexander of Alexandria, *In Petrum ep. Alexandriae* [*AdM* 254, 1–2])

In the specific semantic context of expressing debt, the pattern *uon*-X *e*-Y 'Y has X (lit. exists X to Y)' often appears, although simple possession is attested as well:

(314a) St Paul urges his addressees to live according to the spirit:
*ara=$k^{j}$e na-snêu n-se-ero-n=an e-tre-n-ônh*
PTC=now POSS.P.1S-brother.P NEG-3P-to-1P=NEG to-INFL-1P-live
*kata-sarks*
according-flesh
Therefore, my brethren, we do not owe to live according to the flesh.
($^{S}$Rm 8:12)

(314b) A plea in Lord's Prayer:
*kô=na-n ebol n-n-et-ero-n*
out=for-1P out OBJ-DEF.P-REL-to-1P
*n-t-he hôô-n on ete-n-kô ebol*
in-DEF.F-way self-1P again REL-1P-let out
*n-n-ete-unnta-n erô-u*
OBJ-DEF.P-REL-have-1P to-3P
And forgive us our debt as we forgive our debtors. ($^{M}$Mt 6:12)

(314c) The beings around the throne of the Lord are said to have wings:
*$p^{h}$-uai $p^{h}$-uai ne-uon-2 ero-f pe*
DEF.M-one DEF.M-one PRT-PTC-2 to-3MS PTC
...each of them had two. ($^{B}$Ez 1:23)

An additional pattern to express possession is a verbal construction with the Stative form of the verb $^{S}$*šôpe*/$^{B}$*šôpi*, i.e. *šop*, introducing the possessor via a dative *na-*.

# 4 Negation

## 4.1 Earlier Egyptian

Negation of adverbial sentences in Earlier Egyptian is, firstly, characterised by a diachronic development resembling what can be observed in various verbal future constructions as well as in existential sentences, and, secondly, by an exclusive use of wide-scope predicate negations. Concerning the first of these properties, in texts dating to the Old Kingdom and to the First Intermediate Period, adverbial sentences (including those with the so-called *m* of predication and *r* of futurity, see 3.1.4) are negated by the negative morpheme conventionally transliterated as *n* that occupies the initial position[102]:

(315a) The deceased king takes his place on the side of order and righteousness:
*ỉw* *N=pn* *tp-šms-w* *rꜥ* *n* *N=pn* *tp-nṯr-w* *tḫtḫ*
AUX N=DEM.M upon-follower-P N NEG N=DEM.M upon-god-P confusion
King N is at the helm of the followers of Ra. King N is not at the helm of gods of confusion. (PT 392d)

(315b) The king ascends to heaven:
*n=sw* *ỉr-tꜣ* *ỉw* *N* *ỉr-p-t*
NEG=2MS to-land AUX N to-heaven-F
He is not bound for earth. King N is bound for heaven. (PT 890b/P)

(315c) The king is told of his divine progeny:
*n* *ỉt-k* *m-rmṯ* *n* *mw-t-k* *m-rmṯ*
NEG father-2MS as-human NEG mother-F-2MS as-human
Your father is/was not a human; your mother is/was not a human. (PT 2203b)

102 In spite of the arguments discussed by Loprieno (1995: 168), it does not seem to be the case that in the earlier language the auxiliary *ỉw* could also be used in negated adverbial sentences. The assertion-marking role of *ỉw* was always restricted to affirmative propositions only. In the sole example apparently contradicting this rule, *n ỉw-k m-p-t n-ỉw-k m-tꜣ* (CT VII 35h), the *n* is not, despite its graphemic form, the negative morpheme but rather part of the interrogative marker *(ỉ)nỉw*, as indeed in the variant M2C. Accordingly, the passage translates 'Are you in heaven; are you upon earth?'

https://doi.org/10.1515/9783110409895-005

As can be seen from ex. 315b, personal pronoun subjects take the form of clitic pronouns after *n*. In earlier texts, one also finds instances where the negative particle is followed by the reduplicating (possibly prospective) form of the auxiliary *wn/wnn*; its function seems to be temporal and, more specifically, future reference:

(316) The King is told that he stands apart from spirits ruled by Osiris:
*n=ṯw* *ỉm-sn* *n* *wnn-k* *ỉm-sn*
NEG=2MS in-3P NEG AUX-2MS in-3P
You are not among them, and you will not be among them. (PT 251d)

However, this construction disappears later on. In the classical language, the particle *n* is also replaced by a new negation conventionally transliterated as *nn*, which was to remain the negation of adverbial sentences until post-classical times.[103] The first examples of *nn* in constructions that are certainly analysable as adverbial rather than existential sentences – i.e. constructions negating the locus (or, in the case of *m/r* of predication/futurity, the class-inclusion/membership) rather than the existence of the subject – date to the late First Intermediate Period and the early Middle Kingdom:

(317a) Tef-ib says concerning anyone who may violate his tomb (?):
*nn* *sḫꜣ-f* *ḫr-tp-w* *tꜣ* *nn* *rn-f*
NEG memory-3MS before-upon.RLT-P earth NEG name-3MS
*ḫr-[mr]-t-f*
before-family-F-3MS
His memory shall not be among the living; his renown shall not be among his family. (Siut III, 69)

(317b) Heqanakhte points out that his expectations of harvest yields are realistic:
*nn=s(y)* *m-ʿʿf-t* *qsn-t*
NEG=2FS as-squeeze-F difficult-F
It is not a difficult squeeze. (Heqanakhte I, rº 13)

With one exception (for which see below), from the Eleventh Dynasty onwards *nn* is the sole element used to negate adverbial sentences. Below are some further

103 The careful differentiation between the *n* and *nn* is no longer observed in the Traditional Egyptian of the Third Intermediate Period (and thereafter; see Jansen-Winkeln 1996: 201). Although *nn* is still used sporadically and seems to dominate in existential sentences, the simple *n* is now considerably more common in negated adverbial sentences.

examples with both lexical and phrasal predicates (note the omission of subject in exx. 318d–318e):

(318a) Isis says that her son Horus is burning on the desert, but nothing can be done:
*nn mw ỉm nn=wỉ ỉm*
NEG water there NEG=1S there
No water is there, nor am I there. (pEbers 69, 6)

(318b) Sinuhe argues that his flight was not planned:
*nn=s(y) m-ỉb-ỉ*
NEG=2MS in-heart-1S
It was not in my heart. (Sin B, 223–24)

(318c) In a spell to protect a child against various dangers:
*nn mw-t-k ḥnꜥ-k*
NEG mother-F-2MS with-2MS
Your mother is not with you. (*MuK* v° 2, 3)

(318d) Khakheperraseneb observes the shifting fortunes of people:
*ḫpr-w ḥr-ḫpr nn ø mỉ-sf*
change-P PROG-happen.INF NEG ø like-yesterday
Changes are taking place; nothing is like yesterday.
(Khakheperraseneb r° 10)

(318e) Senwosret III argues that his characterisation of the Nubians is accurate:
*ỉw mꜣ-n=st ḥm-ỉ [nn] ø m-ỉwms*
AUX see-PST=3C majesty-1S NEG ø as-lie
My majesty has seen it. It is not a lie. (Berlin 1157, 11–12)

(318f) A gloss explaining a term in a medical text:
*hrp ỉb-f=pw sꜣ r-ḫrw nn=sw m-s-t-f*
damp heart-3MS=SE go.STA to-down NEG=3MS in-place-F-3MS
It means that his heart is damp and gone down. It is not in its (proper) place. (pEbers 101, 15)

The underlying reason for the change from *n* to *nn*-negations in adverbial sentences is unknown.[104] A parallel development took place also with future verbal sentences, where the particle *n* was similarly replaced by *nn* (see the discussion on negation and adjectival sentences in Part III). In verbal environments, the

104 It seems, however, that the graphemic distinction here and in other uses where *nn* later became standard was already partly made in the Old Kingdom – see Moers (1993: 38–49, 55).

use of *nn* seems to have begun in utterances expressing strong denials and refusals by the speaker, which is well in accord with the analysis suggested in the literature of *nn* as etymologically an 'intensified' version of *n* (Loprieno 1995: 127). However, the spread of *nn* in verbal sentences may also have been motivated by the morphological collapse of specific Prospective form(s) within the so-called *sḏm-f* formation. In Old Egyptian, the standard future negation is the negative element *n* + the so-called Prospective *sḏm-f*,[105] whose paradigm may have become progressively more indistinct from, and more syncretic with, some other paradigm(s) of active *sḏm-f* (Uljas 2011: 161–66). If so, this development resulted in the impossibility to distinguish between the non-past *n sḏm-f*/*mr-f* and the past *n-sḏm-f* both in speech and in writing. The solution to this problem was presumably found in the construction *nn sdm-f*. The *phonological* value of the negative element *nn* was probably not different from the old *n*, but it was *graphemically* sufficiently differentiated to make the negation easily identifiable in writing. At the same time, the old, morphologically defunct Prospective form was replaced by the so-called Subjunctive *sḏm-f*, which appears to have been a uniformly inflected and fully distinct form. This solved also the identifying problem in the spoken language, and henceforth *nn sḏm-f* became the universal future negation in Earlier Egyptian.

Yet if true, the abandonment of *n* and the adoption of *nn* in adverbial sentences must have taken place independently of the formally similar shift in the negation of verbal future constructions. It has been noted that once intensive versions of simple negations are created, the former tend to lose some of their marked character and supplant the latter as the basic negation (Horn 2001: 452–53; cf. Loprieno 1991a: 229). This may have happened in verbal future expressions (and, as will be seen in Part II, partially also in nominal sentences) but hardly so in adverbial sentences, where morphological confusion with another construction cannot have occurred. It has also been argued that the change reflects a shift from a contradictory predicative negation with *n* to contrary term-negation with *nn* (Loprieno 1991a: 228–29; 1995: 169) but this has recently been disputed (Uljas 2013). One theory holds it that the information structure analysis of adverbial sentences might have undergone a change around the end of the Old Kingdom from categorical to thetic (Loprieno 1991a: 227). As noted in 3.1.2.1, the information structure of a thetic *p* is 'even' in that no participant is elevated or promoted,

---

105 For a careful morphological analysis of the data (primarily) from the Pyramid- and the Coffin Texts, see Schenkel (2000). The evidence for the presence in the same environment of the subjunctive *sḏm-f* is limited to rare instances of the *anom.* root *rdi* as *di* (for Pyramid Texts data, see Allen 1984: §330).

nor is the situation profiled as highly salient vis-à-vis associated participants. Existential sentences such as 'God exists/does not exist' are textbook examples of thetic *p* seeing that they simply state the (non-)existence of something. According to the hypothesis of *nn* and theticity, the idea of an entity occupying a locus in space carries the same (or similar) meaning. This would provide a unitary analysis of *nn* as a negation of existential and adverbial sentences and explain why it was *not* used even in Middle Egyptian in adverbial sentences with absolute personal pronouns whose information structure was characterised by very 'anti-thetic' subject focus[106]:

(319a) Sinuhe describes his disorientation after having overheard a royal secret:

| | | | | | | |
|---|---|---|---|---|---|---|
| *b3-i* | *s-w* | *ḥʿ-i* | *3d-w* | *ḥ3-t-i* | *n* | *ntf* |
| soul-1S | flee-STA | body-F-1S | shake-STA | heart-F-1S | NEG | 3MS |
| *m-ẖ-t-i* | | | | | | |
| in-body-F-1S | | | | | | |

My soul was fled, my body shaken and my heart, even *it* was not in my body. (Sin B, 255)

(319b) The king assures Sinuhe that there is absolutely nothing to fear from his part:

| | | | | |
|---|---|---|---|---|
| *sẖr=pn* | *in=n-f* | *ib-k* | *n* | *ntf* |
| plan=DEM.M | bring.PPA=to-3MS | heart-2MS | NEG | 3MS |
| *m-ib(-i)* | *r-k* | | | |
| in-heart[-1S] | against-2MS | | | |

This scheme that took away your mind – even *it* is not in my heart against you. (Sin B, 185)

There are, however, problems with the thetic analysis and the verbal negation *nn sḏm-f*.[107]

Be that as it may, the negation *nn*, and, in Old Egyptian, *n*, are also used in existential negations of the type *n(n) N*, which appear to be abbreviated versions of *n(n) wn N* with an omission of the lexical verb *wn* 'exist':

(320a) The man says of injustice:

| | | |
|---|---|---|
| *nn* | *wn* | *pḥ-wy-fy* |
| NEG | exist | end-DU-3MDU |

It has no end. (Man and Ba 130)

---

**106** As argued in 3.1.2.1, the subject focus here results from the construction [absolute pronoun + adverbial predicate] triggering a special set of presuppositions.

**107** In short, analysing *nn sḏm-f* as thetic presupposes treating it as an existential negation, which is not possible; see Uljas (2013).

(320b) The man laments the prevailing conditions:

| | |
|---|---|
| *nn* | *mꜣʿt-w* |
| NEG | righteous-P |

There are no righteous. (Man and Ba 122)

When the entity whose existence is negated is followed by an adverbial adjunct – a very common state of affairs – the sentence with bare *n/nn* is formally indistinguishable from a negated adverbial sentence. The differences between these two sentence types are semantic rather than syntactic in character and concern the scope of the negative element (cf. here Collier 1991a: 18–19). One may contrast the following two instances the first of which is an existential, the second an adverbial negation:

(321a) Amenemhat I tells that his weakness before his assassins was due to the circumstances:

| | | |
|---|---|---|
| *nn=swt* | *qn* | *grḥ* |
| NEG=PTC | strong.PPA | night |

However, there is none strong at night. (Amenemhat VIIe)

(321b) Ptahhetep notes of a man with recently acquired wealth:

| | | |
|---|---|---|
| *nn=tw* | *ḥꜣ-ky* | *mit-w-k* |
| NEG=2MS | behind-another.M | alike-M-2MS |

You are not behind (i.e. inferior to) others like you. (Ptahhetep 435)

In ex. 321a, the negative *nn* only has scope over the initial noun *qn* 'one strong' and leaves the adverbial(ly used noun) *grḥ* unscathed. There is no predicative relation between *qn* and *grḥ*, and consequently the sentence cannot be read as a negated adverbial sentence *'One strong is not at night'. In ex. 321b, however, *nn* has scope over the entire proposition and there is indeed a predicative relationship between *=tw* and *ḥꜣ-ky mit-w-k*, which the negation 'targets'. An existential translation with the scope over the entire clause after *nn* 'That you are behind others like you does not exist' is semantically strange, but could perhaps be accommodated if *nn* be understood to stand for a negative existential predicate. However, this analysis, which has, in fact, been standard in Egyptological studies ever since the 1920s (Gunn 1924: 198), must be rejected (Uljas 2013).[108] It proposes that the bare adverbial sentence following *nn* is, in fact, a subject complement clause of the latter.

**108** See also the discussion on negation and adjectival sentences in Part III for arguments against analysing *nn* as some kind of a negative 'predicative adjective'.

Yet as seen in 2.1.5, bare adverbial sentences are not used as complements in Earlier Egyptian. In addition, commentators of all philosophical persuasions are unanimous over the view that non-existence does not qualify as predication for the simple reason that nothing can be predicated of something whose existence is denied (Uljas 2013). Here the only way out would seem to be to analyse adverbial sentence negations of the type *nn sš m-pr* 'The scribe is not in the house' as negating the relationship between the subject *sš* and the predicate *m-pr*, – i.e. to view *nn* as a contradictory predicate – rather than contrary term-negation. *nn* would then have a wide scope. Interestingly, this would seem to explain why adverbial sentences are never negated by the discontinuous negation *n...=is*, which, among other things, commonly negates syntactically 'adverbial' expressions (Loprieno 1991a: 216–19):

(322) Senwosret III says that a son who will defend his border was truly born to him, but adds then about a son who will fail in this filial duty:
*n* *ms-t(w)-f=is=n-i*
NEG bear-PASS-3MS=NEG=to-1S
To me he is not born. (Berlin 1157, 18)

In ex. 322, the prepositional phrase *n-i* negated by *n...=is* does not represent the predicate of the proposition, but merely an adjunct. As will be discussed in more detail in connection with nominal sentence negations (Part II), *n...=is* has been analysed as a contrary 'term-negation' that does not affect the predicative relation, and the sentence in which it appears remains affirmative. This could be the reason why *n...=is* was not used to negate adverbial sentences. As will be observed later, the above analysis of *n...=is* has been disputed, but it seems clear that *nn* targets precisely the predicative relation.

Depending on the context, adverbial sentences negated by *n/nn* may be translated as temporally generic or future, as in exx. 317a–317b, or as past:

(323a) The shipwrecked sailor tells of his drowned crew:
*nn* *wḫꜣ* *m-ḥr-ib-sn*
NEG fool in-on-heart-3P
There was no fool among them. (Sh.S. 100–01)

(323b) The snake tells that the members of his family were consumed by fire:
*nn=wi* *m-ḥr-ib-sn*
NEG=1S in-on-heart-3P
...when I was not among them. (Sh.S. 131)

As for clausal syntax, bare negated adverbial sentences may function as initial or coordinated main clauses as in many of the examples above or as unmarked (un-introduced) adjuncts:

(324) Thutmosis III is described:

*nsw=pw* *ꜥḥꜣ* *wꜥ-w* *nn* *ꜥšꜣ-t* *ḥꜣ-ỉb-f*

king=SE fight.PIA one-STA NEG mass-F behind-heart-3MS

He is a king who fights alone, without there being a mass behind him. (*Urk.* IV 1229, 14)

Examples such as this are not particularly common. Instances of negated adverbial sentences introduced by a preposition-conjunction do not seem to be attested at all, and the same holds also for *ntt*-introduced complement clauses. The precise status of the following example with the negative complementiser *ỉwt* is somewhat unclear[109]:

(325) The deceased says to Anubis that his death is only apparent:

*ỉw-k* *rḫ-t(ỉ)* *ỉwt* *wn-t-ỉ* *mm-ỉꜣt-w*

AUX-2MS know-STA COMP.NEG AUX-TERM-1S among-mound.RLT-P

You know that I am not yet among the mound-dwellers. (CT II 125f/G2T)

Finally, instances of negated adverbial sentences in relative clauses are also uncommon. There are some examples of bare *nn*-negated adverbial sentence 'virtual' relative clauses:

(326) The peasant lambasts the high steward:

*mk=tw...* *mỉ-dp-t* *nn* *sḫry* *ỉm*

PTC=2MS like-boat-F NEG captain there

Look, you are like a boat in which there is no captain. (Peas B1, 220–22)

In the following example, already cited earlier on, a *nn*-negated adverbial sentence is used after the relative adjective *nt*-:

(327) The sailor describes the luxury of the Phantom Island:

*nn* *nt-t* *nn=st* *m-ẖnw=s*

NEG REL-F NEG=3C in-interior-3FS

There was nothing that was not within it. (Sh.S. 51–52)

---

109 The analysis here assumes that the complement clause contains a terminative form of the auxiliary *wnn* rather than that *wnt* is existential.

As discussed earlier on, here the negative morpheme intervenes between the adverbial sentence subject and the agreement-carrying relativiser *nt-*, which induces the overt expression of the former even though it is coreferential with the (understood) antecedent of the headless relative clause. The same holds true for the following, already quoted example with a perfective participle form of the auxiliary verb *wn/wnn*:

(328) Senemyah says in reference to the king (?):
*ḫmt-n-f* *smnḫ* *mnw* *wn-w* *nn=st*
plan-PST-3MS restore.INF monument(s) AUX-PPA NEG=3C
*ḥr-pd-w-sn*
on-foot-P-3P
He planned to restore monuments that were no longer standing.
(*Urk.* IV 501, 10)

By contrast, in instances relativised with *ỉwt-*, the negative counterpart of *nt-*, the negation is not a separate morpheme, and the relative clause subject could, if coreferential with the antecedent, be local to the agreement-carrier and remain covert (i.e. zero):

(329) The deceased says that he knows what is missing from the body embalmed by Anubis:
*ỉw* *ø* *m-ỉwt-t* *ḫnt-wsỉr*
AUX ø as-REL.NEG-F before-N
(It) is what is not before Osiris. (CT II 302c)

More commonly, however, the relative clause subject was neither local to the agreement-carrier nor coreferential with the antecedent, and was therefore represented as a resumptive pronoun in the relative clause:

(330a) The deceased is united with divinity:
*nn* *nṯr=nb* *ỉwt(-y)* *kꜣ-f* *ỉm-k*
NEG god=QU.M REL.NEG-M soul-3MS in-2MS
There is no god whose soul is not in you. (CT VI 392n)

(330b) The deceased salutes the judges of the dead:
*ỉnḏḥr-ṯn* *ỉm-w* *wsḫ-t=ṯn* *n-t-mꜣꜥ-ty* *ỉwt-w*
salute-2P in.RLT-P hall-F=DEM.F of-F-truth-FDU REL.NEG-P
*grg* *m-ẖ-t-sn*
falsehood in-body-F-3P
Hail to you, O the ones who are in the Hall of the Double Truth, in whose bodies there is no falsehood. (BD 125/*Nu* pl. 68, 66–67)

The negations *n* and later *nn* were also used to negate semantically possessive adverbial sentences whose predicate is the datival preposition *n*-, although in some cases there is doubt whether the sentence should be understood as existential with the masculine form of the genitival *n(-y)* (Uljas forthcoming):

(331) The peasant reminds the high steward of the rewards of criminal acts:
*nn sf n-wsfw nn ḫnms n-sẖ mꜣꜥ-t*
NEG yesterday to-sluggard NEG friend to-deaf justice-F
*nn hrw nfr n-ꜥwnỉb*
NEG day good to-greedy
The sluggard has no yesterday, he who ignores right has no friend, and the greedy has no holiday. (Peas B2, 109–11)

Examples of negated propositions with the *m* of predication occur as well (see ex. 315c for an early negation of the latter with *n*):

(332) Senenmut tries to persuade his audience to recite the funerary formula on his behalf:
*tꜣw n(-y)-rꜣ ꜣḫ n-sꜥḥ nn nw*
breath of[-M]-mouth beneficial.STA to-spirit NEG DEM.M
*m-wrd-t ẖr-s*
as-weary.PIA-F under-3FS
A mere breath of the mouth benefits the spirit; this is not a thing to be weary about. (*Urk.* IV 415, 11–12)

Examples with the *r* of futurity do not seem to be attested. Singular instances of the patterns *ḥr* and *r* + infinitive negated by *nn* are attested:

(333a) Terrified, the shipwrecked sailor says to the snake:
*ỉw mdw-k=n-ỉ nn=wỉ ḥr-sḏm=st*
AUX speak-2MS-to-1S NEG=1S PROG-hear.INF=3C
You speak to me, but I simply cannot hear it. (Sh.S. 73–75)

(333b) Ankhtify describes himself with outrageous hyperboles:
*nn ḫpr mỉt(-ỉ) nn=sw r-ḫpr*
NEG happen like[-1S] NEG=3MS FUT-happen.INF
My equal will not exist, and nor is he going to exist. (*Moꜥalla*, IIα2)

However, this is anything but standard; in fact, these most 'distant' of grammaticalised extensions of adverbial sentences do not in fact have symmetric negations in Earlier Egyptian. Instead, the *verbal* present/aorist and future constructions *n sḏm-n-f* and *nn sḏm-f* are used as supplementary constructions here, as seen from the parallelisms such as the following[110]:

(334a) The fisherman stalks his prey behind a protective screen on the bank and his spear ready:

| | | | |
|---|---|---|---|
| *iw-i* | *ḥr-m3[3]-f* | *n* | *m3{3}-n-f=wi* |
| AUX-1S | PROG-see.INF-3MS | NEG | see-PST-3MS=1S |

I see it, but it does not see me. (*Lit. Fragm.* pl. 2, 2.7)

(334b) Sinuhe tells his Syrian host about the intentions of the new king Senwosret I:

| | | | | | |
|---|---|---|---|---|---|
| *iw-f* | *r-itt* | *t3-w* | *rs-w* | *nn* | *k3-f* |
| AUX-3MS | FUT-take.INF | land-F.P | southern-P | NEG | think-3MS |
| *ḫ3s-w-t* | *mḥt-t* | | | | |
| foreign land-F-P | northern-F | | | | |

He will seize the southern lands; he will not (even) think about the northern lands. (Sin B, 71–72)

This once again underlines the semantic-pragmatic and grammatical differences between adverbial sentences and the pattern *ḥr/m/r* + infinitive, which is a fully grammaticalised periphrastic verbal construction. Although the latter had its origins in adverbial sentences, it was not negated in a fashion typical to these constructions (or, in fact, at all). Although, as noted, in Later Egyptian, the syntax of adverbial sentences and the patterns subject + *ḥr* + Infinitive/Stative was unified under the same Present I conjugation and *r* + Infinitive was grammaticalised as its own non-isomorphic Future III pattern, the constructions remained essentially verbal in terms of their semantics. In the negative system, the first signs of this later syntactic re-categorisation are seen in Eighteenth Dynasty examples such as the following, where the negation *nn* precedes what is clearly already a Late Egyptian Future III *iw-f r-sḏm* in which the element *iw* is a fixed conjugation-base and no longer an auxiliary:

(335) Words of a woman to her excessively inebriated companion in a banquet-scene:

| | | | |
|---|---|---|---|
| *mt* | *nn* | *iw-i* | *r-w3ḥ-t* |
| PTC | NEG | FUT-1S | to-leave.INF-2FS |

Look, I am not going to leave you. (*Paheri* pl. 7)

**110** See Collier (1994: 76) and Uljas (2009a) for an explanation of this. Another possibility is that, as so often, the grammaticalisation of a symmetric negation lags behind the affirmative – cf. Grossman and Polis (2014: esp. 90).

As will be shown in the next section discussing the diachronic descendants of the Earlier Egyptian adverbial sentence negations, the negation displayed in ex. 335 occurs in Late Egyptian as *bn ἰw-f r-sḏm*, where *bn* is the new graphemic guise of earlier *nn*.

## 4.2 Later Egyptian

### 4.2.1 Late Egyptian

The usual negation of adverbial sentences in Late Egyptian is with the negative element *bn* (< *nn*) preceding the affirmative construction (i.e. S > NEG NP AP):

(336a) The leader of the Libyans absconded at night after the Egyptian victory:
*bn-mḥ-t* *ḥr-tp-f* *rd-wy-f* *dgꜣ-y*
NEG-[plume-F]$_{S}$ [on-head-3MS]$_{P}$ foot-DU-3MS see-STA
There was no plume on his head, and his feet were unshod (lit. visible). (*KRI* IV 14, 10)

(336b) A carpenter corresponds with a customer:
*bn-nꜣy-k-ἰrἰ=ἰm* *r-ḏr-w*
NEG-[POSS.P-2MS-colleagues]$_{S}$=[there]$_{P}$ [to-limit-3P]$_{S}$
None of your colleagues are there. (*KRI* VI 671, 7)

(336c) An entry in the necropolis journal begins directly after the date:
*ἰw-bn-nꜣ-ḫꜣst-w=dy*
DEP-NEG-[DEF.P-foreigner-P]$_{S}$=[here]$_{P}$
*ἰw-mn-dἰw* *n-ꜣbd* *3* *šmw* *ꜣbd* *4* *šmw*
DEP-NEG-rations of-month 3 summer month 4 summer
[Day], the foreigners are not here, while the rations for the third and fourth month of summer are not there. (*KRI* VI 564, 4–5)

(336d) A man reports in court about a ancient tomb, which was given to him after it had been found by chance. Yet other people entered that tomb one day:
*ἰw-bn-ṯ-ἰ* *m-ἰm*
DEP-NEG-PTC-1S in-there
...while I was not there. (oBM EA 5624 v° 4)

(336e) A person is cited in a letter as having said to the author:
*bn-ṯ-k* *m-sš* *bn-ṯ-k* *m-wʿw*
NEG-[PTC-2MS]$_{S}$ [as-scribe]$_{P}$ NEG-[PTC-2MS]$_{S}$ [as-soldier]$_{P}$
You are not a scribe. You are not an officer. ([2]*pAnastasi I* 100, 3)

(336f) Boasting of his prowess, the pupil declares himself to be like a stomping pair of horses:

| | | | | |
|---|---|---|---|---|
| *bw-iy=n-i* | *qd* | *m-ib-i* | *n-hrw* | *bn-sw* |
| NEG.AOR-come=to-1S | sleep | in-heart-1S | in-day | NEG-3MS |
| *mdi-i* | *m-grḥ* | | | |
| with-1S | in-night | | | |

Sleep never enters my heart during the day, and it is not with me at night. (*LEM* 43, 10–11)

(336g) Accusations about a captain of a grain transport contain among other things a deficit of grain:

| | | |
|---|---|---|
| *bn-st* | *m-tꜣ-šn-t* | *n-ẖnm* |
| NEG-[3P] | in-DEF.F-granary | of-N |

It is not in the granary of the god Khnum. (*RAD* 79, 11)

(336h) A woman narrates in court that she had been adopted by her husband and that he had a document drawn up to let her inherit all his belongings:

| | | | | |
|---|---|---|---|---|
| *iw-bn=n-f* | *šri* | *šri* | *r-ḥrw* | *r-ink* |
| DEP-NEG=for-3MS | male_child | female_child | to-except | to-1S |

...since he had no children except me. (*KRI* VI 735, 15)

(336i) Broken context. In a memorandum concerning six donkeys:

| | | | |
|---|---|---|---|
| *wnn-bn-st* | *mdi-prꜥꜣ* | *ꜥ.w.s.* | *pꜣy-w-nb* |
| if-NEG-3P | with-Pharaoh | l.h.p. | POSS.M-3P-lord |

If they are not with Pharaoh, l.h.p., their lord, ...

(*KRI* VI 604, 5)

Note that *im* in 336b shows the same feature as *dy* described above and moves forward to separate the subject NP (*nꜣy-k-iri*) from its quantifier phrase (*r-ḏr-w.*). The older graphemic representation of the negation as *nn* is also attested:

(337a) The author of a letter states that he wrote the following text:

| | |
|---|---|
| *nn-ky* | *ḥnꜥ-i* |
| NEG-other | with-me |

...with no-one being with me. (²*pAnastasi I* 72, 9)

(337b) Longing to see the city of Memphis, the author says: 'I crave for sleep all the time:

| | | |
|---|---|---|
| *ḥꜣty-i* | *nn-sw* | *m-ẖ-t-i* |
| heart-1S | NEG-he | in-body-F-1S |

...but my heart is not in my body'. (*LEM* 39, 13–14)

The following example might speak for an interchangeability of *bn* and *bw*. However, since this is an isolated example and rather inexplicable, it is best seen as a mistake by the scribe:

(338) In a legal case, it is stated:
*iw-bn-pꜣy-f-diw* *m-pꜣ-pr*
DEP-NEG-POSS.M-3MS-ration in-DEF.M-house
*ḫr-bw-pꜣ-ḥꜥti* *mim* *ḫr-bn-pꜣy-i-ḥbs* *mim*
PTC-NEG-DEF.M-bed there PTC-NEG-POSS.M-1S-garment there
...while his ration is not in the house. But the bed is not there, and my garment is not there either. (*KRI* IV 232, 4–5)

Some examples from later Late Egyptian also display the use of *mn* (see 345a and 345b).

It is generally assumed that if a pragmatically focal adverbial phrase is negated, it is followed by the negative element *in* (Winand 1996):

(339a) The answer of a person interrogated about his involvement in thefts with a third person:
*bn-wn-f* *irm-i* *in*
NEG-PST-3MS with-1S NEG
He was not *with me*. (*KRI* VI 810, 13)

(339b) The author of a letter asks the addressee to take care of his father for the following reason:
*ṯ-k* *rḫ-ṯ* *rḏd-rmṯ* *iw-bn-ꜥꜣ-f*
PTC-2MS know-STA.2MS COMP-man DEP-NEG-maturity-3MS
*mdi-f* *in*
with-3MS NEG
You know that he is a man, who lacks experience. (*LRL* 48, 16–49, 1)

(339c) In a broken context:
*iw-bn-tꜣy* *m-tꜣy* *in*
DEP-NEG-DEM.F as-DEM.F NEG
...but this is not this! (oDeM 1221, 1)

(339d) The author of a letter reports that he fell ill on a journey:
*ḫr* *bn-ṯ-i* *m-pꜣy-i-sḫr* *in*
then NEG-PTC-1S in-POSS.M-1S-state NEG
And thus I am not in my usual state. (*LRL* 2, 8–9)

(339e) A thief quarrels with his fellow about the partition of spoils:
*bn-sw* *m-šs* *in* *pꜣ-pš* *i-ir-k=n-i*
NEG-3MS as-good state NEG DEF.M-division REL-make-2MS=for-1S
It is wholly inadequate, the part you allotted to me! (*KRI* VI 515, 3–4)

(339f) The sender opens his letter with the statement:

| | | | | | |
|---|---|---|---|---|---|
| *ptr* | *ṯ-i* | *ꜥmꜣ-k* | *nꜣ-md-t* | *qn* | *ꜥšꜣ* |
| lo | PTC-1S | know-STA.1S | DEF.P-word-F | plenty | many |

| | | |
|---|---|---|
| *nty-bn-mꜣꜥ-t* | *mim-w* | *in* |
| REL-NEG-truth-F | in-3P | NEG |

See, I know the many and numerous issues in which there is no justice.
(*KRI* VII 381, 8–9)

(339g) Robbers list the booty they shared in equal parts stating the amount each of the eight received:

| | | | |
|---|---|---|---|
| *iw-bn-pꜣ-pš* | *n-pꜣy-grg* | *im-f* | *in* |
| DEP-NEG-DEF.M-division | of-DEM.M-equipment | in-3MS | NEG |

... while it does not contain the division of that tomb equipment.
(*KRI* VI 485, 11)

(339h) In regard of the new legal state of former slaves, who were freed and then adopted by the husband of one of their siblings, it is explicitely stated:

| | | | | | |
|---|---|---|---|---|---|
| *iw-bn-st* | *mdi-f* | *m-bꜣk-w* | *mrꜥ* | *in* | *iw-w* |
| DEP-NEG-3P | with-3MS | as-servant-P | still | NEG | DEP-3P |

| | | | | | |
|---|---|---|---|---|---|
| *mdi-f* | *m-sn-w* | *šri-w* | *iw-w* | *m-rmṯ-w* | *nmḥ-w* |
| with-3MS | as-sibling-P | small | DEP-3P | as-man | free |

| |
|---|
| *n-pꜣ-tꜣ* |
| of-DEF.M-land |

...while they are no longer as servants with him but they are with him as younger siblings and they are free people of the country...
(*KRI* VI 737, 15–738,1)

(339i) Interrogated robbers narrate how they discovered the pyramid of King Sobekemsaf:

| | | |
|---|---|---|
| *iw-bn-sw* | *mi-qd-nꜣ-mḥr-w* | *mꜥḥꜥ-w* |
| DEP-NEG-3MS | like-manner-DEF.P-pyramid-P | tomb-P |

| |
|---|
| *n-nꜣ-sr-w* |
| of-DEF.P-official-P |

| | | | | | | | |
|---|---|---|---|---|---|---|---|
| *nty* | *ṯ-n* | *šm* | *r-iṯꜣ-ṯ* | *im-w* | *m-dwn* | *zp-2* | *in* |
| REL | PTC-1P | go | to-take-INF | in-3P | in-else | time-2 | NEG |

...while it was in no way like the pyramids and tombs of the nobles which we got to steal from them usually ... (*KRI* VI 483, 15–484, 1)

As the above examples (and especially the last one) show, the negation *in* is placed after the predicate. However, the use of *in* does not seem to have been obligatory: some examples where the context would seem pragmatically marked show the simple negation *bn*; cf. e.g. 339a with the ex. 340a, or the emphasis that can be assumed for ex. 340b:

(340a) Paneb was accused of having stolen a (wooden?) goose at the funeral of a queen. He swore:

*bn-sw* *mdi-i* *i-ir-tw* *gm-s* *m-p3y-f-pr*
NEG-3MS with-1S ST-make-PASS find-3FS in-POSS.M-3MS-house
'I do not have it!' – although it was found in his house.
(*KRI* IV 413, 15–16)

(340b) In reply to a letter perceived as hostile the sender defends himself:

*ḫr-ir-n3-iḥ-w* *st* *r-ḥ3-t-p3y-w-mniw* *iw-w*
PTC-as-DEF.P-cow-P 3P to-front-F-POSS.M-3P-herdsman DEP-3P
*m-s-t=nb*
in-place-F=QU
*bn-st* *r-ḥ3-t-šms=ink*
NEG-3P to-front-F-retainer=1S
And as for the cattle – they are in charge of their herdsman wherever they are. They are not in charge of a retainer of mine. (*KRI* III 505, 9–10)

As will be shown later, the element *in* was not used as widely in adverbial sentences as, e.g., in nominal sentences (Part II). However, ex. 339b shows that the pattern can be found in dependent clauses used as virtual (non-restrictive) relative clause, whereas 339c is an example of a dependent clause with adversative semantics. Finally, in ex. 339f, a negated clause appears in a 'real' (restrictive) relative clause.

If the subject of the adverbial sentence was indefinite, the negation *bn-wn* + subject was used. Due to a phonetic process (*nw* > *m*, see Peust 1999: 163–165), the combination *bn-wn* regularly appears as *mn*[111]:

(341a) The scribal student's physical form will be soft and effeminate:

*p3wn-mn-qsn* *n-rmṯ* *im-k*
because-NEG-bone of-man in-2MS
...because you have no bone of a man in you. (*LEM* 106, 7–8)

(341b) An entry in the necropolis journal notes that the crew was not working on a certain day:

*iw-mn-lb=dy*
DEP-NEG-Libyan=here
...although there was no Libyan around. (*KRI* VI 564, 14–15)

111 As ex. 339a shows, this process was blocked within the sequence negation *bn-* and preterite operator *wn-*, which did not result into *mn*. The reason might have been to disambiguate the two, i.e. *negation + particle* vs. *negation + operator*.

The same negation *mn* appears in sentences expressing non-existence if the entity in question is indefinite:

(342a) Workmen complain to officials about their unpaid salaries:
*mn-ḥbsw mn-sqnn mn-rmw mn-smw*
NEG-cloth NEG-oil NEG-fish NEG-vegetables
There are no clothes, no oil, no fish, and no vegetables. (*RAD* 53, 16–54, 1)

(342b) An entry in the necropolis journal notes after the date:
*i͗w-bn-nꜣ-ḫꜣst-w=dy i͗w-mn-di͗ n-ꜣbd 3*
DEP-NEG-DEF.P-foreigner-P=here DEP-NEG-ration of-month 3
*šmw ꜣbd 4 šmw*
summer month 4 summer
... when no foreigners were around and there were no rations for the third to the fourth month of summer. (*KRI* VI 564, 4–5)

If the entity whose existence is denied is definite, the negation is with *bn* (Vernus 1985):

(343a) As a final remark in a legal case about a donkey, one of the litigants says:
*ṯ-i͗ ḥms-kwi͗ šw-k(wi͗) r-šꜣ[ꜥ]-pꜣ-hrw*
PTC-1S AUX-STA.1S void-STA.1S to-until-DEF.M-day
*bn-tꜣ-ꜥꜣ-t bn-pꜣy-s-sk*
NEG-DEF.F-donkey-F NEG-POSS.M-2FS-foal
I am still bereft of it today. There is no female donkey or her foal. (*KRI* V 474, 6–8)

(343b) Moral precepts advise:
*mi͗r-gm=n-k bꜣ-w n-nṯr ḏs-k i͗w-bn-šꜥy rnn-t*
NEG.IMP-find=for-2MS might-P of-god self-2MS DEP-NEG-N N-F
Do not account the manifestations of a god for yourself, as if (the gods of fate and omina) Shai and Renenutet are not there. (Amenemope 21, 15–16)

(343c) The author of a letter asks the addressee to send him money:
*mi͗r-di͗t whi͗ pꜣy-i͗-ḥḏ ꜥn m-tꜣ-rnp-t*
NEG.IMP-give.INF miss POSS.M-1S-silver again in-DEF.F-year-F
*wn{-i͗}-bn-nꜣ-bd-t i͗w-bn-pꜣ-bi͗ꜣ*
PST-NEG-DEF.P-wheat-F DEP-NEG-DEF.M-copper
Do not allow my money to be missing again this year. There has not been the wheat, and the copper has neither been there! (*KRI* III 255, 12–14)

A similar distribution is found in the possessive pattern *m-di͗ > mdi͗*, where *mn* is used with indefinite possessees and *bn* with definite ones; as in the affirmative, the predicative A(dverbial)P(hrase) is preposed before the subject:

(344a) The author of a letter has been ordered to supply charcoal but complains:

*mn-mdi-i* *ḫt* *m-wḏ3* *inn* *p3y-i-ḥtr-rnp-t*
NEG-with-1S wood in-storehouse except POSS.M-1S-tax-year-F
I do not have wood in the storehouse, except (for) my annual tax.
(*KRI* VI 67, 10)

(344b) A daughter of a man inherits his slot in the necropolis since:

*iw-mn-di-f* *šri* *ꜥḥ3(ṯ)*
DEP-NEG-with-3MS child male
... since he had no male child. (*KRI* V 476, 3–4)

(344c) Relating to the grain for the offerings for Amun, the author of a letter tells the addressee to join up with another man and discuss the matter with the man in charge:

*y3-bn-sw* *mdi-f* *m-wꜥ-ip-t* *r-p3y-f-ḥtp-nṯr*
PTC-NEG-3MS with-3MS as-IDF.S/1-measure-F for-POSS.M-3MS-offering-god
*m-p3-hrw*
in-DEF.M-day
... because he (Amun) has not even an/one *oipe*-measure for his offering until today! (*LRL* 58, 15–16)

The negation *mn* is sometimes encountered also in adverbial sentences with specific subjects:

(345a) The prince of Byblos answers to Wenamun's ideas of Egypt still being the major power in the Levant:

*in-mn* *20* *n-mnš=dy* *n-t3y-i-mr*
IP-NEG 20 of-boats=here in-POSS.F-1S-harbour
Are there not twenty boats here in my harbour? (*LES* 67, 4–5)

(345b) The prince of Byblos continues his reply to Wenamun regarding the balance of power in the Levantine area, particularly as regards Sidon:

*in-mn-ktṯ* *50* *n-br* *nim*
PTC-NEG-another 50 of-boat there
Are there not fifty further boats? (*LES* 67, 6–7)

An *ad-hoc* explanation for this phenomenon might be that the examples are taken from the speech of the prince of Byblos whose Egyptian supposedly contains mistakes typical to for the user of a foreign language.[112] Another explanation might be that, although semantically definite through being numbered, the boats were considered grammatically indefinite – or maybe better, 'over-marked' – for

**112** As proposed by Satzinger 1997: 171–76, but cf. Peust 2002: 319.

definiteness. Any deviation from simple definiteness (i.e. marking by the article *pꜣ-/tꜣ-/nꜣ-*) such as indefiniteness or the use of demonstratives resulted in the use of the same pattern, as witnessed by the use of the negation *mn* instead of *bn* in the examples. However, as in the case of affirmative sentences, the differentiation between adverbial sentences with indefinite subject and those expressing non-existence of an indefinite entity is possible only on semantic grounds, i.e. there is no distinctive grammatical marking.

### 4.2.2 Demotic

In Demotic, the negation of adverbial sentences is achieved by means of *bn ... ỉn* (also written *ꜥn*). In the following examples, *ỉn/ ꜥn* appears after the first adverbial phrase, which shows that it has no focus-marking function in Demotic:

(346a) The small dog-ape compares turquoise with barley:

| | | | |
|---|---|---|---|
| *bn-nꜣ-tw-w* | *n-mfky=ꜥn* | *m-qdy-t* | *wꜥ-wrs* |
| NEG-DEF.P-mountain-P | of-turqoise=NEG | in-likeness-F | IDF.S-stalk |

*n-ỉt*
of-barley

The mountains of turquoise are nothing compared to a stalk of barley.
(Myth of the Sun's Eye 6, 27–28)

(346b) The author of a letter tries to explain to his correspondent the manners of a third person:

| | | | | | | |
|---|---|---|---|---|---|---|
| *ḫr* | *ḏd-f* | *hyn-md* | *n-rꜣ-f* | *ỉw-bnỉw-st* | *n-ḥꜣty-f* | *ỉn* |
| PTC | say-3MS | IDF.P-word | in-mouth-3MS | DEP-NEG-3P | in-heart-3MS | NEG |

His mouth usually says words that are not in his heart
(pBerlin P 13544, 14–17)

(346c) In a fragmentarily preserved letter the addressee is warned:

| | | | | |
|---|---|---|---|---|
| *bnỉw-pꜣdymḥ* | *ẖn-nꜣ-rmṯ-w* | *ntyỉw-w* | *mḥṯ* | *n-ḏr-ṯ-w* |
| NEG-N | in-DEF.P-man-P | REL-3P | seize | OBJ-hand-F-3P |

*n-md* *ỉn*
in-matter NEG

Padimehi is not among the people whose hand you take in a matter of concern. (pBerlin P 13585, x+3)

The initial negation various between *bn* and *bnỉw*, while the pronominal subjects appear with the initial particle *tw* (with the variant *dy*) or *ỉw* (i.e. *bn-ỉw*-PRN) or, as occasionally in the third plural, follow the negation directly (*bn st*). However, the negation appears as *bn-ỉw* also in front of noun subjects as well as in other surroundings in the syntactically similar Present I pattern (e.g., as *bnỉw dy-k ...*, in which *dy* is a graphemic variant of the initial particle *tw*) and hence it seems to have been reanalysed as *bnỉw*. The combination *bn-ỉỉr-* is used to mark the second tense (see the last example below):

(347a) In a document concerning a short-term marriage, the future husband swears:

*ỉw-bn-tw-y* *msꜣ-t* *n-ʿnḫ* *n-sḥm-t* *ỉn*
DEP-NEG-PTC-1S after-2FS for-oath of-woman-F NEG
...while I have no claim against you regarding a woman's oath...
(oStrasbourg 1845 v° 1)

(347b) King Ptolemy has revealed to mankind that is has been a work of the gods and:

*bnỉw-st* *m-šs* *n-ỉr-mlḫ* *ỉrm-f* *ỉn*
NEG-3P in-order for-do-fight with-3MS NEG
...that is was inapropriate to fight against him. (Raphia decree 25)

(347c) After Merib woke up from his dream in the middle of the night, he expressed his intent to go immediately to the temple of the goddes Hathor and tell the authorities about his revelation:

*ỉw-bn-ỉw-s* *ḫn-pꜣy-s-pr* *ỉn*
DEP-NEG-PTC-3FS in-POSS.M-3FS-house NEG
...although she is not in her house.
(*Saqqâra Demotic Papyri I*, text 02 x+1, 21)

(347d) A woman has sworn an oath at the temple of Jême that a certain man went to the gate of the gods:

*ỉw-bn-ỉw-f* *msꜣ-y* *n-ꜣ(qy)* *ʿn* *msꜣ-ꜣq(y)*
DEP-NEG-PTC-3MS after-1S in-sesame NEG after-sesame
*1/24* *ḥnʿ-pamnṯ* *pꜣy-(y)-hy*
1/24 and-N POSS.M-1S-husband
...having no further claim against me as regards semsame except 1/24 artaba of sesame and (also not against) Pamonthes, my husband.
(*O.Tempeleide* #76, 4–7)

(347e) The statutes of a cultic association stipulate:

*pꜣ-rmṯ* *nỉm-n* *nty-ỉw-f* *ḏd* *n-rmṯ* *nỉm-n* *ỉw-k*
DEF.M-man in-1P REL-FUT-3MS say to-man in-1P PTC-2MS
*ḫr-sḥt* *(r)-bn-ỉw-f* *ḫr-sḥt* *ỉn*
under-leprosy DEP-NEG-PTC-3MS under-leprosy NEG
*pꜣy-f-gns* *ḥḏ* *100*
POSS.M-3MS-fine silver 100
Whoever among us who will say to another one of us: 'You are leprous', although he is not leprous, his fine is 100 silver (*diban*).
(pCG 30605, 20)

(347f) In an encomium on King Ptolemy, the goddess Isis is quoted as saying to him:

| | | | | |
|---|---|---|---|---|
| *iw-k* | *ḥn-n3-nṯr-w* | *bn-iir-k* | *ḥn-n3-rmṯ-w* | *in* |
| PTC-2MS | in-DEF.P-god-P | NEG-ST-2MS | in-DEF.P-man-P | NEG |

You are among the gods. You are not among *the humans*.
(oHor 3, r° 18–19)

The particle *in/ʿn* could also be omitted, although examples are not particularly common:

(348) The small dog-ape evokes the *k3*-food:

| | | | |
|---|---|---|---|
| *bn-gr-tpy-t* | *nḏm* | *ḥr-p3-t3* | *rr-f* |
| NEG-other-taste-F | sweet | on-DEF.M-earth | to-3FS |

There is no taste sweeter than it upon earth.
(Myth of the Sun's Eye 4, 26)

Usually, the position of the element *in* is sentence-final. However, from the Roman period onwards, the particle shows clitic behaviour (see also the ex. 346a):

(349a) The ape reminds the goddess of her festivities and says that he beheld the festival and saw:

| | | | | |
|---|---|---|---|---|
| *r-bn-nṯr-t* | *ḥn-w* | *ʿn* | *m-ʿ3* | *[r-p3y]-t-ʿn* |
| DEP-NEG-goddess-F | inside-3P | NEG | in-way | to-POSS.M-2FS-beauty |
| *n-sḥm-t* | | | | |
| of-woman-F | | | | |

... that there is no goddess among them in the likeness of your female beauty.
(Myth of the Sun's Eye 13, 13–14)

(349b) The small dog-ape resumes the things he said:

| | | | |
|---|---|---|---|
| *bn-p3-nty-šʿdṯ* | *rr-f* | *ḥr-p3-t3* | *ʿn* |
| NEG-DEF.M-REL-cut | to-3MS | on-DEF.M-land | NEG |

Yet nothing is emptier upon earth than it. (Myth of the Sun's Eye 4, 1)

When the subject is indefinite, the negation is *mn*, which could occasionally be written *bn* (see the last example below):

(350a) Setne woke up on the street and wanted to rise but shame prevented him from doing so, because:

| | |
|---|---|
| *mn-ḥbs* | *ḥr-3ṯ-f* |
| NEG-garment | on-back-3MS |

He had no clothes on.
(Setne I 5, 32)

(350b) The troops of the Pharaoh are filled with admiration for Minnebmaat:

| | | | | |
|---|---|---|---|---|
| *mn-mhw-t* | *n-rmt-qnqn* | *ḥn-kmy* | *m-qdy* | *t3-mhw-t* |
| NEG-family-F | of-man-fight | in-Egypt | in-likeness | DEF.F-family-F |

*wsir* *nsw* *itrḥrrrw*
deceased king N
There is no family of warriors in Egypt such as the family of the deceased king Inaros. (pSpiegelberg 17, 15–17)

(350c) In a letter from the Ptolemaic Period:
*st-ḏd=n-y* *[n]im-s* *mḏr-rmt=nb* *nty-(n)-yb* *swn*
3P-say=to-1S OBJ-3FS by-man=QU REL-(in)-N N
*ḏd-mn-sḥm-t* *(n)-pꜣy-k-ꜥwy*
COMP-NEG-woman-F (in)-POSS.M-2MS-house
Everyone (in) Elephantine and Syene tells me: 'There is no woman in your house!' (pBerlin P 13538, 20–23)

(350d) Pharaohs magicians answer to his accusation they could be responsible for his unpleasant state of health and hence would not ask the gods for a longer life time for him:
*pꜣy-i-nb* *ꜥꜣ* *ꜥnḫ* *ḥr-k* *mn-rmṯ* *nim-n* *iw-f*
POSS.M-1S-lord great live face-2MS NEG-man in-1P DEP-3MS
*rḫ-dbḥ* *ꜥḥꜥ* *n-prꜥꜣ*
know-ask life_time for-Pharaoh
Mylord, as your face may live, there is no one among us, who could ask for (more) life time for Pharaoh. (pVandier 1, 9–10)

(350e) The small dog-ape wishes that the sun would shine:
*r-bn-šn* *ḥr-tꜣ-imy-t-spdt*
DEP-NEG-cloud on-DEF.F-way-F-N
... with no cloud upon the way of Sothis. (Myth of the Sun's Eye 16, 6–7)

Note that the pronoun *st* appears to be used impersonally in ex. 350c, anticipating the Coptic use of the third person plural performative *se*-. As the comparison of the first two examples above shows, the distinction between negated adverbial sentences with indefinite subject and non-existential sentences was, as in Late Egyptian, impossible on morpho-syntactic grounds.

The following problematic examples from Papyrus Insinger may also be analysed as examples with a zero subject due to the spurious appearance of an *n* after the initial negation:

(351a) On the relationship between men and women:
*bniw-sḥm-t* *ꜥn-t* *in* *tꜣ-nty-ḥsy*
NEG-woman-F decent-F NEG DEF.F-REL-praise.STA
*n-ḥꜣtṯ* *n-ky*
in-heart of-other
*bniw-tꜣ-lẖ-t* *n-pꜣ-ẖyr* *in* *tꜣ-nty-ir-nḏsy-t* *nim-f*
NEG-DEF.F-fool-F in-DEF.M-street NEG DEF.F-REL-do-whore-F in-3MS

*bniw-n-rmt-rḫ* *in* *pꜣ-nty-ir-sḫne* *nim-w*
NEG-PRP(?)-man-wise NEG DEF.M-REL-AUX-meet in-3P
*tꜣ-wp-t* *n-mw-t* *ḥwtḥr* *tꜣ-nty-ḫpr*
DEF.F-work-F of-N N DEF.F-REL-happen
*iwṯ-nꜣ-sḥm-w-t*
between-DEF.P-woman-P-F
*iir-špšy-t* *wrꜣ-t* *ḥr-pꜣ-tꜣ*
ST-good_fortune-F bad_spirit-F on-DEF.M-land
*ḫn-nꜣ-sḥm-w-t*
in-DEF.P-women-P-F
A decent woman is not she who is praised in the heart of another person. The fool of the street is not she who acts as a whore therein. A wise man is not he who has contacts with both of them. It is the work of Mut and Hathor what happens between women, (and) *in women* are good fortune(?) and bad fortune(?) upon earth. (pInsinger 8, 15–19)

(351b) On a wise man:
*bniw-pꜣ-rmt-rḫ* *nty-sṯny* *pꜣ-nty-gm-sṯny* *in*
NEG-DEF.M-man-wise REL-counsel DEF.M-REL-find-counsel NEG
*bniw-n-pꜣ-lḫ* *irm-pꜣ-ḫn* *in* *ꜥn*
NEG-PRP-DEF.M-fool and-DEF.M-idiot NEG again
*pꜣ-ntyiw-pꜣy-w-sp* *hwš* *iir-sṯny* *ip*
DEF.M- REL-POSS.M-3P-case asperse ST-counsel thought
*irm-ꜥwnḥꜣtṯ* *ꜥwy* *pꜣ-ntr*
and-patience (in)-arms DEF.M-god
A wise man who can give counsel is not he who happens to find counsel. Nor is he whose acts are aspersed a fool or an idiot. Counsel, thought, and patience are *in the hand of god.* (pInsinger 22, 3–5)

However, the semantics rather argue in favour of a cleft sentence pattern. Hence, one would have to accept *bniwn* as a graphic variant for the classical *bn(iw)*. This is perhaps supported by a passage from a late Roman text in which an adverbial sentence analysis can be excluded because of the presence of the element *tꜣy*:

(352) Setne tells his wife to leave him:
*tꜣ-md-t* *ntyiw-ḥꜣṯ-y* *ḏḥrꜣ* *(r)ḏbꜣṯ-s*
DEF.F-matter-F REL-heart-1S grieve because-3FS
*bniwn*$^{(?)}$*-md-t* *iw-šw* *wn-s* *r-sḥm-t* *in* *tꜣy*
NEG-thing-F DEP-fit open-3FS to-woman-F NEG SE.F
The matter over which my heart grieves is not fit to be revealed to a woman. (Setne II 3, 10)

The possessive construction *mtw-* is negated with *mn* if the possessee is indefinite, otherwise the negation is with *bniw* ... *in*:

(353a) The father of Ahure rejects the idea that his two children engage in an incestuous marriage:
*iwfḫpr* *iw-mn-mtw-y* *šr* *msꜣ-šr* *2*
CND DEP-NEG.be-with-1S child after-child 2
*in-pꜣ-hp* *dy-t* *ḥms-wꜥ* *irm-wꜥ* *nim-w*
PTC-DEF.M-law let-INF sit-one with-one of-3P
If I have no children but two, is it lawful that one marries the other?
(Setne I 3, 1)

(353b) In a letter to god Thoth, the author says that he gave up his earlier profession and loves working for the god, noting:
*mn-mtw-(y)* *ḥri* *rmṯ*
NEG-with-1S lord man
I have no human lord. (oChicago OIM 19422, 3)

(353c) In a document concerning a house, a person swears that there will be no recourse to the matter:
*mn-mtw-y* *hp* *wpy* *md=nb* *n-pꜣ-tꜣ*
NEG.be-with-1S law verdict thing=QU in-DEF.M-land
*iirn-t* *(n)-rn-f* *(n)ṯꜣy-pꜣ-hrw* *r-ḥry*
before-2FS in-name-3MS since-DEF.M-day to-above
I have no right, verdict, or anything to ask from you in this world in his name from now on. (pBM 10522, 3)

(353d) Moral precepts suggest:
*mir-qpe* *iw-mn-mtw-k* *ḫr-t*
NEG.IMP-hide DEP-NEG.be-with-2MS food-F
Do not hide when you have no food!
(Onkhsheshonqy 7, 9)

(353e) Moral precepts recommend not to promise to give something to the overlord:
*(r)-bniw-iw-f* *mtw-k* *in*
DEP-NEG-PTC-3MS with-2MS NEG
...although you do not have it at all. (pLouvre N 2414 2, 12)

### 4.2.3 Coptic

The usual way of negating adverbial sentences in Coptic is by means of *(n-)*... *(=)an*, which is the etymological successor of *bn-...(in)* of the earlier stages of Later Egyptian. Yet in Coptic the initial negative morpheme (*n* < *bn*) had become almost obsolete and the second element *an* < *in* was reanalysed as the major negative element. The latter follows the predicate:

(354a) It is said of someone who claims to have know God and yet does not keep his commandments:
*n-t-me* *hm-pai=an*
NEG-DEF.F-truth in-DEM.M=NEG
The truth is not in this one. ($^{S}$1Jn 2:4)

(354b) The patriarch John expands on the issue whether anyone would have been able to enter the heavens before the advent of the son of man. He reasons about Mary, the mother of Jesus, that none would have dared to impede her from entering the heavens being the mother of God and asks who would have dared to say:
*n-t-mau* *m-p-nute* *hn-t-pê=an*
NEG-DEF.F-mother of-DEF.F-god in-DEF.F-heaven=NEG
The mother of God is not in heaven.
($^{S}$*Questions of Theodore* [van Lantschoot 42, 15–16])

(354c) The monk Frange asks another monk in a letter to fetch the codexes containing 1&2 Kings from a third monk but instructs him to insist if the latter would say:
*se-hm-p-ma=[a]n*
3P-in-DEF.M-place=NEG
They are not here. ($^{S}$*O.Frange* #72, 11–12)

(354d) The angel told the women who had come to mourn at Jesus' tomb:
*n-f-m-pei-me=en*
NEG-3MS-in-DEM.M-place=NEG
He is not here. ($^{M}$Mt 28:6)

(354e) Jesus left Lake Tiberias for the mountains, but a crowd looked for him:
*hote=un* *eta-u-nau* *nce-ni-mêš* *ce-i(êsu)s* *mmau=an*
when=now TMP-3P-see PVS-DEF$_2$.P-crowd COMP-N there=NEG
*ude* *ne-f-mathêtês*
or POSS.P-3MS-disciples
When the multitude saw that Jesus was not there, nor were his disciples... ($^{B}$Jn 6:24)

Bohairic again may show the insertion of the dummy verb *k$^h$ê* between the subject and predicate:

(355a) The angel told the women who had come to mourn at Jesus' tomb:
*f-k$^h$ê* *m-pai-ma=an*
3MS-AUX in-DEM.M-place=NEG
He is not here. ($^{B}$Mt 28:6)

(355b) St Anthony argues:

*uon 3 n-hôb $k^{h}$ê ẖen-pi-kosmos uoh se-$k^{h}$ê*
PTC 3 of-thing AUX in-DEF$_2$.M-world and 3P-AUX
*hi-pi-tôu=an*
on-DEF$_2$.M-hill=NEG
There are three things in the world, and they are not in the desert.
($^{B}$*AP St Anthony* [*MG* 25 36, 12–13; collated])

In sentences with indefinite subjects the negation *mn-/mmn-* was used:

(356a) Two monks write to a group of other monks:

*a-u-kui n-šace šôpe hn-te-n-mête a-n-r-anaš*
PST-IDF.S-little of-word happen in-POSS.F-1P-midst PST-1P-make-oath
*ce-mn-sôuh nmmê-tn*
COMP-NEG-gathering with-2P
We had a discussion among us and swore an oath that there will be no gathering with you (anymore). ($^{S}$*O.Ashm.Copt.* 16, 5–7)

(356b) A note in a receipt for some lamps and lampstands:

*p-ke-ua mn-hêbs hiôô-f*
DEF.M-other-one NEG-lamp upon-3MS
There is no lamp upon the other one. ($^{S}$*O.Vind.Copt.* 35, 8–9)

(356c) Gesios strolled along the shore of the sea and found some human bones:

*mmn-fô ude šaar hiô-u alla ne-u-o*
NEG-hair or skin upon-3P but PRT-3P-be.STA
*n-t-he n-u-elaphantion e-mn-lau nhêt-u*
as-DEF.F-way of-IDF.S-ivory DEP-NEG-any in-3P
*hitm-p-rôht n-n-mou-nioue e-u-šei nmma-u*
by-DEF.M-strike of-DEF.P-waters-P DEP-3P-move with-3P
There was neither hair nor skin on them; rather, they were like ivory, while the striking of the waves that came and went with them had left no trace on them. ($^{S}$*Gesios & Isidorus* [*ZÄS* 21, 141, 15])

(356d) Jesus answers to his disciples' objections against visiting the sick Lazarus in Bethany:

*mê mn-mntsnaus n-unu hn-p-hou*
IP NEG-12 of-hour in-DEF.M-day
Does the day not have twelve hours? ($^{L}$Jn 11:9)

(356e) Jesus answers the Pharisees' wish for a sign by saying that whenever an unclean spirit possesses a man:

*ša-f-še ne-f ebal e-hen-me e-mmn-mau nhêt-u*
AOR-3MS-walk for-3MS out to-IDF.P-place DEP-NEG-water in-3P
He has to wander through places that have no water. ($^{M}$Mt 12:43)

(356f) A description of the situation at a palace in Antioch:
*ne-mmon-šêri n-hôut nẖêt-s an pe imêti e-šeri*
IPF-NEG-child.M of-male in-3FS NEG PTC except to-child.F
*2 m-parthenos mmauat-u e-u-šop ẖen-t-agmê*
2 of-virgin alone-3P DEP-3P-be.STA in-DEF.F-point
*n-ti-hylêkia*
of-DEF$_2$.F-youth
There was no male descendant in it; merely two virgin daughters at the point of maturity. ([B]*Mart. Theodore et al.* [*AM* I 35, 19–21])

Note that the use of *mn-/mmn-* usually leads to omission of the indefinite article in the singular. As ex. 356e shows, this affects also the rule of using the indefinite article with substances in indeterminate quantities.

Contrary to the situation in the affirmative pattern, the use of the initial particle *eis* 'behold' did not – for obvious reasons – result in an omission of the initial *mn-* (and thereby the negation) with indeterminate subjects:

(357) Laban and Jakob make an agreement:
*is hêête mmn-lau m-pei-ma nmma-n*
lo behold NEG-any in-DEM.M-place with-1P
Behold, no-one is with us here. ([S]Gn 31:50)

Negative existential sentences have the same outward appearance as negative adverbial sentences in employing the negation *mn-*:

(358a) Jesus asks rhetorically whether the lamp is to be hidden or placed upon a lampstand:
*mn-p-et-hobs=gar n-se-na-k$^j$olp ebol an*
NEG-DEF.M-REL-cover=for NEG-3P-FUT-reveal out NEG
*ude mn-p-et-hêp n-f-na-uônh ebol an*
nor NEG-DEF.M-REL-hide.STA NEG-3MS-FUT-manifest out NEG
There is nothing covered that will not be revealed, nor anything hidden that will not be made manifest. ([S]Mk 4:22)

(358b) The governor tells Apa Ptolemy that he will be tortured unless he offer some incense and say:
*mn-nute nsa-ntok apollôn*
NEG-god exept-2MS N
There is no god but you, O Apollo.
([S]*Mart. Ptolemy* [Till, *KHML* II 33, 16–17])

(358c) St Paul quotes sayings of the Corinthians:
*men-nuti nsa-uei*
NEG-god after-one
There is no god but one. ([F]1Cor 8:4)

(358d) The reason for the argument leading to a division between the Sanhedrin, Pharisees, and Sadducees:
*ni-saddukeos=men=gar se-cô mmo-s ce-mmon-anastasis*
DEF.P-sadducee=PTC=for 3P-say OBJ-3FS COMP-NEG-resurrection
*ude-angelos ude-pn(eum)a*
nor-angel nor-spirit
For the Sadducees say that there is no resurrection, or angel, or spirit.
($^{B}$Acts 23:8)

The expression of inability could be achieved by replacing the particle *un-* of the pattern described in 3.2.4 with its negative counterpart *mn-/mmn-*. As in the affirmative expression, various constructions are attested here:

(359a) Unless a person be born again:
*mmn-k$^{j}$om mmo-f e-nau e-t-mnt-ero m-p-nute*
NEG.PTC-power in-3MS to-see OBJ-DEF.F-ABST-king of-DEF.M-god
...he cannot see the kingdom of God. ($^{S}$Jn 3:3)

(359b) Jesus vows that he will ask the father on behalf of everyone who turns to him to send another comforter:
*p-pn(eum)a n-t-mêe p-ete-mn-k$^{j}$am m-p-kosmos*
DEF.M-spirit of-DEF.F-truth DEF.M-REL-NEG-power in-DEF.M-world
*a-cit-f*
to-take-3MS
...(even) the Spirit of truth, whom the world cannot receive. ($^{L}$Jn 14:17)

(359c) Jesus tells people to fear God rather than those who can kill the body:
*te-tn-psykhê=de mmn-š-k$^{j}$am mmau e-hotb mma-s*
POSS.F-2P-soul=yet NEG.PTC-can-power PTC to-kill OBJ-3FS
...but cannot kill your souls. ($^{M}$Mt 10:28)

(359d) The Ecclesiastes bewails the worn-out nature of words:
*mmn-k$^{j}$am nte-u-rômi seci nhêt-u*
NEG-power CNJ-IDF.S-man speak within-3P
No one can speak in them. ($^{F}$Eccl 1:8 [Schenke 46, 4])

(359e) The apostle warns against participating in pagan feasts:
*mmon-š-com mmô-ten e-sô ebol ḫen-pi-ap$^{h}$ot*
NEG.PTC-can-might in-2P to-drink out in-DEF$_2$.M-cup
*nte-p-c$^{h}$(ôi)s nem-pi-ap$^{h}$ot nte-ni-demôn*
of-DEF.M-lord and-DEF$_2$.M-cup of-DEF.P-demon
You cannot drink from the cup of the Lord and the cup of the demons.
($^{B}$1Cor 10:21)

Finally, the possive construction *un(n)te-* is negated with the help of *mn-* as *mn(n) te-* (note that while the affirmative pattern shows a contracted and an uncontracted pattern, see above 3.2.4), the negative form, at least in Bohairic is limited to the contracted form:

(360a) The monk Frange asks someone per letter for some salt:
*[ce]-mnta-i*
for-NEG.have-1S
...for I don't have any. ([S]*O.Frange* #103, 4–5)

(360b) Clement describes Jesus saying that he was like a child, like a root in thirsting ground:
*au* *na-mn-smat* *ute* *mnt-f-saie* *alla*
and PRT-NEG-form nor NEG.have-3MS-beauty but
*a-t-f-ḫrbe* *šês*
ST-POSS.F-3MS-form despise.STA
And there was no form nor did he possess splendor but despised was his guise. ([A]1Cl 16:3 [Schmidt])

(360c) When the Jews wonder how Jesus would be able to give them his flesh to eat he tells them that unless they would eat the flesh of the Son of man and drink his blood:
*mntê-tn* *mmeu* *m-p-ônh* *hn-têne*
NEG.have-2P PTC OBJ-DEF.M-life in-2P
...you have no life in you. ([L]Jn 6:53)

(360d) Jesus tells a parabel on the heavenly kingdom saying that it would resemble a certain king to whom a man was brought to be judged. This man, who owed him tenthousand talents:
*e-mmnte-f=de* *e-tuia* *ha-f-keleue*
DEP-NEG.have-3MS=yet to-repay PST.3MS-order
*nk[j]ê-pe-f-c(ôi)s* *e-te-f* *ebal*
PVS-POSS.M-3MS-lord to-give-3MS out
But since he had nothing to pay, his lord ordered him to be sold ... ([M]Mt 18:25)

(360e) The apostle answers to those who would question his apostolic mission:
*ce-mman* *uaeet-ø* *mn-barnabas* *mntê-n-eksusia* *mmeu*
or-not alone-1S and-N NEG.have-power PTC
*e-štem-el-hôb*
to-NEG-do-work
Or do only I and Barnabas lack the right to work? ([F]1Cor 9:6)

(360f) Jephthah had vowed to the Lord to offer the first thing to greet him at home if he was victorious against the Ammonites. Now, the first thing to greet him back home is his only daughter:
*ne-mmonte-f-šeri* *mmau* *pe* *ude* *šêri* *ebêl* *ero-s*
PRT-NEG.have-3MS-daughter PTC PTC nor son except to-3FS
He had no daughter or son but her. ([B]Jdg 11:34)

Second tense forms are negated with *n-...=an* as well if the subject is definite (exx. 361a–d). From the similar Present II pattern, i.e. clauses with a verbal predicate, one can infere that sentences with indefinite subject were negated with initial *ete-mmn-* (exx. 361e–f). However, this seems unattested for sentences with adverbial predicate besides the given examples:

(361a) John reasons that the heavens are inhabited by angels since:
*ešce n-ere-nai hn-t-pe=an e-u-hôbs*
CND NEG-ST-DEM.P in-DEF.F-heaven=NEG ST-3P-cover
*m-pe-u-ho etbe-u*
OBJ-POSS.M-3P-face because-what
If these are not in heaven, why do they cover their face?
($^{S}$*Questions of Theodore* [van Lantschoot 40, 15–16])

(361b) After Raphael, the angel of the Lord, revealed himself to Tobit and Tobias, they prostrate themselves on the ground. He tells them to have no fear and says:
*ce-hn-ta-kharis anok=an e-i-nmmê-tn alla hm-p-uôš*
for-in-POSS.F.1S-grace 1S=NEG ST-1S-with-2P but in-DEF.M-wish
*m-p-nute*
of-DEF.M-god
For not on my own grace I am with you, but by the wish of God.
($^{S}$Tb 12:18)

(361c) The people in his hometown Nazareth are astonished as Jesus starts to preach to them and they say among themselves where he received all those wisdom from seeing that he must be that carpenter's son:
*auô ne-f-snêu n-shimi mê n-a-u-hataa-tenen=en*
and POSS.M-3MS-brother.P of-female IR NEG-ST-3P-with-2P=NEG
And his sisters, aren't they here with us? ($^{F}$Mt 13:56)

(361d) The apostle addresses the community like a father and announces that he soon will visit them himself to examine the problems among them:
*ti-met-uro=gar nte-$p^{h}$-(nu)ti n-a-s-ḫen-p-saci=an*
DEF$_2$.F-ABST-king=for of-DEF$_1$.M-god NEG-ST-3FS-in-DEF$_1$.M-word=NEG
*alla a-s-ḫen-u-com*
but ST-3FS-in-IDF.S-power
For the kingdom of God is not in talk but in power. ($^{B}$1Cor 4:20)

(361e) The apostle chides the Corinthians for he has been told about enmity and strife amongst them. In addition, heresies have been reported to him. So he tells them that their gathering as a community is not to feast on the Lord's supper:

*mê* *ete-mntê-tn-êi* *mmau* *e-uôm* *auô* *e-sô*
IR ST-NEG.have-2P-house there to-eat and to-drink
*cn-mmon*
or-not
Don't you have houses to eat and drink, or not? (S1Cor 11:22)

(361f) The Lord asks:
*mê* *ete-mn-kꞌom* *mmo-i* *e-tuce-têutn*
IR ST-NEG-power in-1S to-save-2P
Do I not have the power to rescue you? (SIs 50:2)

Note that many of the Bohairic versions of the quoted instances do not use the Second Tense in the quoted instances.

Unexpected seems the following position of the negation after the subject already:

(362) A series of natural phenomena such as a great storm splitting the mountains or seismic upheaval appears and each time it is said:
*n-ere-p-cois=an* *hm-p-pn(eum)a* ... *n-ere-p-cois=an*
NEG-ST-DEF.M-lord=NEG in-DEF.M-wind ... NEG-ST-DEF.M-lord=NEG
*hm-p-kôht*
in-DEF.M-fire
The Lord is not in the storm. ... The Lord is not in the fire.
(S3Kg 19:11 & 12)

# Part II: **The nominal sentence**

# 1 Internal morpho-syntax

## 1.1 Bipartite nominal sentences without grammaticalised subject element

### 1.1.1 Earlier Egyptian

The structurally simplest type of both Earlier and Later Egyptian nominal sentences, i.e. constructions whose predicate is an expression that can, without further measures being taken, be used as a head of a term (Hengeveld 1992: 58), is the bipartite sentence in which two nominal expressions are directly juxtaposed without any connector or copular element:

S > [NP NP]

In Earlier Egyptian, this construction is attested from the earliest times:

(1a) The king's purification is equated with the divine essence:

| | | | | | |
|---|---|---|---|---|---|
| *snṯr-k* | *snṯr* | *ḏḥwty* | ... | *rꜣ-k* | *rꜣ* |
| purification-2MS | purification | N | ... | mouth-2MS | mouth |
| *n(-y)-bḥs* | *ỉr-t* | | | | |
| of[-M]-calf | milk-F | | | | |

Your purification is Thoth's purification... your mouth is the mouth of a sucking calf. (PT 27b–d)

(1b) The king's physical form is that of the divine:

| | | | | | |
|---|---|---|---|---|---|
| *ḏ-t-k* | *ḏ-t* | *n-t-N=pn* | *ỉf-k* | *ỉf* | *n(-y)-N=pn* |
| body-F-2MS | body-F | of-F-N=DEM.M | flesh-2MS | flesh | of[-M]-N=DEM.M |
| *qs-w-k* | *qs-w* | *N=pn* | | | |
| bone-P-2MS | bone-P | N=DEM.M | | | |

Your body is King N's body, your flesh is King N's flesh, your bones are King N's bones. (PT 193a–b)

(1c) The king is said to be from Heliopolis and to have been born there:

| | | | | | | |
|---|---|---|---|---|---|---|
| *sk* | *rꜥ* | *ḥrytp* | *psḏ-ty* | *ḥrytp* | *rḫw-t* | *nfrtm* |
| PTC | N | leader | ennead-DU | leader | mankind-F | N |

...when Ra was the Double Ennead's leader, and mankind's leader was Nefertem. (PT 483b/W)

Although this type of construction remained functional throughout the history of the Egyptian language, in practise bipartite nominal sentences with two bare nominal elements are not frequent in Earlier Egyptian. They are largely restricted to the earliest texts and/or to a certain number of limited quasi-fossilised uses,

https://doi.org/10.1515/9783110409895-006

such as the closed pairings expressing identity between like nouns as in exx. 1a and 1b.[1] The following semi-formulaic statements with the noun *bw-t* 'abomination' are common in funerary literature (see Frandsen 1986: 150–53):

(2) The deceased proclaims his detestation of urine:

| | | | |
|---|---|---|---|
| *bw-t-ꞽ* | *wsš-t* | *n* | *swrꞽ-ꞽ* |
| abomination-F-1S | urine-F | NEG | drink-1S |

Urine is an abomination of mine; I will not drink (it). (CT III 171f–g/T1C)

Yet, even here, the bipartite pattern *NP NP* varies and is commonly superseded by the more complex and, it seems, diachronically more recent tripartite construction where the nominal constituents are separated by a copular element (see 1.3.1 and ex. 159f). Beyond these uses, nominal sentences of the type *NP NP* are common only with assignment of inalienable attributes, e.g. the personal name of an individual[2]:

(3) Prince Hardjedef tells his father about a great magician:

| | | | | |
|---|---|---|---|---|
| *ꞽw* | *wn* | *nḏs* | *ḏdi* | *rn-f* |
| AUX | exist | freeman | [N | name-3MS] |

There is a freeman whose name is Djedi. (pWestcar 6, 26–7, 1)

The same feature pertains to personal and other names themselves; in the following example, the name of the fortress consists of two bare nouns:

(4) An inundation-record was taken:

| | | | |
|---|---|---|---|
| *ḫft-wnn* | *ḫtmty-bity* | *mr-mšꜥ* | *rnꞽsnb* |
| when-AUX | sealbearer-king | overseer-army | N |

| | | |
|---|---|---|
| *ḥr-ṯs* | *mnw* | *ḫrp-ḫꜥkꜣwrꜥ-mꜣꜥḫrw* |
| PROG-command.INF | fortress | leader-N-justified |

...when the royal sealbearer and general Reniseneb was commanding the fortress (named) 'Khakaura-the-Justified-is-Leader'. (SNM 34370, 3–4)

1 The semantic nature of this sort of pairing will be discussed in 3.1.2.

2 See 2.4.1 for the clausal status of this nominal sentence. It is often argued that the morphemic distance between the possessor and possessed is always smaller in inalienable than in alienable possession (e.g. Haiman 1983: 793–95). If so, Earlier Egyptian would provide a fine example of such a general iconic principle.

Further inalienables often expressed with this construction are kinship- and bodily part-whole relations:

(5a) The king's family consists of divinities:

| | | | | |
|---|---|---|---|---|
| *it-k* | *smꜣ* | *wr* | *mw-t-k* | *ḥnw-t* |
| father-2MS | bull | great | mother-F-2MS | maiden-F |

Your father is the Great Wild Bull and your mother is the Maiden. (PT 809c)

(5b) The king is told to seize a harpoon described in the following terms:

| | | | | | |
|---|---|---|---|---|---|
| *bwn-s* | *ḥnb-w* | *rꜥ* | *qs-wy-s* | *ꜥn-w-t* | *mꜣfdt* |
| barb-3FS | lightning-P | N | point-DU-2FS | claw-P-F | N |

Its barbs are the lightnings of Ra; its points are the claws of (the goddess) Mafdet. (PT 1212c–d)

However, the simple bipartite construction is common when one or, less often, both of the combined nominals are pronouns. The relative ordering of these elements and *vis-à-vis* nouns is strictly hierarchical and can be formulated as follows[3]:

> determinative pronoun > absolute personal pronoun > interrogative pronoun > demonstrative pronoun (> noun) > clitic personal pronoun

Examples with absolute personal pronouns are by far the commonest, particularly when they combine with simple nouns or participles:

(6a) Ankhtify profiles himself in characteristically immodest terms:

| | | | | |
|---|---|---|---|---|
| *ink* | *ḥꜣ-t* | *rmṯ* | *pḥwy* | *rmṯ* |
| 1S | front-F | men | end | men |

I am the beginning of men and the end of men. (*Moꜥalla* IIα2)

(6b) The peasant appropriates standard mortuary phrases in his flattery of the high steward:

| | | |
|---|---|---|
| *ntk* | *it* | *n(-y)-nmḥ* |
| 2MS | father | of[-M]-orphan |

You are a father of an orphan. (Peas B1, 93)

(6c) Neni flatters his addressee:

| | | |
|---|---|---|
| *ntk* | *irr* | *nfr-t=nb-t* |
| 2MS | do.PIA | good-F=QU-F |

It is you who can do everything good. (pUC 32199, 8)

3 For the highest-ranking determinative pronoun, see below.

(6d) Pepinakht profiles himself:
*ink* *mry* *n(-y)-it-f* *ḥzy* *n(-y)-mw-t-f*
1S love.PPP of[-M]-father-3MS praise.PPP of[-M]-mother-F-3MS
*mrr-w* *sn-w-f*
love.PIA-M sibling-P-3MS
I was one beloved of his father, praised of his mother, and loved of his siblings. (*Urk.* I 133, 6–8)

The combination of these personal pronouns with interrogative pronouns occurs as well:

(7a) A question put to the deceased by the guardians of the underworld:
*ṯwt* *m*
2MS WH
Who are you? (CT III 95g/B1L)

(7b) The deceased has just demanded that the guardians of the underworld grant him access. The latter ask:
*ntk* *sy*
2MS WH
What are you? (BD 122/*Nu* pl. 25, 2)

In bipartite sentences of this type, where the second position is occupied by a demonstrative pronoun, the latter displays clitic behaviour. For example, in the following instances the demonstratives *nn*, *nꜣ*, *nfꜣ*, and *nw* separate the indirect genitives built with the element *n-* from their head nouns:

(8a) The author of a letter tries to coax his addressee into supporting him against an enemy:
*zp=swt=nn* *n(-y)-ʿḥʿ* *ḥr-th-t=nb*
occasion=but=DEM of[-M]-stand.INF on-offence-F=QU.M
*n-t-ḥꜣtyʿ=pn*
of-F-mayor=DEM.M
But this is a (proper) occasion to attend to every offence of this mayor. (pBerlin P. 8869, 8–9)

(8b) Heqanakhte exhorts his underlings to greater diligence in troubled times:
*mk* *rnp-t=nꜣ* *n(-y)-irr* *s* *n-nb-f*
PTC year-F=DEM of[-M]-do.GEM man to-lord-3MS
This is a year for a man to take action for his lord. (Heqanakhte I, v° 9)

(8c) The soul says concerning the hereafter:
*s-t=nfꜣ* *n-t-ẖnt*
place-F=DEM of-F-alight.INF
That is a place of alighting upon. (Man and Ba 37)

(8d) A comment on the statement by the deceased that he will pass on 'the high roads of Rosetau':
*wꜣ-w-t=nw* *n-t-wsir*
road-P-F=DEM of-F-N
These are roads of Osiris. (CT VII 282b)

This phenomenon is undoubtedly the result of an analogy with =*pw*, a second position clitic subject or copula element common in Earlier Egyptian nominal sentences and historically derived from an earlier demonstrative pronoun (see 1.2.1 and 1.3.1 for discussion). Further, all the demonstratives used in the above type of constructions belong to the so-called *n*-series (*nn*, *nꜣ*, *nfꜣ*, *nw*), which, together with the singular forms *pꜣ*/*tꜣ*, are the only set of Earlier Egyptian demonstratives regularly used absolutely as nouns (Gardiner 1957: §111).

Constructions of the type *NP NP* with interrogative pronouns are commonest with absolute personal pronouns that occupy the first position (exx. 7a–b), but the former also occur with clitic personal pronouns (ex. 9a), demonstrative pronouns (9b), and nouns and their syntactic equivalents such as relative clauses (9c–9e)

(9a) The deceased has just demanded that the yon ferryman allow him to his boat. The latter asks:
*m=tr=ṯw*
WH=PTC=2MS
Who are you? (CT V 68j/B1C)

(9b) The gods ask the deceased in reference to the overall situation:
*sy=rf=nꜣ*
WH=PTC=DEM
What is this? (CT VI 284l)

(9c) Heqanakhte asks his household, referring to their bad treatment of his new wife:
*ptr* *qy* *n(-y)-wnn-i* *ḥnꜥ-ṯn* *m-ṯ-t* *wꜥ-t*
WH form of[-M]-AUX-1S with-2P in-table-F one-F
What is the point of my staying in one single table with you?
(Heqanakhte II, r° 43)

(9d) In a broken context:
*išst* *ḫ-t* *n-t-irt* *r-nn*
WH thing-F of-F-do.INF to-DEM
What is the thing to be done to this? (CT VII 197i)

(9e) Heqanakhte, stunned by his household's bad treatment of his new wife, asks:
*(i)ḫ* *ir-t-s* *r-ṯn*
WH do.REL.FUT-F-3FS to-2P
What could she do against you? (Heqanakhte I, v° 15)

In some approaches, contructions such as these have been analysed not as nominal, but rather as *adjectival* sentences (e.g. Malaise and Winand 1999: §477; Vernus 2006: 149–51, 154–57; Borghouts 2010: §95.e). The main reason for this is the use in 9a of the clitic personal pronoun *=ṯw* after the initial interrogative pronoun *m*, which, as will be observed later, indeed resembles the adjectival construction (see Part III). This analysis is, however, questionable (see Gundacker 2010: 60–63; Uljas 2012a: 254–56). Ex. 9a does not seem to concern (or inquire about) the *quality* of the referent of the personal pronoun (i.e. the sentence does not mean 'of what sort are you?'), as is prototypically the case in adjectival sentences. Moreover, enquiring a quality was in Earlier Egyptian expressed by interrogative *adverbial* sentences with the preposition *mi* 'like' such as the following:

(10a) A question concerning the yon ferry:
*iw-s{w}=irs* *mi-išst*
AUX-2FS=PTC like-WH
What is she like? (CT V 91d/Sq1Sq)

(10b) The sage laments the shortage of fresh fruit:
*iw* *min* *dp-t* *ir-y* *mi-m* *min*
AUX today taste-F to.RLT-M like-WH today
Today, how is their taste today? (Ipuwer 5, 2)

In addition, the use of the clitic personal pronoun in 9a does not by itself prove that the construction is adjectival in character inasmuch as clitic pronouns are used *whenever* personal pronouns appear after the first prosodic unit of the clause. Besides, and as will be discussed further in 3.1.1, in 9a, the clitic pronoun *=ṯw* represents the *subject* of the construction, whereas sentence patterns are in general classified according to the type of their *predicates*. Finally, it was shown in Part I (1.1) that the same construction also appears with the interrogative adverbial *ṯn* 'where' in the first position:

(11) A question asked concerning the deceased:
*ṯn=sw* *pr*
WH=3MS go.forth.PPA
Where is he who has gone forth? (CT II 292a)

Given the status of *ṯn* as an adverb, this construction obviously cannot be analysed as a nominal sentence, and reading it as an adjectival construction is similarly excluded. Nevertheless, it shall be shown in Part III that adjectival sentences of the type [predicate + clitic personal pronoun] are common; this constructional schema was therefore shared by all the three types of Earlier Egyptian non-verbal sentences. The reasons for this will be discussed later in connection with the adjectival sentences.

In bipartite nominal sentences without a subject element, the combined NPs do not cover the entire set of expressions that can form a part of Earlier Egyptian nominal sentences in general. In fact, only nouns, pronouns, and relative clauses are found in such constructions. In principle, the two expressions can occur in whichever order, but there are pragmatically based and lexically conditioned word-order properties observable here, and the likelihood of certain theoretical combinations in actual discourse must also be taken into account.[4] Save for one exception to be discussed shortly, absolute personal pronouns always occupy the first position, whereas demonstrative and clitic personal pronouns as a rule appear in second position. Overall, and as already noted, the sole truly widespread construction of the type *NP NP* at this stage of the language is the type of sentence where the first element is an absolute personal pronoun and the second a relative clause (as in exx. 6a–6d). Constructions of this type occupy a special status in the grammatical system of Earlier Egyptian inasmuch as they may at times correspond to what in modern languages are called (pronominal) cleft sentences. However, it will be shown later that they cannot be analysed as having been *restricted* to this function. Yet there was also a specialised noun cleft pattern, structurally a simple *NP NP* construction of the type [noun + perfective/imperfective active participle], but with the initial actor introduced by the element *ỉn*, which is an integral part of the construction and marks it as a nominal cleft:

(12a) Sinuhe tells that he received plentiful gifts after his return from exile and adds:

*ỉn* *ḥm-f* *rdi* *ỉr-t(w)-f*

PTC majesty-3MS cause.PPA do.SUB-PASS-3MS

It was his majesty who caused it to be done. (Sin B, 308)

(12b) In order to prevent the peasant from discovering who was giving him rations, the high steward used to give them first to his friends; then:

*ỉn* *ḫnms-w-f* *dd=n-f=st*

PTC friend-P-3MS give.PIA=to-3MS=3C

It was his friends who used to give them to him (the peasant). (Peas R, 18.7)

A corresponding future pattern is also attested, but there the participle is replaced by a fully finite verb form whose paradigm seems to be that of the so-called Prospective *sḏm-f* and the construction was not syntactically a nominal sentence.[5]

4 For example, a predicative relation between a personal pronoun and an infinitive is semantically improbable.

5 See 3.1.3 and 3.1.5. There are also some rare examples that appear to show the Future Participle *sḏm-ty-fy* – form, see ex. 341 below.

The constructions described above represent the structural core of Earlier Egyptian bipartite nominal sentences without a subject element. There are also a number of other patterns that seem to belong to this category but whose grammatical status is more debatable and even controversial. In general, it seems fair to say that clitic personal pronouns did not standardly establish a predicative relation with nouns or absolute personal pronouns without the mediation provided by a copula; i.e. the pattern [*N=sw*] was not part of the main inventory of Earlier Egyptian bipartite nominal sentences of the type *NP NP*. However, there appear to be some rare examples of this pattern:

(13a) A gloss in a mythological text explaining a reference to a 'great cat':
*rˁ=pw ḏs-f ḏd-n-t(w) mỉw r-f m-ḏd sỉꜣ r-f*
N=SE self-3MS say-PST-PASS cat to-3MS in-say N to-3MS
*ỉn mỉw=sw m-nn ỉrr-f*
IP cat=2MS in-DEM.M do.REL-3MS
It is Ra himself; he came to be called 'cat' when Sia said of him: 'Is he cat-like in this that he does?' (CT IV 286/87b–288/89a/Sq1C)

(13b) The deceased asserts his divinity:
*ỉw nṯr ỉwy-f m-ḥtp nb ḥw-t ḏsr-t ỉm*[-y]
AUX god come-3MS in-peace lord mansion-F red-F in.RLT[-M]
*ꜣḫ-t ỉnk=wỉ spsn*
horizon-F 1S=1S twice
A god comes in peace, lord of the red mansion, who is in the horizon. I am of my own kind. (CT VII 495g–h/B5C)

Although the grammaticality of these and comparable examples has been disputed along with their interpretation as nominal sentences (Schenkel 2008; but see e.g. Doret 1990: 55–56), it has been argued that they (or some of them) may represent vestiges of an earlier stage of the Egyptian language where the combination *NP NP* was the standard pattern with *all* nouns or noun-equivalents (Gundacker 2010). Another hypothesis views them as representing one of the cross-categorical types of nominal sentences displaying structural and semantic-pragmatic overlap with one of the 'neighbouring' classes of non-verbal sentences (Uljas 2006, see also 3.1.5). What is certain, however, is that examples of this construction are very rare indeed. Yet the same does not hold for *possessive* nominal sentences of the following type:

(14a) The prenomen of a Fifth Dynasty king best known for his sun-temple at Abu Gurob:
*n-wsr-rˁ*
DPR-might-N
'Might belongs to Ra'

(14b) The physician is in league with the gods:
*n=wi* *rꜥ*
DPR=1S N
I belong to Ra. (pEbers 1, 7–8)

(14c) The sailor describes the enormous snake he encountered on the Phantom Island:
*n=sw* *mḥ* *30*
DPR=3MS cubit 30
He was 30 cubits. (Sh.S. 62–63)

(14d) A question in a mathematical problem:
*n=sw* *wr* *r-wr*
DPR=3MS WH to-WH
How much does it belong to how much? (pRhind math. n.45, 1)

In Egyptological treatments, these constructions have mostly been analysed as *adjectival* sentences with a predicative relational *nisbe*-adjective *n*(*-y*) 'belonging to' formed of the datival element *n* (e.g. Gilula 1968: 55–61; Satzinger 1986: 143–45). Against this analysis, it may be pointed out that possessives with *n* are not negated as is usual for adjectival sentences, but instead display the most characteristic negative pattern of nominal sentences (see 4.1).[6] Moreover, and as shall be shown later, relational adjectives do not standardly seem to be used predicatively in Earlier Egyptian (Part III). Finally, it is semantically difficult to see how such a formation, which in principle expresses semantic *relationality*, could be achieved of a *datival* element, whose meaning characteristically has to do with notions such as recipiency. Alternatively, and following various analyses of analogous constructions in Semitic, it has been suggested that *n* be analysed as etymologically a determinative pronoun 'that of'.[7] There has been much discussion over the years on which element in the compound should be understood as the possessor subject and which as the possessed (part of the) predicate,[8] but no consensus has been reached so far. The analysis of the construction as a nominal sentence with a determinative pronoun is an attempt to avoid the problem altogether. The idea is, in short, that the element *n-* represents merely a relator (or '*nota relationis*') that roughly means '(is) in relation to'. As such it does not in fact select

6 Negation in Earlier Egyptian (and in general) is not always symmetric, but in this case it is isomorphic vis-à-vis the affirmative.
7 See Loprieno (1980: 9); Jenni (2004: 123). For Semitic parallels, see the seminal discussion by Pennacchietti (1968: 1–54, 65, 71ff); cf. also Goldenberg (1995: 4–6); Retsö (2009: 3–33).
8 This is the so-called Lamares-problem discussed most extensively by Westendorf (1959/60: 316–29; 1981: 83–86; 1984: 381–97).

one of the combined NPs as the subject but rather expresses a bidirectional relationship between the two elements. The issue is probably rather more complex than this seeing that relators may e.g. be gender/number-marked and be used with single 'related' participants (see Goldenberg 1995: 4–6). Earlier Egyptian *n* shows the second but not the first of these features.[9] Nevertheless, this analysis cannot be easily dismissed, and were it to be accepted, it would follow that the combined elements would, figuratively speaking, be on an equal ground and thus *either* of them could be understood as the possessor or the possessed. The choice would then depend more on co(n)textual and even extra-linguistic factors than fixed rules of ordering. Taken at face value, this would in turn seem to mean that if predication be understood in the Aristotelian manner as adding relevant information to something chosen as subject,[10] the construction described here should be seen as essentially *non-predicative*. More research is required here and particularly on the character of the element *n*, but it may be noted here that there are other nominal sentence types where the question of predicativity is similarly problematic, and for the same reasons as here.

If one of the combined nominals in the possessive construction with *n* is a personal pronoun, this is normally expressed by a clitic pronoun (for instances with absolute pronouns, see below) occupying the second position in the sentence. Exx. 14b–14d illustrate this; in the following early example, the old second-person masculine clitic pronoun =*kw* (> =*ṯw*) appears:

(15) The twin children of Atum say to the king:
*n=kw* *mn* *nṯr=pw*
DPR=2MS so-and-so god=DEM.M
You belong, O so-and-so, to this god. (PT 147a)

The third-person masculine singular combination *n=sw*, which occurs most frequently, gradually became reanalysed as a single unit. The first signs of this merging occur in Old Egyptian, where *n=sw* is written with an intervening sign  *ns*, showing that it was already prosodically bound (note the anteposition of the subject):

(16) The king is told:
*ḥꜥ-k=pw* *n=sw* *nṯr*
body-2MS=DEM.M DPR=3MS god
(As for) this your body, it belongs to god. (PT N1055+31)

---

9 I.e., *n*- is invariable in gender and number, but it occurs with a single related NP e.g. in personal names such as *n-ptḥ* 'Who belongs to (god) Ptah'.
10 Rather than as argument saturation, as would be required in Fregean predicate logic. See e.g. Geach (1962: 23) as well as section 3.1.2 for some further remarks on this issue.

Later this spelling becomes standard, and in Late Egyptian *n=sw* > *ns* becomes essentially a grammaticalised possessive predicate (1.1.2.1). There was also a variant of this construction with absolute pronoun possessors, first attested in the Sixth Dynasty (Edel 1955/64: §368):

(17a) The resurrected deceased is told:

| | | | |
|---|---|---|---|
| *n* | *ntk* | *hrw* | *wsỉr* |
| DPR | 2MS | day | N |

To you belongs the day, O Osiris. (CT I 254f)

(17b) As above:

| | | | |
|---|---|---|---|
| *N=tn* | *n* | *nts* | *ṯr-t* |
| N=DEM.F | DPR | 3FS | willow-F |

This N, to her belongs the divine willow. (CT III 367c/B3C)

In the first-person singular, the writing *n (ỉ)nk* or *nnk* occurs particularly in earlier material:

(18) The deceased is the ruler of the Ennead:

| | | | |
|---|---|---|---|
| T1Ca: | *nnk* | *sf* | |
| | DPR.1S | yesterday | |
| B1Y: | *n* | *ỉnk* | *sf* |
| | DPR | 1S | yesterday |

Yesterday is mine. (CT IV 192a)

Later, and commonly in the first-person singular, the initial *n* is often elided, so that the sentence has the overall guise of a normal bipartite pattern [absolute pronoun + noun] and is distinguishable from the latter only by the possessive sense (cf. e.g. Allen 2000: 70; Loprieno 1995: 121):

(19a) Sinuhe extols his fortunate position:

| | |
|---|---|
| *ỉnk* | *ḥḏ-pꜣq-t* |
| 1S.POSS | white-linen-F |

I possess fine white linen.[11] (Sin B, 153)

(19b) Sinuhe submits to the will of the king:

| | |
|---|---|
| *ntk* | *ʿnḫ* |
| 2MS.POSS | life |

Yours is life. (Sin B, 263)

11 In principle, one could also understand *ḥḏ* as a participial predicate of *ỉnk*: 'I am one white of linen'. Whether this provides good sense (with the speaker essentially announcing that he is white-coloured) is another issue.

A further pattern is [absolute pronoun + ø] (i.e. zero), which in Earlier Egyptian occurs as a variant of the type of sentence exemplified by 6d and is restricted to mortuary self-presentation formulae, could possibly be added the list of bipartite nominal sentences without grammaticalised subject element (Borghouts 1994: 13–34):

(20a) Rudjahau characterises himself:

| | | | | |
|---|---|---|---|---|
| *ink* | *mr-f* | *nfr-t* | *msḏ-f* | *ḏw-t* |
| 1S | love-3MS | good-F | hate-3MS | evil-F |

I am someone who loves good and hates evil. (BM 159, 11)

(20b) The deceased proclaims:

| | | |
|---|---|---|
| *ink* | *n-rḫ-f* | *dšrw* |
| 1S | NEG-know-3MS | anger(?) |

I am someone who does not know anger (?) (BD 42/*Nu* pl. 17)

These examples seem to express a predication between the absolute pronoun *ink* and the two clauses *mr-f* and *msḏ-f* in ex. 20a, and the negation *n-sḏm-f* in 20b. However, the latter should then have the syntactic status of clausal complements, but at least the negation *n-sḏm-f* is not used thus without an overt complementiser in Earlier Egyptian. Consequently, the constructions above have been analysed as being of the form *ink ø mr-f nfr-t msḏ-f ḏw-t* and *ink ø n-rḫ-f dšrw* 'I am (someone) who loves good and hates evil/who does not know anger', where the second nominal is an indefinite pronoun elided because of its low referentiality (Loprieno 1994: 377–78). In this analysis, the clauses *mr-f*, *msḏ-f*, and *n-rḫ-f* in the examples above function as non-restrictive 'virtual' relative clauses whose antecedent is the covert element (see Part I, 2.1.7 for adverbial sentence 'virtual' relative clauses).

The possessive pattern *n* + absolute pronoun discussed above represents the sole exception to the rule that such pronouns require initial position in Earlier Egyptian. From the mid-Eighteenth Dynasty onwards, examples of nominal sentences with two juxtaposed absolute pronouns are occasionally encountered:

(21) The king says to Ra:

| | | | | |
|---|---|---|---|---|
| *hy* | *rʿ* | *ink* | *ntk* | *tspḫr* |
| VOC | N | 1S | 2MS | vice versa |

Hail Ra; I am you and vice versa. (Litany of Ra 101/Th III)

These examples are symptomatic of the more general revision of the syntactic character of absolute pronouns in Late Egyptian, which will be dealt with in the next section.

### 1.1.2 Later Egyptian

Although the strategy for expressing a predicative relation between two nouns by direct juxtaposition was losing ground in Earlier Egyptian, bipartite constructions of the type *NP NP* experienced a notable revival in Late Egyptian. Yet in Demotic and Coptic, the domain of use of this nominal sentence pattern once again became narrower, being restricted mainly to sentences with pronominal participants and to cleft constructions.

#### 1.1.2.1 Late Egyptian

Although in Earlier Egyptian nominal sentences consisting merely of two juxtaposed NPs without any connector are confined to particular contexts, this pattern becomes much more common in Late Egyptian, where it is the most widely used nominal sentence construction:

(22a) In a series of moral precepts recommending adherence to writings:
*ỉꜣw-w-t nn-wn (m)di-s šri*
office-P-F NEG-exist with-3FS child.P
*pꜣy-sn-nmḥ ḫr-ṯ-f pꜣy-sn-sr mk-ṯ-f*
[POSS.M-3P-man] [provision-F-3MS] [POSS.M-3P-official] [shield-F-3MS]
Offices – they have no children. Their free man is their provision! Their official is their shield! (Ani B 20, 6–7)

(22b) The beautiful appareance of a beloved woman is compared to various things. Among them it is said:
*ḫsbd mꜣꜥ šnw-s*
[lapis lazuli true] [hair-3FS]
Her hair is true lapis lazuli. (Mathieu, *Poésie*, pl. 1, 4)

(22c) The addressee is asked to release a certain man:
*ḫr sn ỉnk pꜣy-[rmṯ]*
PTC [brother 1S] [DEM.M-man]
For this man is a brother of mine. (*LRL* 43, 4)

(22d) A wisdom-text warns the reader:
*mw mḏ bw rḫ-ṯ pḫr-s sḥm-t*
[water deep NEG know-one encircle-3FS] [woman-F
*wꜣi-ṯ (r)-hꜣy-s*
far-STA.3FS (to)-husband-3FS]
A woman far from her husband is deep water impossible to encircle.
(Ani B 16, 14–15)

(22e) A scribe has received a letter from a colleague. Yet his excitement over mail vanished as he started to read. He is answering:

*md* *qb* *nꜣy-k-tptr*
word cool POSS.P-2MS-word
Your words are vain talking. (²*pAnastasi I* 59, 5)

(22f) While working on his own tomb, a man happens to break through into another, older tomb. He inspects the old tomb with a torch and many witnesses and finds a coffin down there:

*pꜣ-nty-im* *wꜥ-ṯꜣy-mḏꜣ-t*
DEF.M-REL-there IDF.S-carrier.PIA-chisel-F
The one who was in there was an engraver. (*KRI* V 479, 8–9)

In 22a, both the combined NPs are definite, whereas in 22b–c and 22e–f an indefinite NP occurs in one (see also example 269d below), and in 22d in both positions. One of them may also be an infinitival construction:[12]

(23a) In a series of moral precepts on anger:

*bw-t* *n-nṯr* *iṯt* *ꜣd*
[abomination-F of-god] [take.INF anger]
The abomination of god is to seize anger! (Ani B 15, 13)

(23b) The mayor of Western Thebes accuses:

*pꜣw-btꜣ* *n-pꜣy-sš* *2* *n-pꜣ-ḫr*
[DEM.M-crime of-DEM.M-scribe 2 of-DEF.M-tomb]
*pꜣy-w-pḥ* *pꜣy-ḥꜣtyꜥ* *n-nw-t* *r-ḏd=n-f* *smy*
[POSS.M-3P-reach.INF DEM.M-mayor of-city-F to-tell=to-3MS report]
That crime of these two scribes of the necropolis is their approaching the said mayor of Thebes to report to him! (*KRI* VI 479, 6–8)

(23c) The lover is praised in many ways and the joy of a stroll of the loving pair is described. In addition, it is said that:

*šdḥ* *pꜣy-i-sḏm* *ḫrw-k*
wine POSS.M-1S-hear.INF voice-2MS
That I hear your voice is like red wine. (*lit:* Red wine is my hearing of your voice). (Mathieu, *Poésie*, pl. 13, 10)

12 These examples have been explained also as patterns with a nominal phrase that is positioned in front of a nominal sentence with deleted subject element, i.e. A – B Ø, see Neveu (1996: 220) for example 23b. However, in example 23c this is semantically unlikely (†Red wine – it is my hearing of your voice.)

Late Egyptian also uses the bipartite construction in expressions of bodily part-whole relations:

(24) In the introduction of the *Strife between Head and Belly*:
*ḏd-t* *ẖ-t* *sn-nw-s* *tp*
say.PPP-F belly-F [two-ORD-3FS] [head]
The belly claimed that the head was second to her. (tTurin 58004, 2–3)

The revival of the use of this pattern for two non-pronominal NPs seems to influence contemporary texts written in Traditional Egyptian:

(25) In a Ramesside magical charm against evil swellings:
*psḏ-t* *ꜥꜣ-t* *ms-w-t* *rꜥ*
[ennead-F great-F] [child-P-F N]
*psḏ-t* *nḏs-t* *ms-w-t* *rꜥ*
[ennead-F small-F] [child-P-F N]
The great ennead is the children of Ra. The small ennead is the children of Ra. (oBerlin P. 1269, 4)

In the majority of examples of bipartite nominal sentences of the type *NP NP*, one of the participants is pronominal. Absolute personal pronouns are particularly common:

(26a) A defendant in a tomb-robbery trial reports that his mother said to a man:
*mntk* *ỉꜣw* *šꜣšꜣ*
[2MS] [old man silly]
You are a silly old man. (*KRI* VI 789, 9)

(26b) The author of a letter says to the addressees:
*mnttn* *tꜣ-ḫ-t* *nty-m-ḥꜣty-ỉ*
[2P] [DEF.F-thing-F REL-in-heart-1S]
You are the thing that is in my heart. (*LRL* 16, 4)

(26c) The bull/Bata replies to his wife's question over his identity revealing himself:
*ỉnk* *bt*
[1S] [N]
I am Bata. (*LES* 25, 11)

As in exx. 22c and 24a, the non-pronominal NP in these examples can be indefinite (26a) or definite (26b and 26c). Examples with interrogative pronouns are also rather frequent:

(27a) The King of Byblos reproaches Wenamun:
*ỉḫ* *nꜣ-mšꜥ* *swgꜣ* *ỉ-dỉ-w* *ỉr-k*
[WH] [DEF.P-journey stupid REL-let-3P do-2MS]
What is the use of these stupid journeys they make you do? (*LES* 69, 4–5)

(27b) The courtiers tell the king:
*ỉṯ* *s-t* *ỉw-bw-mꜣꜣ-k=s*
[WH] [place-F DEP-NEG-see.AOR-2MS=3FS]
Where/What is a place that you cannot see? (*KRI* II 355, 16–356, 1)

(27c) The younger brother turns to his older sibling who is pursuing him and asks:
*ỉḫ* *pꜣy-k-ỉyt* *m-sꜣ-ỉ* *r-ẖdb(-ỉ)* *m-grg*
[WH] [POSS.M-2MS-come.INF in-back-1S to-kill-1S in-lie]
Why do you come after me to kill me treacherously? (*LES* 16, 9–10)

(27d) The divine Ennead gets into turmoil when discussing the question to whom an office should be given:
*ỉḫ* *nꜣ-md-t* *ỉ-ḏd-k* *nty-bn-šꜣw-sḏm=ṯ-w*
[WH] [DEF.P-word-F REL-say-2MS REL-NEG-worth-listen=OBJ-3P]
What are these words you utter which are not worthy of being heard? (*LES* 42, 4–5)

(27e) The author expresses to his son his astonishment at the latter's failure to keep in touch:
[*yꜣ*] *ỉḫ* *tꜣ-md-t* *n-pꜣy-tm-hꜣb* *ỉ-ỉr-k=n-ỉ*
PTC [WH] [DEF.F-thing-F of-DEM.M-AUX.NEG-send REL-do-2MS=to-1S
*pꜣ-nty* *(m)-ḥꜣty-k*
DEF.M-REL in-heart-2MS]
Really, what is the meaning of this failure of yours to write to me what is on your mind? (*LRL* 22, 1–2)

Again, any kind of NP, such as a definite (27a) or an indefinite noun (27c) or an infinitive (27e), is licensed to appear in the second position. As can be seen from the above examples, the pronominal element always occupies the first position. Seeing that in Sahidic Coptic, the personal pronoun usually takes a proclitic form (e.g. *ang*- instead of *anok*, see below), it has been argued that the same differentiation might have existed also at earlier stages of the language (Černý and Groll 1993: 11; Neveu 1996: 220–229). However, there is no evidence in favour of this assumption in Late Egyptian (see 3.1.3 for similar reservations concerning Earlier Egyptian).

Bipartite sentences of the type described here can also consist of two pronouns. Unlike in Earlier Egyptian where absolute pronouns are allowed only initially, in Late Egyptian they can also appear in the second position (see ex. 28a, whose Earlier Egyptian counterpart in 156b displays the form *ỉnk=pw=ṯw ntk=pw=wỉ*, i.e. with clitic pronouns in the non-initial position). In such instances, personal pronouns precede interrogatives (28c):

(28a) It is said in a magical text:
*ink* *mntk* *mntk* *ink*
[1S] [2MS] [2MS] [1S]
I am you and you are me. (pStrasbourg 23, 2)

(28b) The speaker tells that his heart went to see Memphis:
*bsy* *ink* *mntf*
PTC [1S] [3MS]
Would that I were him. (*LEM* 39, 10)

(28c) Two captured Hittite scouts are brought to Pharaoh. He asks them:
*ntwtn* *iḫ*
[2P] [WH]
Who are you? (*KRI* II 110, 3)

One may thus formulate the following positional hierarchy for pronouns:

absolute personal pronouns > absolute interrogative or demonstrative pronouns > nouns.

Interrogative pronouns paired with following nominal phrases are usually directly juxtaposed, as documented by the examples above. Sometimes, however, the interrogative particle *n* may[13] appear between the two constituents, showing that in Late Egyptian, this pronoun is not proclitic, as is the case in Sahidic Coptic:

(29) The bull/Bata tells his former wife that he is still alive. She asks the bull:
*mntk* *n* *nm=tr*
$[2MS]_S$ [IP WH=PTC$]_P$
But who are you? (*LES* 25, 10)

Although direct juxtaposition is the normal pattern when a pronoun is involved, there are some counterexamples where, quite unexpectedly, the copula is used (see 1.3 on tripartite nominal sentences with copula). However, examples are diachronically limited to texts of 18$^{th}$ or 19$^{th}$ dynasty dates mainly and appear later only in royal decorum texts and might be there an attempt to emulate a more elevated language:

(30a) Ramesses IV addresses a god:
*mntk* *pw* *iʿḥ* *im-y* *ḥri(-t)*
2MS COP moon in-RLT sky(-F)
You are the moon in the sky. (*KRI* VI 22, 9)

13 The analysis as particle follows Caminos (1977: 40–1).

(30b) The author of a letter says that he heard of his addressees' having taken action against certain people:

| | | | | |
|---|---|---|---|---|
| *ỉḫ* | *pw* | *pꜣy-ỉ-md-t* | *gr* | ... |
| WH | COP | POSS.M-1S-word-F | PTC | ... |

What then is my argument... (Moscow Bowl 3)

As in Earlier Egyptian, the bipartite pattern *NP NP* historically underlies the expression of predicative possession ('belongs to'). If the possessor is expressed as a noun, the construction *n-s* (< *ny-sw*, the graphemic representation in Late Egyptian shows wide variation) is used. The possessee may precede this expression (pattern (*ỉr*) X *n-s*-Y 'X, it belongs to Y') or follow it (*n-s*-Y *pꜣ*-X 'It belongs to Y, the X'). But unlike in Earlier Egyptian, the Late Egyptian *n-s*-Y always expresses the possessor, i.e. the pattern has been fully grammaticalised as a fixed possessive pattern rather than an expression of relationality (see 1.1.1):

(31a) A letter reports that the metal workers of a *sm*-priest came and said:

| | | |
|---|---|---|
| *ỉr-nꜣy-ḥmt* | *n-s-sm* | *bn-n-s-pꜣ-ḫr* |
| PTC -DEM.P-bronze | POSS-3C-priest | NEG-POSS-3C-DEF.M-tomb |

These bronze objects belong to the *sm*-priest; they do not belong to the necropolis-administration. (*KRI* III 545, 4–5)

(31b) After a description of the despair among the Libyans following their defeat, the power of the king is eulogised:

| | | | | | |
|---|---|---|---|---|---|
| *pꜣ-nb* | *ꜥꜣ* | *n-kmt* | *wsr* | *nḫt* | *ns-sw* |
| DEF.M-lord | great | of-Egypt | strength | victory | POSS-3MS |

The great Lord of Egypt – strength and victory belong to him. (*KRI* IV 15, 12–14)

(31c) The administrative personnel of the royal necropolis raise a complaint that the measure for the crop they receive as provision is too small. The scribe receiving the complaint answers:

| | |
|---|---|
| *n-s-ỉḫ* | *tꜣ-ỉp-t* |
| POSS-3C-WH | DEF.F-measure-F |

To whom belongs the *oipe*-measure? (*KRI* V 467, 16)

As can be seen, in both patterns, the possessee is pronominalised. In the construction with anteposed possesses, the pronoun is anaphoric and refers back to the initial NP. In the pattern *n-s*-Y *pꜣ*-X, the pronoun is cataphoric, and the possessee is added in apposition. Examples of simple *n* + noun seem wholly absent. Thus, one might claim that the pattern is productive only in the bound form *n-s-* with the possessee pronominalised:

(32a) The prince of Byblos denies responsibilty to reimburse Wenamun his money that was stolen in his port:

*hn* *i͗ṯꜣy* *i͗w-n-sw* *pꜣy-i͗-tꜣ*
CFT thief DEP-POSS-3MS POSS.M-1S-land
If it had been a thief who belongs to my land... (*LES* 62, 13)

(32b) A man reports that he went with five other men, the last of whom is identified as:

*tti* *wꜥ-rmṯ* *i͗w-n-sw* *pꜣynḥsi* *sꜣ* *ṯꜣti*
N IDF.S-man DEP-POSS-3MS N son N
Teti, a man who belongs to Pinhas, son of Tjaty. (*KRI* VI 804, 15–16)

(32c) A woman put on trial relates her husband's dealings:

*i͗ni-f* *nhy-n-ḥmti* *i͗w-ns-sw* *pꜣy-pr* *n-sṯꜣ*
bring.PST-3MS IDF.P-of-copper DEP-POSS-3MS DEM.M-house of-draw
He brought copper belonging to this portable shrine. (*KRI* VI 808, 13–14)

(32d) The oracle of the god Seth decrees concerning the wells in the oasis:

*ns-sw* *pꜣ-nmḥ* *nty-i͗w-f* *[i͗]n-ṯ-w* *[r]-bnr* *pꜣ-hꜣw*
POSS-3C DEF.M-free man REL-FUT-3MS bring-INF-3P to-outside DEF.M-day
They belong to the free man who will take them away today.
(Jansen-Winkeln, *IdS* II, 25, 4–5)

If the possessor is coded by a personal pronoun, the absolute pronouns are used. However, until the beginning of the first millennium BC, these are formally the remnants of the Earlier Egyptian *i͗nk*, =*ṯ*(*t*) (< Old Egyptian *ṯwt*), =*sw* (< Old Egyptian *swt*), etc (as introduced in 1.1.1). The last two of these (=*ṯ* and =*sw*) are found in this specific function (i.e. possessive marking) alone and are only marked for person, and not for gender or number. Thus, they can stand for masculine or feminine referents, for singular or plural entities. They are later replaced by the Late Egyptian absolute pronouns *i͗nk*, *mntk*, *mntf*, etc. as is shown by ex. 34. The construction is either PRN DEF-X 'The X belongs to PRN' or (*i͗r*) Y PRN-*sw* 'The X, it belongs to PRN'. Examples echoing the old paradigm are:

(33a) In a list of payments for a statue it is noted that the wood was supplied to the artist and only the making of the statue is accounted for:

*i͗nk* *tꜣ-rpy-t* *m-ḫt*
1S DEF.F-statue-F in-wood
The wood out of which the statue has been made belonged to me.
(*KRI* V 585, 3)

(33b) In a letter to the chief of the security guards the addressee is referred to as follows:

*yꜣ ꞽr-nꜣ-nty-ḥr-ḫꜣs-t ṯw-sn ḫr ṯw*
PTC PTC-DEF.P-REL-on-foreign_land-F 2C-3P PTC 2C
*nꜣ-nty-ḥr-kmt*
DEF.P-REL-on-Egypt
Those in the foreign countries belong to you, and to you belong those in Egypt. (*LEM* 71, 11–12)

(33c) In a court-case, the children of a man who intends to give his belongings to a new wife comment upon their father's intention with a shrug: *Who could argue against it?*

*sw ꜣḫ-ṯ-f*
3S thing.P-F-3MS
His things belong to him. (*KRI* VI 741, 8)

In the following examples, the normal Late Egyptian absolute pronouns appear:

(34a) The prince of Dor denies his responsibility for the theft suffered by Wenamun:

*yꜣ ꞽr-pꜣ-ꞽṯꜣy ꞽ-ṯꜣy=ṯ mntk=sw n-s tꜣy-k-br*
PTC PTC-DEF.M-thief PPA-rob=2MS 2MS=3MS POSS-3C POSS.F-2MS-ship
Well, the thief who has robbed you belongs to you. He belonged to your ship. (*LES* 62, 16–63, 2)

(34b) The addressee of a missive is told to look for some runaways:

*ꞽmꞽ ḥn šmsw ꞽw-mntk=sw msꜣ-f*
give.IMP go retainer DEP-2MS=3C after-3MS
Have a retainer, that belongs to you, go after them (lit. 'him').
(Jansen-Winkeln, *IdS* I, 204, 1–2)

(34c) An oracle states the reason why a certain man has detained a woman:

*ꞽw-mntf pꜣy-17 n-ḏꜣꞽw*
DEP-3MS DEM.M-17 of-garment
...while these seventeen garments belong to him.
(Jansen-Winkeln, *IdS* I, 211, 2)

As can be seen, when the possessee is a pronoun as well, it appears in the clitic form.

The bipartite construction underlies also the so-called cleft sentence, whose semantics and pragmatics will be discussed in more detail in 3.1.3.[14] Structurally, the

14 Not all Earlier Egyptian tripartite constructions of the type 'absolute pronoun + relative clause' are functional clefts. Late Egyptian seems to represent a stage of the language where the clefting function became more inherently associated with this pattern.

pattern is a direct descendent of the Earlier Egyptian cleft sentence noted in 1.1.1. If a noun, the first NP is introduced by the particle *(i)n* (with the graphic variant *m*) and is almost always marked for definiteness (i.e. it either shows the definite or the indefinite article). Pronominal first-position NPs are not specifically marked by a particle. Note that unlike in Earlier Egyptian, analogous constructions with absolute pronouns are now always functionally cleft sentences. The second NP is either an active participle or a relative clause. The cleft construction can be summarised as follows:

**Tab. II.1:** Late Egyptian tense-marked cleft sentence patterns.

| Tense | First NP | Second NP |
|---|---|---|
| Preterite | *(i)n/m* DEF/IDF-NPRN | participle // periphrastic participle (*i-stp*) // (*i-iri qnqn*) |
| Aorist | | periphrastic participle (*i-iri stp*) |
| Prospective | | periphrastic prospective (*i-iri-f stp*) |

For the preterite pattern the participle shows a suppletive paradigm: If the root contains more than three radicals, the periphrastic participle has to be used. In all other cases the simple participle appears. As in Earlier Egyptian, the prospective construction is not a nominal sentence, but rather a suppletive pattern incorporating a clause with a verbal predicate. Although functionally identical with the participial clefts, analysing it as syntactically similar to the latter would entail postulating a predicative relation between the first NP and the following nominalised full clause, which seems semantically improbable.[15] Alternatively, the construction could be viewed as an anteposition pattern with a special function (see Borghouts 2010: §48.d for this analysis).

Below are examples of each of the three tenses:

(35a) A courtier of the prince of Byblos has had a vision and tells the prince to bring Wenamun:
*(i)n* *imn* *i-wḏ=sw*
[PTC N] [PPA-send=3MS]
It was Amun who sent him. (*LES* 65, 5)

15 See 3.1.5 for arguments against this analysis in Earlier Egyptian. The *i*-prefix of the prospective form has been explained as marker of a prospective nominal form (Černý and Groll 1993: 528, non-initial prospective 'that'-clause). This, however, would be almost the only functional domain attested for this form.

(35b) Thutmosis reprimands his addressee for his slackness in carrying out the pharaoh's commissions:
*ḫrỉr wꜥ-mꜣꜥ ỉ-ỉr-mrw ḫꜣ n-ḫt*
PTC [IDF.S-creeper] [AUX-PST-bind 1000 of-wood]
*ḫr ptr mntk ỉ-ỉr-ntf-w*
PTC look [2MS] [AUX-PST-loose-3P]
Now it is a single creeper that can choke a thousand trees; but see, it is you who can disentangle them. (*LRL* 69, 3–4)

(35c) The king tells that a god prophesied of him:
*ntf ỉ-ỉr-f-šsp ỉꜣw-t*
[3MS] [PROSP-AUX-3MS-receive office-F]
He shall receive the office. (pTurin 1882 3, 4–5 [*JEA* 41, pl. 9])

As mentioned above, for verbal roots consisting of more than three radicals, a periphrastic construction is used in the preterite as well:

(36) The wife of the older brother falsely accuses her brother-in-law:
*m pꜣy-k-sn šrỉ ỉ-ỉr-qnqn*
[PTC POSS.M-2MS-brother small] [PPA-AUX-beat]
It was your little brother who beat (me). (*LES* 13, 12)

The participles of certain roots such as *dỉ* 'give' often appear in a form graphemically similar to the infinitive:

(37) The author of the letter noticed two boats belonging to the addressee in the harbour of Memphis:
*ỉw-ṯ ḥr-ḏd=n-ỉ mntk dỉ ỉn-ṯ-w*
DEP-PASS PRP-say=to-1S [2MS] [give.PPA bring-PASS-3P]
...and I was told that it was you who had them brought. (*KRI* III 255, 4)

Since Late Egyptian ordinal numbers have their etymological origin in a construction consisting of a participle of the word *mḥ* 'to fill' followed by the number, examples such as in 38 could be indeed analysed as clefts. But since the degree of grammaticalisation of the construction is not clear, they could also be viewed as bipartite nominal sentences:

(38) Asked about his participation in certain thefts, a man says:
*ṯ-ỉ ḥn-k ỉw(-ỉ) gm pꜣy-5 rmṯ ỉnk mḥ-6*
PTC-1S go-STA.1S DEP-1S find DEM.M-5 man 1S ORD-6
I went out and found these five men. I was the sixth. (*KRI* VI 806, 2–3)

Although it might seem possible to expand the initial NP e.g. by attributes, this construction is unattested. Moreover, mainly personal (the second sentence in exx. 35b and 35c) or interrogative pronouns are attested in the first position in cleft sentences[16]:

(39a) An amorous fowler has forgotten to set his bird trap and sighs:
*iḫ* *kꜣi-i* *n-mwt*
[WH] [say.FUT-1S to-mother]
What shall I tell mother? (Mathieu, *Poésie*, pl. 11, 8)

(39b) The king's courtiers agree that making peace with the Hittites will be favourable:
*mnym* *tꜣy-f=tw* *hrw* *qnd-k*
[WH] [resist.FUT-3MS=2MS day wrath-2MS]
Who will resist you on the day of your wrath? (*KRI* II 97, 9)

(39c) King Ramesses IV praises the gods:
*iṯ* *sṯn-f* *n-ḥm-k*
[WH] [compare.FUT-3MS to majesty-2MS]
Who can be compared to your majesty? (*KRI* VI 23, 3)

As shown in 1.1.1, the second position of cleft sentences was originally occupied by a participle, but due to the growing obsolescence of the latter in Late Egyptian, in this stage of the language headless relative clauses were increasingly used instead. This process, which began with the reanalysis of the pseudo-cleft sentence to be described below, was gradual: no clear-cut chronological boundaries are discernible (Neveu 1994).

Although similar in structure to the cleft sentence, the so-called Late Egyptian pseudo-cleft sentence developed out of a different pattern. In this construction, as it appears in most Late Egyptian material, a bare NP (e.g. noun, personal or demonstrative pronoun, headless relative phrase, or infinitive) is followed by what looks like a relative clause headed by a definite article. The latter agrees with the first NP in gender and number. Tense is marked in the second NP by a relative form (preterite) or a relative clause with a *Present* (aorist) or a *Future III* (future) form. An additional past construction employs the participle of the auxiliary *wnn*. A passive pattern is only attested in the

16 Note that the Late Egyptian interrogative *nym* goes back etymologically to earlier *in* plus *m*, see Vernus (2006: 160–61).

past tense in conjunction with the rare Late Egyptian passive perfective participles constructions:

**Tab. II.2:** Late Egyptian pseudo-cleft sentence patterns.

| **Tense** | **First NP** | **Second NP** |
|---|---|---|
| Preterite | NP<br>(DEF) N<br>PRN<br>INF | COP + relative form/pass. participle<br>(*pꜣ stp-ı͗/pꜣ-dd-yt*) |
| Aorist | | COP + relative clause with Present<br>(*nty* + PRS) |
| Prospective | | COP + relative clause with Future<br>(*nty* + FUT III) |

Of the pseudo-cleft constructions above, those with future reference are rather uncommon. Late Egyptian pseudo-clefts are never of the so-called non-reversed type, where the cleft relative clause precedes the cleft constituent (e.g. 'What I am looking for is gold').[17] The use of the infinitive in the first position foreshadows a common Demotic pattern (see 1.1.2.2). The initial NP can be marked for definiteness[18]:

(40a) An idle scribe is told: 'You are not a true scribe of Thoth':
*pꜣy-f-gsti* *pꜣ-nty* *m-ḏr-t-k*
[POSS.M-3MS-palette] [COP.M-REL in-hand-F-2MS]
His scribal palette is what is in your hand. (*LEM* Caminos 508, 5–6)

(40b) A list of thieves is reported by a police officer of whom it is said:
*mntf* *pꜣ-wn* *ı͗m* *ꜥḥꜥ* *ı͗rm-nꜣ-ı͗ṯꜣ-w*
[3MS] [COP.M-be.PPA there stand.STA with-DEF.P-thief-P]
He is the one who has been standing there with the thieves. (*KRI* VI 803, 16–804, 1)

(40c) In a dispute over two quarreling deities, the other gods ask:
*ı͗ḫ* *pꜣ-nty* *ı͗w-n* *r-ı͗r-f* *n-pꜣ-rmṯ* *2*
[WH] [COP.M-REL FUT-1P FUT-do.INF-3MS to-DEF.M-man 2
*nty* *80* *n-rnp-t* *r-tꜣy* *ı͗w-sn* *m-tꜣ-qnb-t*
REL 80 of-year-F to-DEM.F DEP-3P in-DEF.F-court-F]
What shall we do with these two men who have been standing at the court for 80 years already? (*LES* 39, 13–14)

17 It will be shown in 2.1.3 that such constructions were rare already in Earlier Egyptian.
18 The construction in ex. 40e has been alternatively explained as tripartite clause (*ntf pꜣ-wḏ... pꜣy*). However, the analysis proposed here avoids postulating an aberrant pattern.

(40d) The officials examining thefts in the royal necropolis warn a man not to make a false statement. He replies:

| | | |
|---|---|---|
| *p3-iry-i* | *ˁq3* | *p3y-ḏd-i* |
| [DEF.M-do.REL-1S | accurate] | [COP.M-say-1S] |

What I said is exactly what I did. (*KRI* VI 805, 10–11)

(40e) King Akhenaten proclaims:

| | | | | | |
|---|---|---|---|---|---|
| *ir-p3-wḏ* | *rsy* | *nty* | *ḥr-p3-ḏw* | *i3bty* | *n-3ḫtitn* |
| PTC-DEF.M-stela | southern | REL | on-DEF.M-mountain | eastern | of-N |

| | | | | | | |
|---|---|---|---|---|---|---|
| *ntf* | *p3-wḏ* | *n-3ḫtitn* | *p3y* | *p3-ir-i* | *ˁḥˁ* | *r-ˁ-f* |
| 3MS | DEF.M-stela | of-N | [DEM.M] | [COP.M-AUX-1S | stand | to-arm-3MS] |

As for the southern stela that is on the eastern mountain of Akhetaten, it is the stela of Akhetaten. It is this one which I stand next to.

(*Boundary Stelae*, 90)

Conversely, sometimes the constituent parts of Late Egyptian pseudo-clefts are marked for indefiniteness (exx. 41a–b) or show no marking at all (exx. 41c–e):

(41a) The pharaoh bemoans the amount and quality of black galena sent to him by the viceroy of Kush:

| | | | | |
|---|---|---|---|---|
| *wˁ-dbn* | *wˁty* | *n-msdm-t* | *p3w-gm-yt* | *im-f* |
| IDF.S-deben | single | of-galena | DEF.M-find-PPP | in-3MS |

It was only a single *deben* of galena that has been found there.

(*KRI* VI 519, 2–3)

(41b) An official examines an ancient tomb found by a man working in his own. He confirms what the man had put on record before:

| | | | | |
|---|---|---|---|---|
| *wˁ-wt* | *wˁ(ṯ)* | *p3-nty* | *m-t3-(m)ˁḥˁ-t* | *n-imnmipt* |
| IDF.S-coffin | single | DEF.M-REL | in-DEF.F-tomb | of-N |

It is a single coffin that is inside the tomb of Amenemope.

(*KRI* V 480, 1–2)

(41c) Thieves have bribed a man whose wife tells him: 'You are a silly old man':

| | |
|---|---|
| *irt-iṯ3* | *p3y-i-ir-k* |
| do.INF-take.INF | DEM.M-REL-do-2MS |

Theft is what you have committed. (*KRI* VI 789, 9–10)

(41d) The prince of Byblos replies that the pharaoh would not have paid him if he were his servant:

| | | | | |
|---|---|---|---|---|
| *nn* | *f3y* | *mrk* | *p3-wn-w* | *ir-f* |
| IP | bring.INF | gift | DEF.M-REL.PST-3P | do.INF-3MS |

*n-p3y-i-it*
for-POSS.M-1S-father

Was it just bribery what they used to do for my father? (*LES* 68, 6–7)

(41e) The king has received intelligence on the whereabouts of his opponent's troops. One of his high officials castigates the officials responsible:

*btꜣ* *ꜥꜣ* *pꜣ-irw-nꜣ-imi-w-r-ḫꜣs-wt* *ḥnꜥ-nꜣ-wr-w*
crime great DEF.M-do.REL-DEF.P-title and-DEF.P-great-P
*n-pr-ꜥꜣ* *ꜥws*
of-house-great l.p.h
*pꜣ-tm-di* *smty-ṯ=n-sn* *pꜣ-ḫrw* *n-ḫtꜣ*
DEF.M-AUX.NEG-give inquire-PASS=to-3P DEF.M-foe of-N
*m-pꜣ-nty=nb* *sw* *im*
in-DEF.M-REL=QU 3MS there

It is a great crime that the administrators of the foreign countries and the great ones of Pharaoh, l.p.h., committed, by failing to inquire of the whereabouts of the foe of Hatti. (*KRI* II 116, 7–16)[19]

From a purely syntactic point of view, the constructions in the following examples bear resemblance to pseudo-clefts, but their semantic-pragmatic function of attributing a predication makes an analysis as adjectival sentences similarly possible (see Part III). There is no formal means to decide between these two possibilities:

(42a) Confronted with another man's accusation against him in court, a slave exclaims:

*ꜥḏꜣ* *pꜣy-ḏd-f=nb*
false DEF.M-say.REL-3MS=QU

All that he said is wrong/It is all wrong what he said! (*KRI* VI 798, 3)

(42b) The oracle of a deity is asked to answer whether:

*n* *ꜥḏꜣ* *nꜣ-ḏd-[i/N]*
IP false DEF.P-say.REL-1S/N

Is it wrong what I/NN said? (oIFAO 681 [*BIFAO* 41, 18])

Modifiers such as adjectives or relative clauses can expand the first NP of a pseudo-cleft sentence:

(43a) The crimes of a member of the harem conspiracy against Ramesses III are classified as:

*iw-btꜣ-w* *ꜥꜣ-y* *n-mwt* *nꜣ-bw-t* *ꜥꜣ-y*
DEP-[crime-P great-P of-death DEF.P-abomination-F great-P
*n-pꜣ-tꜣ* *nꜣ-i-ir-f*
of-DEF.M-land] [DEF.P-REL-do-3MS]

19 Alternatively, one might consider an analysis as nominal sentence with ellipsis of the subject index followed by an explicative apposition.

...while it was a great crime worthy of death and the great abominations of the land what he committed. (*KRI* V 361, 9–10)

(43b) The prince of Dor rejects Wenamun's claim for compensation for his stolen goods:

| | | | | |
|---|---|---|---|---|
| *hn* | *iṯ3y* | *iw-n-s* | *p3y-i-t3* | *p3-h3y* |
| CND | [thief | DEP- POSS-3C | POSS.M-1S-land] | [DEF.M-descend.PPA |
| *r-t3y-k-br* | *mṯ-f* | *ṯ3y* | *p3y-k-ḥḏ-nbw* | |
| to-POSS.F-2MS-boat] | CNJ-3MS | take.INF | POSS.M-2MS-silver | |
| *wn* | *iw-i* | *ḏb3-f=n-k* | *m-p3y-i-wḏ3* | |
| PTC | FUT-1S | compensate.INF-3MS=to-2MS | from-POSS.M-1S-storehouse | |

If it had been a thief belonging to my country that went onto your boat and took your money, I would compensate you out of my storehouse. (*LES* 62, 13–15)

For reasons to be discussed later, the pseudo-cleft sentence is often used for WH-questions with an interrogative pronoun in the first position:

(44a) The prince stood at the roof of his house and asked one of his servants:

| | | | | | |
|---|---|---|---|---|---|
| *iḫ* | *p3-nty* | *ḥr-šm* | *m-s3-p3-s* | *ꜥ3* | *nty* |
| WH | COP.M-REL | PRP-walk | in-back-DEF.M-man | big | REL |
| *m-iyt* | *ḥr-t3-mi-t* | | | | |
| PRP-walk.INF | on-DEF.F-road-F | | | | |

What is it that follows the big man who is walking along the street? (*LES* 2, 4–5)

(44b) The author of a letter entreats the addressee to ask from a certain woman:

| | | |
|---|---|---|
| *iḫ* | *n3-dd-yt* | *n-ṯ3wnḏm* |
| WH | COP.P-give-PPP | to-N |

What has been given to Tjawnedjem? (oDeM 10253, r° 3–4)

As can be seen from the above examples, the relative expression or cleft clause is usually preceded by what looks like the definite article with agreement marking (*p3-*/*t3-*/*n3-*). Sometimes, however, the prefixed element takes the graphic guise of the demonstrative *p3y-*/*t3y-*/*n3y-*, cf. exx. 41a and 42a. It can also appear as *p3w* (feminine and plural forms of this sub-pattern are not attested):

(45a) At the end of a note about a priest who had failed to organise food supply for workmen:

| | | |
|---|---|---|
| *bt3* | *ꜥ3* | *p3w-i-ir-f* |
| crime | great | COP.M-REL-do-3MS |

It is a great crime that he committed. (*RAD* 52, 2–3)

(45b) The author of a letter enquires about the cargo of a ship:

*ỉḫ* *pꜣw-ỉr-yt=n-sn*
WH DEF.M-do-PPP=for-3P
What has been done to it? (*KRI* III 500, 14)

The Late Egyptian pseudo-cleft construction was originally a tripartite pattern formed of two NPs connected via a copula (S > NP COP NP). Some early Late Egyptian examples still show this construction (cf. ex. 418b for a possible negated variant):

(46a) The author of a letter has been informed that the addressees have interfered with other peoples' business:

*ỉḫ* *pw* *pꜣy-tn-ỉr* *mỉt-t*
WH COP POSS.M-2P-do.INF likewise-F
What's the meaning of your acting this way? (*KRI* I 322, 7–8)

(46b) The author of a letter asks his addressee:

*ỉḫ* *pw* *n(ꜣ)-nty* *ṯ-k* *ḥr-ỉrỉ-w*
WH COP DEF.P-REL PTC-2MS PRP-do.INF-3P
What are you doing? (*HO* 33.2 r° 6–7)

(46c) In a description of the splendour of a temple it is said of the door-leaves:

*ḥꜥ-w-sn* *pw* *nb-y* *m-ḏꜥm*
body-P-3P COP fashion-PPP in-electrum
Their bodies have been fashioned in electrum. (*KRI* I 47, 10–11)

(46d) In a letter to the gang of workmen the annoyed author goes straight to the point:

*ỉḫ* *nꜣ-nty* *ṯ-tn* *ḥr-ḏd-ṯ-w*
WH DEF.P-REL PTC-2P PRP-say.INF-OBJ-3P
What are you talking about? (*KRI* III 532, 3–4)

(46e) The Elephantine decree of Ramesses III stipulates that should the temple staff complain about inspectors or soldiers interfering with their business, they shall say:

*mntf* *pw* *dỉ-ḫpr* *pꜣ-ꜣq* *ḫpr-w*
3MS COP let.PPA-happen DEF.M-loss happen-PPP
He was the one who caused the loss that happened. (*KRI* V 344, 6)

(46f) In an introductory eulogy to a royal decree:

*ỉn* *rꜥ* *ms* *ḥm-f* *ntf* *pw* *qmꜣ* *nfrw-f*
PTC N bear majesty-3MS 3MS COP create.PPA beauty-3MS
It was the sun-god who gave birth to his majesty. He was the one who created his beauty. (*KRI* I 46, 12)

Although in the first example above the pattern is clearly tripartite, consisting of the copular element *pw* and two NPs (see 1.3), in 46c, one finds a bare definite relative clause in the second position, and ex. 46d shows the pattern without copula. Examples such as these suggest the following line of diachronic development.

The invariant copula *pw* was replaced by an etymologically related copula *pꜣy/tꜣy/nꜣy* marked for gender and number (see 1.3.2.1 ). This morpheme seems in turn to have been reinterpreted as a superfluous double marker of definiteness, because it often coincides with the definite article heading the relative clause. This interpretation, rather than the actualisation of the copula with dropping of the article, can better explain the appearance of *pꜣy* or *pꜣw* in front of the relative clause (*contra* Junge 2008: 182). The use of *pw* in ex. 46e may be an anachronism resulting from imitation of the phraseology of earlier royal decrees.

In addition to the two patterns, we note another cleft construction with a bare initial NP followed by a participle or a relative clause without the determiner (copula), in contrast to the cleft pattern PTC-NP Ø-CLEFT and the pseudo-cleft Ø-NP DET-CLEFT (Vernus 1987: 163–81):

(47) The address of a letter:

| | | | |
|---|---|---|---|
| *[pꜣ-ỉmỉr-mšꜥ]* | *r-ḏd* | *n-nꜣ-rwḏ-w* | *n-pꜣ-ẖr* |
| DEF.M-oversee-army | PPA-say | to-DEF.P-adiministrators-P | of-DEF.M-tomb |

It is the General who addressed the administrators of the necropolis.

(*LRL* 53, 3)

As will be seen shortly, of nominal sentences of the type *NP NP*, only the construction with pronominal elements and the various cleft sentence patterns remained in wide use after Late Egyptian. Thus, the noted revival of this bipartite pattern with two non-pronominal NPs was a short-lived phenomenon of Late Egyptian: in Demotic, the situation had once again become comparable to Earlier Egyptian, and the use of the *NP NP* pattern was largely limited to cases where one of the two members is a pronoun.

#### 1.1.2.2 Demotic

Bipartite nominal sentences consisting of two directly juxtaposed non-pronominal NPs occur in Demotic literature, but they tend to be limited to specific genres, such as religious and wisdom texts or legal formulae in official documents, which may have preserved archaic constructions. When two nouns are combined, less formal texts and discourse display the tripartite pattern to be introduced in 1.3.2.2:

(48a) A series of three sayings from a Ptolemaic wisdom text:

| | | |
|---|---|---|
| *ỉry* | *lḫ* | *lḫ* |
| [friend | idiot] | [idiot] |
| *ỉry* | *rmt-rḫ* | *rmt-rḫ* |
| [friend | man-wise] | [man-wise] |
| *ỉry* | *rmt-swg* | *rmt-swg* |
| [friend | man-fool] | [man-fool] |

A friend of an idiot is an idiot; a friend of a wise man is a wise man; a friend of a fool is a fool. (Onkhsheshonqy 13, 6–7)

(48b) The Great Demotic Wisdom Book states within the part dealing with the burial:
*pꜣ-ḥtp* *n-pꜣ-nṯr* *n-[pꜣ]-rmt-nṯr*
[DEF.M-grace of-DEF.M-god for-DEF.M-man god]
*tꜣy-f-qs-t* *ỉrm-pꜣy-f-ꜥwy* *[n]-ḥtp*
[POSS.F-3MS-burial-F and-POSS.M-3MS-place of rest]
God's grace towards the man of god is his burial and his resting place.
(pInsinger 2, 11)

(48c) Thoth says to a disciple who seeks to make acquaintance with a female deity associated with language:
*pꜣy-k-dy-t* *qy-ḫrw-k* *pꜣy-s-mr* *sḏm-k*
[POSS.M-2MS-give-INF loud-voice-2MS] [POSS.M-3FS-wish hear-2MS
*pꜣy-s-ỉy* *n-tkr* *rr-k*
POSS.M-3FS-come.INF to-quick to-2MS]
Your raising your voice means her wish to hear you and her coming quickly to you. (*Book of Thoth* B02 4, 3)

(48d) From a magical spell:
*bn-pꜥy* *nỉm-f* *r-pꜣ-tꜣ* *ḏd-pꜣy-k-ls*
NEG-spit OBJ-3MS to-DEF.M-land for-[POSS.M-2MS-tongue]
*pꜣ-ls* *n-pꜣ-šꜥy*
[DEF.M-tongue of-DEF.M-fate]
Do not spew it on the ground, for your tongue is the tongue of fate.
(pMag. London & Leiden 20, 12–13)

(48e) The deceased assures in the court of his final judgement to have lived a life according to social rules and that he is clean of all bad things:
*pꜣy-(y)-wꜥb* *pꜣ-wꜥb* *n-pꜣ-nṯr* *nty-ḫn-ḥwtnnzw*
[POSS.M-1S-purity] [DEF.M-purity of-DEF.M-god REL-inside-N]
My purity is the purity of the god that is in Herakleopolis. (pBN 149 2, 1–2)

(48f) A marriage contract stipulates about the respective children:
*pꜣy-t-šr* *ꜥꜣ* *pꜣy-y-šr* *ꜥꜣ* *pꜣ-nb*
[POSS.M-2FS-son great] [POSS.M-1S-son great] DEF.M-lord
*nty-nb* *nkt=nb* *nty-mtw-y*
REL-every thing=QU REL-with-1S
*ḥnꜥ-nꜣ-nty-ỉw-y-dy-t-ḫpr-w*
and-DEF.P-REL-FUT-1S-let-INF-happen-3P
Your eldest son is my eldest son, the owner of everything and anything that I have and all the things that I will acquire.
(pBerlin P. 3109, 4–5 [Lüddeckens, *Eheverträge*, 70][20])

---

20 With the corrections acc. to Pestman (1961: 117–18 note 5 b & d). The stipulation appears in the documents as tripartite nominal sentence (cf. ex. 245b below) or as above as bipartite one.

The only truly productive use of this pattern in Demotic appears to be in constructions with *rn* 'name' as in 49a & b and in wisdom texts in the juxtaposition of two infinitives (49c):

(49a) Description of the power of the Ethiopian cat:
*tw-y ỉrrḫ-s ḏd-tꜣ-ỉmy-t rn-t*
PTC-1S know-3FS COMP-[DEF.F-cat-F] [name-2FS]
I know that your name is 'the she-cat.' (Myth of the Sun's Eye 25, 24)

(49b) The text accompanying the judgement of the deceased scene are given. The deceased has to say to the lord of the judges:
*pꜣ-nb n-wpy-w rn-k*
[DEF.M-lord of-judge-P] [name-2MS]
'Lord of judges' is your name. (pBN 149 1, 27–28)

(49c) The author warns against the squandering of resources:
*ʿse-t n-pr tm-ḥms nỉm-f*
[waste-INF of-house] [AUX.NEG-sit.INF in-3MS]
*ʿse-t sḥm-t tm-rḫ-s*
[waste-INF woman-F] [AUX.NEG-know.INF-3FS]
*ʿse-t ʿꜣ fy-db ʿse-t ḏy*
[waste-INF donkey] [carry.INF-brick] [waste-INF ship]
*fy-dḥ*
[carry.INF-straw]
Not to live in it is waste of a house. Not to know her is waste of a woman. To carry bricks is waste of a donkey. To carry straw is waste of a ship.
(Onkhsheshonqy 20, 22–25)

Finally, the following sequence found in oracular questions seems best analysed as a nominal sentence with an infinitive in the second position:

(50) In an oracle question the god Soknebtunis is asked:
*ỉwfḫpr r-pꜣy(-y)-ʿšsḥn nfr*
CND DEP-[POSS.M-1S-fortune good]
*tm-dyt-ḫpr=n-y sḥm-t n-ḥm-t*
[AUX.NEG-give.INF-become=to-1S woman-F as-wife-F
*ḫn-tꜣy-sḥm-t 2-t*
in-DEM.F-woman-F 2-F
*nty-sẖ r-pꜣy(-y)-bꜣk my ỉn-w=n-y*
REL-write.STA to POSS.M-1S-document] let.IMP bring-3P=to-1S
*pꜣy-bꜣk r-bnr*
DEM.M-document to-outside

If it is my good fortune not to be given a wife from among these two women who are named in my document, let this document be brought out to me! (pCarlsberg 429, 3–8)

In 51a, the first sentence shows the bipartite *NP NP* pattern, but the subsequent variant of the formula in the same text uses the tripartite construction:

(51a) A statement in a document of complaint:
*pꜣ-sp*     *nꜣy-y-mꜣꜥw...*
[DEF.M-remainder]     [POSS.M-1S-justification]
*pꜣ-sp*     *{n}-nꜣy(-y)-mꜣꜥw*     *nꜣw*
[DEF.M-remainder]     [POSS.M[-1S]-justification]     COP.P
...but the remainder is my justification. (pBM 10591, r° 2, 16/r° 5, 12–13)[21]

(51b) As above:
*nꜣy(-y)-md-w*     *nꜣy(-y)-md-w*     *ꜥn*
POSS.M-1S-word-P     POSS.M-1S-word-P     still(ADV)
My words are still my words. (pBM 10591, r° 4, 7)

(51c) A father tells his son to feel at home:
*kꜣ*     *ꜥn*     *tꜣy*     *prspt*     *pꜣy-k-tmy*     *m-qty-ı͗wnw*     *ꜥn*
other     still     SE.F     N     POSS.M-2MS-town     as-well-N     also(ADV)
Further: Pisopdu is your city, as is Heliopolis. (pKrall 6, 3)

(51d) The small dog-ape ends one of his speeches with a paraphrase of a legal formula:
*pꜣy(-y)-ḏd*     *pꜣy(-y)-ḏd*     *ꜥn*     *pꜣy*
POSS.M-1S-word     POSS.M-1S-word     still.ADV     COP.M
My word is still my word. (Myth of the Sun's Eye 8, 4)

In 51b and 51c, the surprising appearance of an adverbial adjunct might suggests that the preposition *n* has been omitted and that the construction should be analysed as an adverbial sentence. However, examples such as (51d), which cannot be interpreted as anything but as tripartite nominal sentences, demonstrate the general possibility of integrating an adverbial into a nominal sentence in Demotic.

In Demotic, as in Earlier Egyptian and later in Coptic, the bipartite construction is most common when one (less often, both) of the combined nominals is a *pronoun*. In the majority of cases, this is an absolute personal pronoun:

**21** The scribe was apparently undecided which sentence pattern he wanted to use in the second instance, which can be read either as an adverbial sentence *pꜣ-sp n-nꜣy(-ı͗)-mꜣꜥw {nꜣw}* (in which case the copula must be emended as erroneous) or, as preferred here, as a nominal sentence *pꜣ-sp {n} nꜣy(-ı͗)-mꜣꜥw nꜣw* (in which case only the preposition *n* must be deleted).

(52a) On his arrival at Heracleopolis, Peteese is asked:
*ỉn* *mtwk* *pꜣdyꜣst*
IP [2MS] [N]
Are you Peteese? (pRylands IX 4, 19)

(52b) An appeal to Isis:
*ỉnk* *pꜣy-(t)-bꜣk* *nfr* *ꜣst*
[1S] [POSS.M-2FS-servant good] N
I am your good servant, O Isis. (grPhilae 416, 20)

(52c) An anonymous person writes to a letter-scribe:
*twys* *pꜣy(-y)-sẖ-wḫꜣ* *ỉnky* *rmt-ꜥꜣ* *wn* *mtw-y*
look POSS.M-1S-scribe-letter [1S] [man-great] AUX with-1S
*nꜣy(-y)-nkt*
POSS.M-1S-thing
See, my letter-scribe, I am a rich man and I have my belongings.
(*Krugtexte* A, text 2, 12)

(52d) An oracle petition addresses the two deities Soknopaios and Isis:
*mtwtn* *nꜣ-ḥry-w* *(n)-nꜣ-ḥry-w*
2P DEF.P-lord-P of-DEF.P-lord-P
You are the lords of the lords. (Bresciani, *Archivio*, #10, 2–3)

(52e) In a contract for the sale of a priestly office written in abnormal hieratic, the vendee begins with the words:
*mtwk* *pꜣ-wꜣḥmw* *n-pꜣ-1/4* *n-tꜣy-y-s-t*
2MS DEF.M-choachyte of-DEF.M-1/4 of-POSS.F-1S-place-F
*n-pꜣ-ḏwi* *ỉ-dy-k=n-y* *ỉbl*
of-DEF.M-mountain REL-give-2MS=to-1S out
You are the *choachyte* of the quarter of my tomb that you sold me.
(pLouvre E 2432, 3 [Malinine, *Choix*, 102])

(52f) A deity is invoked and it is said:
*mtwf* *rꜥ*
3MS N
He is (the Sun-god) Ra. (pLouvre E 10382, 18)

(52g) Magical action is justified with the identification with a powerful being:
*še-ank-to* *si* *n-to* *ank-pu(ê)r* *si* *n-pu(ê)r*
for-1S-N son of-N 1S-N son of-N
*ank-anup* *e-f-bi* *p-klom* *n-ôu* *n-p-rê*
1S-N DEP-3MS-carry DEF.M-crown of-large of-DEF.M-N
*e-f-ti* *nmo-f* *ešen-p-ero* *usiri*
DEP-3MS-give OBJ-3MS upon-DEF.M-king N
*p-ero* *useruenafre*
DEF.M-king N

...for I am To, the son of To; I am Pur (i.e. the great one), son of Pur; I am Anubis, who carries the great crown of Re and who gives it upon the king Osiris, the king Osiris-Wennofre.
(OC Great Mag. P. Paris [*ZÄS* 21, 104, 10–13])

As the last example (52g) shows, the latest Demotic text written in Greek letters shows the unstressed form of the pronouns already. However, it is not clear when this feature can be assumed to have developed and hence the majority of examples is transcribed as not bound.

Although the first uses of the absolute possessive pronouns (i.e. Late Egyptian/Demotic *pꜣy-j* > Coptic *pôi* 'what is mine', etc.) are attested already in Late Egyptian, they seem to have become truly widespread only in Coptic. In Demotic, they are most common in late texts.

As in Late Egyptian, if both NPs are pronouns, the personal pronoun appears first:

(53a) Paklul asks a warrior:
*mtwk iḫ n-rmt ẖn-tꜣy-n-mhꜣw*
[2MS] [WH of man inside-POSS.F-1P-family]S
What kind of a man are you in our family (i.e. what is your relation to our family)? (pKrall 19, 23)

(53b) The magician is told to invoke some demons who will then ask him:
*mtwk nym spsn*
[2MS] [WH] twice
Who are you; who are you? (pMag. London & Leiden 9, 32)

Multiple elements can be coordinated (ex. 54a–c, see also ex. 374c), whereas they must be repeated in disjunction (ex. 54d):

(54a) A slave sold to another person has to agree to the sale saying:
*ink pꜣy-t-bꜣk ḥnꜥ-nꜣy-(y)-ẖrṯ-w*
1S POSS.F-2FS-slave and-POSS.P-1S-child-P
I and all my children are your slave (with all that we have and all we will acquire). (pBN 223, 5)

(54b) The deceased is praised in old-style phraseology:
*mtwk ḥs n-iṯ mnḫ n-mw-t-f*
2MS praise.PPA of-father excellent of-mother-F-3MS
*nḏm-ib sn-w*
sweet-heart brother-P
You are a praised one of the father, an excellent of his mother and a beloved one of the siblings. (CG 31095, 8)

(54c) The little monkey addresses the sun-god:

| | | |
|---|---|---|
| *mtwk* | *pꜣ-ḥry-ẖry* | *pꜣ-ḥry-ḥry-w* |
| 2MS | DEF.M-lord-below | DEF.M-lord-above-P |

You are the lord of the below one and the lord of the above ones.
(pLille 31 A 22)

(54d) After the warrier addressed them, one of the men asks who he would:

| | | | | | | | | |
|---|---|---|---|---|---|---|---|---|
| *ỉn* | *mtwk* | *rmṯ* | *n-ṯꜥny* | *ḫn* | *ỉn* | *mtwk* | *rmṯ* | *n-prbntt* |
| IR | 2MS | man | of-N | or | IR | 2MS | man | of-N |

Are you a man from Tanis or are you a man from Mendes?
(pSpiegelberg 15, 5–6)

There are also some rare cases of two relative clauses combined:

(55) A female warrior says:

| | | | | |
|---|---|---|---|---|
| *pꜣ-nty* | *mtre-w* | *pꜣ-[ntỉw]-ỉw-k* | *ḏd* | *nỉm-f* |
| [DEF.M-REL | correct-STA] | [COP.M-REL-2MS | say | OBJ-3MS] |

What you say is what is correct. (Amazons 7, 41)

A further narrowing of the domain of the bipartite pattern *NP NP* can be observed in Coptic, where it is reserved almost only for sentences with pronominal participants (see 1.1.2.3).

As discussed in the section on Earlier Egyptian (1.1.1), the possessive pattern with *n-s* is probably to be analysed as a nominal sentence. This construction is still attested in Demotic, although it is gradually replaced by the construction *wn-mtw*-POSSESSOR POSSESSEE. If the possessor is a noun, the earlier *n-s* is written *ỉ(w-)s*. This represents an attempt to adapt the graphemic representation to the actual pronunciation. The nature of the latter is clear from Greek renderings of Egyptian names containing the said element, where it usually appears as *εσε-*:

(56a) In the introduction to moral precepts the author is introduced:

| | | | | |
|---|---|---|---|---|
| *ỉp-w* | *ỉdn* | *ṯꜣy-šbd* | *rmṯ* | *na-sꜣpr* |
| assign.PST-3P | lieutenant | carry-staff | man | POSS.P-bodyguard |

| | | |
|---|---|---|
| *ỉ(w-)s* | *prꜥꜣ* | *rr-f* |
| POSS-3C | pharaoh | to-3MS |

A lieutenant, a staff-carrier, and bodyguard belonging to the pharaoh were assigned to him. (Onkhsheshonqy 4, 6–7)

(56b) A priest claims a prebend for himself in the presence of the pharaoh:

| | | | | |
|---|---|---|---|---|
| *ỉnky* | *pꜣ-sꜥnḫ* | *(n)-rn-f* | *ỉ(w-)s* | *pꜣy-y-ỉṯ* |
| 1S | DEF.M-prebend | of-name-3MS | POSS-3C | POSS.M-1S-father |

The said prebend belongs to me; it belonged to my father.
(pSpiegelberg 2, 4)

(56c) In a legal document, a plaintiff states that the opposing party must not touch the property over which the lawsuit is raised:

*ḫpr* *ink=s* *iw* *i-s-p3dywp* *p3y-(y)-šr* *ʿ3*
because 1S=3C DEP POSS-3C-N POSS.M-1S-son great
*irm-n3y-f-sn-w*
with-POSS.P-3MS-sibling-P
Because it belongs to me, while it also belongs to Petophois, my eldest son, and his brothers. (pBM 10591, r° 5, 10)

If the possessor is pronominal, the pattern [absolute pronoun + NP] is used (ex. 57a). If both possessor and possessed are pronominal, the pattern [absolute pronoun + clitic pronoun] is used (ex. 57b–d):

(57a) In a contract on the partition of real estate:
*iw-mtwk* *t3y-w-pš* *ink* *t3y-w-pš*
DEP-[2MS] [POSS.F-3P-part] [2MS] [POSS.F-3P-part]
...while half of it belongs to you and half of it belongs to me.
(pLouvre E 7843, 6)

(57b) The owner of a certain property is to confirm his ownership by stating:
*ink=s*
$[1S]_P$=$[3C]_S$
It is mine. (pRylands IX 18, 8)

(57c) The wife of a man is identified in a marriage contract:
*t3y-y-sn-t* *nty-ink=s*
POSS.F-1S-sibling-F REL-1S=3C
...my sister, who belongs to me.
(pLouvre E 7846, r° 4 [Lüddeckens, *Eheverträge*, 14])

(57d) A legal statement:
*n3-3ḥ-w* *(n)-rn-w* *ink=s*
DEF.P-field.P of-names-3P [1S]=[3P]
The fields in question, they are mine. (pBM 10591, r° 4, 1)

These examples show that there was no grammatical difference between alienable and inalienable possession. The pronouns marking the possessor are those of the absolute series, whereas those marking the possessee are either *s* for the third-person common singular or *st* for third-person plural. In some cases the graphical representation seems to indicate a gradual collapse of all third-person pronouns into the same form *s* [*se]:

(58a) An author's excuse to the addressee for failing to provide a pieve of linen of *byssos*-quality:

| | | | |
|---|---|---|---|
| *ḏd-pꜣ-šsp* | *n-tꜣ-mnḫ-t* | *n-imn* | *mtwk=s* |
| for-DEF.M-reception | of-DEF.F-linen-F | of-N | 2MS=3C |

...because you have the reception of the linen of Amun anyway.

(pRylands IX 14, 14)

(58b) The addressee has asked for an agent of a steward to come to Elephantine. The author replies:

| | | | |
|---|---|---|---|
| *bniw-rḫ-rd* | *iw-mtwf=s* | *ḫpr* | *dy* |
| NEG-can-agent | DEP-3MS=3C | happen | there |

No agent that belongs to him will be able to be there.

(pBerlin P. 13633, v° 9–10)

(58c) In a sale-document of a slave the ownership of the buyer (a woman) is confirmed as follows:

*mtwt=s*

2FS=3C

He belongs to you. (pBN 223, 3)

(58d) In a contract the persons receiving an endowment are assured that no outsiders can make claims to it:

| | | | |
|---|---|---|---|
| *iw-mtwtn* | *tꜣy-tn-s-t* | *ʿn* | *šʿ-ḏ-t* |
| DEP-2P | POSS.F-2P-place-F | again | until-eternity-F |

...while your place belongs to you regardless forever. (pRylands II, 5)

A noun possessee can be either pronominalised and introduced later in apposition (as in ex. 59a) or it may appear immediately after the initial pronoun (59b):

(59a) In a sale document the seller states that he has given everything to the buyer:

| | |
|---|---|
| *mtwk=s* | *tꜣy-k-dny-t* |
| 2MS=3C | POSS.F-2MS-part-F |

Your part belongs to you. (pLouvre E 9294, 3–4)

(59b) A priest has sold half of the income of his office:

| | | | |
|---|---|---|---|
| *iw-mtwk* | *tꜣy-w-pš* | *ink* | *tꜣy-w-pš* |
| DEP-2MS | POSS.F-3P-half | 1S | POSS.F-3P-half |

...while one half belongs to you, and the other half belongs to me.

(pLouvre E 7843, 6)

Multiple possessors can be coordinated by the conjunction *ḥnʿ*:

(60) In a contract of lease the tenant is charged with the task of ploughing a field with three teams of oxen; of these it is said:

*mtwk* *ḥnꜥ-nꜣy-k-ḫbr* *ỉḥ* 5
2MS CNJ-POSS.P-2MS-partner oxen 5
Five oxen belong to you and your partners. (pLouvre E 7837, 4)

A similar situation may pertain to coordinated possessees:

(61a) A priest sells his offices in the temple:
*mtwk=st* *ḥnꜥ-nꜣy-w-ḥtp-w* *ḥnꜥ-nꜣy-w-ꜣḫ-t-w*
2MS=3P CON-POSS.P-3P-revenue-F CON-POSS.P-3P-thing-F
*ḥnꜥ-nꜣ-nty-ỉw-w* *wꜣḥ* *rr-w* *n-ḥ-t-nṯr* ...
CON-DEF.P-REL-FUT-3P put to-3P from-house-F-god ...
They belong to you along with their revenues, their things, and whatever will be added to them from the temple, *from field, from the city and any place thereof in the domain of Amun.* (pRylands I, 2)

(61b) In the deed of sale of some real estate, the seller states:
*mtwk* *nꜣ-sẖ=nb* *qnb=nb* *md=nb* *nty-pḥ*
2MS DEF.P-document=QU stipulation=QU thing=QU REL-reach
*rr-w*
to-3P
*ḥnꜥ-pꜣy-w-hp* *ḥnꜥ-pꜣ-nty-ỉw-y* *mꜣꜥṯ-k* *n[ỉm-w* *rn-w]*
CON-POSS.M-3P-law CON-DEF.M-REL-1S justify-STA.1S in-3P name-3P
To you belong all the documents, all stipulations, everything that pertains to it and their laws, as well as that to which I have right in their name. (pLüddeckens 2, GBS (A) 6–7 [*ZÄS* 115, 52])

(61c) A stipulation in a deed of sale of a real estate says:
*mtwk* *nꜣ-šty-w* *nꜣ-ꜥwy-w* *n-šty-w* *nty=nb* *nty-ḥry*
2MS DEF.P-liturgy-P DEF.P-house-P of-liturgy REL=QU REL-above
*r-ḫ-pꜣ-nty-sẖ* *ḥry*
to-way-DEF.M-REL-write.STA above
The liturgies, the houses of the liturgies, and everything mentioned above belong to you as is written above. (pLouvre N 2409, 5)

Sometimes the coordination is signalled by simple juxtaposition, i.e. without any overt conjunctive element, as shown by the last example quoted above. Demotic is the last stage of the language to employ this pattern, without Coptic survivors.

In Demotic, the earlier cleft sentence pattern with an undetermined participle instead of a relative clause appears rarely, and only in construction with a personal pronoun. Clefts of this type usually have future temporal reference (see

Quack 2009: 235), although some present or past examples are attested in early Demotic texts (see 62d and 62e and 62f and 62g). However, as the participles do not show any distinctive morphology, they are glossed below only as active participles:

(62a) In a land lease written in cursive hieratic, the lessors say:
*ỉnn ỉ-ỉr-ḏd=n-k*
1P PA-AUX-say=*to*-2MS
It is we who will say to you (a quote follows).
(pLouvre E 7852, 4 [*RdE* 48: 86])

(62b) In a land lease it is explicitly stated which party owns which cow; concerning the lessor's cow it is said:
*ỉw-mtwk ỉ-ỉr-ỉr-tȝy(-y)-ỉḥ nty-ḥry n-wpy*
DEP-2MS PA-AUX-do-POSS.F[-1S]-cow REL-above for-work
...and it is you who will use my above-mentioned cow for work.
(pLouvre E 7837, 4–5)

(62c) A marriage document decrees to the husband:
*ỉnỉw mtwk ỉ-ỉr-ḫȝʿ(-y) n-ḥm-t ỉw-k dy=n-y*
CND 2MS PA-AUX-let[-1S] as-woman-F FUT-2MS give=to-1S
*ḥḏ dbn 1*
silver deben 1
If you abandon me as a wife, you will have to give me one *deben* of silver.
(pSaqqara H5–DP 486, 2–3)

(62d) The opening of a piece of correspondence:
*ḏdḥr sȝ ṯȝyḥpnỉmw ỉ-ỉr-ḏd (n)-ḏdḥrbnỉwwthṯf sȝ kȝnfr*
N son N PA-AUX-say to-N son N
Teos, son of Tjahapenimu says to Djedharbeniutahtif, son of Kanuphis.
(pCG 50066, 2–3)

(62e) In a dream text a man says that he spent the night in the courtyard of the god Amunrasonther as he suffered from his eye:
*ỉw-kṯḫ ỉ-ỉr-ṯȝy=n-y my-t*
DEP-other.P PA-AUX-take=to-1S way-F
...since others have to guide me. (oBrooklyn 37.1821E, 10–11)

(62f) A man warns his addressee in a letter that he will sue him and refers to the troubles that he has suffered:
*mtwk ỉ-ỉr-dy ḫpr-w nỉm-y ḏr-w*
2MS PA-AUX-let happen-3P OBJ-1S all-3P
It is you who has made all of them happen to me. (pLoeb 7, 11–12)

(62g) A female claimant accuses two men of fraud and states that even if her opponent held a document done for a certain Timarchos:
*mtww ỉ-ỉr-dỉ ỉr-w=s=n-f ꜥn*
3P PA-AUX-let make-3P=3CS=for-3MS again
...it is they again who had it made for him. (pBM 10591, r° 5, 3)

As can be seen from the examples above, the participle is always of the periphrastic type (with *ỉ-ỉr*). Less common is the simple prefix *ỉ-*:

(63) The Persian satrap Pherendates reprimands the priests of Elephantine for their having chosen their temple's *lesonis*-priest without consulting him. He tells them that he will not accept candidates with dubious reputation:
*sṯbr ỉ-rḫ-pꜣy-wꜣḥ*
N PA-know-DEM.M-order
Satibara knows this order. (pBerlin P. 13540, 8–9)

In addition, this construction seems to have survived in the stereotyped dedication formula 'it is the god X who gives life to Y' as well as in a similar formula in marriage contracts, where the initial element *ỉn/m* appears to be omitted. The form of the verb in the second position is most probably the infinitive (Vleeming 2001: 250–53 and Kruchten 1996: 61–63):

(64a) Dedication formula on a offering table:
*wsỉr nṯr ꜥꜣ dy-t-ꜥnḫ n-pašꜣ sꜣ ḥr*
N god great give-INF-life to-N son N
It is Osiris, the great god, who gives life to Pasha, son of Hor.
(Vleeming, *Short Texts* I, #245)

(64b) The small dog-ape eulogises a certain food:
*mtwf nt-dy-t ỉr-skty my*
[3MS]$_S$ [REL-let-INF make-morning_bark wind
*rỉw-f-dy-t ỉr-mnṯꜥ-t mḥ-t*
DEP-3SM-let-INF make-evening_bark-F north wind-F]$_P$
This is what causes the morning barque to enjoy a good wind, with the evening barque enjoying northern wind. (Myth of the Sun's Eye, 3, 30–31)

(64c) The prospective husband swears to donate property to his wife:
*ỉnk dy-t=n-s pꜣ-nkt nty-sḫ ḥry*
1S give-INF=to-3FS DEF.M-thing REL-write.STA above
I give her the chattels documented above.
(pBerlin P. 3048, v° 19 [Lüddeckens, *Eheverträge*, 10])

The occasional occurrence of the forms *dy* and *nty dyt* instead of the usual *dyt* seems to indicate that the construction was understood as a cleft sentence, as shown by the following dedication:

(65) Dedication formula on a limestone stela:

| | | | | |
|---|---|---|---|---|
| *ḏḥwty* | *wꜣḥ-ꜥḥꜥ(w)* | *pꜣ-ỉỉr-dy-t* | *tꜣ-ẖrꜣ* | *(n)-nꜣ-hb* |
| N | set-lifetime | COP.M-REL.PST-give-INF | DEF.F-food | of-DEF.P-ibis |
| *m-bꜣḥ-ḏḥwty* | | | | |
| in-presence-N | | | | |

Thoth, who sets down lifetime, is the one who has given the food of the ibises before Thoth. (Vleeming, *Short Texts* I, #214, 1–6)

However, an analysis of sentences as in 64a as simple *Present I* (Loprieno 1995: 93) constructions is equally possible (Quack 2009: 233). Indeed, the prevalent cleft pattern in Demotic is structurally identical with the pseudo-cleft sentence of Late Egyptian, which takes over the functions of the Late Egyptian cleft patterns as well. The reason for this lies probably in the gradual loss of the participle as a productive formal word class in Later Egyptian. As in Late Egyptian, an initial NP without any marking particle (as in the earlier cleft pattern) is juxtaposed in Demotic to a relative clause headed by a definite article. The tense marking of the pattern is achieved via relative forms (preterite) or a relative clause with the element *nty* + a present or future construction:

**Tab. II.3:** Demotic Tense-marked (pseudo-)cleft sentence structures.

| **Tense** | **First NP** | **Second NP (subject = antecedent)** | **Second NP (subject ≠ antecedent)** |
|---|---|---|---|
| *Preterite* | | COP + periphrastic participle (*pꜣ-ỉ-ỉr-stp*) | COP + relative form (*pꜣ-r-stp-f*) |
| *Present* | NP | COP + relative clause with *Present I* (*pꜣ-nty-stp*) | COP + relative clause with *Present I* (*pꜣ-nty-ỉw-f stp*) |
| *Future* | | COP + relative clause with *Future III* (*pꜣ-nty-ỉw-f (r)-stp*) | |

In the preterite, graphemic variants show *NP pꜣy-ỉr-stp*, with the auxiliary *ỉr* if the subject of the relative phrase is referentially identical with the antecedent, or the non-periphrastic *NP pꜣy-stp-f*, if it is not. In the Present, the infinitive is never preceded by the preposition *ḥr*. As in Late Egyptian, the second position may also be occupied by a passive participle (in the preterite). Exx. 66a and 66b are temporally preterite, whereas 66c and 66d have present and 66e and 66f future time reference (for the use of the infinitive and its evolution see Quack 1991b: 189–207):

(66a) The priests explain what happened to the sacerdotal prebend of Amun:

*wꜥ-wꜥb* *n-i̓mn* *pꜣ-i̓i̓r-ṯꜣy-ṯ-s* *i̓w-f*
[IDF.S-priest of-N] [COP.M-REL.PST-take-OBJ-3FS] DEP-3MS
*[n]-ḥry* *n-ḥwtnnnsw*
as-leader of-N

A priest of Amun is the one who took it when he was the leader of Heracleopolis. (pRylands IX 3, 18)

(66b) The author of a letter informs the addressee of a reply by a third party concerning some money:

*ḏd-f=n-y* *mtwk* *pꜣ-i̓i̓r-hb=n-y* *nim-w*
said.PST-3MS=to-1S [2MS] [COP.M-REL.PST-send=to-1S in-3P
*r-dy-s=n-y*
to-give.INF-3S=to-1S]

He said to me (that) it was you who wrote to him to give it to him. (pBerlin P. 15521, 5–6)[22]

(66c) The pharaoh awoke and called out:

*nm* *pꜣ-nty-n-bnr*
[WH] [COP.M-REL-in-outside]

Who is outside (lit. who is the one who is outside)? (Onkhsheshonqy 2, x+21)

(66d) A small piece of wisdom in a teaching:

*rmt* *i̓w-nꜣ-ḫm-md-t* *mtws* *tꜣ-nty-ṯꜣy-ṯ-f*
man DEP-ADJ-small-thing-F [3FS] [COP.F-REL-take-INF-3MS]

A man's concern might be small, but it is what occupies him. (Onkhsheshonqy 14, 4)

(66e) Peteese replies to the priests of Teudjoi concerning his prebends:

*mtww* *nꜣ-nty-i̓w-tn-<dy-t>-st=n-y*
[3P] [COP.P-REL-FUT-2P-give-INF-3FS=to-1S]

They are what you should give to me. (pRylands IX 13, 6)

(66f) Peteese replies to the chief of the Ma:

*ꜥnḫ-i̓mn* *i̓nk* *pꜣ-nty-i̓w-f-r-i̓y* *ḥꜥ(-y)*
live-N [1S] [COP.M-REL-FUT-3MS-FUT-come.INF self[-1S]]

By Amun, I shall come myself. (pRylands IX 13, 2–3)

22 Construed as indirect speech with only partial adjustment of pronominal deixis; see Peust (2005: 77–102; 2014: 311–15).

Coordination of elements in the first NP position is attested, but not particularly frequent:

(67) A woman selling herself to a temple pledges to the god:
*mtwk ḥnꜥ-nꜣy-k-rd-w nꜣ-nty-nḥṱy r-md-t=nb*
2MS CON-POSS.P-2MS-agent-P COP.P-REL-entrust to-thing-F=QU
*r-ḏd-ṱ-w ỉrm-y m-md-t=nb nty-ḥry*
to-speak-INF-3P with-1S of-thing-F=QU REL-above
You and your agents are fully authorised to negotiate with me in matters of everything mentioned above. (pBM 10622, 17–18)

In the following examples, a bare relative clause with the relativiser *nty* appears. In these cases, one might be tempted to assume an erroneous omission of the definite article/the copula before the latter, but examples are too frequent for this explanation to be convincing:

(68a) In an oracle question with unclear context, a certain amount of money is mentioned and the gods are asked to send out the present document should the money be given to the author. Then it is stated:
*mtww nty-ỉrrḫ-s*
3P REL-know-3FS
They are informed. (oMallawi 484, x+8)

(68b) A marriage document says concerning the belongings of the woman:
*mtwt nty-nḥṱ rḥr-y nỉm-w ỉwṱ-ḏd qnb-t=nb*
2FS REL-entrust to-1S OBJ-3P without-say court-F=QU
*n-md=nb (n)-pꜣ-tꜣ ỉrm-t*
in-thing=QU in-DEF.M-land with-2FS
You are the one who has authority over them concerning me, without litigating with you in anything in the world. (pAdler 21, 11–12)

(68c) The recipient of a letter is requested to inquire about certain issues with the local god. Among these is the following:
*tḥꜣ=nb nty-ỉw-f ḫn-w ỉnn mtwk nty-gm=n-f bwꜣ*
illness=QU REL-PTC-3MS in-3P IP 2MS REL-find=to-3MS wrong
All the adversities that he is in – is it you (the god) who finds reproach in him? (Cairo JE 95206, 16–17)

(68d) A magical text gives instructions on the preparation of an oracle inquiry:
*ỉwfḫpr ỉw-mtwk nty-nꜣe-šn ỉỉr-k-mḥ-ỉrṱ-k*
CND DEP-2MS REL-FUT-seek FUT-2MS-fill-eye-2MS
*n-wyṱ mstme*
with-green_eye-make_up black_eye-make_up

If it is you who will inquire, you shall anoint your eye with green and black eye-makeup. (pMag. London&Leiden 23, 21–22)

(68e) The author of a letter describes how he found the Ibeion with just a young lad in charge of the sanctuary:

| | | | |
|---|---|---|---|
| *mtwf* | *nty-ḫpr* | *wbꜣ-tꜣ-ḥw-t-nsw* | *tꜣ-s-t-ms* |
| [3MS] | [REL-happen | against-DEF.F-mansion-F-king | DEF.F-place-F-birth] |
| *pꜣy* | | | |
| COP.M | | | |

He is the one responsible for the king's mansion and the birth house. (pLouvre 3334, 14–15)

Instead of an expected cleft sentence (**mtwf pꜣ-nti ḫpr wbꜣ tꜣ-ḥw-t-nsw tꜣ-s-t-ms*), the last example exhibits a tripartite pattern (see 1.3.2.2) with a headless relative clause.

#### 1.1.2.3 Coptic

Examples of bipartite nominal sentences formed by two juxtaposed lexical NPs are almost absent in Coptic. The rare instances appear mainly as bipartite variants of tripartite sentences with copula in other dialects:

(69a) The Lord is the avenger, but

| | | | |
|---|---|---|---|
| *p-cais* | *u-harš-hêt* | | (A) |
| [DEF.M-lord] | [IDF.S-patient-heart] | | |
| *p-cois* | *u-harš-hêt* | *pe* | (S) |
| [DEF.M-lord] | [IDF.S-patient-heart] | COP.M | |

The Lord is slow to anger. ([AS]Na 1:3 [Till vs. Ciasca])

(69b) Jesus says that his testimony of himself would not hold, but there will be another to bear witness of him:

| | | | | | |
|---|---|---|---|---|---|
| *auô* | *ti-soun* | *ce-te-f-mnt-mntre* | *u-me* | | (S) |
| and | 1S-know | COMP-[POSS.F-3MS-ABST-witness] | [IDF.S-truth] | | |
| *et-f-ire* | *mmo-s* | *haro-i* | | | |
| REL-3MS-do | OBJ-3FS | upon-1S | | | |
| *auô* | *ti-emi* | *ce-te-f-met-met^hre* | *u-mêi* | *te* | (B) |
| and | 1S-know | COMP-[POSS.F-3MS-ABST-witness | [IDF.S-truth] | COP.F | |
| *t^hê* | *et-a-f-er-met^hre* | *mmo-s* | *etbêt-ø* | | |
| $DEF_3$.F | REL-3MS-do-witness | OBJ-3FS | because-1S | | |

And I know that his testimony, which he bears concerning me, is true. ([SB]Jn 5:32)

(69c) Jacob blesses his sons:
*nephthalim* *u-laḫem*
N IDF.S-branch
*e-f-p$^{h}$ori* *ebol*
REL-3MS-come out
*e-f-ti* *n-u-met-saie* *ḫen-pi-utah*
REL-3MS-give OBJ-IDF.S-ABST-beauty in-DEF$_{2}$.M-fruit
Naphtali is a sprouting branch, that gives beauty in the fruit. ($^{B}$Gn 49:21)

(69d) The Pharisees and Sadducees wanted Jesus to show them a heavenly sign. He replied:
*ešôp* *afšan-i* *nce-hana-ruhi* *teten-co-s*
CND CND.3MS-come PTC-moment-evening 2P-say-3FS
*ce-t-p$^{h}$e* *u-camê* *e-s-t$^{h}$rošreš*
COMP-DEF.F-sky IDF.S-calm.F DEP-3FS-be_red
*uoh* *hana-toui* *teten-co-s* *ce-p$^{h}$ou* *t-p$^{h}$rô*
and moment-morning 2P-say-3FS COMP-today DEF.F-winter
*et$^{h}$be-pi-t$^{h}$rošreš* *n-t-p$^{h}$e* *nem-ne-s-gnophos*
because-DEF$_{2}$.M-be_red of-DEF.F-sky and-POSS.P-3FS-gloom
When the evening comes you say: 'The sky is calm and red'. And in the morning you say: 'Today is stormy because of the redness of the sky and its gloom'. ($^{B}$Mt 16:2–3)[23]

On the whole, it seems that juxtaposition of nouns is primarily a feature of the Akhmimic dialect, although even there they are rare.[24] The Bohairic examples 69c and 69d might be explained as patterns with an extraposited element in front of a bipartite sentence with deleted subject element, a construction that will be treated shortly. Finally, the Sahidic example might be a cleft sentence subtype (NP REL-, see below). However, the construction *NP NP* is still common in Coptic when one (less often, both) of the combined expressions is a *pronoun* (interrogative,

---

**23** So most witnesses. Although the direct cliticisation of the object to the verb is unusual in the *Present I*, no manuscript seems to employ the Conjunctive here (i.e. *(n)teten-co-s*). Nevertheless, some variants show the copula (J1 and J2).

**24** See Till (1928: §112). Possible examples such as $^{A}$Prv 13:8 *p-sôte n-te-psukhê n-p-rôme te-f-mnt-rmmao* 'The ransom (*p-sôte*) of man's (*n-p-rôme*) soul (*n-te-psukhê*) is his wealth (*te-f-mnt-rmmao*)' are probably better emended (with Böhlig) as *te <t>-f-mnt-rmmao* seeing that *tef-* is not the expected form of the possessive prefix in Akhmimic, which should appear as *tf-* instead.

demonstrative or absolute personal). In Sahidic, the absolute personal pronoun usually appears in its unstressed form *ang-*, *ntk-* (or even *etk-*), *an(n)-* etc.:

(70a) The righteous man calls out to the Lord, but the Lord does not listen:
*anok=de* *ang-u-fnt* *ang-u-rôme=an*
1S=yet 1S-IDF.S-worm 1S-IDF.S-man=NEG
Yet I, I am a worm and not a man. ($^{S}$Ps 21 [22]:6 [7] [Budge])

(70b) The Israelites are reproved:
*ntk-u-laos* *našt-makh*
2MS-IDF.S-people strong-neck
You are stiff-necked people. ($^{S}$Dt 9:6 [Kasser])

(70c) A will contains a quote from Gn 3:19:
*etk-u-kah* *e-k-na-kot-k* *e-p-kah*
2MS-IDF.S-earth ST-2MS-FUT-turn-2MS to-DEF.M-earth
Dust you are and to dust you shall return. ($^{S}$*KRU* #76, 3&21)

(70d) The hegemon has Shnube and Sophia tortured. He asks the young girl:
*nto* *hôô-te* *nte-u* *n-tei-he*
2FS self-2MS 2FS-WH in-DEM.F-way
Now you, what/who are you? ($^{S}$*Mart. Shnube* [*ASAE* 17, 149, 9–10])

(70e) Besa castigates the nun Herai and compares her to Judas Iscariot:
*ce-nto-u-krof* *n-t-he* *m-p-etmmau*
for-2MS-IDF.S-guile in-DEF.F-way of-DEF.M-that
...for you are as guileful as that one. ($^{S}$Besa, *To Herai*, §V.2 [Kuhn 109, 11])

(70f) At the end of the Saviour's revelations, Mary thanks him:
*an-hen-makarios* *anon* *para-rôme* *nim* *n-nei-mnt-nok$^{j}$*
1P-IDF.P-content 1P than-man QU in-DEM.M-ABST-great
*ent-a-k-k$^{j}$olp-u* *na-n* *ebol*
REL-PST-2MS-reveal-3P for-1P out
We are more content than anyone else with these great things that you revealed to us. ($^{S}$*Pistis Sophia* 352, 3 [Schmidt])

(70g) Shenute answers to an accusation that he is too oppressive:
*alla* *ntetn-hen-rôme* *n-krof*
but 2P-IDF.P-man of-guile
But you are guileful people. ($^{S}$Shenute, *Why, O Lord* [L III 134, 23–24])

(70h) When Tobias and the disguised angel Raphael finally arrive at Raguel's house, they are welcomed by him and:
*auô* *hraguêl* *a-f-cnu-u* *ce-ne-snêu* *ntetn-hn-ebol*
and N PST-3MS-ask-3P COMP-DEF.P-brother.P 2P-IDF.P-out
*tôn*
where

*peca-u=na-f* *ce-an-hen-ebol* *hn-n-šêre* *n-(n)ephthalem*
say.PST-3P=to-3MS COMP-1P-IDF.P-out in-DEF.P-son of-N
*ent-a-u-aikhmalôtize* *mmo-u* *e-niniuê*
REL-PST-3P-be_captivated OBJ-3P to-N
And Raguel asked them: 'Brothers, where are you from?' And they said to him: 'We are from the sons of Nephtalim who have been led into captivity in Niniveh.' (STb 7:3)

The situation is similar in the Mesokemic dialect, where the first-person plural pronoun shows some variation between *an-* and *an(n)en-*:

(71a) Jesus asks the disciples who the people say that the Son of Man is. After they have told him, he asks them:
*a-teten-cô* *mma-s* *ce-ank-nim*
PST-2P-say OBJ-3FS COMP-1S-WH
Who did you say I am? (MMt 16:15 mae 2)

(71b) As a voice from above speaks to Saul near Damascus, he answers with a question:
*ntk-nim* *p-c(ai)s*
2MS-WH DEF.M-lord
Who are you, lord? (MActs 9:5)

(71c) As the people of Lystra call them gods, Paul and Barnabas tell them:
*anan* *hô-n* *an-hen-rome* *n-te-tn-hê*
1P self-1P 1P-IDF.P-man of-POSS.F-2P-way
We are men like you. (MActs 14:15)

(71d) Jesus replies to Peter, who had asked him to explain the parable to the disciples:
*a[kmên]* *ntôten* *hô-ten=an* *nteten-hen-anoêto[s]*
still 2P self-2P=again 2P-IDF.P-ignorant
Are you still ignorant? (MMt 15:16 mae 2)

Although examples of first- and second-person pronouns are quite common, third-person instances are rare (here the pattern *X pe* is normally used instead – see below)[25]:

25 It seems that the exx. 72a-b is the sole instance of its kind (cf. the similar construction in B version cited below as 79a. In the M manuscript, the text is unfortunately not preserved, cf. Orlandi 1974: 35). Examples such as BPeter of Alexandria, *On Riches*, *nt$^h$of=de pi-heretikos etemmau* 'Indeed, he is that heretic' (Pearson and Vivian 1993: 134) are better analysed as fronting ('He (*nt$^h$of*), however (=*de*), that heretic (*pi-heretikos etemmau*), said: ...'), since the particle =*de* should not intervene into the predication.

(72a) St Paul urges anyone who claims to belong to the Christ to consider:
*kata-t-he* *e-ntf-pa-pe-kh(risto)s* *anon* *-pô-f*
like-DEF.F-way DEP-[3MS]-[POSS.M-DEF.M-Christ] 1P -POSS.M-3MS
*hôô-n*
self-1P
Just as he belongs to the Christ, so do we. ([S]2Cor 10:7)

(72b) A woman's reply in a certain matter is quoted in a letter as:
*šantê-abu-ali* *i* *ebol* *ntof* *-pa-iôt* *auô* *ntof*
LIM-N go out [3MS] [-POSS.M.1S-father] and 3MS
*p-êt-tôš*
COP.M-REL-decide
Abu Ali will leave. He is my father and he is the one who decides.
([F]*P.Gascou* 24, 11–12)

Other Coptic dialects such as Bohairic, Akhmimic, and Lycopolitan usually display the full forms of the pronouns, but examples with the bound form are attested in all dialects except Bohairic.[26] Although clitic particles cannot intervene between the pronoun and the following expression as well (cf. exx. 73a and b, as well as ex. 75e below) the full forms seem to be separate prosodic units and it seems better not to treat the two NPs as a single unit:[27]

(73a) In a plea to the Lord to be saved the Psalmist exclaims:
*anok* *-u-hêki=de* *uoh* *n-côb* *anok*
1S -IDF.S-poor=yet CNJ of-need 1S
But I, I am poor and needy. ([B]Ps 69 [70]:6 [5])

(73b) Zacharias expresses his incredulity over what the angel of the Lord has told him:
*anok=gar* *anok* *-u-ḫello*
1S=for 1S -IDF.S-old man
...for I am an old man. ([B]Lk 1:18)

(73c) Clement quotes Abraham's words in Gen 18:27:
*anak* *anak* *-u-kah* *anak* *-u-etniḫ*
1S 1S -IDF.S-earth 1S -IDF.S-ashes
As for me, I am earth, I am ashes. ([A]1Cl 7:2 [Schmidt])

26 See e.g. Till (1928: §113c) for Akhmimic or Jn 3:2 and 4:9 (ntk-) as well as 9:40 (an-) for Lycopolitan.

27 However, to mark the syntactic boundness we have chosen the Leipzig glossing rule 2A, i.e. the groups are separated by space yet marked as bound by hyphenation.

(73d) Thekla screamed at an amorous nobleman who tried to embrace her:
*anak -u-nak$^{j}$ hn-hikonios*
1S -IDF.S-great in-N
I am a noblewoman in Iconium! ($^{L}$*Acta Pauli* 15* 21, 5 [Schmidt])

(73e) In the days of the apocalypse, sinners will say:
*o p-et-a-k-ee-f ne-n p-šêre*
WH COP.M-REL-PST-2MS-do-3MS to-1P DEF.M-son
*n-t-anomia e-k-cu mma-s*
of-DEF.F-lawlessness DEP-2MS-say OBJ-3FS
*anak pe p-kh(risto)s e-ntak -p-diabolos*
1S COP.M DEF.M-Christ DEP-2MS -DEF.M-devil
What have you done to us, O son of the lawlessness, saying: 'I am the Christ', although you are the devil?
($^{A}$*ApEl* [Steindorff, *Apokalypse des Elias* 100 40, 4–7)

(73f) Abraham was on his way to Egypt. As he and his wife approached the border, he said to her:
*ti-emi ce-nt$^{h}$o -u-shimi n-saiê e-nesô-s*
1S-know COMP-2FS -IDF.S-woman of-beauty DEP-beautiful-3FS
*ḫen-pe-s-ho*
in-POSS.M-3FS-face
I know that you are a beautiful woman with a fair face. ($^{B}$Gn 12:11)

(73g) Jesus cites from the psalms asking the Jews whether it is not written in their law:
*anak a-i-[c]oo-s ce-ntôten -hen-nu[te]*
1S PST-1S-say-3FS COMP-2P -IDF.P-god
I said: You are gods. ($^{L}$Jn 10:34)

(73h) Although the Antichrist has come into the world, the faithful need not be afraid:
*nt$^{h}$ôten nt$^{h}$ôten -han-šêri ebol ḫen-p$^{h}$-(nu)ti*
2P 2P -IDF.P-child out in-DEF.M-god
You, you are children from God. ($^{B}$1Jn 4:4)

Fayyumic occupies an intermediate position and shows both the reduced (74a–74c) and the unreduced forms (74d–74g) of the pronouns. Especially noteworthy seems example 74d, in which the negation brackets not the whole clause but only the pronoun:

(74a) The Samaritan woman wonders how Jesus could give her water from a deep well without anything with which to draw water:
*mê ntek-u-nak$^{j}$ ntak e-iakôb pe-n-iôt*
IP [2MS]-[IDF.S-great 2MS to-N POSS.M-1P-father]
Are you then greater than our father Jacob, *(who gave that well to us)*?
($^{F}$Jn 4:12)

(74b) Stephen retells the beginning of Exodus where Moses tried to stop the Israelites from quarrelling by saying:
*[n]teten-hen-lômi* *n-snêu*
2P-IDF.P-man of-brother.P
You are brothers. (Why do you hurt one another?)
([F]Acts 7:26 [Kahle, *Balaizah* I, 288])

(74c) John says to the young men of his community:
*ce-ntet[n-he]n-côri*
for-2P-IDF.P-strong
...for you are strong. ([F]1Jn 2:14 [Schenke 126, 19])

(74d) Inhabitants of a city in Phrygia ask a man whether he is a deity. He replies:
*n-anak=en* *-[u]-nuti* *alla* *[an]ak* *-u-lômi* *[n-te]-tn-hê*
NEG-1S=NEG -IDF.S-god but [1S] -[IDF.S-man of-POSS.F-2P-way]
I am no god, but I am a man like you.
([F]*Acts of Philip* [von Lemm I 534, a4–6])

(74e) The first angel refuses to worship the first human and says:
*p-kui* *ela-i* *pe* *u-lômi* *pe* *anak*
DEF.M-small to-1S SE.M IDF.S-man SE.M [1S]
*-u-arkhê-plasma*
-[IDF.S-beginning-creation]
He is inferior to me. He is a man, but I am a first-created being.
([F]John Evangelist, *Investiture of Archangel Michael* [Müller 13, 5])

(74f) In the Song of Songs the Beloved tells the maiden:
*[mpel]-sames* *ela-i* *ce-anak* *-u-kamê*
NEG.IMP-stare OBJ-1S for-[1S] -[IDF.S-black.F]
Do not stare at me because I am dark (*for the sun has burnt my skin).*
([F]Sg 1:6 [Diebner 150])

(74g) Agathonicus addresses other bishops, who now say about themselves:
*anan* *-hen-šaas*
[1P] -[IDF.P-shepherd]
We are shepherds. ([F]Agathonicus of Tarsus, *Apologies* [Erichsen 12, 17])

However, the use of the full forms of the pronouns is also attested in Sahidic texts for all pronouns of the first and second persons, although they are less common than the proclitic forms. Manuscripts often display both patterns side by side:

(75a) When Theodore visits Horsiese, the latter encourages him by saying: *Be confident, for we two are a single man as regards every good work. Actually it is you who appointed me*:

*auô anon -n-šêre n-u-rôme n-uôt*
and 1P -DEF.P-son of-IDF.S-man of-single
...and we are sons of a single man. ($^{S}$*V. Pachom* [Lefort 192, 13])

(75b) As Apa Victor entered the palace to meet the emperor, the latter delivered a speech beginning with:
*anon -hn-makarios*
1P -IDF.P-content
We are content (*that* ...). ($^{S}$*Acts of the Synode of Ephesos* [Bouriant 8, 12])

(75c) Shenute wants to dissuade people from thinking to themselves as follows:
*hamoi ne-anon -ua mmo-u*
PTC PRT-1P -one of-3P
If only we were one of them!
($^{S}$Shenute, *God, Who Alone Is True* [L IV 92, 18])

(75d) Shenute quotes Nestorius:
*ene-u-nute=k$^{j}$e=pe peca-f ne-f-na-coo-s*
CFT-IDF.S-god=then=SE.M say.PPA-3MS PRT-3MS-FUT-say-3FS
*ce-k$^{j}$omk$^{j}$m ero-i*
COMP-touch OBJ-1S
*nte-tn-nau ce-anok -u-pn(eum)a auô anok -u-nute*
CNJ-2P-see that-1S -IDF.S-spirit and 1S -IDF.S-god
'If he had been a god,' he said, 'he would have said: "Touch me and see that I am spiritual and I am divine!"'
($^{S}$Shenute, *I am Amazed* §465 [Cristea 191, 18–25])

(75e) The narrator of the Life of Moses explains why he does not go into detail about certain aspects of Moses' perfect ascetic lifestyle:
*ne-f-polutia=de n-ten-na-š-coo-u=an*
POSS.P-3MS-lifestyle=yet NEG-1P-FUT-can-say-3P=NEG
*anon -hen-hikanos=gar=an e-tre-n-pôh e-n-ši*
1P -IDF.P-able=for=NEG to-INFL-1P-reach to-DEF.P-measure
*n-ne-f-katorthoma*
of-POSS.P-3MS-success
Of his ascetic practises, however, we cannot tell, as we are unable to attain to the measure of his success.
($^{S}$*Life of Moses of Abydos* [Amélineau 692, 4–5])

(75f) After being thrown into the fiery furnace, Timothy prays to the Lord:
*anok -u-šmmo n-at-rôme*
1S -IDF.S-alien of-NEG-man
I am a friendless stranger. ($^{S}$*Mart. Timothy* [Till, *KHML* I 112, 6])

(75g) After she had been tortured, the hegemon asks Sophia who she is. She replies:

| | | | | |
|---|---|---|---|---|
| *anok* | *-u-khrêstianos* | *anok* | *-u-hmhal* | *nte-p-sôtêr* |
| 1S | -IDF.S-Christian | 1S | -IDF.S-servant | of-DEF.M-saviour |

I am a Christian. I am a servant of the Saviour.

([S]*Mart. Shnube* [*ASAE* 17: 149, 10–11])

(75h) Ptolemy is imprisoned after having publicly confessed his Christian faith. The next morning he faces the governor who asks him:

| | |
|---|---|
| *ntok* | *-u-rm-tôn* |
| 2MS | -IDF.S-man-where |

Where are you from? ([S]*Mart. Ptolemy* [Till, *KHML* II 31, 13])

(75i) Gesios found some human bones and lamented the fleeting nature of life:

| | | | | |
|---|---|---|---|---|
| *anok=gar* | *nmma-f* | *anon* | *-u-sôma* | *n-uôt* |
| 1S=for | with-3MS | 1P | -IDF.S-body | of-single |
| *auô* | *u-sarks* | *n-uôt* | *p-ent-a-n-phorei* | *mmo-s* |
| and | IDF.S-flesh | of-single | COP.M-REL-PST-1P-carry | OBJ-3FS |
| *m-pe-snau* | *auô* | *u-pneuma* | *n-uôt* | |
| in-DEF.M-two | and | IDF.S-spirit | of-single | |

| | | | | |
|---|---|---|---|---|
| *p-ent-a-p-nute* | *kharize* | *mmo-f* | *na-i* | *mn-pei-rôme* |
| COP.M-REL-PST-DEF.M-god | grant | OBJ-3MS | for-1S | and-DEM.M-man |
| *nt-a-f-mu* | | | | |
| REL-PST-3MS-die | | | | |

For he and I, we are one single body; it is a single flesh that we both carry, and it is a single spirit that God has granted to this dead man and to me.

([S]*Gesios & Isodorus* [*ZÄS* 21, 142, 15–17)

(75j) The frightened Death asks Jesus in the netherworld:

| | | |
|---|---|---|
| A | *ntok* | *-nim* |
| | 2MS | -WH |
| C | *ntek-nim* | |
| | 2MS-WH | |

Who are you?

([S]*Book of the Resurrection of Christ* [Westerhoff 68, 9 ms. A vs. C])

(75k) The psalmist affirms the might of God:

| | | | |
|---|---|---|---|
| *ce-ntok* | *-u-nok*$^{j}$ | *e-k-ire* | *n-hen-špêre* |
| for-2MS | -IDF.S-great | ST-2MS-do | OBJ-IDF.P-wonder |

Because you are great; it is wondrous things that you do.

([S]Ps 85 [86]:10 [Budge])

(75l) Bachios meets some brethren at the martyrion of St James Intercisus and aks them:
*peca-i=na-u* *ce-nte[tn]-hn-ebol* *tôn*
say.PST-1S-to-3P COMP-2P-IDF.p-out where
*ntou=de* *peca-u* *ce-anon* *-hn-ebol* *hn-sunphora* *t-polis*
3P=yet say.PST-3P COMP-1S -IDF.P-out in-N DEF.F-town
*hn-n-tôš* *n-arduksêruksis* *p-rro* *n-m-persos*
in-DEF.F-territory of-N DEF.M-king of-DEF.F-Persian
I said to to them: 'Where do you come from?' And they said: 'We come from the town of Symphora in the territory of Artaxerxes, king of the Persians, ...
($^{S}$Bachaios of Maiuma, *On the Three Youth of Babylon* [Zanetti 729, 8–9])

(75m) The monk Frange quotes Jn 10:30:
*anok* *mn-pa-iôt* *anon* *-ua*
1S and-POSS.M.1S-father 1S -one
I and my father, we are one.
($^{S}$*O.Frange* #38, 11)

(75n) Frange closes a letter with the wish:
*ari-t-agapê* *n-g-r-pa-meue*
do.IMP-DEF.F-love CNJ-2MS-do-POSS.M.1S-remembrance
*hn-ne-k-šlêl* *etuaab*
in-POSS.P-2MS-prayer holy
*ce-anok* *-u-at-šau*
for-1S -IDF.S-un-worthy
Be so kind and remember me in your holy prayers for I am worthless.
($^{S}$*O.Frange* #58, 10–15)

In general, the use of unreduced forms in Sahidic is most common with *anon* 'we', which also appears in Shenute's writings. In the manuscript from which ex. 75b is taken, a second hand corrected *an-hn-makarios* to *anon -hn-makarios*.[28] In absence of a detailed study on the provenance and date of the manuscripts, it is impossible to decide whether this alternance reflects the scribes' or copyists' dialectal influence or rather a diachronic development. Some sources show both patterns side by side; e.g. the manuscript of the *Martyrdom of Shnube* shows the reduced (in 70d) and full (in 75g) form of the pronoun. Unreduced forms appear

**28** Pointed out by Kraatz (1904: 7 with note 2), and confirmed by H. O. Lange's meticulous collations in his former copy of the edition now in the Royal Library of Copenhagen.

regularly in Sahidic in clauses involving a possessive derivation of the type *pa-/ta-/na-* 'he/she/they of...' with locative expressions:

(76a) John asks a monk:
*pa-cois* *n-iôt* *ntok* *-pa-tôn*
POSS.M.1S-lord of-father 2MS -POSS.M-where
My lord father, where are you from?
($^{S}$*Life of John Calybita* [Budge, *Martyrdoms* 185, 11–12])

(76b) Simeon has just asked to be admitted to a monastic community. The abbot asks him:
*nt*$^{h}$*ok* *-p*$^{h}$*a-t*$^{h}$*ôn* *m-ma*
2MS -POSS.M-where of-place
Where are you from? ($^{B}$*Life & Miracles of St Simeon the Stylites* [Chaîne 22, 17])

(76c) Thekla is taken downstream to Alexandria in a boat with Virgin Mary and Elizabeth, the mother of John the Baptist whom she, however, does not recognise. She asks them:
*ntôtn* *-na-aš* *m-polis*
2P -POSS.P-WH of-city
Which city are you from? ($^{S}$*Mart. Paese & Thekla* [Till, *KHML* I, 80, 6])

(76d) In a reply to the question cited just above (ex. 76c):
*anon* *-na-t-hie(rusa)lm*
1P -POSS.P-DEF.F-N
We are from Jerusalem. ($^{S}$*Mart. Paese & Thekla* [Till, *KHML* I, 80, 8])

The Sahidic texts that provide the examples above employ reduced forms of pronouns also elsewhere in bipartite sentences of this type. This could suggest that they are limited to the construction with *pa-/ta-/na-* 'he/she/they of...'. However, since there are also examples with the possessive pattern *pa-/ta-/na-* 'he/she/they of...' with other expressions, the use of unreduced forms of the pronouns here should be seen as part of a diachronic process.

In the vast majority of cases, the second NP is indefinite, but definite NPs are also attested:

(77a) Mary answered to the angel of the Lord:
*ishêête* *ang-t-hmhal* *m-p-cois*
behold 1S-DEF.F-handmaid of-DEF.M-lord
Behold, I am the handmaid of the Lord. ($^{S}$Lk 1:38)

(77b) The residents of Gibeon came to Joshua and said:
*anon* *-ne-k-hmhal*
1P -POSS.P-2MS-servant
We are your servants. ($^{S}$Jo 9:14 [Thompson])

(77c) As their ship is befallen by a storm, the sailors ask Jonah about his origins. He tells them:

| | | |
|---|---|---|
| *anak* | *-p-ḫmh[el]* | *m-p-cai[s]* |
| 1S | -DEF.M-servant | of-DEF.M-lord |

I am the servant of the Lord. ($^{A}$Jon 1:9 [Malinine])

(77d) The high priest mocked the crucified Jesus for being unable to save himself, although he had said:

| | |
|---|---|
| *ank-p-šêre* | *m-p-n(u)ti* |
| 1S-DEF.M-son | of-DEF.M-god |

I am the Son of God. ($^{M}$Mt 27:43 mae 1)

(77e) When the Lord asked Cain about the whereabouts of his brother Abel, Cain replied:

| | | | |
|---|---|---|---|
| *mê* | *anok* | *-p-urit* | *m-pa-son* |
| IP | 1S | -DEF.M-warden | of-POSS.M.1S-brother |

Am I my brother's keeper? ($^{B}$Gn 4:9)

(77f) When he reached the border of Egypt, Abraham urged his wife Sarah to tell everyone there:

| | |
|---|---|
| *anok* | *-te-f-sôni* |
| 1S | -POSS.F-3MS-sister |

I am his sister. ($^{B}$Gn 12:13)

Most examples show first-person pronouns, but see 4.2.3 (with ex. 438b) for a negative example with a second-person pronoun.

The majority of examples of the pattern *NP NP* with pronouns show personal pronouns in the first position. Demonstrative pronouns are also attested in the same locus, but only rarely; in such cases, variants from other dialects or from manuscripts in the same dialect usually exhibit a tripartite pattern with copula, as in the following examples:

(78a) Wise and good behaviour:

| | | | | |
|---|---|---|---|---|
| *tei* | *t-ḫe* | *et-a-p-cais* | *ee-s* | *ne-n* |
| [DEM.F] | [DEF.F-way | REL-PST-DEF.M-lord | do-3FS | to-1P] |

This is the way in which the Lord has dealt with us. ($^{A}$Zec 1:6 [Till])

(78b) A note concerning the twenty-fourth day of the eleventh month:

| | | | | |
|---|---|---|---|---|
| *pei* | *p-ebat* | *n-sabat* | | A |
| [DEM.M] | [DEF.M-month | of-sabat] | | |
| *$p^{h}$ai* | *pe* | *pi-abot* | *sabat* | B |
| [DEM.M] | COP.M | [DEF$_2$.M-month | sabat] | |

This is the month of Sebat. (Zec 1:7 $^{A}$[Till] vs. $^{B}$[Tattam])

(78c) As Jesus was arrested, he reproached the Jews for treating him like a robber:
*alla t$^{h}$ai te-ten-unu nem-p-er-šiši*
but [DEM.F] [POSS.F-2P-hour CON-DEF.M-do-power
*nte-p-k$^{h}$aki*
of-DEF.M-darkness]
*alla t$^{h}$ai te te-ten-unu nem-p-er-šiši*
but [DEM.F] COP.F [POSS.F-2P-hour CON-DEF.M-do-power
*nte-p-k$^{h}$aki*
of-DEF.M-darkness]
But this is your hour and the authority of darkness. ($^{B}$Lk 22:53 var. lect.)

As can be seen from the examples presented so far, the NP in the second position is usually a noun, but personal, interrogative, and demonstrative pronouns as well as possessive (79a, see ex. 72 for the Sahidic version) and indefinite pronouns (79b and 79c) are also attested:

(79a) St Paul urges anyone who claims to belong to the Christ to consider:
*kata-p$^{h}$-rêti ete-nt$^{h}$of -p$^{h}$a-pe-kh(risto)s pai-rêti anon*
like-DEF.M-way DEP-3MS -POSS.M-DEF.M-Christ DEM.M-way 1P
*hôô-n*
self-1P
Just as he belongs to the Christ, so do we. ($^{B}$2Cor 10:7)

(79b) Jesus told the disciples that he was in heaven and surrounded by angels:
*ôs ce-anak -ue nmma-u ḫn-n-arkhê mn-n-eksusia*
as if that-1S -one with-3P in-DEF.P-power CON-DEF.P-force
...as if I was one of them among the powers and forces.
($^{A}$*Ep. Apostolorum* [Schmidt 4* f. 5, 11–12])

(79c) After having erred, the Psalmist assures the Lord that he will now follow his commandments and adds:
*ntak p-c(ai)s ntk-ue (e)-nanu-f ntk-u-khr(êsto)s*
2MS DEF.M-lord 2MS-one DEP-good-3MS 2MS-IDF.S-friendly
You, Lord, are good and friendly. ($^{M}$Ps 118 [119]:68)

We should observe that although absolute possessive pronouns can appear in the second position (ex. 72), Coptic avoids the bipartite pattern with two such expressions (e.g. †*nu-k nu-i* 'Yours is mine') and employs instead the tripartite pattern to be discussed in 1.3.2.3 (cf. Jn 17:10 *nu-k nu-i ne*). In ex. 79c, what looks graphemically at first like a dependent clause treated as an NP (i.e. *u-e-nanu-f*) should preferably be analysed as the indefinite pronoun *ue* followed by a dependent clause as non-restrictive relative clause (Shisha-Halevy 1983: 317). One of the two *e*'s has been elided; a feature rather common on Coptic. Similar examples will be cited in the section on the tripartite pattern, see ex. 188 in 1.3.2.3.

In Sahidic, constructions with first- or second-person pronouns as the first NP and proper names as the second NP ('I am [NAME]') are avoided. Instead, the tripartite pattern '*anok pe* [NAME]' is used, see ex. 192 in 1.3.2.3:

(80) Jesus had asked his disciples who the people said he is. They reply:
*uan-haini cô [m]ma-s ce-ntek-Iôan[n]ês p-lefticôkem*
PTC-some.P say OBJ-3FS COMP-[2MS]$_S$-[N DEF.M-Baptist]$_P$
*h[e]n-kekaui ce-Hêlias*
IDF.P-others.P COMP-N
*h[e]n-kekaui ce-ui ebal hen-ni-prophêtês=pe*
IDF.P-other.P COMP-one out from-DEF$_2$.P-prophet=SE.M
Some say that you are John the Baptist, others Elias, others still he is one of the Prophets. ($^{F}$Mk 8:28)

In the following example, two absolute pronouns are directly juxtaposed:

(81) The psalmist praises the Lord:
M: *ntak=de ntk-ntak*
2MS=yet 2MS-2MS
S: *ntok=de ntok=on=pe*
2MS=yet 2MS=again=SE.M
B: *nt$^{h}$ok=de nt$^{h}$ok=pe*
2MS=yet 2MS=SE.M
$^{M}$But you, you are you!
$^{S}$But you, you are yourself!
$^{B}$But you, it is you! ($^{MSB}$Ps 101 [102]:28 [27])

Here, the expected construction in the M-variant might have been [PRN SE], as in the Sahidic and Bohairic versions. However, since this example seems to be the only one of its kind, it may be regarded as an *ad-hoc* creation for the Greek σὺ δὲ ὁ αὐτὸς in the process of translation.

Coptic knows a number of patterns in which what is etymologically a prepositional phrase (*e-bol* < *r-bnr*) appears as part of a nominal sentence. As the use of the indefinite article shows, these patterns are apparently treated as NPs:

(82a) Peter insist that he does not know Jesus, but bystanders say:
*alêthôs ntk-u-ebol mmo-u kaigar ntk-u-galilaios*
truly 2MS-IDF.S-out from-3P for 2MS-IDF.S-Galilean
Truly you are one of them, for you are a Galilean. ($^{S}$Mk 14:70)

(82b) The soul is addressed in one of the Manichean psalms:

| | | | | | | |
|---|---|---|---|---|---|---|
| *t-psukhê* | *nto* | *-u-abal* | *to* | *nto* | *-u-abal* | *hi-p-cise* |
| DEF.F-soul | 2FS | -IDF.S-out | where | 2FS | -IDF.S-out | on-DEF.M-height |

O soul, where are you from? You are from up high.

($^{L}$*Psalms of Saracôtôn* [Allberry] 181, 20–21)

(82c) The saints are brought to the seat of the governor who asks their name. After some opening insults, Pirou tells him that they are Christians:

| | | | | |
|---|---|---|---|---|
| *anon* | *-han-ebol* | *ḫen-u-iôt* | *nem-u-mau* | *n-uôt* |
| 1P | -IDF.P-out | in-IDF.S-father | CON-IDF.S-mother | of-single |

We are of a single father and mother.

($^{B}$*Mart. Pirou & Atom* [*AdM* 140, 13])

(82d) Pilate asked Jesus:

| | | |
|---|---|---|
| *nt$^{h}$ok* | *-u-ebol* | *t$^{h}$ôn* |
| 2MS | -IDF.S-out | where |

Where are you from? ($^{B}$Jn 19:9)

Nominal sentences of this type display a positional hierarchy of their constituent parts. If both combined NPs are pronominal, but they belong to different categories such as personal vs. interrogative pronouns, the personal pronoun appears in the initial position, as we already saw in ex. 70d. Some interrogatives such as *u* are treated in Sahidic like a noun and can be augmented by the indefinite article as in ex. 83b:

(83a) God told Moses that he will send him to the pharaoh to free the Israelites. Moses replied:

| | | | | | |
|---|---|---|---|---|---|
| *ang-nim* | *anok=de* | *eie-bôk* | *ša-pharaô* | *p-rro* | *n-kême* |
| 1S-who | 1S=yet | FUT.1S-go | to-pharaoh | DEF.M-king | of-Egypt |

Who am I that I should go unto pharaoh, the king of Egypt?

($^{S}$Ex 3:11 [Maspero, *Et. ég.* I, 266])

(83b) External authorities appear to investigate Shenute's monastery, and their visit seems to have led to physical conflict with one of the officials. Later Shenute claims that he was neither frightened nor troubled; instead:

| | |
|---|---|
| *a-i-cnu-f* | *ce-ntk-u-u* |
| PST-1S-ask-3MS | COMP-2MS-IDF.S-WH |

I asked him: What/Who are you? ($^{S}$Shenute, *In the Night* [L III 38, 17])

(83c) The Angel of Lord explains Zechariah's vision to him by posing a rhetorical question:

| | |
|---|---|
| *ntk-nim* | *ntak* |
| 2MS-WH | 2MS |

Who are you, then?

($^{A}$Zec 4:7 [Malinine])

(83d) A demon said to the sons of a Jewish priest: *I know Jesus and also Paul,*
*nt$^h$ôten=de nt$^h$ôten -nim*
2P=yet 2P -WH
But you, who are you? ([B]Acts 19:15)

Multiple predicates could be attached to a subject pronoun in coordinated structures via asyndesis (ex. 84a) or coordinators such as the particles *nem-* (ex. 84b), *hi-* (ex. 84c) or *au* (ex. 84d):

(84a) In the Gnostic *Gospel of Philip,* the public reaction to the Christian confession is contrasted:
*ekša-coo-s ce-ano[k -u]-hellên u-barbaros*
CND.2MS-say-3FS COMP-1S -IDF.S-pagan IDF.S-barbarian
*u-hmhal [u-eleu]theros mn-lau na-štortr*
IDF.S-servant IDF.S-free man NEG-any FUT-tremble
If you say: 'I am a pagan, a barbarian, a slave or a free man', nobody will tremble.
([SL]*GospPh.* 62, 26–31 [Layton 164, 29–31])

(84b) Abraham pleads to God to spare Sodom: *Since I have undertaken to speak to the Lord,*
*anok=de anok -u-kahi nem-u-kermi*
1S=yet 1S -IDF.S-earth CNJ-IDF.S-ashes
...although I am earth and ashes.
([B]Gn 18:27)

(84c) In his Homily on the Virgin Theophilus narrates how he went into the church on Sunday and addressed the Lord:
*p-nute kô na-i ebol ce-ang-u-kah hi-krms*
DEF.M-god set to-1S out for-1S-IDF.S-earth CNJ-ashes
God, forgive me, for I am dust and ashes.
([S]Theophilus, *Homily on the Virgin* [Worrell 304, 25–305, 2])

(84d) Clement says that past leaders like Moses or the Apostles never avoided strife in their just cause. Hence:
*n-snêu ntôtne -hen-mai-ti-tôn au*
DEF.P-brother.P 2P -DEF.P-love.PIA-give-strife CNJ
*n-ref-kôh etbe-n-et-ci aḫun a-p-ucei*
of-AGT-emulate because-DEF.P-REL-take into to-DEF.M-health
Strife-lovers and zealous you shall be, O brothers, because of that which leads to salvation. ([A]1Cl 45:1 [Schmidt 92])

Instead of juxtaposition or simple connection, the Akhmimic and the Bohairic dialect use the coordinated predicate with CONNECTOR plus *n-* as shown above (*au n-* in Akhmimic in ex. 84d, *uoh/nem n-* in the Bohairic 84b). Stylistic considerations may have sometimes prompted the repetition of the subject:

(85) The psalmist praises the Lord:
*[nt]ak p-c(ai)s p-n(u)ti ntk-u-šan-htê-f*
2MS DEF.M-lord DEF.M-god 2MS-IDF.S-pitiful-heart-3MS
*ntk-u-naêt*
2MS-IDF.S-merciful
*ntk-u-ai-hêt naše-pe-k-nee ntk-u-mee*
2MS-IDF.S-great-heart be plenty-POSS.M-2MS-mercy 2MS-IDF.S-truth
You, Lord God, are compassionate, you are merciful; you are patient, your mercy is plentiful, and you are righteous.
($^{M}$Ps 85 [86]:15)

Although examples are scarce, disjunctive patterns tend to repeat all elements even if these are identical:

(86) The Saint asks the woman calling for his help:
*nt$^{h}$o -u-khrêstianê šan-nt$^{h}$o u-hellênos*
2FS -IDF.S-Christian or-2FS IDF.S-heathen
Are you a Christian or are you a heathen?
($^{B}$*Mart. Theodore Stratelates* [*AM* I 160, 21])

Such a repetition is typical in adversative clauses, even though the Greek *alla* 'but' can be used to coordinate phrasal elements. Bohairic is the only dialect to license regular deletion of the subject, as a comparison of the Sahidic and the Bohairic version in ex. 87b shows:

(87a) Nahrow replies to the accusation that he is a magician:
*anok -u-magos=an alla anok -u-hmhal nte-i(êsu)s*
2P -IDF.S-magician=NEG but 2P -IDF.S-servant of-N
*pe-kh(risto)s*
DEF.M-Christ
I am not a magician, but a servant of Jesus Christ.
($^{S}$*Mart. Nahrow* [Till *KHML* I, 5, 13–14])

(87b) Paul reasons that by sending his son, God freed mankind from the law:
B *hôste nt$^{h}$ok -u-bôk=an=ce alla u-šêri*
so that 2MS -IDF.S-servant=NEG=then but IDF.S-son
S *hôste=k$^{j}$e ntk-u-hmhal=an alla ntk-u-šêre*
so that=then 2MS-IDF.S-servant=NEG but 2MS-IDF.S-son
So you are no longer a slave but a son. ($^{BS}$Gal 4:7)

Note again that the syntactic behaviour of the negation *an* and of the particle =*ce* in ex. 87b shows that the predicative relation is strong enough not to allow these morphemes to be placed between subject and predicate.

Bipartite sentences of the type discussed can be expanded by adverbial extensions:

(88a) Shenute refuses to bless a man, who, agitated by this rebuff, claims to have never sinned:

| | | |
|---|---|---|
| *anok=gar* | *ang-u-khristianos* | *cin-ta-mnt-kui* |
| 1S=for | 1S-IDF.S-Christian | since-POSS.F.1S-ABST-small |

But I am a Christian since my childhood days.
($^{S}$*V. Shenute* [Lubomierski 221, b14–16])

(88b) Moses tells the children of Israel what God had promised them. He warns them not to mingle with other people and tribes that pasture in the Promised Land:

| | | | |
|---|---|---|---|
| *ce-nt$^{h}$ok-u-laos* | *e-f-uab* | *m-p$^{h}$-cois* | *pe-k-nuti* |
| for-2MS-IDF.S-people | REL-3MS-clean | for-DEF.M-lord | POSS-2MS-god |

...for you are a holy people unto the Lord, your God. ($^{B}$Dt 7:6)

(88c) Eusebius confesses publicly:

| | | | |
|---|---|---|---|
| *ce-uêi* | *anok* | *-u-khrêstianos* | *m-parrêsia* |
| for-indeed | 1S | -IDF.S-Christian | in-freedom_of_speech |

...for I am avowedly a Christian. ($^{B}$*Mart. Eusebius* [*AdM* 32, 19])

(88d) Abraham wants to bury Sarah in Hebron; Het's children say to him: *Listen to us, lord,*

| | | | | | | |
|---|---|---|---|---|---|---|
| *nt$^{h}$ok* | *-u-uro* | *ebol* | *hitn-p$^{h}$-(nu)ti* | *nt$^{h}$ok* | *nḫrêi* | *nḫêt-en* |
| 2MS | -IDF.S-king | out | through-DEF.M-god | 2MS | down | inside-1P |

You are, through God, a prince among us. ($^{B}$Gn 23:6)

The so-called cleft sentences are a special type of Coptic bipartite nominal construction. Etymologically a remnant of an earlier pseudo-cleft sentence pattern, Coptic pseudo-cleft sentences are originally tripartite patterns and will be treated in detail below. Anticipating the main point, suffice it to say here that in some treatments Coptic cleft sentences are similarly understood as bipartite patterns consisting of an initial NP followed by the subject element and a relative clause, i.e. as [$NP_i$ $SE_i$ REL]. This analysis, however, raises two very serious questions (Layton 2011: §464). Firstly, according to this view, the initial NP would have to be the predicate, the construction following the alleged subject element being understood as a mere attributive relative clause. But in true cleft sentences the predicate must be a headless relative or participial expression. Secondly, this analysis implies that Coptic only grammaticalised pseudo-cleft, not cleft sentences, which seems typologically unlikely. In view of these problems, Coptic clefts are better analysed as bipartite patterns consisting of an initial NP followed by a headless relative clause, as proposed for the earlier stages of Later Egyptian.

The determiner preceding the second NP usually shows agreement with the first NP in all dialects except Bohairic, where the invariable masculine singular *pe* appears. In all dialects except Bohairic, the determiner sometimes appears graphemically separate, as if representing the subject element or copula followed by the relative expression: *pe ete-*... < *pete-*. This pattern has usually been analysed as reflecting a diachronically earlier stage of the language. However, as will be shown when discussing tripartite patterns, this construction should rather be analysed as a variant of the Coptic pseudo-cleft pattern.

Any relative clause type can be used as the second part of the cleft construction. Below are past examples:

(89a) A man explains why he acted according to an agreement with his brother after the latter had left home:

| | | |
|---|---|---|
| *u-diathykê* | *t-ent-a-i-smnt-s* | *mn-pa-son* |
| IDF.S-treaty | COP.F-REL-PST-1S-agree-3FS | with-POSS.M.1S-brother |

| | | |
|---|---|---|
| *mpate-f-bôk* | *ebol* | *hitoot-f* |
| NCO-3MS-go | out | from-3MS |

It is a treaty that I agreed upon with my brother before he left.

([S]*Gesios & Isodorus* [*ZÄS* 21: 149, 5–6])

(89b) A son advises his mother to take certain medicine stored in her house:

| | | | |
|---|---|---|---|
| *hn-šbêr* | *n-et-a-u-teit-u* | *nê-i* | *e-u-o* |
| IDF.S-friend | COP.P-REL-PST-3P-give-3P | to-1S | DEP-3P-be.STA |

*n-sêine*
as-doctor

It is some friends who gave it to me; they are doctors.

([L]*P.KellisCopt.* 25, 39–40)

(89c) Daughters of a priest of Midian were helped by Moses to drive off some troublesome shepherds. The girls tell their father:

| | | | |
|---|---|---|---|
| *u-rôme* | *n-rm-n-kême* | *p-et-a-f-n[ah]m-ne* | *abal* |
| IDF.S-man | of-man-of-Egypt | COP.M-REL-PST-3MS-save-1P | out |

| | |
|---|---|
| *hitoot-u* | *n-n-šas* |
| from-3P | as-DEF.P-shepherd |

It was an Egyptian who helped us against the shepherds. ([A]Ex 2:19)

(89d) In the parable of the talents the servant to whom two talents were given came and said to his lord:

| | | | | |
|---|---|---|---|---|
| *p-c(ai)s* | *kʲinkʲior* | *sneu* | *n-et-ha-k-te-u* | *etat-ø* |
| DEF.S-lord | talent | two | COP.P-REL-PST-2MS-give-3P | on-1S |

My lord, it was two talents that you gave me *(– look, I have gained two more).* ($^{M}$Mt 25:22 mae 1)

(89e) Stephen speaks about strife among the Israelites, quoting Ex 2:14:
*nim p-et-a-f-ke-k n-arkhôn ie lef-ti-hep*
WH COP.M-REL-PST-3MS-put-2MS as-leader or AGT-give-law
*ehlêi ecô-n*
down on-1P
Who has made you leader or lawgiver over us?
($^{F}$Acts 7:27 [Kahle, *Balaizah* I, 288])

(89f) In the parable of the workers in the vineyard all workers receive equal pay to the dismay of those who came first. The latter complain:
*nai-ḫae-u u-unu n-er-hôb p-et-a-u-ai-s*
DEM.P-last-P IDF.S-hour of-do-work COP.M-REL-PST-3P-do-3FS
These last ones, it is just an hour of work that they did! ($^{B}$Mt 20:12)

Dialects such as Akhmimic differentiate in the past relative form between the coreferent of the subject of the relative clause and the antecedent, using *etah-ø-*VERB when the antecedent is coreferential with the subject of the relative clause vs. *eta*-PRN-VERB when it is not. In these dialects, the difference is marked overtly. Occasionally, the 'normal' form is encountered as well (ex. 90d):

(90a) Clement quotes Jesus as a witness to the his own humbleness when he asked the Lord:
*[p]-cais nim p-et-ah-ø-r-pisteue*
DEF.M-lord WH COP.M-REL-PST-Ø-AUX-believe
*a-p-n-ḫrau* (Schmidt)
OBJ-POSS.F-1P-voice
*[p]-cais nim p-et-a-f-[r-piste]ue*
DEF.M-lord WH COP.M-REL-PST-3MS-AUX-believe
*a-t-n-smi* (Rösch)
OBJ-POSS.F-1P-voice
Lord, who is it that believed our voice?
($^{A}$1Cl 16:3)

(90b) As Moses tries to separate two quarrelling Hebrews, one of them yells at him:
*nim p-et-ah-ø-r-kathista mma-k n-arkhôn uan*
who COP.M-REL-PST-Ø-AUX-set OBJ-2MS as-leader further
*n-ref-ti-hep aḫrêi ecô-n*
as-AGT-give-law down upon-1S
Who is it who appointed you as a leader or even a law-giver over us?
($^{A}$Ex 2:14)

(90c) Elias describes how the word of the Lord occurred to him and that he was told:
*nêstia=de* *e-s-uaabe* *t-et-a-i-sônt* *mma-s*
fasting.F=yet DEP-3FS-clear.STA COP.F-REL-PST-1S-create OBJ-3FS
But it is an immaculate fasting that I created.
([A]*ApEl* [Steindorff, *Apokalypse des Elias* 72 23, 8–9])

(90d) The narrator of the Apocalypse (probably Sophonias) is filled with fear when he sees the sea of flame with its billows of sulphur and pitch:
*anak=kʲe* *na-i-meue* *ce-p-cais* *p-pantokratôr*
1S=then PRT-1S-think COMP -DEF.M-lord DEF.M-almighty
*p-et-a-f-i* *a-kʲm-pa-šine*
COP.M-REL-PST-come to-find-POSS.1S-news
Then I thought that it is the Lord almighty who had come to visit me.
([A]*ApSoph.* [Steindorff, *Apokalypse des Elias* 46 7, 13–15])

Past reference cleft sentences of this type with a relativised preterite are rare and seemingly confined to earlier texts (examples without the determiner can be found below)[29]:

(91a) Wisdom tells that God cherished her from the very beginning:
*anak* *p-e-na-f-reše* *neme-i*
1S COP.M-REL-PRT-3MS-rejoice with-1S
I was the one with whom he was happy. ([A]Prv 8:30)

(91b) Having fed the five thousand, Jesus sent them away and retreated to the mountains to pray alone:
*etha-[ruhê=de]* *šôpê* *ntaf* *u<a>et-f* *p-et-na-f-nmmeu*
TMP-evening=yet happen 3MS sole-3MS COP.M-REL-PRT-3MS-there
As evening came, he was the only one up there. ([M]Mt 14:23 mae 2)

(91c) Jesus was derided not only by those who saw and carried out his crucifixion:
*pei* *p-et-na-u-cô* *mma-f* *ncê-n-ke-sanê*
DEM.M COP.M-REL-PRT-3P-say OBJ-3MS PVS-DEF.P-other-robber
*et-ešê* *nemme-f*
REL-hang with-3MS
This is what even the robbers who hung with him said. ([M]Mt 27:44 mae 2)

29 However, the surviving data are too meagre to reveal whether this might belie a diatopic distribution between relative perfect [*ntaf-/eta-*] vs. relativised preterite [*e-na-/et-na*]. Note that the other manuscript of the Gospel of Matthew in the M dialect (mae 1: Schenke 1981) uses different constructions here. The same can be observed for the other dialectal versions of the cited instances.

For past reference clefts, the dialects M and L (at least in the subvariety L5) also employ a construction incorporating the element *er-*, an etymological participle of the verb *ire* 'to do,' followed by the infinitive of the lexical verb:

(92a) Asked by Pilate whether he is the king of the Jews, Jesus replies:

| | | | | |
|---|---|---|---|---|
| *e-[k]-cô* | *[m-p]ei* | *abal* | *mma-k* | *cn-he[n-kau]ue* |
| ST-2MS-say | OBJ-DEM.M | out | of-2MS | or-IDF.P-others.P |
| *p-er-coo-s=ne-k* | *etbêt-ø* | | | |
| DEF.M-do.PPA-say-3FS=to-2MS | because-1S | | | |

Do you say this out of your own mind or did others
tell you this about me? ([L]Jn 18:34)

(92b) Jesus states that the works he has to accomplish will testify that:

| | |
|---|---|
| *p-iôt* | *p-er-teau-i* |
| DEF.M-father | COP.M-do.PPA-send-1S |

It is the father who sent me. ([L]Jn 5:36)

(92c) God sent Ananias to heal Saul from his blindness. He put his hand upon Saul and said:

| | | | | |
|---|---|---|---|---|
| *saule* | *pa-san* | *p-c(ai)s* | *iê(su)s* | *p-er-taua-i* |
| N | POSS.M.1S-brother | DEF.M-lord | N | DEF.M-do.PPA-send-1S |

Saul, my brother, it is the Lord Jesus who sent me. ([M]Acts 9:17)

(92d) Jesus narrates the parable of the royal wedding in which the king sent envoys to invite people to his son's wedding. Yet the people invited refused to come:

| | | |
|---|---|---|
| *uen* | *p-er-še=ne-f* | *e-pe-f-iohê* |
| IDF.S.ABS | DEF.M-do.PPA-go=to-3MS | to-POSS.M-3MS-field |
| *ue[n=de]* | *p-er-šê* | *n-te-f-iep-šôt* |
| IDF.S.ABS=yet | DEF.M-do.PPA-go | in-POSS.F-3MS-work-take |

There was one who went to his field, and there was one who followed his business. ([M]Mt 22:5 mae 2)

Note that the morph *er-* is also attested in S texts (Sethe 1919; Crum 1939: 57b; Layton 2011: §406), but seemingly not in cleft sentence patterns of the above kind.

Structurally, this pattern with a seemingly headless relative clause in second position is a remnant of Late Egyptian and Demotic cleft sentence with the incorporation of the definite article (thus already Sethe 1919: 145–58). The earlier construction shines through in clefts with relative clauses showing no definite article.

According to the rules of relative clauses with *Present I* constructions, the subject of the relative clause can be deleted if it is coreferential with its antecedent, as in ex. 93b–93d, 93g, and 93h. Otherwise, the subject is expressed, as in exx. 93a and 93e:

(93a) In his episcopal letter, quoted by Shenute, Theophilus argues against Origen and concludes:

*pai=gar* *p-etere-pe-f-meue* *n-akathartos* *sôk*
DEM.M =for COP.M-REL-POSS.M-3MS-thought of-unclean draw
*mmo-f* *ê-coo-f*
OBJ-3MS to-say-3FS
For this is what his unclean thinking pushes him to say.
([S]Shenute, *I am Amazed* §926 [Cristea 220, 16–20])

(93b) A philosopher telling a parable has the heaven say:

*anok* *p-et-ø-hose* *m-pararo-k*
1S COP.M-REL-Ø-suffer.STA in-over-2MS
I am the one who suffers more than you do.
([S]*Sayings of Pagan Philosophers* [Crum 98b])

(93c) The Ecclesiastes states:

*uoiš* *p-et-ø-šoop* *n-uon* *nim*
time COP.M-REL-Ø-be.STA for-one QU
*auô* *u-sêu* *p-et-ø-šoop* *hn-hôb* *nim* *haro-s*
and IDF.S-hour COP.M-REL-Ø-be.STA in-thing QU under-3FS
*n-t-pe*
as-DEF.F-heaven
There is time for everyone and an hour for everything under heaven.
([S]Eccl 3:1 [Ciasca])

(93d) Thekla's fiancé asks her why she only sits by the window and listens to St Paul:

*auô* *eš* *m-pathos* *p-et-ø-emahte* *mmo* *ere-i[ar]m*
and WH of-passion COP.M-REL-Ø-seize OBJ.2FS DEP.2F-stare
And what kind of passion has taken possession of you, since you are dumbfounded? ([L]*Acta Pauli* [Schmidt 7* 11, 22–23])

(93e) God wants to punish Ephraim and Judah and adds:

*u-nae* *p-et-i-uaḫ-f* *u-thusia=en*
IDF.S-mercy COP.M-REL-1S-want-3MS IDF.S-sacrifice=NEG
*au* *u-saune* *n-nute* *n-huo* *a-hen-kʲlil*
and IDF.S-knowledge of-god in-more than-IDF.P-burnt_offering
It is mercy that I want, not sacrifice, and acknowledgement of God more than burnt offerings. ([A]Hos 6:6 [Till])

(93f) Clement recounts from the Biblical story of Rahel how the men of the king came to her door telling her to lead out the Israelite spies sent by Joshua. They tell her:

*p-rro* *p-et-uahsahne* *n-ti-he*
DEF.M-king DEF.M-REL-order in-DEM.F-way
It is the king who orders thusly. ([A]1Cl 12:4)

(93g) Peter goes down to meet the three men asking for him and says:
*hipe anak p-ete-tn-šine nso-i*
look 1S COP.M-REL-2P-look after-1S
Look, I am the one you are looking for. ([M]Acts 10:21)

(93h) In his letter Jeremiah argues against the adoration of idols:
*pei-smat p-et-ø-šaap mma-u n-t-hê*
DEM.M-pattern COP.M-REL-ø-happen.STA in-3P in-DEF.F-way
*n-te-hramnos*
of-DEF.F-thorn
*e-s-hn-u-šê ete-šale-halêt nibi hmaas hicô-s*
DEP-3FS-in-IDF.S-garden REL-AOR-bird QU sit upon-3FS
Thus they equal a thorn hedge that is in a garden and upon which all the birds sit. ([F]Ep. Jer. 70)

(93i) Solomon tells his son to acquire wisdom, as this will lead him to understand the fear of the Lord:
*ce-p-c(oi)s p-et-ti n-u-sophia*
for-DEF.M-lord COP.M-REL-Ø-give OBJ-IDF.S-wisdom
...for it is the Lord who gives wisdom. ([B]Prv 2:6)

Cleft sentences with future reference appear more often with the relativised Future I where the same rules of omission apply, as exemplified by the two clefts in 94b, but similar clauses with the Optative form are also attested:

(94a) At the last supper, Jesus told his disciples:
*ua ebol n-hêt-têutn p-et-ø-na-paradidou mmo-i*
IDF.S.ABS out in-inside-2P COP.M-REL-Ø-FUT-betray OBJ-1S
It is one of you who will betray me. ([S]Mt 26:21)[30]

(94b) The Ecclesiastes bewails the present:
*u p-ent-a-f-šôpe ntof=on p-et-na-šôpe*
what COP.M-REL-PST-3MS-happen 3MS=again DEF.M-Ø-REL-FUT-happen
*u p-ent-a-u-tamio-f ntof=on p-et-u-na-tamio-f*
what COP.M-REL-PST-3P-make-3P 3MS=again COP.M-3P-REL-FUT-make-3P
What is that which has happened? It is that which will happen! What is that which has been done? It is that which will be done!
([S]Eccl 1:9 [Ciasca])

(94c) Filled with astonishment, Peter asks Jesus:
*p-cais ntak p-et-a-ia-na-urite*
DEF.M-lord 2MS COP.M-REL-FUT-wash-POSS.P.1S-foot
Lord, should *you* wash *my* feet? ([L]Jn 13:6)

---

**30** Note that the example has been taken from a variant, not the main text, which shows a verbal sentence pattern here: *un-ua ebol nhêt-têutn na-paradidu mmo-i* "One of you will betray me".

(94d) Clement quotes Is 1:16–20, where the Lord says that those who obey him shall live off the land:
*eša-tetn-tmn-uôẖe a-sôtme nsô-i t-sêfe*
CND-2P-NEG-wish to-listen after-1S DEF.F-sword
*t-et-na-uôm-têne*
COP.F-REL-FUT-eat-2P
If you do not want to obey me, it is the sword that will devour you.
(A1Cl 8:4 [Schmidt])

(94e) A young man approached Jesus, asking:
*[u] n-agathon p-et-i-ne-[e]-f tar-i-kimê [n-uonh]*
WH of-good COP.M-REL-1S-FUT-do-3MS CNJ-1S-find OBJ-life
*n-Ša-en[eh]*
of-for-eternity
*(Rabbi),* what good must I do to achieve the eternal life? (MMt 19:16 mae 2)

(94f) The Ecclesiastes says that man should enjoy his work because that is his lot:
*ce-nim p-et-ne-ent-f e-tama-f*
for-WH COP.M-REL-FUT-bring-3MS to-tell-3MS
*e-p-et-ne-šôpi neme-f*
to-DEF.M-REL-FUT-happen with-3MS
...for who shall bring him to see what will happen to him?
(FEccl 3:22 [Schenke 60, 11–12])

Aorist constructions appear either with the preceding relative particle *ete-ša-* or as aorist relative form *e-ša-*, irrespective of the antecedent's definiteness (cf. 95c *ntos t-e-ša-s-*); in Sahidic texts with Fayyumic influence the form *en-ša-* may appear:

(95a) In claiming Jesus' superiority to the Levitic priests, the author of the Epistle to the Hebrews identifies him as belonging to the line of Melchizedek, to whom even Abraham gave the tenth part of his goods and received the former's blessings. As the superior blesses the inferior, the author pursues his line of reason:
*auô m-pei-ma=men hen-rôme e-ša-u-mu*
and in-DEM.M-place=indeed IDF.P-man REL-AOR-3P-die
*n-e-ša-u-ci n-n-re-mêt*
DEF.P-DEP-AOR-3P-take OBJ-DEF.P-part-ten
*m-p-ma=de etmmau e-u-r-mntre haro-f*
in-DEF.M-place=yet that ST-3P-do-testify towards-3MS
*ce-f-onh*
that-3MS-live
And in one case, mortal men are those who receive the tithes, whereas in the other, he is the one witnessed to live. (SHeb 7:8)

(95b) Pachomius says that if a monk emulates the lives of the saints, grace will blossom in him:

*ne-hmot=gar* *têr-u* *t-mnt-harš-hêt*
DEF.P-grace=for all-3P DEF.M-ABST-slow-heart
*t-ete-ša-s-k$^{j}$olp-u=na-k* *ebol*
COP.F-REL-AOR-3FS-reveal-3P=to-2MS out
For every grace – it is patience that reveals them to you.
($^{S}$Pachom, *Instruction Concerning a Spiteful Monk* 2, 2–3)

(95c) Shenute rejects the view that the Saviour only assumed a body but not a soul. He rephrases the Gospels:

*hôs-rôme* *on* *e-f-cô* *mmo-s* *ce-štortr* *auô* *lupi*
like-man again DEP-3MS-say OBJ-3FS COMP-trouble and grieve
*te-f-mnt-nute=de* *ntos* *me-s-štortr* *ude*
POSS.F-3MS-ABST-god=yet 3FS NEG.AOR-3FS-trouble nor
*me-s-lupi*
NEG.AOR-3FS-trouble
*alla* *ntos* *t-e-ša-s-lupi* *n-hah* *emate* *auô*
but 3FS COP.F-DEP-AOR-3FS-grieve OBJ-many very and
*n-s-štrtr-uon* *nim*
CNJ-3FS-trouble-each QU
Even when they say 'trouble' and 'grieve', his divinity is neither troubled nor grieved, but it is she (the divinity) who troubles very many and makes everyone grieve. ($^{S}$Shenute, *I am Amazed* §491 [Cristea 200, 6–18])

(95d) Urging mankind to enjoy life despite its vanities, the Ecclesiastes reasons:

*pei* *u-ponêron=pe* *hn-p-tamia* *et-sa-p-esêt*
DEM.M IDF.S-evil=COP.M in-DEF.M-creation REL-side-DEF.M-ground
*m-p-re*
of-DEF.M-sun
*ce-pei-tômt* *n-uôt* *p-ete-ša-f-i* *ecô-u*
COMP-DEM.M-event of-single COP.M-REL-AOR-3MS-go upon-3P
*têr-u*
all-3P
This is an evil among the creation under the sun, that there is the very same fate happening to all of them. ($^{F}$Eccl 9:3 [Schenke 90, 24–27])

(95e) The saviour tells Theodore in a dream to narrate the dream to his comrade Leontius the Arab:

*anok* *p-en-ša-u-onomaze* *mmo-f* *hitn-t-hote*
1S COP.M-REL-AOR-3P-call OBJ-3MS by-DEF.F-fear
*m-pe-f-ran* *etuaab*
of-POSS.M-3MS-name holy

| | | | |
|---|---|---|---|
| *e-tre-p-cace* | *pôt* | *hn-u-nokʲ* | *n-šipe* |
| to-CAUS-DEF.M-enemy | flee | in-IDF.S-great | of-shame |

I am the one who is called by name through the fear of his holy name, to cause the enemy to flee in great shame.
(Sf*Mart. Theodore & al.* [Müller and Uljas, *Martyrs & Archangels* §101])

Constructions with *unte-/uonte-* 'to have' show the simple pattern *pete-unte-*. Note also the special construction *un-kʲom/un-š-com* 'to be able' as in 96c:

(96a) The parable of the wayward son begins with the words:

| | | |
|---|---|---|
| *u-rôme* | *p-ete-unt-f-šêre* | *snau* |
| IDF.S-man | COP.M-REL-have-3MS-child | two |

There is a man who has two sons. (SLk 15:11)

(96b) As above:

| | | | | |
|---|---|---|---|---|
| *u-rôme* | *p-e-ne-unta-f* | *mmau* | *n-šêre* | *snau* |
| IDF.S-man | COP.M-DEP-PRT-have-3MS | there | OBJ-child | two |

There was a man who had two sons. (SMt 21:28 var.)

(96c) After Paul had healed a cripple, the inhabitants of Lycaonia thought that he and Barnabas were gods:

| | | | | |
|---|---|---|---|---|
| *epeidê* | *ne-ntaf* | *p-ete-un-š-kʲam* | *mma-f* | *hm-p-sece* |
| for | PRT-3MS | COP.M-REL-have-can-power | OBJ-3MS | in-DEF.M-speech |

*(They called Barnabas Zeus and Paul Hermes)* for he was forceful in speech. (MActs 14:12)

Examples with adverbial sentences (see Part I) show the same rules of subject deletion introduced in the discussion of the *Present I-* and *Future I*-patterns, see exx. 93 and 94:

(97a) Athanasius cites Ps 112:3 in a paragraph of his *Canons*:

| | | | |
|---|---|---|---|
| *f-cô=gar* | *mmo-s* | *ce-p-eou* | *mn-t-mnt-rmmao* |
| 3MS-say=for | OBJ-3FS | COMP-DEF.M-glory | and-DEF.F-ABST-rich |

*n-et-hm-pe-f-êi*
COP.P-REL-in-POSS.M-3MS-house

| | | |
|---|---|---|
| *etbe-pai* | *šše* | *e-tre-te-f-dikaiosynê* |
| because-DEM.M | necessary | to-INFL-POSS.F-3MS-righteousness |

| | |
|---|---|
| *šôpe* | *ša-eneh* |
| happen | until-eternity |

For he says: 'Glory and riches is what is in his house'. Therefore it is necessary that his righteousness exists forever.
(S*Canons of Athanasius* [Crum in Riedel §61])

(97b) Eucharistos tells that after their wedding he and his wife slept separately and wore sackcloths at night:
*hm-p-hou=de* *ne-n-hoite* *n-et-hiôô-n*
in-DEF.M-day=yet POSS.P-1P-garment COP.P-REL-upon-1P
During the day, however, it is our clothes that we wear.
([S]*AP* Chaîne 74, 4–5)

(97c) The proverbs warn:
*u-kʲerôb* *n-šôs* *p-et-ḫn-t-tapro* *n-n-at-hêt*
IDF.S-staff of-scorn COP.P-REL-inside-DEF.F-mouth of-DEF.P-un-heart
A staff of scorn is what is in the mouth of the stupid. ([A]Prv 14:3)

(97d) The advent of the first man is described with naval metaphors: *The ship whose keel is the dawn,*
*n-nauh* *m-p-uaine* *[n]-et-hiôô-f*
DEF.P-rope of-DEF.M-light COP.P-REL-upon-3MS
...the ropes of light are what there is on it.
([L]*Psalms of Thomas* 207, 18–19 [Alberry])

(97e) The Ecclesiastes considers the woman bitterer than death, because:
*[he]n-sneuh* *n-et-hn-ne-s-kʲeu[c]*
IDF.P-fetters COP.P-REL-inside-POSS.P-3FS-hands.P
Fetters is what she has in her hands. ([F]Eccl 7:26 [Schenke 82, 10–11])

(97f) Jesus says that if one's eye causes him stumble, it should be torn out:
*nane-s=gar* *na-k* *nte-k-i* *eḫun* *e-pi-ônḫ*
be good-3FS=for to-2MS CNJ-2MS-go into to-DEF$_2$.M-life
*e-u-bal* *p-ete-mmo-k*
DEP-IDF.S-eye COP.M-REL-in-2MS
For it is better for you that you enter life one-eyed *(than to have two eyes and be thrown into the fire of hell).* ([B]Mt 18:9)

As noted above, the determiner of the second NP regularly displays agreement marking in all dialects except Bohairic. Sometimes, however, an invariable *pe* (MS) is used. In these cases, the other dialects use different patterns:

(98a) The archangel Gabriel tells Mary that she will give birth to a son. To her objection that she is still a virgin, he replies:
*auô* *t-kʲom* *nte-p-et-cose*
and DEF.F-power of-DEF.M-REL-elevate.STA
*p-et-na-r-haibes* *ero-ø*
COP.M-REL-FUT-fo-shadow to-2FS
And it is the power of the Most High that will overshadow you. ([S]Lk 1:35)

(98b) Pilate asks Jesus if he is the king of the Jews. He asks in return whether Pilate thinks so or whether he was only told so. Pilate then says that he is not a Jew; rather:

*pe-k-het[nos]* *auô* *ne-k-arkhiereus*
POSS.M-2MS-people and POSS.P-2MS-high priest
*p-en[t]-a-u-tee-k* *a-toot-ø*
COP.M-REL-PST-3P-give-2MS to-hand-1S
It is your people and your high priests who delivered you into my hands. ([L]Jn 18:35)

(98c) Pilate asks Jesus if he is the king of the Jews. He asks in return whether Pilate thinks so:

*cn-he[n-ka]ue* *p-er-coo-s=ne-k* *etbêt-ø*
or-IDF.P-others.P COP.M-do.PPA-say-3FS=to-2MS because-1S
...or did others tell you this about me? ([L]Jn 18:34)

In coordinated examples, the determiner appears only once if there is continuity in gender and number. If there is a change, the element is repeated:

(99) Shenute opposes some views about the Lord with a quote: *He is ignorant of the word of that voice,*

*p-nute* *n-ša-eneh* *n-f-na-hko=an* *ude*
DEF.M-god of-until-eternity NEG-3MS-FUT-hungry=NEG nor
*n-f-na-hise=an*
NEG-3MS-FUT-suffer=NEG
*alla* *ntof* *p-et-ti* *n-t-kʲom* *n-n-et-hkait*
but 3MS COP.M-REL-give OBJ-DEF.F-power to-DEF.P-REL-hungry.STA
*et-ti-mton* *n-n-et-šp-hise* *etbêêt-f*
REL-give-rest to-DEF.P-REL-receive-suffer because-3MS
The eternal God does not hunger or suffer; rather he is the one who strengthens the hungry and comforts those suffering for him. ([S]Shenute, *I Am Amazed* §316 [Cristea 144, 3–12])

It is difficult to assess at times whether coordinated adversative patterns should be analysed as cleft sentences with ellipsis of the relative clause or as bipartite patterns:

(100a) Gesios has found some human bones and laments the fleeting nature of earthly life:

*m-pai=an* *mauaa-f* *pe-nt-a-f-mu* *alla* *anok*
NEG-DEM.M=NEG self-3MS COP.M-REL-PST-3MS-die but 1S
*nmma-f* *pe*
with-3MS SE.M

It is not only this one that has died, but I with him.
($^{S}$*Gesios & Isodorus* [*ZÄS* 21, 142, 14–15])

(100b) Julian denies having received his reign from the Christ:
*p-kh(risto)s=an* *pe-et-a-f-ti=nê-i*
DEF.M-Christ=NEG COP.M-REL-PST-3MS-give=to-1S
*n-ta-i-met-uro* *alla* *pi-zeus=pe*
OBJ-POSS.F-1S-ABST-king but $\text{DEF}_2$.M-N=SE.M
It was not Christ, but Zeus, who gave me my kingdom.
($^{B}$*Mart. Cyriacus of Jerusalem* [*AM* II 12, 24–25])

Besides this pattern, two (at least in Sahidic) less common cleft constructions with personal pronouns are attested. In one of these, the initial pronoun is directly followed by an undefined relative clause; any kind of formally non-bound pronoun can be used, i.e. personal (*anok* etc.), demonstrative (*pai* etc.), or interrogative. The relative constructions in this pattern are limited to past, present and future, i.e. no examples with an Aorist as for the other patterns above (cf. examples 95a–e) are attested, but bare past forms are of rather low frequency and contrast usually with the more common form *penta-*[31]:

(101a) Jesus prays to God, asking that the world may believe:
*ce-ntok* *ent-a-k-tauo-i*
COMP-2MS REL-PST-2MS-send-1S
...that it was you who sent me. ($^{S}$Jn 17:21)

(101b) Jesus prays to the Lord and assures him that the people believe:
*ntak* *er-tnnau-t*
2MS do.PPA-send-1S
It is you who sent me. ($^{L}$Jn 17:8)

Note that the Lyco-Diospolitan text of the Gospel of John (ex. 101b) shows the remnant of the older cleft sentence with a participle of the verb *ire* 'do.' Bohairic, however, exhibits a certain preference for this construction when the relative clause is a preterite, usually with the pattern *e-na*. Although the latter is etymologically a dependent clause and might thus be interpreted as a different pattern,

31 In Stern's only example (1880: §424 end) $^{B}$Jn 3:32 the reading *p$^{h}$ai et-a-f-er-met$^{h}$re* 'This is what he bore witness to' is a minor variant against *p$^{h}$ai ete-f-er-met$^{h}$re* 'This is what he bears witness to' (with PRS), as well as against the normal cleft patterns *p$^{h}$ai pe et-a-f-er-met$^{h}$re* and *p$^{h}$ai pe ete-f-er-met$^{h}$re*, see Horner (1898–1905: II, 360). Jn 6:60 suggested by Chaîne (1993: §771) is rather to be analysed as temporal clause.

in diachronic perspective it replaced the construction introduced by *ete*. Here, other dialects show alternative structures:

(102a) The disciples remember what Jesus had said to the Jews after casting out the merchants from the temple:
*p*$^{h}$*ai* *e-na-f-cô* *mmo-f*
DEM.M DEP-PRT-3MS-say OBJ-3MS
This is what he said. ($^{B}$Jn 2:22)

(102b) Peter objects to the idea that he will deny Jesus three times:
*pai-rêti=de* *e-na-u-cô* *mmo-s* *nce-ni-ke-mathêtês*
DEM.M-way=yet DEP-PRT-3P-say OBJ-3FS PTC-$DEF_2$.P-other-disciple
*têr-u*
all-3P
And in this same manner all the disciples spoke. ($^{B}$Mt 26:35 var.)

(102c) Macarius of Scetis lived in the inner desert:
*nt*$^{h}$*of* *mmauat-f* *e-na-f-k*$^{h}$*ê* *mmau*
3MS alone-3MS DEP-PRT-3MS-AUX.STA there
*e-f-er-anakhôrin*
DEP-3MS-AUX-live alone
It was he alone who was there, dwelling as an anchorite.
($^{B}$*AP Macarius* B31 [MG 25 230, 16; collated])

This construction is much more common in the present:

(103a) Shenute declares that the way in which other convents are lead is none of his business:
*ntou* *et-rôše*
3P REL-responsible
It is they who are responsible.
($^{S}$Shenute, *God, Who Alone Is True* [L IV 98, 24])

(103b) A brother replies in astonishment to the teachings of an elder:
*u=k*$^{j}$*e* *et-ešše* *e-aa-f*
WH=then REL-fitting to-do-3MS
Now what would be appropriate to do? ($^{S}$*AP* Chaîne 30, 12)

(103c) Pilate asks Jesus if he is the king of Jews; Jesus replies:
*ntak* *et-cô* *mma-s*
2MS REL-say OBJ-3FS
It is you who say so. ($^{L}$Jn 18:37)

(103d) As above:
*ntak* *et-cô* *mma-s*
2MS REL-say OBJ-3FS
It is you who say so. ($^{M}$Mt 27:11 mae 1)

(103e) Jesus has just said that he has food of which the disciples are unaware of. He begins his explanation with the following words:
*mê ntaten=en et-cô mma-s ce-...*
IP 2P=NEG REL-say OBJ-3FS COMP
Is it not you who say...? ($^F$Jn 4:35)

(103f) The psalmist calls to the Lord for help in his dire situation:
*nt$^h$ok=gar et-sôun m-pa-šôš nem-pa-šipi*
2MS=for REL-Ø-know OBJ-POSS.M.1S-shame and-POSS.M.1S-shame
*nem-pa-šp$^h$it*
and-POSS.M.1S-dishonour
It is you who has known my reproach, my shame, and my dishonour.
($^B$Ps 68 [69]:19 [20])

The same holds also with future constructions:

(104a) Jesus reproaches the Jews:
*mpr-meue ce-anok et$^h$-na-katêgori mmô-tn*
NEG.IMP-think COMP-1S REL-FUT-accuse OBJ-2P
*nnahrm-p-iôt*
before-DEF.M-father
Do not think that it is me who will accuse you before the father. ($^S$Jn 5:45)

(104b) The Lord promised Joshua: *If you will walk my ways and keep my charge,*
*ntak et-na-r-krinei m-pa-êi*
2MS REL-FUT-AUX-judge OBJ-POSS.M.1S-house
...you are the one who will judge my house. ($^A$Zec 3:7 [Till])

(104c) After being tortured, St George is imprisoned. At night the Saviour appears and encourages him:
*anok et$^h$-na-ti-com m-pe-k-sôma et$^h$uab*
1S REL-FUT-give-force OBJ-POSS.M-2MS-body holy
*nta-t$^h$re-k-mton mmo-k*
CNJ.1S-INFL-2MS-rest OBJ-2MS
*nem-abraam nem-isaak nem-iakôb*
with-N with-N with-N
It is me who will give strength to your holy body and who will let you rest with Abraham, Isaac, and Jacob. ($^B$*Mart. George* [*AM* II 284, 13–15])

Bohairic provides also some examples with relativised *uon-* 'have':

(105a) Having heard Jesus forgive sins, the scribes wonder:
*nim ete-uon-š-com mmo-f e-k$^h$a-nobi ebol*
WH REL-have-can-power OBJ-3MS to-give-sin out
To whom is it possible to forgive sins *(except God alone)*? ($^B$Mk 2:7)

(105b) In the Sermon on the Mount, Jesus tells people not to worry:
*nim=de ebol-ḫen-t$^h$ênu et-fi-rôuš*
WH=yet out-in-2P REL-take-care
*ete-uon-š-com mmo-f e-tale-u-mahi n-šiê*
REL-have-can-power OBJ-3MS to-mount-IDF.S-cubit of-length
*ecen-te-f-maiê*
upon-POSS-3MS-size
Who among you is one who can add a single cubit to his stature by worrying? ($^B$Mt 6:27)

(105c) The Saint prays over some oil intended for a young girl in labour: *My Lord, Jesus Christ, have mercy on the work of your hands,*
*ce-nt$^h$ok ete-un-š-com mmo-k ḫen-hob niben*
for-2MS REL-have-can-power OBJ-3MS in-work QU
...for it is you who has power over every work.
($^B$*Mart. Epima* [*AM* I 135, 16–17])

This construction is common in introductory formulae of letters (Biedenkopf-Ziehner 1983: 225–26).[32] Although actual letters in Bohairic are rare, epistolographic emulations within other textual sorts make use of this pattern as an introductory construction. Hence, it can be posited that this construction was a peculiarity of 'literary letters':

(106a) Opening of a letter:
*anok sophia et-shai na-korbêne*
1S N REL-write to-N
It is I, Sophia, who writes to Korbe. ($^S$*O.Medin.Habu Copt* #183, 1–3)

(106b) As above:
*anok dauid pe-elakhistos et-tolma et-shai*
1S N DEF.M-least REL-dare REL-write
*na-pe-f-merit n-iôt*
for-POSS.M-3MS-beloved of-father
It is I, David, the humblest, who dares to write to his beloved father.
($^S$*P.Mon.Epiph.* #145, 2–4)

(106c) As above:
*dioskoros pe-k-bôk et-sḫai ša-pe-f-c$^h$(oi)s*
N POSS.M-2MS-servant REL-write to-POSS-3MS-lord
*theodoros pi-stratêlatês*
N DEF$_2$.M-general

32 Fayyumic letters such as those edited by Crum (1893) seem to prefer different opening formulae.

It is Dioscorus, your servant, who writes to his lord Theodore the General. ($^{B}$Theodore of Antioch, *On the Theodores* [*AM* II 129, 20–21])

It needs to be further investigated whether this construction is licensed in all dialects. Some dialectal variants of the Biblical texts cited above employ the more frequent cleft pattern with *pe*.

A further additional cleft pattern consists of an initial pronoun or indefinite NP followed by a copula that agrees in gender and number and a dependent ('circumstantial') clause. Since this pattern is formally a tripartite construction, it will be dealt with in 1.3.2.3.

Finally, a pattern typically found in epistolary introductions is a cleft sentence with a NP followed directly by a dependent clause. This dependent clause may be marked as first or third person, which shows that it cannot be viewed as a simple anteposition of the initial NP:

(107a) Opening of a letter:
*anok pesnte e-i-shai <n>-iôhannês*
1S N DEP-1S-write to-N
It is I, Pesente, who writes <to> John. ($^{S}$*P.Mon.Epiph.* #308, 1–2)

(107b) As above:
*anok tei-at-šau n-ref-r-nobe tsie e-i-shai*
1S DEM.F-NEG-worthy of-AGT-do-sin N DEP-3MS-write
*e-i-šine*
DEP-3MS-seek
*e-pa-merit n-son fragge hn-p-cois*
OBJ-POSS.M.1S-beloved of-brother N in-DEF.M-lord
It is I, the sinful unworthy Tsie, who writes to and greets her beloved brother Frange in the Lord. ($^{S}$*O.Frange* #247, 1–6)

(107c) As above:
*anok frang[e mn]-azarias n-[ref-r]-nobe e-u-s[hai*
1S N and-N DEF.P-AGT-do-sin DEP-3P-write
*e-u]-šine e-te-u-sône*
DEP-3P-seek OBJ-POSS.F-3P-sister
*eulêgie m[n-ne-s]-šêre*
N and-POSS.P-3FS-child
It is I, Frange, and Azarias, the sinners who write to and greet their sister and her children. ($^{S}$*O.Frange* #491, 1–6)

(107d) Peter opens his second letter to Acacius with the words:
*petros pi-arkhêepiskopos nte-rakoti e-f-sẖai n-akaki*
N DEF$_2$.M-archbishop of-N DEP-3MS-write to-N

It is Peter, the archbishop of Alexandria, who writes to Acacius.
([B]*Correspondence of Peter Mongus & Acacius* [Amélineau 199, 2 collated])

(107e) Having failed to kill St Macrobius, the magistrates decide to send him to Alexandria with a letter to the governor asking him to carry out the task:

| | | | | |
|---|---|---|---|---|
| *theophanês* | *nem-ammônios* | *e-u-sẖai* | *n-armenios* | *pi-komês* |
| N | and-N | DEP-3MS-write | to-N | $DEF_2$.M-comes |

It is Theophanes and Ammonius who write to the *comes* Armenius.
([B]*Mart. Macrobius* [*AdM* 232, 7–8])

In summary, all cleft sentences described above display a pattern with the determiner (< copula) alongside one without it. The structure of these constructions may be schematised as follows:

**Tab. II.4:** Distribution of cleft and pseudo-cleft sentence patterns in Coptic.

| Cleft | (Pseudo-)cleft | |
|---|---|---|
| NP DEF-REL | NP COP DEF-REL | NP COP DEP |
| NP REL | NP REL | NP DEP |

At the present stage, it is impossible to fully understand the rules underlying the choice between the constructions with and without an overt copula/determiner.[33] The situation is complicated by the fact that epistolary introductory formulae, our most important set of examples, show a mixture of both patterns: cf. ex. 108a for a cleft with determiner and 108b for one without it, both followed by a dependent clause:

(108a) Opening of a letter:

| | | | |
|---|---|---|---|
| *dioskoros* | *p-elakhist[os* | *m-p]resbyteros* | *p-et-shai* |
| N | DEF.M-least | of-priest | COP.M-REL-write |

| | | | | |
|---|---|---|---|---|
| *e-f[-ši]ne* | *e-pe-f-theosebês* | *n-iô[t* | *a]pa* | *hamoi* |
| DEP-3MS-seek | for-POSS.M-3MS-pious | of-father | Apa | N |

It is the humble priest Dioscorus who writes enquiring after his pious father Father Hamoi. ([S]Crum, *Cat. BM* #1213, 1–4)

33 General tendencies have been pointed out by Shisha-Halevy (2007: 300–05) for Bohairic.

(108b) Opening of a letter:

*anok* *Patermute* *et-shai* *e-f-šine* *e-pe-f-merit*
1S N REL-write DEP-3MS-seek for-POSS.M-3MS-beloved
*n-son* *Paulos*
of-brother N
It is me, Patermute, who writes enquiring after his beloved brother Paul.
(S O.Medin.Habu Copt #134, 1–3)

Coptic cleft sentences differ semantically from other nominal sentences in that they are marked for TAM. The marking pertains to the verbal construction that appears in the second-position relative clause. As the examples above show, almost any sentence pattern can be relativised by an operator and used as a constituent of these constructions.

## 1.2 Bipartite nominal sentences with grammaticalised subject element

The other major category of bipartite nominal sentences in Egyptian-Coptic is a construction in which the second constituent is a specific subject element. Schematically, the pattern may be represented as follows:

S > [NP SE]

### 1.2.1 Earlier Egyptian

In Earlier Egyptian, the subject element in this pattern is the morpheme =*pw*. Here, one should note a specific problem of Egyptological linguistics, where there has been no consensus on a term that would account for all the functions of=*pw* in Earlier Egyptian nominal sentences.[34] Some grammars avoid this problem by referring to=*pw* simply by its transliteration, a procedure which remains functionally neutral, but is hardly linguistically satisfactory. Others use the term 'copula', which appears adequate for tripartite sentences, but, as will be shown, is much less acceptable for bipartite constructions. The same reservation applies to the use of the term 'nexus morph' (Layton 2011: 199), which is occasionally used in Coptic studies for the diachronic descendant of=*pw* and which is ostensibly too jargonic. Yet other grammars prefer the

34 The same holds also for the diachronic descendents of=*pw* in Late Egyptian, Demotic, and Coptic. See the discussion below.

term ‘demonstrative pronoun’, but although=*pw* is indeed historically derived from such a deictic function, in the bipartite sentences of Earlier Egyptian, it no longer conveys demonstrative meaning. The same is true of tripartite sentences, where=*pw* functions as a purely grammatical operator. In this work, no overarching definition of=*pw* is adopted. In bipartite nominal sentences, this element semantically indexes a third-person subject ‘he/she/it/they’, sometimes deictically, and as a residue of its earlier semantic value of ‘this/these’ (cf. Vernus 1994: 333). It only loses its ‘subjecthood’ in constructions with sentential verbal and adverbial predicate complements with anteposition, where the subject of the embedded predication also becomes the subject of the construction and the role of=*pw* changes accordingly (see 3.1.5). Thus, in tripartite sentences, the function of=*pw* can be appropriately understood as a copula, whereas in bipartite sentences, one should preferably refer to=*pw* as the subject element.

In Earlier Egyptian,=*pw* is a second position (or ‘Wackernagel’) clitic, but the concept of ‘second position’ can refer to two different placement-strategies, both of which are displayed by=*pw*.[35] In some cases ‘second position’ may refer to the position immediately after the first prosodic unit or ‘word’ in the phrase, clause, or sentence. This is often the locus occupied by the subject element=*pw*, and in such cases it may break the coherence of noun phrases:

(109a) The peasant is introduced in the Tale:
*sḫty=pw* *n(-y)-sḫtḥmꜣt*
peasant=SE of[-M]-N
He was a peasant of the Wadi el-Natrun. (Peas R, 1.1)

(109b) Ptahhetep reveals the motive behind his advice for husbands to treat their wives well:
*ꜣḥ-t=pw* *ꜣḫ-t* *n-nb-s*
field-F=SE useful-F to-lord-3FS
She is a good field for her master. (Ptahhetep 330)

(109c) An answer to the question ‘who is this Redjedet?’:
*ḥm-t* *wʿb=pw* *n(-y)-rʿ*
wife-F priest=SE of[-M]-N
She is a wife of a priest of Ra. (pWestcar 9, 9)

In ex. 109a, =*pw* separates the head noun from a following indirect genitive, and in 109b it cleaves apart the former from its adjectival attribute. In 109c, the unity of the direct genitive N–N juxtaposition *ḥm-t wʿb* ‘a wife of a priest’, which constitutes a single prosodic group, remains unscathed, but=*pw* precedes the following

35 For what follows, see the discussion in Spencer and Luis (2012: 48–64) and cf. Halpern (1995: 15–17).

indirect genitive with the element *n(y)*.[36] Alternatively, 'second position' can have a more structural meaning and refer to the position after a phrase forming the first constituent daughter (Spencer & Luís 2012: 48; Halpern 1995: 15). The subject element=*pw* shows this placement strategy as well. Relatively common are examples of naming constructions such as 110a below, where, in the first instance, =*pw* appears after the entire complex name because the components of the latter were probably understood as semantically bound, but as the second=*pw*-sentence in the same example shows, this seems to have been a matter of individual choice. However, the first kind of placement is (near-)systematic in instances such as 110b–110i, where the predicate of the bipartite nominal sentence is a full (affirmative or negative) verbal, adverbial, or 'pseudo-verbal' complement clause:

(110a) In a litany of the parts of the yon ferry:
*rn n(-y)-sꜣw-f fnḏ n(-y)-ptḥ=pw*
name of[-M]-loom-3MS nose of[-M]-N=SE
*rn n(-y)-dp-t=tn wʿr-t=pw n-t-ꜣst*
name of[-M]-boat-F=DEM.F leg=SE of-F-N
The name of its loom (?), it is 'Nose-of-Ptah'. The name of this boat, it is 'Leg of Isis'. (CT V 193f–i/B5C)

(110b) A gloss explaining the expression 'his heart is flooded' in a medical text:
*mhh ỉb-f=pw mi-nt-y ḥr-sḫꜣt k-t md-t*
oblivious heart-3MS=SE like-REL-M PROG-recall.INF other-F word-F
This means that his (the patient's) heart is oblivious, like one who is thinking of something else. (pEbers 102, 15–16)

(110c) A gloss explaining the expression 'a wound in his nostril is weak' in a medical text:
*gnn sp-ty wbnw-f=pw*
soft lip-DU wound-3MS=SE
This means that the edges of his wound are soft. (pEdwin Smith 6, 13)

---

**36** Instances of=*pw* breaking up prosodic units are generally rare; they are commonest in Old Kingdom texts (e.g. PT 1127b), where they have sometimes been thought to represent a dialectal feature. A further Middle Kingdom example showing this in a negated nominal sentence is Siut I 288 & 301 *n-ḫ-t=ỉs=pw pr ḥꜣtyʿ* (NEG-thing-F=PTC=SE house mayor) 'They are not possessions of the mayor's office' (see 4.1 for negated nominal sentences). However, immediately before this in both cases one reads *ḫ-t=pw n-w-pr ỉt-ỉ* (thing-F=SE of-P-house father-1S) 'They are possessions of my father's estate' with the indirect genitive *n-w*. It thus seems likely that in the first instance the copyist simply forgot to insert *n-w* in the negative sentence and in the second repeated his error through mechanical copying.

(110d) A gloss explaining an expression in a medical text on veins:

| *ḥbs=sn* | *dḥr-t=pw* |
|---|---|
| cover=3P | N-F=SE |

It means that they cover up the *dḥrt*-disease. (pEbers 100, 18–101, 1)

(110e) A summarising point in an explanation of how god Ra earned his nickname:

| *ḫpr* | *rn-f=pw* | *n(-y)-miw* |
|---|---|---|
| become | name-3MS=SE | of[-M]-cat |

This is how his name of 'Cat' comes about. (CT IV 288b/T1Cb)

(110f) Explanation of a term in a medical text:

| *wnn* | *šf-t-w=pw* | *ḥr-q3b-t-f* |
|---|---|---|
| AUX | swelling-F-P=SE | on-breast-F-3MS |

It means that there are swellings on his (the patient's) breast. (pEdwin Smith 15, 17)

(110g) A gloss explaining the expression 'His heart spreads out' in a medical text:

| *wnn* | *mt-w=pw* | *n-ḥ3ty* | *ẖr-ḥs* |
|---|---|---|---|
| AUX | vein-P=SE | of-heart | under-excrement |

This means that the veins of the heart carry (lit. 'are under') excrement. (pEbers 100, 18)

(110h) Endnote in instructions on preventing damage to orchards by birds:

| *tm=rdi* | *ḫnp* | *ḏrwy-t=pw* |
|---|---|---|
| AUX.NEG=give.NC | rob | kite=SE |

This is how to prevent a kite from doing damage. (pEbers 98, 5–6)

(110i) Endnote in instructions on preventing rodent(?) damage to stored grain:

| *tm=rdi=pw* | *wnm-tw* | *it* |
|---|---|---|
| AUX.NEG=give.NC=SE | eat.SUB-PASS | corn |

This is how to prevent corn from being eaten. (pEbers 98, 10–11)

In the intransitive examples 110b and 110c, =*pw* follows the noun subject of the subordinate clause verb, which in the latter case consists of two nouns in a direct genitive relation where the clitic cannot intervene. In the transitive example 110d, =*pw* is placed after the patient/direct object of the subordinate verb, even though this is a noun. This would seem to suggest that the cliticisation-base of =*pw* is the entire VP, but ex. 110e, where the said element separates the post-verbal subject of the verb *ḫpr* 'to become' from its genitival phrase, shows that this is in fact indeed the 'first constituent daughter'. In the adverbial and pseudo-verbal examples 110f–110g, the predicate complement is headed by a form of the auxiliary verb *wn/wnn*, which hosts the nominal or pronominal subject of the following lexical predicate. In spite of their purely morphological (non-predicative) relationship, together the two serve as the first constituent daughter to which =*pw* cliticises, and the actual predicate of the subordinate clause is, accordingly, cleft off from its subject. However, the subject of the subordinate clause itself is similarly split if it is phrasally complex – i.e. if it, for example, contains an indirect genitive, as in ex. 110g.[37] The only construction of this sort where the placement of =*pw* seems variable between the two second position strategies is seen in the negative examples 110h and 110i, where the predicate complement clause of =*pw* is a complex construction built of a governing matrix clause plus an object complement. In ex. 110h the element follows the entire complex consisting of the negative auxiliary *tm*, the so-called Negatival Complement that carries the lexical meaning and appears to cliticise to the former, and the complement clause of the negated matrix clause. Yet although in ex. 110i, =*pw* does not disturb the unity of the auxiliary + the Negatival Complement, it follows immediately afterwards and before the complement clause, thus apparently conforming to the 'after the first prosodic unit' -placement rule. This sort of double positioning strategy is common for second position clitics in many languages, and although Earlier Egyptian clitics otherwise seem to follow the 'after the first prosodic unit' -principle rather strictly, the subject element =*pw* forms an important exception to this rule. As shall be shown in 1.3.1, the copular =*pw* found in tripartite nominal sentences sometimes behaves in a similar fashion.

In origin, =*pw* was a masculine singular 'distance-neutral' attributive demonstrative adjective 'this', still widely employed in Old Egyptian and the Coffin Texts (Jenni 2009: 119–37). Its development into a subject-indexing element exemplifies the more general (and cross-linguistically recognised) chain of grammaticalisation whereby adnominal demonstratives develop into operators of nominal constituents and third-person pronouns, clitics, and ultimately verb agreement (Diessel 2000: 210). In Earlier Egyptian, the use of =*pw* as a fixed subject-indexing element in bipartite nominal sentences is attested at the latest from the Fifth Dynasty, and there are good reasons to believe that this stage must have been reached considerably earlier, probably well before the Fourth Dynasty (see 1.3.1). However, apart from the just-mentioned lingering use of =*pw* as a demonstrative, there are various graphemic and grammatical phenomena of Old Kingdom Egyptian that show that the grammaticalisation process was not yet complete. In Fifth and Sixth Dynasty texts, and sometimes in the Coffin Texts, =*pw* still occasionally agrees with the preceding noun in gender and number[38]:

---

**37** Cf. Westendorf (1962: §404). Direct genitives in such cases are, of course, kept together – see ex. 119a.

**38** See Doret (1989: 50 n.10) for additional examples. In CT V 273j one reads *kꜣr-w nw n-w-ds* (shrine-P DEM of-P-knife) 'These are the shrines of the knife', with the form *nw* following a plural noun. However, the *n*-series demonstratives are not, strictly speaking, plural, which is also clear from the use of *nw* after singular nouns alongside the example cited (273k, m, n, 274b).

(111) The king is told that his two sisters have been brought to him:
*ꜣst=tw ḥnꜥ-nbtḥwt*
N=SE.F with-N
They are Isis and Nephthys. (PT 577a)

Yet this congruence was in the process of being dropped already in Old Egyptian. Similarly, as when serving as a demonstrative, in early sources, the subject-indexing *=pw* also displays the graphemic variants*=py*, *=pi*, and *=p(w)*:

(112a) The answer by a field-labourer to his companion's question 'Who is strong of heart and firm of hands?':
*i͗nk=py*
1S=SE
It's me. (*Mastaba de Neferirtenef* 59)

(112b) A comment following the evocation of 'The Two Companions':
W: *rꜥ=pi ḥnꜥ-ḏḥwty*
TMN: *rꜥ=pw ḥnꜥ-ḏḥwty*
N=SE with-N
They are Ra and Thoth. (PT 128c)

(112c) The king is received by the gods in perfect form:
T: *i͗r ḫꜣ-t N nḫn-w=pw*
PTC corpse-F N rejuvenate.PPP-P=SE
P: *i͗r i͗f qs-w N=pn nḫni-w=pi*
PTC flesh bone-P N=DEM.M rejuvenate.PPP-P=SE
M: *ḫꜣ-t N nḫni-w=pw*
corpse-F N rejuvenate.PPP-P=SE
N: *sḫꜣ-t-f nḫn-w=pw*
corpse-F-3MS rejuvenate.PPP-P=SE
(As for) the corpse/flesh and bones of King N, they are rejuvenated things. (PT 548b)

(112d) Wepemnefret grants his eldest son a burial shaft and an offering chapel in his own mastaba tomb:
*qrs-t(i͗)-f i͗m-f prtḫrw=n-f i͗m i͗mꜣḫ-w=p(w)*
bury-PASS-3MS in-3MS offering=to-3MS there revered-M=SE
May he be buried in it, with offering there for him. He is a revered one.
(Hassan, *Giza* II, fig. 219)

(112e) After noting that Geb spoke with Atum about giving the king's inheritance to him, the text adds:
M: *i͗-i͗r-t-n-f=p(w)*
P/N: *i͗-i͗r-t-n-f=pw*
PREF-do.REL-F-PST-3MS=SE
That is what he did. (PT 943d)

As exx. 112b–112d show, =*pi*/*p(w)* are the favoured form in the older Pyramid Texts versions (particularly W of late Fifth Dynasty), whereas later variants prefer the more 'modern' spelling=*pw*. Nevertheless, in the above examples=*pw* and its variants function grammatically as third-person subjects rather than deictics modifying nominal heads. A sure sign of erosion of the latter role is the use of other demonstratives, already in the Pyramid Texts, also when =*pw* or some of its earlier forms is present (ex. 113a), as well as of=*pw* as both a demonstrative and subject-index in the same clause (113b)[39]:

(113a) The king is presented with the 'Sound Eye':

*ḏdmdw* *wsir* *N* *ir-t=tn=tw* *n-t-ḥr* *dbḥ-t-n-f*

recitation N N eye-F=DEM.F=SE.F of-F-N ask.REL-F-PST-3MS

*m-ʿ-stš*

from-hand-N

Recitation: Osiris N, this is this Eye of Horus which he demanded from Seth. (PT 65b)

(113b) The deceased warns certain guardian demons to stay away from his soul:

*bꜣ=pw=pw* *n(-y)-wsir*

soul=DEM.M=SE of[-M]-N

It is this soul of Osiris. (CT VI 72h/B9C)

After the Old Kingdom, the use of =*pw* as a demonstrative is basically retained only in the Coffin Texts, and its new role as an element of the nominal sentence takes over more or less completely. Demonstrative=*pw*/*tw* occur henceforth only in particularly elevated language such as in archaising religious texts and in utterances of divine beings.[40] This development is paralleled by loss of gender/number congruence and the regularisation of the orthography of =*pw* into this one fixed form, a development directly motivated by the new roles of the demonstrative as a grammatical subject, rather than an attribute of the preceding NP. As shown above, the so-called *n*-series demonstrative pronouns could also be used in bipartite nominal sentences, e.g. after bare nouns. This seems to be an analogy from =*pw*, which was, however, the sole demonstrative specifically grammaticalised as a general subject-indexing element in bipartite nominal sentences and as a semantically empty copula in tripartite sentences.

In bipartite nominal sentences with =*pw*, the first position 'nominal' that, as will be discussed in 3.1.1, represents the predicate, may be a bare noun or noun phrase:

---

**39** Cf. Doret (1989: 56).

**40** Thus, e.g. in the Book of the Dead, the use of *pw*/*pwy* etc. as a demonstrative is very common in the diachronically most recent material as well. A good example of this sort of use derives from the Eighteenth Dynasty Papyrus Westcar, where the prestigious word 'kingship' is associated with the demonstrative *twy* (9, 11; 9, 25).

(114a) Senwosret III says of a successor who in all instances will defend his conquests:
*s3-i=pw*
son-1S=SE
He is my son. (Berlin 1157, 16)

(114b) This contrasts markedly with the king's opinion of his Nubian adversaries:
*ḥwr-w=pw*
miser-P=SE
They are misers. (Berlin 1157, 11)

(114c) The officials consider it unnecessary to punish the man who stole the peasant's goods:
*sp=pw n(-y)-ẖsf-tw n-nmtynḫt=pn ḥr-nh*
case=SE of[-M]-punish-PASS to-N=DEM.M because-little
*n(-y)-ḥsmn ḥnᶜ-nh n(-y)-ḥm3-t*
of[-M]-salt with-little of[-M]-natron-F
It would be a case of punishing this Nemtynakht for a trifle of salt and natron. (Peas B1, 77–79)

Alternatively, the same position may also be occupied by an absolute personal, interrogative, or demonstrative pronoun:

(115a) The deceased says of a divinity and of himself:
*ntf=pw ink=pw tspẖr*
3MS=SE 1S=SE vice versa
He is he and I am he – and vice versa. (BD 64/*Nebseni* pl. 72, 8)

(115b) After providing an answer to a problem concerning the area of a polygon, a mathematical text adds:
*ntf=pw m-3ḥ-t*
3MS=SE in-area-F
This is it in area. (pRhind math. n.49, 8)

(115c) A gloss explaining a description of a divine being:
*sy=ty=pw tm=pw im(-y) itn-f*
WH=PTC=SE N=SE in.RLT[-M] disc-3MS
Who is he? He is Atum who is in his disc. (CT IV 191c–d)

(115d) A problem in a mathematical text:
*t3 10 100 ḏb3 m-psw 15 wr=pw*
bread 10 100 replace.STA as-baking value 15 WH=SE
*r-ḏb3=s*
to-replace.INF=3FS
A hundred bread of (baking-value) 10 replaced with baking value 15; how many (i.e. bread) replaces it? (pRhind math. n.73, 1)

(115e) A statement after giving an answer to a problem on the number of jugs of beer:
*mk n3=pw*
PTC DEM.M=SE
Look, it is this (i.e. the number). (pMoscow math. n.16, 10)

Also non-attributive relative clauses are found in the same position:

(116a) Sinuhe eulogises Senwosret I with lofty epithets, including:
*swsḫ t3š-w=pw*
extend.PPA border-P=SE
He is one who extends borders. (Sin B, 71)

(116b) Officials brush aside Nemtynakht's beating of the peasant as normal behaviour from men of rank:
*mk irr-t-sn=pw r-sḫty-w-sn*
PTC do.REL.IPF-F-3P=SE to-peasant-P-3P
See, it is what they do to their peasants. (Peas B1, 76)

(116c) A remark following an assertion that the king has been re-established by Geb:
*ir-t-n-f=ḥm=pw*
do.REL-F-PST-3MS=PTC=SE
It is truly what he has done. (PT 1023a)

Note that in ex. 116a, *=pw* is placed after the direct object of the participle *swsḫ* 'who extends', but before the indirect object of the Relative Form *irr-t-sn* 'what they do' in ex. 116b. Examples with the infinitive are also common:

(117a) Khakheperraseneb dismisses attempts for originality in expression:
*ḥḥy=pw r-3q grg=pw*
seek.INF=SE to-disaster falsehood=SE
It is courting with disaster; it is falsehood. (Khakheperraseneb r° 6)

(117b) The author ends his correspondence with a standard epistolary cliché:
*swḏ3-ib=pw ḥr-s*
ease.INF-heart=SE on-3FS
This is to inform about it. (Semnah desp. I, 10)

A remarkable feature of Earlier Egyptian bipartite *pw*-sentence, and unique among nominal sentence patterns, is the possibility of embedding finite, non-relative verbal and adverbial clauses into the same syntactic position as the elements and constructions in exx. 114–117. There are three types of such constructions that fall into two syntactic and semantic-pragmatic types. The best attested of them is found in 'explanatory' sentences with a *sḏm-f* form, which, in root-classes with penultimate weak radical, shows gemination; the negation is built with *tm*. Seeing that examples of these constructions were already cited in 110 above, a single instance of both will suffice here:

(118a) A medical gloss explaining a term:

*ỉr* *nnw* *mwy-t-f* *hȝȝ* *mwy-t=pw*
PTC laziness water-F-3MS descend.GEM water-F=SE
*m-ḥnn-f* *n* *sȝ-n-s=n-f*
from-penis-3MS NEG hold-PST-3FS=to-3MS

As for 'his urine is lazy'; it means urine issues from his penis without control. (pEdwin Smith 10, 21–22)

(118b) As above:

*ỉr* *n* *ʿbȝ-n* *ỉr-w-t-sn* *tm=nbỉbỉw*
PTC NEG sparkle-PST colour-P-F-3P NEG.AUX=shine.NC
*ỉnm-sn=pw*
skin-3P=SE
*ỉr* *nn* *tms* *ḥr-s* *tm=wn* *ḫ-t=pw* *ḥr-s* *dšr*
PTC NEG red on-3FS NEG.AUX=AUX.NC thing-F=SE on-3FS red

As for 'their colouring does not sparkle'; this means their skin does not shine. As for 'there is no reddening on it'; this means there is no red matter on it. (pEdwin Smith 16, 14–16)

As seen above with exx. 110f–110g, with adverbial and verbal constructions with the order S-P, the auxiliary *wn/wnn* appears:

(119a) As above:

*ỉr* *s-t* *hn* *n(-y)-tp-f* *mỉ-bk* *n(-y)-ʿwt*
PTC smell-F chest of[-M]-head-3MS like-urine of[-M]-small_cattle
*wnn* *s-t* *wp-t-f=pw*
AUX smell forehead-F-3MS=SE
*mỉ-wsš-t* *n-t-ʿwt*
like-urine-F of-F-small cattle

As for 'the smell of the "chest" of his head is like (that of) the urine of small cattle'; this means that the smell of his forehead is like (that of) the urine of small cattle. (pEdwin Smith 3, 21–4, 1)

(119b) As above, in a liturgical text:

*ỉr* *ʿr-sn=n-ỉ* *ʿnd* *ỉm-sn* *wnn* *smȝ-w-t* *swty=pw*
PTC ascend-3P=to-1S few in-3P AUX crony-P-F N=SE
*ḥr-tkn* *ỉm-s*
PROG-approach.INF in-3FS

As for 'few of them ascend to me'; it means Seth's cronies were drawing nigh to her. (BD 17/*Nu* pl. 9, 118)

The *sḏm-n-f* is also attested in the same position (note the passive with *-tw*):

(120) A gloss explaining an expression in a liturgical text:

| | | |
|---|---|---|
| *ḥtm-n-tw* | *smꜣ-y-t* | *swty=pw* |
| destroy-PST-PASS | crony-F-P | N=SE |

This means that the cronies of Seth were annihilated. (BD 18/*Nu* pl. 9, 5)

In all the instances above, there is no complementiser before the subordinate clause. Rare examples in which such an element seems to be employed are indeed documented:

(121a) Astonished at having been challenged to a duel by a Syrian strongman, Sinuhe asks:

| | | | | |
|---|---|---|---|---|
| *ỉn* | *nt(t)=pw* | *wn-n-ỉ* | *sꜣ* | *pr-f* |
| IP | COMP=SE | open-PST-1S | back | house-3MS |

Is it that I have prised open the back of his house?[41] (Sin B, 115–16)

(121b) A medical text notes that the pulse of the heart can be felt everywhere in the body and adds:

| | | | |
|---|---|---|---|
| *nt(t)=pw* | *mdw-f* | *ḫnt-m-t-w* | *n-w-ꜥ-t=nb-t* |
| COMP=SE | speak-3MS | before-vessel-F-P | of-P-member-F=QU-F |

This is (i.e. means) that it speaks out of the vessels of each member. (pEbers 99, 5)

(121c) As above:

| | | | | | |
|---|---|---|---|---|---|
| *nt(t)=pw* | *m-t-w-f* | *m-ḥꜣ* | *tp* | *m-s-t* | *ỉb* |
| COMP=SE | vessel-F-P=3MS | in-back | head | in-place-F | heart |

This is (means) that its vessels are at the back of the head and in the position of the heart. (pEdwin Smith 1, 7)

Here, it is probably best to consider the initial *nt(t)* (which is apparently always written in this way in contact with *=pw*) as the standard Earlier Egyptian complementiser separated from the clause it introduces by the clitic *=pw* (i.e. [*nt(t) wn-n-ỉ sꜣ pr-f*][*pw*] → [*nt(t)* [*=pw*] *wn-n-ỉ sꜣ pr-f*] in ex. 121a). Alternatively, one could analyse this construction as a tripartite pattern in which the first position is occupied by a non-attributively used neuter of the relative operator *nt-*, roughly meaning 'what it is' followed by copular *=pw* and, in the third position, a complement clause ([*nt(t)*]*=pw* [*wn-n-ỉ sꜣ pr-f*], lit. 'what it is is that I have opened the back of his house' = 'It is the case that I have...' in 121a). However, this analysis does not seem applicable to ex. 121c, where the assumed complement clause in

41 That is, violated his privacy.

the third position would be a bare adverbial sentence.[42] Such constructions are in Earlier Egyptian seldom used as complements without a complementiser, which here seems to favour the bipartite analysis. This does not mean, however, that bare adverbial sentences could never be used in complement positions or embedded under =*pw*. On the contrary, this often seems to be the case in the third type of clausal embedding under =*pw* illustrated in the following examples:

(122a) The beginning of a mythological narrative:

B1L, B17C, B1C, S1C[a]: *rʿ=pw ḥr-mdt ḥnʿ-imywhmf*
N=SE PROG-speak.INF with-N

S1C[b]: *rʿ=pw mdw-n-f ḥnʿ-imywhmf*
N=SE speak-PST=3MS with-N

Now, Ra spoke to the *imy-whm-f*-snake. (CT II 274/75c–276/77a)

(122b) The sailor begins his narrative to the snake:

*ink=pw hꜣ-kw r-biꜣ m-wpw-t ity*
1S=SE descend-STA.1S to-mine-country in-mission-F sovereign

As for me, I went down to the mine-country on a royal mission. (Sh.S. 89–91)

(122c) The deceased (addressed as 'the magician') is asked beside the solar boat:

*iniw=tr sḫm-k m-tm in=n-k*
IP=PTC power-2MS in-NEG.AUX.PPP bring.NC=to-2MS

*ḥkꜣy=pw*
magician=DEM.M

*dp-t=tn=pw n-wnt mḏꜣb-t-s*
boat-F=DEM.F=SE NEG-AUX bailer-F-3FS

Do you have power over what has not been brought to you, O magician? For this boat – it does not have its bailer. (CT V 109h–j/T1C)

(122d) A new development in a mythological narrative:

*rʿ=pw ḫp-n=sw imyinsf*
N=SE encounter-PST=3MS N

Now Ra, He Who Wears His Bright-red Cloth encountered him. (CT II 280d)

(122e) The king's soul is told to arise before gods and spirits:

*snḏ-k=pw ir-ḥꜣ-t-w-sn... šʿ-t-k=pw ir-ḥꜣ-t-w-sn*
fear-2MS=SE to-heart-F-P-3P dread-F-2MS=SE to-heart-F-P-3P

42 To avoid this problem, the clause following *pw* could be understood as appositional, i.e. 'It$_i$ is the case, (namely) [(that) I have opened the back of his house]$_i$'. In this case the construction would again be bipartite.

The fear of you, it will be in their hearts... the dread of you, it will be in their hearts. (PT 763b–d)

There has been some controversy among scholars over the analysis of examples such as those above. Some have viewed them as simple bipartite sentences with the initial noun/pronoun + =*pw* followed by an attributive adjunct (e.g. Polotsky 2007: 96), whereas others have interpreted the segment subordinated to =*pw* to include also the 'circumstantial' and together with the initial noun/pronoun to form a full verbal (in exx. 122a–122c) or adverbial (in 122e) complement clause (e.g. Gardiner 1957: §§190.1, 325, 332; Junge 1978: 60–62). In defence of the first of these analyses, it could be argued that inasmuch as constructions such as **ink h3-kw* are virtually non-existent in Earlier Egyptian, they can hardly be widely 'embedded' into *pw*-sentences. Yet the clausal analysis is supported by two strong arguments. Firstly, the clauses and phrases following =*pw* are not free 'circumstantials', but display obligatory subject or (as in ex. 122d) object control. They do not alternate with adjuncts lacking this referential linkage with the initial noun/pronoun antecedent:

| | | | | | |
|---|---|---|---|---|---|
| *rˤ*$_i$*=pw* | *mdw-n-f*$_i$ | | **rˤ=pw* | *mdw-n* | *rmṯ* |
| N=SE | speak-PST-3MS | | *N=SE | speak-PST | man |

Secondly, if the alleged 'circumstantials' after =*pw* were mere adjuncts, they should behave accordingly also with respect to their semantic value. Thus, e.g. in *rˤ=pw mdw-n-f* the *sḏm-n-f* should be relative past *'This/he/it is Ra after he spoke...' which is clearly not the case. In more recent analyses, these constructions have been interpreted as bipartite *pw*-sentences with complement clauses of =*pw* showing subject/object ante-position (Loprieno 1995: 111–12; Uljas 2013: 244–46). In case of patterns with the order P–S, the latter is resumed after =*pw* as an overt co-referential pronoun:

| | | | | | | | |
|---|---|---|---|---|---|---|---|
| *rˤ=pw* | *mdw-n-f* | *ḥnˤ-imywhmf* | = | [[*rˤ*$_i$][*mdw-n-f*$_i$ | *ḥnˤ-imywhmf*]] | [*pw*] |
| N=SE | speak-PST-3MS | with-N | | [[N][speak-PST-3MS | with-N]] | [SE] |

In instances with adverbial and verbal patterns with S–P order, one could postulate an analogous covert pronoun in the structure:

| | | | | | |
|---|---|---|---|---|---|
| *rˤ=pw* | *ḥr-mdt* | *ḥnˤ-imywhmf* | = | [[*rˤ*$_i$][ø$_i$ | *ḥr-mdt* |
| N=SE | PROG-speak.INF | with-N | | [[N][ø | PROG-speak.INF |
| *ḥnˤ-imywhmf*]] | [*pw*] | | | | |
| with-N]] | [SE] | | | | |

More straightforwardly, the complements here can be viewed as the basic adverbial/verbal constructions with the initial subject set apart from the rest of the sentence by the syntactic gap created by the clitic =*pw*, i.e. simply as [*rˤ ḥr-mdt*]

[*pw*] → [*rꜥ* [=*pw*] *ḥr-mdt*] without movement of the initial noun/pronoun and 'equi-deletion' after =*pw*. This also renders the use of absolute pronouns quite explicable and removes the above-mentioned objection against the complement clause analysis. Absolute pronouns appear in all subordinate patterns, including adverbial and verbal clauses, simply because these constructions are embedded in bipartite *pw*-sentences where their anteposed pronominal subjects come to occupy the initial position but they cannot be preceded by supporting particles. This means that such constructions are not strictly isomorphic, and the same holds even truer for sentences such as *rꜥ=pw mdw-n-f*.[43] Deconstructing examples such as 122c above, where what follows =*pw* is a negative existential sentence, or 122d, where the anteposed element is the object, is no longer feasible because, on the one hand, no construction of the type *[noun + *n-wnt* N] is documented, and, on the other hand, the initial element of the pattern [noun + suffix-conjugation form] is always the subject. This shows that nominal sentences of this type are not derived from simpler atomic structures, but represent a well-formed and autonomous category of constructions that, as will be shown in 3.1.5, stands at the boundary between nominal and verbal/adverbial sentences, although structurally they are nominal sentences because underlying adverbial or pseudo-verbal sentence is syntactically subordinate to =*pw*. Nevertheless, there are also instances of well-formed bipartite *pw*-sentences in which the clause or construction accompanying =*pw* is not subordinate to the latter. Consider the following example:

(123) After describing certain symptoms on a member of a patient, a medical text instructs the physician:

| | | | |
|---|---|---|---|
| *imi-k=wdy* | *ꜥ* | *r-mit-t=nb-t* | *n-t-nw* |
| AUX.NEG.HORT-2MS=place.NC | hand | to-like-F=QU-F | of-F-DEM.M |
| *tp* | *r-tꜣ=pw* | | |
| head | to-earth=SE | | |

You should not lay (your) hand on anything similar to this: it is (a case of) 'head is to the ground'. (pEbers 109, 17–18)

Here =*pw* does not precede the prepositional phrase *r-tꜣ*, which shows that it is associated with the adverbial sentence *tp r-tꜣ* treated as an indivisible lexicalised block. But rather than 'used', the latter is, in fact, 'mentioned' or 'cited' as in the translation above, and there is no main vs. subordinate (or any kind of predicative) relation between the lexicalised block and =*pw* (cf. Jansen-Winkeln 1996a: 46–47). Corresponding constructions can also be found with similarly

43 That is, unless the underlying construction here is seen as the pattern 'noun + *sḏm-n-f*' as a complement of *pw*.

treated adjectival sentences (ex. 124a), imperatives (124b), and even bipartite *pw*-sentences (124c):[44]

(124a) In a broken context:
*twt=wy=n-f=pw* *ḏd-w* *iri* *m-sḫr-w[-f]*
form=ADM=to-3MS=SE say.PIA-M do.PPA in-plan-P-3MS
'How typical of him' is what is said of him who has acted according to his own plans. (pRamesseum I B1, 10)

(124b) The king clarifies the intent of his friendly letter to exiled Sinuhe:
*mi* *m-s3=pw*
come.IMP in-back=SE
It means 'Come back!'. (Sin B, 160)

(124c) The deceased says that his actions explain his identity:
*ink=pw=pw* *ink* *ḥr* *ink* *wsir* *tm*
1S=SE =SE 1S N 1S N N
It means 'it is me'. I am Horus; I am Osiris and Atum. (CT VI 63h–j)

### 1.2.2 Later Egyptian

#### 1.2.2.1 Late Egyptian

In Late Egyptian bipartite nominal sentences with a grammaticalised subject,[45] the invariable clitic =*pw* of the earlier language is replaced by the gender and number congruent morphemes *p3y/t3y/n3y* [MS/FS/P], which most probably originate in the homographic demonstrative pronouns. However, although this has occasionally been questioned due to the differences in congruence and syntactic position,[46] etymologically, these 'new' morphemes are certainly connected to the earlier =*pw*. Not unexpectedly, the earliest Late Egyptian texts continue to employ =*pw*,[47] which, as the lack of agreement marking in 125a demonstrates, was still invariable:

(125a) The writer of the letter complains about the requisition of a young slave girl and demands compensation:
*ḥr-ntt=r-f* *šri-t=pw*
because-COMP=PTC young-F=SE
...for she is still a girl. (pLouvre 3230b, 4 [*JEA* 12, pl. 17])

---

44 See Vernus (1994: 341–43). Examples like the last one are not rare in the Coffin Texts.

45 This term will here be applied also to elements corresponding functionally to the earlier =*pw*. See 1.2.1 above for issues of terminology.

46 E.g., Sethe (1916: 66). This stance is often more implicit than explicit (see e.g. Erman 1933: §460).

47 It is impossible to decide whether this is a deliberate choice of archaism or dictated by stylistic pragmatics.

(125b) Ramesses II is praised:
*šsꜣ=pw* *mi-ḥm* *n-ḏḥwty*
wise=SE like-majesty of-N
He is one wise like the majesty of Thoth. (*KRI* II 240, 12)

Unlike the earlier =*pw*, the Late Egyptian *pꜣy/tꜣy/nꜣy* is not a second position clitic and usually appears at the end of the sentence (126b). Exx. 126d–126f show that appositions or relative clauses are usually not separated from their antecedent by the subject element:

(126a) The prince, who has never seen a dog, sees one following a man and asks his servant what the animal is. The servant replies:
*ṯsm* *pꜣy*
[dog] [SE.M]
It is a dog. (*LES* 2, 5)

(126b) The older brother has searched for his younger brother's heart for four years. On his last intended day of search he finds a grape:
*is* *ḥꜣty* *n-pꜣy-f-sn* *šri* *pꜣy*
PTC [heart of-POSS.M-3MS-brother small] [SE.M]
It was the heart of his younger brother. (*LES* 23, 10)

(126c) The author of a letter asks the addressee to allow him to make use of his boat:
*pꜣ-hrw* *n-bꜣk-w-f* *pꜣy*
[DEF.M-day of-work-P-3MS] [SE.M]
It is the day of its use. (*KRI* III 255, 8–9)

(126d) The goddess Isis, trying to save her son Horus, has struck him with a harpoon. As he cries for help, she tells the harpoon to let him go:
*mk* *sꜣ* *ḥr* *pꜣy-i-šri* *pꜣy*
PTC [son N POSS.M-1S-young] [SE.M]
Lo, he is Horus, my son. (*LES* 49, 3)

(126e) One of the examining officials remarks to a tomb robber on trial:
*ir-tꜣ-s-t* *i-ḏd-k* *in(-i)* *nꜣ-ṯb-w*
PTC-DEF.F-place-F REL-say-2MS bring.PST[-1S] DEF.P-vessel-P
*n-ḥḏ* *im*
of-silver there
*k-ṯ-s-t* *mḥ-2-t* *tꜣy* *rwi-ṯ*
[other-F-place-F ORD-2-FEM] [SE.F] differ.STA-3FS
*(r)-pꜣy-ḥḏ* *ꜥꜣ*
(from)-DEM.M-treasure great

The tomb of which you reported that you had brought the silver vessels from it – it is a completely different tomb! It is quite distinct from that main treasure. (*KRI* VI 781, 3–5)

(126f) Accused by an official of a theft of some copper tools, the author tells what he said in reply:
*mbỉꜣ n&ꜣ-n-sdbḥ-w n-tꜣ-kꜣ-t wn*
no [DEF.P-of-tool-P of-DEF.F-work-F AUX.PPA
*r-ḫt-pꜣ-ỉt n-pꜣy-ỉ-ỉt nꜣw*
to-authority-DEF.M-father of-POSS.M-1S-father] [SE.P]
No! They are the tools of the work which used to be under my grandfather's supervision. (*HO* 88 r° 11–12)

However, deviations from this rule appear already in Late Egyptian texts, although mostly in later sources: in ex. 127, the subject element *pꜣy* occurs before the adverbial:

(127) A husband abandoned his wife for a younger woman after twenty years of marriage, citing sudden realisation that his wife had only one eye as the reason for his decision. The wife asked:
*n pꜣ-ꜥmꜣ ỉ-ỉr-k pꜣy m-tꜣy-20 n-rnp-t*
IP [DEF.M-knowledge REL-do-2MS]$_a$ [SE] [in-DEM.F-20 of-year-F
*ỉ-ỉr-ỉ m-pꜣy-k-pr*
REL-do-1S in-POSS.M-2MS-house]$_b$
Is this the knowledge that you gained during those 20 years that I spent in your house? (*LRL* 67, 16–68, 1)

However, a diachronic development led to second position cliticisation of the subject element in Demotic and Coptic, as was the case in Earlier Egyptian (see 1.2.2.2–3).

The predicate of a Late Egyptian bipartite nominal sentence with a grammaticalised subject element fills the first syntactic position and can be a bare noun, a noun phrase, a personal name, a personal pronoun, an interrogative phrase, or an infinitive:

(128a) The addressee is told to enquire in matter and:
*ỉnn mꜣꜥ-t tꜣy*
if [truth-F] [SE.F]
If this is true... (pBM 75021, 8 [Demarée, *Bankes Papyri*, pl. 21–22])

(128b) Following the boys request to be told who his father is, his mother said to him: *Do you see the blind man sitting beside the gate?*
*pꜣy-k-ỉt pꜣy*
[POSS.M-2MS-father] [SE.M]
He is your father. (*LES* 33, 4)

(128c) Thoth replies to Ra's question concerning the identity of a headless person approaching:
*pꜣy-i͗-nb* *nfr* *i͗st* *wr-t* *mw-t-nṯr* *tꜣy*
[POSS.M-1S-lord good N great-F mother-F-god] [SE.F]
My good Lord, this is Isis the great, mother of a god. (*LES* 50, 3–4)

(128d) After telling the story of a woman abandoned by her husband after twenty years because he suddenly noticed that she had only one eye, the author of a letter says:
*i͗nk* *pꜣy* *pꜣ-sbi͗* *i͗-i͗r-i͗* *i͗rm-k* *pꜣy*
[1MS] [SE.M] [DEF.M-joke REL-do-1S with-2MS] [SE.M]
This is me! This is the joke I made on you! (*LRL* 68, 1–2)

(128e) King Akhenaten outlines the limits of his newly founded capital and resumes:
*nts* *tꜣy*
[3FS] [SE.F]
This is it. (*Boundary Stelae*, 24, 10 [K 12])

(128f) The author of a letter tries to clarify matters and wants to know:
*i͗ḫ* *m-mdw-t* *tꜣy*
[WH of-thing-F] [SE.F]
What kind of an issue is that? (*LRL* 73, 1)

(128g) The author of a letter quotes the addressee's complaint that he did not receive any gypsum for a month:
*pꜣ-hꜣy-t* *i͗-i͗r-k* *(r)-bꜣk* *pꜣy*
[DEF.M-come-INF REL-do-2MS (to)-work] [SE.M]
(As) that is the reason why you have come down (to) work...
(oDeM 437, r° 2–3)

Instead of being prefixed only by an article, infinitives are often also introduced by the expression *sḫr n-* lit. 'plan of':

(129) A man interrogated in matters of theft declares:
*pꜣ-sḫr* *(n)-šm* *i͗-i͗r-i͗* *ꜥqꜣ* *pꜣy*
[DEF.M-plan of-go.INF REL-do-1S correct] [SE.M]
That is exactly how I went. (*KRI* VI 780, 12)

Although examples are rare, the predicate position may also be occupied by a relative clause (relative form, participle, or *nty*-construction) used absolutely:

(130a) After a woman's denial of accusations against her, a juridical protocol continues:
*ḏd-t-n=n-s* *tꜣ-qnb-t* *nꜣw*
[say.REL-F-PST=to-3FS DEF.F-court-F] [SE.P]
This is what the court said to her (a quote follows). (*KRI* IV 316, 2)

(130b) God Amun has decreed for the lady Neskhons that she will receive food offerings in the netherworld:

| | | |
|---|---|---|
| *m-pꜣ-ḫpr* | *pꜣ-nty-iw-f-nfr=n-s* | *pꜣy* |
| in-DEF.M-happen.INF | [DEF.M-REL-FUT-3MS-be_good=to-3FS] | [SE.M] |

...provided that that is what will be good for her.

(Jansen-Winkeln, *IdS* I, 129, 10)

The Earlier Egyptian method of embedding of complete clauses as predicate complements of the subject element is no longer attested, and perhaps also no longer grammatical.[48]

Overall, Late Egyptian bipartite nominal sentences with a subject element show a relatively strict adherence to the syntactic template S > [NP SE] also documented in Earlier Egyptian, the two major developments being the replacement of the invariable copula *=pw* by the series *pꜣy/tꜣy/nꜣy*, which agrees in gender and number, and its change from second position clitic to sentence-final element. The first of these two features was to be partly revived in Demotic.

#### 1.2.2.2 Demotic

Like Late Egyptian, Demotic displays a lively use of bipartite nominal sentences with a subject element showing agreement for gender and number (singular masculine and feminine vs. plural). However, when compared to Late Egyptian, this subject element shows a graphemically slightly modified form in the plural: instead of the Late Egyptian *pꜣy/tꜣy/nꜣy*, Demotic exhibits the forms *pꜣy/tꜣy/nꜣw*:

(131a) A teaching in a Ptolemaic wisdom text:

| | | | | | |
|---|---|---|---|---|---|
| *mir-ḏd* | *šmw* | *pꜣy* | *wn* | *mtw-f* | *pr-t* |
| NEG.IMP-say | [summer] | [SE.M] | exist | with-3MS | winter-F |

| | | |
|---|---|---|
| *pꜣ-ntyiw-bw-ir-f-ṯꜣy-ḫt* | *(n)-šmw* | *bw-ir-f-ḫm* |
| DEF.M-REL-NEG-AUX-3MS-take-wood | (in)-summer | NEG-AUX-3MS-warm |
| *n-pr-t* | | |
| in-winter-F | | |

Do not say 'it is summer', as it has winter too. He who does not gather wood during the summer cannot warm himself in the winter.

(Onkhsheshonqy 9, 16–17)

48 Some early examples such as *KRI* I 47, 6 *ḥr-ntt pw ʿnḫ-sn im-s* 'because they are living upon it (scil. the truth)' seem suspect given the position of *pw*. Cf. also *KRI* I 113, 1 *ḥr-ntt pw sḫr-w=pw ḏri-w* 'for they are excellent counsels', where the first *pw* looks equally suspicious. A rather trustworthier example is *KRI* I 67, 15 *nttn=pw mi-nṯr-w* 'you (2P) are like gods'.

(131b) The author of a letter says that the addressee should write to a third party, for:

*md-t* *(n)-ky* *t3y*
[thing-F of-other] [SE.F]
It is another man's business. (pLoeb 5 v° 20–21)

(131c) A note in a medical prescription uses also Greek terms to explain parts of its preceding section:

*3nḥ-n-rʿ* *ophrusêliou* *3nḥ-n-iʿḥ* *ophrus-iʿḥ*
eyebrow-of-sun *ophrusêliou* eyebrow-of-moon *ophrus*-moon
*hyn-w-sym-w* *n3w*
[IDF-P-herb-P] [SE.P]
'Eyebrow of the sun' (*ophrus hêliou*) and 'eyebrow of the moon' (*ophrus*-of-the-moon) – they are herbs. (pMag. London&Leiden v° 1, 1–3)

(131d) Meryre asks Pharaoh to send the children of the the court magicians who wish him evil to him. Pharaoh says:

*t3y-k-šbw* *n3w*
POSS.F-2MS-price SE.P
They shall be your price. (pVandier 2, 12)

As the last example above shows, the subject element agrees with the external reference not with the predicate in gender and number.

Otherwise, the morpho-syntax of bipartite sentences of this type has not changed much from Late Egyptian. The subject element usually occupies the sentence-final position. However, in sentences in which the predication is associated with an attributive relative clause, Demotic examples sometimes show insertion of the subject element between the two:

(132a) A note in a medical prescription concerning an ingredient of a drug:

*p3y-f-rn* *n-md-t* *<wynn>* *aphroselênon* *d3ḫ* *n-iʿḥ*
POSS.M-3MS-name in words Greek *aphroselênon* foam of-moon
*wʿ-iny* *p3y* *iw-f-wbḫe*
[IDF.S-stone]$_a$ [SE.M] [DEP-3MS-white]$_b$
Its name in the Greek (?) language is '*aphro selênon*' – 'foam of the moon'; it is a white stone. (pMag. London&Leiden v° 3, 12–13)

(132b) As above:

*phêklês* *wʿ-iny* *iw-f-wbḫe* *p3y* *iw-f-m-qty-gʿrb3nʿ*
*phêklês* [IDF.S-stone DEP-3MS-white]$_a$ [SE.M] [DEP-3MS-in-like-galbanum]$_b$
'*Phêklês*' – it is a white stone, that is like galbanum.
(pMag. London&Leiden v° 3, 4–6)

(132c) The author of a letter agrees with the addressee's choice of a certain person:
*rmṯ* *p3y* *iw-f-rḫ-ir-p3-šn* *n-wꜥ-t-md*
[IDF.S-man]$_a$ [SE.M] [DEP-3MS-know-do-DEF.M-inspection of-IDF-F-thing
*r-tm-dyt-ḥps* *r-n3-wꜥb-w* *irm-p3-nṯr* *ꜥn*
to-AUX.NEG-give.INF-anger to-DEF.P-priest-P and-DEF.M-god again]$_b$
He is a man who knows how to make an inspection of something
without annoying the priests or even the god. (pBerlin P. 13549, 15–17)

(132d) In his rather succinct letter the sender reacts to complaints of the addressee who had expressed his unease about the sender's information policy. He enlightens him now thus:
*wꜥ-msḥ* *n-ds* *nḫṯ* *p3y* *iw-f-ir-špy* *4*
IDF.S-crocodile of-flint strong SE.M DEP-3MS-do-palm 4
*iw-f-mtn* *ḥr-t3y-f-ḫ3s-t* *ḏd-sbk* *nb-mrnfr* *nb-bḫ*
DEP-3MS-engrave.STA on-POSS.F-3MS-base-F COMP-N lord-N lord-N
It is a crocodile of hard flint-stone that measures four palms and is
inscribed on its pedestal with: Sobek, lord of Mernefer, lord of Bakhu.
(pLoeb 10, 4–7)

(132e) A priest begins a story to the pharaoh about a certain man:
*wnn3w-rmṯ-ꜥ3* *mšs* *p3y* *r-ꜥš3-f* *n-sꜥnḫ*
PRT-man-great very SE.M DEP-be plenty-3MS in-nourishment
He was a very rich man who had plenty of income.
(pBM 69532, 6 [Tait, *Enchoria* 31])

(132f) In a magical text, the god Thoth finds his daughter Isis crying and in distress. Being asked what would be the matter with her she reveals to him that she uncovered a secret sexual relationship between her sister Nephthys and her husband Osiris and exclaims:
*u-ment-šairi* *nara-k* *te* *pa-iut*
IDF.S-ABST-cohabitation before-2MS SE.F POSS.M.1S-father
This is adultery against you, my father.
($^{OC}$Great Mag. P. Paris [*ZÄS* 21, 100, 43])

Yet a comparison of exx. 132a and 132b, which are chronologically late, shows that the fronting of the subject element was still rather a tendency than a rule; an impression fostered also by the very late (fourth century AD) example 132f. As shown by 132c, this phenomenon appears as early as the fourth century BC. A similar pattern can be observed occasionally in documentary texts. Here the subject element intrudes into coordinated predicate expressions and is agreement-marked as singular. Note that it does not split attributive constructions as shown by 133c:

(133a) A sale document for a slave states:

*pꜣy-t-bꜣk=pꜣy* *ḥnꜥ-nꜣy-f-ẖrṯ-w* *ḥnꜥ-nty=nb*
POSS.M-2FS-servant=SE.M with-POSS.P-3MS-child-P with-REL=QU
*nty-mtw-w*
REL-with-3P
*ḥnꜥ-nꜣ-nty-ỉw-w-r-dyt-ḫpr-w*
and-DEF.P-REL-FUT-3P-FUT-let.INF-happen-3P
He is your slave with his children and with everything they possess and will acquire. (pBN 223, 3)

(133b) The vendor of a cow states in the sales document:

*tꜣy-k-ỉḥ=tꜣy* *ḥnꜥ-ms=nb* *nty-ỉw-s-ms-w*
POSS.F-2MS-COW=SE.F and-calf=QU REL-FUT-3FS-bear-3P
*n-ṯꜣy-rnp-t* *8* *ỉbd-1* *šmw* *r-ḥry* *šꜥ-ḏ-t*
in-take-year-F 8 month-1 summer to-up until-eternity-F
It is your cow and every calf she shall bear from regnal-year 8, first month of summer, until eternity. (pRylands VIII, 3)

(133c) In a document for a sale of water rights:

*pꜣ(y)-t-mw* *nmḥ=pꜣy* *[ḥnꜥ-pꜣy-f-ḫt*
POSS.M-2FS-water private=SE.M with-POSS.M-3MS-wood
*pꜣy-f-ꜣḥ]* *pꜣy-f-qḥ*
POSS.M-3MS-field POSS.M-3MS-area
*pꜣy-f-wn* *n-ry-t=nb* *n-ṯꜣy-pꜣ-hrw* *[r-ḥry* *š]ꜥ-ḏ-t*
POSS.M-3MS-part of-lot-F=QU in-take-DEF.M-day to-up until-eternity-F
It is your private water with its wood, its field, its area and its part of any allotment from today until eternity.
(oManawir IFAO 5446, 5–7 [Chauveau, *FS Zauzich*])

As in Late Egyptian, the first (predicate) position of a Demotic bipartite nominal sentence with the subject element could be occupied by a definite (134a) or indefinite (134b) noun phrase, a personal name, or an expanded infinitive (134d):

(134a) A juridical manual notes concerning issues over taking over an uninhabited house:

*bw-ỉr-rḫ-pꜣ-rmt* *nty-mḥṯ* *n-pꜣ-ꜥwy* *ḏd*
NEG-AUX-can-DEF.M-man REL-seize OBJ-DEF.M-house say
*pꜣy(-y)-ꜥwy* *pꜣy* *wꜥb-f* *n-y*
[POSS.M[-1S]-house] [SE.M] free-3MS to-1S
The person who seizes the building cannot say: 'It is my house! It is (legally) clear for me.' (*Cod. Herm.* x+2, 17–18)

(134b) To ensure that a lease-contract is not to be prolonged, the lessee has to swear:
*ỉw-bn-ỉw-y-rḫ-ḏd* *sḥn=pꜣy* *ỉw-wtb-f* *rnp-t*
DEP-NEG-FUT-1S-can-say [lease]$_a$=[SE.M] [DEP-turn.PST-3MS year-F]$_b$
I will not be able to say: 'This is a lease that has changed for the year.'
(pTurin Suppl 6107, 22–23)

(134c) A juridical manual instructs that the following words are to be sworn by children whose father is dead:
*nꜣ-sḫ-w* *n-nꜣy-n-ỉṯ-w* *nꜣw*
[DEF.P-writing.P of-POSS.P-1P-father.P] [SE.P]
These are the writings of our fathers.
(pBerlin P. 23757A, r° 2, 11 [Lippert, *Dem. jur. Lehrbuch*, 23])

(134d) A gloss from the pseudo-prophetical text of the *Demotic Chronicle*:
*ršy* *mḏr-nꜣ-ntr-w* *(n)-pꜣy-w-ỉr-ḥry* *pꜣy*
[rejoice.INF by-DEF.P-god-P (for)-POSS.M-3P-do-lord] [SE.M]
...this means 'Rejoicing by the gods over their dominion'. (pBN 215 r° 2, 22)

Coordinated nouns can also appear as the predicate:

(135) A mythological text explains various words and phrases:
*[...pꜣ]-nwn* *r-ḏd-f* *ḥry* *wsỉr* *ḥrsꜣꜣst* *nꜣw*
...DEF.M-abyss REL-say-3MS above N N SE.P
[... the] primeval ocean which he mentioned above, it is Osiris and Harsiese. (Memph. Theology 4, 21)

Absolute personal and interrogative pronouns are similarly found in the same position:

(136a) The Ethiopian cat tells why she is called 'She-of-the-Land':
*tꜣ-šr-t [...]* *nty-n-tꜣ* *ỉnky* *tꜣy*
DEF.F-daughter-F ... REL-in-land [1S] [SE.F]
The daughter of [...], who is on earth – it is me! (Myth of the Sun's Eye 9, 20)

(136b) The pharaoh asked Amun in a procession whether a young priest was the person entitled to certain sacerdotal prebends:
*ỉmn* *ỉw-ṯ* *r-tꜣ-ḥꜣ-t* *n-wꜥ-t-tks-t* *ỉw-s-ys*
N come-STA to-DEF.F-front-F in-IDF.F-step-F DEP-3FS-hurry
*ḏd-mtwf* *pꜣy*
that-[3MS] [SE.M]
Amun came forth with a quick step (and said): 'It is he!' (pSpiegelberg 2, 14)

(136c) The method of calculation concludes with the sentence:
*mtwf* *pꜣy*
[3MS] [SE.M]
This is it. (pBM 10520, A10 [Parker, *Math. Texts*])

(136d) The 'Looking'-bird tells the 'Hearing'-bird that there is something extraordinary about her. The 'Hearing'-bird replies:

*iḫ* *tꜣy*
[WH] [SE.F]
What is it? (Myth of the Sun's Eye 13, 29)

(136e) Setne beheld a beautiful woman on the street and sent one of his servants to speak to one of her maidservant:

*šn-f=s* *ḏd-iḫ̂* *n-rmṯ* *tꜣy*
seek.PST-3MS=3FS that-[WH of-person] [SE.F]
*ḏd-s=n-f* *tabwbw* *tꜣ-šr-t* *n-pꜣ-ḥm-nṯr*
say.PST-3FS=to-3MS N DEF.F-child-F of-DEF.M-servant-god
*n-bꜣst-t* *nb-t-ʿnḫtꜣwi* *tꜣy*
of-N-F lord-F-N SE.F
He asked her: 'What kind of person is this?' She replied: 'She is Tabubu, the daughter of the Prophet of Bastet, the lady of Ankhtaui'.
(Setne I 5, 2–3)

(136f) A former have-not will gain wealth and people will say about him:

*nm* *pꜣy*
[WH] [SE.M]
Who is this? (Lamb of Bocchoris 2, 10)

Relative or participial clauses are found as predicates of Demotic bipartite nominal sentences with the subject element as well:

(137a) The servant explains to Setne the conditions that Tabubu set for their first meeting. Setne answers:

*pꜣ-nty-mtr* *pꜣy*
[DEF.M-REL-correct] [SE.M]
This is fine. (Setne I 5, 10)

(137b) A description of the power of the Ethiopian cat:

*tꜣy-ntyiw-bw-ir-pꜣ-ḏbꜣ* *ir-syḫ̂ꜣṯ* *nim-s* *tꜣy*
[DEM.F-REL-NEG-AUX-DEF.M-avenger do-power OBJ-3FS] [SE.F]
She is the one over whom the avenger has no power.
(Myth of the Sun's Eye 15, 24–25)

(137c) Peteese concludes his discussion with Semtutefnakht:

*ʿnḫ-pꜣrʿ* *pꜣ-iir-ḫpr* *nim(-y)* *irm-nꜣ-wʿb-w* *n-imn*
[live-N ART-AUX.REL-happen OBJ[-1S] with-DEF.P-priest.P of N
*(n)-tꜣywḏy* *pꜣy*
of-N] [SE.M]
By Re, it is that which happened to me with the priests of Amun of Teudjoi. (pRylands IX 11, 21–12, 1)

Examples in which the predicate is an adjectival expression anticipate the pattern which eventually becomes common in Coptic (see 1.2.2.3):

(138) The guests at a banquet see the debauched harpist and think:
*ꜥꜣ pꜣy*
great SE.M
He is great. (Depraved Harpist 2, 7)

Omission of the subject element in coordination is rarely attested:

(139) In a legal document a woman tells that she went to court because her husband had made a property division document for one of his sons:
*šr-iṯ r-bnỉw-šr-mw-t ỉn pꜣy*
[son-father]=ø DEP-NEG-son-mother-F NEG SE.M
...who is the son of (the same) father, but not of (the same) mother.
(pBM 10591 r° 1, 15)

Unlike in Late Egyptian – and also in the majority of Demotic texts – the *Demotic Chronicle* from the third century BC contains examples of glosses with clauses introduced by *ḏd* in the predicate position, thus anticipating the Coptic use of clauses introduced by a marker of dependency:

(140) A gloss from the pseudo-prophetical text of the *Demotic Chronicle*:
*dy-w py n-py*
give.FUT-3P seat to-N
*ḏd-ỉw-w-dyt-pꜣy-f-šr ꜥꜣ ḥr-tꜣy-f-s-t*
[COMP-FUT-3P-give.INF-POSS.M-3MS-son great on-POSS.M-3MS-seat-F
*ḏd-pꜣ-ḥry nty-ỉw-f-ḫpr mḫy-f r-ḥrsꜣꜣst pꜣy*
that-DEF.M-ruler REL-FUT-3MS-happen equal.FUT-3MS to N] [SE.M]
They will give a seat to Pe; this means that they will put his eldest son on his throne and that the future ruler will be similar to Harsiese.
(pBN 215 r° 3, 11)

Finally, a mention should be made of the glossing construction *ntyỉw ... pꜣy/tꜣy/nꜣw* and of its rare variant *rtw ... pꜣy/tꜣy/nꜣw*, which correspond to Coptic *ete ... pe/te/ne* used to introduce a parenthetic gloss (name specification and glossing):

(141a) Whilst narrating Naneferkaptah's misfortunes, Ahwere describes him as:
*nꜣnfrkꜣptḥ pꜣy(-y)-sn ꜥꜣ ntyỉw-sẖ nfr rmt*
N POSS.M[-1S]-brother great [REL-scribe good man
*rḫ mšs pꜣy*
know very] [SE.M]
...Naneferkaptah, my eldest brother, who is a good scribe and a very wise man. (Setne I 4, 3)

(141b) A funerary text describes the actions of the deceased in the hereafter:
*ꜥš-k* *r-pꜣ-nfr* *ntyỉw-wsỉr* *pꜣy* *nty-ḥtp*
recite.FUT-2MS to-DEF.M-good [REL-N] [SE.M] REL-rest
*n-tꜣy-f-ꜥḥꜥyꜣ-t*
in-POSS.F-3MS-tomb-F
You will invoke the Beautiful One, i.e. Osiris, who rests in his tomb.
(pRhind I 5, d6)

(141c) A spell of purification of the deceased contains the wish for the latter:
*ꜥnḫ-by-k* *r-ḫrw-pꜣ-nb* *n-pꜣ-ṯꜣw* *rtw-ỉmn* *pꜣy*
live.FUT-soul-2MS to-voice-DEF.M-lord of-DEF.M-wind REL-N SE.M
May your Ba live alongside the lord of the wind, i.e. Amun.
(pRhind I 6, d4)

(141d) A prescription from the Rosetta decree concerning a statue:
*mtw-w-dy-t-ꜥḥꜥ-wꜥ-twtw* *(n)-prꜥꜣ* *ptlwmys* *ꜥnḫ*
CNJ-3P-let-INF-erect-IDF.S-statue (of)-pharaoh N live
*ḏt* *pꜣ-nṯr* *pr*
eternity DEF.M-god go.PPA
*nty-nꜣ-ꜥn-tꜣy-f-md* *nfr-t* *mtw-w-ḏd=n-f* *ptlwmys*
REL-ADJ-fine-POSS.F-3MS-ABST good-F CNJ-3P-say=to-3MS N
*nḏ* *bqy*
protect.PPA bright land
*ntyỉw-pꜣy-f-wḥm* *ptlwmys* *ỉir-nḫṱ* *km*
REL-POSS.F-3MS-meaning N make.PPA-strong Egypt
...and to set up a statue of King Ptolemy, living forever, the god who appears (i.e. Epiphanes) and whose goodness is great (i.e. Eucharistos), which is to be called ‘Ptolemy who has protected the Bright Land’, the meaning of which is ‘Ptolemy who has preserved Egypt’.
(Rosetta Decree 22–23)

Note the omission of *pꜣy* in the relative clause of the last example.

In conclusion, Demotic bipartite nominal sentences with a subject element follow the Late Egyptian pattern S > [NP SE]. *pꜣy/tꜣy/nꜣw* are still differentiated according to gender and number and show only a graphic change in the plural (Late Egyptian *nꜣy* > Demotic *nꜣw*). However, Demotic shows the first signs of the development of the subject element into a second position clitic, as had been the case in Earlier Egyptian.

### 1.2.2.3 Coptic

In Coptic, bipartite nominal sentences with a subject element, the latter takes in all dialects the form of the morpheme *pe/te/ne* (M also knows the by-forms *pê/tê/nê*), which agrees with the predicate in gender and number:

(142a) Judah tells his brothers not to slay Joseph but to sell him into slavery, for:
*pe-n-son=pe* *uoh* *te-n-sarks=te*
[POSS.M-1P-brother][=SE.M] and [POSS.F-1P-flesh][=SE.F]
He is our brother and our flesh! ($^{B}$Gn 37:27)

(142b) The law of the Israelites prescribes that a man should not have homosexual intercourse:
*u-bote=gar=te*
[IDF.S-abomination.F]=for=[SE.F]
For it is an abomination. ($^{S}$Lev 18:22 [Ciasca])

(142c) The law of the Israelites prescribes that neither men nor women should practise bestiality:
*u-šlof=gar=pe*
[IDF.S-disgrace.M]=for=[SE.M]
For it is a disgrace. ($^{S}$Lev 18:23 [Ciasca])

(142d) Basil of Pemje asks his audience rhetorically whether Longinus and Lucius are the friends of the Lord insofar as they keep his commandments:
*umonon* *ce-šbr* *alla* *hen-son* *hi-sône=ne*
not only COMP-friend but [IDF.P-brother and-sister][=SE.P]
*hi-mau* *m-p-cois*
[and-mother of-DEF.M-lord]
And not only friends, but they are also brothers and sisters and mothers of the Lord! ($^{S}$Basil of Pemje, *Homily on Longinus* [*FS Kasser*, 276, 28–29])

(142e) Clement says of Jesus that the people despised him since his appearance was without glory:
*u-rôme=pe* *e-f-ḫn-u-plêgê* *mn-u-mkah*
IDF.S-man=SE.M DEP-3MS-in-IDF.S-blow and-IDF.S-sorrow
*e-f-saune* *n-fi* *ḫa-laclc*
DEP-3MS-know of-carry under-straits
He was a human, who was beaten and sorrowed, who knows to carry straits. ($^{A}$1Cl 16:3 [Schmidt])

(142f) Jesus tells the disciples how Archangel Michael went instead of Jeremiah:
*a-f-kô* *n-u-leme-sarks* *e-f-ôhi* *elet-b*
PST-3MS-put OBJ-IDF.S-man-flesh DEP-3MS-stand to-3MS
*a-f-maaši* *ntab* *e-u-a-sômatos=pe*
PST-3MS-walk 3MS DEP-IDF.S-un-bodily= SE.M
He let a human stand and went in his stead, although he is bodiless.
($^{F}$John Evangelist, *Investiture of Archangel Michael* [Müller 25, 16–17])

Ex. 142a shows that the subject element agrees with the gender and number marking of the predicative NP and not of the exocentric referent of the statement: the semantic referent 'Joseph' does not determine the gender of the feminine *te*, which agrees with *te-n-sarks* 'our flesh' instead. The lexical gender of the predicate is also responsible for the choice of the form of the subject element when the predicative NP is indefinite. This is the case in 142b, with the feminine *bote* determining the gender of *te*, and in 142c, where the masculine *šlof* prompts the choice of *pe*.

As the above examples show, the subject element develops syntactically into a second position 'Wackernagel' clitic. Although clitic ordering has rarely been studied for Coptic (with the almost sole exception of Shisha-Halevy 1986: 166–67), the interference of *gar* in exx. 142b and 142c seems to suggest an ordering where *gar* ranks higher than the subject index.[49] Coordinated predicates can be construed with a common subject index as in ex. 142d. Yet in cases with coordination involving NPs of different genders (e.g. 142a), two full clauses were normally used. Coptic also provides examples in which the subject element splits a genitive construction, in a manner reminiscent of Earlier Egyptian:

(143a) The Lord orders in his covenant with the Israelites:

| | | | |
|---|---|---|---|
| *hm-p-meh-sašf=de* | *n-hou* | *n-sabbaton=ne* | *m-p-cois* |
| in-DEF.M-ORD-seven=yet | DEF.P-day | of-sabbath= SE.P | of-DEF.M-lord |
| *pe-k-nute* | | | |
| POSS.M-2MS-god | | | |

But on the seventh day – these are the Sabbath days of the Lord, your God! ($^{S}$Dt 5:14 [Ciasca])

(143b) It is said of the crucifixion of Christ:

| | | | | |
|---|---|---|---|---|
| S | *ne-p-nau=de=pe* | *n-cp-šomte* | *auô* | *a-u-stauru* |
| | PRT-DEF.M-moment=yet= SE.M | in-hour-three | and | PST-3P-crucify |
| | *mmo-f* | | | |
| | OBJ-3MS | | | |

| | | | | | |
|---|---|---|---|---|---|
| B | *ne-pʰ-nau=de* | *n-acp-3* | *=pe* | *uoh* | *a-u-aš-f* |
| | PRT-DEF.M-moment=yet | in-hour-three | = SE.M | and | PST-3P-crucify-3MS |

It was the third hour when (lit. 'and') they crucified him. ($^{SB}$Mk 15:25)

49 It should be noted that in Coptic, there seems to be no clitics that affect the phonotactics of the preceding word, by phonotactic reductions, stress movement, or a similar effect. A possible exception to this rule might be the subject element, which in older Coptic manuscripts triggers a double writing of the coda-vowel of monosyllabic words (e.g. *u-šaa=te* 'She is debauched', Prv 7:11 [Worrell]; for further examples see Polotsky 1971: 390–91). However, this effect is purely graphemic (marking the glottal stop only when in non-final position of the word); cf. Polotsky (1971: 232a).

(143c) The Ecclesiastes states that there is a season for everything:
*uoiš=pe m-mise uoiš=pe m-mu*
time= SE.M of-give birth time= SE.M of-die
*uoiš=pe n-tôkʲe uoiš=pe m-pôrk m-p-ent-a-u-tokʲ-f*
time= SE.M of-plant time= SE.M of-pluck OBJ-DEF.M-REL-PST-3P-plant-3MS
It is a time to give birth, and it is a time to die; it is a time to plant, and it is a time to pluck out what has been planted. ([S]Eccl 3:2)

(143d) The angel of the Lord says to Joshua: *You and those near you, sitting in front of you*:
*hen-rôme=ne n-ref-ci-meine*
IDF.P-man= SE.P of-AGT-say-sign
They are diviners! ([A]Zec 3:8 [Till])

(143e) The Lord calls for repentance and that people return to him:
*ce-u-naêt au n-šanhtêf=pe*
for-IDF.S-merciful and of-compassion= SE.M
For he is merciful and compassionate. ([A]Jl 2:13 [Malinine])

(143f) The gospel tells about Joseph of Arimathea:
*ntaf hô-f ne-u-mathêthês=pe nte-i(êsu)s*
3MS self-3MS PRT-IDF.S-disciple= SE.M of-N
He himself was also a disciple of Jesus. ([M]Mt 27:57 mae 1)

(143g) Jesus has addressed seven saints during their martyrdom, who draw strength from their faith; however:
*pi-hagios=de apa panuti nne-u-lômi=pe m-polemarkhês*
$DEF_2$.M-holy=yet apa N PRT-IDF.S-man= SE.M of-warrior
*e-u-atranos=pe hm-pe-f-sôma*
DEP-IDF.S-feeble= SE.M in-POSS-3MS-body
But the holy Apa Papnoute was a warrior, even though he was feeble of body. ([F]*Mart. Papnuti* [Bacot 307b, 16–20])

(143h) God tells Isaiah to write down his words for others to hear:
*ce-u-laos n-at-sôtem=pe hen-šêri n-lef-ci-kʲal=ne*
for-IDF.S-people of- NEG-hear= SE.M IDF.P-son of-AGT-speak-lie=SE.P
For they are a disobedient people and faithless sons. ([F]Is 30:9 [*BIFAO* 2, 176])

(143i) At night, people carried a dead man through the city gates:
*e-u-šêri mmauat-f=pe nte-te-f-mau*
DEP-IDF.S-son alone-3MS= SE.M of-POSS.F-3MS-mother
... who was his mother's only son. ([B]Lk 7:12)

(143j) The emperor will honour the warrior saints when they have reached adulthood:
*ce-han-ref-miši=ne ẖen-pi-polemos*
for-IDF.P-AGT-fight= SE.P in-$DEF_2$.M-war

...for they are warriors in the war.
([B]Theodore of Antioch, *On the Theodores* [*AM* II 91, 3–4])

But these examples show that the same does not necessarily apply to attributes: e.g. in 143a *n-sabbaton* 'of Sabbath' is not separated from *n-hou* 'the days'. Within the same dialect both patterns can be found; cf. the two Akhmimic and Fayyumic examples above with and without clitic intrusion. The same holds true e.g. for constructions with a bene-/malefactive adjunct containing a pronoun[50]:

(144a) Pondering the difference between the sexes, St Paul says concerning a man with long hair:
*u-sôš=na-f=pe*
IDF.S-shame=to-3FS= SE.M
It is a shame for him. ([S]1Cor 11:14)

(144b) Pondering the difference between the sexes, St Paul says concerning a woman with long hair:
*u-ôu=na-s=pe*
IDF.S-glory=to-3FS= SE.M
It is a glory for her. ([B]1Cor 11:15)

(144c) The proverbs describe the features of Wisdom:

| | | | | | | |
|---|---|---|---|---|---|---|
| *u-šên* | *n-ônẖ=te* | *n-uan* | *nim* | *et-ku* | *n-<h>tê-f* | *ara-s* |
| IDF.S-tree | of-life=SE.F | for-one | QU | REL-give | OBJ-heart-3MS | to-3FS |

She is a tree of life for all who trust in her. ([A]Prv 3:18)

The 'leftward movement' of the subject element, however, can also be observed in other phrasal constructions (for a Fayyumic example, see 143g):

(145a) The evil character of some sailors is said to be typical for people from Alexandria; it is then added:

| | | |
|---|---|---|
| *ne-hen-ebol=ne* | *hn-t-polis* | *etmmau* |
| PRT-IDF.P-out= SE.P | from-DEF.F-city | that |

They were from that city. ([S]*Gesios & Isodorus* [*ZÄS* 21: 144, 17–18])

50 Such close connection between the indirect or dative object and e.g. a verbal form that forms a barrier for cliticisation can also be observed elsewhere. E.g., in *eta-f-še=na-f=de* 'Yet, when he had gone...' ([B]Dioscorus of Alexandria, *On Macarius of Tkow* [Amélineau 115, 11 corr. after Moawad 2010: 307]) the expected position of the clitic *=de* is after the first word in the sentence, i.e. *etafše*.

(145b) In a description of the veiled structure housing the Ark of the Covenant:
*mnnsa-p-meh-snau=de* *n-katapetasma*
after-DEF.M-ORD-two=yet of-curtain
*te-skênê=te* *ete-ša-u-mute* *ero-f* *ce-n-et-uaab*
DEF.F-tabernacle= SE.F REL-AOR-3P-call to-3MS COMP-DEF.P-REL-clean
*n-n-et-uaab*
of-DEF.P-REL-clean
But behind the second curtain there is the tabernacle which is called holiest of all. ([S]Heb 9:3)

(145c) The gnostic Gospel of Philip explains the names of Jesus:
*I(êsu)s* *u-ran=pe* *e-f-hêp*
N IDF.S-name= SE.M DEP-3MS-hidden.STA
*pe-kh(risto)s* *u-ran=pe* *e-f-onh*
DEF.M-Christ IDF.S-name= SE.M DEP-3MS-open.STA
Jesus – it is a hidden name. Christ – it is an open name.
([L]*GospPh.* 56, 4–5 [Layton 152])

(145d) When Jesus passed through Jericho, a man named Zacchaeus climbed into a tree to see him:
*ce-ne-u-kuci=pe* *hen-te-f-maiê*
for-PRT-IDF.S-small= SE.M in-POSS.F-3MS-size
He was small of stature. ([B]Lk 19:3)

As in Demotic (see 133a–133c), the subject element, marked as singular, is occasionally followed in Coptic by further coordinated components of the predicate:

(146) The narrator explains his use of the designation 'the trees' for some bellicose generals:
*ete-pi-agios* *theodoros* *pi-anatoleos=pe* *nem-klaudios*
REL-DEF$_2$.M-holy N DEF$_2$.M-Anatolean=SE.M with-N
*nem-apatêr*
with-N
*nem-apa* *biktor* *nem-kuri* *iustos* *nem-eusebios* *nem-basilitês*
with-father N with-lord N with-N with-N
*nem-susinios* *nem-stephanos*
with-N with-N
*nem-apa* *polios* *nem-theodoros* *pi-stratêlatês*
with-Apa N with-N DEF$_2$.M-general
*nem-han-ke-mêš* *e-u-oš*
with-IDF.P-other-multitude DEP-3P-plenty.STA

That is Saint Theodore the Anatolian, Claudios, Apater, Apa Victor, lord Justus, Eusebios, Basilitês, Susinios, Stephan, Apa Polius, Theodore the General, and many others.

($^{B}$Theodore of Antioch, *On the Theodores* [*AM* II 98, 17–22])

Here *pi-agios theodoros pi-anatoleos* is followed by the subject element *pe*, itself followed by no less than eleven further coordinated parts of the predicate. Nevertheless, the subject element is marked for singular as if only the first NP was taken into account.

Besides noun phrases as in the examples above, the predicate position of Coptic bipartite nominal sentences with a subject element could also be occupied by a pronoun. Exx. 147a and 147b show absolute personal pronouns, 147b also an indefinite pronoun, 147c an interrogative pronoun, 147d a possessive pronoun (for the possessive construction in which only the possessed is pronominalized see ex. 276c below), and 147e a demonstrative pronoun:

(147a) Shenute addresses an opponent:

*eršan-t-bašôr* *aškak* *ebol=an* *ete-ntok=pe* *p-hmhal*
CND-DEF.F-fox cry_out out=NEG REL-2MS= SE.M DEF.M-servant
*m-p-mammônas*
of-DEF.M-mammon
*hn-hen-hrou* *e-u-oš* *ere-p-mui* *trre*
in-IDF.P-voice DEP-3P-cry DEP-DEF.M-lion be afraid
*ete-anok=pe* *p-hmhal* *m-pe-kh(risto)s*
REL-1S=SE.M DEF.M-servant of-DEF.M-Christ

Not because a fox barks – which means you, the servant of Mammon – aloud, is the lion – which means me, the servant of the Christ – afraid?

($^{S}$Shenute, *Not because a Fox Barks* [Ch 38, 35–45])

(147b) Theodore went to Egypt, looking for his father. He asked an old man begging for alms in the streets of Paphor whether he knew a certain John. He asked:

*iôannês* *nim* *ete-k-šini* *nsô-f* *iôannês* *pi-turôn=pe*
N WH REL-2MS-look after-3MS N DEF$_2$.M-recruit=SE.M
*šan* *ke-uai=pe*
or other-one=SE.M
*pece-p$^h$ê* *et$^h$-uab=na-f* *ce-aha* *nt$^h$of=pe*
said- DEF$_3$.M REL-clean=to-3MS COMP-yes 3MS=SE.M

'Which John are you looking for? Is it John the recruit or someone else?' The Saint replied: 'Yes, that is him!'

($^{B}$Theodore of Antioch, *On the Theodors* [*AM* II 124, 11–13])

(147c) The Pharisee at whose house Jesus is staying wonders why the latter serves a prostitute:

*ene-u-prophêtês=pe pai ne-f-na-ime ce-u=te*
CFT-IDF.S-prophet=COP.M DEM.M PRT-3MS-FUT-know COMP-WH= SE.F
*auô u-aš m-mine=te te-shime et-côh ero-f*
and IDF.S-WH of-sort=COP.F DEF.F-woman REL-touch OBJ-3MS
*ce-u-ref-r-nobe=te*
for-IDF.S-AGT-do-sin= SE.F
If this one were a prophet he would have known what she is and of what kind this woman who touches him is, for she is a sinner! ([S]Lk 7:39)

(147d) Shenute states that true believers express their amazement at the Lord's holy place:

*se-soun=gar ce-agathon nim nu-f=ne*
3P-know=for COMP-good QU POSS.P-3MS= SE.P
For they know that all good things, they are his!
([S]Shenute, *Continuing to Glorify the Lord* [L III 72, 7–8])

(147e) Frange urges the addressee to fetch an object for him:

*ce-tô-i=te*
for-POSS.F-1S=SE.F
... for it is mine. ([S]*O.Frange* #79, 13–14)

(147f) After Jesus healed a blind man, people asked whether this was not the man who had sat begging:

*haine pa-ce-u ce-pei=pe hen-kaue=[d]e*
some.P PT-say-3P COMP-DEM.M= SE.M IDF.P-others.P=yet
*ce-e-f-ine mma-f*
COMP-DEP-3MS-liken OBJ=3MS
*ntaf=[d]e ne-f-cô mma-s ce-anak=pe*
3MS=yet PRT-3MS-say OBJ-3FS COMP-1S= SE.M
Some said: 'It is this one!' Others said: 'He resembles him'. He himself insisted: 'It is me!' ([L]Jn 9:9)

As in Demotic, especially in the cleft sentence pattern, the infinitive can also be used in the predicate position. The following examples illustrate this with the so-called inflected infinitive which takes the form of an embedded sentence with *e-*:

(148a) A brother asked a wise man: 'What is humility of heart?' He answered:

*e-tre-k-r-p-petnanuf=pe n-n-et-r-pethou na-k*
to-INFL-2MS-do-DEF.M-good= SE.M to-DEF.P-REL-do-bad to-2MS
It is that you do good to those who mistreat you. ([S]*AP* Chaîne 30, 24)

(148b) Stephen asks Cyril whether the fact that Moses' body has not been found indicates that he has been raised from the dead. Cyril replies:

| *u-mnt-saie=te* | *e-coo-s* | *ce-ahe* |
|---|---|---|
| IDF.S-ABST-nice= SE.F | to-say-3FS | COMP-yes |

It would be nice to (be able to) say yes.
([S]Cyril of Alexandria, *Erotapokrisis* [Crum, pCheltenham 5, 29])

In addition, the simple infinitive can be used often expanded by an adverbial phrase. The construction is more often attested with the infinitive marked as indefinite rather than definite:

(149a) A brother asked Apa Allonios: 'What is contempt?' The old man replied:

| *p-kaa-k* | *mauaa-k=pe* | *hi-p-esêt* | *n-en-tbnoue* |
|---|---|---|---|
| DEF.S-put.INF-2MS | self-2MS= SE.M | on-DEF.M-floor | of-DEF.P-animals.P |

It is that you degrade yourself lower than animals. ([S]*AP* Chaîne 25, 10)

(149b) Scriptural instruction to priests says that an offering by a sinner brings atonement:

| *u-ti* | *gar=pe* | *ha-nobe* |
|---|---|---|
| IDF.S-give.INF | for=SE.M | under-sin |

... for it is a sin offering. ([S]Lev 5:12 [*Enchoria* 24: 84, a21])

(149c) In a homily on the miraculous birth of the Christ, it is stated that the Virgin did not originate in heaven:

| *e-ne-u-i* | *gar=te* | *ebol* | *hn-t-p[e]* |
|---|---|---|---|
| DEP-PRT-IDF.S-come | for=SE.F | out | in-DEF.F-heaven |

| *ne-s-na-šôpe=an* | *n-šu-r-špêre* | *mmo-s* | *n-tei-he* | *têr-s* |
|---|---|---|---|---|
| PRT-3FS-FUT-be=NEG | as-worthy-do-marvel | OBJ-3FS | in-DEM.F-way | all-3FS |

| *alla* | *u-i* | *ebol=te* | *hm-p-kah* |
|---|---|---|---|
| but | IDF.S-come | out=SE.F | in-DEF.M-earth |

| *u-cpo=te* | *n-t-he* | *n-uon* | *nim* | *u-ebol=te* |
|---|---|---|---|---|
| IDF.S-give birth=SE.F | in-DEF.F-way | of-each | QU | IDF.S-out=SE.F |

| *hm-p-sperma* | *n-dauid* |
|---|---|
| in-DEF.M-seed | of-N |

For had she come out of heaven, she would not have been so admirable. Instead, she is one out of earth. She is one born like everyone and one out of the seed of David.
([S]*Homily on Christ's Birth* [Elanskaya 367b, 22–33][51])

51 Following Schenke's reading and analysis (1997/98: 169–70).

(149d) The Tripartite Tractate explains that the Father is not like a solitary individual and adds:
*ê mman n-eš n-he u-iôt=pe*
or not in-what of-way IDF.S-father=SE.M
Otherwise, how could he be a father? (ᴸ*Tri. Trac.* 51, 12–13 [*NHS* 22, 192])

(149e) The Tripartite Tractate says about the Father that he is without beginning and without end and adds:
*ce-u-monon u-at-hae=pe*
for-NEG-only IDF.S-un-end=SE.M
*etbe-pei u-at-mu=pe abalce-u-at-cpa-f=pe*
because-DEM.M IDF.S-un-die=SE.M because-IDF.S-un-begot-3MS=SE.M
*alla u-at-rike=an=pe m-p-et-f-šoop mma-f*
but IDF.S-un-bend=NEG=SE.M in-DEF.M-REL-3MS-be.STA in-3MS
*anêhe tmet*
eternity entirety
*auô p-ete-nta-f=pe auô p-et-f-smant*
and DEF.M-REL-with-3MS=SE.M and DEF.M-REL-3MS-establish.STA
*mma-f pe*
in-3MS SE.M
*auô p-et-f-oi n-nokʲ mma-f pe*
and DEF.M-REL-3MS-be.STA as-great in-3MS SE.M
Not only is he without end – He is immortal for this reason, that he is unbegotten – but he is also invariable in his eternal existence, in his identity, in that by which he is established and in that by which he is great. (ᴸ*Tri. Trac.* 52, 7–14 [*NHS* 22, 193–195])

If a complete clause serves as the predicate, it usually has to be introduced by *ce* or *cekas* in the southern and *hina* in the northern dialects (for the B version with deletion of the subject element see 155c); however, examples can also be found without any introductory particle[52]:

(150a) Paul argues that he has to preach the Gospel and asks: *What then is my reward?*
*cekaas=pe e-i-euaggelize ta-ka-p-euaggelion n-ueš*
so_that=SE.M DEP-1S-preach CNJ.1S-give-DEF.M-gospel with-lack
*n-co ebol ero-f*
of-spend out to-3MS
*e-tm-tra-ire m-pa-htor hm-p-euaggelion*
to-AUX.NEG-INFL.1S-do as-POSS.M.1S-accord in-DEF.M-gospel

52 The same phenomenon occurs also in tripartite constructions, see 1.3.2.3.

So that, as I preach, I may offer the Gospel free of charge, and so not make use of the Gospel on my own agreement. ($^{S}$1Cor 9:18)

(150b) A monk was asked 'What is humility?' He answered:
*eršan-pe-k-son* *r-nobe* *ero-k=pe* *n-g-kô* *na-f*
CND-POSS.M-2MS-brother do-sin to-2MS= SE.M CNJ-2MS-put for-3MS
*ebol* *mpate-f-metanoi*
out NCO-3MS-repent
It is that, if your brother sins against you, you forgive him before he repents. ($^{S}$*AP* Chaîne 30, 14–15)

Coptic allows also nominalised phrasal structures such as *u-/hen-ebol* X 'a/some from X' (exx. 151a–c) or *hn-aš n-he* 'of what manner' (ex. 151d) in the predicate position:

(151a) The Jews interrogated a man cured of blindness by Jesus and claimed:
*anan* *tn-saune* *[c]e-a-p-nute* *sece* *mn-[mô]usês*
1P 1P-know COMP-PST-DEF.M-god speak with-N
*pei=de* *ntaf* *tn-saune=en* *ce-u-abal* *to=pe*
DEM.M=yet 3MS 1P-know=NEG COMP-IDF.S-out where= SE.M
We know that God spoke to Moses; but this one, we do not know where he is from. ($^{L}$Jn 9:29)

(151b) The high priests and the Pharisees answer Jesus' question on the origins of John's baptism:
*ten-emi=an* *ce-u-ebol* *$t^{h}$ôn=pe*
1P-know=NEG COMP-IDF.S-out where=SE.M
We do not know where it is from. ($^{B}$Lk 20:7)

(151c) A presbyter named Theodore addresses the patriarch John with the question:
*pa-iôt* *ara* *p-nibe* *n-ônh* *et-šoop* *hm-p-rôme*
POSS.M.1S-father IR DEF.M-breath of-life REL-be.STA in-DEF.M-man
*u-ebol=pe* *hn-u-pn(eum)a* *e-f-uaab*
IDF.S-out=SE.M in-IDF.S-spirit DEP-3MS-pure.STA
My father, the living breath that is inside man, is it from a holy Ghost? ($^{S}$*Questions of Theodore* [van Lantschoot 15, 7–8])

(151d) As Jesus came out of the temple, one of his disciples said:
*p-sah* *a-nau* *e-nei-ône* *ce-hen-aš*
DEF.M-teacher IMP-see OBJ-DEM.P-stone COMP-IDF.P-what
*n-he=ne* *mn-nei-ke-kôt*
of-way=SE.P CNJ-DEM.P-other-building
Master, see the stones and what size they are, and of what sort even these buildings are. ($^{S}$Mk 13:1)

The predication expressed in Coptic bipartite nominal sentences with a subject element can also be modified by attributive adverbs:

(152a) Lady Poemenia travelled with a large entourage including bishops and priests:
*ce-u-orthodoksos=te* *mmate*
for-IDF.S-orthodox=SE.F very
... for she was very orthodox. ($^{S}$*Life of John of Lykopolis* [*AnBoll* 87, 193, 2–3])

(152b) It was a time of heretics:
*p-hagios=de* *aleksandros* *e-ne-u-asteios=pe* *n-u-kui*
DEF.M-holy=yet N DEP-PRT-IDF.S-weak= SE.M for-IDF.S-little
*e-nere-athanasios* *šoop* *[n]a-f* *n-tapro*
DEP-PRT-N be.STA for-3MS as-mouth
Yet when St Alexander was a weak for a while, Athanasius was speaking for him. ($^{S}$Cyril, *In Athanasium* [Orlandi, *Testi copti*, 19, 8–10])

(152c) Frange stresses in a letter the urgency of the delivery of a pricker saying:
*ce-te-khr[i]a=te* *emate*
for-DEF.F-need=SE.F very
... for it is very much needed. ($^{S}$*O.Frange* #44, x+9)

(152d) Travelling with an angel, Sophonias (?) reached a great sea of an altogether unusual sort:
*a-i-k$^{j}$nt-s* *u-thalassa* *n-kôht=te* *têr-s* *n-t-ḫe*
PST-1S-find-3FS IDF.S-sea of-fire=SE.F all-3FS in-DEF.F-way
*n-u-borboros*
of-IDF.S-mud
*e-s-tik-seete* *abal* *e-našô-f* *e-ne-s-haime* *cero*
DEP-3FS-throw-fire out DEP-be many-3MS DEP-POSS.P-3FS-wave glow
*n-then* *mn-u-lamceetp*
of-sulphur with-IDF.S-tar
I found that it was a whole sea of fire like a mire, throwing up much fire and its waves glowing of sulphur and tar.
($^{A}$*ApSoph.*$^{?}$ [Steindorff, *Apocalypse des Elias* 46 7, 8–12])

(152e) Isaac asks his father what and where is the offering that they are going to give to God and concludes:
*arêu* *anok=pe*
perhaps 1S= SE.M
Perhaps it is me. ($^{B}$Amphilochus of Iconium, *De Abraham* [Datema 287, 204])

(152f) Shenute's mother tells the shepherd with whom her son is to stay: *Look, I will give you my son but send him back to me at the evening each day*:
*ce-u-šêri* *mmauat-f=nê-i=pe* *e-[i-r]aši* *e-p$^{h}$-(nu)ti* *nema-f*
for-IDF.S-son self-3MS=to-1S=SE.M REL-1S-rejoice to-DEF.M-god with-3MS

*m-pi-ehou* *nem-pi-ecôrh*
in-DEF$_2$.M-day CON-DEF$_2$.M-night
... for he is my only son over whom I rejoice day and night in God.
(ᴮ*V. Shenute* [Leipoldt 8, 22–23])

Occasionally, the syntactic position of the extension might reflect an attempt by a translator to retain the Greek word or phrase order, sometimes with questionable grammatical success:

(153) The prologue of the Gospel of John tells:
F *nhêt-f* *p-ônh=pe*
in-3MS DEF.M-life=SE.M
S *hrai* *nhêt-f=pe* *p-ônh*
up in-3MS=SE.M DEF.M-life
In him was the life. (Jn 1:4 [ᶠ*AfP* 34:38] vs. [ˢQuecke])

Although in the Fayyumic version of the above example only the prepositional phrase is fronted to copy the Greek ἐν αὐτῷ ζωὴ ἦν, in the Sahidic version, the subject element was moved into the second position of the sentence, making it look like a tripartite pattern with a prepositional phrase in first position.

If a bipartite nominal sentence was introduced by the presentative particle *is* (with nouns) or *is-hêê-te/-pe* (with pronouns) 'lo, behold', the subject element was omitted:

(154a) The philosopher Diogenes saw a young girl being taught to write and remarks:
*is* *u-sêbe* *e-u-côr* *mmo-s*
PTC IDF.S-sword REL-3P-sharpen OBJ-3FS
Look, (it is) a sword that is being sharpened.
(ˢ*Sayings of Pagan Philosophers* [Till 166, 12–13])

(154b) When Thecla's supposed fiancé entered the house, her mother told him about her daughter:
*is* *šamnt=gar* *n-hou* *mn-šamte* *n-ušê*
PTC three=for of-day.M and-three of-night.F
*(e)-mpe-thekla* *tôôn* *abal* *hm-p-šušt* *ute* *a-uôm*
DEP-NEG.PST-N rise out in-DEF.M-window nor to-eat
*ute* *a-su*
not to-drink
Look, (it is) three days and three nights while Thecla has not risen from the window to eat or to drink. (ᴸ*Acta Pauli* [Schmidt 7* 10, 20–24])

(154c) Jesus and the disciples entered a city:
*uoh* *is* *u-rômi* *e-f-meh* *n-seht*
and PTC IDF.S-week REL-3MS-fill.STA with-leprosy
And lo, there (was) a leper. (ᴮLk 5:12)

(153d) Juvenal, the patriarch of Jerusalem, returns with soldiers to his city from Constantinople. Whilst the crowd celebrates the Eucharist at the shrine of the Virgin, the soldiers surround the shrine. As Juvenal shouts that his opponent Paul should be brought out, the latter appears and says:
*ishêête anok*
PTC 1S
Look, I (am here). ($^{SF}$Dioscorus of Alexandria, *On Macarius of Tkow* §7.6 [Johnson 50a, 24–25])

(154g) The Lord tells Ananias to go to a certain street in Damascus and ask for the house of a man from Tarsus named Saul:
*hipe=gar ntaf e-f-proseukhe*
lo=for 3MS DEP-3MS-pray
... for lo, he is praying there. ($^{M}$Acts 9:11)

It should be noted that this sort of deletion only applies to the subject element of bipartite structures, not to the copula of tripartite constructions (see 1.3.2.3). A similar omission occurs with some modal and adjunctive auxiliary constructions (Müller and Uljas 2016; Müller 2014). Bohairic licenses it in affirmative clauses if the subject refers anaphorically to a determiner or an anteposed expression (Shisha-Halevy 1981: 329).[53] This is especially common with the relative construction *ete* + POSS-AGR 'which is his/etc.':

(155a) Having appointed the twelve disciples, Jesus arrived to a house where a large group had gathered:
*uoh et-a-u-sôtem nce-nê ete-nu-f ø a-u-i*
and REL-PST-3P-hear PTC-DEF$_3$.P REL-POSS.P-3MS ø PST-3P-go
*ebol e-amoni mmo-f*
out to-fetch OBJ-3MS
And when those who belonged to him heard (it), they came out to fetch him. ($^{B}$Mk 3:21)

(155b) The apostle urges the Christians of Corinth not to mingle with a fellow Christian of the following kind:
*ešôp e-uon uai e-u-ti-ran ero-f ce-son*
CND DEP-be one DEP-3P-give-name OBJ-3MS COMP-brother
*e-u-pornos ø ie u-ref-ci n-cons ie*
DEP-IDF.S-adulterer ø or IDF.S-AGT-take OBJ-wrath or
*u-ref-šamše-idôlon*
IDF.S-AGT-worship-idol

53 Examples of *pe*-deletion in Sahidic texts have been collected by Kahle 1954: 189 sub 157A. He regards them as 'in most, if not all, cases [...] probably due to the carelessness of the scribe'.

*ie u-ref-hôuš ø ie u-ref-t$^{h}$ihi ie u-ref-hôlem*
or IDF.S-AGT-curse ø or IDF.S-AGT-be drunk or IDF.S-AGT-seize
If there is someone who is called a brother but who is a fornicator, or violent, or an idolator, or a reviler, or a drunkard, or a thief... ([B]1Cor 5:11)

(155c) Paul argues that he has to preach the Gospel and asks: *What is then my reward?*
*hina ø e-i-hi-še-nufi nta-k$^{h}$a-pi-euaggelion acne-tapanê*
so that ø ST-1S-in-case-good CNJ.1S-give-DEF$_2$.M-gospel without-cost
*e-štem-er-khrasthe m-pai-er-šiši ḫen-pi-euaggelion*
to-NEG-do-use much OBJ-DEM.M-use-power in-DEF$_2$.M-gospel
So that, as I preach, I may offer the Gospel free of charge, and so not make use of the Gospel on my own accord. ([B]1Cor 9:18)

(155d) If a person has a skin disease, his clothes must be torn and his hair unbound. He has to cover his moustache and cry 'Unclean! Unclean!':
*n-ni-ehou têr-u ete-pi-c$^{h}$oh hiôt-f e-u-akathartos ø*
in-DEF$_2$.P-days.P all-3P REL-DEF$_2$.M-hurt upon-3MS DEP-IDF.S-unclean ø
As long as he has this affliction, he is unclean. ([B]Lev 13:46)

(155e) Appalled by their attitude towards idolatry, St George says to Dadianos and the seventy rulers:
*mper-co-s e-ne-ete-han-nuti=an=ne ce-nuti ø*
NEG.IMP-say-3FS to-DEF.P-REL-IDF.P-god=NEG=SE.P COMP-god ø
Do not call gods things that are not gods. ([B]*Mart. George* [*AM* II 272, 18–19])

This last example could be also understood as the normal quoting-pattern in which the name of someone or something is introduced simply as *ce*-NAME.

## 1.3 Tripartite nominal sentences

### 1.3.1 Earlier Egyptian

The third major syntactic type of Egyptian nominal sentences is the tripartite pattern in which the predication between two nominals is mediated by a copula:

S > [NP COP NP]

In Earlier Egyptian, the copula is the same element *=pw* which in bipartite sentences serves as subject, but here has the role of a semantically empty, purely functional linking expression between the subject and the predicate. As in bipartite nominal sentences without a connecting element, the expressions linked by *=pw* can be nouns, pronouns, infinitives, or relative clauses, as in the below examples combining these expressions with others of the same kind:

(156a) The soul says:
*pḫr-t=pw* *ʿnḫ*
cycle-F=COP life
Life is a cycle. (Man and Ba 20–21)

(156b) The deceased proclaims his identity with the eye of Horus:
*ink=pw=s(y)* *stt=pw=(w)i*
1S=COP=2FS 2FS=COP=1S
I am it, and it is me. (CT VII 157c)

(156c) Senwosret III expresses his appreciation of warlike qualities:
*qnt=pw* *ꜣd* *ḫst=pw* *ḫmḫt*
attack.INF=COP brave.INF timid.INF=COP retreat.INF
To attack is to be brave; to retreat is to be timid. (Berlin 1157, 8)

(156d) The king says that his proposed building-work is an extension of the Creation:
*irr-t=pw* *wnn-t*
do.PIP-F=COP exist.PIA-F
What is done is what exists. (Berlin Leather Roll I, 19)

(156e) The deceased says to the goddess Sekhmet:
*mrr-t-ṯ=pw* *irr-t-ṯ* *m-nṯr-w*
desire.REL-F-2FS=COP do.REL-F-2FS in-god-P
What you desire is what you do among gods. (CT VI 273b)

The copula *=pw* is almost universally written in this way, although in the Pyramid Texts and the Coffin Texts, there are examples showing a reduced orthography *=p(w)*:

(157a) The king is a manifest god:
*N=p(w)* *ḏḥwty* *ḥr(y)tp* *nwt* *N=pw* *inpw* *ḥr(y)tp* *pr*
N=COP N ruler N N=COP N ruler house
King N is Thoth, ruler of Nut; king N is Anubis, ruler of the house. (PT 2150c)

(157b) The king is almighty:
W: *N=p(w)* *nb* *ḥtp-t*
T: *N=pw* *nb* *ḥtp-t*
N=COP lord offering-F
King N is the lord of offerings. (PT 399c)

In tripartite sentences *=pw* usually cliticises to the first prosodic unit (exx. 158a–158b), but when the first NP in such a construction was a full clause – a state of affairs attested only with relative forms – the copula was placed after the subject of the subordinate clause also when it was a noun (exx. 158c–158e):

(158a) Ptahhetep notes of female wellbeing:
*pẖr-t=pw* *n-t-ḥˁ-s* *mrḥ-t*
remedy-F=COP of-F-body-3FS oil-F
The remedy of her members is oil. (Ptahhetep 328)

(158b) Mentuhetep makes a general point on ethics:
*mnw=pw* *n(-y)-s* *nfrw-f*
monument=COP of[-M]-man goodness-3MS
The monument of a man is his goodness. (UCL 14333, 16)

(158c) King Pepi II makes a general point about the observance of his order:
*mrr-t* *nfrkꜣrˁ=pw* *ỉrt* *ḫt* *ḫft-md-t*
love.REL.IMPF-F N=COP do.INF thing according_to-word-F
*n-t-wḏ=pn*
of-F-decree=DEM.M
What Neferkara desires is acting according to the letter of this decree.
(*Urk.* I 283, 11)

(158d) Senwosret III profiles himself as a man of strong will and action:
*kꜣꜣ-t* *ỉb-ỉ=pw* *ḫpr-t* *m-ˁ-ỉ*
plan.REL.IMPF-F heart-1S=COP happen.IPP-F through-hand-1S
What my mind plans is what comes about through my action.
(Berlin 1157, 5–6)

(158e) Ptahhetep says:
*wḏ-t* *nṯr=pw* *ḫpr-t*
order.REL-F god=COP happen.PIA-F
What god orders is what comes about. (Ptahhetep 116)

Given its stable writing and apparently high degree of grammaticalisation, this function of *pw* could be expected to be a more recent diachronic development than its subject-indexing role in bipartite sentences,[54] although the first example of what is apparently a fully-fledged tripartite *pw*-sentence occurs already in the Fourth Dynasty personal name *kꜣ(-ỉ)=p(w)-nzw* ‘My-*ka*-is-the-king’.[55] There are examples from other languages of demonstratives and third-person pronouns developing into copulas (these are two actually separate processes, see Diessel 2000: 209–11), and it is widely assumed that the tripartite nominal sentence is originally an extension of the bipartite *pw*-sentence. It may have resulted from a reanalysis of an erstwhile appositional third nominal element following a bipartite sentence as a component part of it. That is, a construction such as [*rmṯ=pw*]

54 Indeed, this assumption is implicit in all the numerous descriptions of tripartite nominal sentences that treat them as ‘extensions’ of bipartite patterns (e.g. Edel 1955/64: §965).
55 *Urk.* I 155, 6; cf. Schweitzer (2005: 191). The writing displays honorific anteposition of the word *nzw*.

[*sš*] ‘This is man, (namely) scribe’ (with *=pw* understood as cataphoric) might have undergone re-bracketing as [*rmṯ*]*=pw* [*sš*], with *sš* now corresponding to the subject proper and *=pw* conveying the predicative relation between *rmṯ* and *sš*.[56] However, although the question of differentiating between the grammatical roles in nominal sentences is extremely complex and will be discussed in detail in 3.1.1 and 3.1.2, it can already be noted here that in tripartite constructions the first NP is not necessarily the predicate, as this hypothesis would seem to suggest. Indeed, the reverse order subject–predicate is encountered with some frequency already in the earliest texts and, in fact, seems to be the predominant one in the Pyramid Texts. For this order, a development parallel to that of predicate–subject could be postulated. *=pw* might have been understood as cataphorically anticipating the semantic predicate, so that a sentence such as [*rmṯ=pw*] [*sš*] could have also meant alternatively ‘Man is this: scribe’.[57] The problem with both hypotheses is that no unambiguous instance of cataphoric *=pw* seems to be documented.[58] Ultimately, one must acknowledge that virtually nothing is known about the historical origin of the tripartite nominal sentence, even though it seems that a different mechanism is required for the derivation of the two sequences S–P and P–S. That said, seeing that tripartite nominal sentences often occur without any discernible difference in meaning as variants of bipartite sentences without *=pw* and that in texts surviving in several variants the tripartite pattern is usually found in later sources, the latter does indeed seem to represent a diachronically more recent development of the bipartite construction:

(159a) The deceased stresses his protected status:

| | | | | |
|---|---|---|---|---|
| B4Bo: | *mk-t* | *N=tn* | *mk-t* | *rꜥ* |
| | protection-F | N=DEM.F | protection-F | N |
| B12C & al: | *mk-t-i=pw* | *mk-t* | *rꜥ* | |
| | protection-F-1S=COP | protection-F | N | |

This N’s/My protection is the protection of Ra. (CT VII 279d–80a)

56 This is the most common analysis expressed e.g. by Schenkel (1984: 167).

57 A third conceivable alternative might involve a ‘topicalised’ noun followed by an anaphoric demonstrative *=pw* functioning as the subject of its own clause [*rmṯ*] [*=pw sš*] ‘man, he is scribe’ reanalysed as ‘man is scribe’. Although this development is attested in other languages and sometimes argued to be standard (e.g. Diessel 2000: 210), it can hardly have taken place in Egyptian since it presupposes a *p*-initial position for the demonstrative subject in the original construction, a role that the clitic *=pw* cannot have had.

58 An example such as CT II 383c/S2P showing *išst=pw ꜣḫ=pw* (WH=SE spirit=DEM.M) could be understood as meaning ‘Who is he, (namely) this spirit?’, with a bipartite sentence with a cataphoric *=pw* + co-referential appositional NP (i.e. [*išst=pw*$_1$] *ꜣḫ=pw*$_1$). However, nothing prevents it being read simply as a tripartite sentence [*išst*]*=pw* [*ꜣḫ=pw*] ‘Who is this spirit?’.

(159b) In a spell describing the means of the king's resurrection:

W: *zy* *zp-t(y)-f(y)* *N* *zp-t(y)-f(y)*
WH survive.REL-FUT-AGR N survive.REL-FUT-AGR

T: *zy=pw* *zp-t(y)-f(y)* *N=pw* *zp-t(y)-f(y)*
WH=COP survive.REL-FUT-AGR N=COP survive.REL-FUT-AGR

Who is the one who will survive? King N is the one who will survive. (PT 438c)

(159c) In a gloss explaining a term of a mythical text:

*ptr=rf* *sš-wy* *wr-wy* *ꜥꜣ-wy*
WH=PTC pool-DU great-DU mighty-DU

*sy=ty=pw* *sš-wy* *wr-wy* *ꜥꜣ-wy*
WH=PTC=COP pool-DU great-DU mighty-DU

What are the two great and mighty bird-pools? (CT IV 217a/M8C vs. CT IV 213c/BH1Br)

(159d) The opening phrase in two Letters to Dead:

Qaw Bowl, inside, 2: *ṯnwrꜣ* *nw*
reminder DEM.M

Cairo Linen, 2: *ṯnwrꜣ=pw* *nw*
reminder=COP DEM.M

This is a reminder... (the content follows)

(159e) The deceased says:

L1Li: *ink* *wsir*
1S N

B2L: *ink=pw* *wsir*
1S=COP N

I am Osiris. (CT III 261d)

(159f) The deceased proclaims his detestation of faeces:

B3L: *bw-t-i* *wsš-t* *n* *swri-i*
abomination-F-1S urine-F NEG drink.PROSP-1S

B1L: *bw-t-i=pw* *wsš-t* *n* *swri-i*
abomination-F-1S=COP urine-F NEG drink.PROSP-1S

Urine is an abomination of mine; I will not drink (it). (CT III 201e)

Once established, the tripartite nominal sentence became the usual construction to encode a predication between combinations of nouns, pronouns, infinitives, and relative clauses (see Junge 1981: 456–60):

(160a) Intef assures his audience of the truthfulness of his self-presentation:

*biꜣ-t-i=pw* *nꜣ* *m-wnmꜣꜥ*
character-F-1S=COP DEM.M in-reality

This was truly characteristic of me. (*noun + dem. pron.*) (*Urk.* IV 973, 10)

(160b) The king's identity with a divinity is declared:
*N=pw=ṯw* *ṯwt=pw* *N*
N=COP=2MS 2MS=COP N
King N is you; you are King N. (*noun + pers. pron., pers. pron. + noun*)
(PT 703b/TP)

(160c) The deceased says:
*bw-t-ỉ=pw* *ꜥq* *r-nm-t* *nṯr*
abomination-F-1S=COP enter.INF to-execution place-F god
My abomination is to enter the god's execution-place. (*noun + inf.*)
(CT V 59c)

(160d) Senwosret III profiles the worst failure in royal office:
*ḥm=pw* *mꜣꜥ* *ꜣr-w* *ḥr-tꜣš-f*
coward=COP real drive-PPP on-border-3MS
But he who is driven from his border is a real coward. (*noun + part.*)
(Berlin 1157, 4–5)

(160e) A question before a gloss clarifying an expression in a religious text:
*sy=ty=pw* *nṯr=pn* *ꜥꜣ*
WH=PTC=COP god=DEM.M great
Who, then, is this great god? (*int. pron. + noun*) (CT IV 215b/BH1Br)

(160f) In a broken context[59]:
*[ỉ]šst=pw=ḥm* *nn* *ỉrr-w-ṯn*
WH=COP=PTC DEM.M do.REL-M-2P
What is this that you do? (*int. pron. + dem. pron.*)
(*HP* III pl. 7, Str. Ba v° 6)

(160g) The deceased asks helplessly:
*ỉšst=pw=(w)ỉ=r-ỉ* *ỉrỉ-ỉ* *m*
WH=COP=1S=PTC-1S do-1S WH
What am I? What shall I do? (*int. pron. + pers. pron.*) (CT VII 102g–h)

(160h) In a broken context:
*ỉšst=pw* *mꜣ-t-n-k* *ỉm*
WH=COP see.REL-F-PST-2MS there
What is it that you saw there? (*int. pron. + rel. cl.*) (CT VII 212h/pGard.II)

(160i) A note following the diagnosis in a medical text:
*nw=pw* *ỉꜣ-t* *ꜥ-t*
DEM=COP injury-F member-F
This is the injury of the member. (*dem. pron. + noun*) (pEbers 108, 12–13)

59 The suffix *-ṯn* does not appear in the original publication, but only in Edel (1955/64: §1007).

(160j) The man equates his soul with a praise singer who moves from place to place and adds:
*pɜ=ìs=pw      prr*
DEM.M=PTC=COP  go.PIA
This is the one who goes. (*dem. pron. + rel. cl.*)  (Man and Ba 17)

(160k) Osiris says to Horus:
*ìnk=pw=ḥm   ìt-k*
1S=COP=PTC   father-2MS
I am indeed your father. (*pers. pron. + noun*)  (CT IV 88b)

(160l) The deceased says that gods take care of providing his boat with all the necessary equipment:
*ntsn=pw    šdd-w=n(-ì)=sn         m-šnꜥ*
3P=COP      take.PIA-P=to[-1S]=3P  from-storehouse
They are the ones who take them for me from the storehouse. (*pers. pron. + rel. cl.*)  (CT V 150c)

(160m) The peasant, finding his path blocked, tries to avoid the obstacle:
*prt=pw              ìrì-n-f        r-ḥrw*
go forth.INF=COP     do.REL-PST-3MS to-high
So, he went on higher (lit. 'to go forth is what he did'). (*inf. + rel. cl.*)
(Peas B1, 35)

(160n) An answer to a mathematical problem:
*ḫpr-t=ìm=pw              3*
happen.PIA-F=there=COP    3
What results from it is 3. (*rel. cl. + noun/numeral*)  (pUC 32162 1, 11)

(160o) It is said of the role of certain divinities:
*ìr-t-sn=p(w)       m-dwɜ-t          dwɜw        nṯr=pn         ꜥɜ*
do.REL-F-3P=COP    in-underworld-F  praise-INF  god=DEM.M      great
What they do in the underworld is praise this great god. (*rel. cl. + inf.*)
(Amduat, h12, upper reg./Th III, 8)

Note the cliticisation of the adverb *ìm* 'there' before *=pw* in ex. 160n. The construction in 160m is favoured in classical Middle Kingdom literature for the narrative past. In terms of information structure, it represents (together with ex. 160h) the Earlier Egyptian equivalent of the non-reversed pseudo-cleft constructions of modern Western languages (see 3.1.4). In rare instances, the third position in the construction may be occupied by a finite subject complement clause:

(161a) A sarcastic remark by a man to his adversary amidst a boat-fight:
*ìšst=pw    hɜɜ-k          ḥr-ɜḥ-t*
WH=COP      descend-2MS    on-field-F
Why are you going down onto the field?  (*Reden und Rufe* 58)

(161b) The sage laments that the divine does not accept offerings of men:
*ind=is=pw* *dd-tn=n-f*
misery=PTC=COP give-2P=to-3MS
Your offering to him is a miserable thing. (Ipuwer 5, 9)

As can be seen from the above examples, both in bipartite sentences without a connecting element and in tripartite constructions, the combined nominals can, in principle, occur in multiple orders, the gaps in the data usually resulting from the semantic unlikelihood of certain combinations as well as from idiomatic conventions whose precise nature is difficult to discern.[60] Nevertheless, the order of the elements highlights the general question of the semantic-pragmatic meaning of variations in the linear order of the constituents in the nominal sentence, which often requires an explanation that takes into account both diachrony and semantic-pragmatics. For example, in the great majority of cases absolute personal pronouns occupy the first position in tripartite nominal sentences. Examples contradicting this rule become common only in the Eighteenth Dynasty:

(162a) The deceased says of a divinity and of himself[61]:
*ntf=pw* *ink* *ṯsp*ẖ*r*
3MS=COP 1S vice versa
He is me and vice versa (compare ex. 115a) (BD 64/*Nu* pl. 60, 6)

(162b) The king says about Amun:
*it-i=pw* *ntf*
father-1S=COP 3MS
He is my father. (*Urk.* IV 156, 17)

(162c) King Amenhotep III is characterised:
*rʿ=pw* *ntf*
N=COP 3MS
He is Ra. (*Urk.* IV 1822, 8)

This is probably the symptom of changes in the linear order of absolute pronouns rather than a major revision of the syntax of the tripartite nominal sentence. However, similar examples occur occasionally already in the Pyramid Texts:

---

**60** Once again, this equals such unlikely cases like establishing a predicative relation between an infinitive and a personal pronoun.

**61** 'Vice versa' appears to mean that one should add the reverse version *ink=pw ntk* to what is actually written. This is, in fact, how this passage was cited by Sethe (1916: 97 n.1; cf. Gundacker 2010: 50 n.35). The same passage appears as *ntf=pw ink=pw* in the papyrus of Nebseni (pBM 9900), where it was apparently understood as a pair of bipartite sentences.

(163) A divine being is invoked and told:

| | | | | |
|---|---|---|---|---|
| T/P: | *N=pw=ṯw* | *ṯwt=pw* | *N* | |
| | N=COP=2MS | 2MS=COP | N | |
| N: | *ṯwt=pw* | *N* | *N=pw* | *ṯwt* |
| | 2MS=COP | N | N=COP | 2MS |

King N is you, and you are King N/You are King N, and King N is you.
(PT 703b)

Here, the editor of variant N not only turned around the order of the earlier versions, but in doing so also tampered with the encoding of the pronouns. The first half of his revised version, *ṯwt=pw N*, seems a perfectly legitimate inversion of *N=pw=ṯw*, but for the inversion of the former one might have expected *N=pw=ṯw* as in T/P. However, the N-version writes instead *N=pw ṯwt*, with an absolute pronoun in the third position after *=pw*. Unless the latter variant is a textual corruption (cf. Gilula 1976: 160 n.2 and Sethe 1935–39: 3, 291), this phenomenon would seem to require a semantic or pragmatic explanation. This complex topic will be addressed after the description of the clausal syntax of the nominal sentence patterns.

Tripartite nominal sentences of the sort described above remained in active use until the Eighteenth Dynasty. After this time, changes in the morpho-syntax of its components begin to appear. Early New Kingdom examples such as the following seem to reflect a revision of the basics of the sentence structure:

(164) An interim result in a calculation:

| | | | | |
|---|---|---|---|---|
| *it-šmꜥ* | *ḥqꜣ-t* | *11* | *nꜣ-iri* | *m-ḥnq-t* |
| coarse barley | heqat-F | 11 | DEM.M-do.PPP | as-beer-F |

11 heqat-measures of coarse barley is what is made into beer.
(pMoscow math. n.9, 10–11)

Here, *=pw* is conspicuous by its absence, and instead of the 'classical' *ir-t* 'what has been made', the relative construction shows the analytic form *nꜣ-iri*. It appears that the article *nꜣ* was being reinterpreted as serving the double role as determiner of the following noun and as copula. Examples such as this announce the beginning of the demise of the tripartite nominal sentence and represent harbingers of the rise of bipartite nominal sentences with directly juxtaposed nominals in Late Egyptian (see 1.1.2.1).

## 1.3.2 Later Egyptian

### 1.3.2.1 Late Egyptian

Mirroring the situation in bipartite sentences, Late Egyptian tripartite nominal sentences replace the earlier copula *=pw* by a new series *pꜣy/tꜣy/nꜣy* agreeing in gender (in the singular) and number with one of the nominals. It has been observed in 1.1.2.1. that Late Egyptian favours the direct juxtaposition NP–NP for the expression of a predicative relation between two nominals. By contrast, examples of tripartite constructions are rare and often explicable as bipartite patterns with extensions (cf. Junge 2008: 129):

(165a) Confronted with another man's accusation against him in court, a slave exclaims:
*ꜥḏꜣ* *pꜣy* *ḏd-f=nb*
[wrong]$_P$ COP.M [say.REL-3MS=QU]$_S$
All that he said is wrong. (*KRI* VI 798, 3)

(165b) The ruler of Byblos answers to Wenamun's suggestion to have a stela with an Egyptian inscription erected for himself:
*mtr-t* *ꜥꜣ-t* *n-md-t* *tꜣy* *ḏd-k=n-ỉ*
[testimony-F great-F of-speech-F]$_S$ COP.F [say.REL-2MS=to-1S]$_P$
What you have told me is a remarkable example of oration. (*LES* 73, 5–6)

(165c) A bull is led to the king who is very pleased and offers to him:
*bỉꜣ-t* *ꜥꜣ-t* *tꜣy* *ḫpr-ṯ*
[marvel-F great-F]$_S$ COP.F [happen.PPA-F]$_P$
What has happened is a great marvel. (*LES* 25, 2–3)

(165d) In a hymn to Ramesses VI even animals such as fowl and fish rejoice the king's dominion and say:
*nꜣ-ꜥꜣ-w* *nꜣy* *ḫpr-t=n-n*
[DEF.P-great-P]$_S$ COP.P [happen.PPA-F=to-1P]$_P$
What has happened to us are the momentous things: ....
(pTurin 54031 r° 4, 2)

All these examples have a relative clause in the second position. It is possible that they in fact display a common feature in Demotic, where the articles *pꜣ/tꜣ/nꜣ* introducing a relative verbal form morphologically marked with an initial <*ỉ*>/<*r*> (*ỉ*.REL) are often written *pꜣy/tꜣy/nꜣy* plus an unmarked verbal form. A similar explanation could be proposed for the Late Egyptian ex. 165 (as proposed above for 165a in ex. 42a): rather than tripartite nominal sentences with a copula, they could in fact represent bipartite nominal (actually pseudo-cleft) sentences whose second NP is a relative form or a participle introduced by the article written with a final *-y* as in Demotic.[62] Nevertheless, since the putative copula is written *nꜣw* rather than *nꜣy*, the following could be an example of a genuine Late Egyptian tripartite nominal sentence:

62 However, one might expect *-y*-ending articles to appear more widely before relative verb forms, but unlike in Demotic, this is not the case in Late Egyptian.

(166) The author of a letter states: It is true what you mentioned in my presence:
*dg-w n-ꜥnḫ n-ỉt n-rmṯ n-pꜣy-f-šri nꜣw*
[view-P of-life of-father of-man for-POSS.M-3MS-son]$_S$ COP.P
*hꜣb-k=n-ỉ ḥr-w*
[send.REL-2MS=to-1S on-3P]$_P$
The views of life of a man's father to his son are what you have written to me about. (*KRI* III 505, 4–6)

Otherwise, most Late Egyptian examples seem to consciously emulate the Earlier Egyptian pattern, since the majority of them comes from literary texts. For instance, in the following example, the copula takes the old form =*pw* and the sentence as a whole clearly imitates the tone of the most standard expressions in earlier religious texts:

(167) The reader is advised not to raise his voice in the chapel of a god:
*bw-ṯ-f=pw sbḥ*
[abomination-F-3MS]$_S$=COP [scream.INF]$_P$
Screaming is an abomination for him. (Ani B 17, 2)

The tripartite construction 'infinitive + *pw* + relative form' much favoured in Earlier Egyptian narratives is still sometimes encountered in Late Egyptian literary texts:

(168a) After his dog tried to bite him the prince ran away:
*spr=pw ỉri-n-f r-pꜣ-ym*
[approach.INF]$_S$=COP [do.REL-PST-3MS to-DEF.M-sea]$_P$
Thus he arrived at the sea. (*LES* 8, 12)

(168b) One day when Bata had left his young wife to take care of his daily business:
*pr=pw ỉr-n tꜣ-ꜥḏd r-qd*
[go.INF]$_S$=COP [do.REL-PST DEF.F-girl to-walk.INF
*ḫr-pꜣ-ꜥš nty-r-gs -pꜣy-s-pr*
under-DEF.M-pine REL-to-side-POSS.M-3FS-house]$_P$
The young girl went for a walk underneath the pine that was beside her house. (*LES* 20, 4–5)

Yet even in this case, later texts prefer the bipartite pattern (41b). Possible non-literary examples of 'old-fashioned' tripartite sentences are rare:

(169a) The author opens his letter with a question:
*ỉḫ=pw pꜣy-k-ḏd*
[WH]$_S$=COP [POSS.M-2MS-say.INF]$_P$
What are you saying? (oBerlin 12365, r° 3)

(169b) After the opening lines of a letter, the author complains:
*i͗ḫ=pw* *pꜣy-k-tm-hꜣb=n-i͗* *ḥr-[snb-k=nb*
[WH]$_{S}$=COP [POSS.M-2MS-aux.NEG-send.INF=to-1S on-health-2MS=QU
*mḏrt* *rmṯ=nb* *nty* *ḥr-i͗yt* *dy]* *tnw* *hrw=nb*
with man=QU REL PRP-come.INF here each day=QU]$_{P}$
Why do you not send news about [all your health issues with anyone who comes here] daily? (pMond I, 6–7 [restored after pMond II])

(169c) The author opens his letter with a question:
*i͗ḫ=pw* *pꜣ-sẖr* *bi͗n* *nty-ṯ-k* *i͗m-f*
[WH]$_{S}$=COP [DEF.M-state bad REL-PTC-2MS in-3MS]$_{P}$
What is the meaning of the bad behaviour that you are showing? (*KRI* III 544, 2–3)

(169d) The author wants to correct a wrongly executed order by a subordinate:
*i͗s* *ḏd=pw=n-k* *r-mḥ-ṯ* *i͗m-sn*
PTC [tell.INF]$_{Sa}$=COP=[to-2MS to-fill-2MS with-3P]$_{Sb}$
*pꜣ-i͗r-n-i͗* *i͗s* *bn* *nꜣ-n-[...]-t*
[DEF.M-do.REL-PST-1S]$_{P}$ PTC NEG DEF.P-of-orders-F
*rdi͗-n-i͗=n-k* *m-ḏr-t-k* *m-sš* *nꜣ=pw*
give.REL-PST-1S=to-2MS in-hand-F-2MS in-writing [DEM.P]$_{S}$=COP
*ḏd-n-i͗=n-k* *(r)-mḥ-ṯ* *i͗m-sn*
[say.REL-PST-1S=to-2MS (to)-fill-2MS with-3P]$_{P}$
Did I tell you to apprehend them? Are the [arrest orders] that I gave you in your hand not spelled out in writing? These are the ones I told you to apprehend! (*KRI* I 323, 4–6)

(169e) The report about the preliminary setting of the Battle of Kadesh continues:
*nꜥ-t=pw* *i͗r-n* *ḥm-f* *m-ḫd*
[proceed-INF]$_{S}$=COP [do.REL-PST majesty-3MS in-go north]$_{P}$
His majesty proceeded northwards. (*KRI* II 12, 3)

(169f) The king praises the god Seth:
*wḏ-k=pw* *ḫpr-t=nb-t*
order-2MS=COP happen.PIA-F=QU
Whatever happens you order. (*KRI* II 249, 12)

As noted above, except for 169a–169c, all rare Late Egyptian examples contain a relative clause in the second position and could alternatively be analysed as pseudo-cleft sentences (1.1.2.1). It should also be noted that all examples derive from the earlier phase of Late Egyptian: 169a is from the Eighteenth Dynasty and the remaining instances from the Nineteenth Dynasty. The interrogative pattern *i͗ḫ=pw pꜣy*-PRN-INF in 169a–169c was later replaced by the bipartite construction *i͗ḫ pꜣy*-PRN-INF (see Vernus 2006: 168).

### 1.3.2.2 Demotic

Contrary to Late Egyptian, tripartite nominal sentences are common in Demotic. As in the sentences with a subject indexing element, the copula appears as either *pꜣy* (MS), *tꜣy* (FS) or *nꜣw* (P), thus showing agreement with one of the two NPs, usually the one that precedes (but cf. 171a, 172d & e). The most common construction seems to be the one where the copula appears at the end of the sentence: S > [NP NP COP].

(170a) Setne goes to the Bubasteion, looking for Tabubu's house. Once he sees a large walled mansion with a garden and a bench in front of it, he asks around:

*pꜣy-ˁwy* *pꜣ-ˁwy* *n-nme* *pꜣy*
[DEM.M-house.M]$_S$ [DEF.M-house.M of- WH]$_P$ [COP.M]
*ḏd-w=n-f* *pꜣ-ˁwy* *[n]-tabwbwe* *pꜣy*
say.PST-3P=to-3MS DEF.M-house.M of-N SE.M
'Whose house is this house?' They answered him: 'It is the house of Tabubu.' (Setne I 5, 12)

(170b) In a letter from Elephantine:

*ḥntr* *yb* *ỉrpy* *ˁꜣ* *pꜣy*
[temple.F N]$_S$ [sanctuary.M great]$_P$ [COP.M]
*mỉr-dy-t-ḫpr-nḏnḏ* *n-rmt* *ḫn-f*
NEG.IMP-let-INF happen-strife of-man inside-3MS
The temple of Elephantine is an important sanctuary; do not let human conflicts happen there. (pBerlin P. 15530, x+10–13)

(170c) A precept from a Ptolemaic wisdom text:

*wˁ-sẖ-ls* *n-pr* *prˁꜣ* *wˁ-sẖ-ḥny*
[IDF.S-blow.M-tongue in-house pharaoh]$_S$ [IDF-S-blow.M-helm
*n-pꜣ-ym* *pꜣy*
of-DEF.M-sea]$_P$ [COP.M]
A slip of tongue in the royal house is a slip of (the) helm at the sea. (Onkhsheshonqy 23, 10)

(170d) A gloss from a pseudo-prophetical text (*Demotic Chronicle*):

*pꜣ-ḫpš* *tꜣ-ỉꜣw-t-ḥry* *tꜣy*
[DEF.M-sword.M]$_S$ [DEF.F-office-F-ruler]$_P$ [COP.F]
The sword is the ruler's office; (it means the appearing of the falcon). (pBN 215 r° 5, 5)

As can be seen from the examples above, the combined NPs can be definite or indefinite. This construction has been analysed as an extension of a bipartite pattern showing ante-position of the first element (i.e. $X_i$, Y $SE_i$ 'X, it is Y', see Johnson 1981: 414–30). This might well be true historically, and there are examples such as 171c where the preterite marker *wnnꜣw* points to such an analysis (whereas in 171b one could have expected the interrogative to appear initially). Nevertheless, in many instances this interpretation is semantically unsatisfactory, and overall its primary aim is probably to prevent free positioning of subject and predicate in the tripartite scheme:

(171a) Horus Son of Paneshe is told by Thoth in a dream to find a magical book:

| *tꜣ-mḏy* | *n-ḥyq* | *rn-s* | *tꜣy* |
|---|---|---|---|
| [DEF.F-book | of magic] | [name.M-3FS] | COP.F |

'The book of magic' is its name. (Setne II 5, 13)

(171b) The lion meets a panther that tells him that 'man' is the cause of his injuries. The lion asks:

| *rmt* | *iḫ* | *pꜣy* |
|---|---|---|
| [man.M] | [WH] | COP.M |

What is 'man'? (Myth of the Sun's Eye 17, 15)

(171c) The pharaoh questions Harsiese:

| *ꜥnḫššnqy* | *sꜣ* | *ṯꜣynfr* | *iḫ-rmt* | *rr-k* | *pꜣy* |
|---|---|---|---|---|---|
| [N | son | N] | [WH-man.M | to-2MS] | COP.M |

| *ḏd-f* | *pꜣy-f-iṯ* | *wnnꜣw-pꜣ-iry* | *n-pꜣy(-y)-iṯ* | *pꜣy* |
|---|---|---|---|---|
| say.PST-3MS | [POSS-3MS-father] | [PRT-DEF-M-friend | of-POSS[-1S]-father] | COP.M |

'What kind of man is Onchsheshonqy, son of Tjainefer, to you?' He answered: 'His father was my father's friend.'

(Onkhsheshonqy 3, x+16–17)

The second tripartite pattern shows the copula inbetween the two NPs: S > [NP COP NP]. Either the copula agrees with the preceding element or the invariable *pꜣy* is used, depending on the semantic class of the sentence (see 3.2.2.2). That pattern, with the copula between the NPs, seems to be favoured in Roman Demotic, although earlier examples can also be found (172a). Instances with two non-pronominal NPs are rare, and overall, in most examples of Demotic tripartite nominal sentences, at least one of the participants is an interrogative or a personal pronoun:

(172a) Paqlul, the great chief of the East, answers to the pharaoh's fear of having insulted some people:

| *ḥḥ* | *nꜣw* | *nꜣ-sš* | *ntyiw-iw-k-ir* | *nim-w* | *n-nꜣ-ḫꜥ(m)ẖl-w* | *sp* | *m-sꜣ-pꜣy-f-iri* |
|---|---|---|---|---|---|---|---|
| [million] | COP.P | [DEF.P-insult | REL-PTC-2MS-do | OBJ-3P | to-DEF.P-boy-P | time | in-back-POSS-3MS-fellow] |

Your insults to the boys, one after the other, amount to millions.

(pSpiegelberg 11, 15–16)

(172b) From a wisdom text:
*tꜣ-rhnꜣ-t* *n-pꜣ-rmṯ-ntr* *ẖn-s-t-ḏbꜣ* *pꜣy*
[DEF.F-support-F of-DEF.M-man-god in-ABST-F-trouble] COP.M
*pꜣ-ntr*
[DEF.M-god]
The support of the man of god in trouble is God. (pInsinger 19, 12)

(172c) When the guardian says that he will announce the deceased to the deity in charge, the deceased will say:
*nm* *pꜣy* *pꜣ-ntr* *nty-ẖn-tꜣy-f-wp-t*
[WH] COP.M [DEF. M-god REL-in-POSS.F-3MS-work-F]
Who is the god who is in his duty? (pBN 149 3, 20)

(172d) The disciple asks god Thoth:
*i̭h* *pꜣy* *sẖ* *i̭h* *nꜣw* *nꜣy-f-ꜥwy-w*
[WH] COP.M [writing]$_P$ [WH]$_S$ COP.P [POSS.P-3MS-place-P
*n-wꜣḥ*
of-storage]
*iẖ* *pꜣy* *sẖ* *iẖ* *pꜣy* *pꜣy-f-ꜥwy*
[WH] COP.M [writing]$_P$ [WH]$_S$ COP.M [POSS.M-3MS-place
*wꜣḥ*
(of) storage]
What is writing? What are its places of storage?
(*Book of Thoth* B02 4, 12 vs. L01 2, 22)

(172e) The disciple asks god Thoth:
*i̭h* *tꜣy* *tꜣ-ꜥny-t* *nty-nḏy* *pꜣ-ls*
[WH] COP.M [DEF.F-claw-F REL-seize DEF.M-tongue]
What is the claw which fastens on the tongue?
(*Book of Thoth* B02 3, 16)

(172f) An invocation to the sun recited at dawn:
*mtwk* *pꜣy* *pꜣ-mẖrr* *n-ẖstb* *n-mꜣꜥ-t*
[2MS] COP.M [DEF.M-scarab of-lapislazuli of-truth-F]
You are the scarab of real lapis lazuli. (pMag. London & Leiden 21, 20)

(172g) In a magical texts written in Greek letters the magician addresses the deities and styles himself as:
*sabašḫa* *pe* *pa-ren* *n-mêt*
N COP.M POSS.M.1S-name of-truth
Sabashkha is my real name. ($^{OC}$Great Mag. P. Paris [*ZÄS* 21, 94, 17])

Cf. exx. 171a and 172g.

Demonstrative pronouns and the copula are always graphically distinguished in the Demotic script, and no ambiguity arises in the following examples:

(173a) The concluding words in a plea:

*pꜣy(-y)-ḫrw* *mḥ-1* *pꜣy* *pay*
[POSS.M-1S-plea ORD-1]$_P$ COP.M [DEM.M]$_S$
This is my first plea. (pBM 10591 r° 2, 12)

(173b) Tjainefer runs to the harbour to see if reinforcements are arriving. He asks:

*tꜣ-mr* *nm* *tꜣy* *tꜣy*
[DEF-F-fleet WH]$_P$ COP.F [DEM.F]$_S$
Whose fleet is this? (pKrall 14, 12)

(173c) After writing the Greek version of the invocation, the scribe gives its equivalent in Egyptian:

*pꜣy-f-ʿš* *n-md-t* *rmt-n-kmy* *pꜣy* *pꜣy*
[POSS.M-3MS-reading in-speech-F man-of-N]$_S$ COP(M) [DEM.M
*nty-[ẖr]y* *mir-pdṯ* *msꜣ-y...*
REL-below NEG.IMP-run after-1s]$_P$
Its translation into Egyptian is this which is below: 'Do not run after me'.
(pMag. London & Leiden 15, 28–29)

It will be shown in 3.2.1 that, as in Earlier Egyptian, the ordering of the grammatical roles of subject and predicate is not fixed in Demotic tripartite nominal sentences (see 173a for examples with subject and 173c with predicate in first position). The medial copula can show agreement with either.

Although Coptic displays a diachronic and diatopic distribution of the patterns NP NP COP (< $NP_i$ NP $SE_i$) and NP COP NP, the former being a later and predominantly northern feature, the latter earlier and predominantly southern, no such division is discernible in Demotic, where the second pattern appears more frequently in later texts.

#### 1.3.2.3 Coptic

The two patterns of tripartite nominal sentences already attested in Demotic, i.e. [NP COP NP] and [NP NP COP], show a broad diatopic distribution in Coptic. The first construction is generally preferred in Sahidic (ex. 174), whereas in Bohairic, the copula is more often placed after the two nominal elements (ex. 175)[63]:

63 This is at least the default distribution of the patterns in manuscripts with Sahidic and a Bohairic variants; see Shisha-Halevy 1981: 321.

(174a) Macarius has solved a case of theft on a ship; everyone on board says:
*ontos* *u-hagios* *pe* *pei-rôme*
truly [IDF.S-saint] COP.M [DEM.M-man]
Truly, this man is a saint.
($^{S}$Dioscorus of Alexandria, *On Macarius of Tkow* §3.9 [Johnson 18b, 30–32])

(174b) In the explanation of the parable of the sower and the seed:
*[p-c]ais* *p-nute* *pe* *ta-[k$^{j}$am]*
[DEF.M-lord DEF.M-god] COP.M [POSS.F.1S-power]
The Lord God is my strength. ($^{A}$Hab 3:19)

(174c) Jesus tells the disciples:
*anok* *pe* *p$^{h}$-uôini* *m-pi-kosmos*
[1S] COP.M [DEF.M-light of-DEF$_2$.M-world]
I am the light of the world. ($^{B}$Jn 8:12)

(174d) Jesus explains one of his parables:
*t-šôši=de* *pe* *p-kosmos*
[DEF.F-field=yet] COP.M [DEF.M-world]
*pe-k$^{j}$rak$^{j}$* *et-nanu-f* *ne* *ne-šêli* *n-t-met-rra*
[DEF.F-seed REL-good-3MS] COP.P [DEF.P-child of-DEF.F-ABST-king]
*ni-entêk$^{j}$* *ne* *ne-šêli* *m-p-pethau*
[DEF$_2$.F-weed] COP.P [DEF.P-child of-DEF.M-bad]
The field is the world. The good seed are the children of the kingdom;
the weeds are the children of the wicked one. ($^{F}$Mt 13:38)

(174e) Peter goes to meet three men asking for him and says:
*u* *te* *t-etia* *et-ha-tn-i* *etbêt-s*
[WH] COP.F [DEF.F-reason REL-PST-2P-come because-3FS]
What is the reason for which you came? ($^{M}$Acts 10:21)

(174f) The sentence 'The father reveals his bosom' is explained as:
*pe-f-tap=de* *pe* *pi-pn(eum)a* *et-uaab*
[POSS.M-3MS-bosom=yet] COP.M [DEF$_2$.M-spirit REL-clean]
Now, his bosom is the Holy Spirit. ($^{L}$*EvVer* 24, 10–11)

Besides being predominant in Bohairic, the construction [NP NP COP] is also attested in the other dialects, although less often than [NP COP NP]. Notably, it is not common in Fayyumic, which is otherwise close to Bohairic:

(175a) St Paul tells the Corinthians that Jesus took a cup and said:
*pai-ap$^{h}$ot* *ti-diathêkê* *m-beri=te* *ḫen-pa-snof*
[DEM.M-cup] [DEF$_2$.F-covenant of-new]=COP.F in-POSS.1S-blood
This cup is the new covenant in my blood. ($^{B}$1Cor 11:25)

(175b) The angel of the Lord tells Philip to wait on the road from Jerusalem to Gaza:
*tei=de* *ne-u-erêmos* *te*
[DEM.F=yet] PRT-[IDF.S-lonely COP.F]
This, however, was deserted. ([M]Acts 8:26)

(175c) Finally Jonah obeys the Lord's command and goes to Ninive:
*niniuê=de* *ne-u-nakʲ* *m-polis=te* *m-p-cais*
N=yet PRT-IDF.S-great of-city=COP.F for-DEF.M-lord
*e-s-na-r-u-ḫo* *n-ḫamt* *n-houe* *n-maahe*
DEP-3FS-FUT-make-IDF.S-way of-three of-day of-walk
Now, Ninive was a great city to the Lord, which covered a stretch of a three days walk. ([A]Jon 3:3 [Malinine])

(175d) From a description of the female beloved in the *Song of Songs*:
*nu-bal* *hen-bal* *n-kʲroompe* *ne*
[POSS.P.2FS-eye] [IDF.P-eye of-dove] COP.P
Your eyes are the eyes of a dove. ([S]Sg 1:15)

(175e) John calls his audience to love one another:
*ce-t-agapê* *u-ebol* *hm-p-nute* *te*
for-[DEF.F-love] [IDF.S-out from-DEF.M-god] COP.F
...for the love is from God. ([S]1Jn 4:7)

Nevertheless, exceptions to these tendencies are easy to find: cf. e.g. the pattern NP NP COP in Sahidic (ex. 176a or 176b) or the pattern NP COP NP in Bohairic (176c or 176d):

(176a) Finding his disciples asleep in the garden of Gethsemane, Jesus notes:
*pe-pn(eum)a=men* *rout* *t-sarks=de* *u-asthenês* *te*
DEF.M-spirit=indeed fresh.STA IDF.S-flesh=yet IDF.S-weak SE.F/COP.F
Indeed the spirit is willing, yet the flesh is weak. ([S]Mt 26:41)

(176b) Athanasius declares his conviction that his audience will try to emulate Anthony's life with utter zeal:
*p-bios=gar* *n-antônios* *u-kharaktêr* *pe* *e-f-rôše*
DEF.M-life=for of-N IDF.S-image SE.M/COP.M DEP-3MS-be_fit
*e-m-monakhos* *e-tre-u-askei*
to-DEF.P-monk to-CAUS-3P-practise_asceticism
...for Anthony's way of life is a image, that is befitting for the monks, to make them practise their ascetic way of life.
([S]*Life of Anthony* ed. Garitte 2, 2–3)

(176c) Jesus explains one of his parables:
*pi-iohi=de* *pe* *pi-kosmos*
DEF$_2$.F-field=yet COP.M DEF$_2$.M-world
The field is the world. ($^B$Mt 13:38)

(176d) St Theodore the General tells emperor Diocletian:
*ari-emi=na-k* *ô* *diokklêtianos*
IMP-know=for-2MS VOC N
*ce-te-k-k$^j$rêpi* *u-sêfi* *n-ro* *2* *te*
COMP-POSS.F-2MS-diadem IDF.S-sword of-mouth 2 SE.F/COP.F
*pe-k-k$^h$lom* *u-k$^h$lom* *n-ehbôn* *pe*
POSS.M-2MS-crown IDF.S-crown of-famine SE.M/COP.M
*te-k-phuallê* *u-kholê=te* *nte-p-k$^h$aki*
POSS.F-2MS-beaker IDF.S-gall=SE.F/COP.F of-DEF.M-dark
*n-pi-aêr*
of-DEF$_2$.M-air
*pe-k-êrp* *u-snof* *n-k$^h$rof* *pe*
POSS.M-2MS-wine IDF.S-blood of-guileful SE.M/COP.M
*te-k-trapeza* *u-polemos* *n-ref-ḫôteb* *pe*
POSS.F-2MS-table IDF.S-war of-AGT-kill SE.F/COP.F
*p-arêb* *m-p$^h$-mu* *pe* *pe-k-ariston*
DEF.M-pledge of-DEF.M-death SE.M/COP.M POSS.M-2MS-feast
*pe-k-thronos* *u-taphos* *n-mhau* *pe* *ô*
POSS.M-2MS-throne IDF.S-grave IDF.S-tomb SE.M/COP.M VOC
*p$^h$ê* *et-shuort*
DEF$_3$.M REL-curse.STA
Know, O Diocletian, that your sceptre is a double-edged sword; your crown is a crown of famine; your beaker is gall of darkness of the air; your wine is deceitful blood; your table is murderous war; the pledge of death is your feast, and your throne is sepulchral grave, O accursed one!
($^B$Theodore of Antioch, *On the Theodores* [*AM* II 97, 8–13])

Some grammatical descriptions attempting to preserve the distinction between Sahidic NP COP NP and Bohairic NP NP COP have explained Sahidic examples of NP NP COP as bipartite sentences with an anteposed subject, i.e. NP$_i$ – NP SE$_i$ (see e.g. Layton 2011: §272). In this analysis, the anteposed NP and the subject element are referentially identical and the latter is anaphoric. Some examples do seem to speak in favour of this reading (e.g., example 176b above, since indefinite NPs usually occupy the initial position in the clause), but elsewhere complications arise. For instance, in the examples below, one would have to assume a fronted subject in a conditional protasis (ex. 177a), or assume a double fronting (ex. 177b), which, however, could be explained as an attempt to emulate a Greek syntax pattern in the translation into Coptic:

(177a) Jesus reasons:

| | | | | |
|---|---|---|---|---|
| *ešôpe=de* | *pe-k-bal* | *u-ponêros* | *pe* | |
| CND=yet | POSS.M-2MS-eye | IDF.S-bad | †SE.M/COP.M | |
| *pe-k-sôma* | *têr-f* | *na-šôpe* | *e-f-o* | *n-kake* |
| POSS.M-2MS-body | all-3MS | FUT-happen | DEP-3MS-be.STA | as-black |

If your eye is bad, your whole body will become black. ($^{S}$Mt 6:23)

(177b) Frange seems to quote from an Apophthegmatum to make a point towards a superior monk in his letter to him (partly broken afterwards):

| | | | |
|---|---|---|---|
| *pa-iôt* | *nt-a-i-tôk$^{j}$e* | *hahtê-f* | *pe-f-bios* |
| POSS.M.1S-father | REL-PST-1S-join | with-3MS | POSS.M-3MS-life |
| *têr-f* | *u-paskha* | *pe* | |
| all-3MS | IDF.S-Easter | †SE.M/COP.M | |

My father, with whom I joined, his whole way of life is a Easter.
($^{S}$*O.Frange* #24, 4–7)

The sole criterion that could disambiguate the issue appears to be the position of the preterite operator *ne*, seen in the following examples:

(178a) Having witnessed Jesus' death, a Roman centurion exclaims:

| | | | |
|---|---|---|---|
| *ontôs* | *ne-u-dikaios* | *pe* | *pei-rôme* |
| certainly | PRT-[IDF.S-righteous] | COP.M | [DEM.M-man] |

Certainly, this was a righteous man. ($^{S}$Lk 23:47)

(178b) At Corinth Paul stays with a Jew with whom he shares profession:

| | | |
|---|---|---|
| *ne-te-u-tekhnê=gar* | *pe* | *ref-tamie-skunê* |
| PRT-[POSS.F-3P-occupation=for] | COP.M | [AGT-make-tent] |

For their occupation was that of a tentmaker. ($^{S}$Acts 18:3)

(178c) The Gospel of John begins with the words:

| | | | |
|---|---|---|---|
| *ḫen-t-arkhê* | *ne-pi-saci* | *pe* | |
| in-DEF.F-beginning | PRT-DEF$_2$.M-word | SE.M | |
| *uoh* | *pi-saci* | *na-f-k$^{h}$ê* | *ḫaten-p$^{h}$-(nu)ti* |
| and | DEF$_2$.M-word | PRT-3MS-put.STA | with-DEF.M-god |
| *uoh* | *ne-u-nuti* | *pe* | *pi-saci* |
| and | PRT-[IDF.S-god] | COP.M | [DEF$_2$.M-word] |

In the beginning was the word, and the word was with God, and the word was God. ($^{B}$Jn 1:1)

As operators are thought to be positioned in front of a complete clause, any elements to their left must be viewed as anteposed. This would again lead to the analysis of most Bohairic and of some Sahidic nominal sentences as bipartite with anteposed subject inasmuch as the preterite operator is almost always placed before the second NP:

(179a) Jesus healed ten men in a village. One of them came to thank him:
*ntof=de* *ne-u-samaritês* *pe*
3MS=yet PRT-IDF.S-N SE.M/COP.M
As for him, he was a Samaritan. ($^S$Lk 17:16)

(179b) Shenute explains:
*t-petra=gar* *ne-pe-kh(risto)s* *pe*
DEF.F-rock=for PRT-DEF.M-Christ SE.M/COP.M
For the rock, it was the Christ.
($^S$Shenute, *As I Sat on a Mountain* [L III 51, 28])

(179c) The prophet Malachias has the Lord say:
*êsau* *ne-p-san=en=pe* *n-iakôb*
N PRT-DEF.M-brother=NEG=SE.M/COP.M of-N
Was not Esau Jacob's brother? ($^A$Mal 1:2)

(179d) Noah is introduced intro the account of the flood:
*nôe* *ne-u-rômi* *n-t$^h$-mêi* *pe*
N PRT-IDF.S-man of-DEF.F-truth SE.M/COP.M
Noah was a just man. ($^B$Gn 6:9)

(179e) A characterisation of the Jews of Berea:
*nai=de* *ne-han-eugenês=ne* *ehot-e-nê*
DEM.P=yet PRT-IDF.P-open minded=SE.M/COP.M more-to-DEF$_3$.P
*et-ḫen-thessalonikê*
REL-in-N
These were more open-minded than those in Thessalonica. ($^B$Acts 17:11)

Some Sahidic manuscripts mark anteposed segments with diacritics such as the colon (:):

(180) Saint Elijah quotes of Ps 113 [115]:4 in response to the king's question on why he neglects him:
*n-nute* *têr-u* *n-n-hethnos :*
DEF.P-god all-3P of-DEF.P-heathen
*hn-hat* *hi-nub* *ne* *hn-hbêue=ne* *n-k$^j$ic* *n-rôme*
IDF.P-silver on-gold SE.P IDF.P-work.P=SE.P of-hand of-man
The gods of the heathens – they are silver and gold; they are works of the hands of man. ($^S$*Mart. Elijah* [Sobhy 13, b16–22])

Yet to view every Sahidic example of NP NP COP as displaying subject fronting seems to assign an unlikely frequency to a marked construction. For this reason, it is perhaps better to regard this pattern as a positional variant of the more common NP COP NP and allow for the possibility that *some* instances of NP NP COP may indeed convey subject fronting. However, as the pattern NP NP COP always shows the order [subject – predicate – COP], it could be considered a pragmatic means to disambiguate the function of the constituents against the NP COP NP pattern, in which the first NP can be either subject or predicate. Explaining the unexpected Bohairic examples of NP COP NP as the result of the translator's attempt to maintain unaltered the syntax of the original Sahidic cannot apply to Bohairic scriptural texts, which are less dependent than other genres on Sahidic versions.

The copula often agrees in gender and number with the first or the second NP (M: *pe*; F: *te*; P: *ne*) or appears in the neutral form *pe*. The latter, however, can be identified only if neither of the two NPs is masculine singular (confront, for example, exx. 181a & b with 181c; for an additional example with non-agreement, see 258a):

(181a) The people in Jesus' village wonder how he has gained all his knowledge and ask: '*Is he not the son of the carpenter? And is his mother not the one they call Maria*:

| | | | | | |
|---|---|---|---|---|---|
| *auô* | *ne-f-snêu* | *pe* | *iakôbos* | *mn-iôsês* | *mn-simon* |
| and | POSS.P-3MS-brother.P | COP.M | N | CON-N | CON-N |
| *mn-iudas* | | | | | |
| CON-N | | | | | |

...and his brothers are James, Joseph, Simon, and Judas?' ([S]Mt 13:55)

(181b) Concerning early death taking away the righteous:

| | | | |
|---|---|---|---|
| *t-mnt-hllo* | *pe* | *u-ahe* | *n-at-nobe* |
| DEF.F-ABST-old man | COP.M | IDF.S-lifetime.M | of-NEG-sin |

The true old age is a life without sin. ([S]Sap 4:9)

(181c) Raguel bids his daughter goodbye, who is to move with her husband Tobias to Niniveh. Her father tells her:

| | | |
|---|---|---|
| *tmaie-nu-šmui* | *ce-ntou* | *ne* |
| justify.IMP-POSS.P.2FS-parents_in_law | for-3P | COP.P |
| *nu-iote* | *cin-mpou* | |
| POSS.P.2FS-father.P | since-today | |

Honour your parents in law for they are your parents from today! ([S]Tb 10:12[11])

(181d) On wisdom and foolishness:

| | | | | |
|---|---|---|---|---|
| *pe-klam* | *n-u-ḫllo* | *pe* | *hn-šêre* | *n-šêre* |
| DEF.M-crown | of-IDF.S-old man | COP.M | IDF.P-child | of-child |

Grandchildren are the crown of old men. ([A]Prv 17:6)

(181e) The Christ has enlightened those in darkness and showed them a way:

| | | | |
|---|---|---|---|
| *pi-mait=de* | *pe* | *ti-mnt-mêe* | *ent-a-f-tama-u* |
| DEF$_2$.M-way=yet | COP.M | DEF$_2$.F-ABST-truth | REL-PST-3MS-teach-3P |
| *ara-s* | | | |
| to-3FS | | | |

This way is the truth which he taught them. ($^{L}$*EvVer* 18, 19–21)

(181f) The teacher explains a simile on the good and the bad tree and likens various things to others:

| | | | | |
|---|---|---|---|---|
| *te-f-sbô* | *hôô-s* | *ne* | *n-kaminos* | *n-t-[sete ...]* |
| POSS.F-3MS-teaching | self-3FS | COP.P | DEF.P-furnace | of-DEF.F-fire ... |

His doctrine(s) are the furnaces of [fire ...]. ($^{L}$*Kephalaia* 21, 32)

(181g) The apostle warns the community of Corinth against mingling with unbelievers:

| | | | | | |
|---|---|---|---|---|---|
| *ie* | *u* | *te* | *ti-met-šp$^{h}$êr* | *m-pi-uôini* | |
| or | WH | COP.F | DEF$_2$.F-ABST-friend | of-DEF$_2$.M-light | |
| *nem-pi-k$^{h}$aki* | | | | | |
| CON-DEF$_2$.M-darkness | | | | | |
| *ie* | *u* | *pe* | *p-ti-mati* | *m-p-kh(risto)s* | *nem-beliar* |
| or | WH | COP.M | DEF.M-give-attainment | of-DEF.M-Christ | CON-N |

What is the fellowship of the light with darkness? What is the agreement of the Christ with Beliar? ($^{B}$2Cor 6:14–15)

The question of agreement marking of the copula in Coptic is still unsolved, and explanations have ranged from purely descriptive accounts to structural and semantic approaches. Overall, it seems that the agreement marking is semantically motivated. If the sentence has an identifying function, there appears to be a choice between neutral *pe* or an agreement-marked copula. If the sentence is semantically classifying, the copula agrees with the subject. Variant versions of the same biblical passage sometimes seem to bear testimony to different interpretations of the Greek original by the Coptic translators:

(182) St. Paul tells the Corinthians that Jesus took a cup and said:

| | | | | | |
|---|---|---|---|---|---|
| *pei-apot* | *te* | *t-diathêkê* | *n-brre* | *hm-pa-snof* | |
| DEM.M-cup | COP.F | DEF.F-covenant | of-new | in-POSS.M.1S-blood | (Horner) |
| *pei-apot* | *pe* | *t-diathêkê* | *n-brre* | *hm-pa-snof* | |
| DEM.M-cup | COP.M | DEF.F-covenant | of-new | in-POSS.M.1S-blood | (Thompson) |

This cup is the new covenant in my blood. ($^{S}$1Cor 11:25)

In Sahidic and Bohairic (see also ex. 175a), the copula itself shows clitic tendencies, but clearly less than the subject element. Hence, it has been glossed as clitic only in presence of a clear movement into the phrasal structure of the NP that precedes it. Whilst in earlier texts (ex. 183a–c) the copula usually does not interfere with the structure of nominal phrases (even though the subject element does, see above), later texts (183d) occasionally display such a feature. Yet even Bohairic texts (ex. 183e) often retain the copula in the absolute medial position between the two NPs:

(183a) Shenute explains whom he means by 'snakes and snakes' offspring':
*n-hof=men* *et-sôše* *hicm-p-kah* *ne* *hellên*
DEF.P-snake=indeed REL-crawl upon-DEF.M-earth COP.P heathen
*nim* *mn-hethnos* *nim* *et-uôšt* *m-p-sônt*
QU CON-nation QU REL-worship OBJ-DEF.M-creation
*para-p-ent-a-f-sônt* *p-nute* *p-pantokratôr*
over-DEF.M-REL-PST-3MS-create DEF.M-god DEF.M-almighty
The snakes crawling upon the ground are all the heathens and all the nations who worship the creation over the creator, God the almighty.
($^{S}$Shenute, *Blessed Are They Who Observe Justice* [Ch 139, 32–42])

(183b) The proverbs describe the feature of Wisdom:
*hen-ḫôu* *e-nanu-u* *ne* *ne-s-ḫôu*
IDF.P-way.P DEP-good-3P COP.P POSS.P-3FS-way.P
Her ways are good ways. ($^{A}$Prv 3:17)

(183c) The Manichean teacher explains what are the 'Five Fathers'. Among them is:
*t-mah-tiu=de* *hôô-f* *n-iôt* *pe* *ti-morphê* *n-uaine*
DEF.F-ORD-five=yet self-3MS of-father COP.M DEF$_2$.F-figure of-light
The fifth father, however, is the figure of light.
($^{L}$*Kephalaia* 36, 12)

(183d) Gesios found some human bones in shallow water and brought them to the beach:
*ne-u-ma=gar=pe* *e-f-esukhaze* *p-ma* *etmmau*
PRT-IDF.S-place=for=COP.M DEP-3MS-quiet DEF.M-place that
*e-mn-lau* *n-rôme* *nhêt-f*
DEP-NEG-any of-man inside-3MS
...for that place was a quiet spot, where there was no man.
($^{S}$*Gesios & Isodorus* [*ZÄS* 21, 142, 2–3])

(183e) The virtues of the lives of saints are told:
*alêthôs* *u-paradisos* *e-f-meh* *n-ššên* *niben*
truly IDF.S-garden DEP-3MS-filled.STA with-tree QU
*et$^{h}$-meh* *n-karpos* *et-holc*
REL-filled.STA with-fruit REL-sweet.STA

*pe* *pi-bios* *nem-pi-cin-ônḫ* *nte-nê* *et$^h$-uab*
COP.M DEF$_2$.M-life CON-DEF$_2$.M-NOM-live of-DEF$_3$.P REL-pure.STA
*têr-u*
all-3P
*nê* *et-a-u-iri* *m-p$^h$-uôš* *têr-f* *m-p$^h$-(nu)ti*
DEF$_3$.P REL-PST-3P-do OBJ-DEF.M-wish all-3MS as-DEF.M-god
Truly, the life and times of all the saints who accomplish God's every wish are a garden full of all trees filled with every sweet fruit.
($^B$*Life of Daniel of Scetis* [Guidi 83, 8–11])

The two NPs are usually marked for definiteness by the definite or indefinite articles and only seldom appear as bare nouns (on these see Shisha-Halevy 1984b: 178–80). Any nominal phrase or nominalised expression can be used, including the combination of noun and pronoun (184), noun and infinitive (193), relative clause and noun or pronoun (186), as well as noun and a full clause (187). Combinations of common nouns and pronouns are most frequent. Below are examples with personal pronouns:

(184a) The sixty righteous who oppose the Lawless One say that the latter was not able to raise the dead:
*ḫm-pei* *a-n-suôn-k* *ce-ntak* *pe* *p-šêre*
in-DEM.M PST-1P-know-2MS COMP-2MS SE.M DEF.M-son
*n-t-anomia*
of-DEF.F-lawlessness
By this we have understood that you are the son of lawlessness.
($^A$*ApEl* [Steindorff, *Apokalypse des Elias* 98 38, 4–5])

(184b) Shenute castigates Tahom: *If you say:*
*anon* *pe* *ntof*
1P COP.M 3MS
We are him. ($^S$*Shenute Writes to Tahom* [L III 22, 18])

(184c) Frange asks Isaak to come and visit him to see whether he is content with what Frange will do. He has already written to him:
*ntok* *pe* *p-nok$^j$* *n-son* *ecô-i*
2MS COP.M DEF.M-great of-brother upon-1S
*ntok* *et-keleue* *(n)-hn-hôb* *nim* *kata-p-nute*
2MS REL-order OBJ-IDF.P-thing QU according-DEF.M-god
*kata-p-kosmos*
according-DEF.M-world
You are my superior/older brother. It is you who orders everything whether it pertains to God or the world. (*O.Frange* #14, 10–12)

As in 184a, the absolute personal pronouns usually appear in the initial position. This syntactic distribution does not, however, reflect a positional hierarchy:

(185a) Jesus says that he will pass on a mystery that cannot be spoken of:

*ete-p-mystêrion etmmau pe anok auô anok pe*
REL-DEF.M-mystery that COP.M 1S and 1S COP.M

*p-mystêrion etmmau*
DEF.M-mystery that

...that is, that mystery is me and I am that mystery.

($^{S}$*Pistis Sophia* 232, 14–16 [Schmidt])

(185b) Paul asks does the bread that he and the congregation break not symbolise partaking in the body of Christ:

*ce-u-oik n-uôt pe u-sôma n-uôt pe*
for-IDF.S-bread of-single SE.M IDF.S-body of-single COP.M

*anon têr-n*
1P all-1P

*anon=gar têr-n tn-ci ebol hm-pi-oik n-uôt*
1P=for all-1P 1P-receive out in-DEF$_2$.M-bread of-single

For it is one loaf! We are all a single body, for we all take part of that one bread. ($^{S}$1Cor 10:17)

(185c) Shenute praises the Father and the Son:

*e-ne-k-hbêue ne nu-f auô e-nu-f*
DEP-POSS.P-2MS-works.P COP.P POSS.P-3MS and DEP-POSS.P-3MS

*ne nu-k*
COP.P POSS.ABS.P-2MS

...while your works are his and his are yours.

($^{S}$Shenute, *I Am Amazed* §801 [Cristea 206, 26–29])

(185d) Shenute asks where would a human deed be before the Lord, who is free from evil:

*a-n-r-ua=gar n-uôt mn-n-nobe m-mine nim*
PST-1P-do-one=for as-single CON-DEF.P-sin of-sort QU

*nobe pe pe-n-ran rôme=an*
sin COP.M POSS.M-1P-name man=NEG

For we have become one with every sort of sin, and our name is 'sin', not 'man'.

($^{S}$Shenute, *I Have Been Reading the Holy Gospels* §18 [Moussa 56, 6–10])

The pronoun usually appears in the stressed form (*anok*, *ntok*, etc.); examples with the unstressed forms are rare:

(186a) Emperor Theodosius met an Egyptian monk and asked him whether he knew him. The monk replied that God will know him. To this the emperor said:

*ang* *pe* *theôdosios* *p-rro*
1S COP.M N DEF.M-king
I am emperor Theodosius. ($^{S}$*AP* Chaîne 31, 28–29)

(186b) The devil appeared to a monk disguised as a brother and said:

*ang* *pe* *gabriêl* *nt-a-u-tnnou-t* *šaro-k*
1S COP.M N ST-PST-3P-send-1S to-2MS
I am Gabriel. I have been sent to you. ($^{S}$*AP* Chaîne 32, 6–7)

Although these examples may be simply erroneous – indeed, the manuscript also contains examples of the expected standard construction *anok pe*[64] – they could also represent a late pattern underrepresented in the data.

In the following examples demonstrative pronouns appear:

(187a) Basilides urges Eusebius and Theodore the Anatolian to promise that they will not harm the impious Emperor Diocletian and argues about the latter:

*p*$^{h}$*ai* *u-skeuos* *nte-p-diabolos* *pe*
DEM.M IDF.S-device of-DEF.M-devil COP.M
This one is a device of the devil. ($^{B}$*Mart. Eusebius* [*AdM* 20, 2])

(187b) Jesus explains the role of the wicked in the Parable of the Sower:

*pei* *pe* *pê* *ete-ha-u-ca-f* *hahtn-te-hiê*
DEM.M COP.MS DEF.M REL-PST-3P-take-3MS besides-DEF.F-ways
This is the one who received seed by the wayside. ($^{M}$Mt 13:19 mae 1)

(187c) A letter from a bishop to a cleric who has transgressed begins with the following sentence (possibly a quote):

*pe-n-šlêl=gar* *pe* *pai* *n-uoiš* *nim*
POSS.M-1P-pray=for COP.M DEM.M in-time QU
*e-tre-p-cois* *ti-toot-n* *e-tre-n-bôl* *ebol*
to-INFL-DEF.M-lord give-hand-1P to-INFL-1P-losen out
*n-antilogia* *nim*
OBJ-disagreement QU
*etere-p-satanas* *p-enepibulos* *cin-n-šorp*
REL-DEF.M-Satan DEF.M-plotter since-DEF.P-beginning
*sôr* *mmo-u* *ebol*
spread OBJ-3P out
*e-f-uôš* *e-ti-crop* *m-p-ua* *p-ua*
DEP-3MS-wish to-give-obstacle for-DEF.M-one DEF.M-one
*mmo-n* *hitm-p-et-hituô-f*
OBJ-1P by-DEF.M-REL-beside-3MS

64 E.g. *AP* Chaîne 32, 16.

For this is our prayer at all times, that the Lord help us solve every disagreement that Satan, the plotter against us from the beginning, spreads abroad, striving to set a stumbling-block for each one of us by means of his neighbour. ($^S$Crum, *Varia Coptica*, 45, 1–7)

(187d) Theodosius tells the audience about the topic of his discourse and asks:

*nim pe p$^h$ai p$^h$ai pe pi-arkhêaggelos et$^h$uab*
WH COP.M DEM.M DEM.M COP.M DEF$_2$.M-archangel holy
*Mikhaêl*
N
*p-arkhêgus nte-t-com n-ni-p$^h$êui*
DEF.M-commander of-DEF.F-force of-DEF.P-heaven.P
Who is this? It is Michael, the holy Archangel, commander of the hosts of heaven. ($^B$Theodosius of Alexandria, *In Michaelem* [Budge 2, 14–16])

(187e) Paul tells Andrew that he heard a multitude crying in distress but he could not seem them anywhere. So he asked his guide:

*aš n-topos ne nai*
what of-place COP.P DEM.P
What kind of places are these?
($^S$*Acts of Andrew & Paul* [Jacques 204, 140])

(187f) The proverbs warn the addressed son not to side with bad and evil persons. After vivid descriptions it is resumed:

*nei ne n-ḫôu n-uan nim et-côk abal*
DEM.P COP.P DEF.P-way.P of-one QU REL-complete out
*n-n-nabe*
OBJ-DEF.P-sin
These are the ways of all who accomplish sinful deeds. ($^A$Prv 1:19)

Examples with indefinite pronouns[65]:

(188a) In a story about two men who committed the same crime and were brought before the king:

*ua u-rmmao pe auô p-ke-ua u-hêke*
IDF.S.ABS IDF.S-rich COP.M and DEF.M-other-IDF.S IDF.S-poor
*pe*
COP.M
One was a rich man and the other a poor man.
($^S$*Sayings of Pagan Philosophers* [Crum 98a, 14–15])

65 The construction in 188d has been analysed as *ue (e)-nanu-f*, i.e. consisting of an indefinite pronoun (*ue*), followed by an adjunct circumstantial clause (Shisha-Halevy 1983: 317). The adjacency of the two unstressed *e*'s led to their graphic reduction to a single one.

(188b) The King of the West will rise, and after much bloodshed in Egypt he will bring peace and say:

*ue* *pe* *p-ren* *m-[p-nute]*
IDF.S.ABS COP.M DEF.M-name of-DEF.M-god
God's name is One.
([A]*ApEl* [Steindorff, *Apokalypse des Elias* 78 26, 5])

(188c) In a fragmentary context, a person cries out:

*[hn-u-mê]e* *uei* *pe* *p-nute* *auô* *mn-[ke-nute]*
in-IDF.S-truth IDF.S.ABS COP.M DEF.M-god and NEG-other-god
*šoop* *nsabll[e]-f*
be.STA except-3MS
Truly, God is one, and there exists no other god but him!
([L]*Acta Pauli* [Schmidt 36* 59, 8–10])

(188d) The psalmist encourages others to be loyal to the Lord, telling them how to please him:

*ci-tipe* *<t>areten-neu* *ce-ue* *(e)-nanu-f* *pe*
take-taste CNJ.FUT.2P-see COMP-one (DEP)-good-3MS COP.M
*p-c(ai)s*
DEF.M-lord
Taste, and you will see that the Lord is good.
([M]Ps 33 [34]:9)

(188e) After seeing the miraculous revival of a workman bitten by a snake when digging foundation trenches for a church, the crowd shouts out the Nicene creed:

*uai* *pe* *p$^h$-nuti* *m-pi-ništi* *n-arkhêaggelos* *et$^h$uab*
IDF.S COP.M DEF.M-god of-DEF$_2$.M-great of-archangel holy
*gabriêl*
N
The God of the holy archangel Gabriel is one.
([B]Archelaos of Neapolis, *On Gabriel* [de Vis II 256, 2–3])

Examples with absolute possessive pronouns:

(189a) Shenute quotes from the writings of the heretics:

*auô* *ce* *pô-i* *pe* *pa-sôma*
and COMP POSS.M-1S COP.M POSS.M.1S-body
*mn-te-psykhê* *pa-pa-iôt* *pe* *p-nifi*
CON-DEF.F-soul POSS.M-POSS.M.1S-father COP.M DEF.M-wind
*mn-pe-pneuma*
CON-DEF.M-spirit

And again (they say): Mine are my body and the soul. To my father belong the breath and the spirit.

($^{S}$Shenute, *I Am Amazed* §100 [Cristea 138, 16–20])

(189b) The author quotes Proverbs 8:14–16:

| | | | |
|---|---|---|---|
| *pô-i=gar* | *pe* | *p-šocne* | *mn-p-ôrc* |
| POSS.M-1S-for | COP.M | DEF.M-counsel | CON-DEF.M-firmness |
| *tô-i=gar* | *te* | *t-mnt-rem-en-hêt* | *mn-t-$k^{j}$om* |
| POSS.F-1S-for | COP.F | DEF.F-ABST-man-of-heart | CON-DEF.F-strength |

For mine are counsel and certainty, and mine are understanding and strength. ($^{S}$Ps. Shenute, *On Christian Behaviour* [Kuhn 3, 7–8])

(189c) In the *Apocryphon of James* Jesus explains the meaning of his crucifixion to Peter and James:

| | | | |
|---|---|---|---|
| *n-ent-a[h]-pisteue=[ga]r* | *a-pa-st(au)ros* | *tô-u* | *te* |
| DEF.P-REL-PST-believe=for | to-POSS.M.1S-cross | POSS.F-3P | COP.F |
| *t-mnt-ero* | *m-p-nute* | | |
| DEF.F-ABST-king | of-DEF.M-god | | |

Those who believe in my cross, theirs is the kingdom of God.

($^{L}$*Ap. Jas.* 6, 5–7 [*NHS* 22, 36])

(189d) Jesus glorifies the Father:

| | | | | | | |
|---|---|---|---|---|---|---|
| *auô* | *nô-i* | *têr-u* | *nô-k* | *ne* | *auô* | *nô-k* |
| and | POSS.P-1S | all-3P | POSS.P-2MS | COP.P | and | POSS.P-2MS |
| *nô-i* | *ne* | | | | | |
| POSS.P-1S | COP.P | | | | | |

And all what is mine is yours, and all what is yours is mine. ($^{L}$Jn 17:10)

(189e) The apostle praises the Lord and ends with the words:

| | | | |
|---|---|---|---|
| *pô-f* | *pe* | *p-eou* | *n-ša-ni-enh* |
| POSS.M-3MS | COP.M | DEF.M-glory | for-until-DEF$_2$.P-eternity |
| *hamên* | | | |
| amen | | | |

His is the glory for ever. Amen! ($^{F}$Rm 11:36)

(189f) King David prays to the Lord saying:

| | | | |
|---|---|---|---|
| *$t^{h}$ô-k* | *p-$c^{h}$(ôi)s* | *te* | *ti-met-uro* |
| POSS.F-2MS | DEF$_1$.M-lord | COP.F | DEF$_2$.F-ABST-king |
| *nem-ti-met-ništi* | *nem-ti-com* | | |
| and-DEF$_2$.F-ABST-great | and-DEF$_2$.F-might | | |
| *nem-pi-šušu* | *nem-pi-$c^{h}$ro* | | |
| and-DEF$_2$.M-pride | and-DEF$_2$.F-force | | |

Yours, Lord, is the dominion and the greatness and the might and the boast and the strength. ($^{B}$1Chr 29:11 [de Lagarde])

Examples with interrogative pronouns:

(190a) Sailors find the crying Gesios beside a corpse:

*pe-šbêr u ero-k pe pei-kôôs e-k-hmoos*
DEF.M-friend WH to-2MS COP.M DEM.M-corpse DEP-2MS-sit
*e-k-rime ero-f*
DEP-2MS-cry to-3MS

Friend, what does that corpse mean to you that you should sit and wail about it? ([S]*Gesios & Isodorus* [*ZÄS* 21, 143, 6])

(190b) Paul asks an angel about the four rivers which he sees in the city of the Christ:

*hen-u ne nei-ierôu et-kôte e-te-polis*
IDF.P-WH COP.P DEM.P-rivers.P REL-encircle to-DEF.F-city

What are these rivers that encircle the city?
([S]*ApPaul* [Budge, *Misc.* 564, 21–22])

(190c) Anthony ponders on the words he heard during the reading in the church that the apostles renounced their belongings, whereas others gave their possessions to the apostles so that they would give them to the poor:

*u-aš n-mine ê u-aš n-kʾot te t-helpis*
IDF.S-WH of-kind or IDF.S-WH of-form COP.F DEF.F-hope
*n-nai et-kê=na-u ehrai hn-nem-pêue*
for-DEM.P REL-give.STA=for-3P down in-DEF.P-heaven.P

...what kind or what sort is the hope for those who dwell in heaven.
([S]*Life of Anthony* ed. Garitte 4, 5–6)

(190d) Sophonias (?) asks the angel showing him around:

*nim ne nei*
WH COP.P DEM.P

Who are these? ([A]*ApSoph*[?] [Steindorff, *Apokalypse des Elias* 38 3, 13])

(190e) The sailors ask Jonah:

*o te t-k-iape*
WH COP.F POSS.F-2MS-craft

What is your occupation? ([A]Jon 1:8 [Malinine])

(190f) The narrator bevails that true Christian faith is being slaughtered in Jerusalem by order of the Chalcedonian archbishop:

*ô uêr pe p-agôn n-n-orthodoksos*
VOC WH COP.P DEF.M-struggle of-DEF.P-orthodox
*m-p-nau etmmau*
in-DEF.M-moment that

O how long is the struggle for the orthodox of that day.
([SF]Dioscorus of Alexandria, *On Macarius of Tkow* §7.8 [Johnson 52b, 18–20])

(190g) After her dance, the king asks the daughter of Herod:

*un* *pe* *pu-edêma*
WH COP.M POSS.M.2FS-wish
What is your wish?

($^{F}$John Evangelist, *Investiture of Archangel Michael* [Müller 5, 4–5])

(190h) After Jesus had rebuked the tempest, the people with him marvelled at him:

*u-aš* *n-rêti* *pe* *p$^{h}$ai* *ce-ni-t$^{h}$êu*
IDF.S-WH of-like COP.M DEM.M COMP-DEF.P-wind
*nem-p$^{h}$-iom* *se-sôtm* *na-f*
CON-DEF.M-sea 3P-hear to-3MS
What kind of man is this, that the winds and the sea obey him?

($^{B}$Mt 8:27)

Note that when referring to plural entities, the interrogative pronoun *u* 'who, what' is marked with the indefinite plural article *hen-*. The initial position of the pronoun is certainly due to its higher salience.

The demonstrative pronoun *pai/tai/nai* is regularly used in the explanatory pattern REL DEM COP X 'that means X' (or 'i.e.'), grammatically a relativised tripartite nominal sentence. Both the demonstrative pronoun and the copula agree with the predicate (see 191a for masc., 191b for fem., and 191e for plural):

(191a) Athanasius orders that the readers at Easter celebrations should not eat anything unlawful:

*e-u-uom=gar* *peca-f* *n-u-oik* *m-mokhs*
ST-3P-eat=for said-3MS OBJ-IDF.S-bread of-affliction
*ete-pai* *pe* *p-oik* *e-mn-lau* *n-hêdonê*
REL-DEM.M COP.M DEF.M-bread DEP-NEG-any of-sweetness
*nhêt-f*
inside-3MS
*ete-pai* *pe* *p-oik* *hi-hmu* *mmate* *ê*
REL-DEM.M COP.M DEF.M-bread CON-salt very or
*ke-idos* *n-entêk$^{j}$* *e-mn-hêdonê* *nhêt-f*
other-sort of-herb DEP-NEG-sweetness inside-3MS
'For they eat', he said, 'a bread of affliction', i.e. the bread that contains no sweetness, i.e. there is only bread and salt or another sort of herb, with no sweetness therein.

($^{S}$*Canons of Athanasius* [Crum in Riedel §57])

(191b) Adam's consort was created and called Eve by God:

*adam=de* *a-f-muti* *e-pe-s-len* *ce-zôê*
N=yet PST-3MS-call to-POSS.M-3MS-name COMP-N
*ete-tei* *te* *t-meu* *n-n-et-anh* *têr-u*
REL-DEM.F COP.F DEF.F-mother of-DEF.P-REL-live all-3P
Adam, however, called her Zoë, which is the mother of all that lives.
($^{F}$John Evangelist, *Investiture of Archangel Michael* [Müller 11, 4–5])

(191c) Jesus said to his disciples:

*hareh* *erô-tn* *e-pe-thab* *ete-tai* *te* *t-hypokrisis*
guard to-2P to-DEF.M-leaven REL-DEM.F COP.F DEF.F-hypocrisy
*n-ne-pharissaios*
of-DEF.P-pharisee
Keep yourselves from the leaven, that is, the hypocrisy of the Pharisees.
($^{S}$Lk 12:1)

(191d) Jesus said to the little daughter of Jairus who had just died:

*talitha* *kum* *ete-p*$^{h}$*ai* *pe* *ce-ti-alu* *a-i-ce*
*talitha* *kum* REL-DEM.M COP.M COMP-DEF2.F-child PST-1S-say
*ero-ø* *tôni*
to-2FS rise
'*Talitha koum*', which means 'Little girl; I say to you: arise!' ($^{B}$Mk 5:41)

(191e) In the treatise on the letters of the alphabet the author resumes:

*alef* *beth* *gamel* *daleth* *i* *u* *ete-nai* *ne*
*alef* *beth* *gamel* *daleth* *i* *u* REL-DEM.P COP.P
*n-ša-u-hermêneue* *mmo-f* *ce-...*
REL-AOR-3P-explain OBJ-3P COMP-...
Aleph, Beth, Gimel, Daleth, I, U, that means they are explained as: (...).
($^{S}$*RecTrav* 25, 37)

Ex. 191c shows that the agreement in the relative clause is determined by the gender and number of the explanation, rather than of the preceding NP. If the explanation was delivered in form of a clause, the latter was introduced by *ce* as in 191d. Ex. 191e shows that the second NP could be a relative clause.

As noted earlier (1.1.2.3), most Coptic dialects avoid the direct juxtaposition 'NP–NP' to express name identity and use the tripartite construction instead:

(192a) The birth of John the Baptist is foretold to Zacharias by an angel who introduces himself:

*anok* *pe* *Gabriel*
1S COP.M N
I am Gabriel. ($^{S}$Lk 1:19)

(192b) Ruth's answer to her master's question over her identity:

| | | | |
|---|---|---|---|
| *anok* | *te* | *hruth* | *te-k-hmhal* |
| 1S | COP.F | N | POSS.F-2MS-servant |

I am Ruth, your maiden. ($^{S}$Ru 3:9)

(192c) An area is described as extending from Aroer on the shore of the Arnon:

| | | | | | |
|---|---|---|---|---|---|
| *auô* | *hicm-p-tou* | *n-sêôn* | *ete-ntof* | *pe* | *aermon* |
| and | upon-DEF.M-mountain | of-N | REL-3MS | COP.M | N |

...up to the mountain of Zion, which is the Hermon. ($^{S}$Dt 4:48)

(192d) Jesus assures Peter:

| | | |
|---|---|---|
| *nt$^{h}$ok* | *pe* | *petros* |
| 2MS | COP.M | Peter |

You are Peter (i.e. the rock) ($^{B}$Mt 16:18)

One or both positions in the structure could be occupied by an infinitive. Depending on the need to express the actor, the simple (193a–193h) or the inflected infinitive (193i–193k) was used. However, as Coptic infinitives could be used as nouns (e.g. *ine* 'resemble' vs. *p-ine* 'the likeness'), differentiation of infinitives and nouns is sometimes difficult (cf. 193g):

(193a) The proverbs state:

| | | | |
|---|---|---|---|
| *p-unaf* | *n-n-dikaios* | *pe* | *r-p-hep* |
| DEF.M-joy | of-DEF.P-righteous | COP.M | do.INF-DEF.M-law |

The joy of the just is to do judgement. ($^{A}$Prv 21:15)

(193b) The prophet Micah addresses the heads of the house of Jacob and the princes of Israel:

| | | |
|---|---|---|
| *pô-tne* | *pe* | *sôun-n-hep* |
| POSS.M-2P | SE.M | know-DEF.P-law |

Yours is to know the laws! ($^{A}$Mi 3:1)

(193c) The proverbs state:

| | | | | | |
|---|---|---|---|---|---|
| A | *p-eua* | *m-p-rôme* | *pe* | *sehô-f* | *abal* |
| | DEF.M-honour | of-DEF.M-man | SE.M | remove-3MS | out |
| | *n-sahu* | | | | |
| | from-curse | | | | |
| P | *p-eou* | *m-p-rôme* | *pe* | *sehô-f* | *abol* |
| | DEF.M-honour | of-DEF.M-man | SE.M | remove-3MS | out |
| | *n-hn-sahue* | | | | |
| | from-IDF.P-curse | | | | |
| S | *p-eou* | *m-p-rôme* | *pe* | *sahôf* | *ebol* |
| | DEF.M-honour | of-DEF.M-man | SE.M | remove-3MS | out |
| | *n-hen-sahu* | | | | |
| | from-IDF.P-curse | | | | |

It is man's honour to cease from strife.

(Prv 20:3 [$^{A}$Böhlig 1958, 98] vs. $^{P}$pBodmer 6 vs. [$^{S}$Worrell 1931, 64])

(193d) The Bema-psalms warn the faithful of paying too much attention to bodily instead of spiritual issues:

*t-sete* *et-uôh* *hn-p-sôma* *p-s-hôb* *nta-s*
DEF.F-fire REL-dwell.STA in-DEF.M-body POSS.M-3FS-thing of-3FS
*pe* *uôm* *h[i-s]ô*
COP.M eat CNJ-drink

The fire that dwells in the body, *its* affairs is eating and drinking, (but the soul thirsts for the Word of God always.)

($^{L}$*Psalms of the Bema* 40, 29–30)

(193e) Shenute expresses his disgust at the behaviour of certain people:

*šlof* *pe* *coo-u* *šipe* *pe* *sôtm* *ero-u*
disgrace COP.M say-3P shame COP.M hear to-3P

To mention them is a disgrace. To listen to them is a shame.

($^{S}$Shenute, *Some Kinds of People Sift Dirt/Whoever Seeks God Will Find* [A I 228, 7])

(193f) Shenute teaches his audience:

*ešce* *u-špêre* *pe* *p-soun* *n-n-etuaab*
CND IDF.S-wonder COP.M DEF.M-know of-DEF.P-saint
*hen-moihe* *on* *ne* *ne-hbêue* *et-nanu-u*
IDF.P-marvel again COP.P DEF.P-things.P REL-be good-3P
*nt-a-u-aa-u*
REL-PST-3P-do-3P

If it is a wonder to know the saints (as it is written:), all the good deeds, the accomplished, on the other hand, are marvels.

($^{S}$Shenute, *Acephalous work A14* [Orlandi, *C. Origenistas* 16 §200])

(193g) The narrator of the encomium on the two Theodores points out to the audience that the body of Theodore the General, unlike that of Theodore the Oriental, was not buried at Antioch:

*anok=de* *hô* *p-et-šše* *pe* *e-t$^{h}$ri-tamô-ten*
1S=yet self.1S DEF.M-REL-proper COP.M to-INFL.1S-teach-2P
*ce-et$^{h}$be-u* *a-u-c$^{h}$i* *m-pe-f-sôma* *eḫrêi* *e-k$^{h}$êmi*
COMP-because-WH PST-3P-take OBJ-POSS.M-3MS-body down to-Egypt
*keper* *u-kahi* *n-šemmo=an=pe* *alla* *p-kahi*
CONC IDF.S-land of-alien=NEG=SE.M but DEF.M-land
*m-pe-f-iôt=pe*
of-POSS.M-3MS-father=SE.M

Therefore it is appropriate for me to let you know why his body was taken to Egypt, although it was no foreign country, but his father's land.

($^{B}$Theodore of Antioch, *On the Theodores* [*AM* II 103, 9–11])

(193h) St Paul tells the Roman Christians that he wants to be with them:
*pai=de pe e-tre-n-selsl ne-n-erêu nhêt-têutn*
DEM.M=yet COP.M to-INFL-1P-comfort POSS.P-1P-fellow inside-2P
But this is for us to comfort one another in you. (SRm 1:12)

(193i) After planning to obliterate Jesus' tomb by filling it with waste, Caiphas points out:
*anon=de u-at-kʲom pe e-tre-n-kô nsô-n m-p-nomos*
1P=yet IDF.S-NEG-power COP.M to-INFL-1P-put after-1P OBJ-DEF.M-law
*m-p-arkhê-prophêtês môusês*
of-DEF.M-arch-prophet N
As for us, it is impossible for us to abandon the law of Moses, the first prophet. (S*Eudoxia & the Holy Sepulchre* [Pearson 54, 3–4])

(193j) Shenute calls for repentance: *I say to you*
*n-t-he ete-u-at-kʲom=pe nnahra-n*
in-DEM.F-way REL-IDF.S-NEG-power=COP.M before-1P
*e-tre-n-amahte na-n m-pe-hou hatê-n*
to-INFL-1P-seize to-1P in-DEF.M-day with-1P
*efšan-côk ebol n-ne-f-unoue n-s-šôpe*
CND.3MS-finish out OBJ-POSS.P-3MS-hours.P CNJ-3FS-happen
*nkʲi-te-ušê*
PVS-DEF.F-night
*tai=on te t-he u-at-kʲom pe*
DEM.F=again COP.F DEF.F-way IDF.S-NEG-power COP.M
*e-tre-p-na m-p-nute*
to-INFL-DEF.M-mercy of-DEF.M-god
*i ehrai ecô-n hm-p-ma et-n-na-bôk ero-f*
come down upon-1P in-DEF.M-place REL-1P-FUT-go to-3MS
*hotan enšan-mu hrai hn-ne-n-nobe mn-ne-n-krof*
when CND.1P-die down in-POSS.P-1P-sin con.POSS.P-1P-guile
*mn-ne-n-mnt-asebês têr-u*
CON-POSS.P-1P-ABST-godless all-3P
*nt-a-n-aa-u m-pe-f-mto ebol <e>-n-šoop tenu*
REL-PST-1P-do-3P in-POSS.M-3MS-front out DEP-1P-be.STA now
*hicm-p-kah*
upon-DEF.M-earth
Just as it is impossible for us to keep the day with us – when the hours are complete, the night will fall – so it is impossible that God's mercy come down upon the place where we will go, as soon as we die in all our sins and guiles and godlessness that we committed before him, while living upon earth.
(SShenute, *Why O Lord* [L III 182, 13–19])

Relative clauses in absolute use may also appear in nominal sentences. Whilst in most dialects these are often indistinguishable from relative clauses in cleft structures, classical and later Bohairic[66] employ in this case a headless relative clause in absolute use with a fully stressed (etymological) demonstrative[67] preceding the clause:

(194a) Moses has asked God what to say if the Israelites inquire which god has addressed him. God replies:
S *anok* *pe* *p-et-šoop*
1S COP.M DEF.M-REL-be.STA
B *anok* *pe* *pê* *et-šop*
1S COP.M DEF$_3$.M REL-be.STA
I am who I am. ($^{SB}$Ex 3:14)

(194b) In explaining the Parable of the Sower, Jesus says:
*n-et-hicn-t-petra=de* *ne* *nai* *e-ša-u-sôtm*
DEF.P-REL-upon-DEF.F-rock=yet COP.P DEM.P REL-AOR-3P-hear
*nse-šep-p-šace* *ero-u* *hn-u-raše*
CNJ.3P-receive-DEF.M-word to-3P in-IDF.S-joy
Yet those on the rocky ground are those who listen and receive the word with joy. ($^{S}$Lk 8:13)

(194c) Young Moses of Abydos recited the four Gospels without a single omission. The bishop said:
*alêthôs* *hen-me* *ne* *n-ent-a-i-sotm-u*
truly IDF.P-truth COP.P DEF.P-REL-PST-1S-hear-3P
*etbe-pei-šêre* *šêm*
because-DEM.M-child little
Truly, what I heard of that little boy is true.
($^{S}$*Life of Moses of Abydos* [Amélineau 683, 14])

(194d) Shenute warns the devil:
*nim* *ne* *n-et-k-kʲroit* *ero-u*
WH COP.M DEF.P-REL-2MS-victorious.STA over-3P
*nsa-n-ent-a-k-raht-u* *ehrai* *e-m-paraphusis*
except-DEF.P-REL-PST-2MS-strike-3P down to-DEF.P-perversity
*m-mine* *nim*
of-manner QU

66 In Bohairic, the use of the pseudo-cleft sentence is much more widespread than in the other dialects, which often show the cleft sentence instead; cf. already Polotsky (1971: 427–30). Earlier Bohairic has a preference for simple clefts (Eitan Grossman, pc).

67 The demonstrative has lost its specific deictic function in this pattern, where it rather serves solely as a definite article and hence is glossed here simply as DEF$_3$. Nevertheless, outside this pattern it is still used as a real demonstrative.

Who are those over whom you are victorious if not those whom you struck with all kinds of perversion?

($^{S}$Shenute, *Because of You Too, O Prince of Evil* [Ch 36, 22–27])

(194e) A merchant kept a notebook on his expenses and revenues and has noted down:

*p-nt-a-f-i* *etoot-ø* *nto-thodr* *hn-sun* *n-barôt*
DEF.M-REL-3MS-come to-1S from-N in-worth of-bronze
*pe* *u-halakotte* *mpar-u-kes-u-k$^{j}$os*
COP.M IDF.S-dinar minus-IDF.S-carat-IDF.S-half
What came to me from Theodore in bronze value is one dinar minus 1 ½ carat. (*P. Gascou* 60, A 9–11)

(194f) The Lord punishes Israel by destroying her vineyards and fig trees of which she had said:

*nei* *ne* *n-et-a-i-tḫpa-u=ne-i*
DEM.P COP.P DEF.M-REL-PST-1S-beget-3P=for-1S
This is what I gathered for me. ($^{A}$Hos 2:12)

(194g) A Saracen ruler visits Simeon the Stylite. Whilst talking to him, a worm drops to the ground from Simeon's thigh:

*uoh* *a-f-ti* *n-iat-f* *mmo-f* *nce-uro*
and PST-3MS-give OBJ-eye-3MS OBJ-3MS PVS-king
*plên* *na-f-emi=an=pe* *ḫen-u-tacro*
however PRT-3MS-know=NEG=PTC in-IDF.S-strength
*ce-u-ebol* *t$^{h}$ôn* *pe* *p$^{h}$ê* *et-a-f-hi*
COMP-IDF.S-out where COP.M $DEF_3$.M REL-PST-3MS-fall
*e-p-esêt*
to-DEF.M-ground
And the king looked at it but did not fully understand where the thing that had fallen to the ground had come from.

($^{B}$*Life & Miracles of St Simeon Stylites* [Chaîne 52, 1–4])

(194h) St George prays beside a queen who overhears him. She tells him that she had liked his words and asks:

*nim=de* *ne* *nê* *et-ôš* *ebol*
WH=yet COP.P $DEF_3$.P REL-cry out
*ie* *nim* *ne* *nê* *et-a-u-er-meletan* *ie* *nim*
or WH COP.P $DEF_3$.P REL-PST-3P-AUX-imagine or WH
*pe* *p-kh(risto)s*
COP.M DEF.M-Christ
But who are those who cry out? Or who are those who imagined? Or who is the Christ?

($^{B}$*Mart. George* [*AM* II 299, 12–14])

(194i) The servant whom Abraham had sent out to find a woman for Isaac is praying to the Lord to give him a sign to find the right woman:
*t$^h$ai te t$^h$ê et-a-k-sebtôt-s m-pe-k-alu isaak*
DEM.F COP.F DEF$_3$.F REL-PST-2MS-prepare-3FS for-POSS.M-2MS-boy N
This is the one whom you have prepared for your servant Isaac.
($^B$Gn 24:14)

(194j) A Thessalonian mob accuses Jason and some others before the city council:
*nai ne nê et-a-u-št$^h$orter n-ti-oikumenê*
DEM.P COP.P DEF$_3$.P REL-PST-3P-stir OBJ-DEF$_2$.F-world
These are the ones who stirred up the world. ($^B$Acts 17:6)

(194k) Jesus' favourite disciple asks him:
*p-c$^h$(ôi)s nim pe p$^h$ê et-na-têi-k*
DEF.M-lord WH COP.M DEF$_3$.M REL-FUT-give-2MS
Lord, who is it who will betray you? ($^{B4}$Jn 21:20)

In addition, both NPs can be headless relative clauses:

(195) The heading of a set of Pachomian rules states:
*n-ent-a-u-diakonei=de kalôs ne n-ent-a-u-aherat-u*
DEF.P-REL-PST-3P-serve=yet good COP.P DEF.P-REL-PST-3P-stand-3P
*hm-p-ši n-ne-graphê*
in-DEF.M-measure of-DEF.P-scripture
It is those that fulfilled the service properly who measured up to the scripture. ($^S$Pachom, *Praecepta* [Lefort 33, 30–31])

In a structurally identical pattern, an adjective or an indefinite abstract noun, functionally equivalent to a predicative adjective in Standard European languages, occupies the initial NP position:

(196a) The apostle concludes his first letter to the Thessalonians and says:
*u-pistos pe p-ent-a-f-tahm-n*
IDF.S-faithful COP.M DEF.M-REL-PST-3MS-call-1P
Faithful is he who called us. ($^S$1Th 5:24)

(196b) The proverbs claim that the one who loves discipline loves knowledge:
*u-at-hêt=de pe p-et-maste n-n-cpio*
IDF.S-NEG-heart=yet COP.M DEF.M-REL-hate OBJ-DEF.P-blame
Yet stupid is the one who hates reproof. ($^A$Prv 12:1)

(196c) Jesus says that he did not come on his own initiative:
*alla u-mê pe p-er-taue-i*
but IDF.S-truth COP.M DEF.M-do.PPA-send-1S
...but the one who sent me is true. ($^L$Jn 7:28)

(196d) The prophet foretells Israel that it is ill-advised to put one's trust in the Egyptians:

*u-pik$^j$ei* *pe* *pe-ten-tôbah*
IDF.S-vanity COP.M POSS.M-2P-prayer
This consolation of yours is in vain.

(FIs 30:7)

(196e) John urges to carefully examine any prophets whether they are true or false. Yet the Christians will overcome them:

*u-ništi* *pe* *p$^h$ê* *et-ḫen-t$^h$ênu* *ehot-e-p$^h$ê*
IDF.S-great COP.M $\text{DEF}_3$.M REL-in-2P more-to-$\text{DEF}_3$.M
*et-ḫen-pi-kosmos*
REL-in-$\text{DEF}_2$.M-world
The one who is in you is greater than the one who is in the world.

(B1Jn 4:4)

However, the above examples suggest that the predicate here is the initial NP rather than the headless relative clause. Therefore, these patterns should be analysed as usual nominal sentences and not as pseudo-clefts. In rare cases, the headless relative clause appears in initial position:

(197a) The proverbs describe the benefits of a good wife and add:

*p-et-na-k$^j$ô=de* *mn-u-shime* *n-noik*
DEF.M-REL-FUT-persist=yet CON-IDF.S-woman of-adultery
*u-at-hêt* *pe* *auô* *u-šafte* *pe*
IDF.S-NEG-heart COP.M and IDF.S-iniquitous COP.M
He who remains with an adulterous woman is stupid and iniquitous.

(SPrv 18:22)

(197b) People tilling their own fields are noble:

*p-et-pêt=de* *se-n-et-šuit* *hen-at-sbu*
DEF.M-REL-run.STA=yet after-DEF.P-REL-empty IDF.P-NEG-teaching
*ne*
COP.P
Yet those who chase after vanities are void of teaching.

(APrv 12:11)

(197c) Jesus answers to the question over his identity and points out that he has already answered this:

*alla* *p$^h$ê* *et-a-f-tauo-i* *u-t$^h$mêi* *pe*
but $\text{DEF}_3$.M REL-PST-3MS-send-1S IDF.S-righteous COP.M
...but he who sent me is trustful.

(BJn 7:26)

As is the case in other nominal sentences, the tripartite pattern can incorporate non-etymological NPs treated as such in Coptic when preceded by an article:[68]

(198a) The Lord is good:

| | | |
|---|---|---|
| *ce-u-ša-eneh* | *pe* | *pe-f-na* |
| for-IDF.S-until-eternity | COP.M | POSS.M-3MS-mercy |

| | | | |
|---|---|---|---|
| *auô* | *te-f-me* | *ša-u-côm* | *mn-u-côm* |
| and | POSS.F-3MS-love | until-IDF.S-generation | CON-IDF.S-generation |

...for his mercy is forever and his faithfulness lasts from generation to generation. ([S]Ps 99 [100]:5)

(198b) The father urges his son to pay heed to his counsel and tells him:

| | | | | |
|---|---|---|---|---|
| *ḫn-ereh* | *nim* | *erêh* | *e-p-k-hêt* | *hen-ḫôu=gar* |
| in-guard | QU | guard.IMP | OBJ-POSS.M-2MS-heart | IDF.P-path.P=for |

| | | | |
|---|---|---|---|
| *n-ônḫ* | *ne* | *n-abal* | *ḫn-nei* |
| of-life | COP.P | DEF.P-out | in-DEM.P |

Keep your heart with all vigilance, for out of these things are the paths of life. ([A]Prv 4:23)

(198c) One of the Thomas psalms cries for cure from affliction and disease and praises the physician, whose cure is neither of the earth nor of this world:

| | | |
|---|---|---|
| *pe-k-tlkjo* | *u-abal=pe* | *n-t-khôra* |
| POSS.M-2MS-healing | IDF.S-out=COP.M | of-DEF.F-land |

*n-n-et-anh*
of-DEF.P-REL-live.STA

| | | |
|---|---|---|
| *[ne]-k-pahre* | *et-anit* | *hn-abal=ne* |
| POSS.M-2MS-drug | REL-be_pleasant.STA | IDF.P-out=COP.P |

*n-m-megi[sta]no[s]*
of-DEF.P-prince

Your healing is of the land of the Living ones and your pleasant drugs are of the princes. ([L]*Psalms of Thomas* 221, 3–4)

(198d) As his disciple suffers from thirst in the middle of the desert, St Pisenthius tells him to go to some empty jars that he now finds full of fresh water. He then begs the saint to tell him:

| | | |
|---|---|---|
| *han-ebol-tʰôn* | *ne* | *nai-mu* |
| IDF.P-out-where | COP.P | DEM.P-water |

Where does this water come from?

([B]Moses of Quft, *Vita Pisenthius* 141, 3 collated)

---

68 The construction in 198c could also be analysed as bipartite sentence with a subject element having a fronted element.

(198e) The faithful must not believe every spirit but rather test and the will be able to discriminate them thusly:

*p-n(eum)a niben et-er-omologin ce-iê(su)s p-kh(risto)s*
DEF.M-spirit QU REL-AUX-confess COMP-N DEF.M-N
*a-f-i ḫen-t-sarks*
PST-3MS-come in-DEF.F-flesh
*u-ebol m-p$^{h}$-(nu)ti pe*
IDF.S-out of-DEF.M-god COP.M
*uoh p-n(eum)a niben ete-n-f-uonh n-iê(su)s ebol an*
and DEF.M-spirit QU REL-NEG-3MS-reveal OBJ-N out NEG
*u-ebol m-p$^{h}$-(nu)ti=an pe*
IDF.S-out of-DEF.M-god=NEG COP.M

Every spirit that confesses that Jesus Christ assumed flesh is of God; and every spirit that does not confess Jesus is not of God. ($^{B}$1Jn 4:2–3)

Coptic also allows embedding of full clauses as constituents of nominal sentences. Contrary to what was observed in Earlier Egyptian, such clauses must be introduced by a complementiser such as *ce* (exx. 199a–b, d–f) or *ceka(a)s* (ex. 199c) in southern dialects (SAL) and a conjunction such as *hina* (exx. 199c*bis*) in northern ones (BF):

(199a) Explaining what he means by saying that some people 'run away in the winter' (Mt 12:3), Shenute says:

*te-prô te ce-n-se-noi=an*
DEF.F-winter COP.F COMP-NEG-3P-understand=NEG
*n-ne-graphê*
OBJ-DEF.P-scripture
*ute n-se-soun=an m-p-nute hn-u-me auô*
nor NEG-3P-know=NEG OBJ-DEF.M-god in-IDF.S-truth and
*pe-kh(risto)s*
DEF.M-Christ
*pe-u-pôt pe ce-pi-šmse et-u-ire mmo-f*
POSS.M-3P-run COP.M COMP-DEF$_2$.M-serve REL-3P-do OBJ-3MS

*Winter* means that they neither understand the scriptures nor truly know God and the Christ. Their *flight* means the service which they do.
($^{S}$Shenute, *I am Amazed* §605 [Cristea 204, 31–205, 9])

(199b) Speaking against apocryphal books, Shenute asks his audience:

*u pe ce-p-euaggelion n-i(êsu)s p-šêre m-p-nute*
WH COP.M COMP-DEF.M-gospel of-N DEF.M-son of-DEF.M-god
*pe-cpo ebol hn-n-aggelos*
DEF.M-begot out from-DEF.P-angel

What does it mean: 'The Gospel of Jesus, the son of God, the one begotten by the angels'.

($^{S}$Shenute, *I am Amazed* §309 [Cristea 141, 15–18])

(199c) The disciples want Jesus to eat but he claims to have had food already and answers the disciples' question about who brought him food:

L *ta-hre* *anak* *te* *cek[a]se* *e-i-na-ire* *m-p-uôš*
POSS.F.1S-food 1S COP.F so that ST-1S-FUT-do OBJ-DEF.M-wish
*m-p-ent-a-f-teua-i*
of-DEF.M-REL-PST-3MS-send-1S

B *ta-ḫre* *anok* *te* *hina* *nta-er-p$^h$-uôš*
POSS.F.1S-food 1S COP.F so that CNJ.1S-do-DEF.M-wish
*m-p$^h$ê* *et-a-f-tauo-i*
of-DEF$_3$.M REL-PST-3MS-send-1S

My own food is to do the will of Him who sent me.

(Jn 4:34 L vs. B)

(199d) After telling about the phoenix and its resurrection, Clement asks:

*u-nak$^j$* *m-maihe* *te* *ce-p-ref-sônt*
IDF.S-great of-wonder COP.F COMP-DEF.M-AGT-creation
*m-p-têr-f* *na-ire* *n-n-et-e-n-ḫmhal* *ne-f*
of-DEF.M-all-3MS FUT-do for-DEF.P-REL-do.STA-servant to-3MS
*ne-f* *ḫn-u-m[ie]* *mn-u-emahte* *m-pistis* *e-nanu-f*
to-3MS in-IDF.S-truth CON-IDF.S-prevail in-faith REL-good-3MS
*[hop]u* *f-tamo* *mma-n* *hitn-u-halêt* *[a]-t-mnt-nak$^j$*
when 3MS-tell OBJ-1P through-IDF.S-bird OBJ-DEF.F-ABST-great
*m-p-f-špôp*
of-POSS.M-3MS-promise

Do we consider it a great wonder that the creator of all will act for those who serve him truly and remain in good faith when he shows us his promise through a bird?

($^{A}$1Cl 26:1 [Rösch 87, 26–31])

(199e) The author of the Manichean *Kephalaia* says that also Buddha preached his wisdom and founded churches:

*alla* *pei* *mmete* *pe*
but DEM.M only COP.M
*ce-mp[e-f]-shei-te-f-so[phia* *a-cô]me*
COMP-NEG.PST-3MS-write-POSS.F-3MS-wisdom to-book

But this alone is that he did not write down his wisdom into books.

($^{L}$*Kephalaia* 8, 4)

(199f) Frange writes to the superior hermit Isaac and quotes a passage from 1Kgs 16:7 ('a mortal will look into the face, but God will look into the heart'). He adds the following explanation:
*ete-pai* *pe* *ce-ti-uaš-k* *n-huo* *e-rôme*
REL-DEM.M COP.M COMP-1S-wish-2MS in-more to-man
*e-f-hm-pe-tou*
DEP-3MS-in-DEF.M-mountain
...which means that I love you more than anyone else in the mountain.
([S]*O.Frange* #14, 14–16)

For counterexamples such as 200a and 200b without an embedding particle one might argue that they try to avoid the latter due to the exegetic nature of the passages: As the passage to be expounded is quote in the first place, it would have been pragmatically pointless to mark the quote accordingly again. However, examples such as 200c show that this is probably not necessarily the case and that we rather have to assume two ways of embedding: marked (exx. 199) versus unmarked (exx. 200). Sometimes, a sentence with the conjunctive verb form is employed (200d):

(200a) St Paul explains a passage in the scriptures:
*u=de* *pe* *a-f-bôk* *ehrai* *nsabêl* *rô* *ce-a-f-bôk*
WH=yet COP.M PST-3MS-go up except PTC COMP-PST-3MS-go
*n-šôrp* *e-p-esêt*
as-first to-DEF.M-ground
But what is 'he went up' except that he went down first? ([S]Eph 4:9)

(200b) Christ is explained to be the mediator of the new covenant with the Lord:
*p-kephaleon=de* *n-n-et-u-cô* *mma-u* *pe*
DEF.M-point=yet of-DEF.P-REL-3P-say OBJ-3P COP.M
*uantê-n* *mmeu* *n-u-arkhiereus* *n-tei-mini*
have-1P PTC OBJ-IDF.S-high priest of-DEM.F-sort
Now the point in what they are saying is that we have such a high priest.
([F]Heb 8:1)

(200c) The monk Frange writes to a superior monk asking:
*ekšan-sotm-ne-shai* *n-ta-mnt-elakh(istos)* *mper-ameli*
CND.2MS-hear-DEF.P-writing of-POSS.F.1S-least NEG.IMP-tarry
*n-u-hou* *n-uôt*
for-IDF.S-day of-single
*e-pi-hôb* *ete-pai* *pe* *ari-t-nokʲ* *n-agapê* *nmma-i*
to-DEM.M-thing REL-DEM COP.M do.IMP-DEF.F-great of-love with-1S
*n-g-senau-u-garte* *šêm* *na-i* *e-te-khria*
CNJ-2MS-provide-IDF.S-knife little for-1S for-DEF.F-need

If you listen to the writings of my humbleness, do not tarry for a single day in this matter, i.e. be so utterly kind to me and provide a little knife for me for (my) needs ...

($^{S}$*O.Frange* #48, 14–20)

(200d) After a young servant fearful of his master survived an attempted suicide by drowning, he told his master:

| *u-hêu* | *na-i* | *pe* | *nta-en-pa-mu=na-i* |
|---|---|---|---|
| IDF.S-profit | to-1S | COP.M | CNJ.1S-bring-POSS.M.1S-death=to-1S |

*mauaat-ø*
self-1S

| *n-huo* | *ero-s* | *nta-i* | *ehrai* | *e-ne-k-k$^{j}$ic* |
|---|---|---|---|---|
| in-more | to-3FS | CNJ.1S-go | down | to-POSS.P-2MS-hand |

It is better for me to kill myself than fall into your hands.

($^{S}$*Further Miracles of Apa Mena* [Drescher, *Mena* 21, a29–b1])

Besides these patterns, an alternative strategy consists in employing a demonstrative, usually the masculine singular $^{S}$*pai*/$^{L}$*pei*/$^{B}$*p$^{h}$ai*, as a cataphoric pronoun whose meaning is made explicit in what follows:

(201a) A man is called to the royal court and asks his three dearest friends to accompany him. The second says: *You know that I love and cherish you the most among those whom I love*:

| *p-ete-ša-i-eš-aa-f* | *pe* | *pai* |
|---|---|---|
| DEF.M-REL-AOR-1S-can-do-3MS | COP.M | DEM.M |

| *ša-i-i* | *nmma-k* | *ša-p-[ro* | *m-p-êi* |
|---|---|---|---|
| AOR-1S-go | with-2MS | until-DEF.M-door | of-DEF.M-house |

| *m-p-rro]* | *nta-sto-i* |
|---|---|
| of-DEF.M-king | CNJ.1S-turn-1S |

What I can do is that I come with you to the gates of the palace and then return. ($^{S}$*Sayings of Pagan Philosophers* [Till 169, 24–170, 2])

(201b) St George visits the house of a poor widow with no bread in her house. Asked about her beliefs, she declares that she believes in Apollo. The saint says:

| *alêthos* | *u-hap* | *m-mêi* | *nte-p$^{h}$-(nu)ti* | *pe* | *p$^{h}$ai* |
|---|---|---|---|---|---|
| verily | IDF.S-law | of-truth | of-DEF.M-god | COP.M | DEM.M |

| *ce-mmon-hli* | *n-ôik* | *ḫen-pe-êi* |
|---|---|---|
| that-NEG-any | of-bread | in-POSS.M.2FS-house |

Verily, it is God's just judgement that there is no bread in your house.

($^{B}$*Mart. George* [*AM* II 293, 10–11])

The complementiser *ce* is also found within the exegetic REL DEM COP X construction 'that is' or 'i.e.' when the explanation is a clause (202a). However, sometimes *ce* can also be absent (202b), perhaps documenting a diachronic development from *ce* to zero:

(202a) Dioscorus compares the anti-Chalcedonian party to pike-men in the first line of battle: *So it is also with Father Macarius. And even if Macarius is no pike-man*:

| | | |
|---|---|---|
| *ete-pai* | *pe* | *ce-nn-f-noi=an* |
| REL-DEM.M | COP.M | that-NEG-3MS-understand=NEG |

*e-šace-m-mnt-uainin*
to-speak-DEF.P-ABST-Greek
...that means that he cannot speak Greek (yet he did not rest without going with us to war with Chalcedon).
(SFDioscorus of Alexandria, *On Macarius of Tkow* §1.5 [Johnson 3a, 17–19])

(202b) Athanasius orders that the loaves offered during service should not be stale:

| | | | | |
|---|---|---|---|---|
| *alla* | *hen-oik* | *e-u-hêm* | *ê* | *e-u-rout* |
| but | IDF.P-bread | DEP-3P-warm.STA | or | DEP-3P-fresh.STA |

| | | | |
|---|---|---|---|
| *ete-pai* | *pe* | *emp-u-ôsk* | *ci-nt-a-u-tok$^{j}$-u* |
| REL-DEM.M | COP.M | NEG.PST-3P-delay | since-REL-PST-3P-bake-3P |

...but warm or fresh bread, i.e. ones not delayed since they were baked.
(S*Canons of Athanasius* [Crum in Riedel §64])

Like the other types of nominal sentences, tripartite constructions could also be extended by adverbs or prepositional phrases:

(203a) In the *Gospel according to Philip* the difference between Echamoth and Echmoth is explained as:

| | | | | | |
|---|---|---|---|---|---|
| *ekhamoth* | *te* | *t-sophia* | *haplôs* | *ekhmôth=de* | *te* |
| N | COP.F | DEF.F-wisdom | simply | N=yet | COP.F |

| | |
|---|---|
| *t-sophia* | *m-p-mu* |
| DEF.F-wisdom | of-DEF.M-death |

| | | | | | | |
|---|---|---|---|---|---|---|
| *ete-tai* | *te* | *et-soun* | *m-p-mu* | *tai* | *et-u-mute* | *ero-s* |
| REL-DEM.F | SE.F | REL-know | OBJ-DEF.M-death | DEM.F | REL-3P-call | to-3FS |

| | |
|---|---|
| *ce-t-kui* | *n-sophia* |
| COMP-DEF.F-little | of-wisdom |

Echamoth is simply Wisdom, but Echmoth is the Wisdom of death, i.e. one who knows death, which is called 'the little Wisdom'.
(SL*GospPh.* 60, 11–15)

(203b) Shenute opposes the views of a pagan philosopher and adapts Dt 32:13: *He has nourished them with honey out of rock and oil out of the hardest cliffs*:

*aš=$k^j$e pe p-ebiô nsa-p-šace mn-te-sbô*
WH=now COP.M DEF.M-honey beside-DEF.M-word CON-DEF.F-teach
*n-ne-graphê*
of-DEF.P-scripture
*nim=de petra nsa-pe-kh(risto)s p-nute*
WH=yet rock beside-DEF.M-Christ DEF.M-god
*u pe p-neh ebol hn-u-petra n-sibt*
WH COP.M DEF.M-oil out in-IDF.S-rock of-hill
*imêti e-te-kharis nt-a-ne-khristianos ucai nhêt-s*
except to-DEF.F-mercy REL-PST-DEF.P-Christian safe inside-3FS

Now what is the honey except the word and teaching of the Scripture? What is rock except Christ the God? What is the oil out of a rocky hill except the mercy in which the Christians were safe?
([S]Shenute, *As I Sat On A Mountain* [L III 52, 2–5])

(203c) When Rachel died and was buried near the road to Bethlehem, Jacob erected a stela upon her tomb:

*$t^h$ai te t-stylê m-p-emhau n-rakhêl ša-eḫun*
DEM.F COP.F DEF.F-stele of-DEF.M-tomb of-N to-down
*e-phou n-ehou*
to-today of-day

This is the stela of Rachel's tomb up to the present day. ([B]Gn 35:20)

The Mesokemic dialect shows examples of the use of *ete* as a copula in tripartite sentences (cf. Schenke 1996: 106):

(204a) Pilate asked Jesus:

M *ntak ete p-era n-n-iudai*
2MS COP DEF.M-king of-DEF.P-Jew
S *ntok pe p-rro n-n-iudai*
2MS COP.M DEF.M-king of-DEF.P-Jew

Are you the king of the Jews?
(Mt 27:11 [[M]Schenke mae 1 vs. [S]Aranda Perez])

(204b) In God we trust:

M *serfe tare-tn-neu ce-anak ete p-n(u)ti*
think.IMP CNJ.FUT-2P-see COMP-1S COP DEF.M-god
S *serfe ntetn-nau ce-anok pe p-nute*
think.IMP CNJ.2P-see COMP-1S COP.M DEF.M-god

Think and you will see that I am God!
(Ps. 45 [46]:11 [10] [[M]Gabra vs. [S]Budge])

(204c) Saul preaches in Damascus about the Lord:

| | | | | |
|---|---|---|---|---|
| M | *ntaf* | *ete* | *p-šêre* | *m-p-n(u)ti* |
| | 3MS | COP | DEF.M-son | of-DEF.M-god |
| B | *p$^h$ai* | *pe* | *p-šêri* | *m-p$^h$-(nu)ti* |
| | DEM.M | COP.M | DEF.M-son | of-DEF.M-god |

He is the Son of God! (Acts 9:20 [$^M$Schenke vs. $^B$Horner])

These examples have been analysed as cleft sentences (Shisha-Halevy 1983: 319; Schenke 1991: 53). However, this would entail evoking an otherwise unattested cleft sentence type with a nominal sentence in the relative clause. In addition, one would have to assume that the subject element inside the relative clause has been deleted (i.e. *ete X pe* > *ete X Ø*). One might assume that exx. 204a–204c represent grammaticalised uses of bare *ete*, which sometimes varies with the expected *pe*, as shown by the following witness from M in comparison with the examples above:

(205) The first stanza of Psalm 45 [46]:

| | | | | | |
|---|---|---|---|---|---|
| M | *pe-n-n(u)ti* | *pe* | *pe-n-ma* | *n-pot* | *auô* |
| | POSS.M-1P-god | COP.M | POSS.M-1P-place | of-flight | and |
| | *te-n-k$^j$am* | | | | |
| | POSS.F-1P-power | | | | |
| S | *pe-n-nute* | *pe* | *pe-n-ma* | *m-pôt* | *auô* |
| | POSS.M-1P-god | COP.M | POSS.M-1P-place | of-flight | and |
| | *te-n-k$^j$om* | | | | |
| | POSS.F-1P-power | | | | |

Our god is our refuge and our strength.

(Ps. 45 [46]:1 [$^M$Gabra vs. $^S$Budge])

Another possibility consists in viewing them as bipartite constructions in which the second NP is not marked for definiteness. In favour of such an analysis one can adduce the following examples from dialects SL which exhibit the article, but not the expected unstressed form of the initial absolute pronoun:

(206a) The letter of St Peter to St Philip cites Jesus on the issue of being held in custody. This is because:

| | |
|---|---|
| *ntôtn* | *n-ete-nu-i* |
| 2P | COP.P-REL-POSS.P-1S |

You are mine. ($^S$*EpPt* [NHC VIII, 2] 137, 5)

(206b) St Paul asks the Lord to grant him salvation since:

| | |
|---|---|
| *[anak]* | *p-ete-pô-k* |
| 1S | COP.M-REL-POSS.M-1S |

I am yours. ($^L$*PrecPl* [NHC I, 1] A, 5)

If the nominal expression in the last examples is the result of a process of grammaticalisation of the possessive construction, they might have no longer been considered as relative patterns, but as nominalisations. In this case, the first analysis noted above is probably to be preferred.

Coptic uses both bipartite and tripartite constructions for the predication of qualities:

(207a) Jesus said:
*hen-makarios* *ne* *n-monakhos* *auô* *et-sotp*
IDF.P-blessed COP.P DEF.P-solitary and REL-chose.STA
*ce-tetn-a-he* *a-t-mnt-ero*
for-2P-FUT-find to-DEF.F-ABST-king
Blessed are the solitary and elect, for you will find the Kingdom.
(SL*EvThom* 41:27–29)

(207b) The king wanted two high-ranking officers to find out:
*hen-me* *ne* *ni-šace* *ete-tn-cô* *mmo-u* *na-i*
IDF.P-truth COP.P DEM.P-word REL-2P-say OBJ-3P to-1S
*etbêêt-f* *cin-mmon*
because-3MS or-not
...if these words that you tell me about him are true or not.
(SAcacius of Caesarea, *Encomium on St Mercurius* [Budge, *Misc.* 291, 11–12)

(207c) Isaiah urges Israel not to seek help in Egypt but in believing in the Lord:
*auô* *ntaf* *u-sophos* *pe*
and 3MS IDF.S-wise COP.M
And he is wise. (FIs 31:2)

Here the tripartite construction stands in complementary distribution with the bipartite. Although the latter is the preferred pattern for subjects with pronouns of the first and second persons, the tripartite construction is common with third-person pronouns and with all other nouns or personal pronouns.

The tripartite construction is also used for pseudo-clefts. In Coptic, these consist of an initial NP (of any sort) followed by the copula and an undetermined headless relative clause:

(208a) The Lord tells Moses that he has heard all the things that the children of Israel have told him and asks:
*nim* *pe* *et-na-ti* *m-pe-u-hêt* *e-tre-f-šôpe*
WH COP.M REL-FUT-give in-POSS.M-3P-heart to-INFL-3MS-happen
*hi-nai* *nhêt-u*
on-DEM.P in-3P

*e-tre-u-r-hote* *hêt* *auô* *nse-hareh* *e-na-entolê*
to-INFL-3P-do-fear before-1S and CNJ.3P-hearken to-POSS.P.1S-order
*n-ne-u-hou* *têr-u*
in-POSS.P-3P-day all-3P
Who will give it into their heart so that it stays there in them and so that they will fear me and pay attention to my commandments in all their days?
([S]Dt 5:29 [Budge])

(208b) When Jesus ended his speech, Philippos advanced and laid down the book that he was holding:
*ntof=gar* *pe* *et-shai* *n-šace* *nim* *e-nere-i(êsu)s*
3MS=for COP.M REL-write OBJ-word QU DEP-PRT-N
*cô* *mmo-u* *auô* *mn-n-et-f-ire* *mmo-u* *têr-u*
say OBJ-3P and CON-DEF.P-REL-3MS-do OBJ-3P all-3P
...for he is the one who writes every word that Jesus said and whatever Jesus did. ([S]*Pistis Sophia* 71, 5–7 [Schmidt])

(208c) Philippos asks Jesus:
*pa-cois* *mêti* *anok* *mauaat-ø* *pe*
POSS.M.1S-Lord IP 1S alone-1S COP.M
*ent-a-k-taa-s* *na-i*
REL-PST-2MS-give-3FS to-1S
*e-tra-fi-p-rouš* *m-pi-kosmos* *nta-shai-n-šace*
to-INFL.1S-take-DEF.M-care for-DEF$_2$.M-world CNJ.1S-write-DEF.P-word
*nim* *et-n-a-co-u* *auô* *mn-n-et-n-na-aa-u*
QU REL-1P-FUT-say-3P and CON-DEF.P-REL-1P-FUT-do-3P
My Lord, is it only me to whom you gave it to take care of the world by noting down whatever we will say and whatever we will do?
([S]*Pistis Sophia* 71, 8–11 [Schmidt])

(208d) Context broken: *We should tell them*:
*[ce]-p-nute* *pe* *ent-a-f-tamio-u*
COMP-DEF.M-god COP.M REL-PST-3MS-create-3P
...that Lord was the one who created them. ([S]*V. Pachom* [Lefort 34, 23–24])

(208e) The Lord commands:
*6* *n-ehou* *pe* *ete-k-er-hôb* *mmô-u*
6 of-day COP.M REL-2MS-do-work on-3P
On six days you shall work. ([B]Ex 20:9)

(208f) Threatened by his pagan wife, John wept over his son Theodore and said:
*t-emi=an* *ce-u* *pe* *et-i-na-ai-f*
1S-know=NEG COMP-WH COP.M REL-1S-FUT-do-3MS
I do not know what to do.
([B]Theodore of Antioch, *On The Theodores* [*AM* II 111, 16])

(208g) Peter explains why he sent his letter to Acacius:

| | | | | |
|---|---|---|---|---|
| *hina* | *isce* | *kata-u-met$^h$-mêi* | *nt$^h$ok* | *pe* |
| so that | CND | like-IDF.S-ABST-true | 2MS | COP.M |

| | | | |
|---|---|---|---|
| *et-a-k-ce-nai* | *na-f* | *nte-k-sh̲ai* | *nê-i* |
| REL-PST-2MS-say-DEM.P | to-3MS | CNJ-2MS-write | to-1S |

...so that if it is true that you are the one who told him this so that you might write to me.
([B]*Correspondence of Peter Mongus & Acacius* §I.19 [Amélineau 198, 13–14, collated])

Note that the frequency of the *pe et-* pattern is higher in Bohairic[69] than in the other dialects, where the elided forms (*pet-* etc.) are preferred. As can be seen, the construction is used for subject, object. and adjunct clefts and can be described using the following scheme:

$$NP_i \quad \text{COP} \quad \text{REL}$$

Diachronically, this pattern is reanalysed as bipartite even though it is impossible to decide whether this took place after the vowel elision *pe et- > pet-* that led to the reanalysis or whether the former was the outcome of the latter.[70] The interpretation as a process of reanalysis with vowel elision was favoured in earlier works on Coptic cleft constructions, in which the element *pe* was taken to be the subject element.[71] Yet, as pointed out in the section on the syntactic structure of the clefts (1.1.2.3), this interpretation raises some problems.

We saw that bipartite cleft sentences, unlike tripartite pseudo-clefts, distinguish between a pattern with a relative clause marked for definiteness and one without such marking. Adding now the third pattern with the copula, one might assume the following diachronic process:

NP COP Ø-REL > NP DEF-REL > NP Ø-REL

In the initial stage, cleft sentences are built with an NP, the copula, and a headless relative clause without any determiner. In the second stage, the copula *pe*, *te*,

69 However, *pe et*-examples do not seem to exist in the Early Bohairic manuscript of the Gospel of John in pBodmer III.

70 The latter interpretation (i.e. that the reduction is the actual source of reanalysis) might be supported by the lack of examples of elision in similar environment *pe e-* such as *haps pe e-*. However, the elison might also be considered to be purely graphemic.

71 See Layton (2011: §464). Cf. however Steindorff (1951: 232), who describes it as a tripartite pattern NP COP REL. Polotsky (1971: 418) also calls the element *pe* the copula of the tripartite pattern, designating the analysis as 'wahrscheinlich richtige Annahme'.

and *ne* and the relative clause have merged into a (graphemic) unit that can be interpreted as a headless relative clause with a definite article (i.e. *pe et-* > *pet-*). In the third stage, the determiner is dropped.

It is equally possible that both the second and the third stage actually derive from the initial pattern NP COP Ø-REL. In any case, the latter two constructions exhibit no functional or semantic difference, except in Bohairic where Ø-REL is favoured with personal pronouns and names in the first position and if the cleft sentence does not have past time reference. Occasionally, the patterns appear as variants in different versions of the same text:

(209a) Jesus tells the disciples what to say when charged at court; he begins:

| | |
|---|---|
| *pai* | *p-ete-tn-na-coo-f* |
| DEM.M | COP.M-REL-1P-FUT-say-3MS |

It is this that you should say.

| | | |
|---|---|---|
| *pai* | *pe* | *ete-tn-na-coo-f* |
| DEM.M | COP.M | REL-1P-FUT-say-3MS |

What you should say is this.

($^{S}$Mk 13:11 [Horner vs. Quecke])

(209b) The angel appears to Joseph and foretells him the birth of his son, quoting from the Book of Isaiah, according to which the name of the child shall be Emmanuel:

| | | | |
|---|---|---|---|
| *ete-pai* | *pe-n-ša-u-uahme-f* | *ce-p-nute* | *nmma-n* |
| REL-DEM.M | COP.M-REL-AOR-3P-explain-3MS | COMP-DEF.M-god | with-1P |

...which is translated as “God is with us”

| | | | | |
|---|---|---|---|---|
| *ete-pai* | *pe* | *e-ša-u-uahme-f* | *ce-p-nute* | *nmma-n* |
| REL-DEM.M | COP.M | REL-AOR-3P-explain-3MS | COMP-DEF.M-god | with-1P |

...which is translated as ‘God is with us’.

($^{S}$Mt 1:23 M569 vs. BM Or. 4917)

(209c) Asked whether man has a predestined lifespan, Cyril answers:

| | | | | |
|---|---|---|---|---|
| *ei=men* | *ešôpe* | *u-dikaios=pe* | *n-aggelos* | *ne* |
| CND=indeed | CND | IDF.S-righteous=SE.M | DEF.P-angel | COP.P |

| | | |
|---|---|---|
| *e-ša-u-i* | *nsô-f* | *hn-u-timê* |
| REL-AOR-3P-come | after-3MS | in-IDF.S-honour |

| | | | | |
|---|---|---|---|---|
| *ei=de* | *ešôpe* | *u-ref-r-nobe* | *pe* | *n-et-hicn-kolasis* |
| CND=yet | CND | IDF.S-AGT-do-sin | SE.M | DEF.P-REL-on-punishment |

| | | | |
|---|---|---|---|
| *ne-ša-u-i* | *nsô-f* | *n-se-fit-f* | *hn-u-štortr* |
| DEF.P-AOR-3P-come | after-3MS | CNJ-3P-carry-3MS | in-IDF.S-trouble |

If he is righteous, those who come after him in honour are the angels. If he is a sinner, it is the ones responsible for punishment that come after him and carry him away in turmoil.

($^{S}$Cyril of Alexandria, *Erotapokrisis* [Crum, pCheltenham 5, 3–5])

In other instances, the copula appears as the immutable masculine singular *pe* without agreement marking:

(210) Jacob meets herdsmen from Haran and asks if they know the condition of his uncle Laban. They reply that he is fine and point out that his daughter Rachel is just arriving at the well:

*ntos=gar pe e-ne-s-moone n-n-esou m-pe-s-iôt*
3FS=for COP.M REL-PRT-3FS-herd OBJ-DEF.P-sheep of-POSS-3FS-father
...for it was she who herded her father's sheep. ($^{S}$Gn 29:6 [Maspero])

The tripartite analysis can also easily explain the insertion of an element between the copula and the relative clause:

(211) The children of God were bitten by venomous snakes but were saved only through the mercy of God:

*ute=gar n-u-ntêk$^{j}$=an ute n-u-pahre=an*
neither=for NEG-IDF.S-herb=NEG nor NEG-IDF.S-drug=NEG
*t-ent-a-s-talk$^{j}$o-u*
COP.F-REL-PST-3FS-cure-3P
*alla pe-k-šace pe p-cois et-tuco n-uon nim*
but POSS.M-2MS-word COP.M DEF.M-lord REL-heal OBJ-one QU
For it was neither herb nor medicament that cured them, but what saves everyone is your word, O Lord. ($^{S}$Sap 16:12)

This pattern (*pe e-*) is regular in Bohairic, even though examples of *pe-*, to be cited below, exist as well.

(212a) In a panegyric on John the Baptist, Herod is quoted as wailing:

*u-nobi n-aš m-maiê pe et-a-i-ai-f*
IDF.S-sin of-WH of-kind COP.M REL-PST-1S-do-3MS
What kind of a sin did I commit?
($^{B}$*Panegyric on John the Baptist* [de Vis I 49, 2–3])

(212b) Zachary expands on a passage in the Book of Jonah referring to the destruction of Niniveh:

*u pe e-na-f-mpša n-šôpi*
WH COP.M REL-PRT-3MS-worth of-happen
What was worthy of happening?
($^{B}$Zachary of Sakha, *Consolatory Sermon* [de Vis II, 50, 7])

(212c) General Romanos suggests to Emperor Diocletian that he should publish an edict ordering the whole world to sacrifice to the pagan gods. Delighted by the idea Diocletian asks Romanos:

*u pe ete-k-uoš hina nta-ai-f*
WH COP.M REL-2MS-wish so that CNJ.1S-do-3MS
What do you want me to do? ($^{B}$*Mart. Eusebius* [*AdM* 23, 14–15])

(212d) Having destroyed all the statues of the pagan deities, St George derides the governor Dadianus:

*ešôp nte-k-ini m-pi-araklês*
CND CNJ-2MS-bring OBJ-DEF$_2$.M-N
*nt$^h$of pe et-i-na-uošt mmo-f m-pe-k-mt$^h$o ebol*
3MS COP.M REL-1S-FUT-worship OBJ-3MS in-POSS.M-2MS-front out
If you bring that Herakles, he is the one whom I will worship before you.
([B]Theodotus of Ancyra, *In S. Georgem Diosp.* [*AM* II 248, 16–18])

Again, textual variants occasionally show different patterns in versions of the same text:

(213a) Jesus tells the disciples: *And herein is that saying true:*

*ke-uai pe p$^h$ê et-s[iti uohe] ke-uai*
other-IDF.S.ABS COP.M DEF$_3$.M REL-sow and other-IDF.S.ABS
*pe p$^h$ê et-osẖ* Kasser
COP.M DEF$_3$.M REL-reap
*ke-uai pe et-siti uoh ke-uai*
other-IDF.S.ABS COP.M REL-sow and other-IDF.S.ABS
*pe et-osẖ* Horner var.
COP.M REL-reap
*ke-uai p-et-siti uoh ke-uai*
other-IDF.S.ABS COP.M-REL-sow and other-IDF.S.ABS
*p-et-osẖ* Horner main text
COP.M-REL-reap
It is one who sows and another who reaps.
([B]Jn 4:37)

(213b) The Saint in distress cries out to Jesus: *My Lord, Jesus Christ, help me:*

*nt$^h$ok mmauat-k p-et-a-i-er-helpis ero-k*
2MS self-2MS COP.M-REL-PST-1S-hope OBJ-2MS
*nt$^h$ok mmauat-k pe et-a-i-er-helpis ero-k*
2MS self-2MS COP.M REL-PST-1S-hope OBJ-2MS
It is you whom I hoped for. ([B]*Mart. Apatil* [*AM* I 93, 22])

The context usually provides sufficient information to distinguish cleft sentences and bipartite sentences with subject element followed by an attributive relative clause, but in some cases, there is room for ambiguity (cf. Polotsky 1971: 426):

(214a) Egyptians were idolators before St Mark arrived:

*kaigar ha-t-hê-men mpate-markos ei*
for under-DEF.F-front-indeed NCO-N come
*ne-mn-hou šoop e-p-têr-f pe hn-kême*
PRT-NEG-day happen.STA to-DEF.M-all-3MS PTC in-N

| | | | |
|---|---|---|---|
| *alla* | *ušê=pe* | *et-mên* | *ebol* |
| but | night=SE.M | REL-last.STA | out |

However, before Mark came, day did not exist at all in Egypt, but only endless night prevailed.

($^{S}$John the Hermit, *Enc. on Mark the Evangelist* [Orlandi 16a, 11–17])

(214b) Anna, Tobit's wife, has received a kid and brings it home. Since it starts to bleat then, Tobit surmises that it has been stolen and demands that she returns it. She replies:

| | | |
|---|---|---|
| *u-taio=pe* | *nt-a-u-taa-f=na-i* | *ecm-pa-beke* |
| IDF.S-gift=SE.M | REL-PST-3P-give-3MS=for-1S | upon-POSS.M.1S-wage |

It is a gift that was given to me in addition to my wage. ($^{S}$Tb 2:14[13])

One of the additional cleft patterns introduced above in the chapter on bipartite nominal sentences (1.1.2.3) is probably also best analysed as a tripartite pattern: the construction built with an initial pronoun or indefinite NP followed by an agreeing copula and a dependent ('circumstantial') clause. The last example below may also be analysed as containing two nested circumstantial clauses:

(215a) Macarius of Scetis lived in the inner desert:

| | | | | |
|---|---|---|---|---|
| *e-ne-ntof* | *mauaa-f* | *pe* | *e-f-anakhôri* | *hm-p-ma* |
| DEP-PRT-3MS | alone-3MS | COP.M | DEP-3MS-live alone | in-DEF.M-place |
| *etmmau* | | | | |
| that | | | | |

...while it was he alone who was living there as an anchorite.

($^{S}$*AP* Chaîne 43, 21–22)

(215b) In the Sermon on the Mount, Jesus tells people not to worry:

| | | | |
|---|---|---|---|
| *nim=de* | *hn-tênu* | *pe* | *e-f-fi-rauš* |
| WH=yet | in-2P | COP.M | DEP-3MS-take-care |

| | | |
|---|---|---|
| *e-f-ne-neš-uêh-u-mehe* | *ehrêi* | *ecn-te-f-*$k^{j}$*at* |
| DEP-3MS-FUT-can-put-IDF.S-cubit | up | upon-POSS-3MS-form |

Who among you is one who can add a single cubit to his stature by worrying?

($^{M}$Mt 6:27 mae 1)

(215c) Having heard that Lazarus had died, Jesus went to Bethany. On his arrival:

| | | | |
|---|---|---|---|
| *a-f-cem-f* | *e-pe-f-4* | *pe* | *e-f-*$k^{h}$*ê* |
| PST-3MS-find-3MS | OBJ-POSS.M-3MS-4 | COP.M | DEP-3MS-AUX |
| *ḫen-pi-mhau* | | | |
| in-$DEF_2$.M-grave | | | |

He found that it was his fourth (day) in the grave. ($^{B}$Jn 11:17)

Examples with an indefinite NP show agreement marking of the subject element:

(216a) Shenute begins a parable:

| *u-rôme* | *pe* | *e-f-kôt* | *n-u-topos* | *e-te-f-khria* |
|---|---|---|---|---|
| IDF.S-man | COP.M | DEP-3MS-build | OBJ-IDF.S-place | to-POSS.F-3MS-need |

Once there was a man who was building a place for his own use.

($^{S}$Shenute, *I Answered* [L III 27, 9])

(216b) Shenute begins a parable, which he had learnt from his uncle and predecessor Pk$^{j}$ol:

| *u-rôme* | *pe* | *peca-f* | *e-unta-f* | *mmau* |
|---|---|---|---|---|
| IDF.S-man | COP.M | say.PPA-3MS | DEP-have-3MS | PTC |

| *n-u-šêre* | *auô* | *šeere* | *snte* |
|---|---|---|---|
| OBJ-IDF.S-child.M | and | child.F | two.F |

Once there was a man, he said, who had a son and two daughters.

($^{S}$Shenute, *Acephalous Work A6* [*Or* 44 161, 16–20])

(216c) Theodore mocks Diocletian for his plebeian roots:

| *u-hêu* | *na-k* | *pe* | *e-k-amoni* | *n-ni-baempi* |
|---|---|---|---|---|
| IDF.S-profit | to-2MS | COP.M | DEP-2MS-tend | OBJ-DEF.P-goat |

| *ḫen-t-koi* |
|---|
| in-DEF.F-field |

| *m-p$^{h}$-rêti* | *n-šorp* | *e-hote* | *e-k-oi* | *n-uro* |
|---|---|---|---|---|
| in-DEF.M-way | of-first | to-more | DEP-2MS-be.STA | as-king |

It is more profitable to you to herd the goats in the field as before than to rule.

($^{B}$Theodore of Antioch, *On the Theodores* [*AM* II 97, 6–8])

The last examples resemble the older Earlier Egyptian pattern of the type *s=pw wn* 'There was a man' (see 3.1.5.), and might therefore be analysed simply as bipartite nominal sentences with a dependent clause extension. However, they have been included here due to their parallelism with the other patterns discussed in this section. As with the cleft pattern, the majority of examples of this construction show a subject element with agreement marking, but sometimes the invariable *pe* (MS) is also used:

(217) The preacher laments the worthlessness of wisdom in the world:

| *uaiš* | *hi-apantêma* | *pe* | *e-f-ne-tamie-uan* | *nibi* |
|---|---|---|---|---|
| time | CON-fate | COP.M | REL-FUT-create-IDF.S.ABS | QU |

(For) it is time and fate that will create everything.

($^{F}$Eccl 9:11)

## 1.4 Bipartite nominal sentences with ellipsis of the subject element

In Later Egyptian, one occasionally encounters what appear to be bipartite nominal patterns with omitted subject. Late Egyptian examples such as the following apparently consist of a single nominal phrase without any additional element such as the element *pw/pꜣy/pe*:

(218a) In a letter of complaint regarding slaves, the writer says that he went to the temple of goddess Mut where some people said:

*rḏd-tꜣy-n-sn-t*
COMP-[POSS.F-1P-sister-F]$_P$
She is our sister! (pBM 75015 r° 16 [Demarée, *Bankes Pap.* pl. 2])

(218b) The author of a letter asks the addressee to take care of his father for the following reason:

| *ṯ-k* | *rḫ-ṯ* | *rḏd-rmṯ* | *ꞽw-bn-ꜥꜣ-f* | *mdꞽ-f* | *ꞽn* |
|---|---|---|---|---|---|
| PTC-2MS | know-STA | COMP-[man | DEP-NEG-great-3MS | with-3MS | NEG]$_P$ |

You know that he is a man who lacks experience. (*LRL* 48, 16–49, 1)

(218c) The prince of Syria is told that one of the prospective grooms has reached his daughter's window:

| *wn-ꞽn-pꜣ-wr* | *ḥr-nḏnḏ-f* | *mḏd-šrꞽ* | *nm* |
|---|---|---|---|
| AUX-SEQ-DEF.M-prince | PRP-ask.INF-3MS | COMP-[son | WH |

*m-nꜣ-n-wr-w*
in-DEF.P-of-prince-P]$_P$

| *ꞽw-ṯ* | *ḥr-ḏd=n-f* | *šrꞽ* | *n-wꜥ-snn* |
|---|---|---|---|
| DEP-one | PRP-say.INF=to-3MS | [son | of-IDF.S-charioteer]$_P$ |

The prince asked him: 'He is the son of which of the chieftains?' 'He is the son of a charioteer!' he was told. (*LES* 5, 3–5)

(218d) Moral precepts say:

| *mꞽr-mdy* | *(ꞽ)rm-rmṯ* | *n-ꜥḏꜣ* | *tꜣ-bw-t* |
|---|---|---|---|
| NEG.IMP-speak | with-man | in-falsehood | [DEF.F-abomination |

*n-pꜣ-nṯr*
of-DEF.M-god]$_P$

Do not lie to anyone! It is the abomination of the god.
(Amenemope 13, 15–16)

(218e) In a dispute over two quarreling deities the other gods ask:

| *ꞽḫ* | *pꜣ-nty-ꞽw-n* | *r-ꞽr-f* | *n-pꜣ-rmṯ* | *2* |
|---|---|---|---|---|
| WH | COP.M-REL-FUT-1P | FUT-do.INF-3MS | with-DEF.M-man | 2 |

*nty-80 n-rnp-t r-tꜣy iw-sn m-tꜣ-qnb-t*
REL-[80 of-year-F to-DEM.F DEP-3P in-DEF.F-court-F]$_{P}$
What shall we do with these two men who have now stood in the court for 80 years already?

(*LES* 39, 13–14)

In ex. 218a, the utterance simply consists of the nominal phrase *tꜣy-n-sn-t* 'our sister' framed by quotation markers, whereas in 218b the NP *rmṯ* 'a man' is expanded by a virtual relative clause. Exx. 218c and 218d show a similar use of a genitival construction. Most examples of this type come from quotative contexts; 218e shows the pattern in a relative clause. The expression 'it is X days until now' usually appears without subject element (219a), and the pattern seems obligatory if the interrogative pronoun *nm* is used to inquire identity, i.e. 'who is he?', as in ex. 219b:

(219a) A letter begins without any address:
*ir-pꜣ-ḏd i-ir-k* [...] *ꜣbd n-hrw r-pꜣy*
PTC-DEF.M-say REL-do-2MS ... month of-day to-DEM.M
*mḏr-in-ṯ=n-i qḏ*
since-bring-PASS=to-1S gypsum
*pꜣ-hꜣy i-ir-k (r)-bꜣk pꜣy ptr ṯ-i*
DEF.M-go REL-do-2MS to-work SE.M look PTC-1S
*di-in-ṯ=n-k*
let-bring-PASS=to-2MS
As for the remark which you made, 'It has been a full month till now since gypsum was brought to me', and this is why you have come down (to) work; look, I am sending you some.

(oDeM 437, r° 1–3)

(219b) A boatman is accused of having ferried robbers across the river:
*ḏd-ṯ=n-f nm spsn*
say.PST-PASS=to-3MS [WH] twice
*ḏd-f N N N*
say.PST-3MS [N N N]
He was asked: 'Who were they?'
He said: 'The coppersmith of the necropolis Wares, the priest of the temple of Aakheperure Payres, son of Pawenesh, and the craftsman Itnefer'.

(*KRI* VI 798, 14–16)

The following examples represent alternative yes/no-questions:

(220a) Wermai complains that his old acquaintances do not know him anymore:
*(i)n sp ndndhr mdi-iw-i ḥr-šm*
IP [case greeting] since-come.PST-1S PRP-go.INF
Is it so hard to greet me, since I started coming and going?
(*Tale of Woe* 3, 10–11)

(220b) A question to an oracle:
*(i)n b3-w n-N*
IP [might-P of-N]
Is it Aninakhte's wrath? (oIFAO 857 [*BIFAO* 72, 57])

It has been suggested that examples such as these should be analysed as displaying ellipsis of the subject element *p3y/t3y/n3y* (see Erman 1933: §705; Hintze 1950–52: 306; Callender 1984: 152–56). This seems likely given the restricted use of utterances of the sort, which are found only in the environments just noted as well as in instances showing fronting of an NP by means of the particle *ir* (cf. Gunn 1955: 94 sub §IX.3; Groll 1967: 12–33; Satzinger 1976: 57; Quack 1994: 36):

(221a) The pharaoh stipulates regarding the organisation of gold transport:
*ir-nbw ḥʿw ntr-w bn-n-s-ḫr-t-tn*
PTC-gold [body god-P] NEG-POSS-3S-affair-F-2P
But the gold, it is the body of the gods; it is not of your concern.
(*KRI* I 68, 1–2)

(221b) The general of the pharaoh writes to the necropolis scribe Tjaroy:
*ir-prʿ3 ʿws. i-ir-f-pḥ p3y-t3 mi-iḫ spsn*
PTC-pharaoh l.p.h. ST-AUX-3MS-reach DEM.M-land like-WH twice
*ḫr ir-prʿ3 ʿws. ḥry nm mrʿ*
PTC PTC-pharaoh, l.p.h. [superior WH yet]
As for the pharaoh, l.p.h., how will he reach this land? And as for the pharaoh, l.p.h., whose superior is he still?
(*LRL* 36, 11–12)

(221c) In the *Poem of the king's chariot* certain properties are attributed to its parts:
*ir-n3-dr-w-t n-t3y-k-mrkb-t N N*
PTC-DEF.P-axles-P-F of-POSS.F-2MS-chariot-F [N N]
As for the axles of your chariot – they are Anat and Astarte!
(oEdinburgh 916 vº 12–14 [*JEA* 19, pl. 28])

Possible earlier occurrences of this constructions occur similarly in cases showing *ỉr*-fronting (Wente 1982: 163 n.19; Borghouts 1986: 54):
*Earlier Egyptian*

(222a) The paths of the netherworld are said to be in confusion:
*ỉr rḫ=sn gmm w3-t-sn*
PTC know.PIA=3P [find.PIA way-F-3P]
Who knows them – he is the one who finds their ways!
(*CT* VII 340c/B1C)

(222b) The fields are not productive solely by the inundation. One also needs much labour:
*ỉr ꜥpr ỉm-s spd-ḥr*
PTC equip.PIA in-3FS [sharp- face.PIA]
As for the one equipped with it – he is an attentive one! (*Loyaliste* §11, 8)

Yet in the first of these examples other textual variants show *ỉn rḫ=sn*, i.e. a cleft sentence. The *ỉr rḫ* of the variant B1C might have resulted from an assimilation of the nasal to the following rhotic.

Demotic sources do not seem to provide examples corresponding to the Late Egyptian instances above, but these reappear in Coptic. However, candidates for the deletion of the subject element in bipartite sentences are only found in Bohairic (see also 1.2), where they are common in contexts in which the subject is pragmatically clear (especially when the latter is anteposed), but also within relative clauses:

(223a) The Lord tells Moses to go to the pharaoh and say:
*pa-šorp m-misi p-is(raê)l ø*
POSS.M.1S-first of-birth DEF.M-N Ø
My firstborn, it is Israel. ($^{B}$Ex 4:22)

(223b) If a person has a skin disease, his clothes must be torn and his hair unbound. He has to cover his moustache and cry 'Unclean! Unclean!':
*n-ni-ehou têr-u ete-pi-cʰoh hiôt-f*
in-DEF$_2$.P-days.P all-3P REL-DEF$_2$.M-hurt upon-3MS
*e-u-akathartos ø*
DEP-IDF.S-unclean Ø
As long as he has this affliction, he is unclean. ($^{B}$Lev 13:46)

(223c) The apostle urges the Christians of Corinth not to mingle with a fellow-Christian of the following kind:
*ešôp e-uon-uai e-u-ti-ran ero-f ce-son*
CND DEP-PTC-IDF.ABS DEP-3P-give-name to-3MS COMP-brother

*e-u-pornos* ø
DEP-IDF.S-fornicator ø
*ie u-ref-c$^{h}$in-cons* ø *ie u-ref-šamše-idôlon* ø
or IDF.S-AGT-take-violence ø or IDF.S-AGT-worship-idol ø
*ie u-ref-hôuš* ø
or IDF.S-AGT-revile ø
*ie u-ref-t$^{h}$iḫi* ø *ie u-ref-hôlem* ø
or IDF.S-AGT-get drunk ø or IDF.S-AGT-steal ø
If there is someone who is called a brother but who is a fornicator, or violent, or an idolator, or a reviler, or a drunkard, or a thief... ($^{B}$1Cor 5:11)

In addition, as in Late Egyptian, utterances consisting of a single NP are typically attested in Coptic in naming constructions, as in the following examples:

(224a) Jesus asked his disciples who did the people say that he was:
*nt$^{h}$ôu a-u-co-s na-f e-u-cô mmo-s ce-Iôannês*
3P PST-3P-say-3FS to-3MS DEP-3P-say OBJ-3FS COMP-[N
*pi-reftiôms*
DEF$_{2}$.M-baptist]
*uoh han-kek$^{h}$ôuni ce-Êlias han-kek$^{h}$ôuni ce-uai*
and IDF.P-other.P COMP-[N] IDF.P-other.P COMP-[one
*nte-ni-prophêtês*
of-DAM.P-prophet]
They replied: 'John the Baptist!' But others: 'Elias!' Yet others: 'One of the prophets!' ($^{B}$Mk 8:28)

(224b) As above:
*ntou=de peca-u=na-f ce-hoine ce-Iôhannês=pe*
3P=yet said.PST-3P=to-3MS COMP-some COMP-[N=[SE.M]
*p-baptistis*
DEF.M-baptist]
*hen-koue=de ce-Hêlias=pe hen-koue=de*
IDF.P-other.P=yet COMP-[N]=[SE.M] IDF.P-other.P=yet
*ce-ua=pe n-ne-prophêtês*
COMP-[one=[SE.M] of-DEF.P-prophet]
They replied: 'Some say "He is John the Baptist!" But others: "He is Elias!", and yet others: "He is one of the prophets!"' ($^{S}$Mk 8:28)

(224c) Gesios returned home. Upon entering a church, he asked the porters:
*na-snêu ara n-tetn-soun=an m-pi-son snau*
POSS.P.1S-brother.P IP NEG-2P-know=NEG OBJ-DEF$_{2}$.M-brother two
*nt-a-pe-u-iôt mu ua ce-Gesios ke-ua ce-Isidôros*
REL-PST-POSS.M-3P-father die one COMP-[N] other-one COMP-[N]

My brothers, would you not know these two brothers whose father had died, one named Gesios, the other Isidoros?

(^S*Gesios & Isodorus* [*ZÄS* 21, 148, 17–18])

(224d) Elijah heralds that a king will rise:

| | | | |
|---|---|---|---|
| *hn-t-polis* | *et-ḫar-u-mute* | *ara-s* | *ce-t-polis* |
| in-DEF.F-city | REL-AOR-3P-call | OBJ-3FS | COMP-DEF.F-city |
| *m-p-ri* | | | |
| of-DEF.M-sun | | | |

...in the city called the city of the sun.

(^A*ApEl* [Steindorff, *Apokalypse des Elias* 84 30, 6–8])

(224e) After Paul healed a cripple, the inhabitants of Lycaonia thought that he and Barnabas were gods:

| | | | | |
|---|---|---|---|---|
| *ha-u-mute* | *e-barnabas* | *ce-p-zeus* | *paulos=de* | *ce-p-hermês* |
| PST-3P-call | OBJ-N | COMP-DEF.M-N | N=yet | COMP-DEF.M-N |

They called Barnabas Zeus and Paul Hermes. (^MActs 14:12)

Since utterances like these are clearly restricted to this discourse type and examples such as the Sahidic variant of Mk 8:28 in 224b with an overt *pe*, they are best viewed as either involving ellipsis of the subject element or as non-clausal utterances[72] rather than as examples of an independent 'mono-partite' type of Egyptian nominal sentences.

72 Indeed, both 'John' and 'It was/is John' are valid answers to questions such as 'Who gave you the book?'. The former type, illustrating so-called answer ellipsis, is very common in actual discourse.

# 2 Clausal syntax

## 2.1 Initial and coordinated clauses

### 2.1.1 Earlier Egyptian

Before analysing Earlier Egyptian nominal sentences in initial and coordinated clauses, it is necessary to discuss the use of these constructions with various auxiliaries and comparable elements. As seen in Part I, in this phase of the language auxiliaries are a fundamental feature of the grammar of adverbial sentences. By contrast, nominal sentences are far less often combined with such elements. There are no examples of nominal sentences with the 'narrative' auxiliary *ꜥḥꜥ-n*, and those with the element *wn/wnn* are very rare:

(225) In a broken context:

| | | |
|---|---|---|
| *wnn* | *nꜣ=pw* | *ḏdy-f* |
| AUX | DEM=COP | say.REL.FUT-3MS |

This is what he will say. (pBerlin P. 10081B, 2)

The otherwise ubiquitous auxiliary *ỉw* is also not standardly used with nominal sentences, although some rare examples may be cited[73]:

(226) Sebeki tells of his duties as an official:

| | | | | | |
|---|---|---|---|---|---|
| *ỉw=grt* | *ink* | *ỉri* | *ḥr(y)tp* | *mḏḥ-w* | *rwd-t* |
| AUX=PTC | 1S | do.PPA | head | hewer-P | sandstone-F |

Now, it was me who acted as the head of hewers of sandstone.
(Munich Gl. W.A.F. 31, 6–7)

In the following example, the nominal sentence is preceded by an *ỉr*-anteposed constituent (see below):

(227) A note in a mathematical text:

| | | | | | | |
|---|---|---|---|---|---|---|
| *ỉw* | *ỉr* | *dd-t* | *ḥr-nbw* | *dbn* | *šꜥty* | *12=pw* |
| AUX | PTC | give.PIP-F | on-gold | deben | N | 12=SE |

As for what is given for a deben of gold, it is 12 *šꜥty*. (pRhind math. n.62, 4)

73 This means, of course, *ỉw* in its role as an assertive auxiliary rather than, as was later the case, a subordinator. Some examples of the latter fall within the language period considered in the present chapter; see below.

https://doi.org/10.1515/9783110409895-007

The appearance of *iw* in the example above is puzzling, but there are some exceptional cases where the use of this element in a nominal sentence seems to be perfectly in accord with its very specific semantic-pragmatic function of marking the following proposition as illocutionarily assertive (see 3.1.4).

In contrast to the limited use of auxiliaries, nominal sentences are often combined in Earlier Egyptian with various particles that modify the illocutionary force and information structure of propositions.[74] Combinations with initial particles will be described shortly, but here the various clause-internal clitic particles found in nominal sentences should be noted. Below are examples with the element = *ꜣ*, which often signals speaker incredulity or disbelief, but apparently also elation and surprise, as well as the 'assuring' = *wnnt* 'really', the adversative = *swt* 'but', and the additive = *grt* 'further':

(228a) The king is of divine progeny:
*N=ꜣ=pw* *mtw-t nṯr*
N=PTC=SE seed-F god
King N is the seed of god! (PT 1417a)

(228b) It is said of the milk-goddess:
*stt =wnnt* *ms-t* *N*
3FS=PTC bear.PPA-F N
It is really she who bore King N. (PT 131e)

(228c) The author of a letter tells of his plans:
*mk=swt* *nꜣ=pw* *ḏdy-i*
PTC=PTC DEM.M=SE say.REL.FUT-1S
But look; this is what I shall say. (pUC 32213 r°, 24)

(228d) Sinuhe begins his eulogy of Senwosret I from the basics:
*nṯr=pw=grt* *nn* *sn-nw-f*
god=SE=PTC NEG two-ORD-3MS
Now, he is a god without an equal. (Sin B, 47)

The particle=*tr* is commonly (but not exclusively) used in nominal sentence WH-questions, and the same holds true for the clitic=(*i*)*r* followed by a suffix pronoun, which anaphorically or deictically points out explicitly what or whom the proposition concerns:

(229a) The deceased seeks an entry to the hereafter from a guardian:
*wn=n-i* *ink=tr* *smy*
open.IMP=to-1S 1S=PTC helper
Open for me; I am truly a helper. (CT II 292d–e/S2P)

74 See Oréal (2011) for a synopsis of some of these elements.

(229b) The deceased has just asked for a boat from a divinity, who replies:
*ṯwt=tr m*
2MS=PTC WH
Who are you? (CT VI 314h)

(229c) The magician Djedi notices that King Khufu is saddened; he asks:
*pty=ỉrf pꜣ-ib ỉty ʿws nb-ỉ*
WH=PTC DEM.M-heart sovereign l.p.h. lord-1S
What is this mood, O sovereign my lord? (pWestcar 9, 13)

The 'confirmative' particles=*ms* and=*ḥm* 'truly' are rare:

(230a) Ptahhetep warns against philandering with married women:
*m=ỉrỉ=st bw-t=ms=pw*
AUX.NEG.IMP=do.NC=3C abomination-F=PTC=SE
Do not do it; it is truly an abomination. (Ptahhetep 294)

(230b) Amun says to the future mother of Queen Hatshepsut:
*ḫnmtỉmn ḥꜣtšpst=ḥm rn n(-y)-sꜣ-t=pn*
N N=PTC name of[-M]-daughter=DEM.M
*d-n-ỉ m-ẖ-t[-ṯ]*
place.REL-PST-1S in-womb-F-2FS
Khenmet-Amun Hatshepsut is truly the name of this daughter whom I have placed in your womb. (*Urk.* IV 221, 7)

Also the clitic=*ỉs* appears in nominal sentences, but its function in these constructions seems to relate to clausal syntax, to be discussed below.

Nominal sentences with the element=*pw* can be preceded by a nominal expression anteposed to or otherwise placed outside the sentence nucleus. This phenomenon is attested only with bipartite constructions where=*pw* functions as a subject element, and the anteposed expression is its antecedent and the referent for which=*pw* serves as an anaphoric index. Such expressions are usually introduced by the particle *ỉr*, in so-called left-dislocation:[75]

(231a) A gloss explaining the mythical significance of words:
*ỉr nḥḥ hrw=pw ỉr ḏ-t grḥ=pw*
PTC eternity day=SE PTC everlastingness-F night=SE
As for eternity, it is day; as for everlastingness, it is night. (CT IV 202a/Sq1C)

75 Anteposition is usually split into 'topicalisation' as in 'In Cambridge I spent many happy years' and 'left-dislocation' as in 'That man, he looks suspicious' or 'As for Japanese, it is difficult' (e.g. Foley and Van Valin 1984: 125). The latter is said to be typically associated with a discourse 'topic switch' (e.g. Andrews 2007: 149, 155).

(231b) Khakheperraseneb makes a general point about strength of character:

| | | | | | | |
|---|---|---|---|---|---|---|
| *ir* | *ib* | *qn* | *m-s-t* | *qsn-t* | *sn-nw=pw* | *n-nb-f* |
| PTC | heart | brave | in-place-F | difficult-F | two-ORD=SE | to-lord-3MS |

As for a heart strong in the face of adversity, it is a companion to its lord. (Khakheperraseneb r° 13)

This construction is particularly ubiquitous in explanatory and aetiological texts where it is used to clarify the meaning, etymology etc. of words and expressions (ex. 231a). Sometimes, although less often, *ir* may be absent:

(232a) It is said of the deceased:

| | | |
|---|---|---|
| *ˁnḫ* | *m-sgr* | *rn-f=pw* |
| live.PIA | in-calm | name-3MS=SE |

'He who lives in calm' – it is his name. (CT VII 297b/B1L, B2L)

(232b) Ptahhetep recommends incorruptibility in service:

| | | | | |
|---|---|---|---|---|
| *mtr* | *ḥr-qd* | *ḫr-nb-k* | *iri* | *r-ḏd{n}-f* |
| exact.IMP | on-form | before-lord-2MS | do.IMP | so that-say-3MS |
| *sꜣ-i* | *pfꜣ=pw* | | | |
| son-1S | DEM.M=SE | | | |

Be exact to the fault before your lord. Act so that he may say: 'My son, he is such'. (Ptahhetep 620–21)

In Earlier Egyptian, anteposition of personal pronouns by means of *ir* or using a bare absolute pronoun is not licensed.[76] In adverbial (and some verbal) sentences the same effect could be achieved by subordinating the construction as a complement of=*pw*, which cleaves (ante-, rather than extraposing) the initial subject from the rest of the construction (see 3.1.5.). In nominal sentences bipartite patterns of the type [absolute pronoun + =*pw*] are used for this purpose[77]:

(233) The deceased announces:

| | | | |
|---|---|---|---|
| *ink=pw* | *ink* | *rˁ* | *m-ḫˁ-w-f* |
| 1S=SE | 1S | N | in-appearance-P-3MS |

As for me, I am Ra in his appearances. (CT IV 343b–c)

Examples of right-extraposition, where a referent of a cataphoric pronominal expression is added as an appositional 'tail' or 'afterthought', are rare in nominal

76 This situation changes in Late Egyptian.

77 Cf. Malaise and Winand (1999: §1054). Examples seem to be restricted to first person (but cf. *ibid*. §474 for a possible analogous construction with a noun).

sentences. As noted in 1.3.1, cataphoric use of *=pw* is difficult to demonstrate, and conclusive examples of sentences such as **rmṯ=pw*$_i$ *sš*$_i$ 'He is a scribe, namely the man' are not forthcoming. However, sporadic corresponding examples with clitic pronoun subjects of *=pw*-less bipartite interrogatives such as those below are occasionally encountered:

(234a) King Khufu has been told that a son of a certain Redjedet will bring him a magic charm; he asks:

| | |
|---|---|
| *pty=sy* | *tꜣ-rdḏdt* |
| WH=3FS | DET.F-N |

Who is she, this Redjedet? (pWestcar 9, 8–9)

(234b) The magician Djedi has just brought before king Khufu who asks him:

| | | | |
|---|---|---|---|
| *pty=st* | *ḏdỉ* | *tm=rdỉ* | *mꜣn-ỉ=tw* |
| WH=3C | N | AUX.NEG.INF=give.NC | see.SUB-1S=2MS |

How is it, Djedi, that I have not been allowed to see you? (lit. 'what is it, Djedi, the not letting that I see you') (pWestcar 8, 10–11)

This again raises the issue of the genesis of tripartite constructions, but it also touches on the wider and more intricate question of what exactly is predicated of what in nominal sentences – in simpler terms, which part of the constructions (if any) should be analysed as subject and which one as predicate. This question will be addressed in sections 3.1.1–3.1.2.

Turning now to the question of Earlier Egyptian nominal sentences in initial and coordinated clauses, non-verbal propositions of this type may be loosely characterised as 'main clause constructions' capable of occupying the absolute initial position without any introducing elements:

(235a) Sinuhe succumbs to exhaustion in the desert:

| | | | |
|---|---|---|---|
| *ḏd-n-ỉ* | *dp-t* | *mw-t* | *nn* |
| say-PST-1S | taste-F | death-F | DEM.M |

I said: 'This is the taste of death.' (Sin B, 23)

(235b) Mentuwoser begins his self-presentation:

| | | | | | | |
|---|---|---|---|---|---|---|
| *ỉmꜣḫy* | *mrpr* | *mnṯwwsr* | *ms-n* | *ꜥbw* | *ḏd-f* | *ỉnk* |
| revered | steward | N | bear.REL-PST | N | say-3MS | 1S |

| | | | |
|---|---|---|---|
| *mꜣ-w* | *r-ỉnd* | *qrs-w* | *mty* |
| see.PPA-M | to-miser | bury.PPA-M | dead |

The revered steward Mentuwoser born of Abu says: 'I was one who cared for the afflicted and buried the dead'. (MMA 12.184, vrt. 1)

Occasionally, however, the nominal sentence may be preceded by an initial particle. The most common of these is *mk/mṯ/mṯn*, which, as elsewhere, draws the interest of the hearer and indicates that the information conveyed in the sentence is, according to the speaker, worthy of full attention:

(236a) A note in a mathematical text concerning measures:
*mk mḥ 1=pw*
PTC cubit 1=SE
Look, it is one cubit. (pRhind math. n.57, 3)

(236b) Ahmose says of his king:
*mṯn nṯr=pw m-tꜣ*
PTC god=SE in-earth
See, he is a god upon earth. (*Urk.* IV 20, 14)

Rather less common are *isṯ/isk/ti*, which again signal that the information provided is essential background in the current discourse; the same holds true for the element *isw*, which appears to be a late version of *isṯ* (see Oréal 2011: 252–53):

(237a) Having described his piety towards his ancestors, Khnumhetep remarks:
*isṯ sꜣ=pw mnḫ sr(w)d rn n(-y)-tpwꜥ*
ptc son=COP efficient strengthen.PIA name of[-M]-predecessor
Now, he who strengthens the name(s) of predecessors is an efficient son.
(*Beni Hasan* I, pl. 26, 166–68)

(237b) In a hymn praising King Senwosret III:
*isw ḏw=pw mḏr ḏꜥ*
PTC mountain=SE conquer.PIA storm
Truly, he is a mountain that conquers the storm. (pUC 32157, 2.19)

The particles *smwn* and *ḥꜣ/ḥw* (exx. 238a and 238b), which signal that the situation is a conclusion drawn by the hearer or a desire, are equally rare, as are instances with the interrogative elements *in/iniw* used to mark alternative yes/no questions (238c; see Silverman 1980: 59–64, 82–86):

(238a) Officials suspect the peasant of being merely a runaway tenant of Nemtynakht:
*smwn sḫty-f=pw iw n-k-y r-gs-f*
PTC peasant-3MS=SE go.PPA to-other-M to-side-3MS
It seems that he is his peasant who has run off to someone else.
(Peas B1, 75)

(238b) Amidst his laments, the sage utters in despair:
*ḥꜣ=rf grḥ=pw m-rmṯ*
PTC=PTC end=SE as-man
Would that it were the end as a man! (Ipuwer 5, 14)

(238c) A question put to a female demon intent on harming a child:

| | | |
|---|---|---|
| *ỉnỉw* | *ntt* | *ḥm-t* |
| IP | 2FS | maidservant-F |

Are you the maidservant? (*MuK* v° 2, 8)

Inasmuch as coordination is not overtly marked in Earlier Egyptian, it is often difficult to judge whether nominal sentences appearing amidst longer segments of discourse should be understood as such. For instance, in the following example, the two nominal sentences could be taken to form a paratactic coordinated complex, but this is not the only possible interpretation[78]:

(239) Sinuhe tells about the estate given to him by a Syrian chieftain:

| | | | |
|---|---|---|---|
| *tꜣ=pw* | *nfr* | *ỉꜣꜣ* | *rn-f* |
| land=SE | good | N | name-3MS |

It was a good land, and its name was Yaa. (Sin B, 81)

Yet coordination is clearly present in instances such as the following, where a single overt initial absolute pronoun entertains a predicative relation with several phrasal predicates linked to the former through so-called argument cluster coordination (Haspelmath 2007: 38–39):

(240) The peasant draws from the standard clichés of self-presentation texts in his flattery of the high steward:

| | | | | | |
|---|---|---|---|---|---|
| *ntk* | *ỉt* | *n(-y)-nmḥ* | *hỉ* | *n(-y)-ḫꜣr-t* | *sn* |
| 2MS | father | of[-M]-orphan | husband | of[-M]-widow-F | brother |

| |
|---|
| *n(-y)-wḏꜥ-t* |
| of[-M]-divorcee-F |

| | | |
|---|---|---|
| *šndy-t* | *n-t-ỉwt(-y)* | *mw-t-f* |
| loincloth-F | of-F-REL.NEG[-M] | mother-F-3MS |

You are a father of an orphan, husband of a widow, brother of a divorcee, and a loincloth of a motherless one. (Peas B1, 93–95)

Close to coordination are also constructions such as the following, where an appositional noun follows a bipartite *pw*-sentence:

(241) Sinuhe extols the virtues of king Senwosret I:

| | | | |
|---|---|---|---|
| *nb* | *sꜣ-t=pw* | *ỉqr* | *sḫr-w* |
| lord | wisdom-F=SE | excellent | plan-P |

He is a master of wisdom, one excellent of plans. (Sin B, 48–49)

---

78 Alternatively, the nominal sentence may be read as a 'virtual' relative clause, see 2.4.1.

Despite the generally unmarked nature of coordination, Earlier Egyptian possessed a set of sequential constructions and particles whose function was not to mark coordination *stricto sensu*, but to indicate that the proposition follows somehow from the previous discourse (Vernus 1990: 61–99; Polis 2005). One or two examples of the particles *ḫr* and *k3* signalling this meaning are found with nominal sentences:

(242a) Having greeted the magician Djedi and praised his old age, Prince Hardjedef continues:

*ḫr* *i3w-t* *s-t* *mny* *s-t* *qrs* *s-t* *sm3-t3*
PTC old age-F place-F mooring place-F burial place-F joining-land
For old age is the place of mooring, the place of burial, and the place of landing. (pWestcar 7, 17–18)

(242b) The sage advices to accept food from those higher up on the social ladder and adds:

*k3* *ssf-t=pw*
PTC soothe.PIA-F=SE
Then it will be a soothing thing. (Kagemni I, 10)

Cleft sentences with coordinated second NPs are relatively rare in Earlier Egyptian sources:

(243a) Various deities help King Unas to devour humans:

*in* *ḏsrtp* *z33=n-f=sn* *ḫsf=n-f=sn*
PTC N guard.PIA=to-3MS=3P repell.PIA=to-3MS=3P
It is the Djesertep-snake that guards them for him and repels them for him. (PT 401b)

(243b) Hezi tells of his promotions by successive kings:

*in* *tti* *nb(-i)* *d=w(i)* *m-z3b* *ʿḏmr*
PTC N lord[-1S] put.PPA=1S as-judge district administrator
*d=w(i)* *m-ḫrtp* *nzw*
put.PPA=1S as-chief king
It was Teti, my lord, who appointed me as a judiciary district-administrator and who appointed me as a royal chief. (*Teti Cemetery* V, pl. 59b)

(243c) The peasant notes that their tongues are the balance of men and continues:

*in* *iwsw* *dʿr* *ḏ3-t* *irr* *ḫsf-t*
PTC scale seek.PIA remainder-F do.PIA punishment-F
*r-ḫsf-w=n-f*
to-punish.PIP=to-3MS
It is the handscale that examines the remainder and punishes the one to be punished. (Peas B2, 93–94)

(243d) After an initial invocation of a deity, the deceased acclaims his own achievements:
*in* *wsr-i* *iri* *nḫt* *iri* *qꜣw* *p-t*
PTC strength-1S do.PPA victory do.PPA height heaven-F
It was my strength that achieved victory and reached heaven.
(BD 84/*Nu* pl. 30, 3)

### 2.1.2 Later Egyptian

In Later Egyptian, any type of sentence can freely appear in absolute initial position. The grammatical organisation of coordination remained unchanged. In cases involving complex predicates, these could be coordinated by juxtaposition and omission of repeated information:

(244a) It is said in a magical text:
*ink* *mntk* *mntk* *ink*
1S 2MS 2MS 1S
I am you and you are me. (pStrasbourg 23, 2)

(244b) The sun is addressed in a hymn in the tomb of Apy:
*ntk* *mw-t* *iti* *n-ir-k*
2MS mother-F father to-make.REL-2MS
You are mother and father to those whom you created.
(Davies, *Amarna* IV, pl. 32, 4)

(244c) Hori quotes from his opponent's missive, in which he said:
*ink* *sš* *mhr*
1S scribe officer
I am a scribe and officer. ($^{2}$*pAnastasi I* 123, 1)

(244d) The author of a letter complains about the addressee's apparent slackness regarding the despatch of some flowers to the palace:
*ḫr-iw-pꜣ-hrw* *nꜣ-ib-w* *nꜣ-ꜥnḫ-w* *swḥ-w-t* *ꜣpd-w*
PTC-DEP-DEF.M-day DEF.P-kid-P DEF.P-goat-P egg-P-F bird-P
*sm-w* *pꜣy*
green-P SE.M
For this is the day of the kids, goats, eggs, birds, and vegetables.
(*LEM* 80, 5–6)

(244e) On a bill of sale for a set of 401 *shabti*-figures for the burial equipment, the seller mentions having received the payment and specifies the function of the figures:
*ḥm-w* *ḥm-w-t* *nꜣw*
servant-P servant-P-F SE.P
They are male and female servants. (Jansen-Winkeln, *IdS* II, 460, 9)

(244f) The sender reports that he found two men and repeats what they told him, namely the reason for their return:

*m-pꜣy-n-nb* *r-dỉ* *ỉw-n* *r-pꜣ-nty-ṯ-tn*
PTC-POSS.M-1P-lord PPA-give come.SBJ-1P to-DEF.M-REL-PTC-2P
*ỉm* *ỉw-dỉ-f* *ỉn-n* *wꜥ-šꜥ-t*
there DEP-give.PST-3MS bring.SBJ-1P IDF.S-scroll
It was our lord who made us come to the place where you are and who gave us a letter. (*LRL* 45, 10–11)

The number of examples is relatively limited. The last one, however, shows that unlike in Earlier Egyptian, Late Egyptian coordinated cleft predicates did not consist of a chain of participles or of clauses headed by *nty* in every case. This has been explained with the difference between restrictive and non-restrictive relative clauses (Müller 2016: 123-29).

In Demotic, the coordination of clausal constituents can be achieved through the coordinator *ỉrm*, as in the first of the following examples, or through juxtaposition:

(245a) The Great Demotic Wisdom Book states within the part dealing with the burial:

*pꜣ-ḥtp* *n-pꜣ-ntr* *n-[pꜣ]-rmt-ntr* *tꜣy-f-qs-t*
DEF.M-grace of-DEF.M-god for-DEF.M-man-god POSS.F-3MS-burial-F
*ỉrm-pꜣy-f-ꜥwy* *[n]-ḥtp*
and-POSS.M-3MS-place of rest
The grace of god towards the man of god is his burial and his resting place. (pInsinger 2, 11)

(245b) A marriage contract stipulates about the respective children:

*pꜣy-t-šr* *ꜥꜣ* *pꜣy-y-šr* *ꜥꜣ* *pꜣy* *pꜣ-nb*
POSS.M-2FS-son great POSS.M-1S-son great COP.M DEF.M-lord
*nty=nb* *nty-mtw-y* *ḥnꜥ-nꜣ-nty-ỉw(-y)-dy-t-ḫpr*
REL=QU REL-with-1S and-DEF.P-REL-FUT[-1S]-let-INF-happen
Your eldest son and my eldest son are the owners of everything and all that I have and all the things that I will acquire.
(pLouvre 2433, r° 3 [Lüddeckens, *Eheverträge*, 30])

(245c) In a deed of sale of some real estate, the seller states:

*mtwk* *nꜣ-sḫ=nb* *qnb=nb* *md=nb* *nty-pḥ* *rr-w*
2MS DEF.P-document=QU stipulation=QU thing=QU REL-reach to-3P
*ḥnꜥ-pꜣy-w-hp* *ḥnꜥ-pꜣ-ntyỉw-y-mꜣꜥṯ-k* *n[ỉm-w* *rn-w]*
CON-POSS.M-3P-law CON-DEF.M-REL-1S-justify.STA-1S in-3P name-3P
To you belong all the documents, all stipulations, and everything that pertains to it and their laws, as well as what I have the right to in their name.
(pLüddeckens II GBS 6–7)

(245d) In a gloss explaining a reference to the vulva in a mythical text:

*ink̓y t3y t3-3ty-t nty-šsp t3-mw-t*

1S COP.F DEF.F-vulva-F REL-receive DEF.F-mother-F

*r-ir-sʿnḫ-w n-t3-ẖ-t*

REL-AUX-nourish-3P in-DEF-F-womb-F

I am the vulva that receives and the mother that nourishes them in the womb. (Myth of the Sun's Eye 8, 23)

(245e) In the attempt to prevent Nubian magical spells again to take possession of pharaoh, the Egyptian sorcerer Hor addresses the god Thoth:

*mtwk iir-ʿḫy3 t3-p-t iw-f-smn p3-t3*

2MS PPA-lift DEF.F-sky-F DEP-3MS-create DEF.M-earth

*t3-d(w3)-t*

DEF.F-netherworld

It is you who lifted up the sky and who created the earth and the netherworld. (Setne II 5, 8–9)

Although the restriction on chained *nty*-clauses is no longer strictly adhered to, the last example above shows that clefts can still be internally coordinated with an *iw*-headed clause in second (or later) position.

In Coptic, constructions with 'argument cluster coordination' are common:

(246a) In his Homily on the Virgin Theophilus narrates how he went into the church on Sunday and addressed the Lord:

*p-nute kô na-i ebol ce-ang-u-kah hi-krms*

DEF.M-god set to-1S out for-1S-IDF.S-earth CNJ-ashes

God, forgive me, for I am dust and ashes.

($^{S}$Theophilus, *Homily on the Virgin* [Worrell 304, 25–305, 2])

(246b) Tobit urges in his prayer about the Lord to exalt the Lord and show forth his greatness:

*ce-ntof pe pe-n-cois auô pe-n-nute*

for-3MS COP.M POSS.M-3MS-lord and POSS.M-3MS-god

...for he is our Lord and God. ($^{S}$Tb 13:4)

(246c) Clement says that past leaders like Moses or the Apostles never avoided strife in their just cause. Hence:

*n-snêu ntôtne-hen-mai-ti-tôn au n-ref-kôh*

DEF.P-brother.P 2P-DEF.P-love.PIA-give-strife CNJ of-AGT-emulate

*etbe-n-et-ci aḫun a-p-ucei*

because-DEF.P-REL-take into to-DEF.M-health

Strife-lovers and zealous you shall be, O brothers, because of that which leads to salvation. ($^{A}$1Cl 45:1 [Schmidt 92])

(246d) The sailors ask Jonah:
*[n]tk-u-abal ntak ẖn-eẖ n-khôra au aba[l] ẖn-eẖ n-laos*
2MS-IDF.S-out 2MS in-WH of-land and out in-WH of-people
From what country are you and from what people? ($^{A}$Jon 1:8 [Malinine])

(246e) Clement addresses his audience summing up the aforesaid:
*u-dikaion=kʲe=pe n-rôme n-snêu au*
IDF.S-just=then=SE.M DEF.P-man DEF.P-brother.P and
*p-et-ešše=pe*
DEF.M-REL-fit=SE.M
*a-t-n-sôtme se-p-nute n-huo a-uah-ne*
to-INFL-1P-hear after-DEF.M-god in-more to-put-1P
*se-n-et-ah-ẖôpe n-arkhêgos*
after-DEF.P-REL-PST-be as-leader
*m-p-kôh et-soof ẖn-u-mnt-babe-rôme mn-u-ẖtartre*
in-DEF.M-envy REL-defile.STA in-IDF.S-ABST-boast-man and-IDF.S-trouble
So it is just, o men, brethren, and it is befitting that we hearken to God rather than that we follow those who were leaders of defiled envy in boastfulness and trouble. ($^{A}$1Cl 14:1)

(246f) In the Gnostic *Gospel of Philip*, the public reaction to the Christian confession is contrasted:
*ekša-coo-s ce-ano[k -u]-h[e]llên u-barbaros*
CND.2MS-say-3FS COMP-1S -IDF.S-pagan IDF.S-barbarian
*u-hmhal [u-eleu]theros*
IDF.S-servant IDF.S-free man
*mn-lau na-štortr*
NEG-any FUT-tremble
If you say: 'I am a pagan, a barbarian, a slave, or a free man', nobody will tremble. ($^{SL}$*GospPh.* 62, 26–31 [Layton 164, 29–31])

(246g) The Teacher explains further about the first hunter, who is the king in the realm of darkness:
*pe-f-šne pe te-f-sete mn-te-f-epithumia*
POSS.M-3MS-net COP.M POSS.F-3MS-fire CNJ-POSS.F-3FS-desire
*p-et-a-f-tee-f acn-t-psukhê et-anh*
DEF.M-REL-PST-3MS-give-3MS on-DEF.F-soul REL-live.STA
His his fire and his desire are his net, the one he casted upon the living soul. (L*Kephalaia* 29, 20–21)

(246h) Abraham pleads to God to spare Sodom: *Since I have undertaken to speak to the Lord,*
*anok=de anok -u-kahi nem-u-kermi*
1S=yet 1S -IDF.S-earth CNJ-IDF.S-ashes
...although I am earth and ashes. ($^{B}$Gn 18:27)

(246i) In a plea to the Lord to be saved the Psalmist exclaims:

*anok -u-hêki=de uoh n-côb anok*

1S -IDF.S-poor=yet CNJ of-need 1S

But I am poor and needy. ($^{B}$Ps 69 [70]:6 [5])

In some cases, identical segments in the coordinated clauses could be retained for pragmatic reasons such as stressing (as in 247a and b). Akhmimic and Bohairic can attach the coordinated predicate with CONNECTOR plus *n-*, as in 246c and h (*au n-* in Akhmimic vs. repetition of components in 246c, *uoh n-* in Bohairic). Stylistic considerations may have sometimes prompted subject repetition, as in 247c and 247d:

(247a) Shenute quotes Nestorius:

*ene-u-nute=k$^{j}$e=pe peca-f ne-f-na-coo-s ce-k$^{j}$omk$^{j}$m ero-i*

CFT-IDF.S-god=then=SE.M said-3MS PRT-3MS-FUT-say-3FS COMP-touch OBJ-1S

*nte-tn-nau ce-anok u-pn(eum)a auô anok u-nute*

CNJ-2P-see COMP-1S IDF.S-spirit and 1S IDF.S-god

'If he had been a god,' he said, 'he would have said: "Touch me and see that I am spiritual and I am divine!"'

($^{S}$Shenute, *I am Amazed* §465 [Cristea 191, 18–25])

(247b) The apostle quotes a philosopher who had said:

*ni-krêtês han-ref-ce-met$^{h}$-nuc n-sêu niben han-thêrion*

DEF.P-N IDF.P-AGT-say-ABST-lie in-time QU IDF.P-animal

*e-u-hôu ne han-neci n-argos=ne*

DEP-3P-evil COP.P IDF.P-womb of-lazy=SE.P

The Cretans are always liars, they are evil beasts, and they are lazy gluttons. ($^{B}$Ti 1:12)

(247c) PsCyril praises the Virgin and says that the present day would be the one when she had tasted death like any human:

*ce-u-sarks=te auô u-cpo=te ebol hn-u-iôt*

for-IDF.S-flesh=SE.F and IDF.S-creation=SE.F out in-IDF.S-father

*mn-u-mau n-t-he n-uon nim*

CON-IDF.S-mother in-DEF.F-way of-each QU

... for she is flesh and a creation out of a father and a mother just like everyone. ($^{S}$Ps. Cyril, *On the Virgin* [*Or* 70, 44, 15–16])

(247d) The psalmist praises the Lord:

*[nt]ak p-c(ai)s p-n(u)ti ntk-u-šan-htê-f*

2MS DEF.M-lord DEF.M-god 2MS-IDF.S-pitiful-heart-3MS

*ntk-u-naêt*

2MS-IDF.S-merciful

*ntk-u-ai-hêt naše-pe-k-nee ntk-u-mee*

2MS-IDF.S-great-heart plenty-POSS.M-2MS-mercy 2MS-IDF.S-truth

You, Lord God, are compassionate and merciful; you are patient, your mercy is plentiful, and you are righteous. ($^{M}$Ps 85 [86]:15)

Note in 247b the deletion of the subject element in the first sentence and its repetition in the following sentences.

Although examples are rare, in Bohairic, but not necessarily in Sahidic (see 248b) disjunctive patterns tend to repeat all elements even if these are identical, the polar contrast being usually expressed by an expression 'or not':

(248a) The Saint asks the woman calling for his help:
*nt$^{h}$o u-khrêstianê šan-nt$^{h}$o u-hellênos*
2FS IDF.S-Christian or-2FS IDF.S-heathen
Are you a Christian or are you a heathen?
($^{B}$*Mart. Theodore Stratelates* [*AM* I 160, 21])

(248b) In his closing remarks on the organisation of the church and its service, the apostle says:
B *isce uon-uai e-f-meui ero-f ce-u-prophêtês=pe*
CND PTC-one DEP-3MS-think OBJ-3MS COMP-IDF.M-prohet=SE.M
*ie u-pn(eum)atikos=pe*
or IDF.S-spirit bearer=SE.M
S *p-et-meue ce-u-prophêtês=pe ê u-pneumatikos*
DEF.M-REL-think COMP-IDF.M-prophet=SE.M or IDF.S-spirit bearer
If one considers himself a prophet or a spirit-bearer...
($^{BS}$1Cor 14:37)

(248c) Isaac tells Jacob to come closer so that he can feel him and sense:
*ce-an-nt$^{h}$ok pe pa-šêri êsau šan-mmon*
COMP-IP-2MS COP.M POSS.M.1S-son N or-no
... whether you are my son Esau or not. ($^{B}$Gn 27:21)

Such repetition is typical in Coptic adversative clauses, even though the Greek conjunct *alla* 'but' can also be used to coordinate phrasal elements. Only Bohairic displays regular omission of the subject:

(249a) Nahrow replies to the accusation that he is a magician:
*anok u-magos=an alla anok u-hmhal nte-i(êsu)s*
1P IDF.S-magician=NEG but 1P IDF.S-servant of-N
*pe-kh(risto)s*
DEF.M-Christ
I am not a magician, but a servant of Jesus Christ.
($^{S}$*Mart. Nahrow* [Till *KHML* I, 5, 13–14])

(249b) Paul reasons that by sending his son, God freed mankind from the law:

B *hôste* *nt$^h$ok* *u-bôk=an=ce* *alla* *u-šêri*
so that 2MS IDF.S-servant=NEG=then but Ø-IDF.S-son
S *hôste=k$^j$e* *ntk-u-hmhal=an* *alla* *ntk-u-šêre*
so that=then 2MS-IDF.S-servant=NEG but 2MS-IDF.S-son
So you are no longer a slave but a son. ($^{BS}$Gal 4:7)

Cleft sentence patterns can appear with coordinated entities in the first position (250a–250d) as well as in second position (250e–250h, see also ex. 99 above):

(250a) Athanasius cites Ps 112:3 in a paragraph of his *Canons*:

*f-cô=gar* *mmo-s* *ce-p-eou* *mn-t-mnt-rmmao*
3MS-say=for OBJ-3FS COMP-DEF.M-glory CON-DEF.F-ABST-rich
*n-et-hm-pe-f-êi*
COP.P-REL-in-POSS.M-3MS-house
*etbe-pai* *šše* *e-tre-te-f-dikaiosynê*
because-DEM.M necessary to-INFL-POSS.F-3MS-righteousness
*šôpe* *ša-eneh*
happen until-eternity
For he says: 'Glory and riches is what is in his house'. Therefore it is necessary that his righteousness exist forever.
($^{S}$*Canons of Athanasius* [Crum in Riedel §61])

(250b) The proverbs describe the beauty and other features of Wisdom:

*u-nak$^j$=gar* *n-ahe* *mn-hen-rmpeue* *n-ônẖ*
IDF.S-great=for of-life_time and-IDF.P-year.P of-life
*n-et-hi-t-s-unem* *au* *u-eau*
COP.P-REL-ON-POSS.F-3FS-right_hand and IDF.S-glory
*mn-u-mnt-rmmao* *n-et-hi-t-s-k$^j$bir*
and-IDF.S-ABST-rich COP.P-REL-ON-POSS.F-3FS-left_hand
... for longevity and years of life are what is in her right, and glory and riches are what is in her left hand. ($^{A}$Prv 3:16)

(250c) Pilate asks Jesus whether he is the king of the Jews. He asks in return whether he, Pilate, thinks so or whether he was told this. Pilate replies that he is no Jew and continues:

*pe-k-het[nos]* *auô* *ne-k-arkhiereus*
POSS.P-2MS-people and POSS.P-2MS-highpriest
*p-en[t]-a-u-tee-k* *a-toot-ø*
COP.M-REL-PST-3P-give-2MS to-hand-1S
It is your people and your high priests who delivered you into my hands. ($^{L}$Jn 18:35)

(250d) Dealing with false teachers, the apostle says:

*ḫen-u-ništi=de n-êi han-skeuos n-nub mmauat-u=an*
in-IDF.S-great=yet of-house IDF.P-vessel of-gold self-3P=NEG
*nem-han-hat ete-nḫêt-f*
CON-IDF.P-silver REL-inside-3MS
Now in a wealthy house, it is not only golden and silver vessels that are in it ... ([B]2Ti 2:20)

(250e) The Evangelist quotes from the Book of Isaiah regarding Jesus' works of healing who had said:

*ntof p-ent-a-f-ci-n-n-šône auô a-f-tôun*
3MS COP.M-REL-PST-3MS-take-POSS.P-1P-sickness and PST-3MS-rise
*ha-ne-n-loclec*
under-POSS.P-1P-sickness
It is he who took our infirmities and who bare our sicknesses. ([S]Mt 8:17)

(250f) Tobit praises the Lord in his prayer saying that the Lord may be blessed as well as his kingdom:

*ce-ntof p-et-mastigu auô et-na*
for-3MS COP.M-REL-afflict and REL-show_mercy
... for he afflicts and he shows mercy. ([S]Tb 13:2)

(250g) A man healed of blindness says:

*iê(su)s p-ent-a-f-tena-u-ame a-f-salk*$^{j}$*-f*
N COP.REL-PST-3MS-pound-IDF.S-clay PST-3MS-anoint-3MS
*a-na-bel*
to-POSS.P.1S-eye
It was Jesus who made some clay and anointed with it my eye. ([L]Jn 9:11)

(250h) The saviour tells about himself:

*anok et-sôun m-p-hêt n-uon niben uoh*
1S REL-know OBJ-DEF.M-heart of-each every and
*et-emi e-nu-mokmek*
REL-know OBJ-POSS.P.3P-thought
It is I who knows the heart of everyone and who perceives their thoughts. ([B]Theodosius of Alexandria, *De assumptione Mariae V.* [Robinson 108, 11–12])

As can be seen from the exx. 250 e–h, the coordinated relative clause can appear as headless relative clause (without determiner) or as main clause.

Occasionally, the coordinated elements may follow the whole sentence:

(251) God wants to punish Ephraim and Judah, adding:

*u-nae p-et-i-uaḫ-f u-thusia=en*
IDF.S-mercy COP.M-REL-1S-want-3MS IDF.S-sacrifice=NEG

*au* *u-saune* *n-nute* *n-huo* *a-hen-kʲlil*
and IDF.S-knowledge of-god in-more than-IDF.P-burnt_offering
It is mercy that I want, not sacrifice; and acknowledgement of God more than burnt offering. ($^{A}$Hos 6:6)

In coordinated cleft patterns, the determiner appears only once if there is no change in gender or number. If there is change, the element is repeated (see ex. 446 for a negated example):

(252a) Shenute opposes some views about the Lord with a quote: *He is ignorant of the word of that voice:*
*p-nute* *n-ša-eneh* *n-f-na-hko=an* *ude*
DEF.M-god of-until-eternity NEG-3MS-FUT-hungry=NEG nor
*n-f-na-hise=an*
NEG-3MS-FUT-suffer=NEG
*alla* *ntof* *p-et-ti* *n-t-kʲom* *n-n-et-hkait*
but 3MS COP.M-REL-give OBJ-DEF.F-power to-DEF.P-REL-hungry.STA
*et-ti-mton* *n-n-et-šp-hise* *etbêêt-f*
REL-give-rest to-DEF.P-REL-receive-suffer because-3MS
The eternal God does not hunger or suffer; rather he is the one who strengthens the hungry and comforts those suffering for him.
($^{S}$Shenute, *I Am Amazed* §316 [Cristea 144, 3–12])

(252b) Asked by her astonished father why she and her sisters are at home so early, Sepphora answers:
*u-rômi* *n-rem-n-kʰêmi* *pe* *et-a-f-nahme-n* *ntot-u*
IDF.S-man of-man-of-Egypt COP.M REL-PST-save-1P from-3P
*n-ni-ma-n-esôu*
as-DEF.P-herder-of-sheep.P
*uoh* *a-f-mah-môu* *na-n* *a-f-tsio* *n-ni-esôu*
and PST-3MS-fill-water to-1P PST-3MS-let drink OBJ-DEF.P-sheep.P
It was an Egyptian who saved us from the shepherds and who filled water for us and let the sheep drink. ($^{B}$Ex 2:19)

Another possibility is to mark the coordinated second clause as conjunctive:

(253) Shenute rejects the view that the Saviour only assumed a body but not a soul. He rephrases the Gospels:
*hôs-rôme* *on* *e-f-cô* *mmo-s* *ce-štortr* *auô* *lupi*
like-man again DEP-3MS-say OBJ-3FS COMP-trouble and grieve
*te-f-mnt-nute=de* *ntos* *me-s-štortr* *ude*
POSS.F-3MS-ABST-god=yet 3FS NEG.AOR-3FS-trouble nor

*me-s-lupi*
NEG.AOR-3FS-trouble
*alla* *ntos* *t-e-ša-s-lupi* *n-hah* *emate* *auô*
but 3FS DEF.F-DEP-AOR-3FS-grieve OBJ-many very and
*n-s-štrtr-uon* *nim*
CNJ-3FS-trouble-each QU
Even when they say 'troubled' and 'grieve', his divinity is neither troubled nor grieved, but it is she (the divinity) who troubles very many and makes everyone grieve.
(SShenute, *I am Amazed* §491 [Cristea 200, 6–18)

It is sometime difficult to decide whether coordinated adversative patterns should be analysed as cleft sentences showing ellipsis of the relative clause or as bipartite patterns:

(254a) Gesios has found some human bones and laments the fleeting nature of earthly life:
*m-pai=an* *mauaa-f* *pe-nt-a-f-mu* *alla* *anok*
NEG-DEM.M=NEG self-3MS COP.M-REL-PST-3MS-die but 1S
*nmma-f* *pe*
with-3MS SE.M
It is not only this one that has died, but I with him.
(S*Gesios & Isodorus* [*ZÄS* 21, 142, 14–15])

(254b) In the epilogue of his Life of Antony, Athanasius asks his work to be read to heathens so that they will understand:
*ce-u-monon* *pe-n-cois* *i(êsu)s* *pe-kh(risto)s* *u-nute* *pe*
COMP-NEG-only POSS.M-1P-lord N DEF.M-Christ IDF.S-god COP.M
*alla* *p-šêre* *m-p-nute=pe*
but DEF.M-son of-DEF.M-god=SE.M
... not only that our lord Jesus Christ is divine, but that he is the son of God. (S*Life of Antony* [Garitte 101, 3–4])

(254c) Julian denies having received his kingdom from the Christ:
*p-kh(risto)s=an* *pe-et-a-f-ti* *nê-i* *n-ta-i-met-uro*
DEF.M-Christ=NEG COP.M-REL-PST-3MS-give to-1S OBJ-POSS.F-1S-ABST-king
*alla* *pi-zeus=pe*
but $DEF_2$.M-N=SE.M
It was not Christ who gave me my kingdom, but Zeus.
(B*Mart. Cyriacus of Jerusalem* [*AM* II 12, 24–25])

Both the subject and the predicate position can be occupied by coordinated structures. Although the predicate can be coordinated within a single sentence (i.e. 'X is Y and Z'), the expression of coordinated subjects calls for coordinated clauses (i.e. 'X is Y, and Z is Y'). In Bohairic, predicate expressions are typically coordinated by *uoh n-* (255a) and sometimes by *nem-* (255g). Ex. 255b shows that the subject element could be omitted after its first occurrence if the predicate was a coordinated string of NPs, but it could also be repeated (255c–255e) or appear towards the end of the sentence (255f):

(255a) A saint is described:
*eusebios=de hô-f pi-stratêlatês ne-u-rômi e-f-šêu pe*
N=yet self-3MS DEF$_2$.M-general PRT-IDF.S-man REL-3MS-tall.STA SE.M
*uoh m-polimakhos e-f-cor m-pe-f-com*
and as-warrior DEP-3MS-strong.STA in-POSS-3MS-power
But general Eusebius was a tall man and a strong warrior.
($^B$*Mart. Eusebius* [*AdM* 29, 6–7])

(255b) The apostle urges the Christians of Corinth not to mingle with fellow Christian of the following kind: *If there is someone who is called a brother:*
*ešôpe u-pornos=pe ê n-ref-šmše-idôlon ê*
CND IDF.S-adulterer=SE.M or as-AGT-worship-idol or
*m-mai-to n-huo*
as-love.PAR-share of-more
*ê n-ref-sahu ê n-ref-tihe ê n-ref-tôrp*
or as-AGT-curse or as-AGT-be drunk or as-AGT-rob
... but is an adulterer, or an idolater, or covetous, or a slanderer, or a drunkard, or a thief! ($^S$1Cor 5:11)

(255c) Having seen a man weep over a corpse, sailors ask him what the deceased meant for him:
*ten-nau=gar e-p-rôkh n-ne-k-splakhnon ehun ero-f*
1P-see=for OBJ-DEF.M-fire in-POSS.P-2MS-inward parts inside to-3MS
*hôs e-pe-k-son pe ê pe-k-iôt pe*
as if DEP-POSS.M-2MS-brother SE.M or POSS.M-2MS-father SE.M
For we can see the fire burning inside you for him as if it were your brother or your father. ($^S$*Gesios & Isodorus* [*ZÄS* 21, 143, 7–8])

(255d) The narrator tells how an angel led Sophonias (?) through a door whose parts changed their appearance:
*anak=de a-i-[s]ônt ara-u a-i-kʾnt-s hen-pulê n-hamt ne*
1S=yet PST-1S-look OBJ-3P PST-1S-find-3FS IDF.P-door of-bronze SE.P
*au hen-kl n-ham[t] ne au hen-mokhlos n-banipe ne*
and IDF.P-lock of-bronze SE.P and IDF.P-bolt of-iron SE.P
So, I, looked at them and found that they were bronze doors, locks, and iron bolts. ($^A$*ApSoph*? [Steindorff, *Apokalypse des Elias* 446, 17–7, 1])

(255e) Adam says of his newly created consort:
*tinu u-kêês=te ebal hn-na-kêês*
now IDF.S-bone=SE.F out in-POSS.P.1S-bone

*auô* *u-sarks=te* *ebal* *hn-na-sarks*
and IDF.S-flesh=SE.F out in-POSS.P.1S-flesh
Now, it is a bone out of my bones and a flesh out of my flesh.
($^{F}$John Evangelist, *Investiture of Archangel Michael* [Müller 11, 12–13])

(255f) In the Gnostic *Gospel of Philip* a non-believer is asked 'What will be resurrected?':
*k-cô* *mmo-s* *ce-p-pn(eum)a* *hn-t-sarks* *auô*
2MS-say OBJ-3FS COMP-DEF.M-spirit in-DEF.F-flesh and
*pei-ke-uoin=pe* *hn-t-sarks*
DEM.M-other-light=SE.M in-DEF.F-flesh
You say: 'It is the soul in the flesh and that other light in the flesh'.
($^{SL}$*GospPh.* 57, 14–15)

(255g) A discourse opens with a common cliché explaining the choice of subject:
*uoh* *u-raši* *nem-u-euphrosunê* *na-n* *pe*
and IDF.S-pleasure CON-IDF.S-joy to-1P COP.M
*e-t$^h$re-n-p$^h$iri* *e-ni-saci*
to-INFL-1P-proclaim OBJ-DEF$_2$.P-word
*nte-ni-graphê* *et$^h$uab* *n-sêu* *niben*
of-DEF$_2$.P-scripture holy DEF.P-time QU
Furthermore, it is for us a pleasure and joy to proclaim the words of the Scripture at all times.
($^{B}$John Chrysostom, *In Michaelem et Latronem* [Simon 227, 6–7])

Disjunctive patterns show a repetition of the subject element even in Bohairic:

(256) Theodore observes the brothers at night and has a vision of an angel watching over them. As he rises to approach the angel, the latter says in Theodore's heart what he was about to say:
*nim* *p-et-rôis* *e-ni-snêu* *nt$^h$ok=pe* *šan-anok=pe*
WH COP.M-REL-watch to-DEF$_2$.P-brother.P 2MS=SE.M or-1S=se.M
Who is watching over the brothers? Is it you or is it me?
($^{B}$*V. Pachom* [Lefort 94, 20])

Likewise, adversative coordination does not seem to favour omission in most dialects, which is attested however (ex. 257c):

(257a) Shenute explains the devil's traps to those with little faith. He then explains who are 'those who flee in winter' (Mt 24:29) and reasons that the Lord has not inspired their faith:
*auô* *pe-u-pithe* *n-u-ebol=an=pe* *hm-p-tôhm*
and POSS-3P-obedience NEG-IDF.S-out=NEG=SE.M in-DEF.M-calling

*m-pe-kh(risto)s*
of-DEF.M-Christ
*alla pa-p-et-plana mmo-u=pe*
but POSS.M-DEF.M-REL-deceive OBJ-3P=SE.M
And their obedience does not arise from the invitation of Christ but belongs to the one who leads them astray.
($^{S}$Shenute, *I Am Amazed* §605 [Cristea 205, 13–19])

(257b) Jesus describes St John the Baptist:
*u-kui=pe hem-pe-b-ehi*
IDF.M-small=SE.M in-POSS.M-3MS-lifetime
*alla u-nak$^{j}$=pe nahlem-p$^{h}$-(nu)ti mn-ne-lômi*
but IDF.S-great=SE.M before-DEF.M-god CON-DEF.P-man
*hem-pe-f-tubba*
in-POSS.M-3MS-purity
He was small in his lifetime, but great before God and men in his purity.
($^{F}$John Evangelist, *Investiture of Archangel Michael* [Müller 29, 25–26])

(257c) In a letter, the sender speaks about a third man, who seems distressed because of some business. He characterises him as follows:
*u-anaggeon n-rôme=pe kata-t-sunêtesis alla u-k$^{j}$ôb*
IDF.S-good of-man=SE.M as-DEF.F-conscience but IDF.S-weak
*kata-p-sôma*
as-DEF.M-body
He is a good man according as to conscience but weak as to the body.
($^{S}$*P.RylCopt.* 273, 9–11)

Tripartite nominal sentences do not show a specific coordination pattern: we find examples with repetition of the copula (i.e. A COP B + C COP D; as in ex. 258a), without repetition of the subject and hence with a coordinated bipartite sentence (i.e. A COP B C SE), and coordinated phrases (e.g. A + C COP B + D; as in ex. 258c–258e):

(258a) Jesus explains why all mankind who received the Mystery will reign together with him in his kingdom:
*anok pe ntou auô ntou pe anok*
1S COP.M 3P and 3P COP.M 1S
I am they and they are me. ($^{S}$*Pistis Sophia* 232, 19–20 [Schmidt])

(258b) A servant has stolen a brother's tunic on board of a ship but accuses the brother, saying:
*n-ekyptios têr-u hn-ref-ci-k$^{j}$ol ne hn-ref-ôrk*
DEF.P-Egyptian all-3P IDF.P-AGT-say-lie COP.P IDF.P-AGT-swear
*n-nuc=ne*
of-false=SE.P

All Egyptians are liars and perjurers.
($^{SF}$Dioscorus of Alexandria, *On Macarius of Tkow* §3.7 [Johnson 17a, 28–30])

(258c) Moses taught his congregation about humility and the purification of the body:

| | | | | |
|---|---|---|---|---|
| *pe-šlêl* | *mn-t-ušê* | *n-rois* | *pe* | *p-tbbo* |
| DEF.P-pray | CON-DEF.F-night | of-wake | COP.M | DEF.M-purify |
| *m-p-sôma* | | | | |
| of-DEF.M-body | | | | |

Prayer and nightly vigils are the purification of the body.
($^{S}$*Life of Moses of Abydos* [*Or* 80, 405, b27–406, a2])

(258d) Shenute often spent the forty days of Easter without eating bread:

| | | | | | |
|---|---|---|---|---|---|
| *alla* | *te-f-trophê* | *u-uoti* | *n-uom* | *te* | *nem-u-šbin* |
| but | POSS.F-3MS-food | IDF.S-herb | of-eat | COP.F | CON-IDF.S-grain |
| *et-horp* | | | | | |
| REL-drench.STA | | | | | |

Rather, edible vegetable and moistened grain were his food.
($^{B}$*V. Shenute* [Leipoldt 13, 23])

(258e) Seeing the instruments of torture, St. Macarius prays to the Lord for help:

| | | | |
|---|---|---|---|
| *nt$^{h}$ok* | *pe* | *pa-boêthos* | *nem-pa-našti* |
| 2MS | COP.M | POSS.M.1S-helper | and-POSS.M.1S-strength |

You are my helper and my strength.
($^{B}$*Mart. Macarius of Antioch* [*AdM* 43, 2–3])

In case of several coordinated nouns, these could be either coordinated or divided into several sentences, according to pragmatic or rhetorical needs:

(259a) The prophet Jeremiah foresees the wrath of Lord:

| | | | | |
|---|---|---|---|---|
| *p-cois* | *ntok* | *pe* | *ta-kʲom* | *mn-ta-boêthia* |
| DEF.M-lord | 2MS | COP.M | POSS.F.1S-power | CON-POSS.F.1S-help |
| *auô* | *pa-ma* | *m-pôt* | *hm-pe-hou* | *nm-pethou* |
| and | POSS.M.1S-place | of-flight | in-DEF.M-day | of-evil |

Lord! You are my strength, my fortress, and my refuge in evil times!
($^{S}$Ier 16:19)

(259b) In the Gnostic *Gospel according to Philip* it is said:

| | | | |
|---|---|---|---|
| *p-uoin* | *mn-p-kake* | *p-ônh* | *mn-p-mu* |
| DEF.M-light | CON-DEF.M-darkness | DEF.M-life | CON-DEF.M-death |
| *n-unam* | *mn-n-hbur* | | |
| DEF.P-right | CON-DEF.P-left | | |
| *n-snêu* | *ne* | *n-ne-u-erêu* | |
| DEF.P-brother.P | COP.P | for-POSS.P-3P-fellow | |

The light and the darkness, the life and the death, the ones on the right, and the ones on the left are brethren to each other. ($^{SL}$*GospPh.* 53, 14–16)

(259c) In the Gnostic *Gospel according to Philip*, the female companions of the Lord are Mary, her sister, and Mary Magdalene:
*maria=gar te te-f-sône auô te-f-mau=te*
N=for COP.F POSS.F-3MS-sister and POSS.F-3MS-mother=SE.F
*auô te-f-hôtre=te*
and POSS.F-3MS-companion=SE.F
For Mary is indeed his sister and his mother and his companion.
($^{SL}$*GospPh.* 59, 10–11)

(259d) In the *Gospel of Truth*, the truth is contrasted with anguish, oblivion, and the 'creature of deceit':
*e-ti-mnt-mêe et-smant u-at-šb-s te*
DEP-DEF$_2$.F-ABST-truth REL-establish.STA IDF.S-NEG-change-3FS COP.F
*u-at-štartr te u-at-<t>saia-s te*
IDF.S-NEG-disturb COP.F IDF.S-NEG-make_beautiful-3FS COP.F
... while the established truth is immutable, imperturbable, and perfect in beauty. ($^{L}$*EvVer* 17, 25–28)

(259e) Jacob blesses his sons:
*rubên na-šorp m-misi nt$^h$ok pe ta-com*
N POSS.M.1S-first of-birth 2MS COP.M POSS.F.1S-power
*nem-t-aparkhê nte-na-šêri*
CON-DEF.M-beginning of-POSS.P.1S-child
Ruben, you are my firstborn, my might, and the beginning of my children.
($^{B}$Gn 49:3)

(259f) The hero of the story is introduced:
*uoh p$^h$ai ne-u-diakôn pe uoh n-khrêstianos n-rômi*
and DEM.M PRT-IDF.S-deacon COP.M and of-Christian of-man
This one was a deacon and a Christian.
($^{B}$*Mart. John of Panicôit* [Zaborowski 232–34])

As noted above, Bohairic often makes use of the conjunction *uoh n-* before the second NP, but sometimes *n-* may be omitted. Some writers such as Shenute explicitly use the pattern of repetition as a rhetorical device:

(260) Shenute answers to various accusations by people who left the monastery:
*u pe p-nobe ê aš pe p-ci n-k̉ons*
WH COP.M DEF.M-sin or WH COP.M DEF.M-use of-violence
*p-ent-a-i-ci-têutn*
COP.M-REL-PST-1S-take-2P

*n-kʲons* *nhêt-f* *ntôtn* *n-ref-krmrm*
of-violence inside-3MS 2P DEF.P-AGT-murmur
*n-ref-kʲn-arike*
DEF.P-AGT-find-blame
*imêti* *e-tra-kolaze* *mmô-tn* *hn-u-nokʲ* *n-kʲom*
unless to-INFL.1S-punish OBJ-2P in-IDF.S-great of-violence
*e-tre-tn-kô* *nsô-tn*
to-INFL-2P-put after-2P
*n-t-mnt-cace* *mn-p-titôn* *mn-p-moste*
OBJ-DEF.F-ABST-enemy CON-DEF.M-strife CON-DEF.M-hate
*mn-p-miše* *mn-p-côhm*
CON-DEF.M-fight CON-DEF.M-defile
*mn-p-ciue* *mn-p-kʲol* *mn-t-katalalia* *mn-krof* *nim*
CON-DEF.M-fraud CON-DEF.M-lie CON-DEF.F-calumny CON-guile QU
*mn-hôb* *nim*
CON-thing QU
*e-f-hou* *e-tre-tn-pôt* *ehun* *e-t-agapê* *mn-t-irênê*
DEP-3MS-bad to-INFL-2P-run into to-DEF.F-love CON-DEF.F-peace
*mn-t-me*
CON-DEF.F-truth
*mn-p-tbbo* *mn-thbbio* *nim* *mn-hôb* *nim*
CON-DEF.F-peace CON-humility QU CON-thing QU
*e-nanu-f*
REL-good-3MS
What sin or act of violence did I commit against you, you murmurers and fault-finders, except for my punishing you so as to make you renounce the enmity, and the strife, and the hate, and the quarrel, and the pollution, and the fraud, and the lie, and any guile and any bad thing – so as to make you run to the love, and the peace, and the truth, and the purity, and every humility and every good thing instead?
(ˢShenute, *Why O Lord* [L III 144, 15–22])

Matters of style sometimes lead to repetition of a part of the sentence:

(261) Shenute praises the Lord:
*ntok* *pe* *ntok* *pe* *p-cois* *et-cô*
2MS COP.M 2MS COP.M DEF.M-lord REL-say
*n-t-dikaiosynê* *auô* *et-šace* *n-t-me*
OBJ-DEF.F-justice and REL-speak OBJ-DEF.F-truth
You, only you are the Lord who speaks justice and tells the truth.
(ˢShenute, *Since It Is Necessary to Pursue the Devil* [A I 390, 3–4])

## 2.2 Adjunct clauses

### 2.2.1 Earlier Egyptian

In striking contrast to adverbial sentences, bare nominal sentences are not used as adjunct clauses in Earlier Egyptian. For unmarked adjuncts without an introducing preposition-conjunction and with similar semantics, the language had recourse to adverbial sentences with the so-called *m* of predication (Part I, 3.1.4). Thus, e.g. in present 'circumstantial' (ex. 262a) and final 'so that' clauses (262b):

(262a) The king remembers the early career of Ikhernefret:

| | | | | | |
|---|---|---|---|---|---|
| *ỉw* | *dỉ-n=ṯw* | *ḥm-ỉ* | *r-smr* | *ỉw-k* | *m-ḥwn* |
| AUX | place-PST=2MS | majesty-1S | to-friend | DEP-2MS | as-youth |
| *n(-y)-rnp-t* | *26* | | | | |
| of[-M]-year-F | 26 | | | | |

My majesty appointed you a royal friend when you were a young man of 26 years. (Berlin 1157, 7)

(262b) Goddess Hathor says to Queen Hatshepsut:

| | | |
|---|---|---|
| *ỉỉ-n(-ỉ)* | *wn(-ỉ)* | *m-sꜣḥ-ṯ* |
| come-PST[-1S] | AUX[-1S] | as-protection-2FS |

I have come so that I may be your protection. (*Urk.* IV 239, 16–17)

The same suppletion takes place in conditional protases after the element *ỉr*, where nominal sentences are replaced by *wn/wnn* + adverbial sentence (exx. 263a and 263b) as well as in adjunct clauses introduced by preposition-conjunctions (263c; note also the left-dislocation of the adjunct by means of *ỉr*):

(263a) Ptahhetep gives advise to members of the elite:

| | | | | | |
|---|---|---|---|---|---|
| *ỉr* | *wnn-k* | *m-s* | *ỉqr* | *ỉrỉ-k* | *sꜣ* |
| CND | AUX-2MS | as-man | excellent | make.SUB | son |
| *n-smꜣ* | *nṯr* | | | | |
| to-agreeable | god | | | | |

If you are an excellent man, make (your) son well-disposed towards god. (Ptahhetep 197–98)

(263b) Thutmosis III says that he spoke truthfully:

| | | |
|---|---|---|
| *ḏr-wn* | *ḥm-ỉ* | *m-ỉnpw* |
| since-AUX | majesty-1S | as-youth |

... since my majesty was a young man. (*Urk.* IV 157, 7)

(263c) Sebekemhat tells of his early career:

| | | | | |
|---|---|---|---|---|
| *ỉr* | *m-wn-ỉ* | *m-ẖrd* | *wn-ỉ* | *m-smr* |
| PTC | as-AUX-1S | as-child | AUX-1S | as-friend |

When I was a child, I was already a royal friend. (Hatnub 22, 2)

Like adverbial sentences, nominal sentences could be used in causal adjuncts where the clause serving as complement of the preposition-conjunction was introduced by a complementiser:

(264a) Hapdjefai explains that he has inherited property that he may use in his mortuary fund:

| | | | |
|---|---|---|---|
| *ḥr-ntt* | *ỉnk* | *sꜣ* | *wꜥb* |
| because-COMP | 1S | son | priest |

... because I am a son of a wab-priest. (Siut I, 288)

(264b) The cronies of Seth were destroyed when they approached the eye of Ra:

| | | | |
|---|---|---|---|
| *ḏr-ntt* | *tkn=pw* | *ỉ[m]-s* | *ꜣmm* |
| since-COMP | approach.INF=SE | in-3FS | burn.INF |

... since approaching it is (=means) burning up. (BD 17/*Nu* pl. 9, 8–9)

In the following example, an anteposed segment introduced by *ỉr* precedes the complement consisting of a bipartite nominal sentence:

(265) Senwosret III says that he always answered aggression in kind:

| | | | | |
|---|---|---|---|---|
| *ḏr-ntt* | *ỉr* | *gr* | *mḫt-pḥ* | *ssmḫ* |
| since-COMP | PTC | silent.PIA | after-attack | strengthen.PIA |

| | |
|---|---|
| *ỉb=pw* | *n(-y)-ḫrwy* |
| heart=SE | of[-M]-enemy |

since as for one who remains silent after an attack, he is a strengthener of the enemy's resolve. (Berlin 1157, 7–8)

As already seen with adverbial sentences (Part I, 3.1.3.3), it appears that these three types of adjunct clauses are not free variants, but rather display semantic-pragmatic differences.

In early Eighteenth Dynasty texts (fifteenth century BC), one begins to find examples of nominal sentences subordinated as adjuncts by means of the auxiliary *ỉw*, which by now was assuming the grammatical function of a subordinator (see Part I, 2.2.2.1):

(266) Nakht attributes his success on a mission to turquoise mines to divine providence:

| | | | |
|---|---|---|---|
| *n-pḥ=wỉ* | *k-y* | *mỉtt-ỉ* | *m-ỉỉ=nb* |
| NEG-reach=1S | other-M | like-1S | in-come.PPA=QU.M |

*r-[ḫ3s-t]=ṯn* *iw* *ink* *ḥsy* *n(-y)-ḥwtḥr* *mfk3-t*
to-hill-country=DEM.F DEP 1S praise.PPP of[-M]-N turquoise-F
No-one of my kind who has come to this hill-country has equalled me, because I am one favoured of Hathor of the Turquoise. (Sinai 181, 10–11)

Conversely, in earlier religious texts one finds examples of what appears to be a nominal sentence subordinated as adjunct by means of the clitic particle *=is*:

(267) The deceased is a solar deity:
*iwʿ-n(-i)* *3ḫ-t* *rʿ* *ink=is* *tm*
inherit-PST[-1S] horizon-F N 1S=PTC N
I have inherited the horizon of Ra, because I am Atum.
(CT VII 514c–d/B4L)

However, this construction is no longer common in later material, although it was ostensibly used as a conscious archaism in utterances such as e.g. the following example from a Middle Kingdom literary work, where the speaker is a god:

(268) The sailor has just promised to send the snake myrrh and other valuables. He laughs and says:
*n* *wr=n-k* *ʿntw* *ḫpr-t=nb* *snṯr* *ink=is*
NEG great=to-2MS myrrh form-F=QU.M incence 1S=PTC
*ḥq3* *pwnt*
ruler N
You do not have much myrrh or any form of incense, whereas I am the ruler of Punt. (Sh.S. 150–51)

As elsewhere,*=is* was probably a generalised marker of dependency that could range from syntactic subordination to much looser kinds of semantic and pragmatic linkage between clauses. Therefore, its role as an adjunctor in the examples above is more a contextual implication than a grammatical property.

### 2.2.2 Later Egyptian

In Late Egyptian, nominal (including cleft) sentences can be used in adjunct clauses introduced by the element *iw*, by now a marker of syntactic dependence:

(269a) Wenamun complains to the princess of Cyprus that people from her island have tried to kill him:
*iw-ink* *wpwti* *n-imn*
DEP-1S messenger of-N
...although I am a messenger of Amun. (*LES* 75, 12)

(269b) A suspected tomb robber is quoted as having expressed his indignation at the share of silver that he had received from his accomplices:
*iw-ink i-di ptr-k p3-ḫr*
DEP-1S PPA-give see-2MS DEF.M-tomb
... although it was me who showed you the tomb. (*KRI* VI 786, 7–8)

(269c) An official is told to examine a well:
*iw-ḫnm-t (n)-nmḥ-y*
DEP-well-F [of]-freeman-P
...(it) being a well of the freemen (Jansen-Winkeln, *IdS* II, 25, 3–4)

(269d) A moral treatise paints a negative image of someone who disregards the property rights of others:
*iw-p3y-f-pr ḫft n-p3-dmi*
DEP-POSS.M-3MS-house enemy of-DEF.M-city
... with his house being an enemy of the city. (Amenemope 8, 5)

(269e) The addressee of a letter is asked to report to the vizier in the matter of some money which a third person demands from the sender saying:
*imi-ṯ-f iw-bn-p3y-i-ḥtr in*
give.IMP-OBJ-3MS DEP-NEG-[POSS.M-1S-tax]$_P$ NEG
'Give it', although it is not my tax. (*LEM* 6, 5)

(269f) The author urges the addressee to come to him with some men as soon as possible:
*ir-sḏr-k ꜥ3 n-wḫ3 mk iw-ink iy*
CND-sleep-2MS there in-search PTC DEP-1S come.PIA
*r-in-t-k ḏs-i*
to-bring-INF-2MS self-1S
Should you be idle there searching, well, then it will be me who is coming to fetch you! (pLeiden F 1996/1.1, r° 4–5 [*FS Wente,* 77])

(269g) The addressee of a letter is ordered to send a guard onto the walls, because the author has received an oracle saying:
*mir-di-t-ḥn-rmṯ=nb (r)-sḫ-t iw-f (m)-wꜥw*
NEG.IMP-give.INF-go-man=QU [to]-field-F DEP-3MS (as)-soldier
*iw-f (m)-sḫt iw-f (m)-rmṯ wnḏw=nb*
DEP-3MS (as)-bird catcher DEP-3MS (as)-man common=QU
Do not let anyone go outside to the fields, be it a soldier, a bird catcher, or any person! (pStrasbourg 33, 12–13)

In 269d the analysis of the construction as an adverbial sentence is also possible. None of the attested examples is apparently used as a 'virtual' relative clause (see Part I, 2.2.4.1).

Nominal sentences could also be used after other connectors (usually prepositions used as conjunctions): such as in causal construction after *ḥr-nty*, a Late

Egyptian conjunction based on the Earlier Egyptian construction preposition-conjunction + complementiser (ex. 270a) and, more common it seems, after the conjunction *mi*, which usually expresses accordance (note that the latter construction is limited to early Late Egyptian texts and survives, if at all, only in the Classical Egyptian):

(270a) In a protective spell against snakebites it is said that the protected person cannot be attacked:
*ḥr-nty-ntf* *rw*
because-REL-3MS lion
... because he is a lion. (*KRI* V 264, 11)

(270b) The scribe Hori mocks his impertinent addressee saying:
*wpy-i=n-k* *sḥn-t* *n-nb-k* *ꜥ.w.s.* *mi-mntk*
open.PROSP-1S=for-2MS order-F of-lord-2MS l.h.p. like-2MS
*pꜣy-f-sš-nzw*
POSS.M-3MS-scribe-royal
I will explain the order of your lord, l.h.p., for you, for you are his royal scribe. ([2]*pAnastasi* 108, 7)

(270c) The gods of the netherworld praise the king for his deeds saying that generation might pass:
*iw-ḥm-k* *m-nzw* *m-biti* *mi-ntk* *ir-ꜣḫ-t*
DEP-majesty-2MS as-king as-king as-2MS do.PPA-beneficial_thing-F
... while you are king in Upper and of Lower Egypt for it is you who does what is beneficial. (*KRI* II 330, 10)

(270d) The harpist assures the deceased tomb owner:
*sḫꜣ-ṱ-k* *ḥr-nfr-k*
remember.PROSP-PASS-2MS because-beauty-2MS
*mi-ntk* *pw* *ꜥq* *ḥr-iwn* *rḫ* *sštꜣ* *imi-s*
like-2MS COP.M enter.PIA on-N know.PPA secret.P inside-3FS
You will be remembered for your perfection for you a someone who enters Heliopolis and knows the secrets therein.
(Neferhetep Song 3 [Hari pl. IV] l. 8)

(270e) In the introduction to the inscription dedicated to his father Ramesses I., the common narrative of erstwhile chaos and inactivity at a given area is developed:
*ẖrtnṯr* *n-wn-mḥ-s* *mi-mw=pw* *ꜣs*
necropolis NEG-exist-fill-3FS like-water=SE.M rush.PPA
*[ḥr-w]ꜥr-t*
on-river_bank-F
The necropolis, it was not filled for it was like water rushing by the river bank. (*KRI* I 111, 1–2)

(270f) The assembly court condemns the theft commited by a woman from the village and reports to the vizier urging him to punish her most severly so as to act as a deterrent for the future. They reason:
*ḫr-ỉwsꜣ* *tꜣ-bwṯ* *n-pꜣy-dmỉ* *ṯꜣw* *ḥmtỉ*
and-since DEF.F-abomination of-DEM.M-village taking copper
*mỉm-f*
in-3MS
Since this village's abomination is the theft of copper within it ...
(*KRI* IV 317, 2–3)

Note that the use of *ỉwsꜣ* (< *rsꜣ*) seems to be a development from temporal "since; after" to causal "since".

Nominal sentences are rarely attested in the conditional protasis in Late Egyptian; they are more common in the apodosis:

(271a) The prince of Byblos replies to Wenamun's claim that the pharaoh has control over him:
*ỉr-pꜣ-ḥqꜣ* *n-km-t* *pꜣ-nb* *n-pꜣy-ỉ* *ḫr* *ỉnk*
CND-DEF.M-ruler of-Egypt-F DEF.M-lord of-POSS.M-1S PTC 1S
*pꜣy-f-bꜣk* *m-rꜥ* *n-wn-ỉ-ỉr-f* *dỉ-ỉn-ṯ*
POSS.M-3MS-servant in-state IP-PTC-ST-AUX-3MS give-bring-PASS
*ḥḏ* *nbw*
silver gold
If the ruler of Egypt were the lord of what is mine and I were his servant, he would not have sent silver and gold. (*LES* 68, 3–5)

(271b) The author is disappointed by the content of a jar supposedly containing honey and sends it back:
*ỉnn* *m-ky* *r-dỉ=sw=n-k* *ỉmỉ* *ptr-f=sw*
CND PTC-other PPA-give=3MS=to-2MS give.IMP see-3MS=3MS
If it was someone else who gave it to you, then get him to look at it.
(pLouvre E. 27151, 8 [*JEA* 64, pl. 14])

(271c) After the children of a man agreed to his new settlement of property regarding his new wife, the vizier said:
*ỉr-ỉw-bn* *ḥm-t* *sw* *ỉn* *ỉw-ḫr* *[nḥ]s*
CND -DEP-NEG wife-F POSS.3MS NEG DEP-Syrian Nubian
*ỉw-mrỉ-f=sw* *[ỉ]w-f-dỉ* *n-s* *ꜣḫ-t-f* *[nym*
DEP-love-3MS=3S DEP-3MS-give to-3SF thing-F-3MS WH
*ỉ]-ỉr-f-wsf* *pꜣ-ỉry-f*
REL-AUX-3MS-cancel DEF.M-do.REL-3MS
Even if it were not his wife, but a Syrian or a Nubian whom he loved and to whom he gave his property, who could cancel what he has done?
(*KRI* VI 741, 9–11)

In Demotic, also nominal sentences introduced by the element *ỉw* (sometimes written *r*) are commonly used as adjuncts:

(272a) A petitioner reports that he had been prevented from sowing certain fields:

| *r-ỉnk* | *ỉ-ỉr-skꜣ-nꜣ-ꜣḫ-w* | *n-rn-w* | *n-pr-t* |
|---|---|---|---|
| DEP-1S | PPP-AUX-plough-DEF.P-field-P | of-name-3P | in-winter-F |

... although it is me who ploughed those fields in the winter.

(pBM 10599, 7–8)

(272b) A man is identified in a legal document as the younger brother of the husband of the claimant:

| *šr* | *ỉṯ* | *r-bnỉw-šr* | *mwt* | *ỉn* | *pꜣy* |
|---|---|---|---|---|---|
| child | father | DEP-NEG-child | mother | NEG | SE.M |

He is the son of the (same) father, but not of the (same) mother.

(pBM 10591, r° 5, 14–15)

Examples functioning as 'virtual' relative clause can also be found now[79] as well as *ỉw*-headed complement clauses after certain verbs such as *gm* (see 273d):

(273a) A moral instruction copied on an ostracon:

| *mỉr-nq-sḥm-t* | *ỉw-bn-tꜣy-k* | *ʿn* | *tꜣy* |
|---|---|---|---|
| NEG.IMP-copulate-woman-F | DEP-NEG-POSS-2MS | NEG | SE.F |

| *bw-ỉr-w-gm=n-k* | *lwḥ* | *rḏbꜣṯ-s* |
|---|---|---|
| NEG-do-3P-find=in-2MS | fault | because-3FS |

Do not have sex with a woman who is not yours, lest fault be found with you because of it. (oBM 50627, 3–4)

(273b) The author of a letter objects to consecrating certain people as priests of the temple at Elephantine:

| *wn* | *nỉm-w* | *ỉw-bꜣk* | *n-ky-rmṯ* | *pꜣy* |
|---|---|---|---|---|
| be | in-3P | DEP-servant | of-another-man | SE.M |

Among them is (one,) who is a servant of another man.

(pBerlin P. 13540, 3)

(273c) Naneferkaptah asked why an old priest laughed at him when he was reading old texts in shrines of gods. The priest said that the texts were pointless, but that Naneferkaptah should follow him to the place:

| *ntyỉw-pꜣy-ḏmʿ* | *nỉm-f* | *ỉw-ḏḥwty* | *pꜣ-ỉỉr-sẖ-f* |
|---|---|---|---|
| REL-DEM.M-book | in-3MS | DEP-N | COP.M-REL.PST-write-3MS |

| *n-ḏr-ṯ-f* | *ḥʿ-f* |
|---|---|
| in-hand-F-3MS | body-3MS |

... wherein is that book, which Thoth wrote with his own hands ....

(Setne I 3, 12)

79 Note that *ʿn* in 273a (oHess = oBM 50627) is an unetymological writing of *ỉn*.

(273d) The vultures flew to the desert to see whether their respective stories were true:

*gm-w* *md-t=nb-t* *r-ḏd-w* *n-t3-ẖ-t* *2-t*
find-3P thing-F=QU-F REL-say-3P to-DEF.F-body 2-F
*r-md-t-m3ʿ-t* *ḏr-w* *n3w*
DEP-ABST-F-truth-F all-3P SE.P
They found out that all they had told to each other was true.
(Myth of the Sun's Eye 14, 29)

Demotic conditional clauses with nominal sentences show various patterns. The nominal sentence can be embedded with *inn3w-* (Coptic *ene-*) or *iw-f-ḫpr iw*...:

(274a) The pharaoh tells his scribe to draw up letters conveying the following news:

*my-ir-p3dyist* *wʿb* *nim-w* *inn3w-mtr* *p3y*
give.IMP-do-N priest in-3P CND-right SE.M
May Petese be priest among them, if that is right.
(pRylands IX 8, 18)

(274b) A magical text prescribes how a priest has to act:

*iw-f-ḫpr* *iw-pḥ-nṯr* *p3y* *n3y* *wʿe-ṯ*
DEP-3MS-happen DEP-reach-god SE.M DEM.P single-STA.1S
*n3* *nty-iir-k-ʿš-w*
DEF.P REL-FUT-2MS-call-3P
If it is an oracle question, you should recite these (things) alone.
(pMag. London&Leiden 6, 26–27)

(274c) In a description of an artistically and morally questionable harpist it is stated:

*mtw-f-ḥms* *iw-ḥr-f* *sq* *r-ẖ* *ḫpr*
CNJ-3MS-sit.STA DEP-face-3MS collect.STA to-body happen
*iw-ḥs* *n-m3ʿ-t* *p3y*
DEP-singer of-truth-F SE.M
And there he sits, having pulled himself together as if he were a real singer. (Depraved Harpist 2, 6)

As noted in the previous and will be taken up in the following section, in Demotic the earlier complementiser *ḏd* (< *rḏd*) has acquired the function of a marker of causal clauses also used to introduce nominal sentences (see 2.2.1). The same morpheme is also found with clauses of purpose, but no examples with nominal sentences are known.

In Coptic, the initial particle *e* (earlier *iw/r*) is the standard marker of adjunct clauses:

(275a) Anthony is introduced into the story. He was an Egyptian by birth and his parents were rather wealthy:
*auô e-hen-khristianos ne*
CNJ DEP-IDF.P-Christian SE.P
*ntof hôô-f on a-f-i ehrai*
3MS self-3MS again PST-3MS-come up
*hn-u-mnt-khristianos cine-te-f-mnt-kui*
in-IDF.S-ABST-Christian since-POSS.F-3MS-ABST-small
And them being Christians, he himself was brought up in Christian manner since his childhood. ([S]*Life of Anthony* ed. Garitte 3, 3–5)

(275b) On the day of judgement sinners will accuse the son of lawlessness of having claimed to be the Christ:
*e-ntak -p-diabolos*
DEP-2MS -DEF.M-devil
... although you are the Devil
([A]*ApEl* [Steindorff, *Apokalypse des Elias* 100 40, 6–7])

(275c) After Jesus had asked a woman for water, she wondered why he, being a Jew, should speak to her:
*e-anak -u-shim[e] n-[s]ama[rites]*
DEP-1S -IDF.S-woman of-N
... although I am a Samaritan woman. ([L]Jn 4:9)

(275d) Paul declares to the Athenians that everyone is God's offspring and continues:
*e-anon -u-genos=un nte-p$^h$-(nu)i sše=na-n=an*
DEP-1S -IDF.S-people=then of-DEF$_1$.M-god fitting=for-1P=NEG
*e-t$^h$re-n-meui e-nub ie hat*
to-INFL-1P-think OBJ-gold or silver
*ie ôni m-p$^h$ôth n-tekhnê ie mokmek n-rômi*
or stone of-carve of-craft or think of-man
*ce-a-f-oni mmô-u nce-p$^h$-(nu)ti*
COMP-ST-3MS-liken.STA OBJ-3P PVS-DEF$_1$.M-god
Then, forasmuch as we are the offspring of God, we should not think that God is like gold or silver. ([B]Acts 17:29)

The same pattern is used to mark 'virtual' relative clauses used as non-restrictive relative clauses:

(276a) When people press Jesus to hear the word of God on the shores of the Sea of Galilee, he sees two fisher-boats without their crew, who is washing the nets:
*a-f-ale=de* *e-ua* *n-n-coi* *e-pa-simôn=pe*
PST-3MS-mount=yet OBJ-one of-DEF.P-ship DEP-POSS.M-N=SE.M
He entered one of the ships, which was Simon's, .... ($^{S}$Lk 5:3)

(276b) A man robbed while staying at the shrine of St Colluthos accused his servants of theft:
*hosôn=de* *e-f-mokmek* *mmo-f* *e-basanize* *mmo-u*
as much=yet DEP-3MS-think OBJ-3MS to-punish OBJ-3P
*a-u-šbêr* *e-pô-f=pe* *mooše* *ehun* *ero-f*
PST-IDF.S-friend DEP-POSS.M-3MS=SE.M walk in to-3MS
While he was considering punishing them, a friend of his approached him. ($^{S}$*Miracles of St Colluthus* [Schenke 222, b1–8])

(276c) The Lord says that he saw in Israel's house:
*a-u-pornia* *e-s-naḫt* *e-ta-ephraim=te*
OBJ-IDF.S-fornication DEP-3FS-be_hard.STA DEP-POSS.F-N=SE.F
... a grave act of fornication, which belongs to (i.e. commited by) Ephraim... ($^{A}$Hos 6:10)

(276d) Jesus arrived:
*e-u-polis* *nte-t-samaria* *e-pe-s-len* *pe* *sukhar*
to-IDF.S-town of-DEF.F-N DEP-POSS.M-3FS-name COP.M N
...to a Samaritan town called Sychar. ($^{F}$Jn 4:5)

(276e) Townspeople practising human sacrifice to a dragon had captured
*n-u-kuci* *n-alu* *e-p-šêri=pe* *n-u-khêra*
OBJ-IDF.S-small of-boy DEP-DEF.M-son=SE.M of-IDF.S-widow
*n-shimi* *n-khristianê*
of-woman of-Christian.F
...a young boy, who was the son of a Christian widow.
($^{B}$*Mart. Theodore Stratelates* [*AM* I 160, 2–3])

Nominal sentences functioning as causal clauses are introduced in Coptic by a causal connector such as *epidê*, *ebol-ce*, *ce*, or the like (exx. 277a–e), whereas conditional clauses are marked by an initial conditional particle such as $^{S}$*ešôpe*/$^{B}$*ešôp* "if (it is the case)" (exx. 277f–i) or $^{S}$*ešce*/$^{B}$*isce* "if (it is true)" as real conditions and by *ene-* as hypothetical conditions:

(277a) St John of Lycopolis tells to a father of a possessed boy the reason for his son's plight:
*epidê* *t-mau* *n-p-šêre* *šêm* *u-at-na* *te*
because DEF.F-mother of-DEF.M-son little IDF.S-NEG-mercy COP.F

*e-mn-lau* *m-mnt-šenhtêf* *nhêt-s* *ehun* *e-lau*
DEP-NEG-any of-ABST-compassion inside-3FS in to-any
*n-rôme* *n-talaiporos*
of-man of-miserable
Because the mother of the boy is merciless, having no compassion whatsoever for any miserable man. ($^{S}$*Life of John of Lycopolis* [*AnBoll* 88, 175, b3–11])

(277b) Paul of Tamma points out that the measure of a wise man living in his cell is the Lord:
*e-f-tntôn=gar* *e-p-nute* *ebol-ce-u-at-nau*
DEP-3MS-resemble=for to-DEF.M-god out-for-IDF.S-NEG-look
*ero-f=pe*
to-3MS=SE.M
... for it indeed resembles God because he is invisible.
($^{S}$Paul of Tamma, *De Cella* [Orlandi 94, 48])

(277c) God says that all the other nations will call Israel happy:
*abal-ce-ntôtne* *p-et-na-ḫôpe=ne-i* *n-u-kah*
out-for-2P COP.M-REL-FUT-be=for-1S as-IDF.S-land
*e-a-i-uaḫ-f*
DEP-PST-1S-wish-3MS
... for it is you who will be a land for me that I want. ($^{A}$Mal 3:12)

(277d) Jesus tells the Jews that their father is not God, but the devil whose desires they fulfil:
*hot[an]* *ere-p-ref-ce-k̍al* *na-se[ce]* *šare-f-sece* *abal*
whenever DEP-DEF.M-AGT-say-lie FUT-speak AOR-3MS-speak out
*hn-n-[ete]-nô-f=ne*
in-DEF.P-REL-POSS.P-3MS=SE.P
*ce-u-san-ce-k̍a[l]=pe* *nm-pe-f-ke-iôt*
for-IDF.S-AGT-speak-lie=SE.M CON-POSS.M-3MS-other-father
Whenever the lier speaks, he speaks out of its own, for he is a liar and also the father thereof. ($^{L}$Jn 8:44)

(277e) The apostle says that those who believe have themselves become sons of God and adds:
*oti=de* *ce-nt$^{h}$ôten* *han-šêri*
because=yet COMP-2P IDF.P-son
*a-p$^{h}$-(nu)ti* *tauo* *m-pi-pn(eum)a* *nte-pe-f-šêri*
PST-DEF.M-god send OBJ-DEF$_{2}$.M-spirit of-POSS.M-3MS-son
*eḫrêi* *e-ne-tn-hêt*
down to-POSS.P-2P-heart
And because you are (His) sons, God sent His son's Spirit into your hearts. ($^{B}$Gal 4:6)

(277f) Being asked whether a person who has died would meet God rightaway, patriarch John responds:

*ešôpe u-khrêstianos=pe ša-u-cit-f e-rat-f m-p-nute*
CND IDF.S-Christian=SE.M AOR-3P-take-3MS to-foot-3MS as-DEF.M-god
*nse-tre-f-uôšt n-i(êsu)s*
CNJ.3P-CAUS-3MS-worship OBJ-N
If it is a Christian, he will be brought in front of God and they will make him worship Jesus.
($^{S}$*Questions of Theodore* [van Lantschoot 19, 10–11])

(277g) Jesus preached that the eye is the lamp of the body:

*ešope=un pe-k-bal u-haplus pe pe-k-sôma*
CND=now POSS.M-2MS-eye IDF.S-simple COP.M POSS.M-2MS-body
*têr-f efe-er-uain*
all-3MS FUT.3MS-do-light
If then you eye is pure, your whole body will shine.
($^{M}$Mt 6:22 mae 1)

(277h) The Egyptians tell the midwifes how to treat the newborn babies of the Hebrews:

*ešôp=men u-hôut=pe ḫotbe-f ešôp=de*
CND=indeed IDF.S-male=SE.M kill.IMP-3MS CND=yet
*u-shimi=te ma-tanḫo-s*
IDF.S-female=SE.F IMP-keep_alive
If it is a boy, kill it! If it is a girl, let it live! ($^{B}$Ex 1:16)

(277i) The Pharisees reason that they are aware that God does not listen to the sinner:

*alla ešôp e-u-šamše-nuti pe uai uoh e-f-iri*
but CND DEP-IDF.S-worship-god COP.M one and DEP-3MS-do
*m-pe-f-uôš p$^{h}$ai ša-f-sôtem ero-f*
OBJ-POSS.M-3MS-wish DEM.M AOR-3MS-listen to-3MS
... but if someone is devout and does God's bidding, he will listen to this one. ($^{B}$Jn 9:31)

(277j) The Devils tempts Jesus in the desert:

*isce nt$^{h}$ok pe p-šêri m-p$^{h}$-(nu)ti a-co-s*
CND 2MS COP.M DEF$_{1}$.M-son of-DEF$_{1}$.M-god IMP-say-3FS
*hina nte-nai-ôni er-ôik*
so_that CNJ-DEM.P-stone do-bread
If you really are the son of God, then speak so that theses stone turn to bread. ($^{B}$Mt 4:3)

(277k) Shenute argues that he must be an evil person since:
*e-ne-ang-u-ponêros* *n-rôme=an* *pe* *nere-hoine*
DEP-PRT-1S-IDF.S-bad of-man=NEG PTC PRT-some
*na-krmrm=an* *pe* *ehun* *ero-i*
FUT-murmur=NEG PTC down to-1S
If I would not be an evil person, some would not mutter against me.
($^{S}$Shenute, *Why O Lord* [L III 118, 8–9])

(277l) The Pharisee who had invited Jesus says after he saw that a woman of doubtful reputation anointed Jesus' feet:
*e-ne-u-prophêtês* *pe* *p$^{h}$ai* *na-f-emi* *ce-...*
DEP-PRT-IDF.S-prophet COP.M DEM.M PRT-3MS-know COMP-...
If that one would be a prophet, he would know that ... ($^{B}$Lk 7:39)

(277m) Jesus chides his father Joseph:
*nsabêl* *ce-ntok* *pe* *pa-iôt* *kata-sarks*
except COMP-2MS COP.M POSS.M.1S-father according-flesh
*epei* *ti-na-tamo-k* *ce-a-k-seksek-pa-maace* *n-unam*
then 1S-FUT-tell-2MS COMP-PST-2MS-pull-POSS.M.1S-ear of-right
If you would not be my father according to the flesh, I would let you know what it means that you pulled my right ear.
($^{S}$Death of Joseph [*Aegyptiaca* 17, 30–18, 17])

Note that in Bohairic the clause can be marked additionally as dependent as in ex. 277h.

Greek connectors are widely used in Coptic nominal sentences. They do not usually impose any constraints on the syntactic structure of the following clause:

(278a) Jesus tells the disciples that a man may be born blind without him or his parents having sinned so as to display the works of God:
*šše* *ero-n* *e-r-hôb* *e-ne-hbêue*
fitting to-1P to-do-work to-DEF.P-things.P
*m-p-ent-a-f-tauo-i* *hoson* *pe-hou=pe*
of-DEF.M-REL-PST-3MS-send-1S as much DEF.M-day=SE.M
It is necessary for us to do the works of the one who sent me while it is day.
($^{S}$Jn 9:4)

(278b) Shenute claims that the Jews and those who do not believe in the Lord have ceased to fight against Satan:
*n-se-soun=an* *ce-hoson* *n-cace=ne* *m-pe-st(au)ros*
CNJ-3P-know=NEG COMP-insofar DEF.P-enemy=SE.P of-DEF.M-cross

*n-cace=on=ne* *n-te-f-kʲom*
DEF.P-enemy=again=SE.P of-POSS.F-3MS-might
And they do not know that, insofar as they are enemies of the cross, they are enemies of his might as well.
(^SShenute, *A Beloved One Asked Me Once Years Ago* [Ch 16, 42–47])

(278c) The narrator says about Mark:
*auô kan ešce u-hêke=pe*
and CONC if IDF.S-poor=SE.M
*n-hêke m-p-kosmos ne-nt-a-p-nute sopt-u*
DEF.P-poor of-DEF.M-world COP.P-REL-PST-DEF.M-god choose-3P
Even if he was poor, it are the poor of this world whom God has chosen.
(^SJohn the Hermit, *Enc. on Mark the Evangelist* [Orlandi 44a, 12–17])

(278d) The disciples have asked the Manichean apostle about the signs of greeting and he replies:
*pi-tiu n-sece et-a-tetn-šnt-ø ara-u se-uanh=men*
DEM.M-five of-word REL-PST-2P-ask-1S to-3P 3P-appear=indeed
*abal hm-p-kosmos e-u-o n-t-he*
out in-DEF.M-world DEP-3P-be.STA in-DEF.F-way
*n-n-et-sabk e-u-o n-kui*
of-DEF.P-REL-be_small DEP-3P-be.STA as-small
*kaitoige hn-nakʲ=ne e-u-taiait*
although IDF.P-great=SE.P DEP-3P-be_honoured.STA
These five things about which you asked me, they seem indeed to appear in the world as negligable and small, although they are great and honourable. (^L*Kephalaia* 38, 5–7)

(278e) The author of the encomium points out that the body of Theodore the General, unlike that of Theodore the Oriental, was not buried in Antioch but taken to Egypt:
*keper u-kahi n-šemmo=an=pe alla p-kahi*
CONC IDF.S-land of-alien=NEG=SE.M but DEF.M-land
*m-pe-f-iôt=pe*
of-POSS.M-3MS-father=SE.M
... although it is no foreign country, but his father's land.
(^BTheodore of Antioch, *On the Theodores* [*AM* II 103, 10–11])

(278f) Papnute saw a man approaching him from the desert and climbed on a rock:
*a-i-er-hoti ce-mêpôs u-rem-n-tôu=pe*
PST-1S-do-fear COMP-lest IDF.S-man-of-mountain=SE.M
I was afraid lest he is a Bedouin.
(^BPapnute, *Wanderings* [*RecTrav* 6, 174, 10–11, collated])

## 2.3 Complement clauses

### 2.3.1 Earlier Egyptian

Earlier Egyptian nominal sentences are generally not used as direct clausal complements without a complementiser. As shown in connection with adverbial sentences (Part I, 2.1.5), semantically similar clauses serving as complements of preposition-conjunctions take the form of adverbial sentences headed by *wn/wnn* with the so-called *m* of predication. The same certainly holds true also for complements of verbs, although examples without a complementiser are limited to instances after the causative *rdỉ*:

(279) Thutmosis I says of his conquests:
*ỉrỉ-n-ỉ* *tꜣš-w* *tꜣmrỉ* *r-šnn-t* *ỉṯn...*
make-PST-1S border-P Egypt to-encircle.REL-F sun-disc
*dỉ-ỉ* *wn* *kmt* *m-ḥrttp*
cause.SUB-1S AUX Egypt as-chief
I have set the boundaries of Egypt to what the sun-disc encircles... so that I might cause Egypt to be chief. (*Urk.* IV 102, 11–14)

However, it may once again be noted that nominal sentences could be used in causal adjuncts introduced by preposition-conjunctions where the clause serving as a complement of the latter was introduced by a complementiser:

(280a) Hapdjefa explains that he has inherited property that he may use in his mortuary fund:
*ḥr-ntt* *ỉnk* *sꜣ* *wꜥb*
because-COMP 1S son priest
... because I am a son of a wab-priest. (Siut I, 288)
(280b) The cronies of Seth were destroyed when they approached the eye of Ra:
*ḏr-ntt* *tkn=pw* *ỉ[m]-s* *ꜣmm*
since-COMP approach.INF=SE in-3FS burn.INF
... since approaching it means burning up. (BD 17/*Nu* pl. 9, 118–19)

Instances of nominal sentences serving as complements of verbs and introduced by a complementiser are restricted to clausal objects of the verbs *rḫ* 'know' and *mꜣꜣ* 'see':

(281a) It is said of certain divine beings:
*ỉrỉ-n-sn* *rn* *n(-y)-N=pn* *m-bỉk* *nṯr(-y)* *sk=sn*
do-PST-3P name of[-M]-N=DEM.M as-falcon god[-RLT] PTC=3P

| | | | |
|---|---|---|---|
| *rḫ-y* | *ntt* | *wꜥ* | *ỉm=pw* |
| know-STA | COMP | one | there=SE |

They have made the name of this N as a divine falcon, because they know that he is the one therein. (CT VI 312d–f)

(281b) Amun granted king Thutmosis numerous jubilees:

| | | | |
|---|---|---|---|
| *rḫ* | *ntt* | *sꜣ-f=pw* | *smsw* |
| know.STA | COMP | son-3MS=SE | eldest |

... knowing that he is his eldest son. (*Urk.* IV 592, 1)

(281c) The postscript of Book of the Dead Spell 148 tells of its discovery by prince Hardjedef:

| | | | | |
|---|---|---|---|---|
| *ỉn-n-f=sw* | *mỉ-bỉꜣw* | *n(-y)-nsw* | *ḫft-mꜣꜣ-f* | *ntt* |
| bring-PST-3MS=3MS | like-marvel | of[-M]-king | when-see-3MS | COMP |
| *štꜣ=pw* | *ꜥꜣ* | | | |
| mystery=SE | great | | | |

He brought it (away) like a royal marvel when he saw that it was a great mystery. (BD 148, 21–22)

Yet there is one notable exception to the rule that nominal sentences were not used as complements without an introducing complementiser, namely the verb *gmỉ* 'find, discover', after which bare nominal sentences were indeed used as direct complements:

(282a) The sailor has just heard a frightening noise and covers his eyes in terror; then:

| | | | |
|---|---|---|---|
| *kf-n-ỉ* | *ḥr-ỉ* | *gm-n-ỉ* | *ḥfꜣw=pw* |
| uncover-PST-1S | face-1MS | find-PST-1S | snake=SE |

As I uncovered my face, I found that it was a snake. (Sh.S. 60–62)

(282b) Amenemhat I tells from beyond the grave how he met his assassins:

| | | | | |
|---|---|---|---|---|
| *nhs-n-ỉ* | *n-ꜥḥꜣ* | *ỉw-ỉ* | *n-ḥꜥ-w-ỉ* | *gm-n-ỉ* |
| awake-PST-1S | to-battle | AUX-1S | to-member-P-1S | find-PST-1S |
| *ḥwnyrḥr=pw* | *n(-y)-mwnf* | | | |
| attack=SE | of[-M]-bodyguard | | | |

When I woke up to the battle alone, I discovered that it was an attack of the bodyguard. (Amenemhat VIIa–b)

The *nt* in the following example is probably not the complementiser, but rather an abbreviated writing of the feminine/neuter form of the relative adjective *nt-*:

(283) A remark after the presentation of the solution to a mathematical problem:

| | |
|---|---|
| *g[m]-k* | *nt(-t)=pw* |
| find-2MS | REL-F=SE |

You will discover that this is what it is. (pMoscow math. n. 9, 29)

In the earlier language nominal sentences could also be subordinated as complements by means of the clitic particle =*is*. Of the three examples below, the first is governed by a preposition, the second and third by a verb:

(284a) Ra, in the guise of a heavenly bull, is addressed:

| *nḏ-n=n-f* | N | *sd-k* | *n-N=is=pw* | *nṯr* | *z3* | *nṯr* |
|---|---|---|---|---|---|---|
| seize-PST=to-3MS | N | tail-2MS | because-N=PTC=SE | god | son | god |

King N has seized for himself your tail, because king N is a god, a son of god. (PT 543c)

(284b) Osiris is asked to announce the divine status of the deceased:

| *di-k* | *rḫ* | *imn-t* | *nfr-t* | *s3-k=is=pw* |
|---|---|---|---|---|
| cause-2MS | known | west-F | beautiful-F | son-2MS=PTC=SE |

May you let the Beautiful West know that he is your son.
(CT I 104/105d–e/B1P)

(284c) Osiris acknowledges the status of Horus:

| *ḏd-f* | *s3-f=is=pw* | *iwꜥ-f=is=pw* |
|---|---|---|
| say-3MS | son-3MS=PTC=SE | heir-3MS=PTC=SE |

He says that he is his son and that he is his heir.
(CT III 181b–182a/B2Bo)

As noted in connection with adverbial sentences (Part I, 2.1.3), =*is* is presumably an early marker of general dependence that depending on the broader grammatical or semantic context may impose a complement or adjunctive interpretation on the clause in which it appears. Indeed, as was seen in the previous section, nominal sentences with=*is* also serve as adjuncts in older texts. The diachronically earlier status of=*is* in the Egyptian grammatical system appears to be reflected in its common occurrence in the Coffin Texts (and sometimes already in the Pyramid Texts) in nominal sentence complements where the complementiser *ntt* is equally present either in the same witness or in variants (cf. Gilula 1978: 47; 1986: 161):

(285a) The king is given provisions:

| *n-ntt* | *swt=is* | *k3* | *wr* |
|---|---|---|---|
| because-COMP | 3MS=PTC | bull | great |

... because he is the Great Bull. (PT 121b)

(285b) It is said of the deified deceased and gods:

| CT VI 348r–s | *isṯ* | *rḫ-n-sn* | | *N=tn=is* | *ḥḏt3* |
|---|---|---|---|---|---|
| | PTC | know-PST-3P | | N=DEM.F=PTC | dawn god |
| CT VI 349m | *rḫ* | *rꜥ* | *ntt* | *N=tn=is* | *ḥḏt3* |
| | know | N | COMP | N=DEM.F=PTC | dawn god |
| CT VI 348l | *isṯ* | *rḫ-n-sn* | *ntt* | *N=tn* | *ḥḏt3* |
| | PTC | know-PST-3P | COMP | N=DEM.F | dawn god |

They/Ra knows that this N is the Dawn-god.

Nevertheless, it will be seen later that there are also important pragmatic differences between the two. In the later language, *=ỉs* no longer appears with any regularity, but occasionally it seems to have been used for a specially archaic or elevated register. Of the following Eighteenth Dynasty examples, the first is a solemn proclamation by the king, the second a statement of a deceased high official (note the simultaneous use of *ntt* in 286b):

(286a) Thutmosis III explains his motives for increasing the daily offerings in Karnak:

| | | | | |
|---|---|---|---|---|
| *rḫ-n-ỉ=ỉs* | *nḥḥ=pw* | *wꜣst* | *ḏ-t=pw* | *ỉmn* |
| know-PST-1S=PTC | eternity=SE | N | everlastingness-F=SE | N |

I have learnt that Thebes is an eternal place and Amun is forever.
(*Urk.* IV 164, 5–6)

(286b) Amenhotep Son of Hapu addresses future generations:

| | | | | |
|---|---|---|---|---|
| *ỉr-w=n-ỉ* | *ỉrỉ-tw=n-tn* | *ḥr-ntt=ỉs* | *ỉnk* | *ỉwꜥ* |
| do.IMP-P=to-1S | do-PASS=to-2P | because-COMP=PTC | 1S | heir |
| *grg* | *nw-t-f* | | | |
| found.PPA | city-F-3MS | | | |

Provide for me, and one will provide for you, because I am the heir who founded his city. (*Urk.* IV 1824, 10–11)

Yet the artificiality of this use in this phase of the language is suggested by the placement of *=ỉs* before *nḥḥ=pw* in ex. 286a and after *ntt* in 286b, neither of which was probably wholly 'correct' (cf. exx. 248b and 285a). Moreover, at the time the two examples were written, a *new* complementiser *rḏd* had already become a fully established part of the Egyptian grammatical repertoire. This morpheme, the result of the grammaticalisation of *r* 'to' + the infinitive of *ḏd* 'say', was used to introduce direct speech and survived as *ϫe* until Coptic, after having made its first appearance in First Intermediate Period texts of informal kind.[80] In the early Eighteenth Dynasty, sporadic instances begin to appear in monumental texts, and then also in complement clauses functioning as object of the verb *rḫ* 'know':

(287a) Thutmosis III explains why he has embellished the temple of Amun:

| | | | |
|---|---|---|---|
| *[ỉw]-ỉ* | *rḫ-kw* | *rḏd* | *ḫnw[-f]=pw* |
| AUX-1S | know-STA.1S | COMP | resting place-3MS=SE |

I know that it is his resting place. (*Urk.* IV 736, 16)

80 Complementiser-grammaticalisation of this kind is very common in other languages; a representative sample is provided in Heine and Kuteva (2002: 261–65).

(287b) The Great Sphinx of Giza says to the future king Thutmosis IV:
*rḫ-kw* *rḏd* *ntk* *sꜣ-ỉ* *nḏty-ỉ*
know-STA.1S COMP 1S son-1S protector-1S
I know that you are my son and my protector. (*Urk.* IV 1543, 10)

### 2.3.2 Later Egyptian

In Late Egyptian, the use of the complementiser *rḏd* has become obligatory to introduce nominal sentence complement clauses, however, some early texts do not use any complementizer as in ex. 288d:

(288a) The author of a letter reminds the recipient:
*yꜣ* *ṯ-k-rḫ-ṯ* *rḏd-mntk* *pꜣy-n-ỉt* *r-ḏr-w* *spsn*
PTC PTC-2MS-know-STA.2MS COMP-2MS POSS.M-1P-father to-limit-3P twice
You know that you are the father of us all. (*LRL* 29, 15)

(288b) The author of a letter asks his recipients to take care of his father:
*ṯ-n-rḫ-ṯ* *rḏd-rmṯ* *mr* *ỉw-bwpw-f-ỉr-t-mḫn*
PTC-1P-know-STA COMP-man sick DEP-NEG.PST-3MS-do-INF-journey
We are aware that he is a sick man who has never made a journey.
(*LRL* 16, 8–9)

(288c) A woman takes an oath that she did not steal chisels from the workmen:
*mṯ-ṯ-gm* *rḏd-ỉnk* *ỉṯꜣy* *pꜣ-ḫꜣ*
CNJ-PASS-find COMP-1S take.PPA DEF.M-chisel
... and if it will be discovered that it was me who stole the chisel...
(*KRI* IV 316, 6–7)

(288d) A man confirms an accusation of larceny against another man and takes an oath that the stolen objects belong to Pharaoh:
*mṯ-ṯ* *smt* *m-dwꜣ* *rsꜣ-dwꜣ* *rḏd-bn-ns-prꜥꜣ*
CNJ-one learn in-morrow after-morrow COMP-NEG-POSS-Pharaoh
*ꜥ.w.s.*
l.h.p.
... and should one learn in the future that it does not belong to Pharaoh, l.h.p., ... (*KRI* IV 319, 6–7)

(288e) The author of the letter noticed two boats belonging to the addressee in the harbour of Memphis:
*ỉw-ṯ* *ḥr-ḏd=n-ỉ* *mntk* *dỉ* *ỉn-ṯ-w*
DEP-PASS PRP-say=to-1S [2MS] [give.PPA bring-PASS-3P]
... and I was told that it was you who had them brought.
(*KRI* III 255, 4)

As can be seen, complementation of nominal sentences is attested for bipartite sentences with deletion of the subject element, for bipartite sentences, and for cleft sentences. This shows that there were no syntactic constraints on the chosen construction.

In Demotic, the earlier complementiser *rḏd*, now regularly written *ḏd*, has acquired the function of a specific marker of causal clauses (see 2.2.2), but is also used to introduce complement clauses, including nominal sentences:

(289a) The lady Tabubu tells the servant:
*m-šm r-ḏd-s n-stne ḏd-ink-wꜥb bn-ink-rmṯ ḫm in*
IMP-go IMP-say-3FS to-N COMP-1S-priest NEG-1S-man small NEG
Go and tell Setne, that I am a of priestly rank and not a common person.
(Setne I 5, 8–9)

(289b) The pharaoh sent a boatman to Daphnai, and he returned on the same day:
*msꜣ-ḥn-s r-ir-prꜥꜣ ḏd-iwn iw-s-ys pꜣy*
after-order-3FS REL-do-pharaoh COMP-freight DEP-3FS-hurry SE.M
...after pharaoh had ordered that it should be an urgent freight.
(pBN 215 v° a, 17)

Coptic complement clauses, including nominal sentences, are typically introduced by the element *ce*, a direct descendent of the earlier *rḏd* > *ḏd* without constraints on the syntax of the following clause:

(290a) Paul of Tamma urges the audience to search for humility:
*anau ce-u-aš n-kʲot pe pe-thbbio*
look.IMP COMP -IDF.S-WH of-form COP.M DEF.M-humility
See what humility is like.
([S]Paul of Tamma, *De Humilitate* [Orlandi 126, 5])

(290b) The hegemon urges his *logistes* who are beating a saint to show restraint:
*n-g-soun=an ce-na-tei-mine têr-u hen-sah*
NEG-2MS-known=NEG COMP-POSS.P-DEM.F-kind all-3P IDF.P-teacher
*m-magos ne*
of-magic COP.P
Do you not know that all people of this kind are masters of magic?
([S]*Mart. Panesnew* [Till, *KHML* I 95, 18–20])

(290c) The teacher tells one of the disciples that he, the teacher, will explain his own deeds to him:
*ti-htê-k hitn-pei ce-anak -u-man(i)kh(aio)s*
give-heart-2SM through-DEM.M.ABS COMP-1S IDF.S-Manichean
*n-uôt*
of-single
Pay heed through this that I am a single Manichean ...
([L]*Kephalaia* 100, 23)

(290d) Jesus answers to pharisees who accuse His disciples of breaking the Sabbath rules:
*enne-ha-tetn-ime* *ce-u* *pe* *u-nee* *p-et-i-ueš-f*
CFT-PST-2P-know COMP-WH COP.M IDF.S-mercy COP.M-REL-1S-wish-3MS
*n-u-thusia=en=te*
NEG-IDF.S-sacrifice=NEG=SE.F
If you had known what 'It is mercy I want. It is not sacrifice' means...
($^{M}$Mt 12:7 mae 1)

(290e) John explains to his disciples that not he, but Jesus is Christ:
*pê* *et-a-f-ci* *n-te-f-met-metrê*
DEM.M REL-PST-3MS-take OBJ-POSS.F-3MS-ABST-witness
*a-f-el-sphragizin* *mma-f* *ce-*$p^{h}$*-(nu)ti* *u-mei* *pe*
PST-3MS-AUX-certify OBJ-3MS COMP-DEF.M-god IDF.S-true COP.M
He who has accepted his testimony has confirmed that God is true.
($^{F}$Jn 3:33)

## 2.4 Relative clauses

### 2.4.1 Earlier Egyptian

Nominal sentences were not used in relative clauses except as *bare* constructions that have been termed 'virtual' relative clauses, discussed in connection with adverbial sentences (Part I, 2.1.7). Although not rare, this clausal type is typologically homogenous and apparently restricted to bipartite patterns without *=pw* of the type *N rn-f* 'his name is/was N':

(291a) The opening lines of the story of The Eloquent Peasant:
*s=pw* *wn* *ḫwninpw* *rn-f* *sḫty=pw* *n(-y)-sḫtḥmꜣt*
man=SE exist.STA N name-3MS peasant=SE of[-M]-N
*ỉst* *wn* *ḥm-t-f* *mrt* *rn-s*
PTC exist wife-F-3MS N name-3FS
There was a man whose name was Khuenanupe. He was a peasant of the Wadi el-Natrun. He also had a wife, whose name was Merit. (Peas R, 1.1–2)

(291b) The peasant has just arrived in the neighbourhood of the town Mednit:
*gm-n-f* *s* *ỉm* *ʿḥ̣ʿ* *ḥr-mry-t* *nmtynḫt*
find-PST-3MS man there stand.STA on-riverbank-F N
*rn-f* *sꜣ* *s=pw* *ỉsry* *rn-f*
name-3MS son man=SE N name-3MS
And there, standing on the riverbank, he encountered a man whose name was Nemtynakht. He was a son of a man whose name was Isry.
(Peas Bt, 19–21)

Most notably, and again in stark contrast to adverbial sentences, nominal sentences are not relativised by means of the relative adjective *nt-* or a participle or relative form of the auxiliary *wn/wnn*. The only exception seems to be the negative construction *nfr=pw x* '*x* is complete', from which the meaning '*x* does not exist' or 'there is no *x*' is derived (see 4.1 for this construction):

(292) An administrative memorandum speaks of providing rations to people:

| | | | | |
|---|---|---|---|---|
| *ỉmỉ* | *fꜣ-tw* | *n-nꜣ-n-rmṯ* | *[mnꜥ-t]* | *nty* |
| cause.IMP | lift.SUB-PASS | to-DEM.P-of-people | nursery-F | REL |
| *nfr=pw* | *fꜣ-tw=n-sn* | *m-sf* | | |
| NEG=COP | lift-PASS=to-3P | in-yesterday | | |

See to it that one pays the people of the nursery who were not paid yesterday. (pBoulaq 18 XIX, 2.2–3)

Nevertheless, this unique example is rather late, and *nty* is already an immutable relativiser. Overall, in relative clauses semantically similar to nominal sentences, the adverbial sentence with the *m* of predication is employed instead. Examples are not common, and those with *wn/wnn* appear restricted to headless relative clauses without overt antecedent, as in 293b:

(293a) Thoth proclaims to other gods about Queen Hatshepsut:

| | | | | | | |
|---|---|---|---|---|---|---|
| *mꜣꜥtkꜣrꜥ* | *nt-t* | *m-nsw* | *ḫꜥ-ti* | *ḥr-s-t* | *ḥr* | *ḏt* |
| N | REL-F | as-king | appear-STA | on-throne-F | N | forever |

Maatkara, who is the king, has appeared on the throne of Horus eternally! (*Urk.* IV 289, 10)

(293b) The sage bemoans the demise of the elite:

| | | | |
|---|---|---|---|
| *wn* | *m-wpty* | *ḥr-hꜣb* | *k-y* |
| AUX.PP | as-messenger | PROG-send.INF | other-M |

He who was a messenger is now sending another. (Ipuwer 8, 3)

### 2.4.2 Later Egyptian

Later Egyptian maintains the dichotomy of *nty*-headed relative clauses for restrictive and *ỉw*-headed 'virtual' relative clauses for non-restrictive clauses (see 2.2.2 for non-restrictive examples).[81] In addition, relative clauses are not coordinated by

81 Usually, the difference between the two patterns is explained alongside a definiteness split of the antecedent. For an explanation based on a restriction dichotomy, see Korostovtsev (1973: 446–447) for Late Egyptian, Simpson (1996: 54–57) for Demotic, and Reintges (2004: 425–29). See also Müller (2015b).

means of *nty…nty*, but by means of a 'virtual' relative clause headed by *ỉw*, i.e. *nty…ỉw*.[82] This rule does not apply to Demotic.

In Late Egyptian, the Earlier Egyptian constraint on the use of nominal sentences in relative clauses introduced by the relativiser *nty* is still largely valid. However, first isolated examples of this construction are now attested:

(294) In a dispute over two quarreling deities the other gods ask:

| | | | | |
|---|---|---|---|---|
| *ỉḫ* | *pꜣ-nty-ỉw-n* | *r-ỉr-f* | *n-pꜣ-rmṯ* | 2 |
| WH | COP.M-REL-FUT-1P | FUT-do.INF-3MS | with-DEF.M-man | 2 |

| | | | | |
|---|---|---|---|---|
| *nty-80* | *n-rnp-t* | *r-tꜣy* | *ỉw-sn* | *m-tꜣ-qnb-t* |
| REL-80 | of-year-F | to-DEM.F | DEP-3P | in-DEF.F-court-F |

What shall we do with these two men who have now stood in the court for 80 years already? (*LES* 39, 13–14)

Yet in the majority of cases one still encounters the earlier suppletive pattern *nty* + adverbial sentence with the '*m* of predication':

(295a) A love song starts with the yearning to be as close to the beloved woman as her servant girl:

| | | |
|---|---|---|
| *ḥl=n-ỉ* | *tꜣy-st-nḥsy* | *nty-m-ỉrỉ-rd-wỉ-st* |
| PTC=to-1S | POSS.F-3FS-Nubian.F | REL-as-do-feet-DU-3FS |

Would that I were her Nubian servant who is her attendant.
(Mathieu, *Poésie*, pl. 19, 18)

(295b) In a fragmentary set of notes a group of Sea-peoples are described as follows:

| | | | |
|---|---|---|---|
| *š<r>dn* | *[n-]wꜣḏ<wr>* | *nty-m-ḥꜣq-w* | *ḥm-f* |
| N | of-sea | REL-as-prisoner-P | majesty-3MS |

The Sherden of the sea who are prisoners of his majesty. (*LEM* 20, 2)

The subject of the relative clause is regularly omitted if co-referential with the antecedent. Texts from the first millennium BC tend to omit the *m* in writing. The constraint on the use of *nty* with nominal sentences has been lost in Demotic, where relativisation of nominal sentences with this element becomes standard as example 296c shows.[83]

(296a) Description of the afterlife in a funerary papyrus:

| | | | |
|---|---|---|---|
| *tw-w-šm-pꜣy-k-by* | *ỉrm-swḥ* | *rtw-wsỉr* | *pꜣy* |
| give.FUT-3P-go-POSS.M-2MS-soul | with-N | REL-N | SE.M |

82 Due to the lack of examples with nominal sentences this cannot be exemplified here, see Müller (2015b: 123–29).

83 Note that *ntyỉw* and *rtw* are simply diachronic graphemic variants of the relative particle. They are not bound to specific environments.

*ỉrm-nꜣ-syw-w* *nty-šms* *n-spd-t*
with-DEF.P-stars-P REL-follow OBJ-N-F
Your soul will be allowed to travel with Orion, i.e. Osiris, together with the stars that follow Sothis. (pRhind I 6, d5)

(296c) The narrator contrasts his modest abilities with those of his elder brother Naneferkaptah:
*ntyỉw-sẖ* *nfr* *rmṯ* *rḫ* *mšs* *pꜣy*
REL-scribe good man know very SE.M
... who is a good scribe and a very wise man. (Setne I 4, 3)

(296a) An epiteth of Anubis:
*pꜣ-ntyỉw-pꜣy-f* *pꜣy-qḥ*
DEF.M-REL-POSS-3MS DEM.M-earth
The one to whom this earth belongs. (pMag. London&Leiden 21, 7)

This evolution apparently went hand in hand with the receding use of sentences with the '*m* of predication.'

In Coptic, nominal sentences are also regularly attested with the relativiser *ete-*:

(297a) Shenute calls for repentance: *I say to you*:
*n-t-he* *ete-u-at-kʲom=pe* *nnahra-n*
in-DEM.F-way REL-IDF.S-NEG-power=COP.M before-1P
*e-tre-n-amahte* *na-n* *m-pe-hou* *hatê-n*
to-INFL-1P-seize to-1P in-DEF.M-day with-1P
*efšan-côk* *ebol* *n-ne-f-unoue* *n-s-šôpe*
CND.3MS-finish out OBJ-POSS.P-3MS-hours.P CNJ-3FS-happen
*nkʲi-te-ušê*
PVS-DEF.F-night
*tai=on* *te* *t-he* *u-at-kʲom* *pe*
DEM.F=again COP.F DEF.F-way IDF.S-NEG-power COP.M
*e-tre-p-na* *m-p-nute*
to-INFL-DEF.M-mercy of-DEF.M-god
*i* *ehrai* *ecô-n* *hm-p-ma* *et-n-na-bôk* *ero-f*
come down upon-1P in-DEF.M-place REL-1P-FUT-go to-3MS
*hotan* *enšan-mu* *hrai* *hn-ne-n-nobe* *mn-ne-n-krof*
when CND.1P-die down in-POSS.P-1P-sin con.POSS.P-1P-guile
*mn-ne-n-mnt-asebês* *têr-u*
CON-POSS.P-1P-ABST-godless all-3P
*nt-a-n-aa-u* *m-pe-f-mto* *ebol* *<e>-n-šoop* *tenu*
REL-PST-1P-do-3P in-POSS.M-3MS-front out DEP-1P-be.STA now
*hicm-p-kah*
upon-DEF.M-earth

Just as it is impossible for us to keep the day with us – when the hours are complete, the night will fall – so it is impossible that God's mercy come down upon the place where we will go, as soon as we die in all our sins and guiles and godlessness that we committed before him, while living upon earth. ([S]Shenute, *Why O Lord* [L III 182, 13–19])

(297b) The Lord says he will have pity with Hosea's child called Not-pitied and he will speak to the other child called:

*p-ete-pa-laos=en=pe*
DEF.M-REL-POSS.M.1S-people=NEG=SE.M
Not-my-people ([A]Hos 2:23)

(297c) In the introduction to the *Gospel of Truth*, the main character is introduced as the one who is in the thought and the mind of the father:

| | | | | |
|---|---|---|---|---|
| *ete-pei* | *pe* | *et-u-šece* | *ara-f* | *ce-p-sôter* |
| REL-DEM.M | SE.M | REL-3P-call | OBJ-3MS | COMP-DEF.M-saviour |

| | | | |
|---|---|---|---|
| *e-p-ren* | *m-p-hôb* | *et-f-na-ei-f* | *pe* |
| DEP-DEF.M-name | of-DEF.M-work | REL-3MS-FUT-do-3MS | SE.M |

| | | |
|---|---|---|
| *a-p-sôte* | *n-nei* | *nt-ah-r-at-sôun-p-iôt* |
| to-DEF.M-redemption | of-DEM.P | REL-PST-do-NEG-know-DEF.M-father |

That is the one who is addressed as the Saviour, although that is only the name of the work which He will perform for the redemption of those who were ignorant of the Father. ([L]*EvVer* 16, 36–17, 1)

(297d) Jesus' body was buried and guarded by Mary Magdalene and the other Mary. Then:

| | |
|---|---|
| *m-pe-f-reste=de* | *ete-mnnsa-t-paraskêue=te* |
| in-POSS.M-3MS-morrow=yet | REL-after-DEF.F-preparation=SE.F |

The next morning, which was the day after the preparation...
([M]Mt 27:62 mae 1)

(297e) Claiming that nothing can keep him from telling the eternal truth, Peter says that he has freedom of speech:

| | | |
|---|---|---|
| *ete-p*$^h$*ai* | *pe* | *p-k*$^h$*(risto)s* |
| REL-DEM.M | COP.M | DEF.M-Christ |

... which is the Christ.
([B]*Correspondence of Peter Mongus & Acacius* [Amélineau 209, 1, collated])

Note that Coptic nominal sentence relative clauses occasionally seem to contain anteposed expressions:

(298) After prasing the Lord, Shenute beseeches him to bestow his peace upon those eirenic and meek and to give trouble to troublesome people in return. Shenute continues:

| | | | | |
|---|---|---|---|---|
| *n-tei-he* | *on* | *t-orgê* | *n-na-t-orgê* | *ete-ntou* |
| in-DEM.F-way | again | DEF.F-wrath | to-POSS.P-DEF.F-wrath | REL-3P |

*ntou=on=ne*
3P=again=SE.P
*n-et-kô* *n-htê-u* *e-hen-eidôlon* *n-daimonion*
DEF.P-REL-set OBJ-heart-3P to-IDF.P-idol of-demon
Likewise also the wrath to the wrathful, who are always the same, those who trust in demonic idols.
([S]Shenute, *I Have Been Reading the Holy Gospels* §23 [Moussa 67b, 7–13])

However, it appears here that a previous anteposition structure has become grammaticalised as a fixed pattern [PRN PRN ON SE] conveying the notion 'X is always the same', where the initial element no longer shares the pragmatic functions characteristically associated with anteposed NPs.

# 3 Semantics and pragmatics

## 3.1 Earlier Egyptian

### 3.1.1 Grammatical relations: subject and predicate I

The semantic and pragmatic characteristics of Earlier Egyptian nominal sentences are very complex, and the difficulties already begin with the basic level of grammatical relations. It is fair to say that no other problem pertaining to the meaning of nominal sentences in this language has so preoccupied scholars as the question of differentiating between the subject and predicate roles.[84] In addition to difficulties with defining what exactly constitutes 'subjecthood' vs. 'predication' that have prompted some scholars to abandon 'subject' as a valid linguistic concept,[85] complications arise first and foremost from the lack of *marking* of grammatical relations in Earlier Egyptian nominal sentences. Put simply, there are no formal criteria that could be used to decide whether e.g. a tripartite construction such as *sš=pw rmṯ* (scribe=COP man) should be understood as communicating a proposition of the type 'scribe is man' or 'man is scribe'. As noted in Part I, 1.1, it is here assumed as a working hypothesis that 'subject' in particular is a valid grammatical category that (its possibly language-specific character notwithstanding) can be defined broadly and semi-informally as the most 'prominent' and least oblique participant of a state of affairs that scores highest on the hierarchies of definiteness (definite > other specific > nonspecific), person (first > second person > third person), agentivity (agent > goal > recipient > instrumental > locative > temporal), and animacy (human > other animate > inanimate) as well as pragmatically commands the main vantage point and perspective from which the state of affairs is described.[86] Overall, the mutual ordering of grammatical relations is *not fixed* in Earlier Egyptian nominal sentences, and there is no one-to-one relation between this and sentence construction – even though a number of strong correlations

84 See e.g. Sethe (1916: 23); Gardiner (1957: §§126–27, 130); Edel (1955/1964: §§939, 947, 965, 971); Gilula (1976); Junge (1981: 439–43); Westendorf (1981; 1989); Callender (1984: 120–23); Schenkel (1984; 1985; 1987); Borghouts (1986: 56–57); Depuydt (1986); Frandsen (1986); Roeder (1986: 31–70); Loprieno (1988b: 37–41); Vernus (1994: 335); Malaise and Winand (1999: §§456, 471, 473, 1059); Allen (2000: 73–76); Gundacker (2010: 42–44).
85 For nominal sentences in particular, see e.g. Polotsky (1971: 419–21, 425); Depuydt (2009: 37).
86 See references in n.3 of Part I.

https://doi.org/10.1515/9783110409895-008

are observable.[87] Yet here too the grammatical role of 'subject' is assigned to the element which is contextually allocated the highest degree of semantic-pragmatic accessibility, individuation, definiteness, referentiality, and cognitive prominence. That is, the subject of a nominal sentence corresponds to the expression that adheres most closely to the subject prototype outlined above – except that, since nominal sentences are non-verbal propositions, factors such as agentivity do not play a role. However, this is not only a matter of intuition. Rather, there are a number of formal and functional facets that partake in the process of identifying the subject, some of which involve considering the broader communicative function of the nominal sentence proposition.

Broadly speaking, there are two complementary strategies or rules by which the subject of an Earlier Egyptian nominal sentence can be identified: a *formal* one and a *formal-functional* one. The formal rule concerns sentences with pronouns and with the element *=pw*. The subject of the nominal sentence is most straightforwardly identifiable in bipartite constructions with *=pw*, which is specifically grammaticalised to serve as such. Consequently, in nominal sentences of this sort, the predicate may belong to a class of grammatical items that are otherwise highly atypical in this role, e.g. demonstrative or personal pronouns (see also exx. 115a, 115b, and 115e above):

(299a) The yon ferryman receives clarification of a name that the deceased has uttered:

| | | | |
|---|---|---|---|
| *pꜣ=pw* | *m-ꜥnḫ* | *m-grḥ* | *ḫnt-rnp-t* |
| DEM.M=SE | in-life | in-night | before-year-F |

He is this one alive on the night of the New Year's Eve. (CT V 94e/T1Be)

(299b) The king's reply to his children who had argued that the Syrian before them was not Sinuhe:

| | |
|---|---|
| *ntf=pw* | *m-mꜣꜥ-t* |
| 3MS=SE | in-truth-F |

It is really him. (Sin B, 267–68)

Pronouns differ in the degree of their definiteness and referentiality, and thus, in Earlier Egyptian, form a hierarchy with respect to their potential to function as

87 Nevertheless, there have been several attempts to analyse nominal sentences as associated with a single ordering of grammatical roles, with some favouring the universal order S–P, at least outside bipartite *pw*-sentences (Westendorf 1981: 78, 88–99; Borghouts 2010: §101.a) or in other selected environments (Schenkel, 1984: 159–60), others the order P–S (e.g. Junge 1981: 443; Roeder 1986: 32, 36, 61–62).

subjects.[88] By their nature, interrogative pronouns describe referentially undetermined and often highly indefinite concepts.[89] As a result, they almost invariably serve as predicates in Earlier Egyptian nominal sentences:

(300a) The deceased has just demanded a ferryboat; the yon ferryman replies:
*ṯwt=tr* *m*
2MS=PTC WH
And who are you? (CT V 121e/M5C)

(300b) A gloss in a mythological text after a reference to 'Land of the Horizon-dwellers':
*pw=tr=rf* *tꜣ=pn*
WH=PTC=PTC land=DEM.M
What is this land? (CT IV 222c/Sq1C)

The so-called cleft constructions are almost the only exception to the near-universal predicativity of interrogative pronouns in Earlier Egyptian nominal sentences (see 3.1.3). In contrast to interrogatives, demonstrative pronouns point to referents that are assumed to be more or less contextually accessible either in terms of spatial proximity/remoteness or more generally in the universe of discourse. Accordingly, in Earlier Egyptian, demonstrative pronouns are almost always subjects:

(301a) It is said of the deceased:
*wsir=pw* *nn*
N=COP DEM
This one is Osiris. (CT VI 163b)

(301b) A note after presenting the result in a calculation for the *sqd* of a pillar:
*pꜣ=pw* *sqd* *n-f-im-y*
DEM.M=COP N to-3MS-in.RLT-M
This is its *sqd*. (pRhind math. n.60, 3–4)

The sole exception here is formed by bipartite sentences with the element *=pw* such as *nꜣ=pw* 'it is this' in ex. 115e above, where *=pw* outranks the demonstrative pronoun in subjecthood qualities. Yet as can be seen, although the status of the interrogative and demonstrative pronouns as predicates and subjects remains

88 This does not imply that a similar hierarchy must exist universally in languages, particularly if the subject turns out to be a language-specific role.

89 Hence the often noted formal (and often also derivative) similarity between interrogative and indefinite pronouns in many languages (cf. Haspelmath 1997: 24–27, 170–79).

unchanged, the mutual order of these grammatical roles in the sentence is not constant. The reasons for this variation will be discussed shortly.

Personal pronouns fall between interrogative and demonstrative pronouns in terms of their subjecthood potential,[90] but overall, they are in this respect much closer to demonstratives than to interrogatives and show a strong tendency to serve as subjects rather than as predicates in Earlier Egyptian nominal sentences. Only in combination with demonstratives or with the subject clitic *=pw* they can be 'out-subjected' and function as predicates. Examples with *=pw* such as 302a are common enough, whereas instances with demonstratives such as 302b are extremely rare (other variants have *ink/N=pw*):

(302a) Thoth is addressed and told that the deceased has appeared in glory:

| | | | |
|---|---|---|---|
| S14C: | *ink=pw* | *iw-i* | *m-rn-i* |
| | 1S=SE | AUX-1S/3MS/3FS | in-name-1S |
| B1Bo: | *ntf=pw* | *iw-f* | *m-rn-f* |
| | 3MS=SE | AUX-3MS | in-name-3MS |
| B3Bo: | *N=tn=pw* | *iw-s* | *m-rn-s* |
| | N=DEM.F=SE | AUX-3FS | in-name-3FS |

This is me/he/this N, and I am/he/she is in my/his/her name.
(CT V 236d–e)

(302b) The deceased arrives in vindication:

| | | | | | |
|---|---|---|---|---|---|
| *sk* | *imn-t-t* | *nfr-t* | *m-ḥʿ-w-t* | *mꜣꜣ-sn* | *ʿ-t* |
| PTC | west-F | beautiful-F | in-jubilation-P-F | see-3P | member-F |
| *m-nṯr* | *ink* | *nw* | | | |
| in-god | 1S | DEM | | | |

The beautiful West is in jubilation at seeing the members of the god. Such am I. (CT V 24a–c/B2L[b])

Complications arise, however, when both combined nominals are personal pronouns – a not too infrequent phenomenon in tripartite sentences:

(303) The deceased says:

| | | | | | |
|---|---|---|---|---|---|
| *ink* | *ʿfnw-t=pw* | *im-y* | *dp* | *ink=pw=sw* | *ink* |
| 1S | headcloth.RLT-F=DEM.M | in.RLT-M | N | 1S=COP=3MS | 1S |
| *ʿfnw-t* | *im-y* | *kkw* | | | |
| headcloth.RLT-F | in.RLT-M | darkness | | | |

I am this wearer of a head-cloth who is in Dep... I am he; I am the wearer of a head-cloth who is in the darkness. (CT VII 478g–j/B5C)

90 There are also internal divisions in this respect between the various personal pronouns, see 3.1.3.

Here the identification of subject and predicate – insofar as it is possible at all – is dependent on the interpretation and analysis of the proposition's meaning as a whole. This is, in fact, the case in all the remaining types of nominal sentences, where the assignment of grammatical roles is intimately tied to the semantic *type* of predication that the sentence expresses and how this is decoded.

### 3.1.2 Semantic typology of Earlier Egyptian nominal sentences: subject and predicate II

In verbal and adverbial sentences, the predicate typically corresponds to a situation schema in which the subject is embroiled. Nominal sentence predication is semantically of a sort that cannot be easily characterised as describing a 'situation', but rather it mostly concerns the classification and identification of the subject.[91] The predicate corresponds to an element that fulfils one of these semantic functions *vis-à-vis* the subject. Although, as will be shown later, this characterisation does not actually cover the entire semantic scope of Earlier Egyptian nominal sentences, it does describe their core meanings. Classifying nominal sentences often portray some entity as a member of some class whose constituents are less defined than the former. They define one or more semantic properties of the subject without, however, profiling it exhaustively. Thus, in ex. 304, the referent of the subject 'I' is presented as an example of the class of 'followers':

(304) Sinuhe begins his narrative by characterising himself:

| | | | | |
|---|---|---|---|---|
| *šms[w* | *sꜣn]ht* | *ḏd-f* | *ink* | *šmsw* |
| follower | N | say-3MS | 1S | follower |

The royal follower Sinuhe says: 'I was a follower'. (Sin R, 2–3)

Alternatively, when the two constituent parts have equally indefinite referential properties, as e.g. in 'cats are (among other things) mammals', classifying

91 The division proposed below follows closely Hengeveld (1992: 80–91). See also e.g. Dik (1997: 205–06); Langacker (1991: 64–71); Stassen (1997: 100–06). For the Earlier Egyptian nominal and cleft sentences, semantics, concepts, and terminology differ widely between scholars. The terms adopted here are largely those employed in Loprieno (1995: 104–09, 114–18). For alternative formulations, see also e.g. Junge (1978: 45, 52–54, 57; 1981: 443–47); Schenkel (1984: 162); Depuydt (1986: 110); Roeder (1986: 66–69); Doret (1990: 50; 1991: 42); Vernus (1994: 325–27); Loprieno (1988b: 39); Malaise and Winand (1999: §§454, 457, 459, 463); Winand (2006: 154–55).

sentences do not concern the membership of an entity in a class, but rather its characterisation as a subcategory of it:

(305) The peasant profiles the ideal of responsible governance:
*ḫsr-w* *ḏw-t=pw* *sr-w*
dispel.PIA-P evil-F=COP official-P
Officials are dispellers of evil. (Peas B1, 319)

By contrast, identifying sentences generally establish a relation of complete or co-extensive semantic equity between entities. By so doing they may have a specifying function if the identification concerns (or is intended to concern) the sole identity of the identified entity, as in 'The capital of the UK is (none other than) London' or in the following Egyptian example:

(306) The eye of the sun-god is addressed:
*N=pw=ṯw* *ṯwt=pw* *N*
N=COP=2MS 2MS=COP N
King N is you, and you are King N. (PT 703b/TP)

As the above example shows, this relation is reversible without affecting the meaning.[92] Yet identifying sentences may also express non-reversible characterisation if the identity assigned is not the only identity of the identified, as in 'London is (among other things) the capital of the UK', or in the following Egyptian instance:[93]

(307) In a litany assigning various identities to the deceased king:
*N=pi* *bꜣ* *ꜥnḫ* *zpꜣ* *ḥr*
N=COP soul living centipede face
King N is the living soul with the face of a centipede. (PT 1098c/P)

This semantic division, incomplete and problematic as it may be,[94] breaks further the unity of the syntactic classes of Earlier Egyptian nominal sentences, already

92 The same holds true in the case of the so-called classifying-specifying sentences such as 'A bachelor is an unmarried man', which define the meaning of a term against some member of some class. Earlier Egyptian examples of this do not seem to be attested.

93 Note, however, that deciding on the interpretation of a sentence is normally a co(n)textual matter. For example, the precise reading of an instance such as PT 1810a *zꜣ-k=pw wsir N=pn* (son-2MS=SE N N=DEM.M) 'Your son is this Osiris N' depends on matters such as whether the addressee is thought to have more than one son.

94 For example, a sentence such as Ptahhetep 328 *pḫr-t=pw n-t-ḥꜥ-s mrḥ-t* (healing-F=SE of-F-member-3FS oil-F) 'The healing of her (a woman's) members is oil' (ex. 158a) would seem to express an identifying-specifying relation singling out the only identity of 'the healing of her members', which is 'nothing but' oil. However, the relation cannot be reversed without changing the sense. Does this then mean that the sentence is actually characterising?

damaged by the subject-predicate groupings in 3.1.1. Nevertheless, it also aids in identifying the grammatical roles in the sentence when formal criteria fail. That is, the second rule for identifying the subject in nominal sentences is that, except in constructions involving pronouns or the subject element *=pw*, the semantic function of the Earlier Egyptian nominal sentence correlates with the mutual ordering of its grammatical roles.[95] When such a sentence is of a classifying type, the order of the subject and predicate is P–S; when it is identifying, the order is the reverse (S–P) or, alternatively, no assignment of grammatical relations is possible at all. In isolation, a sentence such as *rmṯ=pw sš* simply establishes a relation between 'man' and 'scribe' that is in principle reversible, i.e. it may variously express the proposition 'man is scribe' or 'scribe is man'. Yet in Earlier Egyptian, reading *rmṯ* 'man' as the subject would mean that 'scribe', the predicate, were not profiled as a term for a class of which 'man' is an example either through membership or inclusion, but rather as an indivisible whole identified with 'man'. That is, 'man' and 'scribe' would refer to one and the same entity, regardless of whether the identity assigned is the only one or not. In English the difference between these alternatives may be expressed e.g. by marking *scribe* for definiteness: identification of 'man' as 'scribe' corresponds to 'the man is *the* scribe', whereas classifying 'man' as a member or a subcategory of the class of 'scribes' is equal to the proposition 'the man is *a* scribe'. In Earlier Egyptian, the differentiating factor is the order of the grammatical roles. The possible interpretations of such sentences are checked against context for consistency. For example:

(308a) The soul says:
*dmỉ=pw* *ỉmn-t*
harbour=COP West-F
The West is a harbour. (Man and Ba 38)

(308b) The beginning of a description in an administrative document:
*ḥm-t=pw* *n-t-ḏ-t* *n-t-rmṯ* *n-t-ꜣbw* *snbt*
maidservant-F=COP of-F-tenant-F of-F-people of-F-N N
Senbet is a maidservant of the tenants of the people of Abydos.
(pBerlin P. 10470 I, 10–11)

In ex. 308a, reading *dmỉ* 'harbour' as the subject not only produces rather curious semantics ('Harbour is identical to West') but also fits ill with the fabric of the co-text, which concerns life and death and the material world versus the realm of the dead, not 'harbours'. Thus, *ỉmn-t* is most naturally read as the subject, whose one property – namely that it is 'harbour' – is then profiled. More precisely, the unique entity 'West' is classified as belonging to the class of

95 What follows represents a modified version of Loprieno (1995: 104–09).

'harbours'. In ex. 308b, there is no previous discourse, and the decision cannot be based on co(n)textual clues derived from what precedes. Thus in principle, it cannot be known whether the purpose of the sentence is to classify an individual called Senbet as having a certain social status or to identify 'the maidservant of the tenants' as being that person. However, in this instance a classifying reading is established by the following discourse, which turns out to be a memorandum on administrative decisions made concerning the woman named. That is, the semantic decoding is not a purely anaphoric process but rather involves the entire discourse co(n)text.

In the following examples, the situation is slightly different:

(309a) The father of King Merikara describes the devious enemy of the Egyptians:
*ꜥ3mw=pw* *msḥ* *ḥr-mry-t-f*
Asiatic=COP crocodile on-riverbank-F-3MS
The Asiatic is crocodile on its riverbank. (Merikara E, 97–98)

(309b) A explanatory note in a religious spell:
*[nw]=pw* *it* *nṯr-w*
N=COP father god-P
Nun is the father of gods. (BD 17/*Nebseni* pl. 38, 6)

In ex. 309a, the text describes the Asiatic enemy of the king, not crocodiles, and in any case reading *msḥ* as the subject would result in a proposition that classifies some (or 'the') crocodile as an Asiatic. A more likely interpretation is to read 'Asiatic' as subject profiled as being identical to a crocodile, albeit in a classifying way without implying that this is his only identity. In 309b, the co-text does not allow the subject to be inferred by pragmatic bridging. Nevertheless, the classifying P–S seems excluded due to the semantically unique nature of the initial NP 'Nun', which describes the only entity of its kind and with which any notion of class-inclusion is ostensibly impossible.[96] The sentence must therefore express identification of 'Nun' as 'father of gods', probably again in a characterising way (i.e. paternity of gods is not Nun's sole identity). The order of the grammatical roles is thus S–P.

Examples of the following sort are, however, rather more problematic:

(310) The deceased claims to be a member of a family of divinities:
*sn-t-i=pw* *tfnwt*
sister-F-1S=SE N
My sister is (the goddess) Tefnut. (CT II 22b/B1P)

96 This is the case unless one accepts 'classes with a single member' (Doret 1990: 50).

The issue here is again clearly that of the mutual identification of the sentence participants, but now it seems to be more precisely specifying its sole identity (i.e. 'My sister is none other than Tefnut'), which can be seen from the reversibility of the relation. If predication is understood in the Aristotelian manner as adding relevant information to something chosen as subject (see 1.1.1), as seems to be almost required in view of the fact that nominal expressions do not project arguments and 'predication' in nominal sentences can therefore scarcely be viewed as saturation of argument positions,[97] specifying-identifying propositions would then seem to be non-predicative in character (see e.g. Lyons 1977: 185; Stassen 1997: 101–02). That is, in an utterance such as 'My sister is Tefnut', neither 'my sister' nor 'Tefnut' is specifically chosen as something of which something else is predicated. Instead, what is communicated is merely a relation of complete identity between two expressions, neither of which is elevated as a subject or predicate. It was seen above (1.1.1.) that the same may be argued of possessive constructions of the type *n=sw* if these be understood as bipartite patterns with an earlier determinative pronoun expressing mere abstract relationality between two NPs. The basic difficulty here is of course to establish a solid definition of predication, a problem that has puzzled logicians and philosophers for millennia and cannot be elaborated further here. Suffice it to say that in specifying-identifying nominal sentences there are good reasons to doubt whether the establishment of the order of grammatical relations is at all feasible. Nevertheless, it may be generally maintained that in absence of pronouns and of the subject element *=pw*, the subject of the nominal sentence is, at first, undetermined. In case of constructions such as A(*=pw*) B where neither A or B is a pronoun, the recipient of the communication must begin by evaluating the semantic *raison d'être* of a proposition. In this s/he will be aided by the rule that the order $A^S$ $B^P$ identifies A, whereas $A^P$ $B^S$ classifies

**97** The other major view of what constitutes predication arises from Fregean predicate logic, where a predicate is a function that accepts a referential subject as its argument. Prior to this, the function is said to be unsaturated and awaiting saturation. This done, one obtains a certain output that represents the value of the function, and the outcome is predication. However, natural languages know expressions that do not project arguments but appear to behave predicatively, and here nominal predication is a particular case in point. The problem has been often noted in linguistics, and in approaches following the Fregean model various solutions thereto have been proposed. Some simply assume that all predicative expressions project arguments (e.g. Hengeveld 1992: 3–4), others claim that this projection is of a special non-thematic type (e.g. Grimshaw 1990: 49–57) or maintain that non-verbal predicates are associated with indexical characteristics that allow their predicative use (e.g. Borsley 1996: 101). None of these hypotheses is particularly convincing.

B. This rule will then also decode the grammatical roles in the sentence, insofar as this is logically possible.

The mechanism for subject-identification just described does not function in cases where personal and demonstrative pronouns, as well as =*pw* in its subject element role, enter the scene – even if sometimes this would seem to be the case:

(311a) PT Spell 416 consists merely of the following statement:

| | | | | | |
|---|---|---|---|---|---|
| *wḏꜣ-t=pw* | *nw* | *iri-n* | *ḥr* | *n-it-f* | *wsir* |
| intact garment-F=COP | DEM.M | do.REL-PST | N | to-father-3MS | N |

This is an intact garment that Horus made for his father Osiris. (PT 740)

(311b) In a calculation of the height of a pyramid whose side is said to be 140, the same figure is referred to again; a commentary adds:

| | |
|---|---|
| *pꜣ=pw* | *wḫꜣ-ṯbt* |
| DEM.M=COP | base |

This is the base. (pRhind math. n.57, 4)

(311c) Senwosret III says of his Nubian adversaries:

*ḥwr-w=pw*
wretch-P=SE
They are wretches. (Berlin 1157, 11)

(311d) The deceased says to Osiris:

| | | | |
|---|---|---|---|
| *ṯwt* | *it-i* | *ink* | *sꜣ-k* |
| 2MS | father-1S | 1S | son-2MS |

You are my father; I am your son. (CT I 207d)

(311e) The deceased has just demanded that the guardians of the underworld grant him access. The latter ask:

| | |
|---|---|
| *ntk* | *sy* |
| 2MS | WH |

What are you? (BD 122/*Nu* pl. 25, 2)

In exx. 311a and 311b, both examples involve a demonstrative pronoun as one of the sentence constituents. Since demonstratives can be 'out-subjected' only by the element =*pw*, there is no difficulty in identifying the subject, but the rule P–S = classifying, S–P = identifying works here as well. The sentences above do not convey the same meaning. In 311a, the referent of *nw* appears to be profiled as a *sort* of thing, not any actual thing at hand – i.e. it is profiled as a member of a class – and the order is P–S. Conversely, in 311b, the referent of *pꜣ* is presented as a 'substance', i.e. as the actual, particular 'base' to which reference was made earlier. It is, in other words, identified with the latter, and the order is S–P. Similarly, in 311c the Nubian enemies are clearly classified as wretches with the order P–S, whereas in 311d the sentence concerns (one of) the identities of the speaker and his addressee, and the order is the 'expected' S–P. Finally, nominal sentence WH-questions are, in turn, always identifying,[98] although they do not, of course, state but rather question the identity. In 311e, this correlates, as expected, with the order S–P. Consider now the following examples:

(312a) Heqaib begins his self-presentation:
*i͗nk nḏs i͗qr ḏd m-rꜣ-f*
1S subject excellent speak.PPA with-mouth-3MS
*i͗ri m-ḫpš-f*
do.PPA with-foreleg-3MS
I was an excellent subject who spoke with his mouth and achieved with his arm. (BM 1671, 1–2)

(312b) Ankhtify ends his self-adulation with a characteristic boast:
*i͗nk=pw ṯꜣy i͗wt(-y) wn k-y*
1S=COP male REL.NEG[-M] exist.STA other-M
I was a man without equal. (*Moʿalla*, Iβ4–5)

(312c) A question in a glossary to a religious text:
*sy=pw wꜥ m-nw n(-y)-i͗m-w ḫt-ḥr*
WH=COP one in-DEM of[-M]-in.RLT-P behind-N
Who is the one among these who are in the retinue of Horus? (CT IV 252a/Sq1C)

(312d) A divine being wakes up and asks:
*i͗šst=pw*
WH=SE
What is it? (CT V 108a)

(312e) A gloss following a section in a religious spell referring to 'great god':
*ptr=rf=sw rꜥ=pw ḏs-f*
WH=PTC=3MS N=SE self-3MS
Who is he? He is Ra himself. (CT IV 214b–c/Sq1C)

(312f) The deceased equates himself with the eye of Horus:
*i͗nk=pw stt=pw ṯspẖr*
1S=SE 3FS=SE vice versa
It is me, and it is it – and vice versa. (CT IV 99h)

(312g) Intef assures his hearers of the accuracy of his self-presentation:
*biꜣ-t-i͗=pw nꜣ m-wnmꜣꜥ-t*
character-1S=SE DEM.M in-truth-F
This was my character in truth. (*Urk*. IV 973, 10)

98 Semantically classifying interrogative constructions are not formally nominal, but rather adverbial sentences; see ex.s 23b and 246 of Part I.

In ex. 312a, the third-person anaphoric pronouns in *rꜣ-f* and *ḫpš-f* show that the sentence classifies its subject as a representative example of 'excellent subjects', but the order of the grammatical roles is S–P. The same holds with the tripartite ex. 312b. Conversely, 312c questions the identity of the referent of the NP following the copular *=pw*, but the order is P–S. The same holds also for 312d and 312e with the subject element *=pw*. In the latter case, as in 312f, a classifying sense seems excluded given the unique character of the initial predicate noun. Finally, in 312g, it is certainly not the case that the referent of *nꜣ* is classified as 'my character', but rather 'this' is identified as being the actual, specific character of the speaker, and yet the order of grammatical constituents is P–S.

The key to this behaviour lies in the word order properties of the relevant expressions. Absolute pronouns (almost) regularly occupy, in Earlier Egyptian, the sentence-initial position,[99] and this requirement holds whatever the semantic purport of the sentence. By contrast, the subject element *=pw* is a second position clitic, and must take this position in all instances. Of the interrogative pronouns, *sy* and *m* are more flexible here,[100] but *išst* and *ptr* again regularly occupy the first position. Finally, it was noted earlier (1.1.1) that in nominal sentences the so-called *n*-series demonstratives such as *nn* and *nꜣ* show a tendency to behave like clitics and do not normally occur in initial position.[101] As can be seen from examples 312a–312g, these word-order requirements are observed in each case even though this breaks the correspondence between semantic function and the order of grammatical roles. Nevertheless, the price to be paid for this violation of the rule is small. As discussed above, in nominal sentences where no pronouns or subject element *=pw* appear, the order of grammatical roles is not fixed, and the hearer must infer it on the basis of his understanding of the proposition's semantic function and the rule stipulating a correlation between the two. By contrast, pronouns and the subject element *=pw* form a scale of potential subjecthood, and with elements belonging to this group the subject of the nominal sentence is, with one exception to be discussed in the next section, readily identifiable. Decoding of the sentence, in other words, begins here with the identification of the grammatical roles and then proceeds to the semantic interpretation. In cases where no pronouns or subject element *=pw* are present, the process is reversed.

---

**99** The one exception here are constructions with the determinative pronoun *n* described in 1.1.1.
**100** One finds both *m=tr=ṯw* (WH=PTC=2MS, CT V 68j/B1C, ex. 9a) and *twt m* (2MS WH, CT III 95g/B1L, ex. 7a) for 'Who are you?' as well as *sy=rf nꜣ* (WH=PTC DEM, CT VI 284l, ex. 9b) 'What is this' and *ntk sy* for 'Who are you?' (BD 122/*Nu* pl. 25, ex. 7b). The reasons for the variant placement of these interrogatives are discussed in Uljas (2012a: 262–65).
**101** Exceptions are bipartite constructions such as *nꜣ=pw* (pMoscow math. n.16, 10; ex. 115e) and cleft constructions, see 3.1.3.

In the first instance, there is naturally no need for the rule stipulating correspondence between semantic function and grammatical roles, and no such rule is observed. Conversely, in the second instance the rule is an essential component of the decoding process.

The mechanisms for analysing the organisation of grammatical roles and the semantic nature of nominal sentences are observable in most of the Earlier Egyptian data. However, there are instances where their applicability is rather open to question. The problematic status of specifying-identifying propositions *vis-à-vis* predicativity was already noted above. In addition, in bipartite constructions of the type described in 1.2.1, where the predicate of *=pw* is a fully finite clause, the categories 'classifying', 'identifying' etc. lose their significance more or less completely. That is, a sentence such as *hꜣꜣ mwy-t-f=pw* in ex. 118a above clearly does not classify or identify the complement sentence as anything. This shows that the less prototypically 'nominal' the predicate and the less concrete and tangible the referent of *=pw* are, the less the construction actually represents a true nominal predication (see 3.1.5 for further discussion).

### 3.1.3 Nominal sentences with non-canonical information structure

The final group of Earlier Egyptian affirmative nominal sentences requiring a detailed discussion are bi- and tripartite constructions that combine initial nouns or absolute personal pronouns with relative clauses and display non-canonical information structure that since the early days of Egyptological linguistics have been seen as equivalent to what is known as cleft and pseudo-cleft sentences.[102] This equation is still mostly valid, but there are certain facets that must be revised.

In Earlier Egyptian, the equivalent of the English pseudo-cleft sentence such as 'Jack is the one who loved Jill' is structurally a tripartite nominal sentence with an initial noun or a personal, demonstrative, or interrogative pronoun plus a relative clause (a relative form, participle, the future participle *sḏm-ty-fy*) after the copula *=pw* (cf. Loprieno 1995: 106):

(313a) The deceased asserts his divine parentage:

| | | |
|---|---|---|
| *ink=pw* | *ms-n* | *nṯrtḥm-t* |
| 1S=COP | bear.REL-PST | goddess-F |

I am the one whom the goddess bore. (CT VII 487b/B1P)

---

**102** In Egyptology, the (English) term 'cleft sentence' goes back to Polotsky (1971: 418 n.1). The most extensive discussion of constructions traditionally grouped under this heading is Doret (1991); see also Vernus (1991: 338–39, 343–47, 355). For a bibliography of Egyptian cleft sentences, see Doret (1991: 57 nn.1–5) and Schenkel (1990: 169–70).

(313b) A concluding remark after presenting a method of finding the number of cows:
*nꜣ=pw* *ỉn-(n)-f*
DEM.P=COP bring.REL-[PST]-3MS
These are the ones that he brought. (pRhind math. 67, 22)

(313c) The author lists the duties of certain serfs:
*sꜣ-t* *ḏꜣ=pw* *ỉrr-t* *pꜣq-t*
daughter-F N=COP do.PIA-F fine linen-F
The daughter of Dja is the one who makes fine linen. (pBerlin P. 10030A, 9)

(313d) The deceased asserts his immortality:
*ỉnk=pw* *wnn-t(y)-f(y)* *m-tꜣ=pn* *n(-y)-ꜥnḫ-w*
1S=COP exist-REL.FUT-AGR in-land=DEM.M of[-M]-living-P
I am the one who shall exist in this land of the living. (CT I 171d/B16C)

(313e) In a spell describing the means of the king's resurrection:
*zy=pw* *zp-t(y)-f(y)* *N=pw* *zp-t(y)-f(y)*
WH=COP survive-REL.FUT-AGR N=COP survive-REL.FUT-AGR
Who is the one who will survive? King NN is the one who will survive. (PT 438c/T)

More particularly, this construction is formally identical with the so-called reversed pseudo-clefts in which the cleft constituent precedes the cleft clause ('X is the one who…'). Formally (if not quite functionally) similar is the construction [infinitive + *=pw* + relative clause] with the verb *ỉri* 'do', a favourite narrative construction in Middle Egyptian classical literature, used particularly with verbs of motion to present a new and outstanding turn in the narrative:

(314a) The shipwrecked sailor departs from the Phantom Island in a new boat with a new crew:
*nꜥt=pw* *ỉri-n-n* *m-ḫd*
sail.INF=COP do.REL-PST-1P in-downstream
So we sailed downstream (lit. 'sailing is what we did'). (Sh.S. 172)

(314b) Prince Hardjedef lands at Djed-Sneferu:
*ḫr* *mḫt* *nꜣ-n-ꜥḥꜥ-w* *mni* *r-mry-t* *šꜣs=pw*
PTC after DET.P-of-barque-P moor.STA to-bank travel.INF=COP
*ỉri-n-f* *m-ḥrty*
do.REL-PST-3MS in-overland
Then after the barques had been moored to the riverbank, he travelled overland. (pWestcar 7, 11–12)

As in the above examples, in this narrative pattern the relative clause after *=pw* is normally a past relative form. Corresponding cases with passive participles are much less frequent:

(315) Redjedet's maidservant has just been seized by a crocodile:
*šꜣs=pw* *ỉry* *r-ḏd=st* *n-rdḏdt* *ỉn* *pꜣy-s-sn*
travel=COP do.PPP to-say.INF=3C to-N AGT POSS.M-3FS-brother
Then her brother went off to tell it to Redjedet (lit. 'a travelling is what was done… by her brother'). (pWestcar 12, 19–20)

Non-reversed pseudo-clefts ('The one who… is X') are not particularly common in Earlier Egyptian, and most examples derive from Old Kingdom texts (cf. Edel 1955–64: §971):

(316a) After a statement informing that the king has been granted towns and nomes by god Atum:
*mdw* *ḥr-s=pw* *gb*
speak.PIA on-3FS=COP N
The one who speaks of it is Geb. (PT 961d/P)

(316b) Inti makes a generic point on ethics:
*mrr-t* *nṯr=pw* *ỉrt* *ḫt* *mꜣꜥ*
love.REL-F god=COP do.INF thing just
What god loves is doing the right thing. (*Urk.* I 71, 10)

(316c) King Pepi II makes a general point about the observance of his order:
*mrr-t* *nfrkꜣrꜥ=pw* *ỉrt* *ḫt* *ḫft-md-t*
love.REL.IMPF-F N=COP do.INF thing according_to-word-F
*n-t-wḏ=pn*
of-F-decree=DEM.M
What Neferkara desires is acting according to the letter of this decree. (*Urk.* I 283, 11)

(316d) An answer in a mathematical text:
*hꜣꜣ-t=pw* *r-f* *m-ḥqꜣt* *sš* *ḥqꜣt* *48*
descend.PIA-F=COP to-3MS as-heqat grain heqat 48
What goes into it in *heqat*-measures is 48 *heqats* of grain. (pRhind math. n.41, 4)

In early sources there are some instances of what appear to be (reversed and non-reversed) proto-pseudo-cleft sentences without *=pw*:

(317a) The king is told at an offering ritual:
*wnm-t-n-k* *ỉr-t*
eat.REL-F-PST-3MS eye-F
What you have eaten is an eye. (PT 192b/W)

(317b) The king is presented offerings with the following utterance:

| | | | | |
|---|---|---|---|---|
| *ḥtp-t* | *ꞽn-t=n-k* | *ḥtp-t* | *mꜣꜣ-t-k* | *ḥtp-t* |
| offering-F | bring.PPP-F=to-2MS | offering-F | see.REL-F-2MS | offering-F |
| *sḏm-t-k* | | | | |
| hear.REL-F-2MS | | | | |

Offerings is what is brought to you; offerings is what you see; offerings is what you hear. (PT 34c/W)

Yet such examples are rare already in the Pyramid Texts. Overall, the reversed order is dominant and, in line with the grammaticalisation of *=pw* as a copula in tripartite nominal sentences, the construction without *=pw* is common only in personal and other names.[103] It should be noted that constructions of the following kind are not, as has sometimes been argued, cleft sentences of any kind (Borghouts 2010: §80.b):

(318) A new section in the dialogue between a man and his soul sets off:

| | | | |
|---|---|---|---|
| *ḏd-t-n=n-ꞽ* | *bꜣ-ꞽ* | *n-ntk=ꞽs* | *rmṯ* |
| say.REL-F-PST-to-1S | soul-1S | NEG-2MS=NEG | man |

What my soul said to me: 'You are not a man'. (Man and Ba 30–31)

Here, the initial headless relative clause is not the subject (or, for that matter, the predicate) of the following direct quote, which instead stands in apposition to the former.[104] Similarly, a caveat should be made with tripartite sentences where also the first NP is a relative clause. These constructions are not pseudo-clefts but rather ordinary nominal sentences, and they occur frequently in fossilised set phrases such as the following variant of the 'Appeal to the Living' – a common formulaic call to readers of tomb inscriptions to make an offering – combining two relative clauses without *=pw*:

(319) Qay begins his Appeal to the Living with the following statement:

| | | | | |
|---|---|---|---|---|
| *mrr* | *ḥss=sw* | *ḫntyꞽmntw* | *ḏd-t(y)-f(y)* | *ḫꜣ* |
| love.PIA | favour=3MS | N | say-REL.FUT-AGR | thousand |
| *m-ḫt=nb* | *n-ꞽmꜣḫ* | *qꜣy* | | |
| in-thing=QU.M | to-revered | N | | |

He who desires that Khentyamenty favour him is the one who will say: 'A thousand of everything for the revered Qay'. (CG 20567, 1–2)

103 E.g. *rꜣ-ms-sw* 'Ramses', i.e. 'Ra-is-the-one-who-bore-him'.

104 This is obvious from the fact that the direct quote need not be a 'linguistic' expression (What he said was 'Aargh!') or even in the same language as the relative clause (What he said was 'Guten Tag').

Yet even in this highly register-particular usage, *=pw* is sometimes employed:

(320a) The Appeal to the Living of Khui:

| | | | | |
|---|---|---|---|---|
| *mrr* | *nzw=pw* | *mrr* | *ỉnpw* | *tp-ḏw-f=pw* |
| love.REL | king=COP | love.REL | N | on.RLT-mountain-3MS=COP |

| | | | |
|---|---|---|---|
| *ḥryẖbt=nb* | *ỉw-t(y)-f(y)* | *r-ỉr(t)=n(-ỉ)* | *sꜣẖ-w* |
| lector priest=QU.M | come-REL-FUT-AGR | to-do.INF=to[-1S] | transfiguration-M |

One whom the king loves, and one whom Anubis-upon-his-Mountain loves, is any lector priest who will come to perform transfiguration for me. (*ASAE* 43, 503–04, b1)

(320b) In the Appeal to the Living of Djau:

| | | | | |
|---|---|---|---|---|
| *mrr-w* | *nzw=pw* | *ḥ[zz]-w* | *nṯr-sn* | *nw-t-y* |
| love.REL-P | king=COP | praise.REL-P | god-3P | town.RLT-F-M |

| | | | |
|---|---|---|---|
| *ḏd-t(y)-sn* | *ẖꜣ* | *tꜣ* | *ḥnq-t* |
| say-FUT.REL-AGR | thousand | bread | beer-F |

Those whom the king loves and their local god praises are those who will say 'A thousand bread and beer...' (*Urk.* I 147, 10–11)

The subject of Earlier Egyptian reversed pseudo-cleft sentences has sometimes been taken to be not the initial cleft constituent but rather the clause following *=pw* (Loprieno 1995: 106). However, there are morpho-syntactic and semantic-pragmatic factors suggesting that this view is not correct. As can be seen from ex. 313c, the relative clause *ỉrr-t pꜣq-t* after *=pw* shows gender-agreement with the initial cleft constituent *sꜣ-t ḏꜣ*, 'the daughter of Dja'. It is clearly the lexical gender of the latter that determines the grammatical gender of the relative clause, not vice versa. The same phenomenon is observable in the following example:

(321) Mentuhetep makes a generic comment on just behaviour:

| | | |
|---|---|---|
| *dr-t=pw* | *ỉꜣm-t* | *mrr-t* |
| hand-F=COP | gentle-F | love.PIP-F |

A gentle hand is what is loved. (UCL 14333, 13)

Similarly, it shall be shown shortly that the order of the grammatical roles in cleft sentences is S–P, and thus it would be strange if Earlier Egyptian pseudo-clefts had a different order in this respect. Further, also Late Egyptian pseudo-cleft sentences display the S–P-order (see 3.2.1). The analysis proposed here for Earlier Egyptian thus harmonises the situation between the earlier and later stages of the language and entails no assumption of a reversal of the grammatical roles in what is functionally one and the same sentence type. In pseudo-cleft constructions, the initial expression can be the demonstrative pronoun *nꜣ* that usually, in nominal sentences, does not occupy the first position:

(322) In a broken context:

| | | | |
|---|---|---|---|
| *mk=swt* | *nꜣ=pw* | *ḏdy-ỉ* | *r-tnw-sp-gmm=sw* |
| PTC=PTC | DEM.M=COP | say.REL.FUT-1S | to-every-occasion-find=3MS |
| *bꜣk-ỉm* | | | |
| servant-there | | | |

Look, moreover, this is what I shall say every time yours truly finds him.
(pUC 32213 rº 24–vº 2)

The initial placement of *nꜣ* here is based on the requirement that in the pseudo-cleft sentence the subject occupy the first position. The order S–P is, in other words, a constructional feature of nominal sentences of this particular semantic-pragmatic type. Finally, the Earlier Egyptian pseudo-cleft sentence is formally a tripartite *pw*-sentence, where, as seen, the order S–P is the signal of an identifying role (certain word-order-related exceptions notwithstanding). Not only has the function of (true) cleft constructions long been considered to be identifying,[105] but, as can be seen from the examples above, the relationship between the initial cleft constituent and the following clause is identifying in all instances. This is so even in cases of [non-relative NP + =*pw* + relative clause], where one might be tempted to reverse the order of grammatical roles:

(323a) Having described his piety towards his ancestors, Khnumhetep remarks:

| | | | | | |
|---|---|---|---|---|---|
| *ỉsṯ* | *sꜣ=pw* | *mnḫ* | *sr(w)d* | *rn* | *n(-y)-tpwꜥ* |
| PTC | son=SE | efficient | strengthen.PIA | name | of[-M]-ancestors |

Now, an efficient son is the one who strengthens the name(s) of ancestors. (*Beni Hasan* I, pl. 26, 166–68)

(323b) Senwosret III profiles the worst failure in royal office:

| | | | |
|---|---|---|---|
| *ḥm=pw* | *mꜣꜥ* | *ꜣr-w* | *ḥr-tꜣš-f* |
| coward=COP | real | drive-PPP | on-border-3MS |

But the true(st) coward is he who is driven from his border.
(Berlin 1157, 4–5)

105 For the character of cleft and pseudo-cleft sentences as identifying, see e.g. Halliday (1985: 40); Collins (1991: 2). In Egyptology, despite varying terminology (Doret 1989: 50 n.16), this has similarly been often noted; see e.g. Junge (1978: 52; 1981: 445–46); Vernus (1991: 338); Doret (1989: 59). For Schenkel (1984: 164–66) and Loprieno (1988a: 83–89) cleft sentences may be specifying or qualifying. In Loprieno (1995: 106–09), pseudo-cleft sentences are identifying, cleft sentences more particularly specifying.

(i.e. not 'He who strengthens the names... is an efficient son' or 'He who is driven from his border is a real coward').

The pseudo-cleft sentence subject often carries the role of a patient of the verbal situation described in the relative clause, but it may also be associated with some other role such as the experiencer in ex. 313d or the agent in 313c. Pragmatically, the cleft constituent is associated with specific 'highlighting' or participant focus that can create a sense of exclusiveness (John alone is the one), contrast (John is the one, not you), replacement (Not you, but John is the one), and so forth.[106] Copious quantities of ink have been spilled in attempts to identify the mechanisms by which 'focussing' is achieved in cleft constructions, and much of the argument has revolved around the notions 'given' vs. 'new' information[107] and 'topic' vs. 'comment'.[108] Here, it is maintained that the key to the 'focussing' effect of pseudo-clefts and cleft constructions is best understood as related to their being used to create particular kinds of presuppositions (Lambrecht 1994: 228–33). Consider, e.g. the proposition such as 'The daughter of Dja is the one who prepares fine linen' in ex. 313c above. The primary presupposition here is an existential 'There is someone who prepares fine linen', and the actual 'news' (often termed 'assertion') communicated is the relationship between the presupposition and the cleft constituent, i.e. '*x* prepares fine linen; *x* = daughter of Dja' rather than simply the relationship between 'daughter of Dja' and 'prepares fine linen'. Although entailed by '*x* prepares fine linen, and *x* = daughter of Dja', 'Daughter of Dja prepares fine linen' is not what is presented to the audience as the most important piece of information and could have been expressed by just such a non-cleft construction. This is, of

**106** Much discussion has been devoted in the past to the precise characteristics of the 'focus' associated with cleft constructions. In Earlier Egyptian, as, it seems, elsewhere, cleft constructions are not specialised for any one of the proposed (and often rather *ad-hoc*) classes of 'focus'. Rather, they represent a group of patterns used for the generalised 'highlighting' of participants whose exact pragmatic function depends on the nature of the discourse in which they appear.

**107** For a somewhat selective summary, see Johansson (2001: 554–60); cf. also Collins (1991: 98–109). An exception here is Chafe (1976: 38).

**108** An overview of the use of these concepts in Egyptology will appear in Uljas, in preparation. Overall, if (a sentence level) topic (or 'theme' or 'logical predicate' etc.) is conceived e.g. as an element which the *p* 'is about' and/or 'the first element in the sentence', in cleft and (reversed) pseudo-cleft sentences this can be argued to be the cleft constituent. Many linguists accept this analysis (see e.g. Halliday 1967: 226; Givón 2001: 2, 228–30; Collins 1991: 84, 151). Yet in linguistic approaches where a 'topic' or 'theme' is incompatible with the 'focus' associated with clefts, and commonly so amongst Egyptologists, in cleft sentences the topic has instead been argued to be the cleft clause (Gundel 1977: 552–53; Dik 1980: 219; Gardiner 1957: §227.2; Borghouts 1972: 273–74; Loprieno 1988b: 49 ('demoted topic'); Junge 1989: 62; Vernus 1991: 336, 338–39; Ritter 1994: 246; 1995: 38).

course, merely to stress the well-known fact that pseudo-clefts and cleft constructions in general are among the best examples of presupposition triggers.[109] In these constructions the hearers are invited to treat the predication of the proposition as part of the common ground shared with the speaker, and this invitation is made in a very consistent manner. The presupposition is a built-in automaton and an inherent property of the used linguistic expression, in this instance the triggering cleft construction itself. This means that by using a cleft construction, the speaker's illocutionary intention is not so much to cast focus on something as to downplay the communicative relevance of one part of the sentence by turning it into a presupposition (cf. Loprieno 1988b: 48; Schenkel 1990: 143). This might (and usually does) have the effect of putting extra 'focus' on the cleft constituent, but the latter is, figuratively speaking, not so much focused as the rest of the information is de-focused. The overall effect of this then depends on the character of the cleft constituent. In most instances the downgrading of the non-cleft material leaves the latter in relief, which may then be loosely said to result in 'focussing' of the latter. There is one caveat to this, however. With interrogative expressions, which are presupposition triggers themselves, the use of cleft constructions would seem rather superfluous. However, Earlier Egyptian pseudo-cleft, and, as shall be shown below, cleft sentences, are often used with interrogatives:

(324a) In a broken context:
*ỉšst=pw* *mꜣ-t-n-k* *ỉm*
WH=COP see.REL-F-PST-2MS there
What is it that you saw there? (CT VII 212h/pGard.II)

(324b) The queen says to Amun:
*ỉšst=pw* *mr-t-n-k* *ḫpr* *ỉry-ỉ=ỉ(s)=s(y)*
WH=COP want.REL-F-PST-2MS happen.INF do-1S=PTC=3FS
*ḫft-wḏ-t-n-k*
before-order.REL-F-PST-2MS
What is it that you have wanted to happen? I will carry it out according to what you have ordered. (Red Chapel 99, 13)

It could be said that here the cleft structure does not so much create but rather marks explicitly that the proposition displays the presuppositional structure typical of WH-questions. That is, when used with interrogatives the construction signals that their introduction has changed the canonical information structure into one in which everything else but the interrogative is presupposed. In a sense,

109 The original note here is due to Keenan (1971: 47).

using a cleft construction here serves the same purpose as WH-fronting in English, where the idea behind the 'movement' of the WH-expression is not 'focussing', but rather marking the non-canonical information structure of the proposition (see e.g. Lambrecht 1994: 285). Note also that in examples 324a and 324b above, the interrogative pronoun *ꞽšst* functions as the subject. As seen in 3.1.1, in ordinary nominal sentences involving interrogatives, the latter serve always as predicates. Cleft constructions such as pseudo-cleft sentences are, however, a special class of nominal sentences where the pronoun hierarchy of subjecthood described earlier does not apply. These constructions have a non-canonical information structure and are used for special purposes, which correlates with their fixed ordering of grammatical roles.

In Earlier Egyptian, there are also constructions that correspond to cleft sentences proper (English 'it'-clefts), but the number of patterns belonging to this group is somewhat smaller than what has been thought hitherto. In the only Earlier Egyptian construction truly *specialised* for this role, the subject is a noun or a pronoun, but not a personal pronoun, introduced by the element *ꞽn* and followed by a masculine singular active participle predicate, whence its Egyptological label 'participial statement' (thus S > [*ꞽn* + *Noun* + *active participle*]:

(325a) A reply of an Asiatic servant caught stealing honey from his Egyptian master:

| | | | | |
|---|---|---|---|---|
| *mk* | *ꞽn* | *bnr-t* | *rdꞽ* | *ꞽry-ꞽ=st* |
| PTC | PTC | sweetness-F | cause.PPA | do.SUB-1S=3C |

Look, it was the sweetness that made me do it. (pUC 32124, 2.10)

(325b) Ptahhetep says that good speech is more difficult than anything; so:

| | | | |
|---|---|---|---|
| *ꞽn* | *wḥꜥ=s(y)* | *dd=s(y)* | *r-ẖt* |
| PTC | loosen.PPA=3FS | place.PIA=3FS | to-stick |

It is only he who has mastered it who can make it useful. (Ptahhetep 369)

(325c) A dedication to the deceased in a tomb:

| | | | |
|---|---|---|---|
| *ꞽn* | *zꜣ-f* | N | *ꞽrꞽ=n-f nw* |
| PTC | son-3MS | N | do.PPA=to-3MS DEM.M |

It was his son N who made this for him. (*Urk.* I 228, 16)

(325d) A note in a medical text explaining what causes deafness in the two ears:

| | | | |
|---|---|---|---|
| *ꞽn* | *m-t* | 2 | *ꞽrr=st* |
| PTC | vein-F | 2 | do.PIA=3C |

It is two vessels that do it. (pEbers 99, 14)

(325e) The peasant says to the high steward:

| | | | |
|---|---|---|---|
| *ꞽn* | *sḏr-w* | *mꜣꜣ* | *rsw-t* |
| PTC | sleep.PIA-M | see.PIA | dream-F |

It is the sleeper who dreams. (Peas B1, 247)

In the Pyramid Texts, and occasionally still in the Coffin Texts, the relative clause shows gender agreement with the cleft constituent, but this feature is later dropped; cf.:

(326a) The king belongs to the divine offspring:

| | | | | | | | |
|---|---|---|---|---|---|---|---|
| *ỉwr* | *N* | *ỉn* | *sḫmt* | *ỉn* | *šzmtt* | *ms-t* | *N* |
| conceive.PASS | N | AGT | N | PTC | N | bear.PPA-F | N |

King N was conceived by Sekhmet; it was Shezmetet who gave birth to King N. (PT 262b)

(326b) The author of the letter to dead asks whether his correspondent is not missing something essential in his failure to protect his former maidservant:

| | | | | | |
|---|---|---|---|---|---|
| *(ỉ)n-wnn* | *n* | *rḫ-n-k* | *ntt* | *ỉn* | *tꜣ-bꜣk-t* |
| IP-AUX | NEG | know-PST-2MS | COMP | PTC | DEM.F-maidservant-F |
| *ỉrr* | *pr-k* | *m-rmṯ* | | | |
| do.PIA | house-2MS | in-people | | | |

Could it really be that you do not know that it is this maidservant who runs your house among the people? (Cairo Bowl, inside 7–8)

In the Pyramid Texts, there are some instances that appear to show that *ỉn* had had the role of a generalised actor clefting element in nominal (ex. 327a) and even verbal (327b) sentences:

(327a) The king is born of the celestial goddess:

| | | | | |
|---|---|---|---|---|
| *ỉn* | *N=pn* | *zꜣ* | *smꜣ-t-ḥm-t* | *wr-t* |
| PTC | N=DEM.M | son | cow-F-female-F | great-F |

It is this king N who is the son of the Great Wild Cow. (PT 1370a)

(327b) The king, as Osiris, is restored to life by his heir:

| | | | | |
|---|---|---|---|---|
| *ỉn* | *zꜣ-k* | *mry-k* | *snṯ-n-f=n-k* | *ỉr-ty-k* |
| PTC | son-3MS | beloved-2MS | fix.REL-PST-3MS=to-2MS | eye-DU-2MS |

It is your beloved son who has set in place your eyes for you. (PT 644c)

Some Pyramid Texts examples also suggest the existence of an earlier form of cleft sentence where the noun cleft constituent was not introduced, but rather juxtaposed directly to the following relative clause (cf. the 'proto-pseudo-cleft sentence' examples above):

(328) It is said concerning the eye of Horus:

| | | |
|---|---|---|
| *ḏḥwty* | *ỉn=sw* | *ẖr-s* |
| N | bring.PPA=3MS | under-3FS |

It is Thoth who has brought himself carrying it. (PT 58b)

Yet the grammaticalisation of *i͗n* in participial cleft sentences must have taken place relatively early. It has been argued that some examples of cleft sentences without *i͗n* are to be found in Earlier Egyptian textual material after the Pyramid Texts (Vernus 1987: 179–81), but a closer examination of the alleged instances does not support this hypothesis:

(329) The deceased is in the service of the Lord of Life (CT I 393e–394a):

| | | | | |
|---|---|---|---|---|
| S1C: | *i͗nk* | *smn* | *ḥꜣ-w* | *kꜣr-f* |
| | 1S | establish.PPA | behind.RLT-P | shrine-3MS |
| B2L: | *i͗nk* | *smn=n-f* | *ḥꜣ-w* | *kꜣr-f* |
| | 1S | establish.PPA=to-3MS | behind.RLT-P | shrine-3MS |
| T3C: | *i͗nk* | *smn(=n)-f* | *ḥꜣ-w* | *kꜣr-f* |
| | 1S | establish.PPA[=to]-3MS | behind.RLT-P | shrine-3MS |
| B1Bo: | *ntf* | *smn=n-f* | *ḥꜣ-w* | *kꜣr-f* |
| | 3MS | establish.PPA=to-3MS | behind.RLT-P | shrine-3MS |
| B3C: | *N=tn* | *smn=n-f* | *ḥꜣ-w* | *kꜣr-f* |
| | N=DEM.F | establish.PPA=to-3MS | behind.RLT-P | shrine-3MS |
| B1C: | *N* | *smn=n-f* | *ḥꜣ-w* | *kꜣr-f* |
| | N | establish=to-3MS | behind.RLT-P | shrine-3MS |
| B1P: | *N=pn* | *smn=n-f* | *ḥꜣ-w* | *kꜣr-f* |
| | N=DEM.M | establish=to-3MS | behind.RLT-P | shrine-3MS |

| | | |
|---|---|---|
| S1C: | *ḫft-wḏ-t-n-f=n-i͗* | |
| | order.REL-F-PST-3MS=to-1S | |
| B2L: | *ḫft-wḏ=n-i͗* | |
| | as-order=to-1S | |
| T3C: | *ḫft-wḏ=n-i͗* | |
| | as-order=to-1S | |
| B1Bo: | *ḫft-wḏ-f* | *n-N=pn* |
| | as-order-3MS | to-N=DEM.M |
| B3C: | *ḫft-wḏ* | *n-N=pn* |
| | as-order | to-N=DEM.M |
| B1C: | *ḫft-wḏ=n-i͗* | |
| | as-order=to-1S | |
| B1P: | *ḫft-wḏ=n-i͗* | |
| | as-order=to-1S | |

The general sense of this passage seems to be 'It is me who established the ones who are behind his (= the Lord of Life) shrine, as he ordered to me'. However, the variants from the sources known as B3C, B1C, and B1P apparently do not represent grammatical cleft sentences with a bare noun head, but result from a mechanical replacement of the first-person singular absolute pronoun *ink* with the name of the deceased. Particularly notable is the incomplete manner in which this is carried out in the variants B1C and B1P, which actually translate *'It is this N who established for him the ones who are behind his shrine as ordered to *me*'. Hence, examples such as these hardly represent genuine examples of cleft sentences without *in*. In Earlier Egyptian, this archaic pattern is encountered only in highly standardised expressions such as the epistolary greeting in ex. 330a below, in the dedication formula 'it is N who did this for him' (330b) found on numerous funerary memorials from the Old Kingdom onwards, or sometimes in accounting, where brevity is essential (330c):

(330a) The author to the letter to dead begins his communication:

| | | | |
|---|---|---|---|
| *špsi* | *ḏd* | *n-mw-t-f* | *iy* |
| N | say.PPA | to-mother-F-3MS | N |

It is Shepsi who writes (lit. 'says') to his mother Iy. (Qaw Bowl, outside 1)

(330b) A dedication inscription on a statue of Nika-ankh:

| | | | |
|---|---|---|---|
| *z3-t-f* | *z3-f* | *iri=n-f* | *nw* |
| daughter-F-3MS | son-3MS | do.PPA=to-3MS | DEM.M |

It was his daughter and son who made this for him. (*Urk.* I 32, 6)

(330c) An answer to the question 'how many people it takes' (*in m ꜥḥꜥ ḏd=sw*):

| | | |
|---|---|---|
| *mk* | *3* | *ḏd=sw* |
| PTC | 3 | say.PIA=3MS |

Look, it is three that it takes (lit. 'who say it'). (pMoscow math. n.25, 4)

With personal pronoun subjects, the structurally corresponding construction is [absolute pronoun + masculine singular active participle]:

(331a) The author designates himself as the one responsible for rations of a workforce:

| | | | | |
|---|---|---|---|---|
| *ink* | *dd=n-sn* | *ꜥq-w* | *r-ṯnw* | *rnp-t* |
| 1S | give.PIA=to-3P | ration-P | to-every | year-F |

It is me who gives them rations every year. (pBerlin P. 10033, 5)

(331b) In a text describing human anatomy:

| | | | | | | |
|---|---|---|---|---|---|---|
| *iw* | *m-t* | 2 | *n-špty-t* | *ntsn* | *dd* | *mwy-t* |
| AUX | vein-F | 2 | to-bladder-F | 3P | give.PIA | water-F |

The bladder has two veins; it is them that produce urine. (pEbers 100, 11)

This construction, however, is just an ordinary bipartite nominal sentence without *=pw*, that, unlike the *in*-sentence, is not specialised for the kind of information structure typical of cleft constructions. There are several indicators of this. Firstly, in true cleft sentences the participial predicate does not agree with the subject introduced by *ỉn* heading the construction (except in earliest texts). When the initial expression is an absolute pronoun, there is again no agreement per se, but the participle is independently declined as either masculine or feminine. The following example where the speaker is a female deity is instructive:

(332) Goddess Hathor announces:
*ỉnk ỉr-t=tw n-t-ḥr wpt-t nb wꜥ... ỉnk=ỉgrt*
1S eye-F=DEM.F of-F-N messenger-F lord unique 1S=PTC
*ỉr-t rn-f*
do.PPA-F name-3MS
I am this eye of Horus, the female messenger of the Unique Lord. I am, moreover, she who made his name. (CT IV 173f–h/G1T)

As can be seen, here the participle *ỉr-t* is feminine, reflecting the gender of the speaker. Secondly, after absolute pronouns the following relative clause is not necessarily an active participle, but it can also be a corresponding passive (exx. 333a and 333b) or even a relative form with its own subject (exx. 333c and 333d):

(333a) The gods who will protect the king's pyramid are fortunate:
*ntsn rdi-w=n-sn ḥtpdinzw... ntsn stpp=n-sn stp-w-sn*
3P give.PPP-P=to-3P offering formula 3P choose.PIP=to-3P cut-P-3P
*ntsn i-ỉri-w=n-sn ꜥꜣb-w-t-sn*
3P PREF-do.PPP-P=to-3P offering-P-F-3P
They are the ones to whom the offering-formula will be read... they are the ones for whom their choicest cuts will be chosen; they are the ones to whom their offerings will be made. (PT 1651a–d/M)

(333b) The deceased proclaims:
*ỉnk msy m-rstꜣw*
1S bear.PPP in-N
I am one born in Rosetau. (CT VII 289a/B9C)

(333c) Henqu maintains his worth:
*ỉnk=ḥm wꜥb-w-n nṯr rꜣ-f*
1S=PTC purify.REL-M-PST god mouth-3MS
I was truly one whose mouth the god purified. (*Urk.* I 79, 26a)

(333d) The deceased demands respect from other divinities:
*ỉnk ỉri-n nb wꜥ*
1S do.REL-PST lord unique
I am one whom the Unique Lord made. (CT III 382e/S2Cª)

Corresponding constructions with *ỉn* + noun do not occur. Thirdly, the cleft clause in the construction with *ỉn* cannot be negated (see 4.1), whereas this restriction does not apply with the absolute pronoun pattern:

(334) The deceased announces:
*ỉnk nt-y n-ỉp-ø*
1S REL-M NEG-count.PASS-ø
I am one who has not been counted. (BD 7/*Nu* pl. 64, 5)

Fourthly and most importantly, with first- and second-person absolute pronouns the construction often lacks the characteristic actor focus found in all *ỉn*-clefts. Compare the following examples:

(335a) Amenemhab tells of an elephant-hunt during which one bull put up a fight before being felled; then:
*ỉnk šˁd dr-t-f*
1S cut.PPA hand-F-3MS
It was me who cut off his trunk (lit. 'hand'). (*Urk.* IV 894, 1)

(335b) Having set out a plan to keep the peasant speaking, the king orders Rensi to provide him with rations; yet:
*wnn-k ḥr-rdỉt dỉ-tw=n-f ˁq-w nn*
AUX-2MS PROG-give.INF give-PASS=to-3MS ration-P NEG
*rdỉt rḫ-f ntt ntk rdỉ=n-f=st*
cause.INF know-3MS COMP 2MS give.PPA=to-3MS=3C
You are to keep making sure that he is given rations, but without letting him know that it is you who has given them to him. (Peas B1, 114–15)

(335c) Intef characterises himself:
*ỉnk rḫ sbꜣ=sw r-rḫ*
1S know.PPA teach.AP=3MS to-know.INF
I am one who knew and who taught himself to know. (Leiden V6, 11)

(335d) The deceased king is told:
*pr ỉr-ḫfti-k ṯwt wr ỉr-f m-rn-k*
go.IMP against-enemy-2MS 2MS great.PP to-3MS in-name-2MS
*n(-y)-pr-wr*
of[-M]-house-great
Go against your enemy; you are one stronger than him in your name of 'Great Shrine'. (PT 648d/T)

Unlike 335a and 335b, exx. 335c and 335d apparently do not identify the subject but only classify it. In addition, no specific pragmatic contrastive, distinctive, or other 'highlighting' effect seems to be associated with it. It was argued above that the actor focus typical of pseudo-cleft sentences was due to the kind of presuppositions that these constructions trigger. The same holds also for cleft sentences. In a sentence such as ‘It was his son who made this for him’, the triggered presupposition is ‘someone did this for him’ and the actual information conveyed is the identity between the variable ‘someone’ and the cleft constituent (i.e. *x* did this for him; *x* = his son). This downgrading of the predicate part into the presupposed base of the proposition results in the characteristic focus assigned to the subject/actor. However, in true cleft sentences, as in pseudo-clefts, triggering presuppositions is associated with the particular construction and is one of its most fundamental features. Yet in Earlier Egyptian sentences of the type [*ink/ntk* + participle], this feature is not constant. The reason for this lies in the peculiar and non-uniform pragmatic status of absolute personal pronouns. In appropriate co(n)texts, absolute pronouns of the interlocutive first and second persons may at times be read as focal. Consider the following example:

(336) Sinuhe contrasts his fortunate position with that of other fugitives:

| | | | | | | |
|---|---|---|---|---|---|---|
| *btꜣ* | *s* | *n-gꜣw* | *hꜣb-f* | *ink* | *ʿšꜣ* | *mr-w-t* |
| hurry | man | for-lack | send.REL.FUT(?)-3MS | 1S | many | serf-P-F |

A man may need to hurry due to lack of an envoy, but *I* am one rich of serfs. (Sin B, 154–55)

There is a clear contrastive sense expressed here, which may be described in a similar vein as above. In ex. 336, the relationship between the subject ‘I’ and the predicate is part of the presupposition ‘someone is rich of serfs’, which is not the actual news conveyed by the proposition. This is, instead, establishing an identity between the referent of the subject and the variable slot in the presupposition (i.e. ‘someone is rich of serfs, and that someone is me’). The result is a focus cast on the subject expression. Similar examples can be found of second person as well. Now, if this focussing were a regular feature of absolute pronouns, one might analyse them as presupposition triggers, but as can be seen e.g. from the clearly non-focal instances 335c and 335d above, this is not the case. That is, presupposition triggering does not occur regularly with first- and second-person absolute personal pronouns. By contrast, the corresponding delocutive third-person pronouns always function as presupposition triggers; thus they are always focal and contrast with *=pw* used in non-focal allo-sentences:

(337) It is said of the king/of the deceased:

| | | | | | |
|---|---|---|---|---|---|
| *zꜣ-k=pw* | *n(-y)-ḏ-t-k* | *n-ḏt* | *ntf* | *sꜣ* | *wsir* |
| son=3MS=SE | of[-M] body-F-2MS | to-eternity | 3MS | son | N |

He is your (Ra-Atum’s) bodily son forever. (PT 160c)

*He* is Osiris’ son. (CT IV 37f/Sq6C)

This difference between the absolute pronouns also explains why the third person does not combine with interrogative pronouns. As is well known, the latter are also presupposition triggers by nature, and combining them with third-person absolute pronouns would result in a complex containing nothing but presupposition triggers and with a very strange information structure. However, corresponding sentences with the second person, which is not per se markedly focal, do occur; see 1.1.1 and 3.1.1 for examples. What all this shows then is that nominal sentences with absolute personal pronoun subjects and participial (or, indeed, any other type of) predicates do not actually trigger the relevant presupposition as constructions. Rather, when present, presuppositions are triggered by the pronouns, but because the first- and second-person absolute pronouns do not trigger them regularly, they are not regularly present. In corresponding third-person constructions, presuppositions are regular, because these pronouns always trigger them. It follows then that unlike the construction [*in* + noun + participle], the construction [absolute personal pronoun + participle] is not a 'cleft sentence' in the sense that it *always* serves this function. Rather, it is more correct to say that this construction does so only when it is of the third person and that if it is of the first or second person it *may* function thus if the discourse co(n)text allows such a reading. In the latter case, the 'focus' perhaps represents a contextual implicature of a particular sort.

The reason why there should be a difference such as this between the various absolute pronouns is unclear. It has often been suggested that the 'non-focal' first- and second-person examples might represent instances of proclitic absolute pronouns similar to the later Sahidic Coptic *ang*- and *ᵉntk*- that were used alongside the prosodically fuller forms *anok* and *ᵉntok* (e.g. Gilula 1976: 168–69; Borghouts 1986: 62–63; Doret 1989: 55). This proposal is attractive seeing that in Coptic the proclitic forms are similarly formed only of the first- and second-person absolute pronouns.[110] Yet it is not without problems. The said division is in Coptic largely a feature of the southern dialects (particularly Sahidic and Achmimic but also Fayyumic) and then of mostly earlier material; in Bohairic, no corresponding difference is found (see 1.1.2.3). Furthermore, there is no conclusive evidence from Late Egyptian or Demotic for a similar division as in (some) Coptic. Consequently, the varying behaviour of absolute pronouns in the earlier language may have been due to a difference in prosodic values, but this hypothesis cannot be proven.

**110** Loprieno (1988a: 93) has suggested that the division could be based on the scale of 'topicality' (first person is more 'topical' than second and both are more so than third). The 'cutting-off point' between persons 1/2 and 3 is justified by the cognitive immediacy of the interaction (first-second person) as opposed to the narration (third person).

Be that as it may, the question is whether there are some fixed parameters conditioning where and when a first- or second-person absolute pronoun may be read as focal. It would appear that, in principle, this was the case whenever the pronouns were used in allo-sentences contrasting with constructions in which clitic- or suffix pronouns were 'normally' used. One such instance was seen in connection with adverbial sentences, where the rare construction [absolute pronoun + adverbial predicate] (e.g. *ỉnk m-pr*, 1S in-house) was used instead of the more standard pattern with (particle-introduced) clitic or suffix pronouns to focalise the subject (Part I, 3.1.2.1). In nominal sentences, there are rare (pre-New Kingdom) examples such as 163 above, where an absolute pronoun replaces a clitic pronoun in the third position of a tripartite *pw*-sentence.[111] Below is the only other early example of this same phenomenon:

(338) The king is united with the sungod:
*N=pw ntf N=pw wꜥ n(-y)-p-t*
N=SE 3MS N=SE unique of[-M]-heaven-F
King N is he; King N is one unique of heaven. (PT 2041)

It has been argued that here the ordering of the constituents reflects a pragmatic organisation where the pronominal predicate corresponds to the sentence 'rheme' rather than the 'theme' (in Prague School terms), coded by clitic pronouns (Gundacker 2010: 47). Alternatively, the construction could be viewed as an allo-sentence associated with a specific presuppositional structure similar to the one achieved by phonetic stress on the predicate (if this is what it is) in 'King N is *he*'.

There is a partial semantic division of labour between cleft- and pseudo-cleft sentences. Although in the latter the cleft constituent may be semantically agentive, patients are more common in this position. By contrast, in cleft sentences the cleft constituent is always the actor. The principal *raison d'être* of this construction is, of course, to focalise the latter. However, interrogative expressions, which, as noted, are presupposition triggers themselves and hence 'focal' by nature, are even more common with cleft sentences than with their pseudo-cleft counterparts:

(339a) A question put to the deceased concerning the ferry to the yon realm:
*ỉn m=ỉrf ꜥḥꜥ ḥr-s*
PTC WH=PTC stand.PIA on-3FS
Who stands upon her? (CT V 98a)

111 That is, unless these examples are corrupt.

(339b) A question in a mathematical problem with an unknown *x*:

*in* *m* *ḏd=sw*
PTC WH say.PIA=3MS
What corresponds to (lit. 'says') it? (pUC 32134A, 2)

Here too the use of a presupposition-triggering 'focalising' construction seems redundant. Yet it could again be said that the cleft structure is here an explicit signal that the proposition has a presuppositional structure typical of WH-questions.

Cleft constructions provide a fine example of iconicity in Earlier Egyptian grammar. In both cleft- and pseudo-cleft sentences, the highlighted participant is set syntactically apart from the relative clause. In the semantically less isolating pseudo-cleft sentences, the predicate agrees with the cleft constituent in gender but not number; cleft sentences show neither type of agreement. Thus, morpho-syntax mirrors the informational contour of these sentences: the more the focal participant stands apart from the situation in which it is involved, the greater its pragmatic salience and isolation. Cleft constructions and the 'participial statement' more broadly also constitute one of the many bridges covering the gap between nominal sentences and other grammatical patterns in Earlier Egyptian. Although syntactically they belong to the class of nominal sentences, the discourse-pragmatic role of clefts in Egyptian and elsewhere is to highlight semantic roles of the 'underlying' *verbal* propositions. This interaction between cleft sentences and verbal situation descriptions is most apparent in the so-called Gunn's construction.[112] This is functionally the future equivalent of the cleft sentence, but instead of the expected future participle *sḏm-ty-fy*, the predicate following the noun introduced by *in* or the bare absolute personal pronoun takes the guise of a fully finite clause with the so-called Prospective *sḏm-f* verb form:

(340a) The king is a star and brings about his own resurrection:

*in* *ḏr-t* *N* *wṯz-s=sw*
PTC hand N raise.PROSP-3FS=3MS
It is the hand of King N that will lift him up. (PT 537c)

(340b) The deceased says to gods:

*ink* *iw-i=n-ṯn* *m-bꜣ=pn* *sḥd*
1S come.PROSP-1S=to-2P as-soul=DEM.M shine.STA
It is me who will come to you as this shining soul. (CT IV 145m)

**112** See Doret (1991: 57 n.4) for a bibliography up to early 1990s. The seminal discussion here is Gunn (1924 [2012]: chapter 5).

(340c) In a question-answer sequence between the deceased and a divinity:
*in* *m=irf* *sšm-f=ṯw*
PTC WH=PTC lead.PROSP-3MS=2MS
*in* *sꜣ-ty* *bity* *sšm-w-sn=wi*
PTC son-DIM king lead-PROSP-3P=1S
Who will lead you? It is the two sons of the king of Lower Egypt who will lead me. (CT V 105i–106a/Sq2Sq)

There are also a small number of instances where the *sḏm-ty-fy* appears:

(341) In an obscure context:
*in* *wnm-t(y)-f(y)=sw* *wnm-t(y)-f(y)=wi*
PTC eat-REL.FUT-AGR=3MS eat-REL.FUT-AGR=1S
It is the one who will eat it who will (also) eat me. (CT V 32k)

Yet since most examples of this sort derive from sources not earlier than the Coffin Texts,[113] the attestations probably do not represent an archaic version of the future cleft sentence. The normal *sḏm-f* shows person, gender and number agreement with the initial absolute pronoun or other element introduced by *in*. Although this construction is always actor-focalising (that is, apparently a constructional presupposition-trigger) and the actor is cleft to the leftmost position, there is no predicative relation between the initial (pro)noun and the following full clause. Similarly, although the actor stands in an antecedent-resumptive relation with the *sḏm-f*, it is structurally outside the sentential frame, which only comprises the verb.[114] The future cleft sentence is structurally not a nominal, but essentially a verbal construction that can be thought of as standing at the crossroads of verbal and nominal sentences.[115] It is one manifestation of the more global phenomenon of nominal sentences merging semantically and structurally with other sentence patterns which will be considered in more detail in 3.1.5. Prior to this, however, it is necessary to investigate the temporal features of these constructions and their remaining pragmatic characteristics, which seem to be primarily responsible for the properties of the clausal syntax of nominal sentences described above.

---

**113** An Eighteenth Dynasty example is *Urk.* IV 221, 14 *swt ḥqꜣ-t(y)-s(y) tꜣ-wy* (3MS rule-REL-AGR land-DU) 'It is (s)he who will rule the Two Lands'; probably also *Urk.* IV 257, 17. But see Doret (1989: 61).

**114** A rather similar view has been most recently expressed by Borghouts (2010: §48.d).

**115** *Contra* e.g. Jansen-Winkeln (1996b: §458), who argues for the nominal sentence analysis on basis of the paradigmatic alternance of the *sḏm-f* and participles.

### 3.1.4 Tense and modality

Earlier Egyptian nominal sentences are, generally speaking, neutral in terms of illocutionary value(s) and temporal deixis. As for the former, many of the examples cited thus far may fairly be said to represent statements of fact that present the situation described as something to which the speaker is wholly committed and which is portrayed as relevant information. Yet in both bipartite and tripartite constructions, one of the combined expressions may also be an interrogative pronoun and the sentence as a whole expressive of a WH-question. In addition, nominal sentences do not profile the relation described in any temporally limited, contingent, or defined way. That is, although in individual instances they may refer to past states of affairs, nominal sentences are insensitive to temporal deixis and portray the semantic relation described as beyond the confines of time.[116] This conceptual neutrality explains many of the grammatical differences they display if compared with patterns such as adverbial sentences, which, although equally non-verbal, nevertheless describe situations inherently sensitive to change and development. The incompatibility of nominal sentences with auxiliaries is perhaps the most obvious reflection of this. These constructions do not profile the relation described as acquired, bounded, or prospective, but simply as associated with some entity.[117] If the status was intended as being somehow limited in these respects, Earlier Egyptian had recourse to verbal and adverbial allo-constructions. Consider the following examples:

(342a) Sinuhe tells Ammunenshi about the character of the new king Senwosret I:

| | | | | | | |
|---|---|---|---|---|---|---|
| *ỉw-f* | *m-nsw* | *ỉt-n-f* | *m-swḥ-t...* | *wꜥ=pw* | *n(-y)-dd* | *nṯr* |
| AUX-3MS | as-king | take-PST-3MS | in-egg-F | one=SE | of[-M]-give | god |

He is (now) a king, although he conquered already in egg... He is one unique, God-given. (Sin B, 68–70)

(342b) As above:

| | |
|---|---|
| *nb* | *ssꜣ-t=pw* |
| lord | wisdom-F=SE |

He is a lord of wisdom. (Sin B, 48)

116 The most succinct discussion of this to date is Winand (2006: 159–63). See also e.g. Gardiner (1957 §133); Assmann (1974: 66–67); Callender (1984: 129–33); Allen (2000: 78); Loprieno (1995: 103); Malaise and Winand (1999: §456), among others.

117 The latter may mean that the quality or status is an inherent and inseparable attribute thereof, or that mention and suggestion of the developmental or other character of it is simply omitted.

(342c) The sage laments the reversal of social roles:

| | | | | |
|---|---|---|---|---|
| *iw=ms* | *šwꜣ-w* | *ḫpr-w* | *m-nb-w* | *špss-w* |
| AUX=PTC | beggar-P | become-STA | as-lord-P | valuable-P |

Alas, beggars have become lords of riches. (Ipuwer 2, 4)

(342d) The loyalist teacher says concerning the king:

| | | | |
|---|---|---|---|
| *iw* | *ḥsy-f* | *r-nb* | *ꜥꜣb-w-t* |
| AUX | favour.REL.FUT-3MS | to-lord | offering-P-F |

One whom he will favour will be a lord of offerings. (*Loyaliste* §3, 9)

In ex. 342a, the adverbial sentence profiles the kingship of Senwosret I as something that he has acquired subsequent to his father's death, even though he also had kingly traits before: 'He now is/has become a king'. By contrast, the following nominal sentence *wꜥ=pw n(-y)-dd nṯr* conveys the idea of the same person's temporally unlimited uniqueness and divinity. Similarly, in 342b the king's role as 'lord of wisdom' is in no way temporally restricted, whereas in 342c with the verb *ḫpr* 'become', the 'beggars' are lords of riches only because of the breakdown of social order. In 342d with the verbal construction *r* + infinitive, the king's favourite will acquire the status of 'lord of offerings' in the future. That is, in 342c and 342d, the relation described is profiled as limited, acquired, bounded, or forthcoming, whereas the nominal sentence portrays the state of affairs in a strictly atemporal fashion and as not susceptible of development or change over time. This is because the predicative expression, a noun, is associated with maximum conceptual time-stability (see e.g. Givón 2001: I, 50–54; Stassen 1997: 15–16). Consequently, a relation involving such an expression may – but does not need to – be profiled as outside temporal or spatial deixis, and this is precisely what the nominal sentence construction does. Yet as can be seen in examples 342c and 342d, the adverbial and verbal constructions combine with the auxiliary *iw*, whereas nominal sentences do not. This is because in states of affairs not profiled as undergoing sudden or gradual development, resulting from anything, or having a beginning or an end, there is less room for features such as nuances of illocution and modality than in more contingent and transitory situation-descriptions. Modality, for example, concerns the speaker's attitude towards propositions and the information they convey. Its grammatical expression is more likely to be associated with descriptions of situations where (real or imaginary) participants interact with others, function in a real or possible world, or exist and occupy a locus in time and space that is open to change. As seen with adverbial sentences, the role of the auxiliary *iw* appears to be inherently modal: it signals assertive illocution. The role of *wn/wnn* is less clear, but its strong association with non-assertion seems to suggest that it also had a modal-illocutionary function. These elements combine with verbal and adverbial constructions because the latter express meanings that locate them at or close to the conceptual core for communicating speaker attitudes and opinions. This core consists of descriptions of states of affairs that contain an idea of dynamics, of development, progress, and change either in real or in potential terms. Nominal sentences are in antithesis to such situation profiling, and consequently they do not partake in the system of expressing modality by means of auxiliaries. There is, however, one apparent exception to this rule, which, incidentally, also proves the assertive role of *iw* beyond doubt. It seems that even nominal sentences could be preceded by this element in the special context of oaths. Consider the following example with the possessive construction *n=sw*, which can be analysed as a nominal sentence (1.1.1):

(343) Queen Hatshepsut swears:

| | | | | | | |
|---|---|---|---|---|---|---|
| *ꜥnḫ=n-i* | *mry=wi* | *rꜥ...* | *iw* | *ir* | *pꜣ-tḫn-wy* | *wr-wy* |
| live=to-1S | love=1S | N | AUX | PTC | DEM.M-obelisk-DU | great-DU |

| | | | | |
|---|---|---|---|---|
| *bꜣk-n* | *ḥm-i* | *m-ḏꜥm* | *n-it-i* | *imn...* |
| work.REL-PST | majesty-1S | from-fine gold | to-father-1S | N |

| | | | | | |
|---|---|---|---|---|---|
| *iw* | *n=st* | *inr* | *wꜥ* | *m-mꜣ-t* | *rwḏ-t* |
| AUX | DPR=3C | stone | one | in-granite-F | hard-F |

As Ra lives for me and loves me... as for these two great obelisks which my majesty has hewn of fine gold for my father Amun... they are of a single block of hard red granite. (*Urk.* IV 365, 14–366, 17)

Oaths are a special category of statements which instead of asserting something, are sworn by the speakers to represent the categorical truth to which they are utterly committed (in a sense, they are super-assertions). In Earlier Egyptian, the ban on employing *iw* before a nominal sentence could be deliberately broken in such cases to mark the strongest possible assertivity of the proposition by means of the element that serves as a prototypical assertion-marker.

Assertivity would also seem to determine the grammar of some of the subordinate clause patterns in which nominal sentences are found, although much is still unclear. For example, it is not clear why nominal sentences apparently cannot be subordinated by means of the relative adjective *nt-*, after which the adverbial sentence is used as a supplementary construction.[118] This has presumably nothing to do with the (possible) difference between restrictive *nt*-constructions and non-restrictive 'virtual' relative clauses. One thing that it does show, however, is that the element *nt-* is not a simple syntactic converter. Its incompatibility with nominal sentences is, as will be seen in Part III, also

**118** Constructions of this sort appear only in Demotic and Coptic, see 2.4.2.

paralleled by corresponding absence before *adjectival* sentences. What these two constructions share, and what distinguishes them from adverbial sentences, is the conceptual inertia and temporal-modal insensitivity of the states of affairs they describe. This feature perhaps somehow prevented their co-occurrence with the relativiser *nt*-, but more work is needed to understand why this should be so. In complementation, the situation is not quite as obscure, although here too there are issues that still await explanation. Nominal sentences may appear in complement clauses if accompanied by the complementiser *ntt* or, in earlier material, by the clitic particle *=ꞽs*. The diachronically later strategy with the complementiser is limited to cases when the complement is asserted (for what follows, see Uljas 2007c: 24 and *passim*):

(344a) Queen Hatshepsut explains why she has favoured the temple of Amun:

| *ꞽw-ꞽ* | *rḫ-kw* | *ntt* | *ꜣḫ-t=pw* | *ꞽptswt* | *tp-tꜣ* |
|---|---|---|---|---|---|
| AUX-1S | know-STA.1S | COMP | horizon-F=SE | N | upon-earth |

I know that Karnak is a horizon upon earth. (*Urk*. IV 364, 1–2)

(344b) The king smites his enemies ignorant of his might; however:

| *mꜥr* | *sp* | *r-ṯnw* | *rḫ-w* | *ntt* | *sꜣ-f=pw* | *mꜣꜥ* |
|---|---|---|---|---|---|---|
| sweet | fate | to-number | know-STA | COMP | son-3MS=SE | true |

Fate is lenient to multitudes who know that he is his (Amun's) true son. (*Urk*. IV 1293, 1–3)

(344c) The author of the letter to the dead asks whether his correspondent is not missing something essential in his failure to protect his former maidservant:

| *(ꞽ)n-wnn* | *n* | *rḫ-n-k* | *ntt* | *ꞽn* | *tꜣ-bꜣk-t* |
|---|---|---|---|---|---|
| IP-AUX | NEG | know-PST-2MS | COMP | PTC | DEM.F-maidservant-F |
| *ꞽrr* | *pr-k* | *m-rmṯ* | | | |
| do.PIA | house-2MS | in-people | | | |

Could it really be that you do not know that it is this maidservant who runs your house among the people? (Cairo Bowl, inside 7–8)

(344d) Having set out a plan to keep the peasant speaking, the king orders Rensi to provide him with rations; yet:

| *wnn-k* | *ḥr-rdꞽt* | *dꞽ-tw=n-f* | *ꜥq-w* | *nn* |
|---|---|---|---|---|
| AUX-2MS | PROG-give.INF | give-PASS=to-3MS | ration-P | NEG |
| *rdꞽt* | *rḫ-f* | | | |
| cause.INF | know-3MS | | | |
| *ntt* | *ntk* | *rdꞽ=n-f=st* | | |
| COMP | 2MS | give.PPA=to-3MS=3C | | |

You are to keep making sure that he is given rations, but without letting him know that it is *you* who has given them to him. (Peas B1, 114–15)

In all these instances with the same verb *rḫ* 'know', the complement clause is definitely presented by the speakers as important information which they know and to which they are fully committed. It is clear from ex. 344b, where it is left open whether the referents of the sentence subject knew the complement state of affairs, as well as from 344c, where this is questioned, and from 344d where it is definitely excluded, that the relevant participant is once again the *real* speaker. It was seen in connection with the adverbial sentences that instances where the complement was not asserted, *ntt* could not be used and the clause was instead replaced by a construction with *wn/wnn* (Part I, 3.1.3.3). The same probably held for nominal sentences as well, but examples with non-assertive governing verbs are lacking. This is probably due to the statistical unlikelihood of propositions such as 'He ordered/desired that you be an X'. However, examples do appear with causatives:[119]

(345) Goddess Nut has spread herself above the deceased:

| | | |
|---|---|---|
| *rdi-n-s* | *wn-k* | *m-nṯr* |
| cause-PST-3FS | AUX-2MS | as-god |

She has caused you to be(come) a god. (Turin 4262)

The replacement of the nominal sentence with an adverbial construction after *wn* follows directly from the incompatibility of the former pattern with auxiliaries discussed above. There are, however, two special cases of complementation where the putative rule asserted > complementiser and un-asserted > no complementiser are not observed. The first of these involves the verb *gmi* 'find, discover'. Nominal sentence complements occur after this verb without a complementiser, and they also seem to do so regardless of whether the complement is asserted or not. Examples are more abundant with verbal clauses, but the following instance with the possessive pattern *n-* seems instructive:

(346) A piece of Machiavellian advice on how to deal with a dangerously popular local potentate begins:

| | | | |
|---|---|---|---|
| *ir=grt* | *gm-k* | *n=sw* | *nw-t-w* |
| CND=PTC | find-2MS | DPR=3MS | town.RLT-F-P |

If you discover that he belongs to the townspeople (i.e. has urban support)... (Merikara E, 25–26)

119 It was proposed earlier that the use of the auxiliary (and particularly the non-reduplicating form *wn*) here might be based on the material implication 'He caused that X → X', which renders marking the complement for assertion unnecessary (cf. Uljas 2007c: 139, 148–51).

The governing verb and its complement clause are here part of a conditional protasis and thus not asserted. It is unknown why complementisers are not used after *gmỉ*, a fundamentally assertive verb.[120] Nevertheless, its strange behaviour shows that these elements were not used for purely syntactic reasons. The other special case of complementation is clauses with the clitic *=ỉs*. The use of this element in complement clauses appears to belong to an earlier stage of the language and also to stand outside its system of marking assertion. In examples 284c and 286b, the *=ỉs*-complements fulfil the requirements for assertive status, but this is not the case e.g. in the following instances:

(347a) Isis has claimed that her unborn child is Osiris' seed and divine;
Ra-Atum replies:
*sꜣ* *ỉb-ṯ* *ḥm-t* *ỉ-rḫ-ṯ{n}=rf* *mỉ-ỉšst* *nṯr=ỉs=pw*
guard.IMP heart-2FS wife-F PREF-know-2FS=PTC like-WH god=PTC=SE
Be prudent, woman! How do you know if he is a god?
(CT II 215b–216a/S1Cª)

(347b) The ritualist disclaims responsibility of his address to the deceased:
*ỉmỉ-k=ḏd* *ỉnk=ỉs* *ḏd=n-k* *nw* *ỉn*
AUX.NEG.JUSS-2MS=say.NC 1S=PTC say.PPA=to-2MS DEM.M PTC
*gb* *ḏd=n-k* *nw*
N say.PPA=to-2MS DEM.M
Say not that it is me who says this to you. It is Geb who says this to you.
(CT I 302d–f/B10C)

In ex. 347a, *=ỉs* occurs in a complement whose propositional content is subject to speaker doubt and which is under an interrogative scope. In 347b, the speaker shows non-commitment to the complement proposition, whose falsity he goes on to substantiate in the following sentence.[121] The role of *=ỉs* had clearly nothing to do with the illocutionary status of the complement. However, it was not a complementiser (or nominaliser) either, as can be sen from its use

---

120 The verb *gmỉ* and its descendants in Later Egyptian have several other unusual features as regards their complement-selection properties. In Late Egyptian, only *gmỉ* can take complements of the form [noun/pronoun + *ỉw*-less 'circumstantial'] as well as [object + *r-ḏd* + sentence]; see Sweeney (1986: 355). In Coptic, *kʲine* 'find' is the only verb that, when negated and appearing in the *status constructus* form *kʲn-* can take bare second tense and interrogative object complements of the type *ang-nim* 'Who am I?' and *e-i-na-er-u* 'What shall I do?' (see Layton 2011: 363, 426). The peculiarities of the verb *gmỉ* have been recently discussed in full by Vernus (2012).

121 However, of the other variants T2C has *ỉnk ḏd=n-k nw* without *=ỉs* and in the two other witnesses the clause is in the negative (*n ỉnk=ỉs*). It could also be that B10C has simply missed the negative *n*.

in adjunct clauses as well. Instead, as already noted, it probably represents an archaic means of marking the clause as semantically and syntactically dependent. Finally, it is not clear why nominal sentences seemingly had to be replaced by adverbial sentences in unmarked adjunct clauses not introduced by preposition-conjunctions. A straightforward syntactic explanation would be to argue that they were not adverbial by nature and thus could not be used thus without an adverbialising preposition-conjunction. This may be true, but such a purely structural account is more a description than an explanation. As things stand presently, adjunction of nominal sentences adds another item to the list of phenomena pertaining to these constructions whose semantic-pragmatic basis is still unclear.

### 3.1.5 The limits of the nominal sentence

Owing to the difficulties in recognising the grammatical roles of subject and predicate as well as their complex semantics, nominal sentences represent perhaps the most problematic class of Earlier Egyptian non-verbal patterns. However, they appear to exhibit at least one redeeming feature, namely their seemingly easily definable and well-delimited character as a sentence type, free from the intertwining of meaning and form characteristic of adverbial and adjectival sentences. Yet this closed character of nominal sentences as a formal-functional category is, at least in Earlier Egyptian, largely illusory. Rather, these constructions are better described as a semantic-pragmatically and morpho-syntactically fuzzy category that overlaps with verbal, adjectival, and adverbial sentences in form and function. One of the points of convergence with verbal sentences, i.e. future clefts, was noted above. As observed, the 'Gunn's construction' resembles the 'participial statement' [independent personal pronoun/*in* + noun + active participle] to a notable extent, its only apparent difference *vis-à-vis* the latter being the replacement of the participial predicate by a prospective verbal *sḏm-f* form:

(348a) A question-answer sequence in a magical spell concerning a missing head:

*in* *m=irf* *in-f=sw* *gm-f=sw*
PTC WH=PTC bring.PROSP-3MS=3MS find.PROSP-3MS=3MS
*ink* *in-i=sw* *ink* *gm-i=sw*
1S bring.PROSP-1S=3MS 1S find.PROSP-1S=3MS

Who then will bring it and find it? It is me who will bring it; it is me who will find it. (pEbers 58, 10–11)

(348b) Part of a question-answer sequence:

| | | | | |
|---|---|---|---|---|
| *in* | *m=ỉrf* | *s3-y-f=n-n* | *dp-t=pn* (sic)... | *swt* |
| PTC | WH=PTC | protect-PROSP-3MS=to-1P | boat-F=DEM.M | 3MS |

*s3-y-f=s(y)*
protect-PROSP-3MS=3FS
Who will guard this boat for us? ... It is he who will guard it.
(CT V 89d–90a/T1C)

Yet the only predication expressed in the complex is clearly the one between the *sḏm-f* and its suffixed subject.[122] Therefore, in absence of a predicative relation between its two constituent parts, the future cleft is not in fact a nominal sentence construction at all. It is rather an essentially verbal construction. A similar merger between nominal and adjectival sentences may perhaps be recognised in the rare constructions where dependent pronouns are used as subjects of nouns and pronouns in bipartite nominal sentences. Examples were already presented (see 13a and 13b), but one further instance may be cited here:

(349) Hori and Suty sing praise to the sun god:

| | | |
|---|---|---|
| *ptḥ=tw* | *nb-k* | *ḥʿ-k* |
| N=2MS | fashion-2MS | limb-2MS |

You are Ptah-like when you fashion your (own) limb(s)! (*Urk.* IV 1944, 1)

Assuming again that this and similar examples are not corrupt or otherwise defective, this construction could be seen to bridge the structural and semantic gap between Earlier Egyptian nominal and adjectival sentences (Uljas 2006; rather differently Gundacker 2010: 106–10). The structural similarities with e.g. *ptḥ=tw* in ex. 349 and adjectival constructions such as *nfr=tw* 'You are good' (see Part III) are obvious. In terms of meaning as well, *ptḥ=tw* appears to state that the subject has certain properties of Ptah and manifests the qualities characteristic to the Memphite creator god. The semantic nature of the predication is thus again not as in prototypical nominal sentences, but rather echoes the properties of adjectival sentences.

Perhaps the most elaborate examples of nominal sentences converging with other sentence types structurally and semantically are instances where the latter are subordinated to the element *=pw*. These constructions form a scale of increasing convergence with verbal sentences, whose beginnings may be recognised in

**122** As clearly realised by Gunn (1924 [2012]: 58) and most recently stressed by Borghouts (2010: §48.d); cf. also Allen (1994: 2 n.4), who notes that the Gunn's construction is apparently never negated.

constructions in which a fully clausal (geminating) *sḏm-f* verb form serves as a clausal predicate complement:

(350) A gloss in a medical text:

| | | | | | |
|---|---|---|---|---|---|
| *ỉr* | *rwt* | *n-t-ḥꜣ-t* | *rww-f=sw=pw* | *ḥr-mnḏ-f* | *ỉꜣb-y* |
| PTC | move.INF | of-F-heart-F | move-3MS=3MS=SE | on-breast-3MS | left.RLT-M |

As for 'the movement of the heart'; this means that it moves itself upon his (the patient's) left breast. (pEbers 101, 11–12)

Here the subject element *=pw* indexes, as normal, the expression *rwt n-t-ḥꜣ-t* 'movement of the heart' left-dislocated by *ỉr*,[123] and there appears to be a predicative relation between *=pw* and *rww-f*. Yet this relation is apparently not of a classifying or identifying nature; the referent of *=pw* is not identifiable or classifiable as the clausal predicate 'it moves itself', but only shows the same semantic denotation. In other words, nominal sentences such as these are not prototypical examples of the category, but represent a sub-class where the basic semantic typology of this type of predication begins to break down. This process is more advanced in nominal sentences of the type exemplified in examples 122a–122e above and 351 below, where, as argued in 1.2.1, entire verbal and adverbial sentences are embedded as predicates of *=pw* and the subject of the former is anteposed:

(351) A new turn in a mythological narrative of the battle between Horus and Seth:

| | | | | | |
|---|---|---|---|---|---|
| *stẖ=pw* | *ỉri-n-f* | *ḫprw* | *r-f* | *m-šꜣỉ* | *km* |
| N=SE | do-PST-3MS | form | to-3MS | as-pig | black |

Now Seth, he then transformed himself into a black pig against him. (CT II 342b)

As in the roughly literal translation of ex. 351 as 'It is so that Seth, he transformed himself…' the sentence after the complementiser *that* is not classified or identified as anything else. But in addition, the element *=pw* no longer semantically indexes anything. In the English 'It is so that Seth, he transformed himself…' the pronoun *it* functions as an expletive and is co-indexed with the *that*-clause. However, unlike *it*, the Earlier Egyptian *=pw* does not have any anaphoric or cataphoric referent, which causes the often-noted difficulties in finding a fixed translation for this type of construction and the

123 Note, incidentally, the grammatical treatment of the infinitive *rwt* as feminine. The example dates to the Eighteenth Dynasty; earlier infinitives were treated as grammatically masculine.

inappropriateness of the translational device 'it is that...', for example in absolute initial environments:

(352) The Tale of the Eloquent Peasant begins:

| | | | |
|---|---|---|---|
| *s=pw* | *wn* | *ḫwninpw* | *rn-f* |
| man=SE | exist.STA | N | name-3MS |

There was a man whose name was Khuenanupe. (Peas R, 1.1)

*=pw* has here completely lost what may be called its semantic subjecthood, i.e. its status as a referential, semantically identifiable landmark of which something is predicated. As a consequence, the only remaining predication in the complex is actually that of the embedded proposition. Put another way, although e.g. the clause [*s wn*] in ex. 352 is indeed syntactically subordinate to *=pw*, it is not the latter's predicate. This level of predication has now disappeared: whereas in nominal sentences such as the one in ex. 350 there are still two predications in the complex, in *s=pw wn* there is only one, namely that between the subordinate clause subject *s* and its predicate *wn*. However, in 122a–122 and 351–352, the overall structure, as it were, lags behind semantics. Syntactically, these constructions are well-formed bipartite nominal sentences with *=pw*, but semantically they are no longer sentences with a nominal predicate. Instead, they are more properly viewed as verbal and adverbial sentences whose subjects have been anteposed by means of *=pw*, which, therefore, is not meaningless, but has a crucial syntactic and semantic-pragmatic role, albeit one that differs considerably from its more characteristic functions in prototypical nominal sentences (Loprieno 1995: 111–12; Uljas 2013: 244–46). On the one hand, *=pw* provides a way of anteposing subjects of S–P patterns and represents the only way to antepose pronominal subjects as well as verbal patterns with VSO-order such as the *sḏm-n-f*, which in Earlier Egyptian cannot be introduced by the element *ir*.[124] On the other hand, *=pw* serves the pragmatic function of signalling that the described situation has a high degree of informative novelty and relevance in the co(n)text. This communicative role, called 'presentative-apocritic', 'Sachverhalts-Aktualisierung', and 'exposition' (Junge 1978: 60; Shisha-Halevy 1987: 174. See also Polotsky 2007: 95; Malaise and Winand 1999: §469), could be described informally as resulting from the role of *=pw* not in the meaning '*x* is something', but rather '*x* is', with *x* being the complement situation. That is, *=pw* lays stress

124 Although no examples of adverbial sentences with pronominal subjects are known, verbal constructions of the type *ink=pw ḥr-sḏm* and *ink=pw hꜣ-kw* are widely attested (see Uljas 2007c: 290, 291 n.8, 292–93). In instances where *=pw* is followed by *sḏm-n-f*, object anteposing also occurs: see ex. 122d from CT II 280d.

on the actuality and occurrence of the situation described and signals its high degree of relevance and novelty. In addition to its anteposing function, it indeed 'presents' the situation and has virtually no independent meaning beyond this. As such, its role belongs to the domain of verbal semantic-pragmatics and is far from the core meaning of *=pw* in nominal sentences.

## 3.2 Later Egyptian

### 3.2.1 Subject and predicate

The identification of the subject and predicate in nominal sentences is a thorny issue also in Later Egyptian. Here again, one faces the lack of overt marking of grammatical roles, which results in the absence of formal criteria for deciding whether, e.g. a Coptic tripartite sentence such as **p-sah pe p-rôme* should be understood as communicating a proposition 'The scribe is the man' or 'The man is the scribe'. It is commonly accepted that, as in earlier stages of the language, the analysis requires a combination of structural rules and contextual considerations, but scholars disagree on the precise mechanisms.

As in Earlier Egyptian, the key to decoding the identities of the grammatical roles in the nominal sentence lies in the identification of the sentence subject, which then allows the predicate to be isolated. The subject is the noun phrase that adheres most closely to the subject prototype described in 3.1.1. The various types of nominal sentences found in the later language can be divided into three groups depending on how the subject is identified. These groups cut across the syntactic categories of 1.1–1.3:
- Bipartite sentences with subject element (*pꜣy/pe*)
- Sentences with pronominal elements
- Other nominal sentence patterns

In bipartite sentences with the subject element, recognising the subject does not present any difficulty. As in Earlier Egyptian, the element *=pw* > *pꜣy/pe* is grammaticalised for the subject role, which allows a formal identification. In most instances, *pꜣy/pe* is the sole candidate for the subject role, whereas the predicate can also be a demonstrative or personal pronoun:

*Late Egyptian*

(353a) The prince, who has never seen a dog, sees one following a man and asks his servant what the animal is. The servant replies:
*ṯsm pꜣy*
dog SE.M
It is a dog. (*LES* 2, 5)

(353b) King Akhenaten outlines the limits of his newly founded capital and resumes:
*nts* *tꜣy*
3FS SE.F
That is it (i.e. the city). (*Boundary Stelae*, 24, 10)

*Demotic*

(353c) Siosire tells his father Setne to bring a book of his own choice, and he will tell:
*iḫ* *n-ḏmꜥ* *pꜣy*
WH of-book SE.M
... what kind of a book it is. (Setne II 3, 20)

(353d) The pharaoh asked Amun in a procession whether a young priest was the person entitled to certain sacerdotal prebends:
*imn* *iw-ṯ* *r-tꜣ-ḥꜣ-t* *n-wꜥ-t-tks-t* *iw-s-ys*
N come-STA to-DEF.F-front-F in-IDF-F-step-F DEP-3FS-hurry
*ḏd-mtwf* *pꜣy*
COMP-[3MS] [SE.M]
Amun came forth with a quick step (and said): 'It is he!'
(pSpiegelberg 2, 14)

*Coptic*

(353e) Jesus tells the Jews that it is only the Father that honours him, who is the same of whom they say:
*pe-n-nute=pe*
POSS.M-1P-god=SE.M
He is our god. ($^{S}$Jn 8:54)

(353f) Village inhabitants press a pregnant girl to name the father of her child; she implicates St Macarius:
*pi-anakhôri=pe*
DEF$_2$.M-hermit=SE.M
It is the hermit. ($^{B}$*AP Macarius* B1 [MG 25 203, 8–9; collated])

Unlike Earlier Egyptian, Later Egyptian does not usually allow bare clausal verbal or adverbial sentence complements in the nominal sentence predicate position (see 1.2.1 and 3.1.3). For example, Coptic often uses here subordinating particles such as *ce-* or *ceka(a)s*, as was discussed in the section on tripartite nominal sentences in 1.3.2:

(354a) Paul argues that he has to preach the Gospel and asks: *What then is my reward?*
*cekaas=pe* *e-i-euaggelize* *ta-ka-p-euaggelion* *n-ueš*
so that=SE.M DEP-1S-preach CNJ.1S-give-DEF.M-gospel with-lack
*n-co* *ebol* *ero-f*
of-spend out to-3MS

*e-tm-tra-ire* *m-pa-htor* *hm-p-euaggelion*
to-AUX.NEG-INFL.1S-do as-POSS.M.1S-accord in-DEF.M-gospel
So that, as I preach, I may offer the Gospel free of charge, and so not make use of the Gospel on my own accord. (S1Cor 9:18)

(354b) Speaking against apocryphal books, Shenute asks his audience:
*u* *pe* *ce-p-euaggelion* *n-i(êsu)s* *p-šêre* *m-p-nute*
WH COP.M COMP-DEF.M-gospel of-N DEF.M-son of-DEF.M-god
*pe-cpo* *ebol* *hn-n-aggelos*
DEF.M-begot out from-DEF.P-angel
What does it mean: 'The Gospel of Jesus, the son of God, the one begotten by the angels'? (SShenute, *I am Amazed* §309 [Cristea 141, 15–18])

In other bipartite and in all tripartite nominal sentences where one of the participant elements is pronominal, subject and predicate are differentiated on basis of the degree of semantic thematicity, topicality, definiteness, and referentiality of the combined nominals. As discussed in 3.1.1, interrogative pronouns score low on this scale, and hence almost invariably serve as predicates in Later Egyptian nominal sentences as well:

*Late Egyptian*

(355a) After Bata had assumed the form of a bull, his former wife asked him:
*ntk* *n* *nm=tr*
2MS PTC WH=PTC
But who are you? (*LES* 25, 10)

(355b) After having been mocked for not having a father, a young boy asked his mother:
*nm* *rn* *n-pꜣy-i-it*
WH name of-POSS.M-1S-father
What is my father's name? (*LES* 32, 16–33, 1)

*Demotic*

(355c) The ghosts asked the magician:
*mtwk* *nym* *spsn*
2MS WH twice
Who are you? Who are you? (pMag. London&Leiden 9, 32)

(355d) When the guardian says that he will announce the deceased to the deity in charge, the deceased will say:
*nm* *pꜣy* *pꜣ-nṯr* *nty-ẖn-tꜣy-f-wp-t*
WH COP.M DEF.M-god REL-in-POSS.F-3MS-work-F
Who is the god who is in his duty? (pBN 149 3, 20)

*Coptic*

(355e) The Jews ask John the Baptist:
*ntk-nim*
2MS-WH
Who are you? ($^S$Jn 1:19)

(355f) The Jesus asks a man possessed by demons:
*nim pe pe=k-ran*
WH COP.M POSS.M-2MS-name
What is your name? ($^B$Lk 8:30)

An exception to the predicativity of interrogative pronouns in nominal sentences can be found in cleft and pseudo-cleft sentences, where the non-canonical pragmatic status assigned to the subject also allows these pronouns to assume a predicative role (3.1.3). Demonstrative pronouns deictically point to referents that are portrayed as situationally or contextually accessible to the audience; for this reason, they also function as subjects in Demotic and Coptic (Late Egyptian examples are lacking):

*Demotic*

(356a) The concluding words in a plea:
*pꜣy(-y)-ḫrw mḥ-2 pꜣy pay*
POSS.M-1S-plea ORD-2 COP.M DEM.M
This is my second plea. (pBM 10591 r° 5, 11)

(356b) The animals of the desert ask for their mother and say:
*ʿn tꜣy-n-mw-t tꜣy tꜣy*
IP POSS.F-1P-mother COP.F DEM.F
Is this our mother? (pLouvre N 2420c, 5)

*Coptic*

(356c) St. Paul cites Jesus' words at the Eucharist:
*pai pe pa-sôma*
DEM.M COP.M POSS.M.1S-body
This is my body. ($^S$1Cor 11:24)

(356d) The opening phrase of the Book of Baruch:
*nai ne pi-saci nte-pi-côm nê*
DEM.P COP.N $DEF_2$.M-word of- $DEF_2$.M-book $DEF_3$.P
*et-a-f-sḫêt-u nce-Barukh ...*
REL-PST-3MS-write-3P PVS-N ...
*ḫen-tʰ-babylon*
in-DEF.F-N
These are the words of the book that Baruch... wrote in Babylon. ($^B$Bar 1:1)

Examples of tripartite nominal sentences with personal and demonstrative pronouns as subject and predicate (e.g. 'This is me') are not attested. The bipartite pattern [pronoun + subject element] is used instead:

*Late Egyptian*

(357a) After telling the story of a woman abandoned by her husband after twenty years because he suddenly noticed that she had only one eye, the author of a letter says:

*ink* *pꜣy*
1MS SE.M
This is me! (*LRL* 68, 1)

*Demotic*

(357b) The method of calculation concludes with the sentence:

*mtwf* *pꜣy*
3MS SE.M
This is it. (pBM 10520, A10 [Parker, *Math. Texts*])

*Coptic*

(357c) The apostles are disturbed by Jesus' announcement that one of them will betray him, and each one asks:

*mê* *anok=pe*
IP 1S=SE.M
Is it me? ($^{S}$Mk 14:19)

(357d) A prophet proclaimed that the Lord will grant the king of Israel the victory in battle:

*pece-akhab=na-f* *ce-nim* *p-et-na-r-šorp* *ebol* *e-p-polumos*
say.PST-N=for-3MS COMP-who COP.M-REL-FUT-do-first out to-DEF.M-war
*pece-p-prophêtês=na-f* *ce-ntok=pe*
say.PST-DEF.M-prophet=for-3MS COMP-2MS=SE.M
Achab said to him: 'Who will start the fight?' The prophet said: 'It is you.' ($^{S}$3Kg 21[20]:14)

(357e) St Peter speaks in Joppa about the resurrection of Jesus which God showed to him openly:

*m-pi-laos* *têr-f=an* *alla* *n-ni-met$^{h}$reu* *nê*
to-DEF$_2$.M-people all-3P=NEG but to-DEF.P-witness.P DEF$_3$.P
*et-a-f-er-šorp* *n-sotp-u* *nce-p$^{h}$-(nu)ti* *ete-anon=pe*
REL-PST-3MS-do-first as-chose-3P PVS-DEF.M-god REL-1P=SE.M
... and not to all the people, but unto witnesses chosen before by God, that is us. ($^{B}$Acts 10:41)

This is due to the specifying semantic character associated with the order S–P in nominal sentences discussed in 3.1.1, which also holds for Later Egyptian and is most frequent when two personal pronouns form a predicative relation (see 1.2.1):[125]

*Late Egyptian*

(358a) It is said in a magical text:
*i͗nk mntk mntk i͗nk*
1S 2MS 2MS 1S
I am you and you are me. (pStrasbourg 23, 2)

*Coptic*

(358b) The psalmist praises the Lord:
*ntak=de ntk-ntak*
2MS=yet 2MS-2MS
But you, you are yourself! ($^{M}$Ps 101 [102]:28 [27])

In the remaining types of Later Egyptian nominal sentences, the identification of the subject is more complex. Unlike in the latter two cases, the difference between grammatical roles does not depend on syntactic position or on lexical characteristics; in the majority of Late Egyptian examples of the bipartite juxtaposition pattern (see 1.2.1), the NP in the first position appears to represent the predicate:

*Late Egyptian*

(359a) The author of a letter starts with an issue of a letter sent to another man that he considered to be insulting and asks:
*i͗s pꜣy-k-bꜣk mrmꜣꜥt i͗w-i͗nk pꜣy-k-rwḏ*
IP POSS.M-2MS-servant N DEP-1S POSS.M-2MS-inspector
Is Merymaat really your servant, with me being your inspector? (*KRI* III 232, 15)

(359b) The heroes of a story are introduced as brothers:
*i͗np rn-pꜣ-ꜥꜣ i͗w-bt rn-pꜣ-šri͗*
N name-DEF.M-great DEP-$N_2$ name-DEF.M-young
The name of the elder was Anubis, while the name of the younger was Bata. (*LES* 9, 10–11)

(359c) A love song identifies parts of a pond with deities:
*ptḥ pꜣy-f-i͗sy sḫmt tꜣy-f-srpt*
N POSS.M-3MS-reed N POSS.F-3MS-lotus leaf

125 Coptic also shows a very specific sense for the pattern *anok pe* 'I am someone (important)', see Layton 2011: §283; Müller in prep. §3.6.1.2.

*ỉ3dt* *t3y-f-nḥm* *nfr-tmmw* *p3y-f-[sšn]* *prš*
N POSS.F-3MS-lotus bud N POSS.M-3MS-lotus blossom.STA
Its reed is Ptah, and its lotus leaf is Sakhmet; its lotus bud is Jadet, and its blossoming lotus is Nefertem. (Mathieu, *Poésie*, pl. 9, 7–8)

(359d) Officials are described who were maimed or handicapped but nevertheless occupied important positions in the administration as examples not to mock humans suffering from bodily detriments. Among them a scribe called Ray, who neither ever moved nor ran since his birth:
*bw-t-f* *k3-t* *pr-ꜥ*
abomination-3MS work-F go_out-arm
Active work was an abomination to him. ([2]*pAnastasi I* 88, 1)

In the first example, the author complains that in his previous letter the addressee had asked about the whereabouts of a servant called Merymaat but not of the addressee's. He uses the interrogative particle *ỉs* to mark the sentence as an inverted polar question (see Collier 2014: 7–40) and takes up the issue about Merymaat by asking whether this person is really the addressee's servant. In the second example above, the narrator elaborates on two heroes who were already introduced at the beginning of the story, and their names are now added to the stock of information concerning them. Finally, in 359c, the various plants and flowers of the pond under discussion are equated with deities that represent contextually new information. However, examples such as 359d might be interpreted in either way, i.e. with "his abomination" being predicate or subject.

In contrast to Late Egyptian, Demotic examples of this same pattern display in the majority of cases the order S–P:

*Demotic*

(360a) Moral precepts state:
*sb-t-dmy* *n3y-f-sre*
wall-F-city POSS.P-3MS-council
The walls of a city are its council-members. (pLouvre N 2414 1, 4)

(360b) As above:
*mn-t-dmy* *ḥry* *ỉw-f-ỉr-wpy-t* *mn-t-ḥ-t-nṯr*
boon-F-city superior DEP-3MS-do-judgement-F boon-F-house-F-god
*wꜥb* *mn-t-ẖ-t* *tp-f* *n-ỉr-wp-t*
sanctuary boon-F-estate be_accustomed.INF-3MS of-do-work
*mn-t-wḏ3* *swṯt-f* *mn-t-prḥḏ* *wꜥ-t-ḏr-t*
boon-F-granary supply.INF-3MS boon-F-treasury IDF.S-F-hand-F

| | | | |
|---|---|---|---|
| *mn-t-nkt* | *sḥm-t-rmṯ-rḫ-t* | *mn-t-rmṯ-rḫ* | *rꜣ-f* |
| boon-F-possession | woman-F-man-wise-F | boon-F-man-wise-F | mouth-3MS |

The boon of a city is a superior who judges justly. A boon of a temple is a sanctuary. A boon of an estate is to get it accustomed to be tilled. A boon of a granary is to supply it. A boon of a treasury is a (single) hand. A boon of possession is a wise woman. A boon of a wise man is his mouth. (Onkhsheshonqy 8, 17–23)

In the first example above, the author of the wisdom text elaborates on issues of the city, and therefore the city's walls can be understood as the subject. The same applies to the repetition of constructions with *mn-t* in the second set of examples. However, the sequence P–S is also attested in Demotic (the topic of the discourse is not stone statuary but man's progeny):

*Demotic*

(361) In the tenth teaching about the education of one's own progeny, the moral precepts start with the insight:

| | | | | | |
|---|---|---|---|---|---|
| *twtw* | *(n)-ỉny* | *šr* | *lḫ̂* | *ỉw-bnp-pꜣy-f-iṯ̂* | *mtr-f* |
| statue | [of]-stone | son | stupid | DEP-NEG.PST-POSS.M-3MS-father | teach-3MS |

A stupid son who has not been educated by his father is a stone statue. (pInsinger 8, 22)

In Coptic, the bipartite pattern is no longer used unless with pronouns.

### 3.2.2 The core semantic functions of Later Egyptian nominal sentences

The standard Egyptological categorisation of the functions of nominal sentences, partially adopted but expanded in the description of Earlier Egyptian (3.1.2), is based on the difference between classifying and identifying sentences.[126] In this model, the subject is either included in a group of entities denoted by the predicate ('X is a scribe') or equated with it ('X is my father'). These different classes, however, seldom have direct formal equivalents in discrete syntactic patterns, and in Coptic any nominal sentence pattern can be used in classifying as well as identifying function. The distinction between the two hinges mainly on the marking of definiteness of the entity of which

126 Polotsky 1971: 421–422, whose remarks go back to Praetorius's description of Ethiopian nominal sentences (Praetorius 1871: 755).

a statement is made and which is identifiable as the subject.[127] Consider the following examples:

*Coptic*

(362a) Bewailing his own calamities, Jeremiah states:

| | | | |
|---|---|---|---|
| *ang-p-rôme* | *anok* | *et-nau* | *e-t-mnt-hêke* |
| 1S-DEF.M-man | 1S | REL-see | OBJ-DEF.F-ABST-poor |

I am the man who has seen the affliction. ($^{S}$Lam 3:1)

(362b) The Jews tell Jesus that they will not stone him because of his good deeds, but they are still angry:

| | | | | |
|---|---|---|---|---|
| *ntok* | *e-ntk-u-rôme* | *k-ire* | *mmo-k* | *n-nute* |
| 2MS | DEP-2MS-IDF.S-man | 2MS-make | OBJ-2MS | as-god |

...because you, although a human, make yourself God. ($^{S}$Jn 10:33)

While in the first example Jeremiah gives his identity as the man who has experienced affliction, as opposed to the rest of mankind who presumably has not, in 362b, the Jews classify Jesus as a human being and therefore consider him a blasphemer deserving death. Yet the grammatical construction is the same in both instances, i.e. a bipartite nominal sentence. Sometimes, however, different diachronic or diatopic variants of the same text display different patterns:

(363a) Jesus asks angry Jews whether they accuse him of blasphemy because he had said:

| | | | | |
|---|---|---|---|---|
| S | *ang-p-šêre* | *m-p-nute* | | |
| | 1S-DEF.M-son | of-DEF.M-god | | |
| B | *anok* | *pe* | *p-šêri* | *m-p$^{h}$-(nu)ti* |
| | 1S | COP.M | DEF.M-son | of-DEF.M-god |

I am the Son of God. ($^{SB}$Jn 10:36 [$^{S}$Quecke vs. $^{B}$Kasser])

(363b) A pagan priest caught by Christians appeals to his deity for help, pointing out:

| | | | | |
|---|---|---|---|---|
| *anok* | *pe* | *pe-k-arkhiereus* | *n-hak* | Ms. M609 |
| 1S | COP.M | POSS.M-2MS-highpriest | of-sober | |
| *anok-pe-k-nok$^{j}$* | *n-arkhiereus* | | | Ms. Ham B |
| 1S-POSS.M-2MS-great | of-highpriest | | | |

I am your sober/great high priest. ($^{S}$Dioscorus of Alexandria, *On Macarius of Tkow*, §5.10 [Johnson 38, 2 vs. 38, 11)

127 As shown unintentionally by Polotsky (1971: 421). It should be noted that indefiniteness does not need to be specified in the 'head' in these cases, as a sentence such as German 'Ich bin *ein* Sohn eines Gärtners/eines Gärtners Sohn' is as classifying as 'Ich bin *der* Sohn eines Gärtners'.

Ex. 363a appears to be an identifying sentence, and although both dialects possess both the bipartite and the tripartite pattern, they use different constructions here. Therefore, the difference cannot be founded on semantic differences inherent to the constructions.

Charting the distribution of nominal sentences with and without a copula in combinations of nouns and (personal) pronouns yields the following table:

**Tab. II.5:** Distribution of copular and non-copular nominal sentence patterns in Later Egyptian

| | −COP | | +COP |
|---|---|---|---|
| | A-B | A-SE | |
| Late Egyptian | | | |
| Pronoun | + | + | – |
| Noun | + | + | – |
| Demotic | | | |
| Pronoun | + | + | + |
| Noun | – | + | + |
| Coptic | | | |
| Pronoun *(personal)* | + | + | + |
| Noun | – | + | + |

As can be seen, the simple juxtaposition of two nouns is falls out of use after Late Egyptian. Hence, any function connected with this pattern must have been taken over by the tripartite construction with a copula. Furthermore, in Coptic, the second position in pronoun+noun combinations is mainly (although not exclusively) occupied by nouns marked for indefiniteness. However, in presence of pronouns the construction A COP B seems to be restricted to definite NPs in the second position. In addition, no examples of IDF-A COP PRN are attested. One could, therefore, formulate the basic rule that in Later Egyptian the pattern A–B is reserved for classifying, and the pattern A COP B for identifying function if pronouns of first and second person are involved. Few attestations with definite nouns in the simple juxtaposition pattern A–B represent an exception to this rule. Moreover, with third-person pronouns, this construction is attested with identifying as well as classifying function.

If both combined participants of a Later Egyptian nominal sentence are nouns, the rule subject-initial > identifying, predicate-initial > classifying, which accounts for most Earlier Egyptian examples (3.1.2), holds reasonably well:

(364) The apostle argues that an outward Jew is not a Jew and outward circumcision is not circumcision:

| | | | | | |
|---|---|---|---|---|---|
| *alla* | *p-iudai* | *et-hêp* | *pe* | *p-iudai* | |
| but | DEF.M-Jew | REL-hidden.STA | COP.M | DEF.M-Jew | |

| | | | | |
|---|---|---|---|---|
| *auô* | *p-sbbe* | *pe* | *p-sbbe* | *m-p-hêt* |
| and | DEF.M-circumcision | COP.M | DEF.M-circumcision | of-DEF.M-heart |

| | |
|---|---|
| *hn-u-pn(eum)a* | *hn-u-shai=an* |
| in-IDF.S-spirit | in-IDF.S-letter=NEG |

... but the inward Jew is the Jew and the circumcision is the circumcision of the heart in spirit and not in the letter. ($^{S}$Rm 2:29)

However, although most predicate-initial examples express classification, counterexamples are also documented:

(365a) An old man is asked to name the child; he writes upon a writing board:

| | | |
|---|---|---|
| *iôhannês* | *pe* | *pe-f-ran* |
| N | COP.M | POSS.M-3MS-name |

His name is John. ($^{S}$Lk 1:63)

(365b) The proverbs warn:

| | | | | |
|---|---|---|---|---|
| *p-bote* | *m-p-cois* | *pe* | *ši* | *snau* |
| DEF.M-abomination | of-DEF.M-lord | COP.M | measure | two |

A double weight is the Lord's abomination. ($^{S}$Prv 20 [23]:17)

The distribution of form and function may again be expressed by means of a table:

**Tab. II.6:** Form vs. function in Coptic nominal sentences

| | | Identification | Classification |
|---|---|---|---|
| Bipartite | | (+) | + |
| Bipartite with subject index | | + | + |
| Tripartite | P–S | (+) | + |
| | S–P | + | – |

It should be added to this distribution that, at least in Coptic, only personal pronouns allow a choice between the bipartite and the tripartite pattern, since nouns do not appear in bipartite patterns of the A–B type. The reason behind this syntactic behaviour seems to be that the two participants of the bipartite pattern constitute a single phonetic unit in most Coptic dialects, which leads to elimination of any vowels except in the main stressed syllable. The outcome of this phonetic evolution may have generated grammatical ambiguity. An examination of data such as the corpus of the Coptic New Testament for a distribution of the two patterns shows that PERS.PRN-DEF-NP (with PERS.PRN largely restricted to first and second persons) appears much less frequently than PERS.PRN COP DEF-NP. Considering only affirmative constructions, the ratio between the two is roughly 1:4 in favour of constructions with a copula against those without such an element. Assuming that a more frequently attested pattern is less marked than its less common counterpart, one might argue that patterns with copula are a less marked option for sentences involving pronouns and definite NPs. Accordingly, despite their conceptually problematic character, the terms 'classifying' and 'identifying' will still be used to describe the semantics of Late Egyptian and Demotic nominal sentences.

Thus, the major functions of nominal sentences in Later Egyptian can be summarised in the following way. *Quality assigning* nominal sentences ascribe a quality to an entity, whereas *identifying* sentences signal that an entity *A* is co-referential and co-extensive with entity *B*. *Classifying* sentences posit an entity as a member of the class exemplified by entity *B*, and *specifying* sentences explicitly restrict the reference to some particular entity.[128] This last function can be equated with the formal pattern of the so-called cleft sentence (see 3.2.2.1–3). The other semantic types are only partially documented in Later Egyptian nominal sentences. Some of their properties are shared by adjectival and adverbial sentences.

### 3.2.2.1 Late Egyptian

*Quality assigning* is the main function of Late Egyptian adjectival sentences (Part III). Since this pattern is recessive, nominal sentences begin to intrude into its functional domain:[129]

(366a) The author of a letter begins his request that the addressee take care of his father with the words:
*yꜣ* *mntk* *nfr*
PTC 2MS good
Indeed you are kind. (*LRL* 48, 15)

128 Note that this use of the term is different from the one employed in Hengeveld 1992: 86.
129 Apparently via the extension 'I am a great one' > 'I am great'.

(366b) In arguing against mocking of the inflicted the author list prime examples of men burdened with bodily afflictions, yet important positions in the administrative hierarchy. He assures his addressee of the latters superiority in strength over them (to mock him instead):
*mntk nḫt-ꜥ ı͗w-k r-ḥdb-w*
2MS strong-arm FUT-2MS FUT-overthrow-3P
You are strong and you will overthrow them. ([2]*pAnastasi I* 96, 3)

For the expression of *classification*, the preferred Late Egyptian construction is the adverbial sentence pattern with the preposition *m*, which has a graphemic variant *n*:

(367a) The man sings the praise of the beauty of his beloved by ascribing floral qualities to parts of her body:
*mnd-s n-rrm-t*
breast-3FS as-mandrake-F
Her breasts are mandrake. (Mathieu, *Poésie*, pl. 8, 11)

(367b) The king of the Hittites addresses his court with a description of the prevailing sad state of affairs:
*ḫꜣs-t=nb m-ḫrw-y ḥr-ꜥḥꜥ-n twt*
land-F=QU as-enemy-P PRP-stand-1P gather.STA
Every land is hostile and jointly opposes us. (*KRI* II 246, 10–13)

(367c) A song of praise to the pharaoh states that the kingship of Horus has been established forever:
*ı͗w-k m-nsw mı͗-(ı͗)mn*
DEP-2MS as-king like-N
...while you are a king like Amun. (*KRI* II 380, 2–3)

As in Earlier Egyptian, classifying nominal sentences are common in Late Egyptian:

(368a) A defendant in a tomb-robbery trial reports that his mother said to a man:
*mntk ı͗ꜣw šꜣšꜣ*
2MS old man silly
You are a silly old man. (*KRI* VI 789, 9)

(368b) Wenamun tells the prince of Byblos:
*mntk mrꜥ mntk bꜣk n-ı͗mn*
2MS as well 2MS servant of-N
And you too are a servant of Amun. (*LES* 70, 4–5)

(368c) Asked about his origins, the disguised prince from Egypt says:
*ı͗nk šrı͗ (n)-wꜥ n-snny n-pꜣ-tꜣ n-kmt*
1S son (of)-IDF.S of-charioteer of-DEF.M-land of-Egypt
I am a son of an Egyptian charioteer. (*LES* 6, 6)

It is noteworthy that in classifying nominal sentences, the noun functioning as predicate is never morphologically marked for indefiniteness, i.e. it never shows the indefinite article.

The expression of *identity* is the exclusive domain of the nominal sentence in Late Egyptian:

(369a) Following the boys request to be told who his father is, his mother said to him: Do you see the blind man sitting beside the gate?:
*p3y-k-it* *p3y*
POSS.M-2MS-father SE.M
He is your father. (*LES* 33, 4)

(369b) The pupil uses nautical metaphors to acknowledge the role of his teacher:
*ink* *p3-imw* *ntk* *p3-ḥmw*
1S DEF.M-boat 2MS DEF.M-oar
I am the boat, you are the oar.
(Teaching of Amunnakht 27 [*ZÄS* 131, 40, 38–39])

(369c) Hori is boasting with his knowledge about Levantine coastal towns mentioning:
*st* *ḥr-ḏd* *ky-dmi* *m-p3-ym* *ḏr-n-mrw* *rn-f*
3P PRP-say other-town in-DEF.M-sea N-of-harbour name-3MS
They say another town is by the sea, Tyros-harbour is its name.
([2]*pAnastasi I* 131, 4–5)

As already noted, Later Egyptian *specifying* nominal sentences are formally the so-called cleft constructions. In Late Egyptian, the structural difference between subject clefts (cleft sentences) and any other clefts, such as object clefts (pseudo-cleft sentences) is maintained:

(370a) A thief testifies:
*ink* *i-wn* *p3y-ḫr*
1S PPA-open DEM.M-tomb
It was me who opened that tomb. (*KRI* VI 811, 3)

(370b) During interrogation, a thief is asked whether he took part in plundering of several tombs; he replied:
*wꜥ-s-t* *wꜥ-ṯ* *t3-wn-n*
IDF.S-place-F single-STA DEF.F-open-1P
It is only a single place that we opened. (*KRI* VI 781, 6)

(370c) The author of a letter tells the addressee not to worry about the people at home, because:
*mntk* *p3-nty-ib-n* *ptr-k*
2M COP.M-REL-heart-1P see-2MS
It is you whom we wish to see. (*LRL* 27, 16)

(370d) The king states that the stela on which his words are written is on the eastern mountain of Akhetaten, and:

| | | | |
|---|---|---|---|
| *pꜣy* | *pꜣ-ir-i* | *ꜥḥꜥ* | *r-ꜥ-f* |
| DEM.M | COP.M-AUX-1S | stand | to-arm-3MS |

It is this one next to which I stand. (*Boundary Stelae*, 90)

The Late Egyptian distribution of patterns and functions may thus be charted as follows:

**Tab. II.7:** Form vs. function in Late Egyptian
(Patterns of lesser frequency are in smaller font size).

| | | |
|---|---|---|
| *Quality assignment* | Adjectival sentence | Nominal sentence |
| *Classification* | Adverbial sentence | Nominal sentence |
| *Identification* | Nominal sentence | |
| *Specification* | Cleft and pseudo-cleft | |

However, the common dropping of the preposition *m/n* in adverbial sentences might signal the start of a diachronic development that eventually led to the demise of the use of this sentence type to express classification (see 3.2.2.2).

#### 3.2.2.2 Demotic

The distribution of patterns and semantic functions in Late Egyptian largely applies to Demotic as well. However, in this stage of the language, the adjectival sentence has been more or less lost from the grammatical system and partially replaced by the residual class of adjectival verbs (see Part III). The nominal sentence now takes over the predication of qualities, continuing the process that had begun in Late Egyptian:

(371a) The guests at a banquet see the debauched harpist and think:

| | |
|---|---|
| *ꜥꜣ* | *pꜣy* |
| great | SE.M |

He is great. (Depraved Harpist 2, 7)

(371b) The lion leaves the jackals, because:

| | | | | |
|---|---|---|---|---|
| *ḥry* | *ꜥꜣ* | *nꜥ* | *pꜣy* | *m-qdy-t-ḏd* |
| lord | great | mercy | COP.M | in-likeness-F-say |

A great lord is merciful, as they say. (Myth of the Sun's Eye 16, 28)

(371c) A mummy label says of a woman who had died at the age of twenty:
*ẖm-ꜥḥꜥ tꜣy*
short-lifetime SE.F
She was short-lived. (Vleeming, *Short Texts* II, #513 B11)

The classifying function is still associated with adverbial sentences with the preposition *m* or *n*. However, the preposition is now often elided, and sentences expressing this particular type of semantics are no longer as common as before:

(372a) A document is dated to the regnal year of the pharaoh:
*ỉw-tmtrys sꜣ-ꜣpyrꜣ n-wꜥb-(n)-ꜣrgsntrs ꜥws ỉrm-nꜣ-nṯr-w-sn-w*
DEP-N son-N as-priest-[of]-N l.p.h. with-DEF.P-god-P-brother-P
*nꜣ-nṯr-w mnḫ-w*
DEF.P-god-P splendid
... while Demetrios, the son of Apelles, was priest of Alexander, l.p.h., with the beneficent sibling gods. (pHauswaldt VI, 1)

(372b) The magician asks:
*nꜣw-pꜣ-16 n-nꜣw-tbew-w*
IP-DEF.M-16 as-DEF.P-avenger-P
Are the 16 the avengers? (pMag. London&Leiden v° 33, 5)

One also witnesses here the intrusion of nominal sentence patterns. In 373, the absolute pronoun in subject position shows that the pattern is not an adverbial sentence with elided *m*:

(373) The queen of the Amazons says to Inaros who has come to her land:
*mtk wꜥ-nṯr ỉỉrḥr-y pꜣ-rmṯ-kmy*
2MS IDF.S-god before-1S DEF.M-man-Egypt
You are a god before me, O Egyptian. (Amazons 6, x+28)

Identifying nominal sentences are common in Demotic, but show a syntactic difference with respect to the earlier stages: in sentences with pronouns, the bipartite pattern is still in use:

(374a) When the hero threatens to report the misdemeanour of the local priests to the regional authorities, one of the priests retorts that this will be to no avail, as he will be put under the speaker's command:
*[ḏd]-bn-mtwk rmṯ ỉn*
for-NEG-2MS man NEG
... for you are no man. (pRylands IX 1, 18)

(374b) A man suffering from an eye disease prays to his god:
*ỉ ỉmn tw-y-gby ḏr-ṯ ỉnk pꜣy-k-bꜣk*
VOC N PTC-1S-weak hand-F.1S 1S POSS.M-2MS-servant

*mir-dy-ʿq-y* *mir-ꜣbḫ* *iḥr-y*
NEG.IMP-let-perish-1S NEG.IMP-forget to-1S
O Amun, I am wretched, but I am your servant. Do not let me perish; do not forget me! (Vleeming, *Short Texts I*, #135, 14–15)

(374c) The deceased is identified with the five members of the divine corporation headed by god Thoth:
*mtwt wʿ irm-2 mtwt 2 irm-3 mtwt 3 irm-4 mtwt 4 irm-5*
2FS 1 with-2 2FS 2 with-3 2FS 3 with-4 2FS 4 with-5
You are one and two. You are two and three. You are three and four. You are four and five. (pHarkness 4, 16)

(374d) Instructions for an amulet against the evil eye call for a depiction of an eye with rays and the caption:
*mtwk pꜣy-byl n-tꜣ-p-t*
2MS DEM.M-eye of-DEF.F-sky-F
You are this eye of the sky. (pMag. London&Leiden v° 20, 7)

When two nouns are combined, the tripartite structure with a copula is now obligatory:

(375a) The main protagonist of a literary text is introduced:
*pꜣdyꜣst sꜣ-ʿnḫššq pꜣ-ʿꜣ-n-mr wn[nꜣ]w-šr n-wʿb-(n)-imnrʿ*
N son-N DEF.M-great-of-ship PRT-son of-priest-of-N
*nsw-nṯr pꜣy*
king-god COP.M
Peteese, son of Onkhsheshonqy the shipmaster, was the son of a priest of Amun-Ra, king of the gods. (pRylands IX 5, 15–16)

(375b) In a marriage document, the future husband declares to his wife:
*pꜣy-t-šr ʿꜣ pꜣy-(y)-šr ʿꜣ pꜣy*
POSS.M-2FS-son great POSS.M-1S-son great COP.M
*ḫn-nꜣ-ḫrṱ-w ntyiw-t-r-ir-ms-ṱ-w=n-y*
in-DEF.P-child-P REL-2FS-FUT-do-bear.INF-3P=to-1S
Your eldest son is my eldest among the children whom you will bear for me. (pChicago OI 25256, 4)

(375c) Glosses explain the sentence 'Left will be exchanged for right':
*wnmy kmy pꜣy smḥ pꜣ-tꜣ-ḫr pꜣy*
right Egypt COP.M left DEF.M-land-Syria COP.M
Right is Egypt. Left is Syria. (pBN 215 r° 2, 12)

(375d) The breath of life and the breath of death unite and take all that there is upon earth:
*mtw-pꜣ-ʿnḫ irm-pꜣ-mwt nꜣw*
REL-DEF.M-life with-DEF.M-death SE.P
... that is to say, life and death. (*Primeval Ocean* fr. 13 2, 5)

(375e) The magician identifies himself as powerful magical being via naming himself:

| | | | | | | |
|---|---|---|---|---|---|---|
| *ank-barbariôth* | *barbariôth* | *ank-peskut* | *iaḫo* | *adônai* | *elôai* | *sabaôth* |
| 1S-N | N | 1S-N | N | N | N | N |

| | | | | | | |
|---|---|---|---|---|---|---|
| *amu* | *eḫun* | *e-pi-kui* | *npou* | *še-anok* | *pe* | *barbariôth* |
| come.IMP | into | to-DEM.M-little | today | for-1S | COP.M | N |

I am Barbariôth, Barbariôth. I am Peskut, Iakho, Adonai, Elôai, Sabaôth. Come to this child today for *I* am Barbariôth!

(OCGreat Mag. P. Paris [*ZÄS* 21, 99, 30–32])

However, the last example, with its difference between bipartite (*ank-barbariôth*) and tripartite patterns (*anok pe barbariôth*), shows already a development visible in full in Coptic and to be described below. Residual uses of bipartite sentences occur only in literary texts:

(376a) Moral precepts warn:

| | | | | |
|---|---|---|---|---|
| *ḫrw-ỉ* | *ḫrw-k* | *ḫr-f* | *n-pꜣ-gby* | *(n)-ḏr-t* |
| voice-1S | voice-2MS | say-3MS | as-DEF.M-weak | of-hand |

'My voice is your voice', says the weakling. (Onkhsheshonqy 23, 16)

(376b) A warning not to speak freely at all times:

| | | | | | |
|---|---|---|---|---|---|
| *ls* | *ḫn* | *rmṯ-swg* | *tꜣy-f-sfy* | *n-šꜥṯ* | *ꜥḥꜥ* |
| tongue | fool | man-stupid | POSS.F-3MS-sword | of-cut | lifetime |

The fool's and the idiot's tongue is his sword for cutting his lifetime.

(pInsinger 4, 5)

Since adverbial sentences with *m*/*n* are rather underrepresented in the data, it is probable that nominal sentences had already usurped their function, anticipating its takeover in Coptic:

(377a) The author of a letter gives advise for proper conduct of the temple business at Elephantine:

| | | | | | |
|---|---|---|---|---|---|
| *ḥtnṯr* | *yb* | *ỉrpy* | *ꜥꜣ* | *pꜣy* | *mỉr-dy-ḫpr-nḏnḏ* |
| temple | N | sanctuary | great | COP.M | NEG.IMP-let-happen-strife |

| | |
|---|---|
| *n-rmṯ* | *ḫn-f* |
| of-man | in-3MS |

The temple of Elephantine is a great sanctuary. Do not let human strife happen within it! (pBerlin P. 15530, x+10–11)

(377b) The author of a letter denies his paternity of a boy and adds:

| | |
|---|---|
| *wꜥ-ḫl-rse* | *pꜣy* |
| IDF.S-boy-foster? | SE.M |

He is a foster-child. (*Krugtexte* A, text 2, 11)

(377c) A note in a medical text explains the character of a medical ingredient:
*wꜥ-ỉny* *pꜣy* *ỉw-f-wbḫe*
IDF.S-stone SE.M DEP-3MS-white
It is a white stone. (pMag. London&Leiden v° 3, 13)

These rather late examples also document the first uses of predicate nouns with the indefinite article in nominal sentences. Apparently due to this reorganisation of functions, late Demotic texts now show tripartite constructions with pronouns alongside the juxtaposition pattern:

(378a) In a recitation over a scarab the magician is to say:
*mtwk* *pꜣy* *pꜣ-mḫrr* *n-ḫstb* *n-mꜣꜥ-t*
2MS COP.M DEF.M-scarab of-lapis_lazuli of-truth-F
You are the scarab of real lapis lazuli. (pMag. London&Leiden 21, 32–33)

(378b) In a gloss explaining a reference to the vulva in a mythical text:
*ỉnky* *tꜣy* *tꜣ-ꜣty-t* *nty-šsp* *tꜣ-mw-t*
1S COP.F DEF.F-vulva-F REL-receive DEF.F-mother-F
*r-ỉr-sꜥnḫ-w* *n-tꜣ-ẖ-t*
REL-AUX-nourish-3P in-DEF-F-womb-F
I am the vulva that receives and the mother that nourishes them in the womb. (Myth of the Sun's Eye 8, 23)

Specification is still expressed in Demotic by means of cleft constructions. The productive cleft pattern has become the former pseudo-cleft sentence, now used for all types of clefts:

(379a) Tabubu's requests were fulfilled when Setne caused a deed of maintenance and a payment of money to be made for her:
*wꜥ-t-wnw-t* *tꜣ-ỉỉr-ḫpr* *ỉr-w* *ꜥn-smy* *nỉm-s*
IDF-F-hour-F DEF.F-REL.PST-happen do.PST-3P report OBJ-3FS
*ỉỉrḥr-stne* *ḏd*
before-N COMP
Shortly afterwards (*lit.* It was an hour that passed), they reported it before Setne, saying... (Setne I 5, 21)

(379b) Moral precepts warn against rushing headlong into an argument with someone more powerful:
*pꜣ-nty-ḥwy-tw-f* *r-pꜣ-nw* *pꜣ-ntyỉw-pꜣ-sḫ̮*
DEF.M-REL-throw-chest-3MS to-DEF.M-lance COP.M-REL-DEF.M-blow
*šm* *nỉm-f*
go in-3MS
He who throws his chest towards the lance is hit by the blow. (pInsinger 4, 3)

(379c) A mythological text states about god Thoth:
*mtwf pꜣ-nty-ṯꜣy* *mtwf pꜣ-nty-dy-t*
3MS DEF.M-REL-take 3MS DEF.M-REL-give-INF
It is he who takes and it is he who gives. (*Primeval Ocean* fr. 13 2, 14)

(379d) In a legal document, the husband grants his future wife:
*mtwt tꜣ-nty-nḥṯ* *r-tꜣ-wḏꜣ* *n-pꜣy-t-ʿqḥbs*
2FS DEF.F-REL-vouch.STA to-DEF.F-rest of-POSS.M-2FS-sustenance
*ntyiw-s-(r)-ḫpr* *ʿwi-i* *mtw-y-dy-s=n-t*
REL-3FS-FUT-happen to-arm-1S CNJ-1S-give-3FS=to-2FS
You have authority over the remains of your sustenance that are on my account and that I will give to you. (pChicago OI 25388, 3)

**Tab. II.8:** Form vs. function in earlier and middle Demotic.

| | | |
|---|---|---|
| *Quality assignment* | | |
| | Adjectival verbs | Nominal sentence |
| *Classification* | | |
| | Adverbial sentence | Nominal sentence |
| *Identification* | | |
| | Nominal sentence | |
| *Specification* | | |
| | Cleft | |

Table II.8 shows that in earlier and middle Demotic, patterns and functions resemble the Late Egyptian situation. Late Demotic, however, anticipates the situation in Coptic (cf. tabs. II.9–10):

**Tab. II.9:** Form vs. function in late Demotic (i = coindexed, S = subject, P = predicate).

| | | |
|---|---|---|
| *Quality assignment* | | |
| | Nominal sentence | |
| Adjectival verbs | PRN-NP<br>$NP_i$-$SE_i$ | $NP_P$-COP-$NP_S$ |
| *Classification* | | |
| | Nominal sentence | |
| Adverbial sentence | PRN-NP<br>$NP_i$-$SE_i$ | $NP_P$-COP-$NP_S$ |
| *Identification* | | |
| | Nominal sentence | |
| NP-*pꜣy* (?) | | $NP_S$-COP-$NP_P$ |
| *Specification* | | |
| | Cleft | |

### 3.2.2.3 Coptic

In Coptic, classifying adverbial sentences with the preposition *m* are no longer productive, and the functions of this construction have been taken over by nominal sentences. We saw above that the use of the adverbial sentence in Coptic is limited to a semantically restricted class of predicates expressing stative location (Part I, 3.2.1), whereas nominal sentences are used elsewhere. Similarly, although residual forms of adjective verbs still exist and are commonly used, they are few in number. Indeed, the expression of qualities had also been taken over by nominal sentences. Also, stative forms of quality verbs are increasingly used.

Both *classification* and *quality assignment* are expressed by means of the same nominal sentence construction, but a split based on the nature of constituents has now evolved within the pattern. In presence of pronouns, the construction takes the form PRN-NP if the pronominal referents are the first and second person:

(380a) The Samaritan woman says to Jesus:
*ntok=de ntk-u-prophêtês*
2MS=yet 2MS-IDF.S-prophet
You are a prophet. ($^{S}$Jn 4:19)

(380b) When God urged Moses to go and report his words to the pharaoh, the prophet demurred:
*anak -u-hak$^{j}$b-smêi*
1S -IDF.S-weak-voice
I am weak-voiced. ($^{A}$Ex 6:30)

(380c) The sons of inferior knowledge are urged:
*ire=k$^{j}$e ntôtn m-p-uôš m-p-iôt ce-ntôtn*
do.IMP=then 2P OBJ-DEF.M-wish of-DEF.M-father for-2P
*-hn-abal mma-f*
-IDF.P-out in-3MS
So you, do the will of the Father, for you are from him. ($^{L}$*EvVer* 33, 30–32)

(380d) Jesus blames the Jews:
*ntetn-n-šêre n-n-er-hotb n-ne-prophêtês*
2P-DEF.P-child of-DEF.P-do.PPA-kill OBJ-DEF.P-prophet
You are children of those who killed the prophets. ($^{M}$Mt 23:31 mae 1)

(380e) The first-created angel Mastêma, i.e. Satan, refuses to worship Adam:
*n-ti-ne-uôšt=en m-pei ce-p-kui=ela-i=pe*
NEG-1S-FUT-worship=NEG OBJ-DEM.M for-DEF.M-small=to-1S =SE.M
*u-lômi=pe anak -u-arkhêplasma*
IDF.S-man=SE.M 1S -IDF.S-first creation
I will not worship this one, for he is beneath me and he is human. I am a first creation. ($^{F}$John Evangelist, *Investiture of Archangel Michael* [Müller 13, 4–5])

(380f) Cain replies to God's demand to be told of the whereabouts of Abel:
*mê anok -p-urit m-pa-son*
IP 1S -DEF.M-warden of-POSS.M.1S-brother
Am I my brother's keeper? ([B]Gn 4:9)

With third-person pronoun referents, the pattern NP–SE is used:

(381a) Shenute argues that during the summer heat people will spend the hottest time in their houses resting. After they have rested, they will resume their work in their houses:
*ešôpe=de te-prô te mogis nse-er-te-u-aprête*
CND=yet DEF.F-winter SE.F hardly CNJ.3P-do-POSS.F-3P-time_span
*n-er-hôb nse-tiuô*
of-do-work CNJ.3P-stop
But if it is winter, they will hardly spend their time of work and rest.
([S]Shenute, *God Who Alone Is True* [L IV 111, 1–3])

(381b) Jesus urges not to swear at all and especially not by Jerusalem:
*ce-t-polis m-p-nak$^{j}$ n-era te*
for-DEF.F-city of-DEF.M-great of-king SE.F
...for it is the city of the great King. ([M]Mt 5:35 mae 1)

(381c) Context broken. Mani must have entered the town of Belapat. Then:
*m-magusaios ntar-u-r-aisth[a]n[e] a[ra-u] e-u-šine*
DEF.P-magicians TEMP-3P-AUX-notice OBJ-3P DEP-3P-ask
*ce-nim=rô pe pei et-a-f-i ahu[n]*
COMP-who=then COP.M DEM.M REL-PST-3MS-come into
*[pace-u]=ne-u ce-p-manikhaios pe*
say.PST-3P=for-3P COMP-DEF.M-N SE.M
When the Magicians noticed that they (the people) were asking: "Who is this one who entered?", they said: "He is Mani."
([L]*Man. Homilien* 45, 11–13)

(381d) Judah tells his brothers not to slay Joseph but to sell him into slavery, for:
*pe-n-son=pe uoh te-n-sarks=te*
POSS.M-1P-brother=SE.M and POSS.F-1P-flesh=SE.F
He is our brother and our flesh. ([B]Gn 37:27)

If, however, nouns are involved, the regularly used pattern was the one of the tripartite one, i.e. $NP_P$-COP-$NP_S$ or $NP_S$-$NP_P$-COP:

(382a) The proverbs state that knowledge of the law is a sign of sound mind:
*u-tako=de ne ne-hioue n-m-para-nomos*
IDF.S-destruction=yet COP.P DEF.P-ways.P of-DEF.P-beyond-law
...but the ways of the lawless are destruction. ([S]Prv 13:15)

(382b) The angel of the Lord tells Tobias and Tobit:
*u-agathon pe smu e-p-nute auô e-cise*
IDF.S-good COP.M bless OBJ-DEF.M-god and to-lift
*m-pe-f-ran*
OBJ-POSS.M-3MS-name
It is good to bless God and exalt his name ... ([S]Tb 12:7)

(382c) In his vision of the Day of the Lord, the prophet lists awe-inspiring phenomena:
*au u-nakʲ pe p-houe m-p-cais*
and IDF.S-great COP.M DEF.M-day of-DEF.M-lord
For great is the day of the Lord. ([A]Jo 2:11 [Malinine])

(382d) The disciples express their gratitude to Mani for explaining to them his advent:
*a-n-cit-s hn-u-aieute a-n-nahte ce-ntak pe*
PST-1P-take-3FS in-IDF.S-increase PST-1P-believe COMP-2MS COP.M
*pprkls=an*
paraclete=again
*pei-abal m-p-iôt p-ref-kʲôlp abal*
DEM.M-out in-DEF.M-father DEF.M-AGT-reveal out
*n-n-et-hêp têr-u*
of-DEF.P-REL-hidden.STA all-3P
We are increasingly acceptive and believe that you are still the 'Paraclete', the one out of the Father and the one who reveals all secrets. ([L]*Kephalaia* 16, 29–31)

(382e) The Psalmist tells that the Lord rescued him from lion cubs. Troubled do the sons of men sleep:
*ne-u-nece hen-hoplon ne men-hen-sate*
POSS.P-3P-tooth IDF.P-weapon COP.P and-IDF.P-arrow
*auô ne-u-les u-sêfe e-s-têm pe*
and POSS.P-3P-tongue IDF.S-knife DEP-3SF-be_sharp.STA COP.M
Their teeth are weapons and arrows and their tongues a sharp dagger. ([M]Ps 56[57]:5[4])

(382f) The righteous and the sinners will each receive their share:
*ce-u-dikaios pe p-c(ai)s auô f-mêie n-t-dikaiosunê*
for-IDF.S-righteous COP.M DEF.F-lord and 3MS-love OBJ-DEF.F-righteousness
... for the Lord is righteous and he loves righteousness... ([M]Ps 10[11]:7)

(382g) God will show his leniency and mercy:
*ce-u-kritês pe p-c(ai)s pe-n-nuti*
for-IDF.S-judge COP.M DEF.M-lord POSS.M-1P-god
... because the Lord our God is a judge. ([F]Is 30:18)

(382h) Pharaoh's daughter found a basket in the Nile with a crying baby inside and said:

| | | | | |
|---|---|---|---|---|
| *u-abal* | *ẖn-ni-alôui* | *nte-ni-hebraios* | *pe* | *p$^h$ai* |
| IDF.S-out | in-DEF$_2$.P-children.P | of-DEF$_2$.P-Hebrew | COP.M | DEM.M |

This is one of the Hebrew children. ($^B$Ex 2:6)

*Identification* is expressed with the tripartite pattern $NP_S$-COP-$NP_P$ if nouns are involved. If the identified entity is a pronoun, the same pattern is used ($PRN_S$-COP-$NP_P$), unless the identification is to a clause-external entity, in which case PRN-*pe* is used:

(383a) As Joab laid siege to Abel Beth Maakah, a wise woman standing on the walls called out to him:

| | | | | | |
|---|---|---|---|---|---|
| *peca-s* | *na-f* | *nk$^j$i-te-shime* | *ce-ene-ntok* | *pe* | *iôab* |
| said-3FS | to-3MS | PVS-DEF.F-woman | COMP-IP-2MS | COP.M | N |

| | |
|---|---|
| *peca-f* | *ce-anok=pe* |
| said-3MS | COMP-1S=SE.M |

The woman said: 'Are you Joab?' He said: 'I am.' ($^S$1Kg 20:17)

(383b) The angel of the Lord reveals himself to Tobit and Tobias saying:

| | | | | | | |
|---|---|---|---|---|---|---|
| *anok* | *pe* | *hraphaêl* | *ua* | *ebol* | *hm-p-sašf* | *n-aggelos* |
| 1S | COP.M | N | one | out | in-DEF.M-seven | of-angel |

| | |
|---|---|
| *et-fi* | *ehrai* |
| REL-carry | up |

| | | | | | |
|---|---|---|---|---|---|
| *auô* | *et-bêk* | *ehun* | *m-p-mto* | *ebol* | *m-p-eou* |
| and | REL-go.STA | into | in-DEF.M-front | out | of-DEF.M-glory |

*m-p-et-uaab*
of-DEF.M-REL-pure.STA

I am Raphael, one of the seven angels who carry up and enter into the presence of the glory of the holy one. ($^S$Tb 12:15)

(383c) After the alleged dead man revealed the plot of the city's Jews against the apostles, Andrew addresses them asking:

| | | | |
|---|---|---|---|
| *nim* | *[t]enu* | *p-et-sôrm* | *m-p-mêêše* |
| who | now | COP.M-REL-lead_astray | OBJ-DEF.M-multitude |

| | |
|---|---|
| *[a]non=pe* | *ce-ntôtn=pe* |
| 1S=SE.M | or-2P=SE.M |

Who now leads the people astray? Is it us or is it you?
($^S$*Acts of Andrew & Paul* [Jacques 212, 231])

(383d) When God asked Moses what he held in his hand, the prophet replied:

*u-k$^j$erôb=pe*
IDF.S-rod=SE.M

It is a rod. ($^A$Ex 4:2)

(383e) The author of the tractate reviles pagan philosophers, who thought that they had attained wisdom although they were only deceived. He says that they not simply did so in minor issues such as appellations or designations, but that the powers themselves seemed to hinder them:
*hôs* *e-ntau* *pe* *p-têr-f* *abol*
like DEP-3P COP.M DEF.M-all-3MS out
... as if they were the totality. ($^{L}$*Tri. Trac.* 110, 4–5 [*NHS 22*, 290])

(383f) In the *Psalms of Thomas*, the temple built by Solomon is described:
*n-ekate* *et-a-u-kat-f* *ne* *n-dikaios*
DEF.P-builders.P REL-PST-3P-build-3MS COP.P DEF.P-righteous
*n-l[a]ksos* *et-šôt-ône* *araf* *ne* *n-aggelo[s]*
DEF.P-mason REL-hew-stone for-3MS COP.P DEF.P-angel
*p-kah* *[m]-p-êi* *pe* *t-mêe*
DEF.M-earth of-DEF.M-house COP.M DEF.F-truth
The builders who built it are the righteous; the masons who hewed stones for it are the angels; the floor$^{(?)}$ of the house is the truth.
($^{L}$*Psalms of Thomas* 222, 20–22)

(383g) In the Sermon on the Mount, Jesus said to his audience:
*ntotn* *pe* *p-hmu* *m-p-kehe*
2P COP.M DEF.M-salt of-DEF.M-earth
You are the salt of the earth. ($^{M}$Mt 5:13 mae 1)

(383h) Isaiah argues that salvation lies in wisdom, knowledge, and piety towards God:
*nei* *ne* *ne-ahôôr* *nte-dikeosunê*
DEM.P COP.P DEF.P-treasures.P of-righteousness
These are the treasures of righteousness. ($^{F}$Is 33:6)

(383i) Gregory has Sarah say:
*p$^{h}$ai* *pe* *pa-šorp* *m-misi* *uoh* *pa-ḫae* *hi-u-sop*
DEM.M COP.M POSS.M.1S-first of-birth and POSS.M.1S-last on-IDF.S-time
This is my first and my last giving birth at the same time.
($^{B}$Ps. Gregory of Nyssa, *De Sacrificio Abraham* [*ROC* 17 406, 5–6])

(383j) In the Catenae, a word from the Gospel is explained:
*pi-soc* *pe* *pi-at-hêt* *ie* *pi-at-kati*
DEF$_2$.M-fool COP.M DEF$_2$.M-un-heart or DEF$_2$.M-un-knowledge
The fool is the stupid or the dumb. ($^{B}$*Catenae* 9)

Thus, the patterns with pronominal entities are not linked to a specific function, whereas those with nouns still differentiate between quality assignment and identification. However, within the pronominal patterns, some constructions seem to contrast in the same function. The patterns PRN-NP and NP=SE apparently contrast with the structure PRN-COP-NP. One could be inclined to explain this co-existence of three opposing patterns as the result of a diachronic evolution: since Coptic displays a general tendency to agglutinative patterns, the PRN-NP-pattern eventually supersedes the other domains. However, an analysis that assumes the spread of the PRN-NP-pattern into other domains would represent a counterexample to developments such as those described above (see 1.1.2.3), in which reduced forms of the pronouns are discarded in favour of the full forms in the PRN-NP-pattern, e.g. *anok -u-rôme* 'I am a human' instead of *ang-u-rôme*. Moreover, it leaves unexplained the occasional *ang=pe* NP examples, which would have to be considered as mistakes. Hence, we should look for a better solution elsewhere.

The simplest way would be to view the patterns as suppletive. Occasionally, texts show contrastive examples such as the following:

(384a) Jesus explains that as long as he is upon earth:

| | |
|---|---|
| *ang-p-uoin* | *m-p-kosmos* |
| 1S-DEF.M-light | of-DEF.M-world |

I am the light of the world ([S]Jn 9:5)

(384b) As above:

| | | | |
|---|---|---|---|
| *anok* | *pe* | *p-uoin* | *m-p-kosmos* |
| 1S | COP.M | DEF.M-light | of-DEF.M-world |

*I* am the light of the world. ([S]Jn 8:12)

(384c) After his punishment of his chosen flock will eventually lead to their repentence, the Lord promises:

| | | |
|---|---|---|
| *au* | *ti-na-coo-s* | *m-p-ete-pa-laos=en=pe* |
| and | 1S-FUT-say-3FS | to-DEF.M-REL-POSS.M.1S-people=NEG=SE.M |

| | |
|---|---|
| *ce-ntak* | *-pa-laos* |
| COMP-2MS | -POSS.M-people |

| | | | | | | |
|---|---|---|---|---|---|---|
| *au* | *ntaf* | *f-na-coo-s* | *ce-ntak* | *pe* | *p-cais* | *pa-nute* |
| and | 3MS | 3MS-FUT-say-3FS | COMP-2MS | COP.M | DEF.M-lord | POSS.M.1S-god |

And I will say to Not-my-people: 'You are my people' and he will say: '*You* are the Lord, my God'. ([A]Hos 2:23)

(384d) The Pharisees revile a blind man healed by Jesus who had asked them if they too were Jesus' disciples:

| | | | | | |
|---|---|---|---|---|---|
| *ntak* | *pe* | *p-mathêtês* | *m-p-etmmeu* | *anan=de* | *anan* |
| 2MS | COP.M | DEF.M-disciple | of-DEF.M-there | 1P=yet | 1P |

| | |
|---|---|
| *m-mathêtês* | *m-môusês* |
| DEF.P-disciples | of-N |

You are the disciple of that one! We, however, are the disciples of Moses. ([L]Jn 9:28)

(384e) Close to his death the patriarch Isaac deliveres a speech and says in it turning to the Lord:
*anok -pe-k-šêri anok -pe-k-bôk anok*
1S -POSS.M-2MS-son 1S -POSS.M-2MS-servant 1S
*-p-šêri nte-te-k-boki*
-DEF1.M-son of-POSS.F-2MS-maid-servant
*anok pe pi-ref-nobi nt$^{h}$ok pe pi-ref-k$^{h}$ô ebol*
1S COP.M DEF$_2$.M-AGT-sin 2MS COP.M DEF$_2$.M-AGT-give out
I am your son, I am your servant and I am the son of your maid-servant. *I* am the sinner and *you* are the forgiver.
($^{B}$Ps. Athanasius, *TestPatr: Isaac* [Guidi 233, 14–16])

Here the difference could well be one between the unmarked pattern in the first example and a marked one that pragmatically focalises the subject in the second. In the fourth example, the syntactic pattern of the first exclamation puts an identifying stress on the initial pronoun, whereas in the following opposing statement a comparable effect is achieved through the left-dislocation of the subject and the use of the clitic *=de.*

For third-person pronominal referents, the bipartite pattern with subject index agreeing in gender and number with the predicative NP is used as the unmarked construction (as in 385a). This contrasts with the tripartite pattern with an initial pronoun (385b). Rare examples of bipartite sentences with an initial third-person pronoun may also be cited (385c, which is actually the only example of this pattern with a third-person pronoun):

(385a) Jesus reasons that the Son has received the authority to give judgement from the Father, for:
*p-šêri m-p-rômi pe*
DEF.M-son of-DEF.M-man SE.M
He is the son of man. ($^{S}$Jn 5:27)

(385b) Jesus exhorts his disciples not to reveal the fact that:
*ntof pe pe-khristos*
3MS COP.M DEF.M-Christ
*He* is the Christ. ($^{S}$Mt 16:20)

(385c) St Paul urges anyone who claims to belong to the Christ to consider:
*kata-t-he e-ntf-pa-pe-kh(risto)s anon pô-f hôô-n*
like-DEF.F-way DEP-3MS-POSS.M-DEF.M-Christ 1P POSS.M-3MS self-1P
Just as he belongs to the Christ, so do we. ($^{S}$2Cor 10:7)

The functional difference between sentences with agreement-marked subject index or copula, such as above, and those with invariable *pe* below may be explained along similar lines, i.e. assuming that the latter are used to put additional pragmatic stress on the predicate:

(386a) St Paul asks the Corinthians rhetorically whether they need letters of recommendation and assures them:
*te-n-epistolê ntôtn=pe*
POSS.F-1P-letter 2P =SE.M
Our letter, it is *you*. ($^{S}$2Cor 3:2)

(386b) Shenute accuses the prince of evil of being wont to announce among his followers:
*ce-t-hae=te e-ntos=an=pe*
COMP-DEF.F-end=SE.F DEP-3FS=NEG=SE.M
... that this is the end, when it is not.
($^{S}$Shenute, *Because of You Too, O Prince of Evil* [Ch 23, 5–7])

(386c) The patriarch John expands on the issue whether anyone would have been able to enter the heavens before the advent of the son of man. He reasons about Mary, the mother of Jesus:
*nim p-et-na-š-kôlu mmo-s ntos pe t-mau*
who COP.M-REL-FUT-can-hinder OBJ-3FS 3FS COP.M DEF.M-mother
*m-p-nute ce-mper-bôk ehun*
of-DEF.M-god COMP-NEG.IMP-go into
Who could have impeded her, – *she* is the mother of God –, saying: 'Do not enter!'? ($^{S}$*Questions of Theodore* [van Lantschoot 42, 14–15])

(386d) The Teacher explains about the four days and four nights, which are likened to light and darkness:
*t-mah-snte n-ušê pe t-hulê*
DEF.F-ORD-two of-night COP.M DEF.F-Hyle
The second night is *the Hyle* (i.e. matter). ($^{L}$*Kephalaia* 26, 11)

(386e) The prophet describes the Chaldeans as a scourge of God and announces:
*t$^{h}$ai pe ti-com nte-pa-nuti*
DEM.F COP.M DEF$_{2}$.F-might of-POSS.M.1S-god
The might of my god is *this*. ($^{B}$Hab 1:11)

As noted above, the diachronic distribution is occasionally uneven, with earlier sources showing the agreement-marked pattern:

(387a) In the background narrative of a story:
*ne-t-p$^{h}$rô=pe*
PRT-DEF.F-winter=SE.M
It was winter. ($^{B}$Jn 10:22)

(387b) As above:
*ne-t-prô=te*
PRT-DEF.F-winter=SE.F
It was winter. ([S/L]Jn 10:22)

In addition, it should be pointed out that whilst examples with coordinated predicates are attested with the copular construction, similar instances with the bipartite pattern in identification function are rare:

(388a) Jesus proclaims to John:
*anok pe alpha auô ô p-šorp auô p-hae*
1S COP.M alpha and omega DEF.M-first and DEF.M-last
*t-arkhê auô p-côk*
DEF.F-beginning and DEF.M-completion
I am Alpha and Omega: the beginning and the end; the first and the last. ([S]Rev 22:13)

(388b) The angel of the Lord speaks to Tobias and Tobit telling them:
*u-agathon pe u-šlêl mn-u-nêstia*
IDF.S-good COP.M IDF.S-prayer and-IDF.S-fasting
*mn-u-mnt-na mn-u-dikaiosunê*
and-IDF.S-ABST-mercy and-IDF.S-righteousness
Prayer and fasting and almsgiving and righteousness are good. ([S]Tb 12:8)

(388c) Clement says that past leaders like Moses or the Apostles never avoided strife in their just cause. Hence:
*n-snêu ntôtne hen-mai-ti-tôn au n-ref-kôh*
DEF.P-brother.P 2P IDF.P-love.PIA-give-strife CNJ of-AGT-emulate
*etbe-n-et-ci aḫun a-p-ucei*
because-DEF.P-REL-take into to-DEF.M-health
Strife-lovers and zealous you shall be, O brothers, because of that which leads to salvation. ([A]1Cl 45:1 [Schmidt 92])

(388d) The psalmist calls out to God to come to his aid:
*ntk-pa-boêthos auô ta-našte* (S ed. Budge)
2MS-POSS.M.1S-helper and POSS.F.1S-strength
*ntak pe pa-boêthos auô ta-nešte* (M ed. Gabra)
2MS COP.M POSS.M.1S-helper and POSS.F.1S-strength
*ntok pe pa-boêthos nem-pa-ref-nahme-t* (B ed. de Lagarde)
2MS COP.M POSS.M.1S-helper and-POSS.M.1S-AGT-safe-1S
You are my help and my strength. (Ps 69 [70]:5 [6])

Note that the Bohairic and Mesokemic versions of ex. 388c above prefer the tripartite pattern. Occasionally, however, syntactic variation cannot be adequately explained:

(389a) On his return with a stranger, who in reality is the archangel Michael, Abraham called out to Isaac and told him to bring a bowl of water in which to wash the stranger's feet, because his heart told him:
*pi-ḫae* *n-sop* *pe* *p$^h$ai*
DEF$_2$.M-end of-time COP.M DEM.M
*ere-pe-k-iôt* *na-hiui* *n-u-môu* *e-u-lakanê*
DEP-POSS.M-2MS-father FUT-put OBJ-IDF.S-water to-IDF.S-bowl
The last time this is that your father will pour water into a bowl.
($^B$Ps. Athanasius, *TestPatr: Abraham* [Guidi 160, 19–20])

(389b) Abraham spoke to his son Isaac again after washing the stranger's feet and said:
*p$^h$ai* *pe* *pi-ḫae* *n-sop*
DEM.M COP.M DEF$_2$.M-end of-time
*ete-k-na-nau* *e-pe-k-iôt* *n-ḫello* *et$^h$-nane-f*
REL-2MS-FUT-see OBJ-POSS.M-2MS-father of-old man REL-good-3MS
This is the last time that you will see your good old father.
($^B$Ps. Athanasius, *TestPatr: Abraham* [Guidi 160, 23–161, 1])

The difference between these two examples is probably one between classification (389a) and identification (389b). The main function of Coptic cleft sentences is specification:

(390a) Both Jews and the gentiles are under sin:
*u-matu* *n-hof* *t-et-ha-ne-u-spotu*
IDF.S-venom of-snake COP.F-REL-under-POSS.P-3P-lip
It is the venom of the asps that is on (lit. 'under') their lips. ($^S$Rm 3:13)

(390b) Future prophets will be expelled from the country, and if one is found, he will deny being a prophet, saying:
*au* *u-rôme* *p-et-a-f-tḫpa-i*
and IDF.S-man COP.M-REL-PST-3MS-beget-1S
... and it was a human who brought me forth. ($^A$Zec 13:5)

(390c) The teacher starts his explanation with the words:
*tiu* *n-iôt* *n-et-šoop*
5 of-father COP.P-REL-be.STA
It is five fathers that exist ... ($^L$*Kephalaia* 34, 19–20)

(390d) The Devil urged Herod to have John the Baptist beheaded:
*ce-ntaf* *p-et-pôlc* *n-hêrôtês* *ela* *e-b-cô*
for-3MS COP.M-REL-split OBJ-N from.2FS DEP-3MS-say
*mma-s* *nê-f*
OBJ-3FS for-3MS

*ce-uk* *eksesti* *nê-k* *n-k-ci* *n-te-shimi*
COMP-NEG possible to-2MS CNJ-2MS-take OBJ-DEF.F-woman
*m-pe-k-san*
of-POSS.M-2MS-brother
... for it is he who separates Herod from you saying: 'It is not meet for you to take your brother's wife!'
([F]John Evangelist, *Investiture of Archangel Michael* [Müller 3, 22–24])

(390e) Jesus states that the works he has to accomplish will testify that:
*p$^h$-iôt* *p-et-a-f-tauo-i*
DEF.M-father COP.M-REL-PST-3MS-send-1S
It was the father who sent me. ([B]Jn 5:36)

As in earlier stages of the Egyptian language, cleft sentences are especially common in interrogative constructions:[130]

(391a) Claiming to be the Messiah, the Devil summons one of his demons to worship him. As he approaches him the Devil shouts at him:
*nim* *p-ent-a-f-nt-k* *e-pi-ma* *ê*
WH COP.M-REL-PST-3MS-bring-2MS to-DEF$_2$.M-place IP
*nt-a-k-i* *ebol* *tôn*
ST-PST-2MS-come out where
*ê* *e-k-kôte* *nsa-nim* *m-pei-ma*
IP ST-2MS-turn after-WH in-DEM.M-place
Who has sent you here? Where do you come from? Whom do you seek here? ([S]*Legend of Jeremia* [*Or* 67, 42 [13], 12–18])

(391b) The doorkeeper finds Marina, disguised as a monk Marinos, lying on the floor of her cell. He asks:
*u* *p-ent-a-f-šôpe* *mmo-k* *pa-son* *marinos*
WH COP.M-REL-PST-3MS-happen OBJ-2MS POSS.M.1S-brother N
What happened to you, my brother Marinos?
([S]*Life of Marina* [Till, *KHML* I, 30, 9–10])

---

**130** Note also the use of cleft sentences with an additional interrogative adverbial expression in the sentence-initial position:

(FNa) The descendants of Joseph address Joshua:
*etbe-u* *u-klêros* *n-uôt* *auô* *u-sk-nuh* *n-uôt*
because-WH [IDF.S-lot of-single and IDF.S-draw-rope of-single
*p-ent-a-k-taa-f=na-n* *e-u-klêronomia*
COP.M-REL-PST-2MS-give-3MS=to-1P to-IDF.S-heritage]
Why is it only a single lot and a single portion that you gave us as inheritance?
([S]Jo 17:14 [Thompson])

(391c) The men of the city counter Samson's riddle with a riddle of their own:

| | | | | |
|---|---|---|---|---|
| *u* | *p-et-holk$^{j}$* | *e-p-ebiô* | *auô* | *u* |
| WH | COP.M-REL-sweet.STA | to-DEF.M-honey | and | WH |

| | |
|---|---|
| *p-et-coor* | *e-p-mui* |
| COP.M-REL-strong.STA | to-DEF.M-lion |

What is sweeter than honey? And what is stronger than a lion? ($^{S}$Jdg 14:18)

(391d) The Lord, angered by humanity's lack of heed, asks his chosen flock:

| | | | |
|---|---|---|---|
| *ô* | *p-et-i-na-ee-f* | *ne-k* | *ephraim* |
| WH | COP.M-REL-1S-FUT-do-3MS | to-2MS | N |
| *ô* | *p-et-i-na-ee-f* | *ne-k* | *iuda* |
| WH | COP.M-REL-1S-FUT-do-3MS | to-2MS | N |

What shall I do to you, O Ephraim? What shall I do to you, O Judah? ($^{A}$Hos 6:4 [Till])

(391e) After a description of God's awe-inspiring might, the Book of Nahum asks:

| | | | | |
|---|---|---|---|---|
| *nim* | *p-et-na-ḫ-ôhe* | *a-ret-s* | *m-p-mto* | *abal* |
| WH | COP.M-REL-FUT-can-stand | to-foot-3FS | in-DEF-M-face | out |

*n-t-f-orgê*
of-POSS.F-3MS-wrath

| | | | |
|---|---|---|---|
| *au* | *nim* | *p-et-na-ḫ-fi* | *ḫa-t-f-orgê* |
| and | WH | COP.M-REL-FUT-can-bear | under-POSS.F-3MS-wrath |

*m-p-f-k$^{j}$ônt*
of-POSS.M-3MS-anger

Who shall endue before his wrath? And who shall withstand the wrath of his anger? ($^{A}$Na 1:6 [Till])

(391f) Jesus asks the high priests and a presbyter:

| | | |
|---|---|---|
| *u* | *p-ete-ten-cô* | *mma-f* |
| WH | COP.M-REL-2P-say | OBJ-3MS |

What do you say? ($^{M}$Mt 21:28 mae 2)

(391g) The narrator tells of a saint who was helped by a stranger in a fight against barbarians:

| | | | |
|---|---|---|---|
| *alla* | *mpe-f-ime* | *hn-u-akribia* | *ce-nim* |
| but | NEG.PST-3MS-know | in-IDF.S-precision | COMP-WH |

| | |
|---|---|
| *p-et-miše* | *ecô-f* |
| COP.M-REL-fight | upon-3MS |

But he had no clear idea of who was fighting for him.
($^{F}$*Mart. Mercurius* [M589 f. 9 v° a24–27 collated])

(391h) St George appears at night to Andrew, asking whether he recognises him. Andrew replies:

| | | |
|---|---|---|
| *u* | *p-et-šop* | *pa-c$^{h}$(oi)s* |
| WH | COP.M-REL-happen.STA | POSS.M.1S-lord |

What is it, my Lord? ($^{B}$*First Wonder of St George* [Budge 44, 22])

(391i) Pisenthius condemns those who are negligent to their own salvation and continue in their sins until their death:

| | | | | | |
|---|---|---|---|---|---|
| *nta-nim* | *kôlu* | *mmo-k* | *e-ci-shime* | *ô* | *p-rôme* |
| PST.ST-WH | hinder | OBJ-2MS | to-take-wife | VOC | DEF.M-man |

| | |
|---|---|
| *šante-k-kô* | *e-k-porneue* |
| LIM-2MS-put | DEP-2MS-fornicate |

| | | | | | |
|---|---|---|---|---|---|
| *ê* | *nim* | *p-ent-a-f-kôlu* | *mmo-ø* | *ô* | *te-shime* |
| or | WH | COP.M-REL-PST-3MS-hinder | OBJ-2FS | VOC | DEF.F-woman |

| | |
|---|---|
| *e-ci-shai* | *kata-p-nomos* |
| to-take-husband | like-DEF.M-law |

| | | |
|---|---|---|
| *ce-nne-r-he* | *e-u-loik$^{j}$e* | *m-pornia* |
| FIN-NEG.OPT-2FS-find | OBJ-IDF.S-excuse | of-fornication |

Who has hindered you to take a wife, a man, so that you stop fornicating? Or who was it who has hindered you, o woman, to take a husband according to the law, so that you do not find an excuse for fornication?
($^{S}$Pisenthius of Quft, *On Onnofrius* [*ROC* 20: 54, 25–27])

Note the parallelism between the socalled Second tense pattern and the cleft sentence pattern in the last example (ex. 391i).

The construction is also used at the inception of pastoral letters[131] and in the expression 'The Lord knows...' instead of the more common *p-nute soun* 'God knows' of private letters:

(392a) Opening of a letter by Besa:

| | | |
|---|---|---|
| *bêsa* | *p-et-shai* | *n-antinoi* |
| N | COP.M-REL-write | to-N |

It is Besa who writes to Antinoe. ($^{S}$*Besa to Antinoe* [Kuhn 95, 14])

(392b) Opening of a letter by Shenute:

| | | | |
|---|---|---|---|
| *sinuthios* | *pi-elakhistos* | *p-et-shai* | *m-pe-f-merit* |
| N | DEF$_2$.M-humblest | COP.M-REL-write | to-POSS.M-3MS-beloved |

| |
|---|
| *n-iôt* |
| of-father |

| | | | | |
|---|---|---|---|---|
| *n-theo-philestatos* | *auô* | *m-makariôtatos* | *apa* | *timotheos* |
| of-God-beloved | and | of-most blessed | Apa | N |

| |
|---|
| *p-arkhi-episkopos* |
| DEF.M-arch-bishop |

It is the most humble Shenute who writes to his dear father Archbishop Apa Timothy, beloved by God and most blessed.
($^{S}$*Shenute Writes to Timothy* II [Munier 95, 6–12])

131 Actual letters, especially from Thebes, seem to prefer the second pattern discussed below.

(392c) Opening of a letter:
*hatre ...* *p-et-shai* *(n)-pe-f-iôt* *paiêu ...*
N ... COP.M-REL-write to-POSS.M-3MS-father N
It is Hatre who writes (to) his father Paiêu.
($^{S}$Crum in Bell, *Jews & Christians*, 92, 1–2)

(392d) The author bewails the lack of a trusted person. He asks the addressee to send someone to him:
*p-cois* *p-et-soun* *ce-nsabl-ce-a-i-tha<r>rei*
DEF.M-lord COP.M-REL-know COMP-except-COMP-PST-1S-trust
*e-te-k-mnt-son*
to-POSS.F-MS-ABST-brother
*ene* *ua-i-hmoos* *kata-ma* *k-na-hee* *ero-s* *e-i-ai* *ebol*
PTC FUT-1S-sit as-place 2MS-FUT-find OBJ=3FS DEP-1S-go out
The Lord knows that had I not put my trust in your brotherliness and lived elsewhere, you would discover that I was leaving. ($^{S}$KSB II #893, 17–21)

(392e) Opening of a letter:
*paniske* *p-et-shei* *m-pa-iot* *apa* *philokse*
N COP.M-REL-write to-POSS.M.1S-father Apa N
It is Paniske who writes to my father Apa Philokse. ($^{M}$KSB II #849, 1–3)

(392f) The *Life* of Apa Hor begins with a letter from Hor to Apa Jeremy:
*hôr* *pi-elakhistos* *p-et-sh̲ai* *erat-f* *m-pa-menrit*
N DEF$_2$.M-least COP.M-REL-write unto-3MS as-POSS.M.1S-beloved
*n-iôt* *et*$^{h}$*uab* *nem-rômi* *nte-p*$^{h}$*-(nu)ti* *apa* *ieremias*
of-father holy CON-man of-DEF.M-god Apa N
It is Hor, the humblest, who writes unto my beloved holy Father, the man of God, Apa Jeremy. ($^{B}$*Life of Hor* [*Mon. Wadi Natrun* I 169, a1–4])

Here is the distribution of nominal sentence types and semantic functions in Coptic:

**Tab. II.10:** Form vs. function in Coptic (i = coindexed, S = subject, P = predicate).

| | | |
|---|---|---|
| *Quality assignment and classification* | | |
| | Nominal sentence | |
| | PRN-NP // NP-SE | $NP_P$-$COP_i$-$NP_{Si}$ |
| *Identification* | | |
| | Nominal sentence | |
| | NP-SE | $NP_S$-COP-$NP_P$ |
| *Specification* | | |
| | Cleft | |

Although still extant in Coptic, adjectival verbs are rather marginalised and limited to an ever receding stock of lexical expressions (see Part III). For this reason, they have not been included in the above table. Similarly, as no distinctive pattern for the expression of the classification function existed anymore (see the introduction to this chapter), characterisation and classification have been merged above.

### 3.2.3 Temporal modification

As in the earlier stages of the language, Later Egyptian nominal sentences are temporally unmarked. However, from Late Egyptian on it gradually became possible to assign past reference to nominal constructions by means of the initial preterit operator *wn-* > *wnnꜣw-* > *ne-*. In Late Egyptian, the use of *wn* is limited in principle to adverbial sentences (as in 393a), but one can find first examples of it with cleft sentences (393b):[132]

*Late Egyptian*

(393a) Disguised as a beautiful woman, Isis tells the lecherous Seth about her supposed background:

| | | | | | |
|---|---|---|---|---|---|
| *kꜣ-y* | *pꜣy-ỉ-nb* | *ꜥꜣ* | *ỉr-ỉnk* | *wn-ỉ* | *m-ḥm* |
| say-1S | POSS.M-1S-lord | great | PTC-1S | PRT-1S | as-wife |

*mdꜣy-wꜥ-mnỉ-ỉḥ*
with-IDF.S-herdsman-cow

Let me tell, my great lord; as for me, I was a wife of a herdsman of cattle... (*LES* 44, 16–45, 1)

132 In view of examples such as FNc below, instances such as FNb appear to involve elision of the *m* rather than of the subject element:

(FNb) The author of a letter urges his addressee not to neglect a certain woman in a manner of one Khonspatjau:

| | | | | |
|---|---|---|---|---|
| *wn-(m)-rmṯ* | *ỉw-f-ḫꜥꜣ* | *nn* | *n-tꜣy-f-sn-t* | *n-ḥꜥ-t* |
| PRT.REL-[as]-man | DEP-3MS-put | neglect | to-POSS.F-3MS-sister-F | of-body-F-3MS |

... who was someone who showed neglect to his own sister. (*LRL* 15, 3–4)

(FNc) People of the royal household involved in a conspiracy against the pharaoh are listed. Among them:

| | | | |
|---|---|---|---|
| *ḫrw* | *ꜥꜣ* | *pꜣybs* | *wn-m-wdpw* |
| enemy | great | N | PRT.REL-as-cupbearer |

The great criminal Paybes who had been a cupbearer. (*KRI* V 360, 3)

(393b) In a fragmentary report dealing with inheritance, a person seems to have paid for a coffin for his stepfather's burial. After a lacuna the text continues:
*ı͗w-wn-ı͗nk ı͗-dd [...]-w m-ḏr-t-f ḫr wn-ı͗nk ı͗-ı͗r [...]*
DEP-PRT-1S PPA-give [...]-3P in-hand-F-3MS PTC PRT-1S PPA-do [...]
... while it was me who had given [...longer lacuna...] they/them in his hand and it was me who had done [...] (KRI IV 161, 3–4)

In Demotic, the use of this operator is extended to all nominal sentences:

*Demotic*

(394a) The pharaoh asks Harsiese about his relationship with Onkhsheshonqy. He replies:
*pꜣy-f-ı͗ṯ wnnꜣw-pꜣ-ı͗ry n-pꜣy-(y)-ı͗ṯ pꜣy*
POSS.M-3MS-father PRT-DEF.M-friend of-POSS.M-1S-father COP.M
His father was my father's friend. (Onkhsheshonqy 3, x+17)

(394b) A priest begins a story to pharaoh about a certain man by introducing him:
*wnnꜣw-rmṯ-ꜥꜣ mšs pꜣy r-ꜥšꜣ-f n-sꜥnḫ*
PRT-man-great very SE.M DEP-be_plenty-3MS as-nourishment
He was a very rich man who had plenty of income.
(pBM 69532, 6 [Tait, *Enchoria* 31])

*Coptic*

(394c) Gesios discovered some old bones washed up to the shore. At night the bones began to talk and related to him the story of their deceased owner, beginning with:
*na-eiote=men n-šorp ne-hen-ebol ne hn-t-lekaonia*
POSS.P-1S-fathers.P=PTC of-first PST-IDF.P-from COP.P in-DEF.F-N
Originally my parents were from Lycaonia.
([S]*Gesios & Isidorus* [*ZÄS* 21, 148, 3–4])

(394d) Anguish and terror made error powerful, but this did not humiliate the Supreme Being:
*ne-u-laue=gar pe pi-nušp mn-ti-bše*
PRT-IDF.S-any=for COP.M DEF$_2$.M-anguish CON-DEF$_2$.F-oblivion
*mn-pi-plasma nte-p-kʲal*
CON-DEF$_2$.M-creature of-DEF.M-deceit
... for the anguish and the oblivion and the creature of deceit were nothing. ([L]*EvVer* 17, 23–25)

(394e) The crowd demanded that Pilate should release Barabbas instead of Jesus; however:
*pai-barrabas ne-u-soni pe*
DEM.M-N PRT-IDF.S-robber COP.M
This Barabbas was a robber. ([B]Jn 18:40)

Note that in the Bohairic pattern A–B COP, the preterite marker *ne-* is almost always placed before the second NP, which betrays the etymological origin of this construction as a bipartite pattern with extraposed NP.

In Coptic, nominal sentences could be temporally defined or modified by embedding them as dependent clauses of the syntactically superordinate form of the verb *šôpe* 'become':

(395a) Jesus Sirach advises people to be firm in understanding:

| | | | |
|---|---|---|---|
| *auô* | *pe-k-šace* | *mare-f-šôpe* | *e-uaa=pe* |
| and | POSS.M-2MS-word | JUSS-3MS-be | DEP-one=SE.M |

And your word, let it be one. ([S]Sir 5:10 [12])

(395b) In a description of the extent of the area settled by the tribe of Manasse it is stated:

| | | | | |
|---|---|---|---|---|
| *auô* | *pe-f-i* | *ebol* | *e-f-na-šôpe* | *e-te-thalassa=te* |
| and | POSS.M-3MS-come | out | DEP-3MS-FUT-be | DEP-DEF.F-sea=SE.F |

And the seas will be its limit. ([S]Jo 17:9 [Thompson])

Examples of this construction are, however, not particularly frequent and apparently limited to the Sahidic dialect.

### 3.2.4 Pragmatics of subordinated nominal sentences

Later Egyptian nominal sentences marked as adjunct clauses by means of the element *ỉw* > *e* are mostly, but not only, limited to concessive clauses:

*Late Egyptian*

(396a) The conjured seed of Horus is told to leave the head of Seth through his ear. With indignation it answers:

| | | | | | | | |
|---|---|---|---|---|---|---|---|
| *isṯ* | *ỉ-ỉr-ỉ* | *pry* | *r-bnr* | *m-msḏr-t-f* | *ỉw-ỉnk* | *mw* | *nṯri* |
| IP | ST-AUX-1S | go | to-outside | in-ear-F-3MS | DEP-1S | water | divine |

Shall I leave through his ear, although I am divine fluid? (*LES* 54, 3–4)

*Demotic*

(396b) The administrative chief of a temple says to a man expecting his revenues from there:

| | | | | | | | |
|---|---|---|---|---|---|---|---|
| *tws* | *ỉw-ỉbd* | *3* | *prt* | *pꜣy* | *mn-bd-t* | *n-tꜣ-šnw-t* | *n-ỉmn* |
| PTC | DEP-month | 3 | summer | SE.M | NEG-barley-F | in-DEF.F-barn-F | of-N |

| | | |
|---|---|---|
| *mn-ḥḏ* | *n-tꜣ-ꜥft* | *n-ḥtnṯr* |
| NEG-silver | in-DEF.F-chest | of-temple |

Behold, even though it is the third month of summer, there is no barley in the barn of Amun, and there is no money in the chest of the temple. (pRylands IX 1, 4–5)

(396c) Moral precepts warn:
*tm-ẖn* *iw-bniw-pꜣ-tꜣ* *in* *pꜣy*
NEG.IMP-enter DEP-NEG-DEF.M-proper moment NEG SE.M
*mtw-pꜣy-k-ḥry* *msd-k*
CNJ-POSS.M-2MS-superior hate-2MS
Do not enter when it is not the proper moment and your superior would hate you! (pInsinger 10, 12)

*Coptic*

(396d) Emperor Diocletian created seventy idols:
*a-f-ti-ran* *ero-u* *ce-nute* *(e)-n-hoine=an=ne*
PST-3MS-give-name OBJ-3P COMP-god DEP-NEG-IDF.P =NEG=SE.P
He called them gods although they are nothing of the sort.
($^{S}$*Mart. St Victor the General* [Budge, *Martyrdoms* 1, 21])

(396e) Shenute argues for proper conduct of life and cites negative examples, including:
*te-shime* *et-cô* *mmo-s* *ce-ang-u-parthenos* *e-uei=an=te*
DEF.F-woman REL-say OBJ-3FS COMP-1S-IDF.S-virgin DEP-one.F=NEG=SE.F
... the woman who says 'I am a virgin', even though she is not.
($^{S}$Shenute, *I See Your Eagerness* [A II 62, 3–4])

(396f) Jesus praises his mother Virgin Mary after her death:
*naiat-u* *n-nu-kibe* *ô* *ta-mau*
blessed-3P as-POSS.P.2FS-breast VOC POSS.F.1S-mother
*ce-a-i-saanš* *ebol* *nhêt-u*
for-PST-1S-feed out in-3P
*e-anok* *p-et-saanš* *m-p-sônt* *têr-f*
DEP-1S COP.M-REL-feed OBJ-DEF.M-creation all-3MS
Blessed are your breasts, O my mother, for I received nourishment from them, although I am the one who nourishes all creation.
($^{S}$*Dormition of the Virgin* [Robinson, *ApGosp* 76, 27–29])

(396g) After Jesus had asked a woman for water, she wondered why he, being a Jew, should speak to her:
*e-anak* *u-shim[e]* *n-[s]ama[ritês]*
DEP-1S IDF.S-woman of-N
... although I am a Samaritan woman. ($^{L}$Jn 4:9)

(396h) Jesus' supplication to save him from death has been heard by the Lord, for he had cherished the Lord:
*keper* *e-u-šêri=pe* *a-f-emi* *e-ti-met-ref-sôtem*
CONC DEP-IDF.S-son=SE.M PST-3MS-know OBJ-DEF$_2$.F-ABST-AGT-hear
*ebol* *ẖen-ni-mkauh* *et-a-f-*$c^{h}$*it-u*
out in-DEF.P-pains.P REL-PST-3MS-take-3P

Although he is the Son, he learned the obedience from the sufferings he underwent. ([B]Heb 5:8)

The concessive function could also be conveyed by a Greek connector such as *kaiper* 'although' or *kaitoi* 'although' without any additional marking of syntactic dependency, whereas the connector *kan* marks both clauses of alternative concessive conditionals. These can be additionally marked as syntactically subordinated (by *e-*):

(397a) John urges his audience to turn to the Virgin and the Apostles regarding the resurrection, because Jesus had appeared to them first:

| | | |
|---|---|---|
| *a-f-uônh=gar* | *e-te-f-mau* | *n-šôrp* |
| PST-3MS-appear=for | to-POSS.F-3MS-mother | as-first |

| | | | |
|---|---|---|---|
| *kaiper* | *p-et-prepei* | *pe* | *pai* |
| CONC | DEF.M-REL-appropriate | COP.M | DEM.M |

In fact, he appeared first to his mother; although this is appropriate.
([S]John Chrysosthom, *On Resurrection & the Apostles* [Depuydt, *Homiletica* 64, 29–30])

(397b) Clement says that the Christ did not emerge in boastful splendour:

| | | |
|---|---|---|
| *kaiper* | *e-un-kʲam* | *mma-f* |
| CONC | DEP-PTC-force | in-3MS |

... although he could have... ([A]1Cl 16:2 [Schmidt])

(397c) The author of the encomium points out that the body of Theodore the General, unlike that of Theodore the Oriental, was not buried in Antioch but taken to Egypt:

| | | | | |
|---|---|---|---|---|
| *keper* | *u-kahi* | *n-šemmo=an=pe* | *alla* | *p-kahi* |
| CONC | IDF.S-land | of-alien=NEG=SE.M | but | DEF.M-land |

| |
|---|
| *m-pe-f-iôte=pe* |
| of-POSS.M-3MS-father=SE.M |

... although it is not a foreign land, but it is his father's land.
([B]Theodore of Antioch, *On the Theodores* [*AM* II 103, 10–11])

(397d) Constantine urges against bad or false measures as God knows about it:

| | | | |
|---|---|---|---|
| *kan* | *e-u-sukôstatês=pe* | *kan* | *u-pragmateutês=pe* |
| CONC | DEP-IDF.S-public_weigher=SE.M | CONC | IDF.S-merchant=SE.M |

| | | | | |
|---|---|---|---|---|
| *kan* | *u-boêthos=pe* | *kan* | *u-apaitêtês=pe* | *kan* |
| CONC | IDF.S-helper=SE.M | CONC | IDF.S-claimant=SE.M | CONC |

| | | | |
|---|---|---|---|
| *ua=pe* | *n-time* | *e-f-hmoos* | *e-f-sunallasse* |
| one=SE.M | of-village | DEP-3MS-sit | DEP-3MS-change |

| | | | | |
|---|---|---|---|---|
| *kan* | *ua=pe* | *e-f-ti-lau* | *n-eidos* | *ebol* |
| CONC | one=SE.M | DEP-3MS-give-any | of-payments | out |

... be it a public weigher, a merchant, an auxiliary, a claimant, a villager who sits and changes, or one who sells some payment...
([S]Constantine of Assiut, *On Athanasius* ed. Orlandi 34, 19–22)

(397e) An invoked magical power is told to protect a woman and the child she is pregnant with:

| | | | |
|---|---|---|---|
| *kan* | *u-haot=pe* | *kan* | *u-simi=te* |
| CONC | IDF.S-male=SE.M | CONC | IDF.S-female=SE.F |

... be it male or female... (FKropp, *Zaubertexte* I, 17, 5)

(397f) Theodore reacted to Pachom's injunction:

| | | | | | |
|---|---|---|---|---|---|
| *kan* | *u-kuci* | *pe* | *pai-hôb* | *kan* | *u-ništi=pe* |
| CONC | IDF.S-small | COP.M | DEM.M-thing | CONC | IDF.S-great=SE.M |

| | |
|---|---|
| *nn-a-uah-tot-ø=ce* | *e-ai-f* |
| NEG.FUT-1S-put-hand-1A=PTC | to-do-3MS |

Whether this thing is small or great, I will never do it again.

(B*V.Pachom* [Lefort 86, 2–3])

# 4 Negation

## 4.1 Earlier Egyptian

The negation of the Earlier Egyptian nominal sentences could be achieved simply by prefixing the negator *n* to the construction:

(398a) A diagnosis in a medical text after a description of certain symptoms:
*n-ḫ-t=pw*
NEG-thing-F=SE
It is not anything. (pEdwin Smith 15, 15)

(398b) After promising to perform a certain task, the author of a letter adds a self-mocking comment:
*n-qs(n)=pw* *m-rꜣ* *ḏd*
NEG-difficulty=SE in-mouth speaker
It is not a difficult thing in the mouth of the speaker. (pUC 32213, r° 17)

(398c) Sinuhe questions the motives of the Goliath of Retenu who has challenged him to a duel[133]:
*[n]-rḫ-i͗=sw* *n-i͗nk=tr* *smꜣ-f*
NEG-know-1S=3MS NEG-1S=PTC acquaintance-3MS
I do not know him; I am not even his acquaintance. (Sin B, 114)

(398d) Sinuhe is brought before the king and the royal children, but has changed greatly:
*ḏd-i͗n-sn* *ḫft-ḥm-f* *n-ntf=pw* *m-mꜣꜥ-t*
say-SEQ-3P before-majesty-3MS NEG-3MS=SE in-truth-F
*i͗ty* *nb-i͗* *ḏd-i͗n* *ḥm-f* *ntf=pw* *m-mꜣꜥ-t*
sovereign lord-1S say-SEQ majesty-3MS 3MS=SE in-truth-F
Thereupon they said to his majesty: 'It is not him in reality, O sovereign our (lit. 'my') lord!'. But his majesty said: 'It is really him'.
(Sin B, 266–68)

In ex. 398c the second position clitic particle *=tr* does not intervene between *n* and the following absolute pronoun, probably showing that the negative element

133 It should be noted that the negation *n* before the absolute pronoun could also represent an alternative writing of the interrogative element (*i͗*)*n*; this was the interpretation adopted by the New Kingdom editor of the text in the Ashmolean Ostracon version of Sinuhe (AO 45, *i͗ni͗w i͗nk pꜣ-wn smꜣ*).

https://doi.org/10.1515/9783110409895-009

formed a prosodic unit with the following lexeme. Examples such as the above are, however, relatively rare. Much more commonly, the negation of nominal sentences was effected by using the discontinuous negation *n...=is*, where *=is* is apparently the same element used as a marker of generic semantic dependency in the early language (see e.g. 2.3.1). Like *=pw*, *=is* is a second position clitic and precedes the latter. The constituent parts of this negation enclose the first prosodic unit of the sentence, e.g. in bipartite sentences with the subject element *=pw* (for the prefix status of *n*, see below):

(399a) The king is told to throw off his bonds at rebirth:
*n-q3s-w=is=p(w)* *n3p-w=pi* *n-w-nbtḥwt*
NEG-bond-P=NEG=SE tress-P=SE of-P-N
For they are not bonds; they are tresses of Nephthys. (PT 1363c)

(399b) Meryra-nefer ends his account of his agricultural achievements:
*n-gm-t-n(-i)=is=pw* *m-ˁ-ḥr(w)tp* *wn*
NEG-find.REL-F-PST[-1S]=NEG=SE in-hand-chief:P AUX.PP
*m-sp3-t=tn* *ḥr-ˁ-w(y)*
in-nome-F=DEM.F on-arm-DU
It is not what I found (done) by other chiefs who had lived in this nome earlier. (*Urk.* I 254, 10)

(399c) The deceased says that he knows the magical essence of a certain object:
*ḥ3y-t=tw=pw* *n-t-skr* *n-t-nbt-f* *ḏs-f*
skin-F=DEM.F=SE of-F-N of-F-smelt.INF-3MS self-3MS
*n-nby-t* *ḥm-w-t-f=is=pw*
NEG-smelt.REL-F craftsman-P-F-3MS=NEG=SE
It is this 'skin' of Sokar of his own smelting; it is not what his craftsmen smelt. (CT VI 284a–b)

(399d) The author of a letter to the dead protests his innocence of injuring a certain third party:
*in=is* *qd-f* *dr=sw* *ḏs-f* *sk*
PTC=PTC character-3MS suppress.PPA=3MS self=3MS PTC
*n-ḫpr-n=is* *ḫpr* *r-f*
NEG-happen-PST=NEG happen.PPA to-3MS
*n-ˁ-n(-y)-b3k-im* *n-ḏr=is=pw*
through-arm-of[-M]-servant-there NEG-limit=NEG=SE
*n(-y)-ḫpr-t=nb* *sk* *n-ink=is* *p3-wdt*
of[-M]-happen.IP-F=QU.M PTC NEG-1S=NEG DET.M-inflict.PPA
*sṯ[3w-f]* *iw* *ir-n* *k-w* *ḫr-ḥ3t-b3k-im*
injury-3MS AUX do-PST other-P under-front-servant-there

It was his own character that brought about his suppressing; what happened to him happened not through the agency of yours truly. This is not the end of all that may happen, however – but it was not me who inflicted his injury. Others acted before yours truly.

(Nagaʿ ed-Deir 3737, 3–5)

(399e) The road next to the house of the villain Nemtynakht is described:

*ḥns=pw*    *n-wsḫ=is=pw*
narrow=SE    NEG-wide=NEG=SE
It was a narrow one; it was not a wide one.    (Peas R, 7.4)

In the following unique instance the negative relative adjective *iwt-* 'which (is) not' appears with *=is*:

(400) Nika-ankh ordains his funerary-priest not to use his property for other purposes; however:

*ir*    *iṯ-f=sn*    *(r-)kꜣ-t=nb-t*    *iwt(-t)*    *prtḫrw=n(-i)=is=pw*
CND    take-3MS=3P    [to]-task-F=QU-F    REL.NEG[-F]    oblations=to[-1S]=NEG=SE
*n*    *rdi-n(-i)*    *sḫm-f*    *m{m}-ḥm-kꜣ-ipn*
NEG    give-PST[-1S]    powerful-3MS    in-priest-soul-DEM.P
*r-kꜣ-t=nb-t*    *ḫꜣw-prtḫrw(-i)*
to-work-F=QU-F    above-oblations[-1S]
If he takes it for any other purpose than to make funerary oblations to me, I do not allow him to have authority over these soul-priests in any work in addition to my funerary oblations.    (*Urk.* I 162, 16–18)

Examples of bipartite sentences with absolute personal and demonstrative pronoun subjects and without *=pw* occur as well:

(401a) The deceased asserts his preparedness for the afterlife:

*n-ink=is*    *mt*    *ḫm*    *rꜣ-f*    *ink*    *rḫ*
NEG-1S=NEG    dead    ignorant.PPA    spell-3MS    1S    know.PIA
*tp-tꜣ{-f}*    *sḫꜣ*    *imn-t*
upon-earth    remember.PPA    west-F
I am not one dead who is ignorant of his spell; I was one knowledgeable on earth and who remembered the West.

(CT VII 18w–y)

(401b) Heqanakhte exhorts his folk to greater diligence in troubled times:

*n-rnp-t=is*    *nꜣ*    *n-t-bꜣg*    *in*    *s*    *ḥr-nb-f*
NEG-year-F=NEG    DEM.M    of-F-lax.INF    AGT    man    on-lord-3MS
This is not a year for a man to be lax concerning his lord.

(Heqanakhte I, rº 14)

Examples of tripartite sentences are less frequent:

(402a) The peasant chastises the high steward:
*n-wr=is=pw* *wr* *im* *ꜥwn-ib*
NEG-chief=NEG=COP chief there greedy-heart
A chief who is greedy is not (really) a chief. (Peas B1, 196)

(402b) The peasant asks the high steward:
*n-iw=is* *iwsw* *gsꜣ-w*
NEG-wrong=NEG balance tilt.PPA-M
Is a balance that tilts not an aberration? (Peas B1, 126–27)

(402c) Mereri says that the achievements that he has described are not simply something that is commonly purported to be true in tomb inscriptions:
*n-nw=is=pw* *ḏd* *m-iꜣ[wt* *ẖrtnṯr]*
NEG-DEM.P=NEG=COP say.INF as-offices necropolis
This is not to speak as 'necropolis offices'. (*Dendereh* pl. 8, top 5)

Notice the P–S vs. S–P order in the first and last sentences. Of the possessive pattern with *n-* there exists one negated example each with a clitic personal pronoun and an absolute personal pronoun:

(403a) In an obscure context:[134]
*n-n=wi=is* *spꜣ-t*
NEG-DPR=1S=NEG district-F
I do not belong to the district. (CT III 390e/S1C)

(403b) The deceased addresses a hostile entity[135]:
*n{n}-ink=is* *rꜣ-k*
NEG -1S=NEG mouth-2MS
Your spell is certainly not mine. (BD 40/*Tb* II, 40, 8/Ba)

This seems to show that the construction is indeed a nominal rather than an adjectival sentence (see 1.1.1). Abnormal positioning of the element *=is* is rare;

134 *n-n=wi* is spelled , i.e. *n* + *nw* + *wi*, showing the phonological merging of the negation and the clitic pronoun. Cf. the practise of writing the corresponding third-person *n=sw* with the extra 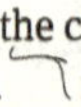 *ns* in the same position (1.1.1 and ex. 16 above).

135 This example, which derives from a Nineteenth Dynasty source, is probably slightly corrupt, but the same holds also for the variants of this passage. E.g. the excellent Eighteenth Dynasty papyrus of Nu (BM EA 10477) has here *nn ink nb r-k*, which appears quite garbled.

in the following example, both clitics =*is* and =*pw* exceptionally split up a direct genitive:

(404) Hapdjefa stresses his legal right to the property he is distributing in his funerary contract:

*mṯn* *ḫ-t-i=pw* *n-w-pr* *it-i* *n-ḫ-t=is=pw*
PTC thing-F-1S=SE of-P-house father-1S NEG-thing-F=NEG=SE
*pr* *ḥꜣtyꜥ*
house mayor
Look, this is my property of my paternal inheritance; it is not property of the mayor's office. (Siut I, 288)

Sometimes =*pw* is omitted in the negative:

(405a) Having said that defenders of his boundary are his true heirs, Senwosret III adds:

*ir=grt* *fḫ-t(y)-fy=sw* *tm-t(y)-f(y)=ꜥḥꜣ*
PTC=PTC abandon.REL-FUT-AGR=3MS NEG.AUX.REL-FUT-AGR=fight.NC
*ḥr-f* *n-sꜣ-i=is* *n-ms-t(w)-f=is=n-i*
on-3MS NEG-son-1S=NEG NEG-bear-PASS-3MS=to-1S
But who will abandon it and not fight for it; he is not my son and not born to me. (Berlin 1157, 17–18)

(405b) Senwosret III gives his assessment of Nubians in general:

*n-rmṯ=is* *n-t-šft=st*
NEG-people=NEG of-F-respect.INF=3C
They are not people deserving respect. (Berlin 1157, 11)

There are no examples of *n*...=*is* co-occurring with second position clitics other than =*pw*. It is thus unknown whether the negation *n* was prefixed to the following word or not – or, to put it another way, whether a hypothetical construction with such a particle would have appeared as **n*=PTC *N*=*is*=*pw* or as **n* *N*=PTC=*is*=*pw*. Yet in Later Egyptian there is evidence of the prefixal character of the diachronic successor of *n* (4.2.1). Perhaps the latter had this status in the earlier language as well.

The variation in nominal sentences (and elsewhere) between the simple *n* and the discontinuous negation *n*...=*is* has been much discussed among Egyptological linguists. Until recently, the most widely accepted theory connected this to the assumed character of *n* as a wide scope *contradictory* negation that reversed the polarity of the predicative relation expressed by the proposition, as opposed to *n*...=*is*, which was seen as a limited scope *contrary* negation.[136] It was argued, mostly on basis of verbal sentences such as that in ex. 405a above, that the negative scope of *n...=is* did not include the relation between the subject and predicate, but that the sentences actually maintained their affirmative polarity. To use classical terminology, the negation was a 'term negation', i.e. the negative predicate of an affirmative sentence (Horn 2001: 14–18). Accordingly, e.g. in 405a, the literal translation of the proposition would have been 'he is a not-my-son', but a son of someone else, and similarly in ex. 404 'It is not-property of the governor', but rather some other type of property. Since the polarity of the proposition was not reversed, *n...=is* created a ready sense of pragmatic contrariety, which could be further elaborated co-textually:

(406a) The deceased is told:
*n-ḥs* *rn-k=is* *rꜥ* *rn-k*
NEG-excrement name-2MS=NEG N name-2MS
'Excrement' is not your name; your name is Ra. (CT V 30b–c)

(406b) The deceased says to a divinity:
*irw-k=pw* *n-irw-i=is=pw*
form-2MS=SE NEG-form-1S=NEG=SE
It is your form, not mine. (CT VI 332k–l)

(406c) A statement by the tomb owner:
*ink* *mrr-i* *wnm* *dg-f* *n-ink=is* *wnm* *ꜥfn-w*
1S love.PIA-M eat.INF see-3MS NEG- 1S=NEG eat.PIA blind-STA
I am one who wants to eat when he sees. I am not one who eats blindfolded. (*Dendereh* pl. 25B)

The contrary effect may at times be of a rather subtle pragmatic variety:

(407) The soul deplores the man's submissive attitude:
*n-ntk=is* *s* *iw-k=tr* *ꜥnḫ-t(i)*
NEG-2MS=NEG man DEP-2MS=PTC live-STA
You are not really a man ('you are a not-man'), although you are, oddly, alive. (Man and Ba 31–32)

The argument was, in other words, that in Earlier Egyptian nominal sentences with the negation *n...=is* were, in fact, affirmative propositions whose predicate was a negative term. This analysis has been recently disputed, and

136 See Loprieno (1991a) as well as Horn (2001: 6–35) for a discussion of this difference.

it is now argued that in nominal (and verbal) sentences negated with *n...=is* the predicative relation is indeed under the scope of the negation, but that the element *=is*, analysed now as a pragmatic restrictor, represents a formal means of inviting hearers to infer the focal contrary reading from the contradictory predicative negation (Collier 2016). That is, e.g. in 401b, the semantic value of the construction is ['This is a year of laxness' is false], but the restrictor *=is* represents a grammatical signal that the pragmatic pivot of the proposition is the genitival phrase *n-t-bꜣg* 'of laxness' on which the sense of contrariety rests. On the whole, the new hypothesis of *n...=is* in general and its use in nominal sentences in particular seems persuasive seeing that the earlier analysis of this negation must argue that more than 85% of apparently negated Earlier Egyptian nominal sentences are in fact affirmative. This seems somewhat unlikely. Similarly, the presence at the head of the construction of the negator *n*, which is the most common Egyptian negation, renders the earlier view intuitively unattractive. Nevertheless, many questions remain unsolved and the issue is far from being settled. For example, the new analysis of *n...=is* would seem to give reasons to expect that *adverbial* sentences be negated using this pattern, since their predicate is surely the pivot on which the (truth value of the) proposition hinges. Yet as seen in Part I, 4.1, this is not the case. The earlier hypothesis would seem to get over this difficulty by the idea that *n...=is* does not negate the predicative relation. As for nominal sentences in particular, sometimes the earlier analysis still appears to make better predictions on the data. For example, although there are, strangely, no examples of negated pseudo-cleft or future cleft sentences, *n...=is* is also the negation of present and past cleft sentences and the 'participial statement' in general:

(408a) Osiris is addressed on behalf of the king:

| *n-in=is* | *N* | *dbḥ* | *mꜣ-f=ṯw...* | *in* | *zꜣ-k* |
|---|---|---|---|---|---|
| NEG-PTC=NEG | N | ask.PIA | see.SUB-3MS=2MS | PTC | son-2MS |

| *dbḥ* | *mꜣ-f=ṯw* |
|---|---|
| ask.PIA | see.SUB-3MS=2MS |

It is not this King N who asks whether he may see you... it is your son who asks whether he may see you. (PT 1128a–1129a/P)

(408b) In a broken context:

| *n-in=is* | *rʿ* | *pr* | *m-ḥtrw* |
|---|---|---|---|
| NEG-PTC=NEG | N | go.PPA | from-yoke |

It is not Ra who went forth from the yoke. (CT VII 241k)

In cleft sentences negated with *n…is* the actor marker *in* may at times be omitted[137]:

(409) The deceased says:

*n=is* *it-i* *rdi=n-i* *n=is* *mw-t-i*
NEG=NEG father-1S give.PPA=to=1S NEG=NEG mother-F-1S
*rdi=n-i*
give.PPA=to-1S
*in* *iwʿ=pw {pw}* *ʿꜣ* *knst* *swt* *rdi=n-i=s(y)*
PTC heir=DEM.M great N 3MS give.PPA=to-1S=3FS
It was not my father who gave (something) to me; it was not my mother who gave (something) to me. It was rather this great heir of Kenset; it was he who gave it to me. (CT III 336f–i)

In one Pyramid Texts passage, simple *n* occurs in what appears to be a negated example of the sort of archaic cleft sentence with an un-introduced noun subject discussed in 3.1.3[138]:

(410) The king has the means of passing the waterways of the hereafter:

*n* *ḥr* *sḏr* *ḫꜣ-mr* *n* *ḏḥwty* *iw-y*
NEG N sleep.PIA behind-canal NEG N stranded-STA
*n=ḥm* *iwi-w* *N=pn*
NEG=PTC stranded-PROSP N=DEM.M
It is not Horus who has to sleep behind the canal; it is not Thoth who is stranded. Truly this King N will not be stranded (either). (PT 1429d–e/P)

It is notable that the participial predicate is never negated by the auxiliary verb *tm* (or *nt-y n*) otherwise used to negate participles and other relative verb forms (i.e. there are no examples of a construction such as **in N tm sḏm*). This appears to be in keeping with the hypothesis that in a sentence negated by *n…=is* the predicate is a negative term, which is tantamount to saying that a cleft sentence such as *in n N=is sḏm* is already of the form 'It is X who not-hears'. However, as seen in 3.1.3, in participial statements with absolute pronouns that are not functional clefts, the clause following the pronoun could be negated.

137 A rather different analysis is proposed by Loprieno (1991a: 219; 1995: 128). The view expressed here follows Borghouts (2010: §104.e.ii).

138 Alternatively, the construction may be analysed as containing stative predicates negated 'directly' with *n*.

In texts dating to the Seventeenth and early Eighteenth Dynasties, the *n-* of *n…=is* is often written *nn*:

(411a) King's words at the installation of the vizier:

*mk ir ṯꜣty mk nn-bnri=is=pw mk dḥr=pw mi-wšdf*
PTC PTC vizier PTC NEG-sweet=NEG=SE PTC bitter=SE like-gall
Now, as for the vizierate, it is not a sweet one. Rather, it is bitter as gall. (*Urk.* IV 1087, 7–9)

(411b) The magician has just told of a powerful charm certain to interest the king; however:

*ḏd-in ḏdi ity ꜥws nb-i mk nn-ink=is*
say-SEQ N sovereign l.p.h. lord-1S PTC NEG-1S=NEG
*inn=n-k=sy ḏd-in ḥm-f in m=rf*
bring.PIA=to-2MS=3FS say-SEQ majesty-3MS PTC WH=PTC
*in-f=n-i=sy*
bring.PROSP-3MS=to-1S=2MS
*ḏd-in ḏdi*
say-SEQ N
*in smsw n(-y)-pꜣ-ẖrd-w 3 nty m-ẖ-t n-rdḏdt*
PTC old of-DEM.M-child-P 3 REL in-womb-F of-N
*in-f=n-k=sy*
bring.PROSP-3MS=to-2MS=2FS
But then Djedi said: 'O sovereign l.p.h. my lord, it is not me who can bring it to you'. 'Who then will bring it to me?' replied his majesty. Then said Djedi: 'It is the eldest of the three children who are in the womb of Redjedet who will bring it to you'. (pWestcar 9, 5–8)

(411c) Ptahhetep's advice concerning the treatment of a disobedient heir:

*rwi-k=sw nn-sꜣ-k=is=pw*
depart.SUB-2MS=3MS NEG-son-2MS=NEG=SE
*nn-ms-n-tw-f=is=n-k*
NEG-bear-PST-PASS-3MS=NEG=to-2MS
You should exclude him; he is not your son and was not born to you (cf. ex. 405). (Ptahhetep 213–14/$L_2$)

The first examples of this change are found already in the Coffin Texts:

(412) The deceased states his mastery over the waters of the yon realm:

*nn-ink=is=pw iw*
NEG-1S=NEG=COP stranded.PPA
I am not one stranded. (CT III 76h/$\mathrm{S10C}^{a}$)

It has been argued that this shift provides an example of the so-called O–E drift affecting 'weak' contradictory negations such as *nn* (which, although sometimes viewed as contrary, is surely contradictory in character) that merely represent the polar opposite of the affirmative 'A is not B'. These have a tendency of being replaced by 'strong' contrary negations 'A is not-B' that logically entail contrariety ('A is not-B' entails 'A is not B' but not vice versa; Horn 2001: 17; Loprieno 1991a: 221, 229–30).[139] Nevertheless, the correctness of this claim depends on whether or not *n...=is* be analysed as a specialised negation of contrariety. In fact, in nominal sentences the form *nn...=is* is undoubtedly simply a new way of writing of an old negation. *n* is often written *nn* also in bipartite *pw*-sentences where the element *=is* is absent:

(413a) Paheri maintains that his autobiography is edifying and has a soothing effect:
*nn* *sḫwrỉ* *nn* *sḫwn* *ỉm-f* *nn-ꜥḥꜣ=pw*
NEG vilification NEG dispute in-3MS NEG-fight.INF=SE
*ḥnꜥ-k-y*
with-another-M
In it there is no vilification, no dispute in it; it is not fighting with another. (*Urk.* IV 122, 13–14)

(413b) Thutmosis III assures his audience of the exactitude of his words:
*nn-ỉwms=pw*
NEG-untruth=SE
It is not a lie. (*Urk.* IV 808, 13)

In some approaches, constructions such as these are viewed as lexicalised or directly quoted paratactic elements not syntactically subordinate to *=pw* (e.g. 413b would read 'this means: "there is no lie"'), in others as bipartite nominal sentences with negative adverbial or existential sentences subordinated as the predicate complement of *=pw* ([*nn NP* (*m-pr*)]=*pw*), and in others still as complexes where bipartite nominal sentences serve as a subject complement of the 'negative existential predicate' *nn* (*nn* [*NP=pw*]; see Jansen-Winkeln 1996a: 46–47; Vernus 1994: 344; Gilula 1970: 209, respectively). However, it has been argued that these analyses involve a number of syntactic and logico-philosophical defects, and that the simplest interpretation of the examples as merely equalling the earlier negation *n-NP=pw* with a 'modernised' orthography as *nn-NP=pw* is likely to be correct (Uljas 2013).

Besides particle negations such as *n* (in nominal sentences at least) and *n...=is*, Earlier Egyptian also possessed a number of negative lexemes. Some of

139 The term 'O–E drift' refers to the two right-hand corners of the classical Aristotelian square of negative opposites where O = contradiction and E = the contrary of 'A is B'.

these were negative verbs whose negativity lies in their lexical semantics. The best attested expression here is the auxiliary *tm*, already mentioned several times above. This is used to negate the predicate complement clause of bipartite nominal sentences of the type discussed in 3.1.5[140]:

(414a) A medical gloss explaining a term:

*ỉr ꜥnd ỉb tm=mdt ḥꜣty=pw*
PTC dumb heart AUX.NEG=speak.INF heart-SE
As for 'The heart is dumb', this means that the heart does not speak.
(pEbers 100, 14)

(414b) As above:

*ỉr rꜣ-f mr... tm-f=wn rꜣ-f=pw*
PTC mouth-3MS tie.STA AUX.NEG-3MS=open.NC mouth-3MS=SE
As for 'His mouth is tied'... This means that he cannot open his mouth.
(pEdwin Smith 4, 2–3)

(414c) As above:

*ỉr n šsp-n ỉf-f w-t tm=šsp*
PTC NEG receive-PST flesh-3MS bandage-F AUX.NEG=receive.NC
*ỉf-f pẖr-t=pw*
flesh-3MS remedy-F=SE
As for 'His flesh does not accept bandage', this means that his flesh does not respond to treatment. (pEdwin Smith 14, 13–14)

Here the predicative relation between *=pw* and the *tm*-clause is, of course, affirmative, so that these constructions are genuine cases of nominal sentences whose predicate is a negative term. A further negative lexeme is *nfr*, 'to be good', from where the meaning 'to have reached perfection' and hence 'to be at end' or 'be not' seems to have been derived (see Gardiner 1923, but cf. Reintges 1997: 348–49). *nfr* is occasionally used as a term negation in tripartite nominal sentences with the meaning 'X is one at end/complete', from which one obtains 'X has been perfected' or 'there is no X':

(415a) The sage envisages a hopeless situation where social roles have been reversed and says:

*nfr=pw pẖr-t=ỉr-y*
NEG=COP remedy-F=to.RLT-M
There is no remedy to it. (Ipuwer 4, 11–12)

---

**140** See also ex. 118b. Originally *tm* perhaps denoted 'finish', which may refer to both completion/success and failure/premature cessation.

(415b) Lady Redjedet has asked her maidservant why jars for beer-making have not been brought:

*ꜥḥꜥ-n ḏd-n tꜣ-wbꜣ-t nfr=pw smnḫ ꜥꜣ*
AUX say-PST DEF.F-maidservant-F NEG=COP establish.INF here
Then the maidservant said: 'There is no way to make (it) good'.
(pWestcar 11, 22–23)

(415c) The concluding remarks of Thutmosis III's description of his re-endowment of offerings in the temple of Ptah in Karnak:

*[wḏ ḥm]-ỉ ỉri-tw ỉrr-t=nb m-rpr=pn*
order majesty-1S do-PASS do.PIP-F=QU in-temple=DEM.M
*m-tꜣ-ꜣ-t*
in-DEF.F-hour-F
*nfr=pw mꜣꜥ tkꜣ ỉm*
NEG=COP offer.INF taper there
My majesty ordered everything that used to be done in this temple to be done at once; for there was no offering of even a taper there.
(*Urk.* IV 772, 4–6)

(415d) The writer reports a failure in a processing of foodstuffs:

*swḏꜣ ỉb=pw n-nb ꜥws [r-ntt ḏd-n] bꜣk-ỉm*
ease.INF heart=SE to-lord l.p.h. to-COMP say-PST servant-there
*n-mr šnꜥ wsr mk di-ỉ=n-k pꜣ-diw*
to-overseer store N PTC give-1S=to-2MS DEF.M-ration
*tꜣ-bnr-t n-t-ỉmny-t ꜥḥꜥ-n ḏd-n-f*
DEF.F-date-F of-F-daily offerings-F AUX say-PST-3MS
*nfr=pw ỉri-ỉ=st*
NEG=COP do.SUB-1S=3C
This is to inform the lord l.p.h. that yours truly had said to the overseer of the storehouse User: 'Look, I can give you the grain-rations and the confections for (lit. of) the daily offerings'. But then he said: 'I will not handle them'.
(pBerlin P. 10016, r° 4–6)

Note the full complement clause subject of *nfr=pw x* in ex. 415d. *nfr* might here be a participle, but otherwise the construction [participle + *=pw*] is not common. Accordingly, it might be better to view *nfr* simply as a grammaticalised negative lexeme. The construction *nfr=pw* is not attested before the Middle Kingdom, and even then it seems initially to belong to lower registers of textual use. As the examples above show, it is typically found in direct speech recording colloquial, informal parlance, sometimes perhaps reflecting the speaker's low social standing. In the New Kingdom, its use spreads to monumental inscriptions, but both then and before *nfr=pw* seems to carry a rather specific pragmatic flavour. It appears to be favoured in contexts where it is believed that something should be or should have been the case, but, astonishingly or regrettably, is or was not. This background assumption is clearly present in all the examples above and seems to be part of the discourse profile of *nfr=pw*.

## 4.2 Later Egyptian

### 4.2.1 Late Egyptian

All Late Egyptian nominal sentence constructions are negated by the same negation *bn…ỉn* (the latter usually transliterated *ỉwnꜣ*)[141], which justifies their being treated jointly. This discontinuous negation, which resembles the Earlier Egyptian *n…ỉs* but is not its formal descendent, surrounds the predicative NP. No particle can intervene between *bn* and the immediately following word, which shows that the former was a negative prefix. The clitic status of *ỉn* is less clear, and in what follows it will not be glossed as such. The simplest construction with this negation consists merely of a single NP enveloped by the negative (schema S > [NEG NP NEG]):

(416a) The addressee of a letter is asked to report to the vizier in the matter of some money which a third person demands from the sender saying:

| | | |
|---|---|---|
| *ỉmỉ-ṯ-f* | *ỉw-bn-pꜣy-ỉ-ḥtr* | *ỉn* |
| give.IMP-OBJ-3MS | DEP-NEG-[POSS.M-1S-tax]$_{P}$ | NEG |

'Give it', although it is not my tax. (*LEM* 6, 5)

(416b) In response to rumours about his wife's adulterous conduct, an anonymous writer exclaims:

| | | | | | |
|---|---|---|---|---|---|
| *ḫr* | *bn-tꜣy-ỉ-ḥm-t* | *ỉn* | *n* | *mnts* | *tꜣy-ỉ-ḥm-t* |
| PTC | NEG-[POSS.F-1S-wife-F]$_{P}$ | NEG | IP | 3FS | POSS.F-1S-wife-F |

But she is not my wife! Or is she? (oDeM 439, r° 1–3)

141 The transliteration *bn* is conventional and reflects the graphemic form of the negation written with an apparent <b>. However, Coptic shows that the true phonological value thereof was always /n/ (see below). The etymology of the negative particle *ỉn* (*ỉwnꜣ*) is unknown. The graphical representation might represent a loan word, which could be the Akkadian *janu*. The latter, however, negates existential clauses in Akkadian.

(416c) The author of a letter states that earlier correspondence from his addressee is no cause for concern:
*bn-md-t* *n-mwt* *ỉn*
NEG-[thing-F of-death]$_{P}$ NEG
It is not a matter of death. (*KRI* III 505, 6)

(416d) Children of a man who intends to give his belongings to his new wife react to the words of the Vizier directed to them:
*ỉrỉw-bn-ḥm-t* *sw* *ỉn* *ỉw-ḫꜣ[r-t]* *nḥsy*
COND-NEG-woman-F POSS.M NEG DEP-Syrian-F Nubian
*ỉw-mrỉ-f=s* *ỉw-f* *dỉ=n-s* *ꜣḫ-t-f*
DEP-love.PST-3MS=3C DEP-3MS give=to-3FS thing-F-3MS
Even of she would not be his wife, but a Syrian or Nubian woman, whom he loves and whom he gives his belongings ... (*KRI* VI 741, 9–10)

The following examples show that the use of *ỉn* was initially optional. Its absence or presence has been explained as scope or focus marking (see below)[142], but the semantic differences are not always easy to discern:

(417a) Abandoned by his troops, Ramesses II addresses the god Amun amidst the enemy forces:
*bn-kꜣ-t* *n-rmṯ-w* *qn-w* *ꜣḫ* *ỉmn* *r-sn*
NEG-work-F of-people-P many-P useful N as-3P
It is not the work of many people. Amun is more help then they are. (*KRI* II 42, 2)

(417b) A letter starts with the greeting formulae. Then the sender comes straight to the point asking: *What's up? What crime did I commit against you?*
*bn-ỉnk* *pꜣy-k-ỉrw* *n-wm* *n-ꜥq-w* *ỉs*
NEG-1S POSS.M-2MS-fellow of-eat of-bread-P old
Am I not your old table companion? (*KRI* VI 265, 2)

A remarkable feature of these examples is the absence of any kind of subject expression, and they may be seen as negative versions of the 'monopartite' nominal sentences analysed here as bipartite constructions with an omitted subject element (see 1.4). Earlier Egyptian bipartite sentences with *=pw* negated by *n...ỉs* are common. By contrast, corresponding constructions are very rare in

142 See Winand (1997: 223–26) for a convenient overview of the positions.

Late Egyptian; indeed, the following instances appear to be the sole examples attested:

(418a) In a letter to the viceroy of Nubia, Amenhotep II warns him about the Nubians:

*ptr* *pꜣ-bꜣk* *n-nmḥ-yw* *in-n-k*
look.IMP DEF.M-servant of-man-P bring.REL-PST-2MS
*r-di-t-f* *r-sr* *iw-bn-sr=pw*
to-give-INF-3MS as-official DEP-NEG-$[\text{official}]_{\text{Pa}}$=$[\text{SE}]_{\text{S}}$
*n-pꜣy-k-smi-ṯ-f* *n-ḥm-f*
[of-POSS.M-2MS-report-INF-3MS to-majesty-$3\text{MS}]_{\text{Pa}}$
*rpw* *r-dit* *sḏm-ṯ*
or to-let.INF hear-PASS

Keep an eye on that servant of nobodies whom you brought to be appointed as official, because he is not an official whom you would recommend to His Majesty, nor let him be heard.

(*Urk.* IV 1344, 13–15)

(418b) In the narrative of the Battle of Kadesh, the Hittites are reported as having exclaimed of Ramesses II:

*wꜥ* *ḥr-ꜥš* *im-sn* *n-snnw-f* *ḥr* *bn-rmṯ=pw*
one PRP-scream.INF of-3P to-second-3MS QUOT NEG-man=SE
*pꜣ-nty-m-ẖnw-n* *swtẖ* *ꜥꜣ-pḥti* *bꜥl* *m-ḥꜥ-f*
DEF.M-REL-in-inside-1P N great-power N in-body-3MS

One screamed to the other thus: ‘This is no human!
The one who is among us is powerful Seth, Baal himself!’

(*KRI* II 52, 13–53, 2)

Both the use of =*pw* (instead of expected Late Egyptian *pꜣy*) and its position point towards Earlier Egyptian influence here. However, in a later copy of the text of the *Battle of Kadesh* the sentence has been re-interpreted as a negated pseudo-cleft sentence in an indirect speech (cf. ex. 424b). Thus, it could be argued that 418b above represents a negated version of one of the developmental stages of Late Egyptian pseudo-cleft sentences. Overall, it would seem that both varieties of bipartite nominal sentences (with *pꜣy/tꜣy/nꜣy* and with the latter's ellipsis) shared the same negation [*bn NP in*] characterised, in the latter instance, by the recurrent omission of the subject element.

Bipartite nominal sentences of the type NP NP are also negated by *bn*...(*in*), but some early texts still employ the older graphemic form *nn* for the later *bn*. If the element *in* is present, it appears after the predicative NP. Thus, in 419c, it cleaves to the first, predicative NP *pr mꜣw* whereas in 420a it follows *rmṯ* in second position:

(419a) The author of a letter complains that a young female servant has been taken away from him:
*iniw nn-ink pꜣy-k-bꜣk ḥr-sḏm wp-w-t-k*
IP NEG-[1S]$_S$ [POSS.M-2MS-servant]$_P$ PRP-hear message-P-F-2MS
*m-grḥ mi-hrw*
in-night like-day
Am I not your servant and hearken to your errands night and day?
(pLouvre 3230b, 2–3 [*JEA* 12, pl. 17])

(419b) Complaints about a scribe:
*bn-ntk iꜣw ḫm-f r-nṯr*
NEG-[2MS]$_S$ [old man ignore.REL-3MS to god]$_P$
*bn-ntk ꜥḏd swgꜣ ḫm-f ꜥnḫ*
NEG-[2MS]$_S$ [lad stupid ignore.REL-3MS life]$_P$
You are not an old man who does not care about god or a stupid lad who is ignorant about life.
(pTurin A 4, 10–5, 1 [Fischer-Elfert, *Lesefunde*, 26])

(419c) The author of a letter gives orders regarding certain estates:
*bn-pr n-mꜣw in nꜣ-pr-w*
NEG-[estates of-new]$_P$ NEG [DEF.P-house.P]$_S$
The estates are not new estates. (pBM 10373, r° 5–6)

As seen in 4.1, it has been argued that in Earlier Egyptian, the negation *n...is* represents a narrow-scope term negation that leaves the predicative relation out of scope. If true, this could mean that the Late Egyptian *bn...in* first functioned similarly and in opposition to the bare *bn*. Nevertheless, in view of the fact that it also negates adverbial sentences (Part I, 4.2.1), it is almost certain that by this stage of the language *bn...in* functioned as a wide-scope negation of predicative relation generalised for the use in both types of non-verbal sentences:

(420a) The author of a letter questions the virility of his addressee:
*bn-mntk rmṯ in*
NEG-[2MS]$_S$ [man]$_P$ NEG
*yꜣ bw-ir-k di-iwr-tꜣy-k-ḥm-t*
PTC NEG-AOR-2MS let-be_pregnant-POSS.F-2MS-wife
*mi-qd-pꜣy-k-iry*
like-way-POSS.M-2MS-fellow
You are not a man; actually you are not even able to make your wife pregnant like your friend. (*KRI* VI 155, 12–14)

(420b) The author of a letter complains to his addressee that the latter is in charge of some cattle:

*bn-mntk* *pꜣy-ỉ-ḥry* *bn-mntk* *pꜣ-mniw*
NEG-[2MS]$_S$ [POSS.M-1S-superior]$_P$ NEG-[2MS]$_S$ [DEF.M-herdsman
*n-nꜣ-ỉꜣw-t*
of-DEF.P-cattle-F]$_P$
Are you not my superior? Are you not the herdsman of the cattle?
(*KRI* III 506, 15–16)

(420c) The author of a letter tries to elicit a response from his addressee:

*ḫr* *ink* *pꜣy-tn-nfr* *bn-ink* *pꜣy-tn-bin* *in*
PTC [1S]$_S$ [POSS.M-2P-good]$_P$ NEG-[1S]$_S$ [POSS.M-2P-bad]$_P$ NEG
...for I am your benefit; I am not your disadvantage. (*LRL* 2, 1)

In the following examples, bare *bn* seems to have the same function:

(421a) A reply to a claim for an identity in a magical incantation:

*m-biꜣ* *bn-mntk* *sf* *bn-[mntk* *p]ꜣ-hrw*
NEG NEG-[2MS]$_S$ [yesterday]$_P$ NEG-[2MS]$_S$ [DEF.M-day]$_P$
*bn-mntk* *dwꜣ* *bw-iy-f*
NEG-[2MS]$_S$ [tomorrow NEG-come-3MS]$_P$
No! You are not yesterday, you are not today and you are not tomorrow, which has not yet come. (Roccati, *Mag. Taur.*, 75, 8–9)

(421b) As above:

*mbiꜣ* *bn-mntk* *s* *n-ḥḥ* *n-mḥ* *nn-rḫ-ṯ*
NEG NEG-[2MS]$_S$ [man of-million of-cubit NEG-know-PASS
*iwn-f*
character-3MS]$_P$
No! You are not the man of millions of cubits in length with unknown character. (Roccati, *Mag. taur.*, 75, 12)

Yet some of the apparent examples of nominal sentences seemingly negated by the bare *bn* actually involve the interrogative particle *is-bn* and thus represent inverted polar questions (best translated as tag-question)[143]:

(422a) A woman denounces her brother-in-law as a seducer. She claims to have answered to his advances:

*is-bn-ink* *tꜣy-k-mwt*
PTC-PTC-[1S]$_S$ [POSS.F-2MS-mother]$_P$
I am your mother, am I not? (*LES* 14, 6)

**143** Satzinger (1976: 265 n.2 to 1.2.1.3). Černý and Groll (1994: 151), suggest treating it as a marker of 'rhetorical questions expecting the answer yes'. See now the treatment by Collier (2014: 7–40). In Coptic, this function is expressed by the Greek loanwords *mê or mêti*.

(422b) A man complains to his son that he feels neglected by the latter although he is severely ill:
*ỉs-bn-ỉnk* *pꜣy-k-ỉt*
PTC-PTC-[1S]$_S$ [POSS.M-2MS-father]$_P$
I am your father, am I not? (*KRI* III 533, 7)

Interestingly, Late Egyptian cleft sentences are usually negated by *bn* only; the use of *bn…ỉn* (423c) is very rare:

(423a) The angry author of a letter asks his addressee:
*n* *bn-ntk* *ỉ-ḏd=n-ỉ*
IP NEG-[2MS]$_S$ [PPA-say=to-1S]$_P$
Is it not you who spoke to me? (oIFAO 1328 v° ii, 2)[144]
(423b) The author of a letter has angered his correspondent with an off-hand joke and defends himself:
*bn-m-sr* *ꜥꜣ* *ỉ-ỉr-šsp* *qbꜥ* *n-wꜥ=nb* *spsn*
NEG-[PTC-official great]$_S$ [PPA-AUX-receive joke of-one=QU]$_P$ twice
*ḫr* *ỉrm-n-pꜣy-f-sn* *ꜥꜣ*
PTC with-of-POSS.M-2MS-brother great
It is no high official who tolerates ridicule from just anyone, not even his elder brother! (*LRL* 68, 4–5)[145]
(423c) Officials refuse to supply the crew of necropolis workmen with grain:
*ỉyꜣ* *bn-ỉnn* *ỉ-ỉr-ḫn-w* *m-dwn* *ỉn*
PTC NEG-[1P] [PPA-AUX-ferry-3P regularly] NEG
Indeed, it is not us who transport them regularly!
(pTurin 1978/208 v° 1–2 [*HOP* 97])
(423d) Accused of the theft of a chisel, lady Heriya says:
*m-bỉꜣ* *bn-ỉnk* *r-ṯꜣy=sw*
PTC NEG-[1S] [PPA-take=3MS]
No, it was not me who took it. (*KRI* IV 316, 2)
(423e) The author of a letter denies all responsibility for an accident, blaming divine intervention instead:
*bn-ỉnn* *ỉ-ỉr-pꜣ-mw-t*
NEG-[1P] [PPA-do-DEF.M-death-F]
It was not us who commited murder.
(pBerlin P. 10497, 19–20 [*ZÄS* 129, 76])

144 According to Černý and Groll (1994: 539, ex. 1528).
145 See the corrections in Černý and Groll (1994; 539–540, ex. 1530).

Pseudo-cleft sentences are mostly negated by *bn…in* bracketing the initial NP:

(424a) Wenamun's retort to the suggestion by the prince of Byblos that he has been sent on foolish trips:

| | | | | |
|---|---|---|---|---|
| *bn-mšꜥ* | *swgꜣ* | *in* | *n(ꜣ)-nty-ṯ-i* | *im-w* |
| NEG-[travel.P | foolish] | NEG | [COP.P-REL-PTC-1S | in-3P] |

It is not foolish travels on which I am! (*LES* 69, 5–6)

(424b) In the narrative of the Battle of Kadesh, the Hittites are reported having exclaimed of Ramesses II (cf. 418b above):

| | | | |
|---|---|---|---|
| *iw-wꜥ* | *ḥr-ꜥš* | *m-im-sn* | *n-snnw-f* |
| DEP-one | PRP-scream.INF | in-of-3P | to-second-3MS |

| | | | | |
|---|---|---|---|---|
| *m-ḏd-bn-rmṯ* | *in* | *pꜣ-nty-mḫnw-sn* | *swtḫ* | *ꜥꜣ-pḥti* |
| in-saying-NEG-man | NEG | COP.M-REL-among-3P | N | great-power |

| | |
|---|---|
| *bꜥl* | *m-ḥꜥ-f* |
| N | in-body-3MS |

Thus one screamed to another that the one who among them was not a man – but powerful Seth and Baal himself.

(*KRI* II 52, 15–53, 5)

Note that in pseudo-cleft sentences with a *tm*-negated infinitive in subject position the predicative relation has affirmative polarity and the predicate is in fact a negative term[146]:

(425a) In a set of instructions on repairing a barque:

| | | | |
|---|---|---|---|
| *tm-dit=n-f* | *ḥry-t* | *qꜣi* | *pꜣ-iry* |
| AUX.NEG-give.INF=to-3MS | gunwale-F | high | DEF.M-do.PPP |

However, a high gunwale was not given to it. (*LEM* 42, 12)

(425b) Accused of having failed to write, the author of a letter says that he had given two letters to be delivered by certain men:

| | |
|---|---|
| *tm-di-w=n-k* | *pꜣ-ir-w* |
| AUX.NEG-give.INF-3P=to-2MS | DEF.M-do.REL-3P |

They failed to give them to you (just as those I had caused to be taken to the scribe Tjaroy, which they neither delivered).

(*LRL* 64, 14–15)

146 The renderings here have been adjusted somewhat to avoid translations such as 'Not giving them to you was what they did' (425b).

(425c) The god Amun-Ra clears Dhutmose from any suspicion of guilt:

*tm-iri-gbi* *mḫnw-nwt* *p3y-k-dmi*
AUX.NEG-do.INF-damage inside-N POSS.M-2MS-town
*p3-iry* *ḏḥwtyms*
DEF.M-do.REL N
Dhutmose committed no misdemeanour in Thebes, your city.
(Jansen-Winkeln, *IdS* I, 176, 18–19)

As in Earlier Egyptian, the negation of the relative expression in clefts and pseudo-clefts is unattested, and probably unknown before Coptic (see 4.2.3).

In ex. 426, the negation *bw*, which is usually employed only in verbal patterns, seems to be a mistake:

(426) Wermai complains that he had to leave his town and had to roam throughout the whole of Egypt:

*bw-ink* *di-st* *iw-i-m3wḏ-k(i)* *ḥr-šm*
NEG-1S give.PPA-3FS DEP-1S-force-STA.1S PRP-go.INF
I did not do so of my own free will, for I was forced to leave.
(*Tale of Woe* 3, 6–7)

The possessive patterns *n-s/ink* are similarly negated with *bn*:

(427a) Falsehood sees among his cattle the ox of the son of truth and wants to eat it. The herdsman replies:

*bn-ink=sw*
NEG-1S=3C
It is not mine. (*LES* 34, 10)

(427b) A woman accused of stealing some tools makes an oath including:

*mṯ-ṯ* *gm* *rḏd* *bn-ink* *n3-ḫ3-w* [...]
CNJ-PASS find COMP NEG-1S DEF.P-chisel-P
And if one finds out that the chisels do not belong to me...
(*KRI* IV 319, 13–14)

(427c) Foreman Paneb is accused of having entered a tomb:

*iw-bn-sw=sw*
DEP-NEG-3S=3MS
...that does not belong to him. (*KRI* IV 410, 4)

(427d) Pharaoh stipulates regarding the organisation of gold transport:

*ir-nbw* *ḥ*ʿ*-nṯr-w* *bn-n-s-ḫr-t-tn*
PTC-gold body-god-P NEG-POSS-3S-affair-F-2P
But the gold, it is the body of the gods; it is not of your concern.
(*KRI* I 68, 1–2)

Rarely, the negation *bn…in* appears:

(428) In a court-case a person reports that his adversary had given him a storehouse:

| | | | | | |
|---|---|---|---|---|---|
| *iw-bn-ink=sw* | *in* | *n-s-imnḥtp* | *ʿws* | *pꜣ-nb* | *(n)-pꜣ-dmi* |
| DEP-NEG-1S=3C | NEG | POSS-3C-N | l.p.h. | DEF.M-lord | of-DEF.M-village |

…which does not belong to me, but belongs to Amenhotep l.p.h., the lord of the village. (*KRI* V 572, 1–2)

Occasionally also the question-tag-pattern with initial *is-bn* is attested:

(429) In a Letter to Dead, the addressee is urged to have a woman come to him, and he should ask her:

| | | |
|---|---|---|
| *is-bn-ink* | *psš* | *n-t-t[t]* |
| PTC-PTC-NEG-1S | part | of-F-N |

Tet's part is mine, is it not? (Moscow Bowl 2)

As seen above, tripartite nominal sentences are very rare in Late Egyptian (1.3.2.1). It is not surprising, therefore, that corresponding negated constructions are even less frequent. The following instance seems to be the only candidate:

(430) The mayor of Thebes had accused the workmen of tomb robbery but his accusation turned out to be false:

| | | | | | | |
|---|---|---|---|---|---|---|
| *ḫr* | *bn-md* | *šri-t* | *in* | *tꜣy* | *i-ḏd-pꜣy-ḥꜣtyʿ* | *n-nwt* |
| PTC | NEG-thing | small-F | NEG | COP.F | PPA-say-DEM.M-mayor | of-N |

However, what this mayor of Thebes mentioned is no small matter! (*KRI* VI 478, 1–2)

However, this example could alternatively be analysed as a negated pseudo-cleft sentence (see exx. 424 and 425), but the position of the negation *in* after the first NP does not help to solve the ambiguity, since this particle is otherwise attested only once with clefts (423c).

In sum, Late Egyptian nominal sentences by and large share the negation *bn…in*. The less common *bn* represents a Late Egyptian version of the earlier *nn*. It may be that *bn…in* was in origin a narrow-scope negator that diachronically extended its scope and developed into a wide-scope contradictory, but the correctness of this hypothesis depends on the final analysis of its Earlier Egyptian predecessor *n…is*. In any case, the relationship between the negative and affirmative constructions is not strictly isomorphic, but rather shows a degree of reduction in complexity that may be charted in the following manner:

**Table II.11:** Distribution of Late Egyptian Nominal sentence pattern (affirmative vs. negative).

| Pattern | Affirmative | Negative |
|---|---|---|
| Bipartite w. SE | NP SE | NEG NP (NEG) |
| w. ellipis | NP ø | |
| Bipartite | NP NP | NEG NP NP (NEG) |
| Clefts | PTC-NP REL | NEG NP NEG REL |
| Pseudo-Clefts | NP DEF.REL | NEG NP NEG DEF-REL |
| Tripartite | (NP COP NP) | (NEG NP NEG COP NP) |

### 4.2.2 Demotic

In Demotic, nominal sentences are negated by *bn*(*iw*)...*in*, which is the same discontinuous morpheme as the earlier *bn*...*in*. As in Late Egyptian, the element *in* usually appears after the predicative NP. No particle can intervene between *bn*(*iw*) and the following word, which apparently documents the proclitic status of the negation. Conversely, the element *in* does not seem to display any clitic behaviour.[147]

In bipartite sentences, *bn* appears at the beginning and *in* at the end of the sentence. Exx. 431a and 431b show a negated sentence with a personal pronoun in subject position, whereas 431c shows two common noun phrases:

(431a) Tabubu stresses her high status as a lady and tells a servant to return to Setne and say to him:

| | | | | |
|---|---|---|---|---|
| *ink* | *wꜥb* | *bn-ink* | *rmt-ḫm* | *in* |
| 1S | priest | NEG-[1S] | [man-small] | NEG |

I am of priestly rank and not a common person. (Setne I 5, 8–9)

(431b) A warrior addressed a priest who in return asked him where he was from. As he admitted that he was not from the north, the priest replied:

| | | | | |
|---|---|---|---|---|
| *iw-f-ḫpr* | *iw-bniw-mtwk* | *rmṯ* | *pr* | *tꜣ-mḥṯ* |
| DEP-3MS-happen | DEP-NEG-[2MS] | [man | house | (of) land-north] |

147 The element *in* does show emergent clitic behaviour in other sentence patterns such as the adverbial sentences. See the example from the *Myth of the Sun's Eye* 13, 12–13 in example I.349a.

*in i-ir-f-pšn nim-k r-pꜣ-w-imn iw-ḏbꜣ-iḫ*
NEG ST-do-3MS-call OBJ-2MS to-DEF-M-barque-N to-because-WH
So, if you are not a northerner, why should he (the pharaoh) call you for the barque of Amun? (pSpiegelberg 15, 9–11)

(431c) The author of a letter defends himself against accusations:
*bniw-rn-y rn-wsirwr sꜣ-ḏdḥr in*
NEG-[name-1S] [name-N son-N] NEG
My name is not the name of Osoroeris, son of Teos.
(pBerlin P. 13549, v° 15–16)

As in Late Egyptian, the negation usually wraps the first (subject) NP in cleft sentences (note that the latter are the remnants of the earlier pseudo-clefts):

(432a) The chief of the Ma tells Peteese:
*in bn-pꜣy-n-ḥry in pꜣ-iir-sꜥnḫ-n*
IP NEG-[POSS-1P-superior] NEG [COP.M-AUX.REL-nourish-1P]
Is it not our superior who has allowed us to live?
(pRylands IX 12, 11)

(432b) A remark in a wisdom text:
*bniw-sḥm-t ꜥn-t in tꜣ-nty-ḥsy n-ḥꜣtṯ*
NEG-[woman-F decent-F] NEG [COP.F-REL-favour.STA in heart
*n-ky*
of-other]
It is not a decent woman who is favoured in the heart of another (man).
(pInsinger 8, 15)

(432c) The writer of a letter defends himself against accusations:
*bniw-nꜣ-rmṯ-w nty-kpy in*
NEG-[DEF.P-people-P REL-hide.STA] NEG
*nꜣ-nty-ḏd-nꜣ-šs-w*
[COP.P-REL-say.INF-DEF.P-slander-P]
It is not the hidden people who express slander.
(pBerlin P. 13549, v° 16–17)

Note, however, counterexamples such as 433a, where *in* appears in sentence-final position, or 433b and 433c, where it is absent:

(433a) The pharaoh defends himself against the claim that he had insulted troops:
*bniw-inky pꜣ-nty-sš nim-w in*
NEG-[1S] [COP.M-REL-insult.INF OBJ-3P] NEG
It is not me who insults them! (pSpiegelberg 11, 18)

(433b) Moral precepts state:

| | | |
|---|---|---|
| *bniw-p3-rmṯ-rḫ* | *nty-sq* | *p3-nty-gm-wḏ3-t* |
| NEG-[DEF.M-man-wise | REL-save.INF] | [COP.M-REL-find.INF-remainder-F] |
| *in* | | |
| NEG | | |

It is not the parsimonious wise man who finds profit. (pInsinger 7, 15)

(433c) In a series of characterisations of the fool:

| | | |
|---|---|---|
| *bniw-wꜥ-t-yt* | *t3-ntyiw-iw-f-ir-šfṯ* | *nim-s* |
| NEG-[IDF-F-way-F] | [COP.F-REL-FUT-3MS-do-fall | OBJ-3FS] |

It is not in one way alone that the fool errs! (pInsinger 5, 19)

As in Late Egyptian, the subject position may also be filled by an infinitive, which may be negated by *tm*. In these cases, the predicative relation in the proposition remains affirmative:

(434a) A warrior addresses his opponents that they should unblock the way:

| | | |
|---|---|---|
| *in* | *tm-ir-s* | *p3-nty-iw-tn-ir-f* |
| IP | [AUX.NEG-do-3FS] | [COP.M-REL-FUT-2P-do.INF-3MS] |

Are you not willing to do it? (pSpiegelberg 15, 19)

(434b) A legal manual explains how to phrase a note of protest:

| | | | |
|---|---|---|---|
| *tm-gmṯ-f* | *p3y-ir-y* | *r-ir-šꜥr* | *iir-ḥr-f* |
| [AUX.NEG-find.INF-3MS] | [COP.M-do.REL.PST-1S | to-do-protest | to-face-3MS] |

I did not find him to protest in his presence. (Cod. Herm. x+2, 16)

(434c) Moral precepts urge a father to take care of his son:

| | | |
|---|---|---|
| *tm-dyt-ir-f* | *3yṯy* | *p3-nty-iw-k-ir-f* |
| [AUX.NEG-let.INF-do-3MS | lack] | [COP.M-REL-FUT-2MS-do-3MS] |

You should not let him suffer from lack. (pLouvre N 2414 3,5)

Negation of the relative expression is unattested (and probably impossible) in Demotic.

In bipartite sentences with the subject element, the predicate appears between the constituents of the negation *bn* and *in*; the subject element *p3y/t3y/n3y* occupies the sentence-final position:

(435a) A statement in a letter from Elephantine:

| | | | | |
|---|---|---|---|---|
| *bniw-md* | *iw-ḥn-k=(s)* | *n-y* | *in* | *t3y* |
| NEG-[thing.F | DEP-order.PST-2MS=[3FS] | to-1S] | NEG | [SE.F] |

It is nothing that you ordered to me. (pBerlin P. 15617, v° 2)

(435b) A group of priests explain how they bribed a person with a share of the temple revenue:

| | | | | |
|---|---|---|---|---|
| *bn-dny-t* | *iw-wnn3w* | *mtw-f=s* | *in* | *t3y* |
| NEG-[part-F | DEP-have | with-3MS=3C] | NEG | [SE.F] |

It is not a share he holds. (pRylands IX 17, 5)

(435c) Advice in a wisdom text:
*mir-ḏd-md-t* *iw-bniw-pꜣy-s-ṯꜣ* *in* *pꜣy*
NEG.IMP-say-matter-F DEP-NEG-[POSS-3FS-time] NEG [SE.M]
Do not say something when it is not its time. (Onkhsheshonqy 12, 24)

(435d) A stepfather claims to have taken care of a boy; however:
*twi-s* *pꜣ-sẖ-wḫꜣ* *pꜣ-ẖl* *rn-f*
PTC DEF.M-scribe-letter [DEF.M-boy name-3MS]$_S$
*bniw-pꜣy(-y)-šr* *in* *pꜣy*
NEG-[POSS-1S-son]$_P$ NEG COP/SE
Look, O letter writer, the said boy – he is not my son! (or: 'the said boy is not my son). (*Krugtexte* A, text 2, 11)

As 435a and 435b show, the predicate is bracketed in its entirety. Examples such as 436 look at first glance like the Late Egyptian negative pattern for bipartite nominal sentences with elided subject element (thus *bniw-md-t rmṯ-qnqn in ø*). Yet their rarity and, as in this case, occasional late appearance has led most scholars to assume that they need to be emended by adding a sentence-final *nꜣw*:

(436) The count Petechons says to the queen of the Amazons:
*bniw-md-t* *rmṯ-qnqn* *in*
NEG-[matter-F man-strife] NEG
These are not the words of a warrior. (Amazons, A2, x+20)

There are no negated examples of the possessive patterns *n-s/ink* in Demotic. The productivity of these constructions was already limited and they could only be used in the affirmative.

Examples of negated tripartite sentences are surprisingly rare; the only certain instance seems to be the following (note that the negation again brackets the predicate):

(437) Month-Baal prevents Pami from taking immediate revenge with the following words: *No, my brother Pami. Draw your hand back, until we will take again revenge*:
*r-bniw-ꜣḫy* *in* *pꜣy* *pꜣ-rmt* *ḏd-iw-w-šꜥt-f*
DEP-NEG-[reed]$_P$ NEG COP.M [DEF.M-man]$_S$ that-DEP-3P-cut.INF-3MS
*iw-f-rt*
FUT-3MS-grow.INF
...because (the) man is not a reed, so that it will grow again when it is cut. (pKrall 23, 11)

Accordingly, like their Late Egyptian predecessors, Demotic nominal sentences by and large share the same negation *bn(iw)…in*, and the relationship between the negative and affirmative constructions is not strictly isomorphic:

**Table II.12:** Distribution of Demotic Nominal sentence pattern (affirmative vs. negative).

| Pattern | Affirmative | Negative |
|---|---|---|
| Bipartite w. SE | NP SE | NEG NP NEG SE |
| Bipartite | NP NP | NEG NP NP NEG |
| Clefts | NP DEF-REL | NEG NP NEG DEF-REL |
| Tripartite | NP NP COP | *NEG NP NEG COP NP |

Note that the negation of the tripartite pattern is only attested once, and it is marked by an * in the table above.

### 4.2.3 Coptic

All nominal sentence constructions in Coptic are negated by the discontinuous negation *(n)...an/en*, which is a direct descendent of the earlier *bn...in* > *bn(iw)...in*. If still present,[148] *n* occupies the initial position, whereas *an* appears usually after the predicate (but see example 438g). The latter now increasingly shows clitic behaviour, but unlike the Earlier Egyptian *=is* in the negation *n...is*, *an/en* does not yet seem to have become fully grammaticalised as such. Below are examples with bipartite structures of the type [NP – NP] > (NEG) [NP – NP] NEG:

(438a) David said to Abner:

*mê* *ntk-u-rôme=an* *n-dynatos* *ntok*
IP 2MS-IDF.S-man=NEG of-strong 2MS
Are you not a valiant man? ($^{S}$1Kg 26:15 [Drescher])

(438b) The apostle quotes from Genesis and concludes about his addressees and himself

*etbe-pai=kʲe* *ne-snêu* *n-anon* *-n-šêre*
because-DEM.M=then DEF.P-brother.P NEG-1P -DEF.P-son
*n-t-hmhal=an*
of-DEF.F-servant=NEG

148 Nominal sentences provide no means to decide whether the disappearance of the *n-* leaves any trace in form of a zero morpheme as proposed for other syntactic environments in Upper Egyptian dialects by Funk (1987: 101–02).

| | | |
|---|---|---|
| *alla* | *anon* | *-na-t-rmhê* |
| but | 1P | -POSS.P-DEF.F-free.F |

Therefore, brethren, we are not the children of the slave woman, but of the free one. ([S]Gal 4:31)

(438c) The frightened Death says to Jesus in the netherworld:

| | | |
|---|---|---|
| A | *ntok* | *-u-hllo=an* |
| | 2MS | -IDF.S-old man=NEG |
| C | *auô* | *ntek-u-hllo=an* |
| | and | 2MS-IDF.S-old man=NEG |

You are not an old man.

([S]*Book of Resurrection of Christ* [Westerhoff 70, 1 ms. A vs. C])

(438d) The Lord urges his chosen flock to contend against their mother for:

| | | | | |
|---|---|---|---|---|
| *ntas* | *ta-shime=en=te* | *anak* | *hu-t* | *anak* |
| 3FS | POSS.F.1.S-wife=NEG=SE.F | 1S | self-1S | 1S |
| *-p-s-hei=en* | | | | |
| -POSS.M-3FS-husband=NEG | | | | |

She, she is not my wife, and I, however, I am not her husband.

([A]Hos 2:2 [Till])

(438e) The psalmist feels abandoned by the Lord:

| | | |
|---|---|---|
| *anak=de* | *ank-u-fent* | *n-ank-u-rome=en* |
| 1S=yet | 1S-IDF.S-worm | NEG-1S-IDF.S-man=NEG |

But I am a worm; I am not a man. ([M]Ps 21 [22]:6 [7])

(438f) The apostle asks:

| | | | | | |
|---|---|---|---|---|---|
| *ešce* | *n-anak* | *-u-apostolos=en* | *n-hn-kekaui* | *alla* | *anak* |
| if | NEG-1S | -IDF.S-apostle=NEG | for-IDF.P-other.P | but | 1P |
| *-uei* | *nê-tn* | | | | |
| -one | to-2P | | | | |

If I am not an apostle to the others, I am at least one to you.

([F]1Cor 9:2 [Zoega])

(438g) Inhabitants of a city in Phrygia ask a man whether he is a deity. He replies:

| | | | | | |
|---|---|---|---|---|---|
| *n-anak=en* | *[u]-nuti* | *alla* | *[an]ak* | *-u-lômi* | *[n-te]-tn-hê* |
| NEG-1S=NEG | IDF.S-god | but | [1S] | -[IDF.S-man | of-POSS.F-2P-way] |

I am no god, but I am a man like you.

([F]*Acts of Philip* [von Lemm I 534, a4–6])

Note that in the southern dialects (certainly in S and A; partly in L and in M, the northernmost of these dialects) *an/en* can appear after the first prosodic unit of the sentence, which creates the impression of a Wackernagel clitic. Yet in view of examples such as 438b, it may be that the cliticisation was a diachronic feature. A similar general rule does not seem to exist in Bohairic (see the B version in 439d).[149] However, occasional movement of *an/en* is observed even in Bohairic (cf. 447c). The reason for this might be the need to mark the scope of the negation, but the examples above hardly speak in favour of such an analysis. Be that as it may, the appearance of the initial element *n* had become facultative in Coptic, as is the case in colloquial French with *ne...pas*; cf. 438a and 438b with the following examples, of which 439b and 439c have an indefinite predicate NP, whereas 439d shows a definite NP in predicate position:

(439a) Victor refuses to obey his father's command to worship pagan gods and says after citing Tit 3:5:
*etbe-pai* *ntk-pa-iôt=an*
because-DEM.M 2MS-POSS.M.1S-father=NEG
Therefore you are not my father.
($^{S}$*Mart. St Victor the General* [Budge, *Martyrdoms*, 9, 6–7])

(439b) St Andrew has heard that the inhabitants of a city have been jailed because of him. He goes to the street and says:
*n-u-hôb=an=pe* *e-hypokrini*
NEG-IDF.S-thing=NEG=SE.M to-arrest
There is no need to arrest. ($^{S}$*Acta Andreae* [Prieur 657, 6])

(439c) As God's anger abates, he decides not to annihilate his chosen flock all together:
*ce-anak* *-u-nute* *anak* *e-f-uaabe* *ẖn-t-k-mête*
for-1S -IDF.S-god 1S DEP-3MS-pure.STA in-POSS.F-2MS-midst
*au* *anak* *-u-rôme=en*
and 1S -IDF.S-man=NEG
...for I am a god, who is holy amidst you, and I am not a human.
($^{A}$Hos 11:9)

(439c) Jesus prays to the Lord asking him to forgive men: I gave them your word. But the world hated them because they are not out of this world:
*kata-t-he* *anak-u-abal=en* *hn-p-kosmos*
like-DEF.F-way 1S-IDF.S-out=NEG in-DEF.M-world
...even as I am also not of the world. ($^{L}$Jn 17:14)

(439d) The Jews object to Pilate's plan to release Jesus:
B *ešôp* *akšan-k*$^{h}$*a-p*$^{h}$*ai* *ebol* *nt*$^{h}$*ok* *p-šp*$^{h}$*êr*
if CND.2MS-put-DEM.M out 2MS DEF.M-friend
*m-p-uro=an*
of-DEF.M-king=NEG

149 Also, the Old Boharic and Lycopolitan versions show the negation in the final position after the genitive.

S *ekšan-ka-pai* *ebol* *ntk-pe-špʰêr=an* *m-p-rro*
CND.2MS-put-DEM.M out 2MS-DEF.M-friend=NEG of-DEF.M-king
If you release this one, you are not the friend of the emperor.
(BSJn 19:12)

(439e) The count pities the martyr whom he had been ordered to torture:
*ce-ntʰok* *u-rômi=an* *n-šu-ti-šoš=na-f*
for-2MS IDF.S-man=NEG of-worthy-give-humiliation=to-3MS
...for you are not a man worthy of humiliation.
(B*Mart. Eusebius* [*AdM* 33, 1–2])

If two sentences are coordinated, the negation appears in both coordinands:

(440a) After the priest of Beth-El told Amos to go away and stop his prophesies, he replied:
*ne-anak* *-u-prophêtês=en=pe* *anak* *ude* *anak* *-u-šêre=en*
PRT-1S -IDF.S-prophet=NEG=PTC 1S nor 1S -IDF.S-son=NEG
*m-prophêtês* *alla* *ne-anak* *-u-mane-bampe* *e-i-puuce*
of-prophet but PRT-1S -IDF.S-herdsman-goat DEP-1S-break
*n-hen-lku*
OBJ-IDF.P-sycamore fruit
I was not a prophet nor am I a prophet's son. I was a goatherd gathering sycamore fruit. (AAm 7:14 [Till])

(440b) In the description of natural phenomena after the death of the father of a nun, it is stated that a thunderstorm raged:
*ude* *n-u-ušê=an=te* *ude* *n-u-hou=an=pe*
either NEG-IDF.S-night=NEG=SE.F neither NEG-IDF.S-day=NEG=SE.M
It was neither night nor day. (S*AP* Chaîne 55, 9)

(440c) Athanasius argues that when Jesus died on the cross, he took his human body with him as a gift to his father. About this gift he says:
*u-nub=an=pe* *ude* *u-hat=an=pe*
IDF.S-gold=NEG=SE.M nor IDF.S-silver=NEG=SE.M
*alla* *p-rôme* *p-ent-a-f-tamio-f* *kata-pe-f-ine*
but DEF.M-man COP.M-REL-PST-3MS-make-3MSlike-POSS.M-3MS-picture
*mn-te-f-hikôn*
CON-POSS.F-3MS-image
It is neither gold nor silver, but it was man whom he created according to his likeness and image.
(SAthanasius of Alexandria, *De Anima et corpore* [Budge, *Homilies* 131, 32–34])

(440d) Hosea is told by the Lord to call his second-born son Not-my-people:

*ce-nt$^{h}$ôten -pa-laos=an uoh anok hô anok*
for-2P -POSS.M.1S-people=NEG and 1S self.1S 1S
*-p$^{h}$ô-ten=an*
-POSS.M-2P=NEG
...for you are not my people and I am not yours. ($^{B}$Hos 1:9)

Below are examples of negated bipartite sentences with a subject element. The element *an* appears in second position after the predicate, i.e. before the subject element. The occurrence of initial negation *n* is variable, as elsewhere, so the basic structure is (NEG) NP=NEG=SE:

(441a) Shenute argues against heretics:

*nim p-ent-a-f-tamie-p-rê mn-p-ooh mn-n-siu*
WH COP.M-REL-PST-3MS-create-DEF.M-sun and-DEF.M-moon and-DEF.P-star
*mê p-nute=an=pe*
IP DEF.M-god=NEG=SE.M
Who created the sun, the moon, and the stars, if not God?
($^{S}$Shenute, *Well Did You Come* [A II 407, 9–10])

(441b) Shenute, drawing on Ps 90:10 (LXX) that says who makes the Lord a place of refuge for him will be untouched by evil and not be approached by scourges, denies any suggestion that even though the community has a refuge in God they would be suffering from great scourges of every sort of disease with a succinct:

*m-pai=an=pe*
NEG-DEM.M=NEG=SE.M
This is not so!
($^{S}$Shenute, *I Have Been Reading the Holy Gospels* §24 [Moussa 90a, 23])

(441c) The narrator, John, reacts to the argument Barnabas might have spoken in favour of Mark only due to their family relations:

*n-tei-he=an=te n-tei-he=an=te ô*
NEG-DEM.F-way=NEG=SE.F NEG-DEM.F-way=NEG=SE.F VOC
*p-merit*
DEF.M-beloved_one
*alla ne-u-rôme=pe n-šnhtêf ehun e-rôme nim*
but PRT-IDF.S-man=SE.M of-compassionate into to-man QU
*phusei pe p-apostolos barnabas*
nature PTC DEF.M-apostle N
It is not so, it is not so, o beloved one!! But he was naturally a compassionate man towards everyone, the apostle Barnabas.
($^{S}$John the Hermit, *Enc. on Mark the Evangelist* [Orlandi 38, 3–6])

(441d) The Lord announces Israel's punishment for he will raise the belligerent Chaldeans, a bitter and swift nation, that goes over the breadth of the earth:

| | | | |
|---|---|---|---|
| *et-r-klêronomi* | *n-hen-ma* | *n-ḫope* | *e-nô-f=en=ne* |
| REL-AUX-inherit | OBJ-IDF.P-place | of-dwell | DEP-POSS.P-3MS=NEG=SE.P |

...who inherit dwellings not of their own. ($^{A}$Hab 1:6 [Malinine])

(441e) Anguish and terror came into being:

| | |
|---|---|
| *pei=k$^{j}$e* | *ne-u-thbbio=ne-f=en=pe* |
| DEM.M=PTC | PRT-IDF.S-humiliation=for-3MS=NEG=SE.M |

But this, it was no humiliation to him (the Supreme Being) ($^{L}$*EvVer* 17, 21–22)

(441f) Herod made an oration to his people who say:

| | | | |
|---|---|---|---|
| *u-hrau* | *n-n(u)ti=pe* | *n-u-hrau* | *n-rome=en=pe* |
| IDF.S-voice | of-god=SE.M | NEG-IDF.S-voice | of-man=NEG=SE.M |

It is a voice of god; it is not a voice of a man! ($^{M}$Acts 12:22)

(441g) Agathonicus says that a Christian must oppose any non-Christian view:

| | | |
|---|---|---|
| *a-f-š<t>em-apologize=nê-s* | *kan* | *u-arkhê-episkopos=pe* |
| CND-3MS-NEG-oppose=for-3FS | even if | IDF.S-arch-bishop=SE.M |

| | |
|---|---|
| *n-u-khrêstianos=en=pe* | *e-p-têl-f* |
| NEG-IDF.S-Christian=NEG=SE.M | to-DEF.M-all-3MS |

If he does not oppose it, even if he is an archbishop, he is not a Christian at all. ($^{F}$Agathonicus of Tarsus, *De incredulitate* [Erichsen 26, 7–11])

(441h) Isaiah urges Israel not to seek help in Egypt but in believing in the Lord:

| | | | |
|---|---|---|---|
| *u-romi* | *n-rem-n-kêmi* | *auô* | *n-u-nuti=en=pe* |
| IDF.S-man | of-man-of-Egypt | and | NEG-IDF.S-god=NEG=SE.M |
| *hen-sarks* | *n-ehta* | *auô* | *n-hen-boêthia=en=ne* |
| IDF.P-flesh | of-horse | and | NEG-IDF.P-help=NEG=SE.P |

An Egyptian and not divine he is; equine flesh and of no help they are. ($^{F}$Is 31:3 [*BIFAO* 2])

(441i) The governor refuses to belief that the man addressing him is St George, whom he had recently executed:

| | | |
|---|---|---|
| *nt$^{h}$ok=an=pe* | *alla* | *te-f-ḫêibi=te* |
| 2MS=NEG=SE.M | but | POSS.F-3MS-shadow=SE.F |

It is not you but his shadow. ($^{B}$*Mart. George* [AM II 282, 17])

Any NP can occupy the predicate position before the subject element, such as possessive (ex. 442a) or personal pronouns (exx. 442b & c) or nominalised expressions (ex. 442d). An addition, clauses can be contain adverbial adjuncts (ex. 442c & e):

(442a) A paragraph in the *Canons of Athanasius* begins with:
*nne-lau* *n-klêrikos* *tôh* *mn-shime*
NEG.FUT-any of-cleric mix with-woman
*(e)-n-tô-f=an=te*
(DEP)-NEG-POSS.F-3MS=NEG=SE.F
No cleric shall mix with a woman that is not his own.
(S*Canons of Athanasius* [Crum in Riedel §42])

(442b) Speaking to the Jews of Antioch, St Paul quotes John the Baptist's words *Why do you say it is me?*:
*n-anak=en=pe*
NEG-1S=NEG=SE.M
It is not me (but the one who will come after me). (MActs 13:25)

(442c) The disciples are told about the resurrection, but they do not believe the news:
*anan=de* *a-n-i* *šara-f* *e-n-r-distaze* *ẖ[n-p-n]-het*
1P=yet PST-1P-go to-3MS DEP-1P-AUX-doubt in-POSS.M-1P-heart
*ce-meẖek* *ntaf=en=pe*
COMP-maybe NEG-1S=NEG=SE.M
We went to him still doubting in our hearts: 'Maybe it is not him'.
(A*Ep. Apostolorum* [Schmidt 3* f. 3, 14–15])

(442d) Jesus prays to the Lord asking him to forgive men: I gave them your word, but the world hated them:
*ce-n-hen-ebol=an* *hm-p-kosmos=ne*
for-NEG-IDF.P-out=NEG in-DEF.M-world=SE.P
...for they are not of this world *(even as I am also not of this world).*
(SJn 17:14)

(442e) Mark is sent to tell something to the apostles and especially also St. Peter. The narrator reminds the audience:
*mpertre-f-meue=gar* *peca-f* *n$k^j$i-petros* *ce-uketi*
NEG.JUSS-3MS-think=for say.PST-3MS PVS-N COMP-no_longer
*n-u-apostolos=an=pe* *etbe-t-kui* *m-parabasis*
NEG-IDF.S-apostle=NEG=SE.M because-DEF.F-small of-transgression
*nt-a-s-šôpe*
REL-PST-3FS-happen
'He must not think,' said Peter, 'that he would be no apostle any longer because of this little transgression that has happened.
(SJohn the Hermit, *Enc. on Mark the Evangelist* [Orlandi 40a, 5–13])

Occasionally, *an/en* may appear as *am/em* before the initial bilabial plosive of the masculine subject element:

(443a) Archbishop Cyril condemns the heretics in his *Discourse on the Cross*:
*ešce u-r[ôme] mmate pe pe-[kh(risto)s] auô*
CND IDF.S-man only COP.M DEF.M-Christ and
*n-u-nute=am=pe*
NEG-IDF.S-god=NEG=SE.M
*ô p-heretikos i e-k-šmše ntok n-u-rôme*
VOC DEF.M-heretic then ST-2MS-worship 2MS OBJ-IDF.S-man
If the Christ is a mere man and no god, O heretic, you worship a man yourself.
([S]Ps.Cyril of Jerusalem, *On the Cross* §110 [Budge, *Misc.* 227, 18–20])

(443b) Clement exhort to humility by saying:
*p-kh(risto)s=gar pa-n-et-thbbiait=pe*
DEF.M-Christ=for POSS.M-DEF.P-REL-humble.STA=SE.M
*pa-n-et-tône=em=pe ahrêi acm-p-f-ôhe*
POSS.M-DEF.P-REL-raise=NEG=SE above upon-POSS.M-3MS-flock
For the Christ belongs to those who are humble, he does not belong to those who place themselves above his flock.
([A]1Cl 16:1 [Schmidt])

(443c) In an address to a healer, the person begging for healing states:
*ce-pe-k-tlkʲo u-abal=em=[pe m-p-kah]*
for-POSS.M-2MS-healing IDF.S-out=NEG=SE.M of-DEF.M-earth
*ne-k-pahre hn-abal=en=ne m-pei-ko[s]mos*
POSS.P-2MS-cure IDF.P-out=NEG=SE.P of-DEM.M-world
For your healing is not of the earth, your cures not of this world.
([L]*Psalms of Thomas* 221, 1–2)

This would point to a close phonological juncture between the two (with both *an* and *pe* constituting a single prosodic unit with the preceeding noun), as assimilatory processes across word boundaries are not very common in Coptic.

Cleft sentences are likewise negated by *(n)...a/en*, which surrounds the initial NP. Note again the 'movement' of the negation *an* in 444c, 444d, and 444g. As with the affirmative patterns, there appears to be no limitation in the relative constructions used: one finds perfect relative clauses (exx. 444a and 444b), imperfective (ex. 444c), present (ex. 444d), aorist (ex. 444e) and future ones (exx. 444f and 444g) as well as relative clause with an adverbial sentence (ex. 444h and 444i).

(444a) Shenute stipulates:
*tenu=de ti-cô mmo-s n-tei-he ce-ne-nt-a-n-krine*
now=yet 1S-say OBJ-3FS in-DEM.F-way COMP-DEF.P-REL-PST-1P-judge

*auô* *a-n-diakrine* *e-taho-u* *erat-u* *ecn-nei-topos*
and PST-1P-separate to-stand-3P at-3P upon-DEM.P-place
*nne-u-eš-er-hôb* *ecô-i*
NEG.FUT-3P-can-do-work upon-1S
*ude* *nne-u-eš-ci-u-hnau* *e-uom-f* *ntoot-u*
nor NEG.FUT-3P-can-take-IDF.S-thing to-eat-3MS by-3P
*n-n-et-diakoni* *e-n-anok=an* *p-ent-a-i-taa-f* *na-u*
as-DEF.P-REL-serve DEP-NEG-1S=NEG COP.M-REL-PST-1S-give-3MS to-3P
I now say thus: those whom we judge and whom we separated to stand on these places will neither be able to work for me nor to receive anything to eat from the servers, without me being the one who has given it to them. (SShenute, *God Who Alone Is True,* [L IV 113, 14–18])

(444b) The psalmist says that it was not people's own doing that made them receive the land:
*auô* *m-pe-u-cneh=en* *p-ete-ha-f-nehm-u*
and NEG-POSS.P-3P-arm=NEG COP.M-REL-PST-3MS-save-3P
*nsa-te-k-uinem=te* *p-c(ai)s* *nem-pe-k-cneh*
after-POSS.F-2MS-right=SE.F DEF.M-lord with-POSS.M-2MS-arm
*nem-p-uain* *m-pe-k-ha*
with-DEF.M-light of-POSS.M-2MS-face
And it was not their arm that saved them but your right hand, O Lord, and your arm and the light of your countenance.
(MPs 43 [44]:4)

(444c) Jesus learns that the Pharisees are looking for him, as he is said to have baptised more disciples than John. The author of the Gospel inserts a parenthesis:
*kaitoi* *i(êsu)s=an* *p-e-ne-f-baptize* *alla*
although N=NEG COP.M-REL-PRT-3MS-baptize but
*ne-f-mathêtês=ne*
POSS.P-3MS-disciples=SE.P
...although it was not Jesus who baptised but it was rather his disciples.
(SJn 4:2)

(444d) Shenute argues that Gen 1:26 shows that Christ was with the Father already in the beginning:
*mê* *p-iôt=an* *p-et-šace* *mn-pe-f-šêre*
IP DEF.M-father=NEG COP.M-REL-talk with-POSS.M-3MS-son
*pe-f-mono-genês* *etuaab*
POSS.M-single-born holy
Is it not the Father who speaks with his son, his holy only-begotten son?
(SShenute, *It Happened One Day* [*ZÄS* 80, 42, 28–29])

(444e) Asked whether a Christian who has fallen into sin would be put before the Lord once he dies, the archbishop answers positively and goes on to say that Jesus is going to sentence him and punish him according to the measure of his sin:

| | | | |
|---|---|---|---|
| *alla* | *n-amnte=an* | *p-ete-ša-u-noc-f* | *ero-f* |
| but | NEG-hell=NEG | COP.M-REL-AOR-3P-throw-3MS | to-3MS |
| *alla* | *e-ša-u-noc-f* | *e-n-kolasis* | *ša-p-ehou* |
| but | ST-AOR-3P-throw-3MS | to-DEF.P-punishment | until-DEF.M-day |
| *ete-f-na-meh-ne-f-nobe* | *ebol* | *nse-ti-mton* | *na-f* |
| REL-3MS-fut-fill-POSS.P-3MS-sin | out | CNJ.3P-give-rest | to-3MS |

But not to Hell (alone) will he be cast, but to punishments until the day he will have redeemed his sin and will be given rest.
($^{S}$*Questions of Theodore* [van Lantschoot 22, 1–3])

(444f) Jesus says in the Sermon on the Mount:

| | | | | | |
|---|---|---|---|---|---|
| *n-uan* | *nim=en* | *et-ne-ce-s* | *ne-i* | *ce-p-c(ai)s* | *p-c(ai)s* |
| NEG-each | QU=NEG | REL-FUT-say-3FS | to-1S | COMP-DEF.M-lord | DEF.M-lord |
| *p-et-nnêu* | *ehun* | *e-t-mnt-era* | *n-m-pêue* | | |
| DEF.M-REL-go.STA | into | to-DEF.F-ABST-king | of-DEF.P-heaven | | |

Not everyone who will say to me 'Lord, Lord', shall enter into kingdom of heaven. ($^{M}$Mt 7:21 mae 1)

(444g) Paul answers to one who will ask how the body will be resurrected and what will it be like: *You fool, what you sow will not live, except it dies*:

| | | |
|---|---|---|
| *m-p-sôma=an* | *et-na-šôpe* | *p-e-ša-k-co-f* |
| NEG-DEF.M-body=NEG | REL-FUT-happen | COP.M-REL-AOR-2MS-sow-3MS |

It is not the future body that you sow. ($^{S}$1Cor 15:37)

(444h) Shenute discusses Mt 25:31–32 mentioning the separation of sheep from goats:

| | | | | |
|---|---|---|---|---|
| *ê* | *ene-u-psukhê=an* | *n-zôon* | *t-et-nhêt-u* | *ne-u-na-oš* |
| or | CFT-IDF.S-soul=NEG | of-animal | COP.F-REL-inside-3P | PRT-3P-FUT-cry |
| *ebol=an=pe* | *ce-...* | | | |
| out=NEG=PTC | COMP-... | | | |

So, if it were not an animal's soul that is in them, would they not cry out saying...
($^{S}$Shenute, *I Have Been Reading the Holy Gospels* §1 [L III 220, 7–8])

(444i) The prophet asks:

| | | | | |
|---|---|---|---|---|
| *mê* | *u-[nut]te=en* | *n-uôt* | *p-et-a-[f-s]mn-têne* | |
| IR | IDF.S-god=NEG | of-single | COP.M-REL-PST-3MS-establish-2P | |
| *mê* | *u-iôt=en* | *[n]-uôt* | *p-et-hicô-tn[e]* | *têr-têne* |
| IR | IDF.S-father=NEG | of-single | COP.M-REL-upon-2P | all-2P |

Is it not a single God who created us? Is it not a single father who is above us all? ($^{A}$Mal 2:10)

As in the affirmative, most negative examples of cleft sentences show agreement in gender and number between the initial NP and the relative clause. Only Bohairic shows a regular use of the invariable masculine form of the copula/definite article with the relative clause. There are, however, rare examples of the invariable masculine form in Sahidic as well (445d)[150]:

(445a) Jesus tells the disciples not to hesitate when preaching the gospel but to say what comes first to mind:

*nt$^h$ôten=gar=an p-et$^h$-na-saci alla pi-pn(eum)a et$^h$uab=pe*
2P=for=NEG COP.M-REL-FUT-speak but DEF$_2$.M-ghost holy=SE.M
...for it is not you who speak but the Holy Spirit. ($^B$Mk 13:11)

(445b) Theodore tells his soldiers that it is useless to pursue a stag that they had just seen:

*ce-anon=an p-et$^h$-na-c$^h$op-f*
for-1P=NEG COP.M-REL-FUT-seize-3MS
*alla nt$^h$of pe et$^h$-na-taho-n ḫen-ni-šnêu*
but 3MS COP.M REL-FUT-reach-1P in-DEF$_2$.P-net.P
*nte-te-f-met-agathos*
of-POSS.F-3MS-ABST-good
...for it is not we who will seize him but he will catch us in the nets of his goodness. ($^B$Theodore of Antioch, *On the Theodores* [*AM* II 120, 11–13])

(445c) The prophet addresses Israel:

*mê u-nuti n-uôt=an pe ete-ntô-ten têr-u*
IP IDF.S-god of-single=NEG COP.M REL-with-2P all-3P
Is it not a single god who is with you all? ($^B$Mal 2:10)

(445d) The author of the first epistle of John stresses the necessity of love:

*ere-t-agapê m-p-nute šoop hm-pai*
ST-DEF.F-love of-DEF.M-god happen.STA in-DEM.M
*ce-anon=an p-ent-a-n-meri-p-nute alla ntof*
COMP-1P=NEG COP.M-REL-PST-1P-love-DEF.M-god but 3MS
*p-ent-a-f-merit-n*
COP.M-REL-PST-3MS-love-1P
The love of God means that it is not we who loved God; rather, it is He who loved us. ($^S$1Jn 4:10 [Schüssler])

Coordinated patterns often repeat the negation, but not in all cases. Note that the second example below shows repetition of the subject element due to the difference in gender and number of the respective predicates:

150 The fact that they all appear in adversative coordination is probably merely accidental.

(446a) The children of God were bitten by venomous snakes but were saved only through the mercy of God:

*ute=gar* *n-u-ntêkʲ=an* *ute* *n-u-pahre=an*
nor=for NEG-IDF.S-herb=NEG nor NEG-IDF.S-drug=NEG
*t-ent-a-s-talkʲo-u*
COP.F-REL-PST-3FS-cure-3P
*alla* *pe-k-šace* *pe* *p-cois* *et-tuco* *n-uon* *nim*
but POSS.M-2MS-word COP.M DEF.M-lord REL-heal OBJ-each QU
For it was neither herb nor drug that cured them, but (it is) your word, O Lord, which heals everything. ($^{S}$Sap 16:12)

(446b) Shenute argues against heathens:

*nim=de* *p-ent-a-f-r-hôb* *e-t-ete-tn-mute* *ce-êse*
WH=yet COP.M-REL-PST-3MS-do-work OBJ-DEF.F-REL-2P-call COMP-N
*šante-f-mong-s* *nte-tn-šmše=na-s*
LIM-3MS-form-3FS CNJ-2P-serve=to-3FS
*mê* *u-rôme=an=pe* *ê* *hen-rôme=an=ne*
IP IDF.S-man=NEG=COP.M or IDF.P-MAN=NEG=COP.P
*nt-a-u-r-hôb* *e-eidos* *nim* *p-še* *mn-p-ône*
REL-PST-3P-do-work to-shape QU DEF.M-wood and-DEF.M-stone
*mn-n-koue* *têr-u* *šant-u-aa-u* *n-hen-eidolon* *auô*
and-DEF.P-other.P all-3P LIM-3P-do-3P OBJ-IDF.P-image and
*hen-kô*
IDF.P-idol
But who produced her whom you call Isis so that he fashioned her and that you should worship her? Is it not man, or rather men, who produce any shape, wood, stone, and all the rest of it so that they make images and idols? ($^{S}$Shenute, *Well Did You Come* [A II 407, 10–13])

(446c) Jesus says that Simon Peter is blessed because he said that Jesus was the Christ:

*ce-n-sarks=an* *hi-snof* *p-ent-a-f-kʲelp-pai=na-k*
for-NEG-flesh=NEG on-blood COP.M-REL-PST-3MS-reveal-DEM.M=to-2MS
*ebol* *alla* *pa-iôt=pe* *et-hn-m-pêue*
out but POSS.M.1S-father=SE.M REL-in-DEF.P-heaven.P
...for not flesh and blood have revealed this to you, but my father who is in heaven. ($^{S}$Mt 16:17)

See also the Mesokemic version of Matthew 16:17 cited as 449a where the negation follows the coordinated NPs.

The other cleft constructions described earlier are similarly negated by *an/en*; cf. the following examples with the pattern NP + bare relative clause:

(447a) The apostle warns against boasting:

*ešce k-šušu=de mmo-k ntak=en et-bi ha-t-nuni*
CND 2MS-boast=yet OBJ-2MS 2MS=NEG REL-bear under-DEF.F-root
*alla t-nuni t-et-bi hala-k*
but DEF.F-root COP.F-REL-bear under-2MS
If you do boast, (remember) it is not you who bears the roots, but it is the root that bears you. ($^{F}$Rm 11:18 [Wessely])

(447b) Theodore hears a voice telling him: 'Theodore, Theodore, my beloved':

*nt$^{h}$ok=an et$^{h}$-na-taho-i alla anok et$^{h}$-na-taho-k*
2MS=NEG REL-FUT-take-1S but 1S REL-FUT-take-2MS
*ḫen-ni-šnêu nte-ta-met-nuti*
in-DEF$_{2}$.P-net.P of-POSS.F.1S-ABST-god
It is not you who will catch me, but it is me who will catch you in the nets of my divinity.
($^{B}$Theodore of Antioch, *On the Theodores* [*AM* II 118, 27–29])

(447c) Jesus says in the Sermon on the Mount:

*uon niben=an et-cô mmo-s nê-i ce-p-c$^{h}$(oi)s*
one QU=NEG REL-say OBJ-3FS to-1S COMP-DEF.M-lord
*p-c$^{h}$(oi)s*
DEF.M-lord
*et$^{h}$-nai ehun e-ti-met-uro nte-ni-p$^{h}$êui*
REL-go.STA into to-DEF$_{2}$.F-ABST-king of-DEF.P-heaven
Not everyone who will say to me 'Lord, Lord' will enter the kingdom of heaven. ($^{B}$Mt 7:21)

Negative examples of the other cleft types are rare:

(448a) Shenute wonders whether the people taking care of him and sending him clothes that he does not need are being sincere and asks:

*ê m-pai=an pe e-f-šoop e-u-mkah*
or NEG-DEM.M=NEG COP.M DEP-3MS-happen.STA to-IDF.S-sorrow
*n-hêt*
of-heart
Is it not the following matter that causes distress?
($^{S}$Shenute, *Who But God Is the Witness* [Boud'hors 176, a9–13])

(448b) Gesios replies to the thankful words of the sick man in his care:

*p-nute p-et-soun pa-son*
DEF.M-god COP.M-REL-know POSS.M.1S-brother

*ce-n-u-agapê=an te e-n-ire mmo-s nmma-k*
COMP-NEG-IDF.S-love=NEG COP.F DEP-1P-do OBJ-3FS with-2MS
*alla u-khreôs=pe*
but IDF.S-duty=SE.M
God knows, my brother, that it is not affection we grant to you, but duty.
($^{\mathrm{S}}$*Gesios & Isodorus* [*ZÄS* 21, 151, 1–2])

(448c) The Lord ordains Moses to tell the people when they are allowed to eat meat:
*n-u-ehou=an pe ere-ten-na-uôm nḫêt-f ude 2 an*
NEG-IDF.S-day=NEG COP.M DEP-2P-FUT-eat inside-3MS nor 2 NEG
*ude 5 n-ehou an=ne ude 10=an=ne ude 20*
nor 5 of-day NEG=SE.P nor 10=NEG=SE.P nor 20
Not one day, nor two, nor five days, nor ten nor twenty you shall eat...
($^{\mathrm{B}}$Nm 11:19)

Negated cleft sentences with the etymological participle *er-* are attested only in Mesokemic and Old Bohairic (so-called B4)[151]:

(449a) Jesus says that Simon Peter is blessed because he said that Jesus was the Christ:
*ce-n-sarks hi-snaf=en er-kʲelp-pei=ne-k ebal*
for-NEG-flesh on-blood=NEG do.PPA-reveal-DEM.M=to-2MS out
*alla pa-iot=pe et-hn-m-pê*
but POSS.M.1S-father=SE.M REL-in-DEF.P-heaven
...for not flesh and blood have revealed this to you, but my father who is in heaven. ($^{\mathrm{M}}$Mt 16:17 mae 1)

(449b) Jesus asks the Jews:
*an m-môusês=an er-ti-pi-nomos nô-ten*
IP NEG-N=NEG do.PPA-give-DEF$_2$.M-law to-2P
Did not Moses give you the law? ($^{\mathrm{B}}$Jn 7:19 [Kasser])

(449c) Jesus teaches the disciples:
*ntʰôten=an er-sôtep mmo-i alla anok a-i-setp-tʰênu*
2P=NEG do.PPA-choose OBJ-1S but 1S PST-1S-choose-2P
It was not you who chose me, but I have chosen you. ($^{\mathrm{B}}$Jn 15:16 [Kasser])

Although examples are relatively uncommon, unlike the earlier phases of the language Coptic allows the negation of the relative clause of cleft sentences. Note

151 Even though the element *er-* is attested also in some early Sahidic Gnostic texts, it does not appear in clefts even in these sources; see Müller (2011a: 267).

that in 450a, the Sahidic variant uses the cleft pattern, whereas the Bohairic text shows omission of the subject element:

(450a) Those victorious over the beast sing Moses' songs of praises about the Lord and his deeds:

S *nim* *p-ete-n-f-r-hote* *hêt-k=an* *p-c(oi)s*
WH COP.M-REL-NEG.FUT-3MS-do-fear before-2MS=NEG DEF.M-lord
Who does not fear you, o Lord. ($^{S}$Rev 15:4)

B *nim* *ete-nne-f-er-hoti* *ḫa-t-hê* *m-p-c*$^{h}$*(ôi)s*
WH REL-NEG.FUT-3MS-do-fear under-DEF.F-front of-DEF.M-lord
Who shall not fear the Lord. ($^{B}$Rev 15:4)

(450b) The torturer Dionysos has been healed by the hot water in which St Ptolemy is boiled and converts to Christianity. The hegemon is enraged but Dionysus tells him to look around and see:

*nim* *p-et-n-f-na-pisteue=an* *e-ne-kʲom* *m-p-nute*
WH COP.M-REL-NEG-3MS-FUT-believe=NEG to-DEF.P-power of-DEF.M-god
Who will not believe in God's might?
($^{S}$*Mart. Ptolemy* [Till, *KHML* II 37, 12–13])

(450c) Jesus preaches to the disciples:

*ephoson* *mpe-tn-ire* *n-ue* *n-nei-elakhistos*
inasmuch NEG.PST-2P-do to-one of-DEM.P-humblest
*anak* *p-ete-mpe-tn-e-s* *ne-i*
1S COP.M-REL-NEG.PST-2P-do-3MS to-1S
Inasmuch as you did not do (it) to one of the least of these, it is me to whom you did not do it. ($^{M}$Mt 25:45 mae 1)

The earlier possessive patterns *n-s/ink* no longer exist in Coptic.

Finally, the same negation is employed for tripartite sentences. No constraints on the participant structures seem apparent, i.e. all NPs are allowed:

(451a) Paul says that the question of flesh is irrelevant when resurrection is considered:

*n-u-sarks* *n-uôt=an* *te* *sarks* *nim*
NEG-IDF.S-flesh of-single=NEG COP.F flesh QU
All flesh is not a single (kind of) flesh. ($^{S}$1Cor 15:39)

(451b) Clerics should not spoil their wives with gold, silver, jewels, etc.

*is* *skhêma=gar* *n-tei-mine* *n-na-n-šêre=an=ne*
PTC guise=for of-DEM.F-sort NEG-POSS.P-of-son=NEG=COP.P
*n-t-ekklêsia*
of-DEF.F-church
...for lo, apparel like this is not for the children of the church.
($^{S}$*Canons of Athanasius* [Crum in Riedel §44])

(451c) Peter tells Cornelius:
*hn-u-mee* *ti-saun* *ce-n-u-ref-ci-ha=en* *pe*
in-IDF.S-truth 1S-know COMP-NEG-IDF.S-AGT-take-face=NEG COP.M
*p-n(u)ti*
DEF.M-god
Verily, I know that God is not someone who respects persons.
($^{M}$Acts 10:34)

(451d) The Lord rebukes Satan and says:
*au* *pei* *u-šeu* *n-ẖe=en* *pe* *e-a-u-takme-f*
and DEM.M IDF.S-log of-wood=NEG COP.M DEP-PST-3P-pluck
*abal* *ẖn-p-kôht*
out in-DEF.M-fire
And is this not a log taken out of the fire? ($^{A}$Zec 3:2 [Till])

(451e) Agathonicus condemns people reading books of pagan Greek authors:
*nei* *n-tei-hê* *hen-khrêstianos=en* *ne*
DEM.P of-DEM.F-kind IDF.P-Christian=NEG COP.P
People like this are not Christians.
($^{F}$Agathonicus of Tarsus, *De incredulitate* [Erichsen 28, 2–4])

(451f) There is comfort even for the hopeless fallen:
*n-u-a-dikos=gar=en* *pe* *p-(nu)ti* *e-el-p-ôbeš*
NEG-IDF.S-un-righteous=for=NEG COP.M DEF.M-god to-do-DEF.M-forget
*m-pe-ten-hôb*
of-POSS.M-2P-work
For God is not unrighteous so as to forget your work. ($^{F}$Heb 6:10 [Zoega])

(451g) The people of Nazareth wonder about Jesus:
*mê* *te-f-mau=an* *te* *mariam*
IP POSS.F-3MS-mother=NEG COP.F N
Is not Mary his mother? ($^{B}$Mt 13:55)

(451h) After Domnus' father had died he begged John to resurrect him as well. John replied:
*mper-er-hoti* *p$^{h}$-mu=gar* *m-pe-k-iôt*
NEG.IMP-AUX-fear DEF.M-death=for of-POSS.M-2MS-father
*u-mu=an* *pe* *alla* *u-ônẖ=pe*
IDF.S-death=NEG COP.M but IDF.S-life=SE.M
Fear not! For the death of your father is not death, but it is life.
($^{B}$*Apocr. Acts of the Apostles* [*FS Crum* 313, 1–3])

As can be seen from the above examples, the negation brackets the initial NP, which here happens to be the predicate. Sometimes, however, it seems that the position of the negation obeys a structural rather than a semantic rule, as there are cases in which the initial NP cannot be identified as the predicate, but rather seems to function as subject:

(452a) John the Baptist is introduced in the *Gospel of John* as a man who testified about the light. Yet:

| | | |
|---|---|---|
| *ne-p-etmmau=an* | *pe* | *p-uoin* |
| PRT-DEF.M-there=NEG | COP.M | DEF.M-light |

This one was not the light. (SJn 1:8)

| | | |
|---|---|---|
| *ntaf=en* | *pe* | *p-uain* |
| 3MS=NEG | COP.M | DEF.M-light |

He is not the light. (FJn 1:8 [*AfP* 34: 38])

(452b) Asked whether a blasphemer would be from a holy spirit, patriarch John of Alexandria denies the idea and says:

| | | | | | |
|---|---|---|---|---|---|
| *alla* | *rôme* | *nim* | *e-f-cô* | *mmo-s* | *ce-n-i(êsu)s=an* |
| but | man | QU | DEP-3MS-say | OBJ-3FS | COMP-NEG-N=NEG |

| | | | | |
|---|---|---|---|---|
| *pe* | *p-šêre* | *m-p-nute* | *e-f-ciua* | *e-pe-pn(eum)a* |
| COP.M | DEF.M-son | of-DEF.M-god | ST-3MS-blaspheme | to-DEF.M-spirit |

| |
|---|
| *et-uaab* |
| REL-clean.STA |

...but every man, who says that Jesus is not the son of God, blasphemes against the Holy Ghost.

(S*Questions of Theodore* [van Lantschoot 16, 16–18])

(452c) Barnabas wants to take Mark along when they return to the city, but Paul is unwilling to do so. Hence they argue:

| | | | |
|---|---|---|---|
| *pece-barnabas* | *ce-n-u-diakion=an* | *pe* | *e-štam* |
| say.PST-N | COMP-NEG-IDF.S-just=NEG | COP.M | to-shut |

| | | |
|---|---|---|
| *m-p-ro* | *n-t-metanoia* | *hn-t-arkhê* |
| OBJ-DEF.M-mouth | to-DEF.F-repentance | in-DEF.F-beginning |

| |
|---|
| *m-p-tašeoiš* |
| of-DEF.M-preaching |

| | | | |
|---|---|---|---|
| *pece-paulos* | *ce-n-u-eulogon=an* | *pe* | *e-tre-u-ti-kʲnon* |
| say.PST-N | COMP-NEG-IDF.S-proper=NEG | COP.M | to-INFL-3P-give-softness |

| | |
|---|---|
| *n-m-pistos* | *e-tre-u-slaate* |
| to-DEF.P-faithful | to-INFL-3P-slip |

Barnabas said: 'It is not right to shut the door for repentance at the beginning of the preaching.' And Paul said: 'It is not proper to slacken the faithful so as to make them slip.'

(SJohn the Hermit, *Enc. on Mark the Evangelist* [Orlandi 30, 1–5])

(452d) People will flee from the son of the lawlessness saying:

| | | |
|---|---|---|
| *pei=en* | *pe* | *p-kh(risto)s* |
| DEM.M=NEG | COP.M | DEF.M-Christ |

This one is not the Christ.

(A*ApEl* [Steindorff, *Apokalypse des Elias* 98 38, 11])

(452e) Saul preaches the glory of Jesus in Damascus to the effect that everyone is astonished and asks:

*mê m-pei=en pe pê et-ha-f-core ebal*
IP NEG-DEM.M=NEG COP.M DEF$_3$.M REL-PST-3MS-disperse out
*n-uan nim et-epikali m-pei-ren hn-t-hi(rusa)lêm*
OBJ-each QU REL-invoke OBJ-DEM.M-name in-DEF.F-N
Is this not the one who in Jerusalem persecuted all those who invoked that name? ($^{M}$Acts 9:21)

(452f) The author of a gnostic treatise answers in advance to possible objections. Among them is the question how entities coming into existence later could name preceding entities. He reflects on what a name is:

*ntaf pe p-ren mamêe*
3MS COP.M DEF.M-name really
*ntaf=en=$k^j$e pe p-ren abal m-p-iôt*
3MS=NEG=PTC COP.M DEF.M-name out of-DEF.M-father
It is the name in truth; it is therefore not the name from the Father.
($^{L}$*EvVer* 40, 5–7)

(452g) A pagan resurrected by St George tells of his suffering in Hell, where Apollo had told him:

*anok=an pe $p^h$-(nu)ti alla anok u-idôlon n-at-psykhê*
1S=NEG COP.M DEF.M-god but 1S IDF.S-idol of-NEG-soul
I am not God but a soulless idol.
($^{B}$Theodotus of Ancyra, *In S. Georgem Diosp.* [AM II 227, 8–9])

(452h) John the Baptist answers the question of his identity:

*anok=an pe p-kh(risto)s*
1S=NEG COP.M DEF.M-Christ
I am not the Christ. ($^{B}$Jn 1:20)

It would thus appear that the negation simply surrounds the first NP, regardless of grammatical roles. Yet counterexamples do exist (see 453c).

Coordinated structures exhibit *an* after the first element:

(453a) An angel leads Paul through the abyss and shows him a pit of fire holding people who refused bread and wine in the service. The angel explains the reason for their fate:

*ntou=an te t-sarks m-pe-kh(risto)s mn-pe-f-snof*
3P=NEG COP.F DEF.F-flesh in-DEF.M-Christ with-POSS.M-3MS-blood
They are not the flesh of Christ or his blood.
($^{S}$*ApPaul* [Budge, *Misc.* 546, 22–23])

(453b) Paul warns the Roman congregation against letting good things be spoken as evil:

*t-mnt-ero=gar=an* *m-p-nute* *pe* *uôm* *hi-sô*
DEF.F-ABST-king=for=NEG of-DEF.M-god COP.M eat on-drink
*alla* *u-dikaiosunê=te* *mn-u-eirênê* *mn-u-raše*
but IDF.S-righteousness=SE.F with-IDF.S-peace with-IDF.S-joy
*hm-pe-pn(eum)a* *et-uaab*
in-DEF.M-soul holy

For the kingdom of God is not to eat and drink, but righteousness and peace and joy in the Holy Spirit. ($^{S}$Rm 14:17)

(453c) David sends word to ask Amasa:

*mê* *ntok* *pe* *na-kees=an* *ntok* *auô* *na-sarks*
IP 2MS COP.M POSS.P.1S-bone=NEG 2MS and POSS.P.1S-flesh

Are you not also my bone and my flesh? ($^{S}$2Kg 19:13)

(453d) Shenute stresses the importance of good administration:

*na-rôme=an* *ne* *nei-hbêue*
POSS.P-man=NEG COP.P DEM.P-things.P
*ce-e-n-na-tet-pe-n-hêt* *ero-n* *n-tn-kaa-u*
COMP-ST-1P-FUT-please-POSS.M-1P-heart to-1P CNJ-1P-put-3P
*n-t-he* *et-uo* *mmo-s* *alla* *na-p-noute=ne*
in-DEF.F-way REL-cease OBJ-3FS but POSS.P-DEF.M-god=SE.P

These tasks do not belong to people, so that we may please ourselves and let it go, but they are those of God.

($^{S}$Shenute, *God Who Alone Is True* [*WZKM* 88: 288, ff. 213, 50–214, 5])

In negated sentences of the type [A B COP], the element *an* is positioned after the predicate but before the copula. Note here especially ex. 454c, which shows clitic movement of the negation int the phrase structure but sentence-final position of the copula:

(454a) Father Sisoes tells how he once went to Father Hor begging him for a wise saying. Father Hor sent him away saying:

*p-nute* *m-pa-p-et-o=an=pe* *m-mai-huo*
DEF.M-god NEG-POSS.M-DEF.M-REL-be.STA=NEG=COP.M for-love.PIA-more
*alla* *p-et-ci* *mmo-f* *n-kʼons* *smamaat* *hn-hôb* *nim*
but DEF.M-REL-take OBJ-3MS as-violence blessed.STA in-work QU

God is not one for the greedy, but whoever constraints himself is blessed in every work. ($^{S}$*AP* Chaîne 115, 7–9)

(454b) Upon Paul's question on the identity of a certain person in Hell, an angel replies:

| | | | |
|---|---|---|---|
| *pai* | *u-diakanos* | *pe* | *e-f-porneue* |
| DEM.M | IDF.S-deacon | COP.M | DEP-3MS-fornicate |

| | |
|---|---|
| *mn-ne-hiome* | *n-nu-f=an=ne* |
| with-DEF.P-woman.P | NEG-POSS.P-3MS=NEG=SE.P |

That one is a deacon who fornicated with women that were not his.

([S]*ApPaul* [Budge, *Misc.* 541, 5–6])

(454c) Jesus argues that his kingdom is not of this world and concludes:

| | | | | |
|---|---|---|---|---|
| *tinu[=kʲe* | *t]a-mnt-rro* | *u-abal=en* | *hen-[pe]i-ma* | *te* |
| now=then | POSS.F-ABST-king | IDF.S-out=NEG | in-DEM.M-place | COP.F |

Thus now, my kingdom is not from hence. ([L]Jn 18:36)

(454d) No one who relies on the law is justified before God:

| | | | |
|---|---|---|---|
| *pi-nomos=de* | *n-u-ebol* | *ḫen-pi-nahti=an* | *pe* |
| $DEF_2$.M-law=yet | NEG-IDF.S-out | from-$DEF_2$.M-faith=NEG | COP.M |

The law is not based on (lit. 'of') the faith. ([B]Gal 3:12)

However, as most of the examples of the pattern A B COP can be derived from a pattern with anteposition (i.e. $A_i$ – B $COP_i$, an extension of the bipartite pattern with subject element with an explicit referent before the sentence), these instances do not contradict the observation that the negation brackets the initial NP. Although in Bohairic the pattern A B COP is prevalent, any semantic-pragmatic markedness as an anteposition construction (i.e. A – it is the B) has been lost. Yet the construction still abides to the rules characteristic to its structural properties.

Finally, the same negation appears in the specific case of nominal sentences with an adverbial phrase:

(455a) Shenute recommends paying attention to all the words and saying of earlier leaders of the congregation. He reasons about their impeccable reputation:

| | | |
|---|---|---|
| *kata-u-eou=an* | *ute* | *n-kata-u-kʲin-šace=an=ne* |
| like-IDF-S-fame=NEG | nor | NEG-like-IDF.S-AGT-talk=NEG=SE.P |

They were neither thirsty for fame nor talkative.

([S]Shenute, *You, God, The Eternal* [L IV 65,12–13])

(455b) Jesus tells his disciples that the last days will be preceded by news of war and turmoil:

| | | | |
|---|---|---|---|
| *alla* | *satot-f=an* | *pe* | *pi-côk* |
| but | through-3MS=NEG | COP.M | $DEF_2$.M-complete |

But the end is not by this. ([B]Lk 21:9)

(455c) The Egyptians notice that the Hebrew women still give birth to male children. As they accuse the midwives, the latter midwives tell the pharaoh why they were not able to kill the male offspring of the Hebrews at birth:

*m-p$^h$-rêti=an* *n-ni-hiomi* *nte-k$^h$êmi* *ne*
in-DEF.M-way=NEG of-DEF$_2$.P-women.P of-Egypt COP.P
*ni-hiomi* *nte-ni-hebreos*
DEF$_2$.P-women.P of-DEF$_2$.P-Hebrew
The Hebrew women are unlike the women of Egypt. ($^B$Ex 1:19)

# Part III: **The adjectival sentence**

# 1 Internal morpho-syntax

The third and final type of Ancient Egyptian non-verbal predication is the so-called *adjectival* sentence. The internal syntax of these constructions remained virtually unchanged throughout the diachronic period in which they are attested in the language, conforming to the following generic schema:

$$S > [AdjP_P\ NP_S]$$

Nevertheless, the adjectival sentence is, from a diachronic point of view, primarily an Earlier Egyptian phenomenon. Widely attested in Old and Middle Egyptian, adjectival sentences play a rather minor role in the linguistic system of Late Egyptian and disappeared in Demotic and Coptic, when they are superseded in their function by new patterns.

## 1.1 Earlier Egyptian

In Earlier Egyptian, the predicate of an adjectival sentence can be an expression denoting a quality such as *štꜣ* 'difficult', *ḥ(w)ꜥ* 'short', *ꜣw* 'long', *ꜥšꜣ* 'many', *ꜥnd* 'scarce', *wš* 'barren', *ꜥꜣ* 'great', *ktt* 'small', *wr* 'great', and *nfr* 'good, content' in the following examples:

(1a) In a description of hauling a colossal statue:
*isṯ* *štꜣ=wr-t* *wꜣ-t* *ii-t-n-f*
PTC difficult=very-ADV road-F come.REL-F-PST-3MS
*ḥr-s* *r-ḫ-t=nb-t*
on-3FS to-thing-F=QU-F
Now, the road on which it came was more difficult than anything.
(*El Bersheh* I, pl. 14, 1)

(1b) The peasant makes a general observation about the ways of men:
*ḥ(w)ꜥ* *ḫsf* *ꜣw* *iy-t*
short redress long evil-F
Redress is short, but evildoing is long. (Peas B1, 139–40)

https://doi.org/10.1515/9783110409895-010

(1c) Neferty describes Egypt's political fragmentation and the prevailing misery:
*ʿnd t3 ʿš3 ḫrp-w-f wš ø ʿ3*
scarce land many controller-P-3MS barren ø great
*b3k-w-f ktt it wr ip-t*
due-P-3MS meagre grain great measure-F
Land is scarce, but its controllers are many; (it) is barren, but its taxes are great; grain is lacking, but the (tax-collector's) measure is large.
(Neferty XIb–c)

Derived adjectives, which in Egyptological linguistics are termed *nisbe* ('relation') and are formed from nouns or from prepositions,[1] are not generally used as predicates in Earlier Egyptian.[2] However, it is possible that in the oldest language, where *nisbe*-formation was probably more widely employed than later,[3] the predicative use was still grammatical. Examples such as the following are suggestive in this respect:

(2a) The deceased king is told:
*ḫnt(-y)=ṯw pr-w wr-w*
before[-RLT.M]=2MS house-P great-P
You are pre-eminent (of) the great houses. (PT 1288a)

(2b) The deceased is a raging god:
*ḫt(-y) mw-i tp-r3-i*
fire[-RLT-M] water-1S upon-mouth-1S
The water in my mouth is fiery. (CT VI 342e)

Yet *nisbe*-adjectives are very commonly used as predicates in nominal sentences in later sources, which emphasises the difference between adjectival and nominal sentences:

(3) The deceased says:
*ink ḫnt(-y) 3bḏw*
1S front[-RLT.M] N
I am one pre-eminent of Abydos. (CT VII 480j/B5C)

Common are examples where the predicate of an adjectival sentence is morphologically or semantically recognisable as an active or passive participle,

1 For Earlier Egyptian, *nisbe*-adjectives in general, see e.g. Schenkel (1966); Satzinger (1986); Jansen-Winkeln (1993). The standard work on *nisbe*-morphology is Osing (1976: 309–20).
2 A similar view on the predicativity of *nisbe*-adjectives is also expressed e.g. by Satzinger (1986: 141) and Malaise and Winand (1999: §121). Against their view, *n* is analysed here as a determinative pronoun, see Part II Section 1.1.1 above. A different opinion is held by e.g. Borghouts (2010: §95.b.1 NB 2).
3 See Allen (2013: 87) for some remarks.

such as *sḥḏ* 'illuminating', *swḏ3* 'rejuvenating', *ḏsr* 'secluded', and *ḥ3p* 'hidden' in the following examples:

(4a) The king is a life-giving force:

| | | | |
|---|---|---|---|
| *sḥḏ-w=sw* | *t3-wy* | *r-itn* | *sw3ḏ-w=sw* |
| illuminate.PPA-M=3MS | land-DU | to-sun disc | freshen.PPA-M=3MS |

| | |
|---|---|
| *r-ḥʿp(y)* | *ʿ3* |
| to-flood | great |

He is more illuminating of the two lands than the sun-disc; he is more rejuvenating than a high Nile. (*Loyaliste* §2, 9–10/St)

(4b) Thutmosis I says of the divine images which he ordered to be made:

| | | | |
|---|---|---|---|
| *ḏsr=st* | *r-ḫpr-t* | *m-p-t* | *ḥ3p=st* |
| hide.PPP=3C | to-happen.PIA-F | in-heaven-F | hide.PPP=3C |

| | |
|---|---|
| *r-sḫr-w* | *dw3t* |
| to-plan-P | underworld |

They are more secluded than what happens in the heaven; they are more hidden than the plans of the underworld. (*Urk.* IV 99, 15–16)

Note here the use of the preposition *r* to express the standard of comparison (*nfr X r Y* 'X is good in relation to Y'). The same way of expressing the comparative is also found in verbal sentences with quality concept root predicates (see Section 3.1).

Predicative adjectives do not show agreement with the subject but rather appear in an unmarked form, morphologically identical with the masculine singular. This can be seen, e.g., in the difference in gender between the predicate *št3* 'difficult' and the feminine subject *w3-t* 'road' in (1a) above. The same holds for participles used as adjectival predicates: these also appear invariably in the perfective masculine singular form (which, in case of the so-called mutable roots, shows no gemination of the penultimate or reduplication of the final radical):

(5a) Thutmosis III says of his relationship to Amun:

| | | | | |
|---|---|---|---|---|
| *ḥʿ=sw* | *im-i* | *r-nsw=nb* | *ḫpr-w* | *m-t3* |
| joy.PPA=3MS | in-1S | to-king=QU.M | happen.PPA-P | in-earth |

He is more joyful in me than (in) any king that has existed on earth. (*Urk.* IV 162, 5)

(5b) Henu characterises himself in third person:

| | | | | |
|---|---|---|---|---|
| *iri=sw* | *ḏd-t* | *3ḫ=sw* | *m-ib* | *n(-y)-nb-f* |
| do.PPA=3MS | say.PIA-F | efficient.PPA=3MS | in-heart | of[-M]-lord-3MS |

He is one who performs what is said; he is efficient in the mind of his lord. (*Hammamat* 114, 7)

Participial predicates sometimes show the masculine singular ending *-w*:[4]

(6) The Foremost of Westeners says of the deceased:
*ꜣḫ-w=sw* *nṯr=pn*
transfigure.PPP-M=3MS god=DEM.M
He is transfigured, namely, this god. (CT II 248b/S1P)

This ending is usually taken to represent a 'defective' writing of the clitic element *=wy*, 'how X is...', which is common in adjectival sentences, including ones with participle predicates:

(7a) Ptahhetep praises paternal eduction:
*nfr=wy* *dwꜣ-n* *it-f*
good=ADM teach.REL-PST father-3MS
How fine is one whom his father taught! (Ptahhetep 629)

(7b) In a hymnic poem dedicated to the king:
*wr=wy* *nb* *n(-y)-nw-t-f*
great=ADM lord of[-M]-city-F-3MS
How great is the lord of his city! (pUC 32157, 2.11)

(7c) The deceased addresses divinities:
*qd=wy* *pr-k* *tm* *snt=wy* *ḥw-t-k* *rwty*
build.PPA=ADM house-2MS N found.PPA=ADM mansion-F-2MS N
How well-built is your house, O Atum; how well-founded is your mansion, O Ruty! (BD 17/*Nu* pl. 8, 105)

The clitic is indeed often, and in Old Egyptian, always, written without the final 𓏭. However, as shown by exx. 4a and 6 above, the putative *=w(y)* is written *before* the classifier, the word-final sign that provides a graphemic 'pointer' to the meaning of the word ( and  respectively), which is regular for the participial ending *-w*. By contrast, the fully spelled *=wy* regularly follows the classifier, if there is any:

(8a) The snake implies that the survival of the sailor was most fortunate:
*rš=wy* () *sḏd* *dp-t-n-f*
joyful.PPA=ADM relate.PIA taste.REL-F-PST-3MS
How joyful is one who can relate what he has experienced! (Sh.S. 124)

(8b) The peasant laments to the high steward:
*nḫ=wy* () *mꜣir* *sky-k*
miserable=ADM wretch destroy.REL.FUT-2MS
How miserable is a wretch whom you would destroy! (Peas B1, 148–49)

4 For the following analysis see Uljas (2007a: 235 n.27).

In addition, reading a stray *-w* as *=w(y)* is sometimes semantically impossible, as in the following interrogative example:

(9) King Pepi asks his emissary:

| | | | |
|---|---|---|---|
| *ỉn=tr* | *rḫ-w=ṯw* | *ỉrt* | *mrr-t* |
| IP=PTC | know.PPA-M=2MS | do.INF | love.REL-F |

| | |
|---|---|
| *ḥzz-t* | *nb-k* |
| praise.REL-F | lord-2MS |

Now, are you truly knowledgeable to do what your lord loves and praises?
(*Urk.* I 129, 5)

*=wy* is an 'admirative' element used to make so-called exclamative speech acts.[5] Outwardly, it resembles a dual nominal ending and it is likely that it had its diachronic origin in the latter: 'twice X is...'.[6] As such it can be seen as an abbreviation of examples such as the following:

(10) It is said that Queen Hatshepsut renovated a fortress in Thebes; then:

| | | | |
|---|---|---|---|
| *nfr* | *nfr=sy* | *r-sḫr-w-s* | *tpʿ* |
| good | good=2SF | to-plan-P-2FS | before |

It was twice more beautiful than (in) its former state. (*Urk.* IV 312, 12)

However, in historical Egyptian *=wy* is already a fully grammaticalised element, as is shown by its placement after the classifier that contrasts with the nominal dual ending *wi/wy/w(y)*, which is written before it.[7] It is a constitutive component of the expression *ỉỉ=wy* 'welcome', where *ỉỉ* is a Stative and the second-person subject is omitted as a rule (cf. Oréal 2008; 2010):

(11) Ptahhetep says:

| | | | | |
|---|---|---|---|---|
| *ỉr* | *ḫpr* | *sp-w* | *n-w-ḥs-w-t* | *ỉn* |
| CND | happen | occasion-P | of-P-favour-P-F | PTC |

| | | | |
|---|---|---|---|
| *ʿq-w* | *ḏd* | *ỉỉ=wy* | ø |
| enter.PIA-P | say.PIA | come.STA=ADM | ø |

When lucky events take place, it is the intimate friends who say 'Welcome!'
(Ptahhetep 346–47)

In Earlier Egyptian, the *subject* of an adjectival sentence follows the predicate, but can be separated from it by clitics such as the element *=wy*, a pronominal

5 See Michaelis (2001) as well as König and Siemund (2007: 316–17). For examples of similar clitics in other languages, see Sadock and Zwicky (1985: 163).

6 Thus e.g. Gardiner (1957: §49 Obs.) and Heckel (1957: 40). There does not seem to be any reason to revise this old hypothesis.

7 E.g. *twt-wi*, 'two divine images', PT Nt 838.

dative with the preposition *n* (see below), or the clitic-like degree adverb *wr-t* 'very' seen in ex. 1a as well as in the following instance:

(12) An exclamation in a description of a dragging of a colossal statue by a workforce:
*nfr=wr-t* *mꜣꜣ* *r-ḫ-t=nb-t*
good=very-ADV see.INF to-thing-F=QU-F
It was very much better to look at than anything. (*El Bersheh* I, pl. 14, 10)

When the subject is a bare noun and there are no clitics intervening between it and the predicate, the adjectival sentence is formally indistinguishable from the so-called *sḏm-f* verbal formation with a nominal subject. Yet when the subject of an adjectival sentence is a personal pronoun, the difference between the two is more apparent. In the *sḏm-f* personal pronoun subjects take the form of suffix pronouns, whereas, as can be seen from the examples above, in adjectival sentences the clitic personal pronouns are employed instead (insofar as these differ – see below). The use of the adjectival pattern is not equally common in all persons.[8] In general, it is most widespread in the third person (*nfr=sw*, good=3MS 'He is good'), whereas in the second person, it varies with the nominal sentence construction [absolute pronoun + participle], as was already discussed in Part II[9]:

(13a) The divine mother of the king says to him:
*nfr=w(y)=ṯw*
beautiful=ADM=2MS
How beautiful you are! (PT 1450a)

(13b) Osiris is told at his resurrection:
*nfr=w(y)=ṯw* *ꜥḥꜥ-t(i)* *m-min* *m-ḥr* *dwꜣt*
good=ADM=2MS stand-STA today as-N netherworld
How happy you are when you stand today as Horus of the Netherworld. (CT I 311g/T1C)

(13c) The king is told of his enemy:
*ṯwt* *wr* *ir-f*
2MS great.PIA to-3MS
You are (one) greater than him. (PT 648d)

In the first person, adjectival examples such as ex. 14a below are rare (see Vernus 1994: 329–32), and the nominal sentence such as in exx. 14b and 14c is mostly used instead (note in 14c the negation *n*...=*is* characteristic of nominal sentences):

8 See Section 3.1 below for the possible semantic-pragmatic reasons for this.
9 In exx. 13a and 13b it is also possible to read *nfr-w=ṯw*, good-M=2MS 'You are good', with -*w* analysed as a masculine participial ending.

(14a) Khakheperraseneb bewails his general weariness:
*snni=wi* *ḥr-ib-i*
sad=1S on-heart-1S
I am sad in my heart. (Khakheperraseneb r° 13)

(14b) Hapdjefa profiles himself:
*ink* *wr* *ḏfꜣ-w* *ꜥꜣ* *ḥb-w*
1S great.PPA oblation-P great.PPA festival-P
I am one great of oblations and manifold of festivals. (Siut I, 228)

(14c) Sinuhe protests his humility:
*n-ink=is* *qꜣ-sꜣ*
NEG-1S=NEG high-back
I was not an overweening person. (Sin B, 230)

Conversely, in the third person, occurrences of the nominal sentence construction such as the following are rare:

(15) The king's resourcefulness in building work is extolled:
*ntf* *mnḫ* *ḥr-šꜣ(-t)-n-f* *ḥr-kꜣ-t*
3MS efficient.P on-begin.REL[-F]-PST-3MS on-work-F
*rwd-t* *n-t-ḏt*
enduring-F of-F-eternity
He is one efficient in what he has initiated and in enduring works of eternity. (*Urk.* IV 861, 8)

Thus, the adjectival sentence forms a paradigm with the nominal sentence in different persons:

| | | | |
|---|---|---|---|
| 1P | *ink nfr* | 'I am (a) good (one)' | NomS |
| 2P | *nfr=ṯw/ntk nfr* | 'You are good/(a) good (one)' | AdjS/NomS |
| 3P | *nfr=sw* | 'He is good' | AdjS |

Besides clitic personal pronouns, the subject of an adjectival sentence may also be some of the so-called *n*-series demonstrative pronouns (formed with an initial *n*-), although examples are relatively infrequent:

(16) The king is resurrected:
*nfr=w(y)* *nn* *wr=w(y)* *nn* *iri-n=n-k*
good=ADM DEM great=ADM DEM do.REL-PST=to-2MS
*it-k* *wsir*
father-2MS N
How beautiful is this; how great is this thing which your father Osiris has done for you! (PT 2022a)

More often, the subject of the adjectival sentence is one of the forms and constructions seen to serve this syntactic role also in Earlier Egyptian adverbial sentences – namely the infinitive as in ex. 17a, an active or passive perfective or imperfective participle (17b–c), or a headless *sḏm-f* or *sḏm-n-f* relative clause (17d–e):

(17a) Ptahhetep makes a general point about the usefulness of acquiring and passing on education:
*nfr sḏm nfr mdt*
good hear.INF good speak.INF
It is good to listen and it is good to speak. (Ptahhetep 537)

(17b) Words of praise to Amenyseneb after his success in a religious/fiscal undertaking:
*wꜣḏ=wy ỉrỉ nꜣ n-nṯr-f*
flourish.PPA=ADM do.PPA DEM.M to-god-3MS
How flourishing is he who has done this for his god!
(Louvre C12, 13–14)

(17c) The author makes an oblique reference to trouble at the highest governmental level:
*mt qsn ỉrr-t m-ẖnw r-ḫ-t=nb-t*
PTC miserable do.PIP-F in-residence to-thing-F=QU-F
What is done in the residence is more miserable than anything.
(pUC 32200, 5–7)

(17d) Ammulanenshi assures Sinuhe of his good intentions:
*nfr ỉrr-t-ỉ=n-k*
good do.REL-F-1S=to-2MS
What I can do for you is good. (Sin B, 77)

(17e) It is said that Horus has set the king at the helm of gods; then:
*nfr=w(y) ỉr-t-n ḥr n-N=pn*
good=ADM do.REL-F-PST N to-N=DEM.M
How good is what Horus has done for this king N! (PT 903c/P)

Yet unlike in adverbial sentences, but in accordance with nominal sentences, the subject of an Earlier Egyptian adjectival sentence can also be a finite *sḏm-f* complement clause:

(18a) A piece of hate-mail (?) makes mockery of standard salutary clichés:
*bỉn=wy ỉỉỉ-k ꜥḏ-tỉ wḏꜣ-tỉ*
bad=ADM come-2MS safe-STA sound-STA
How very unfortunate that you should come safe and sound.
(pUC 32204, 2)

(18b) Thutmosis I says to Amun after purportedly having asked him to appoint Queen Hatshepsut as his heir:

| | | | |
|---|---|---|---|
| *ỉst* | *wr=wy* | *ỉrr-k* | *ḫr-ḥm-t-s* |
| PTC | great=ADM | do-2MS | before-majesty-F-3FS |

How great it is that you should act for her majesty! (*Urk.* IV 274, 3)

(18c) The writer asks for help also from her dead addressee's mother and adds:

| | |
|---|---|
| *nḏm=w(y)* | *fꜣ-k=s(y)* |
| sweet=ADM | lift-2MS=3FS |

It would be most pleasant if you supported her.

(Haskell Museum 13945, 3–4)

The use of different *sḏm-f* forms as complements here is semantic-pragmatically based (Uljas 2007c: 184–87). In instances with geminating and reduplicated forms, the complement situations are presupposed as factual. For instance, in ex. 18b, with the geminating form *ỉrr-k* of the root *ỉrỉ*, which belongs to the so-called *3inf* root-class characterised by occasional reduplication (or 'gemination') of the penultimate radical, the 'point' of the sentence is not to inform the addressee that Amun acts for his chosen heir, but rather to comment on this piece of encyclopaedic information.[10] In contrast, the non-geminating (and thus probably subjunctive) *sḏm-f* form *fꜣ-k* of the similarly *3inf* root *fꜣỉ* is used in ex. 18c because the situation described in the subordinate clause is a mere prospect; cf. also the following example:

(19) The courtiers express their opinion on the king's grandiose building-plan:

| | | |
|---|---|---|
| *twt=wr-t* | *ỉrỉ-k* | *mnw-k* |
| perfect=very-ADV | do-2MS | monument-2MS |

It would be wonderful if you were to make your monument!

(Berlin Leather Roll II, 4)

There also exists a rare tripartite nominal sentence variant of this construction (see Part II, Section 1.3.1):

(20) The sage laments the non-acceptance of men's offerings by the divine and says:

| | | |
|---|---|---|
| *ỉndw=ỉs=pw* | *dd-tn=n-f* | ø |
| miserable=PTC=COP | give-2P=to-3MS | ø |

Your offering to him is a miserable thing. (Ipuwer 5, 9)

10 A very similar situation obtains in, e.g., Spanish, where the subjunctive is used in subject complements whenever the latter is a presupposed state of affairs commented upon (Butt and Benjamin 2000: 250–51).

As noted briefly above, sometimes a generic or referentially opaque subject of the adjectival sentence could be non-overt, but examples of this are rather infrequent (cf. Gardiner 1957: §145):

(21) A note accompanying a depiction of captured desert-animals being inspected:
*ist* *ꜥšꜣ-ø=wr-t* *r-ḫ-t=nb-t*
PTC manifold-ø=great-ADV to-thing-F=QU-F
(They) were much more numerous than anything. (*El Bersheh* I, pl. 7)

However, subject omission is fairly common in instances where the semantic experiencer of the adjectival quality is coded as a grammatical dative of the covert subject expression:

(22a) The sage expresses his general despair of the prevailing situation:
*bin=wy=n-i* ø
bad=ADM=to-1S ø
How ill it is with (lit. 'to') me! (Ipuwer 6, 8)

(22b) Words of praise for a successful taskforce:
*nfr=w(y)* ø *n-ḏꜣmw* *iri-n* *nb-f*
good=ADM ø to-battalion do.REL-PST lord-3MS
How well it goes with a battalion that its lord has founded!
(*El Bersheh* I, pl. 15, 3. reg.)

The omission of the subject may be motivated by its status as semantically non-referential, as in the examples above, or as situational as in exx. 23a–23b below, but as seen from ex. 23c, it may also be expressed overtly even then:

(23a) After a retrospect to his own exemplary life, Ineni turns to his audience:
*iri-w* *mit-t=ir-w* *ꜣḫ=n-ṯn* ø
do.IMP-P like-F=to.RLT-P useful=to-1P ø
Do the like yourselves; it is beneficial to you. (*Urk.* IV 65, 16–17)

(23b) After asking the visitors to his stela to recite the offering formula, Nefernaiy says:
*ꜣḫ* ø *n-irr* ø *r-irr-w=n-f* ø
useful ø to-do.PIA ø to-do.PIP-M=to-3MS ø
It is more beneficial for him who does it than to the one to whom it is done. (Florence 2590, 4–5)

(23c) Intef asks passers-by to raise their hands and pronounce his name:
*ꜣḫ=st* *n-irr=st* *r-irr-w=n-f=st*
useful=3C to-do.PIA=3C to-do.PIP-M=to-3MS=3MS
It is more beneficial for him who does it than to the one to whom it is done. (*SEH* 152, 8)

The following example could in principle be understood as incorporating a clausal subject, but it may also be that the subject is covert and that *ỉri-tn* is an unmarked conditional adjunct:

(24) Paheri finishes his plea for offerings to the visitors to his tomb:
*nfr=n-tn* *ỉri-tn=st*
good=to-2P do-2P=3C
It is good for you if you do it. (*Urk.* IV 123, 4)

There is also, once again, a nominal sentence variant of the same construction, where the element *=pw* provides the overt indeterminate or situational subject:

(25a) The father of King Merikara recommends keeping religious establishments in good order:
*ꜣḫ-t=pw* *n-ỉrr=sy*
useful.PIA-F=SE to-do.PIA=3FS
It is a beneficial thing for him who does it. (Merikara E, 66)

(25b) The father of king Merikara expresses his views on Egypt's Asiatic foes:
*ỉs* *ꜥꜣmw* *ḫs-y* *qsn=pw* *n-bw* *nt(-y)-f* *ỉm*
PTC Asiatic vile-M difficult=SE to-place REL[-M]-3MS there
Ah, the vile Asiatic! He is a misfortune to the place where he is.
(Merikara E, 91)

The overt subject version of the construction adjective + dative can also exhibit possessive sense, thanks to the dative expressing the recipient of the referent of the sentence subject:

(26) Sinuhe says of his Syrian estate:
*wr=n-f* *ỉrp* *r-mw*
great=to-3MS wine to-water
It had more wine than water. (Sin B, 82)

As discussed in Part II Section 1.1.1, possessive constructions of the type *n=sw N* 'He belongs to N', which are often analysed as adjectival sentences with a predicative *nisbe*-adjective *n(-y)*, should rather be interpreted as nominal sentences. Yet besides the pattern exemplified in ex. 26, another undoubtedly adjectival construction is used to express possession with pronominal possessors. It consists of the preposition *n* + suffix possessor + *nisbe* form *ỉm(-y)/ỉm-y* of the preposition *m*, which together build the predicate and are followed by a nominal or (less often) pronominal possessee (see Satzinger 1986: 150–53; Loprieno 1995: 120–21):

(27a) The resurrected deceased is told:
*wsi͗r* *N=pn* *n-k-i͗m(-y)* *mꜣꜥḫrw*
N N=DEM.M to-2MS-in[-RLT.M] justification
Osiris N; to you belongs justification. (CT I 79i–j/T9C)

(27b) Hori praises King Senwosret I:
*n-f-i͗m(-y)* *šnn-t* *i͗tn*
to-3MS-in[-RLT.M] encircle.REL-F sun_disc
To him belongs what the sun-disc encircles. (*ASAE* 39, 189, 9)

(27c) Sinuhe says to the king concerning Syria:
*n-k-i͗m(-y)=s(y)* *mi͗tt-ṯsm-w-k*
to-2MS-in[-RLT.M]=3FS like-dog-P-2MS
It belongs to you like your dogs. (Sin B, 222–23)

Although its internal structure is still recognisable, the expression *n-k-i͗my* constitutes a non-segmentable pattern functioning as adjectival predicate to the possessee as subject.[11] This is clear from the possibility of using *n* + suffix + *i͗my* as an attributive term:

(28a) The generals of Thutmosis III object to his idea of entering battle with the troops in a single file:
*i͗ni͗w* *wnn* *[t]ꜣ-ḥꜣ-t* *n-n-i͗m-y* *ḥr-ꜥḥꜣ*
IP AUX DEM.F-front-F to-1P-in-RLT.M PROG-fight.INF
*i͗w* *nꜣ-n-[pḥwy]-w* *ꜥḥꜥ* *ꜥꜣ* *m-ꜥꜣrwnꜣ*
DEP POSS.P-of-end-P stand.STA here in-N
Will our vanguard be fighting while the rear-guard stands here in Aruna?
(*Urk.* IV 650, 5–7)

(28b) The high steward asks the peasant in reference to his having been robbed by one of his employees:
*i͗ni͗w* *ꜥꜣ-t=pw* *n-k-i͗m-y* *ḥr-i͗b-k*
IP great.PPA-F=SE to-2MS-in-RLT.M on-heart-2MS
*r-i͗t-tw* *šmsw-i͗*
to-take-PASS retainer-1S
Is what you have so important in your opinion that my retainer should be arrested? (Peas B1, 134–35)

11 As such, it could perhaps be transliterated and glossed as a single lexeme, but the original internal division is maintained here for the sake of ease of recognition.

In addition, in exx. 27a–27c, *n-k/-f-ỉm-y* precedes the possessee NP and thus syntactically does not behave as an adverbial phrase. Finally, as shown by ex. 27c, the clitic pronoun =*s*(*y*) cliticises to the entire complex *n-k-ỉm-y* instead of only *n-k*, which provides further proof that the pattern cannot be analysed as an adverbial sentence. Nevertheless, given the use of suffix pronouns, it is clear that *n* + noun/pronoun is indeed etymologically an adverbial phrase. It would appear that the derived *nisbe*-expression *ỉm-y* provides a dummy element whose function was originally to de-adverbialise the phrase both syntactically and semantically. More particularly, *ỉm-y* assigns the datival expression morphological weight that allows it to occur initially and to express adjectival rather than adverbial locative meaning. *n-k-ỉm-y* is a latecomer in the Earlier Egyptian grammatical system: there are no examples of its predicative use before the First Intermediate Period and the Early Middle Kingdom, and there is but one Old Egyptian example of its attributive use.[12]

Apart from the element =*wy*, the use of clitic particles is rather restricted in adjectival sentences, although some examples of the rather obscure elements =*ꜣ* and =*tr* as well as the additive =*grt* 'also, moreover' are attested (see Oréal 2011: 25–60, 437–85, 487–515 for an overall discussion):

(29a) The beginning of PT Spell 474:

*nfr=w(y)=ꜣ* *mꜣꜣ* *ỉt* *ỉn* *ꜣst* *ḥtp=w(y)=ꜣ*
good=ADM=PTC see.INF QUOT AGT N pleasant=ADM=PTC
*ptr* *ỉt* *ỉn* *nbtḥwt*
behold.INF QUOT AGT N

'How good it is to see', says Isis; 'How pleasant it is to behold', says Nepthys. (PT 939a–b)

(29b) The king tells his vizier:

*rḫ=ṯw=tr* *ḏd* *mrr-t* *ḥm(-ỉ)* *r-ḫ-t=nb*
know=2MS=PTC say.INF love.REL-F majesty[-1S] to-thing-F=QU

You really have the knowledge to say what my majesty loves more than anything. (*Urk.* I 179, 17)

(29c) Sinuhe says concerning his becoming rich abroad:

*ꜥꜣ=grt* *dmỉ-t* *r-ỉ* *m-ỉỉ* *n-mr-t-ỉ*
great=PTC touch.PPA-F to-1S as-come.PPA through-love-F-1S

Moreover, what was due to me as income through love of me was great. (Sin B, 85–86)

12 *Urk.* I 77, 16 *rmṯ n-s-ỉm(-y)* 'man belonging to it (scil. the nome)'.

In the following example with the clitic =*ḥm* 'truly', the possible adjectival sentence is preceded by the initial particle *ḫr* used to mark atemporal sequentiality:

(30) Sinuhe wonders how he could have been pardoned and says:
*ḫr=ḥm* *nfr* *wꜣḥib* *nḥm=wi* *m-ʿ-mt*
PTC=PTC good clemency save.PPA=1S from-hand-death
So, the clemency that has saved me from death is indeed good.
(Sin B, 202–03)

There are some instances of adjectival sentences with extraposed sentence constituent outside (in front of) the sentence nucleus:

(31a) Ptahhetep laments the ills of old age:
*dp-t=nb-t* *ꜣq=sy*
taste-F=QU-F destroy.PPP=3FS
All taste – it is perished. (Ptahhetep 25)

(31b) The snake says that he controls the access to the coveted raw material for incense:
*ink=is* *ḥqꜣ* *pwnt* *ʿntw* *n-i-im(-y)=sw*
1S=PTC ruler N myrrh to-1S-in[.RLT-M]=3MS
I am the ruler of Punt, and myrrh – it belongs to me. (Sh.S. 151)

However, examples with the element *ir*, the usual Earlier Egyptian marker of extraposition, do not seem to occur, and extraposition is generally rather rare with adjectival sentences. More common is what is, in a sense, the reverse of this phenomenon: namely the use of adjectival sentences with semantically cataphoric pronoun subjects followed by the referent of the latter as an appositional 'tail' (see also the pre-New Kingdom ex. 6 above):

(32a) Khakheperraseneb feels compelled to share his Weltschmerz:
*wḫd-w=sw* *ḥꜣp* *ẖ-t-i* *ḥr-f*
difficult.PPA-M=3MS hide.INF belly-F-1S on-3MS
It is difficult – namely to hide my innermost because of it.
(Khakheperraseneb r° 13)

(32b) A boastful comment of a man bringing back a pole used to carry grain baskets:
*rwd=wy=sw* *ib-i*
strong=ADM=3MS heart-1S
How strong it is, namely, my heart! (*Paheri*, pl. 3, top register)

(32c) A harpist sings to Rekhmira:

| | | | | |
|---|---|---|---|---|
| *ḥḏ=wy=st* | *nꜣ-n-rnp-w-t* | *wḏ* | *nṯr* | *ḫr-k* |
| brilliant=ADM=3C | DET.P-of-year-P-F | order.REL | god | before-2MS |

How bright they are – these years, which god assigns to you.

(*Urk.* IV 1166, 10)

Although the examples cited thus far may be reasonably considered to represent adjectival sentences, it has to be noted that more often than not this judgement is not based on formal criteria but rather on deductions based on syntax and semantics. Indeed, as was hinted above, adjectival sentences are often difficult to distinguish from verbal constructions on formal grounds. When the subject of a seemingly 'adjectival' construction is not a clitic singular personal pronoun, the construction is indistinguishable from a *sḏm-f* verb form with a similar subject expression. For example, compare the following pair of constructions:

(33a) Kagemni stresses the benefits of tranquillity:

| | | |
|---|---|---|
| *wsḫ* | *s-t* | *n-t-hr* |
| wide | place-F | of-F-content.PIA |

The abode of a content man is wide. (Kagemni I, 2)

(33b) Thutmosis III expresses his intention to embellish the temple of Amun:

| | | | |
|---|---|---|---|
| *di-i* | *wsḫ* | *s-w-t* | *iri=wi* |
| cause.SUB-1S | wide.SUB | place-P-F | make.PPA=1S |

I will make wide the abode of my maker. (*Urk.* IV 163, 6)

Ex. 33b is analysed as involving a subjunctive *sḏm-f* because it follows the causative *rdi*, a diagnostic environment for this verb form in Earlier Egyptian, but there are no formal differences between it and what is assumed to be an adjectival sentence in ex. 33a – at least insofar as *written* morphology is concerned. Similarly, in the following example, a geminating *sḏm-f* verb form serves as a subject complement of a semantically adjectival expression, but given the apparent adjunct status of the entire complex *qsn mss-s*, it more probably represents a finite *sḏm-f* than a predicative adjective:

(34) Reddjedet's travails are described:

| | | | | | | |
|---|---|---|---|---|---|---|
| *wꜥ* | *m-nn* | *hrw* | *ḫpr* | *wn-in* | *rdḏdt* | *ḥr-šnt-s* |
| one | in-DEM | day | happen.STA | AUX-SEQ | N | PROG-suffer-3FS |
| *qsn* | *mss-s* | | | | | |
| difficult | bear-3FS | | | | | |

One of these days, Redjedet was suffering, because her childbearing was difficult. (pWestcar 9, 21–22)

Even with personal pronouns, the analysis of the construction is not necessarily always clear. Although adjectival sentences with first- and second-person clitic pronoun subjects are easily distinguished from corresponding *sḏm-f* forms with suffixes, this difference vanishes when plural personal pronouns (which do not differentiate between suffix and clitic pronouns) appear, and unless contextually clear, the opposition between these two patterns is opaque:

(35) Sehetepibra advises or characterises his audience:
*šw-/=ṯn* *m-sp* *n(-y)-bgsw*
empty-/=2P from-case of[-M]-laxness
You are/you should be free from moments of laxness. (*Loyaliste* §6, 2/St)

Furthermore, the third-person singular feminine clitic pronoun =*sy* is often (in Old Egyptian, always) spelled as =*s*(*y*), which again may cause problems, as shown by ex. 93a below. Ultimately, Earlier Egyptian adjectival sentences are formally distinguishable from *sḏm-f* with a noun subject only in the following four instances (for a broad discussion of this problem, see Edel (1955/1964: §466):

a) The subject is a fully written first-, second-, or third-person singular clitic pronoun (e.g. *nfr=sw*)
b) The clitic =*wy* appears (e.g. *nfr=wy N*)
c) The predicate is clearly an active or passive participle (e.g. *sḥḏ-w N*)
d) The sentence is a possessive construction of the type *n-f-im-y N*

Other possible indicators such as comparatives with the preposition *r* or the presence of the adverbial expression =*wr-t* 'greatly' (thus Allen 1986a: 11) or of the dative preposition *n* are not unequivocal, as can be seen from the following verbal examples with the *sḏm-f* and Stative forms:

(36a) Rediu-Khnum says in reference to his performance at the service of the queen:
*iw* *ꜣḫ=wr-t* *irr* *s* *ꜣḫ-t* *n-ib-f*
AUX beneficial=great-ADV do man useful.PIA-F to-heart-3MS
*n-nb-t-f*
to-mistress-F-3MS
It is very beneficial for a man to do what in his mind seems useful for his mistress. (CG 20543, 18)

(36b) Ptahhetep says that it is advisable to laugh when someone in a higher position laughs:
*wnn* *ø* *nfr-w* *ḥr-ib-f* *wr-t*
AUX ø good-STA on-heart-3MS great-ADV
(It) will be greatly pleasant in his heart. (Ptahhetep 132)

(36c) The king explains why Sinuhe should return home:

| | | | | |
|---|---|---|---|---|
| *ỉw* | *nꜣ* | *ꜣw* | *r-ḥ(w)t* | *tꜣ* |
| AUX | DEM.M | wide.STA | to-roam.INF | earth |

This is more important than roaming the earth. (Sin B, 198–99)

(36d) An assurance in the introduction of a mortuary spell:

| | | | | |
|---|---|---|---|---|
| *ỉw* | ø | *ꜣḫ* | *n-ỉrr=st* | *tp-tꜣ* |
| AUX | ø | useful.STA | to-do.PIA=3C | upon-earth |

It is useful for him who does it upon earth. (BD 17/*Nu* pl. 3, 3)

Here something should be said of the categorial status of adjectives and of the adjectival sentence as a grammatical class in Earlier Egyptian. A functionalist definition of adjective characterises it as a 'quality concept' expression that, without further measures, can be used as an attribute (modifier) of a nominal head, as in 'a *beautiful* song' or 'a *weird* idea, or predicatively, as in 'This song *is beautiful*' or 'His idea *is weird*' (Hengeveld 1992: 58).[13] However, the justification for viewing adjectives as an autonomous grammatical category has often been challenged for Egyptian and other languages. In linguistics, adjectives have commonly been characterised as expressions falling between verbs and nouns and as associated with characteristics of both these apparently better definable categories (i.e. as [+V] [+N], see Bhat 1994: 248–49 and cf. Introduction to the present volume, Section 5.3). Elsewhere, it has been commonplace to either isolate a group of allegedly universal primary adjectives that have certain fixed semantic characteristics and uses (e.g. Dixon 2004: 3–5, 9–12), or to speak of languages as having 'adjectival verbs' or 'adjectival nouns' besides or instead of 'true' adjectives, or, as a variant, to view the grammatical behaviour of adjectives as reflective of their character as either more 'nouny' or 'verby', depending on the language in question (e.g. Wetzer 1996: 43–69, resp. Stassen 1997: 344, 612). Some view the modifying use of adjectives as more central and the predicative and referential ('nominal') employment as more peripheral (Bhat 1994: 19, 92), and a yet further alternative formulation has been to argue that languages differ in whether they are 'rigid' in their formal and structural separation of lexemes as representatives of the various parts of speech Adj/V/N or 'flexible', in which case they eschew morpho-syntactic differentiation of two or more of these classes (Hengeveld 1992: 63–68).

---

**13** For the idea of adjectives as 'quality concept expression', see e.g. Schachter (1985: 13); Stassen (1997: 16); Givón (2001 vol. 1: 53, 81–84).

This same impression of adjectives as a rather hazy category has also characterised Egyptological discussions from early on,[14] and this has also been reflected in the manner in which adjectival sentences have been understood. A very common view has been to view adjectival sentences not as an autonomous sentence type, but as bipartite *nominal* sentences without the element *=pw*. It is true that the syntax of the two constructions seems suspiciously similar, particularly when the predicate of the nominal sentence is an interrogative pronoun:

**Tab. III.1:** Comparison of nominal and adjectival sentence structures in Earlier Egyptian.

| **Nominal Sentence** | **Adjectival Sentence** |
|---|---|
| Subject = Noun | |
| [*pty*] [*ꜣh-t-f*]<br>What is its area? (pRhind math. n.49, 2) | [*nfr*] [*mtn-i͗*]<br>My path is right (Peas B1, 34) |
| Subject = Personal (clitic) Pronoun | |
| [*ptr*] [*=sw*]<br>Who is he? (CT IV 188b) | [*nfr*] [*=tw*]<br>You are fine (Sin B, 31) |
| Subject = Infinitive | |
| – | [*nfr*] [*sḏm*]<br>It is good to listen (Ptahhetep 537) |
| Subject = Finite Complement Clause | |
| – | [[*nf*]*r =wy*] [*i͗w sḫ-t*]<br>How good it is that the lady of the marshland comes!<br>(*Deir el-Gebrawi* II, pl. 5, right) |
| Subject = Participle | |
| [*pty*] [*hꜣꜣ-t r-f m-sš*]<br>What goes into it in grain?<br>(pRhind math. n.43, 1) | [*rš =wy*] [*sḏd dp-t-n-f*]<br>How fortunate is one who can tell what he has experienced! (Sh.S. 124) |
| Subject = Relative Form | |
| [*ptr*] [*ḏd-t=n-i͗ nb-i͗*]<br>What does my lord say to me? (Sin B, 261) | [*nfr*] [*i͗r-t-n-sn*]<br>What they did was good (Sin R, 52) |

14 For example, in Sethe's seminal work on Egyptian non-verbal sentence patterns, adjectival sentences are treated as a subtype of the 'nominaler Nominalsatz' (1916: 29–31). By contrast, Gardiner, albeit considering most Middle Egyptian adjectives as participles, separated adjectival and nominal sentences in Middle Egyptian (1957: §135) and in Heckel's thorough study of adjectival sentences and various other 'quality-assigning' sentences, the former have a fully independent status (1957: 19–47). Edel, however, returned to the Sethean model and viewed Old Egyptian adjectival sentences as a subcategory of bipartite nominal sentences (1955/1964: §§466, 637, 944, 946). The same analysis appears in Junge's work on the syntax of Middle Egyptian literature (1978: 56, 59).

Nevertheless, despite stressing the supposedly fuzzy status of adjectives, it has recently become customary to draw a relatively clear line between adjectival and nominal sentences as constructions.[15] The reasons for this are both structural and semantic-pragmatic. As for structure, the omission of indeterminate or situational subjects is, as seen, permitted in adjectival but not in bipartite nominal sentences[16]: for example, compare the adjectival sentences in exx. 23b–23c above with the nominal nominal sentences in ex. 25, which would be ungrammatical without *=pw*. In addition, adjectival sentences, unlike nominal sentences, are extremely rare with first-person pronominal subjects. It will also be observed in Section 4.1 that adjectival sentences are not negated by *n…=is*, the usual nominal sentence negation. Accordingly, these and the various semantic differences between adjectival and nominal sentences (see Section 3.1) suggest that adjectival sentences should neither be removed from the inventory of Earlier Egyptian sentence patterns nor subsumed under other construction types. Nevertheless, it is undeniable that they constitute a class of non-verbal constructions that in Earlier Egyptian displays perhaps the greatest overlap and intersection with nominal and verbal patterns (see Sections 3.1 and 4.1 for further discussion).

Finally, it should be re-emphasised that negations of verbal and adverbial sentences with the negative element *nn* have nothing to do with adjectival sentences (see Part I Section 4.1). The hypothesis of *nn* as some sort of 'adjectival predicate' – which goes back to an influential analysis proposed in the 1920s (Gunn 1924 [2014]: 141, 198) and has been repeated numerous times ever since (most recently by Malaise and Winand 1999: §506 and Schenkel 2012: 155–57) – is very uncertain (for what follows, see Jansen-Winkeln 1996b: §459 and particularly Uljas 2013: 246–51). Unlike actual Earlier Egyptian quality concept lexemes, the negation *nn* cannot be used attributively or referentially, and it cannot have a recipient introduced by *n*. *nn*-sentences do not co-occur with the

---

**15** Thus, e.g., Vernus (1994: 330–32) noted that adjectives and participles shared functional and formal features, but expressed reservations towards equating the two and treated nominal and adjectival sentences as two different types of proposition (cf. also Loprieno 1995: 112). Malaise and Winand (1999: §§494–95) analyse 'adjectives of quality' as 'etymologically participles' that have, nevertheless, come to function as 'true adjectives' e.g. in adjectival sentences. Also Allen (2000: 59, 67–70) and Borghouts (2010: §95.a) view Middle Egyptian adjectives as active participles, but make a relatively clear distinction between adjectival and nominal sentences. Schenkel analyses adjectives essentially as participles or *nisbe*-formations, but treats adjectival sentences apart from nominal sentences (2012: 96–97, 154–61). Peust (2008) has argued that adjectives are, after all, a formally recognisable category whose member lexemes are identifiable by their ability to form 'abstract nouns' with the prefix *bw-* (literally 'place') and that adjectival sentences are one special type of constructions formed of these but also other, e.g., participial expressions.

**16** For omission under relevance, see Collier (1991b: 36–37).

particle =*wy*, nor can they be used in comparative constructions, but unlike adjectival sentences they *can* be used directly as adjuncts. At the root of the adjectival analysis of *nn* lies the view of it as a negative predicate followed by a subject that can be, e.g., an affirmative clausal complement (i.e, *nn N/sḏm-f* = [*is non-existent* [*N/he-hears*]], see Gunn 1924 [2014]: 198). However, as already discussed in connection with the adverbial sentences in Part I Section 4.1, in full clauses *nn* clearly serves to negate the predicative relation, which means that it cannot stand for a term-negation 'is non-existent'. When used to negate a following full clause, the semantic contribution of *nn* to the situation also differs dramatically from that of true adjectival predicates (see Section 4.1) in terms of semantic-pragmatic features. In addition, viewing 'negative existence' as a predicative property runs against a long logico-philosophical tradition that has doubts about the predicativity of affirmative existence and is more or less unanimous in rejecting this honour from the expression of non-existence (see Uljas 2013: 249–50 for discussion).

## 1.2 Later Egyptian

### 1.2.1 Late Egyptian

It is generally accepted that adjectival sentences are a recessive grammatical class in Late Egyptian (Junge 2008: 182–183). This is mainly based on the observation that these constructions had become confined to textual genres such as literary texts and monumental inscriptions, which are more likely to preserve vestiges of the grammatical patterns of Classical Egyptian. The syntax of the attested examples adheres to the earlier generic scheme:

$$S > [AdjP_P \ NP_S]$$

Identification of the construction is possible only in sentences with a pronominal subject; as in Earlier Egyptian, adjectival sentences with nominal subjects are indistinguishable from verbal constructions with adjective verbs. Personal pronoun subjects are clitic:

(37a) A master-scribe castigates an idle pupil:

| | | |
|---|---|---|
| *bin=tw* | *r-smn* | *n-wḏb* |
| bad=2MS | than-goose | of-shore |

You are worse than the goose on the shore (i.e. busy with mischief).

(*LEM* 102, 5–6)

(37b) A scribe is admonished:

| | | | | |
|---|---|---|---|---|
| *snsn=n-k* | *tꜣ-ꜥty* | *pꜣ-gsti* | *nḏm=sw* | *r-šdḥ* |
| befriend=to-2MS | DEF.F-roll | DEF.M-palette | sweet=3C | to sweet_wine |
| *ỉr-sš* | *n-pꜣ-nty* | *rḫ=sw* | *ꜣḫ=sw* | |
| PTC-writings | for-DEF.M-REL | know=3MS | beneficient=3MS | |
| *r-ỉꜣw-t=nb-t* | | | | |
| than-office-F=QU-F | | | | |

Make friends with the bookroll and the scribal palette: they are sweeter than sweet wine. As for writing, it is more beneficent than any other office for him who knows it. (*LEM* 100, 12–13)

(37c) It is said about the city of Tyre:

| | | |
|---|---|---|
| *wrs=sw* | *m-rm-w* | *r-šꜥ-t* |
| strong=3MS | in-fish | to-sand-F |

It is richer in fish than in sand. ([2]*pAnastasi I* 131, 8)

In a number of examples, the subject is introduced first as a cataphoric pronoun, with a coreferential noun phrase in apposition (cf. also exx. 32a–c above and ex. 43c below):

(38a) The god Amun is addressed:

| | |
|---|---|
| *nḏm=sn* | *pꜣ-dm-rn-k* |
| sweet=3C | DEF.M-pronounce-name-2MS |

It is sweet to utter your name. (*JEA* 14, pl. 5, 12)

(38b) King Ramesses II tries to encourage his troops, but also chides them:

| | | |
|---|---|---|
| *ḫsy=wi=sw* | *ḥꜣty-tn* | *tꜣy-i-nṯ-ḥtr-w* |
| feeble=ADM=3C | heart-2P | POSS.F-1S-of-horse-P |

How faint are your hearts, O my charioteers. (*KRI* II 56, 13)

(38c) The hero laments the unjust character of a former superior:

| | |
|---|---|
| *nḫt=sw* | *tꜣy-f-wḏ-y* |
| hard=3C | POSS.F-3MS-order-PPP |

His allocation was hard. (*Tale of Woe* 4, 13)

(38d) The sage recommends philanthrophy towards the weak since all humankind is god's creation:

| | | | |
|---|---|---|---|
| *rš=wiꜣ=sw* | *pꜣ-ir-pḥ-imnt-t* | *iw-f* | *wḏꜣ* |
| happy=ADM=3MS | DEF.M-PST-reach-west-F | DEP-3MS | sound.STA |
| *m-ḏr-t-pꜣ-nṯr* | | | |
| in-hand-F-DEF.M-god | | | |

How happy is the one who has reached the West, being safe in the hand of god. (Amenemope 24, 19–20)

(38e) An adorant promises to spread the fame of a deity so that people everywhere will say:

*ꜥꜣ=yw=sw* *nꜣ-i͗-i͗r-ḏḥwty*
great=ADM=3C DEF.P-REL-do-N
Great are the things that Thoth achieves. (*LEM* 60, 12)

In the last example, noteworthy are the apparent plural marking of the adjective (which, however, stands probably just for the misunderstood admirative particle) and the use of the shared form *=sw* for third person pronouns. However, examples such as the following with a noun in the subject position are ambiguous and discussed above might alternatively be analysed as examples of the verbal use of adjectival roots, depending on how much Earlier Egyptian use one is inclined to accept at work in these texts:

(39a) An opening of a letter to a lady:

*nfr* *ḥy*
good N
Haja is well. (*HO* 46.3, 1)

(39b) A graffito by a visitor to a tomb praises the god Amun:

*nfr* *ḥr-k* *nb* *nṯr-w*
good face-2MS lord god-P
Your face is fair, O lord of the gods. (gTT 63, 6)

(39c) A eulogy of the city of Thebes begins:

*nḏm* *nw-t* *ms<d>* *ḫd*
sweet city-2MS hate.PPA going upstream
Sweet is your city, detestable is leaving (it). (oDeM 1232, 1)

As before, this ambiguity can be resolved on formal grounds only when the admirative particles *=wi͗* or *=wsi͗* appear. Earlier texts seem to have a preference for *=wi͗*:

(40a) The victorious King Merenptah is praised after his defeat of the Libyans:

*nṯry=wi͗=sw*
divine=ADM=3MS
How divine he is! (*KRI* IV 10, 7)

(40b) The king says:

*qsn=wi͗* *wꜣ-t*
miserable=ADM way-F
How miserable is the way! (*KRI* I 66, 2)

The particle *=wsi* is usually explained as a merger of *=wi* and a following third-person pronoun (Erman 1933: §684; Junge 2008: 181):

(41a) A hymn to Ramesses VI praises his building works:

| | | | | | |
|---|---|---|---|---|---|
| *nḏm=wsi* | *ḫrw* | *pꜣ-ḫp* | *n-qn* | *nb* | *ḫpš* |
| sweet=ADM | voice | DEF.M-hammer | of-hero | lord | sword |

How sweet is the sound of the hammer of the hero, the lord of the sword! (*KRI* VI 334, 3)

(41b) King Merenptah is praised:

| | | |
|---|---|---|
| *nḏm=wsi* | *pꜣy-k-šm* | *r-wꜣst* |
| sweet=ADM | POSS.M-2MS-go | to-N |

How sweet is your moving to Thebes! (*LEM* 15, 2–3)

(41c) As above:

| | | | | | |
|---|---|---|---|---|---|
| *nfr=wsi* | *hrw* | *n-hꜣw-k* | *nḏm-wsi* | *ḫrw-k* | *ḥr-mdt* |
| good=ADM | day | of-time-2MS | sweet-ADM | voice-2MS | PRP-speak.INF |

How good is the day of your time; how sweet is your voice speaking. (*LEM* 28, 10–11)

(41d) The hero laments the injustice of crops being measured with a false measure:

| | | |
|---|---|---|
| *ꜥḏꜣ=wsy* | *pꜣ-ḥm* | *i-ir=sw* |
| false=ADM | DEF.M-workman | REL-do=3MS |

How despicable is the workman who made it! (*Tale of Woe* 4, 14)

(41e) Hori castigates his opponent:

| | | | |
|---|---|---|---|
| *ḥḏ=wsy* | *pr=nb* | *ḥr-ns-t-k* | *wiꜣwiꜣ=wsy* |
| damaged=ADM | come.PPA=QUA | on-tongue-F-2MS | confused=ADM |
| *ṯs-w-k* | | | |
| utterance-P-2MS | | | |

How damaged is everything that comes forth from your tongue, how confused are your utterances. (²*pAnastasi I* 155, 7)

The examples would thus be similar to exx. 38a–d with cataphoric pronouns.

The NP in the subject position is usually a common noun (ex. 42a), a demonstrative pronoun (42b), a headless relative clause (42c–d), or an infinitive (42e):

(42a) King Ramesses II is praised on his first jubilee:

| | | | |
|---|---|---|---|
| *nḏm* | *ib* | *n-Kmt* | *m-hꜣw-k* |
| sweet | heart | of-Egypt | in-surrounding-2MS |

Egypt's heart is content in your time. (*KRI* II 378, 6–7)

(42b) The sister-in-law tries to seduce the younger brother:

| | |
|---|---|
| *ꜣḫ=n-k* | *pꜣy* |
| beneficent=to-2MS | DEM.M.ABS |

This is beneficent for you. (*LES* 12, 11)

(42c) Osiris reacts to a letter from god Ra:

| | | | | |
|---|---|---|---|---|
| *nfr* | *r-ỉqr* | *spsn* | *pꜣw* | *ỉ-ỉr-k=nb* |
| good | to-excellence | twice | DEM.M.ABS | REL-do-2MS=QU |

| | | |
|---|---|---|
| *pꜣ-gm* | *tꜣ-psḏ* | *m-ỉ-rt* |
| DEF.M-find | DEF-ennead.F | in-do-INF |

How absolutely splendid is everything that you did and what the Ennead found appropriate to do! (*LES* 57, 16–58, 1)

(42d) The author of a letter tells the addressee that he has taken care of certain issues:

| | | |
|---|---|---|
| *ḫr-ỉw-mꜣꜥ* | *pꜣ-ỉ-ḏd-k* | *m-bꜣḥ-ỉ* |
| PTC-DEP-true | DEF.M-REL-say-2MS | in-presence-1S |

Although what you said in my presence is true... (*KRI* III 505, 4)

(42e) A scribe praises his master saying that he obeyed the latter's advice while the master was alive and was beating the pupil's back:

| | | |
|---|---|---|
| *ỉst-nḏm* | *qnqn* | *m-ꜥ-t-sbꜣ-t* |
| IP-sweet | beating.INF | in-room-F-teaching-F |

Is the beating at school sweet?

(*Teaching of Amunnakht* 35 [*ZÄS* 131, 41, 13–15])

Ex. 42a is remarkable in that, rather than an absolute demonstrative pronoun extended by a relative form, one might have expected the subject to appear as a relative form (such as *pꜣ-ỉr-k nb*) or a complement clause, as in Earlier Egyptian. However, when a headless relative clause appears in the subject position, the construction resembles a cleft sentence structurally and semantically. The same example also shows that the predicate can be extended.

The use of what are formally or semantically distinctive participles in the predicate position continues to be licensed:

(43a) In the Great Aten hymn the god is praised:

| | | | |
|---|---|---|---|
| *smnḫ=wysy* | *sḫr-w-k* | *pꜣ-nb* | *nḥḥ* |
| efficient.PPA=ADM | plan-P-2MS | DEF.M-lord | eternity |

How efficient are your plans, O lord of eternity.

(*Great Aten Hymn* [Sandman, 95, 6–7])

(43b) The younger brother tries to convince his elder sibling that the latter's wife had tried to seduce him and not vice versa:

| | |
|---|---|
| *pnꜥ=sw=n-k* | *m-ktḫ* |
| turn.PPA=3MS=to-2MS | in-other.P |

You got it all wrong! (lit. 'it is upturned to you as another') (*LES* 16, 13–14)

(43c) The opening of a stanza in a cycle of love songs:

| | | |
|---|---|---|
| *ỉfd=sw* | *ỉb-ỉ* | *ꜣs* |
| flee.PPA=3MS | heart-1S | fast |

My heart is beating fast. (Mathieu, *Poésie*, pl. 2, 9)

(43d) The scribe invokes Thoth, the god of wisdom and all scribes, saying that the office of the scribe is far better than any other:
*sꜥꜣ=sw*
enlarge.PPA=3MS
It makes important. (*LEM* 60, 7)

(43e) A love song begins with the praise of the woman adored:
*rḫ=wsy* *m-ḫꜣꜥ* *il*
know.PPA=ADM in-lay rope
How skilled is she at throwing the rope! (Mathieu, *Poésie*, pl. 7, 2)

(43f) God Thoth in his manifestation as a dog and his positive effects are praised:
*nḏm* *ib* *n-tꜣy-i-rwy-t* *ḏr-ꜥq-iw* *r-s*
sweet.PPA heart of-POSS.F-1S-quarter-F since-enter.PST-dog to-3FS
My living quarter is happy since 'the dog' entered it. (*LEM* 25, 13)

(43g) A visitor's graffiti invokes the god Amun:
*ršw* *dm=nb* *rn-k*
happy.PPA proclaim.PPA=QU name-2MS
Whoever proclaims your name is happy. (*KRI* III 347, 15)

(43h) The priests of Armant welcome the portable barque of the god Month and exclaim that the local populace is exceedingly happy about his arrival[17]:
*rš=wi=sw* *iw-k* *m-ḫnw-s* *wꜣḏ=wi*
happy.PPA=ADM=3MS DEP-2MS in-inside-3FS flourish.PPA=ADM
*inb-w-s*
wall-P-3FS
*nṯr-w* *im-w-s* *ḥt<p>-w* *psḏ-t-s* *m-ḥꜥꜥ*
god-P in.RLT-P-3FS content-STA ennead-F-3FS in-jubilation
How happy is it (the city of Armant), that you are inside it and how flourishing are its walls. The gods within it are content and its ennead is in jubilation. (*KRI* III 403, 2–3)

(43i) The difficulty of the passing of a place in southern Lebanon is compared in the following way:
*iw-k* *r-ḏd* *[w]bd=sw* *r-ḏdb-w* *mr=wsy* *mhr*
FUT-2MS FUT-say burning.PPA=3MS to-sting-P sick.PPA=ADM soldier
You will say: It burns more than stings,
how the soldier suffers. ($^2$*pAnastasi I* 132, 3)

However, Late Egyptian participles are a recessive category, only past forms surviving in standard use. In contrast to their attributive use, they never show the standard *i*-prefix in predicative use (for the morphology of Late Egyptian participles see Winand 1992: 343–64).

17 Following Sethe's restoration on the Zettel DZA 26.078.810.

The predicate can be extended by adjuncts (cf. also 42c):

(44a) Generals tell the king:
*nfr* *r-ỉqr* *ḥrt* *ỉty* *nb-n*
good to-excellent peace sovereign lord-1P
Very excellent is peace, O sovereign, our Lord! (*KRI* II 97, 7)

(44b) The tomb-owner tells about his life and how he chose his personal deity, the goddess Mut:
*nhy=sw* *m-ꜣ-t* *ḏw-t*
lack=3C in-moment-F evil-F
She lacks a moment of evil. (*KRI* III 336, 11–12)

(44c) In a story about the king Neferkare and general Sisene, the following appears in broken context:
*nḏm=sw* *ꜥꜣ* *wr*
sweet=3MS great very
It was exceedingly pleasant. (Sisene Story [tDeM 1214 v° x+4])

(44d) In a fragmentary love-song the following is said of the male lover:
*nḏm* *tẖ* *ỉw-ỉ* *r-gs-f*
sweet drinking DEP-1S to-side-3MS
Sweet is drunkenness when I am by his side. (Mathieu, *Poésie*, pl. 27, 3)

Examples with omission of the subject[18] have occasionally been viewed as sentences with a Stative verbal form and zeroed subject. Despite the lack of morphological distinction, this analysis is impossible. Unlike in Earlier Egyptian, Late Egyptian statives cannot appear without an overt subject in main or subordinated clauses, the pattern $[\emptyset]_{S}$ $[\text{STATIVE}]_{P}$ being ungrammatical. The only exceptions are to be found in very specific syntactic environments such as relative clauses whose omitted subject is coreferential with the antecedent. Another environment is after some verbs of control whose object complement is not introduced by a complementiser. In these cases, the object pronoun of the matrix clause functions at the same time as subject of the complement clause:

(45a) The author has received notice of the death of a man and his children and now enquires:
*n-mꜣꜥ* *[n]-ꜥḏꜣ*
IP-true-ø IP-false-ø
Is (it) true or false? (*KRI* III 500, 9)

**18** Such omissions are also typical in the omen texts such as the Dreambook of Chester Beatty III (Gardiner 1935: 7–23 and pl. 5–8) in which a case such as 'When a man sees himself in his dream copulating with a cow' (v° 16) is first mentioned and then evaluated as either good or bad (in this particular example as *nfr-ø* 'Good; (it means) making festivals in his house').

(45b) A man was told to sell a sack at the market but:
*iw-ṯ* *ḥr-ḫȝʿ-f* *rḏd-bin*
DEP-one PRP-put-3MS COMP-bad-ø
It was refused (saying): it is bad. (*KRI* V 2, 3)

(45c) A man charged of theft denies the accusation against him:
*ʿḏȝ*
false-ø
It is false. (*KRI* VI 781, 5)

This omission seems regular in the expression *nfr n*-X 'It is/goes well with X', which, however, is more common in Earlier Egyptian (see 1.1 above):

(46) Victorious king Merenptah proclaims after the defeat of the Libyans:
*nfr* *n-kmt*
good-ø to-Egypt
It goes well with Egypt. (*KRI* IV 10, 4)

The use of complement clauses in the subject position is rare in Late Egyptian, but when this occurs, the clause is introduced by the element *iw*. Instances of this construction have usually been explained as involving constructions known as Sequential, Continuative, or Non-initial main sentences.[19] However, ex. 47b with *iw* before the Future III pattern (for which see Loprieno 1995: 91 and 94; Winand 1992: 481–517) shows that this is not always the case.[20] In addition, similar constructions are found also in Demotic, where the earlier Late Egyptian Sequential has disappeared. Hence, an analysis as a dependent clause is preferred here (as proposed in Polis 2009: 225–226):

(47a) An author of a graffito laments the incompetent scribbles left by others on a wall of a chapel:
*fdq-ib-i* *iw-i* *ḥr-mȝȝ* *bȝk* *n-ḏr-t-sn*
sever-heart-1S DEP-1S PRP-see work of-hand-F-3P
It is heartbreaking to me that I have to see their handiwork.
(Graffito M.2.3.P.18.15 [Navrátilová 156])

(47b) In an oracular question the deity is asked:
*n-nfr* *iw-iw-f-ḫpr* *mdi-st*
IP-good DEP-FUT-3MS-happen with-3FS
Is it good that it will happen to her? (oDeM 10264)

19 For instance, Černý and Groll (1993: 547–48), although the authors label it as *iw.f* (*ḥr*) *stp.f* pattern that seems to refer to their chapters 37–41; similarly Groll 1967: 40 bottom. For the form/pattern itself, see Loprieno (1995: 225–29).

20 A similar analysis has been proposed even without this clear example by Neveu (1996: 234).

(47c) The addressee was supposed to go on an errand involving a third party but apparently failed to do so. In the meantime the third man has spoken to the author of a letter, saying:

*i͗s-nfr* *i͗w-i͗-ḥr-ḏd=n-f* *n-ky-ḏri͗*
IP-good DEP-1S-PRP-say=to-3MS to-other-alien
Is it proper that I should tell him on behalf of some third party?
(oDeM 554, r° 5–6)

(47d) The author of a letter says that he has brought water to a deity and tells his addressee not to worry about the matter any longer:

*ḫr-nfr* *i͗w-k* *di͗-ḥꜣty-k=n-f*
PTC-good DEP-2MS give-heart-2MS=to-3MS
Now it is appropriate for you to be considerate of him (i.e. so that he is considerate of you in return without being angry). (*LRL* 32, 4)

(47e) Instead of fowling, the female lover would rather be alone with her lover and says:

*nfr=wi͗* *i͗w-k* *i͗m* *ḥnꜥ-i͗* *i͗w-i͗* *ḥr-grg* *pḫꜣ*
good=ADM DEP-2MS here with-1S DEP-1S PRP-set trap
How good it is that you are here with me, while I set up a trap.
(Mathieu, *Poésie*, pl. 11, 6)

The sentence in the subject position can be marked by *wn* as counterfactual but that seems limited to early Late Egyptian texts:

(48a) The author of a letter gives instructions on the construction of a house and exhorts the addressee and the workmen to hurry up:

*nfr=wi͗* *wn-pꜣy(-i͗)-sn* *mdi͗-k*
good=ADM PRT-POSS.M-1S-brother with-2MS
How good would it be if my brother were with you! (pBM 10102 r° 17)

(48b) Ramesses II addresses his deceased father saying:

*nfr=n-k* *wnn-i͗* *m-nsw* *r-nḥḥ*
good=to-2MS PRT-1S as-king for-eternity
It would be good for you if I were to be king for eternity. (*KRI* II 334, 5)

No formal distinction seemed to exist between counterfactual and hypothetical/imaginative states of affairs, as shown by a comparison of 48a and 49:

(49) The harper sings of the gods welcoming the deceased and says:

*nfr* *wn-k* *ḫr-nṯr-w*
good be-2MS among-god-P
It is good that you will be with the gods. (Neferhotep Song 3 [Hari pl. IV 1.8])

There are some examples whose status is less easy to decide. Among them are the following standard phrases appearing at the end of letters:

(50a) The author ends his letter with wishes:
*nfr* *snb-k*
good health-2MS
Your health shall be good./?It is good that you are healthy.
(*KRI* I 240, 6)

(50b) The author finishes his admonitions to the addressee with:
*nfr* *sḏm-k*
good hear-2MS
Your obedience would be good./It is/will be good that/if you obey.
(oBM 5627 v° 3)

The subjects in examples of this sort could be analysed as infinitives, nouns, or as full complement clauses. Instances such as the following might speak in favour of the first two interpretations:

(51a) At the end of a graffito praising a lover:
*nfr=wi* *pꜣy-i͗-mꜣꜣ-k*
good=ADM POSS.M-1S-see.INF-2MS
How good is my beholding you! (TTS 5, 26, 11)

(51b) The author tells the addressee not to worry about a sacred standard of the god Thoth:
*ḫr-i͗w-nfr* *pꜣy-k-di͗* *i͗n-ṯ-f=n-i͗*
PTC-DEP-good POSS.M-2MS-give bring-SUB-3MS=to-1S
*di͗-i͗-šms-f*
give-1S-follow-3MS
...although it would be better if you sent it to me so that I may have it partake in a procession. (*KRI* IV 80, 16)

(51c) The author advises his correspondent to have some other person send a letter first:
*i͗w-nfr* *pꜣy-k-tm-[hꜣb* *tꜣ]-šꜥ-t* *r-ḥꜣ-t*
DEP-good POSS.M-2MS-NEG-send DEF.F-letter-F to-beginning-F
*i͗-i͗r-ṯ-f-hꜣb=n-tn*
to-AUX-TERM-3MS-send=to-2P
...as it is better that you do not send the letter first, before he has sent one to you. (*LRL* 73, 16–74, 1)

A peculiar case is provided by examples with an initial *ḫy*, usually associated with the interrogative *ḫy* 'how?' (Grapow 1941: III, 63–64) but more probably connected with *ḫy* 'to be high' (<*ꜥḫi* 'lift')[21]:

(52a) When the army of the king saw him fighting the Hittites all on his own, his charioteers cried out:

| *ḫy* | *pꜣ-ꜥḥwty* | *nfr* | *smn* | *ḥꜣty* |
|---|---|---|---|---|
| high | DEF.M-fighter | good | establish | heart |

Elevated is the perfect fighter who makes the heart firm! (*KRI* II 75, 12–16)

(52b) Context not known:

| *ḫy* | *pꜣ-ḥms* | *nfr* | *m-nw-t* | *rs-t* |
|---|---|---|---|---|
| high | DEF.M-sit | good | in-city-F | southern-F |

Elevated is the dwelling in the southern city (Thebes)!
(Berlin 6768 [acc. to Grapow 1941: 63])

Often the subject position after *ḫy* is occupied by the expression *sp nfr n* 'perfect case of' followed by another nominal phrase

(53a) The king prays to Amun, wishing to be in Egypt rather than alone on the battlefield:

| *ḫy* | *pꜣ-sp* | *nfr* | *n-pꜣ-ḫrp* | *mn-w* | *qn-w* |
|---|---|---|---|---|---|
| high | DEF.M-case | good | of-DEF.M-guide | monument-P | many-P |
| *r-wꜣst* | *nw-t* | *imn* | | | |
| to-N | city-F | N | | | |

Elevated is he who provided many monuments to Thebes, the city of Amun! (*KRI* II 62, 1–3)

(53b) Amun makes those who approach his city say:

| *ḫy* | *pꜣ-sp* | *nfr* | *n-pꜣ-dmi-k* |
|---|---|---|---|
| high | DEF.M-case | good | of-DEF.M-touch-2MS |

Elevated is he whom you touched! (*KRI* V 223, 1–2)

Another construction shows an infinitive of *wꜣḏ* 'prosper' with the definite article after *ḫy*:

(54a) The deceased addresses the goddess of the West:

| *ḫy* | *pꜣ-wꜣḏ* | *pꜣ-ꜥq* | *m-bꜣḥ-t* | *pꜣ-ḥtp* |
|---|---|---|---|---|
| high | DEF.M-prosper | DEF.M-enter | in-presence-2FS | DEF.M-rest |

21 See Peust (1999: 104) for the development. Recently, however, examples with *ḫy* have once more been analysed as interrogatives; see Vernus (2006: 157).

*m-ḫnw(-t)*
in-inside(-2FS)
Elevated is the prospering of him who enters into your presence, he who rests inside you! (TT 23 [acc. to Grapow 1941: 64])

(54b) The god Atum says to the other gods:
*ḫy* *pꜣ-wḏ* *n-sꜣ-w-n* *ḏr-ḫwi-sn* [...] *psḏ-t*
high DEF.M-prosper of-son-P-1P since-guard-3P [...] ennead-F
*n-wꜣst* *ꞽwnw* *ḥwtkꜣptḥ*
of-N N N
Elevated is the prospering of our sons since they guard the enneads of Thebes, Heliopolis, and Memphis! (*KRI* VI 5, 9–10)

### 1.2.2 Demotic

Adjectival sentences of the type found in Earlier and, to some extent, Late Egyptian are uncommon in Demotic, and none of the few attested examples postdates the first century BC:

(55a) The administrative standards of an authority receive official approval:
*nfr* *pꜣy-f-ꞽp*
good POSS.M-3MS-accounting
His accounting is good. (pRylands IX 10, 12)

(55b) The author of a letter writes to a lady, telling how he and others reached an official on a certain day:
*r-nfr* *ḥꜣty-t* *n-nꜣ-md-w* *ꜥn-w* *nty-ꞽw-w*
DEP-good heart-2FS for-DEP.P-thing.F-P nice-P REL-FUT-3P
*r-ḫpr* *n-pꜣ-mr-kꜣ-t*
FUT-happen for-DEF.M-oversee-work-F
...while your heart is content about the good things that will happen to the overseer of works. (pCG 50067 + 50087, 3)

(55c) Drunk with good wine, the pharaoh enjoyed a manly form of entertainment:
*ꜥn-ḥr* *prꜥꜣ* *ꞽrm-nꜣy-f-sḥm-w*
beautiful-face pharaoh with-POSS.P-3MS-woman.F-P
The pharaoh delighted himself with his women. (pBN 215 vº a4)

(55d) In an encomium on the king:
*ꜥꜣ* *ḥꜣti-k* *nfr* *nꜣy-k-sḏy*
great heart-2MS good POSS.P-2MS-affair
May you be steadfast. May your issues be good. (*Archive of Hor* #3, 19)

(55e) The author of a letter expresses his joy and excitement at having received four letters:

*nfr* *ḥ3ṯ-y* *m-šs* *ḏb3-ḫpr* *iw-bnp-w-3bḫe*
good heart-1S in-excess because-happen DEP-NEG.PST-3P-forget
*r-ḥr-n* *šꜥ-t3-wnw-t*
to-face-1P until-DEF.F-hour-F
My heart rejoices greatly because we have not yet been forgotten.
(pBerlin P. 23629, 4–6)

The emerging pattern in Demotic is a new construction of adjectival predication built of the etymologically opaque (Fecht 1960: §398 note 540 deriving it from a geminated verbal form of *wnn* governing verbal form of a predicative verb vs. Quack 1991a: 96 without a proposed derivation but arguments against the former hypothesis) initial element *n3* (or *n3w* in texts from the Roman era) followed by the predicative adjective and the subject, which in most cases is a suffix, and not a clitic pronoun as in the earlier stages of the language. Note that both forms, with or without *n3*, may appear in the same text:

(56a) Moral precepts demand:
*mir-ḏd* *n3-sb3-y*
NEG.IMP-say ADJ-educated-1S
Do not say: 'I am educated'. (Onkhsheshonqy 8, 3)

(56b) To obtain wisdom from Anubis, the magician has to ask his questions to a boy. The outcome depends on the ear with which the boy hears:
*iw-f-ḫpr* *iw-p3y-f-msḏr* *n-wnmy* *p3y* *n3w-nfr-f*
DEP-3MS-happen DEP-POSS.M-3MS-ear of-right SE.M ADJ-good-3MS
If it is his right ear, it is good. (pMag.London and Leiden 3, 19–20)

(56c) An epistolary formula implies that more detailed information will be given orally:
*n3-ꜥš3-w* *r-hb* *nim-w*
ADJ-plenty-3P to-send OBJ-3P
They (the issues) are too numerous to write. (pBerlin P. 13537, 21)[22]

(56d) In the setting of a story the pharaoh is described as gluttonous:
*iw-n3-ꜥ3y* *ir-t* *n-prꜥ3* *ꜥ.w.s.* *m-šs*
DEP-ADJ-great eye-F of-pharaoh l.p.h. in-excess
...while the eye of the pharaoh l.p.h. was exceedingly large.
(pVandier 1, 3)

22 See Depauw (2006: 278–80), for further examples.

(56e) A lion tells his mate to stay away from the man for:
*nꜣw-swk-f*
ADJ-despicable-3MS
He is despicable. (Myth of the Sun's Eye 18, 2)

(56f) Moral precepts exhort against losing faith in times of need, for:
*nꜣ-ꜥ(ꜣ)   tꜣ-wpw-t   n-pꜣ-nṯr*
ADJ-great   DEF.F-work-F   of-DEF.M-god
God's deeds are great. (pInsinger 20, 4)

(56g) Amun is manifest as a bull:
*nꜣw-sbk   nꜣy-f-ꜥb-w*
ADJ-short   POSS.P-3MS-horn-P
His horns are short. (*Primeval Ocean*, fr. 3, 12)

(56h) An encomium on pharaoh Ptolemy VI starts with the wishes and blessings:
*nꜣ-nfr=n-k   tꜣ-rnp   tꜣy-k-rnp   nfr-t   rnp=nb*
ADJ-good=for-2MS   DEF.F-year   POSS.F-2MS-year   good-F   year=QU
*nty-i͗w-w   i͗y*
REL-FUT-3P   come
*nꜣ-nfr=n-k   tꜣy   i͗rm-w   nfr-s   (n)-pꜣy-k-šy*
ADJ-good=for-2MS   DEM.F   with-3P   good-3FS   for-POSS.M-2MS-fate
*nꜣ-nfr-s   (n)-tꜣy-k-špšy   nfr-s   n-nꜣ-rmṯ-w*
ADJ-good-3FS   for-POSS.F-2MS-nobility   good-3FS   for-DEF.P-human-P
*nty-ršy   i͗w-w   nw   ri͗r-k*
REL-be_happy   DEP-3P   see   OBJ-2MS
The year may be good for you. Every year that will come is your good year. This one may be good for you with them. It may be good for your fate and it may be good for your good fortune. It may be good for the humans who are happy when they behold you.
(*Archive of Hor* #3, 2–5)

Sometimes the initial element is shortened to *n*:

(57) The author of a letter states:
*ꜥsm   tꜣ-md-t   nty-sṱ   r-pꜣdyḥrpꜣrꜥ*
PTC   DEF.F-thing-F   REL-3FS   to-N
*n-dḥr-hb   i͗i͗r-ḥr-pꜣ-sẖ-ḥwtnṯr   ni͗m-s*
ADJ-painful-send.INF   to-face-DEF.M-scribe-temple   OBJ-3FS
Lo, the issue that pertains to Peteharpres, it is too painful to inform the temple-scribe about it. (pLeiden I 382, 22–25)

This same morpheme appears with adjectives both in attributive and predicative use. It can be used to build adjectives from verbs (ex. 56a above), nouns as well as from prepositional phrases (ex. 58):

(58a) In a fragment of translation from Middle Egyptian to Demotic, the following sentence appears in the Demotic part:
*n3-wnš-f* *p3y-ḥry-mni*
ADJ-wolf-3MS DEM.M-overseer-herdsman
This overseer of herdsmen is wolf-like.
(pBM EA 69574 B 2 ed. *JEA* 85: 156)

(58b) Moral precepts state:
*n3-m-šs* *n3-nfy-w* *n-p3-ḥf* *r-[n3-]hwhw-w*
ADJ-in-order DEF.P-hiss-P of-DEF.M-snake than-DEF.P-braying-P
*n-p3-ʿ3*
of-DEF.M-donkey
The hissing of the snake is more important than the donkey's braying.
(Onkhsheshonqy 20, 9)

Like the older adjectival sentence construction *nfr=sw*, the pattern *n3-nfr-f* is not temporally marked:

(59a) After a woman noticed the absence of her periods, she told the pharaoh that she was pregnant. Then:
*n3-nfr* *ḥ3ṯ-f* *m-šs*
ADJ-good heart-3MS in-order
His heart was very happy. (Setne I 3, 7)

(59b) A letter begins with a wish:
*n3-nfr=n-k* *t3-rnp-t*
ADJ-good=to-2MS DEF.F-year-F
May the year be happy for you! (pLoeb 4, 2)

This shows that the construction is not connected to other Demotic verbal patterns of the type VERB-SUFFIX such as the past and future *sḏm-f*. In addition, the adjectives with *n3* do not seem to conform to the rule that roots beyond three radicals have to make use of the analytic auxiliary pattern *ir-f-sḏm*, as examples such as *n3-tgtg* 'to be hasty' (de Cenival 1985: pl. 12 top right, 6) show. Apart from this, they were treated as other verbal roots and could appear, e.g., after imperatives, vetitives, or in the Limitative form where usually the infinitive of the lexical verb appears:

(60a) The addressee is urged:
*my* *ꜥꜣ-s* *mtw-nꜣy-k-ḫyr*
let.IMP great-3FS with-POSS.P-2MS-enemy
Let it be an obligation to you. (pLouvre E 7854, 4)[23]

(60b) In a prescription for the treatment of a dog-bite:
*mtw-k-md-t* *rr-f* *n-mne* *šꜥmtw-f-nꜣw-nfr*
CNJ-2MS-speak-INF to-3MS in-daily LIM-3MS-ADJ-good
...and you should speak to it daily until it is well.
(pMag.London and Leiden 19, 9)

Syntactically, the *nꜣ*-formations can also be used as infinitives (as just seen) or appear in the Stative:

(61) Advice on ethical conduct:
*iw-k* *ḫpr* *irm-rmṯ* *mtw-k* *nfr* *irm-f*
DEP-2MS happen with-man CNJ-2MS be_good with-3MS
*iw-f* *nꜣ-b(i)n* *mir-ḫꜣꜥ-f*
DEP-3MS ADJ-bad.STA NEG.IMP-leave-3MS
If you are with a man and doing fine with him, while he is doing bad, do not leave him! (Onkhsheshonqy 17, 18)

The subject position of *nꜣ*-forms can in principle be filled by any nominal phrase, including a headless relative clause or an infinitive:

(62a) A Nubian official extols his proper conduct in all business assigned to him by his lord. He says that he went to the island of Philae with some priests:
*nꜣw-nw* *nꜣ-šꜥšꜥ-w* *ntyiw-wꜣḥ-nꜣ-ḥm-nṯr-w*
ADJ-nice DEF.P-honour-P REL-AUX.PST-DEF.P-servant-god-P
*irm-nꜣ-wꜥb-w*
with-DEF.P-priest-P
*irm-pꜣ-mšꜥ* *n-pꜣ-tyme* *ir-f* *n{ꜣ}-i*
with-DEF.M-multitude of-DEF.M-town do-3MS for-1S
Nice were the honours that were demonstrated to me by the prophets, the priests, and the multitude of the city. (grPhilae 416, 7)

(62b) A steward replies to a suggestion by his correspondent to detain some children until the arrival of the pharaoh:

23 An apotropaic expression using *nꜣy-k-ḫir* 'your enemies' for 'you'.

*n3-nfr* *n3y-ḏd-k*
ADJ-be good DEM.P-say.REL.PST-2MS
What you have said is good. (*Saqqara Dem. Papyri* I #2 x+1, 31)

(62c) Moral precepts state:
*n3-ʿn* *ḥms* *n-p3y-k-pr* *ẖm*
ADJ-nice sit.INF in-POSS.M-2MS-house small
*r-ḥms* *n-p3-pr* *ʿ3* *n-ky*
to-sit.INF in-DEF.M-house great of-other
It is nicer to sit in your own small house than in the great house of another. (Onkhsheshonqy 23, 8)

(62d) The author of a letter suggests that a god be returned to his home, for:
*n3-dḥr* *ẖ3ʿ-f* *p3-bnr* *n-p3y-f-m3ʿ*
ADJ-painful let.INF-3MS DEF.M-outside of-POSS.M-3MS-place
It would be painful to leave him outside of his place. (pLoeb 8, 37–38 = v° 4–5)

In the case of clausal complements, the subject position is occupied by a cataphoric expletive pronoun co-indexed with the clause in apposition and marked as dependent by the element *iw*:

(63a) The author of a letter expresses his gratitude for his addressee's care:
*iir-ʿn-f* *iw-n* *mtw-k* *n-sn* *ẖm*
ST-nice-[3MS]$_i$ [DEP-1P with-2MS as-brother small]$_i$
It is nice that we are to you like a younger brother. (pBerlin P. 13544, 9–11)

(63b) A request in a short message:
*n3-ʿn-f* *iw-k* *ir-f* *mtw-k-dy-in-w* *šśw* *mw* *1* *n-N*
ADJ-nice-3MS DEP-3MS do-3MS CNJ-2MS-let-bring-3P jar water 1 to-N
It would be nice if you could be so kind and have a jar of water brought to N. (oKöln 184, 2)

(63c) The author of a letter begs the addressee:
*ʿn-f* *iw-k* *ir-f*
nice-3MS DEP-3MS do-3MS
It would be nice if you did it. (pBerlin P. 3093, 12)

It is unclear whether examples such as the following should be analysed as displaying subject omission of the type seen in Late Egyptian (Section 1.2.1 above):

(64) A legal document contains the following stipulation:
*bn-iw(-y)-rḫ-ḏd* *ʿḏ* *r-md-t=nb-t* *nty-ḥry*
NEG-FUT[-1S]-can-say false to-thing-F=QU-F REL-above
I will not be able to say 'false' concerning anything above.
(pRylands I, 7)

### 1.2.3 Coptic

The adjectival construction with *na-*, which continues Demotic *nꜣ*, stands outside the regular verbal system of Coptic both morphologically and syntactically. The order of grammatical constituents is VS instead of the normal SV; constructions with *na-* cannot syntactically replace the infinitive, and do not alternate with a Stative form. They are often treated alongside other finite constructions that differ structurally from the main verbal constructions of Coptic such as *peca-f* 'he said', etc. The difficulty raised by the classification of this pattern is illustrated by the wide variety of labels used for it in the literature, *na*-constructions being referred to as 'nominal verbs' (Stern 1880: §308; Steindorff 1951: §297), verbs with suffixed subjects (Chaîne 1993: §704), quality (Till 1970: §284; Vergote 1973: Ia, §70.2) or adjectival verbs (Mallon 1956: §292–98; Reintges 2004: 394–96), and 'suffixally conjugated verboids' (Layton 2011: §376). For the sake of clarity, we shall label them 'adjective verbs'. However, since their function is majorly to express the predicative use of adjectives they are glossed as adjectives below. This is also follows the observation that Greek adjectives can be used in the very position and the very syntactic pattern otherwise showing 'adjective verbs', see ex. 78c below.

Of the more than fifty attestations of *nꜣ*-patterns in Demotic, Coptic retains only a handful of adjective verbs. This shows that the pattern was no longer productive and that the forms had been lexicalised. Some of them only allow pronominal subjects:

**Tab. III.2:** Coptic adjective verbs.

| Form | | Translation | Etymology |
|---|---|---|---|
| **Prenominal** | **Prepronominal** | | |
| $^{SB}$*naa-* | $^{SB}$*naa*(a)- | | |
| $^{A}$*nee-* | $^{A}$*nee-* | 'be great' | (<*nꜣ-ꜥꜣ*) |
| – | *naiat-* | 'be blessed' | (<*nꜣ-ꜥꜣ-i͗r-t-*) |
| $^{SAF}$*nanu-* | $^{SAF}$*nanu-* | | |
| $^{B}$*nane-* | $^{B}$*nane-* | 'be good' | (<*nꜣ-ꜥn*) |
| *nese-* | *nesô-* | 'be beautiful' | |
| – | $^{S}$*nesbôô-* | 'be intelligent | (<*nꜣ-sbꜣ*) |
| *naše-* | *naSô-* | 'be many, plentiful' | (<*nꜣ-ꜥšꜣ*) |
| $^{S}$*nefr-* | – | 'be pleasant' | (<*nꜣ-nfr*) |
| – | $^{S}$*nahlô/ok*$^{j}$*-* | 'be pleasant' | (<*nꜣ-ḥlq*) |
| – | $^{S}$*nek*$^{j}$*ô-* | 'be ugly' | (<*nꜣ-gꜣ*) |

A form *nefr-* without *na-* is attested only once in Sahidic[24]:

(65) Jesus says that no one drinking old wine will exchange it for new, but he will rather say:
*nefr-p-erp as*
good-DEF.M-wine old
The old wine is good. ($^{S}$Lk 5:39)

The subject can be either a suffix pronoun or a noun, except with lexemes with only a pre-pronominal form. In most cases and dialects (insofar as the pattern is attested), the form of the predicative adjective varies according to rules of prosodic stress when a suffix pronoun is attached.[25] In Bohairic, however, the predicative adjective 'good' has an identical pronominal and pre-pronominal form (*nane-*). Only with the first-person singular pronoun it appears as *nanê-i*. In the presence of pronouns, Akhmimic shows a form *nee-* instead of *naa-* in the other dialects:

(66a) Shenute quotes from the Song of Songs (Sg 1:16):
*ishêête nanu-k pa-son auô nesô-k e-kʲôšt nsô-k*
behold good-2MS POSS.M.1S-brother and beautiful-2MS to-look after-2MS
Behold, you are fair, my brother, and beautiful to gaze upon.
($^{S}$Shenute, *As I Sat on a Mountain* [L III 53, 6–7])

(66b) Holofernes answers to Judith:
*tenu=kʲe nto nesô-ø hrai hm-pu-ine*
now=then 2FS beautiful-2FS down in-POSS.M.2FS-image
*auô nanu-ø hrai hn-(n)u-šace*
and good-2FS down in-POSS.P.2FS-word
And now you are both beautiful in your countenance and witty in your words. ($^{S}$Jdt 11:23)

24 Witnesses in all other dialects make use of different constructions here.

25 If pronominal forms consisting of a single (all singular forms and 3P) or two consonants (1P) are attached to the predicative adjective, the stress falls onto the ultimate (single consonant) or penultimate syllable (two consonants); hence, *ne-sôf* or *ne-sô-tn*. All nouns as well as the pronoun of the second plural (*têutn*) have a syllabic structure in which the stress falls on one of the syllables within their structures. As Coptic allows only a single stressed syllable per word, the predicative adjective becomes de-stressed and appears in a 'reduced' form (*nese-*). The topic will be treated in detail in a fortchcoming volume on phonology in this series; for the time being, see Müller (2011b: 523–26).

(66c) The Canons order that a young man wishing to become a Christian must provide a reference from his superior:

*eršan-tm-pe-f-cois* *er-mntre* *haro-f*
CND-AUX.NEG-POSS.M-3MS-lord do-witness about-3MS
*ce-nanu-f* *mar-u-noc-f* *ebol*
COMP-good-3MS JUSS-3P-throw-3MS out
If his master does not testify about him that he is good, he shall be expelled.
($^{S}$*Can. Eccl.* [de Lagarde, *Aeg.* 251, 26–27])

(66d) Jethro bids farewell to Moses and the story adds:

*mnnse-n-houe* *et-našo-u* *etmmo* *a-f-mu* *nk$^{j}$i-p-rro*
after-DEF.P-day REL-great-3P that PST-3MS-die PVS-DEF.M-king
*n-kême*
of-Egypt
Many days thereafter the king of Egypt died. ($^{A}$Ex 4:18 [Lacau 1911])

(66e) The proverbs assure the addressed son of the positive effects of wisdom:

*aša-t-sophia=gar* *i* *a-p-k-hêt*
CND-DEF.F-wisdom=for go to-POSS.M-2MS-heart
*au* *k-meue* *a-t-aisthêsis* *ce-nanu-s*
and 2MS-think OBJ-DEF.F-perception COMP-good-3FS
*n-t-k-psukhê*
for-POSS.F-2MS-soul
For if wisdom enters heart, you perceive that it is good for your soul.
($^{A}$Prv 2:10)

(66f) God said: 'Let there be light', and there was light:

*a-f-nau* *nce-p$^{h}$-(nu)ti* *e-pi-uôini* *ce-nane-f*
PST-3MS-see PVS-DEF.M-god OBJ-DEF$_{2}$.M-light COMP-good-3MS
And God saw that the light was good. ($^{B}$Gn 1:4 [Kasser])

Direct attachment of nouns is less common than pronouns, the examples listed below are almost exhaustive. It is uncertain whether this is due to a general diachronic replacement of pre-nominal by pre-pronominal forms. The difference in frequency might simply reflect the statistical preponderance of pronominal subjects in Coptic (or in languages in general):

(67a) Shenute opens his discourse with the words:

*a-i-uôšb* *e-i-cô* *mmo-s* *na-u*
PST-1S-answer DEP-1S-say OBJ-3MS to-3P
*ce-nanu-pe-tn-urot* *ô* *m-merate*
COMP-good-POSS.M-2P-zeal VOC DEF.P-beloved
I answered, saying to them: 'Your zeal is excellent, O beloved ones.'
($^{S}$Shenute, *I Answered* [L III 27, 5–6])

(67b) Shenute says:
*nanu-tre-p-rôme mu n-huo e-ônh*
good-INFL-DEF.M-man die in-more than-live
*e-f-r-nobe m-p-mto ebol n-n-et-na-sonh-f*
DEP-3MS-do-sin in-DEF.M-presence out of-DEF.P-REL-FUT-bind-3MS
It is better that a man should die than live committing sin before those who will bind him. ($^{S}$Shenute, *Is It Not Written* [A I 52, 9–10])

(67c) Wisdom begs the Light not to leave her in darkness:
*sôtm ero-i p-uoin ce-nanu-pe-k-na*
hear OBJ-1S DEF.M-light for-good-POSS.M-2MS-mercy
Listen to me, O light, for your mercy is good.
($^{S}$*Pistis Sophia* 49, 13 [Schmidt])

(67d) A song about the rich and the poor begins with a proverbial statement:
*nanu-u-hêke hi-pe-f-êi para u-rmmao*
good-IDF.S-poor on-POSS.M-3MS-house more IDF.S-rich
*n-ref-cin-*$c^{h}$*[oons]*
of-AGT-take-violence
*e-f-katalalei n-ciue nsa-p-et-hituô-f hn-u-krof*
DEP-3MS-revile in-stealth after-DEF.M-REL-near-3MS in-IDF.S-guile
Better a poor man in his hut than a violent rich man who stealthily reviles his neighbour through guile. ($^{S}$Junker, *Poesie* II, 88, 3–6)

(67e) The angel of the Lord tells Tobit and Tobias:
*p-mustêrion m-p-rro nanu-hop-f*
DEF.M-secret of-DEF.M-king good-hide.INF-3MS
*ne-hbêue=de m-p-nute e-*$k^{j}$*olp-u ebol hn-u-mpša*
DEF.P-things=yet of-DEF.M-god to-reveal-3P out in-IDF.S-worth
As to the secret of the king, it is good to conceal it but to reveal gloriously the things of God. ($^{S}$Tb 12:11)

(67f) God says that the Israelites make sacrifices under trees:
*ce-nanu-t-ḫaibe*
for-good-DEF.F-shadow
...because the shadow is good. ($^{A}$Hos 4:13 [Till])

(67g) The teacher urges the devotees to preserve the Manichean revelations in written form:
*epeidê naše-t-sophia et-a-[i-t]eua-s [arô-ten]*
because plenty-DEF.F-wisdom REL-PST-1S-send-3FS to-2P
...because the wisdom that I handed down to you is plentiful.
($^{L}$*Kephalaia* 6, 26)

(67h) The Ecclesastes says: *Since those days I learned*:
*ce-nanu-p-et-er-hati* *ha-t-hê* *m-p-nuti*
COMP-good-DEF.M-REL-do-fear under-DEF.F-front of-DEF.M-god
...that whoever fears God is good. ($^{F}$Eccl 8:12)

(67i) Jesus tells that everyone must be 'salted with fire':
*nane-pi-hmu*
good-DEF$_2$.M-salt
The salt is good. ($^{B}$Mk 9:50)

(67j) Basil warns:
*naše-nê* *et-a-u-mu* *et$^{h}$be-ti-cin-saci*
plenty-DEF$_3$.P REL-PST-3P-die because-DEF$_2$.F-NOM-talk
*uoh* *mp-u-côk* *n-ni-hbêui* *ebol*
and NEG.PST-3P-fulfil OBJ-DEF$_2$.P-works.P out
Numerous are those who died because of talking and did not accomplish the works. ($^{B}$Basil of Caesarea, *On Noah's Ark* [De Vis II 215, 2])

As can be seen, any kind of NP can appear in the subject position. However, the direct cliticisation of an NP is almost lexicalised in the expression *naše-su(e)nt-* 'costly':

(68a) After Diocletian reinstalled the pagan gods, he and his nobles furnished the temples with riches.
*a-f-ti-šomnt* *n-ône* *m-me* *e-pe-klom* *m-p-apollôn*
PST-3MS-give-three of-stone of-truth to-DEF.M-crown of-DEF.M-N
*e-naše-suent-u*
DEP-great-price-3P
He (the emperor) gave three real precious stones for the crown of Apollo. ($^{S}$*Mart. St Victor the General* [Budge, *Martyrdoms* 3, 31–33])

(68b) When Jesus was in Bethany in Simon's house, a leprous woman came to him:
*e-un-u-alabastron* *n-sak$^{j}$n* *n-tat-s*
DEP-PTC-IDF.S-alabaster of-ointment in-hand-3FS
*e-naše-sunt-f*
DEP-great-price-3MS
...with an alabaster box of very precious ointment. ($^{M}$Mt 26:7)

(68c) When Jesus stayed with Lazarus:
*mari[a=de* *a-s]-ci* *n-u-litra* *n-sak$^{j}$n* *n-nardos*
N=yet PST-3FS-take OBJ-IDF.S-pound of-ointment of-nard
*e-s-nhat* *e-naše-sunt-s*
DEP-3FS-real.STA DEP-great-price-3FS
Mary took a pound of real and very costly ointment of nard. ($^{L}$Jn 12:3)

(68d) Jesus likens the kingdom of heavens to a merchant seeking pearls:

| | | | | |
|---|---|---|---|---|
| *ete-a-f-cimi=de* | | *n-u-markitês* | *e-naše-suent-f* | |
| REL-PST-3MS-find=yet | | OBJ-IDF.S-pearl | DEP-great-price-3MS | |
| *a-f-šê* | *a-f-ti* | *n-hôb* | *nibi* | *ete-ntê-f* |
| PST-3MS-go | PST-3MS-give | OBJ-thing | QU | REL-POSS-3MS |
| *abal* | *šante-f-šap-f* | | | |
| out | LIM-3MS-buy-3MS | | | |

When he found a costly pearl, he went, sold all that he had, and bought it. ($^{F}$Mt 13:46)

(68e) David declares what he brought for the temple. Amongst other things there were:

| | | |
|---|---|---|
| *nem-han-ništi* | *n-ôni* | *e-naše-suen-u* |
| CON-IDF.P-great | of-stone | DEP-great-price-3P |

...many costly stones. ($^{B}$1Chr 29:2 [de Lagarde])

Another special case is *naiat-*, which goes back etymologically to a construction with a predicate *naa-* 'be great' + *eiat-* 'eye' and only allows pronominal subjects. Nominal subjects must be attached periphrastically.

(69a) After Jesus revealed a further mystery to the disciples, they fell on their knees and said:

| | | | | |
|---|---|---|---|---|
| *naiat-n* | *anon* | *para-rôme=nim* | | |
| blessed-1P | 1P | more-man=QU | | |
| *ce-a-k-k$^{j}$ôlp* | *na-n* | *ebol* | *n-nei-nok$^{j}$* | *n-špêre* |
| for-PST-2MS-reveal | for-1P | out | OBJ-DEM.P-great | of-wonder |

We are more blessed than any other man because you have revealed to us these great wonders. ($^{S}$*Pistis Sophia* 357, 19–20 [Schmidt])

(69b) Tobit says about Jerusalem:

| | | | |
|---|---|---|---|
| *naiat-u* | *n-n-et-me* | *mmo-ø* | *se-na-raše* |
| blessed-3P | as-DEF.P-REL-love | OBJ-2FS | 3P-FUT-rejoice |
| *ecn-tu-eirênê* | | | |
| over-POSS.F.2FS-peace | | | |
| *naiat-u* | *n-n-ent-a-u-mkah* | *n-hêt* | |
| blessed-3P | as-DEF.P-REL-PST-3P-grieve | in-heart | |
| *ecn-nu-mastigks* | *têr-u* | | |
| over-POSS.P.2FS-affliction | all-3P | | |
| *ce-se-na-raše* | *ehrai* | *ecô-ø* | *e-a-u-nau* |
| for-3P-FUT-rejoice | down | upon-2FS | DEP-PST-3P-see |
| *e-pu-eou* | *têr-f* | | |
| OBJ-POSS.M.2FS-glory | all-3P | | |

| | | |
|---|---|---|
| *auô* | *se-na-euphrane* | *ša-eneh* |
| and | 3P-FUT-be_delighted | for-eternity |

Happy are those who love you; they will rejoice over your peace. Happy are those who grieved over all your afflictions, for they will rejoice over you upon seeing all your glory and the will be made glad forever.

($^{S}$Tb 13:14)

(69c) The proverbs state:

| | | | |
|---|---|---|---|
| *neiet-f* | *m-p-rôme* | *et-a-f-k$^{j}$ine* | *n-t-sophia* |
| blessed-3MS | as-DEF.M-man | REL-PST-3MS-find | OBJ-DEF.F-wisdom |
| *auô* | *p-rôme* | *et-a-f-k$^{j}$ine* | *n-t-mnt-sabe* |
| and | DEF.M-man | REL-PST-3MS-find | OBJ-DEF.F-ABST-wise |

Blessed is the man who found wisdom, and the man who found understanding. ($^{A}$Prv 3:13)

(69d) Jesus tells the disciples:

| | | | | |
|---|---|---|---|---|
| *ešpe* | *tetn-saune* | *n-[ne]i* | *neietn-têne* | *ereš[a]-tetn-eet-u* |
| CND | 2P-know | OBJ-DEM.P.ABS | blessed-2PS | CND-2P-do-3P |

If you know these things, you are happy if you do them. ($^{L}$Jn 13:17)

(69e) Jesus begins his Sermon on the Mount with the words:

| | | |
|---|---|---|
| *naiet-u* | *n-ni-hêke* | *hm-pe-pn(eum)a* |
| blessed-3P | as-DEF$_2$.P-poor | in-DEF.M-spirit |
| *ce-to-u=te* | *t-mnt-era* | *n-m-pêue* |
| for-POSS.F-3P=COP.F | DEF.F-ABST-king | of-DEF.P-heaven.P |

Blessed are the poor in spirit, for theirs is the kingdom of heaven.

($^{M}$Mt 5:3 mae 1)

(69f) The prophet quotes the Lord with the word:

| | | | |
|---|---|---|---|
| *naiet-f* | *m-p-ete-uantê-f* | *nn-u-sperma* | *hn-siôn* |
| blessed-3MS | as-DEF.M-REL-have-3MS | OBJ-IDF.S-seed | in-N |
| *auô* | *hen-rem-n-êi* | *hn-t-hie(rusal)em* | |
| and | IDF.P-man-of-house | in-DEF.F-N | |

Happy is the one who has seed in Zion and kinsmen in Jerusalem.

($^{F}$Is 31:9)

(69g) On Peter's question whether he would preach to the disciples or to everyone, Jesus answers: Who then is that faithful and wise steward, whom his lord shall make ruler over his household, to give them their portion of meat in due season?

| | | | | |
|---|---|---|---|---|
| *ôu* | *niat-f* | *m-pi-bôk* | *etemmau* | *p$^{h}$ê* |
| length | blessed-3MS | as-DEF$_2$.M-servant | that | DEF$_3$.M |
| *et-afšan-i* | | | | |
| REL-CND.3MS-come | | | | |

*nce-pe-f-c$^h$(oi)s* *nte-f-cem-f* *e-f-iri*
PVS-POSS.M-3MS-lord CNJ-3MS-find-3MS DEP-3MS-do
*m-pai-rêti*
in-DEM.M-manner
Blessed is the servant whom his lord finds doing thus when he returns.
(BLk 12:43)

Note that Bohairic Biblical texts make use of *ôu niat-* rather than simple *niat* (Crum 1939: 74a). However, as mentioned above, not all predicative adjectives retain the ability to attach nouns. In these cases, the subject must first be introduced as a cataphoric pronoun. Some Coptic authors and translators use a similar pattern with lexemes that actually allow noun attachment. The pattern with resumption of the referent of a cataphoric pronominal subject by means of the postverbal subject marker *nk$^j$i-/nce-* is rare, and perhaps stylistically motivated:

(70a) Shenute argues:
*ontos* *ti-na-coo-s* *ce-u-monon* *naše-n-et-r-hôb*
verily 1S-FUT-say-3FS COMP-not-only many-DEF.P-REL-do-work
*etbe-te-hre* *m-pn(eum)atikon*
because-DEF.F-food of-spiritual
*e-u-ire* *n-na-t-khreia* *m-p-sôma* *e-u-ire=de*
DEP-3P-do OBJ-POSS.P-DEF.F-need of-DEF.M-body DEP-3P-do=yet
*on* *n-na-te-psukhê*
again OBJ-POSS.P-DEF.F-soul
*alla* *našô-u* *on* *nk$^j$i-n-argos* *u-monon* *ce-n-se-ire*
but plenty-3P again PVS-DEF.P-lazy not-only for-NEG-3P-do
*an* *n-na-t-khreia* *m-p-sôma*
NEG OBJ-POSS.P-DEF.F-need of-DEF.M-body
*ude* *na-te-psukhê* *e-u-sroft* *e-hen-pethou*
nor OBJ-POSS.P-DEF.F-soul DEP-3P-have leisure.STA for-IDF.P-bad
*auô* *e-u-šaar* *e-ne-u-sarks* *hn-u-mnt-at-šipe*
and DEP-3P-smite OBJ-POSS.P-3P-flesh in-IDF.S-ABST-un-shame
*hrai* *hn-hen-akatharsia*
down in-IDF.P-impure
Verily, I will say that numerous are not only those who work for spiritual food, doing the things of need of the body and also the things of the soul, but numerous are also those who are lazy, not only because they neither do the things of need of the body nor the things of the soul, having leisure for evil and shamelessly smiting their flesh with impurities.
(SShenute, *Reading Today from the Proverbs* [L III 114, 27–115, 5])

(70b) The serpent asks Eve why she does not eat fruit from the forbidden tree amidst the paradise:
*ce-e-nesô-u* *nk$^{j}$i-ne-f-karpos*
for-ST-nice-3P PVS-POSS.P-3MS-fruit
...since its fruits are very fine.
($^{S}$Timothy of Alexandria, *On Abbaton* [Budge, *Martyrdoms* 237, 10–11])

Another possibility is to place the nominal subject in initial position and attach an anaphoric pronoun to the stem:

(71a) Clement says that children should be brought up in fear of the Lord so that they will recognise:
*ce-n-eẖ* *n-ẖe* *t-f-hnôôhe* *nanu-s* *au*
COMP-in-WH of-manner POSS.F-3MS-fear good-3FS and
*u-nak$^{j}$=te*
IDF.S-great=SE.F
...how the fear of Him is good and great. ($^{A}$1Cl 21:8 [Schmidt])

(71b) The apostle warns of people who depart from the faith and e.g. proscribe eating meat:
*ce-sônt=niben* *nte-p$^{h}$-(nu)ti* *nane-f*
for-creation=QU of-DEF.M-god good-3MS
...because every creation of God is good. ($^{B}$1Ti 4:4)

Clausal subjects are not attached directly to the predicate. Instead, the cataphoric expletive pronoun *-s* (3FS) appears on the predicate, co-indexed with a following appositional clause. The latter can take the form of an *e* + infinitive phrase, a dependent clause, the Conjunctive form, or a complement clause introduced by *ce*. In the pattern with *e* plus infinitive, a contextually obvious actor of the subject clause can be omitted:

(72a) Shenute cuts a lengthy sermon short with the words:
*nanu-s* *e-hô* *n-tei-he* *ê* *ša-pei-ma*
good-3FS to-suffice in-DEM.F-way or until-DEM.M-place
*ere-pe-f-snof* *tltl* *n-huo* *e-tre-f-sôk*
DEP-POSS.M-3MS-blood drop in-more to-INFL-3MS-flow
*n-t-he* *n-u-mou*
in-DEF.F-way of-IDF.S-water
It is good to let it suffice thus, or rather until here, while his blood drops rather than flows like water. ($^{S}$Shenute, *Is It Not Written* [A I 55, 3–4])

(72b) The apostle takes up a topic from an earlier letter sent by the community to him and quotes:
*nanu-s* *m-p-lômi* *e-štem-côh* *e-shimi*
good-3FS for-DEF.M-man to-NEG-touch OBJ-woman
It is good for a man not to have sexual relations with a woman. ($^{F}$1Cor 7:1)

(72c) The apostle admonishes the Galatians:
*nane-s=de* *e-k$^h$oh* *ḫen-pi-pet$^h$nanef* *n-sêu* *niben*
good-3FS=yet to-emulate in-DEF$_2$.M-good in-time QU
It is good to be zealous in good thing at all times. ($^B$Gal 4:18)

(72d) The apostle exhorts the strong to help the weak:
*nane-s* *e-štem-uem-af* *ude* *e-štem-se-êrp*
good-3FS to-NEG-eat-meat nor to-NEG-drink-wine
*nem-p$^h$ê* *ete-pe-k-son* *na-c$^h$i-c$^h$rop* *nḫêt-f*
CON-DEF$_3$.M REL-POSS.M-2MS-brother FUT-take-stumble inside-3MS
It is good not to eat meat or drink wine, or to do anything that causes your brother to stumble. ($^B$Rm 14:21)

In cases in which the actor of the subject clause is deemed to have contextual relevance, it is introduced by the inflection marker *tre-* (*e-tre-*SUB-INF):

(73a) Shenute states that if one is unworthy of wearing God's garments:
*eie* *nanu-s* *na-f* *e-tm-tre-f-ti* *hiôô-f*
then good-3FS to-3MS to-AUX.NEG-INFL-3MS-put upon-3MS
*n-huo* *e-tre-f-ti*
in-more to-INFL-3MS-put
...then it is better for him not to wear than to wear.
($^S$Shenute, *Who But God Is The Witness* [Young 26, 64–67])

(73b) The Israelites complain that their Promised Land is already inhabitated:
*tinu=un* *nane-s* *na-n* *e-t$^h$re-n-kot-ten* *eḫrêi* *e-k$^h$êmi*
now=PTC good-3FS for-1P to-INFL-1P-turn-1P down to-Egypt
Now, would it not be better if we returned to Egypt? ($^B$Nm 14:3)

In the following examples, the clausal subject is coded as a dependent clause:

(74a) The Israelites wandered through the desert, and soon people started to grumble:
*nanu-s* *e-a-n-mu* *ehrai* *hm-p-kah* *n-kême*
good-3SF DEP-PST-1P-die down in-DEF.M-land of-Egypt
*e-a-u-šok$^j$-n* *ebol* *hitoot-f* *m-p-cois*
DEP-PST-3P-smite-1P out by-3MS as-DEF.M-lord
*(e-)n-hmoos* *ehrai* *ecn-ne-khalkion* *n-af* *auô*
DEP-1P-sit down upon-DEF.P-pots of-meat and
*(e-)n-uem-oik* *e-u-sei*
DEP-1P-eat-bread DEP-3P-full
It would be better if we had died in the land of Egypt, having been smitten by the Lord, when we sat by the fleshpots and ate bread to the full.
($^S$Ex 16:3)

(74b) Jesus curses his would-be betrayer:

| | | | |
|---|---|---|---|
| *ne-nanu-s* | *m-p-rome* | *etmme* | *e-mp-u-cpa-f* |
| PRT-good-3FS | for-DEF.M-man | that | DEP-NEG.PST-3P-born-3MS |

It would be better for that man if he had not been born. ([M]Mt 26:24 mae 1)

The subject clause can be marked as counterfactual by *e-ne* (<*wn*):

(75a) Besa castigates sister Herai:

| | | | |
|---|---|---|---|
| *nanu-s=gar* | *ne* | *e-ne-mpe-i* | *ehun* |
| good-3FS=for | for.2FS | DEP-PRT-NEG.PST.2FS-come | into |

| | |
|---|---|
| *e-n-sunagôgê* | *m-p-cois* |
| to-DEF.P-assembly | of-DEF.M-lord |

| | | |
|---|---|---|
| *ehuero-s* | *e-tre-arna* | *n-tu-hupomonê* |
| more-3FS | to-INFL.2FS-deny | OBJ-POSS.2FS-perseverance |

| | | | |
|---|---|---|---|
| *mn-t-entolê* | *etuaab* | *ent-a-u-taa-s* | *etoot-e* |
| CON-DEF.F-order | holy | REL-PST-3P-give-3FS | to-2FS |

It would have been better for you if you had not entered the assemblies of the Lord than to deny your perseverance and the holy order that has been delivered to you. ([S]Besa, *To Herai*, V.2 [Kuhn 109, 6–9])

(75b) Paul moves to another topic:

| | | | |
|---|---|---|---|
| *nanu-s* | *e-ne-tetn-a-anekhe* | *mmo-i* | *n-u-kui* |
| good-3FS | DEP-PRT-2P-FUT-bear | OBJ-1S | for-IDF.S-little |

*m-mnt-at-hêt*
of-ABST-NEG-heart

It would be good if you were patient with me in a little foolishness. ([S]2Cor 11:1)

(75c) The psalmist regrets his earlier misconduct:

| | | |
|---|---|---|
| *nanu-s* | *e-nnare-na-hiaue* | *ne-sauten* |
| good-3FS | DEP-PRT-POSS.P.1S-ways.P | FUT-straight |

It would have been better if my ways had been straight. ([M]Ps 118 [119]:5)

A similar effect is achieved by using a conditional clause:

(76a) The apostle urges the community not to think high of their achievements as all merit comes from God:

| | | | | | |
|---|---|---|---|---|---|
| *nanu-s=de* | *ešce* | *a-tetn-r-rro* | *cekaas* | *ene-r-rro* | *hôô-n* |
| good-3SF=yet | CND | PST-2P-do-king | so that | FUT.1P-do-king | self-1P |

*nmê-tn*
with-2P

It would be better if you had reigned so that we also might reign with you. ([S]1Cor 4:8)

(76b) The apostle says concerning the unmarried and the widows:
*nane-s=nô-u* *aušan-šôpi* *m-pai-rêti*
good-3SF=for-3P CND.3P-happen in-DEM.M-way
It would be better for them if they stayed this way. ([B]1Cor 7:8)

Examples of the subject clause marked as the Conjunctive are:

(77a) A righteous couple prays to the archangel Michael to entreat God to have mercy with mankind:
*auô* *nanu-s* *ntn-mu* *nhuo* *ero-s* *ntn-r-p-ôbš*
and good-3FS CNJ.1P-die more to-3FS CNJ.1P-do-DEF.M-neglect
*n-te-k-thusia* *mn-te-k-prosphora*
of-POSS.F-2MS-sacrifice CON-POSS.F-2MS-offering
And it is better that we die than we forget your sacrifice and your offering.
([S]Theodosius of Alexandria, *In Michaelem* [Budge 371, 8–9])

(77b) Peter says to Jesus:
*p-c(ai)s* *nanu-s* *ne-n* *nt-n-kʲô* *m-pei-me*
DEF.M-lord good-3FS to-1P CNJ-1P-stay in-DEM.M-place
Lord, it is good for us that we stay here. ([M]Mt 17:4 mae 1)

(77c) The proverbs advise to avoid boldness in the presence of the king and his nobles:
*nanu-s=gar* *f-coo-s* *ne-k* *ce-amu* *ahrêi* *ne-i*
good-3FS=for CNJ.3MS-say-3MS to-2MS COMP-come.IMP up to-1S
*n-huo* *a-t-k-thbbio* *m-p-mto* *abal*
in-more than-INFL-2MS-humiliate in-DEF.M-presence out
*n-hen-côre*
of-IDF.P-noble
For it is better that it is said to you: 'Come up here to me!' than that you are humiliated in the presence of nobles. ([A]Prv 25:7)

(77d) Dorotheus tells his wife that God requires only what the faithful can give:
*nane-s* *nte-n-ti* *n-u-kuci* *ehote* *nte-n-štem-ti-hli*
good-3FS CNJ-1P-give OBJ-IDF.S-little more CNJ-1P-NEG-give-any
*e-p-têr-f*
to-all-3MS
It is better that we should give a little than that we should give nothing at all.
([B]Theodosius of Alexandria, *In Michaelem* [Budge 33, 3–4])

Examples of the subject clause coded as a complement introduced by *ce*; rarely the subject clause appears without any complement marking as in ex. 78d.

Noteworthy is the use of a Greek adjective in ex. 78c (note that in Coptic the difference between the endings -ος and -ως was neglected and both forms can be found for both functions, adjective or adverbial):

(78a) In a diatribe against Jews, Shenute reminds the audience:

| | | | |
|---|---|---|---|
| *nanu-s-men* | *ce-tn-elegkhe* | *m-p-iudai* | *auô* |
| good-3FS-indeed | COMP-1P-reprove | OBJ-DEF.M-Jew | and |

| | |
|---|---|
| *p-ke-hellên* | *mn-n-et-ine* |
| DEF.M-other-heathen | and-DEF.P-REL-equal |

| | | | | | |
|---|---|---|---|---|---|
| *mmo-u* | *alla* | *name* | *tn-šipe* | *hêt-u* | *n-nei-šace* |
| OBJ-3P | but | truly | 1P-be ashamed | before-3P | as-DEM.P-word |

It is indeed good that we reprove the Jew and the heathen and their kind, but truly we are ashamed before them in these words.
([S]Shenute, *There is Another Foolishness* [A II 380, 64–67])

(78b) The psalmist confesses:

| | | |
|---|---|---|
| *nanu-s* | *ne-i* | *ce-ha-k-thebbia-i* |
| good-3FS | to-1S | COMP-PST-2MS-humiliate-1S |

| | | |
|---|---|---|
| *cekes* | *eie-tsaba-i* | *e-ne-k-dikaiôma* |
| so that | FUT.1S-teach-1S | OBJ-POSS.P-2MS-statutes |

It is good for me that you have humiliated me so that I may learn your statutes. ([M]Ps 118 [119]:71)

(78c) The monk Frange reproaches another monk, who had promised to provide him with some linen but failed to meet the delivery speed standards of Frange:

| | | | |
|---|---|---|---|
| *tenu* | *kakôs* | *na-k* | *ce-a-k-tako-p-šace* |
| now | bad | for-2MS | COMP-PST-2MS-destroy-DEF.M-word |

Now, it is bad for you that you broke the agreement.
([S]*O.Frange* #61, 9–11)

(78d) The inhabitants of the town in which the SS Peter and Phillip preach tell their local pagan priest:

| | | | | |
|---|---|---|---|---|
| *nanu-s* | *tn-s[ô]tm* | *nsa-ne-apos[to]los* | *petros* | *mn-[phi]lippos* |
| good-3FS | 1P-listen | after-DEF.P-apostle | N | CON-N |

| | |
|---|---|
| *e-hua* | *ela-tn* |
| to-more | than-2P |

It is better that we listen to the apostles Peter and Philip than to you. ([F]*Acts of Peter and Philip* [von Lemm 536, 19–23])

However, such examples as 78d are so underrepresented that one might argue for an emendation into one of the above patterns.

# 2 Clausal syntax

## 2.1 Initial and coordinated clauses

### 2.1.1 Earlier Egyptian

In Part II Section 2.3.1 above, Earlier Egyptian nominal sentences were loosely characterised as being primarily 'main clause constructions'. The same can also be said of adjectival sentences, which are common in initial clauses without any introductory particle or other expression:

(79a) Sinuhe tells of his Syrian host:

| | | | | | |
|---|---|---|---|---|---|
| *ḥqꜣ=pw* | *n(y)-(r)tnw* | *ḥr-t* | *ḏd-f=n-ỉ* | *nfr=tw* | *ḥnꜥ-ỉ* |
| ruler=SE | of[-M]-N | upon.RLT-F | say-3MS=to-1S | good=2MS | with-1S |

He was a chief of Upper Retenu, who said to me: 'You are well with me'. (Sin B, 30–31)

(79b) Queen Hatshepsut argues that future generations will not accuse her of lying about her deeds:

| | |
|---|---|
| *wpwḥr-ḏd* | *twt=wy=n-s=st* |
| except-say.INF | typical=ADM=to-3FS=3C |

...but rather say: 'How typical of her it is!' (*Urk.* IV 368, 4–5)

Nevertheless, like all verbal and non-verbal sentence patterns, adjectival sentences too may be preceded by initial particles that modify the illocutionary and informational character of the following proposition. Examples are relatively infrequent and most do not occur with singular pronominal subjects, but possible attestations are with the attention-calling *mk*, the background-signalling *ỉsṯ*, and the atemporal sequential element *ẖr*. The last two particles are found with a distinctive adjectival construction (see ex. 18b above for *ỉst wr=wy*):

(80a) The sailor asks his captain to listen and adds:

| | | | |
|---|---|---|---|
| *mk* | *nfr* | *sḏm* | *n-rmṯ* |
| PTC | good | hear.INF | to-people |

Look, listening is good for people. (Sh.S. 182)

https://doi.org/10.1515/9783110409895-011

(80b) In a description of hauling a colossal statue:

*ist štꜣ=wr-t wꜣ-t ii-t-n-f ḥr-s*
PTC difficult=very-ADV road-F come.REL-F-PST-3MS on-3FS
*r-ḫ-t=nb-t*
to-thing-F=QU-F
Now, the road on which it came was more difficult than anything.
(*El Bersheh* I, pl. 14, 1)

(80c) Heqanakhte says to his deputy, whom he suspects of hoarding good grain in his absence:

*ḫr (i)n nfr=ṯw ḥr-wnm itmḥ nfr iw-i r-tꜣ*
PTC IP good=2MS PROG-eat.INF barley good DEP-1S to earth
So, are you well off eating good barley while I am cast out?
(Heqanakhte I, v° 2)

In the following example, the interrogative particle *iniw* precedes an adjectival sentence whose predicate is a perfective passive participle of the verb *mri* 'desire' and the subject a full complement clause[26]:

(81) Nekhebu asks visitors to his tomb:

*iniw mry=n-ṯn ḥz=ṯn nzw wnn imꜣḫ-ṯn*
IP desire.PPP-M=to-2P favour=2P king AUX reverence-2P
*ḫr-nṯr ꜥꜣ*
before-god great
Is it desirable to you that the king may favour you and your reverence may remain before the great god? (*Urk.* I 218, 16–17)

By contrast, auxiliaries are generally not used before adjectival sentences. The only real exception is *wn/wnn*, which shows a restricted compatibility with these constructions, e.g., in the past sequential pattern *wn-in* + clause[27]:

(82) The high steward presented the king with copies of the peasant's petitions:

*wn-in nfr=st ḥr-ib-f r-ḫ-t=nb-t nt-t*
AUX-SEQ good=3C on-heart-3MS to-thing-F=QU-F REL-F
*m-tꜣ=pn r-ḏr-f*
in-land=DEM.M to-limit-3MS
And so it pleased him more than anything in this entire land.
(Peas B2, 131–32)

26 See *Urk.* I 205, 2 and 12; 217, 16; 218, 8 (*ir wn*) for further examples of this peculiar construction. Cf. also Edel (1955/1964: §509).

27 See Section 3.1 below for further remarks.

The auxiliary *ꞽw* in particular is not used before adjectival sentences; counter-examples are of late date and can be interpreted as being influenced by the Late Egyptian use of *ꞽw* as a generalised marker of dependence, including adjunction:

(83) It is said of Nebamun, an official of Thutmosis IV:

*wn* *pḥ-n-f* *ꞽꜣw-t* *ꞽw-f* *ḥr-šms* *pr'ꜣ*
AUX reach-PST-3MS old age-F DEP-3MS PROG-follow.INF pharaoh
*ꞽw* *nfr=sw* *m-pꜣ-hrw* *r-sf*
DEP good=3MS in-DEM.M-day to-yesterday
He has reached old age following the pharaoh... while he is healthier today than yesterday. (*Tombs of Two Officials*, pl. 26)

In many instances with *ꞽw* and omitted subject, the construction turns out to be either a *sḏm-f* verb form or, more often, the Stative[28]:

(84) The man laments his dreary disposition:

*ꞽw* *nꜣ* *wr* *r-ꞽ* *m-mꞽn* *ꞽw* *ø=grt*
AUX DEM.M great.STA to-1S in-today AUX ø=PTC
*wr* *r-ʿbʿ*
great.STA to-boast.INF
This is too much for me today... (it) is also too much to boast about. (Man and Ba 5–6)

As in the case of nominal sentences, coordinated adjectival sentences are difficult to identify with certainty given the generally unmarked and paratactic character of coordination in Earlier Egyptian. Nevertheless, there are some relatively certain examples of this, e.g., when two predicates share a common subject:

(85) Khakheperraseneb expresses his Weltschmerz:

*ꜣw=w(y)*[29] *wdn* *mn-ꞽ*
long=ADM heavy malady-1S
How long and heavy is my malady! (Khakheperraseneb v° 4)

### 2.1.2 Later Egyptian

Following the typological change that transformed Egyptian into a dependent-clause-marking language, from Late Egyptian onwards any kind of sentence type

---

**28** The grammatical identity of *wr* here as the Stative is shown by the positioning of the clitic particle *=grt*.

**29** Again, an alternative reading here might be *ꜣw-w wdn*, with the first participle showing the ending *-w*.

could stand on its own in absolute initial position and the earlier distinction between bare initial clauses and patterns introduced by a particle was no longer productive. Thus, in Late Egyptian coordinated adjectival predicates could share the subject, as in the following examples:

(86a) The author praises his master and the beatings he suffered at school:
*ptr ꜣḫ mnq=sw r-ḫnm sšny*
look beneficial reward=3MS than-smell lotus
Look, it is more beneficial and rewarding than smelling a lotus-flower.
(*Teaching of Amunnakht* 36 [*ZÄS* 131, 41, 16–18])

(86b) In a eulogy on the city of Thebes, the local god Amun is praised:
*mr ꜥꜣ ỉmn*
beloved great N
Beloved and great is Amun. (oDeM 1232, 1)

Shared subjects of a single predicate can be treated similarly:

(87) The beloved is called to the lover:
*ršw it mw-t*
happy father mother-F
Father and mother will be happy. (Mathieu, *Poésie*, pl. 2, 3–4)

In Demotic, unambiguous cases of coordinated adjective verbs are rare, although some instances show subject sharing between two predicates as in ex. 88a; otherwise the clauses are coordinated by juxtaposition as in 88b:

(88a) In a draft for a petition the writer styles himself as poor:
*nꜣ-sb<q> nꜣ-ḫm <nꜣ>-nkt-w*
ADJ-be_tiny ADJ-be_small DEF.P-things-P
*nty-ḫn-tꜣy(-y)-ry*
REL-inside-POSS.F-(1S)-chamber.F
Tiny and small are the things in my chamber. (oIFAO D 632, 9)

(88b) The one who praises wisdom says about the ibises:
*nꜣw-qns tꜣy-w-wnmy-w nꜣw-ḫtḫt nꜣy-w-ꜥnḫ*
ADJ-pain POSS.F-3P-food-P ADJ-cut POSS.P-3P-life
Their food is arduous and their lifes are difficult.
(*Book of Thoth* B06 1,1/F01 11)

In Coptic, coordination of adjective verbs is more widely attested and seems to be done by juxtaposition. Coordinated predicates can be repeated:

(89a) Shenute is speaking about the patriarchs:
*naše-n-tbnoue et-šoop na-u m-mine nim*
plenty-DEF.P-animal.P REL-happen.STA for-3P of-kind QU

*naše-p-nub* *naše-p-hat* *naše-ne-u-huparkhonta*
plenty-DEF.M-gold plenty-DEF.M-silver plenty-POSS.P-3P-governance
*têr-u* *hm-mnt-rmmao* *nim*
all-3P in-ABST-rich QU
Plentiful were the animals of every kind that they had, plentiful was the gold, plentiful the silver, and plentiful their governance in all riches.
($^{S}$Shenute, *Truly, When I Think* [L IV 22, 10–12])

(89b) Theodore has three books. When he asks Macarius' advice on what to do with them, the latter replies:
*nanu-p-hôb-men* *alla* *nanu-t-mnt-hêke* *pararo-u* *têr-u*
good-DEF.M-thing-indeed but good-DEF.F-ABST-poor to-3P all-3P
The matter is indeed good, but poverty is better than all of these.
($^{S}$*AP* Elanskaya 13a, 27–30)

In Bohairic, coordinated subjects are connected with *uoh n-*:

(90) The Lord is praised as gracious, merciful and slow to anger:
*naše-pe-k-nai* *uoh* *n-t$^{h}$-mêi*
plenty-POSS.M-2MS-mercy and as-DEF.F-truth
Your mercy and truth are plentiful. ($^{B}$Ps 85 [86]:15)

Causal coordination can be expressed by means of the clitic *=gar* (for causal clauses with *ce-* see below 2.2.2):

(91) The prophet laments that the children of Israel set their hopes to the horses and chariots of the Egyptians:
*našô-u=gar*
plenty-3P=for
...for they are a great multitude. ($^{F}$Is 31:1)

## 2.2 Adjunct clauses

### 2.2.1 Earlier Egyptian

In adjunct environments, the grammar of Earlier Egyptian adjectival sentences closely parallels that of nominal sentences (Part II Section 2.2.1). Like nominal sentences, but unlike adverbial sentences (Part I Section 2.1.2–4), adjectival sentences were not used as adjunct clauses without preposition-conjunctions. When preceded by such elements, they had to be introduced by a complementiser. Unequivocal examples of this construction are uncommon:

(92) Horus' lament when subjected to a homosexual rape by Seth:

| | | | | | | | |
|---|---|---|---|---|---|---|---|
| *ỉw* | *ø* | *qsn* | *r-ỉ* | *ḥr-qd* | *ḥr-ntt* | *dns=tw* | *r-ỉ* |
| AUX | ø | difficult | to-1S | on-form | because-COMP | heavy=2MS | to-1s |

It is altogether too hard for me, because you are heavier than me!
(pUC 32158, 2.5)

In most cases, the construction following the complementiser is formally ambiguous:

(93a) The peasant exhorts the high steward to carry out his duty as an official:

| | | | | | |
|---|---|---|---|---|---|
| *ḏd* | *mꜣꜥ-t* | *ỉri* | *mꜣꜥ-t* | *ḏr-ntt* | *wr-s/=s(y)* |
| speak.IMP | right-F | do.IMP | right-F | since-COMP | great-/=3FS |
| *ꜥꜣ-s/=s(y)* | *wꜣḥ-s/=s(y)* | | | | |
| mighty-/=3FS | endure-/=3FS | | | | |

Speak righteousness, perform righteousness – because it is great, it is mighty, it is enduring! (Peas B1, 351–52)

(93b) Iyemiatib tries to elicit a response to his letter from his superior and adds:

| | | | | |
|---|---|---|---|---|
| *ḥr-[n]tt* | *nfr* | *ỉb* | *n(-y)-bꜣk-ỉm* | *sḏm-n-f* |
| because-COMP | good | heart | of[-M]-servant-there | hear-PST-3MS |
| *ꜥ.w.s.* | *nb* | *ꜥ.w.s.* | | |
| l.p.h. | lord | l.p.h. | | |

...because the heart of yours truly is happy once he has heard that the lord l.p.h. is alive, prosperous, and healthy. (pUC 32198, 11–12)

Earlier Egyptian quality concept lexemes could be inflected as suffix conjugation forms, although the extent to which this was possible in the different root-classes is unclear,[30] or appear as an infinitive or a Stative verb form. These patterns normally replace the adjectival sentence in all other types of adjunction except the construction with preposition-conjunction + complementiser seen above. Thus, in un-introduced adjuncts with a relative present sense, the simple *sḏm-f* (exx. 94a–94b) or, more often, the bare subjectless Stative form (exx. 94c–94f) appears:

(94a) The king is told:

| | | |
|---|---|---|
| *m=n-k* | *snṯr-k* | *nṯr-k* |
| take.IMP=to-2MS | incense-2MS | divine-2MS |

Take to yourself your incense, because you are divine. (PT 765b)

**30** In Uljas (2007a), it is proposed that the degree to which different root-classes could be inflected as adjectives might have been generally low. The issue, however, remains controversial.

(94b) In a medical instruction on examining a patient with a wound in his armpit:
*ỉr=swt gm-k s=pf šmm-f*
CND=PTC find-2MS man=DEM.M hot-3MS
If, however, you find that man having fever... (pEdwin Smith 17, 12)

(94c) Ineni promises those who will follow his example:
*wꜣḥ ꜥnḫ-ṯn tp-tꜣ wḏꜣ-twny*
prosper life-2P upon-earth flourish-STA.2P
Your life will prosper upon earth, you being flourishing. (*Urk.* IV 66, 1–2)

(94d) In a medical instruction describing a case involving a patient with stomach pains:
*gmm-k ḏrw-f šm ḫ-t-f qb-ti*
find.GEM-2MS side-2MS hot.STA skin-F-3MS cool-STA
Whenever you find his side hot and his skin cool (then you say...)
(pEbers 37, 3)

(94e) The snake bids farewell to the sailor and reveals his sole request to him:
*ỉmỉ rn-ỉ nfr m-nw-t-k*
do.IMP name-1S good.STA in-town-F-2MS
Make my name good in your town. (Sh.S. 159)

(94f) The deceased addresses unidentified deities:
*m-y=n-ỉ m-ksw snḏ-twn=n(-ỉ) wr-t*
come.IMP-P=to-1S in-bowing afraid-STA.2P=to[-1S] very-ADV
Come to me in bowing, because you are very afraid of me. (CT VII 232k–l)

As can be seen from the examples above, the bare subjectless Stative is typically used when the actor of the adjunct is semantically controlled by some overt or covert element in the preceding cotext, e.g., the subject, as in ex. 94c, the direct object, as in 94d, or the implicit subject of the imperative, as in exx. 94e–94f. In final clauses without an introducing preposition-conjunction, the subjunctive *sḏm-f* form appears:

(95a) Sobek has taken possession of the Eye of Horus:
*dỉ-n-k=sy m-tp-k wr-k ỉm-s qꜣ-k*
put-PST-2MS=3FS in-head-2MS mighty-2MS in-3FS high-2MS
*ỉm-s ꜥꜣ šfšf-t-k ỉm-s*
in-3FS great repute-F-2MS in-3FS
You have placed it on your brow so that you can be mighty by means of it, that you can be exalted by means of it, and that your repute can be great by means of it. (Hymn to Sobek [Erman 1911 16, 1–2])

(95b) The deceased assists the gods:
*ỉw psg-n N=pn smꜣ=pn n(-y)-tm qb-f*
AUX spit-PST N=DEM.M forehead=DEM.M of[-M]-N cool-3MS
This N has spat on this forehead of Atum so that he may become cool.
(CT VI 224m–n)

In the conditional protasis, a *sḏm-f* verb form is the usual construction, but there are also rare examples of the progressive construction *ḥr* + infinitive preceded by the auxiliary *wn/wnn*:

(96a) Ptahhetep advises:

| *ỉr* | *ẖs-k* | *šms* | *s* | *ỉqr* |
|---|---|---|---|---|
| CND | poor-2MS | follow.IMP | man | excellent |

If you are poor, follow a successful man. (Ptahhetep 175)

(96b) Neferhetepu utters the transfiguration formula:[31]

| *ỉr* | *wnn* | *ꜣḫ-w* | *ḥr-ꜣḫ* | *ỉw* | *bꜣ-ỉ* |
|---|---|---|---|---|---|
| CND | AUX | spirit-P | PROG-spiritual.INF | AUX | soul-1S |

| *r-šms* | *ḥwtḥr* |
|---|---|
| FUT-follow.INF | N |

If the blessed dead become spiritual, my soul will follow Hathor. (CG 34057, 12)

In adjuncts introduced by preposition-conjunctions and without a complementiser, adjectival sentences are, like nominal sentences, replaced by a form of *sḏm-f* or by *wn/wnn* + the Stative or the *ḥr* + infinitive progressive construction:

(97a) Weni says that the king appointed him as town-governor and overseer of Upper Egypt:

| *n-ỉqr(-ỉ)* | *ḥr-ỉb* | *n(-y)-ḥm-f* | *n-wꜣb(-ỉ)* |
|---|---|---|---|
| for-excellent[-1S] | on-heart | of[-M]-majesty-3MS | for-rooted[-1S] |

| *ḥr-ỉb* | *n(-y)-ḥm-f* |
|---|---|
| on-heart | of[-M]-majesty-3MS |

| *n-mḥ* | *ỉb* | *n(-y)-ḥm-f* | *ỉm(-ỉ)* |
|---|---|---|---|
| for-fill | heart | of[-M]-majesty-3MS | in[-1S] |

...because I was excellent in his majesty's heart, because I was well-rooted in his majesty's heart, and because his majesty's heart was confident in me. (*Urk.* I 105, 14–16)

(97b) Ahmose tells how, after having founded a household, he set out to pursue a career in the navy:

| *ꜥḥꜥ-n-ỉ* | *ỉt-kw* | *r-pꜣ-ꜥḥꜥ* | *mḥty* | *ḥr-qnn-ỉ* |
|---|---|---|---|---|
| AUX-1S | take-STA.1S | to-DET.M-ship | N | because-brave-1S |

Then I was taken to the ship called 'Northerner' because I was so brave. (*Urk.* IV 3, 3–4)

---

31 For the formula in this example, see Grapow (1942: 57–69).

(97c) A medical handbook describes the correct application of an ointment:

*r-snb-f*     *ḥr-ꜥ-wy*
to-healthy-3MS     on-arm-DU
...so that he might become healthy immediately. (pEdwin Smith 22, 14)

(97d) The author seeks support to his appeal for the office of his dead father by citing the latter:

*ꞽw=grt*     *ḏd-n=n-ꞽ*     *pꜣ[y]-ꞽ-ꞽt*     *ḫft-wn-f*     *mr*
AUX=PTC     say-PST=to-1S     POSS.M-1S-father     when-AUX-3MS     ill.STA
Moreover, my father said to me when he was ill... (a quote follows).
(pUC 32055, x+14)

(97e) Ukhhotep explains his reasons for depicting previous nomarchs in his tomb:

*ꞽrꞽ-n-ꞽ*     *nw*     *n-mrwt-wnn*     *rn-w-sn*     *mn*
do-PST-1S     DEM     through-love-AUX     name-P-3P     stable.STA
*n-ḏ-t*
through-eternity-F
I have done this in order that their names may remain stable for eternity.
(*Meir* III, pl. 11)

(97f) Queen Hatshepsut refers to her obelisks as something that she has prepared:

*n-mrwt-wn*     *rn-ꞽ*     *mn*     *wꜣḥ*
through-love-AUX     name-1S     stable.STA     endure.STA
*m-rpr=pn*
in-temple=DEM.M
...so that my name may become stable and enduring in this temple.
(*Urk.* IV 366, 15)

### 2.2.2 Later Egyptian

In Late Egyptian, undisputable examples of adjectival sentences subordinated as adjuncts by means of the element *ꞽw* are relatively rare; in most instances, the subject expression is a noun and the construction, therefore, formally oscillates between an adjectival sentence and *sḏm-f*. Nevertheless, in some cases, clitic pronouns appear or, alternatively, the subject is omitted[32]:

---

**32** Note that examples without explicit subjects cannot be analysed as Statives, which in Late Egyptian do not allow deletion of the subject after the marker of dependency, i.e. *ꞽw*-PRN-STA > †*ꞽw*-ø-STA.

(98a) King Akhenaten refers to a situation in the area of his newly founded town Akhetaten:

| iw-bin=st | r-nꜣ-sḏm-i | m-rnp-t | 4 |
|---|---|---|---|
| DEP-bad=3FS | than-DEF.P-hear.REL-1S | in-year-F | 4 |
| iw-[bin=s]t | r-[nꜣ]-sḏm-i | m-rnp-t | 3 |
| DEP-bad=3FS | than-DEF.P-hear.REL-1S | in-year-F | 3 |
| iw-bin=st | r-nꜣ-sḏm-i | [m-rnp-t | 2] |
| DEP-bad=3FS | than-DEF.P-hear.REL-1S | in-year-F | 2 |

...being worse than what I heard in regnal year four, worse than what I heard in regnal year three, and worse than what I heard in regnal year two, ....
(*Boundary Stelae*, 26, 4–7 [K 20])

(98b) The relationship between Ramesses II and the Hittite king Hattusili was peaceful:

| iw-nfr-sw | r-pꜣ-ḥtp | r-pꜣ-snsn | hꜣwty |
|---|---|---|---|
| DEP-good-3MS | than-DEF.M-peace | than-DEF.M-brotherhood | earlier |

...being better than the earlier peace and brotherhood.
(Edel, *Vertrag*, 25*, 7)

(98c) The author of a letter is asking for a quiver capable of holding hundred arrows:

| iw-s | irm-tꜣy-s-pḏ-t | iw-nfr | m-sš |
|---|---|---|---|
| DEP-3SF | with-POSS.F-3SF-bow-F | DEP-good-∅ | in-excess |

...together with its bow, which is very good.
(pBM EA 75019+10302 v° 5–6 [Demarée])

In Demotic, adjective verbs with *nꜣ-* could also be used as adjuncts when preceded by the dependency marker *iw*:

(99a) The hero of the story is introduced: *His name was the magician Merire*:

| iw-nꜣ-šry-f | n-[ms]-w | iw-nꜣ-nfr-f | n-sš | m-šs |
|---|---|---|---|---|
| DEP-ADJ-young-3MS | of-birth-P | DEP-ADJ-good-3MS | in-write | in-excess |

...and although young of years, he was well-versed in writing.
(pVandier 1, 1)

(99b) While in a temple, Setne saw:

| wꜥ-t-sḥm | iw-nꜣ-ꜥn-s | m-šs |
|---|---|---|
| IDF-F-woman.F | DEP-ADJ-nice-3FS | in-excess |

...a very beautiful woman (lit: a woman, that is very beautiful) ...
(Setne I 4, 38–39)

In Coptic, adjunctive subordination of adjectival constructions with *e-* (<*iw*) is common:

(100a) Shenute says that he will denounce opponents in his congregation to a higher church leader, who will then decide on an appropriate punishment:

*ešôpe=de e-f-uôš e-uôh ehrai ecn-nei-sêše*
CND=yet ST-2MS-wish to-add down upon-DEM.P-blow
*f-rôše u-hôb e-nanu-f p-et-f-na-aa-f*
3MS-suffice IDF.S-thing DEP-good-3MS COP.M-REL-3MS-FUT-do-3MS
Now, if he wishes to add to these blows, he may; it is a good thing that he should do so. ($^{S}$Shenute, *Why O Lord* [Young 106, 22–29])

(100b) Shenute speaks of a man led astray by evil thoughts who prostrated before God. Then:

*a-f-hmoos ehrai e-f-onš ebol e-f-amahte*
PST-3MS-sit up DEP-3MS-dazed.STA out DEP-3MS-seize
*n-te-f-ape e-našô-u nk$^{j}$i-ne-f-meue*
OBJ-POSS.F-3MS-head DEP-plenty-3P PVS-POSS.P-3MS-thought
He sat up confused and holding his head while his thoughts were manifold.
($^{S}$Shenute, *Canon I* [A I 452, 9–10])

(100c) Mark advises in a letter Papnute and Elisabeth again:

*ce-ntetn-na-snêu n-ti-uoš=an e-setm-lau n-hôb*
2P-POSS.P.1S-brother.P NEG-1S-wish=NEG to-hear-any of-thing
*e-nek$^{j}$ô-f harô-tn*
DEP-ugly-3MS about-2P
For you are my siblings and I do not wish to hear anything unpleasant about you. ($^{S}$*O.Crum* Ad. 13, 4–7)

(100d) The monk Frange asks in letter politely for a small knife and a matching sheath and adds:

*sena-s e-nanu-s n-g-cou-s na-i hn-u-k$^{j}$epê*
provide-3FS DEP-good-3FS CNJ-2MS-send-3FS for-1S in-IDF.S-hurry
Provide it quickly for me in good quality (lit. while it is good)!
($^{S}$*O.Frange* #48, 23–25)

(100e) Jonah prays to God and admits that he fled knowing His grace and mercy:

*au ntk-u-[har]š-hêt e-naše-p-k-nae*
and 2MS-IDF.S-slow-heart DEP-plenty-POSS.M-2MS-kindness
...and that you are slow to anger, whereas your kindess is manifold.
($^{A}$Jon 4:2 [Till])

(100f) Jesus teaches:

*pai-rêti ššên=niben et$^{h}$-nane-f ša-f-en-utah*
DEM.M-way tree=QU REL-good-3MS AOR-3MS-bring-fruit
*e-nane-f ebol*
DEP-good-3MS out
Just as every good tree brings forth good fruit... ($^{B}$Mt 7:17)

The adjective verb adjunct often represents a 'virtual' relative clause used to mark a non-restrictive relative clause (ex. 100a and d above).[33] Adjective verbs can be used in conditional clauses introduced by *ešce* (ex. 101a below). When marked by *ce-*, they can be used in causal clauses (100b–c; for causal coordination with *=gar* see above Section 2.1.2).

(101a) Shenute ponders:

| | | | | | | |
|---|---|---|---|---|---|---|
| *auô* | *ešce* | *nanu-s* | *e-unta-n* | *e-rôme* | *nhuo* | *e-unta-n* |
| and | CND | good-3FS | DEP-have-1P | to-man | more | DEP-have-1P |

| | | | | | |
|---|---|---|---|---|---|
| *ero-n* | *nanu-s* | *an* | *on* | *e-sôrm* | *n-ne-hnau* |
| to-1P | good-3FS | NEG | again | to-loose | OBJ-DEF.P-thing |

| | |
|---|---|
| *n-t-koinônia* | *m-p-nute* |
| of-DEF.F-communion | of-DEF.M-god |

| | | |
|---|---|---|
| *etbe-ti-ha-ebra* | *ê* | *sort* |
| because-give-under-seed | or | wool |

And even if it is good that we have against man more than we have against us, it is again not good to lose the things of the communion of God because of selling seed or wool.

($^{S}$Shenute, *God Who Alone Is True* [MMAF IV.1 278, 5–7])

(101b) God has the prophet tell how the maiden Zion will seek her lovers. She will not find them, and thus she will reconsider returning to her husband:

| | | |
|---|---|---|
| *ce-nane-ni-ouaiš* | *ne-[i]* | *a-tinu* |
| for-good-DEF.P-time | for-1S | to-now |

...for that time was better for me than now. ($^{A}$Hos 2:7 [Till])

(101c) The Prophet says that the Lord will give forth his voice before his host:

| | |
|---|---|
| *ce-naše-t-f-parembolê* | *mpša* |
| for-plenty-POSS.F-3MS-encampment | greatly |

...because his encampment is very large. ($^{A}$Jl 2:11 [Malinine])

## 2.3 Complement clauses

### 2.3.1 Earlier Egyptian

It is probable that Earlier Egyptian adjectival sentences could, like nominal sentences, appear in complement clauses introduced by a complementiser after

33 Occasionally, this is also employed as an adverbial expression, e.g., in *CO* Ad 57, 8–10. The use here is equivalent the one of the Greek *kalôs* later in the same letter in a similar sentence.

preposition-conjunctions, but no clear example is attested in the textual corpus. In some instances, the complementiser *ntt* introduces a *sḏm-f* verb form of a quality concept lexeme:

(102) Thutmosis III explains why he has built a temple for Amun:
*rḫ-kw* *ntt* *ḥtp-f* *ḥr-s*
know-STA.1S COMP content-3MS on-3FS
I know that he is content with it. (*Urk.* IV 835, 16)

However, there are examples that, by analogy with nominal sentences, could be adjectival sentence complements with the clitic element *=ỉs* (see Part II Section 2.3.1):

(103) The deceased extols to the gods the triumph of Horus:
*dỉ(-ỉ)* *rḫ-sn* *wr=ỉs* *nrw-f* *spd=ỉs*
cause[-1S] know-3P great=PTC dread-3MS sharp=PTC
*ḥnw-t-f* *r-stẖ*
horn-F-3MS against-N
I will let them know that the dread of him is greater and that his horn sharper than Seth's. (CT IV 84i)

As discussed in connection with adverbial (Part I Section 2.1.5) and nominal sentences (Part II Section 2.3.1), *=ỉs* appears to be an early marker of general dependence rather than a complementiser or adjunctor per se. Nevertheless, it is found in one instance alongside *ntt* in what is probably an adjectival sentence object complement clause of the verb *ḏd* 'say':

(104a) A messenger of a demon is told:
*ỉ* *sḫm* *ỉs* *ḏd-k* *n-hꜣb=ṯw*
VOC N go.IMP say-2MS to-send.PPA=2MS
*ꜣḫ=ỉs* *rꜣ* *n(-y)-N=pn* *r-ds-f*
powerful=PTC spell of[-M]-N=DEM.M to-flint-3MS
O mighty one, go and tell the one who sent you that the spell of this N is more powerful than his knife. (CT V 49b–c/B6C)

(104b) As above:
*[ỉ]* *sḫm* *ỉs* *ḏd-k* *n-hꜣb=ṯw*
VOC N go.IMP say-2MS to-send.PPA=2MS
*ntt* *ꜣḫ=ỉs* *rꜣ* *n(-y)-wsỉr* *N* *r-ds-f*
COMP powerful=PTC spell of[-M]-N N to-flint-3MS
O mighty one; go and tell the one who sent you that the spell of Osiris N is more powerful than his knife. (CT V 49b–c/B4C)

However, instances where the complement clause is a conjugated *sḏm-f* verb form used as a complement without an overt complementiser are much more common.

Below are three examples of clausal complements of prepositions of this type, where the *sḏm-f* of reduplicating and geminating roots shows reduplication of the final or gemination of the penultimate radical:

(105a) Yamu-Nedjeh sings praise to the sun god:
*twt=n-k* *ỉꜣw* *mỉ-wrr-k*
perfect=to-2MS adoration like-great-2MS
Adoring you is fitting in accordance with how great you are. (*Urk.* IV 943, 5)

(105b) The deceased addresses a divinity:
*qꜣ-k* *ḫft-qꜣꜣ-ỉ* *ṯspḫr*
high-2MS corresponding to-high-1S vice versa
Be exalted as much as I am exalted – and vice versa. (CT II 156b)

(105c) A note concerning the legal treatment of two children:
*ỉrỉ* *ꜥꜣ* *r-ꜥꜣꜣ-f* *šr* *r-šrr-f*
treat.PASS great to-great-3MS small to-small-3MS
The older was treated according to how old, and the younger according to how young he was. (pBerlin P. 9010, 3)

Common are also similarly construed object clauses of governing verbs:

(106a) Amun gives thanks to Thutmosis III for his enthusiasm for building:
*rḫ-n-f* *ḥtp(-ỉ)* *ḫnt-f*
know-PST-3MS content[-1S] before-3MS
He had come to know how content I would be before him.
(*Urk.* IV 883, 14)

(106b) An instruction on determining the effects of an ulcer on the health of a bull from the discharge:
*sỉꜣ-k* *snb-f* *ḥr-ỉw* *ḥsꜣ*
perceive-2MS healthy-3MS on-come semi-solids
You will be able to perceive whether he is healthy on the basis of how semi-solids emerge. (pUC 32036, 1.x+14)

(106c) Ptahhetep advises against undue hostility when debating with an inferior orator:
*m=ꜣd* *ỉb-k* *r-f* *rḫ-tỉ* *ḫss-f*
AUX.NEG.IMP=hostile.NC heart-2MS against-3MS know-STA feeble-3MS
Do not show hostility against him if you know how weak he is.
(Ptahhetep 76/$L_2$)

No examples of analogous subject complement clauses appear to exist. Medical texts show many instances of clauses with a *sḏm-f* with gemination and reduplication, subordinated as predicate complements of bipartite nominal sentences with the subject element *=pw* (see Uljas 2007c: 287–89):

(107a) A gloss explaining a medical term:
*ỉr wbn m-šr-t-f ỉsdb gnn sp-ty wbn=pw*
PTC wound in-nostril-F-3MS weak.STA soft lip-DU wound=SE
As for 'a wound in his nostril is weakened', this means that the edges of his wound are soft. (pEdwin Smith 6, 12–13)

(107b) A gloss explaining an expression in a medical text:
*ỉr ỉb-f mḥ mhh ỉb-f=pw mỉ-nt-y*
PTC heart-3MS fill.STA forgetful heart-3MS=SE like-REL-M
*ḥr-sḫꜣt k-t md-t*
PROG-recall.INF other-F thing-F
As for 'his heart is filled', this means that his heart is oblivious, like one who is thinking of something else. (pEbers 102, 15–16)

The *sḏm-f* varies with the Stative introduced by a reduplicating form of the auxiliary *wn/wnn*:

(108a) Glosses explaining an expression in a medical text:
*ỉr mt-w n-w-nḥb-t-f dwn-y*
PTC muscle-P of-P-neck-F-3MS stretch-STA
*wnn mt-w=pw n-w-nḥb-t-f dwn nḫt*
AUX muscle-P=SE of-P-neck-F-3MS stretch.STA hard.STA
*mꜥ-ỉh-f*
through-pain-3MS
As for 'the muscles of his neck are stretched'; this means that the muscles of his neck are stretched (i.e. cramped) and hard due to his pain. (pEdwin Smith 3, 19–20)

(108b) Another gloss in a medical text:
*ỉr ỉw ỉb-f wḫ-f dp-f ḥꜣ-t-f*
PTC AUX heart-3MS dark-3MS taste-3MS heart-F-3MS
*wnn ỉb-f=pw gꜣw kkw m-ẖ-t-f*
AUX heart-3MS=SE narrow.STA darkness in-body-F-3MS
*mꜥ-ḏnwd*
through-anger
As for 'his heart is so dark that he can taste his heart', this means that his heart is constricted, since there is darkness in his body due to anger. (pEbers 102, 9–10)

### 2.3.2 Later Egyptian

Late Egyptian adjectival sentences functioning as complement clauses can be introduced by the complementiser *rḏd*:

(109a) The author of a letter deals with troubles between his addressee's retainers:

| *ḫr-ỉr-ỉw-ỉ* | *ꜥmꜣ* | *rḏd-mꜣꜥṯ* | *pꜣy-ỉ-[šms]* |
|---|---|---|---|
| PTC-CND-DEP-1S | know | COMP-true | POSS.M-1S-retainer |

Yet if I should discover that my servant is right ([and that] he beat your retainer...) (*LRL* 42, 4–5)

(109b) The author of a letter blames another person of certain crimes; asserting that he has witnessed this personally, he adds:

| *ꜥmꜣ-k* | *rḏd-mꜣꜥt* | *[pꜣ-]ỉ-ḏd-ỉ* |
|---|---|---|
| know-2MS | COMP-true | COP.M-REL.PST-say-1S |

You will realise that all I have said is true. (*KRI* III 506, 11–12)

(109c) The author of a letter gives orders on how to proceed in the matter of two policemen and says that they should be interrogated:

| *ỉr-ỉrỉ-ṯ-w* | *ꜥmꜣ* | *ḏd-mꜣꜥ* |
|---|---|---|
| CND-AUX.ST-3P | know | COMP-true |

If they determine that it is true (you shall put them in two baskets and they shall be thrown to the river). (*LRL* 36, 9)

As noted above (Part I Section 2.2.3 on complementation with adverbial sentences), verbs such as *gmỉ* 'find' can signal the difference between the speaker's evaluation of the proposition in terms of perceptual and conceptual discovery, i.e. whether the speaker actually witnessed the find or merely assesses the truth value of the proposition. In the first instance, the complement is introduced by the dependency marker *ỉw*, in the second by the complementiser *rḏd*:

(110) In a model letter the author complains about the poor quality of grain that has been sent. He had gone to inspect the grain himself:

| *ỉw-ỉ-ḥr* | *gm-ṯ-w* | *ỉw-bn-nfr=ỉn* | *m-mꜣꜥ-t* |
|---|---|---|---|
| DEP-1S-PRP | find-INF-3P | DEP-NEG-good=NEG | in-truth-F |

...and I found that it really was not good. (*LEM* 94, 7)

Examples like these are, nevertheless, relatively rare. With verbs of real or implied perception such as *gmỉ* 'find', oblique constructions with the subjectless Stative were used instead:

(111a) A visitor to an old tomb was amazed:

| *[ỉ]w-gm-f=sw* | *nfr-tỉ* | *[m]-ỉb-f* | *r-ḥw-t-nṯr=nb* |
|---|---|---|---|
| DEP-find-3MS=3CS | good-STA | in-heart-3MS | to-temple-F-god=QU |

...for he found it more beautiful inside than any other temple. (gTT 63, 1–2)

(111b) A ringlet was brought to the pharaoh, and:

| *gm-<pꜣy-st>-sti* | *nḏm* | *r-iqr* | *spsn* |
|---|---|---|---|
| find.PASS-POSS.M-3FS-scent | sweet.STA | to-excellent | twice |

<Its> scent was found to be very sweet. (*LES* 21, 2)

One example shows coordinated adjectival sentences after *rḫ* 'know' (disjunction)[34]:

(112) The author mocks his opponent for his apparent false erudition, saying that he is merely quoting a text:

| *bw-rḫ-k* | *[n]-n[fr* | *m]rpw* | *bin* |
|---|---|---|---|
| NEG.AOR-know-2MS | IP-good.STA | or | bad.STA |

But you do not know whether it is good or bad. (²*pAnastasi I* 97, 8)

Complemention of *rḫ* introduced by *(i)n* must be a diachronic development of Late Egyptian. In analogous contexts, Earlier Egyptian would probably have suffix conjugation complements not introduced by a particle (Uljas 2007c: 81–82).

In complement environments without a complementiser, adjectival sentences were, as in Earlier Egyptian, usually replaced by a *sḏm-f* form:

(113a) In a graffito, a man prays to Hathor, the goddess of love:

| *imi-nḫt-ṯ* | *ḥnn-f* | *r-sḥm-t=nb-t* |
|---|---|---|
| give.IMP-strong | penis-3MS | to-woman-F=QU-F |

Let his penis be strong with every woman. (gDeir el-Bahari #6, 4–5)

(113b) The tomb-owner tells about his life and how he chose his personal deity:

| *iw(-i)-rḫ-kwi* | *ꜣḫ-s* | *m-ḥr-i* | *mnḫ=sw* |
|---|---|---|---|
| DEP[-1S]-know-STA.1S | beneficent-3FS | in-face-1S | excellent=3C |
| *wꜥ-t-y* | | | |
| single-F-RLT | | | |

I knew that she is beneficent to me, for she is uniquely excellent.
(*KRI* III 336, 10–11)

Although the first example above shows no specific marking,[35] in ex. 113b the suffix pronoun *-s* is used alongside the clitic pronoun *=sw*. Since in Earlier Egyptian adjectival sentences were not used as direct complements of governing verbs, the second clause in ex. 113b should probably be analysed as an unmarked causal clause rather than as a complement clause. Yet in contrast with earlier phases of

34 Further examples of *in*-complementation after *rḫ* can be found in *Tale of Woe* 4, 16, with a verbal clause as complement, or *LES* 69, 12–13, with an adverbial clause. Note that the last instance shows repetition of *n*.

35 The *ṯ* in *nḫt-ṯ* probably merely indicates that the final *t* of the word had not been reduced to a glottal stop but was still pronounced.

the language, Late Egyptian shows undisputable cases of adjectival sentences used as direct complements without a complementiser. In the following instances after the verbs of perception *m33* and *ptri*, the clauses following the verbs must be complements, their status as adjectival sentences being signalled by the particle =*wi*:

(114a) A man admits to having sworn falsely before god Thoth, who then retaliated:
*iw-f* *ḥr-rdi-t* *m33-i* *ꜥ3=wi* *pḥ-ty-f*
DEP-3MS PRP-give-INF see-1S great=ADM strength-DU-3MS
*m-b3ḥ-p3-t3* *r-ḏr-f*
in-presence-DEF.M-land to-limit-3MS
...and he made me see how great is his strength before the entire land.
(Turin 50044, 3–4)

(114b) A man prays to the moon and exclaims:
*ptr-i* *ꜥ3=wi* *[ḥt]p-k*
see-1S great=ADM grace-2MS
I see how great is your grace. (Turin 50046, 3)

In Demotic, the recessive adjectival sentences of the Earlier Egyptian type are also found as complements of the causative verb *di* 'give':

(115a) The recipient of a letter is told of a certain matter:
*my* *ꜥ3-s* *mtw-n3y-k-ḫyr*
let.IMP great-3FS with-POSS.P-2MS-enemy
Let it be an obligation to you. (pLouvre E 7854, 4)[36]

(115b) The author of a letter tells how he prays for his addressee's well-being:
*i* *dy-p3-rꜥ* *qy-p3y-f-ꜥḥꜥ*
VOC give-DEF.M-N high-POSS.M-3MS-lifetime
O may the sun god cause his lifetime to be long. (pBerlin P. 13544, 4–5)

Demotic attests also the use of adjective verbs as complements after the complementiser *ḏd* or as dependent clauses with *iw* (or its graphic variants) after verbs such as *gm* 'find':

(116a) The magician is advised to say over the child for whom he seeks divine help:
*tw-y-ḏd* *nim-s* *ḏd-n3y-n3w-ꜥn* *p3y-šn-hne*
PTC-1S-say OBJ-3FS COMP-ADJ-ADJ-nice DEM.M-enquiry-vessel
*n-p3-ḫbs* *r-p3-ḫrp*
of-DEF.M-light than-DEF.M-first
I claim that this vessel-enquiry of the light is better than the first one.
(pMag.London and Leiden 17, 20)

36 An apotropaic expression using *n3y-k-ḫir* 'your enemies' for 'you'.

(116b) The sentence 'I love the first day of the month more than the last one' is explained with the words:

*pꜣ-ntyiw-f-ḏd* *nim-f* *ḏd-nꜣ-ꜥn* *tꜣ-rnp* *ḥṱ-t*
DEF.M-REL-3MS-say OBJ-3MS COMP-ADJ-nice DEF.F-year.F first.F
*r-tꜣ-rnp-t* *ẖꜥ-t*
than-DEF.F-year-F last-F
*n-nꜣ-ssw* *ntyiw-w* *ir-w* *ḏd-nꜣ-mdw*
of-DEF.P-time REL-FUT-3P do-3P COMP-DEF.P-N
What it means is that the first year is better than the last year in times that they, namely the Medians, will spend.
(pBN 215 rº 5, 1)

(116c) In a fragmentary story, a person narrates how he fought against an opponent:

*gm-i=s* *r-nḫtṱ-f* *m-sš*
find-1S=3MS DEP-strong-3MS in-excess
I discovered that he was very strong. (*Petese Stories*, fr. C3, 1)

As noted already in the earlier chapters (see sections I.2.2.3.3 and II.2.3.2 above), the Coptic complementiser *ce-* can introduce any kind of sentence as a complement. Below are examples with adjective verbs:

(117a) Paul warns against false teachers:

*tn-soun=de* *ce-nanu-p-nomos* *eršan-ua* *aa-f*
1P-know=yet COMP-good-DEF.M-law CND-one do-3MS
*hi-te-f-mnt-me*
under-POSS.F-3MS-ABST-true
But we know that the law is good if used justly. ([S]1Ti 1:8)

(117b) In the story narrating the birth of Moses:

*a-u-no=de* *ara-f* *ce-neso-f* *a-u-hap-f*
PST-3P-see=yet OBJ-3MS COMP-beautiful-3MS PST-3P-hide-3MS
*n-ẖ[am]t* *n-ebat*
for-three of-month
But they saw that he was fair and they hid him for three months. ([A]Ex 2:2)

(117c) Paul resumes his argument and says:

*ti-mêui* *on* *ce-nanu-pei* *e-tre-f-šôpi*
1S-think again COMP-good-DEM.M.ABS to-INFL-3MS-happen
*n-tei-hê* *etbe-t-anagkê* *et-šoop*
in-DEM.F-way because-DEF.F-need REL-happen.STA
Therefore I think that in the present crisis, it is better that you stay as you are. ([F]1Cor 7:26)

(117d) Speaking about marriage, Paul says:
*ti-cô=de* *mmo-s* *n-nê* *ete-mp-u-c*ʰ*i*
1S-say=yet OBJ-3FS to-DEF$_3$.P REL-NEG.PST-3P-take
*nem-ni-ḫêra*
CON-DEF.P-widow
*ce-nane-s=nô-u* *aušan-šôpi* *m-pai-rêti*
COMP-good-3FS=for-3P CND.3P-happen in-DEM.M-way
To the unmarried and widows I say that it is best if they stay this way.
([B]1Cor 7:8)

## 2.4 Relative clauses

### 2.4.1 Earlier Egyptian

Adjectival sentences were probably never used in relative clauses in Earlier Egyptian, which instead uses participles, relative forms, and the Future Participle *sḏm-ty-fy* alongside adverbial sentences and SV-order verbal constructions preceded by the relative operator *nt-* or a relativised version of the auxiliary *wn/wnn*. In particular, it should be observed that, like nominal sentences but unlike adverbial sentences, adjectival sentences apparently could not be relativised by means of *nt-* or *wn/wnn*. Counterexamples are extremely rare and not wholly reliable; in the following pair of textual variants, the apparent adjectival sentence of the first witness appears as a Stative in the second, earlier variant:

(118a) A note at the end of a magico-medical incantation:
*ḏdmdw* *ḫft-wꜣḥ* *pẖr-t* *ḥr-ꜥ-t=nb-t* *nt-y*
recitation when-apply.INF medicine-F on-limb-F=QU-F REL-M
*mr=sy*
ill=3FS
Recitation when administering a medicine on any limb that is ill.
(pHearst 6, 10)

(118b) As above:
*ḏdmdw* *ḫft-wꜣḥ* *pẖr-t* *ḥr-ꜥ-t=nb-t* *n-t-s*
recitation when-apply.INF medicine-F on-limb-F=QU-F of-F-man
*nt-t* *mr-ti*
REL-F ill-STA
Recitation when administering a medicine on any human limb that is ill.
(pEbers 1, 10–11)

A handful of examples are conventionally analysed as adjectival sentences used as 'virtual' and possibly non-restrictive relative clauses (e.g. Malaise and Winand 1999: §1023). Yet the putative instances, all of which have noun subjects, are formally ambiguous and could alternatively be viewed as involving a *sḏm-f* verb form rather than adjectival sentences:

(119a) The courtiers describe the sage Neferty to the king:

| | | | |
|---|---|---|---|
| *špss=pw* | *ꜥ3=n-f* | *ḫ-t* | *r-mity-f=nb* |
| rich=SE | great=to-3MS | thing-F | to-peer-3MS=QU.M |

He is a rich man who has more possessions than any of his peer.
(Neferty IId)

(119b) A title of a medical prescription:

| | | | | |
|---|---|---|---|---|
| *ḥ3-t* | *m-pẖr-t* | *n-t-msḏr* | *nḏs* | *sḏm-f* |
| head-F | in-prescription-F | of-F-ear | poor | hear-3MS |

Beginning of the treatment of an ear whose hearing is impaired.
(pEbers 91, 2)

(119c) As above:

| | | | |
|---|---|---|---|
| *k-t* | *n-t-dr* | *mwy-t* | *ꜥš3-s/=s(y)* |
| another-F | of-F-dispel.INF | water-F | numerous-/=3FS |

Another prescription for stopping excessive urine. (pEbers 50, 6)

### 2.4.2 Later Egyptian

As in Earlier Egyptian, the sole instances of morphologically unambiguous subordinated adjectival sentences in Late Egyptian are those in which the subject is a singular personal pronoun. Unless emended as *<ḥr>-nty*, ex. 120a is the only case of an adjectival sentence introduced by the relativising element *nty*, whereas 120b could be a possible case of deleted subject (see Section 1.2.1 above)[37]:

(120a) In a magical spell certain entities pour out substances:

| | |
|---|---|
| *nty-dḥr=st* | *r-ḥmy* |
| REL-bitter=3P | than-bitter almond |

...that are more bitter than bitter almond. (pLeiden I 343+345 r° 4, 2–3)

37 However, in the light of *ir md-t=nb nty-iw-w nfr n-N* 'as to everything that will be good for N', example 120b might be analysed as a relative clause with deleted subject and *3ḫ* being the infinitive.

(120b) The god Amun grants to the lady Neskhons in his decree in her favour to save her from any evil that might befall her in the netherworld. In addition, he assures:
*iw-i* *di* *ḫpr* *iw-pꜣ-nty-ꜣḫ=n-s* *<m>-qꜣ=nb*
FUT-1S cause happen to-DEF.M-REL-beneficient=to-3FS in-state=QU
I will make what is beneficient for her happen in every manner ...
(Jansen-Winkeln, *IdS* I, 137, 19)

The situation is rather different in Demotic, where the *nꜣ*-pattern is used in both relative clauses (ex. 121a–c) and 'virtual' relative clauses (ex. 122d; cf. also 99b above):

(121a) A statue of the king will be named as follows:
*ptlmis* *ḥr-nḏ-iṯ-f* *nty-nꜣ-ʿn* *nꜣy-f-qnqn*
N N-avenger-father-3MS REL-ADJ-beautiful POSS.P-3MS-victory
Ptolemy, Horus avenger of his father, whose victories are glorious.
(Raphia Decree 32)

(121b) The deceased must say before god Thoth:
*tw-i* *wʿb* *r-md-bn-t* *nb* *nty-nꜣ-bn-s*
PTC-1S pure to-thing-bad-F QU REL-ADJ-bad-3FS
*nty-ḫn-nꜣy-s-hrw-w* *nty-lk* *rḥr-y*
REL-in-POSS.P-3FS-day-P REL-remove.STA to-1S
I am clean of every evil thing that is evil and that has been at times remote in me but has been removed from me. (pBN 149 3, 22–23)

(121c) Moral precepts state:
*pꜣ-lḫ* *nty-nꜣ-ḫm-ḥꜣṯ-f* *nꜣ-ḫm* *pꜣ-nṯr* *msꜣ-f*
DEF.M-fool REL-ADJ-small-heart-3MS ADJ-small DEF.M-god after-3MS
The god will be impatient with the impatient fool. (pInsinger 21, 18)

(121d) Moral precepts state:
*sy* *iw-nꜣ-sbꜣ-f* *iw-ir-f-mwy* *mwy* *n-ʿḏ*
man DEP-ADJ-teach-3MS DEP-do-3MS-think thought of-wrong
*nꜣw-ir-f*
COP.P-do-3MS
Even an educated and thoughtful man has wrong thoughts.
(Onkhsheshonqy 15, 9)

(121e) Moral precepts state:
*rmṯ-ḫm* *iw-nꜣ-ʿꜣ-tꜣy-f-bꜣ-t*
man-small DEP-ADJ-great-POSS.F-3MS-character-F
*nꜣ-ʿšꜣ-tꜣy-f-ḫnšt-t*
ADJ-plenty-POSS.F-3MS-stench-F
A commoner of great attitude will be utterly detested.
(Onkhsheshonqy 7, 19)

(121f) Ahure trying to keep Setne from taking the secret divine book narrates him her story. She, her husband, who was looking for the said book as well, and their child went by boat to Coptos. Upon their landing:

*ṯꜣy-w* *ṯ-n* *r-wʿ-ʿwy* *ỉw-nꜣw-ʿn-f* *m-šs*
take.PST-3P OBJ-1P to-IDF.S-house DEP-ADJ-beautiful-3MS in-excess
We were taken to a very beautiful house (lit: a house, which has very beautiful). (Setne 3, 26)

A similar relativisation of adjective verbs by means of the relativiser *et-* is very common in Coptic, and these relative clauses can appear as adjuncts or in headless absolute use (e.g., in cleft sentences). Once again, adjective verbs are used both in relative clauses (ex. 122c–e) and in 'virtual' relative clauses (ex. 122a–b):

(122a) John argues that monks should rejoice in God and strive for His honour:

*mn-laau* *e-nekʲôô-f* *ê* *e-f-sêš* *n-t-he*
NEG-any DEP-ugly-3MS or DEP-3MS-despise.STA in-DEF.F-way
*n-te-psykhê* *et-mêh* *m-pathos*
of-DEF.F-soul REL-fill.STA with-passion
There is nothing so ugly or despicable as the soul filled with passion.
([S]John of Constantinople, *On Repentance and Continence* [Budge, *Homilies*, 2, 19–20])

(122b) The prophet Micah foresees that in the last days the mountain of the Lord will become visible:

*se-mahe* *nkʲi-hen-hethnos* *e-našô-u*
3P-walk PVS-IDF.P-people DEP-plenty-3P
And countless peoples will come. ([A]Mi 4:2 [Till])

(122c) The disciples ask the master about Saklas and his forces:

*nt-a-u-kʲn-ti-hikôn* *to* *et-nesô-s*
2P-PST-3P-find-DEM.F-image where REL-fair-3FS
Where did they find this beautiful image? ([L]*Kephalaia* 137, 17)

(122d) People recognised the leper whom Peter and Andrew had healed as the one who usually sat by the entrance:

*e-f-tbh-eleêmosyne* *ahtn-t-pylê* *et-neso-s* *m-p-hieron*
DEP-3MS-ask-alms at-DEF.F-gate REL-fair-3FS of-DEF.M-temple
...begging for alms at the beautiful gate of the temple. ([M]Acts 3:10)

(122e) Jesus begins his parable on the tares among the wheat with the word: The heavenly kingdom is like a man

*e-a-f-siti* *nn-u-kʲrakʲ* *e-nanu-f* *e-te-f-šôši*
DEP-PST-3MS-SOW OBJ-IDF.S-seed DEP-good-3MS to-POSS.M-3MS-field
...who sowed good seed onto his field. ([F]Mt 13:24)

The relativisation of *nanu-* resulted in a lexicalised form *et-nanu-* 'good, fair' > *p-et-nanu-f* 'that which is good' (cf. Crum 1939: 227–28). The latter was eventually reanalysed as a noun and hence appears often marked for definiteness twice, i.e. *p-petnanuf*.

# 3 Semantics and pragmatics

## 3.1 Earlier Egyptian

The semantic and pragmatic features of Earlier Egyptian adjectival sentences are best observable through a comparison with verbal and other non-verbal sentence patterns, with which they show notable structural and semantic overlap. The general semantic function of adjectival sentences is the assignment of qualities. In this they differ from nominal sentences, which, as discussed in Part II Section 3.1.2, concern the classification or identification of the subject. They also differ from adverbial sentences, whose prototypical function is the description of location. However, predication of qualities and classification are related notions. Although the other semantic function of nominal sentences, identification, is potentially exclusive in the sense that it may single out the identified entity as the unique participant to whom the status described is applicable, classification is always inclusive in that it does not set the classified participant apart from others sharing the same properties. Quality assignment is rather similar in this respect. Classification through membership or characterisation (e.g., 'Judas was a disciple' and 'cats are mammals' respectively) do not provide an exhaustive definition of the classified entity, but rather select one of its features for a specific mention (i.e. 'Judas' was also 'a man', 'a traitor', etc.). The same is also true of adjectival qualifications. The frequent use of adjectival and classifying nominal sentences in close parallel is a reflection of these shared properties:

(123a) The author makes an oblique reference to trouble at the highest governmental level:

| | | | | |
|---|---|---|---|---|
| *mt* | *qsn* | *ỉrr-t* | *m-ẖnw* | *r-ḫ-t=nb-t* |
| PTC | miserable | do.PIP-F | in-residence | to-thing-F=QU-F |

What is done in the residence is more miserable than anything.

(pUC 32200, 5–7)

(123b) Ptahhetep notes that a certain amount of sycophancy is commendable:

| | | |
|---|---|---|
| *qsn=pw* | *ỉtn-w* | *m-ḥr(y)tp* |
| miserable=SE | opponent-M | in-superior |

He who opposes a superior is a miserable person. (Ptahhetep 446)

Nevertheless, the sentences above do not have exactly the same meaning. In ex. 123a, the subject is assigned a quality, whereas in ex. 123b it is in fact profiled as a member of a class characterised by a certain quality. The partial structural similarities between the patterns noted in Section 1.1 above should not blind

https://doi.org/10.1515/9783110409895-012

one from recognising the clear semantic differences between them. In addition, features that often appear to be overlapping may ultimately reflect complementary functions. As seen earlier above in Section 1.1, when the subject is a personal pronoun, the adjectival sentence forms a paradigm with nominal sentences with initial absolute pronoun subject. This phenomenon probably originates in the latter's information structure properties, but details remain slightly unclear. It was observed in connection with nominal sentences with non-canonical information structure (Part II Section 3.1.3) that absolute pronouns differ in their ability to trigger presuppositions. The first and second persons are not triggers, although they may function as such if there exist an allo-sentence where the said pronouns are not used. By contrast, third-person absolute pronouns are always focal presupposition triggers. This model works well insofar as assignment of qualities applies to third-person subjects. In a standard adjectival sentence, the information structure is what may be called canonical: the predicate represents the communicative high point of what is said, and the subject is not particularly elevated. Yet when such an effect was intended in the third person, the adjectival sentence could be replaced by the nominal sentence pattern [absolute pronoun *ntf* + participle], but the rarity of this construction points to its strongly marked value:

(124a) It is said of the resurrected and divine king:

| | | | | | |
|---|---|---|---|---|---|
| *ntf* | *ꜥꜣ* | *im-y* | *p-t* | *iw-f* | *mdw-f* |
| 3MS | great.PPA | in.RLT-M | heaven-F | AUX-3MS | speak-3MS |

*m-bꜣḥ-imn-t*
in-front-underworld-F

*He* is the great one who is in heaven; he speaks before the underworld.
(Litany of Ra 123–24/R IV)

(124b) The king's resourcefulness in building work is extolled:

| | | | |
|---|---|---|---|
| *ntf* | *mnḫ* | *ḥr-šꜣ(-t)-n-f* | *ḥr-kꜣ-t* |
| 3MS | excellent.PPA | on-begin.REL(-F)-PST-3MS | on-work-F |

| | |
|---|---|
| *rwd-t* | *n-t-ḏ-t* |
| enduring-F | of-F-eternity-F |

*He* is one excellent in what he has initiated and in enduring works of eternity. (*Urk.* IV 861, 8)

However, problems arise with first- and second-person subjects. Given the existence of the nominal sentence pattern, one might expect this to be the pragmatic focal means of quality assignment as is the case in the third person, in contrast with the adjectival sentence. Yet in the second person, the ratio of occurrences of the two constructions *nfr=ṯw* and *ntk/ṯwt nfr* is roughly even, and no obvious pragmatic (as opposed to semantic) difference between the two is discernible:

(125a) Nehesi sings praise to the sun god:

| | | |
|---|---|---|
| *nfr=tw* | *m-rꜥ* | *rꜥ=nb* |
| beautiful=2MS | as-N | day=QU.M |

You are beautiful as Ra every day. (Berlin 7317, 17)

(125b) The author of a Letter to Dead tries to convince his deceased addressee to be active on his behalf:

| | | | | | |
|---|---|---|---|---|---|
| *ntk* | *i͗qr* | *tp-tꜣ* | *ntk* | *mnḫ* | *m-ẖrtnṯr* |
| 2MS | excellent.PPA | on-earth | 2MS | efficient.PPA | in-necropolis |

You were one excellent upon earth; you are (also) one efficient in the necropolis. (Louvre Bowl 8)

Even more surprising is the fact that instances of the first-person nominal pattern *i͗nk nfr* far outnumber the examples of *nfr=wi͗*, which, if anything, seems to have carried some special pragmatic value, but whose exact character is difficult to gauge due to scarcity of data:

(126) The deceased announces his survival after death:

| | | |
|---|---|---|
| *ꜣḫ-w=wi͗* | *nḫt* | *sꜣ-i͗* |
| spiritual.PPA-M=1S | strong | son-1S |

I am spiritual and my son (i.e. heir) is strong. (CT II 242c/S1P)

It has been pointed out that the division here rather seems to follow the split between what have been called interlocutive (first and second) and delocutive (third) persons, the former of which show strong preference for nominal sentences, whereas the latter are characteristically found in adjectival sentences (Loprieno 1995: 114). In fact, it seems that the idea of focalising versus canonical allo-sentences should rather be assumed to obtain only if such pairs exist within the *same* morpho-syntactic sentence pattern. It was seen in Part I Section 3.1.2.1 that adverbial sentences with absolute pronouns are subject-focalising, and this seems to be the case because they contrast with similarly adverbial constructions with suffix and clitic pronouns. In the same vein, the variant with absolute pronouns of the possessive nominal sentence pattern [*n* + pronoun] (Part II Section 1.1.1) is focalising because it contrasts with the construction with clitic pronouns, which is also, grammatically speaking, a nominal sentence. Adjectival sentences know no similar pairing of allosentences within the grammatical category itself: *nfr=ṯw* (good=2MS 'you are good') does not contrast with **nfr ntk*, which might be what a 'truly' focalising adjectival sentence could have looked like. Accordingly, to look for differences between *nfr=ṯw* (ex. 125a) and *ntk i͗qr* (ex. 125b) in the focality of the subject might be misguided: this is not real variation between allosentences, which takes place only *within* morpho-syntactic categories. The difference between the latter two constructions might then indeed somehow relate to the interlocutive vs. delocutive split, although details remain obscure. The fact that the third-person construction *ntf nfr* seems to be focalising should not lead one astray. It does so simply because third-person absolute pronouns are, as noted, inherently focal presupposition-triggers, not because the construction varies with an allosentence in the same grammatical category. An indication that this reasoning may be correct is provided by another case of variation between nominal sentences with absolute pronouns and adjectival sentences. In possessive clauses the adjectival pattern *n-k-im-y* sometimes occurs in parallel with the nominal sentence construction *n* + absolute pronoun (the *n* may display haplography with an initial *n* of the latter):

(127) The council of nobles praises the successful plunder of king Thutmosis I:

| | | | |
|---|---|---|---|
| *ntk* | *nbw* | *n-k-im-y* | *ḥḏ* |
| 2MS.POSS | gold | to-2MS-in.RLT-M | silver |

Yours is gold; to you belongs silver. (*Urk.* IV 96, 6–7)

Again the variation here does not appear to be based on the greater focality of the absolute pronoun subject; instead, it may have been motivated by stylistic considerations. This is almost certainly the case in the following example, which shows an alternation between the two adjectival and nominal possessive patterns just noted and the adverbial construction with the dative marker *n* 'to':

(128) The gods say of Queen Hatshepsut:

| | | | | |
|---|---|---|---|---|
| *iw=n-s* | *tꜣ-w* | *nt(s)* | *ḫꜣs-w-t* | *n-s-im(-y)* |
| AUX=to-3FS | land-P | 3FS.POSS | hill country-P-F | to-3FS-in.REL[-F] |

| | |
|---|---|
| *ḥbs-t=nb-t* | *p-t* |
| conceal.REL-F=QU-F | heaven-F |

She owns the lands; hers are hill-countries; to her belongs all that heaven conceals. (*Urk.* IV 244, 10–12)

The final, possible, overlap between adjectival and other sentence patterns is perhaps observable in the constructions already discussed in Part II Section 3.1.5. Assuming that they are not corrupt, in these cases the use of simple nouns in the adjectival construction coerces a 'quality' reading on the former, illustrating an overlap and merging of adjectival and nominal sentences as semantic as well as syntactic categories (so Uljas 2006)[38]:

(129) Hori and Suty sing praise to the sun god:

| | | |
|---|---|---|
| *ptḥ=tw* | *nb-k* | *ḥꜥ-k* |
| N=2MS | fashion-2MS | limb-2MS |

You are Ptah-like when you fashion your own limb! (*Urk.* IV 1944, 1)

38 The hypothesis is disputed by Schenkel (2008). The syntactic, but not the semantic analysis proposed here is broadly accepted by Gundacker (2010: 106–10).

Already with regular adjectival sentences where the predicate is semantically a quality concept expression, it is difficult to decide whether the construction should be seen as an adjectival or nominal sentence, particularly when the predicate is a participle. In *ptḥ=tw* of ex. 129 above the predicate is a common noun, but in this particular context it expresses a quality, because it is used in the construction [predicate + clitic pronoun subject] characteristic to the predication of quality. Examples such as these could provide the mediating link between adjectival and nominal sentences that unifies them into a linguistic continuum covering both the syntactic and semantic spheres:

**Tab. III.3:** The proposed linguistic continuum of adjectival and nominal sentences in Earlier Egyptian.

| |
|---|
| ***Core Adjectival Sentence*** |
| *nfr=sw* |
| 'He is good' |
| *ḥʿ=sw* |
| 'He is (one) rejoicing' |
| *ptḥ=tw* |
| 'You are Ptah-like' |
| *ptḥ=pw* |
| 'He is Ptah' |
| ***Core Nominal Sentence*** |

Generally speaking, adjectival sentences are neutral with respect to tense, aspect, and modality (see, e.g., Heckel 1957: 38; Allen 1986a: 11; Malaise and Winand 1999: §494; Winand 2006: 160; Reintges 1997: 94, 97, among many others). They do not profile the quality assigned to the subject as transitory or acquired, nor suggest that there is any potential for it to evolve. Instead, the quality predicated is presented as unchanging and without a suggestion of development, origin, or end. In this capacity, adjectival sentences again resemble the similarly unbounded nominal sentences and are equally incompatible with auxiliary elements such as *ỉw* or *ʿḥʿ-n* (cf. Heckel 1957: 41–44; Malaise and Winand 1999: §500). It was noted in the preceding parts that these morphemes combine with predications that are temporally limited or contingent and susceptible to change or development over time.

Nevertheless, the adjectival predication also shares characteristics with verbal and even adverbial situations to a greater extent than nominal sentences. As a predicate as well as an attribute, a quality may be viewed as inherent to an entity, but unlike identity, it can also easily represent something transitory, temporary, or acquired, which in turn sets it more within the sphere of speakers' attitudes and opinions. More abstractly, in adjectival predication the predicate expression is not necessarily associated with a similarly high degree of time-stability as a noun, and consequently the adjectival quality may be set more within the range of temporal and spatial deixis and speaker evaluation (cf. e.g. Givón 2001 vol. 1: 53; Stassen 1997: 16–18). In Earlier Egyptian, the grammatical consequences of this conceptual profile of adjectival predication are wide-ranging. For example, in adjectival sentences where the predicate is a participle, roots with unambiguous written morphology show that the participle occurs in the perfective form:

(130a) Sinuhe says that the people of the king's city love him and adds:
*ḥꜥ=st* *ꞽm-f* *r-nṯr-w-sn*
jubilant.PPA=3C in-3MS to-god-P-3P
They are more jubilant in him than in their gods. (Sin B, 66–67)

(130b) Ptahhetep says concerning someone who has the privilege of hearing his instruction:
*rš=wy* *ḏdd-y=n-f* *nn*
joyful.PPA=ADM say.PPP-M=to-3MS DEM
How joyful is the one to whom this has been said! (Ptahhetep 557)

This behaviour corresponds to expectations if perfective aspect is viewed as presenting a situation in its totality as bounded, without attention to its internal structure and development.[39] Meanwhile, adjectival sentences, although not found with the auxiliaries *ꞽw* and *ꜥḥꜥ-n*, show limited compatibility with the complex auxiliary *wn/wnn*. The inertia or immutability of the adjectival state of affairs could apparently be removed if the adjectival sentence is introduced by the past sequential narrative construal *wn-ꞽn* (see also ex. 82 above):

(131) The brethren of Kagemni accepted their teaching:
*wn-ꞽn* *nfr=st* *ḥr-ꞽb-sn* *r-ḫ-t=nb-t* *nty*
AUX-SEQ good=3C on-heart-3P to-thing-F=QU-F REL
*m-tꜣ=pn* *r-ḏr-f*
in-land=DEM.M to-limit-3MS
Then it was more pleasant in their heart(s) than anything in this entire land. (Kagemni II, 6–7)

39 *Locus classicus* is Comrie (1976: 18). However, opinions on this matter vary greatly.

There are also some rare examples of *wn/wnn* used to project the adjectival predication to the future:

(132) In a broken context:

| | | | |
|---|---|---|---|
| *mk* | *wnn* | *nḏm=sy* | *ḥr-ib-f* |
| PTC | AUX | sweet=3C | on-heart-3MS |

See, it will be pleasing in his mind. (pUC 32158, 2.8)

However, it is noteworthy that occurrences of these two constructions are all of the type *wn-in nfr=st ḥr-ib-f* and *nfr/nḏm=st ḥr-ib* X '(Then) it was/will be pleasing in his mind', which suggests that they have presumably acquired an idiomatic character. More remarkably, adjectival quality concept lexemes could also be associated with verbal TAM-properties by inflecting them as verb forms of the so-called suffix conjugation as well as in the Stative and the infinitive as part of the grammaticalised progressive and future patterns [preposition + infinitive]. The use of the suffix conjugation forms in adjunct and complement clauses was illustrated in Sections 2.2.1 and 2.3.1 above. Below are further examples of finite forms (the simple *sḏm-f* in ex. 133a, the subjunctive *sḏm-f* in 133b, the *sḏm-n-f* form in 133c–d, the Stative in 133e, and the future construction *r* + infinitive in 133f) of adjectival roots[40]:

(133a) An appeal to the addressee:

| | | | | |
|---|---|---|---|---|
| *m3n-k* | *ḥm-t-k* | *iw* | *mr* | *rmm-s=ṯw* |
| see.SUB-2MS | wife-F-2MS | AUX | painful | cry-3FS=2MS |

You should see your wife. It is painful how she weeps for you. (Kemyt 9/TC)

(133b) Thutmosis III tells why he rebuilt the temple of Senwosret III:

| | |
|---|---|
| *di-i* | *sḫm-f* |
| cause.SUB-1S | mighty.SUB-3MS |

(I did it...) so that I could cause him to be mighty. (*Urk.* IV 198, 7)

(133c) Sinuhe waxes lyrical in his description of how he plundered the goods of his vanquished foe:

| | | | |
|---|---|---|---|
| *wsḫ-n(-i)* | *m-ꜥḫꜥ-i* | *ꜥš3-n(-i)* | *m-mnmn-t-i* |
| wide-PST[=1S] | in-property-1S | many-PST[-1S] | in-cattle-F-1S |

I made my property more extensive, I made my cattle more numerous. (Sin B, 146–47)

40 Cf. also Winand (2006: 163–64). For a superb discussion and collection of examples of the *sḏm-n-f* of 'quality' roots, see Vernus (1984: 171–84).

(133d) Sebekkhu tells what happened after he had been assigned to do soldiering for the king:

*ꜥḥꜥ-n spd-n-ỉ r-gs-f*
AUX sharp-PST-1S to-side-3MS
Then I strove for excellence beside him. (*Lesestücke* 83, 3)

(133e) The peasant points out the status of the high steward, which contrasts with his own:

*ỉw-k=swt sꜣ-t(ỉ) m-tꜣ-k*
AUX-2MS=PTC sated-STA in-bread-2MS
You are, on the contrary, sated with your bread. (Peas B1, 155–56)

(133f) After giving advice concerning sycophancy before officials, Ptahhetep notes:

*ỉw ḏd-t-k r-nfr ḥr-ỉb*
AUX say.REL.FUT-F-2MS FUT-good.INF on-heart
What you shall say will be pleasing to the heart. (Ptahhetep 130)

The different nuance obtained by this verbal profiling of the qualities as opposed to adjectival sentences is clearest in exx. 133b and 133c, the first of which portrays the situation described as having been dependent on the realisation of the causative main clause verb *rdi*, the second as an endpoint of a processual development, whose role in the overall structure of information is not pivotal (the so-called Second Tense construction, see Part II Section 3.1.3.1.2 above for some remarks on these constructions) and culminates in the speaker's current deictic centre. Similarly, in complement clauses without a complementiser, the use of the geminating *sḏm-f* form implies that the development or the degree of the quality are taken into the speaker's account; this form can also present the predicative relation itself as presupposed information of secondary contextual importance, as in ex. 133a, with a subject complement (Uljas 2007c: 84–90):

(134a) Ahmose says of his valour in battles against foreign foes:

*ỉst=wỉ m-tp n(-y)-mšꜥ-n mꜣ-n ḥm-f qnn-ỉ*
PTC=1S in-head of[-M]-army-1P see-PST majesty-3MS brave-1S
I was at the vanguard of our army, and his majesty saw how brave I was. (*Urk.* IV 9, 15–16)

(134b) In an instruction about preparing certain ingredients of a medical potion by washing them in a jar:

*rḫ-tw ỉꜥꜥ-sn ḥr-dp-tw dp-t nꜣ-n-mw*
know-PASS clean-3P on-taste-PASS taste-F DEM.PL-of-water
*nty m-pꜣ-ꜥnḏw*
REL in-DET.M-jar
One may tell how clean they are by tasting the taste of the water in the jar. (pEdwin Smith 21, 20–21)

(134c) Queen Hatshepsut claims to have abided by Amun's will at all time:

*ἰw* *ḥm-t-ἰ* *rḫ-tἰ* *nṯrr-f*
AUX majesty-F-1S know-STA divine-3MS
My majesty knows how divine he is. (*Urk.* IV 363, 6)

Instances of equivalent verbal and adjectival variants are also illustrative:

(135a) Ptahhetep makes a general point about a petitioner whose case is attained to:

*ḥʿ=sw* *ἰm* *r-sprw=nb*
rejoice.PPA=3MS there to-petitioner=QU.M
He rejoices thereupon more than any petitioner. (Ptahhetep 270)

(135b) Thutmosis III says of Amun's reception of religious observance:

*ḥʿ-f* *m-dwꜣw-f*
rejoice.SUB-3MS in-adoration-3MS
He will rejoice in adoration for him. (*Urk.* IV 167, 12)

In ex. 135a, the adjectival sentence again profiles the quality assigned to the subject as a non-dynamic property lacking all suggestion of progress, change, or temporal position. By contrast, in ex. 135b 'rejoicing' is something that apparently still lies in the future and is potentially subject to the speaker's epistemic evaluation. In case of alternation with the simple *sḏm-f* form, the difference between adjectival and verbal profiling is not particularly clear given the 'timeless' character of the latter:

(136a) In a medical text on diagnosing a fracture by asking the patient to look at his shoulder:

*qsn* *mꜣꜣ* *ḫpr* *ø* *mʿ-f*
difficult see.INF happen.SUB(?) ø through-3MS
It is difficult to see whether (anything) happens as a result. (pEdwin Smith 10, 10)

(136b) A description of symptoms on a patient seemingly suffering from tetanus:

*ἰw* *qsn* *r-f* *wn* *rꜣ-f* *ẖr-s*
AUX difficult to-3MS open.INF mouth-3MS under-3FS
It is difficult for him to open his mouth because of it. (pEdwin Smith 3, 3)

Here most semantic differences between adjectival and verbal constructions seem to be almost neutralised.

Adjectival sentences are relatively featureless not only in terms of properties of TAM, but also, as already noted briefly above, in terms of their information structure. This is also the case with adverbial and the nominal sentences, which are also not particularly marked in this respect. However, adverbial and nominal sentences display special patterns for the expression of non-canonical information structure, such as constructions with absolute pronouns in the former and cleft constructions in the latter case. By contrast, adjectival sentences do not display a similar variation between canonical and non-canonical allo-sentences. Rather, a marked information structure in the predication of quality is signalled by the use of a finite verb form – such as the geminating *sḏm-f* in the so-called Second Tenses, which convey a non-canonical low information status of the verb – instead of the adjectival sentence. It has also been argued that with specifically 'thematic' subjects, adjectival sentences are replaced by the Stative (Loprieno 1995: 113):

(137a) Amun says to the king:
*nḏm=wy* *ỉ3m-t-k* *r-šnb-t-ỉ*
sweet=ADM charm-F-2MS to-breast-F-1S
How pleasant is your charm against my bosom! (*Urk.* IV 612, 4)

(137b) Amun says to Queen Hatshepsut at seeing her works in his name:
*ỉw* *ỉb-ỉ* *nḏm* *wr-t*
AUX heart-1S sweet.STA great-ADV
My heart is very pleased. (*Urk.* IV 297, 5)

Whatever the exact meaning of 'thematic' may be, examples such as 138a below, where the Stative subject is contextually strongly established, might be called in support of this analysis, but in ex. 138b the subject of the Stative is an impersonal subject, which naturally cannot be 'thematised':

(138a) The resurrected king is told:
*ʿ3* *rd-k* *rd-k* *wr-ỉ*
mighty foot-2MS foot-2MS great-STA
Mighty is your foot; your foot is great! (PT 658c)

(138b) Amenyseneb carried out his restoration work successfully:
*ʿḥʿ-n-tw* *ḥʿ-w* *ỉm* *wr* *r-ḫ-t=nb-t*
AUX-PST-PASS rejoice-STA there greatly to-thing-F=QU-F
Then one rejoiced therewith more than anything'. (Louvre C12, 17)

Adjectival sentences do not occur with impersonal subjects. The variation between them and Stative constructions could be based on the temporal profiling of the respective constructions. Although the adjectival sentence merely assigns a quality to the subject, the Stative characteristically portrays it as a result of a process[41]: in ex. 137a above the king's 'charm' is simply said to be

**41** Cf. Winand (2006: 226–29). However the author cites counterexamples to this standard state of affairs.

'pleasant', whereas in 137b, the speaker's intention stresses that his 'heart is pleased' as a result of the Queen's pious actions. In addition, the subject of the adjectival predicate could also be anteposed, a frequent sign of topicalisation or thematisation[42]:

(139) The sailor describes the appearance of the fantastic snake-deity:
*ḫbsw-t-f* *wr=s(y)* *r-mḥ* *2*
beard-F-3MS great=3FS to-cubit 2
His beard – it was greater than two cubits. (Sh.S. 63–64)

In many examples above, the degree of the quality expressed by the adjectival predication is set into a comparative construction by means of the preposition *r* 'in relation to'. Further instances are:

(140a) Having told the shipwrecked sailor that he will see his home again, the snake adds:
*nfr=st* *r-ḫ-t=nb-t*
good=3C to-thing-F=QU-F
It is better than anything. (Sh.S. 134)
(140b) The deceased is told:
*ḫ3ḫ=ṯw* *r-ṯ[m]* *n(-y)-ỉr-t*
fast.PPA=2MS to-blink.INF of[-M]-eye-F
You are faster than the blink of an eye. (CT I 266g)
(140c) The father of king Merikara remarks on offering to gods:
*šsp* *bỉ-t* *n-t-ʿq3-ỉb* *r-ỉw3-w*
receive.PPP cake-F of-F-exact-heart to-bull-P
*n(y)-ỉr(r)* *ỉsf-t*
of[-M]-do.PIA evil-F
A cake of a righteous person is more acceptable than bulls of an evildoer. (Merikara C, V.1–2)

By contrast, the superlative is apparently not expressed within the framework of the adjectival sentence pattern. This semantic nuance was conveyed by the

42 However, it should be noted that for many Egyptologists who accept the hypothesis of 'double thematic structure' derived from Functionalist literature (e.g. Dik 1980: 15–16; Downing 1991: 127–28; Siewierska 1991: 149–51), anteposition equals *p*-external thematisation, with 'theme' understood along the Chafean lines as the 'setting' or 'framework' 'against which the following predication holds' (cf. Chafe 1976: 50). Thus it represents a phenomenon different from topicalisation, which allegedly has more to do with singling what the *p* 'is about' and concerns arguments rather than adjuncts.

corresponding nominal sentence, where the superlative sense seems to have been left on the level of contextual inferences:

(141b) The King is told:

| *ṯwt* | *wrỉ* | *ỉm(-y)* | *ms-w-s* |
|---|---|---|---|
| 2MS | great.PPA | in.RLT[-M] | child-P-3FS |

You are the greatest among her (goddess Nut's) children. (PT 638d)

(141b) The inhabitants of the underworld are told of the deceased:

*wr-ṯn=pw*
great-2P=SE
He is the greatest among you (lit. 'your great one'). (CT VII 51s)

(141c) Senmut boasts:

| *ỉnk* | *wr* | *wr-w* | *m-tꜣ* | *r-ḏr-f* |
|---|---|---|---|---|
| 1S | great.PPA | great-P | in-land | to-limit-3MS |

I was greatest of the great in the entire land. (*Urk.* IV 410, 11)

In sum, adjectival sentences display strong syntactic and semantic parallels with verbal and nominal sentences. This is one of the reasons why they are frequently analysed as somehow secondary or viewed as a subclass of other construction types. However, notable as the links between predication and patterns may be, the morpho-syntactic and semantic blending of adjectival and verbal predication is in fact strongest in the negative patterns (see Section 4.1), which completely neutralise the formal and semantic opposition between verbal and non-verbal predication.

## 3.2 Later Egyptian

In Later Egyptian, non-verbal patterns were subject to various semantic changes. Late Egyptian adjectival sentences share quality assignment with nominal sentences:

**Tab. III.4:** Form vs. function in Late Egyptian (patterns of lesser frequency are given in smaller font size).

| | | |
|---|---|---|
| *Quality assignment* | | |
| | Adjectival sentence | Nominal sentence |
| *Classification* | | |
| | Adverbial sentence | Nominal sentence |
| *Identification* | | |
| | Nominal sentence | |
| *Specification* | | |
| | Cleft and pseudo-cleft | |

As a diachronically recessive pattern, adjectival sentences are attested mainly in more formal textual genres, rarely if ever in lower registers such as epistolary sources, where the use of nominal sentences takes over. Compare ex. 142a from a literary text with an adjectival sentence and ex. 142b from a letter with a nominal sentence:

(142a) The bovine friends of the younger brother used to guide him to the best pastures, saying:
*nfr* *pꜣ-sm* *n-s-t* *ḥmn-t*
good DEF.M-green in-place-F so and so-F
The greenery in such-and-such a place is good. (*LES* 10, 13–14)

(142b) The author of a letter begins his request that the addressee take care of his father with the words:
*yꜣ* *mntk* *nfr*
PTC 2MS good
Indeed, you are kind. (*LRL* 48, 15)

Thus, the overlapping of semantic functions described above for Earlier Egyptian is organised within a stylistic hierarchy in which adjectival sentences are preferred in more formal textual genres and nominal sentences elsewhere. A residual environment for adjectival sentences in documentary texts is provided by constructions with omission of the subject[43]:

(143) The author urges the addressee to keep him informed about the condition of the people at home:
*n-nfr* *n-bin*
IP-good-ø IP-bad-ø
...whether good or bad. (*LRL* 3, 12)

In Demotic, the adjectival sentence of earlier stages has been completely lost from the grammatical system. Its function is partly taken over by adjective verbs or nominal sentences:

(144a) In a lamentative prayer to Amun, the god is asked not to turn to those calling unto him:
*nꜣ-wh-ḥꜣty-w* *nꜣ-b(y)n-ỉr-t-w* *nꜣ-ʿšꜣ-nꜣy-w-rmt-byn-w*
ADJ-mean-heart-3P ADJ-bad-eye-F-3P ADJ-plenty-POSS.P-3P-man-bad
*nꜣ-nḏm-rꜣ-w* *ẖn-ꜣyt* *nꜣ-why-w* *ỉw-w-ỉr-bnr*
ADJ-sweet-mouth-3P in-need ADJ-mean-3P DEP-3P-to-outside

43 A way out would be to assume that these are actually nominal sentences with subject omission as described above in Section 1.4. However, it seems impossible to decide between the two alternatives.

Their hearts are mean. Their eyes are bad. Their bad people abound.
They are sweet only in need. They are mean, running away.
(pRylands IX 24, 6–7)

(144b) A mummy label says of a woman who died at the age of twenty:
*ḫm-ꜥḥꜥ* *tꜣy*
short-lifetime SE.F
She was short-lived. (Vleeming, *Short Texts* II, #513 B11)

The Stative of verbs of quality can express the same function. In ex. 145 below, it is used alongside a remnant of the adjectival sentence, i.e. an adjective verb with the prefix *nꜣ*:

(145) The author of a letter greets his addressee:
*nꜣ-nfr=n-k* *tꜣ-rnp* *tꜣy-k-rnp* *nfr-t*
ADJ-good=to-2MS DEF.F-year.F POSS.F-2MS-year.F good-STA.3FS
May the year be good for you. Your year is good. (pLoeb 6, 2–3)

The distribution of functions is thus broadly similar to Late Egyptian, except for the substitution of adjective verbs for the old adjectival sentence:

**Tab. III.5:** Form vs. function in earlier and middle Demotic.

| | | |
|---|---|---|
| *Quality assignment* | | |
| | Adjective verbs | Nominal sentence |
| *Classification* | | |
| | Adverbial sentence | Nominal sentence |
| *Identification* | | |
| | Nominal sentence | |
| *Specification* | | |
| | Cleft | |

Late Demotic texts exhibit a Coptic-like pattern, where one finds the split system for the quality-assignment function with nominal sentences and adjective verbs described in Part II Section 3.2.2.2.

Finally, in Coptic, adjective verbs are fading away, and despite the high frequency of specific lexical items, the lexical inventory (and thus the type frequency) is gradually reduced. This effect is compensated by the growing use of nominal sentences, and to a lesser extent by the rise of Stative forms of quality verbs of the type *o n-X* 'being X'. The examples below illustrate the different patterns with *caie* 'ugly' (146a–b) and *nok*$^{j}$ 'great' (146c–e).

(146a) The two daughters of Laban, Leia and Rachel, are introduced:
*lia=de ne-u-caie n-iat-s=te rakhêl=de*
N=yet PRT-IDF.S-ugly of-eye-3FS=SE.F N=yet
*ne-nane-s=pe ḫen-pe-s-smot*
PRT-good-3FS=PTC in-POSS.M-3FS-figure
*uoh e-nesô-s=pe ḫen-pe-s-ho emašô*
and DEP-fair=PTC in-POSS.M-3FS-face very
Leia was weak-eyed, but Rachel was beautiful in figure and very fair of face.
($^{B}$Gn 29:17)

(146b) After St Theodore had slain the dragon, a demon revealed himself to him:
*m-p-smot n-u-et$^{h}$ôš e-f-oi n-caie*
in-DEF.M-form of-IDF.S-Ethiopian DEP-3MS-be.STA as-ugly
...in the guise of an ugly Ethiopian.
($^{B}$Theodore of Antioch, *On the Theodores* [*AM* II 153, 6–7])

(146c) In a gnostic treatise, the personified wisdom addresses the light:
*kô ebol n-ta-parabasis ce-u-nok$^{j}$=te*
let out OBJ-POSS.F.1S-trespass for-IDF.S-great=SE.F
Forgive my transgression, for it is great. ($^{S}$*Pistis Sophia* 80, 12 [Schmidt])

(146d) A text dealing with the deeds of Pilate end with glorifications of the Lord; among them:
*ntk-u-nok$^{j}$ ntok auô u-nok$^{j}$ pe pe-k-ran*
2MS-IDF.S-great 2MS.ABS and IDF.S-great COP.M POSS.2MS-name
You are great, and great is your name.
($^{S}$*Ev. Nicodemus* §210 [Orlandi 38, 9–10])

(146e) The author of a sermon refers to an animal called Camelopard (i.e. giraffe), which resembles a camel, but:
*pe-f-mate o n-nok$^{j}$ emate*
POSS.M-3MS-neck be.STA as-great very
...its neck is very long. ($^{S}$Ps. Cyril, *On the Cross* [Campagnano 146, 1])

(146f) Jesus invites the troubled and heavy burdened telling them:
*pa-nahb=gar nahlôk$^{j}$-f auô s-asôu*
POSS.M.1S-yoke=for sweet-3MS and 3FS-light.STA
*nk$^{j}$i-ta-etpô*
PVS-POSS.F.1S-load
...for my yoke is sweet and light is my burden. ($^{S}$Mt 11:30)

(146g) Jesus invites the troubled and heavy burdened telling them:
*pa-nahb=gar hlôk$^{j}$ auô s-asôu*
POSS.M.1S-yoke=for sweet.STA and 3FS-light.STA
*nk$^{j}$i-ta-etpô*
PVS-POSS.F.1S-load
...for my yoke is sweet and light is my burden. ($^{S}$Mt 11:30 var.)

(146h) The Devil intends to tempt Antony leading him away from his path to God:

| | | | | |
|---|---|---|---|---|
| *auô* | *e-p-hae* | *n-nai* | *a-f-nuce* | *e-pe-f-hêt* |
| and | to-DEF.F-end | of-DEM.P | PST-3MS-throw | to-POSS.M-3MS-heart |

| | | | |
|---|---|---|---|
| *m-pe-nšot* | *n-t-aretê* | *auô* | *ce-u-nokj* |
| OBJ-DEF.M-hardness | of-DEF.F-virtue | and | COMP-IDF.S-great |

| | | | |
|---|---|---|---|
| *pe* | *pe-s-mkah* | *auô* | *on* |
| COP.M | POSS.M-3FS-pain | and | again |

*ce-naše-pe-s-hise*
COMP-plenty-POSS.M-3FS-suffering

And at the end of these things he threw the hardship of the virtue into his heart and that its pains are great and its sufferings are plenty.
(S*Life of Antony* §5 [Garitte 7, 24–26])

However, as noted above, the use of the adjective verbs is limited in Coptic to fewer lexical items than in Demotic. Quality assignment is now most often expressed by the nominal sentence, with the Stative as a less frequent alternative. The factors determining the choice between these two constructions are not particularly clear. The table below summarises the functional spread of the constructions:

**Tab. III.6:** Form vs. function in Coptic (patterns of lesser frequency are in smaller font size).

| | |
|---|---|
| *Quality assignment and classification* | |
| Nominal sentence | |
| PRN-NP // NP-SE | $NP_P$-COP-$NP_S$ |
| Adjective verbs | Stative forms |
| *Identification* | |
| Nominal sentence | |
| PRN-NP // NP-SE | $NP_S$-COP-$NP_P$ |
| *Specification* | |
| Cleft | |

Comparison of qualities is construed by means of the preposition *mi* 'like' in case of their equality (ex. 147a–b) and with *r* 'more than' in instances of inequality (147c–h). However, occasionally such marking can be missing and the comparison must be inferred from the context as in ex. 147i:

(147a) The pharaoh reports to the gods about the vineyards he founded in the north of Egypt:

| | | |
|---|---|---|
| *sꜥšꜣ=st* | *m-tꜣmḥy* | *mi-ḥfn-w* |
| increase=3P | in-N | like-millions-P |

They are in Lower Egypt as numerous as millions. (pHarris I 7, 10)

(147b) A part of the chariot called *ꜥrq* is connected with the homographic root *ꜥrq*:

*ꜥrq=ṯ*  *mi-ḏḥwṯ*
wise=2MS  like-N
You are as wise as Thoth. (oEdinburgh 916 vº 8–9)

(147c) Moral precepts assert:

*ꜣḫ*  *pꜣw-w-t*  *ỉw-ḥꜣty*  *nḏm*  *r-wsr*
beneficient  offering bread-P-F  DEP-heart  sweet.STA  than-riches
*ẖr-šnn*
under-pain
Better are offering breads when the heart is merry than riches under pain. (Amenemope 16, 13–14)

(147d) The author addresses his opponent by quoting examples of other officials – among them a certain Paheripedjet from Heliopolis:

*šri=st*  *r-my*  *ꜥꜣ=sw*  *r-gf*
small=3MS  than-cat  great=3MS  than-monkey
He is smaller than a cat but bigger than a monkey. ([2]*pAnastasi I* 92, 2)

(147e) The scribe invokes Thoth, the god of wisdom and of all scribes:

*nfr*  *ỉꜣw-ṯ-k*  *r-ỉꜣw-t=nb-t*
good  office-F-2MS  than-office-F=QU-F
Your calling is better than any other calling. (*LEM* 60, 6)

(147f) In a eulogy for King Ramesses IV, all of Egypt exclaims:

*ꜥn*  *ḥr*  *r-s-t*  *it-f*  *ỉmnrꜥ*
nice  N  than-seat-F  father-3MS  N
Horus is more beautiful than the throne of his father, Amun-Ra. (oTurin 57001 rº 8)

(147g) In a eulogy on the city of Thebes those far away from it exclaim:

*nḏm*  *pꜣ-ꜥq*  *nty-m-ẖnw-s*  *r-šꜥy-t*  *n-ꜥḏ-sri*
sweet  DEF.M-food  REL-in-inside-3FS  than-cake-F  of-fat-goose
The food inside it is sweeter than the cakes made of goose fat. (*KRI* V 646, 7–8)

(147h) The author quotes examples of officials chosen as role models by his opponent, such as a certain Nakht:

*ꜣḫ=sw=n-k*  *r-nn*  *10*  *n-sp*
beneficient=3MS=to-2MS  than-DEM.P.ABS  10  of-time
He is ten times more beneficient to you than these others. ([2]*pAnastasi I* 91, 1)

(147i) The sender of a letter tries to find out what he did to enrage his friend.

*nḏm*  *rmṯ*  *ỉw-f*  *ỉrm-pꜣy-f-ỉrw*  *(n)-wm*  *ỉs*
sweet  man  DEP-3MS  with-POSS.M-3MS-fellow  of-eat  old
*nfr*  *nkt*  [...]  *n-mꜣwt*  *nfr*  *ỉri*  *n-ỉs*
good  thing  [...]  of-new  good  fellow  of-old

A person is delighted when he is together with an old table companion.
Some [...] things are good, but an old friend is better. (*KRI* VI 265, 6–8)

(147j) A woman is taking an oath by adjuring Amun and the ruler:
*nty bin pꜣy-f-bꜣ-w r-mwt*
REL bad POSS.M-3MS-might-P than-death
...whose might is more evil than death. (*KRI* IV 316, 5–6))

(147k) The king describes the olive orchards he laid out and says about them:
*ꜥšꜣ nḥḥ im-sn r-šꜥ-t n-wḏb*
plenty oil in-3P to-sand of-shore
The olive-oil therein is more abundant than sand at the shore.
(pHarris I 8, 6)

(147l) A certain place in Israel/Palestine is described as full of horrors such as:
*ꜥšꜣ mꜣi-w r-ꜣby-w ḥtm-w*
plenty lion-P to-panther bear.F-P
Lions are more abundant than panthers and bears. (²*pAnastasi I* 126, 1)

As the last instance shows, comparision with different entities shows no marking either.

No specific morpho-syntactic means marks degrees of quality, which are inferred from the context:

(148) King Ramesses II suddenly finds himself alone in battle with the Hittite forces and prays to Amun, justifying his war against them:
*ꜥꜣ=wsy nb ꜥ.w.s. ꜥꜣ n-kmt r-di ẖꜥm*
great=PTC lord l.p.h. great of-Egypt to-give approach
*ḫꜣs-t-w m-r-wꜣ-t-f*
foreign_land-ADJ-P in-mouth-way-F-3MS
Too great is the great Lord of Egypt, may he life, prosper and be healthy, to allow aliens to step on his path. (*KRI* II 35, 10)

Although examples of this sort are not particularly abundant, they are not restricted to specific textual genres.

Demotic sentences with adjective verbs expressing a comparative relation introduce the standard of comparison by means of the preposition *r*:

(149a) Moral precepts state:
*nꜣ-nḏm pꜣ-mw n-pꜣ-i-ir-dy-s*
ADJ-sweet DEF.M-water of-DEF.M-PPA-AUX-give.INF-3FS
*r-pꜣ-irp n-pꜣ-[i-ir-šsp]-f*
than-DEF.M-wine of-DEF.M-PPA-AUX-receive-3MS

The water of him who gave it is sweeter than the wine of him who received it. (Onkhsheshonqy 19, 3)

(149b) Retaliating evil with evil should be avoided:

*nꜣ-hrš* *pꜣy-f-btw* *r-pꜣ-btw* *sḫmy*
ADJ-heavy POSS.M-3MS-punishment than-DEF.M-punishment N
*ỉw-s* *ẖꜥr-w*
DEP-3FS wrath-STA
Its punishment is heavier than the punishment by Sakhmet in wrath. (pInsinger 34, 4)

(149c) The hearing-bird says to the looking-bird:

*nꜣw-ḏq* *ỉr-ṯ̂-t* *r-ỉr-ṯ̂-y* *nꜣw-nfr* *n[ꜣy-t]-nww*
ADJ-sharp eye-DU-2FS than-eye-DU-1S ADJ-good POSS.P-2FS-sight
*r-nꜣy-y* *ꜥn*
than-POSS.ABS.P-1S again
Your eyes are sharper than mine, and your sight is also better than mine. (Myth of the Sun's Eye 14, 1–2)

(149d) The author of a letter complains about the attitude of the addressees towards him and his fellow-priest:

*nꜣ-wḏꜣ* *ḥꜣṯ-n* *ỉỉr-pꜣ-nṯr* *(n-)ḥw* *rḥr-tn*
ADJ-healthy heart-1P towards-DEF.M-god [as-]addition to-2P
Our heart is sounder than yours towards god. (pBerlin P. 15527 v° 14–15)

The examples show that the standard of comparison is usually overtly expressed. Occasionally, it may be left unexpressed, as in 150 below, where the understood comparison is between staying here and going somewhere else:

(150) In a letter to an oracle, the author wants to know whether it is better to go to the countryside to receive money for grain:

*gr* *in* *nꜣw-nfr-[s]* *ḫpr* *dy* *n-yb*
PTC IP ADJ-good-3FS happen here in-N
Or is it better to stay here in Elephantine? (pBerlin P. 15637+15803, x+6–7)

There are no specific morpho-syntactic means for marking degrees of a quality, which have to be understood from the context:

(151) Moral precepts state:

*šṯ̂* *ỉw-nꜣ-ꜥ(ꜣ)* *rꜣ-f* *nꜣ-ꜥšꜣ*
window DEP-ADJ-great mouth-3MS ADJ-many

*nꜣy-f-šhb-w* *r-nꜣy-f-qbb-w*
POSS.P-3MS-hot_wind than-POSS.P-3MS-cool-P
A window whose yawning is too big has its hot winds outnumbering its cool ones. (Onkhsheshonqy 20, 14)

In Coptic, the comparative could be expressed by a variety of prepositional phrases. Most dialects mark comparison of inequality by introducing the standard of comparison with *e-*, the direct descendent of the earlier *r*:

(152a) Shenute compares animal behaviour to the devil and his demons.
*homaios on un-ke-zôon šoop n-akatharton*
likewise again PTC-other-creature happen.STA of-unclean
*e-nanu-p-mui ero-f*
DEP-good-DEF.M-lion to-3MS
*p-côôre hn-ne-thêrion têr-u ebol-ce ntof-men*
DEF.M-strong in-DEF.P-animal all-3P because 3MS-indeed
*ša-f-r-hoten nn-rôme*
AOR-3MS-do-fear OBJ-DEF.P-man
There is also another filthy creature, in comparison to which the lion, the strongest of all wild animals, is better because he is afraid of people.
(SShenute, *Acephalous Work A1* [Young 153, 15–22])

(152b) The Ecclesiastes disputes the idea that a stillborn child is worse off than a living rich man who cannot enjoy the fruit of his labours:
*pei nae-f e-pei*
DEM.M.ABS great-3MS than-DEM.M.ABS
This is greater than that. (FEccl 6:5)

(152c) On the morrow after the queen made Agrippitos a Roman emperor, the devil appeared to him and offered him to do as he wishes:
*uoh kh-na-nau e-nê et-naa-u e-nai*
and 2MS-FUT-see OBJ-DEF$_3$.P REL-great-3P to-DEM.P
And you will see things greater than these.
(B*Mart. Theodore et al.* [*AM* I 38, 17])

Sometimes the Greek preposition *para* occurs:

(153a) Two notables trying to persuade Leontius to sacrifice according to the emperor's bid ask him:
*mê nanu-k pararo-n*
IP good-2MS more-1P
Are you better than us?
(S*Mart. Leontius the Arab* [von Lemm 11, a13–14])

(153b) Besa quotes utterances by monks jealous of other monks' food:

*ce-pai* *nanu-f* *ehue-pô-n*
COMP-DEM.M.ABS good-3MS more-POSS.M-1P
*ê* *ce-pa-pai* *nanu-f* *para-pa-pai*
or COMP-POSS.M-DEM.M.ABS good-3MS more-POSS.M-DEM.M.ABS
...saying: 'That is better than ours' or 'This one's is better than what belongs to me'. ($^S$Besa, *Reproofs and Monastic Rules*, X.3 [Kuhn 36, 35–36])

(153c) The Ecclesiastes stresses the benefits of being alive:

*[ce-p-uh]r* *et-anh* *nanu-f* *para-p-mui*
for-DEF.M-dog REL-live.STA good-3MS more-DEF.M-lion
*et-maut*
REL-die.STA
...for the living dog is better than the dead lion. ($^F$Eccl 9:4)

(153d) Basil praises his audience:

*ne-ten-sp$^h$otu-de* *on* *nai* *et-a-u-šôui*
POSS.P-2P-lips-yet again DEM.P REL-PST-3P-dry
*hiten-ti-met-at$^h$-uôm*
through-DEF$_2$F-ABST-un-eat
*nane-u* *nê-i* *emašô* *para-u-mêš* *e-u-lobi*
good-3P to-1S very more-IDF.S-multitude DEP-3P-mad.STA
*ḫen-pi-t$^h$iḫi* *nte-ni-êrp* *et$^h$-nêu* *ebol*
in-DEF$_2$.M-drunkenness of-DEF$_2$.M-wine REL-come.STA out
*ḫen-rô-u*
in-mouth-3P
Yet your lips, dried by fasting, are more beautiful to me than a multitude mad of drunkenness of wine that comes out of their mouth.
($^B$Basil of Caesarea, *On Noah's Ark* [De Vis II 207, 3–5])

The comparison may be stressed with the phrase *e-/n-huo e-* or $^F$*ehua(i)st e-* 'in excess to':

(154a) After making a quote, Shenute asks to whom and what it pertains and says:

*eišan-hast* *ê* *eršan-hast-e* *nto* *ere-šine*
CND.1S-trouble.1S or CND.2FS-trouble-2FS 2FS DEP.2FS-seek
*te-na-ime=an* *ebolce* *sop-men*
2FS-FUT-KNOW=NEG because time-indeed
*nanu-šine* *tar-n-k$^j$ine* *n-t-he* *et-sêh*
good-seek FIN-1P-find in-DEF.F-way REL-write.STA
*hen-sop-de* *on* *nanu-p-tm-šine* *n-huo* *e-šine*
IDF.P-time-yet again good-DEF.M-AUX.NEG-seek in-more to-seek

*ebolce* *eršan-p-rôme* *hast-f* *e-f-šine*
because CND-DEF.M-man trouble-3MS DEP-3MS-seek
*n-f-na-*$k^{j}$*ine=an*
NEG-3MS-find=NEG
*kata-t-he* *ent-a-p-ekklêsiastês* *coo-s*
like-DEF.M-way REL-PST-DEF.M-Ecclesiastes say-3FS
If I trouble myself or you trouble yourself seeking, you will not understand, because sometimes – as it is written – it is good to search so that we find and, at other times, it is better not to seek for the sake of seeking because – as the Ecclesiastes says – if man troubles himself with seeking, he will not find.
($^{S}$Shenute, *Is It Not Written* [A I 37, 12–38, 3])

(154b) The angel of the Lord tells Tobit and Tobias:
*nanu-p-kui* *et-aa-f* *hn-u-dikeiosunê*
good-DEF.M-small REL-do-3MS in-IDF.S-righteousness
*ehue-p-nok*$^{j}$ *et-aaf* *hn-u-ci-n-*$k^{j}$*ons*
more_than-DEF.M-great REL-do-3MS in-IDF.S-use-of-force
*nanu-s* *e-r-mnt-na* *n-huo* *e-seuh-nub* *ehun*
good-3FS to-do-ABST-mercy in-more than-gather-gold into
The small that is done in righteousness is better than the great that is done in violence. It is better to give alms than to gather gold.
($^{S}$Tb 12:8)

(154c) The proverbs state:
*nane-u-rôme* *e-f-e* *n-ḫmḫel* *ne-f* *uaheet-f*
good-IDF.S-man DEP-3MS-be.STA as-servant to-3MS alone-3MS
*e-f-ḫn-u-šos*
DEP-3MS-in-IDF.S-scorn
*nhuo* *a-p-et-ti-eau* *ne-f* *uaheet-f* *e-f-šaat*
more to-DEF.M-REL-give-glory to-3MS alone-3MS DEP-3MS-cut.STA
*m-p-aik*
OBJ-DEF.M-bread
A man despised but with a servant is better off than he who honours himself and lacks bread. ($^{A}$Prv 12:9)

(154d) The Ecclesiastes maintains that the life of man is brief and his death is certain:
*nanu-p-ehau* *m-pe-f-mu* *ehuast* *e-p-ehau*
good-DEF.M-day of-POSS.M-3MS-death more than-DEF.M-day
*nt-a-u-cpa-f*
REL-PST-3P-beget-3MS
The day of his death is better than the day he was born. ($^{F}$Eccl 7:2)

In Bohairic, the comparison of inequality can be marked via *e-hote*:

(155a) Dioscorus writes a letter to St Theodore who is in Egypt and tells him about the war with the Persians, adding:

| | | | |
|---|---|---|---|
| *nane-p-polemos* | *n-ni-persês* | *e-hote-p-polemos* | *n-k$^h$rof* |
| good-DEF.M-war | of-DEF$_2$.P-Persian | to-more-DEF.M-war | of-guile |
| *n-diokklêtianos*$^{sic}$ | | | |
| of-N | | | |

...the warfare of the Persians is better than the crafty warfare of Diocletian.
($^B$Theodore of Antioch, *On the Theodores* [*AM* II 130, 3–4])

(155b) Jesus advises everyone to pluck out an offending eye:

| | | | | |
|---|---|---|---|---|
| *nane-s* | *na-k* | *nte-k-i* | *eḫun* | *e-ti-met-uro* |
| good-3FS | for-2MS | CNJ-2MS-go | into | to-DEF$_2$.F-ABST-king |
| *nte-p$^h$-(nu)ti* | *e-u-bal* | *mmauat-f* | *et-ero-k* | |
| of-DEF.M-god | DEP-IDF.S-eye | alone-3MS | REL-for-2MS | |
| *e-hote* | *e-uon-bal* | *2* | *mmo-k* | *nse-hit-k* | *e-ti-geenna* |
| to-more | DEP-have-eye | 2 | OBJ-2MS | CNJ.3P-throw-2MS | to-DEF$_2$.F-hell |

It is better for you that you enter the kingdom of God having one eye only than having two eyes and being cast into Hell. ($^B$Mk 9:47)

Multiple compared entities can be coordinated with conjuncts:

(156) Shenute warns not to develop blasphemous thoughts from the biblical verse 'My father is greater than me' (Jh 14:28) as the heretics do when they claim:

| | | | |
|---|---|---|---|
| *pantôs* | *e-naa-f* | *hm-p-taio* | *mn-p-eou* |
| then | ST-great-3MS | in-DEF.M-honour | CON-DEF.M-glory |

Thus he is greater in honour and in glory.
($^S$Shenute, *I Am Amazed* §807 [Cristea 209, 1–3 (A)])

# 4 Negation

## 4.1 Earlier Egyptian

It has already been observed above that in Earlier Egyptian the negation of non-verbal sentences cannot be treated wholly independently of verbal negations. In adverbial sentences the negation *nn*, earlier *n*, is used for the negation of the predicative relation, and the same negations also occur in verbal sentences where they are used for the same function. In nominal sentences one finds either the negative element *n* or the negation *n... =ỉs*, perhaps depending on the scope of the negation. The former is employed when the predicative relation is definitely included within the scope of the negation and the latter when this is not the case or when the hearer is invited to draw a pragmatic inference that the target of the negation lies elsewhere. Yet in nominal and adverbial sentences, the formal relationship between the affirmative is symmetric: the affirmative and negative constructions display no structural differences except for the presence and absence of the negative expression. In adjectival sentences, this is not the case. Earlier Egyptian adjectival sentences are not negated directly: the negation of qualities assumes the form of a regular *n*- or *nn*-negated *verbal* sentence, where the adjectival quality concept lexeme appears either as part of the bound negation *n-sḏm-f* or as *sḏm-n-f* or, rarely, Stative verb form. As verbal constructions, these negations are also sensitive to tense distinctions and observe the normal rules of verbal negations in this respect. The construction *n sḏm-n-f* has present or aorist reference, sometimes with a dynamic modal overtone of ability:

(157a) The father of King Merikara remarks about wreaking havoc in times of war:

| | | | | | | |
|---|---|---|---|---|---|---|
| *ỉw* | *mr* | *wšš* | *ḫ-t* | *ḫrwy* | *n* | *qb{b}-n* |
| AUX | harmful | destroy.INF | thing-F | enemy | NEG | cool-PST |

| | |
|---|---|
| *ḫrwy* | *m-ẖnw-kmt* |
| enemy | in-inside-Egypt |

Destroying the property of the enemy is harmful, for (then) the enemy cannot remain calm in Egypt. (Merikara E, 68)

(157b) Ptahhetep advices against approaching married women in the houses of friends:

| | | | | | | |
|---|---|---|---|---|---|---|
| *n* | *nfr-n* | *bw* | *ỉrr-w=st* | *ỉm* | *n* | *spd-n* |
| NEG | good-PST | place | do.PIA-M=3C | there | NEG | sharp-PST |

| | |
|---|---|
| *ḥr* | *ḥr-pḫꜣ=st* |
| face | PROG-open.INF=3C |

A place where such is done is not good, and a mind (lit. 'face') penetrating them cannot be sharp. (Ptahhetep 282–83)

https://doi.org/10.1515/9783110409895-013

(157c) Satep-Yehu characterises a blessed dead:

| | | |
|---|---|---|
| *n* | *šw-n* | *drp-w-f* |
| NEG | empty-PST | oblation-P-3MS |

His oblations are not lacking. (*Urk.* IV 519, 11)

Ex. 158 below represents the negative equivalent of the possessive construction [adjective + dative + (overt or covert) subject], but here the subject is a subjunctive complement clause *dgꜣ-f* 'that he look'[44]:

(158) A paraphrase for expression 'he finds no way to look at his breast' in a medical text:

| | | | |
|---|---|---|---|
| *n* | *nḏm-n=n-f* | *dgꜣ-f* | *n-qꜣb-t-f* |
| NEG | sweet-PST=to-3MS | look-3MS | to-breast-F-3MS |

It is not pleasant for him to look at his breast. (pEdwin Smith 1, 26)

The negation *n-sḏm-f* has an invariably past sense:

(159a) The deceased states before one of the magistrates of the dead:

| | | |
|---|---|---|
| *i* | N | *n-dꜣdꜣ-i* |
| VOC | N | NEG-unchaste-1S |

O N, I have not been unchaste. (BD 125/*Nebseni* pl. 90, 44)

(159b) As above:

| | | | |
|---|---|---|---|
| *i* | N | *n-qꜣ* | *ḫrw-i* |
| VOC | N | NEG-high | voice-1S |

O N, my voice has not been high. (BD 125/*Nebseni* pl. 91, 61)

44 The following example would at first sight appear to represent a *n sḏm-n-f* negating the same construction:

(FNc) The snake ridicules the sailor's promise to send him luxury goods:

| | | | | |
|---|---|---|---|---|
| *n* | *wr=n-k* | *ꜥntw* | *ḫpr-t=nb* | *snṯr* |
| NEG | great=to-3MS | myrrh | form-F=QU | incense |

You do not have much myrrh or any (type) of incense. (Sh.S. 150)

Yet the writing *n wr n-k ꜥntw* without a second *n* (i.e. **n wr-n=n-k*) is problematic, since it cannot be analysed as a negation of a hypothetical adverbial sentence **iw=n-k ꜥntw wr* 'You have much myrrh', whose negation would acquire the form **nn=n-k ꜥntw wr* (with the negation *nn*; see Part I Section 4.1 above). This example has been thoroughly discussed by Scalf (2009, with a review of previous views). Following many previous commentators, Scalf reads the apparent negative *n* as the interrogative particle *(i)n* ('Do you have much myrrh?) but also understands the rest of the sentence as Stative *ḫpr-t(i) (m) nb ꜥntw* '[you] being a possessor of myrrh'. This, however, requires inserting a missing *m* of predication.

(159c) Harwerra says that he carried out his mining mission with exemplary zeal:

*n-bdš* *ḥr-i* *m-ḥꜣt-bꜣk*
NEG-weary face-1S in-front-work
I was not daunted by (lit. 'my face was not weary before') the task.
(Sinai 90, 15–16)

In ex. 160a below, the negation follows the relative operator *nt-* (see Section 2.4 above), whereas in 160b one finds *iwt-*, the negative counterpart of *nt-*[45]:

(160a) A note concerning the effects of the application of certain medications:

*snb-ḫr-f* *ḥr-ꜥ-wy* *mi-nt-y* *n-mr-f*
healthy-SEQ-3MS on-hand-DU like-REL-M NEG-ill-3MS
He (the patient) becomes healthy immediately, just like one who has not been ill. (pEbers 47, 17–18)

(160b) Ini characterises himself:

*mnḫ-ib* *iwt-y* *bꜣgg-f* *rs-tp* *ḥr-wnw-t-f*
strong-heart REL.NEG-M tire-3MS upright-head on-hour-F-3MS
One strong of heart who did not tire, but was vigilant in his moment.
(BM 334, vertical 3–5)

The negation *nn* + the subjunctive *sḏm-f* verb form has, as elsewhere, a future sense:

(161a) Ptahhetep says that his legacy will be enduring:

*nn* *šr* *ir-t-n-i* *tp-tꜣ*
NEG few.SUB do.REL-F-PST-1S upon-earth
What I have done upon earth will not decrease. (Ptahhetep 640)

(161b) An offering-bearer promises to the deceased User:

*nn* *šw-k* *ḥr-iꜥ-t* *ib-k*
NEG empty.SUB-2MS on-refreshment-F heart-2MS
*m-ḫnw-pr-k* *nfr*
in-inside-house-2MS good
You will not be devoid of your heart's refreshment in your beautiful house. (*Five Th. T.* pl. 26, left, 3–6)

45 Similar examples are BM 334, vertical 7; *Urk.* IV 410, 6; 959, 15 (all with *bgg-f*).

In Old Egyptian, where *n* and *nn* are not differentiated, *n* is also used with the Prospective *sḏm-f* associated with a recurrent future time-reference:

(162) The resurrected king is a star:

*n* *šw* *p-t* *m-N=pn* *n* *šw*
NEG empty.PROSP heaven-F from-N=DEM.M NEG empty.PROSP
*tꜣ* *m-N=pn* *ḏt*
land from-N=DEM.M forever
The sky will not be lacking of King N, nor will earth ever be lacking of King N. (PT 1455c/P)

The following example has sometimes been thought to be the only known instance of an adjectival sentence negated directly by *nn* (e.g. Allen 2000: 122):

(163) Hapdjefa stresses the permanent nature of his funerary foundation:

*mṯn* *nn* *šrr* *pꜣ-tꜣ* *ḥnq-t* *irr-w=n-i*
PTC NEG few DEM.M-bread beer-F do.REL-M=to-1S
*tꜣ-qnb-t* *n-t-ḥwtnṯr*
DEM.F-council-F of-F-temple
These bread and beer, which the council of the temple gives to me, will not decrease. (Siut I, 295)

Yet it is more likely that this example is an error for *nn šr pꜣ-t ḥnḳ-t* with a *nn sḏm-f* form 'This bread and beer will not decrease' (i.e. must not be pilfered by future temple administrators). However, there are some examples of qualities expressed by the construction [subject + Stative verb form] negated with *nn*:

(164) The father of king Merikara advises against violent purges:

*m=sqri* *nn=st* *ꜣḫ=n-k*
NEG.AUX.IMP=kill.NC NEG=3C useful.STA=to-2MS
Do not kill: it is not useful to you. (Merikara E, 48)

Symmetric negation of sentences with a Stative predicate is very rare. In negative contexts, the suffix conjugation construction *n sḏm-n-f* usually occurs. Since two of the approximately five known instances involve the lexeme *ꜣḫ* 'be beneficial', as in the example above,[46] the choice of negation here might have been lexically conditioned.

---

46 The other examples are Ptahhetep 291, *nn=st ꜣḫ m-irt* (NEG=3C useful.STA in-do.INF) 'It is not useful to do'; CT III 76g, *nn ir-t ḥr iw-t(i)* (NEG eye-F Horus be stranded-STA) 'The Eye of Horus is not stranded'; Man and Ba 126–27, *nn=sw wn* (NEG=3MS exist.STA) 'He does not exist'; *Urk.* IV 1109, 12, 'documents... *nty nn=st ḥbs* (REL NEG=3C cover.STA) which are not covered (=closed?)'.

The reason for the use of verbal rather than adjectival constructions in negation of qualities is not known.[47] Its semantic effect appears to be to a shift away from reversing the polarity of a quality predicated to denying it as an *occurrence* or a *process*. Overall, the phenomenon represents a peculiar anomaly in the general grammar of Earlier Egyptian, where grammaticalisation of TAM-features tends to be highest in prototypical or cognitively 'simpler' expressions, which in practise means affirmative active situations descriptions with canonical information structure (see Collier 1994: 76–77 and Uljas 2009a, where this phenomenon is labelled 'radiality'). In the case of adjectival predication, this principle does not seem to be observed; in fact, negative sentences such as those in the examples above actually carry *more* TAM-information than the affirmative adjectival sentences. However, something akin to this resisting of negation and reversal of polarity that is characteristic of qualities may be observable in nominal sentences as well. As seen earlier on (Part II Section 4.1), negation of these constructions by means of the negator *n* is rather exceptional and the standard negation here is the pattern *n...=is*. If the latter is truly a narrow-scope contrary negation that leaves the predicative relation affirmative, it again looks as if here too there had been some sort of reluctance to negate the latter. By contrast, in adverbial sentences, negation is always of the predicative sort. The three non-verbal constructions perhaps then form a scale in terms of whether the polarity of the predicative relation could be reversed. In adverbial sentences this was the sole option, whereas in nominal sentences this strategy was, perhaps, avoided, and in adjectival sentences it was not an option at all. Overall, it seems that the more the predicate had the characteristics of what has been termed 'time-stability' and the less it was susceptible to change (see Givón 2001 vol. 1: 50–52), the less reversible was the polarity of the predicative relation. Nevertheless, certain parts of the analysis (particularly the status of *n...=is*) are still debated. There is as yet no satisfactory explanation for the differences between the three non-verbal negative patterns or for the 'processual' treatment of qualities in the domain of negation in Earlier Egyptian.

## 4.2 Later Egyptian

Unlike in Earlier Egyptian, which displays no symmetric negation of adjectival sentences, in Late Egyptian, these constructions could be negated by *bn-* or *bn-...in*.

47 The argument that this might reflect an Egyptian 'cultural' aversion against negating an inherent quality (Malaise and Winand 1999: §510) should be considered with care.

Instances of these constructions are not particularly common. Below are examples with the negation *bn-* alone[48]:

(165a) The author of a letter castigates his addressee for failing to carry out an errand:

*bn-nfr* *p3y-i-ir-k*

NEG-good DEF.M-REL-do-2MS

What you have done is not good! (*LRL* 6, 7–8)

(165b) The divine Ennead gets into turmoil when discussing the question to whom an office should be given:

*iḫ* *n3-md-t* *i-ḏd-k* *nty-bn-š3w-sḏm=ṯ-w*

WH DEF.P-word-F REL-say-2MS REL-NEG-worth-listen=OBJ-3P

What are these words you uttered which are not worthy to be heard? (*LES* 42, 4–5)

(165c) An accused robber swears an oath:

*iw-bn-m3ʿ* *p3-ḏd-i=nb* *iw-i-di-k* *tp-ḫt*

DEP-NEG-true DEF.M-say.REL-1S=QU FUT-1S-give-STA upon-wood

If all I said is not true, I will be put upon a stake. (*KRI* VI 758, 16–759, 1)

(165d) A magical text threatens that the magician will enter a person's body as a fly and make his face turn to the back of his head and the toes to his back of feet. All counterspells will be ineffective:

*bn-3ḫ* *md-w-t-k* *bn-sḏm-ṯ-f*

NEG-beneficient word-P-F-2MS NEG-hear.FUT-PASS-3MS

Your speech will not be beneficient and it will not be heard. (oArmytage 8 [*JEA* 22])

However, since the subjects of all the examples above are nouns, it is impossible to decide whether they represent negated verb forms or negated predicative adjectives.

The discontinuous *bn…in* encloses the predicate part of the sentence. Sometimes, this allows the construction with noun subjects to be recognised as adjectival rather than verbal with the *sḏm-f*, since in the latter case, the element *in* should not intervene between the verb and its subject, i.e. the construction should appear as *bn-nfr-f in*:

48 The possible instance from the *Lament of Menna* (*HO* 79 edge l.1, see Davies 1973: 42) might actually be a case of *[is]-bn* seeing that there is a small break in front of the *bn*. This would seem to fit the semantics better than a negated sentence.

(166a) The author of a letter expresses his disapproval of the way in which the addressee has treated him:

*bn-nfr=ỉn* *pꜣ-ỉ-ỉr-k* *r-ỉ* *m-dwn* *spsn* *spsn*
NEG-good=NEG DEF.M-REL-do-2MS to-1S in-extend twice twice
What you have been doing against me is not good! (*KRI* VI 266, 8–9)

(166b) Horus accuses Seth of a false testimony before a divine tribunal and exclaims:

*bn-nfr=ỉn* *pꜣy-gbỉ-ṯ* *m-bꜣḥ-tꜣ-psḏ*
NEG-good=NEG DEM.M-weaken-1S in-presence-DEF.F-ennead.F
It is not good to defraud me in the presence of the Ennead.
(*LES* 42, 5–6)

(166c) The sage advises to live according to one's economic means[49]:

*bn-nfr=ỉn* *šm* *m-ḥr-f*
NEG-good=NEG go in-face-3MS
To rush in is not good. (Ani B 21, 11)

(166d) A high court-offical sent to examine issues in the royal necropolis asks the foreman of the gang of workmen to give a report about the state of the necropolis. He replies:

*bn-mtr=ỉn* *pꜣ-ḥry-šsqd* *ỉw-f-m*
NEG-correct=NEG DEF.M-overseer-draughtsman DEP-3MS
*pꜣ-ḫr*
in-DEF.M-tomb
*ḫr* *bn-mtr=ỉn* *tꜣ-dnỉ* *2* *ỉw-w* *mdỉ-f*
PTC NEG-correct=NEG DEF.F-register 2 DEP-3P with-3MS
The chief draughtsman, who is in the royal necropolis, is not correct, and the two registers, which are in his hands, are not correct.
(*KRI* VI 579, 14–16)

Examples with subject omission mostly show *bn…ỉn*,[50] although simple *bn* is attested as well (see ex. 167e):

(167a) In a court case a claimant reports to having bought a donkey, which he sent back because it was sick. He received another one:

*ḫr* *bn-nfr=ỉn*
PTC NEG-good-Ø=NEG
…but it was not good either. (*KRI* V 524, 8)

49 A textual variant to this example shows the Earlier Egyptian construction *n nfr-n*.

50 Again, these cannot be analysed as Statives, because in Late Egyptian, Statives appear only with overt subject in independent clauses (i.e. *bn sw nfr ỉn*).

(167b) The author of a letter tells his addressee that it is good to be considerate towards a god, who then will be considerate of him:
*bn-ꜣty=in*
NEG-angry=NEG
...without being angry. (*LRL* 32, 4–5)

(167c) Even after been interrogated with the help of a stick, a suspected tomb-robber denies his involvement in any crimes:
*m-ir-gꜣ(-i)* *bn-mꜣꜥ=in*
NEG.IMP-do-need[-1S] NEG-true=NEG
Do not torture me! It is not true. (*KRI* VI 792, 13)

(167d) The author of a letter reports that the chiefs of the granaries complained about the low quality of grain delivered by the letter's recipient. He went to examine the issue:
*iw-i* *ḥr-gmṯ-w* *iw-bn-nfr=in* *m-mꜣꜥ-t*
PTC-1S PRP-find.INF-3P DEP-NEG-good-ø=NEG in-truth
...and I found that it is not good at all. (*LEM* 94, 7)

(167e) The author mocks his addressee and tells him that although he might be a learned scribe with much knowledge, his previous letter was impossible to read and a waste of papyrus:
*bsy-k* *rḫ-ṯ* *ẖr-ḥꜣt* *rḏd-bn-nfr*
CFT-2MS know-STA under-heart COMP-NEG-good
If only you had known that its content is not good. ([2]*pAnastasi I* 69, 3)

It is impossible to decide whether the following example displays an isolated remnant of the Earlier Egyptian use of negated verb form:

(168) The author of a letter asks the addressee to take care of his father for the following reason:
*ṯ-k* *rḫ-ṯ* *rḏd-rmṯ* *iw-bn-ꜥꜣ-f* *mdi-f*
PTC-2MS know-STA COMP-man DEP-NEG-great-3MS with-3MS
*in*
NEG
You know that he is a man who lacks experience! (*LRL* 48, 16–49, 1)

Yet occasionally, the form cannot be anything but verbal as in the examples below: The third-person plural pronoun in ex. 169a below must be a suffix, whereas in exx.169b–d, the pattern used is clearly the Stative. However, ex. 169d is rather early, and albeit displaying some Late Egyptian features, its grammatical mould is still unmistakably Middle Egyptian:

(169a) The pupil is warned:

*m-dy-ḥꜣt-k* *n-ky* *nfr* *s* *ỉrr*
NEG.IMP-give-heart-2MS to-other good man act.PIA
*m-dy-ḥꜣt-k* *msꜣ-ꜣb-w* *wgꜣ* *bn-ꜣḫ-w*
NEG.IMP-give-heart-2MS after-dance-P weak NEG-beneficient-3P

Do not put your heart in others – the acting man is good! Do not set your heart into silly entertainments – they will not be beneficient!

(*LEM* 82, 7–8)

(169b) The author of a letter complains that an earlier correspondence from his addressee made no sense:

*[bn]-tptrꜣ-w-k* *bnr* *bn-st* *dḥr*
NEG-utterance-P-2MS sweet.STA NEG-3P bitter.STA

Your utterances are neither sweet nor bitter. (²*pAnastasi I* 57, 5)

(169c) King Haremhab remarks in a decree about a possible report of officials having confiscated the boat and cargo of a freeman working for the royal and priestly administration:

*bn-sw* *nfr-w* *pꜣy-smỉ* *sp* *gꜣb* *r-ỉqr*
NEG-3MS good-STA DEM.M-report case deprivation to-excellence

This report is not good. It is a case of extreme depravation.

(*Urk.* IV 2146, 1–2)

(169d) The god Amun assures that he will provide the Lady Neskhons with everything that befits her in the netherworld and states:

*ỉw-bn-sw* *šrỉ* *ỉn*
DEP-NEG-3MS small.STA NEG

...while it is not small. (Jansen-Winkeln, *IdS* I, 129, 10–11)

Clear negated examples of adjective verbs do not occur in Demotic. One may surmise that, as in Earlier Egyptian, suppletive patterns – e.g., a negated Stative as in ex. 170b – was used instead. However, there are instances in which adjective verbs are syntactically used like an infinitive:

(170a) Moral precepts claim:

*ỉỉr* *sḥm-t* *ḥtp* *(n)-pꜣy-s-hy* *bnỉr-w*
CND woman-F rest in-POSS.M-3FS-husband NEG.AOR-3P
*n-bn* *ꜥn* *spsn*
ADJ-bad NEG twice

When a woman lives in peace with her husband, they can never have it bad. (Onkhsheshonqy 25, 18)

(170b) A laconic note on a mummy label of a woman maltreated by her husband:

*bnỉw-ḥ3ṯ-s* *n3-nfr* *n-ḏr-ṯ-f* *ỉn*
NEG-heart-3FS ADJ-good.STA in-hand-F-3MS NEG
She was not happy with him. (Vleeming, *Short Texts* II, #909 v° 1–2)

The Coptic predicative adjective construction with *na-* is negated by using the discontinuous negation *n...an*. The initial element *n* becomes progressively more optional:

(171a) Shenute says that he is doing a favour to those whom he castigates of fornication:

*ene-našô-u=an* *nk*$^{j}$*i-n-et-na-r-bol* *n-t-he*
CFT-plenty-3P=NEG PVS-DEF.P-REL-FUT-do-out in-DEF.F-way
*n-n-ent-a-p-euaggelion* *tntôn-u* *e-pe-suo*
of-DEF.P-REL-PST-DEF.M-gospel liken-3P to-DEF.M-wheat
*et-u-na-souh-f* *ehun* *e-t-mnt-ero*
REL-3P-FUT-gather-3MS into to-DEF.F-ABST-king
*anti-apothêkê* *ne-u-šipe=an=pe*
instead-magazine PRT-IDF.S-shame=NEG=SE.M
*mn-u-nok*$^{j}$*nek*$^{j}$ *n-n-ete-n-se-na-r-bol*
CON-IDF.S-reproach for-DEF.P-REL-NEG-3P-FUT-do-out
*ero-s=an* *n-t-he* *n-n-e(n)t-a-f-tntôn-u*
OBJ-3FS=NEG in-DEF.F-way of-DEF.P-REL-PST-3MS-liken-3P
*e-p-tôh* *et-u-na-rokh-f* *hm-p-kôht*
to-DEF.M-chaff REL-3P-FUT-burn-3MS in-DEF.M-fire
*ete-me-f-ôšm*
REL-NEG.AOR-3MS-quench
If they were not so numerous, those who are going to elude as those whom the Gospel likened to the wheat that will be gathered into the kingdom instead into the store-house, then it would not be a shame and a reproach to those who are not going to elude it (i.e. the wrath) as those it likened to the chaff that will be burned in the fire that does not quench. ($^{S}$Shenute, *God Is Blessed* [Ch 173, 7–27])

(171b) Chastised for following an alleged Christian custom and raising his head when speaking to a superior, the saint answers to the hegemon:

*alla* *nanu-i=an* *n-t-he* *m-pe-khrêstianos*
but good-1S=NEG in-DEF.F-way of-DEF.M-Christian
But I am not a very good Christian.
($^{S}$*Mart. Ptolemy* [Till, *KHML* II 32, 30])

(171c) Jesus answers a woman who had asked him to heal her possessed daughter:

| | | |
|---|---|---|
| *n-nanu-ci-p-aik* | *n-n-šêre=en* | *e-te-f* |
| NEG-good-take-DEF.M-bread | of-DEF.P-child=NEG | to-give-3MS |
| *n-ne-uhar* | | |
| for-DEF.P-dog | | |

It is not good to take away the children's bread and give it to the dogs. ($^{M}$Mt 15:26)

(171d) After the first man was created, God said to himself:

| | | | | |
|---|---|---|---|---|
| *nanu-p-lômi=en* | *e-tre-b-k$^{j}$ôôt* | *uaeet-b* | | |
| good-DEF.M-man=NEG | to-INFL-3MS-persist | alone-3MS | | |
| *alla* | *male-n-tamia* | *n-u-bôithia* | *nê-f* | *katala-b* |
| but | JUSS-1P-create | OBJ-IDF.S-aid | for-3MS | according-3MS |

It is not good that man should persist alone – so let us create a helper for him in his likeness.
($^{F}$John Evangelist, *Investiture of Archangel Michael* [Müller 11, 3–4])

(171e) The apostle scolds the Christian community of Corinth:

*nane-pe-ten-šušu=an*
good-POSS.M-2P-glorify=NEG
Your glorifying is not good. ($^{B}$1Cor 5:6)

Similarly, in cases with an expletive pronoun followed by a clause, the negation *an* appears after the first prosodic unit:

(172a) Shenute reasons that if those who say things were bad and those who hide them were good, then there would be no bad person amongst them down to the man who speaks to the community:

| | | | |
|---|---|---|---|
| *ebolce-ešce* | *nanu-s=an* | *ce-f-cô* | *mmo-s* |
| because-CND | good-3SF=NEG | COMP-3MS-say | OBJ-3FS |

...because if it is not good that he says...
($^{S}$Shenute, *God Who Alone Is True* [A II 511, 2–3])

(172b) The proverbs state:

| | | |
|---|---|---|
| *nanu-tre-u-rôme=an* | *n-dikaios* | *ti-ose* |
| good-CAUS-IDF.S-man=NEG | of-righteous | give-loss |

It is not good that a righteous man is being punished. ($^{S}$Prv 17:26)

(172c) The Lord said after he had created Adam:

| | | | |
|---|---|---|---|
| *nane-s=an* | *e-t$^{h}$re-pi-rômi* | *šôpi* | *mmauat-f* |
| good-3FS=NEG | to-INFL-DEF$_{2}$.M-man | happen | alone-3MS |

It is not good that the man should be alone. ($^{B}$Gn 2:18)

# Bibliography

NB: Demotic examples derive from the electronic database Thesaurus Linguae Aegyptiae (TLA = http:// http://aaew.bbaw.de/tla/). All references to these texts are given merely as *see TLA sub Texte > Demotisch*.

All books of the Bible, including the Apocrypha, have been listed under Bible in the sequence of the LXX and the Coptic New Testament.


Acacius of Caesarea, *Encomium on St Mercurius* = Budge 1915.

*Acta Andreae* = Prieur 1989.

*Acta Pauli* = Schmidt 1905.

*Acts of Andrew and Paul* = Jacques 1969.

*Acts of Peter and Philip* = von Lemm 1890.

*Acts of Philip* = von Lemm 1890.

*Acts of the Synod of Ephesos* = Bouriant 1892.

pAdler 21 *see TLA sub Texte > Demotische Textdatenbank.*

Adrom, Faried. 2006. *Die Lehre des Amenemhet* (Bibliotheca Aegyptiaca 19). Turnhout: Brepols.

Agathonicus of Tarsus, *Apologies* & *De incredulitate* = Erichsen 1932.

Alexander of Alexandria, *In Petrum ep. Alexandriae* = Hyvernat 1886.

Allberry, Charles Robert Cecil. 1938. *A Manichean Psalm-Book Part II*, with a Contribution by Hugo Ibscher (Manichäische Handschriften der Sammlung A. Chester Beatty II). Stuttgart: Kohlhammer.

Allam, Shafik. 1973. *Hieratische Ostraka und Papyri aus der Ramessidenzeit* (Urkunden zum Rechtsleben im Alten Ägypten 1). Tübingen: Shafik Allam.

Allen, James P. 1986a. Features of nonverbal predicates in Old Egyptian. In Gertie Englund & Paul John Frandsen (eds.), *Crossroad. Chaos or the Beginning of a New Paradigm* (CNI Publications 1), 9–44. Copenhagen: Carsten Niebuhr Institute of Ancient Near East Studies.

Allen, James P. 1986b. Tense in Classical Egyptian. In William Kelly Simpson (ed.), *Essays on Egyptian Grammar* (Yale Egyptological Studies 1), 1–21. New Haven, CT: Yale Egyptological Seminar.

Allen, James P. 1994. Pronominal rhematization. In David Silverman (ed.), *For His Ka: Essays Offered in Memory of Klaus Baer* (Studies in Ancient Oriental Civilizations 55), 1–13. Chicago: Oriental Institute.

Allen, James P. 2000. *Middle Egyptian. An Introduction to the Language and Culture of Hieroglyphs*. Cambridge: Cambridge University Press.

Allen, James P. 2002. *The Heqanakht Papyri* (Publications of The Metropolitan Museum of Art 27). New York: The Metropolitan Museum of Art.

Allen, James P. 2013. *The Ancient Egyptian Language. An Historical Study*. Cambridge: Cambridge University Press.

Amazons *see TLA sub Texte > Demotisch.*

Amélineau, Emile. 1885. Voyage d'un moine égyptien dans le desert, in: *Recueil de Travaux relatifs a la Philologie et l'Archéologie égyptiennes et assyriennes* 6. 166–194.

Amélineau, Emile. 1888 & 1895. *Monuments pour servir à l'histoire de l'Égypte chrétienne aux IVe et Ve siècles* (Mémoires publiés par les membres de Mission archéologique française au Caire IV). Paris: Ernest Leroux.

Amélineau, Emile. 1889. Étude sur le Christianisme en Égypte au septième siècle. *Mémoires de l'Institut Égyptien* 2. 261–424 (also published separately with page-numbers 1–164).


https://doi.org/10.1515/9783110409895-014

Amélineau, Emile. 1894. *Histoire des Monastères de la Basse-Égypte. Vies des Saints Paul, Antoine, Macaire, Maxime et Domèce, Jean le Nain, &ª, Texte copte et traduction française.* (Annales du Musée Guimet 25). Paris: Ernest Leroux.

Amélineau, Emile. 1907 & 1914. *Œuvres des Schenoudi* I & II. *Texte copte et traduction française*, Paris: Ernest Leroux.

Amenemhat = Adrom 2006.

Amduat = Hornung 1987–92.

Amenemope = Laisney 2007.

Amphilochius of Iconium, *On Abraham* = Datema 1978.

[2]*pAnastasi I* = Fischer-Elfert 1992.

Andrews, Avery D. 2007. The major functions of the noun phrase. In Timothy Shopen (ed.), *Language Typology and Syntactic Description vol. I: Clause Structure*, 132–223. Cambridge: Cambridge University Press.

Ani = Quack 1994.

Anthes, Rudolf. 1928. *Die Felsinschriften von Hatnub* (Untersuchungen zur Geschichte und Altertumskunde Ägyptens 9). Leipzig: J.C. Hinrichs.

*AP* Chaîne = Chaîne 1960.

*AP* Elanskaya = Elanskaja 1994.

*AP Macarius* = Amélineau 1894.

*AP St Anthony* = Amélineau 1894.

*ApEl* = Steindorff 1899.

*Ap. Jas.* = Attridge 1985.

*ApPaul* = Budge 1915.

*ApSoph.* = Steindorff 1899.

*Apocr. Acts of the Apostles* = Hatch 1950 & Evelyn White 1926.

Aranda Perez, Gonzalo. 1984. *El evangelio de San Mateo en Copto Sahídico, Texto de M 569, estudio preliminar y aparato crítico* (Textos y estudios 'Cardenal Cisneros' 35). Madrid: Departamento de Filología Bíblica y de Oriente Antiguo.

Aranda Perez, Gonzalo. 1988. *El evangelio de San Marcos en Copto Sahídico, Texto de M 569 y aparato crítico* (Textos y estudios 'Cardenal Cisneros' 45). Madrid: Departamento de Filología Bíblica y de Oriente Antiguo.

Archelaos of Neapolis, *On Gabriel* = [B]de Vis 1929 & [S]Müller & Uljas in press.

*Archive of Hor see TLA sub Texte > Demotische Textdatenbank.*

oArmytage = Shorter 1936.

*ASAE* 39 = Rowe 1939.

*ASAE* 43 = Drioton 1943.

O.Ashm.Copt. = Biedenkopf-Ziehner 2000.

Assmann, Jan. 1974. Ägyptologie und Linguistik. *Göttinger Miszellen* 11. 59–76.

Athanasius of Alexandria, *De Anima et corpore* = Budge 1910.

Attridge, Harold W. (ed.). 1985. *Nag Hammadi Codex I (The Jung Codex). Introductions. Texts. Translations, Indices* (Nag Hammadi Series 22). Leiden: Brill.

Bachios of Maiuma, *On the Three Youth of Babylon* = Zanetti 2004.

Bacot, Seÿna. 1999. Une nouvelle «passion» copte fayoumique (Paris, BNF, Copte 163[1], f.1). *Le Muséon* 112, 301–315.

Bakir, 'Abd el-Moḥsen. 1970. *Egyptian Epistolography from the Eighteenth to the Twenty-first Dynasty* (Bibliothèque d'Étude 48). Cairo: Institut Français d'Archéologie Orientale.

Balestri, Giuseppe & Hyvernat, Henri 1907 & 1924. *Acta Martyrium* I & II (Corpus Scriptorum Christianorum Orientalium 43 & 86/Scriptores Coptici 3 & 6). Paris: Typographeo Reipublicae.
Barnes, John W. B. 1956. *Five Ramesseum Papyri*. Oxford: The Griffith Institute.
Basil of Caesarea, *On Noah's Ark* = De Vis 1929.
Basil of Pemje, *Homily on Longinus* = Depuydt 1994.
BD *Nu* = Lapp 1997.
BD *Tb* I & II = Naville 1886.
BD *Nebseni* = Lapp 2004.
Bell, Harold Idris. 1924. *Jews and Christians in Egypt. The Jewish Troubles in Alexandria and the Athanasian Controversy, Illustrated by Texts from Greek Papyri in the British Museum*, with Three Coptic Texts edited by Walter E. Crum. London: The British Museum.
*Beni Hasan* I = Newberry 1893.
Berlin 1157 = Generalverwaltung Museum Berlin 1913 & Roeder 1924.
Berlin 1199 = Generalverwaltung Museum Berlin & Roeder 1924.
Berlin 1204 = Generalverwaltung Museum Berlin 1913 & Roeder 1924.
Berlin 6768 = Grapow 1941.
Berlin 7317 = Generalverwaltung Museum Berlin 1913 & Roeder 1924.
Berlin Bowl = Gardiner & Sethe 1928.
Berlin Leather Roll = de Buck 1938.
oBerlin P. 1269 = unpublished.
oBerlin P. 12365 = unpublished.
pBerlin P. 3048 = Lüddeckens 1960.
pBerlin P. 3080 *see TLA sub Texte > Demotische Textdatenbank.*
pBerlin P. 3093 *see TLA sub Texte > Demotische Textdatenbank.*
pBerlin P. 3109 *see TLA sub Texte > Demotische Textdatenbank.*
pBerlin P. 8869 = Smither 1942.
pBerlin P. 9010 = Sethe 1926.
pBerlin P. 10012 = Sethe 1928: 96–97.
pBerlin P. 10016 = Luft 2006.
pBerlin P. 10030A = Luft 2006.
pBerlin P. 10033 = Luft 1992.
pBerlin P. 10074 = Luft 1992.
pBerlin P. 10081B = Luft 2006.
pBerlin P. 10470 = Smither 1948.
pBerlin P. 10497 = Sabek 2002.
pBerlin P. 13537 *see TLA sub Texte > Demotische Textdatenbank.*
pBerlin P. 13538 *see TLA sub Texte > Demotische Textdatenbank.*
pBerlin P. 13540 *see TLA sub Texte > Demotische Textdatenbank.*
pBerlin P. 13544 *see TLA sub Texte > Demotische Textdatenbank.*
pBerlin P. 13548 *see TLA sub Texte > Demotische Textdatenbank.*
pBerlin P. 13549 *see TLA sub Texte > Demotische Textdatenbank.*
pBerlin P. 13563 *see TLA sub Texte > Demotische Textdatenbank.*
pBerlin P. 13579 *see TLA sub Texte > Demotische Textdatenbank.*
pBerlin P. 13585 *see TLA sub Texte > Demotische Textdatenbank.*
pBerlin P. 13633 *see TLA sub Texte > Demotische Textdatenbank.*
pBerlin P. 13637 *see TLA sub Texte > Demotische Textdatenbank.*

pBerlin P. 15521 *see TLA sub Texte > Demotische Textdatenbank.*

pBerlin P. 15527 *see TLA sub Texte > Demotische Textdatenbank.*

pBerlin P. 15530 *see TLA sub Texte > Demotische Textdatenbank.*

pBerlin P. 15617 *see TLA sub Texte > Demotische Textdatenbank.*

pBerlin P. 15637 + 15803 *see TLA sub Texte > Demotische Textdatenbank.*

pBerlin P. 23629 unpublished, sequence quoted after Depauw 2006, 200.

pBerlin P. 23757A = Lippert 2004.

pBerlin med. = Grapow 1958.

Besa = Kuhn 1956.

Bhat, Darbhe Naravana Shankara. 1994. The *Adjectival Category: Criteria for Differentiation and Identification* (Studies in Language Companion Series 24). Amsterdam/Philadelphia: Benjamins.

The Bible

Gn = $^{B}$de Lagarde 1867 & Kasser 1958; $^{S}$Ciasca 1885 & Maspero 1892.

Ex = $^{A}$Lacau 1911; $^{B}$de Lagarde 1867; $^{S}$Ciasca 1885, Maspero 1892 & Kasser 1961.

Lev = $^{B}$de Lagarde 1867; $^{S}$Ciasca 1885 & Maspero 1892.

Nm = $^{B}$de Lagarde 1867; $^{S}$Ciasca 1885 & Maspero 1892.

Dt = $^{B}$de Lagarde 1867; $^{S}$Ciasca 1885, Maspero 1892 & Kasser 1962a.

Jo = $^{S}$Thompson 1911; Kasser 1962b & Shorter 1963.

Jdg = $^{S}$Thompson 1911.

Ru = $^{S}$Thompson 1911.

1Kg = $^{S}$Drescher 1970.

2Kg = $^{S}$Drescher 1970.

3Kg = $^{S}$Ciasca 1885 & Maspero 1892.

1Chr = $^{B}$de Lagarde 1879.

2Chr = $^{B}$de Lagarde 1879.

Jdt = $^{S}$Thompson 1911.

Tob = $^{S}$Ciasca 1885 & Maspero 1892.

Job = $^{B}$Porcher 1924.

Ps = $^{B}$Burmester & Dévaud 1925; $^{M}$Gabra 1995; $^{S}$Budge 1899.

Prv = $^{A}$Böhlig 1958; $^{B}$Burmester & Dévaud 1930; $^{P}$Kasser 1960; $^{S}$Worrell 1931.

Eccl = $^{F}$Diebner & Kasser 1989 & Schenke 2003; $^{S}$de Lagarde 1880 & Ciasca 1889.

Sg = $^{F}$Diebner & Kasser 1989.

Sap = $^{S}$de Lagarde 1880.

Sir = $^{S}$de Lagarde 1880.

Is = $^{B}$Tattam 1852; $^{F}$Chassinat 1902 & Zoega 1810; $^{S}$Ciasca 1889.

Ier = $^{B}$Tattam 1852; $^{S}$Feder 2002.

Lam = $^{B}$Tattam 1852; $^{F}$Diebner & Kasser 1989; $^{S}$Feder 2002.

Bar = $^{S}$Feder 2002; $^{B}$Brugsch & Kabis 1872–74.

EpJer = $^{F}$Diebner & Kasser 1989; $^{S}$Feder 2002.

Ez = $^{B}$Tattam 1852; $^{S}$Ciasca 1889.

Jl = $^{A}$Malinine 1950 & Till 1927; $^{A}$Malinine 1950 & Till 1927; $^{B}$Tattam 1836.

Hos = $^{A}$Malinine 1950 & Till 1927; $^{B}$Tattam 1836.

Am = $^{A}$Malinine 1950 & Till 1927; $^{B}$Tattam 1836.

Jon = $^{A}$Malinine 1950 & Till 1927; $^{B}$Tattam 1836.

Mi = $^{A}$Malinine 1950 & Till 1927; $^{B}$Tattam 1836.

Na = $^{A}$Malinine 1950 & Till 1927; $^{B}$Tattam 1836.

Hab = ᴬMalinine 1950 & Till 1927; ᴮTattam 1836.
Zec = ᴬMalinine 1950 & Till 1927; ᴮTattam 1836.
Mal = ᴬMalinine 1950 & Till 1927; ᴮTattam 1836.
Mt = ᴮHorner 1898–1905; ᶠChassinat 1902 & Zoega 1810; ᴹSchenke 1981; 2001; ˢAranda Perez 1984.
Mk = ᴮHorner 1898–1905; ᶠChassinat 1902 & Zoega 1810; ˢQuecke 1972.
Lk = ᴮHorner 1898–1905; ˢQuecke 1977.
Jn = ᴮHorner 1898–1905 & Kasser 1958; ˢQuecke 1984.
Acts = ᴮHorner 1898–1905; ᶠKahle 1956: I 288; ᴹSchenke 1981; ˢThompson 1932.
Rm = ᴮHorner 1898–1905; ᶠWessely 1908; ˢThompson 1932.
1Cor = ᴮHorner 1898–1905; ᶠZoega 1810; ˢThompson 1932.
2Cor = ᴮHorner 1898–1905; ᶠWessely 1908; ˢThompson 1932.
Gal = ᴮHorner 1898–1905; ˢThompson 1932.
Eph = ᴮHorner 1898–1905; ᶠZoega 1810; ˢThompson 1932.
1Ti = ᴮHorner 1898–1905; ˢThompson 1932.
2Ti = ᴮHorner 1898–1905; ˢThompson 1932.
Ti = ᴮHorner 1898–1905; ˢThompson 1932.
Heb = ᴮHorner 1898–1905; ᶠWessely 1908; & Zoega 1810; ˢThompson 1932.
Col = ᴮHorner 1898–1905; ˢThompson 1932.
1Th = ᴮHorner 1898–1905; ˢThompson 1932.
1Jn = ᴮHorner 1898–1905; ᶠSchenke 2003; ˢSchüssler 1991.
Rev = ˢHorner 1924; ᴮHorner 1898–1905.

Biedenkopf-Ziehner, Anneliese. 1983. *Untersuchungen zum koptischen Briefformular unter Berücksichtigung ägyptischer und griechischer Parallelen*. Würzburg: Gisela Zauzich.

Biedenkopf-Ziehner, Anneliese. 2000. *Koptische Ostraka II: Ostraka aus dem Ashmolean Museum in Oxford*, Wiesbaden: Harrassowitz.

Blackman, Aylward M. 1915. *The Rock Tombs of Meir* III: *The Tomb-Chapel of Ukh-Ḥotp and Mersi (B, No. 4)* (Archaeological Survey of Egypt 24). London: Egypt Exploration Fund.

Blackman, Aylward. 1931. The Stela of Thethi, Brit. Mus. No. 614. *The Journal of Egyptian Archaeology* 17, 55–61.

Blackman, Aylward. 1933. *Middle Egyptian Stories* (Bibliotheca Aegyptiaca 3). Brussels: Fondation Égyptologique Reine Élisabeth.

Blackman, Aylward M. 1988. *The Story of King Kheops and the Magicians transcribed from Papyrus Westcar (Berlin Papyrus 3033)*. Reading: J. V. Books.

BM EA 101 = Budge 1912a.
BM EA 152 = Budge 1912a.
BM EA 159 = Faulkner 1951.
BM EA 334 = Budge 1912b.
BM EA 572 = Budge 1912a.
BM EA 574 = Budge 1912a.
BM EA 581 = Budge 1912a.
BM EA 614 = Blackman 1931.
BM EA 1671 = Polotsky 1930.
BM EA 23186 *see TLA sub Texte > Demotische Textdatenbank.*
BM EA 35464 *see TLA sub Texte > Demotische Textdatenbank.*
oBM EA 5627 = Demarée 2002.
oBM EA 50627 *see TLA sub Texte > Demotische Textdatenbank.*

pBM EA 10102 = Glanville 1928.
pBM EA 10373 = Janssen 1991.
pBM EA 10416 = Janssen 1991.
pBM EA 10520 *see TLA sub Texte > Demotische Textdatenbank.*
pBM EA 10522 *see TLA sub Texte > Demotische Textdatenbank.*
pBM EA 10524 *see TLA sub Texte > Demotische Textdatenbank.*
pBM EA 10591 *see TLA sub Texte > Demotische Textdatenbank.*
pBM EA 10599 *see TLA sub Texte > Demotische Textdatenbank.*
pBM EA 10622 *see TLA sub Texte > Demotische Textdatenbank.*
pBM EA 69532 *see TLA sub Texte > Demotische Textdatenbank.*
pBM EA 69574 = Quack 1999.
pBM EA 73785 *see TLA sub Texte > Demotische Textdatenbank.*
pBM EA 73786 *see TLA sub Texte > Demotische Textdatenbank.*
pBM EA 75015 = Demarée 2006.
pBM EA 75016 = Demarée 2006.
pBM EA 75019 + 10302 = Demarée 2006.
pBM EA 75021 = Demarée 2006.
pBN 149 *see TLA sub Texte > Demotische Textdatenbank.*
pBN 215 *see TLA sub Texte > Demotische Textdatenbank.*
pBN 223 *see TLA sub Texte > Demotische Textdatenbank.*
pBN 226a + pLouvre N 2412 *see TLA sub Texte > Demotische Textdatenbank.*
Böhlig, Alexander. 1958. *Der achmimische Proverbientext nach Ms.Berol.orient.oct. 987* I: *Text und Rekonstruktion der sahidischen Vorlage* (Studien zur Erforschung des christlichen Ägyptens 3). München: Robert Lerche.
Boeser, Pieter Adriaan. 1909. *Beschreibung der Aegyptischen Sammlung des Niederländischen Reichsmuseums der Altertümer in Leiden. Die Denkmäler der Zeit zwischen dem Alten und Mittleren Reich und des Mittleren Reiches I: Stelen.* The Hague: Martinus Nijhoff.
pBologna 3173 *see TLA sub Texte > Demotische Textdatenbank.*
Bombeck, Stefan. 2001. Pseudo-Kyrillos *In Mariam virginem.* Text und Übersetzung von Pierpont Morgan M 597 fols. 46–74. *Orientalia* nova series 70. 40–88.
*Book of Resurrection of Christ* = Westerhoff 1999.
*Book of Thoth* = Jasnow & Zauzich 2005.
Borghouts, Joris F. 1972. A special use of the emphatic *sḏm.f* form in Late Egyptian. *Bibliotheca Orientalis* 29. 271–276.
Borghouts, Joris F. 1986. Prominence constructions and pragmatic functions. In Gertie Englund & Paul John Frandsen (eds.), *Crossroad. Chaos or the Beginning of a New Paradigm* (CNI Publications 1), 45–70. Copenhagen: Carsten Niebuhr Institute of Ancient Near East Studies.
Borghouts, Joris F. 1994. *jnk mr(i) = f*: an elusive pattern in Middle Egyptian. *Lingua Aegyptia* 4. 13–34.
Borghouts, Joris F. 2010. *Egyptian. An Introduction to the Writing and Language of the Middle Kingdom* I. *Grammar, Syntax and Indexes* (Egyptologische Uitgaven 24.1). Leuven: Peeters/Leiden: NINO.
Borsley, Robert D. 1996. *Modern Phrase Structure Grammar* (Blackwell Textbooks in Linguistics 11). Oxford: Blackwell.
Bosticco, Serge. 1959. *Museo Archeologico di Firenze. Le stele egiziane dall'Antico al Nuovo Regno.* Rome: Istituto Poligrafico dello Stato.

Boud'hors, Anne. 2013. *Le Canon 8 de Chénouté d'aprés le manuscript IFAO copte 2 et les fragments complémentaires* (Bibliothèque d' Études Coptes 21). Cairo: Institut Français d'Archéologie Orientale.
Boud'hors, Anne & Chantal Heurtel. 2010. *Les ostraca coptes de la TT 29. Autour du moine Frangé* (Études d'Archéologie Thébaine 3). Brussels: CreA Patrimoine.
pBoulaq 18 = Scharff 1922.
*Boundary Stelae* = Murnane & van Siclen 1993.
Bouriant, Urbain. 1892. *Actes du Concile d'Éphèse. Texte copte* (Mémoires publiés par les membres de Mission archéologique française du Caire). Paris: Ernest Leroux.
Bresciani, *Archivio see TLA sub Texte > Demotische Textdatenbank.*
pBresciani 33 *see TLA sub Texte > Demotische Textdatenbank.*
Brooklyn 16.645 *see TLA sub Texte > Demotische Textdatenbank.*
oBrooklyn 37.1821E *see TLA sub Texte > Demotische Textdatenbank.*
pBrooklyn 37.1781 *see TLA sub Texte > Demotische Textdatenbank.*
pBrooklyn 37.1839A *see TLA sub Texte > Demotische Textdatenbank.*
Brugsch, Heinrich & Mark Kabis. 1872–74. Das Buch Baruch. *Zeitschrift für Ägyptische Sprache und Altertumskunde* 10. 134–136; 11. 18–21 & 12. 46–49.
de Buck, Adriaan. 1935–61. *The Egyptian Coffin Texts* I–VII (Oriental Institute Publications 34, 49, 64, 67, 73, 81 & 87). Chicago: Oriental Institute Press.
De Buck, Adriaan. 1938. The building inscription of the Berlin Leather Roll. *Studia Aegyptiaca* I (Analecta Orientalia 17), 48–57. Rome: Pontificium Institutum Biblicum.
Budge, Ernest Alfred Wallis. 1888. *The Martyrdom and Miracles of Saint George of Cappadocia* (Oriental Text Series I). London: Nutt.
Budge, Ernest Alfred Wallis. 1894. *Saint Michael The Archangel: Three Encomiums by Theodosius, Archbishop of Alexandria, Severus, Patriarch of Antioch, and Eustathius, Bishop of Trake.* London: Kegan Paul, Trench, Trübner & Co.
Budge, Ernest Alfred Wallis. 1899. *The Earliest Known Coptic Psalter. The Text, in the Dialect of Upper Egypt, edited from the Unique Papyrus Codex Oriental 5000 in the British Museum.* London: Kegan Paul, Trench, Trübner & Co.
Budge, Ernest Alfred Wallis. 1910. *Coptic Homilies in the Dialect of Upper Egypt edited from the Papyrus Codex Oriental 5001 in the British Museum* (Coptic Texts I). London: The British Museum.
Budge, Ernest Alfred Wallis. 1912. *Coptic Biblical Texts in the Dialect of Upper Egypt* (Coptic Texts II). London: The British Museum.
Budge, Ernest Alfred Wallis. 1912a. *Hieroglyphic Texts from the Egyptian Stelae &c., in the British Museum Part II.* London: British Museum.
Budge, Ernest Alfred Wallis. 1912b. *Hieroglyphic Texts from the Egyptian Stelae &c., in the British Museum Part III.* London: British Museum.
Budge, Ernest Alfred Wallis. 1913. *Coptic Apocrypha in the Dialect of Upper Egypt* (Coptic Texts III). London: The British Museum.
Budge, Ernest Alfred Wallis. 1914. *Coptic Martyrdoms etc. in the Dialect of Upper Egypt* (Coptic Texts IV). London: The British Museum.
Budge, Ernest Alfred Wallis. 1915. *Miscellaneous Coptic in the Dialect of Upper Egypt* (Coptic Texts V). London: The British Museum.
Burmester, Oswald H. E. 1932. The Homilies or Exhortations of the Holy Week Lectionary. *Le Muséon* 45. 21–70.

Burmester, Oswald H. E. & Eugène Dévaud. 1925. *Psalterii versio memphitica e recognitione Pauli de Lagarde. Réédition avec le texte copte en caractères coptes*, Louvain: J. B. Istas.
Burmester, Oswald H. E. & Eugène Dévaud. 1930. *Les proverbes de Salomon (Ch. 1, v. 1–14, v. 26*, Ch. 24, v. 24–v.29 et v. 50*–v. 77 et Ch. 29, v. 28–v. 38). Texte bohairique du Cod. 8 de la Rylands Library, Manchester, du Cod. 53 et 98 de la Bibliothèque Vaticane et du Cod. 1051 du Musée Copte au Caire avec les variantes de 24 autres manuscrits et index des mots coptes et des mots grecs*, Vienna: Successors A. Holzhausen.
Butt, John & Carmen Benjamin. 2000. *A New Reference Grammar of Modern Spanish*. 3rd ed. London: Arnold.
Cairo Bowl = Gardiner & Sethe 1928.
Cairo JE 49566 = Černý 1969.
Cairo JE 95206 *see TLA sub Texte > Demotische Textdatenbank.*
Cairo Linen = Gardiner & Sethe 1928.
Callender, John. 1984. *Studies in the Nominal Sentence in Egyptian and Coptic* (Near Eastern Studies 24). Berkeley/Los Angeles/London: University of California Press.
Caminos, Ricardo A. 1954. *Late Egyptian Miscellanies* (Brown Egyptological Studies 1). London: Oxford University Press.
Caminos, Ricardo A. 1956. *Literary Fragments in the Hieratic Script.* Oxford: The Griffith Institute.
Caminos, Ricardo A. 1977. *A Tale of Woe, from a Hieratic Papyrus in the A. S. Pushkin Museum of Fine Arts in Moscow.* Oxford: The Griffith Institute & The Ashmolean Museum.
Campagnano, Antonella. 1980. *Ps. Cirillo di Gerusalemme: Omelie copte sulla passione, sulla croce e sulla vergine* (Testi e documenti per lo studio dell'antichità 65). Milano: Istituto Editoriale Cisalpino – La Goliardica.
*Can. Eccl.* = de Lagarde, *Aeg.*
*Canons of Athanasius* = *ASAE* 19, 239.
Canopus Decree A *see TLA sub Texte > Demotische Textdatenbank.*
Canopus Decree B *see TLA sub Texte > Demotische Textdatenbank.*
pCarlsberg 159 + PSI inv. D 10 v° = Ryholt 2012: 1–21.
pCarlsberg 429 *see TLA sub Texte > Demotische Textdatenbank.*
Carnarvon Tablet = Gardiner 1916.
Cassonet, Patricia. 2000. *Études de Néo-Égyptien : Les Temps Seconds i-sḏm.f et i-iri.f sḏm. Entre syntaxe et sémantique* (Études et Mémoires d'Égyptologie 12). Paris: Cybèle.
*Catenae* = De Lagarde 1886.
CG 8631 = Crum 1902b.
CG 20001 = Lange & Schäfer 1902.
CG 20057 = Lange & Schäfer 1902.
CG 20538 = Lange & Schäfer 1909.
CG 20539 = Lange & Schäfer 1909.
CG 20543 = Lange & Schäfer 1909.
CG 20567 = Lange & Schäfer 1909.
CG 25206 = Daressy 1902.
CG 25725 = Černý 1935.
CG 34057 = Lacau 1909.
CG 42210 = Legrain 1914.
pCG 30605 *see TLA sub Texte > Demotische Textdatenbank.*
pCG 30692 *see TLA sub Texte > Demotische Textdatenbank.*

pCG 50058 *see TLA sub Texte > Demotische Textdatenbank.*

pCG 50066 *see TLA sub Texte > Demotische Textdatenbank.*

pCG 50067 + 50087 *see TLA sub Texte > Demotische Textdatenbank.*

pCG 58060 = Bakir 1970.

Černý, Jaroslav. 1935. *Ostraca Hiératiques: N^os 25501–25832* (Catalogue général des antiquités égyptiennes du Musée du Caire). Cairo: Institut Français d'Archéologie Orientale.

Černý, Jaroslav. 1939. *Late Ramesside Letters* (Bibliotheca Aegyptiaca 9). Brussels: Fondation égyptologique Reine Élisabeth.

Černý, Jaroslav. 1942. Nouvelle série de questions adressées aux oracles. *Bulletin de l'Institut Français d'Archéologie Orientale* 41. 13–24 & pl. I–III.

Černý, Jaroslav. 1951. *Catalogue des Ostraca Hiératiques Non Littéraires de Deîr el-Médînéh* V: *N^os 340 à 456* (Documents de Fouilles de l'Institut Français d'Archéologie Orientale 7). Cairo: Institut Français d'Archéologie Orientale.

Černý, Jaroslav. 1969 The stela of Emhab. *Mitteilungen des Deutschen Archäologischen Instituts Kairo* 24. 87–92.

Černý, Jaroslav. 1970. *Catalogue des Ostraca Hiératiques non littéraires de Deîr el-Médînéh* VII: *N^os 624–705* (Documents de Fouilles de l'Institut Français d'Archéologie Orientale 14). Cairo: Institut Français d'Archéologie Orientale.

Černý, Jaroslav. 1972. Troisième série de questions adressées aux oracles. *Bulletin de l'Institut Français d'Archéologie Orientale* 72. 49–69 & pl. XV–XXV.

Černý, Jaroslav. 1978. *Papyrus Hiératiques de Deîr el-Médînéh* I: *N^os 1–17*, catalogue complété et éd. par Georges Posener (Documents de Fouilles de l'Institut Français d'Archéologie Orientale 8). Cairo: Institut Français d'Archéologie Orientale.

Černý, Jaroslav & Alan Henderson Gardiner. 1957. *Hieratic Ostraca* I. Oxford: Griffith Institute.

Černý, Jaroslav & Sarah Israelit Groll. 1993. *A Late Egyptian Grammar*, assisted by C. Eyre (Studia Pohl: Series Major 4). Rome: Pontificio Istituto Biblico.

Chafe, Wallace. 1976. Givenness, contrastiveness, definiteness, subjects, topics, and point of view. In Charles N. Li (ed.), *Subject and Topic*, 25–56. New York: Academic Press.

Chaîne, Marius. 1912 & 1913. Une homélie de Saint Gregoire de Nysse traduite en copte attribuée à Saint Gregoire de Nazianze. *Revue de l'Orient Chrétien* 17. 395–409 & 18. 36–41.

Chaîne, Marius. 1933. *Éléments de grammaire dialectale copte : Bohairique, Sahidique, Achmimique, Fayoumique.* Paris: Geuthner.

Chaîne, Marius. 1948. *La vie et les miracles de Saint Syméon stylite l'ancien.* (Bibliothèque d'Études Coptes III). Cairo: Institut Français d'Archéologie Orientale.

Chaîne, Marius. 1960. *Le manuscrit de la version copte en dialecte sahidique des 'Apophthegmata Patrum'.* (Bibliothèque d'Études Coptes VI). Cairo: Institut Français d'Archéologie Orientale.

Chassinat, Émile. 1902. Fragments des manuscrits coptes en dialecte fayoumique. *Bulletin de l'Institut Français d'Archéologie Orientale* 2. 171–206.

Chassinat, Émile. 1911. *Le quatrième livre des entretiens et épîtres de Shenouti.* (Mémoires publiés par les membres de l'Institut français d'archéologie orientale du Caire 23). Cairo: Institut Français d'Archéologie Orientale.

Chauveau, Michel. 1990. Glorification d'une morte anonyme (P. dém. Louvre N 2450 c). *RdÉ* 41. 3–8.

pChester Beatty III = Gardiner 1935.

oChicago OIM 19422 *see TLA sub Texte > Demotische Textdatenbank.*

pChicago OI 25256 *see TLA sub Texte > Demotische Textdatenbank.*

pChicago OI 25388 *see TLA sub Texte > Demotische Textdatenbank.*

Ciasca, Augustino 1885 & 1889. *Sacrorum Bibliorum Fragmenta Copto-Sahidica Musei Borgiani iussu et sumptibus S. Congregationias de Propaganda Fide* I & II, Rome: S. Congregatio de Propaganda Fide.
Cod. Herm. *see TLA sub Texte > Demotische Textdatenbank.*
Collier, Mark. 1990. The circumstantial *sḏm(.f)/sḏm.n(.f)* as verbal verb-forms in Middle Egyptian. *The Journal of Egyptian Archaeology* 76. 73–85.
Collier, Mark. 1991a. Constructions with *ḫꜣ* revisited. *Göttinger Miszellen* 120. 13–32.
Collier, Mark. 1991b. The relative clause and the verb in Middle Egyptian. *The Journal of Egyptian Archaeology* 77. 23–42.
Collier, Mark. 1991c. 'Circumstantially adverbial'? The circumstantial *sḏm(=f)/sḏm.n(=f)* reconsidered. In Stephen Quirke (ed.), *Middle Kingdom Studies*, 21–50. New Malden: SIA Publishing.
Collier, Mark. 1996. The language of literature: on grammar and texture. In Antonio Loprieno (ed.), *Ancient Egyptian Literature. History and Forms* (Probleme der Ägyptologie 10), 531–553. Leiden: Brill.
Collier, Mark. 1999. Of verbs and times past. In Anthony Leahy & John Tait (eds.), *Studies on Ancient Egypt in Honour of Harry S. Smith* (EES Occasional Publications), 49–58. London: Egypt Exploration Society.
Collier, Mark. 2005. Reading *ir wnn* conditionals in the Heqanakhte documents. *Lingua Aegyptia* 13. 1–29.
Collier, Mark. 2007 Facts, situations and knowledge acquisition: *gmi* with *iw* and *r-ḏd* in Late Egyptian. In Thomas Schneider & Kasia Szpakowska (eds.), *Egyptian Stories. A British Egyptological Tribute to Alan B. Lloyd on the Occasion of His Retirement* (Alter Orient und Altes Testament 347), 33–46. Münster: Ugarit Verlag.
Collier, Mark. 2014. Antiphrastic Questions with *ist* and *is* in Late Egyptian. In Eitan Grossmann, Stéphane Polis, Andréas Stauder & Jean Winand (eds.), *On Forms and Functions: Studies in Ancient Egyptian Grammar* (Lingua Aegyptia Studia Monographica 15), 7–40. Hamburg: Widmaier Verlag.
Collier, Mark. 2016. Alternatives and the grammar of Earlier Egyptian: negations with low-end indefinites and negation with *n…is*. In James P. Allen, Mark A. Collier & Andréas Stauder (eds.), *Coping with Obscurity. The Brown Workshop on Earlier Egyptian Grammar* (Wilbour Studies in Egyptology and Assyriology 3), 151–168. Atlanta: Lockwood Press.
Collier, Mark & Stephen Quirke. 2002. *The UCL Lahun Papyri: Letters* (BAR International Series 1083). Oxford: Archeopress.
Collier, Mark & Stephen Quirke. 2004. *The UCL Lahun Papyri: Religious, Literary, Legal, Mathematical and Medical* (BAR International Series 1209). Oxford: Archeopress.
Collins, Peter C. 1991. *Cleft and Pseudo-Cleft Constructions in English* (Theoretical Linguistics Series). London/New York: Routledge.
Comrie, Bernard. 1976. *Aspect* (Cambridge Textbooks in Linguistics). Cambridge: Cambridge University Press.
Condon, Virginia. 1978. *Seven Royal Hymns of the Ramesside Period: Papyrus Turin CG 54031* (Münchner Ägyptologische Studien 37). Munich/Berlin: Deutscher Kunstverlag
*Correspondence of Peter Mongus & Acacius* = Amélineau 1888.
Couyat, Jean & Pierre Montet. 1913. *Les inscriptions hiéroglyphiques et hiératiques du Ouâdi Hammamat* (Mémoires publiés par les membres de l'Institut Français d'Archéologie Orientale du Caire 34). Cairo: Institut Français d'Archéologie Orientale.

Cristea, Hans-Joachim 2011. *Schenute von Atripe: Contra Origenistas. Edition eines koptischen Textes mit annotierter Übersetzung und Indizes einschließlich einer Übersetzung des 16. Osterfestbriefes des Theophilus in der Fassung des Hieronymus (ep. 96)* (Studien & Texte zu Antike & Christentum 60). Tübingen: Mohr Siebeck.

Cristofaro, S. 2003. *Subordination* (Oxford Studies in Typology and Linguistic Theory). Oxford: Oxford University Press.

Crum, *Cat. BM* = Crum 1905.

Crum, in Bell, *Jews & Christians* = Bell 1924.

Crum, Walter Ewing. 1893. *Coptic Manuscripts Brought from the Fayyum by W. M. Flinders Petrie, together with a Papyrus in the Bodleian Library*. London: David Nutt.

Crum, Walter Ewing. 1902a. *Coptic Monuments: N^os^ 8001–8741* (Catalogue générale des antiquités égyptiennes du Musée du Caire 4). Cairo: Institut Français d'Archéologie Orientale.

Crum, Walter Ewing. 1902b. *Coptic Ostraca from the Collections of the Egypt Exploration Fund, the Cairo Museum and Others*, with a contribution by the Rev. F. E. Brightman (Special Extra Publication of the Egypt Exploration Fund). London: Egypt Exploration Fund.

Crum, Walter Ewing. 1905. *Catalogue of the Coptic Manuscripts in the British Museum*, London: The British Museum.

Crum, Walter Ewing. 1909. *Catalogue of the Coptic Manuscripts in the Collection of the John Rylands Library Manchester*, Manchester & London: The University Press, Bernard Quaritch and Sherratt & Hughes.

Crum, Walter Ewing. 1915. *Der Papyruscodex saec. VI–VII der Phillippsbibliothek in Cheltenham. Koptische theologische Schriften*, mit einem Beitrag von A. Ehrhard (Schriften der wissenschaftlichen Gesellschaft in Straßburg 18). Strassburg: Trübner.

Crum, Walter Ewing. 1915–17. Discours de Pisenthius sur Saint Onnophrius, *ROC* 20: 38–67.

Crum, Walter Ewing. 1935. *Varia Coptica, Texts, Translations, Indexes*, Aberdeen: The University Press.

Crum, Walter Ewing. 1939. *A Coptic Dictionary*. Oxford: Clarendon Press.

Crum, Walter Ewing & Georg Steindorff. 1912. *Koptische Rechtsurkunden des achten Jahrhunderts aus Djême (Theben)*. Leipzig: J. C. Hinrichs.

Crum, *Varia Coptica* = Crum 1935.

*CO* = Crum 1902b.

CT I–VII = De Buck 1935–61.

Cyril of Alexandria, *De Hora Mortis* = Amélineau 1888.
*In Athanasium* = Orlandi 1968b.
*Erotapokrisis* = Crum 1915.
*Miracles of the Three Youth* = de Vis 1929.

Datema, Cornelis 1978. *Amphilochii Iconiensis Opera. Orationes, pluraque alia quae supersunt, nonnulla etiam spuria* (Corpus Christianorum. Series Graeca 3). Turnhout & Leuven: Brepols.

Daressy, Georges. 1992. *Ostraca: N^os^ 25001–25385* (Catalogue général des antiquités égyptiennes du Musée du Caire 1). Cairo: Institut Français d'Archéologie Orientale.

Davies, *Amarna* IV = Davies 1906.

Davies, Norman de Garis. 1902. *The Rock-Tombs of Deir el-Gebrawi* Part II: *Tomb of Zau and Tombs of the Northern Group* (Archaeological Survey of Egypt 12). London: Egypt Exploration Fund.

Davies, Norman de Garis. 1906. *The Rock-Tombs of El-Amarna* IV: *The Tombs of Penthu, Mahu and Others* (Archaeological Survey of Egypt 16). London: Egypt Exploration Fund.

Davies, Norman de Garis. 1913. *Five Theban Tombs, Being Those of Mentuherkhepeshef, User, Daga, Nehemawāy and Tati* (Archaeological Survey of Egypt 21). London: Egypt Exploration Fund.
Davies, Norman de Garis & Nina de Garis Davies. 1923. *The Tombs of Two officials of Tuthmosis the Fourth (Nos. 75 and 90)* (The Theban Tomb Series 3). London: Egypt Exploration Society.
Davies, Norman de Garis & Nina de Garis Davies. 1933. *The Tombs of Menkheperrasonb, Amenmose and Another (TT 86, 112, 42, 226)* (The Theban Tombs Series 5). London: Egypt Exploration Society.
Davies, Norman de Garis, Alan Henderson Gardiner & Nina de Garis Davies. 1920. *The Tomb of Antefoker, Vizier of Sesostris I, and of his Wife, Senet* (The Theban Tombs Series 2). London: Egypt Exploration Society.
Davies, Virginia Lee. 1973. *Syntax of Negative Particles bw and bn in Late Egyptian* (Münchner Ägyptologische Studien 29). Munich/Berlin: Deutscher Kunstverlag.
Dawson, Warren R. & Thomas Eric Peet. 1933. The so-called Poem of the King's Chariot. *The Journal of Egyptian Archaeology* 19. 167–174 & pl. 25–28.
de Cenival, Françoise. 1985. Les nouveaux fragments du mythe de l'œil du soleil de l'Institut de Papyrologie et d'Égyptologie de Lille. *Cahier de Recherches de l'Institut de Papyrologie et d'Égyptologie de Lille* 7. 95–115.
gDeir el-Bahari = Marciniak 1974.
*Deir el-Gebrawi* II = Davies 1902.
oDeM 437 = Černý 1951.
oDeM 439 = Černý 1951.
oDeM 554 = Sauneron 1959.
oDeM 663 = Černý 1970.
oDeM 1079 = Posener 1938.
oDeM 1221 = Posener 1951–72.
oDeM 1232 = Posener 1951–72.
oDeM 10253 = Grandet 2010.
oDeM 10264 = Grandet 2010.
pDeM 8 = Černý 1978.
pDeM 39 = Sauneron 1980.
Demarée, Robert J. 1999. A Letter of Reproach. In Emily Teeter & J. A. Larson (eds.), *Gold of Praise. Studies on Ancient Egypt in Honor of Edward F. Wente* (Studies in Ancient Oriental Civilization 58), 75–82. Chicago: Oriental Institute.
Demarée, Robert J. 2002. *Ramesside Ostraca*. London: The British Museum Press.
Demarée, Robert J. 2006. *The Bankes Late Ramesside Papyri*, with contributions by Bridget Leach & Patricia Usick (The British Museum Research Publication 155). London: The British Museum Press.
*Dendereh* = Petrie 1898.
Depauw, Mark. 2006. *The Demotic Letter: A Study of Epistolographic Scribal Traditions Against Their Intra- and Intercultural Background* (Demotische Studien 14). Sommerhausen: Gisela Zauzich.
Depraved Harpist *see TLA sub Texte > Demotische Textdatenbank.*
Depuydt, Leo. 1983. The Standard Theory and the 'emphatic' forms in Classical (Middle) Egyptian: a historical survey. *Orientalia Lovaniensia Periodica* 14. 13–54.
Depuydt, Leo. 1986. The emphatic nominal sentence in Egyptian and Coptic. In Gertie Englund & Paul John Frandsen (eds.), *Crossroad. Chaos or the Beginning of a*

*New Paradigm* (CNI Publications 1), 91–117. Copenhagen: Carsten Niebuhr Institute of Ancient Near East Studies.
Depuydt, Leo (ed.). 1991. *Homiletica from the Pierpont Morgan Library. Seven Coptic Homilies Attributed to Basil the Great, John Chrysostom, and Euodius of Rome*, edited by David Brakke, Paul Chapman, Zlatko Pleše, James Ross Smith, Mark C. Stone, Craig S. Wansink & Frederick Weidmann (Corpus Scriptorum Christianorum Orientalium 424/Scriptores Coptici 43), Leuven: Peeters.
Depuydt, Leo. 1993. *Conjunction, Contiguity, Contingency. On Relationships between Events in the Egyptian and Coptic Verbal Systems*. Oxford: Oxford University Press.
Depuydt, Leo. 1994. A Homily on the Virtues of Saint Longinus Attributed to Basil of Pemje. In Søren Giversen, Martin Krause & Peter Nagel (eds.), *Coptology: Past, Present, & Future, Studies in Honour of Rodolphe Kasser* (Orientalia Lovaniensia Analecta 61), 267–291. Leuven: Peeters.
Depuydt, Leo. 1998. The meaning of Old and Middle Egyptian *jw* in light of the distinction between narration and discussion. In Irene Shirun-Grumach (ed.), *Jerusalem Studies in Egyptology* (Ägypten und Altes Testament 40), 19–36. Harrassowitz: Wiesbaden.
Depuydt, Leo. 1999. *Fundamentals of Egyptian Grammar* I: *Elements*. Norton, MA: Frog Publishing.
Depuydt, Leo. 2009. Towards the full digitalization of grammar. The case of the Egyptian nominal sentence. *Lingua Aegyptia* 17. 27–50.
Devos, Paul. 1969. La « servante de dieu » Pœmenia d'après Pallade, la tradition copte et Jean Rufus. *Analecta Bollandiana* 87. 189–212.
Diebner, Bernd Jørg & Rodolphe Kasser. 1989. *Hamburger Papyrus Bil. 1. Die alttestamentlichen Texte des Papyrus Bilinguis 1 der Staats- und Universitätsbibliothek Hamburg: Canticum canticorum (coptice), Lamentationes Ieremiae (coptice), Ecclesiastes (graece et coptice)* (Cahiers d'Orientalisme 18). Geneva: Cramer.
Diessel, Holger. 2000. Demonstratives. In Keith Allan & Keith Brown (eds.), *Concise Encyclopedia of Semantics*, 207–212. Amsterdam: Elsevier.
Dik, Simon C. 1980. *Studies in Functional Grammar*. London: Academic Press.
Dik, Simon C. 1997. *The Theory of Functional Grammar Part I: The Structure of the Clause* (Functional Grammar Series 20). Berlin/New York: Mouton de Gruyter.
Dioscorus of Alexandria, *On Macarius of Tkow* = $^{B}$Amélineau 1888 & $^{S}$Johnson 1980.
Dixon, Robert M. W. 2004. Adjective classes in typological perspective. In Robert M. W. Dixon & Alexandra Y. Aikhenvald (eds.), *Adjective Classes. A Cross-linguistic Typology* (Explorations in Linguistic Typology 1), 1–49. Oxford: Oxford University Press.
Donadoni Roveri, Anna Maria (ed.), 1988. *Museo Egizio di Torino. Civilta' degli egizi: le credenze religiose*. Turin: Istituto Bancario San Paolo di Torino.
Donker van Heel, Koenrad. 1997. Papyrus Louvre E 7852. A Land Lease from the Time of Taharka. *Revue d'Égyptologie* 48. 81–93.
Doret, Éric. 1979. The reading of the negation . *The Journal of Egyptian Archaeology* 65. 161–163.
Doret, Éric. 1980. A note concerning the Egyptian construction Noun + *sḏm.f*. *Journal of Near Eastern Studies* 39. 37–45.
Doret, Éric. 1986. *The Narrative Verbal System of Old and Middle Egyptian* (Cahiers d'Orientalisme XII). Geneva: Patrick Cramer.
Doret, Éric. 1989. Phrase nominale, identité et substitution dans les Textes des Sarcophages, première partie. *Revue d'Égyptologie* 40. 49–63.

Doret, Éric. 1990. Phrase nominale, identité et substitution dans les Textes des Sarcophages, deuxième partie. *Revue d'Égyptologie* 41. 39–56.

Doret, Éric. 1991. Cleft-sentence, substitutions et contraintes sémantiques en égyptien de la première phase (V-XVIII Dynastie). *Lingua Aegyptia* 1. 57–96.

Doret, Éric. 1992. Phrase nominale, identité et substitution dans les Textes des Sarcophages, troisième partie. *Revue d'Égyptologie* 43. 49–74.

*Dormition of the Virgin* = Robinson 1896.

Dorn, Andreas. 2004. Die Lehre Amunnachts. *Zeitschrift für Ägyptische Sprache und Altertumskunde* 131. 38–55 & Taf. 2–7.

Downing, Angela. 1991. An alternative approach to theme: a systemic-functional perspective. *Word* 42(2). 119–143.

Drescher, James. 1946. *Apa Mena. A Selection of Coptic Texts Relating to St. Menas* (Publications de la Société d'Archéologie Copte: Textes et Documents). Cairo: Société d'Archéologie Copte.

Drescher, James. 1970. *The Coptic (Sahidic) Version of Kingdoms I, II (Samuel I, II)* (Corpus Scriptorum Christianorum Orientalium 35/Scriptores Coptici 313). Louvain: Secrétariat du Corpus Scriptorum Christianorum Orientalium.

Drioton, Étienne. 1943. Description sommaire des chapelles funéraires de la V$^{e}$ dynastie récemment découvertes derrière le mastaba de Mérérouka à Sakkarah. *Annales du Service des Antiquités de l'Égypte* 43. 487–513.

Dziobek, Eberhard & Mahmoud Abdel Raziq. 1990. *Das Grab des Sobekhotep: Theben Nr. 63*, mit Beiträgen von Betsy Bryan & Günter Burkhard (Archäologische Veröffentlichungen 71). Mainz: van Zabern.

pEbers = Grapow 1958.

Edel, Elmar. 1955/64. *Altägyptische Grammatik* (Analecta Orientalia 34/39). Roma: Pontificium Institutum Biblicum.

Edel, Elmar. 1997. *Der Vertrag zwischen Ramses II. von Ägypten und Ḫattušuli III. von Ḫatti* (Wissenschaftliche Veröffentlichungen der Deutschen Orient-Gesellschaft 95). Berlin: Gebrüder Mann.

Edel, *Vertrag* = Edel 1997.

oEdinburgh 916 = Dawson & Peet 1933.

pEdwin Smith = Grapow 1958.

Egypt Exploration Society. 1932. *Studies Presented to F. Ll. Griffith*. London: Egypt Exploration Society.

Elanskaja, Alla Ivanovna. 1994. *The Literary Coptic Manuscripts in the A. S. Pushkin State Fine Arts Museum in Moscow* (Supplements to Vigiliae Christianae XVIII), Leiden, New York & Köln: Brill.

*El Bersheh* I = Newberry 1895.

Enmarch, Roland. 2006. *The Dialogue of Ipuwer and the Lord of All*. Oxford: Griffith Institute.

*Ep. Apostolorum* = Schmidt 1919.

*EpPt* (NHC VIII, 2) = Sieber 1991.

Erichsen, Wolja. 1932. *Faijumische Fragmente der Reden des Agathonicus Bischofs von Tarsus* (Det Kgl. Danske Videnskabernes Selskab. Historisk-filologiske Meddelelser 19.1). Copenhagen: Andr. Fred. Høst & søn.

Erichsen, Wolja. 1933. *Papyrus Harris I. Hieroglyphische Transkription* (Bibliotheca Aegyptiaca 5). Bruxelles: Fondation égyptologique Reine Élisabeth.

Erman, Adolf. 1897. *Bruchstücke koptischer Volksliteratur*. Berlin: Königliche Akademie der Wissenschaften.

Erman, Adolf. 1911. Hymnen an das Diadem der Pharaonen aus einem Papyrus der Sammlung Golénischeff. *Abhandlungen der Königlich-Preußischen Akademie der Wissenschaften zu Berlin, Philosophisch-historische Klasse*, 1–58.

Erman, Adolf. 1918. Reden, Rufe und Lieder auf Gräberbildern des Alten Reiches. *Abhandlungen der Königlich-Preußischen Akademie der Wissenschaften zu Berlin, philosophisch-historische Klasse*, NR 15, 1–62.

Erman, Adolf. 1933. *Neuägyptische Grammatik*. Zweite, völlig umgestaltete Auflage. Leipzig: Engelmann.

Emmel, Stephen. 2004. *Shenoute's Literary Corpus*. (Corpus Scriptorum Christianorum Orientalium. Subsidia 111 & 112). Leuven: Peeters.

The Epigraphic Society. 1979. *The Temple of Khonsu* I: *Scenes of King Herihor in the Court* (Oriental Institute Publications 100). Chicago: Oriental Institute.

Erman, Adolf. 1883. Die ägyptischen Beschwörungen des grossen Pariser Zauberpapyrus. *Zeitschrift für Ägyptische Sprache und Altertumskunde* 21. 89–109.

van Esbroeck, Michel. 1998. La légende d'Apa Jeremias et Apa Johannes et les fragments Chester Beatty Copte 829. *Orientalia* nova series 67. 1–63 & pl. I–IV.

*Eudoxia and the Holy Sepulchre* = Orlandi, Pearson & Drake 1980.

Evelyn White, Hugh Gerard. 1926. *The Monasteries of the Wadi 'n Natrûn* I: *New Coptic Texts from the Monastery of Saint Macarius* (Publications of The Metropolitan Museum of Art, Egyptian Expedition), New York: The The Metropolitan Museum of Art.

*EvNicodemus* = Orlandi 1966.

*EvThom* = Layton 1989.

*EvVer* = Attridge 1985.

Faulkner, Raymond. 1951. The stela of Rudjahau. *The Journal of Egyptian Archaeology* 37. 47–52.

Fecht, Gerhard. 1960. *Wortakzent und Silbenstruktur. Untersuchungen zur Geschichte der ägyptischen Sprache* (Ägyptologische Forschungen 21). Glückstadt, Hamburg & New York: J. J. Augustin.

Feder, Frank. 2002. *Biblia Sahidica: Ieremias, Lamentationes (Threni), Epistula Ieremiae et Baruch* (Texte und Untersuchungen zur Geschichte der altchristlichen Literatur 147). Berlin & New York: de Gruyter.

*First Wonder of St George* = Budge 1888.

Fischer-Elfert, Hans-Werner. 1992. *Die satirische Streitschrift des Papyrus Anastasi I. Textzusammenstellung* (Kleine Ägyptische Texte). Wiesbaden: Harrassowitz.

Fischer-Elfert, Hans-Werner. 1997. *Lesefunde im literarischen Steinbruch von Deir el-Medineh* (Kleine Ägyptische Texte 12). Wiesbaden: Harrassowitz.

*Five Th. T.* = Davies 1913.

Florence 2590 = Bosticco 1959.

pFlorence PSI D 88 *see TLA sub Texte > Demotische Textdatenbank.*

Förster, Hans. 2006. *Transitus Mariae. Beiträge zur koptischen Überlieferung mit einer Edition von P. Vindob. K 7589, Cambridge Add 1876 8 und Paris BN Copte 129*[17] *ff. 28 und 29* (Die griechischen christlichen Schriftsteller der ersten Jahrhunderte. Neue Folge 14: Neutestamentliche Apokryphen 2). Berlin: de Gruyter.

Foley, William A. & Robert D. Van Valin. 1984. *Functional Syntax and Universal Grammar* (Cambridge Studies in Linguistics 38). Cambridge: Cambridge University Press.

Fournet, Jean-Luc & Arietta Papaconstantinou (eds.). 2016. *Mélanges Jean Gascou. Textes et études papyrologiques (P.Gascou)* (Travaux et Mémoires 20/1). Paris: Association des Amis du Centre d'Histoire et Civilisation de Byzance.

Frandsen, Paul John. 1986. On the relevance of logical analysis. In Gertie Englund & Paul John Frandsen (eds.), *Crossroad. Chaos or the Beginning of a New Paradigm* (CNI Publications 1), 145–159. Copenhagen: Carsten Niebuhr Institute of Ancient Near East Studies.

Funk, Wolf-Peter. 1987. Zur Negation des Präsens in den oberägyptischen Dialekten. *Zeitschrift für Ägyptische Sprache und Altertumskunde* 114. 101–102.

*Further Miracles of Apa Mena* = Drescher 1946.

Gaballa, Gaballa A. 1977. *The Memphite Tomb-Chapel of Mose*. Warminster: Aris & Philips.

Gabra, Gawdat. 1995. *Der Psalter im Oxyrhynchitischen (mesokemischen/mittelägyptischen) Dialekt*, mit Beiträgen von Nasry Iskander, Gerd Mink und John L. Sharp (Abhandlungen des Deutschen Archäologischen Instituts Kairo. Koptische Reihe 4). Heidelberg: Heidelberger Orientverlag.

Gardiner, Alan Henderson. 1916. The defeat of the Hyksos by Kamōse: The Carnarvon Tablet, No. I. *The Journal of Egyptian Archaeology* 3. 95–110.

Gardiner, Alan Henderson. 1923. A hitherto unnoticed negative in Middle Egyptian. *Recueil de Travaux relatifs à la philologie et à l'archéologie égyptiennes et assyriennes* 40. 79–82.

Gardiner, Alan Henderson. 1928. The Graffito in the Tomb of Pere. *The Journal of Egyptian Archaeology* 14. 10–11 & pl. V–VI.

Gardiner, Alan Henderson. 1930. A new Letter to the Dead. *The Journal of Egyptian Archaeology* 16. 19–22.

Gardiner, Alan Henderson. 1932. *Late-Egyptian Stories* (Bibliotheca Aegyptiaca 1). Brussels: Fondation égyptologique Reine Élisabeth.

Gardiner, Alan Henderson. 1935. *Chester Beatty Gift*. 2 vols. (Hieratic Papyri in the British Museum III). London: British Museum.

Gardiner, Alan Henderson. 1937. *Late-Egyptian Miscellanies* (Bibliotheca Aegyptiaca 7). Brussels: Fondation égyptologique Reine Élisabeth.

Gardiner, Alan Henderson. 1946. The instruction addressed to Kagemni and his brethren, *The Journal of Egyptian Archaeology* 32. 71–74.

Gardiner, Alan Henderson. 1948. *Ramesside Administrative Documents*. London: Oxford University Press.

Gardiner, Alan Henderson. 1955/56. A Pharaonic encomium. *The Journal of Egyptian Archaeology* 41. 30 & pl. VII–XI and 42. 8–20.

Gardiner, Alan Henderson. 1957. *Egyptian Grammar*. 3rd ed. Oxford: Griffith Institute.

Gardiner, Alan Henderson & Kurt Sethe. 1928. *Egyptian Letters to the Dead, Mainly from the Old and Middle Kingdoms*. London: The Egypt Exploration Society.

Gardiner, Alan Henderson & Peet, Thomas Eric. 1952. *The Inscriptions of Sinai*. 2nd ed. Oxford: Oxford University Press.

Gardner, Iain, Anthony Alcock & Wolf-Peter Funk. 1999. *Coptic Documentary Texts from Kellis I, P. Kell. V (P. Kell. Copt. 10–52; O. Kell. Copt. 1–2)*, with a contribution by C. A. Hope and G. E. Bowen (Dakhleh Oasis Project: Monograph 9). Oxford: Oxbow Books.

Gardner, Iain, Anthony Alcock & Wolf-Peter Funk. 2014. *Coptic Documentary Texts from Kellis II, P. Kellis VII (P. Kellis Copt. 57–131)* (Dakhleh Oasis Project: Monograph 16). Oxford: Oxbow Books.

Garitte, Gerard. 1967. *S. Antonii Vitae Versio Sahidica* (Corpus Scriptorum Christianorum Orientalium 117/Scriptores Coptici 13). Louvain: Secrétariat du Corpus Scriptorum Christianorum Orientalium.

*P. Gascou 60* = Richter 2016.

Gasse, Annie & Rondon, Vincent. 2007. *Les inscriptions de Séhel* (Memoires publiés par les membres de l'Institut Français d'Archeologie Orientale). Cairo: Institut Français d'Archéologie Orientale.

Geach, Peter Thomas. 1962. *Reference and Generality. An Examination of some Medieval and Modern Theories* (Contemporary Philosophy). Ithaca, NY: Cornell University Press.

Generalverwaltung Museum Berlin. 1913 & Roeder, Günther. 1924. *Aegyptische Inschriften aus den königlichen Museen zu Berlin*. 2 vols. Leipzig: J.C. Hinrichs.

*Gesios & Isidorus* = Steindorff 1883.

Gilula, Mordechai. 1968. An adjectival predicative expression of possession in Middle Egyptian. *Revue d'Égyptologie* 20. 55–61.

Gilula, Mordechai. 1970. Review of Satzinger, Helmut. 1968, *Die negativen Konstruktionen im Alt- und Mittelägyptischen*. *The Journal of Egyptian Archaeology* 56. 205–214.

Gilula, Mordechai. 1971. Coffin Texts spell 148. *The Journal of Egyptian Archaeology* 57. 14–19.

Gilula, Mordechai. 1972. Enclitic particles in Middle Egyptian. *Göttinger Miszellen* 2. 53–59.

Gilula, Mordechai. 1976. An unusual nominal pattern in Middle Egyptian. *The Journal of Egyptian Archaeology* 62. 160–175.

Gilula, Mordechai. 1978. *Pyr.* 604C–D and *Westcar* 7/17–19. *The Journal of Egyptian Archaeology* 64. 45–51.

Gilula, Mordechai. 1986. Sentence system in Middle Egyptian. In Gertie Englund & Paul John Frandsen (eds.), *Crossroad. Chaos or the Beginning of a New Paradigm* (CNI Publications 1), 161–166. Copenhagen: Carsten Niebuhr Institute of Ancient Near East Studies.

Givón, Talmy. 2001. *Syntax*. 2 vols. Amsterdam: Benjamins.

Glanville, Stephen Ranulph Kingdon. 1928. The Letters of Aḥmose of Peniati. *The Journal of Egyptian Archaeology* 14. 297–302 & pl. XXXI–XXXII.

Goedicke, Hans. 1970a. The Story of the Herdsman. *Chronique d'Égypte* 45. 244–266.

Goedicke, Hans. 1970b. *The Report about the Dispute of a Man with His Ba*. Baltimore: Johns Hopkins Press.

Goldenberg, Gideon. 1995. Attribution in Semitic languages. *Langues Orientales Anciennes : Philologie et Linguistique* 5/6. 1–20.

*GospPh* = Layton 1989.

Gracia Zamacona, Carlos. 2010. Space, Time and Abstract Relations in the Coffin Texts. *Zeitschrift für Ägyptische Sprache und Altertumskunde* 137. 13–26.

Graefe, Erhardt. 2001. *Mittelägyptische Grammatik für Anfänger*. 6th ed. Wiesbaden: Harrassowitz.

Graffito M.2.3.P.18.15 = Navrátilová 2015.

Grandet, Pierre. 2010. *Catalogue des Ostraca Hiératiques Non Littéraires de Deîr el-Médînéh* XI: *Nos 10124–10275* (Documents de Fouilles de l'Institut Français d'Archéologie Orientale 48). Cairo: Institut Français d'Archéologie Orientale.

Grapow, Hermann. 1941. *Wie die alten Ägypter sich anredeten, wie sie sich grüßten und wie sie miteinander sprachen* III: *Zur Verwendung von Anrufen, Ausrufen, Wünschen und Grüßen* (Abhandlungen der Preußischen Akademie der Wissenschaften, Phil. Hist. Klasse 11). Berlin: Verlag der Akademie der Wissenschaften.

Grapow, Hermann. 1942. Ägyptische Jenseitswünsche in Sprüchen ungewöhnlicher Fassung aus dem Neuen Reich. *Zeitschrift für Ägyptische Sprache und Altertumskunde* 77. 57–78.
Grapow, Hermann. 1958. *Die medizinischen Texte in hieroglyphischer Umschreibung autographiert* (Grundriss der Medizin der Alten Ägypter V). Berlin: Akademie Verlag.
Great Aten Hymn = Sandman 1938.
Great Mag. P. Paris = Erman 1883.
Green, Michael. 1987. *The Coptic* share *Pattern and its Ancient Egyptian Ancestors*. Warminster: Aris & Phillips.
Griffith, Francis Llewellyn. 1889. *The Inscriptions of Siût and Dêr Rîfeh*. London: Trübner.
Grimshaw, Jane. 1990. *Argument Structure* (Linguistic Inquiry Monographs 18). Cambridge, MA: MIT Press.
Groll, Sarah Israelit. 1967. *Non-Verbal Sentence Patterns in Late Egyptian*, London: Oxford University Press.
Grossman, Eitan. 2007. Protatic *ỉir = f sḏm* in the Report of Wenamun: a 'proto-demotic' feature? *Göttinger Miszellen* 215. 49–55.
Grossman, Eitan & Stéphane Polis. 2014. On the pragmatics of subjectification. The emergence and grammaticalization of a verbless allative future in Ancient Egyptian. *Acta Linguistica Hafniensia* 46. 25–63.
Grossman, Eitan, Guillaume Lescuyer & Stéphane Polis. 2014. Contexts and inferences. The grammaticalization of the Later Egyptian Allative Future. In Eitan Grossman, Stéphane Polis, Andréas Stauder & Jean Winand (eds.), *On Forms and Functions: Studies in Ancient Egyptian Grammar* (Lingua Aegyptia Studia Monographica 15), 87–136. Hamburg: Widmaier Verlag.
Guidi, Ignazio. 1900a. Il testo copto del Testamento di Abramo. *Rendiconti Accademia dei Lincei* 9. 157–180.
Guidi, Ignazio. 1900b. Il Testamento di Isacco e il Testamento di Giacobbe. *Rendiconti Accademia dei Lincei* 9. 223–264.
Guidi, Ignazio. 1901. Texte copte. In Léon Clugnet (ed.), *Vie (et récits) de l'Abbé Daniel le scétiote (VI^e siècle)* (Bibliothèque hagiographique orientale I), 83–114. Paris: Picard & fils.
Gundacker, Roman. 2010. Eine besondere Form des Substantivalsatzes. Mit besonderer Rücksicht auf ihre dialektale und diachrone Bedeutung. *Lingua Aegyptia* 18. 41–117.
Gundel, Jeanette K. 1977. Where do cleft sentences come from? *Language* 53(3). 543–559.
Gunn, Battiscombe. 1924 [2012]. *Studies in Egyptian Syntax*. Oxford: Griffith Institute.
Gunn, Battiscombe. 1955. The Decree of Amonrasonthĕr for Neskhons. *The Journal of Egyptian Archaeology* 41. 83–105.
Habachi, Labib. 1972 *The Second Stela of Kamose and His Struggle against the Hyksos Ruler and His Capital* (Abhandlungen des Deutschen Archäologischen Instituts, Abteilung Kairo 8). Glückstadt: Augustin.
Haiman, John. 1983. Iconic and economic motivation. *Language* 59(4). 781–819.
Halliday, Michael Alexander Kirkwood. 1967–1968. Notes on transitivity and theme in English (Parts 1–3). *Journal of Linguistics* 3(1). 37–81; 3(2). 199–244; 4(2). 179–215.
Halliday, Michael Alexander Kirkwood. 1985. *An Introduction to Functional Grammar*. 2nd ed. London: Arnold.
Halpern, Aaron. 1995. *On the Placement and Morphology of Clitics* (Stanford Dissertations in Linguistics). Stanford: Center for the Study of Language and Information.
*Hammamat* = Couyat & Montet. 1913
*Hamra Dom* = Säve-Söderbergh 1994.

Hari, Robert. 1985. *La tombe thébaine du père divin Neferhotep* (Collection Epigraphica). Geneva: Éditions de Belles-Lettres.
Hardjedef = Helck 1984.
pHarkness *see TLA sub Texte > Demotische Textdatenbank.*
Harris, Alice & Campbell, Lyle. 1995. *Historical Syntax in Cross-Linguistic Perspective* (Cambridge Studies in Linguistics 74). Cambridge: Cambridge University Press.
pHarris I = Erichsen 1933.
Hasitzka, Monika. R. M. 2004. *Koptisches Sammelbuch* II (Mitteilungen aus der Papyrussammlung der Österreichischen Nationalbibliothek [Papyrus Erzherzog Rainer]. Neue Serie XXIII/2). Wien: Hollinek.
Haskell Mus. 13945 = Gardiner 1930.
Haspelmath, Martin. 1997. *Indefinite Pronouns* (Oxford Studies in Typology and Linguistic Theory). Oxford: Oxford University Press.
Haspelmath, Martin. 2007. Coordination. In Timothy Shopen (ed.), *Language Typology and Syntactic Description vol. II: Complex Constructions*, 1–51. Cambridge: Cambridge University Press.
Hassan, *Giza* II = Hassan, Selim. 1936. *Excavations at Gîza II 1930–1931*. Cairo: Government Press.
Hatch, William H. P. 1950. Three Hitherto Unpublished Leaves from a Manuscript of the *Acta Apostolorum Apocrypha* in Bohairic. In *Coptic Studies in Honor of Walter Ewing Crum* (= The Bulletin of the Byzantine Institute 2), 305–317. Boston/MA: The Byzantine Institute.
Hatnub = Anthes 1928.
pHauswaldt VI *see TLA sub Texte > Demotische Textdatenbank.*
Hayes, William. 1947. Horemkhaʿuef of Nekhen and his trip to I̱t-Towe. *The Journal of Egyptian Archaeology* 33. 3–11.
Hayes, William. 1953. *The Scepter of Egypt. A Background fort he Study oft he Egyptian Antiquities in The Metropolitan Museum of Art. Part I: From the Earliest Times to the End of the Middle Kingdom*. Cambridge (MA): Harward University Press.
pHearst = Grapow 1958.
Heckel, Ursula. 1957. Studien zum Eigenschaftsverbum und zum prädikativen Adjektivum im Altägyptischen (Fortsetzung). *Zeitschrift für Ägyptische Sprache und Altertumskunde* 82. 19–47.
Heine, Bernd. 2006. *Possession. Cognitive Sources, Forces, and Grammaticalization* (Cambridge Studies in Linguistics 83). Cambridge: Cambridge University Press.
Heine, Bernd & Tania Kuteva. 2002. *World Lexicon of Grammaticalization*. Cambridge: Cambridge University Press.
Helck, Wolfgang. 1970. *Die Prophezieung des Nfr.tj* (Kleine Ägyptische Texte). Wiesbaden: Harrassowitz.
Helck, Wolfgang. 1984. *Die Lehre des Djedefhor und die Lehre eines Vaters an seinen Sohn* (Kleine Ägyptische Texte). Wiesbaden: Harrassowitz.
Helck, Wolfgang. 2002. *Historisch-biographische Texte der 2. Zwischenzeit und neue Texte der 18. Dynastie. 3., unveränderte Auflage* (Kleine Ägyptische Texte). Wiesbaden: Harrassowitz.
Hengeveld, Kees. 1992. *Non-Verbal Predication. Theory, Typology, Diachrony* (Functional Grammar Series XV). Berlin/New York: Mouton de Gruyter.
Heqanakhte = Allen 2002.
Herdsman = Goedicke 1970a.

Hezi = Silverman 2000.
Hintze, Fritz. 1950–1952. *Untersuchungen zu Stil und Sprache neuägyptischer Erzählungen*. 2 vols. Berlin: Akademie-Verlag.
Hintze, Fritz & Reineke, Walter-Friedrich. 1989. *Felsinschriften aus dem sudanesischen Nubia*. 2 vols. Berlin: Akademie Verlag.
*HO* = Černý & Gardiner 1957.
*Homily on Christ's Birth* = Elanskaya 367b
Hooper, Joan & Tracy Terrell. 1974. A semantically based analysis of mood in Spanish. *Hispania* 57. 484–494.
Hopper, Paul J. 1981. Aspect and Foregrounding in Discourse. In T. Givón (ed.), *Discourse and Syntax* (Syntax and Semantics 12), 213–241. New York/San Francisco/London: Academic Press.
Hopper, Paul J. & Elizabeth Closs Traugott. 1993. *Grammaticalization* (Cambridge Textbooks in Linguistics). Cambridge: Cambridge University Press.
oHor *see TLA sub Texte > Demotische Textdatenbank.*
Horn, Laurence R. 2001. *The Natural History of Negation* (The David Hume series of philosophy and cognitive science reissues). Stanford: Center for the Study of Language and Information.
Horner, George. 1898–1905. *The Coptic Version of the New Testament in the Northern Dialect otherwise called Memphitic and Bohairic*, 4 vols. Oxford: Clarendon Press.
Horner, George. 1924. *The Coptic Version of the New Testament in the Southern Dialect otherwise called Sahidic and Thebaic* VII: *The Catholic Epistles and the Apocalypse*, Oxford: Clarendon Press.
Hornung, Erik. 1975–76. *Das Buch der Anbetung des Re im Westen (Sonnenlitanei) nach den Versionen des Neuen Reichs I–II* (Ægyptiaca Helvetica 2 & 3). Basel & Geneva: Ägyptologisches Seminar der Universität Basel & Faculté des Lettres de l'Université de Genève.
Hornung, Erik. 1987–92. *Texte zum Amduat* I–III (Ægyptiaca Helvetica 3, 14 & 15). Basel & Geneva: Ägyptologisches Seminar der Universität Basel & Faculté des Lettres de l'Université de Genève.
*HP* III = *Hieratische Papyrus Berlin*, herausgegeben von der Generalverwaltung III: *Schriftstücke der VI. Dynastie aus Elephantine. Zaubersprüche für Mutter und Kind. Ostraka*. Leipzig: J. C. Hinrichs, 1911.
Hymn to Sobek = Erman 1911.
Hyvernat, Henri. 1886. *Les Actes des Martyrs de l'Égypte tirés des manuscrits coptes de la Bibliothèque Vaticane et du Musée Borgia*, Paris [reprint Hildesheim & New York: Oldenburg 1977].
oIFAO D 632 *see TLA sub Texte > Demotische Textdatenbank.*
oIFAO 681 = Černý 1942.
oIFAO 857 = Černý 1972.
oIFAO 1328 unpublished, see Černý & Groll 1994 : 539 Example 1528.
*Inscr. of Mose* = Gaballa 1977.
Imhausen, Annette. 2003. *Ägyptische Algorithmen. Eine Untersuchung zu den mittelägyptischen mathematischen Aufgabentexten* (Ägyptologische Abhandlungen 65). Wiesbaden: Harrassowitz.
pInsinger *see TLA sub Texte > Demotische Textdatenbank.*
pInv. Sorbonne 1248 *see TLA sub Texte > Demotische Textdatenbank.*

Ipuwer = Enmarch 2006.
Jacoby, Adolf. 1903. Studien zur koptischen Literatur. *Recueil de Travaux relatifs à la philologie et à l'archéologie égyptiennes et assyriennes* 25. 37–49.
Jacques, Xavier. 1969. Les deux fragments conservés des « Actes d'André et de Paul » (Cod. Borg. Copt. 109, fasc. 132). *Orientalia* nova series 38. 187–213.
Jansen-Winkeln, *IdS* I & II = Jansen-Winkeln 2007a & 2007b.
Jansen-Winkeln, Karl. 1993. Nisbe-adjektiv und Partizip. *Lingua Aegyptia* 3. 7–16.
Jansen-Winkeln, Karl. 1996a. Zitierform und Kontextform. *Göttinger Miszellen* 154. 45–48.
Jansen-Winkeln, Karl. 1996b. *Spätmittelägyptische Grammatik der Texte der 3. Zwischenzeit* (Ägypten und Altes Testament 34). Wiesbaden: Harrassowitz.
Jansen-Winkeln, Karl. 2007a. *Inschriften der Spätzeit* I: *Die 21. Dynastie*. Wiesbaden: Harrosswitz.
Jansen-Winkeln, Karl. 2007a. *Inschriften der Spätzeit* II: *Die 22.–24. Dynastie*. Wiesbaden: Harrosswitz.
Janssen, Jac. J. 1991. *Late Ramesside Letters and Communications* (Hieratic Papyri in the British Museum VI9. London: The British Museum Press.
Jasnow, Richard & Karl-Theodor Zauzich. 2005. *The Ancient Egyptian Book of Thoth. A Demotic Discourse on Knowledge and Pendant to the Classical Hermetica*. Wiesbaden: Harrassowitz.
*JEA* 14 = Gardiner 1928.
Jenni, Hanna. 2004. Sätze zum Ausdruck von Zugehörigkeit und Besitz im Ägyptischen. *Lingua Aegyptia* 12. 123–131.
Jenni, Hanna. 2009. The Old Egyptian demonstratives *pw*, *pn* and *pf*. *Lingua Aegyptia* 17. 119–137.
Johansson, Mats. 2001. Clefts in contrast: a contrastive study of *it* clefts and *wh* clefts in English and Swedish texts and translations. *Linguistics* 39/3. 547–582.
John Chrysostom, *In Michaelem et Latronem* = Simon 1934/35.
John Chrysostom, *On the Resurrection & Apostles* = Depuydt 1991.
John of Constantinople, *On Repentance and Continence* = Budge 1910.
John Evangelist, *Investiture of Archangel Michael* = Müller 1962.
John the Hermit, *Encomium of Mark the Evangelist* = Orlandi 1968a
Johnson, David W. 1980. *A Panegyric on Macarius Bishop of Tkôw Attributed to Dioscorus of Alexandria* (Corpus Scriptorum Christianorum Orientalium 415/Scriptores Coptici 41), Leuven: Peeters.
Johnson, Janet. 1981. Demotic nominal sentences. In Dwight W. Young (ed.), *Studies presented to Hans Jakob Polotsky*, 414–430. East Gloucester, MA: Pirtle & Polson.
Junge, Friedrich. 1978. *Syntax der Mittelägyptischen Literatursprache. Grundlage einer Strukturtheorie* (Sonderschriften des DAI Kairo 4). Mainz: Philipp von Zabern.
Junge, Friedrich. 1981. Nominalsatz und Cleft Sentence im Ägyptischen. In Dwight W. Young (ed.), *Studies Presented to Hans Jakob Polotsky*, 431–462. East Gloucester, MA: Pirtle & Polson.
Junge, Friedrich. 1989. *"Emphasis" and Sentential Meaning in Middle Egyptian* (Göttinger Orientforschungen IV/20). Wiesbaden: Harrassowitz.
Junge, Friedrich. 2008. *Neuägyptisch. Einführung in die Grammatik*, 3., verbesserte Auflage. Wiesbaden: Harrassowitz.
Junker, *Giza* VI = Junker 1943
Junker, *Giza* XI = Junker 1953

Junker, *Poesie* = Junker 1908–1911.
Junker, Hermann. 1908–1911. *Koptische Poesie des 10. Jahrhunderts*. Hildesheim/NY: Georg Olms.
Junker, Hermann. 1943. *Gîza VI. Die Mastabas des Nfr (Nefer), Ḳdfjj (Kedfi), Ḳ3ḥjf (Kahjef) und die westlich anschließenden Grabanlagen* (Österreichische Akademie der Wissenschften in Wien, philosophisch-historische Klasse Denkschriften 72.1). Vienna: Hölder-Piehler-Tempsky.
Junker, Hermann. 1953. *Gîza XI. Der Friedhof südlich der Cheopspyramide, Ostteil* (Österreichische Akademie der Wissenschften in Wien, philosophisch-historische Klasse Denkschriften 74.2). Vienna: Rudolf Rohrer.
Kagemni = Gardiner 1946.
Kahle, Paul Eric. 1954. *Bala'izah. Coptic Texts from Deir el-Bala'izah in Upper Egypt*, 2 vols. London/Oxford: Oxford University Press.
Kammerzell, Frank. 1990. Funktion und Form. Zur Opposition von Perfekt und Pseudopartizip im Alt- und Mittelägyptischen. *Göttinger Miszellen* 117/118. 181–202.
Kammerzell, Frank. 1991. Personalpronomina und Personalendungen im Altägyptischen. In Daniela Mendel & Ulrike Claudi (eds.), *Ägypten im afro-orientalischen Kontext. Aufsätze zur Archäologie, Geschichte und Sprache eines unbegrenzten Raumes. Gedenkschrift Peter Behrens* (Afrikanistische Arbeitspapiere, special issue), 177–203. Cologne: University of Cologne.
Kammerzell, Frank. 1998. The Sounds of a Dead Language. Reconstructing Egyptian Phonology. *Göttinger Beiträge zur Sprachwissenschaft* 1. 21–41.
Kamose Stela = Habachi 1972.
Kanawati, Naguib & Abder-Raziq, Mahmoud. 1999. *The Teti Cemetery at Saqqara III: The Tombs of Nefersheshemre and Seankhuiptah* (The Australian Centre for Egyptology Reports 11). Oxford: Aris & Phillips.
Kanawati, Naguib & Abder-Raziq, Mahmoud. 2000. *The Teti Cemetery at Saqqara V: The Tomb of Hezi* (The Australian Centre for Egyptology Reports 13). Oxford: Aris & Phillips.
Kaplony-Heckel, Ursula. 1963. *Die demotischen Tempeleide* (Ägyptologische Abhandlungen 6). Wiesbaden: Harrassowitz.
Kasser, Rodolphe. 1958. *Papyrus Bodmer III: Evangile de Jean et Genèse I–IV,2 en bohaïrique* (Corpus Scriptorum Christianorum Orientalium 177/Scriptores Coptici 25). Louvain: Secrétariat du Corpus Scriptorum Christianorum Orientalium.
Kasser, Rodolphe. 1960. *Livre de Proverbes; Papyrus Bodmer VI* (Corpus Scriptorum Christianorum Orientalium 194/Scriptores Coptici 27). Louvain: Secrétariat du Corpus Scriptorum Christianorum Orientalium.
Kasser, Rodolphe. 1961. *Papyrus Bodmer XVI: Exode I–XV,2 en sahidique*, Cologny/Genève: Bibliotheca Bodmeriana.
Kasser, Rodolphe. 1962a. *Papyrus Bodmer XVIII: Deutéronome I–X, 7 en sahidique*. Cologny–Geneva: Bibliotheca Bodmeriana.
Kasser, Rodolphe. 1962b. *Papyrus Bodmer XXI: Josué VI, 16–25, VII, 6–XI, 23, XXII, 1–2, 19–XXIII, 7, 15–XXIV, 23 en sahidique*. Cologny–Geneva: Bibliotheca Bodmeriana.
Keenan, Edward L. 1971. Two kinds of presupposition in natural language. In Charles John Fillmore & Donald Terrence Langendoen (eds.), *Studies in Linguistic Semantics*, 45–54. New York: Holt, Rinehart and Winston.
*P.KellisCopt.* = Gardner, Alcock & Funk 1999.
Kemyt = Posener 1951–1972.
*Kephalaia* = Polotsky 1940.

Khakheperraseneb = Parkinson 1997.
Kitchen. Kenneth A. 1975–1990. *Ramesside Inscriptions: Historical & Biographical* I–VII Oxford: Blackwells.
Koch, Roland. 1990. *Die Erzählung des Sinuhe* (Bibliotheca Aegyptiaca 19). Brussels: Fondation égyptologique Reine Élisabeth.
oKöln 184 *see TLA sub Texte > Demotische Textdatenbank.*
König, Ekkehard & Peter Siemund. 2007. Speech act distinctions in grammar. In Timothy Shopen (ed.), *Language Typology and Syntactic Description vol. 1: Clause Structure*, 276–324. Cambridge: Cambridge University Press.
Kom el-Koffar = Mostafa 1984–85.
Korostovtsev, Mikhail. 1973. *Grammaire du Néo-egyptien*. Moscow: Edition Nauka.
Kraatz, Wilhelm. 1904. *Koptische Akten zum ephesinischen Konzil vom Jahre 431. Übersetzung und Untersuchungen* (Texte und Untersuchungen zur Geschichte der altchristlichen Literatur 26.2). Leipzig: J.C. Hinrichs.
pKrall *see TLA sub Texte > Demotische Textdatenbank.*
*KRI* = Kitchen 1975–1990.
Kroeber, Burkard. 1970. *Die Neuägyptizismen vor der Amarnazeit. Studien zur Entwicklung der ägyptischen Sprache vom Mittleren zum Neuen Reich*. Diss. Universität Tübingen.
*KRU* = Crum & Steindorff 1912.
Kruchten, Jean-Marie. 1994. *ir wnn śḏm.f* (*śḏm.n.f*) et *ir śḏm.f* (*śḏm.n.f*) : une approche structuraliste. *The Journal of Egyptian Archaeology* 80. 97–108.
Kruchten, Jean-Marie. 1996. Deux cas particuliers de phrase coupée sans l'opérateur énonciatif *in*. *The Journal of Egyptian Archaeology* 82. 51–63.
*Krugtexte see TLA sub Texte > Demotische Textdatenbank.*
*KSB* II = Hasitzka 2004.
Kuhn, Karl-Heinz. 1956. *Letters & Sermons of Besa*. (Corpus Scriptorum Christianorum Orientalium 157/Scriptores Coptici 21). Louvain: Imprimerie orientaliste L. Durbecq.
Kuhn, Karl-Heinz. 1960. *Pseudo-Shenoute: On Christian Behaviour* (Corpus Scriptorum Christianorum Orientalium 206/Scriptores Coptici 29). Louvain: Secrétariat du Corpus Scriptorum Christianorum Orientalium.
Lacau, Pierre. 1908. Textes coptes en dialectes akhmimique et sahidique. *Bulletin de l'Institut Français d'Archéologie Orientale* 8. 43–109.
Lacau, Pierre. 1909. *Stèles du Nouvel Empire: N$^{os}$ 34001–34189* (Catalogue générale des antiquités égyptiennes du Musée du Caire 45). Cairo: Institut Français d'Archéologie Orientale.
Lacau, Pierre & Chevrier, Henri. 1977. *Une chapelle d'Hatshepsout à Karnak*. Cairo: IFAO.
de Lagarde, Paul. 1867. *Der Pentateuch koptisch*, Leipzig: Teubner.
de Lagarde, Paul. 1879. Bruchstücke der koptischen Übersetzung des Alten Testaments. *Abhandlungen der historisch-philologischen Classe der Königlichen Gesellschaft der Wissenschaften zu Göttingen* 24. 63–96 [reprinted Osnabrück: Zeller 1973].
de Lagarde, Paul. 1880. *Aegyptiaca*, Göttingen: D. A. Hoyer.
de Lagarde, Paul. 1886. *Catenae in evangelia aegyptiacae qua supersunt*, Göttingen: D. A. Hoyer.
Laisney, Vincent Pierre-Michel. 2007. *L'enseignement d'Aménémopé* (Studia Pohl: Series Major 19). Rome: Pontificio Istituto Biblico.
*Lamb of Bocchoris see TLA sub Texte > Demotische Textdatenbank.*

Lambrecht, Knud. 1994. *Information Structure and Sentence Form. Topic, Focus and the Mental Representations of Discourse Referents* (Cambridge Studies in Linguistics 71). Cambridge: Cambridge University Press.
Langacker, Ronald W. 1991. *Foundations of Cognitive Grammar II: Descriptive Application*. Stanford: Stanford University Press.
van Lantschoot, Arnold. 1957. *Les "Questions de Théodore". Text sahidique, Recensions arabes et éthiopienne* (Studi e Testi 192). Vatican City: Biblioteca Apostolica Vaticana.
Lapp, Günther. 1997. *The Papyrus of Nu* (Catalogue of the Books of the Dead in the British Musum I). London: British Museum.
Lapp, Günther. 2004. *The Papyrus of Nebseni* (Catalogue of the Books of the Dead in the British Museum III). London: British Museum.
Layton, Bentley (ed.). 1989. *Nag Hammadi Codex II, 2–7 Together With XIII*, Brit. Lib. Or.4926(1), and P. Oxy. 1, 654, 655*, with contributions by many scholars (Nag Hammadi Studies 20). 2 vols. Leiden, New York, København & Köln: Brill.
Layton, Bentley. 2011. *A Coptic Grammar*. 3rd ed., revised (Porta Linguarum Orientalium 199). Wiesbaden: Harrassowitz.
Lefort, Louis Théophile. 1952. *S. Pachomii Vitae, Sahidicae Scriptae* (Corpus Scriptorum Christianorum Orientalium 99 & 100/Scriptores Coptici 9 & 10). Louvain: Imprimerie orientaliste L. Durbecq [reprint of the 1933/34 edition].
Lefort, Louis Théophile. 1953. *S. Pachomii Vita, Bohairice Scripta* (Corpus Scriptorum Christianorum Orientalium 89/Scriptores Coptici 7). Louvain: Imprimerie orientaliste L. Durbecq [reprint of the 1925 edition].
Lefort, Louis Théophile. 1955. Catéchèse christologique de Chenoute. *Zeitschrift für ägyptische Sprache und Altertumskunde* 80. 40–45.
Lefort, Louis Théophile. 1956. *Œuvres de S. Pachôme et de ses disciples* (Corpus Scriptorum Christianorum Orientalium 159/Scriptores Coptici 23). Louvain: Imprimerie orientaliste L. Durbecq.
*Legend of Jeremia* = van Esbroeck 1998.
Legrain, Georges. 1909. *Statues et statuettes des rois et de particuliers: Nos 34001–34189* (Catalogue générale des antiquités égyptiennes du Musée du Caire 45). Cairo: Institut Français d'Archéologie Orientale.
Leiden V6 = Boeser 1909.
pLeiden I 343 + 345 = Massart 1954.
pLeiden I 371 = Gardiner & Sethe 1928.
pLeiden I 379 *see TLA sub Texte > Demotische Textdatenbank.*
pLeiden I 382 *see TLA sub Texte > Demotische Textdatenbank.*
pLeiden I F 1996/1.1 = Demarée 1999.
Leipoldt, Johannes. 1906. *Sinuthii Vita Bohairice* (Corpus Scriptorum Christianorum Orientalium 41/Scriptores Coptici 1). Paris & Leipzig: Poussielge & Harrossowitz.
Leipoldt, Johannes. 1908 & 1913. *Sinuthii archimandritae vita et opera omnia* III & IV (Corpus Scriptorum Christianorum Orientalium 42 & 73/Scriptores Coptici 4 & 5). Paris & Leipzig: Poussielge & Harrossowitz.
*LEM* = Gardiner 1937.
*LEM* Caminos = Caminos 1954.
von Lemm, Oskar. 1890 & 1894. Koptische apokryphe Apostelacten I & II. *Bulletin de l'Académie Impériale des Sciences de St.-Pétersbourg* NS 1 (33). 509–581 & 3 (35). 233–326.

von Lemm, Oskar. 1913. Bruchstücke Koptischer Märtyrerakten I–V. *Mémoires de l'Académie Impériale des Sciences de St.-Pétersbourg, VIIIe série* 12 (1). 1–84.
*LES* = Gardiner 1937.
*Lesestücke* = Sethe 1928.
*Life and Miracles of St Simeon the Stylite* = Chaîne 1948.
*Life of Antony* = Garitte 1967.
*Life of Daniel of Scetis* = Guidi 1901.
*Life of Hor* = Evelyn White 1926.
*Life of John Calybita* = Budge 1914.
*Life of John of Lycopolis* = Devos 1969.
*Life of Macarius of Alexandria* = Amélineau 1894.
*Life of Marina* = Till 1935.
*Life of Moses of Abydos* = Amélineau 1895 & Uljas 2011c.
Lippert, Sandra Luisa. 2004. *Ein demotisches juristisches Lehrbuch. Untersuchungen zu Papyrus Berlin P 23757* (Ägyptologische Abhandlungen 66). Wiesbaden. Harrassowitz.
Litany of Ra = Hornung 1975–76.
*Lit. Fragm.* = Caminos 1956.
pLoeb 1 *see TLA sub Texte > Demotische Textdatenbank.*
pLoeb 4 *see TLA sub Texte > Demotische Textdatenbank.*
pLoeb 5 *see TLA sub Texte > Demotische Textdatenbank.*
pLoeb 6 *see TLA sub Texte > Demotische Textdatenbank.*
pLoeb 7 *see TLA sub Texte > Demotische Textdatenbank.*
pLoeb 8 *see TLA sub Texte > Demotische Textdatenbank.*
pLoeb 17 *see TLA sub Texte > Demotische Textdatenbank.*
pLondon med. = Grapow 1958.
López, Jesús. 1978. *Ostraca ieratici N. 57001–57092* (Catalogo del Museo Egizio di Torino. Serie seconda – Collezioni III/1). Milano: Cisalpino La Goliardica.
López, Jesús. 1984. *Ostraca ieratici N. 57450–57568, Tabelle lignee N. 58001–58007* (Catalogo del Museo Egizio di Torino. Serie seconda – Collezioni III/4). Milano: Cisalpino La Goliardica.
Loprieno, Antonio. 1980. Osservazioni sullo sviluppo dell'articolo prepositivo in egiziano e nelle lingue semitiche. *Oriens Antiquus* 19. 1–27.
Loprieno, Antonio. 1988a. Der ägyptische Satz zwischen Semantik und Pragmatik: die Rolle von *jn*. In Silvia Schoske (ed.), *Akten des vierten internationalen Ägyptologen Kongresses* 3 (Studien zur altägyptischen Kultur. Beihefte 3), 77–98. Hamburg: Helmut Buske.
Loprieno, Antonio. 1988b. On the typological order of constituents in Egyptian. *Journal of Afroasiatic Linguistics* 1. 26–57.
Loprieno, Antonio. 1991a. Topics in Egyptian negations. In Daniela Mendel & Ulrike Claudi (eds.), *Ägypten im Afroasiatischen Kontext. Aufsätze zur Archäologie, Geschichte und Sprache eines unbegrenzten Raumes. Gedenkschrift Peter Behrens* (Afrikanistische Arbeitspapiere, special issue), 213–235. Cologne: University of Cologne.
Loprieno, Antonio. 1991b. Focus, mood, and negative forms: Middle Egyptian syntactic paradigms and diachrony. *Lingua Aegyptia* 1. 201–226.
Loprieno, Antonio. 1994. As a summary: new tendencies in Egyptological linguistics. *Lingua Aegyptia* 4. 369–382.
Loprieno, Antonio. 1995. *Ancient Egyptian. A Linguistic Introduction*. Cambridge: Cambridge University Press.

Loprieno, Antonio. 2006. On fuzzy boundaries in Egyptian syntax. In Gerald Moers, Heike Behlmer, Katja Demuß und Kai Widmaier (eds.), *jn.t ḏr.w. Festschrift für Friedrich Junge*, 429–441. Göttingen: Seminar für Ägyptologie und Koptologie.
Louvre AF 10076 *see TLA sub Texte > Demotische Textdatenbank.*
Louvre C3 = Simpson 1974.
Louvre C11 = Simpson 1974.
Louvre C12 = Simpson 1974.
pLouvre E 2432 = Malinine 1953.
pLouvre E 2433 = Lüddeckens 1960.
pLouvre E 3230b = Peet 1926.
pLouvre E 3334 *see TLA sub Texte > Demotische Textdatenbank.*
pLouvre E 7837 *see TLA sub Texte > Demotische Textdatenbank.*
pLouvre E 7843 *see TLA sub Texte > Demotische Textdatenbank.*
pLouvre E 7846 = Malinine 1983.
pLouvre E 7852 = Donker van Heel 1997.
pLouvre E 7854 *see TLA sub Texte > Demotische Textdatenbank.*
pLouvre E 7855 *see TLA sub Texte > Demotische Textdatenbank.*
pLouvre E 9294 *see TLA sub Texte > Demotische Textdatenbank.*
pLouvre E 27151 = Posener-Kriéger 1978.
pLouvre N 706 *see TLA sub Texte > Demotische Textdatenbank.*
pLouvre N 2409 *see TLA sub Texte > Demotische Textdatenbank.*
pLouvre N 2414 *see TLA sub Texte > Demotische Textdatenbank.*
pLouvre N 2420c *see TLA sub Texte > Demotische Textdatenbank.*
Louvre Bowl = Gardiner & Sethe 1928.
*Loyaliste* = Posener 1976.
*LRL* = Černý 1939.
Lubomierski, Nina. 2007. *Die Vita Sinuthii. Form- und Überlieferungsgeschichte der hagiographischen Texte über Schenute den Archimandriten* (Studien & Texte zu Antike & Christentum 45). Tübingen: Mohr Siebeck.
pLüddeckens 2 *see TLA sub Texte > Demotische Textdatenbank.*
pLüddeckens 13 *see TLA sub Texte > Demotische Textdatenbank.*
Lüddeckens, Erich. 1960. *Ägyptische Eheverträge* (Ägyptologische Abhandlungen 1). Wiesbaden. Harrossowitz.
Luft, Ulrich. 1992. *Das Archiv von Illahun* (Hieratische Papyri aus den Staatlichen Museen zu Berlin, Preussischer Kulturbesitz 1). Berlin: Akademie Verlag.
Luft, Ulrich. 2006. *Urkunden zur Chronologie der späten 12. Dynastie: Briefe aus Illahun* (Österreichische Akademie der Wissenschaften. Denkschriften der Gesamtakademie XXXIV = Contributions to the Chronology of the Eastern Mediterranean VII). Vienna: Österreichische Akademie der Wissenschaften.
Lyons, John. 1977. *Semantics*, vol. 1. Cambridge: Cambridge University Press.
pMag. London&Leiden *see TLA sub Texte > Demotische Textdatenbank.*
Malaise, Michel. 1985, La conjugaison suffixale dans les propositions conditionelles introduites par *ir* en ancien et moyen égyptien. *Chronique d'Égypte* 60. 152–167.
Malaise, Michel & Jean Winand. 1999. *Grammaire raisonnée de l'égyptien classique* (Ægyptiaca Leodiensia 6). Liège: Centre d'Informatique de Philosophie et Lettres.

Malinine, Michel. 1950. Fragment d'une version achmimique des petits prophètes. In *Coptic Studies in Honor of Walter Ewing Crum* (= The Bulletin of the Byzantine Institute 2), 365–415. Boston/MA: The Byzantine Institute.
Malinine, Michel. 1953. *Choix de textes juridiques en hiératique « anormal » et en démotique (XXVe et XXVIe dynasties* I: *Traduction et commentaire philologique* (Bibliothèque de l'École des Hautes Études 300). Paris: Champion.
Malinine, Michel. 1983. Transcriptions hiéroglyphiques de quatre textes du Musée du Louvre écrits en hiératique anormal. *Revue d'Égyptologie* 34. 93–100.
oMallawi 484 *see TLA sub Texte > Demotische Textdatenbank.*
Mallon, Alexis. 1956. *Grammaire copte, bibliographie, chrestomathie et vocabulaire*, 4th ed. Beirut: Imprimerie catholique.
Man and Ba = Goedicke 1970b
oManawir IFAO 5446 *see TLA sub Texte > Demotische Textdatenbank.*
*Man. Homilien* = Polotsky 1934.
Marciniak, Marek. 1974. *Les inscripitions hiératiques du temple de Thoutmosis III* (Deir el-Bahari I). Warsaw: Éditions Scientifiques de Pologne.
*Mart. Apatil* = Balestri & Hyvernat 1924.
*Mart. Ari* = Hyvernat 1886.
*Mart. Cyriacus of Jerusalem* = Balestri & Hyvernat 1924.
*Mart. Elijah* = Sobhy 1919.
*Mart. Epima* = Balestri & Hyvernat 1924.
*Mart. Eusebius* = Hyvernat1886.
*Mart. George* = Balestri & Hyvernat 1924.
*Mart. John of Panicôit* = Zaborowski 2005.
*Mart. Leontius the Arab* = von Lemm 1913.
*Mart. Macarius of Antioch* = Hyvernat 1886.
*Mart. Macrobius* = Hyvernat 1886.
*Mart. Mercurius* unpublished, quoted after M589.
*Mart. Nahrow* = Munier 1919 & Till 1935.
*Mart. Paese & Thekla* = Till 1935.
*Mart. Panesnew* = Till 1935.
*Mart. Papnuti* = Bacot 1999.
*Mart. Pirou & Atom* = Hyvernat 1886.
*Mart. Ptolemy* = Till 1936.
*Mart. Shnube* = Munier 1917.
*Mart. St Victor the General* = Budge 1914.
*Mart. Theodore & al.* = ᴮBalestri & Hyvernat 1924 & ˢMüller & Uljas, *Martyrs & Archangels* I.
*Mart. Theodore Stratelates* = Balestri & Hyvernat 1924.
*Mart. Timothy* = Till 1935.
Maspero, Gaston 1892. *Fragments de Manuscrits coptes-thébains provenant de la Bibliothèque du Deir Amba-Shenoudah. Fragments de l'Ancien Testament* (Mémoires publiés par les membres de Mission archéologique française au Caire VI/1), Paris: Ernest Leroux.
Massart, Adhémar. 1954. *The Leiden Magical Papyrus I 343 + 345* (Oudheidkundige Mededelingen uit het Rijksmuseum van Oudheden te Leiden). Leiden: Brill.
*Mastaba de Neferirtenef* = van den Walle 1973.

Mathieu, Bernard. 1996. *La poésie amoureuse de l'Égypte ancienne. Recherches sur un genre littéraire au Nouvel Empire* (Bibliothèque d'Étude 115). Cairo: Institut Français d'Archéologie Orientale.

Mathieu, *Poésie* = Mathieu 1996.

Matthiessen, Christian & Sandra A. Thompson. 1988. The structure of discourse and 'subordination'. In John Haiman & Sandra A. Thompson (eds.), *Clause Combining in Grammar and Discourse* (Typological Studies in Language 18), 275–329. Amsterdam/Philadelphia: Benjamins.

*Meir* III = Blackman 1915.

*Memph. Theology see TLA sub Texte > Demotische Textdatenbank.*

Merikara = Quack 1992.

Michaelis, Laura A. 2001. Exclamative constructions. In Martin Haspelmath, Ekkehard König, Wulf Oesterreicher & Wolfgang Raible (eds.), *Language Typology and Language Universals* (Handbücher zur Sprach- und Kommunikationswissenschaft 20), 1038–1050. Berlin/New York: Walter de Gruyter.

Mikhail, Maged S. M. & Tim Vivian. 2010. *The Holy Workshop of Virtue. The Life of John the Little by Zacharias of Sakhā* (Cistercian Studies Series 234). Collegeville/MN: Liturgical Press.

*Miracles of St Colluthos* = Schenke 2013.

MMA 12.184 = Hayes 1953.

MMA 35.7.55 = Hayes 1947.

Moawad, Samuel. 2010. *Untersuchungen zum Panegyrikos auf Makarios von Tkōou und zu seiner Überlieferung* (Sprachen und Kulturen des Christlichen Orients 19). Wiesbaden: Reichert.

Moers, Gerald. 1993. Freie Varianten oder funktional gebundene Morpheme? Zu den Graphien der altägyptischen Negation *n*. *Lingua Aegyptia* 3. 33–58.

pMond I = Newberry 1930.

*P.Mon.Epiph.* = Crum & Evelyn White 1926.

Moscow Bowl = Gardiner & Sethe 1928.

pMoscow math. = Imhausen 2003.

*Moꜥalla* = Vandier 1950.

Moses of Quft, *Vita Pisenthius* = Amélineau 1889.

Mostafa, Maha F. 1984–85. Erster Vorbericht über einen Ersten Zwischen-Zeit Text aus Kom el-Koffar. *Annales du Service des Antiquités de l'Égypte* 70. 419–429 with pl. I–II.

Moussa, Mark. 2010. *I Have Been Reading the Holy Gospels by Shenoute of Atripe (Discourses 8, Work 1): Coptic text, translation, and commentary*. Ann Arbor: UMI Dissertations.

Müller, Caspar Detlef Gustav. 1962. *Die Bücher der Einsetzung der Erzengel Michael und Gabriel* (Corpus Scriptorum Christianorum Orientalium 31/Scriptores Coptici 225). Louvain: Secrétariat du Corpus Scriptorum Christianorum Orientalium.

Müller, Matthias. 2011a. Die ultimative Grammatik des Koptischen? Generelles und Marginales zur 3. Auflage von Laytons *A Coptic Grammar*. *Lingua Aegyptia* 19. 251–285.

Müller, Matthias. 2011b. Ägyptische Phonologie? Möglichkeiten und Grenzen linguistischer Modelle bei der Beschreibung des Lautsystems einer extinkten Sprache. In Alexandra Verbovsek, Burkhard Backes & Catherine Jones (eds.), *Methodik und Didaktik in der Ägyptologie. Herausforderungen eines kulturwissenschaftlichen Paradigmenwechsels in den Altertumswissenschaften* (Ägyptologie und Kulturwissenschaften IV), 509–531. München: Fink.

Müller, Matthias. 2014. Expressing necessity in Sahidic Coptic. In Eitan Grossman, Stéphane Polis, Andréas Stauder & Jean Winand (eds.), *On Forms and Functions: Studies in Ancient Egyptian Grammar* (Lingua Aegyptia Studia Monographica 15), 137–172. Hamburg: Widmaier Verlag.

Müller, Matthias 2015a. Empirie vs. Kategorienbildung. *Fuzzy boundaries* und *fuzzy categories* in der ägyptisch-koptischen Syntax. In Hans Amstutz, Andreas Dorn, Matthias Müller, Miriam Ronsdorf & Sami Uljas (eds.), *Fuzzy Boundaries – Festschrift für Antonio Loprieno* I, 89–118. Hamburg: Widmaier Verlag.

Müller, Matthias. 2015b. Relative Clauses in Later Egyptian. *Lingua Aegyptia* 23. 107–173.

Müller, Matthias. *in prep. Einführung in die Grammatik des Bohairischen. Ms.*

Müller, Matthias & Sami Uljas. 2016. 'He almost heard'. A Case Study of diachronic reanalysis in Coptic syntax. In Philippe Collombert, Dominique Lefèvre, Stéphane Polis & Jean Winand (eds.), *Aere Perennius. Mélanges égyptologiques en l'honneur de Pascal Vernus* (Orientalia Lovaniensia Analecta 242), 465–491. Leuven, Paris/Bristol: Peeters.

*MuK* = Yamazaki 2003.

Munich Gl. W.A.F. 31 = Simpson 1974.

Munier, Henri. 1916. *Manuscrits Coptes: Nos 9201–9304* (Catalogue général des antiquités égyptiennes du Musée du Caire). Cairo: Institut Français d'Archéologie Orientale.

Munier, Henri. 1917. Fragments des actes du martyre de l'Apa Chnoubé. *Annales du Service des Antiquités de l'Égypte* 17. 145–159.

Munier, Henri. 1919. Nahroou et les actes de son martyre. *Annales du Service des Antiquités de l'Égypte* 19. 69–80.

Murnane, William J. & Charles van Siclen III. 1993. *The Boundary Stelae of Akhenaten* (Studies in Egyptology). London: Kegan Paul.

*Mysteries of St John Evangelist* = Budge 1913.

Myth of the Sun's Eye *see TLA sub Texte > Demotische Textdatenbank.*

Nag'a ed-Deir 3737 = Simpson 1966.

Naville, Edouard. 1886. *Das Aegyptische Todtenbuch der XVIII. bis XX. Dynastie.* Vols I–II. Berlin: von Asher & Co.

Naville, Edouard & John Joseph Tylor. 1894. *Ahnas el Medineh (Herakleopolis magna) & The Tomb of Paheri at El Kab* (Excavation Memoirs 11). London: The Egypt Exploration Fund.

Navrátilová, Hana. 2015. *Visitors' Graffiti of Dynasties 18 and 19 in Abusir and Northern Saqqara, with a Survey of the Graffiti at Giza, Southern Saqqara, Dahshur and Maidum.* Wallasey: Abercrombie Press.

Neferhetep Song 3 [TT 50] = Hari 1985.

Neferty = Helck 1970.

Neveu, François. 1994. Vraie et Pseudo Cleft Sentence en Néo-Égyptien. *Lingua Aegyptia* 4. 191–212.

Neveu, François. 1996. *La langue des Ramsès : Grammaire du néo-égyptien.* Paris: Éditions Khéops.

Newberry, Percy E. 1893. *Beni Hasan* I (Archaeological Survey of Egypt). London: Egypt Exploration Fund.

Newberry, Percy. 1895. *El Bersheh Part* I (Archaeological Survey of Egypt). London: Egypt Exploration Fund.

Nyord, Rune. 2010. The radial structure of some Middle Egyptian prepositions. *Zeitschrift für Ägyptische Sprache und Altertumskunde* 137. 27–44.

*O.Ashm.Copt.* = Biedenkopf-Ziehner 2000.

*O.Crum* = Crum 1902b.
*O.Frange* = Boud'hors & Heurtel 2010.
*OIP* 100 = The Epigraphic Society 1979.
*O.Medin.Habu Copt.* = Stefanski & Lichtheim 1952.
Onkhsheshonqy *see TLA sub Texte > Demotische Textdatenbank.*
Oréal, Elsa. 2008. 'Bienvenue!' (Ptahhetep, maxime 22): répartition des biens et salut individuel. *Revue d'Égyptologie* 59, 335–356.
Oréal, Elsa. 2010. 'Bienvenue en paix!': la réception rituelle du mort aux funérailles. *Revue d'Égyptologie* 61, 135–150.
Oréal, Elsa. 2011. *Les particules en égyptien ancien : De l'ancien égyptien à l'égyptien classique* (Bibliothèque d'Étude 152). Cairo: Institut Français d'Archéologie Orientale.
Orlandi, Tito. 1966. *Vangelo di Nicodemo* I (Test e Documenti per lo Studio dell'Antichità 21). Milano & Varese: Istituto Editoriale Cisalpino.
Orlandi, Tito. 1968a. *Studi copti. 1) Un encomio di Marco Evangelista 2) Le fonti copte della Storia dei Patriarchi di Alessandria 3) La leggenda di San Mercurio* (Test e Documenti per lo Studio dell'Antichità 22). Milano & Varese: Istituto Editoriale Cisalpino.
Orlandi, Tito. 1968b. *Testi copti. 1) Encomio di Atanasio 2) Vita di Atanasio* (Test e Documenti per lo Studio dell'Antichità 15). Milano & Varese: Istituto Editoriale Cisalpino.
Orlandi, Tito. 1974. *Lettere di San Paolo in copto-ossirinchita* (Papiri dell'Università degli Studi di Milano 5). Milano: Goliardica.
Orlandi, Tito. 1985. *Shenute Contra Origenistas* (Corpus dei Manoscritti Copti Letterari), Rome: C.I.M.
Orlandi, Tito. 1988. *Paolo di Tamma – Opere* (Corpus dei Manoscritti Copti Letterari), Rome: C.I.M.
Orlandi, Tito, Birger A. Pearson & Harold A. Drake. 1980. *Eudoxia & the Holy Sepulchre. A Constantine Legend in Coptic* (Testi e Documenti per lo Studio dell'Antichitá LXVII). Milano: Cisalpino La Goliardica.
Osing, Jürgen. 1976. *Die Nominalbildung des Ägyptischen* (Sonderschriften des DAI Kairo 3). Mainz: Philipp von Zabern.
Osing, Jürgen. 1977. Zur Syntax der Biographie des *Wnj*. *Orientalia* 46. 165–182.
*O.Tempeleide* = Kaplony-Heckel 1963.
*O.Vind.Copt.* = Till 1960.
Pachom, *Instructions Concerning a Spiteful Monk* = Lefort 1956.
Pachom, *Praecepta* = Lefort 1956.
*Paheri* = Naville & Tylor 1894.
Palmer, Frank Robert. 2000. *Mood and Modality*, 2nd ed. (Cambridge Textbooks in Linguistics). Cambridge: Cambridge University Press.
*Panegyric on John the Baptist* = de Vis 1922.
Papnute, *Wanderings* = Amélineau 1885.
*Paraph. Shem* = Pearson 1996.
Parkinson, Richard B. 1991. *The Tale of the Eloquent Peasant.* Oxford: The Griffith Institute & The Ashmolean Museum.
Parkinson, Richard. 1997. The text of *Khakheperraseneb*: new readings of EA 5645, and an unpublished ostracon. *The Journal of Egyptian Archaeology* 83. 55–68.
Paul of Tamma, *De Cella* = Orlandi 1988.
Paul of Tamma, *De Humilitate* = Orlandi 1988.
Peas = Parkinson 1991.

Pearson, Birger A. 1996. *Nag Hammadi Codex VII* (Nag Hammadi and Manichean Studies 30). Leiden, New York & Cologne: Brill.
Pearson, Birger A. & Tim Vivian. 1993. *Two Coptic Homilies Attributed to Saint Peter of Alexandria: I. On Riches, II. On the Epiphany*, with the assistance of Donald B. Spanel (Corpus dei Manoscritti Copti Letterari), Rome: C.I.M.
Peet, Thomas Eric. 1926. Two Eighteenth Dynasty Letters. Papyrus Louvre E 3220. *The Journal of Egyptian Archaeology* 12. 70–74 & pl. XVII.
Peet, Thomas Eric. 1930. Two Letters from Akhetaten. *Annals of Archaeology and Anthropology* 17. 82–97.
Pennacchietti, Fabrizio A. 1968. *Studi sui pronomi determinativi semitici* (Pubblicazioni dal Seminario di Semitistica 4). Napoli: Istituto Orientale di Napoli.
Peter of Alexandria, *On Riches* = Pearson & Vivian 1993.
*Petese Stories* = Ryholt 2005.
*Petubastis Cycle* tCambridge 5 *see TLA sub Texte > Demotische Textdatenbank.*
Petrie, William Matthew Flinders. 1898. *Dendereh*. London: The Egypt Exploration Fund.
Peust, Carsten. 1996. *Indirekte Rede im Neuägyptischen* (Göttinger Orientforschungen IV/33). Wiesbaden: Harrassowitz.
Peust, Carsten. 1999. *Egyptian Phonology: An Introduction to the Phonology of a Dead Language* (Monographien zur Ägyptischen Sprache 2). Göttingen: Peust & Gutschmidt.
Peust, Carsten. 2002. Objektspronomen im Ägyptischen. *Lingua Aegyptia* 10. 309–333.
Peust, Carsten. 2005. Weiteres zur Personenverschiebung in der ägyptischen indirekten Rede. *Lingua Aegyptia* 13. 77–102.
Peust, Carsten. 2008. Adjektive und Adjektivverb im Mitteläqyptischen. In C. Peust (ed.), *Miscellanea in Honorem Wolfhart Westendorf* (Göttinger Miszellen Beihefte 3), 58–82. Göttingen: Seminar für Ägyptologie und Koptologie.
Peust, Carsten. 2014. Doch keine Einaktantenverschiebung in der neuägyptischen indirekten Rede. *Lingua Aegyptia* 22. 311–315.
*P.Gascou* = Fournet & Papaconstantinou 2016.
pPhiladelphia 1 *see TLA sub Texte > Demotische Textdatenbank.*
grPhilae 416 *see TLA sub Texte > Demotische Textdatenbank.*
Pisenthius of Quft, *On Onnofrius* = Crum 1915–17.
*Pistis Sophia* = Schmidt 1925.
*P.KellisCopt* = Gardner, Alcock & Funk 1999 & 2014.
Polis, Stéphane. 2005. Les formes 'contingentes' en ancien égyptien : une catégorisation en question. In Christian Cannuyer (ed.), *La langue dans tous ses états. Michel Malaise in honorem* (Acta Orientalia Belgica 18), 301–322. Brussels: Société belge d'études orientales.
Polis, Stéphane. 2009a. *Étude de la modalité en néo-égyptien*. Unpublished PhD dissertation, University of Liège.
Polis, Stéphane. 2009b. Interaction entre modalité et subjectivité en néo-égyptien. Autour de la construction *mri* + *iw*$_{circ}$. « souhaiter que ». *Lingua Aegyptia* 17. 201–229.
Polotsky, Hans Jakob. 1930. The stela of Heka-Yeb. *The Journal of Egyptian Archaeology* 16. 194–199.
Polotsky, Hans Jakob. 1934. *Manichäische Homilien*, mit einem Beitrag von Hugo Ibscher (Manichäische Handschriften der Sammlung A. Chester Beatty I). Stuttgart: Kohlhammer.
Polotsky, Hans Jakob. 1940. *Kephalaia – 1. Hälfte*, mit einem Beitrag von Hugo Ibscher (Manichäische Handschriften der Staatlichen Museen Berlin I). Stuttgart: Kohlhammer.
Polotsky, Hans Jakob. 1971. *Collected Papers*. Jerusalem: Magnes Press.

Polotsky, Hans Jakob. 2007. *Scripta Posteriora on Egyptian and Coptic*, ed. Verena M. Lepper & Leo Depuydt (Lingua Aegyptia Studia Monographica 7). Hamburg: Widmaier Verlag.
Porcher, Emile. 1914. *Vie d'Isaac, Patriarche d'Alexandrie de 686 à 689* (Patrologia Orientalis XI/3). Turnhout: Brepols.
Porcher, Emile. 1924. *Le Livre de Job, Version copte bohaïrique* (Patrologia Orientalis XVIII/2, N° 87), Turnhout: Brepols (reprint 1990).
Posener, Georges. 1938. *Catalogue des Ostraca Hiératiques Littéraires de Deîr el-Médînéh* I: *N^os 1001–1108* (Documents de Fouilles de l'Institut Français d'Archéologie Orientale 1). Cairo: Institut Français d'Archéologie Orientale.
Posener, Georges. 1951–72. *Catalogue des Ostraca Hiératiques Littéraires de Deîr el-Médînéh* I: *N^os 1109–1266* (Documents de Fouilles de l'Institut Français d'Archéologie Orientale 18). Cairo: Institut Français d'Archéologie Orientale.
Posener, Georges. 1957. Recherches littéraires VI: Le conte de Néferkarê et du général Siséné. *Revue d'Égyptologie* 11. 119–137.
Posener, Georges. 1976. *L'Enseignement Loyaliste. Sagesse égyptienne du Moyen Empire* (Hautes Études Orientales 5). Geneva: Librairie Droz.
Posener, Georges. 1985. *Le Papyrus Vandier* (Bibliothèque Générale 7). Cairo: Institut Français d'Archéologie Orientale.
Posener-Kriéger, Paule. 1978. A Letter to the Governor of Elephantine. *The Journal of Egyptian Archaeology* 64. 84–87 & pl. XIV–XIVA.
Praetorius, Franz. 1871. Review of Stern, *Koptische Grammatik*. *Zeitschrift der Deutschen Morgenländischen Gesellschaft* 35. 750–761.
*PrecPl* (NHC I, 1) = Attridge 1985.
Prieur, Jean-Marc. 1989. *Acta Andreae – Textus* (Corpus christianorum. Series apocryphorum 6). Turnhout: Brepols.
*Primeval Ocean see TLA sub Texte > Demotische Textdatenbank.*
*Psalms of the Bema* = Allberry 1938.
*Psalms of Saracôtôn* = Allberry 1938.
*Psalms of Thomas* = Allberry 1938.
Ps. Athanasius, *TestPatr* = Guidi 1900a & b.
Ps. Cyril, *On the Cross* = Campagnano 1980 & Budge 1915.
Ps. Cyril, *On the Virgin* = Bombeck 2001.
Ps. Gregory of Nyssa, *De Sacrificio Abraham* = Chaîne 1912 & 1913.
Ps. Shenute, *On Christian Behaviour* = Kuhn 1960.
oPSBA 35, pl. 27 = Thompson 1913.
PT = Sethe 1908–22.
Ptahhetep = Žabá 1956.
Quack, Joachim Friedrich. 1991a. Über die mit *ʿnḫ* gebildeten Namenstypen und die Vokalisation einiger Verbalformen. *Göttinger Miszellen* 123. 91–100.
Quack, Joachim Friedrich. 1991b. Die Konstruktion des Infinitivs in der Cleft Sentence. *Revue d'Égyptologie* 42. 189–207.
Quack, Joachim Friedrich. 1992. *Studien zur Lehre für Merikare* (Göttinger Orientforschungen IV/23). Wiesbaden: Harrassowitz.
Quack, Joachim Friedrich. 1994. *Die Lehren des Ani: Ein neuägyptischer Weisheitstext in seinem kulturellen Umfeld* (Orbis Biblicus et Orientalis 141). Freiburg: Universitätsverlag/ Göttingen: Vandenhoeck & Ruprecht.

Quack, Joachim Friedrich. 1999. A New Bilingual Fragment from the British Museum. *The Journal of Egyptian Archaeology* 85. 153–164 & pl. XXII–XXIII.
Quack, Joachim Friedrich. 2009. Zum Partizip im Demotischen. *Lingua Aegyptia* 17. 231–258.
Qaw Bowl = Gardiner & Sethe 1928.
Quecke, Hans. 1972. *Das Markusevangelium Saïdisch. Text der Handschrift PPaulau Rib. Inv.-Nr. 182 mit den Varianten der Handschrift M 569* (Papyrologica Castroctaviana, Studia et textus 4). Barcelona: Papyrologica Castroctaviana.
Quecke, Hans. 1977. *Das Lukasevangelium Saïdisch. Text der Handschrift PPaulau Rib. Inv.-Nr. 181 mit den Varianten der Handschrift M 569* (Papyrologica Castroctaviana, Studia et textus 6). Barcelona: Papyrologica Castroctaviana.
Quecke, Hans. 1984. *Das Johannesevangelium Saïdisch. Text der Handschrift PPaulau Rib. Inv.-Nr. 183 mit den Varianten der Handschriften 813 und 814 der Chester Beatty Library und der Handschrift M 569* (Papyrologica Castroctaviana, Studia et textus 11). Rome & Barcelona: Papyrologica Castroctaviana
*Questions of Theodore* = van Lantschoot 1957.
Raphia Decree *see TLA sub Texte > Demotische Textdatenbank.*
*RAD* = Gardiner 1948.
pRamesseum I = Barnes 1956.
*RecTrav* 25 = Jacoby 1903.
Red Chapel = Lacau & Chevrier 1977.
*Reden und Rufe* = Erman 1918.
Reintges, Chris. 1997. *Passive Voice in Older Egyptian. A Morpho-Syntactic Study* (HIL Dissertations 28). The Hague: Holland Institute of Generative Linguistics.
Reintges, Chris. 2004. *Coptic Egyptian (Sahidic Dialect). A Learner's Grammar* (Afrikawissenschaftliche Lehrbücher 15). Köln: Rüdiger Köppe.
Retsö, Jan. 2009. Nominal attribution in Semitic. Typology and diachrony. In Janet C. E. Watson & Jan Retsö (eds.), *Relative Clauses and Genitive Constructions in Semitic* (Journal of Semitic Studies Supplement 25), 3–33. Oxford: Oxford University Press.
pRhind I *see TLA sub Texte > Demotische Textdatenbank.*
pRhind II *see TLA sub Texte > Demotische Textdatenbank.*
pRhind math. = Imhausen 2003.
Richter, Tonio Sebastian. 1999. Spätkoptische Rechtsurkunden neu bearbeitet: BM Or. 4917(15) und P. Med. Copto inv. 69.69. *Journal of Juristic Papyrology* 29. 85–92.
Richter, Tonio Sebastian. 2016. Ein fatimidenzeitliches koptisches Rechnungsheft aus den Papieren Noël Girons. In Jean-Luc Fournet & Arietta Papaconstantinou (eds.). *Mélanges Jean Gascou. Textes et études papyrologiques (P. Gascou)* (Travaux et Mémoires 20/1), 381–402. Paris: Association des Amis du Centre d'Histoire et Civilisation de Byzance.
Ritter, Thomas. 1992. On particles in Middle Egyptian. *Lingua Aegyptia* 2. 127–137.
Ritter, Thomas. 1994. On cleft sentences in Late Egyptian. *Lingua Aegyptia* 4. 245–269.
Ritter, Thomas. 1995. *Das Verbalsystem der königlichen und privaten Inschriften XVIII. Dynastie bis einschließlich Amenophis III* (Göttinger Orientforschungen IV/30). Wiesbaden: Harrassowitz.
Roccati, *Mag. taur.* = Roccati 2011.
Roccati, Alessandro. 2011. *Magica Taurinensia. Il grande papiro magico di Torino e i suoi duplicati* (Analecta Orientalia 56). Rome: Gregorian & Biblical Press.
Robinson, Forbes. 1896. *Coptic Apocryphal Gospels.* (Texts & Studies. Contributions to Biblical & Patristic Literature IV.2) Cambridge: Cambridge University Press.

Roeder, Hubert. 1986. Die Prädikation im nominalen Nominalsatz – Ein logisch-semantischer Ansatz. *Göttinger Miszellen* 91. 3–77.

Rösch, Friedrich. 1910. *Bruchstücke des Ersten Clemensbriefes nach dem achmimischen Papyrus der Strassburger Universitäts- und Landesbibliothek mit biblischen Texten derselben Handschrift.* Strassburg: Schlesier & Schweickhardt.

Rosengren, Inger. 1997. The thetic/categorical distinction revisited once more. *Linguistics* 35/3. 439–479.

Rosetta Decree *see TLA sub Texte > Demotische Textdatenbank.*

Rowe, Alan. 1939. Three new stelæ from the south-eastern desert. *Annales du Service des Antiquités de l'Égypte* 39. 187–194 with pl. XXV–XXVI.

Ryholt, Kim. 2002. *The Carlsberg Papyri 10: Narrative Literature from the Tebtunis Temple Library* (CNI Publications 35). Copenhagen: Carsten Niebuhr Institute of Ancient Near East Studies & Museum Tusculanum Press.

Ryholt, Kim. 2005. *The Carlsberg Papyri 6: The Petese Stories* II (CNI Publications 29). Copenhagen: Carsten Niebuhr Institute of Ancient Near East Studies & Museum Tusculanum Press.

pRylands I *see TLA sub Texte > Demotische Textdatenbank.*

pRylands II *see TLA sub Texte > Demotische Textdatenbank.*

pRylands VIII *see TLA sub Texte > Demotische Textdatenbank.*

pRylands IX *see TLA sub Texte > Demotische Textdatenbank.*

*P.RylCopt.* = Crum 1909.

Sabek, Yasser. 2002. Der hieratische Papyrus Berlin P 10497. *Zeitschrift für Ägyptische Sprache und Altertumskunde* 129. 75–84 & pl. XV–XVI.

Säve-Söderbergh, Torgny. 1994. *The Old Kingdom Cemetery at Hamra Dom (El-Qasr wa es-Saiyed).* Stockholm: The Royal Academie of Letters/History and Antiquity.

Sadock, Jerrold M. & Arnold M. Zwicky. 1985. Speech act distinctions in syntax. In Timothy Shopen (ed.), *Language Typology and Syntactic Description I: Clause Structure*, 155–196. Cambridge: Cambridge University Press.

Sandman, Maj. 1938. *Texts from the Time of Akhenaten* (Bibliotheca Aegyptiaca 8). Brussels: Fondation égyptologique Reine Élisabeth.

*Saqqâra Dem. Papyri I see TLA sub Texte > Demotische Textdatenbank.*

pSaqqara I 1 *see TLA sub Texte > Demotische Textdatenbank.*

pSaqqara H5-DP 265 *see TLA sub Texte > Demotische Textdatenbank.*

pSaqqara H5-DP 486 *see TLA sub Texte > Demotische Textdatenbank.*

pSaqqara 71/2 DP 145 *see TLA sub Texte > Demotische Textdatenbank.*

pSaqqara-Sekhemkhet *see TLA sub Texte > Demotische Textdatenbank.*

Sasse, Hans-Jürgen. 1987. The thetic/categorical distinction revisited. *Linguistics* 25. 511–580.

Satzinger, Helmut. 1968. *Die negativen Konstruktionen im Alt- und Mittelägyptischen* (Münchner Ägyptologische Studien 12). Berlin: Bruno Hessling.

Satzinger, Helmut. 1976. *Neuägyptische Studien: Die Partikel ir. Das Tempussystem* (Beihefte zur Wiener Zeitschrift für die Kunde des Morgenlandes 6). Wien: Verband der wissenschaftlichen Gesellschaften Österreichs.

Satzinger, Helmut. 1986. Syntax der Präpositionadjektive ('Präpositionsnisben'). *Zeitschrift für Ägyptische Sprache und Altertumskunde* 113. 141–153.

Satzinger, Helmut. 1993. Die Protasis *jr sḏm.f* im älteren Ägyptisch. *Lingua Aegyptia* 3. 121–135.

Satzinger, Helmut. 1997. How good was Tjeker-Baʿal's Egyptian? Mockery at foreign diction in the Report of Wenamun. *Lingua Aegyptia* 5. 171–176.
Sauneron, Serge. 1959. *Catalogue des Ostraca Hiératiques Non Littéraires de Deîr el-Médînéh* VI: *N^os 550–623* (Documents de Fouilles de l'Institut Français d'Archéologie Orientale 13). Cairo: Institut Français d'Archéologie Orientale.
Sauneron, Serge. 1980. Deux pages d'un texte littéraire inédit. Papyrus Deir el-Médineh 39. In Jean Vercoutter (ed.), *Livre du Centenaire 1880–1980* (Mémoires publiés par les Membres de l'Institut Français d'Archéologie Orientale du Caire 94), 135–141 & pls. X–XIa. Cairo: Institut Français d'Archéologie Orientale du Caire.
*Sayings of Pagan Philosophers* = Crum 1905 & Till 1934.
Scalf, Foy D. 2009. Is that a rhetorical question? Shipwrecked Sailor (pHermitage 1115), 150 reconsidered. *Zeitschrift für Ägyptische Sprache und Altertumskunde* 136. 155–159.
Schachter, Paul. 1985. Parts of speech systems. In Timothy Shopen (ed.), *Language Typology and Syntactic Description I: Clause Structure*, 3–61. Cambridge: Cambridge University Press.
Scharff, Alexander. 1922. Ein Rechnungsbuch des königlichen Hofes aus der 13. Dynastie. *Zeitschrift für Ägyptische Sprache und Altertumskunde* 57. 51–68 & 1*–24*.
Schenke, Gesa. 2013. *Das koptisch hagiographische Dossier des Heiligen Kolluthos, Arzt, Märtyrer und Wunderheiler* (Corpus Scriptorum Christianorum Orientalium. Subsidia 132). Leuven: Peeters.
Schenke, Hans-Martin. 1981. *Das Matthäus-Evangelium im Mittelägyptischen Dialekt des Koptischen (Codex Scheide)* (Texte und Untersuchungen zur Geschichte der altchristlichen Literatur 127). Berlin: Akademie.
Schenke, Hans-Martin. 1991. *Apostelgeschichte 1,1–15, 3 im Mittelägyptischen Dialekt des Koptischen (Codex Glazier)* (Texte und Untersuchungen zur Geschichte der altchristlichen Literatur 137). Berlin: Akademie.
Schenke, Hans-Martin. 1996. Die Psalmen im mittelägyptischen Dialekt des Koptischen (der Mudil-Codex). *Enchoria* 23. 86–144.
Schenke, Hans-Martin. 1997–1998. Review of Elanskaya, *The literary Coptic manuscripts in the A.S. Pushkin State Fine Arts Museum in Moscow*. *Enchoria* 24. 163–170.
Schenke, Hans-Martin. 2001. *Das Matthäus-Evangelium im mittelägyptischen Dialekt des Koptischen (Codex Schøyen)* (Manuscripts in the Schøyen Collection I: Coptic Papyri 1). Oslo: Hermes.
Schenke, Hans-Martin. 2003. *Papyrus Michigan 3520 und 6868(a): Ecclesiastes, Erster Johannesbrief und zweiter Petrusbrief im Fayumischen Dialekt*, in Zusammenarbeit mit Rodolphe Kasser (Texte und Untersuchungen zur Geschichte der altchristlichen Literatur 151). Berlin & New York: de Gruyter.
Schenkel, Wolfgang. 1966. Die mittelägyptischen Nisben als Nuklei in präpositionaler, limitierender und Genitiv-Relation. *Chronique d'Égypte* 41. 50–59.
Schenkel, Wolfgang. 1984. Fokussierung. Über die Reihenfolge von Subjekt und Prädikat im klassisch-ägyptischen Nominalsatz. In Friedrich Junge (ed.), *Studien zu Sprache und Religion Ägyptens zu Ehren von Wolfhart Westendorf* I, 157–174. Göttingen: Hubert & Co.
Schenkel, Wolfgang. 1985. „Spezifität" – der Schlüssel zum ägyptisch-koptischen Nominalsatz? *Bibliotheca Orientalis* 42. 255–265.
Schenkel, Wolfgang. 1987. Zur Struktur des dreigliedrigen Nominalsatzes mit der Satzteilfolge Subjekt–Prädikat im ägyptischen (mit disproportionalen Bemerkungen zu einigen Pyramidentext-Stellen, insbesondere zu Pyr. § 131a–d). *Studien zur altägyptischen Kultur* 14. 265–282.

Schenkel, Wolfgang. 1990. *Einführung in die altägyptische Sprachwissenschaft* (Orientalistische Einführungen). Darmstadt: Wissenschaftliche Buchgesellschaft.

Schenkel, Wolfgang. 2000. Die Endungen des Prospektivs und Subjunktivs (*śč̣m=f, śč̣m.w=f, śč̣m.y=f*) nach Befunden der Sargtexte. *Lingua Aegyptia* 7. 30–61.

Schenkel, Wolfgang. 2007. Die Partikel *iw* und die Intuition des Interpreten. Randbemerkungen zu Antonio Loprieno, 'On fuzzy boundaries in Egyptian Syntax'. *Lingua Aegyptia* 15. 161–201.

Schenkel, Wolfgang. 2008. Substantiv/selbständiges Personalpronomen + enklitisches Personalpronomen, eine grammatische Konstruktion des älteren Ägyptischen? *Göttinger Miszellen* 217. 97–109.

Schenkel, Wolfgang. 2010. Die Clèresche Relativform. Belege für ihre Existenz und Nachweis ihrer Verschiedenheit von einem passivischen Partizip und der Futurischen Relativform. *Zeitschrift für Ägyptische Sprache und Altertumskunde* 137. 66–90.

Schenkel, Wolfgang. 2012. *Tübinger Einführung in die klassisch-ägyptische Sprache und Schrift*. Tübingen: Selbstverlag.

Schmidt, Carl. 1905. *Acta Pauli aus der Heidelberger koptischen Papyrushandschrift Nr. 1*, 2nd edition, Leipzig: J. C. Hinrichs.

Schmidt, Carl. 1908. *Der erste Clemensbrief in altkoptischer Übersetzung* (Texte und Untersuchungen zur Geschichte der altchristlichen Literatur 3. Reihe, 2. Band [= 32. Band Gesamtreihe], 1. Heft). Leipzig: J.C. Hinrichs.

Schmidt, Carl. 1919. *Gespräche Jesu mit seinen Jüngern nach der Auferstehung. Ein katholisch-apostolisches Sendschreiben des 2. Jahrhunderts nach einem koptischen Papyrus des Institut de la Mission Archéol. Française au Caire unter Mitarbeit von Herrn Pierre Lacau derzeitigem Generaldirektor der ägypt. Museen, nebst drei Exkursen*, Leipzig.

Schmidt, Carl. 1925. *Pistis Sophia*. (Coptica II). Hauniae: Gyldendalske Boghandel – Nordisk Forlag.

Schüssler, Karlheinz 1991. *Die katholischen Briefe in der koptischen (sahidischen) Version* (Corpus Scriptorum Christianorum Orientalium 157/Scriptores Coptici 21). Louvain: Peeters.

Schweitzer, Simon. 2005. *Schrift und Sprache der 4. Dynastie* (MENES 3). Wiesbaden: Harrassowitz.

Searle, John. 1969. *Speech Acts*. Cambridge: Cambridge University Press.

Seele, Keith C. 1959. *The Tomb of Tjanefer at Thebes* (Oriental Institute Publications 86). Chicago: Oriental Institute Press.

*SEH* 152 = Gasse & Rondon 2007.

Sethe, Kurt. 1908–22. *Die Altägyptischen Pyramidentexte nach den Papierabdrücken und Photographien des Berliner Museums*. 4 vols. Leipzig: J.C. Hinrichs.

Sethe, Kurt. 1916. *Der Nominalsatz im Ägyptischen und Koptischen* (Abhandlungen der sächsischen Akademie der Wissenschaften 33/3). Leipzig: B.G. Teubner.

Sethe, Kurt. 1919. *Die relativischen Partizipialumschreibungen des Demotischen und ihre Überreste im Koptischen in zwei Ausdrücken der hellenistischen Mysteriensprache* (Nachrichten von der Gesellschaft der Wissenschaften zu Göttingen, Philologisch-historische Klasse 1919), 145–158. Göttingen: Vandenhoeck & Ruprecht.

Sethe, Kurt. 1926. Ein Prozessurteil aus dem Alten Reich. *Zeitschrift für Ägyptische Sprache und Altertumskunde* 61. 67–79.

Sethe, Kurt. 1928. *Ägyptische Lesestücke zum Gebrauch im akademischen Unterricht zusammengestellt. Texte des Mittleren Reiches*. 2nd edition. Leipzig: J.C. Hinrichs.

Sethe, Kurt. 1932. *Urkunden des Alten Reichs* (Urkunden des ägyptischen Altertums 1). 2nd edition. Leipzig: J. C. Hinrichs.

Sethe, Kurt. 1935–1939. *Übersetzung und Kommentar zu den altägyptischen Pyramidentexten.* 6 vols. Glückstadt/Hamburg/New York: J. J. Augustin.

Sethe, Kurt & Wolfgang Helck. 1906–1988. *Urkunden der 18. Dynastie: Historisch-biographische Urkunden* (Urkunden des ägyptischen Altertums 4). Leipzig: J.C. Hinrichs & Berlin: Akademie Verlag.

Semnah desp. = Smither & Gunn 1945.

Setne I *see TLA sub Texte > Demotische Textdatenbank.*

Setne II *see TLA sub Texte > Demotische Textdatenbank.*

Shenute,

*A Beloved One Asked Me Once Years Ago* = Chassinat 1911.
*Acephalous Work A1*= Young 1993.
*Acephalous Work A6* = Shisha-Halevi 1975.
*Acephalous Work A14* = Orlandi 1985.
*As I Sat on a Mountain* = Leipoldt 1908.
*Because of You too, O Prince of Evil* = Chassinat 1911.
*Blessed Are They Who Observe Justice* = Chassinat 1911.
*Canon I* = Amélineau 1907.
*Continuing to Glorify the Lord* = Leipoldt 1908.
*God Is Blessed* = Chassinat 1911.
*God Who Alone Is True* = Amélineau 1888; 1914; Leipoldt 1913; Young 1988.
*I Am Amazed* = Cristea 2011.
*I Answered* = Leipoldt 1908.
*I Have Been Reading the Holy Gospels* = Leipoldt 1908 & Moussa 2010.
*In the Night* = Leipoldt 1908.
*I See Your Eagerness* = Amélineau 1914.
*Is It Not Written* = Amélineau 1907.
*It Happened One Day* = Lefort 1955.
*Not because a Fox Barks* = Chassinat 1911.
*Reading Today from the Proverbs* = Leipoldt 1908.
*Shenute Writes to Tahom* = Leipoldt 1908.
*Shenute Writes to Timothy* II = Munier 1916.
*Some Kinds of People Sift Dirt/ Whoever Seeks God Will Find* = Amélineau 1907.
*Since It Is Necessary to Pursue the Devil* = Amélineau 1907.
*There is Another Foolishness* = Amélineau 1914.
*Truly, When I Think* = Leipoldt 1913.
*Well Did You Come* = Amélineau 1914.
*Who But God Is the Witness* = Boud'hours 2013 & Young 1993.
*Why, O Lord* = Leipoldt 1908 & Young 1993.
*You, God, The Eternal* = Leipoldt 1913.
*Le Muséon* 45 = Burmester 1932.
Shenute? (attribution doubtful) = Leipoldt 1908.

Shisha-Halevy, Ariel. 1974. Protactic *efsôtm*: a hitherto unnoticed Coptic tripartite conjugation-form and its diachronic connections. *Orientalia* nova series 43. 369–381.

Shisha-Halevy, Ariel. 1975. Two New Shenoute Texts from the British Library. *Orientalia* nova series 44. 149–185 & 469–484 with Tab. IX–X.

Shisha-Halevy, Ariel. 1981. Bohairic-Late Egyptian diaglosses: a contribution to the typology of Egyptian. In Dwight W. Young (ed.), *Studies presented to Hans Jakob Polotsky*, 314–338. East Gloucester, MA: Pirtle & Polson.
Shisha-Halevy, Ariel. 1983. 'Middle Egyptian' gleanings: grammatical notes on the 'Middle Egyptian' text of Matthew. Review of Schenke 1981. *Chronique d'Égypte* 58. 311–329.
Shisha-Halevy, Ariel. 1984a. Existential statements in the Sahidic New Testament: work notes. *Göttinger Miszellen* 77: 67–79.
Shisha-Halevy, Ariel. 1984b. Notes on some Coptic nominal sentence patterns. In Friedrich Junge (ed.), *Studien zu Sprache und Religion Ägyptens: zu Ehren von Wolfhart Westendorf* I, 175–189. Göttingen: Hubert & Co.
Shisha-Halevy, Ariel. 1987. Grammatical discovery procedure and the Egyptian-Coptic nominal sentence. *Orientalia* 56. 147–175.
Shisha-Halevy, Ariel. 2007. *Topics in Coptic Syntax: Structural Studies in the Bohairic Dialect* (Orientalia Lovaniensia Analecta 160). Leuven/Paris/Dudley: Peeters.
Sh.S. = Blackman 1933.
Shorter, Alan W. 1936. A Magical Ostracon. *The Journal of Egyptian Archaeology* 22. 165–168.
Shorter, Alan W. 1963. *Joshua I–VI and Other Passages in Coptic, Edited from a Fourth-century Sahidic Codex in the Chester Beatty Library, Dublin* (Chester Beatty Monographs 9), Dublin: Hodges Figgis & Co. Ltd.
Sieber, John H. (ed.). 1991. *Nag Hammadi Codex VIII. Introductions. Texts. Translations, Indices* (Nag Hammadi Series 31). Leiden: Brill
Siewierska, Anna. 1991. *Functional Grammar* (Linguistic Theory Guides). London/New York: Routledge.
Silverman, David. 1980. *Interrogative Constructions with JN and JN-JW in Old and Middle Egyptian* (Bibliotheca Aegyptia I). Malibu: Undena.
Silverman, David. 2000. The threat-formula and biographical text in the tomb of Hezi in Saqqara, *Journal of the American Research Center in Egypt* 37. 1–13
Simon, Jean. 1934/35. Homélie copte inédite sur S. Michel et le bon larron attribuée à S. Jean Chrysostome. *Orientalia* nova series 3. 217–242 & 4. 222–234.
Simpson, Robert. 1996. *Demotic Grammar in the Ptolemaic Sacerdotal Decrees*. Oxford: Griffith Institute.
Simpson, William Kelly. 1966. The Letter to the Dead from the tomb of Meru (N 3737) at Nagʿ ed-Deir. *The Journal of Egyptian Archaeology* 52. 39–52.
Simpson, William Kelly. 1974. *The Terrace of the Great God at Abydos: The Offering Chapels of Dynasties 12 and 13* (Publications of the Pennsylvania-Yale Expedition to Egypt 5). New Haven/Philadephia: The Peabody Museum of Natural History of Yale University/The University Museum of the University of Pennsylvania.
Sin = Koch 1990.
Sinai = Gardiner & Peet 1952.
Sisene Story (tDeM 1214 v°) = Posener 1957.
Siut I = Griffith 1889.
Siut III = Griffith 1889.
Siut IV = Griffith 1889.
Siut V = Griffith 1889.
Smither, Paul Cecil. 1942. An Old Kingdom Letter Concerning the Crimes of Count Sabni. *The Journal of Egyptian Archaeology* 28. 16–19.

Smither, Paul Cecil†. 1945. The Semnah Despatches. *The Journal of Egyptian Archaeology* 31. 3–10 & pl. II–VII.

Smither, Paul Cecil†. 1948. The Report Concerning the Slave-Girl Senbet. *The Journal of Egyptian Archaeology* 34. 31–34.

SNM 34370 = Hintze & Reineke 1989.

Sobhy, P. G. 1919. *Le martyre de Saint Hélias et l'encomium de l'évêque Stéphanos de Hnès sur Saint Hélias* (Bibliothèque d'Études Coptes 1). Cairo: Institut Français d'Archéologie Orientale.

Spencer, Andrew & Ana Luís. 2012. *Clitics. An Introduction* (Cambridge Textbooks in Linguistics). Cambridge: Cambridge University Press.

Stassen, Leon. 1997. *Intransitive Predication* (Oxford Studies in Typology and Linguistic Theory). Oxford: Oxford University Press.

Stauder, Andréas. 2013. *Linguistic Dating of Middle Egyptian Literary Texts* (Lingua Aegyptia Studia Monographica 12). Hamburg: Widmaier Verlag.

Stauder, Andréas. 2014. Splitting the *sḏm-n=f*? A discussion of written forms in Coffin Texts, parts 1 and 2. *Zeitschrift für Ägyptische Sprache und Altertumskunde* 96. 83–96, 195–208.

Stauder, Andréas & Sami Uljas. *in prep*. Thetic sentences in Earlier Egyptian.

Stauder-Porchet, Julie. 2009. *La préposition en égyptien de la première phase. Approche sémantique* (Aegyptiaca Helvetica 21). Basel: Schwabe.

Steindorff, Georg. 1883. Gesios und Isidoros. Drei sahidische Fragmente über "die Auffindung der Gebeine Johannes des Täufers". *Zeitschrift für Ägyptische Sprache und Altertumskunde* 21. 137–158.

Steindorff, Georg. 1899. *Die Apokalypse des Elias. Eine unbekannte Apokalypse & Bruchstücke der Sophonias-Apokalypse*, Leipzig: J. C. Hinrichs.

Steindorff, Georg. 1913. *Das Grab des Ti*. Leipzig: J.C. Hinrichs.

Steindorff, Georg. 1951. *Lehrbuch der koptischen Grammatik*. Chicago: University of Chicago Press.

Stefanski, Elizabeth & Miriam Lichtheim. 1952. *Coptic Ostraca from Medinet Habu* (Oriental Institute Publications 71). Chicago: Oriental Institute Press.

Stern, Ludwig. 1880. *Koptische Grammatik*. Leipzig: Weigel.

Stewart, Harry Milne. 1979. *Egyptian Stelae, Reliefs and Paintings from the Petrie Collection Part 2: Archaic Period to the 2nd Intermediate Period*. Warminster: Aris & Phillips.

pSt Petersburg 1118 = Bakir 1970.

pSt Petersburg 1119 = Bakir 1970.

oStrasbourg 1845 *see TLA sub Texte > Demotische Textdatenbank.*

pStrasbourg 23 unpublished.

pSpiegelberg *see TLA sub Texte > Demotische Textdatenbank.*

Sweeney, Deborah. 1986. The nominal object clause of verbs of perception in non-literary Late Egyptian. In Gertie Englund & Paul John Frandsen (eds.), *Crossroad. Chaos or the Beginning of a New Paradigm* (CNI Publications 1), 337–388. Copenhagen: Carsten Niebuhr Institute of Ancient Near East Studies.

*Studies Griffith* = Egypt Exploration Society 1932.

*Tale of Woe* = Caminos 1977.

Tattam, Henry. 1836. *Duodecim prophetarum minorum libri in lingua aegyptiaca vulgo coptica seu memphitica ex ms. parisiensi descripti et cum ms. Johannis Leo comparati*, Oxford: Oxford University Press.

Tattam, Henry. 1852. *Prophetae maiores in dialecto linguae aegyptiacae memphitica seu coptica* I: *Esaias et Jeremias cum Lamentationes Jeremiae* & II: *Ezeciel et Daniel*, Oxford: Oxford University Press.
*Teaching of Amunnakht* = Dorn 2004.
*Teti Cemetery* III = Kanawati & Abder-Raziq 1999
*Teti Cemetery* V = Kanawati & Abder-Raziq 2000.
*Texte 2. Zwischenzeit* = Helck 2002.
grThebes 3156 *see TLA sub Texte > Demotische Textdatenbank.*
Theodotus of Ancyra, *In S. Georgem Diosp.* = Balestri & Hyvernat 1924.
Theodore of Antioch, *On the Theodores* = Balestri & Hyvernat 1924.
Theodosius of Alexandria, *De assumptione Mariae V.* = Robinson 1896.
Theodosius of Alexandria, *In Michaelem* = Budge 1894.
Theophilus of Alexandria, *Homily on the Virgin* = Worrell 1923.
Thompson, Sir Herbert. 1908. *The Coptic (Sahidic) Version of Certain Books of the Old Testament from a papyrus in the British Museum*, Oxford: Henry Frowde.
Thompson, Sir Herbert. 1911. *A Coptic Palimpsest Containing Joshua, Judges, Ruth, Judith, and Esther in the Sahidic Dialect, Coptic Text, edited from a seventh century manuscript in the British Museum with a short critical introduction and textual notes*, London et al.: Henry Frowde & Oxford University Press.
Thompson, Sir Herbert. 1913. A Demotic Ostracon. *Proceedings of the Society of Biblical Archaeology* 35. 95–96 & pl. XXVII.
Thompson, Sir Herbert. 1924. *The Gospel of St. John According to the Earliest Coptic Manuscript* (British School of Archaeology in Egypt and Egyptian Research Account 36). London: British School of Archaeology in Egypt & Bernard Quaritch.
Thompson, Sir Herbert. 1932. *The Coptic Version of The Acts of the Apostles & The Pauline Epistles in the Sahidic Dialect.* Cambridge: University Press.
*Ti* = Steindorff 1913.
Till, Walter Curt. 1927. *Die achmîmische Version der Zwölf Kleinen Propheten* (Coptica 4). Hauniae: Gyldendalske Boghandel – Nordisk Forlag.
Till, Walter Curt. 1928. *Achmimisch-koptische Grammatik mit Chrestomathie und Wörterbuch.* Leipzig: J.C. Hinrichs.
Till, Walter Curt. 1934. Griechische Philosophen bei den Kopten. In *Mélanges Maspero* II (Mémoires publiés par les Membres de l'Institut Français d'Archéologie Orientale du Caire 67), 165–175. Cairo: Institut Français d'Archéologie Orientale du Caire.
Till, Walter Curt. 1935 & 1936. *Koptische Heiligen- und Märtyrerlegenden*, 2 vols. (Orientalia Christiana Analecta 102 & 108), Rome: Pont. Institutum Orientalium Studiorum.
Till, Walter Curt. 1960. *Die koptischen Ostraka der Papyrussammlung der Österreichischen Nationalbibliothek* (Denkschriften der Österreichischen Akademie der Wissenschaften. Philosophisch-historische Klasse 78/1). Vienna: Hermann Böhlaus Nachfahren
Till, Walter Curt. 1970. *Koptische Grammatik (Saïdischer Dialekt), mit Bibliographie, Lesestücken und Wörterverzeichnissen*, 4th ed. (Lehrbücher für das Studium der orientalischen und afrikanischen Sprachen I). Leipzig: VEB Verlag Enzyklopedie.
Timothy of Alexandria, *On Abbaton* = Budge 1914.
*Tomb of Antefoqer* = Davies, Gardiner & Davies 1920.
*Tomb of Tjanefer* = Seele 1959.
*Tombs of Two Officials* = Davies & Davies 1923.

Tosi, Mario & Alessandro Roccati. 1972. *Stele e altre epigrafi di Deir el Medina, n. 50001 – n. 50262* (Catalogo del Museo Egizio di Torino, Serie Seconda – Collezioni I). Turin: Edizioni d'Arte Fratelli Pozzo.
*Trans. Mariae* = Förster 2006.
*Tri. Trac.* = Attridge 1985.
TT 23 = Grapow 1941.
gTT 63 = Dziobek & Abdel Raziq 1990.
TTS 5 = Davies & Davies 1933.
Turin 1447 = Donadoni Roveri 1988.
Turin 4262 = Donadoni Roveri 1988.
Turin 50044 = Tosi & Roccati 1972.
Turin 50046 = Tosi & Roccati 1972.
Turin 50050 = Tosi & Roccati 1972.
oTurin 57001 = López 1978.
pTurin 1882 = Gardiner 1955.
pTurin 1977 = Bakir 1970.
pTurin 1978/208 = Allam 1973.
pTurin 54031 = Condon 1978.
pTurin Suppl 6107 *see TLA sub Texte > Demotische Textdatenbank.*
pTurin A = Fischer-Elfert 1997.
tTurin 58004 = López 1984.
UCL 14333 = Stewart 1979.
pUC 32036 = Collier & Qirke 2004.
pUC 32037 = Collier & Qirke 2004.
pUC 32055 = Collier & Qirke 2004.
pUC 32057 = Collier & Qirke 2004.
pUC 32058 = Collier & Qirke 2004.
pUC 32124 = Collier & Quirke 2002.
pUC 32134A = Collier & Qirke 2004.
pUC 32157 = Collier & Qirke 2004.
pUC 32158 = Collier & Qirke 2004.
pUC 32162 = Collier & Qirke 2004.
pUC 32163 = Collier & Qirke 2004.
pUC 32198 = Collier & Quirke 2002.
pUC 32199 = Collier & Quirke 2002.
pUC 32200 = Collier & Quirke 2002.
pUC 32201 = Collier & Quirke 2002.
pUC 32204 = Collier & Quirke 2002.
pUC 32205 = Collier & Quirke 2002.
pUC 32213 = Collier & Quirke 2002.
Uljas, Sami. 2006. Noun/personal pronoun + personal pronoun as a grammatical construction in Earlier Egyptian. *The Journal of Egyptian Archaeology* 92. 245–248.
Uljas, Sami. 2007a. The Earlier Egyptian adjective reconsidered. *Lingua Aegyptia* 15. 231–250.
Uljas, Sami. 2007b. Why (not) leave it 'virtual'? More on grammar and texture in Earlier Egyptian. *Lingua Aegyptia* 15. 251–262.

Uljas, Sami. 2007c. *The Modal System of Earlier Egyptian Complement Clauses. A Study in Pragmatics in a Dead Language* (Probleme der Ägyptologie 26). Leiden/NY: Brill.

Uljas, Sami. 2009a. Radiality in Earlier Egyptian grammar. *Lingua Aegyptia* 17. 277–290.

Uljas, Sami. 2009b. Adverbial sentence WH-questions in Earlier Egyptian. *Revue d'Égyptologie* 60. 147–158.

Uljas, Sami. 2010a. Grammar as a mirror of mind: more on fuzzy boundaries in Egyptian syntax. *Göttinger Miszellen* 224. 93–100.

Uljas, Sami. 2010b. Formally Speaking: observations on a recent theory of the Earlier Egyptian *sḏm.n=f*. *Lingua Aegyptia* 18. 253–261.

Uljas, Sami. 2011a. Syncretism and the Earlier Egyptian *sḏm=f*. Speculations on morphological interconnections across paradigms. *Lingua Aegyptia* 19. 155–174.

Uljas, Sami. 2011b. On adverbial ante-position and operator scope in Coptic. *Zeitschrift für Ägyptische Sprache und Altertumskunde* 139. 93–102.

Uljas, Sami. 2011c. The IFAO Leaves of the *Life* of Moses of Abydos. *Orientalia* nova series 80. 373–422.

Uljas, Sami. 2012a. Begging the question. Earlier Egyptian WH-questions and the marking of information structure. *Lingua Aegyptia* 20. 253–266.

Uljas, Sami. 2012b. Agreement domains and resumption in Earlier Egyptian. *Zeitschrift für Ägyptische Sprache und Altertumskunde* 140. 78–83.

Uljas, Sami. 2013. Some remarks on a negated Earlier Egyptian nominal sentence and related constructions. *The Journal of Egyptian Archaeology* 99. 241–251.

Uljas, Sami. 2014. On control constructions in Earlier Egyptian. In Eitan Grossman, Stéphane Polis, Andréas Stauder & Jean Winand (eds.), *On Forms and Functions: Studies in Ancient Egyptian Grammar* (Lingua Aegyptia Studia Monographica 15), 233–256. Hamburg: Widmaier Verlag.

Uljas, Sami. Forthcoming. Possessive and existential constructions in Earlier Egyptian. In Eitan Grossman & Stéphane Polis (eds.), *Possession in Ancient Egyptian* (The Mouton Companions to Ancient Egyptian 1). Berlin: De Gruyter Mouton.

Uljas, Sami. *in prep*. The Grammar of Pragmatics in Earlier Egyptian Independent Clauses.

*Urk.* I = Sethe 1932.

*Urk.* IV = Sethe & Helck 1906–1988.

pVandier = Posener 1985.

Vandier, Jacques. 1950. *Mo'alla. La tombe d'Ankhtifi et la tombe de Sébekhotep* (Bibliothèque d'Étude 18). Cairo: Institut Français d'Archéologie Orientale.

Van Valin, Robert D. Jr. 2010. Role and Reference Grammar as a framework for linguistic analysis. In Bernd Heine and Heiko Narrog (eds.), *The Oxford Handbook of Linguistic Analysis* (Oxford Handbooks of Linguistics), 703–738. Oxford: Oxford University Press.

Vergote, Jozef. 1973. *Grammaire copte. Tome Ia: Partie Synchronique – Introduction, phonétique et phonologie, morphologie synthématique (structure de sémantèmes); Tome Ib: Partie Diachronique – Introduction, phonétique et phonologie, morphologie synthématique (structure de sémantèmes)*. Leuven: Peeters.

Vernus, Pascal. 1981. Formes 'emphatiques' en fonction non 'emphatiques' dans la protase d'un système corrélatif. *Göttinger Miszellen* 43. 73–88.

Vernus, Pascal. 1984. Études de philologie et de linguistique III. *Revue d'Égyptologie* 35. 159–188.

Vernus, Pascal. 1985. Études de philologie et de linguistique IV. *Revue d'Égyptologie* 36. 153–168.

Vernus, Pascal. 1987. Études de philologie et de linguistique VI. *Revue d'Égyptologie* 38. 163–181.

Vernus, Pascal. 1990. *Future at issue. Tense, mood and aspect in Middle Egyptian: studies in syntax and semantics* (Yale Egyptological Studies 4). New Haven, CT: Yale Egyptological Seminar.
Vernus, Pascal. 1991. Le rhème marqué : typologie des emplois et effets de sens en Moyen Égyptien (temps seconds, cleft sentences et constructions apparentées dans les stratégies de l'énonciateur). *Lingua Aegyptia* 1. 333–355.
Vernus, Pascal. 1994. Observations sur la prédication de classe ('nominal predicate'). *Lingua Aegyptia* 4. 325–348.
Vernus, Pascal. 1997. *Les parties du discours en moyen égyptien. Autopsie d'une théorie* (Cahiers de la Société 5). Genève: Société d'Égyptologie Genève.
Vernus, Pascal. 1998. Processus de grammaticalisation dans la langue égyptienne. *Comptes rendus de l'Académie des Inscriptions et Belles-Lettres*. 191–210.
Vernus, Pascal. 2006. Pronoms interrogatifs en égyptien de la première phase. *Lingua Aegyptia* 14. 145–178.
Vernus, Pascal. 2012. Le verbe *gm(j)*: essai de sémantique lexicale. In Eitan Grossman, Stéphane Polis & Jean Winand (eds.), *Lexical Semantics in Ancient Egyptian* (Lingua Aegyptia Studia Monographica 9), 387–438. Hamburg: Widmaier Verlag.
Vernus, Pascal. 2014. La non représentation segmentale du (premier) participant direct ('sujet') et la notion de ø. In Eitan Grossman, Stéphane Polis, Andréas Stauder & Jean Winand (eds.), *On Forms and Functions: Studies in Ancient Egyptian Grammar* (Lingua Aegyptia Studia Monographica 15), 257–308. Hamburg: Widmaier Verlag.
pVienna D 70 *see TLA sub Texte > Demotische Textdatenbank.*
pVienna D 10000 *see TLA sub Texte > Demotische Textdatenbank.*
pVienna D 12006 *see TLA sub Texte > Demotische Textdatenbank.*
*O.Vind.Copt.* = Till 1960.
de Vis, Henri. 1922 & 1929. *Homélies coptes de la Vaticane* I & II (Coptica I & V). Hauniae: Gyldendalske Boghandel – Nordisk Forlag.
Vleeming, *Short Text* I = Vleeming 2001.
Vleeming, *Short Text* II = Vleeming 2011.
Vleeming, Sven P. 2001. *Some Coins of Artaxerxes and Other Short Texts in the Demotic Script Found on Various Objects and Gathered from Many Publications* (Studia Demotica 5). Leuven: Peeters.
Vleeming, Sven P. 2011. *Demotic and Greek-Demotic Mummy Labels and Other Short Texts Gathered From Many Publications – Short Texts II: 278–1200* (Studia Demotica 9). Leuven: Peeters.
*V. Pachom* = $^{S}$Lefort 1952 & $^{B}$Lefort 1953.
*V. Shenute* = $^{B}$Leipoldt 1906 & $^{S}$Lubomierski 2007.
van den Walle, Baudouin. 1973. *La Mastaba de Neferirtenef* (Guide de Départment Égyptien). Brussels: Musées Royaux d'Art et Histoire
Wente, Edward Frank. 1982. Mysticism in pharaonic Egypt? *Journal of Near Eastern Studies* 41. 161–179.
Wessely, Carl. 1908. Ein Sprachdenkmal des mittelägyptischen (baschmurischen) Dialekts. *Sitzungsberichte der Kaiserlichen Akademie der Wissenschaften in Wien. Philosophisch-historische Klasse* 158/1. 1–46.
pWestcar = Blackman 1988.
Westendorf, Wolfhart. 1959/1960. Hieß Lamares Lamares? *Mitteilungen des Instituts für Orientforschung* 7. 316–329.

Westendorf, Wolfhart. 1981. *Beiträge zum altägyptischen Nominalsatz* (Nachrichten der Akademie der Wissenschaften in Göttingen, I. phil.-hist. Klasse 3). Göttingen: Vandenhoeck & Ruprecht.
Westendorf, Wolfhart. 1984. Lamares und Rathures als Kronzeugen für die mit *nj-* gebildeten Namen? *Studien zur altägyptischen Kultur* 11. 381–397.
Westendorf, Wolfhart. 1989. Der dreigliedige Nominalsatz Subjekt-*pw*-Prädikat: konstatierend oder emphatisch? *Göttinger Miszellen* 109. 83–94.
Westerhoff, Matthias. 1999. *Auferstehung & Jenseits im koptischen „Buch der Auferstehung Jesu Christi, unseres Herrn"* (Orientalia Biblica et Christiana 11). Wiesbaden: Harrassowitz.
Wetzer, Harrie. 1996. *The Typology of Adjectival Predication* (Empirical Approaches to Language Typology 17). Berlin/New York: Mouton de Gruyter.
Winand, Jean. 1992. *Études de néo-égyptien 1. La morphologie verbale* (Ægyptiaca Leodiensia 2). Liège: Centre d'Informatique de Philosophie et Lettres.
Winand, Jean. 1996. Les constructions analogiques du Futur III en Néo-Égyptien. *Revue d'Égyptologie* 47. 117–145.
Winand, Jean. 1997. La négation *bn...ἰwnꜣ* en néo-Egyptien. *Lingua Aegyptia* 5. 223–236.
Winand, Jean. 2006. *Temps et aspect en égyptien. Une approche sémantique* (Probleme der Ägyptologie 25). Leiden/Boston: Brill.
Winand, Jean. 2016. Traces d'indices actantiels en Néo-Égyptien. In Philippe Collombert, Dominique Lefèvre, Stéphane Polis & Jean Winand (eds.), *Aere Perennius. Mélanges égyptologiques en l'honneur de Pascal Vernus* (Orientalia Lovaniensia Analecta 242), 861–894. Leuven, Paris/Bristol: Peeters. Worrell, William Hoyt. 1931. *The Proverbs of Solomon in Sahidic Coptic According to the Chicago Manuscript* (Oriental Institute Publications 12). Chicago: Oriental Institute Press.
Worrell, William Hoyt. 1923. *The Coptic Manuscripts in the Freer Collection* (University of Michigan Studies – Humanistic Series X). New York & London: The Macmillan Company.
Yamazaki, Naoko. 2003. *Zaubersprüche für Mutter und Kind. Papyrus Berlin 3027* (Achet: Schriften zur Ägyptologie 2). Berlin: Dr Norbert Dürring.
Young, Dwight Wayne. 1998. Two Leaves from a Copy of Shenoute's Ninth Canon. *Wiener Zeitschrift zur Kunde des Morgenlandes* 88. 281–301.
Young, Dwight Wayne. 1993. *Coptic Manuscripts from the White Monastery: Works of Shenute* (Mitteilungen aus der Papyrussammlung der Österreichischen Nationalbibliothek [Papyrus Erzherzog Rainer]. Neue Serie XXII). Wien: Komm. Hollinek.
Žabá, Zbyněk. 1956. *Les Maximes de Ptaḥḥotep*. Prague: Académie Tchécoslovaque des Sciences.
Zaborowski, Jason R. 2005. *The Coptic Martyrdom of John of Phanijōit. Assimilation and Conversion to Islam in Thirteenth-Century Egypt* (The History of Christian-Muslim Relations 3). Leiden & Boston: Brill.
Zachary of Sakha, *De Presentatione* = de Vis 1929.
*Consolatory Sermon* = de Vis 1929.
*V. John Kolobos* = Mikhail & Vivian 2010.
Zanetti, Ugo. 2004. Le roman de Bakhéos sur les trois jeunes saints de Babylone. Fragments coptes. In B. Janssens, B. Roosen & P. van Deun (eds.), *Philomathestatos. Studies in Greek & Byzantine Texts presented to Jacques Noret for his Sixty-Fifth Birthday* (Orientalia Lovaniensia Analecta 137), 713–747. Leuven, Paris & Dudley/MA: Peeters.
Zoega, Georg 1810. *Catalogus codicum Copticorum manu scriptorum qui in Museo Borgiano Velitris adservantur.* Rome: S. Congregatio de Propaganda Fide.
1Cl = Rösch 1910 & Schmidt 1908.

# Index of cited sources


Acacius of Caesarea, *Encomium on St Mercurius*
– Budge, *Misc.* 291, 11–12 II.207b
*Acta Andreae*
– Prieur 657, 6 II.439b
*Acta Pauli*
– Schmidt 7* 10, 17–18 I.287c
7* 10, 20–24 II.154b
7* 11, 22–23 II.93d
15* 21, 5 II.73d
22* 31, 12–13 I.151c
23* 32, 21 I.302d
36* 59, 8–10 II.188c
40* 46, 23–24 I.304c
*Acts of Andrew and Paul*
– Jacques 202, 127–128 I.283c
204, 129 I.254f
204, 140 II.187e
212, 231 II.383c
*Acts of Peter and Philip*
– von Lemm 536, 19–23 III.78d
*Acts of Philip*
– von Lemm I 524, 22–23 I.179d
– von Lemm I 534, a4–6 II.74d, 438g
*Acts of the Synod of Ephesos*
– Bouriant 8, 12 II.75b
pAdler 21, 11–12 II.68b
Agathonicus of Tarsus, *Apologies*
– Erichsen 12, 17 II.74g
– *De incredulitate*
– Erichsen 26, 7–11 II.441g
28, 2–4 II.451e
Alexander of Alexandria, *In Petrum ep. Alexandriae*
– *AdM* 254, 1–2 I.313c
Amazons A2 x+17 I.270b
A2, x+20 II.436
6, x+28 II.373
7, 41 II.55
Amenemhat VIIa–b II.282b
VIIe I.321a
Amduat, h12, upper reg./Th III, 8 II.160o
Amenemope 8, 5 II.269d
13, 15–16 II.218d
16, 13–14 III.147c
18, 10–11 I.278b
21, 9–12 I.38b
21, 15–16 I.343b
24, 19–20 III.38c
Amphilochius of Iconium, *On Abraham*
– Datema 275, 5–7 I.66d
287, 204 II.152e
*pAnastasi I*
– [2]Fischer-Elfert
56, 3–4 I.160
57, 5 III.169b
59, 5 II.22e
69, 3 III.167e
72, 9 I.337a
88, 1 II.359d
91, 1 III.147h
92, 2 III.147d
97, 8 III.112
96, 3 II.366b
100, 3 I.336e
101, 6–7 I.156c
108, 7 II.270b
123, 1 II.244c
126, 1 III.147l
131, 3–4 I.33a
131, 4–5 II.369c
131, 8 III.37c
132, 3 III.43i
155, 7 III.41e

Ani
– Quack B 15, 13 II.23a
B 16, 14–15 II.22d
B 17, 2 II.167
B 19, 13–14 I.31
B 20, 6–7 II.22a
B 21, 11 III.166c
B 22, 4 I.270a
*AP* Chaîne 25, 10 II.149a
30, 12 II.103b


https://doi.org/10.1515/9783110409895-015

30, 14–15 II.150b
30, 24 II.148a
31, 28–29 II.186a
32, 6–7 II.186b
33, 22 I.284b
43, 21–22 II.215a
55, 9 II.440b
67, 18–19 I.63b
74, 4–5 II.97b
80, 5 I.58a
81, 1–2 I.65
115, 7–9 II.454a
*AP* Elanskaya 13a, 27–30 III.89b
*AP Macarius*
– Amélineau, *MG* 25
– #1 203, 8–9 II.353f
– #9 212, 15 I.64a
– #30 226, 4 I.61e
– #34 230, 16 II.102c
230, 16–231, 2 I.n.97
*AP St Anthony*
– Amélineau, *MG*
25, 36, 12–13 I.66e
*ApEl*
– Steindorff, *Apokalypse des Elias*
67 19, 6–7 I.177c
72 23, 8–9 II.90c
74 23, 15–24, 1 I.289e
78 26, 5 II.188b
83 29, 5–6 I.291b
84 30, 6–8 II.224c
98 38, 4–5 II.184a
98 38, 11 II.452d
100 40, 4–7 II.73e
100 40, 6–7 II.275b
*Ap. Jas.* 6, 5–7 II.189c
*ApPaul*
– Budge, *Misc.*
541, 5–6 II.454b
546, 22–23 II.453a
564, 12–22 II.190b
*ApSoph.*
– Steindorff, *Apokalypse des Elias*
37 2, 2–4 I.255d
38 3, 13 II.190d
44 6, 17–7, 1 II.255d
46 7, 8–12 II.152d
46 7, 13–15 II.90d
50 9, 19–10, 11 I.63c
52 11, 8 I.n.55
53 10, 21–11, 1 I.165
58 14, 15–16 I.151b
*Apocr. Acts of the Apostles*
– *FS Crum* 313, 1–3 II.451h
– *Mon. Wadi Natrun* I 22, 28 I.143a
Archelaos of Neapolis, *On Gabriel*
– de Vis II 256, 2–3 II.188e
– Müller & Uljas §15 I.288h
*Archive of Hor* 3, 2–5 III.56h
3, 8–9 I.40d
3, 19 III.55d
oArmytage 8 III.165d
*ASAE* 39, 189, 9 III.27b
43, 503–04, b1 II.320a
Athanasius of Alexandria,
*De Anima et corpore*
Budge, *Homilies* 131, 32–34 II.440c
Bachios of Maiuma,
– *On the Three Youth of Babylon*
– Zanetti 729, 8–9 II.75l
Basil of Caesarea,
*On Noah's Ark*
– De Vis II 207, 3–5 III.153d
215, 2 III.67j
Basil of Pemje,
*Homily on Longinus*
*FS Kasser* 276, 28–29 II.142d
BD 7/*Nu*, pl. 64, 5 II.334
17/*Nebseni*, pl. 38, 6 II.309b
17/*Nu*, pl. 3, 3 III.36d
17/*Nu*, pl. 8, 105 III.7c
17/*Nu*, pl. 9, 118 II.119b
17/*Nu*, pl. 9, 118–19 II.280b
17/*Nu*, pl. 9, 8–9 II.264b
18/*Nu*, pl. 9, 5 II.120
40/*Tb* II, 40, 8/Ba II403b
42/*Nu*, pl. 17 II.20b
64/*Nebseni*, pl. 72, 8 II.115a
64/*Nu*, pl. 60, 6 II.162a
72/*Nu*, pl. 20, 14 I.90b, 237
72/*Nu*, pl. 20, 8–9 I.241a
84/*Nu*, pl. 30, 3 II.243d
89/*Nu*, pl. 51, 2–3 I.119b

90/*Nu*, pl. 22, 7 I.68c
122/*Nu*, pl. 25, 2 II.7b, 311e, n.100
125/*Nebseni*, pl. 90, 44 II.159a
125/*Nebseni*, pl. 91, 61 III.159b
125/*Nu*, pl. 68, 66–67 I.330b
144/*Nu*, pl. 75, 33–34 I.219d
148, 21–22/*Tb* I II.281c
149/*Nu*, pl. 83, 34 I.121
189/*Nu*, pl. 55, 11 I.233b
190/*Nu*, pl. 45 13 I.213b
*Beni Hasan* I, pl. 25, 46–47 I.99c
pl. 25, 62–63 I.185b
pl. 25, 96–99 I.223
pl. 26, 166–68 II.237a, 323a
pl. 44, 7 I.99c
Berlin 1157, 5–6 II.158d
7–8 II.265
8 II.156c
8–9 II.160d, 323b
11 II.114b, 311c, 405b
11–12 I.318e
16 II.114a
17–18 II.405a
18 I.322
1199, 8–9 I.239c
1204, 7 II.262a
7–8 I.95a
6768 III.52b
7317, 17 III.125a
Berlin Bowl, 2 I.93b
Berlin Leather Roll I, 19 II.156d
II, 4 III.19
oBerlin P. 1269, 4 II.25
P. 12365, r° 3 II.169a
pBerlin P. 3048, v° 19 II.64c
P. 3080, 25 I.138b
P. 3093, 12 III.63c
27 I.174a
P. 3109, 4–5 II.48f
P. 8869, 8–9 II.8a
P. 9010, 3 III.105c
P. 10012, 4–5 I.74b
P. 10016, r° 4–6 II.415d
P. 10030A, 9 II.313c
P. 10033, 5 II.331a
P. 10081B, 2 II.225
P. 10470 I, 10–11 II.308b
P. 10497, 19–20 II.423e
P. 13537, 21 III.56c
P. 13538, 20–23 I.350c
P. 13540, 3 II.273b
8–9 II.63
P. 13544, 4–5 III.115b
9–11 III.63a
14–17 I.346b
P. 13548, 2–3 I.311b
P. 13549, 15–17 II.132c
16–17 II.432c
v° 15–16 II.431b
P. 13563, 14–15 I.150b
P. 13579, x+9 I.48c
P. 13585, x+3 I.346c
P. 13633, v° 9–10 II.58b
P. 13637, 13–15 I.298h
P. 15521, 5–6 II.66b
P. 15522, 20–21 I.149a
P. 15527 v° 14–15 III.149d
P. 15530, x+10–13 II.170b
x+10–11 II.377a
P. 15617, 3 I.148c
5 I.170a
v° 2 II435a
P. 15637+15803, x+6–7 III.150
P. 23629, 4–6 III.55e
P. 23757A, r° 2, 11 II.134c
pBerlin med. 14, 7 I.132a
Besa,
*Reproofs & Monastic Rules*, X.3
– Kuhn 36, 35–36 III.153b
– *To Antinoe*
– Kuhn 95, 14 II.392a
– *To Herai* V.2
– Kuhn 109, 6–9 III.75a
109, 11 II.70e
The Bible
– Gn 1:4 III.66f
2:11 I.179a
2:18 III.172c
4:9 I.270d, II.77e, 380f
6:9 II.179d
12:11 II.73f

| | | |
|---|---|---|
| | 12:13 | II.77f |
| | 18:27 | II.84b, 246h |
| | 22:7 | I.287a |
| | 22:11 | I.257e |
| | 23:6 | II.88d |
| | 24:14 | II.194i |
| | 26:24 | I.66a |
| | 27:12 | II.248c |
| | 29:6 | II.210 |
| | 29:17 | III.146a |
| | 31:50 | I.357 |
| | 34:25 | I.298k |
| | 35:4 | I.257h |
| | 35:20 | II.203c |
| | 37:27 | II.142a, 381d |
| | 38:5 | I.284j |
| | 44:18 | I.273b |
| | 49:3 | II.259e |
| | 49:21 | II.69c |
| – Ex | 1:5 | I.284f |
| | 1:16 | II.227h |
| | 1:19 | I.273c, II.455c |
| | 2:2 | III.117b |
| | 2:6 | II.382h |
| | 2:14 | II.90b |
| | 2:19 | II.89c, 252b |
| | 3:11 | II.83a |
| | 3:14 | II.194a |
| | 4:2 | II.383d |
| | 4:16 | I.283d |
| | 4:18 | III.66d |
| | 4:22 | II.223a |
| | 5:19 | I.164b |
| | 6:30 | II.380b |
| | 7:17 | I.178b |
| | 16:3 | III.74a |
| | 20:9 | II.208e |
| – Lev | 5:12 | II.149b |
| | 13:46 | II.155d, 223b |
| | 11:23 | I.261e |
| | 18:22 | II.142b |
| | 18:23 | II.142c |
| – Nm | 11:19 | II.448c |
| | 14:3 | III.73b |
| | 14:9 | I.263e |
| | 22:29 | I.290g |
| – Dt | 2:36 | I.178c |
| | 4:48 | II.192c |
| | 5:14 | II.143a |
| | 5:29 | II.208a |
| | 7:6 | II.88b |
| | 9:6 | II.70b |
| | 11:30 | I.61b |
| – Jo | 1:9 | I.153a |
| | 2:11 | II.382c |
| | 3:7 | I.283h |
| | 9:14 | II.77b |
| | 9:31[24] | I.298i |
| | 17:4 | II.FNa |
| | 17:9 | II.395b |
| | 22:31 | I.164a |
| – Jdg | 11:34 | I.360f |
| | 14:18 | II.391c |
| – Ru | 3:9 | II.192b |
| | 4:11 | I.177b |
| – 1Kg | 20:17 | II.383a |
| | 26:15 | II.438a |
| – 2Kg | 19:13 | II.453c |
| – 3Kg | 19:11 & 12 | I.362 |
| | 19:12 | I.285c |
| | 21[20]:14 | II.357d |
| – 1Chr | 29:2 | III.68e |
| | 29:11 | II.189f |
| – 2Chr | 5:9 | I.66c |
| – Jdt | 11:23 | III.66b |
| – Tb | 2:10 | I.164c |
| | 2:14[13] | II.214b |
| | 3:6 | I.58b |
| | 7:3 | II.70h |
| | 10:12[11] | II.181c |
| | 12:7 | II.382b |
| | 12:8 | II.388b, III.154b |
| | 12:12 | I.284d |
| | 12:15 | II.383b |
| | 12:18 | I.361b |
| | 13:2 | II.250f |
| | 13:4 | II.246b |
| | 13:11 | I.288i |
| | 13:14 | III.69b |
| | 14:2 | I.301d |
| – Job | 1:7 | I.141b |
| – Ps | 10 [11]:4 | I.54e, 285a |
| | 10 [11]:7 | II.382f |
| | 15 [16]:8 | I.61d |
| | 17 [18]:10 [9] | I.151a |

| | | |
|---|---|---|
| | 21 [22]:6 [7] | II.70a, 438e |
| | 33 [34]:9 | II.188d |
| | 37[38]:18[17] | I.262k |
| | 41 [42]:4[3] | I.287d |
| | 43 [44]:4 | II.444b |
| | 45 [46]:1 | II.205 |
| | 45 [46]:11 [10] | II.204b |
| | 49 [40]:3 | I.262i |
| | 50 [51]:5 [3] | I.54d, 141a |
| | 56 [57]:5 [4] | II.382e |
| | 68 [69]:19 [20] | II.103f |
| | 69 [70]:6 [5] | II.73a, 246i, 388d |
| | 70 [71]:6 | I.293b |
| | 76 [77]:20 | I.285e |
| | 85 [86]:10 | II.75k |
| | 85 [86]:15 | II.85, 247d, III.90 |
| | 88 [89]:25 [24] | I.56a, 254e |
| | 99 [100]:5 | II.198a |
| | 101 [102]:28 [27] | II.81, 358b |
| | 104 [105]:7 | I.54a |
| | 118 [119]:5 | III.75c |
| | 118 [119]:68 | II.79c |
| | 118 [119]:71 | III.78b |
| | 134[135]:16–17 | I.313a |
| | 134 [135]:17 | I.26a |
| – Prv | 1:19 | II.187f |
| | 2:6 | II.93i |
| | 2:10 | III.66e |
| | 3:13 | III.69c |
| | 3:16 | II.250b |
| | 3:17 | II.183b |
| | 3:18 | II.144c |
| | 3:28 | I.302a |
| | 4:23 | II.198b |
| | 7:11 | II.n.49 |
| | 8:27 | I.284g |
| | 8:30 | II.91a |
| | 10:11 | I.285d |
| | 11:24 | I.26e |
| | 12:1 | II.196b |
| | 12:9 | III.154c |
| | 12:11 | II.197b |
| | 13:8 | II.n.24 |
| | 13:14 | I.58c |
| | 13:15 | II.382a |
| | 14:3 | II.97c |
| | 17:6 | II.181d |
| | 17:26 | III.172b |
| | 18:22 | II.197a |
| | 20:3 | II.193e |
| | 20 [23]:17 | II.365b |
| | 21:15 | II.193a |
| | 25:7 | III.77c |
| – Eccl | 1:8 | I.359d |
| | 1:9 | I.300l, II.94b |
| | 1:16 | I.58g |
| | 3:1 | II.93c |
| | 3:2 | II.143c |
| | 3:22 | II.94f |
| | 6:5 | III.152b |
| | 7:2 | III.154d |
| | 7:26 | II.97e |
| | 8:12 | III.67h |
| | 9:3 | II.95d |
| | 9:4 | III.153c |
| | 9:11 | II.217 |
| – Sg | 1:6 | II.74f |
| | 1:15 | II.175d |
| – Sap | 4:9 | II.181b |
| | 16:12 | II.211, 446a |
| – Sir | 5:10 [12] | II.395a |
| – Is | 30:4 | I.58f |
| | 30:7 | II.196d |
| | 30:9 | II.143h |
| | 30:18 | II.382g |
| | 30:33 | I.255e |
| | 31:1 | III.91 |
| | 31:2 | II.207c |
| | 31:3 | II.441h |
| | 31:9 | III.69f |
| | 33:2 | I.151d |
| | 33:6 | I.288j, II.383h |
| | 36:8 | I.303b |
| | 40:2 | I.361f |
| – Ier | 16:19 | II.259a |
| – Lam | 3:1 | II.362a |
| – Bar | 1:1 | II.356d |
| – Ep. Jer. | 70 | II.93h |
| – Ez | 1:23 | I.314c |
| – Hos | 1:9 | II.440d |
| | 2:2 | II.438d |
| | 2:7 | III.101b |
| | 2:12 | II.194f |
| | 2:23 | II.297b |

| | | |
|---|---|---|
| | 4:13 | III.67f |
| | 5:4 | I.153b |
| | 6:4 | I.268b, 269a, II.391d |
| | 6:6 | II.93e, 251 |
| | 6:10 | II.276c |
| | 10:4 | I.67c |
| | 11:9 | II.439c |
| | 13:10 | I.287b |
| | 13:14 | I.270c |
| – Am | 6:4 | I.300k |
| | 7:14 | II.440a |
| – Mi | 3:1 | II.193b |
| | 4:2 | III.122b |
| – Jl | 2:11 | I.292b, III.101c |
| | 2:13 | II.143e |
| | 2:27 | I.62b |
| – Jon | 1:8 | III.190e, 246d |
| | 1:9 | II.77c |
| | 2:1 [1:17] | I.284h |
| | 3:3 | II.175c |
| | 4:2 | III.100e |
| – Na | 1:3 | I.285f, II.69a |
| | 1:6 | II.391e |
| – Hab | 1:6 | II.441d |
| | 1:11 | II.386e |
| | 3:8 | I.256 |
| | 3:19 | II.174b |
| – Zec | 1:7 | II.78b |
| | 2:1 | I.179b |
| | 3:2 | II.451d |
| | 3:7 | II.104b |
| | 3:8 | II.143d |
| | 4:2 | I.60b |
| | 4:7 | II.83c |
| | 10:5 | I.264e |
| | 13:5 | II.390b |
| – Mal | 1:2 | II.179c |
| | 2:10 | II.444i, 445c |
| | 3:12 | II.277c |
| – Mt | 1:23 | II.209b |
| | 2:16 | I.177e |
| | 5:3 | III.69e |
| | 4:3 | II.277j |
| | 5:13 | II.383g |
| | 5:25 | I.152b |
| | 6:12 | I.314b |
| | 6:22 | II.277g |
| | 6:23 | II.177a |
| | 6:27 | II.105b, 215b |
| | 7:17 | III.100f |
| | 7:21 | II.444g, 447c |
| | 8:2 | I.303a |
| | 8:17 | II.250e |
| | 8:27 | II.190h |
| | 9:9 | I.179c |
| | 10:28 | I.359c |
| | 11.30 | III.146f, 146g |
| | 12:6 | I.55a |
| | 12:7 | II.290d |
| | 12:42 | I.55b |
| | 12:43 | I.356e |
| | 13:19 | II.187b |
| | 13:24 | III.122e |
| | 13:38 | II.174d, 176c |
| | 13:42 | I.283g |
| | 13:55 | II.181a, 451g |
| | 13:56 | I.361c |
| | 14:23 | II.91b |
| | 15:16 | II.71d |
| | 15:26 | III.171c |
| | 16:2–3 | II.69d |
| | 16:15 | II.71a |
| | 16:17 | II.446c, 449a |
| | 16:18 | II.192d |
| | 16:20 | II.385b |
| | 17:4 | III.77b |
| | 18:9 | II.97f |
| | 18:24 | I.261c |
| | 18:25 | I.360d |
| | 19:12 | I.26d |
| | 19:16 | II.94e |
| | 20:12 | II.89f |
| | 21:28 | II.96b, 391f |
| | 22:5 | II.92d |
| | 23:31 | II.380d |
| | 25:22 | II.89d |
| | 25:45 | II.450c |
| | 26:7 | III.68b |
| | 26:9 | I.303c |
| | 26:21 | II.94a |
| | 26:24 | III.74b |
| | 26:35 | II.102b |
| | 26:41 | II.176a |

| | | |
|---|---|---|
| | 26:42 | I.304d |
| | 27:11 | II.103d, 204a |
| | 27:43 | II.77d |
| | 27:44 | II.91c |
| | 27:56 | I.56b |
| | 27:57 | II.143f |
| | 27:62 | II.297d |
| | 28:6 | I.354d, 355a |
| – Mk | 1:13 | I.284a |
| | 2:7 | II.105a |
| | 2:19 | I.304a |
| | 3:21 | II.155a |
| | 4:22 | I.358a |
| | 5:41 | II.191d |
| | 5:42 | I.301f |
| | 8:18 | I.289d |
| | 8:28 | II.80, 224a&b |
| | 9:50 | III.67i |
| | 13:1 | II.151d |
| | 13:11 | II.209a, 445a |
| | 13:21 | I.57a |
| | 13:46 | III.68d |
| | 14:19 | II.357c |
| | 14:70 | II.82a |
| | 15:25 | II.143b |
| | 15:40 | I.263d |
| | 17:21 | I.57c, 64b |
| | 17:23 | I.61a |
| | 19:20 | I.67a |
| – Lk | 1:18 | II.73b |
| | 1:19 | II.192a |
| | 1:35 | II.98a |
| | 1:38 | II.77a |
| | 1:63 | II.365a |
| | 5:3 | II.276a |
| | 5:21 | II.154c |
| | 5:39 | III.65 |
| | 7:12 | II.143i |
| | 7:39 | II.147c, 277l |
| | 8:13 | I.291a, II.194b |
| | 8:30 | II.355f |
| | 11:31 | I.60d |
| | 12:1 | II.191c |
| | 12:43 | III.69g |
| | 15:11 | II.96a |
| | 17:16 | II.179a |
| | 19:3 | II.145d |
| | 20:7 | II.151b |
| | 21:9 | II.455b |
| | 22:27 | I.263f |
| | 22:53 | II.78c |
| | 23:38 | I.284c |
| | 23:47 | II.178a |
| | 24:21 | I.273a |
| – Jn | 1:1 | II.178c |
| | 1:4 | II.153 |
| | 1:8 | II.452a |
| | 1:19 | II.355e |
| | 1:20 | II.452h |
| | 2:1 | I.284i |
| | 2:22 | II.102a |
| | 3:2 | II.n.26 |
| | 3:3 | I.359a |
| | 3:32 | II.n.31 |
| | 3:33 | II.290e |
| | 4:2 | II.444d |
| | 4:5 | II.276d |
| | 4:9 | II.275c, 396g, n.26 |
| | 4:12 | II.74a |
| | 4:14 | I.283e |
| | 4:19 | II.380a |
| | 4:20 | I.n.97 |
| | 4:34 | II.199c |
| | 4:35 | II.103e |
| | 4:37 | II.213a |
| | 5:13 | I.151e |
| | 5:27 | II.385a |
| | 5:32 | II.69b |
| | 5:36 | II.92b, 390e |
| | 5:45 | II.104a |
| | 6:24 | I.354e |
| | 6:53 | I.360c |
| | 6:60 | II.n.31 |
| | 7:19 | II.449b |
| | 7:26 | II.197c |
| | 7:28 | II.196c |
| | 7:49 | I.300m |
| | 8:12 | II.174c, 384b |
| | 8:44 | II.277d |
| | 8:52 | I.291c |
| | 8:54 | II.353e |

| | | | | | |
|---|---|---|---|---|---|
| | 9:4 | II.278a | | 9:38 | I.164e |
| | 9:5 | II.384a | | 10:21 | II.93g, 174e |
| | 9:9 | I.268a, II.147f | | 10:41 | II.357e |
| | 9:11 | II.250g | | 12:22 | II.441f |
| | 9:28 | II.384d | | 13:11 | I.283f |
| | 9:29 | II.151a | | 13:15 | I.58e |
| | 9:31 | II.277i | | 13:25 | II.442c |
| | 9:40 | II.n.26 | | 14:12 | II.96c, 224e |
| | 10:22 | II.387a, 387b | | 14:15 | II.71c |
| | 10:33 | II.362b | | 16:1 | I.271 |
| | 10:34 | II.73g | | 17:6 | II.194j |
| | 10:36 | II.363a | | 17:11 | II.179e |
| | 11:9 | I.356d | | 17:29 | II.275d |
| | 11:17 | II.215c | | 18:3 | II.178b |
| | 12:3 | III.68c | | 19:15 | II.83d |
| | 12:9 | I.164d | | 19:16 | I.176b |
| | 13:6 | II.94c | | 23:8 | I.358d |
| | 13:17 | III.69d | – Rm | 1:12 | II.193h |
| | 14:10 | I.164f | | 2:25 | I.313b |
| | 14:11 | I.61c | | 2:29 | II.364 |
| | 14:17 | I.359b | | 3:13 | II.390a |
| | 15:16 | II.449c | | 6:15 | I.57b |
| | 16:4 | I.284e | | 8:12 | I.261a, 314a |
| | 17:8 | II.101b | | 8:34 | I.177a |
| | 17:10 | II.189d | | 9:2 | I.142a |
| | 17:14 | II.439d, 442d | | 11:18 | II.447a |
| | 17:21 | II.101a | | 11:36 | II.189e |
| | 18:34 | II.92a, 98c | | 12:10 | I.152c |
| | 18:35 | II.98b, 250c | | 14:17 | II.453b |
| | 18:36 | II.454c | | 14:21 | III.72d |
| | 18:40 | II.394e | – 1Cor | 4:8 | III.76a |
| | 19:9 | II.82d | | 4:20 | I.361d |
| | 19:12 | II.439e | | 5:6 | III.171e |
| | 21:11 | I.289f | | 5:11 | II.155b, 223c, 255b |
| | 21:20 | II.194k | | | |
| – Acts | 1:10 | I.269b | | 7:1 | III.72b |
| | 2:44 | I.258c | | 7:8 | III.76b, 117d |
| | 3:2 | I.293c | | 7:21 | I.302e |
| | 3:10 | III.122d | | 7:26 | III.117c |
| | 7:26 | II.74b | | 8:4 | I.358c |
| | 7:27 | II.89e | | 9:2 | II.438f |
| | 8:8 | I.292c | | 9:6 | I.360e |
| | 8:26 | II.175b | | 9:18 | II.150a, 155c, 354a |
| | 9:11 | II.154g | | | |
| | 9:17 | II.92c | | 10:17 | II.185b |
| | 9:20 | II.204c | | 10:21 | I.359e |
| | 9:21 | II.452e | | 11:14 | II.144a |

| | | |
|---|---|---|
| | 11:15 | II.144b |
| | 11:22 | I.361e |
| | 11:24 | II.356c |
| | 11:25 | II.175a, 182 |
| | 14:37 | II.248b |
| | 15:37 | II.444h |
| | 15:39 | II.451a |
| – 2Cor | 3:2 | II.386a |
| | 6:14–15 | II.181g |
| | 10:7 | II.72a, 79a, 385c |
| | 11:1 | III.75b |
| – Heb | 3:4 | I.62d |
| | 5:8 | II.396h |
| | 6:10 | II.451f |
| | 7:8 | II.95a |
| | 8:1 | II.200b |
| | 9:2 | I.176e |
| | 9:3 | II.145b |
| | 13:25 | I.254g |
| – Gal | 3:12 | II.454d |
| | 4:6 | II.277e |
| | 4:7 | II.87b, 249b |
| | 4:18 | III.72c |
| | 4:31 | II.438b |
| – Eph | 4:9 | II.200a |
| – Col | 3:1 | I.180a |
| – 1Th | 3:3 | I.67d |
| | 5:24 | II.196a |
| – 1Ti | 1:8 | III.117a |
| | 4:4 | III.71b |
| – 2Ti | 2:20 | II.250d |
| – Ti | 1:12 | II.247b |
| – 1Jn | 2:4 | I.354a |
| | 2:14 | II.74c |
| | 2:24 | I.283a |
| | 4:2–3 | II.198e |
| | 4:4 | I.291d, II.73h, II.196e |
| | 4:7 | II.175e |
| | 4:10 | II.445d |
| – Rev | 2:13 | I.178a, 255f |
| | 15:4 | II.450a |
| | 22:13 | II.388a |
| BM EA | 101, horizontal 2 | I.203b, 219c |
| | 152, 3–4 | I.219b |
| | 159, 11 | II.20a |
| | 334, vertical 3–5 | III.160b |
| | vertical 7 | III.n.45 |
| | 572, 8 | I.92b |
| | 574, 4 | I.202 |
| | 581, 16 | I.122 |
| | 614, 13–14 | I.124d |
| | 1671, 1–2 | II.312a |
| | 5661 | I.n.97 |
| | 23186, a6 | I.301b |
| | 35464, 19–20 | I.138c |
| oBM EA | 5624, v° 4 | I.336d |
| | v° 6 | I.167e |
| | 5627, v° 3 | III.50b |
| | 50627, 3–4 | II.273a |
| pBM EA | 10102 r°, 17 | III.48a |
| | 10373, r°, 5–6 | II.419c |
| | 10416 r°, 9–10 | I.289a |
| | 10520, A10 | II.136c, 357b |
| | 10522, 3 | I.353c |
| | 10524, 3 | I.281c |
| | 10591, r° 1, 12–13 | II.51a |
| | r° 1, 15 | II.139 |
| | r° 2, 12 | II.173a |
| | r° 2, 16 | II.51a |
| | r° 4, 1 | II.57d |
| | r° 4, 7 | II.51b |
| | r° 5, 3 | II.62g |
| | r° 5, 10 | II.56c |
| | r° 5, 11 | II.356a |
| | r° 5, 14–15 | II.272b |
| | 10599, 7–8 | II.272a |
| | 10622, 17–18 | II.67 |
| | 69532, 6 | II.132e, 394b |
| | 69574 B 2 | III.58a |
| | 73785, 4 | I.171b |
| | 73786, 4 | I.310c |
| | 75015 r° 16 | II.218a |
| | 75016 r° x+1 | I.300c |
| | 75019+10302 v° 3 | I.276d |
| | v° 5–6 | III.98c |
| | 75021, 8 | II.128a |
| pBN 149, | 1, 18 | I.262i |
| | 1, 20–21 | I.41c |
| | 1, 27 | I.170e |
| | 1, 27–28 | II.49b |

2, 1–2 II.48e
3, 20 II.172c, 355d
3, 22–23 III.121b
215, r° 2.12 II.375c
r° 2, 22 II.134d
r° 3, 11 II.140
r° 5, 1 III.116b
r° 5, 5 II.170d
v° a4 III.55c
v° a11 I.45
v° a12–13 I.44b
v° a17 II.289b
223, 3 II.58c, 133a
5 II.54a
226a + pLouvre N 2412, 2 I.n.97
pBologna 3173 I.53a
*Book of Resurrection of Christ*
– Westerhoff 68, 9 II.75j
70, 1 II.438c
*Book of Thoth*
– B02 3, 16 II.172e
4, 3 II.48c
4, 12 II.172d
– B06 1,1/F01 11 III.88b
– L01 2, 22 II.172d
pBoulaq 18 XIX, 2.2–3 II.292
*Boundary Stelae*
24, 10 II.353b
24, 16 I.146a
26, 4–7 (K 20) III.98a
90 II.40e, 370d
Bresciani, *Archivio*, #10, 2–3 II.52d
pBresciani 33, 7–8 I.49c
oBrooklyn 37.1821E, 10–11 II.62e
pBrooklyn 37.1781, 2 I.296a
37.1839A, r° 8 I.148a

Cairo Bowl, inside 7–8 II.326b, 344c
Cairo JE 49566, 11 I.14b
JE 95206, 16–17 II.68c
Cairo Linen, 2 II.159d
*Can. Eccl.*
– de Lagarde, *Aeg.* 251, 26–27 III.66c
*Canons of Athanasius*
– *ASAE* 19, 239, 5–10 I.59
– Crum in Riedel §42 II.442a
§44 II.451b
§50 I.306
§57 II.191a
§61 II.97a, 250a
§64 II.202b
§66 I.305b
Canopus Decree A, 17 I.262f, 282c
B, 62–63 I.282d
pCarlsberg 159+PSI inv. D10
v° 1, 13 I.171e
pCarlsberg 429, 3–8 II.50
Carnarvon Tablet 7 I.14a
15 I.240
*Catenae* 9 II.383j
CG 8631, 2–3 I.26c
20001, 5–6 I.190c
20057s I.116a
20538ii, 18–19 I.245b
20539ii, b12 I.228a
20543, 9 I.69a
18 III.36a
20567, 1–2 I.68b, II.319
25206, 10 I.28b
31095, 8 II.54b
34057, 12 III.96b
42210, d1–2 I.FNa
42254, left 9–10 I.FNb
pCG 30605, 20 I.347e
30692, 4 I.177b
50058 5 & 6 I.272c
6 I.48a
50066, 2–3 II.62d
50067 + 50087, 3 III.55b
58060 r° 12 I.n.51
pChester Beatty III v° 16 III.n.18
oChicago OIM 19422, 3 I.353b
pChicago OI 25256, 4 II.375b
OI 25388, 3 II.379d
Cod. Herm. x+2, 16 II.434b
x+2, 17–18 II.134a
*Correspondence of Peter Mongus & Acacius*
– Amélineau 199, 2 II.107d
209, 1 II.297e
Crum, *Cat. BM* #1213, 1–4 II.108a
– in Bell, *Jews & Christians*,
92, 1–2 II.392c
– *Varia Coptica* 45, 1–7 II.187c
Constantine of Assiut,
*On Athanasius*
Orlandi 34, 19–22 II.397d

| | | |
|---|---|---|
| CT I | 55b | I.247c |
| | 77f–78a/B6C | I.90e |
| | 79i–j/T9C | III.27a |
| | 104/105d–e/B1P | II.284b |
| | 162e | I.18 |
| | 171d/B16C | II.313d |
| | 207d | II.311d |
| | 227c | I.70c |
| | 254f | II.17a |
| | 266g | III.140b |
| | 302d–f/B10C | II.347b |
| | 311g/T1C | III.13b |
| | 393e–394a | II.329 |
| – II | 22b/B1P | II.310 |
| | 34b/B1C | I.218b |
| | 108c | I.84 |
| | 125f | I.325 |
| | 156b | III.105b |
| | 215b–216a/S1C[a] | II.347a |
| | 222b–c | I.219e |
| | 242c/S1P | III.126 |
| | 248b/S1P | III.6 |
| | 274/5c–276/77a | II.122a |
| | 280d | II.122d, n.124 |
| | 292a | I.3b, II.11 |
| | 292d–e/S2P | II.229a |
| | 302c | I.329 |
| | 342b | II.351 |
| | 359c–360a/S2P | I.102b |
| | 375c–377c/S2P | I.209a |
| | 383c/S2P | II.n.58 |
| – III | 49b–e/B1C | I.101b |
| | 76g | III.n.46 |
| | 76h/S10C[a] | II.412 |
| | 95g/B1L | II.7a, n.100 |
| | 171f–g/T1C | II.2 |
| | 181b–182a/B2Bo | II.284c |
| | 201e | II.159f |
| | 261d | II.159e |
| | 300d | I.247b |
| | 334d | I.229b |
| | 336f–i | II.409 |
| | 348a–b/S1C[b] | I.186c |
| | 367c/B3C | II.17b |
| | 382e/S2C[a] | II.333d |
| – IV | 37f/Sq6C | II.337 |
| | 48d | I.22 |
| | 59l | I.205a |
| | 75d–f/B6C | I.90c |
| | 75f/B6C | I.238a |
| | 79p–q | I.89b |
| | 84i | III.103 |
| | 88b | II.160k |
| | 99h | II.312f |
| | 145m | II.340b |
| | 173f–h/G1T | II.332 |
| | 188b | III.tab.1 |
| | 191c–d | II.115c |
| | 192a | II.18 |
| | 202a/Sq1C | II.231a |
| | 207b/T3L | I.208a |
| | 210b–212a/T1C[b] | I.113a |
| | 213c/BH1Br | II.159c |
| | 214b–c/Sq1C | II.312e |
| | 215b/BH1Br | II.160e |
| | 217a/M8C | II.159c |
| | 222c/Sq1C | II.300b |
| | 252a/Sq1C | II.312c |
| | 286/87b–288/89a/Sq1C | II.13a |
| | 288b/T1C[b] | II.110e |
| | 292a/T1C[b] | I.196 |
| | 310a/M54C | I.92a |
| | 312b–313a/M4C | I.117d |
| | 343b–c | II.233 |
| – V | 24a–c/B2L[b] | II.302b |
| | 30b–c | II.406a |
| | 32k | II.341 |
| | 49b–c/B6C | III.104a |
| | 49b–c/B4C | III.104b |
| | 59c | II.160c |
| | 68c | I.6b |
| | 68j/B1C | II.9a, n.100 |
| | 89d–90a/T1C | II.348b |
| | 91d/T1Be | I.24, 199b |
| | 91d/Sq1Sq | II.10a |
| | 94e/T1Be | II.299a |
| | 98a | II.339a |
| | 105i–106a/Sq2Sq | II340c |
| | 108a | II.312d |
| | 109h–j/T1C | II.122c |
| | 121e/M5C | II.300a |

150c II.160l
187d/B7C I.71
193f–i/B5C II.110a
236d–e II.302a
259c/B2Bo I.133a
387b–f I.209b
– VI 57e/S1C I.187
63h–j II.124c
72h/B9C II.113b
80g/B3L I.214b
86c–d/B9C I.205b
163b II.301a
208g–h I.77b
212b/S11C I.17a
218k I.118
224m–n III.95b
259b–c I.185c
273b II.156e
273j II.n.38
273k II.n.38
273m II.n.38
273n II.n.38
274b II.n.38
284a–b II.399c
284l II.9b, n.100
312d–f II.281a
314h II.229b
332g–h I.183d
332k–l II.406b
333a I.76b, 211
342e III.2b
348l II.285b
348r–s II.285b
349m II.285b
353l–m I.127b
392n I.330a
393h I.104a
398f I.68a
– VII 18w–y II.401a
51s III.141b
96l I.21
102g–h II.160g
105o–p I.188b
105q I.201b
157c II.156b
197i II.9d
212h/pGard. II II.160h, 324a
232k–l III.94f
241k II.408b
282b II.8d
279d–80a II.159a
289a/B9C II333b
297b/B1L, B2L II.232a
340c/B1C II.222a
385b–c/B3C I.91c
398c–399a/B3C I.91d
401b–c/B3L I.241b
478g–j/B5C II.303
480j/B5C III.3
487b/B1P II.313a
495g–h/B5C II.13b
514c–d/B4L II.267
Cyril of Alexandria,
*De Hora Mortis*
– *MMAF* IV.1 187, 13–14 I.272d
– *In Athanasium*
Orlandi,
*Testi Copti* 19, 8–10 II.152b
– *Erotapokrisis*
Crum,
pCheltenham 5, 3–5 II.209c
5, 29 II.148b
6, 3 I.287g
10, 1 I.67b
– *Miracles of the Three Youth*
de Vis II 169, 8–9 I.269c

Davies, *Amarna* IV, pl. 32, 4 II.244b
*Death of Joseph*
– *Aegyptiaca* 17, 30–18, 17 II.277m
– gDeir el-Bahari #6, 4–5 III.113a
*Deir el-Gebrawi* II, pl. 5, right III.tab.1
– oDeM 437, r° 1–3 II.219a
r°2–3 II.128g
439, r° 1–3 II.416b
554, r° 5–6 III.47c
1221, 1 I.339c
1232, 1 III.39c, 86b
10253, r° 3–4 II.44b
10264 III.47b
pDeM 8 r° 9 I.272b
39 r° 7 I.167a
*Dendereh*, pl. 8, top 5 II.402c
pl. 25B II.406c

Depraved Harpist 2, 5 I.267b
2, 6 II.274c
2, 7 II.138, 371a
3, 13 I.174b
Dioscorus of Alexandria, *On Macarius of Tkow*
– $^{B}$Amélineau 97, 14–98, 1 I.290e
115, 11 II.n.50
– $^{S}$Johnson 50a, 24–25 II.153d
52b, 18–20 II.190f
17a, 28–40 II.258b
*Dormition of the Virgin*
– Robinson, *ApGosp* 76, 27–29 II.396f
– pEbers 1, 7–8 II.14b
1, 10–11 III.118b
37, 3 III.94d
40, 14–15 I.133b
47, 17–18 III.160a
50, 6 III.119c
51, 19–20 I.131a
58, 7–8 I.78c
58, 10–11 II.348a
69, 6 I.318a
76, 12 I.124a
88, 4 I.132b
89, 20 I.234d
91, 2 III.119b
98, 5–6 II.110h
98, 10–11 II.110i
99, 4 I.91a
99, 5 II.121b
99, 14 II.325d
100, 11 II.331b
100, 14 II.414a
100, 17–18 I.107a
100, 18 II.110g
100, 18–101, 1 II.110d
101, 11–12 II.350
101, 15 I.318f
102, 9–10 II.110b, III.108b
102, 15–16 III.107b
108, 12–13 II.160i
109, 17–18 II.123
Edel, *Vertrag* 23*, 6 I.298a
25*, 7 III.98b
28*, 1–3 I.39b
oEdinburgh 916 v° 8–9 III.147b
916 v° 12–14 II.221c
pEdwin Smith 1, 7 II.121c
1, 26 III.158
3, 3 III.136b
3, 19–20 III.108a
3, 21–4, 1 I.107b; II.119a
4, 2–3 II.414b
6, 12–13 III.107a
6, 13 II.110c
10, 10 III.136a
10, 21–22 II.118a
14, 13–14 II.414c
15, 15 II.398a
15, 17 I.220, II.110f
16, 14–16 II.118b
17, 12 III.94b
18, 15 I.192
21, 20–21 III.134b
22, 14 III.97c
*El Bersheh* I, pl. 7 III.21
pl. 14, 1 III.1a, 80b
pl. 14, 10 III.12
pl. 15, 2. reg. I.184b
pl. 15, 3. reg. III.22b
p. 33 I.100b
*Ep. Apostolorum*
Schmidt 3* f. 3, 14–15 II.442c
4* f. 5, 11–12 II.79b
*EpPt* (NHC VIII, 2) 137, 5 II.206a
*Eudoxia and the Holy Sepulchre*
Pearson 54, 3–4 II.193i
*EvNicodemus*
Orlandi 38, 9–10 III.146d
*EvThom* 41:27–29 II.207a
*EvVer* 16, 37–17, 1 II.297c
17, 21–22 II.441e
17, 23–25 II.394d
17, 25–28 II.259d
18, 19–21 II.181e
24, 10–11 II.174f
33, 30–32 II.380c
40, 5–7 II.452f
*First Wonder of St George*
Budge 44, 22 II.391h
*Five Th. T.* pl. 26, left, 3–6 III.161b

Florence 2590, 4–5 III.23b
pFlorence PSI D 88, 7 I.266e
*Further Miracles of Apa Mena*
– Drescher, *Mena* 21, a29–b1 II.200c
81, b21–25 I.290f

*Gesios & Isidorus*
– *ZÄS* 21, 141, 15 I.356c
142, 2–3 II.183d
142, 14–15 II.100a, 254a
142, 15–17 II.75i
143, 6 II.190a
143, 7–8 II.255c
143, 10 I.302c
144, 17–18 II.145a
148, 3–4 II.394c
148, 17–18 II.224c
149, 5–6 II.89a
151, 1–2 II.448b
*GospPh.* 53, 14–16 II.259d
56, 4–5 II.145c
57, 14–15 II.255f
57, 27–28 I.58d
59, 10–11 II.259c
59, 13–16 I.143b
59, 16–18 I.62c
60, 11–15 II.203a
62, 26–31 II.84a, 246f
Graffito M.2.3.P.18.15
– Navrátilová, pl. 24 III.47a
*Great Aten Hymn*
– Sandman 95, 6–7 III.43a

Great Mag. P. Paris
[*ZÄS* 21, 94, 17] II.172g
[*ZÄS* 21, 99, 30–32] II.375e
[*ZÄS* 21, 100, 34] I.300i
[*ZÄS* 21, 100, 43] II.132f
[*ZÄS* 21, 104, 10–13] II.52g
[*ZÄS* 21, 104, 15] I.171f

*Hammamat* 114, 7 III.5b
10–11 I.20b
*Hamra Dom*, pl. 47, 5 I.128b
Hardjedef II.1/Mü I.216
pHarkness 2, 34–35 I.140
3, 22 I.262h
4, 16 II.374c
4, 29 I.288f
5, 29 I.266b

pHarris I 6, 1 I.28f
7, 6 I.262e
7, 10 III.147a
8, 6 III.147k
9, 5 I.259b
26, 1 I.295e
75, 2 I.146b
77, 2 I.146c
Haskell Mus. 13945, 3 I.n.47
3–4 III.18c
Hassan, *Giza* II fig. 219 I.184a, 231
II.111d
Hatnub 16, 9–10 I.201a
20, 5–6 I.75
22, 2 II.263c
pHauswaldt VI, 1 II.372a
pHearst 6, 10 III.118a
Heqanakhte I, r° 13 I.317b
r° 14 II.401b
v° 2 I.81a, III.80c
v° 9 II.8b
v° 15 II.9e
II, r° 3 I.224b
r° 40–41 I.197c
r° 43 I.109a, II.9c
III, r° 3 I.7
Herdsman 7 I.5b
Hezi A4–5 I.226b
*HO* 33.2 r° 6–7 II.46b
46.3, 1 III.39a
70.2, 6–7 I.308a
79 edge 1.1 III.n.48
88 r° 4 I.28e
r° 11–12 II.126f
r° 14 I.167e
*Homily on Christ's Birth*
– Elanskaya 367b, 22–33 II.149c
oHor1, 2 I.258b
3, r° 18–19 I.347f
*HP* III, pl. 7, Str. Ba v° 6 II.160f
Hymn to Sobek
– Erman 1911 16, 1–2 III.95e
– oIFAO D 632, 3 I.170f
9 III.88a
– oIFAO 681 II.42b
857 II.220b
1328 v° ii, 2 II.423a

*Inscr. of Mose* S13
– Gaballa, pl. 63 I.n.97
pInsinger 2, 11 II.48b, 245a
4, 3 II.379b
4, 5 II.376b
5, 19 II.433c
7, 15 II.433b
8, 5 I.297
8, 15 II.432b
8, 15–19 I.351a
8, 22 II.361
10, 12 II.396c
17, 4 I.310b
19, 12 II.172b
20, 4 III.56f
21, 18 III.122c
21, 20 I.42c
22, 3–5 I.351b
34, 4 III.149b
pInv. Sorbonne 1248, 7–8 I.257d
Ipuwer 2, 4 II.342c
2, 8 I.23d
3, 12 I.199c
4, 11–12 II.415a
5, 2 II.10b
5, 9 II.161b, III.20
5, 14 II.238b
6, 4–5 I.4d
6, 8 III.22a
6, 14 I.215a
7, 10 I.181b
8, 3 II.293b
9, 5 I.244c
15,2 I.23c

Jansen-Winkeln, *IdS* I, 129, 10 II.130b
I, 129, 10–11 III.169d
I, 137, 19 III.120b
I, 176, 18–19 II.425c
I, 183, 1–2 I.38e
I, 199, 8–9 I.166a
I, 200, 12–14 I.38d, II.269g
I, 203, 9–10 I.167h
I, 203, 12 I.38c
I, 204, 1–2 II.34b
I, 211, 2 II.34c
II, 25, 3–4 II.269c
II, 25, 4–5 II.32d
II, 296, 7–8 I.274a
II, 460, 9 II.244e
*JEA* 14, pl. 5, 12 III.38a
12–14 I.265b
John Chrysostom,
*In Michaelem et Latronem*
– Simon 227, 6–7 II.255g
– On the Resurrection & Apostles
Depuydt, *Homiletica*
64, 29–30 II.397a
John the Elder,
*Vita Pisenthius*
– Budge, *Apocrypha*,
77, 27–29 I.290c

John of Constantinople,
*On Repentance and Continence*
– Budge, *Homilies*, 2, 19–20 III.122a
John Evangelist,
*Investiture of Archangel Michael*
– Müller 3, 22–24 II.390b
5, 4–5 II.190g
11, 3–4 III.171d
11, 4–5 II.191b
11, 12–13 II.255e
13, 4–5 II.380e
13, 5 II.74e
25, 16–17 II.142f
29, 25–26 II.257b
31, 12 I.301e
39, 15–16 I.287e
John the Hermit,
*Encomium of Mark the Evangelist*
– Orlandi 16a, 11–17 II.214a
30, 1–5 II.452c
38, 3–6 II.441c
40a, 5–13 II.442e
44a, 12–17 II.278c
Junker, *Giza* VI, fig. 43 I.2a, 182b, 199a
XI, fig. 105 I.16b
Junker, *Poesie* II
88, 3–6 III.67d
96, e13–14 I.298j

Kagemni I, 2 III.33a
I, 10 II.242b
II, 6–7 I.114a, III.131

| | | | |
|---|---|---|---|
| Kamose Stela II, 23 | | | I.182a |
| *P.KellisCopt.* 25, 39–40 | | | II.89b |
| Kemyt 9/TC | | | III.133a |
| *Kephalaia* 6, 26 | | | III.67g |
| | 8, 4 | | II.199e |
| | 16, 29–31 | | II.382d |
| | 21, 32 | | II.181f |
| | 26, 11 | | II.386d |
| | 29, 20–21 | | II.246g |
| | 34, 19–20 | | II.390c |
| | 36, 12 | | II.183c |
| | 38, 5–7 | | II.278d |
| | 100, 23 | | II.290c |
| | 137, 17 | | III.122c |
| Khakheperraseneb | r° 6 | | II.117a |
| | r° 10 | | I.318d |
| | r° 13 | | II.231b, III.14a, 32a |
| | r° 13–14 | | I.70b |
| | v° 4 | | III.85 |
| oKöln 184, 2 | | | III.63b |
| Kom el-Koffar A9 | | | |
| | *ASAE* 70, 419–29 | | I.90a |
| pKrall | 6, 3 | | II.51c |
| | 14, 12 | | II.173b |
| | 18, 32 | | I.170 |
| | 19, 23 | | II.53a |
| | 23, 11 | | II.437 |
| *KRI* | I | 38, 4–5 | I.254a |
| | | 46, 12 | II.46f |
| | | 47, 6 | II.n.48 |
| | | 47, 10–11 | II.46c |
| | | 66, 2 | III.40b |
| | | 67, 3 | I.136f |
| | | 67, 15 | II.n.48 |
| | | 68, 1–2 | II.221a, 427d |
| | | 70, 3–4 | I.274d |
| | | 111, 1–2 | II.270e.,mm |
| | | 113, 1 | II.n.48 |
| | | 238, 12 | I.307c |
| | | 239, 4 | I.267a |
| | | 239, 10–11 | I.169a |
| | | 239, 14–15 | I.144d |
| | | 240, 6 | III.50a |
| | | 322, 7–8 | II.46a |
| | | 323, 4–6 | II.169d |
| | – II | 12, 3 | II.169e |
| | | 29, 1–7 | I.300a |
| | | 35, 10 | III.148 |
| | | 42, 2 | II.417a |
| | | 44, 12 | I.137 |
| | | 52, 13–53, 2 | II.418b |
| | | 52, 15–53, 5 | II.424b |
| | | 56, 1–6/K1 | I.288b |
| | | 56, 13 | III.38b |
| | | 61, 4 | I.279 |
| | | 62, 1–3 | III.53a |
| | | 71, 16–72, 9 | I.154b |
| | | 75, 11–16 | III.52a |
| | | 87, 12 | I.n.15 |
| | | 87, 13 | I.n.15 |
| | | 97, 7 | III.44a |
| | | 97, 9 | 39b |
| | | 102, 8 | I.35a |
| | | 108, 6 | I.154c |
| | | 110, 3 | II.28c |
| | | 110, 15 | I.154a |
| | | 116, 7–16 | II.41e |
| | | 240, 12 | II.125b |
| | | 244, 6 | I.35b |
| | | 246, 4 | I.299c |
| | | 246, 10–13 | II.367b |
| | | 249, 1 | I.278a |
| | | 249, 12 | II.169f |
| | | 326, 8–9 | I.258a |
| | | 330, 10 | II.270c |
| | | 334, 5 | III.48b |
| | | 355, 3–4 | I.n.97 |
| | | 355, 16–356, 1 | II.27b |
| | | 378, 6–7 | III.42a |
| | | 380, 2–3 | II.367c |
| | – III | 231, 7 | I.147a |
| | | 232, 15 | II.359a |
| | | 252, 8–9 | I.276a |
| | | 255, 4 | II.37, 288e |
| | | 255, 8–9 | II.126c |
| | | 255, 12–14 | I.343c |
| | | 283, 6–7 | I.136g |
| | | 336, 10–11 | III.113b |
| | | 336, 11–12 | III.44b |
| | | 347, 15 | III.43g |
| | | 403, 2–3 | III.43h |

| | | |
|---|---|---|
| | 500, 9 | III.45a |
| | 500, 14 | II.45b |
| | 504, 3–5 | I.288d |
| | 505, 4 | III.42d |
| | 505, 4–6 | II.166 |
| | 505, 6 | II.416c |
| | 506, 11–12 | III.109b |
| | 506, 15–16 | II.420b |
| | 532, 3–4 | II.46d |
| | 533, 7 | II.422b |
| | 544, 2–3 | II.169c |
| | 545, 4–5 | II.31a |
| – IV | 3, 11 | I.30b |
| | 10, 4 | III.46 |
| | 10, 7 | III.40a |
| | 14, 4 | I.28d |
| | 14, 10 | I.336a |
| | 14, 16 | I.288a |
| | 15, 1 | I.298c |
| | 15, 3–5 | I.295c |
| | 15, 5 | I.274c |
| | 15, 12–14 | II.31b |
| | 23, 6 | I.25c |
| | 80, 10–11 | I.299e |
| | 80, 16 | III.51b |
| | 161, 3–4 | II.393b |
| | 232, 4–5 | I.338 |
| | 316, 2 | II.130a, 423d |
| | 316, 5–6 | III.147j |
| | 316, 6–7 | II.288c |
| | 317, 2–3 | II.270f |
| | 317, 5–7 | I.289b |
| | 318, 6 | I.308c |
| | 319, 6–7 | II.288d |
| | 319, 13–14 | II.427b |
| | 330, 13–14 | I.168d |
| | 408, 13–14 | I.168a |
| | 410, 4 | II.427c |
| | 410, 14–16 | I.169b |
| | 412, 15–16 | I.135b |
| | 413, 1 | I.166b |
| | 413, 15–16 | I.340 |
| | 416, 8–10 | I.39a |
| | 417, 7 | I.n.15 |
| | 417, 12–13 | I.168c |
| – V | 2, 3 | III.45b |
| | 33, 8 | I.265a |
| | 33, 12 | I.299a |
| | 223, 1–2 | III.53b |
| | 239, 5–6 | I.144c, 254b |
| | 245, 2 | I.259a |
| | 264, 11 | II.270a |
| | 344, 6 | II.46e |
| | 351, 9–10 | I.263b |
| | 352, 2 | I.298b |
| | 360, 3 | II.FNc |
| | 361, 9–10 | II.43a |
| | 450, 5–6 | I.262d |
| | 467, 16 | II.31c |
| | 474, 6–8 | I.343a |
| | 475, 6–9 | I.288c |
| | 476, 3–4 | I.344b |
| | 479, 8–9 | II.22f |
| | 480, 1–2 | II.41b |
| | 480, 2–3 | I.275d |
| | 524, 8 | III.167a |
| | 527, 1–2 | II.428 |
| | 533, 16–534, 1 | I.157a |
| | 565, 5–6 | I.146d |
| | 585, 3 | II.33a |
| | 646, 7–8 | III.147g |
| – VI | 5, 9–10 | III.54b |
| | 22, 9 | II.30a |
| | 23, 3 | II.39c |
| | 67, 10 | I.344a |
| | 142, 8 | I.307a |
| | 155, 12–14 | II.420a |
| | 237, 15 | I.266a |
| | 253, 3 | I.300d |
| | 265, 2 | II.417b |
| | 265, 6–7 | I.264b, III.42f |
| | 266, 2–3 | I.276e |
| | 266, 8–9 | III.166a |
| | 267, 6–7 | I.154e |
| | 334, 3 | III.41a |
| | 343, 13–14 | I.288e |
| | 431, 8 | I.274e |
| | 470, 8–9 | I.144e |
| | 471, 2–3 | I.158 |
| | 473, 8 | I.168b |
| | 478, 1–2 | II.430 |
| | 479, 6–8 | II.23b |
| | 483, 13–484, 1 | I.156a |
| | 483, 15–484, 1 | I.339i |

485, 11 339g
515, 3–4 I.339e
519, 1 I.157b
519, 2–3 II.41a
564, 4–5 I.336c; 342b
564, 14–15 I.341b
579, 14–16 III.166d
604, 5 I.336i
671, 7 I.336b
735, 15 I336h
737, 5–6 I.294d
737, 15–738, 1 I.339h
738, 3–6 I.290a
738, 7–8 I.295d
741, 8 II.33c
741, 9–10 II.416d
741, 9–11 II.271c
758, 16–759, 1 III.165c
769, 12 I.275a
770, 7 I.25a
770, 8–9 I.156b
776, 2–3 I.29a
780, 12 II.129
781, 3–5 II.126e
781, 5 III.45c
781, 5–6 I.277
781, 6 II.370b
786, 7–8 II.269b
789, 9 II.26a, 368a
789, 9–10 II.41c
792, 13 III.167c
798, 3 II.42a, 165a
798, 14–16 II.219b
803, 16–804, 1 II.40b
804, 15–16 II.32b
805, 10–11 II.40d
806, 2–3 II.38
807, 6–7 I.275c
808, 9 I.n.15
808, 13–14 II.32c
810, 1–3 I.154d
810, 13 I.339a
811, 3 II.370a
823, 12 I.275b
824, 15 I.155
– VII 381, 8–9 I.339f

Kropp, *Zaubertexte* I
15, 12 I.257g
17, 5 II.397e
*KRU* #76, 3&21 II.70c
*Krugtexte* A, text 2, 11 II.377b, 435d
12 II.52c
KSB II #849, 1–3 II.392e
#893, 17–21 II.392d

Lamb of Bocchoris 2, 10 II.136f
*Legend of Jeremia*
*Or* 67, 42 [13], 12–18 II.391a
Leiden V6, 11 II.335c
pLeiden I 343+345 r° 4, 2–3 III.120
371, 3–4 I.276b
379, 3 I.170c, 300g
382, 22–25 III.57
F 1996/1.1, r° 4–5 II.269f
*LEM* 5, 6 I.274b
6, 5 II.269e, 416a
7, 8–9 I.275e
12, 8 I.272a
15, 2–3 III.41b
17, 4–5 I.257a
17, 7 I.257b
20, 2 II.295b
25, 13 III.43f
28, 10–11 III.41c
39, 10 II.28b
39, 13–14 I.337b
42, 12 II.425a
43, 5 I.166c
43, 5–6 I.144b
43, 6–7 I.n.53
43, 10–11 I.336f
59, 4 I.32b
60, 6 III.147e
60, 7 III.43d
60, 12 III.38e
62, 13–14 I.136a
65, 13–14 I.276c
71, 11–12 II.33b
80, 5–6 II.244d
82, 7–8 III.169a
90, 9 I.300b
90, 12 I.260a
94, 7 III.110

100, 12–13 III.37b
101, 12–13 I.295a
102, 5–6 III.37a
106, 7–8 I.341a
*LEM* Caminos, 508, 2 I.299d
508, 5–6 II.40a
*LES* 2, 2–3 I.169d
2, 4–5 II.44a
2, 5 II.126a, 353a
3, 1–2 I.264a
3, 8–9 I.298d
5, 3–5 II.218c
6, 5 I.25b, 36
6, 6 II.368c
8, 12 II.168a
9, 10–11 II.359b
10, 13–14 III.142a
12, 8 I.30a
12, 11 III.42b
12, 15 I.32a
13, 12 II.36
14, 6 II.422a
16, 9–10 II.27c
16, 13–14 III.43b
19, 14–15 I.38a
20, 4–5 II.168b
20, 12 I.28a
21, 2 III.111b
21, 14 I.263a
23, 10 II.126b
25, 2–3 II.165c
25, 10 II.29, 355a
25, 11 II.26c
25, 13 I.295b
32, 16–33, 1 II.355b
33, 4 II.128b, 369a
33, 7–8 I.29b, 135a
34, 10 II.427a
39, 13–14 II.40c, 218e, 294
42, 4–5 II.27d, III.165b
42, 5–6 III.166b
43, 8–9 I.145b, 262a
44, 16–45, 1 I.275f, II.393a
49, 3 II.126d
50, 3–4 II.128c
54, 3–4 II.396a
57, 16–58, 1 III.42c
58, 2–3 I.167b
59, 11–12 I.136d
60, 7 I.299b
62, 13 II.32a
62, 13–15 II.43b
62, 16–63, 2 II.34a
63, 9 I.167g
65, 5 II.35a
66, 7 I.167d
66, 9–10 I.33b
67, 3–4 I.308d
67, 4–5 I.345a
67, 6–7 I.345b
68, 3–5 II.271a
68, 6–7 II.41d
69, 4–5 II.27a
69, 5–6 II.424a
69, 12–13 III.n.34
69, 13 I.161a
70, 4–5 II.368b
73, 5–6 II.165b
75, 12 II.269a
85, 6–7 I.144a
*Lesestücke* 74, 13–14 I.114b
74, 16–17 I.8b
83, 3 III.133d
87, 7 I.19, 242a
*Life and Miracles of St Simeon the Stylite*
– Chaîne 22, 17 II.76b
52, 1–4 II.194g
*Life of Antony*
– Garitte 2, 2–3 II.176b
3, 3–5 II.275a
4, 5–6 II.190c
7, 24–26 III.146h
101, 3–4 II.254b
*Life of Daniel of Scetis*
– Guidi 83, 8–11 II.183e
*Life of Hor*
– *Mon. Wadi Natrun* I 169, a1–4 II.392f
*Life of John Calybita*
– Budge, *Martyrdoms* 185, 11–12 II.76a
*Life of John of Lycopolis*
– *AnBoll* 87, 193, 2–3 II.152a
88, 175, b3–11 II.277a
*Life of Macarius of Alexandria*
– MG 25 254, 6 I.261d

*Life of Marina*
– Till, *KHML* I, 30, 9–10 II.391b
*Life of Moses of Abydos*
– Amélineau 683, 14 II.194c
692, 4–5 II.75e
– *Or* 80, 405, b27–406, a2 II.258c
pLille 31 A 22 II.54c
Litany of Ra 101/Th III II.21
123–24/R IV III.124a
*Lit. Fragm.*, pl. 2, 12 I.229a
pl. 2, 2.7 I.334a
pl. 3, 4.6 I.1b
pLoeb 1, 9–10 I.149b
4, 2 III.59b
10–11 I.311a
5, 11–12 I.300h
20–21 II.131b
6, 2–3 III.145
7, 11–12 II.62f
8, 37–38 III.62d
17, 47–48 I.42b
pLondon med. 7, 12 I.74a
Louvre AF 10076, 5 I.301a
C3, 7 I.12b
C11, 5–6 I.234b
7 I.214a
C12, 13–14 III.17b
17 III.138b
pLouvre E 2432, 3 II.52e
E 2433, r° 3 II.245b
E 3230b, 2–3 II.419a
4 II.125a
E 3334, 14–15 II.68e
E 7837, 4 II.60
4–5 II.62b
E 7843, 6 II.57a
E 7846, r° 4 II.57c
E 7852, 4 II.62a
E 7854, 4 III.60a, III.115a
E 7855, 11–12 I.264d
E 9294, 3–4 II.59a
E 10382, 18 II.52f
E 27151, 8 II.271b
N 706 v° 2 I.264c
N 2409, 5 II.61c
N 2414 1, 4 II.360a
2, 12 I.353e
3, 5 II.434c
N 2420c, 5 I.51, II.356b
Louvre Bowl 8 III.125b
*Loyaliste* §2, 9–10/St III.4a
§3, 9 II.342d
§3, 9–10 I.8e
§6, 2/St III.35
§11, 8 II.222b
*LRL* 2, 1 II.420c
2, 8–9 I.339d
3, 12 III.143
6, 7–8 III.165a
9, 10–11 I.134b
10, 8–9 I.30c
15, 3–4 II.FNb
15, 6 I.307b
16, 4 II.26b
16, 8–9 II.288b
19, 15 I.308b
22, 1–2 II.27e
27, 16 II.370c
28, 11 I.n.15
29, 15 II.288a
32, 4 III.47d
32, 13 I.294b
34, 11–12 I.33c
36, 9 III.109c
36, 11–12 II.221b
42, 4–5 III.109a
43, 4 II.22c
45, 10–11 II.244f
46, 15 I.294e
48, 15 II.366a, III.142b
48, 16–49, 1 I.339b, II.218b, III.168
53, 3 II.47
58, 15–16 I.344c
59, 1–2 I.157c
64, 14–15 II.425b
67, 16–68, 1 II.127
68, 1 II.357a
68, 1–2 II.128d
68, 4–5 II.423b
69, 3–4 II.35b
73, 1 II.128f
73, 16–74, 1 III.51c

pLüddeckens 2, GBS (A) 6–7 II.61b, II. 254c
13 B19 I.46b

pMag. London&Leiden
3, 19–20 III.56a
4, 8 I.163a
6, 26–27 II.274b
9, 18–19 I.138d
9, 32 II.53b, 355c
15, 28–29 II.173c
17, 20 III.116a
19, 3–4 I.263c
19, 9 III.60b
20, 12–13 II.48d
21, 4 I.171d
21, 7 II.296c
21, 20 II.172f
21, 32–33 II.378a
23, 21–22 II.68d
v° 1, 1–3 II.131c
v° 3, 4–6 I.173c, II.132b
v° 3, 12–13 II.132a
v° 20, 7 II.374d
v° 33, 5 II.372b
oMallawi 484, x+8 II.68a
Man and Ba 5–6 III.84
17 II.160j
20–21 II.156a
30–31 II.318
31–32 II.407
33–34 I.82
37 II.8c
38 II.308a
122 I.320b
126–27 III.n.46
130 I.8a, 320a
oManawir IFAO 5446, 5–7 II.133c
*Man. Homilien*
– ed. Polotsky 45, 11–13 II.381c
*Mart. Apatil*
– *AM* I 193, 22 II.213b
*Mart. Ari*
– *AdM* 203, 10–11 I.176f
*Mart. Cyriacus of Jerusalem*
– *AM* II 12, 24–25 II.100b, 254c
*Mart. Elijah*
– Sobhy 13, b16–22 II.180
*Mart. Epima*
– *AM* I 135, 16–17 II.105c
*Mart. Eusebius*
– *AdM* 20, 2 II.187a
23, 14–15 II.212c
29, 6–7 II.255a
32, 15–16 I.287f
32, 19 II.88c
33, 1–2 II.439f
*Mart. George*
– *AM* II 272, 18–19 II.155e
282, 17 II.441i
284, 13–15 II.104c
293, 10–1 II.201b
299, 12–14 II.194h
*Mart. John of Panicôit*
– Zaborowski 232–34 II.259f
*Mart. Leontius the Arab*
– von Lemm 11, a13–14 III.153a
*Mart. Macarius of Antioch*
– *AdM* 40, 17 I.66b
43, 2–3 II.258e
*Mart. Macrobius*
– *AdM* 232, 7–8 II.107e
*Mart. Mercurius*
– M589 f. 9 v° a24–27 II.391g
*Mart. Nahrow*
– *ASAE* 19, 78, 18–21 I.302b, 305a
– Till, *KHML* I, 5, 13–14 II.87a, 249a
*Mart. Paese & Thekla*
– Till, *KHML* I 80, 6 II.76c
80, 8 II.76d
*Mart. Panesnew*
– Till, *KHML* I 95, 8–20 II.290b
*Mart. Papnuti*
– Bacot 307b, 16–20 II.143g
*Mart. Pirou & Atom*
– *AdM* 140, 13 II.82c
*Mart. Ptolemy*
– Till, *KHML* II 31, 13 II.75h
32, 30 III.171b
33, 16–17 I.358b
37, 12–13 II.450b
*Mart. Shnube*
– *ASAE* 17, 149, 9–10 II.70d
149, 10–11 II.75g
150, 4–7 I.262j

*Mart. St Victor the General*
– Budge, *Martyrdoms* 1, 21 II.396d
3, 31–33 III.68a
9, 6–7 II.439a
31, 19–22 I.63a
*Mart. Theodore & al.*
– *AM* I 35, 19–21 I.356f
38, 17 III.152c
– Müller & Uljas, *Martyrs & Archangels*
§4 I.292a
§37 I.293a
§99 I.152a
§101 II.95e
*Mart. Theodore Stratelates*
– *AM* I 160, 2–3 II.276e
160, 21 II.86, 248a
*Mart. Timothy*
– Till, *KHML* I 112, 6 II.75f
*Mastaba de Neferirtenef* 59 II.112a
Mathieu, *Poésie*, pl. 1, 4 II.22b
pl. 2, 3–4 III.87
pl. 2, 9 III.43c
pl. 7, 2 III.43e
pl. 8, 11 II.367a
pl. 8, 12–pl. 9, 1 I.136b
pl. 9, 7–8 II.359c
pl. 11, 6 III.47e
pl. 11, 8 II.39a
pl. 13, 7–8 I.262c
pl. 13, 10 II.23c
pl. 16, 3 I.134a
pl. 19, 18 II.295a
pl. 27, 3 III.44d
*Meir* III, pl. 8 I.245d
pl. 11 III.97e
*Memph. Theology* 4, 21 II.135
Merikara C, V.1–2 III.140c
E, 25–26 II.346
48 III.164
66 III.25a
68 III.157a
91 III.25b
97–98 II.309a
*Miracles of St Colluthos*
– Schenke, 222, b1–8 II.276b
MMA 12.184, vertical 1 II.235b
35.7.55, 7–8 I.98
10 I.210
pMond I, 6–7 II.169b
P.Mon.Epiph.#145, 2–4 II.106a
#308, 1–2 II.107a
Moscow Bowl 2 II.429
3 II.30b
pMoscow math. n.9, 10–11 II.164
n.9, 29 II.283
n.16, 10 II.115d, n.101
n.23, 5 I.6a
n.25, 4 II.330c
*Mo'alla*, Iβ4–5 II.312,b
IIα2 I.333b,II.6a
Moses of Quft,
*Vita Pisenthius*
Amélineau 115, 13–116, 1 I.273e
141, 3 II.198d
*MuK* v° 2, 3 I.318c
v° 2, 8 II.238c
Munich G1. W.A.F. 31, 6 –7 II.226
*Mysteries of St John Evangelist*
– Budge, *Apocrypha* 59, 7–8 I.176a
60, 33–61, 1 I.27
61, 23–24 I.255c
Myth of the Sun's Eye
3, 30–31 II.64b
4, 1 I.349b
4, 26 I.348
6, 27–28 I.346a
7, 21–22 I.282b
8, 4 II.51d
8, 16–17 I.296b
8, 18 I.309c
8, 23 II.245d, 378b
9, 5 I.48b
9, 20 II.136a
9, 21–22 I.40a
11, 3–4 I.53b
11, 4 I.300e
11, 5 I.n.97
12, 3 I.254d
13, 13–14 I.349a, II.n.145
13, 29 II.136d
14, 1–2 III.149c

14, 29 II.273d
15, 24–25 II.137b
16, 5–7 I.148g
16, 6–7 I.350e
16, 15 I.281b
16, 28 II.371b
16, 30 I.46d
17, 15 II.171b
18, 2 III.56e
22, 28 I.170d
25, 24 II.49a
Nag'a ed-Deir 3737, 3–5 II.399d
Neferhetep Song 3 [Hari pl. IV]
1.8 II.270d, III.49
Neferty If I.112a
Ii I.73, 212
IId III.119a
IIIg I.244b
IVc I.8d
IXf I.100a
XIb–c III.1c
*O.Ashm.Copt.* 3, 4–5 I.257f
16, 5–7 I.356a
*O. Crum* Ad. 13, 4–7 III.100c
Ad. 57, 8–10 III.n.34
*O.Frange* #14, 10–12 II.184c
14–16 II.199f
#24, 4–7 II.177b
#38, 11 II.75m
#44, x+9 II.152c
#48, 14–20c II.200c
23–25 III.100d
#58, 10–15 II.75n
#61, 9–11 III.78c
#72, 11–12 I.354c
#74, 1–8 I.290d
#79, 13–14 II.147e
#103, 4–5 I.360a
#247, 1–6 II.107b
#491, 1–6 II.107c
*OIP* 100, pl. 20 I.136e
*O.Medin.Habu Copt.*
#134, 1–3 II.108b
#183, 1–3 II.106a
Onkhsheshonqy
2, x+17 I.281a
2, x+21 II.66c
3, x+16–17 II.171c
3, x+17 II.394a
4, 6–7 II.56a
6, 22 I.310a
7, 9 I.353d
7, 19 III.121e
8, 3 III.56a
8, 17–23 II.360b
9, 16–17 II.131a
10, 12 I.254c
12, 24 II.435d
13, 6–7 II.48a
14, 4 II.66d
15, 9 III.122d
17, 18 III.61
18, 16 I.312c
19, 3 III.149a
19, 13 I.172
20, 9 III.58b
20, 14 III.151
20, 22–25 II.49c
22, 13 I.266c
23, 8 III.62c
23, 10 II.170c
23, 16 II.376a
25, 18 III.170a
27, 10 I.47b
28, 10 I.312b
*O.Tempeleide* 76, 4–7 I.347d
*O.Vind.Copt.* 35, 8–9 I.356b

Pachom,
*Instructions Concerning a Spiteful Monk*
– Lefort 2, 2–3 II.95b
*Praecepta*
– Lefort 33, 30–31 II.195
*Paheri*, pl. 3, top register III.32b
pl. 3, middle register I.n.15
pl. 7 I.335
*Panegyric on John the Baptist*
– de Vis I 49, 2–3 II.212a
Papnute,
*Wanderings*
*RecTrav* 6, 169, 3 I.177f
174, 10–11 II.278f
177, 15 I.142c
185, 7–9 I.63d
*Paraph. Shem* 1, 25–28 I.255b

Paul of Tamma,
*De Cella*
Orlandi 94, 48 II.277b
*De Humilitate*
– Orlandi 126, 5 II.290a
Peas B1, 26 I.181c
34 III.tab.1
35 II.160m
57–58 I.250b
75 II.238a
76 II.116b
77–79 II.114c
93 II.6b
93–95 II.240
102 I.252a
114–15 II.335b, 344d
126–27 I.246b, II.402b
134–35 III.28b
139–40 III.1b
148–49 III.8b
155–56 III.133e
196 II.402a
199–200 I.249a
220–22 I.326
246 I.191a
247 II.325e
248–49 I.233a
249 I.6c
278–79 I.185d
319 II.305
332–33 I.253e
338 I.23a, 252c
351–52 III.93a
B2, 39–42 I.253h
65–66 I.77a, 197b
93–94 II.243c
109–11 I.331
131–32 III.82
Bt, 19–21 II.291b
27–28 I.86
R, 1.1 II.109a, 352
1.1–2 II.291a
7.4 II.399e
7.5–6 I.78a
18.7 II.12b
Peter of Alexandria,
*On Riches*
– Pearson & Vivian, 134 II.n.25
*Petese Stories* fr. C3, 1 III.116c
*Petubastis Cycle* tCambridge 5 I.139a
*P.Gascou* 24, 11–12 II.72b
60, A 9–11 II.194e
pPhiladelphia 1, 3–4 I.309d
2–3 I.149d
grPhilae 416, 7 I.288g, III.62a
13 I.298g
20 II.52b
Pisenthius of Quft,
*On Onnofrius*
– *ROC* 20: 54, 25–27 II.391i
*Pistis Sophia*
Schmidt 49, 13 III.67c
71, 5–7 II.208b
71, 8–11 II.208c
80, 12 III.146c
232, 14–16 II.185a
232, 19–20 II.258a
352, 3 II.70f
357, 19–20 III.69a
*P.KellisCopt* 64, 9–11 I.54c
26–27 I.60c
72, 19–22 I.261b
*PrecPl* (NHC I, 1) A, 5 II.206b
*Primeval Ocean*
fr. 3, 12 III.56g
fr. 13 2, 5 II.375d
fr. 13 2, 14 II.379c
*Psalms of the Bema*
40, 29–30 II.193d
*Psalms of Saracôtôn*
181, 20–21 II.82b
*Psalms of Thomas*
207, 18–19 II.97d
209, 28 I.176d
211, 15–16 I.142b
221, 1–2 II.443c
221, 3–4 II.198c
222, 20–22 II.383f
223, 3 I.26c
Ps. Athanasius,
*TestPatr*
– *Abraham* Guidi 160, 19–20 II.389a
160, 23–161, 1 II.389b
*Isaac* 233, 14–16 II.384e
238, 18 I.286b

| | |
|---|---|
| *Jacob* 255, 5–8 | I.301g |
| Ps. Cyril, | |
| *On the Cross* | |
| – Campagnano 146, 1 | III.146e |
| – Budge, *Misc.* 227, 18–20 | II.443a |
| – *On the Virgin* | |
| *Or* 70, 44, 15–16 | II.247c |
| Ps. Gregory of Nyssa, | |
| *De Sacrificio Abraham* | |
| – *ROC* 17 406, 5–6 | II.383i |
| Ps. Shenute, | |
| *On Christian Behaviour* | |
| – Kuhn 3, 7–8 | II.189b |
| oPSBA 35, pl. 27, 2–3 | I.44a |
| PT 27b–d | II.1a |
| 34c/W | II.317b |
| 52a/N | I.188a |
| 58b | II.328 |
| 65b | II.113a |
| 121b | II.285a |
| 121c | I.111 |
| 128c | II.112b |
| 131e | II.228b |
| 147a | II.15 |
| 160c | II.337 |
| 192b/W | II.317a |
| 193a–b | II.1b |
| 248b | I.1a |
| 251d | I.316 |
| 262b | II.326a |
| 270a | I.250a |
| 304a/W | I.185a |
| 363f | I.245a |
| 366c | II.327b |
| 377b | I.200c |
| 392d | I.315a |
| 396a–b | I.181g |
| 399c | II.157b |
| 401b | II.243a |
| 414a–b | I.FNc |
| 438c/WT | II.159b, 313e |
| 483b/W | II.1c |
| 537c | II340a |
| 543c | II.284c |
| 548b | II.112c |
| 577a | II.111 |
| 638d | III.141a |
| 644c | II.331b |
| 648d/T | II.335d, III.13c |
| 658c | III.138a |
| 681a | I.3a |
| 703b/TPN | II.160b, 163, 306 |
| 719a–b | I.247a |
| 740 | II.311a |
| 763a–d | I.108, 195a |
| 763b–d | II.122e |
| 765b | III.94a |
| 809c | II.5a |
| 884 | I.94 |
| 890b/P | I.315b |
| 903c/P | III.17e |
| 939a–b | III.29a |
| 943d | II.111e |
| 961d/P | II.316a |
| 1023a | II.116c |
| 1092d–1093a/P | I.186b |
| 1098c/P | II.307 |
| 1102a | I.123 |
| 1114a–b/P | I.12a, 186a |
| 1127b | II.n.36 |
| 1128a–1129a/P | II.408a |
| 1212c–d | II.5b |
| 1288a | III.2a |
| 1363c | II.399a |
| 1370a | II.327a |
| 1417a | II.228a |
| 1429d–e/P | II.410 |
| 1436d/P | I.119a |
| 1450a | III.13a |
| 1455c/P | III.162 |
| 1489b–1490a | I.110 |
| 1544c–d | I.129 |
| 1810a | II.n.93 |
| 2022a | III.16 |
| 2041 | II.338 |
| 2085a–b | I.236a |
| 2150c | II.157a |
| 2200a–b | I.113b |
| 2203b | I.315c |
| N1055+31 | II.16 |
| Nt 838 | III.n.7 |
| Ptahhetep 25 | III.31a |
| 53 | I.91b |
| 76/$L_2$ | III.106c |

116 II.158e
130 III.133f
132 III.36b
137–37 I.208b
142 I.8c
175 III.96a
197–98 II.263a
213–14/$L_2$ II.411c
216 I.6e
232–33 I.232
270 III.135a
282–83 III.157b
291 III.n.46
294 II.230a
328 II.158a, n.94
330 II.109b
346–47 III.11
369 II.325b
435 I.321b
446 III.123b
486 I.99b
494 I.245e
537 III.17a, tab.1
557 III.130b
569 I.6d
620–21 II.232b
629 III.7a
640 III.161a
Qaw Bowl, inside, 2 II.159d
inside, 8 I.181f
outside 1 II.330a
outside 3 I.n.47
*Questions of Theodore*
– van Lantschoot 15, 7–8 II.151c
16, 15–17 II.452b
19, 10–11 II.277f
22, 1–3 II.444f
40, 15–16 I.361a
42, 14–15 II.386c
42, 15–16 I.354b
68, 20–21 I.285b

Raphia Decree 25 I.347b
32 III.121a
*RAD* 14, 9 I.28c
52, 2–3 II.45a
53, 16–54, 1 I.342a
59, 16–60, 1 I.145a
77, 3 I.n.15
79, 11 I.336g
pRamesseum I, A15 I.23b, 246
B1, 10 II.124
*RecTrav* 25, 37 II.191e
Red Chapel 99, 13 II.324b
126, 16–17 I.72
*Reden und Rufe* 58 II.161a
pRhind I 2, d9 I.148b
3, d9 I.260b
5, d5 I.262g
5, d6 II.141b
6, d4 II.141c
6, d5 II.296b
8, d1 I.40c
II 5, d3 I.163b
pRhind math. n.22, 9 I.227
n.41, 4 II.316d
n.43, 1 III.tab.1
n.45, 1 II.14d
n.49, 2 III.tab.1
n.49, 8 II.115b
n.56, 3 I.249b
n.57, 3 II.236a
n.57, 4 II.311b
n.58, 1 I.131c
n.60, 3–4 II.301b
n.62, 2 I.194
n.62, 4 II.227
n.67, 3 I.17b
n.67, 22 II.313b
n.73, 1 II.115d
Roccati, *Mag. taur.*, 24, 2–3 I.37
24, 6 I.167c
25, 5 I.262b
25, 5–7 I.169c
26, 14 I.168e
75, 8–9 II.421a
75, 12 II.421b
Rosetta Decree 13 I.175c
22–23 II.141d
27 I.41a
pRylands I, 2 II.61a
7 I.171a; III.64
II, 5 II.58d
VIII, 3 II.133b
9 I.148d

IX 1, 4–5 II.396b
1, 6–7 I.290b
1, 18 II.374a
2, 8–9 I.175a
3, 2 I.173a
3, 18 I.300f, II.66a
4, 19 II.52a
5, 15–16 II.375a
5, 17 I.309b
5, 20–6, 1 I.309a
8, 18 II.274a
10, 3 I.312a
10, 12 III.55a
10, 21 I.49d
11, 21–12, 1 II.137c
12, 11 II.432a
13, 2–3 II.66f
13, 6 II.66e
14, 2 I.46c
14, 14 II.58a
15, 4 I.49a
16, 6–7 I.139b
16, 13 I.170h
17, 5 II.435b
18, 8 II.57b
24, 6–7 III.144a
24, 12–13 I.298e

*P.RylCopt.*
#267, 7 I.283b
#273, 9–11 II.257c

*Saqqâra Dem. Papyri I*,
#1 9, 17 I.173b
#2 x+1, 21 I.347c
x+1, 31 III.62b
6, 30 I.49b

pSaqqara I 1 9, 16 I.162c
H5-DP 265, 1–2 I.138a
H5-DP 486, 2–3 II.62c
71/2 DP 145, 21–22 I.298f

pSaqqara-Sekhemkhet, 5 I.170b

*Sayings of Pagan Philosophers*
– Crum 98a, 14–15 II.188a
98b II.93b
– Till 166, 12–13 II.154a
169, 24–170, 2 II.201a

*SEH* 152, 8 III.23c

Semnah desp. I, 10 II.117b

Setne I 3, 1 I.353a
3, 7 III.59a
3, 12 II.273c
3, 14 I.280
3, 17–18 I.257c
3, 26 III.121f
3, 37 I.43b, 289c
4, 3 II.141a, 296c
4, 7 I.46a
4, 35–36 I.149e
4, 38–39 III.99b
4, 39 I.41b, 149c
5, 2–3 II.136e
5, 8–9 II.289a, 431a
5, 9 I.42a
5, 10 II.137a
5, 12 II.170a
5, 16 I.43a
5, 21 I.40b, II.379a
5, 32 I.350a
6, 3 I.162b
6, 11 I.47a
6, 13 I.282a

Setne II 3, 10 I.352
3, 20 II.353c
5, 8–9 II.245e
5, 13 II.171a

Shenute,
*A Beloved One Asked Me Once Years Ago*
Ch 16, 42–47 II.278b
– *Acephalous Work A1*
Young 153, 15–22 III.152a
– *Acephalous Work A6*
*Or* 44 161, 16–20 II.216b
– *Acephalous Work A14*
Orlandi, *C. Origenistas*
16 §200 II.193f
– *As I Sat on a Mountain*
L III 44, 18–20 I.300j
51, 28 II.179b
52, 2–5 II.203b
53, 6–7 III.66a
– *Because of You too, O Prince of Evil*
Ch 23, 5–7 II.386b
36, 22–27 II.194d
– *Blessed Are They Who Observe Justice*
Ch 139, 32–42 II.183a

– *Canon I*
A I 452, 9–10 III.100b
– *Continuing to Glorify the Lord*
L III 72, 7–8 II.147d
– *God Is Blessed*
Ch 173, 7–27 III.171a
– *God Who Alone Is True*
A II 511, 2–3 III.172a
L IV 92, 18 II.75c
98, 24 II.103a
111, 1–3 II.381a
113, 14–18 II.444a
161, 2–3 I.60a
MMAF IV.1 278, 5–7 III.101a
*WZKM* 88, 288,
ff. 213, 50–214, 5 II.453d
– *I Am Amazed*
§100 [Cristea 138, 16–20] II.189a
§309 [Cristea 141, 15–18] II.199b, 354b
§316 [Cristea 144, 3–12] II.99, 252a
§465 [Cristea 191, 18–25] II.75d, 247a
§491 [Cristea 200, 6–18] II.95c, 253
§605 [Cristea 205, 13–19] II.257a
[Cristea 204,
31–205, 9] II.199a
§801 [Cristea 206, 26–29] II.185c
§807 [Cristea 209, 1–3 A] III.156
§926 [Cristea 220, 16–20] II.93a
– *I Answered*
L III 27, 5–6 III.67a
L III 27, 9 II.216a
– *I Have Been Reading the Holy Gospels*
§1 L III 220, 7–8 II.444h
§18 Moussa 56, 6–10 II.185d
§23 67b, 7–13 II.298
§24 90a, 23 II.441b
– *In the Night*
L III 38, 17 II.83b
– *I See Your Eagerness*
A II 62, 3–4 II.396e
– *Is It Not Written*
A I 37, 12–38, 3 III.154a
52, 9–10 III.67b
55, 3–4 III.72a
– *It Happened One Day*
*ZÄS* 80, 42, 28–29 II.444d
– *Not because a Fox Barks*
Ch 38, 35–45 II.147a
– *Reading Today from the Proverbs*
L III 114, 27–115, 5 III.70a
– *Shenute Writes to Tahom*
L III 22, 18 II.184b
– *Shenute Writes to Timothy II*
Munier 95, 6–12 II.392b
– *Some Kinds of People Sift Dirt/ Whoever Seeks God Will Find*
A I 228, 7 II.193e
– *Since It Is Necessary to Pursue the Devil*
A I 390, 3–4 II.261
– *There is Another Foolishness*
A II 380, 64–67 III.78a
– *Truly, When I Think*
L IV 22, 10–12 III.89a
– *Well Did You Come*
A II 407, 9–10 II.441a
407, 10–13 II.446b
– *Who But God Is the Witness*
Boud'hours 176, a9–13 II.448a
Young 26, 64–67 III.73a
– *Why, O Lord*
L III 118, 8–9 II.277k
134, 23–24 II.70g
144, 15–22 II.260
182, 13–19 II.193j, 297a
Young 106, 22–29 III.100a
– *You, God, The Eternal*
L IV 65, 12–13 II.455a
– *Le Muséon* 45 26 #4, 7–8 I.179e
Shenute? (attribution doubtful)
L III 101, 6–7 I.62a
Sh.S. 15–16 I.79a
32–33 I.191
47–50 I.189
50–51 I.4a, 327
51–52 I.115
60–62 II.282a
62–63 II.14c
63–64 III.139
67–68 I.81b
70–72 I.97
73–75 I.333a
75 I.5a, 181e
84–86 I.117c
89–91 II.122b
100–01 I.323a
108 I.10a, 181d

117–19 I.253g
119–21 I.79b
124 III.8a, tab.1
125–26 I.215b
130 I.4c
131 I.323b
131–32 I.95c
134 III.140a
135–36 I.127a
150 III.FNc
150–51 II.268
151 III.31b
156 I.116b
159 III.94e
172 II.314a
182 III.80a
Sin AO 45 II.n.133
B, 23 II.235a
30–31 III.79a
31 III.tab.1
33–34 I.112c
43–44 I.76a
44–45 I.126
47 II.228d
48 342b
48–49 II.241
66–67 III.130a
68 I.244d
68–70 II.342a
71 II.116a
71–72 I.334b
74–75 I.125
77 I.2b, 203c, III.17d
81 II.239
81–84 I.197a
82 III.26
85–86 III.29c
114 II.398c
115–16 II.121a
117–18 I.70a, 230
125 I.93a
146–47 III.133c
153 II.19a
154–55 II.336
156 I.1c
160 II.124b
166 I.112b
173–74 I.117a, 234c
185 I.319b
198–99 III.36c
202–03 III.30
222–23 III.27c
223–24 I.318b
224–25 I.16a
230 III.14c
243–44 I.79c
246 I.252c
254 I.5c
255 I.319a
261 III.tan.1
263 II.19b
266–68 II.398d
267–68 II.299b
280–81 I.245c
286 I.131b
287–88 I.20a
308 II.12a
309–10 I.10c
R, 2–3 I.253b, II.304
8 I.198a
8–9 I.78b
11–13 I.190a
22–23 I.124c
52 III.tab.1
54 I.204a
Sinai 90, 15–16 III.159c
181, 10–11 II.266
Sisene Story
tDeM 1214 v° x+4 III.44c
Siut I, 228 III.14b
269 I.224a
288 II.264a, 280a, 404, II.n.36
295 III.163
301 II.n.36
317 I.234a
III, 69 I.317a
IV, 23–24 I.248
V, 9 I.83
SNM 34370, 3–4 II.4
oStrasbourg 1845 r° 7 I.148f
v° 1 I.347a
pStrasbourg 23, 2 II.28a, 244a, 358a

pSpiegelberg 2, 4 II.56b
2, 14 II.136b, 353d
11, 15–16 II.172a
11, 18 II.433a
12, 23 I.50b
15, 5–6 II.54d
15, 9–11 II.431b
15, 19 II.434a
17, 14–17 I.162a
17, 15–17 I.350b
pSt Petersburg 1118, 6 I.34
1119, 12 I.147c
*Studies Griffith*, pl. 39, 16 I.213a
*Tale of Woe*, 3, 6–7 II.426
3, 10–11 II.220a
4, 13 III.38c
4, 14 III.41d
4, 16 III.n.34
*Teaching of Amunnakht*
27 *ZÄS* 131, 40, 38–39 II.369b
35 41, 16–18 III.42e
36 41, 13–15 III.86a
*Teti Cemetery* III, pl. 18 I.76c
pl. 18, middle
jamb left, 1 I.200b
V, pl. 59b II.243b
*Texte 2. Zwischenzeit*
n.122, 24 I.200a
n.131, 2 I.238b
grThebes 3156, i, 11 I.52
Theodotus of Ancyra,
*In S. Georgem Diosp.*
*AM* II 184, 22–23 I.180b
227, 8–9 II.452g
248, 16–18 II.212d
Theodore of Antioch,
*On the Theodores*
*AM* II 91, 3–4 II.143j
97, 6–8 II.216c
97, 8–13 II.176d
98, 17–22 II.146
103, 9–11 II.193g
103, 10–11 II.278e, 397c
111, 16 II.208f
116, 20 I.151f
118, 27–29 II.447b
120, 11–13 II.445b
124, 11–13 II.147b
124, 14–15 I.298l
129, 12–13 I.285g
129, 20–21 II.106c
130, 3–4 III.155a
136, 4–5 I.298m
139, 21 I.164g
153, 6–7 III.146a
Theodosius of Alexandria,
*De assumptione Mariae V.*
Robinson 108, 11–12 II.250h
*In Michaelem*
Budge 2, 14–16 II.187d
33, 3–4 III.77d
371, 8–9 III.77a
Theophilus of Alexandria,
*Homily on the Virgin*
Worrell 304, 25–305, 2 II.84c, 246a
*Ti*, pl. 116 I.15a
Timothy of Alexandria,
*On Abbaton*
Budge, *Martyrdoms*
237, 10–11 III.70b
*Tomb of Antefoqer*, pl. 8 I.209c
*Tomb of Tjanefer*, pl. 10, 1 I.159
*Tombs of Two Officials*, pl. 26 III.83
*Trans. Mariae*
13–14, r° a3–13 I.301c
49, r° a1–4 I.255a
*Tri. Trac.*
51, 12–13 [*NHS* 22, 192] II.149d
52, 7–14 [*NHS* 22, 193–195] II.149e
110, 4–5 [*NHS* 22, 290] II.383e
TT 23
Grapow 1941, 64 III.54a
gTT 63, 1–2 III.111a
6 III.39b
*TTS* 5, 26, 11 III.51a
Turin 1447, 23 I.217
4262 I.221b, II.345
50044, 3–4 III.114a
50046, 3 III.114b
50050, 8–9 I.147b
oTurin 57001 r° 8 III.147f
r° 9 I.259c
pTurin 1882, 3, 4–5 II.35c
1977, 5–6 I.39c
9–10 I.136c

1978/208, r° 2–3 I.161b
v° 1–2 II.423c
54031 r° 4, 2 II.165d
Suppl 6107, 22–23 II.134b
A 4, 10–5, 1 II.419b
tTurin 58004, 2–3 II.24

UCL 14333, 4 I.204b
13 II.321
16 II.158b
pUC 32036, 1.x+14 III.106b
32037, r° 3–4 I.253d
32055, x+14 III.97d
32057, 3.14 I.294c
32058, 4 I.183b
32058, 7 I.294a
13 I.203a
32124, 2.10 II.325a
32134A, 2 II.339b
32157, 2.11 III.7b
2.19 II.237b
32158, 2.5 III.92
2.8 III.132
32162, 1, 11 II.160n
32163, r° 2 I.193
32198, 11–12 III.93b
32199, 8 II.6c
32200, 5–7 III.17c, 123a
32201, 20–21 I.228b
32204, 2 III.18a
32205, v° 4 I.253a
32213, r° 17 II.398b
r° 24 II.228c
r° 24–v° 2 II.322
v° 10–11 I.105b, 221a
*Urk.* I 23, 12–14 I.183a
32, 6 II.330b
61, 9 I.102a
71, 10 II.316b
77, 16 III.n.12
79, 26a–28a I.219a
84, 3 I.101a
100, 6–7 I.87a
101, 2–3 I.226a
102, 9–10 I.85a
102, 11–14 II.279
104, 12 I.103
105, 11–18 I.206a
105, 14–16 III.97a
116, 6 I.253f
129, 5 III.9
130, 6–8 I.124b
130, 16–131, 1 I.85b
133, 6–8 II.6d
133, 14–16 I.225b
147, 10–11 II.320b
162, 16–18 II.400
168, 9–10 I.218a
179, 17 III.29b
197, 18 I.251a
202, 11 I.251b
204, 9–10 I.104b
205, 2 III.n.26
205, 12 III.n.26
211, 5–11 I.128a, 215c
216, 1 I.96
217, 15–17 I.106
217, 16 III.n.26
218, 8 III.n.26
218, 16–17 III.81
222, 8–9 I.253c
228, 16 II.325c
253, 18 I.244a
254, 8 I.105a
254, 10 II.399b
283, 11 II.158c, 316c
299, 6 I.198c
IV 2, 12–14 I.191b
3, 3–4 III.97c
9, 15–16 III.134a
17, 14–15 I.242c
20, 14 II.236b
54, 4 I.244e
65, 16–17 III.23a
66, 1–2 III.94c
96, 6–7 III.127
99, 15–16 III.4b
119, 3 I.99a
122, 13–14 II.413a
123, 4 III.24
123, 10 I.243
132, 16 I.105c
137, 16–138, 1 I.225a
139, 2–3 I.9

| | | | |
|---|---|---|---|
| 156, 17 | II.162b | | |
| 157, 2–3 | I.80a | | |
| 157, 7 | I.239b, II.263b | | |
| 157, 8–9 | I.69b | | |
| 162, 5 | III.5a | | |
| 163, 6 | III.33b | | |
| 164, 5–6 | II.286a | | |
| 167, 12 | III.135b | | |
| 198, 7 | III.133b | | |
| 221, 7 | II.230b | | |
| 221, 14 | II.n.113 | | |
| 239, 16–17 | I.89a, II.262b | | |
| 244, 10 | I.242b | | |
| 244, 10–12 | III.128 | | |
| 257, 17 | II.n.113 | | |
| 274, 3 | III.18b | | |
| 289, 10 | I.235, II.293a | | |
| 297, 5 | III.137b | | |
| 312, 12 | III.10 | | |
| 347, 2–3 | I.195b | | |
| 363, 6 | III.134c | | |
| 364, 1–2 | II.344a | | |
| 365, 14–366, 17 | II.343 | | |
| 366, 15 | III.97f | | |
| 368, 4–5 | III.79b | | |
| 385, 3–4 | I.11, 207 | | |
| 390, 6–7 | I.90d | | |
| 410, 6 | III.n.45 | | |
| 410, 11 | III.141c | | |
| 415, 11–12 | I.332 | | |
| 497, 9–10 | I.109b | | |
| 501, 4–5 | I.206b | | |
| 501, 10 | I.130, 328 | | |
| 519, 11 | III.157c | | |
| 547, 8–10 | I.239a | | |
| 592, 1 | II.281b | | |
| 612, 4 | III.137a | | |
| 650, 5–7 | III.28a | | |
| 736, 16 | II.287a | | |
| 772, 4–6 | II.415c | | |
| 776, 13–14 | I.222 | | |
| 808, 13 | II.413b | | |
| 835, 14 | I.4b | | |
| 835, 16 | III.102 | | |
| 861, 8 | III.15, 124b | | |
| 883, 14 | III.106a | | |
| 892, 7 | I.10b | | |
| | 894, 1 | | II.335a |
| | 897, 11–12 | | I.80b |
| | 898, 14 | | I.95b |
| | 943, 5 | | III.105a |
| | 959, 15 | | III.n.45 |
| | 973, 10 | | II.160a, 312g |
| | 1020, 7–9 | | I.88 |
| | 1024, 11–12 | | I.218c |
| | 1087, 7–9 | | II.411a |
| | 1090, 3 | | I.15b |
| | 1092, 9–10 | | I.224c |
| | 1109, 5–8 | | I.102c |
| | 1109, 12 | | III.n.46 |
| | 1111, 9–13 | | I.236b |
| | 1166, 10 | | III.32c |
| | 1229, 14 | | I.324 |
| | 1291, 1–3 | | I.236c |
| | 1293, 1–3 | | II.344b |
| | 1344, 13–15 | | II.418a |
| | 1543, 10 | | II.287b |
| | 1822, 8 | | II.162c |
| | 1824, 10–11 | | II.286b |
| | 1944, 1 | | II.349, III.129 |
| | 2146, 1–2 | | III.169c |
| pVandier | 1, 1 | | III.99a |
| | 1, 3 | | III.56d |
| | 1, 9–10 | | I.350d |
| | 2, 1 | | I.266d |
| | 2, 12 | | II.131d |
| pVienna D | 70, 10 | | I.150a |
| | 10000 | 2, 20–21 | I.148e |
| | | 3, 4–5 | I.50a |
| | 12006 | 3, 30 | I.171c |
| *V. Shenute* | | | |
| Leipoldt | 8, 22–23 | | II.152f |
| | 13, 23 | | II.258d |
| Lubomierski | | 221, b14–16 | II.88a |
| *V. Pachom* | | | |
| SLefort | | 34, 23–24 | II.208d |
| | | 192, 13 | II.75a |
| BLefort | | 86, 2–3 | II.397f |
| | | 94, 20 | II.256 |
| Vleeming, | | | |
| – *Short Text* I, | | #135, 14–15 | II.374b |
| | | #214 | II.65 |
| | | #245 | II.64a |

| | | |
|---|---|---|
| II, | #513 B11 | II.371c, III.144b |
| | #909 v° 1–2 | III.170a |
| pWestcar | 6, 10–11 | I.13, 233c |
| | 6, 26–7, 1 | II.3 |
| | 7, 11–12 | II.314b |
| | 7, 17 | I.198b |
| | 7, 17–18 | II.242a |
| | 8, 4–5 | I.117b |
| | 8, 10–11 | II.234b |
| | 9, 3–4 | I.120 |
| | 9, 4–5 | I.16c |
| | 9, 5–8 | II.411b |
| | 9, 8–9 | II.234a |
| | 9, 9 | II.109c |
| | 9, 11 | II.n.40 |
| | 9, 13 | II.229c |
| | 9, 21–22 | III.34 |
| | 9, 25 | II.n.40 |
| | 9, 27–10, 1 | I.190b |
| | 11, 22–23 | II.415b |
| | 11, 24 | I.181a |
| | 12, 19–20 | II.315 |

| | | |
|---|---|---|
| Zachary of Sakha, | | |
| *De Presentatione* | de Vis II 7, 2–7 | I.288k |
| – *Consolatory Sermon* | de Vis II 50, 7 | II.212b |
| – *V. John Kolobos* §63 | Mikhail & Vivian 176, 31–32 | I.273d |
| 1Cl | 7:2 | II.73c |
| | 8:4 | II.94d |
| | 10:4 | I.176c |
| | 10:5 | I.304b |
| | 11:2 | I.177d |
| | 12:4 | II.93f |
| | 14:1 | II.246e |
| | 16:1 | II.443b |
| | 16:2 | II.397b |
| | 16:3 | I.360b, II.90a, 142e |
| | 21:8 | III.71a |
| | 22:6 | I.54b |
| | 26:1 | II.199d |
| | 45:1 | II.84d, 246c, 388c |

# Index of topics

*Absolute personal pronoun, see personal pronoun*
additive 35, 470, 661
ad-nominal 101, 102, 150, 185, 371
adjective, attributive 682
adjunct clause
– *marked* 77–81, 183–84
– *unmarked* 70–76, 100, 101, 148, 183–84, 493, 556
admirative 653, 670
adverb
– *dy* 37, 46, 53, 112, 209
– interrogative 23–25, 34, 43, 44, 146, 294, 590n.130
– primary 24, 25
– secondary 25
– spatial 24, 25, 201, 211
– temporal 24, 62
adversative 271, 348, 360, 470, 483, 486, 488, 636n.150
agentive, agentivity 23, 519, 547
agreement 10, 14, 19, 29, 91–93, 99, 101, 167, 176, 263, 315, 350, 359, 371, 381, 385, 388, 418, 421, 427–28, 438, 458, 461, 535, 540, 543, 548, 549, 586, 587, 636, 651
*alienable possession, see possession*
allo-sentence 146, 545, 547, 550, 724, 725, 732
alternative questions 66, 177, 464, 474
analytic 1, 3, 7, 212, 414, 682
anaphoric 14, 32, 306, 405, 409n.57, 424, 470, 471, 526, 530, 558, 693
animacy 23, 519
ante-position 31, 178, 379, 418
antecedent 19, 27, 91–93, 97, 99–101, 125, 128–31, 133, 134, 137, 150–51, 169, 179, 263, 300, 329, 351, 353, 356, 379, 382, 471, 514, 515, 549, 674
anterior form (*sḏm-n-f*) 172
Aorist/aorist 167, 264, 309, 312, 356, 361, 633
apposition 43, 180, 306, 314n.19, 325, 379n.42, 382, 408, 409n.58, 472, 475, 534, 662, 669, 684, 693
article
– definite 2, 3, 8, 273, 309, 311, 315, 317, 329, 331, 353, 384, 414, 415, 430, 442n.67, 446, 453, 457, 636, 678
– indefinite 3, 8, 13, 36, 41, 48, 50, 57, 106, 110, 114, 129, 281, 309, 345, 346, 430, 437, 573, 578
aspect
– imperfective 11, 96, 167, 181, 295, 634, 656
– perfective 10, 11, 20, 96, 167, 168, 173, 180, 182, 263, 295, 312, 651, 656, 700, 728
assertion, assertive 142–46, 153, 154–57, 169, 171, 180, 181, 183–84, 255n.102, 469n.73, 470, 537, 551, 552–55
asyndetic 69, 103, 108
auxiliary 12, 23, 24, 30, 33, 63, 65, 76, 82, 90, 100, 101, 102, 106, 108, 117, 141, 152–73, 220, 226, 245, 246, 255n.102, 265, 329, 371, 405, 469, 494, 551, 554n.119, 608, 611, 682, 701, 727
– *wn/wnn* 28, 29, 30, 67, 76, 77, 78, 80, 82, 87, 89, 96, 97, 99, 127, 157–73, 176, 177, 178, 181, 183, 187, 190, 212, 216, 256, 262n.109, 263, 311, 370, 376, 514, 706, 713, 718, 728

Background information 66, 72, 74, 76n.33, 174, 474, 699
bodily part-whole relations 291, 303

Cataphoric 33, 43, 255, 306, 409, 450, 472, 473, 558, 662, 669, 671, 684, 692, 693
causal clause 78, 85, 111, 115, 182, 184, 494, 496, 498, 500, 503, 507, 512, 703, 710, 715
causal connector
– *(r)-ḏbꜣ-ḫpr* 115
– *ce-* 117, 503
– *ḏd* 115
– *ebolce-* 117, 503
causative 6, 87, 171, 507, 554, 663, 716, 730
characterisation 524, 526, 594, 665, 723

https://doi.org/10.1515/9783110409895-016

circumstantial 18, 70, 133, 365, 379, 433n.65, 460, 493, 555n.120
classification 24, 27, 45, 186, 189, 236, 238, 523, 570, 572, 574, 579, 580, 589, 593, 594, 723, 734, 736, 738
classifier 4, 7, 652, 653
cleft sentence 15, 23, 277, 295, 301, 308–11, 317, 326, 329, 332, 333, 349–50, 352, 353–55, 360–61, 365–67, 400, 442, 459–61, 465, 476, 478–79, 483, 485, 486, 495, 512, 521, 523n.91, 530n.101, 531–49, 563, 571, 573, 574, 578, 579, 589–90, 592, 593, 594, 607, 608, 618, 620, 621, 622, 623, 626, 633, 636, 638–40, 672, 721, 732, 734, 736, 738
– with *in* 295, 309, 539–41, 546
– future 295, 548–49, 556–57, 607
– pseudo-cleft 311–16, 349–50, 415, 417, 442n.66, 445, 453, 454, 456–57, 531–49, 563, 573, 574, 578, 607, 615, 619, 620, 621, 622, 623, 734
  – reversed 532, 535, 537n.108
  – non-reversed 312, 412, 533
clitic 9, 25, 29–30, 31, 33, 34, 35, 37, 46, 53, 72, 79, 80, 82, 84, 89, 90, 94, 109, 141, 256, 275, 291, 292–94, 295, 296, 298, 308, 324, 333n.23, 336, 368, 370, 371, 377, 379, 381, 382, 383, 385, 392, 394, 396, 407, 409n.57, 412, 428, 470, 471, 473, 495, 509, 522, 530, 547, 553, 555, 586, 601, 604, 605, 613, 622, 626, 627, 644, 652–54, 655, 661–62, 663, 664, 666, 668, 680, 689, 701n.28, 703, 707, 711, 715, 725, 727
  – *=ꜣ* 35, 470, 661
  – *=wy/=wỉ* 652, 653, 661, 664, 668, 670, 716
  – *=wnnt* 'really' 470
  – *=wr-t* 654, 664
  – *=wsỉ* 670–71
  – *=ỉs* 35, 80, 89, 471, 495, 509, 553
  – *=(ỉ)r* 35, 470
  – *=ms* 'truly' 35, 471
  – *=ḥm* 'truly' 471, 662
  – *=swt* 'but' 35, 470
  – *=grt* 'further' 35, 470, 661
  – *=tr* 35, 470, 601, 661
– second position 29–30, 109, 112, 293, 368, 392, 394, 530, 601, 627
– *clitic pronoun, see pronoun*
colloquial 612
comparative 15, 207, 351, 664, 668, 733, 738, 740–43, 745
– standard of comparison 351, 741, 742
– superlative 733–34
complement clause
– object 82, 86–87, 118–19, 169, 171, 180–81, 183–84, 499, 507, 510, 553–55, 674, 711, 714–17, 748
– oblique 119, 122, 124
– of genitival *n-* 89
– of prepositions 78, 85, 90, 159, 172, 177, 181–84, 494, 497, 507–08, 703–06, 711–12
– predicate 88–89, 151, 170, 177, 300, 368, 369–71, 379–80, 385, 472, 558, 561, 610, 611, 713
– subject 86, 88, 260, 412, 610, 612, 656–57, 663, 666, 668, 672, 675, 677, 684, 693, 696, 700, 712, 730
complementiser 78, 79n.35, 82, 85, 90, 95, 96, 118, 121, 122, 124n.55, 152, 177, 178, 180–81, 183–84, 262, 377, 378, 447, 451, 494, 497, 500, 507–12, 553–55, 558, 703, 704, 710–11, 714–17, 730
concessive 161, 175, 230, 596, 598
conditional 80, 161, 177, 183, 231, 247, 424, 493, 498, 500, 659, 695, 710
– particle 177, 231, 502
– protasis 80, 177, 231, 247, 248, 424, 493, 498, 555, 706
Conjunctive form 39, 333n.23, 449, 485, 693, 696
connector 76, 78n.34, 96, 107, 115, 289, 301, 347, 481, 496, 502, 505, 598
contingent clause 66
Continuative 675
continuous state of affairs 188n.92, 191
coordination 14, 18–19, 70, 103, 148, 326, 331, 391, 475–76, 478–79, 488, 489, 636n.150, 701–03, 710
– argument cluster 475, 479

coordinator
– *irm-* 478
– *auô/au/uoh* 347
– *hi-* 347
– *mn-/nem-* 347
– *uoh n-* 481, 487, 491, 703
copula 16, 23, 289, 290, 293, 296, 305, 316–17, 320n.21, 331, 332, 333n.23, 343, 350, 365, 366, 367–68, 371, 373, 377, 385, 405, 406–08, 414–16, 418–21, 427–29, 437, 452, 454, 456, 458, 460, 489, 530, 531, 534, 569, 571, 576, 586, 588, 636, 644
– agreement marking of 365, 385, 414, 421, 427–28, 437, 458, 460, 586, 636
– *ete* 452
– *nꜣw* 415, 418, 419
co-reference of subject with antecedent 93, 99, 515,
counterfactual 182, 676, 695

Dative 33, 92n.46, 143, 185, 253, 264, 297, 396n.50, 654, 658–59, 661, 664, 726, 748
defective writing 652
*definite article, see article*
definiteness/indefiniteness 23, 28, 40, 48, 55, 100, 125n.56, 129, 150, 238, 248, 251, 273, 309, 312, 313, 317, 356, 430, 453, 456, 514n.81, 519, 520, 525, 562, 567, 568n.127, 570, 573, 722
deixis 6, 330n.22, 550, 551, 728
delocutive 545, 725, 726
*demonstrative pronoun, see pronoun*
deontic 143, 153, 155, 158, 165
dependency 18, 19, 73, 80, 81, 90, 117, 225, 231, 391, 495, 598, 602, 707n.32, 708, 714
– clitic *=is* 35, 80–81, 89–90, 471, 495, 509–10, 553, 555, 602, 711
desiderative 35, 142, 143, 176
dialect 3–4, 6, 57, 59, 62, 63, 64, 116, 133, 196, 223, 245, 332, 333, 335, 336, 341, 343, 347, 348, 350, 351, 352n.29, 353, 359, 362, 365, 369n.36, 392, 396, 401, 422, 438, 442, 447, 452, 453, 456, 488, 546, 569, 571, 596, 626n.148, 627, 686, 742
*direct genitive, see genitive*
directive 142, 143
*discontinuous negation n...=is, see negation*
disjunctive 348, 482, 488
doubt 555
dual 7, 13, 91, 653
dummy predicate *kʰê* 63, 135, 279
'dummy' verb 162, 163

Ellipsis 32, 54n.19, 56, 314n.19, 360, 462–67, 486, 615
elision 456, 594n.132
emphatic 90, 162–65, 172, 173n.82, 188
epistemic 731
exclamative speech acts 143, 153, 155, 653
exhortative 142
existential 28, 37, 39, 41–42, 50, 58, 79n.35, 121n.53, 255, 256, 259, 260, 261n.109, 264, 276, 281, 380, 537, 610, 613n.141
extra-position 177, 178

Feminine 7, 8, 9, 10, 14, 43n.15, 59, 91, 93, 95, 98, 180, 307, 315, 385, 394, 508, 543, 558n.123, 651, 664
final clause 30, 76, 152, 169, 705
focality, focus 14, 145–46, 162–63, 165, 259, 268, 273, 537–39, 544–49, 586, 607, 614, 724–26
free positioning 62, 419
Functional Grammar 23
functional scope 152, 173
future 12, 16, 30, 76, 97, 100, 109n.50, 141, 155, 156, 158–60, 165, 168, 171, 172–73, 176, 181–82, 186, 191, 194, 212, 217, 219, 221, 225, 233, 255, 256, 257–58, 261, 264, 295, 311, 312, 326, 329, 355, 361, 363, 391, 531, 548, 549, 556, 557, 607, 633, 683, 729, 731, 749, 750,
Future III (Optative) 212, 235, 236, 265, 311, 312, 329, 675
future participle 97, 100, 168, 295n.5, 531, 548, 718

Gemination 7, 99, 160, 172, 173, 212, 376, 558, 651, 657, 663, 680, 712, 732
gender 2, 6, 8, 10, 13, 14, 27, 41, 91, 96, 99, 298, 307, 311, 317, 360, 365, 371, 373, 381, 385, 386, 392, 393, 394, 415, 427, 438, 485, 535, 540, 543, 548, 549, 586, 636, 651
generic state of affairs 67, 163
genitive 10, 13, 34, 628n.149
– direct 185, 370, 394, 605
– indirect 292, 368, 369, 371
given-new – contrast 537
*gmi* 'find, discover' 81, 119, 508, 554, 555, 714
government 19, 26, 27, 81, 82, 85, 171, 188, 190, 191, 371, 509, 554, 555, 680, 712, 715
grammaticalisation 18, 42n.14, 77, 158, 173, 186, 190, 191, 212, 235, 252, 265, 289, 299, 300, 306, 310, 317, 382, 510, 520, 534, 541, 612, 626, 653, 729, 751
*Gunn's Construction, see cleft sentence, future*

*Headless relative clause, see Relative clause*
hierarchy 14, 521, 521n.88, 539, 735
– positional 305, 346, 431
hypothetical 183, 231, 502, 676

Iconicity 4, 290n.2, 548
identification 150, 189, 524, 526, 570, 574, 579, 583, 584, 588, 589, 593, 668, 723, 724, 736, 738
illocution 34, 69, 73, 141, 143, 154, 155, 157, 158, 160, 172, 173, 470, 538, 550, 551, 555
*Imperfect, see Preterite*
imperative 11, 381, 705
*inalienable possession, see possession*
*indefinite article, see article*
*indefinite subject, see subject*
*indirect genitive, see genitive*
infinitive 11, 14, 16, 18, 28, 39, 190–93, 235, 246, 264, 265, 295n.4, 304, 310, 311, 312, 319, 328, 329, 330, 353, 375, 383, 384, 388, 399, 400, 406, 410, 413b.60, 416, 430, 439, 510, 532, 558n.123, 619, 624, 656, 666, 671, 677, 678, 682, 683, 685, 693, 704, 706, 719n.37, 729, 755
– inflected 12, 399, 439
information structure 29, 34, 65, 69, 73, 141, 142, 143, 146, 153, 155, 158, 159, 160, 165, 172, 174n.84, 188n.92, 212–17, 258, 259, 412, 470, 531–38, 542, 546, 548, 724, 730, 732
initial element *n-/nꜣ-/nꜣw* 628, 680–81, 756
initial, initiality 6, 14, 16, 18, 19, 25, 26, 30, 31, 33, 34, 35, 36, 40, 55, 57, 62, 66–69, 70,102–08, 109n.50, 110, 115, 132, 133, 141, 146, 152, 153, 161, 162, 163, 165, 173–74, 176, 212, 217, 221, 255, 262, 273, 276, 278, 281, 284, 294, 295, 299, 300, 304, 306, 309n.15, 311, 312, 317, 325, 328, 329, 346, 349, 350, 361, 365, 377, 379, 380, 409n.57, 415, 419, 424, 431, 437, 444, 445, 453, 454, 457, 460, 469–74, 477, 501, 502, 518, 526, 530, 531, 534, 535, 536, 543, 549, 559, 569, 570, 586, 590n.130, 594, 619, 621, 626, 628, 630, 632, 636, 641, 645, 655, 662, 675, 678, 680, 681, 693, 699–702, 724, 726, 756
*initial particles, see particles*
injunction 176
interlocutive 545, 725
*interrogative adverb, see adverb*
*interrogative particle, see particles*
*interrogative pronoun, see pronoun*
*iw*-support 30, 72–73, 100, 149, 153, 226, 235, 265

Juxtaposition 14, 16, 45, 289, 300, 301, 305, 317, 319, 326, 329, 332, 333, 345, 347, 368, 414, 415, 438, 477, 478, 540, 565, 569, 578, 702

Kinship terms 291

Left periphery 31
left-dislocation 146, 471, 493, 558, 586
Limitative 682
location 23, 24, 37, 62, 185, 198, 201, 209, 211, 723

locative 23, 37, 52, 53, 62, 93, 94, 139–41, 186, 191, 196, 210, 211, 235, 238, 252, 342, 520
locus 30, 139, 141, 156, 159, 160, 185, 186, 191, 196, 211, 238, 256, 259

Marked vs. unmarked 70–81, 100–02, 147–48, 184, 226, 449, 586
*m* of predication 27, 28, 45, 81, 83, 186, 188–91, 236–38, 255, 264, 493, 507, 514, 748
main clause 14, 19, 30, 43, 69, 71, 75, 76, 102, 106, 107, 109, 111, 114, 117, 148, 174, 181, 183, 217, 234, 262, 380, 473, 484, 674, 699
masculine 7–10, 14, 43, 51–52, 91, 264, 298, 307, 350, 371, 385, 394, 427, 450, 458, 539, 542–43, 632, 636, 651–52, 654
matrix verb 81–85
matrix clause 169, 227, 371, 674
modifier 23, 27, 30, 314, 665
modality 18, 76, 153, 155, 156–57, 160, 173, 176, 179, 187, 217, 245, 405, 550–56, 727, 747,

Negation 12, 172, 183, 255–85, 297, 300, 337, 349, 376, 601–46, 667–68, 747–57
– *=an* 626–46, 756–57
– *bn/bniw* 266–270, 614, 617, 618, 620, 752
– bound 747
– *bw* 268, 620
– contradictory predicative 12, 258, 261, 605, 610
– contrary term-negation 258, 261, 605–07, 610, 751
– discontinuous *bn/bniw...=in* 268–69, 270–75, 276–78, 613–22, 622–26, 751–56
– discontinuous *n- ...=an* 278–80, 283–85, 626–46, 756–57
– discontinuous *n...=is* 261, 602–10, 654, 667
– *mn-* 270–73, 275–76
– *mn(n)-/mmon-* 280–83, 285
– *mn(n)te-* 283
– *mtw-...* 278
– *n* 255–56, 259–60, 601, 747–49
– negative complementiser *iwt-* 263–66, 603, 749
– negative lexemes 610–11
– *nfr=pw* 611–13
– *nn* 256–66, 749–51
– *nn* (as variant of *n*) 609, 750
– present/aorist 264–65
– scope of 255, 260–61, 605–07, 614, 616, 621, 628, 747, 751
– symmetric 264–65, 747, 750, 751
– *tm/tm/štem* 376, 610–11, 619–20, 624
– negative verbs 610–11
neuter 8, 93, 95, 180, 377, 508
*nisbe*-adjectives 27, 297, 650, 659, 661, 667
– *n(-y)* 297, 659
non-assertion 142–46, 153, 155, 169, 171, 180–81, 183–84, 551, 554
– non-assertive speech acts 142–43
non-existence 259, 261, 271, 273, 668
Non-initial main sentence (NIMS) 675
non-predicative 162, 164–65, 298, 370, 527
– -adverbials 62
non-restrictive relative proposition 100, 125, 128, 129, 131, 133, 136, 150, 270, 300, 344, 478, 501, 514, 552, 710, 719
noun 7–8, 9, 12, 13, 14 16, 17, 28, 30, 31, 36–37, 62, 65, 69, 71, 74, 76, 102, 109n.50, 112, 115, 133, 152, 157, 188, 190–91, 201, 225, 236, 238, 273, 290–93, 295–96, 299, 301, 304–06, 309, 311, 317, 323, 325, 333, 344, 346, 370–71, 371n.38, 373, 380, 383, 389, 404, 406, 407, 409n.57, 410–12, 414, 430, 439, 444, 454, 472n.77, 475, 490, 530, 531, 539, 541, 544, 546, 548–49, 551, 555n.120, 556–57, 560, 569–70, 573, 576, 578, 582, 583–84, 608, 650, 654, 661, 664, 665, 666, 667n.15, 669–71, 677, 682, 686, 686n.25, 687, 692, 707, 719, 722, 726, 728, 752
– preposition-derived relational 27
– simple 291, 726
noun phrase 26, 34, 373–74, 383–84, 388–89, 560, 669

number 2, 6, 7, 8, 10, 13, 27, 91, 96, 99, 298, 307, 311, 317, 360, 365, 371, 373, 381, 385–86, 392–93, 414, 427, 438, 485, 548–49, 586, 636
numbers 13, 14, 50, 251, 272
- cardinal 13
- ordinal 13, 310

Oaths 552
object 9, 12, 81–85, 86, 122, 171, 333, 371, 375, 379–80, 456, 507, 510, 555, 559, 674, 711–12
- direct 83–84, 370, 705
- indirect 375, 396
omission 45, 54, 92, 94, 101, 121, 235, 250, 259–260, 275, 281, 320, 328, 331, 380, 392, 477–78, 488, 491–92, 608
- of subject 14, 32, 60, 70, 83, 95–96, 105, 108, 122–23, 125, 129, 130–31, 135–36, 257, 302, 333, 348, 353–56, 358–59, 391, 404–06, 453, 462–67, 482–83, 487–88, 515, 605, 614–15, 640, 653, 658, 667, 674–75, 684, 693–94, 701, 707, 719, 735, 753–54
operators 73, 80–81, 152–55, 162, 174, 196, 212–26, 235–36, 270, 367–71, 377, 425–26, 594–96
- relative operators
- *nty-* 125–29, 514–15, 718–20, 749
- *ntyiw-* 129–33, 515–16, 720–21
- *et(e)-* 133–37, 516–18, 721–22
*Optative, see Future III*
overt expression of subject 83, 99, 263

Participle 7, 13, 17, 27, 28, 96–97, 100, 127–28, 129–30, 157, 180, 291, 295, 309–12, 317, 327–29, 353, 361, 384, 415, 478, 514, 531, 539, 542–46, 556, 608, 612, 639, 650–56, 656, 664, 666, 667, 672–73, 718, 724, 727–28
- future 97, 100, 168, 531, 533, 548, 718
- imperfective active 167, 656
- imperfective passive 656
- perfective active 167, 263, 656, 672–73
- perfective passive 88, 656, 700
- periphrastic 309

particles 10, 12, 14–15, 19, 24, 30–31, 34–37, 41, 43, 49–50, 55, 57, 65–67, 69, 72–73, 80–81, 89, 92, 102, 105–07, 112, 114–15, 121, 127, 129–31, 141, 152, 173–78, 217, 231, 234, 245, 249, 251–52, 256–57, 273, 275, 282, 305, 309, 329, 336, 347, 349, 356, 380, 401, 404, 449, 470–71, 473–74, 476, 495, 501–02, 509, 547, 553, 561, 566, 601, 605, 610, 613, 617, 621–22, 661–62, 668, 670, 699–702, 715–16, 748
- *(e)is* 'behold' 58, 281, 404,
- *iw* 15, 68–69, 72–73, 701
- *ir* 177, 471, 662
- *clitic particle, see clitic*
- initial particle 57, 65, 107, 109n.50, 273–74, 473–75, 501, 662
  - *iḫ* 67, 175–76
  - *isṯ/ist/isk* 66, 72–73, 175, 474, 699
  - *wn-/un-/uon-* 41, 49–50, 57, 106–07, 114, 129–31, 249, 251–52, 282
  - *wn-in* 700
  - *mk/mṯ/mtn* 65, 174, 473, 699
  - *nḥmn* 66, 177
  - *ḥꜣ/ḥw* 35, 66, 474
  - *ḫr* 67, 175–76, 476, 662, 699
  - *smwn* 474
  - *kꜣ* 67, 175–76, 476
  - *ti* 72
- interrogative particle
  - *in/n* 121, 177, 305, 309
  - *iniw* 66, 177, 474–75, 700
  - *is-bn* 617–18, 621
past 30, 67, 118, 133, 141, 155–56, 158–59, 161–62, 166–67, 171–73, 182, 188, 194, 213, 215, 217, 221, 233, 258, 261, 311–12, 327, 350–53, 361, 379, 412, 457, 533, 550, 594, 607, 673, 682, 700, 728, 748
perfective aspect 19, 182
perfective form 11, 173, 728
*perfective relative form, see relative form*
periphrasis 3, 18, 190, 265, 309–10, 328–29, 690
person 23, 29, 42–43, 51–52, 59, 79, 94–95, 117, 127, 145, 159, 163, 276, 298–99, 307, 324, 335, 343, 345, 365, 368, 371,

373, 408, 454, 472n.77, 519, 526, 530, 542, 544–47, 549, 569, 580–81, 586, 604n.134, 653–55, 664, 667, 670–71, 686, 724–26, 754
personal pronoun datives 33, 92n.46
*personal pronoun, see pronoun*
plural 6–8, 10, 11, 13, 36, 41, 42, 43n.15, 48, 51, 59, 91, 93, 95, 110, 112, 116–17, 214, 218, 223, 273, 276, 307, 315, 324, 335, 371n.38, 385, 392, 437, 664, 670, 868n.25, 754
polarity 605–06, 619, 751
possession 185, 200, 248, 253, 306, 324, 659
– alienable 185, 290n.2, 324
– inalienable 290n.2, 324
– possessed/possessee 185, 248–51, 271, 278, 290n.2, 297–98, 306, 308, 323–26, 660–61
– possessor 8, 185, 248, 251, 253, 290n.2, 297–99, 306–07, 323–25, 659
*possessive pronouns, see pronouns*
predicate 15–18, 23–26, 32–34, 36–37, 39, 42, 43–44, 46n.16, 47, 52–54, 55–56, 60–61, 63, 67, 88–89, 90n.44, 135, 139–141, 144, 146, 158n.73, 160, 164–65, 170, 174n.84, 189, 209, 212, 216, 218, 245, 248, 255, 257, 259n.106, 260–61, 264, 269, 279, 284, 289, 294, 297, 299, 309, 347, 349, 368–71, 373, 383–85, 386–91, 392, 394, 397–402, 406, 409, 419, 421, 427, 437, 445, 473, 475, 477–81, 487, 519–31, 534, 537n.108, 539, 542, 545–48, 556, 558–59, 560–67, 567–71, 573, 578–79, 580, 587–88, 593, 606–08, 610–11, 619, 624–25, 626–31, 636, 641, 644, 649–54, 659–60, 664, 666, 667–68, 672, 674, 690, 693, 700–01, 702, 713, 724, 727–28, 733, 750–51, 752
– multiple 322, 347
predication-level operator 73, 153
*predicative adjective, see adjective*
predicative adjunct 81, 83–84, 165
*prefix personal pronouns, see pronoun*
*prefixed 'preformative' personal pronoun, see personal pronoun*
preposition 10, 12–16, 19, 24–27, 33, 45, 54, 77–78, 79n.35, 85, 90, 139, 141, 143, 159, 172, 177, 181, 183–84, 185–88, 190–91, 196, 198–99, 201, 204–07, 209, 235, 249, 252, 264, 294, 320, 329, 509, 572, 574–75, 580, 650, 651, 654, 659, 664, 712, 729, 733, 738, 740, 742
preposition-conjunction 70, 77–78, 85, 152, 178, 181, 182, 262, 493–94, 507, 556, 704–06, 711
– *ḏr* 'since' 77
– *m* 'when' 77
– *mi* 'like' 77
– *n-mrwt* 'so that' 77
– *r* 'in order' 77
*preposition-derived relational noun, see noun*
prepositional phrase 13–16, 26, 33, 36, 45, 52, 61, 139, 219, 245, 251, 261, 380, 404, 451, 682, 742
– used as NP 210–11
present 17, 30, 70, 141, 155, 181, 264, 327, 329, 361–62, 493, 607, 633, 704, 747
Present I 31, 39, 51, 58, 105, 124, 131, 235, 265, 273, 311–12, 329, 333, 353, 358
*present/aorist negation, see negation*
presupposition 144–47, 155, 164, 174, 259, 537–38, 545–49, 724, 726
– accommodation of 161–62
– trigger 147, 538, 545–49, 724, 726
Preterite 10, 221, 223, 231, 309–12, 329, 352, 361, 425–26, 596
– preterite marker *wn-* 118, 270n.11
– preterite marker *wnnꜣw-* 217, 418
promissive speech acts 142
pronoun 36–37, 125, 127, 133, 152, 201, 249, 276, 291, 305, 308, 317, 322, 333, 347, 365, 379–80, 396, 398, 404, 406, 410, 430, 520, 525, 527, 555, 558, 569, 571, 583, 585–86, 663, 674, 687, 757
– anaphoric 14, 306, 530, 693
– cataphoric 33, 43, 225, 306, 450, 662, 669, 671, 684, 692–94
– demonstrative 3, 8, 14, 32, 54, 291, 292–93, 295, 305, 343–44, 368, 373, 374, 381, 398–99, 408, 420–21, 432–33, 437–38, 450, 520–22, 528, 531, 536, 560, 563, 603, 655, 671–72

– determinative 8, 10, 291, 297, 527, 650
– indefinite 300, 344, 398–99, 433–34
– interrogative 10, 27, 32, 42, 207, 291–94, 303–05, 311, 315, 346, 374, 389–90, 398–99, 419-20, 436–37, 463, 521–22, 530, 531, 539, 546, 550, 562–63, 666
– personal 9–10, 16, 25, 29–31, 33, 292–95, 298, 311, 322, 326, 343, 346, 361, 383, 420, 457, 472, 520, 522, 528, 531, 539, 569–70, 622, 654, 719–20, 724
  – 1st and 2nd 145–46, 299, 335–36, 343, 345, 454, 542, 544, 546–47, 580–81, 654–55, 664, 686
  – 3rd person 127, 322, 335–36, 371, 408, 454, 530, 545, 581, 586, 655, 670–71, 724, 726, 754
  – absolute 9, 65, 145, 151, 251, 259, 291, 295–96, 298–300, 303–05, 307–08, 320–22, 324, 336–41, 345, 361, 374, 389–90, 398–99, 413–14, 419–20, 431, 453, 460, 472, 475, 530, 531, 542–49, 556, 560–61, 564–65, 575, 578, 601–04, 608, 631–32, 724–26, 732
    – proclitic (unstressed) 304, 334–37, 431–32, 453, 585–86
  – clitic 9, 25, 29–31, 72, 79, 82, 84, 256, 291, 293–96, 298, 304, 324, 473, 547, 557, 604, 654–55, 661, 664, 666, 668–69, 680, 715, 725, 727
  – preformative 31, 43–45, 50–52, 55, 59–60, 102, 110–11, 112–14, 116–17
  – proclitic 304–05, 338, 546
  – suffixed 10, 26, 29–31, 33, 51, 72–73, 79, 100, 149, 153, 157, 159, 215–16, 218, 223, 226, 470, 547, 654, 661, 664, 680–81, 686, 715, 725
– possessive 322, 324
  – absolute 322, 344, 398–99, 434–35, 631–32
  – derivative (*pꜣ-n-/pa-* etc.) 342
prosodic unit(s) 33, 92, 294, 336, 368–69, 371, 407, 602, 627, 633, 757
Prospective 309, 312
– periphrastic 309
– prospective form 11, 172–73, 258, 256, 258, 548, 556
– prospective *sḏm-f* 172–73, 258, 548, 556, 750
*– prospective relative form, see relative form*
protasis 247–48, 424, 498, 706
protatic 161–62, 172
*pseudo-clefts, see cleft sentence*
'Pseudo-Verbal' 16, 369–70, 380
purpose/-ive 246, 500
– *e-* plus infinitive 246–47

Quality 207, 294, 571–74, 579, 580–81, 584, 593, 649–51, 658, 665, 667, 704, 711, 723–45, 747, 751
– predication of 649–51, 723–45
quality verbs 685
quantifier 13, 14, 50, 267
question marker *iniw* 66, 177, 474–75, 700

*R* of futurity 27–28, 83, 186–87, 189–91, 255–56, 264, 551, 729
radial, radiality 24, 139, 751
re-bracketing 409
recipiency 297
reduplication 7, 11, 88–89, 96–97, 99, 158–161, 172, 177, 256, 651, 657, 712–13
relationality 297–98, 306, 527
– relator 297–98
relative clause 9, 90–99, 100–02, 125–37, 147, 179, 263, 295, 308n.14, 309–13, 317, 326, 329–32, 349–367, 384–85, 386–87, 415, 417, 430, 438, 442, 445, 453, 456–61, 463, 484, 486, 513–18, 532–37, 540, 543, 548, 633–40, 656, 671, 710, 719
– headless 180, 262, 311, 332, 349, 350, 353, 442, 444, 445, 454, 457, 484, 514, 534, 656, 671–72, 683, 721
– *nt-/et*-introduced 90–96, 125–27, 129–31, 133–36, 309–13, 329–32, 350–61, 384–85, 386–87, 415, 417, 430, 438, 442, 445, 453, 456–60, 463, 484, 486, 514–18, 633–38, 671
– 'virtual' 100–02, 128–29, 131–33, 136–37, 344–45, 361–66, 460–61, 463, 475n.78, 496, 499, 515, 638–639, 710, 719
– *see also operators*

relative form 27, 97–99, 127, 129, 167–68, 172, 311–12, 329, 351, 356, 375, 384, 415, 416, 514, 531, 533, 543, 666, 672
– perfective 99, 167–68, 172
– prospective 168
*relative particle, see operators*
restrictive relative proposition 19, 100, 125–37, 168, 178–79, 478, 514–18, 552
resumption 92–95, 99, 102, 134, 263, 549, 692
resumptive pronoun 92–95, 99, 134, 263
*rḫ* 'know' 246, 507–08, 553–54, 715

Salience 155, 161, 437, 548
second position clitic 33, 46–47, 292–293, 295, 298, 304–05, 368–71, 382–83, 385, 392, 394, 530, 601–02, 605, 616, 630–31
Second Tense 18, 89–90, 157, 161–62, 166, 188, 212, 218, 223–26, 274, 284–85, 555, 592, 730
Sequential 675
sequential clause 60–61, 166, 175–76, 476, 662, 699–700, 728
*sequential particle, see particles*
similes 141, 205
situation descriptions 548
situation-thetic 144, 146, 153, 165, 170
space 23, 141, 156, 185, 191, 211, 238, 259, 551
*spatial adverb see adverb*
speaker assessment 176
speaker evaluation 14, 35, 119, 143, 154–56, 176, 177, 180–81, 258, 470, 474, 538, 550–55, 714, 728, 731, 733
speaker expectation 176
specification 150, 189, 391, 574, 578–79, 589–90, 593, 734, 736, 738
speech acts 142, 153, 155, 158
Stative verb form 9, 11, 29, 39, 63, 81, 83, 87, 159, 163, 196, 207–08, 210, 238, 253, 265, 580, 608, 653, 664, 674, 683, 685, 701, 704–07, 713, 714, 718, 729, 732, 736, 738, 747–50, 753–55
subject 9–10, 14–15, 17, 23–25, 27, 28–34, 36–37, 40–45, 48–52, 55–60, 63, 65, 69, 70–74, 76, 79, 81–84, 86, 88, 92–93, 95, 97, 99–100, 102, 105, 108, 109–10, 112–14, 115–16, 119–20, 122, 125, 128–29, 130–32, 134–36, 141, 144–46, 149, 151–52, 157, 160, 168, 169, 172, 177, 181, 188–89, 191, 214, 218–19, 223, 225, 235–36, 238, 249, 251, 256–57, 259–61, 263, 265, 267, 272, 273, 279, 284–85, 293, 294, 297–98, 300, 329, 347–51, 353, 358, 368, 370–71, 373, 379–80, 405, 406–09, 412, 419, 421, 424, 426–29, 454, 456, 462, 465, 482, 486–89, 515, 519–23, 525–30, 534–37, 539, 542–47, 554–55, 556–59, 560–69, 573, 575, 586, 603, 606, 608, 610, 612, 614, 619, 622–25, 630, 641, 651, 653–60, 662–64, 666–72, 674–78, 680, 683–86, 689–90, 692–96, 699–703, 705, 707, 712, 719, 723–27, 730–35, 748, 750, 752–53
– definition of 24, 519–31, 560–67
– focalisation of 145–56, 725
– indefinite 36, 41, 48–50, 57–59, 63, 102–03, 106, 107–08, 114, 215, 250, 270–71, 275–76, 280–81, 284
– relativisation of 97, 168
– sharing of 56–57, 701
subject element 367–406, 418
– agreement marking of 381, 385
– omission of 462–467, 512, 615, 640
– *=pw* 88, 151, 171, 177–78, 193, 367–82, 385
– *pꜣy/tꜣy/nꜣy* 317, 381–82, 385, 624
– *pꜣy/tꜣy/nꜣw* 385, 391–92
– *pe/te/ne* 391–92
subjunctive 87, 169, 171–73, 176, 179, 181, 258, 657, 663, 705, 729, 748, 749
subordination 18–19, 80, 102, 183, 495, 708
– subordinate clause 19, 30, 43, 73, 77, 81, 89, 102, 109, 147–52, 167, 174–75, 177, 183, 217, 226–35, 370–71, 377, 379–80, 407, 494–95, 509, 552, 557, 559, 596–99, 610, 657, 674, 708–10
– subordinator *e-* 115–18, 598–99
– subordinator *iw* 108–15, 494, 707–09
*suffixed personal pronoun, see personal pronoun*
*superlative, see comparison*

superordinate clause 71
suppletive 220, 251, 309, 515, 585, 755
SVO-syntax 3, 11, 18

TAM (tense, aspect, mood) 24, 141, 156, 212, 367, 729, 731, 751
tempus 217
– temporal 10, 18, 23–24, 39, 69, 76, 148, 153, 155–57, 158–60, 166–67, 172–73, 181–82, 186–87, 190–91, 193–94, 196, 209, 212–26, 227, 234, 256, 261, 326, 329, 361, 498, 519, 549, 550–56, 594–96, 682, 727–28, 731–32
– *-adverb, see adverb*
– -operator 155, 212–26, 270, 425–26, 594–96
tense 6, 10, 17, 27, 118, 167, 171, 217, 233–34, 309–12, 329, 550–56, 727, 747
– tenseless 141
*term-negation, see negation*
thematic 69, 74, 732–33
thematisation 733
theme-rheme – contrast 547
thetic 143–45, 155, 165, 258–59
time-reference 188, 750
topic vs. comment 537
topical 546, 562
topicalisation 151–52, 170, 177, 409, 471, 733
truth-value 119–21, 552, 607, 714

*Unte-/uonte-* 248–53, 358

Verbal future construction 12, 173, 255, 257–58, 264–65, 295–96, 548–49, 557, 682, 749–50
verbs of cognition 81–82, 180
verbs of government 85–86, 554–55, 715
verbs of locution 180
verbs of perception 81–83, 86, 100, 119, 180, 716
vetitive 682–83

*Wackernagel clitic, see clitic, second position*
WH-movement 146–47
wide-scope negation 255, 616, 621
word-order 23, 25, 33, 295, 530, 536

Zeroing 263, 276, 300, 451, 626, 674
– absence of 82

www.ingramcontent.com/pod-product-compliance
Lightning Source LLC
Chambersburg PA
CBHW032130010526
44111CB00034B/333
* 9 7 8 3 1 1 0 6 5 1 5 7 7 *